Utopia
and
Revolution

Melvin J. Lasky

Utopia and Revolution

*On the Origins of a Metaphor,
or Some Illustrations of the Problem
of Political Temperament and
Intellectual Climate
and
How Ideas, Ideals, and Ideologies
Have Been Historically
Related*

The University of Chicago Press

Chicago and London

MELVIN J. LASKY was born in New York City and
was educated at City College, the University of
Michigan, and Columbia University. During World
War II he was a U.S. combat historian in France
and Germany. He was the founding editor and
publisher of the international Berlin review, *Der
Monat*. Since 1958 he has been the coeditor and publisher of *Encounter Magazine*. He is the author of many
articles in newspapers and periodicals and of two
books, *Africa for Beginners* and *The Hungarian Revolution*.

The University of Chicago Press, Chicago 60637
The University of Chicago Press, Ltd., London

Library of Congress Cataloging in Publication Data

Lasky, Melvin J
    Utopia and revolution.

    Includes index.
    1. Utopias.   2. Revolutions.   I. Title.
HX806.L37   321'.07   75-27893
ISBN 0-226-46909-3

To the memory of my grandfather

Eli Meyer Kantrowitz

a learned man, who patiently tried to teach me the importance of relevant and appropriate passages, and used to remind me (from the legends of the Jews) that

The angels were not all of one opinion.
The Angel of Love favored the creation of man,
because he would be affectionate and loving;
but the Angel of Truth opposed it, because he would be full of lies.
And while the Angel of Justice favored it,
because he would practice justice,
the Angel of Peace opposed it, because he would be quarrelsome.

To invalidate his protest,
God cast the Angel of Truth down from heaven to earth,
and when the others cried out against
such contemptuous treatment of their companion,
He said, "Truth will spring back out of the earth ... "

Everything belongs together in the human understanding; the obscurity of one idea spreads over those that surround it. An error throws shadows over neighboring truths, and if it happens that there should be in society men interested in forming, as it were, centers of shadow, even the people will find itself plunged into a profound darkness.

—Diderot, *Encyclopédie*

Contents

Preface ix

Part 1 Ideals

1. The Utopian Longing 2
2. The Revolutionary Commitment 34
3. The Heretic's True Cause 96

Part 2 Images and Ideas

4. Martyrs of Reason and Passion 174
5. The Birth of a Metaphor: I 218
6. The Birth of a Metaphor: II 238
7. The Metaphysics of Doomsday 260
8. The Novelty of Revolution 288
9. The Great Intelligencers: I 320
10. The Great Intelligencers: II 348

Part 3 Ideologies

11. To Armageddon and Back 384
12. The Politics of Paradise 416
13. The Prometheans 470
14. The English Ideology: I 494
15. The English Ideology: II 528
16. The Sweet Dream 576

Notes 603

Index 709

Preface

This book constitutes the text, with substantial revisions and additions, which I prepared at the invitation of The University of Chicago for the *Encyclopaedia Britannica* Lectures in 1965. In delivering them in May of that year, I condensed the argument, omitted much of the illustrative material, and without benefit of ventriloquy made no attempt to deal with footnotes and addenda. I am aware that the pages which follow bear the marks of their origin, and I ask indulgence for those little stylistic peculiarities which are born of a lecturer's temptation to please the listening ear rather than the reading eye. But it could be that this fuller manuscript will more effectively meet some of the questions and challenges which were put to me in subsequent debates and seminars. In any case, I am grateful to the faculty and student audience of The University of Chicago (and especially to my friends on the aisle, Edward Shils and Saul Bellow) without whose arched eyebrows and quizzical attention in Breasted Hall a lecturer's courage would have gone untested.

My theme was Utopia and Revolution, and these lectures represented a connected series of studies in an intellectual climate. They began in the spirit of Tocqueville, who observed,

> Effrayant spectacle! car ce qui est qualité dans l'écrivain est parfois vice dans l'homme d'Etat, et les mêmes choses qui souvent ont fait faire de beaux livres peuvent mener à de grandes révolutions ...

They conclude in the spirit of Camus, who understood that, "Tout révolutionnaire finit en oppresseur ou en hérétique."

I say "intellectual climate," for what I am engaged in is less a formal exercise in intellectual history than a kind of meteorological report, and as such it attempts deliberately to stay pretty close to the weather, to Spinoza's "heat, cold, storm, and thunder."[1]

The first lecture began with utopia and ended with revolution; that is, it started with the utopian longing and moved to the systematic attempt to realize the dream of a good society by political action and violent upheaval.

The second lecture began with revolution and ended with dogma; that is, it moved from the revolutionary commitment to a dogmatic faith in violence and total control.

The third lecture began with dogma and ended with heresy; that is, it began with the precarious and untenable structure of orthodoxy and concluded with the emergence of doubt, dissent, and the curious beginnings of a new return, da capo, to ... utopia and revolution. (In that Chicago springtime of the mid-1960s, it was not difficult to observe, before one's own eyes, yet another turn on a historic spiral.)

In the years since those lectures were originally given, I have restlessly tampered with the texts, expanding, recasting, reconsidering.[2] My work will be in its final form (for there is a sequel still to come) a study of the ideological extension of the human personality over some five centuries of history; and its primary interest is now less in the exponents of utopia or the proponents of revolution than in those ideologues who came to believe that the noble dream and the great deed have no real effective life without each other. My concern is not with the vision of the perfect society alone, nor with the movement, by itself, toward violent social change: it is with the fateful point in human history at which the two meet.

For if utopia and revolution are too much with us today,[3] it was not always so. If ideology appears to have become in our time an anthology culled from a vest-pocket dictionary of *idées reçues,* and if in every ideological phrase there lies buried the etymological lore of centuries, there was a time when the words were new, the sentiments fresh, the ideas original and unprecedented.

The history of ideas is, I feel, a form of dialogue with the past in which the essential lines have already been spoken. I can fully understand A. O. Lovejoy's exasperation at finding in his reading paraphrases where he "desiderated the actual language of ideas," and his temptation (in his masterpiece, *The Great Chain of Being*) toward overabundant citations of illustrative passages and even toward a corpus of texts in which the central and related ideas dealt with occur. The present study in comparative ideology often verges on becoming an analytical compilation, and I ask the benevolent reader to make allowance for its chrestomathic character. I have quoted so much and so persistently because I have wanted to catch the relationship of utopia and revolution as it actually comes through in "the conversation of mankind." The paraphrase is the blur and the blot in the rendering of historical immediacy.

The historian's précis of a poetic vision is less revealing than the extravagant metaphors themselves; anger and passion are best left in the original expletives; the process of doubt and disenchantment is both moving and meaningful only when the echoes of the questing mind are directly rendered. I am pursuing here that elusive ideal: history as experience. There are, I am convinced, lessons at once instructive and chastening in the reading of history; but it may be that we fail to learn from experience because we do not effectively experience what we learn. We are often condemned to repeat the past not merely because we do not remember it but because the memories fail to function in the deep shaping of the imagination. What history is remembered has a limited quality as a mere abstracted accuracy or a formal antiquarianism, falling short of both the vitality of Croce's "contemporary history" and the relevance of a "usable past."

Still, what more selective and interpretive method is there in historical writing than the exhibition of texts and contexts? And what more illuminating patterns emerge in the history of ideas than those that derive from the study of words and their phraseological variations,[4] from the analysis of images and their real and rhetorical deployment? Thus, there are times when the historian is quoting least when he is quoting most: the fragments which he brings back from his search among books and documents were perhaps strung together long before in his own mind. This could be the essential solipsism of the intellectual historian; one must look if one is to find, but one may be always finding what one is looking for. Historical interpretations of the chaotic multifarious past are often a personal form of retrospective self-fulfilling prophecies. The inverted commas and the footnote references are only the conventional and approved devices for assuring his readers—and himself—that what he has long suspected and what he is now suggesting is really and truly so. The truth remains in the detail. I can only regret that the form of these published lectures has made it necessary to put so much of what I found relevant and illuminating in the back as addenda or notes. But then, as Pascal observed, "the last thing one discovers when writing a book is what ought to have come first . . . "

Yet some first things are simple and obvious. I know that to treat this subject historically (as I have, after a fashion, tried to do), rather than philosophically, is necessarily to do it in breadth rather than depth. I am, consequently, grateful for those traditions and achievements of modern scholarship which make such eclecticism both possible and useful. I can only hope that, in some way or another, men of letters reading quickly and widely (and hawking and hunting so avidly en route),[5] are repaying scholars and specialists for their single-minded devotion to original research. If these pages offer some intellectual pleasure and general suggestiveness, it would be a token of my own gratitude. Footnotes are debts and promises.

One other thing needs to be said. These lectures were, in their way, a kind of ideological autobiography. I have myself identified my views, at various times in the past, with many of the main intellectual currents which figure so prominently in the following pages. I have often found myself caught—and perhaps still am—in utopias and revolutionary commitments, orthodoxies and heresies: between (in the recurrent image of what follows) the fire and the ant. Where history has taken, I feel, a profound tragic turn is in the triple error: utopia conceived as a sterile monolithic harmony; revolution as a dogmatic commitment to total change and violent reconstruction; principles of hope and belief transmogrified into an orthodoxy incompatible with heretical dissent or critical opposition. Where history provides consolation (and I, at least, feel so consoled) is in the triple hope: when utopian longing is a supple changing ideal of diverse virtues and dreams; where revolution represents a reformer's open-eyed recourse to a difficult path of fundamental social reorganization, without conspiratorial self-delusion and bewitching metaphor; and where, whatever the devotion to principles of political action and ethical aspiration, there is present "the heretic's true cause"—dissent, tolerance, and a respect for humane reason.

Here the past is a spur, for men in history have been known to be such utopians, revolutionaries, and heretics, and they have succeeded—in the sense of their magnificent and timeless relevance—more than they ever had reason to surmise.

And yet, and yet: I remain deeply troubled by one puzzling aspect of the human condition as it has exhibited itself in the history of man's political affairs. It is, I suspect, an underlying anthropological leitmotiv which, for all my efforts to refrain from ultimate judgments, will not escape the reader. Candor calls for its open formulation at the very outset of our inquiry into the splendors and miseries of utopia and revolution.

Man, for all the occasional easy comings and goings, is born *in extremis* and dies *in extremis,* and his liveliest moments of joy, pleasure, and excitement are in the extreme emotions of sex, affection, and combat. He has learned to survive as a thoughtful animal by means of cunning compromise and shrewd reconsiderations: dangers are assessed, prospects of safety and sustenance vigilantly reevaluated. But because of his very nature it has never been easy for him to conceive of ecstasy in terms of moderation, love as a form of balance, a splendored victory as an ally of prudence or a heroic loyalty as a patchwork thing.

> How show, in spite of all the rhetoric ...
> Proportion, not as something calm congealed

> From lack of fire, but ruling such a fire
> As only such proportion could contain?[6]

There have always been deep, and doubtless inexpugnable, sources for the immemorial war between Passion and Reason, between man the Dionysian extremist and the reasonable, reasoning creature. His heart leads him on to utopian dreams and revolutionary aspirations; his reflectiveness teaches him care, caution, and a course which must beware of seductive simplicities. It is understandable that he tends to confound the imperatives of private pleasures and public virtues. He sings of the fire but knows the fear of being burned; and a storm (or an earthquake, or a flood) which, under most circumstances in the experience of man on earth, would compel him to take to his heels in flight for safe refuge, arouses him on certain historic occasions to make grand disproportionate gestures and otherwise inexplicable sacrifices. The foolhardy lies close to the tragic, and man often embraces his complex fate in the recurrent vivifying hope that in the embrace some of life's ultimate meaning can be found. He is, at times, unavoidably confused by what is profane and what sacred, and jumbles the various sensations and satisfactions which make up his essential nature. He longs for immortal loyalties and imperishable deeds, but lives out most of his years trying to learn how not to reach for more than he can grasp or to bite off more than he can chew. He is tempted by intimations of vague Apollonian nobility, but something between the humdrum and the penultimate is what he usually comes to settle for. Or is the chief end of man to be found in what lies between?

> Between extremities
> Man runs his course;
> A brand, or flaming breath,
> Comes to destroy
> All those antinomies
> Of day and night;
> The body calls it death,
> The heart remorse ...[7]

London/New York,   M. J. L.
Summer 1975

Part 1

Ideals

1

What is a merit in the writer may
well be a vice in the statesman, and the
very qualities which go to make great
literature can lead to catastrophic
revolutions.

—Tocqueville (1856)

Politics calls for both passion and
perspective. All historical experience
confirms the truth that man would not have
attained the possible unless time and again
he had reached out for the impossible.

—Max Weber (1918)

The Utopian Longing

1. Green Stick and Ant Brotherhood
Tolstoy's Vision: " ... all mankind under the wide dome of heaven"—The Double Metaphor—Imagists of Myrmecoid Discipline: Plato, Milton, Bismarck, Nkrumah—Lapses of the Human Imagination—Standards of the Anthill: Dostoevsky, Maeterlinck, Alexander Pope—"Natural Civics": The Formicary as an Ideal Republic

2. The Distorting Mirror
Toynbee and the Insectarian Potential—Utopian Ambivalence—Sources of Compulsion and Regimentation—Hateful Diversity or the Miracle of Coherence—Campanella's "City of the Sun"—Temptations of Total Control—Balance-Sheet of More's "Utopia" (1516)—The Eternal Post-utopian Problem

3. The Utopian as Fabian
Hexter's Three Views of More—Escape, Reform, or Radicalism—Montaigne's Tension of the Two Halves—"What Is to be Done?"—The Prospects for Improvement—More's Difficulties with "Clean Contrary Minds"—Between the Moderately Good and the Very Bad

4. Columbus's New World: From Dante to More
Emperor Frederick's Question to Michael Scot: "Where was Paradise?"—Columbus as a Millennial Messenger—Vespucci and Botticelli—Dante's Shining Prophet: Joachim of Flora—Joachimism and Resisting Evil to the End—The Mission of the Faithful—The Promise

of the Future in a Transitional Era—Dante and the Common Good—
Imminent Doom and Immanent Order—"Universalis Civilitas Humani Generis"—The Messianic Emperor's World Liberation—Dante's
Theory of Dual Power: The Two Paradises—Judge Quiroga and
More's Utopia in New Spain—Mendieta's Mystical Hope for a Perfect
Indian Commonwealth—"Hythlodaeus," Ardent Visionary

---

5. Practical Reformers or Rebels in a Hurry
The Lure of Gradualism and Reasonableness—Karl Popper's
Empiricism—David Hume's "Perfection and Gentle Alterations"—
When Patience Runs Out—"The Heart of Time": Milton, Paine,
Robespierre—Utopian and Anti-utopian Revolutionaries—The
Double-Tongued Tradition—Philo and the Interpretation of Dreams

---

1. Green Stick and Ant Brotherhood

There is somewhere in Tolstoy—or so I was led to believe by a passage
which I had, long ago, in a burst of utopian enthusiasm, scribbled into
an old notebook—the story of a green stick buried by the road at the
edge of a ravine in the Zakaz Forest. On this green stick, his brother
Nikolai had told him when he was a child, was written the greatest of all
secrets: namely, how all men would become happy, how one day there
would be no more disease, no trouble: no one would be angry with
anybody, all would love one another. All his life Tolstoy believed in
this—"a little green stick whereon was written the message which could
destroy all evil in men and give them universal welfare." At Yasnaya
Polyana, in the days before his death, with tear-filled eyes, he asked to
be buried there near the ravine; and by the path in the forest he lies.

The passage in my notebook was reassuring, for the utopian longing
has always been touched by something of this Tolstoyan quality, its
large humanism, its generous impulse and noble vision. But the passage
was, curiously (and perhaps characteristically) incomplete. There were a
few phrases missing; a metaphor had dropped out, and small wonder,
for it was the dark image which no innocent utopian gladly confronts.
Acting out their happy game of the good society, Tolstoy and his
brothers decided to call themselves, in their surprising, upsetting
phrase, the "Ant-Brothers." If the chief secret was not yet theirs, at least
"the Ant-Brotherhood was revealed to us," and it was a revelation

which in a long life was never to recede. When he was over seventy, Tolstoy explained that "the ideal of ant-brothers lovingly clinging to one another ... all mankind under the wide dome of heaven, has remained the same for me."[1]

I make this confession, for it seems to me now that this delinquent transcription is symbolic: the moving finger does not write, and moves on. We search, enchanted, for the green stick; we turn away (surely it is irrelevant, accidental) from the prospect of the ant brotherhood. Yet the human longing for universal welfare has always been characterized by the double metaphor, and by now the one-eyed utopian has recovered a fuller sight. In my own case (if I may be allowed another personal remark about my notebooks), there are now passages of more perceptive response. Next to the green stick, and happy entries from all the blessed isles, the cities of the sun, and worlds beyond the seas, there are the dark surmises of a tragic flaw in the longing for an enlarged humanity, a perfected mankind. "Go to the ant," we are told in Proverbs (6:6), "consider her ways and be wise." But the consideration may be complicated, and the wisdom ambiguous. Let me turn at random to a number of other great imagists of the ant brotherhood.

When Socrates contemplated in the *Phaedo* the future of those wandering souls in Hades, ceaselessly pursued by a craving for the corporeal, he felt certain that they would be ultimately reattached to the same sort of character or nature which they developed during life. Those who cultivated gluttony or selfishness or drunkenness would be likely to assume the form of donkeys and other brutish animals; and those who deliberately preferred a life of injustice, tyranny, and violence would become wolves and hawks and kites. As for "the happiest people"— namely, those who cultivated the goodness of an ordinary citizen: self-control and integrity, acquired by habit and practice—Socrates suggested that "they will probably pass into some other kind of social and disciplined creature like bees, wasps, and ants; or even back into the human race again, becoming decent citizens."[2] This notion of human civic virtue as a form of myrmecoid discipline, or the ant as hero, is an idea which crawls through all of Western thought.

In a moment of political desperation, John Milton, whose gaze was seldom so earthbound, hurled the biblical injunction—"Go to the Ant, thou sluggard (saith Solomon)"—at those faithless backsliders who, with the breakup of the Cromwellian protectorate, were slipping toward royalism. "They who think the nation undone without a King," Milton writes in his last political pamphlet (1660), "have not so much true spirit and understanding in them as a Pismire." He was a little worried about the analogical precision; and in a second edition, published some weeks

later, he eagerly explained that no suggestion had been intended that
"these diligent creatures ... live in lawless anarchie"; rather, they are
"the examples to imprudent and ungoverned men, of a frugal and self-
governing democratie or Commonwealth; safer and more thriving in the
joint providence and counsel of many industrious equals, than under
the single domination of one imperious Lord." Hobbes, whom Milton
disliked, had, in a powerful page of his *Leviathan* (1651), relentlessly
demonstrated the superficiality and irrelevance of the analogy between
the sociability of ants and the political complexity of men who were at
least capable of speech and reason, susceptible to envy and hatred, and
sorely tempted by power and domination.[3] But neither Milton nor his
contemporaries could easily manage such sovereign Hobbesian coolness, and the easy metaphor provided a shortcut to hope. Creatures
could be diligent, frugal, and purposeful; and when one historian
sketched the *Brief Character of the Low Countries* (1652), he noted with
deep satisfaction that "they are the pismires of the world, and having
nothing but what grass affords them, are yet, for almost all provisions,
the storehouse of whole Christendom ... Everyone is busy, and carries
his grain." How easily could the ant adapt itself, at least in intellectual
metaphorics, to Platonic, Protestant, and indeed Prussian contexts!
There is a recorded conversation with Prince Otto von Bismarck, when
he was still the Iron Chancellor in Berlin, in which he made a remarkable
confession. "If I had to choose the form in which I would prefer to live
again," he said, "I am not so sure that I should not like to be an ant. You
see," he added, "that little insect lives under conditions of perfect political organization. Every ant is obliged to work—to lead a useful life;
everyone is industrious; there is perfect subordination, discipline, and
order. They are happy, for they work." What Bismarck, not unlike Plato,
consigned to the realm of metempsychosis (although some will find in it
more than *ein Körnchen* of Prussian reality), others have given a more
immediate, this-worldly pertinence. Kwame Nkrumah (or the *Osagyefo*,
the Great Liberator, as he once preferred to be known), told in his
Autobiography of sitting and watching the ants one day in Ghana, then
the old Gold Coast, where he was active in organizing an African revolutionary movement. " 'Nothing will stop them,' I thought, as I watched
those minute creatures running purposefully backwards and for-
wards ... 'They will always succeed in their objective because they are
disciplined and organized.' There was not a single slacker among
them."[4]

It must surely be taken as one of the great lazy lapses of the human
imagination that a utopian vision of a future man, at last erect and
godlike, should be reduced to a hunched-over peering at Russian floor-
boards, African verandas, and the sandy fields of Mark Brandenburg.
The ants are always with us, even in our antiseptic American

laboratories. In Professor B. F. Skinner's scientific utopia, called (in a mild slander on Thoreau) *Walden Two*, there is a brief, ineffectual challenge by a dissenting observer: "So far as I can see," the utopian scientist is told, "you've blocked every path through which man was to struggle upward toward salvation. Intelligence, initiative—you have filled their places with a sort of degraded instinct, engineered compulsion. Walden Two is a marvel of efficient coordination—as efficient as an ant-hill!"[5] The point is promptly, blithely, ignored.

It had been most forcefully put once by Dostoyevsky, writing in his *Summer Impressions*, a disenchanting record of his voyage (1862) of European discovery:

> [T]here is a curious paradox. A man is offered full security, promised food and drink, and found work, and as against this he is merely required to give up a tiny grain of his personal freedom for the sake of the common good—just a tiny, tiny grain. But man does not want to live on these conditions; he finds even the tiny grain too irksome. He thinks that he is being put in gaol, poor fool, and that he would be better off by himself, because then he would have full freedom. And when he is free he is knocked about and refused work, he starves to death and has no real freedom. But all the same, the strange fellow still prefers his own freedom. Naturally enough, the socialist is simply forced to give him up and tell him that he is a fool, that he is not ready yet, not ripe enough to understand what is good for him; that a dumb little ant, a miserable ant is more intelligent than he is because everything is so lovely in an ant-hill, so well-ordered, no one goes hungry and all are happy, everyone knows what he has to do; in fact, man has a long way to go before he can hope to reach the standards of an ant-hill.[6]

Indeed, ever since Maeterlinck's rehabilitation of the ant and the ant heap from the calumnies of Aesop and La Fontaine, the formicary has had its defenders, not only as "a replica in little of our own destinies" but as an inspiring model of organization and purposefulness.[7] Maeterlinck himself was convinced that modern myrmecology had proved the ant to be "one of the noblest, most courageous, most charitable, most devoted, most generous, and most altruistic creatures on earth." Its government was "superior to any that man will ever be able to realize"; socially, there was "peace and abundance and perfect fraternity"; as for its religion, "more Good Samaritans pass along the tracks of the formicary than along the road from Jerusalem to Jericho." Here, indeed, was a utopia for mankind, the prospect of a happy life "in all and for all." But: "We have lost the sense of the collective. Shall we recover it? The Socialism and Communism toward which we are advancing marks a step in this direction."[8]

Apparently, for the ants, it was a road already taken. Nothing less than a tempting variant of collectivist communism—"surely this is an ideal republic: no idlers, no tramps, no citizen-parasites, no misers, no spendthrifts, no paupers!"—was what one American formicologist, studying "natural civics," found in the government of ant communities. "Is this socialism?" Dr. Henry McCook asked, "nature's type of a practical socialism? Learn this, then: if socialism as a form of human government would be equally or even approximately successful, it must first attain that perfect individual discipline and absolute self-control, self-abnegation, self-surrender, and self-devotion to the good of the whole community that one sees in a Commonwealth of Ants." Nor was it merely a matter of socialism in one anthill. The celebrated Swiss naturalist, Auguste Forel, looking hopefully toward Geneva, was convinced that the new League of Nations could represent the true utopian beginnings of "a supernational human formicary"; and, as a matter of fact, a British naturalist, reporting from Central America, had already announced that there among the Nicaraguan anthills he had found at last a usable model and a just analogue to Sir Thomas More's description of Utopia.[9] It is all very much in the spirit of Alexander Pope's famous injunction:

> Thus then to Man the voice of Nature spake—
> "Go, from the Creatures thy instructions take: ...
> Learn each small People's genius, policies,
> The Ant's Republic, and the realm of Bees;
> How those in common all their wealth bestow,
> And Anarchy without confusion know.... "
> Great Nature spoke; observant Men obey'd;
> Cities were built, Societies were made.[10]

2. The Distorting Mirror

I want to suggest no more than the insectarian potential in the utopian model, although Arnold Toynbee has gone further than simple anthropomorphic hints. In the third volume of his *Study of History*, he tries ingeniously to compare the social structure of those imaginary human societies called utopias not only with that of the social insects but also with the "arrested civilisations" of the Spartans, the Eskimos, and the nomads. He discerns in an ant heap (and in a beehive) the same outstanding features: "the two phenomena of caste and specialisation, and the fatally perfect adaptation of the society to its particular environment ... " He finds these features equally true for Plato's *Republic*, Aldous Huxley's *Brave New World*, and H. G. Wells's various fantasies; and he goes on, adventurously, to argue:

These fictitious descriptions of imaginary human societies that have never existed are really programmes of action masquerading in the disguise of descriptive sociology; and the action which they are intended to evoke is the "pegging," at a certain social level, of an actual society which has broken down and has entered upon a decline that must end in a fall unless the downward movement can be artificially arrested. To arrest a downward movement is the utmost to which a Utopia can aspire, since Utopias seldom begin to be written in any society until after its members have lost the expectation and ambition of making further progress and have been cowed by adversity into being content if they can succeed in holding the ground which has been won for them by their fathers.

This is, as so often in Toynbee, more stimulating than sound. He himself has to concede that his theory is true only for "almost all Utopias," the most noteworthy exception being "that work of English genius which has given this whole genre of literature its modern Western name," namely, Sir Thomas More's *Utopia*. Like many a theoretician who has taken the trouble to search More's text, he finds it "surprising," quite different from Hellenic predecessors and modern Western successors: there is little static social rigidity, almost no caste and specialization. If this is "really extraordinary"—More's adoption of an ideal of elasticity and growth—then it is "an enigma which has to be explained." He suggests, finally, that "perhaps the true explanation may be that More was subconsciously aware of being a member of a lustily growing society all the time, notwithstanding his conscious conviction that the world in which he had grown up was falling to pieces . . . " This flight into depth psychology won't quite do, for have not the societies of Huxley and Wells, Godwin and Bellamy and William Morris, proved to be "lustily growing" as well?[11]

More than this: what single-minded critics of utopia appear to miss is the "double metaphor," the ambivalent and often dialectical character of the utopian inspiration. Utopias are written out of both hope and despair. They are models of stability conceived in the spirit of contradiction. They are actions—a kind of "action dreaming"—in the name of ideal values: neglected or betrayed in the present, once enjoyed in the past, or yet to be fulfilled in the future. They are interpretations of the existing order, and as often as not programs for change. Utopia's hortatory implication, in the form of a secret injunction, is always there, for all political ideals are implicitly revolutionary: their critical elements lead to dissent, their perfect projections to a longing to construct anew. The utopian dream of the future, with its sources in fantasy and alienation, implies the nightmare of the present. And yet, as we have seen, the conceivable and desirable future is never free of this nightmarish escape.

Let us concede the enigma. The rigidity of almost all utopias, their authoritarianism and paternal perfectionism, are almost incomprehensible, seen against the whole record of the human imagination. Where life and literature have been usually so various, could there never have been a less inflexible dream of freedom and man's destiny? Walter Bagehot once suggested "how hateful variation" could be, with the very innovators inventing the most rigid mechanisms for crushing new and anomalous social forms. Facing this "puzzle" more recently, Lewis Mumford has asked, similarly: "How could the human imagination, supposedly liberated from the constraints of actual life, be so impoverished? ... Where did all the compulsion and regimentation that mark these supposedly ideal commonwealths come from?"[12]

This is, perhaps, only explicable if utopia is seen as a predictably desperate diversion from what has characterized almost all but a small modern sector of known human societies—namely, chaos, arbitrariness, waste, uncertainty, license. To confront an age-old spectacle of incorrigible human indolence is to be led to dream of a society where all labored duly and had no excuse for vagrancy. To see the wild, thoughtless irresponsibility of both ruler and ruled throughout brutal and treacherous centuries is to be driven to a high-minded fantasy of how and when and where men could gain a sense of solidarity, of discipline and loyalty in their everyday duties and customs. I remember once standing on the desolate bank of an upper branch of the Nile; around me were primitive lands and tribes, lost in timelessness; and I was seized by wonder at how a farm or a town or a market had ever come to pass, how the "neolithic revolution" had ever happened in history. A response to what challenge? a flood? a conqueror? a mountaineer's discovery of a fertile valley? Then I dreamt, in a utopian burst, of a Pharoah (may the prophets forgive me), and that was a kind of solution.

Utopias, I suggest, were these kinds of solution. The utopians rarely went on to conceive of a free, differentiated man because in an elemental sense they felt men were too devilishly, wastefully, pointlessly free. They hardly hoped for diversity, for differentness among men in society, because their deepest longing was for the miracle of a coherence which could give a measure of purpose, dignity, and meaning to the empty randomness that marked and marred the life they were criticizing.

> Werft die Angst des Irdischen von euch,
> Fliehet aus dem engen dumpfen Leben
> In des Ideales Reich!*
>
> Schiller[13]

*"Cast aside the anxieties of this earth, / Flee from the narrow gloom of life / Into the realm of the ideal!"

It was in a rare spirit of Victorian forgiveness that Bagehot contemplated the faults of what he called "the preliminary ages," dominated by "the need of a fixed life when all else was unfixed life." The quantity of life was much more important than its quality. What one wanted, he imagined, was "a comprehensive rule binding men together, making them do much the same things, telling them what to expect of each other—fashioning them alike, and keeping them so. What this rule is does not matter so much. A good rule is better than a bad one, but any rule is better than none ... How to get the obedience of men is the hard problem; what you do with that obedience is less critical." If this is so, then to understand may well be to excuse. Otherwise, we must conclude, with Mumford and some others, that the body of utopian literature constitutes the most wretched, barren, mindless, and uninspired genre in the story of letters. But where life has been so poor, is it any wonder that it produces poverty-stricken ideals? Utopia is a looking glass: and a mirror, no matter how creatively it distorts, can reflect only the shapes and shadows that are there.

There is, for example, much that is admirable in Campanella's *City of the Sun*.[14] They honored greatness there, including Moses, Osiris, and Jupiter ("even Mahomet whom nevertheless they hate as a false and sordid legislator"). They were clean and healthy, bathed in wine, and knew a secret for renovating life after seventy. They were above keeping slaves, and were moved to help their oppressed neighbors in a struggle for liberty. But there was also a basic docility among them, understandable perhaps in the vision of a Dominican monk who had peered out into the harshness of a Spanish prison yard for almost thirty years. The City of the Sun was not without its shadow of monastic patterns. "It is wonderful," Campanella writes, "to see how men and women march together collectively, and always in obedience to the voice of the king." This traditional ideal of a collectivity of obedience also influenced Andreae in his picture of what would constitute an "absolutely free commonwealth," and he was deeply impressed by the authoritarian moral strictness he found in Geneva.[15] This is what we have come to think of as the Orwellian component in political astigmatism: absolute freedom means absolute control. Or, put another way, here again is our green stick buried among the ant brothers.

In Thomas More, too, there are these lingering mirror images of reality, this time inverted reflections of the anarchy and decadence which More must have found so estranging in his own society. He was not unaware of the phenomenon: the crack in the conception, the flaw in the vision. Recall his own touching confession of the temptation of power lust (in a letter to Erasmus, who had seen the manuscript of *Utopia* through the presses in Louvain).[16] "You cannot think how elated I am," he wrote, "how I have grown in stature and hold my head higher: so constantly do I imagine myself in the part of sovereign of Utopia: in fact, I fancy I am walking with the crown of corn ears upon my head, wearing a Franciscan cloak, and carrying the corn sheaf as a sceptre, attended by a great throng of the people." After all, Dante, when he passed through the wall of flame separating Purgatory from the Earthly Paradise (in Canto 27), had given himself both the crown and the mitre. Just so had Campanella imagined himself to be the Great Metaphysician in his City of the Sun; Bacon, the Father in his Solomon's House; John Milton, the God-inspired orator whose eloquence converted a listening Europe; Cabet, the Lawgiver of his Icaria; and Wilhelm Weitling, the revolutionary sword-carrying Messiah of a worldwide Communia. Few utopian revolutionaries in history ever show the species of spiritual self-discipline which would, in view of mankind's immemorial record of arrogant authority, propose only the humblest role for themselves in the future polity. As Johann Valentin Andreae frankly concedes in the opening pages of his *Christianopolis* (1619), "Inasmuch as I myself do not like to be corrected, I have built this city for myself where I may exercise the dictatorship."[17] No, the temptations of aggrandized power among the intellectual spokesmen of utopian excellence have proved hard to resist. Their natural imperious egoism, compounded by a sense of charismatic self-confidence and messianic purposefulness, always puts them at the utopian center of things.

More's dream of being King in Utopia was short-lived. "The break of day dispersed the vision, deposing poor me from my sovereignty and recalling me to prison." Where he failed to transcend the modalities of the past, harsh traces remain in his utopian future. There is the dreary uniformity of sights and sounds. The cities lack variety and the person "whoso knoweth one of them knoweth them all, they be all so like one to another"; the public dress (shades of the "blue ants" of our own day!) is a standard cape, "a garment of one colour throughout the island."[18] Then one worries too about the extirpation of all "domestical dissension" so that "perfect concord remaineth"; surely, it would take an unwise father or a short-sighted son to wish for it all to be "like a single family." Worse than that: "nowhere is there any license to waste time, nowhere any pretext to evade work—no wine-shop, no ale-house, no brothel anywhere, no opportunity for corruption, no lurking hole, no secret meeting-place. On the contrary, the people are under the eyes of all."

Still, on balance, who would not be tempted to live among the citizens of this Utopia? Who would not be attracted by their seductive virtues? They condemned the miseries of war ("War, as an activity fit only for beasts and yet practiced by no kind of beast so constantly as by man, they regard with loathing; against the usage of almost all nations they count nothing so inglorious as glory sought in war"). They rejected the horrors and follies of brutal punishments for petty crimes. They chose ambassadors and governors out of the company of scholars, and were committed to the freedom and culture of the mind ("the citizens withdraw from bodily service to the free liberty of the mind and its culture, for herein they suppose the felicity of this life to consist"). They introduced good literature to children, and their intellectual and literary curiosity went so far as to insist that learned visitors give public lessons in Greek, so devoted were they to the texts of Plato and Aristotle (that is, where "an ape on the voyage" hadn't damaged the shipment of books). Their fondness and delight with fools mixed with their general temper ("merry, quick, and fine-witted"). They banished all cunning and manipulating lawyers from the land. Theirs was a good neighborliness (and more than that, for this was not utopia in one country: "their neighbors are free and independent since many of them were long ago delivered from tyrants by the Utopians"). They derided vain superstitions and were proud of their religious tolerance. Their enlightened attitude toward prisoners of war was evinced in the humanitarian role of their priests on the battlefield. Almost last, but not least, was their sovereign attitude toward money, wealth, and material acquisitions, and their opposition to greed, exploitation, and pride.

Most of all—there was the open-endedness of the whole experiment.[19] It will be recalled that when Raphael Hythlodaye, who had accompanied Amerigo Vespucci on some of his travels, finishes his story, the author entertains some possible objections against absurdities in Utopia's laws and customs: the methods of waging war, the religious ceremonies, and especially their communistic attitude toward money. But would, at this weary moment, Raphael "brook any opposition"? The author takes him by the hand and leads him into supper, for "there would be another chance to think about these matters more deeply and to talk them over with him more fully." Still, he cannot help getting in a word of his own: "I cannot agree with all that he said. But I readily admit that there are very many features in the Utopian commonwealth which it is easier for me to wish for in our countries than to have any hope of seeing realized."

There is, then, at the very birth of the classical utopia the accompanying elements of opposition and disagreement, of reconsideration, deeper reflection, and the continuing dialogue. The essential utopian text has very little in common with that mythologized version of a sterile, changeless perfectionism,[20] a monolithic harmony, a tranquil, permanent paradise. True, what is outlined is not a good, or a better, but "The Best State of a Commonwealth," or, in the verses of Utopia's poet laureate:

> Wherefore not Utopie, but rather rightly
> My name is Eutopie: a place of felicity.

Yet the point of departure was not apocalyptic, but pragmatic; the mission was not eschatological, but an empirical search for remedies and reforms.

Even in his most orthodox religious works (in, for example, the furious polemic against Martin Luther), there is to be found More's English and humanistic aversion to political eschatology and, especially, the fiery apocalyptic temperament. He dismisses the German Protestant as "a firebrand of hell"; quotes his simple-minded juxtapositions of good and evil ("I ask about liberty and slavery; I fight for liberty") and even implies that this is a species of simple-minded utopianism; warns against "a new Esdras" (an apocalyptic book of the Apocrypha); attacks the element of *anarchos* in his political thought; and goes on patiently to explain how dangerous naïveté can be in devising new social arrangements.

> If you take away the laws and leave everything free to the magistrates, either they will command nothing and they will forbid nothing, and then the magistrates will be useless; or they will rule by the leading of their own nature and imperiously prosecute anything they please, and then the people will be in no way freer, but, by reason of a condition of servitude, worse, when they will have to obey, not fixed and definite laws, but indefinite whims changing from day to day. And this is bound to happen even under the best magistrates, whom, although they may enjoin the best laws, nevertheless the people will oppose and murmur against as suspect, as though they govern everything, not according to what is just and fair, but according to caprice.[21]

A humane and just society required a rule of laws, not of men. Utopia was not to be marred by the unworldly utopian illusion, namely, that a faith in good souls and hearts and their ideal intentions was sufficient for the new order. Institutional arrangements were to form the structural basis, and even these were never without shaky foundations.

> To find citizens ruled by good and wholesome laws, that is an exceeding rare and hard thing. But as he marked many fond foolish laws in those new found lands, so he rehearsed divers acts and constitutions whereby these our cities, nations, and kingdoms may take example to amend their faults, enormities, and errors.[22]

Here is the eternal post-utopian problem: after the dream, there comes the rude, mind-troubled, question-ridden awakening. Would, in point of fact, the "example" take? Would it always be easier "to wish" than "to have any hope"? Who would have the strength or the wisdom to introduce "good and wholesome laws"? How, in the here-and-now, were the faults of an ailing society to be mended, its errors corrected, its enormities removed? We are at the very heart of modern politics: the problem of means and ends, of reform and revolution.

3. The Utopian as Fabian

But, at this point, to our host of puzzles and enigmas we must, alas, add another, for the most ingenious student of More's *Utopia* appears to be of several (and most contradictory) minds on the subject of whether and how these questions were actually faced. Was More's *Utopia* a historic fantasy of political escape, or a suggestive program of reform and reconstruction, or a desperate manifesto of total radicalism? Professor J. H. Hexter has made three resourceful attempts at these questions, and the answers have been consistently different each time.[23]

The case for More as a complete revolutionary, with the communism of *Utopia* as a basis for "modern egalitarian radicalism," is formally put in the Yale edition of the *Works*. Utopia is presented as "a sort of anti-Europe," as an indictment of "the sins of the whole ruling class of the West." All reforms are "transitory" and "ultimately futile." There is no hope in "mild measures" or "ameliorations": they could at best only stave off utter disaster. If men are to give a sane and superior stamp to their institutions, it is basically a drastic matter of "the structure of society," not of "futile moralistic incantation"; and Hexter insists here that "the idea of eradicating, deracinating, pulling up by the roots—the starting point of radicalism—is not only implicit in *Utopia*, it is sporadically explicit." A textual reference or two (from More, from R. H. Tawney) is supplied, but not very convincingly, even for the author who, at one point, unwittingly confirms what he is at pains to deny, namely, that this thesis is perhaps "a bit of *trompe-l'oeil*, a trick of perspective, the results of staring too long at a sixteenth-century book from some place in the twentieth century ... "

Indeed, the perspective of a previous stare was another breathtaking trick. In a perceptive study of both Machiavelli and More, Professor Hexter has argued that the possibilities latent in their visions were not at all grasped; in More's case, there was only evasion and escape. "How are men to pass from this world of alienation and bondage to that world of reconciliation and freedom? To this question More gives no answer, but only tells a tale of Utopus, a king who never was, who seventeen hundred years ago brought this blessed consummation to Utopia, a land that never was. *Utopia* is literally nowhere." He goes on to suggest that the true link "between the Machiavellian actuality and the utopian dream was not a mythical King Utopus; it was class war, seizure of power, revolution," and that this "potpourri of conceptions ... was concocted in the milieu of Paris between 1840, the publication date of Pierre Proudhon's *What is Property?* and 1848, that of the *Communist Manifesto* of Karl Marx and Friedrich Engels." Yet this melodramatic notion of a nineteenth-century breakthrough to revolution, or from More to Marx in one move, was matched in still another reading of *Utopia* as a more modest sixteenth-century breakthrough to reform.

For the author of *Utopia*, as Professor Hexter argued in a third place, was neither a revolutionary nor a utopian. No Christian humanist could evade offering guidance to a Europe fallen on evil ways. He was the warden of true standards, the enlightened adviser of perfect princes and knights, and the confident propagandist of the authentic good whose Words would in truth become Flesh.[24] He was the teacher and preacher of the age, and even when, like Erasmus, he despaired of the prevailing wickedness, he would rebuke the world by the revelation of the ideal, the best state of commonwealth.

But revelation was not all. There was always the prospect of rebellion (if not revolution, in our sense of the word) as well as the hope of reform; these have always been man's proposed roads to freedom. I have spoken earlier of utopia's secret injunction, its implicit exhortation for change and renovation. Even in the ancient world—with those limiting Hellenic notions of time and cyclical human destiny which, as some thinkers insist, precluded progressive political purpose—there was "action dreaming."[25] According to an ancient chronicler, the third-century Hellenistic utopia of Iambulus was set in a group of islands in the Indian Ocean and was called a "Sun State." And according to the historian Tarn, the "Sun State" of Iambulus was the inspiration of an attempted revolution at Pergamum, led by Aristonicus and his "Heliopolitans" (among whom were slaves whom he had pledged to liberate).[26] In More's own time, Montaigne makes the following remark in one of his utopian discourses:

> They have a way in their language of speaking of men as if they were halves of one another—they had noticed among us some men gorged to the full with things of every sort while their other halves were beggars at their doors, emaciated with hunger and poverty. They found it strange that these poverty-stricken halves should suffer such injustice, and that they did not take the others by the throat or set fire to their houses.[27]

Nor was More himself oblivious to the violent tensions between "the two halves," or what was later to be called "the two nations." In his *Utopia* we read: "Who be more desirous of new mutations and alterations, than they that be not content with the present state of their life? Or who be bolder stomached to bring all in a hurly burly (thereby trusting to get some windfall) than they that have now nothing to lose?" There has always been a new world to win; and, as a consequence, the perennial question—phrased in identical words from More to Burke to Owen to Lenin—*"What is to be done?"*[28]

For More what had to be done was for him to go into politics, and it was a fateful decision: in 1517, a year after *Utopia*'s publication, he became a member of the King's Council; in 1529 he became Lord Chancellor; and in 1535 he was beheaded on the scaffold. In the history of the intelligentsia, More's decision stands, it seems to me, at a memorable midpoint between Aristotle's call to instruct Alexander[29] and Max Weber's explanation (in *Politik als Beruf*) to the modern intellectuals of the complex nature of the public interest.[30] And, in the final additions to the manuscript of *Utopia,* written (according to Hexter) when he was still wrestling with the pros and cons of accepting Henry VIII's offer, More had already formulated the splendors and miseries of a utopian in public affairs, a philosopher among kings, a reformer in his political calling.

"Much against my will," he once confessed in a letter,[31] "did I come to Court (as everyone knows, and as the King himself in joke sometimes likes to reproach me). So far I keep my place there as precariously as an unaccustomed rider in his saddle ... " In a harsh and almost inflexible age of royal absolutism and courtly conformity, an intellectual's political commitment could in the very nature of things be only a faith without illusions. "For I must either give a different opinion from the rest there," he recognizes, "and for what good that would do I had as well give no opinion at all. Or I must give the same opinion as they, and ... help to further their madness." For, in a circle of royal councillors he knows that

there is no place to dissemble in, nor to wink in. Naughty counsels must be openly allowed and very pestilent decrees must be approved. He shall be counted worse than a spy, yea, almost as evil as a traitor, that with a faint heart doth praise evil and noisome decrees ... If he remain good and innocent, yet the wickedness and folly of others shall be imputed to him and laid on his neck. So that it is impossible with that crafty wile and subtle train to turn anything to better.

Yet turn things to better he must. Kings and princes are often "deaf hearers" to new counsels—"How can they be beaten into their heads whose minds be already prevented with clean contrary persuasions?" Yet craftily, subtly, into their heads he must. "This," he says, "is the philosophy you must use." Let me cite the whole, memorable passage:

> Whatsoever part you have taken upon you, play that as well as you
> can and make the best of it . . . . So the case standeth in a common-
> wealth, and so it is in the consultations of kings and princes. If evil
> opinions and naughty persuasions cannot be utterly and quite
> plucked out of their hearts, if you cannot even as you would remedy
> vices which use and custom hath confirmed, yet for this cause you
> must not leave or forsake the commonwealth; you must not forsake
> the ship in the tempest because you cannot rule and keep down the
> winds. No, nor you must not labour to drive into their heads new and
> strange information which you know well shall be nothing regarded
> with them that be of clean contrary minds. But you must with a crafty
> wile and a subtle train study and endeavour yourself as much as in
> you lieth to handle the matter wittily and handsomely for the pur-
> pose, and that which you cannot turn to good, so to order it that it be
> not very bad.[32]

If Milton's poetry was (in Blake's famous phrase) of the party of the
Devil, More's utopianism was in the service now of Quintus Fabius
Maximus: King Utopus had turned Fabian.

4. Columbus's New World: From Dante to More

But there is yet another ancient route to the new world of politics, and
although it may well be as long as a transatlantic voyage, our map would
be full of blank spaces if we did not mark, at least in passing, the role of
such adventurous souls as Dante and Joachim of Flora, Columbus and
Amerigo Vespucci, Quiroga and Mendieta,[33] in the formation of the
modern utopian and revolutionary spirit.

If, as I will be arguing throughout this book, the idea of utopia and
revolution is involved in a movement from astrology to astronomy, and
from theology to politics, then this transvaluation occurs against the
widest backdrop of European thought; and at this point I feel compelled
to look backward again to an earlier, medieval scene, beyond More to
the Dantesque epoch of the Holy Roman Emperors, in order to record
the emergence of a secular this-worldly drama in place of what had
always been a matter of religious and eschatological climax. How did the
passion for new social ideals supplant the traditional dedication to the
quest for paradise? When did the immemorial longing for the Garden of
Eden give way to a modern search for utopia? In what way would dream
and fantasy be combined with political action and terrestrial adventure?

"Where was Paradise?" Presumably, Emperor Frederick II (1194–1250)
knew most of the conventional answers when he put a series of intricate

questions to Michael the Scot, the Hohenstaufen court astrologer. Paradise was in the Middle East (for, after all, it derived originally from the old Persian *pairidaēza,* a park or orchard); or it was in Africa, in the land of Prester John; or perhaps in Asia, or across the seas, or on an enchanted island. If Paradise had been lost, could Paradise be regained? And what was he supposed to do about it: merely find it, or to re-create it? If he was the Messiah Emperor, was his leadership to be only backward looking? Was there no trace—in the stars, on a map, in an ambiguous prophecy—of future prospects at all? Would it be a return to the ancient Eden or, perhaps, the coming of a new and different future?[34] A historical observer may be tempted to think that the European mind was here almost on the great borderline between old nostalgia and new hope, between a golden restoration and a revolution of the new.

When Columbus crossed the ocean sea to find an *otro mundo,* an Other World, he was convinced (as he wrote in his journal) that he had rediscovered the Garden of Eden. The terrestrial paradise had been placed "where all land and islands end" at the farthest point of the far east, as Columbus had reassured himself by reading the medieval commentators on Genesis 2:8 ("The Lord God planted a garden eastward in Eden") in his copy of *Imago mundi.* It would be, he knew, "like a woman's breast, and this nipple part is the highest and closest to heaven." Now, at long last, it had been found. "This land," Columbus wrote in his journal of October 1492, "is the best and most fertile and temperate and level and good that there is in the world." According to Peter Martyr, the first historian of the *mundus novus,* it seemed to be "that golden world of which old writers speak so much, wherein men lived simply and innocently without enforcement of laws, without quarreling, judges, and libels, content only to satisfy nature ... "

Sick and troubled in the Indies, Columbus turned his thoughts to the Christian hope of rebuilding Jerusalem and Mount Zion, and the prediction of the Abbot Joachim that a redeemer would come from Spain; indeed, if he, Columbus, were to return to Spain, the holy work could begin. When he had a strangely high sea without wind, he noted that "such a thing had not been seen save in the time of the Jews." When he wrote to the Catholic monarchs, he fervently confessed that he was still "animated by a heavenly fire," and that light from the holy scripture illuminated both the Admiral of the Seas and the Catholic monarchs with "rays of marvellous brightness." When he found the fresh waters brought down by the Orinoco, he exultantly identified it as one of the four ancient rivers Adam and Eve had known, for "the roar, as of thunder," could only come from a source in Paradise.

Columbus presented himself as a millennial messenger, echoing the apocalyptic tones of Joachim of Flora (whom he had cited in his *Book of*

Prophecies written just before his last voyage to America). And, in fact, Columbus was often so seen and heard, as, for example, by Lope de Vega, in whose drama (1614) Columbus is regarded as a Christ figure whose discovery was "to begin to achieve the redemption of the whole human race," thus preparing the way for the millennium. This only dramatized Columbus's own millennial inspiration. "God made me the messenger," he wrote, "of the new heaven and the new earth, of which He spoke in the Apocalypse by St. John, after having spoke of it by the mouth of Isaiah; and He showed me the spot where to find it."[35]

Amerigo Vespucci's conception of the Eden he had discovered in the New World was less apocalyptic, more Dantesque. Like Dante a wandering Florentine exile, Vespucci quoted the cantos of *"nostro Poeta Dante"* when he crossed the seas, and when he savored the paradisaical elements of the American landscape he was reminded of scenes by Botticelli (who had illustrated the *Divine Comedy* and had indeed once painted Amerigo's own portrait).

Thus, both church fathers and Renaissance humanists played their role as guiding spirits at the birth of a new world. Such inspiration as adventurous admirals needed beyond the call of profitable service for great empires was part theological and part humanistic. Even the golden treasure[36] had its higher justification, as Columbus himself had argued, for "he who possesses it may do what he will in the world, and may so attain as to bring souls to Paradise." The pattern of interrelated associations[37] would seem to be inescapable. Columbus had thought of Joachim of Flora, whom Dante had put close to himself in one of the inner circles of souls in *Paradiso*;[38] Vespucci had thought of Dante, who had captured the ultimate vision of enchantment. And Thomas More, who had been inspired by his reading of Vespucci's *Mundus novus* (with its report of a native Indian form of ideal communism), had his Utopia discovered by "Raphael Hythlodaeus," a learned Portuguese traveler, a circumnavigator of the globe who was said to have accompanied Vespucci on three of his voyages.[39]

The outlines of our imaginative cycles are, I think, clear. Dante considered Joachim his intellectual mentor (although they had one fundamental political difference: whether the Emperor had a messianic mission or was part of the designs of the Beast); and the lines of the *Divine Comedy* which place the Calabrian abbot in Paradise were to become part of the liturgical honors for Joachim, *"il Calabrese abate Gioacchino / di spirito prophetico dotato."*[*][40] It was an unusual tribute, for although Joachim had been favored by four popes he also had been officially condemned. St.

---

*" ... and shining at my side, / Joachim the Calabrian abbot, great / in gift, through whom the spirit prophesied."

Thomas Aquinas dismissed him as a man of mere "conjectures," and for St. Bonaventura he was an ignoramus. He was hated by the Cistercian order as a runaway brother and a renegade; and he was denounced as a "converted Jew." Yet he became a source of inspiration to Renaissance prophets and Reformation rebels, and something of a cult figure among religious dissenters and peasant insurgents. He upset John Foxe, who found his work "detestable and blasphemous"; and he troubled John Donne, who, in a sermon at St. Paul's on Whitsunday in 1628, had anxieties about the influence of Joachitism, "this torrent, this inundation, this impetuousness."[41]

Joachim, we are told, had "a kaleidoscopic mind," bewildering in its richness of changing images; and we know of his bursting literary compulsiveness from Lucas, his scribe, who has recorded that "I used to write day and night in copy-books, what he dictated and corrected on scraps of paper, with two other monks who he employed in the same work."[42] It will not be easy, then, to make a beginning with Dante's shining prophet without doing violence to the obscure and enigmatic texts and the varying historical contexts of Joachite emergence and theological dispute: the Trees of History and the Tables of Concord, the end of the Anti-Christ, the coming of Gog and Magog, the conversion of the Jews, the gnosis of Last Things.[43] But perhaps, taking a cue from Joachim's own numerological obsession (especially his pattern of "three," the *tertius status*: from which "Third Reich"),[44] we can make the following points, bearing on our present purposes.

1. *The Evil.* The present state of earthly affairs is, from top to bottom, evil, sinful, and corrupt. "We shall not be what we have been," Joachim prophesied in his *Psalter of Ten Strings*, "but we shall begin to be other."[45]

2. *The Resistance.* The evil forces (as Joachim's followers came to insist) must be resisted and they shall be destroyed; and all will be subsequently converted to authentic principles.

3. *The Decline.* Things will get worse before they get better. An "abomination of Desolation" leads to the Last Tranquility, and a terrible time of tribulation will precede the *renovatio mundi*. "One thing we can say with certainty," Joachim writes in his *Exposition of the Apocalypse:* "the sixth age will be worse than the previous five ages, and the seventh age will be worse than the sixth, and both will be filled with the evil doings of the dragon of the Apocalypse."[46]

4. *The Faithful.* A small band of the faithful, the best of a new salvational generation, will serve as the heart of the resistance and the nucleus of an austere renewal, a *reformacio*, and the harbinger of a new communal era of universal love. "They shall increase," Joachim continues in his *Exposition*, and "their fame shall be spread abroad; they

shall preach the faith and defend it until the consummation of the world . . . . They shall be an order of hermits living like angels, whose life shall be as a burning fire."[47]

5. *The Doctrine.* There is a true and everlasting general doctrine that can guide the remnant on the unique mission, the *evangelium aeternum*, an "eternal gospel." (Certain extreme doctrinal elements were officially condemned in 1215, and a leading scholar on Joachimist ideas has written: "Joachim's philosophy of history, it was now realized, constituted an incitement to subversive thought and action that was dangerously infectious. It is always beliefs which provide a basis for action that must be watched.")[48]

6. *The Transition.* The present age is only one of transition, a dramatic mid-passage, an untenable interim, a provisional moment in time. (Commenting on "the expectation of the Kingdom of God on earth after the terror of the end," one authority has noted: "And wherever Joachist ideas led to communist-chiliastic movements, like the Taborites in Bohemia or the Anabaptists or Thomas Münzer in the Peasant Revolt, their pamphlets are filled with quotations and reflections on the Apocalypse." And another has observed: "A Joachimist view of history produced a mood somewhat akin to that of an early Marxist, a mood of certainty and urgency. The Spiritual Franciscan knew he was right because he had the clue to history; he could expect the imminent crisis confidently, since history was on his side.")[49]

7. *The End.* A final messianic stage is about to begin, wherein an end is put to the old eras of persecution, the ultimate drama of salvation commences, and perfect freedom is inaugurated. "Life should be changed because the state of the world will be changed" (*Concordia*). "To each will be given in such manner that he will rejoice less on his own account than because his neighbour has received something. He will count a thing less as his own as given to others through him" (*Expositio*).[50]

8. *The Promise.* The future will surpass the known past in a glorious consummation, a crescendo of illumination, the true apotheosis of history. "Clear the eyes of the mind from all dusts of earth," Joachim called out in his *Concordia*, "leave the tumults of crowds and the clamour of words; follow the angel in spirit into the desert; ascend with the same angel into the great and high mountain; there you will behold high truths hidden from the beginning of time and from all generations . . . . For we, called in these latest times to follow the spirit rather than the letter, ought to obey, going from illumination to illumination, from the first heaven to the second, and from the second to the third, from the place of darkness into the light of the moon, that at last we may come out of the moonlight into the glory of the full Sun."[51]

Dante, in his Tenth Epistle (to Can Grande), sketched the basic movement of the *Divine Comedy*: "at the beginning it was horrible and fetid, for it is Hell; and at the end it is prosperous, desirable and gracious, for it is Paradise." Comparing More's work with Dante's, a recent scholarly editor of *Utopia* has observed: "The Hell in More's masterpiece is Western Christendom; the paradise is utopia. Dante ends in Paradise. More returns the reader to hell upon earth."[52] But how long would any true utopia-minded reader, properly instructed in the grand vision, consent to remain there? Nor was there any reason, if he knew the political Dante Alighieri—the refugee, the uncompromising exile, the embittered pamphleteer (and the Pope ordered the heretical *De monarchia* burned in the Bologna marketplace)—to accept an other-worldly paradise as the only alternative for man in suffering Christendom.

For Dante himself had offered a practical down-to-earth route to utopia, that is, to a universal order of peace and freedom, "when the land would be gay with the spring green ... " He promised an end to "the darkness of our prolonged calamity" and offered indeed the prospect of a tomorrow with milk and honey (*"lacte ac melle manatem*, Deut. 6:3"). He explained that he was devoted to "the well-being of the world," and that nothing would so serve his love of truth as to "contribute to the common good" and to "work for the benefit of future generations." Man could live a life of happiness and justice in this world, for he was endowed with a free will, a precious ability to choose, an immutable liberty to pronounce on good and evil. "And the human race is at its best when most free [*Et humanum genus, potissime liberum, optime se habet*]."

If this was of an almost unprecedented intellectual audacity—and Dante confessed that he was driven to "demonstrate truths that no one else has considered"—it was not intended to be idle speculation or a mere imaginative escape for oppressed spirits. These were matters which called for a unity of theory and practice: "not only can we speculate about them, but also we can do something about them ... " He repeats the point: "speculation is for the sake of action, because the aim in such matters is action." And then underscores it again:

> Since the present subject is political—indeed, the source and principle of all just governments—and anything political lies within our power, it is obvious that the matter in hand is not primarily directed towards speculation but towards action. Again, since in practical affairs the ultimate end is the principle and cause of all that is done ... it follows that the formulation of means is derived from the end in view.[53]

Here, then, was a manifesto on behalf of a grand world-political conception, a universal civil order of mankind (*universalis civilitas humani generis*), and its cosmopolitanism has been called "really the first known expression of the modern idea of Humanity."[54] It also expressed a whole range of radical rhetorical strategies which, as we shall see, would accompany all subsequent ideological efforts to prepare the way for global change:

1. Root and Branch. Dante warned that what he had in mind was no superficial alteration, but an operation that was basic, deep, fundamental.

> For to kill a tree the mere lopping of branches does not serve; they form new branches with redoubled virulence so long as the roots remain undamaged to supply them with sap ... until the cause of this exuberance is rooted out. When the root of this monstrous perversion is extracted, the prickly branches will wither with the trunk.

2. Storm and Shipwreck. He offered some slim hope that the violent uprooting which appeared so necessary and inevitable could still be stayed:

> O humanity, in how many storms must you be tossed, how many shipwrecks must you endure, so long as you turn yourself into a many-headed beast lusting after a multiplicity of things! You are ailing in both your intellectual powers, as well as in heart.

3. Imminent Doom. But he did not disguise the catastrophe that was looming (as in his letter to Florence from "a Florentine in undeserved exile"):

> To your sorrow you will see your palaces, which you have not raised with prudence to meet your needs but have thoughtlessly enlarged for your pleasures, fallen ... fallen under the battering-ram or consumed by fire. You will see your populace, now a raging mob, disorganized and divided against itself, part for, part against you, soon united against you in howls of fury, since a starving mob can know no fear. You will see with remorse your churches, now thronged every day by crowds of your ladies, pillaged, and your children doomed to pay for their fathers' sins in bewilderment and ignorance. And if my prophetic soul is not deceived in delivering a message brought home to me by unmistakeable omens as well as by incontrovertible arguments, your small remnant, when the greater part has perished by slaughter or been taken prisoner, will witness with tears, before it passes into exile, the final delivery of your city, worn out with prolonged grief, into the hands of strangers.

4. Immanent Order. What a far cry was this prophetic fury from the impersonal transitive coolness of a remark which Dante had borrowed from Aristotle: "Things resent being badly ordered."[55]

How, then, were "things" to be rightly ordered?

As he had said, "the formulation of means is derived from the end in view." And the proper means were in the hands of the messianic Emperor, Henry VII, a successor to the Hohenstaufens, crowned in Aix-la-Chapelle in 1309, the divine Henry (*divi Henrici faustissimi* ...) on his splendid way to establish peace, justice, and happiness, Dante's longed-for world liberator. This was the historic moment: "Awake therefore, all of you, and rise."[56]

Dante's theory of the rising was contained in his *De monarchia*, and it is clearly a direct political confrontation with the *Unam sanctam*, Pope Boniface's classic statement in 1302 of the supremacy of the spiritual over the temporal power. No medieval mind would have ventured to argue the converse, or to suggest that a sound temporal authority representing the *humana civilitas* had within itself a legitimating spirituality. Dante, a loyal son of a true *ecclesia*, split the difference by rendering unto the Pope that which was his, namely, the other-worldly paradise, and rendering unto the this-worldly liberation that which was its own empire of political responsibility, namely, an earthly paradise. Dante's manifesto against the Papacy and on behalf of the Emperor is, in this embryonic sense, the prelude to modern utopian revolution. The startling imagery with which he thought it proper and persuasive to clothe his audacious breakthrough—the notion of "the two suns"—has been called "a blatant astronomical absurdity"; but mixed metaphors have always given revolutionary language that extra dimension of wild, unexpected strength it needed to move beyond the existing circles of power.

It is, then, a theory of dual power: and the dualism embraced two suns, two goals, two kinds of happiness, two forms of paradise. Man is set

> to attain two goals: the first is happiness in this life, which consists in the exercise of his own powers and is typified by the earthly paradise; the second is the happiness of eternal life, which consists in the enjoyment of the divine countenance (which man cannot attain to of his own power but only by the aid of divine illumination) and is typified by the heavenly paradise. These two sorts of happiness are attained by diverse means, just as one reaches different conclusions by different means.[57]

Nor did Dante hesitate, having gone this far, to indicate how the means were to be related with the ends, thus uniting (as he had promised) social theory and political practice.

> This explains why two guides have been appointed for man to lead him to his twofold goal: there is the Supreme Pontiff who is to lead mankind to eternal life in accordance with revelation; and there is the

Emperor who, in accordance with philosophical teaching, is to lead
mankind to temporal happiness.[58]

"The world," Dante once avowed in a burst of Florentine cosmopolitanism, "is our native country."[59] If, then, this was to be a world
revolution (with one sun outcircling the other), it was inevitably to be a
revolution from above, from on high. There would, in times to come, be
enough opportunities to find guides to a path from below.

My essential point here is that new paths to paradise were opening
up. Dante had shown one, an empire of earthly peace and justice; Columbus and Amerigo Vespucci had shown another, green lands of exotic
hope and good fortune; and More had shown yet another, a secular
society with virtuous human arrangements. Still other pathfinders were
to come, dreamers and visionaries, explorers and adventurers,
humanists and prophets, all seeking a new way of life for man in the
here and now. Utopia was an other world, a new world, a distant but
now discovered reality, truly out there beyond the seas. Utopia was an
"America," possibly an Eden (and so it was to remain, even to Scott
Fitzgerald's "fresh green breast of the new world [that] had once pan-
dered in whispers to the last and greatest of all human dreams ... the
orgiastic future").[60]

Not a few learned men of More's own time received his tale as if it
were "a true storie"; and many were prepared to make the great ocean
voyage to the Utopians, to learn from them and perhaps to convert
them. Indeed, when one Spanish judge (Quiroga),[61] aglow in the spirit
of the European Renaissance, arrived in New Spain in the 1530s, he
outlined in the manner of More's *Utopia* a new system of government for
the Indians which was seriously considered by the Council of the Indies.
"For not in vain," Quiroga wrote, "but with much cause and reason is
this called the New World, not because it was newly found, but because
it is in its people and in almost everything as was the first and golden
age ... " It was, after all, a piece of daring for Waldseemüller to have
called it on his maps "a new world," for general opinion held it to be a
traditional part of the old and known world. It was almost rash for
Columbus to have claimed that the lands he was exploring belonged to a
region "of which the world has never had any knowledge." Now the
implication was that man could establish a new and golden age. This
was a drastic notion which went beyond the orthodox quest for a lost
Eden or the sentimental nostalgia for enchanted islands. The where-
abouts of Quiroga's original manuscript, outlining his Indian utopia, is
still unknown; but we do know that this assiduous student of More
(whom he called "an illustrious and ingenious man, more than human")

drafted laws and ordinances as the secular Bishop of Michoacan which aimed at both economic well-being and a rational political system, that he continued to argue against overwhelming opposition for their systematic and practical execution, and insisted that he would "not yield at any point ... "[62]

And when, in the same generation, a Spanish missionary (Mendieta), guardian of Franciscan monasteries among the Aztecs, returned to Madrid, inflamed with the mystical hope of establishing a perfect Indian commonwealth, pious, happy, unique, he was full of jeremiads to the royal court. He was as "unyielding" as Quiroga: if the cruelties and oppressions of a rapacious empire did not cease all would go under in a well-deserved apocalyptic ruin.[63] Half-begging and half-warning that "it is still not too late" (1587) for a messianic monarch to intervene and save the promise of the New World, Mendieta pleaded for an end to the rule of Mammon and for the Joachimite fulfillment of Spain's destiny to build a new Jerusalem wherein men would live "virtuously and peacefully, as in a terrestrial paradise," free from want, violence, and injustice.[64]

In this movement from paradise to utopia, from terrestrial adventure to political commitment, from old fantasies to new dreams, "Raphael Hythlodaeus" would take his own place in the inner circle of Europe's guiding spirits. Raphael, from the biblical texts, was a salvation-bringer; and Hythlodaye, according to a Greek-Latin lexicon of 1512, signified a *glühender Phantast*, an "ardent visionary."[65] How long would it be before utopians—"like those that under hot ardent zeal would set whole realms on fire"[66]—would come to make revolutions?

They would not be the same breed of men who had come to make a Renaissance; and here, in passing, it is revealing to note the role of classical Greco-Roman intellectual sources in producing a certain quality of "ancient coolness" over many modern centuries of political debate. If one takes Renaissance thought in its final Florentine flights of ideology and rhetoric, one is struck by an unusual incombustibility, by a temperate present-mindedness. There are here no politics of paradise, for politics are not promises but present performance. The future is no obsessive problem, for libertarian ideals are for each generation to create, fashion, and defend with honor. Dante's Caesarean dream is rudely—by most representative critics of the Trecento (Bruni, Salutati, et al.)—rejected. Neither Guelph nor Ghibelline visions catch fire. There has been here, as Professor Hans Baron has documented,[67] a remarkable secularization of sentiment, and no religious passion or theological precept intrudes on the new humanist civic ideals, at least for this extraordinary Quattrocento generation of Florentines.

5. Practical Reformers or Rebels in a Hurry

It is not without some symbolic importance that in this first classical
century of utopian longing, the English utopian should fear "hurly-
burly" and opt for handling matters "wittily and handsomely for the
purpose," the French utopian should hint at the coming rebellion of the
just in anger and violence, the Spanish utopian should have his text
misplaced in a disorderly Iberian archive, and the Italian utopian should
languish pathetically in a foreign prison, vaguely and vainly hoping for a
conspiracy, a cardinal's hat, or the miracle of a Universal Republic.
These patterns were to persist: we were never again to be without our
protagonists of utopian reform, utopian rebellion, utopian quixoticism,
and utopian flamboyance. But I hold it essential to emphasize that at the
very birth of our modern utopian tradition, it was associated with a very
English sense of the gradual and the practical.[68] Even the most uncompromising enemies of the concept and spirit of utopia can be seen, in
England today, to proceed, paradoxically enough, from this very same
Fabian tradition, this *Urquelle* of patient empiricism.

Thus, Sir Karl Popper insists that the idea of utopia is dangerous,
pernicious, and self-defeating—"if only," he says, "we could give up
dreaming about distant ideals and fighting over our utopian blue-prints
for a new world and a new man ... "[69] Reacting with a violence to the
idea of utopia that would have perplexed Thomas More (who surely
would have shared his belief that "we cannot make heaven on earth"),
Popper goes on to state, with verbal echoes from *Utopia* which are as
unwitting as they are unmistakable: "What I believe we can do instead is
to make life a little less terrible and a little less unjust in each generation." The utopianist, Popper feels, "must win over, or else crush, his
utopianist competitors who do nor share his utopian aims, those who do
not profess his own Utopianist religion." More would indeed have been
puzzled. If tolerance is a human virtue, cannot—must not—the utopian
vision incorporate it? Why should the prize of tolerance, achieved
slowly, painfully, fitfully in history, not be vouchsafed for competing
political religions? King Utopus, More tells us, "was certain in thinking
it both insolence and folly to demand by violence and threats that all
should think to be true what you believe to be true ... " The utopianist,
Popper contends, inspired and impassioned by the prophecies of distant
ideals, must be "opposed to the attitude of reasonableness."[70] More
would have found it passing strange that the humane attempt to work
out an arrangement of reasonable institutions for men in society should
ever be accounted unreasonable. It is an old question in the history of
the European political debate, and there are many old answers. In his

essay on the "Idea of a Perfect Commonwealth" (1742), David Hume attempted to reconcile the utopian and the empirical traditions:

> As one form of government must be allowed more perfect than another, independent of the manners and humours of particular men, why may we not enquire what is the most perfect of all, though the common botched and inaccurate governments seem to serve the purposes of society, and though it be not so easy to establish a new system of government as to build a vessel upon a new construction? The subject is surely the most worthy curiosity of any the wit of man can possibly devise. And who knows, if this controversy were fixed by the universal consent of the wise and the learned, but, in some future age, an opportunity might be afforded of reducing the theory to practice, either by a dissolution of some old government, or by the combination of men to form a new one, in some distant part of the world? In all cases, it must be advantageous to know what is most perfect in the kind, that we may be able to bring any real constitution or form of government as near it as possible, by such gentle alterations and innovations as may not give too great disturbance to society.[71]

Popper's difficulty—and the dilemma of all wise and fearful philosophers—is that he wishes to hold fast to attractive and humanizing social ideals, to those "important and far-reaching political reforms" which would combat human misery, and at the same time he prefers to remain unemotionally aloof from utopian clarity about ultimate aims and the kind of commonwealth we should consider best. More's difficulty—the dilemma of all noble and cautious visionaries—is in the tragic tension between the utopian's clear-eyed perception of the good and the reformer's heavy-hearted burden of practical compromise and recurring defeat.[72] More often shrank even from the dangers of publication. "Now, as I think the matter over," he wrote in 1520, "I see that it would be safer if you would wait a while, at least until I revise . . . . In my remarks upon peace and war, upon morality, marriage, the clergy, the people, etc., perhaps what I have written has not always been so cautious and guarded that it would be wise to expose it to captious critics."[73]

History, alas, is no great respecter of the dilemmas of sensitive spirits. More's Utopia, once it made its mark on intellectual affairs, took on an independent and erratic life of its own. In the mind of the man of letters, the utopian longing was an imaginative achievement, and hence loose, untidy, contradictory, liberal. Liberty could live in the interstices of a deeply imagined social order, in its aesthetic complexity, its verbal openness. But in the desperate soul of religious impatience, or the impassioned heart of political demand, there was neither time nor space for any ambivalence. Fundamentalism allows for no inessentials. An abstracted theoretical idealism is of a more rigorous web. And it is at this point, where patience runs out, that the idea of revolution arrives. It is the point at which the sense of the perfect combines with the mood of the immoderate.

If utopia is by its very nature compounded of revulsion from present reality and attraction for a better world, how much of that horror and hope could a saintly court reformer effectively express? How much closer could the Lord Chancellor actually bring us to the place of true felicity? What successes could he show for all his craft and subtlety? If words were not enough to change the world, even for Christian humanists who believed in the Word, the wit and wile of the Fabian would scarcely suffice for utopians in a hurry, intolerant of the vaunted complications of this imperfect life. We are faced by a rising tide of main force.

> To ruine the great Work of time,
> And cast the Kingdome old
> Into another mould.*

The revulsion from reality is fed by the slowness of pace; the powerlessness of well-meaning innovators fires the general impatience. In mounting political excitement, ideas grow more abstract and absolute.[74] The utopian longing for a republic of virtue or for the "new earth, wherein dwelleth righteousness," becomes irresistible, as an apocalyptic ecstasy seizes the hearts and minds of men. Thus does revolution displace reform on the historical agenda. In 1641, John Milton, searching as he was for "high strains in new and lofty Measures to sing and celebrate," proclaimed "a good time, our time of Parliament, the very jubily and resurrection of the State ... and all creatures sigh to be renewed."[75]

"We have it in our power to begin the world over again," Thomas Paine announced in 1776:[76] "The birthday of a new world is at hand." "We have reached the heart of time," is the cry before the Bastille in 1789, "the tyrants are ready to fall."[77]

In this "heart of time," the utopian opportunity had come: at least for the revolutionary who had cultivated (in Camus's phrase) "the taste for the apocalypse and a life of frenzy." For Robespierre, living frenziedly in the midst of one, the revolution was the means to a blessed end; it would at long last bring to mankind those reasonable and felicitous institutions which were its due. For Karl Marx, living rather in apocalyp-

---

*Andrew Marvell, "An Horation Ode upon Cromwell's Return from Ireland" (1650).

tic hope, the longed-for means was the end; the revolution was itself utopia.[78]

The point was put in another, yet essentially related, way when Schiller made his subtle effort to comprehend the psychology of an absolute enthusiasm, and its hidden complexities of an "eagerness" and an "impetuosity" which presses for rapid and definitive results. "The unhappiness of his generation," Schiller writes (and it may, in part, be taken as a confession of his own political romanticism), "speaks urgently to the sensitive man, its degradation still more urgently. Enthusiasm is kindled, and glowing desire strives in vigorous souls impatiently for action." And yet, in the final analysis,

> The pure moral impulse is directed towards the Absolute. Time does not exist for it, and the Future is its present.... In the eyes of a Reason which knows no limits, the Direction is at once the Destination, and the Way is completed from the moment it is trodden.[79]

Translated into the vocabulary of a Marxian generation, this would suggest that the bourgeois democrat, unscientific and hence irrelevant, could dream on; the proletarian socialist need not concern himself with devising programs for the future, for (as Marx wrote) it "is not a matter of bringing some utopian system or other into being but of consciously participating in the historical revolutionary process of society which is taking place before our very eyes ... " The future is the present; and the present contains an absolute which transcends the normal requirements of time.

A final observation about the twin enthusiasts—both full of ardor and audacity, and equally impatient in their sense of outrage—with whom we will be dealing throughout in the analysis of the utopian and revolutionary impulse. We can discern here the same dualism that previously bifurcated our image of the reformer—now we have both the utopian revolutionary and the anti-utopian revolutionary. For the one (in the words of Saint-Just), "our purpose is to set up an honest government, so that the people may be happy ... " And may we (Robespierre added) "whilst we seal our work with our blood, see at least the first rays of the dawn of universal felicity. That is our ambition: that is our aim ... " For the other (in Marx's famous and fateful phrase), the revolution "has no ideals to realize, it has only to set free ... " It wants no part of utopian fantasy. "That which was an inner light," Marx writes, "becomes a consuming flame, turned outward."[80] For the anti-utopian, holding fast to it "in permanence," the revolution was the apocalypse.

In that ancient utopia of Iambulus (to which I referred earlier), there is a description of the "happy island" and of the blessed inhabitants of the Sun State: "They were good-looking and had a good carriage; they had wide open ears and exceptionally quick hearing; their tongues were double, down to the root, which enabled them to imitate every human language and the notes of all birds—and even to carry on two conversations at once ... " In a sense, all the utopians have been double-tongued and have, in what Michael Oakeshott has called the conversation of mankind, spoken to us in two voices. One, the voice of the enchanter; the other, the prophet. One induces to dreams, the other to action. One is Athenian, in the abstract contemplation of the good; the other is Hebraic, in the translation of ideal values into reality. I conclude with their meeting point in the Judeo-Greek tradition, in the words of Philo Judaeus of Alexandria which have been the true points of departure for all I have been saying:

> I will venture frankly to say that the statesman is beyond any doubt an interpreter of dreams ... a man accustomed to estimate at its true worth the common, universal great dream which is dreamed not only by the sleeping, but also by the waking. This waking dream, to speak truly, is human life itself .... Inasmuch as life is laden with all confusion and chaos and obscurity, the statesman must come forward and like some wise interpreter of dreams he must sit in judgment on the day-dreams and fantasies of his fellows who think that they are awake—using likely conjectures and reasonable persuasions, on such occasions, to show them that this is beautiful and that the reverse; this good and that bad; this just and that unjust. And so, too, with other qualities: he will try to show what is prudent, what courageous, what pious, what sacred, what beneficial, what profitable; and again what is unprofitable, what unreasonable, what ignoble, what impious, what profane, what disadvantageous, what injurious and what selfish. And besides these he will also teach other lessons .... Be prepared for change. You have often stumbled: hope now for a better time. For with men things turn to their opposite.[81]

2

Morbleu, let us revolutionize! It is the
only good thing, the only reality in life.

—P. J. Proudhon (1848)

A research firm in Cambridge, Massachusetts,
has been given a contract to see if computers and
techniques of systems analysis can be used to predict
revolutions.
    It is part of the American Army's "Project Camelot,"[1]
a study of revolution, insurgency, and counter-insurgency.
    Dr. Clark Abt, president of the company, said:
"A computer can, in a few minutes, consider, evaluate,
compare and relate unlimited numbers of facts, a task
that would require years of effort by historians and
political scientists."

—*Daily Telegraph* (London), 8 May 1865

Knowledg, why didst thou come, to wound, and not to cure . . .
O power where art thou, that must mend things amiss?

—Gerrard Winstanley (1652)

The Revolutionary
Commitment

1. **The Salvation of Society**
   Toward a Golden Future—Revolution without Revolutionaries?—
   Condorcet's "Unbreakable Chain": Truth, Happiness, and Virtue—
   Tocqueville's "Hitherto Unknown Breed"—Marx as a Connoisseur of
   the Apocalypse—The Esotericism of Ultimate Aims—Buonarroti,
   Babeuf, Bronterre—Clarity about Ends and Means—The Apocalyptists Reject the Prophets—Nietzsche's Ambiguous Nostalgia—Where
   are "the Astronomers of the Ideal"?—Bonapartist Touches in the Rage
   against Utopians—Proudhon's Dark Future—Exchanging the Visionary Dream for the Secret Millennium

2. **The Secret Millennium**
   The Retreat from Horizons—Marx's Alternative: "a Distant Land" or
   "on the Streets"—"In the Midst of Darkness"—Buber and the Magic
   Wand of Politics—"Salvation behind Society's Back"—A Mystical Pattern: Direct Access to Devout Abstractions—Secular Reasonableness
   and Theological Absolutes—Political Gynecology: Hours of Begetting
   and Hours of Birth—A Day in the Life of Utopia—Marx or Plato: the
   Amateurization of Society—Lenin and Destroying the Old: "a Heap of
   Ruins"—The Syndicate State—Proudhon's Protest

3. **Temptations of Good and Evil**
   Byron's "Overwhelming Eloquence," Novalis's "Absolute Urge,"
   Marx's "Russian Extremism"—The Revolutionification of Utopia—
   Tree of Evil, Tree of Knowledge—Hegel's "Depravity in Revolt against

Depravity"—Thomas Mann's Naphta—Georg Lukacs and "a Dialectical Theory of Wickedness"—Brecht on Changing the World—Bonaparte's "Vilest Dunghills, Noblest Plants"—Kierkegaard on Interpretation—The Confusion of Motives and Meanings

4. Magico-Religious Paraphernalia
Political Questions and Theological Answers—Eliade's Sacred Forms
and Secular Types—Ideology and Pseudo-Religion—The Relevance of
Apocalyptic—Links in the Great Chain of Human Hope—Triumphant
Enthusiasm—Messianic Complexes—Ideological Plagiarism—Lassalle
between Hebrew Confidence and Hegelian Certainty—Heine and
Engels on "the Modern Saviour"—The Proletariat as the Rock of the
Church—Revolutionary Religiosity—The Christological Pattern—Dr.
Fromm's Syncretism—Engels on Christians and Communists

5. The Fall
Tragedy, Failure, Betrayal—Biographical Explanations—The Lure of
Mixed Metaphors—The Revolution as Dynamite—The Best and the
Worst—Consequences of a Radical Disorder—The Elements of Malaise
—Sex, Neurosis, and Personality Conflicts

6. The Vow
The True Revolutionary Commitment: Paradise at a Stroke—The
Miracles of the Means and the Miracle of the Ends—Reformatio Sigismundi (1438) and the Rhine Revolutionary—The Tragedy of the
Desperado—Tocqueville's Paradox (1856)—The Unnecessary Ex-
plosion—Three Engagements: England, France, Russia—Morley on
the Weakness of Doctrinaire Meliorism—Marx's Prophecy (1879)—
The Reformer in the Eyes of the Militant—The Revolutionary in the
Eyes of the Moderate—Burke's Radicalism—Gentz on "the Deadly Passion"—The Mill-Bentham Strategy of Energy and Pressure—Engels
and Tocqueville—Superiors and Inferiors—Anglo-French Contrasts—
Burke on "Splendid and Perilous Extremes"—The Point Between

1. The Salvation of Society

Although we have spoken of a sixteenth-century breakthrough to reform and an eighteenth-century breakthrough to revolution, we are re-

minded by the historian who has studied "the pursuit of the millennium" that the original context for some, if not all, of these elements was set even earlier, in the fourteenth century. "When did people cease to think of a society without distinctions of status or wealth simply as a Golden Age irrecoverably lost in the distant past, and begin to think of it instead as preordained for the immediate future?" Norman Cohn's reply is: "So far as can be judged from the available sources, this new social myth came into being in the turbulent years around 1380." He is thinking of John Ball, the insurrectionary violence of the English Peasants' Revolt of 1381, and the whole naïve revolutionary eschatology of the later Middle Ages. Another historian, who has studied revolutionary organizations in sixteenth-century France and the Netherlands, has asked a related question: whether the origins of both Jacobin and later utopian-revolutionary parties could not be found among the Huguenots and the Holy League of France, the Water Beggars and Calvinists of Holland, and (to a lesser degree) among Knox's Brethren and the Lords of the Congregation of Scotland.

"You know, sir," an English agent reported in 1559, "how difficult it is to persuade a multitude to revolt of established authority." Yet the perceptive Venetian ambassador, reporting from Paris in 1569 about the widespread and efficient Huguenot organization of cadres, could write: "Thus, they could, in one day, at one definite hour, and with all secrecy start a rising in every part of the kingdom and unleash a cruel and perilous war." These various revolutionary parties were highly organized minorities which, in places, amounted to states-within-a-state; their dedicated members infiltrated public offices; their officers were in a position skillfully to take over parts of the governmental machinery (impose taxes, mint coins, etc.); and their ruthless leaders had "learned the political value of terror and mob violence."[2]

Only one detail is missing from this picture: the genuine revolutionary. These "revolutionary parties" were mostly conservative forces of religious dissent and political disaffection, led usually by aristocratic rebels, with no essential program for either the subversion or reorganization of the traditional social order. Our historian concedes the point: "It was the paradox," he writes, "of the revolutionary movements of the sixteenth century that they were led by men who were not revolutionaries."

Yet, as we have seen, the dynamism of radical social fantasy was being accelerated in several ways. The utopians contributed a vivifying clarity to the picture of the Golden Age, and the militant reformers offered new hope for practical, this-worldly change. But, with the coming of the first modern generation of utopian revolutionaries, we are faced, in Tocqueville's phrase, with "a hitherto unknown breed . . . the

first of a new race of men." Condorcet had insisted that "'revolu-
tionnaire' ne s'applique qu'aux révolutions qui ont le liberté pour ob-
jet ... " and that in "la chaine éternelle des destinées humaines" truth,
happiness, and virtue were linked in an "unbreakable chain." The
dream of liberty, then, could be transformed for the first time into a
systematic program of action which was no longer involved in amend-
ments and corrections to an existing order in the tentative spirit of a
distant model, but would, today or tomorrow at dawn, destroy all and
build anew. This was, Tocqueville claimed (and with some exaggeration,
but with no pride at all), a peculiarly French achievement. "If," he
speculated, "the French, like the English, had succeeded in gradually
modifying the spirit of their ancient institutions without destroying
them, perhaps they would not have been so prompt to clamour for a
new order."[3]

Revolutionary man tends either to be a connoisseur of the apocalypse
or a visionary of the terrestrial paradise. Mere prophetic dreamers like
Saint-Simon, Fourier, Robert Owen, were cursorily dismissed by Karl
Marx: "Those new social systems were from the outset doomed to be
utopias; the more their details were elaborated, the more they necessarily receded into pure fantasy .... "

That "necessarily" was a characteristic touch: pretending to a certainty
when the question was clearly problematical. For Marx was, at times,
not at all certain of the necessary identity of detail and doom. As a
matter of fact, the differences between the first and final draft of his *Civil
War in France* (1871) exhibit a most dramatic resolution of the ambivalence of his thought on the relationship between utopia and revolution.
The two relevant passages need to be looked at closely.[4]

In the original version—and the crossed-through pages were only
found among his papers after his death—Marx had been tempted to say
that the new revolution was essentially the practical means with which
to realize the old utopian ends. The men of the utopian sects—Fourier's
phalanstère, Cabet's *Icarie*—were magnificent but irrelevant. The ripe historic moment had not yet come.

> They attempted to compensate for the missing historical precondi-
> tions of the movement with fantastic pictures and plans of a new
> society in the propaganda for which they saw the true means of salva-
> tion. From that moment on, when the working-class movement be-
> came a reality, the fantastic utopias disappeared: not because the
> working class abandoned the objective for which these utopians had
> reached, but because the true means had been found for its realiza-
> tion, and in place of fantastic utopias there now was a true insight into
> the movement's historical conditions and an increasing accumulation
> of the forces for a fighting organization of the working class. Still, both

the ultimate aims [*Endziele*] of the movement had been announced by the utopians (*i.e.*, the end of the system of wage-labour and class domination) are also the ultimate aims of the Paris Revolution and, of the International. Only the means are different . . .

This friendly, fraternal concession to the noble dreamers—and, more important, this recognition of the historic interdependence of political means and imaginative ends—disappears completely in the final and published text. This is the passage now as it moves from the world of prophecy to the mood of apocalyptic:

> The working class did not expect miracles from the Commune. They have no ready-made utopias to introduce *par décret du peuple*. They know that in order to work out their own emancipation, and along with it that higher form to which present society is irresistibly tending by its own economical agencies, they will have to pass through long struggles, through a series of historic processes, transforming circumstances and men. They have no ideals to realize but to set free the elements of the new society with which old collapsing bourgeois society itself is pregnant.

Marx held fast as best he could to this esotericism of ultimate aims. Few spokesmen for a new heaven and a new earth ever kept themselves so systematically free from images of paradise and utopia. Was it that public ideals make for passive spirits? He seemed to be certain of it: "The doctrinaire and necessarily fantastic anticipations of the program of action for a revolution of the future only divert us from the struggle of the present." But was not the anticipatory fantasy throughout history the motor force for heroes and martyrs? He doubted it. True, "the dream that the end of the world was at hand inspired the early Christians in their struggle with the Roman Empire and gave them confidence in victory." But today the source of inspiration and confidence lay elsewhere, and were fecund enough to yield what Marx considered "a sufficient guarantee."

> Scientific insight into the inevitable disintegration of the dominant order of society continually proceeding before our eyes, and the ever-growing passion into which the masses are scourged by the old ghosts of government—while at the same time the positive development of the means of production advances with gigantic strides—all this is a sufficient guarantee that with the moment of the outbreak of a real proletarian revolution there will also be given the conditions (though these are certain not to be idyllic) of its next immediate *modus operandi*. [5]

It was not only the formal utopians with whom Marx was breaking. That, for all its emotional (and logical) difficulties, was less problematical

than his secession from a cumulative radical tradition which for two
centuries, from the Levellers to the Mountain, had been identifying itself
more and more with a detailed sense of pragmatic openness. Men, in the
struggle for the new, would no longer necessarily be condemned to
struggle blindly. They could rise to new heights in the full awareness of
the things they would be prepared to die for; they need never again be
sacrificial martyrs for a vague and ambiguous cause which inevitably
would make for deceptions and betrayals.

Thus, when Buonarroti recorded the history of Babeuf's Conspiracy
for Equality and the post-Jacobin plans for "a new revolution" which
would finally institute the true "regeneration of man," he emphasized
this essential, indispensable clarity about both ends and means.

> It was the wish of all that each member might not only be convinced of
> the justice of the enterprise, but that he should also have formed a
> clear and complete idea of the political system he would substitute for
> the one whose annihilation was contemplated [une idéa complète de
> l'ordre politique qu'il convenait de substituer à celui dont on
> méditait l'anéantissement]. They sincerely desired the happiness of
> the people; and with this impression, they felt that it was contrary to
> the people's true interests to rashly expose it to convulsions, the only
> result of which might be to build up a new tyranny on the ruins of the
> existing one, to create new privileges, and to favour new ambitions.
> The Committee was, at first, a sort of political Lyceum, or school, in
> which, after unraveling the causes of the calamities that afflict na-
> tions, they at length arrived at the knowledge of determining with
> precision the principles of social order the best calculated, in their
> belief, to deliver mankind from them, as well as to prevent their re-
> currence. [Le comité fut d'abord un lycée politique, ou, après avoir
> démêlé les causes des maux qui affligent les nations, on parvint à
> poser avec précision les principes d'ordre social que l'on crut les plus
> propres à les en délivrer et à en empêcher le retour.]

And when Bronterre O'Brien, the great Irish Chartist leader, translated
Buonarroti's *Conspiration pur l'égalité dite de Babeuf*, he added to the text
an even more emphatic warning as a footnote to this passage: "A
stronger proof could not be offered of their integrity and good intentions. Men that would merely *knock down*, without having clear and just
ideas of the edifice they would substitute, are not Reformers, but mere
speculators in anarchy. They are either robbers or the tools of robbers."[6]

But what Bronterre O'Brien viewed as robbery Marx saw as a historic
deed of expropriation. Had the Chartists known any Hegel, they would
have understood that the clear and just ideas of the future needed no
personal, subjective embodiments in the minds and fantasies of men;
they were incorporated in the very logic of events and immanence of

history. Knocking down was the prelude to setting free: this was the dialectic of liberation. The precision was not in the principles of reconstruction but in the sociological inevitabilities of the revolutionary movement. The distinction was not between speculation in anarchy and a reformed social order, but between speculation in fantasy and the laws of a social process: or, as Marx and Engels insisted on drawing it, between "Utopia" and "Science." The radical break which Engels sketched in his *Entwicklung des Sozialismus von der Utopie zur Wissenschaft* (1878) was indeed one of the great modern turning points. The apocalyptists rejected the prophets, and neither utopia nor revolution was ever to be the same again.

These difficult and drastic alternatives, so often darkened by nervous doubts and intellectual hesitations, are by no means confined to the troubled political psyche of the socialist tradition.[7] In Nietzsche, as might be expected, the overwhelming demands of both present and future are kept in dramatic contradictory balance. He was, by nature, suspicious of all "altruism" and could not help feeling that what mankind tended to idolize so much was merely that which it enjoyed so little. Utopian promises were only a kind of hedonist's inflation to make up for everyday deficits. As Nietzsche dourly observes, "let a poet for once show, in the picture of a Utopia, the existence of universal philanthropy [*die allgemeine Menschenliebe*]," and what would emerge would only be "a grievous and ridiculous state [*einen qualvollen und lächerlichen Zustand*]." Society would be condemned to the boredom of a total love, and this, in turn, would be "as fiercely insulted and cursed as selfishness had been by ancient humanity . . . " When the dream becomes a nightmare, the dreamers suddenly awake to a new sense of old realities. Nietzsche ventured to predict:

> . . . and the poets of that state, if we grant them leisure for their compositions, will be dreaming of nothing but the blissful, loveless past, the divine selfishness, the solitude once upon a time possible on earth.

Needless to say, enjoying his own leisurely composition, Nietzsche, some four hundred aphorisms further on, shows himself desperately concerned about "future virtues." Now he mourns the present loss of "the kind of courage which is akin to extravagant generosity," indeed, of the charm and mystery of the inconceivable.

> Oh, that the poets would again be such as they used to be: seers, foretelling us something of our possibilities! . . . Did they wish to make us anticipate future virtues? or virtues that will never be met on earth, though they might exist somewhere in the world?—purple-

glowing stars and whole galaxies of the beautiful? Where are ye, astronomers of the ideal [*Wo seid ihr, ihr Astronomen des Ideals*]?[8]

If the virtues were in the stars, why, then, was it a fault in ourselves to
reach out for them?

By making a clear, if desperate and belated choice, Marx succeeded in
escaping the dilemma. Indeed, there was more than an accidentally
Bonapartist touch to Marx's impatience with utopian dreamers who
could only get in the way of the natural forces of revolutionary change
and power. Napoleon, in his own time, roared against "the ideologists,"
the "idea seekers." As he told young de Staël, pleading in vain on behalf
of his famous mother, "your planners are putting utopias on paper.
They are imbeciles who read these daydreams; they are circulated, they
are believed, everybody talks about universal welfare." Even in his
deathbed fever, Napoleon was still registering his hostility to those who
failed to "understand" him, "with their utopias, their English notions,
their bills of grievances." All they saw in revolution was "a mere reform
of abuses," and they refused to admit that "it constituted, all in itself, a
complete social rebirth."[9]

There was, I suggest, something of this Napoleonic rage in Marx
when, in 1877, he discovered a new outbreak of "utopian socialism,"
with radicals again "playing with fancy pictures of the future structure
of society." A "rotten spirit" was making itself felt, represented by "a
whole gang of half-mature students and super-wise doctors who want to
give socialism a 'higher ideal' orientation, that is to say, to replace its
materialistic basis (which demands serious objective study from anyone
who tries to use it) by modern mythology with its goddesses of Justice,
Freedom, Equality and Fraternity . . . " The previous anti-utopianism of
the Germans made them "theoretically, and therefore also practically,
superior to the French and the English." Of course, the contributions of
"the great French and English utopians" had some validity: but only
before Marx. "Naturally," Marx writes, "utopianism, which *before* the
time of materialistic-critical socialism concealed the germs of the latter
within itself, coming now *after* the event can only be silly—silly, stale,
and basically reactionary." Nothing was to be said about the shape of
things to come. The future was secret. Communism, in one of the most
apodictic of Marx's maxims, "is the solution to the riddle of history and
knows itself to be this solution."[10]

But so well kept the secret was not. Proudhon wrote this definition of
communism in 1864:

A compact democracy having the appearance of being founded on the
dictatorship of the masses, but in which the masses have no more
power than is necessary to ensure a general serfdom in accordance

with the following precepts and principles borrowed from the old absolutism: indivisibility of public power, all-consuming centralization, systematic destruction of individual, corporative, and regional thought (regarded as disruptive), inquisitorial police.

To Karl Marx himself Proudhon had written:

> Let us, if you wish, seek together the laws of society, the way in which they work out and the process by which they will be successfully discovered; but, for God's sake, after having cleared away all the a priori dogmatisms, let us not fall into the contradiction of your countryman Martin Luther, who, having overthrown the Catholic theology, immediately set about founding a Protestant theology of his own amid a great clamor of excommunications and anathemas.... I welcome with all my heart your idea of bringing to light all opinions; let us carry on a good and loyal polemic; and let us give the world an example of learned and far-sighted tolerance [*une tolérance savante et prévoyante*]. But let us not, because we are at the head of a new movement, make ourselves the leaders of a new intolerance; let us not pose as the apostles of a new religion, even if it be the religion of logic, the religion of reason. Let us welcome and encourage all protests, and condemn all exclusiveness and mysticisms. Never let us think of any question as closed, and when we have exhausted our very last argument, let us begin again, if necessary, with eloquence and irony. On that condition I will gladly collaborate with you—*sinon, non!*[11]

This, then, was the apocalyptic utopian's bad bargain: the exchange of the visionary dream for the secret millennium.

2. The Secret Millennium

It can, I suppose, be argued that the laurels of the prophet in despair are only too easy to earn—glimpse the dark horizon, shrink back before decline and fall, cry havoc! Were those not easy triumphs that Proudhon, Burckhardt, Tocqueville, Nietzsche, Kierkegaard all registered with their dark surmises of terror and tyranny? This is arguable. But for the moment I am only inquiring whether the abandonment of utopia does not entail a disorienting loss of horizons. In some verses of the young Marx, he contrasts himself with those who "were fond of flying off into the upper air, seeking there a distant land; I only try valiantly to understand what I find on the streets...."[*12] It is, I feel, no casual astigmatic oversight that Marx did not find on the streets what Proudhon (among others) found there.

---

*Kant und Fichte gern zum Äther schweifen, / Suchten dort ein fernes Land, / Doch ich such' nor tüchtig zu begreifen / Was ich—auf der Strasse fand.

Carnage will come and the enfeeblement that will follow these blood-baths will be terrible. We shall not live to see the work of the new age, we shall fight in the darkness; we must prepare ourselves to endure this life without too much sadness, by doing our duty. Let us help one another, call to one another in the gloom, and practice justice wher-ever opportunity offers. . . .

Today civilization is in the grip of a crisis for which one can only find a single analogy in history—that is the crisis which brought about the coming of Christianity. All the traditions are worn out, all the creeds abolished; but the new program is not yet *ready* . . . . This is the cruellest moment in the life of societies. . . .

I am under no illusion and do not expect to wake up one morning to see the resurrection of freedom. . . . No, no; decay, and decay for a period whose end I cannot fix and which will last for not less than one or two generations—is our lot . . . I shall witness the evil only, I shall die in the midst of darkness.

Where there is no dream of a distant land, there is perhaps no despair; but where there is no vision there is no proper preparation for the real or the desired course of human events. It is a matter not only of foresight but of fore-planning. In a sense, the tradition of empirical experimenta-tion among the prophetic utopians is linked with the utopian prag-matism of the traditional reformers. I refer to the consumer-and-producer cooperatives in England (Owen's New Lanark, etc.); the "na-tional workshops" of Louis Blanc; the adventurous settlements in America (New Harmony in Indiana, Brook Farm in Massachusetts). True, often these reformers, instead of trying to assimilate and humanize the new industrial order, dissipated their energies in efforts to escape it. Marx had a point here when he (in the *18th Brumaire*) spoke about "searching for salvation behind society's back." Still, as Martin Buber has countered, "what is more practical in the last analysis: to try to create social reality through social reality, with its rights defended and extended by political means, or to try and create by the magic wand of politics alone?"[13]

The religious parallels are worth pursuing here, for they offer more than a mere historian's analogy: specific case studies would, I am con-vinced, show notable structural similarities in the temperaments in-volved and their emotional and intellectual consequences. Accordingly, if one inquires into the sources of the destructiveness which did away with all images and pictures during the triumphant days of the Radical Reformation in sixteenth- and seventeenth-century Europe, one ob-serves a familiar pattern of rigor and mysticism. All distractions had to be eliminated in order to protect the authentic thrust of sacred devotion. The human soul had to find direct access to God. Some radical reformers (*e.g.*, the so-called Quietists) "declared war even on mental pictures, even on mental images."[14] In a strikingly similar fashion, the strict Marxian antipathy to utopia and to all diverting imagery of a fancied new society shares a related spirit of protest against any deviations from a devout abstraction. The true movement, in its genuine moments of historic purity, has direct access to the future by its identification with the word incarnate: the Revolution.

Even Martin Buber was entangled in difficulties on this point: for there was an inescapable contradiction between his secular faith in a humanist socialism and his transcendental faith in the God of Israel. As he writes of Jeremiah in his study of *The Prophetic Faith*, "this was not the appropriate hour to obtain a picture of the future order ... there was no place to foretell the forms in which the changed heart would express itself ... The pure prophet is not imaginative ... [his truth] can never be depicted beforehand."[15] Thus, Marx, whose apocalyptic character we have contrasted with prophetism, could curiously become in this reading a type of pure and true prophet, a "quivering magnet needle" pointing the way, since the actual picture of arrangements and institutions is a problem for another time and place, indeed for other and later prophetic spirits. The so-called false prophets are the dreamers of dreams, misled by "the deceit of their own heart" toward the fulfillment of human wishes. Buber wavers here between a secular reasonableness and a theological absolute: he wants his socialists to be practical but his prophets to be existentially pure. Freed from the responsibilities of man's wishes and dreams, separated from pictures of forms and details, the apocalyptist can only hold to his esoteric vision by representing his message as "something to be kept from general knowledge and to be handed down in secret ... "[16]

Public, on the other hand, is the commitment of the school of imaginative prophecy, concerned as it is not only with foretelling and depicting beforehand but also with unambiguous practical action. It is our final utopian turn: reform not as an alternative to revolution, but the reformer as revolutionary, who (with Landauer, with Kropotkin) insists on prerevolutionary progress, the maturing of a true communal spirit accompanying a gradual creation of new institutions and a new society. These prophets are the apostles of "the changed heart" now. They sense the tragic encumbrances of all other proposed paths forward; and they insist especially on the difficulties of the utopian revolutionaries:

> As regards their positive goal they will always result in the exact opposite of what the most honest revolutionaries strive for, unless and until this has so far taken shape *before* the revolution that the revolutionary act has only to wrest the space for it in which it can

develop unimpeded. . . . It can only perfect, set free something that
has already been foreshadowed in the womb of the pre-revolutionary
society. . . . The hour of revolution is not an hour of begetting but an
hour of birth—provided there was a begetting beforehand.[17]

Despite the easy turn to homely inbred metaphor (and it often gives the
impression of a midwives' dispute in political gynecology), a serious
question is raised: Is this, as Buber seems to believe, what Marx had in
mind? This must be seriously doubted. Marx rejected utopia and all its
games, and so long as he refused to tip his own hand his position was
invulnerable. (To show no cards is, perhaps, not to play the game; but
only the greatest gamblers dare it.) One may well debate forever what it
was that Marx really meant. Was he being merely flippant when he
quipped that he had no intention of composing menus for the cafés of
the future? This was, again, dialectical evasion by flight into metaphor.
For what, after all, was being reasonably asked was not the complete
table d'hôte of the new establishment, but merely what (if anything) was
going to be served and what the costs were likely to be.

By scouring all the Marxian texts, from the youthful Hegelian poetry
written in Berlin to that curious correspondence with Vera Zasulich (in
which Marx was hard-pressed to find a very special answer for very
special Russian problems: and he composed three different drafts), it is
barely possible to get some vague hints of Marx's own utopia, otherwise
so sedulously repressed.[18] With some generosity these can, I suppose,
be taken to indicate a belief in a kind of federalism of communes and
cooperatives (but this would be to ignore, of course, the strong under-
current of state centralism). For the rest, there is only that touching
glimpse in *Die deutsche Ideologie* (1845) of a day in the life of Utopia

> where nobody has one exclusive sphere of activity but each can be-
> come accomplished in any branch he wishes ... thus it is possible for
> me to do one thing today and another tomorrow, to hunt in the
> morning, fish in the afternoon, rear cattle in the evening, criticize after
> dinner, just as I have a mind to, without ever becoming hunter,
> fisherman, shepherd, or critic.[19]

Indeed, an after-dinner critic could, with some understandable impatience, airily dismiss this as a caricature of Leonardo da Vinci in a summer holiday camp. At least old King Utopus—which is to say, Sir
Thomas More and his Renaissance contemporaries—knew that the accomplishment of true human excellence was not so easily arranged. Yet
the temptations of what might be called the amateur's paradise are a
seductive and often irresistible element in human affairs, and the serious place of young Marx's dream in the long fantasy of utopian
response should not be overlooked. Men have always wanted to know,
even if they have not always been told, how the happy hours of Golden

Time would pass; and from Plato's *Republic* to Mao's *Red Book* a number of simple and stock answers have never been in short supply. How would the new man use his unprecedented opportunities for total felicity? Would he, a communal creature at last, busy himself with social duties and truly human obligations? Or would he, erect and god-like for the first time, fulfill his sovereign personal potential? It could even be that now, as never before, private interests would emerge as public virtues, personality and community having become so deeply interfused that the most various individuality would be seen to be the flower of man's estate.

The annals of utopian longing, like the history of human ideals in general, are replete with such attempts to confront the One and the Many, to choose between harmony and diversity, or perhaps to coalesce the eclectic aspirations of the differentiated individual with the social functions of the collectivized mass. Although the variations are consid-erable, they appear to be, given the limits of the ideological imagi-nation and the vantage point of historical hindsight, fairly predictable. Two examples may help to suggest the place of Marx's brief utopian excursion in the long perspective of ancient Greece and contemporary China.

For Plato, nothing could be more characteristic of life in a democratic city than the longing for the unfettered fulfillment of variegated hopes and desires. The opportunity for social liberation comes with the triumph of democracy: "when the poor have gained the day," killing or banishing some of their opponents, sharing with all the rest equal rights and opportunities. The young "democratic man" of the *Republic* grew up in "an uncultured and niggardly atmosphere"; in him, desires "of all kinds and tones and varieties" had been suppressed. But what is the reign of liberty and equality for, if not to free his spirit, to help him transcend "a self divided against itself"? There is (in A. D. Lindsay's rendering) "the beginning of the revolution within him," for "where the permissive principle rules, each man will arrange his own life to suit himself . . . " The result is a "many-colored" society, judged by many to be the "fairest of all." Its greatest distinction is "the wonderful variety of men in it."

This vision of human felicity and social bliss is as distasteful for Plato as it is, in his own slightly different presentation, agreeable for Marx. No two pages in political literature appear to be so close in formulation and so apart in evaluation. In a mordant transvaluation of values, Plato concludes his portrait of "democratic man" and his faith in "liberty and equality" with this vignette:

And this is his life. Day after day he gratifies the pleasures as they come—now fluting down the primrose path of wine, now given over to teetotalism and banting; one day in hard training, the next slacking and idling, and the third playing the philosopher. Often he will take to politics, leap to his feet and do or say whatever comes into his head; or he conceives an admiration for a general, and his interests are in war; or for a man of business, and straightway that is his line. He knows no order or necessity in life; but he calls life as he conceives it pleasant and free and divinely blessed, and is ever faithful to it. [*Republic*, 8.561][20]

Marx's day in Utopia, short-lived as it was, left too many open questions, and an even greater blankness when it disappeared. Was the hunting and fishing for pleasure or for provender, and what standards of banter or insight (if any) should the practice of after-dinner criticizing attain? To leave the committed future so vague and empty is to invite all the follies of ambiguity and misunderstanding. The amorphous heterogeneity cannot but lead to the disastrous no-man's-land where rambling armies of hapless words are set against each other and, inevitably, one—or the other—calls "insolence good breeding, license liberty, extravagance generosity, and shamelessness courage ... " (*Republic*, 8.560). Utopian abstractions need sharper definition if they are to be of use in shaping things to come.

Here was a case of Marx standing not Hegel, but Plato, on his head: the reversal of a classic ancient doctrine is perfect and complete. What Marx saw as the desirable life-style of postrevolutionary man had been long before rejected by Plato as the absurd, undisciplined eclecticism of a democratic idea which confounded insolence with good breeding, lawlessness with liberty, profligacy with munificence, and violence with valor. The transvaluation of values was deemed progressive or decadent, godlike in its own dignity or devilish in its prodigality, according to one's inspiration. So far as Plato (and a whole ancient philosophical tradition) was concerned: nothing could be worse than the ideal which impressed Marx as the ultimate in human opportunity in an authentically free society. It is as if the debate echoed through twenty-five centuries of utopian political projections.

Did Marx, then, mean that in the new social order freedom will have so utterly replaced necessity that all hitherto known standards of professional excellence or specialization would be obsolete? Here the vision of what could be considered the humanistic utopia of the Amateur stands in severe contrast to the technocratic utopia of the Professional. It would appear to be a basic conflict between the ideals of the whole man and the perfect specialist. But it can also be seen—especially in the light of later Marxian developments—as a difference between old and narrow life-styles and a new vocational diversity. Thus, Mao Tse-tung—in a

Chinese echo of Marx's adolescent ideal of "hunter, fisherman, shepherd, or critic"—has proclaimed the People's Army as "at the same time a fighting force, a political force, and a production force." The true liberator (or Red Guard) is equally involved in "politics, military affairs, and culture." Indeed, according to an official injunction (*Jenmin Jih Pao*, 1 August 1966), "the whole country should become a great school in Mao Tse-tung's thought." If the army "can concurrently study, engage in agriculture, run factories and do mass work," then workers and peasants and students, too, are obliged not only to study but to work in the factories, help on the farms, assist in the army, and do their share of criticizing the bourgeoisie.

> This brilliant idea of Comrade Mao Tse-tung's is of great historic importance. . . . The idea set forth by Comrade Mao Tse-tung that every field of work should be made into a great revolutionary school, where people take part both in industry and agriculture, in military as well as civilian affairs—such is our programme. . . . With hammer in hand they will be able to do factory work, with hoe or plough they will be able to do farming, with the gun they will be able to fight, and with the pen express themselves in writing.

This scheme has been aptly referred to by one commentator as "the total amateurization" of society.[21]

I leave it to disputatious students of Marxist dialectics to decide whether or not it was Marx's seed that produced Mao's flower. In any event, this outlandish development—prompted by isolated tidbits of dogmatic theory, itself an improvised fragment of a *Weltanschauung* which systematically refused to confront the problems of a revolutionized future—only underscores the tragic abandonment of the utopian imperative. This is, I am convinced, more significant than the conventional arraignment of Marxism on the charge of not being empirical. It is true that Marxism made no serious attempt to promote, influence, direct, coordinate, and federate social experiments; that it created no "cell groups" or "associations" for the new living community; that it had turned its attention away from the community; that it refused to interest itself in the specific evolution of the new social form. Still, was this not primarily a failure of vision? Wasn't this less the result of a pragmatic lethargy than a speculative poverty, an abject refusal to dream? In the camp of the revolutionary utopians, only the partisans of the speculative or prophetic solution have been able to keep themselves warm by the sparks of their initial inspiration. For the others, there is only the cold substitution of vague rhetoric, fanatical activity, or belated bureaucratic blueprints for what was, ever since More's imaginative leap forward, the humanizing strength of the ideal of a good society.

Marx's greatest student, Lenin, was in this sense a legitimate heir indeed, for he came along to compound the fault into one of the great narrownesses of history. "In Marx," he cries, "you will find no trace of Utopianism in the sense of inventing the 'new' society and constructing it out of fantasies." So disappeared idea, direction, goal. In 1918, Lenin confessed, "What Socialism will be we just don't know." Result: the vision floundered somewhere between an amorphous notion of the "withering away of the State" and buzzing systems of nationwide electrification. The revolution had arrived, but the anti-utopian revolutionaries had no clear or consistent conception of how the new society was to be constructed or, for that matter, even why. Only one thing was certain: what was old would be destroyed, what was new would remain abstract. In Lenin's words,

> really great revolutions grow out of the contradictions between the old, between what is directed towards analysing the old, and the abstract striving for the new, which must be so new that not a particle of the old remains.... The old is destroyed, as it deserved to be destroyed; it has been transformed into a heap of ruins as it deserved to be.[22]

How far we have come from the wise utopian warnings of the past! In September 1917, Lenin speaks of the transformation of all citizens into workers and employees of one big "syndicate," namely, the state as a whole—"the whole of society will turn into one office and one factory with equal work and equal pay." And, in a protest of 1848, Proudhon writes:

> A dictatorial, authoritarian, doctrinaire system starts from the axiom that the individual is subordinate, in the very nature of things, to the collectivity; from it alone does right and life come to him; the citizen belongs to the state as the child to his family, he is in its power and possession, and he owes it submission and obedience in all things.... Labor would be regimented and ultimately enslaved through a state policy of brotherhood.... What would freedom, universal happiness, civilization have gained? Nothing. We would merely have changed our chains and the social idea would have made no step forward; we would still be under the same arbitrary power, not to say under the same economic fatalism.[23]

What is surprising is only that Lenin, apparently exhibiting a greater sensitivity than Western critics are usually prepared to concede to Russian Bolsheviks, could manage to say with some bitterness shortly before he died, "We have become a Bureaucratic Utopia." Some time before, he had stated (answering objections from Bukharin): "We cannot outline socialism. What socialism will look like when it takes on its final forms we do not know and cannot say."

This is, as we have been arguing, the very heart of the failure. It is not a matter of "knowing" what socialism is to look like, but rather what one wants it to look like. This knowing and willing, as Martin Buber wisely concluded, "this conscious willing itself influences what is to be ... " The future is a perilous vacuum if the present does not bring forward to it humane and inspired images of excellence and beauty. Strange that it was in that fateful year of the *Manifesto* that the man who appears to have been one of the first to have used the word *socialism*, Pierre Leroux, should have cried out—"If you have no will for human association, I tell you that you are exposing civilization to the fate of dying in fearful agony!" The authentic utopian today, now as then, remains persuaded that this fearful agony cannot be redeemed by anything less than a new will fired by the longing for a better society and by a reasonable vision of human capabilities.

3. Temptations of Good and Evil

There is, then, an idea of utopia and revolution which confines its social force, modestly and safely, to a manageable happy minimum. The process of maximization over the centuries of modern history involves the conversion of the modest good into the absolute perfect, occasional force into principled violence, pertinent change into spectacular upheaval, measured hope into immeasurable rage, all in a new spirit expressed by Byron in *Childe Harold's Pilgrimage:*

> ... self-torturing sophist, wild Rousseau
> The apostle of affliction, he who threw
> Enchantment over passion, and from woe
> Wrung overwhelming eloquence.

Novalis put it another way when he wrote, "an absolute urge toward perfection and completeness is a kind of disease, as soon as it adopts a destructive and hostile attitude towards the imperfect, the incomplete."[24] In either case, we have reached the point at which the vision of a better life becomes enlisted in the revolution for a final solution. Dream becomes dogma; fears become fanaticized; ideas become the signal for ultimate action.

My theme in these pages is the conversion of the utopian longing to a revolutionary commitment, and I should like to follow the course of this new engagement from Cromwell and Robespierre to Marx and Lenin, from Paris and London (or Trier and Berlin, if you will) to Moscow and beyond. It is not an academic exercise, for I feel myself part of that "whole generation"[25] for whom Albert Camus wrote in his book *The Rebel*, "lost in loneliness, with weapons in our hands and a lump in our throats ... "[26] If it is a course full of surprising turns, it has something of that irony which Karl Marx himself sensed when he suddenly heard that his *Kapital*, so hurriedly written in order to appear before the European *déluge*, would have its first translated edition—in St. Petersburg. "It is an irony of fate," he wrote from London to Kugelmann (12 October 1868), "that the Russians, whom I have fought for twenty-five years, and not only in German but in French and English, have always been my 'patrons.' My work against Proudhon was nowhere more popular than in Russia; and now it is the Russians who are to publish the first foreign translation of *Das Kapital*."[27] But then, as Marx said, the Russians "always run after the most extreme ideas that the West has to offer ... "[28] The word is his: *extremism*. They needed it; he offered it. We move disastrously from the revolutionification of utopia to the Russification of revolution.

Ironies of fate abound. It was not merely that a book was translated, but that it was "written large" (as Robespierre said of the book of Machiavelli) in the course of cataclysmic events. Could Marx himself have had any illusions about the outcome? "Since the time of Adam," he once remarked, "is not the tree of evil also the tree of knowledge?" He had read in Lorenz von Stein about "that kind of communism which knows very well that it leads only to an upheaval but does not know what will follow." In this so-called raw communism, on the morrow of the revolution, greed would not be overcome, only generalized; labor would not be abolished, but extended to all men. Marx's premise (as it has been put in Professor Tucker's reading of the texts)[29] is that "the revolution is itself a colossal acquisitive act of violence performed in a spirit of greed, envy, hate and resentment." Before it can construct, it comes to destroy, and it must necessarily be caught up in what Engels referred to as "the wicked passions of men" and Marx as "infinite degradation." It was, in a phrase which Marx borrowed from Hegel, "a depravity in revolt against depravity." Marx himself saw this paradoxical element in his own thought. In a letter to Engels he explained that by "demonstrating hidden progress even where modern economic conditions are being accompanied by horrifying immediate consequences," he had given—"perhaps *malgré lui*," as he says—a final blow to all "utopianism."[30] The whole conception amounted to "a doctrine of the historical beneficence of moral evil."

A curious thing has happened to this doctrine: it has all but disappeared. Some elements of it remained extant until the death of Lenin: there were more than a few traces of it in the proud amorality of early Bolshevik theory and practice. But, since Marx, only one Marxist has dared to continue in the original spirit of the revolutionary anti-utopian tradition—George Lukacs, and he only fleetingly before his formal ex-communication. This is the young Lukacs who wrote that strange masterpiece, *Geschichte und Klassenbewusstsein*, then recanted all its arguments and never allowed the book to be republished again. This is the young dialectician whose dark brilliance inspired Thomas Mann to the portrait of Naphta, the Jesuitical Jewish revolutionary, in *The Magic Mountain* (and Lukacs, who was a close reader of Mann, never, curiously enough, recognized himself). Naphta, it will be recalled, tells Settembrini, "the man of progress, liberalism, and middle-class revolution," that his Utopia is "monstrous," that "the task of the proletariat is to strike terror into the world for the healing of the world, that man may finally achieve salvation and deliverance, and win back freedom from law and from distinction of classes." When Settembrini protests, "and now you profess a socialism pushed to the point of dictatorship and terrorism, how do you reconcile the two things?," Naphta replies: "Opposites may be consistent with each other." This is what I remember the late Franz Borkenau calling "the secret, dialectical theory of wickedness," and he called my attention to a little-known document of the early 1920s which recorded the following fascinating and historic incident:

> A representative theoretician [unnamed in the document] who was perhaps the sole brain behind Hungarian communism, at a decisive moment answered my quesion as to whether lying and cheating of the members of the party by their own leaders were admissible, by this statement: Communist ethics make it the highest duty to accept the necessity to act wickedly. This, he said, was the greatest sacrifice revolution asked from us. The conviction of the true communist is that evil transforms itself into bliss through the dialectics of historical evolution. (That this morality of the type of Nechayev is, inter alia, based upon admiration of Dostoyevsky, will surprise nobody.) This dialectical theory of wickedness has never been published by the theoretician mentioned, nevertheless this communist gospel spread as a secret doctrine from mouth to mouth, until it was finally regarded as the semi-official quintessence of "true communism,"as the one criterion of a "true communist."[31]

The theoretician in question was George Lukacs. He was, as Marx once said of Mandeville's open defense of evil in the *Fable of the Bees*, only being "more audacious and more honest than the narrow-minded apologists." After his recantation, there was to be no more philosophical audacity.[32] The propaganda of ideology and apologia was to rule the day—with the single possible exception of the ingenious cynicism of Bert Brecht.[33]

I am thinking especially of Brecht's "didactic play," *Die Massnahme* (1930), which Herbert Luethy has called "the most significant, perhaps even the only, Bolshevik drama."[34]

> What meanness would you not commit, to
> Stamp out meanness!
> If, at last, you could change the world, what
> Would you think yourself too good for?
> Who are you?
> Sink into the mire
> Embrace the butcher, but
> Change the world: it needs it!*

The victim, a revolutionary idealist with an individual conscience ("in the twilight we saw his naked face, open, human, innocent"), is thrown into the lime pit; and the *Kontrollchor*, or the Party's conscience, intones:

> He who fights for Communism must be able to fight and not to fight; to speak the truth and not to speak the truth; to render services and to refuse services; to keep promises and not to keep promises; to incur danger and to avoid danger; to be recognizable and unrecognizable. He who fights for Communism has of all virtues only one: that he fights for Communism.

How much was audacity here, and how much apologia? In Marx there was still an element of philosophical and moral mystery; with Brecht it became an icy inhuman discipline, *Ja-sagend zur Revolutionierung der Welt*. For Marx, communism was "the riddle of history resolved." In Brecht's verses, written in East Germany a century later, it still remained:

> not the riddle
> but the solution.
> It is the simple thing
> That is hard to accomplish.†

I remember once accompanying W. H. Auden to the East-West borderline in Berlin, but he refrained from going on to visit Brecht in his

---

*"Welche Niedrigkeit begingest du nicht, um / Die Niedrigkeit auszutilgen? / Könntest du die Welt endlich verändern, wofür / Wärest du dir zu gut? / Wer bist du? / Versinke in Schmutz / Umarme den Schlächter, aber / Ändere die Welt: sie braucht es!"

†Er ist nicht das Raetsel, / Sondern die Loesung. / Er ist das Einfache / das schwer zu machen ist."

Theater am Schiffbauerdamm. It was, perhaps, the same hesitation which kept him from adding (as he told me) the dedication "for B. B." to his poem entitled *Vespers*, in which the remarkable confrontation between the two poets—"And it is now that our two paths cross"—actually took place.[35]

> Both simultaneously recognize his Anti-type: that I am an Arcadian, that he is a Utopian.
>
> He notes, with contempt, my Aquarian belly: I note, with alarm, his Scorpion's mouth.
>
> He would like to see me cleaning latrines: I would like to see him removed to some other planet.
>
> Neither speaks. What experience could we possibly share?
>
> Glancing at a lampshade in a store window, I observe it is too hideous for anyone in their senses to buy: He observes it is too expensive for a peasant to buy.
>
> Passing a slum child with rickets, I look the other way: He looks the other way if he passes a chubby one.
>
> I hope our senators will behave like saints, provided they don't reform me: He hopes they will behave like *baritoni cattivi*, and, when lights burn late in the Citadel,
>
> I (who have never seen the inside of a police station) am shocked and think: "Were the city as free as they say, after sundown all her bureaus would be huge black stones":
>
> He (who has been beaten up several times) is not shocked at all but thinks: "One fine night our boys will be working up there."
>
> You can see, then, why between my Eden and his New Jerusalem, no treaty is negotiable . . .

If this is so, if "no treaty is negotiable," then the spectacle of revolutionary faith and enthusiasm in our own time must embody some deep human confusion, some failure of the mind and the heart. Moral and ideological blindness belongs to the peculiar tragedies of our age. For who would, with free will and an open eye, opt for the worse rather than the better? who would choose rawness or wickedness or degradation?

Napoleon had asserted that the Revolution, in spite of (and not *because of*) all its horrors, had nonetheless been "the true cause of our moral regeneration . . . just as the vilest dunghills feed the noblest plants."[36] Indeed, there may be "some soul of goodness in things evil" (*Henry V*, 4.1. 4–5); and there are always those who, in the biblical formulation, would "do evil, that good may come." But much that is evil in modern totalitarian practice is not a regrettable means to a preferable end but the end itself, and held to be good at that. The moving ideals of Hitler's *Mein Kampf* or Alfred Rosenberg's *Mythos des 20 Jahrhundert* are those of war, not peace; of hate, not love; of exploitation, not equality; of oppression and superiority, not liberty and fraternity. The visions of New Jerusalem of the latter-day followers of Marx and Lenin, and, indeed, of most revolutionary movements, are quite different. The good by which, and for which, they live is presented as an amalgam of the most classical values of human idealism. Their cause is the cause of peace, brotherhood, freedom, welfare, culture, garden cities, mental health, not to mention science and reason. Is this a matter only of words? or of a mere ideology of a utopia which refuses to commit itself in true detail? "The most terrible fight," Kierkegaard reminds us,[37] "is not when there is one opinion against another; the most terrible is when two men say the same thing—and fight about the interpretation, and this interpretation involves a difference of quality."

This is precisely the character of the debate in contemporary world politics: it is a struggle over interpretations, an exercise which is carried out in the same language but in which every word is defined differently and every active verb is conjugated with irregular endings.

No one dictionary can help. In one, a Marxist definition of communism would read: a philosophy based on scientific laws, a form of society rooted in the dignity of man. Consult another, and one would find: a system of dogmatic principles, held together by a pseudoreligious fanaticism, a form of society in which man is degraded to an instrument of the state and a monolithic political party. The encyclopedic entries for, say, "Russia," would exhibit the same total divergence. In one, we could find a glowing epic of expanding progress and power, from Peter the Great to the current chairman of the Party, from Lomonósov to Lysenko, from Pushkin to Sholokhov. Poets sang of freedom, novelists bemoaned dead souls and dreamed of beautiful ones, peace was praised and war condemned, the people groaned under tyranny and planned their blow for emancipation. But there is another version: Russia as the unfortunate projection of Asia onto the European continent, a backward, semi-civilized area never blessed by Latin culture and institutions, and hence alien to the essence of liberty and forever marked by the natural, cursed affinity between Slav and slave.... Similarly in the case of "Revolution." In one grammar of politics, it is: I make a revolution to do a noble deed for humanity; we make a revolution to end all tyranny and usher in an era of human harmony. The opposing conjugation reads: We make a revolution because we are bewitched by leaders who will betray us; they make a revolution because they are possessed by hate, envy, and power lust.

One does not have to be a semanticist or psycholinguist to know that words have weight, that words are weapons. The dialogue of our time takes place in an echo chamber of meanings; and if and when evil is chosen, sworn by, voted for, it is less the work of the devil than the spirit of sheer ambiguity. All of our concepts—Marxism, Revolution, Russia—have a double character, two faces, and the features change and vary according to perspective. Let me make an attempt to bring, if I can, both faces into focus, into a combined clarity, without blurring the image. For, if reality is not relative, then there is only one image "out there," waiting to be caught.

For there is (if I may leave this already unclear, overexposed metaphor) an element in Marxism which is profoundly useful in social science and remains intellectually stimulating; there is, also, a Russia which is rich in humanist traditions, which deserves respect and admiration; and in Revolution there is a moment which touches on something authentically great in the human spirit. Not to see and recognize this is to condemn the contemporary dialogue to an endless, fruitless altercation in which all truth is lost. For, when evil is seen only as evil, one overlooks its special quality to present itself as the good. Where the Prince of Darkness succeeded it was not so much through his satanic powers as through that touch of tragic nobility about him as a fallen Angel of Light. Like the great globe itself, born in a chaos of the universe, the decisive acts of human history emerge out of a confusion of motives and meanings.

One of Goethe's maxims suggests that a false doctrine is not contradictable, for it is based on the conviction that the false is the true.[38] Is it not, rather, based on an ambivalence? And isn't there, within that ambivalence, a firm point somewhere from which to hold back the confounding of values? For it would seem to be a strange thing that in the present conflict of ideas, the Marxist *Weltanschauung* should be taken to be both a vulgar materialism and a fanaticized idealism, both a godless scientism which denies the transcendental and a religious absolutism which subverts human reason. It is no less remarkable that the international Communist movement is held to be the uncompromising representative of the radical left as well as the bulwark of an almost unmovable reaction. Thus, in our double focus, we have: Marxism, at once religion and science; Russia, at once liberator and enslaver; Revolution, at once creative and destructive.

4. Magico-Religious Paraphernalia

When Karl Marx died, Friedrich Engels gave the funeral oration at the cemetery in London's Highgate. He could offer no more glowing tribute to the achievement of his friend's life than to say: "*So war dieser Mann der Wissenschaft!* (So was this man of science!)." He argued that Marx, like

Darwin and his discovery of the great laws of organic evolution, had revealed the essential pattern of historical change. He had studied past and present and had formulated their secrets. No doubt about it, the genius who worked for so long in the British Museum had found a secret or two; few social scientists in the age of Keynes and Max Weber are thinkable without the context of Marxism. How outraged Marx would have been—he who had called religion "the opium of the people"—to have found himself put down as the founder of a "new religion" (or, even worse, a pseudoreligion). Yet intentions do not control consequences, and the character of both ideas and events—in this case, the drama of a political religion—is always more complex than authors and actors know. Nietzsche had once referred to the French Revolution as the daughter of Christianity; and Spengler, trying his own hand at the family tree, thought he recognized Christianity as the grandfather of Bolshevism. (Toynbee has branched off in another but not unrelated direction in his insistence that Marxism-Leninism was a variant of Christian heresy.) Earlier on—and in a mood too agonized for quips, for he was watching the upsurge of a rival faith—Kierkegaard had observed:

> Even now, in 1848, it certainly looks as though politics were everything; but it will be seen that the catastrophe [the Revolution] corresponds to and is the obverse of the Reformation: then everything pointed to a religious movement and proved to be political; now everything points to a political movement, but it will become a religious movement.[39]

And, writing of the same events in his *Confessions of a Revolutionist* (1849), Proudhon had been frank enough to note, "It is surprising how constantly we find all our political questions complicated with theology." He carried his confession even further: "All the metaphysico-theological systems, brought into being by dreams of the absolute and the ideal, are, in short, but the archaeology of Justice, the apocalypse of the Revolution."[40]

In Marx's own tradition there were elements of both the old and the new Testaments. The point is, as I say, not new and the parallel has often been drawn. Mircea Eliade has put it forcefully in *The Sacred and the Profane:* "the great majority of the irreligious are not liberated from religious behavior, from theologies and mythologies. They sometimes stagger under a whole magico-religious paraphernalia." In the specific case of Marx he observes:

> Marx takes over and continues one of the great eschatological myths of the Asiatico-Mediterranean world—the redeeming role of the Just (the "chosen," the "anointed," the "innocent," the "messenger"; in our day, the proletariat), whose sufferings are destined to change the onto-

logical status of the world. In fact, Marx's classless society and the consequent disappearance of historical tensions find their closest precedent in the myth of the Golden Age that many traditions put at the beginning and the end of history. Marx enriched this venerable myth by a whole Judaeo-Christian messianic ideology: on the one hand, the prophetic role and soteriological function that he attributes to the proletariat; on the other, the final battle between Good and Evil, which is easily comparable to the apocalyptic battle between Christ and Antichrist, followed by the total victory of the former. It is even significant that Marx takes over for his own purposes the Judaeo-Christian eschatological hope of *an absolute end to history*.[41]

This argument is often taken over in a pejorative manner by anti-Marxist pamphleteers. Curiously enough, the recognition of the parallel between sacred forms of religion and secular types of ideology has endeared Marxism to certain Christian thinkers. For others, engaged in cruder polemics, the point is made invidiously; the analysis of its unacknowledged religious aspect is felt to be its unmasking.

Both Reinhold Niebuhr and Karl Löwith have made strenuous and subtle attempts to delimit the role of religiosity in the revolutionary Marxian faith; evidently, a secular ideology cannot constitute any kind of true belief, for it "manages to evade the tragic realities of life and to obscure the moral ambiguity in all political positions . . . " In his *Faith and History*, Dr. Niebuhr writes:

> Marxism is a secularized version of messianism without the knowledge of the prophets that the judgement of God falls with particular severity upon the chosen people . . . . Its non-prophetic messianism endows a particular social force in history with unqualified sanctity and its post-Christian utopianism prompts the illusion of a kingdom of perfect righteousness (*i.e.*, a classless society and an anarchistic brotherhood) in history . . . . Its materialism is, on the whole, a justified reaction to pietistic religions which do not understand the social character of life . . . . Its ostensible atheism is less significant than its idolatry. It worships a god who is the unqualified ally of one group in human society against all others.[42]

Similarly, Professor Löwith has made a serious qualification of the thesis of Marxism as a secular political religion by arguing:

> The Communist creed, though a pseudo-morphosis of Jewish-Christian messianism, lacks the fundamentals of it: the free acceptance of humiliation and of redemptive suffering as the condition of triumph. The proletarian Communist wants the crown without the cross; he wants to triumph by earthly happiness . . . [43]

This would appear to be at best only half-true: because the tragic element in the course of Marxist revolutions may well consist precisely in the humiliation of the idealists and the suffering of the masses. This has not, to be sure, been "freely accepted," except to the extent that some Marxist philosophers[44] have attempted to assimilate the idea and the fact of tragedy (as I have already indicated) to an otherwise optimistic conception of human hope and social progress.

But this much, at least, is clear. At one place in his *Capital,* Marx writes: "Just as it was written upon the brow of the chosen people, that they were Jehovah's property, so does the division of labour brand the manufacturing worker as the property of capital." In the place of a "chosen people" Marx put the idea of a chosen class. This chosen class—the carriers of the chiliastic hope, not unlike the prophets of ancient Israel or of the medieval Waldensians and Taborites—was to lead the way to the millennium.

Here we must turn to what one historian has called the relevance of apocalyptic. I abstract, for the special purposes of this context, a number of essential elements which link apocalyptic thought in both the religious and secular traditions of the West. There is indeed a point at which there would seem to be no major distinction, as in Martin Buber's interpretation of *The Prophetic Faith* in which "the living God and eternal King"

> desires no religion, He desires a human people, men living together, the makers of decision vindicating their right to those thirsting for justice, the strong having pity on the weak, men associating with men.

Why this should (or perhaps only could) be so, is implied in a reading of the Jeremianic spirit:

> The prophet has to proclaim just this, that God seeks something other than religion. Out of a human community He wills to make His kingdom; community there must be in order that His kingdom shall come; therefore here, where He blames a people for not having become a community, man's claim upon man takes precedence of God's claim.[45]

These are the links, then, which are part of the great chain of human hope, taken either in their theological or secular connections.

1. *Crisis.* The intolerability of the miseries of the present time of suffering, tribulation, humiliation, and woe.

2. *Vengeance.* The inspired prospect of vindication and flaming deliverance from the currently afflicted age.

3. *Catastrophe.* The imminence of the messianic day of universal terror and destruction when the righteous cause of martyrs will be redeemed.

4. *Promise.* The ultimate inevitability of a fairer world of enduring peace and justice, brotherhood and bliss, joy and virtue.

5. *Climax.* A supreme denouement of history which follows the contest between light and darkness, ending in the disastrous ruin of evil, wicked oppression, and all worldly abominations.

6. *Dawn.* The grand inauguration of a new and golden Age, a brighter earthly future, an absolute glory.

In point of fact, Judeo-Christian messianism was more deeply interfused in the dream of the social revolution than the new prophets were prepared to concede. One wonders whether the Jesuit in Robespierre wasn't secretly flattered when one admirer called him "the Messiah promised by the Eternal Being, to reform everything" ("*Je vous regarde comme le Messie que l'Etre éternel nous a promis pour réformer toute chose,*" 17 June 1794).[46] Bonaparte, as so often, was more candid and explicit. In a conversation in 1816 (as transcribed by Las Cases), he went into a paean of praise for "the grand principles of our Revolution" and said:

> These truths will rule the world. They will be the creed, the religion, the morality of all nations. And, no matter what has been said, this memorable era will be linked to my person, because, after all, I have carried its torch and consecrated its principles, and because persecution now has made me its Messiah.[47]

A critical sense of the fatality of the messianic complex as it burgeons in militant movements for peace or liberation was already present in the first English epoch of modern revolution. Compiling in 1656 his dismal record of *Enthusiasmus triumphatus*, Dr. Henry More has left us a vivid and valuable, if somewhat donnish, portrait of a European political zealot for whom peace was war and victory his personal predestination:

> Whether there might not be as much of *Villany* and *Melancholy* in some of these false *Messiases*, if it be suspected, it will be hard to take off the suspicion. But there was a *German*, in whom we may more safely instance, not many years ago here in *England*. He styl'd himself a *Warriour of God, David the Second*, and in deep compassion of the sufferings of his Country, would very fain have got some few Forces here to carry over; with which, he was confident, he could have silenced the enemy, and settled all *Germany* in peace.

It is probably quite impossible to make out after three centuries who this was; it could have been almost anyone in the Comenius-Dury-Hartlib circle, among whom we will be moving in a later chapter. Possibly (allowing for a certain gossipy margin of error, for he was no "German," but then Dr. More, down from Cambridge to London, only glimpsed the man from a distance) it was Comenius himself. In his *Lux in tenebris,*

Comenius collected a whole variety of prophetical visions of the downfall of "Tyranny and Oppression" in Europe.

> The man seemed [Dr. More continued] to be a very religious man, and a great hater of Tyranny and Oppression, and very well in his wits to other things; only that he was troubled with this infirmity, that he fancied himself that *David* the prophets foretell of, who should be that peaceable Prince, and great Deliverer of the *Jews*. He published a short writing of his, which I had the opportunity of seeing, which was full of Zeal and Scripture-eloquence: I saw his person in *London*, if he that shewed me him was not mistaken. He was a tall proper man, of a good age, but of a very pale, wasted, Melancholy countenance.[48]

So would men of zeal and compassion come, again and again, to give inspired leadership to the oppressed in a sacred struggle against their tyrants. As among the first utopians—Campanella had thought of sixteenth-century Spain and, later, seventeenth-century France, as the servant of the Messiah and sometimes even of himself as a suffering and victorious Messiah[49]—the ancient eschatological note, now mixed with the *furor teutonicus* of one epoch and now with a little Napoleonic hero worship of another, was struck very early in the nineteenth-century Communist movement. "I see a new Messiah coming with the sword," Wilhelm Weitling had prophesied in a work (*Guarantees of Harmony and Freedom*, 1842), which Marx had greeted as the "brilliant debut" of the German proletariat as "the theoretician of Europe."

"By his courage," Weitling continued, "he [the new Messiah] will be placed at the head of the revolutionary army, and with its help he will crumble the decayed structure of the old social order, and drown the sources of tears in the ocean of forgetfulness, and transform the earth into a paradise."[50] Marx subsequently changed his mind about Weitling and demanded more "strictly scientific ideas and concrete doctrine"; *Weitlingerei* might do only for Russia. Indeed, Plekhanov describes in his memoirs the forging of the revolutionary faith in Russia and recalls how he and his colleagues "impatiently waited for the proletariat to appear on the stage of history like a promised Messiah ... "[51] Touchingly transplanted to the New World, the promise lost none of its force and sentiment, as in Michael Gold's *Jews Without Money* (1930), a tale of a poor, despairing immigrant boy on the streets of Manhattan who "prayed on the tenement roof in moonlight to the Jewish Messiah who would redeem the world ... "

> A man on an East Side soap-box, one night, proclaimed that out of the despair, melancholy and helpless rage of millions, a world movement had been born to abolish poverty.
> I listened to him.

O Worker's Revolution, you brought hope to me, a lonely, suicidal boy. You are the true Messiah. You will destroy the East Side when you come, and build there a garden for the human spirit.

O Revolution, that forced me to think, to struggle and to live.

O great Beginning![52]

The proletariat, thus, became a kind of collective Messiah, and to it belonged the future as inevitably as in predestination. Man was to be reborn, and the genius of mankind resurrected; exploitation was the original sin; a new Adam was to come from the ranks of the poor and persecuted. It is almost as if every central idea in the history of religion had been plagiarized—*e.g.*, the final contest between the forces of good and evil, as among the Manichees; between the light and the darkness, as among the Zoroastrians—to prepare the way for the hosts of the faithful, strong in their orthodoxy, redeeming and reconciling all mankind.

"I will proclaim freedom to the nations, though I should perish in the attempt." This is the youthful Lassalle writing in his schoolboy's diary. "I will come before all nations, and summon them with burning words to fight for freedom." But the proclamation and the summoning were inescapably couched in old and familiar accents, fragments of Judeo-Christian traditions and echoes of other ancient lore. "Why should I, of all people, become a martyr? Why? Because God has put a voice in my heart that calls me to battle . . . . Because I can fight and suffer for a noble cause." Nor was the consecrated calling too general or vague for specific marching orders. "Whenever I indulge in childish dreams," Lassalle confessed, "I prefer to picture myself sword in hand, at the head of the Jews, leading them to recover their independence." When Hegelian certainty began to replace Hebrew confidence, he felt himself on surer grounds with the revolution than with the apocalypse. "If there should ever be a revolution, what could be a juster one than that the Jews in the city should rise, start incendiary fires everywhere, blow up the powder magazine, and destroy themselves together with their persecutors." Still, victory was preferable to tragedy, "for we must triumph in the battle which I intend to fight! Light must conquer, and darkness withdraw!" Now, he wrote, "now is the time to struggle for humanity's most sacred ends."[53]

Marx, who by tradition and temperament shared some of these fantasies, was sensitively aware of this psychic process; indeed, he had a keen critical eye for all religiosity but his own. "From the very start," Marx wrote (after Lassalle's death in a duel in 1864, at the age of thirty-nine), "like every one who believes that he has in his pocket a panacea for the sufferings of the masses, he gave his agitation a religious and sectarian character." Marx declined to write an obituary for "the Modern Saviour" (and Engels joined him in mocking *der moderne Erlöser!*"). Lassalle had always tried to reassure Marx of his orthodox credentials: "Since 1840 I have been a revolutionist, and since 1843 a convinced socialist." And, for the most part, his ardor and ambition found expression in the acceptably conventional revolutionary stereotypes, as in this comment on the 1844 disturbances among the German weavers:

> This is serious, bloody serious [Lassalle wrote to his father]. Do you notice anything? Do you hear the distant thunder? Don't be afraid. It will pass this time, and will pass yet again; but in the end the storm will break! . . . "The time is out of joint," but the new Hamlet, unlike the old one, says, "I am glad that I was born to set it right."—Or are you really so blind, so deaf, so bereft of your senses, that you do not realize what all this means? They are petrels, I tell you, stormy petrels, heralding the storm of the new spirit [*Sturmvögel, die da verkünden dass der Sturm des neuen Geistes im Anzug sei*] . . . Don't deceive yourselves. This is the beginning of that war of the poor against the rich which is imminent. These are the first rumblings of communism. . . . These are the first convulsions of the embryo towards independence and the light of day. These are the birth pangs [*Das sind die ersten Wehen*] . . .

But beyond these standard images of war, womb, and weather, there was another metaphorical dimension; for if Lassalle was a "sectarian," he was the leader of the sect, its priest and prophet, endowed with godlike powers. In his Breslau text, his "war manifesto against the world," he announced:

> Knowing myself to be lord of the earth, one before whose fiery breath nothing finite can persist, I look around me, see that the earth is my footstool, and that heaven is the throne of my glories . . . . I am servant and master of the idea, priest of the god I myself am . . . .* I have the will to destroy, and I have the means for spreading woe and disaster over those on whom I breathe.[54]

For Heinrich Heine, young Lassalle was the hero of "the new generation which wants to make itself seen and heard," which disdains the "scent of blue flowers" (and would put an end to "the thousand-year reign of romanticism"), and which "like a stern gladiator advances so proudly to the death struggle . . . ." More than that, he was once moved to refer to Lassalle (in a letter to his father, Heyman Lassal) as "the Messiah of the nineteenth century."[55] And in the spirit of that supreme apostolic certitude—something more than even the Hegelian confidence

---

*"Ich bin Diener und Herr des Begriffs, Priester des Gotts, der ich selber bin."

which led him to claim, "And see, I cannot say a word to which History does not immediately shout back its Yes ... "—Lassalle came to give sanctifying assurance to the working class (in his *Arbeiter-Programm* of 1862), "You are the rock upon which the Church of the present is to be built!"*[56]

None of this, I submit, was mere imagistic decoration of a thought which could have been expressed otherwise (*e.g.*, "You are the heart of a new society," or "You are the foundation of a new world," etc.). The style was consistent with the intellectual mood; the phrase was part of a deeper predisposition. For at least another century, religious *Metaphorik* was to remain a constant sign of the temperamental reality. "A meeting of the Party," the Italian Communist writer, Cesare Pavese, wrote in his *Diary* for June 1947, "has all the characteristics of a religious rite. We listen to be assured of what we already think, to be exalted by our common faith and confession."[57]

The constituent elements of the temper of revolutionary religiosity to which I have drawn attention by a variety of historical illustrations are, then, fourfold: (1) the rites of common exaltation; (2) the expectation of the Messiah; (3) the dark vision of the apocalypse; and (4) the bright hope of final redemption.

This last, as one scholar has acutely pointed out, came to Marxism directly from the original Christian conceptions of Hegelian philosophy. The vocabulary has become rationalized (except for revealing traces), but the structure and drama of the Christological narratives has been preserved. Where Hegel writes (in his *History of the Philosophy of Religion*), "Christ has risen. Negation is consequently surmounted, and the negation of the negation is thus a moment of the Divine nature," Marx writes (in *Capital*), "capitalist production begets its own negation; communism is a negation of a negation," and again, in the *Economic and Philosophical Manuscripts:* "Communism is the phase of negation of the negation and is, consequently, for the next stage of historical development, a real and necessary factor in the rehabilitation and emancipation of man." As Professor Olssen has argued, both Hegel and Marx modulated a prototypal Christological pattern: the New Testament's basic narrative of a journey of departure, transformation, and return.[58] Hegel's theory of politics is "a well-nigh eerie transposition" of this Christological movement of departure (thesis), transformation (antithesis), and return (synthesis); the dialectic is a transcription into rationalistic terms of the movement informing the life of the Trinity, which Hegel described as "the axis on which the history of the world turns." Marx's thought, he contends, "is

---

*"Sie sind der Fels, auf welchen die Kirche der Gegenwart gebaut werden soll!"

shaped and controlled in its most intimate expressions by this same departure-transformation-return rhythm." Just as Marx had claimed to lay bare the "rational kernel" concealed within the "mystical shell" of Hegel's political theory, so did Hegel claim to have disclosed the "rational kernel" concealed within the Christological narratives. We have in both cases to do with a modulated resurrection drama following a sacrificial transformation and announcing the apocalyptic "fulfillment of time."

It was surely a sense of these dialectical transpositions that led Erich Fromm to make that unusual admission: "Marx's atheism is the most advanced form of rational mysticism, closer to Meister Eckhart or to Zen Buddhism than are most of those fighters for God and religion who accuse him of 'godlessness.'" For the scientific socialist of a certain orthodoxy, this might appear to be a case of joining the false gods instead of defeating them; but the loneliness of revolutionary man has propelled him into strange alliances and new casuistical compromises. "Thus," continues Dr. Fromm, warming to the task of theological syncretism, "Marxist and other forms of socialism are the heirs of prophetic Messianism, Christian Chiliastic sectarianism, thirteenth-century Thomism, Renaissance Utopianism, and eighteenth-century enlightenment."[59] The first Marxists may have thought they were breaking radically with the past; the last Marxists feel richer with the relics of all the ages.

Perhaps, then, Marx would not have been so outraged after all by being given his due place in the history of secular religion. I have often in London walked past his headstone and have long felt it to be a serious mistake that he lies in an unbeliever's plot at Highgate cemetery. What Marx criticized in religion was its tendency to strengthen and sanctify the existing social order, to make the powers that be ordained of God. But what of a religion that would tend to upset, undermine, and overthrow the existing social order? Again, religion was objectionable because it consoled the exploited masses with the prospect of milk and honey in a heavenly paradise and diverted them from the struggle for justice in the here-and-now. But what of a religion that aroused the masses, gave them new hope for tomorrow or the day after tomorrow, for their grandchildren? Could there, then, be an objection in principle? Engels himself once compared Christians and Communists in the following passage:

> The history of early Christianity has many characteristic points of contact with the present working-class movement. Christianity was also, in the beginning, a movement of the oppressed. It began as a religion of the enslaved and the outlawed, of the poor and the de-

feated victims of Roman violence. Both Christianity and proletarian socialism preach the coming deliverance from slavery and poverty.[60]

And when Che Guevera, that martyred and hence most beloved revolutionary Marxist of his day, thought of man's political failures, that long record of ineffectiveness and treason to the dream of a liberated humanity (and he savagely rejected by name the heritage of Joan of Arc, George Washington, Napoleon, Hitler, Mussolini, and Stalin), he felt that "only Christ was the exception to the rule that liberators are always betrayers . . . "[61]

There are thus, I suggest, ambiguities within ambiguities. First, Marx established both a science and a religion; second, he is both for and against religion; third, religion can be both reactionary and revolutionary; fourth, Marx's own science, which is in reality a political religion, begins in revolution and ends in reaction. His own words describing the religious ideology of his day are the best formulation of the major secular religion of our day:

> It is the universal theory of our world, its encyclopedic compendium, its popularized logic, its spiritual *point d'honneur*, with enthusiasm as its moral sanction, its ceremonial justification.[62]

5. The Fall

It would appear that throughout all of history man has tried to fulfill some of his highest moral and political aspirations through some form of revolutionary act. There is a line, no doubt, which can be drawn from the anger of the biblical prophets to the modern storminess, associated with 1917 and after. Few can remain untouched, unmoved, in the face of such a vivifying gallery of Promethean figures. And yet, during this long and ever-recurring process of revolt and rebellion something extraordinary has always happened—a tragic failure, a surprising turn and twist, an unexpected decline and fall—which led away from fulfillment to a sense of betrayal.

Engels understood this, when he wrote in a revealing letter: "People who boasted that they had made a revolution have always seen the next day that they had no idea what they were doing, that the revolution made did not in the least resemble the one they would have liked to make. . . . That is what Hegel calls the irony of history, an irony which few historic personalities escape." But among those happy few, presumably, he included himself. Herman Melville, puzzling in his preface over the meaning of *Billy Budd*, asked how it was possible that after "the rectification of the old world's hereditary wrongs . . . straightway the

Revolution itself became a wrong-doer, one more oppressive than the kings"? Was it only what the Greeks condemned as hubris, the excessive ambition and pride of men who would live like the gods, with their stolen fire and on their mountain peaks? Pascal formulated the conventional theological explanation: "Man is neither angel nor brute, and the unfortunate thing is that he who would act the angel acts the brute." William Butler Yeats has set the poetic mood in his quatrain:

> Hurrah for revolution! Let the cannon shoot,
> The beggar upon horseback lashes the beggar on foot.
> Hurrah for revolution! Cannon once again,
> The beggars have changed places but the lash goes on.

But if this is either too metaphysical, or too poetical, we have the more empirical workaday reflections of historians, psychologists, and sociologists, on the unhappy course of revolutionary hope.[63]

Historical analysis pays great attention to the biographical details, to the differences in character and talent among the revolutionaries themselves. Conrad put it as incisively as anyone in his remarkable novel, *Under Western Eyes:*

> In a real revolution the best characters do not come to the front. A violent revolution falls into the hands of narrow-minded fanatics and of tyrannical hypocrites at first. Afterwards come the turn of all the pretentious intellectual failures of the time. Such are the chiefs and the leaders. You will notice that I have left out the mere rogues. The scrupulous and the just, the noble, humane and devoted natures, the unselfish and the intelligent may begin a movement—but it passes away from them. They are not the leaders of a revolution. They are its victims: the victims of disgust, of disenchantment—often of remorse. Hopes grotesquely betrayed, ideals caricatured—that is the definition of revolutionary success. There have been in every revolution hearts broken by such success.[64]

But brokenheartedness is only the ailment of the utopian revolutionary. For the anti-utopian revolutionary who has, as we have seen, "no ideals to realize," who has only contempt for the stages of change and pragmatic innovation, the onrushing course of events is not a degenerating but literally a regenerating movement.

Engels's letter (which I referred to above) is replete with instructive imagery:

> What I know or believe about the situation in Russia impels me to the opinion that the Russians are approaching their 1789. The revolution *must* break out there in a given time; it *may* break out there any day. In these circumstances the country is like a charged mine which only

needs a fuse to be laid to it. . . . Once the spark has been put to the powder, once the forces have been released and national energy has been transformed from potential into kinetic energy (another favourite image of Plekhanov's and a very good one)—the people who laid the spark to the mine will be swept away by the explosion, which will be a thousand times as strong as themselves.

A moment later Engels has changed his metaphor.

Supposing these people imagine they can seize power, what does it matter? Provided they make the hole which will shatter the dyke, the flood itself will soon rob them of their illusions . . . there, when 1789 has once been launched, 1793 will not be long in the following.

As a man of both '89 and '93, Napoleon himself had some thoughts on the subject; and, just as Marx (as we have seen) seemed to be echoing his views on the utopians, Engels here appears to be paralleling Bonapartist certainties and rhetoric.[65] "General rule:" ran Napoleon's formulation,

No social revolution without terror. Every revolution is, by its nature, a revolt which success and the passage of time legitimize but in which terror is one of the inevitable phases.

The metaphor is only a slight variant of the versions of natural catastrophe. A Jacobin before him, Collot d'Herbois, had once shouted, "Some wish to moderate the revolutionary movement. What! Can a tempest be steered? The Revolution is one. We cannot and we must not check its motion." And a revolutionary man of letters, Shelley, imagined this scene when, in his vision of *The Revolt of Islam* (1818), the oath to be free was taken:

The very darkness shook, as with a blast
  Of subterranean thunder, at the cry;
The hollow shore its thousand echoes cast
  Into the night, as if the sea, and sky,
And earth, rejoiced with new-born liberty. . . .
Yet soon bright day will burst—even like a chasm
  Of fire, to burn the shrouds outworn and dead,
Which wrap the world; a wide enthusiasm,
To cleanse the fevered world as with an earthquake's spasm![66]

The image-ridden revolutionary, whether poet, plotter, or proconsul, exuberates in his language. For Napoleon, Revolution is a "convulsion"

as irresistible in its effects as a volcanic eruption. When the mysterious molten substance in the entrails of the earth has reached its explosive point, the lava escapes and the eruption takes place. The hidden travail of the masses follows an identical course: when their sufferings are ripe, they explode in revolution.[67]

Wilhelm Weitling (whom Max Beer called "the only really great Communist of pre-Marxian times") wrote of the revolution coming "like a thunderstorm" and of communism spreading "like a flow of lava." And Che Guevera, a century later, still listening for the "rumblings" of "the new world which is coming," predicted that "to the horror of the old world, the volcano will hurl its lava up to the heights of the heavens . . . " It was a fearful image of Vesuvian perversity, and it also appealed to Marx, who quoted with satisfaction a journalist's reference in 1850 to *die glühende Lava der Revolution* (the glowing lava of the revolution)." For Bakunin, with rather more Russian temperament, it would roll "like a raging avalanche, devouring and destroying. . . ."

Mixed metaphors in the language of revolution were almost inevitable: for there are, in truth, only very limited verbal resources available.[68] One turns either to the elemental forces of nature (as, with Milton and Shelley, most poets tended to do) or to the instrumental powers of man (as, with Harrington, most ideologists tended to do); or sometimes, in stylistic chaos but temperamental consistency, to both. Plekhanov's faith allied itself less with the natural than with the man-made. The anarchists, after all, had been throwing bombs for the revolution, and this drastic anarchistic commitment was skillfully countered by Plekhanov in a famous and ingenious formulation which showed the true cunning of revolutionary semantics; the word took the place of the thing. "An idea that is revolutionary in its internal content is a kind of dynamite for which no other explosive in the world may be substituted."[69] Revolution was the only true dynamite. And when, at long last, it came to explode—in order, as Alexander Blok said, "to make everything over . . . to make everything different, to change our false, filthy, boring hideous life into a just, clean, gay, and beautiful life"—the political poet's language itself burst into metaphorical fireworks:

> When such an intent, concealed since the dawn of time in the heart of man, the heart of the people, breaks its confining bonds and rushes forth in a stormy torrent, tearing down the last dams, carrying off chunks of riverbank, this is called revolution. Lesser, tamer, lowlier things are called insurrection, riot, coup d'etat. But *this* is called *revolution*.
>
> It is akin to Nature. Woe to those who expect a revolution to fulfill merely their own dreams, however high-minded and noble. A revolution, like a hurricane, like a blizzard, always brings something new and unexpected. It cruelly deceives many, it easily maims the deserving in its vortex, it often carries the undeserving unharmed to dry land; but these are details, they change neither the main direction of the torrent nor its awesome, deafening roar. The roar is still about something *grand*—always.

The sweep of the Russian Revolution, which wants to engulf the whole world (no genuine revolution can desire less; whether the wish will come true isn't ours to forecast), is such that it hopes to raise a world-wide cyclone, which will carry warm winds and the sweet scent of orange groves to snow-covered lands, moisten the sun-scorched steppes of the South with cool northern rain.

"Peace and the brotherhood of nations" is the sign under which the Russian Revolution runs its course. This is what its torrent roars. This is the music that all who have ears must hear.[70]

Thus, whether flood or explosion or tempest or eruption, the true revolution is in the maximum intensity. But what happens when the roaring pressure mounts?

Psychological analysis suggests that it is not merely that the best gives way to the worst, but, in the heat of revolutionary passion, that it *becomes* the worst. Things move (and here I am inverting Saint-Just's epigram) from courage to weakness, from virtue to crime.

There is in Anatole France's *The Gods Athirst* a portrait of a young Jacobin who can hardly wait for the noble abolition of hated capital punishment but soon will be demanding the most ruthless destruction of all enemies. There is something of both best and worst in Robespierre, who believed once that "there is no more formidable enemy to liberty than fanaticism" and came to believe later that "the terror is nothing more than prompt, strict, undeviating justice"; and in Marat, who was the organizer of the massacres of September 1792, yet once, a few years earlier, excused himself, on grounds of sensitiveness, from attending a postmortem.

"When the virile generation," as Tocqueville pointed out, "which had launched the revolution had perished, as usually befalls a generation engaging in such ventures, its first fine energy had dwindled ... " We are claiming just a bit more: that all life changes men, and the revolutionary life changes men most radically. Remembering, no doubt, his own Jacobin time of virile engagement, a disenchanted Coleridge wrote of the moment when he knew men to be

> ... least themselves in the mad whirl of crowds
> Where folly is contagious, and too oft
> Even wise men leave their better sense at home
> To chide and wonder at them when returned.[71]

One vivid moment of contagious transformation is caught by Chateaubriand, and it concerns Malesherbes, a relation of his for whom he had affection. In his *Memoirs*, Chateaubriand records:

He was full of knowledge, courage, and integrity, but so violent and hot-blooded that one day, talking to me about Condorcet, he said:

"That man was a friend of mine; today I would have no scruples about killing him like a dog." The tide of the Revolution swept over him.[72]

A half-century later, Walter Bagehot, stopping on a Paris street to watch the barricades going up, caught another moment in the tumid career of principled violence:

> I saw them myself, men whose physiognomy and accoutrements exactly resembled the traditional Montagnard, sallow, stern, compressed, with much marked features which expressed but resisted suffering, and brooding one-ideaed thought, men who from their youth upward had for ever imagined, like Jonah, that they did well—immensely well—to be angry, men armed to the teeth, and ready, like the soldiers of the first Republic, to use their arms savagely and well in defence of theories broached by a Robespierre, a Blanqui, or a Barbes, gloomy fanatics, over-principled ruffians. I may perhaps be mistaken in reading in their features the characters of such men, but I know that when one of them disturbed my superintendence of barricade-making with a stern *allez vous-en*, it was not too slowly that I departed, for I *felt* that he would rather shoot me than not.[73]

Sociological analysis comes to illuminate our problem with a breakdown of ideal (and not-so-ideal) types whose minds and spirits have a natural affinity with revolutions, who are drawn invariably into the movement. As John Stuart Mill used to say with that characteristic English finickiness about temperament and character, "it really is of importance, not only what men do, but also what manner of men they are that do it . . . ." A character in *Dr. Zhivago* saw "the vast figure of Russia bursting into flames like a light of redemption for all the sorrows and misfortunes of mankind." But Pasternak knew his manner of men:

> . . . revolutions are made by fanatical men of action with one-track minds, geniuses in their ability to confine themselves to a limited field. They overturn the old order in a few hours or days, the whole upheaval takes a few weeks or at most years, but the fanatical spirit that inspired the upheavals is worshipped for decades thereafter, for centuries.

Yet, mourning for Lara, he also mourned "that distant summer in Meliuzeievo when the revolution had been a god come down to earth from heaven."

There are, to be sure, the idealists whose sincere indignation and compassion catches them up in a struggle against injustice and suffering; if they are often intemperate we would do well not to ignore Renan's reminder that "it is often the fanatics, and not always the delicate spirits, that are found grasping the right thread of the solutions required by the future ... " But there are others in the ranks. There are cynical and arrogant intriguers; there are romantics for whom it is tingling pleasure to be involved in underground conspiracy; there are youths who are exhilarated by the free outlet for hitherto purposeless energies. A woman historian has sketched for us the role of bored wives of businessmen before the French Revolution: "They were devastated with boredom and given to fits of the vapors; restlessly, they applauded innovators." "Vanity," said Napoleon, "made the Revolution; liberty was only a pretext." We know, too, the angry man who would (as a Karamazov confessed) persist in indignation even if he were wrong. There is also the enthusiast and his loyal friend; the neurotic with his pliable accomplice; the outsize man of energy who strides through events (like Bakunin with "satanic pride"). In a word: all the masks of human nature.[74] Here, then, is another putative source of the fall: for if all of humanity is there, how will men succeed in transforming themselves by their own collective effort? Will not human weakness always tend to reproduce social failure?

Pondering the problem of the failure of the Brook Farm utopian (for all his "heroic devotion to the cause of human welfare"), Hawthorne sought in *The Blithedale Romance* to ascribe it to "a stern and dreadful peculiarity." There was, he observed, something "not altogether human" about the so-called celestial spirit.

> This is always true of those men who have surrendered themselves to an overruling purpose. It does not so much impel them from without, nor ever operate as a motive power within, but grows incorporate with all that they think and feel, and finally converts them into little else save that one principle.... They have no heart, no sympathy, no reason, no conscience. They will keep no friend, unless he make himself the mirror of their purpose; they will smite and slay you, and trample your dead corpse under foot, all the more readily, if you take the first step with them, and cannot take the second, and the third, and every other step of their terribly strait path.

Hawthorne's insight went further than Conrad's, deeper than Pasternak's. "They have an idol," he wrote of "our little army of saints and martyrs,"

> to which they consecrate themselves high-priest, and deem it holy work to offer sacrifices of whatever is most precious; and never once seem to suspect—so cunning has the Devil been with them—that this false deity, in whose iron features, immitigable to all the rest of

mankind, they see only benignity and love, is but the spectrum of
the very priest himself, projected upon the surrounding darkness.
And the higher and purer the original object, and the more un-
selfishly it may have been taken up, the slighter is the probability
that they can be let to recognize the process by which godlike benevolence has been debased into all-devouring egotism.[75]

How would a Bakunin of generous soul bridge the chasm between the
creative and the destructive passions once he came under the influence
of a Nechayev? He plunged headlong into an enthusiasm for the *Principles of Revolution* (1869), in which Nechayev wrote:

We recognize no other activity but the work of extermination, but we
admit that the forms in which this activity will show itself will be
extremely varied—poison, the knife, the rope, etc. In this struggle
revolution sanctifies everything alike.

Bakunin joined the call for a crusade of destruction, and he, too, became
a robber baron in a holy cause. The good life was only to be found
beyond the law. When he was once asked what his aims and beliefs
were, he burst out: "I believe in nothing, I read nothing, I think of only
one thing: break their necks, smash their heads, leave nothing left of
them!" And when he was asked what he would do if he succeeded in
realizing all his plans and creating everything he had dreamed of, he
replied: "Then I should at once begin to pull down again everything I
had made."[76]

Yet, after all this, I still would want to claim that there remains an
ambivalence, a double focus, and if I return to this it is not merely to
revive a casual metaphor. For this same Michael Bakunin was the gigantic and heroic figure whom Richard Wagner had met on the streets of
Dresden during the revolutionary events of 1848—and who inspired
him (according to Bernard Shaw) to the grand conception of Siegfried.

"Half his lifetime," Nietzsche wrote, "Wagner believed in the *Revolution* as only a Frenchman could have believed in it . . . . He thought he
had found a typical revolutionary in *Siegfried.*" When Wagner asked
himself where all the world's evil came from and what could be done to
liberate mankind, his reply was that of *"alle Revolutions-Ideologen."*
Wagner would (as Nietzsche explained) declare war on the old society,
its laws, institutions, customs, and morals. He would struggle for "the
dawn of the golden age," for *die Götterdämmerung der alten Moral* when all
evil would be abolished, and would in the meantime "console the world
with the hope of a socialistic Utopia in which *'alles gut wird'* . . . "[77]

Nietzsche was guilty here of some polemical oversimplification;
Wagner was nothing like an orthodox socialist; and in his most youthful
effusions on behalf of utopia he insisted on the half-Christian, half-

Apollonian ideal in which brotherhood and community would be wedded to beauty and joy. His mind was insensitive to economics but oversensitive to the rhetoric which united a like-minded international. Europe was "a huge volcano," and Wagner's musical ear heard a resounding "fearsome roar," and he imagined how

> crater columns of black smoke ascend to heaven big with storm, and mantle all the earth with darkness, while here and there a lava stream, a fiery harbinger, breaks through the hard-set crust and bears destruction to the vale below ...

He was certain of his own place and role in the enfolding drama: "I will destroy the existing order of things." In the central egoistic tradition of the great utopian revolutionaries, he naturally put himself at the center of the stage:

> Two peoples, only, are there from henceforth: the one that follows me, the other that withstands me. The one I lead to happiness; over the other grinds my path: for I am Revolution, I am the ever-fashioning Life, I am the only God, to whom each creature testifies, who spans and gives both life and happiness to all that is!

Here is the godlike Revolution as it reaches its Wagnerian crescendo:

> Ay, we behold it; the old world is crumbling, a new will rise therefrom; for the lofty goddess Revolution comes rustling on the wings of storm, her stately head ringed round with lightnings, a sword in her right hand, a torch in her left, her eye so stern, so punitive, so cold; and yet what warmth of purest love, what wealth of happiness streams forth toward him who dares to look with steadfast gaze into that eye! Rustling she comes, the e'er-rejuvenating mother of mankind; destroying and fulfilling, she fares across the earth; before her soughs the storm, and shakes so fiercely at man's handiwork that vast clouds of dust eclipse the sky, and where her mighty foot steps falls in ruins what an idle whim had built for aeons, and the hem of her robe sweeps its last remains away. But in her wake there opens out a ne'er-dreamed paradise of happiness, illumined by kindly sunbeams; and where her foot had trodden down, spring fragrant flowers from the soil, and jubilant songs of free mankind fill full the air scarce silent from the din of battle.[78]

In that world of "battle," Wagner found Bakunin to be "a most witty and wonderful man." And Bakunin found in Wagner's world a moment of humane hesitation. He was present in the Opera House when Wagner conducted Beethoven's Ninth Symphony, and apparently the performance led Bakunin to introduce a reservation into the doctrine of pan-destruction. When he congratulated Wagner, Bakunin declared that "should all the music that had ever been written perish in the world conflagration, they must pledge themselves to rescue this symphony ... " Once, a half-century before, Babeuf had insisted: "We will pay any price ... If need be let all the arts perish ... " Lenin, a half-century later, turning away from Beethoven's *Appassionata*, told Gorky:

> But I can't listen to music too often. It affects your nerves, makes you want to say nice stupid things and stroke the heads of people who could create such beauty while living in this vile hell. And now you mustn't stroke anyone's head—you might get your hand bitten off. You have to hit them on the head, without any mercy.[79]

We are left with this historical irony. When Bakunin left Dresden, the Opera House was in flames and ruins. Wagner went on to Switzerland and many years later wrote his *Siegfried*, wherein the young hero forged the sword, slew the dragon, and passed through fire. It was an ambiguous victory of the utopian imagination over reality.

In that reality, as I have been strongly hinting, there was an element of *malaise* which, if it fed the creative instincts of great art, also fired the destructive habits of revolutionary political passion. "Revolution," one wise anarchist (Gustave Landauer) has confessed, "comes like a convalescent fever, between two spells of sickness; it would not exist at all if it were not preceded by fatigue and followed by exhaustion." This prompts a consideration of what, after all, our other analysts of revolutionary momentum, the pathologists, are likely to offer.

I am reluctant to broach this subject because it has in our time become so fashionable to reduce all motivations to the unconscious, to associate radicalism with regression, socialism with psychiatry, religious reform with "excremental visions." Such a view is narrow and unsympathetic and mean-spirited; and, to be sure, it is not really new. Thoreau said in *Walden* that "if anything ail a man so that he does not perform his functions, if he have a pain in his bowels even ... he forthwith sets about reforming—the world." The trouble with this is that the political scientist has yet to set the proper correlation between, say, conservatism and constipation. If the revolutionary has his rash, the liberal, too, is not without his libido, nor the reactionary without his ration of repression and anxiety. Still, the matter would appear to be a serious one, and we should not be tempted to throw the diagnosis out with the quack.

In point of fact, it was a serious student of France, J. M. Thompson, who proposed that more attention be paid to "the medical history of the Revolution." He observed Marat's "yellow aspect" (the skin disease that might have saved Charlotte Corday the trouble of killing him); Mirabeau's ruined eyesight; the paleness of Saint-Just; and Robespierre's "sea-green" complexion. "Are they not," he asks, "all symptoms of physical ill-health due to overwork, nervous strain, and lack of sleep and exercise? Do they not go far to explain the atmosphere of personal and party passion in which the early promise of the Revolution was unfulfilled?" A not unsympathetic biographer of Babeuf concedes that a modern psychologist would "doubtless describe Babeuf as a paranoiac"; and he goes on to cite a bit of evidence:

> he was wont to work himself into a frenzy of excitement before he could write his inflammatory, rhetorical outbursts. He would pace nervously up and down the room, walking faster and faster until his eyes blazed and he snarled phrases from clenched teeth. After kicking the furniture and emitting cries of *Aux armes! L'insurrection!* he would seize a pen and write furiously until he was bathed in sweat and his whole body trembled as if in a frenzy.[80]

Bakunin himself once admitted that "there was in my character a radical defect," but he went on to specify only "love for the fantastic, for out-of-the-way unheard-of adventures, for undertakings which open up an infinite horizon and whose end no man can foresee"—nothing worse here than the usual elements of romanticism, adventurism, and Faustian longing. His biographer, E. H. Carr, however, makes a more revealing admission:

> ... his sexual development is strangely arrested. In later life, Michael was certainly impotent. When he was in his twenties, some of his contemporaries already suspected an incapacity of this kind; he is not known to have had sexual relations with any women. No explicit statement on the subject, medical or other, has been preserved. But it seems probable that his incapacity dated from adolescence, and was the psychological product of that hatred of a dominating mother of which he afterward spoke in such passionate terms. His tumultous passions, denied a sexual outlet, boiled over into every personal and political relationship of his life, and created that intense, bizarre, destructive personality which fascinated even where it repelled, and which left its mark on half nineteenth-century Europe.[81]

I am not arguing on behalf of the validity of such an interpretation of revolutionary neurosis. I am only suggesting the persistence of the pathological theme in the cycles of ideology. We are surely very far from having discovered a method of making a true and final evaluation of the medical details which sympathetic biographers have soberly recorded and hostile contemporaries have invidiously charged. How much should one make of Saint-Simon's mental illness or Robert Owen's decline into madness? And what is the balance between poetic, political, and pathological insight in, say, this characteristic outburst among the dissidents? Jacobinism, wrote Proudhon, with the peculiar ruthlessness that only revolutionaries can have for each other, "is above all an affection, a malady, a kind of moral pestilence, special to the French temperament . . . "[82]

There is additional (and less ethnocentric) evidence from three recent historians of the English, the German, and the Russian revolutionary movements.

The historian of "the revolution of the saints" was moved to ask: What connection is there between the political radicalism and the psychology of Puritanism's "unsettled" men? He denies that "holiness was an impractical dream" or that it was "the program of neurotic, muddled, or unrealistic men"; but he does suggest that "the 'unsettledness' which Knox, Cartwright and Cromwell experienced, with all its attendant fearfulness and enthusiasm" was "disfiguring" as well as ennobling, and hints that "saintly vigor had its own pathology."

"The intellectual revolt of Mehring and Luxemburg," we have been told by Rosa Luxemburg's careful and balanced biographer, "was neither wholly objective nor altruistic; it was also in part a remedy for their own personality conflicts." This would be, he recognizes, "a dangerous statement if the evidence were not so overwhelming." For both of them, he suggests, "the recovery from a period of excessive alienation from society was something of a relief; alienation which could be cured as much by fiercer opposition as by any revisionist attempt at integration."

In the Russian movement, too, and even exacerbatingly more so, the revolutionary temperament was shaped in the personality conflict between alienation and integration, between the temptations of revisionism and oppositional ferocity. A leading follower of Bukharin and Plekhanov conceded (if only in private correspondence) that in his opinion Bernstein's followers "have no less right to exist than the ultra-revolutionaries: [for] the whole thing is a matter of temperament." Pavel Axelrod went on to admit that the reformist road to socialism "even has some advantage over the methods of *Sturm und Drang*: at least it will cost less blood." The main point against it, we are told, is that "it would be exceedingly boring."[83]

Let me not be misunderstood. I am not suggesting that the natural history of revolution is determined by the unnatural spirit of the revolutionary. Quite the contrary, for both are the product of a more general, basic ailment: a disordered society. The objective sources of revolution are in a world's misery. The revolutionary is born in despair and hopelessness, out of the hateful conflict between powerless men and powerful institutions. His desperation is always mixed with a dawning sense of human justice. He comes—sometimes with a dream, sometimes with a malady—to confront the sheer immobility of the reactionary mass that for so much of history has been the oppressive *status quo ante revolutionibus*. Chip away at it? How absurd. Reform it and improve it? How self-defeating and dull. Move it slowly, gradually, moderately? Impossible. It has to be undermined. Destroyed. Split, subverted, and disintegrated.

> To achieve great things, great changes are needed.
> Little changes are the enemies of great changes.[84]

6. The Vow

The ambiguities we have been considering may well have blurred the true double nature of the revolutionary vow: the true revolutionary is committed to his cause both as means and ends. Revolution, taken only as means, suggests that there are situations of political and social crisis where, all available methods of change—peaceful or gradual or reasonable, or any other approach associated with concessions, compromise, and reconciliation—having proved futile, only a sharp break and basic overturn can now serve to defend justice and establish a tolerable order. So it is that not only radicals but also moderates, reformers, liberals, and even conservatives, find themselves enlisted in a revolution. Revolution, as an end, suggests that a new society is conceivable, and is indeed possible, only on the basis of fundamentally different social, political and cultural principles. All utopians are revolutionary (though not all revolutionaries are utopian); many reformers are revolutionary, in the sense that the ultimate end of all their reforms and renovations transcends the existing patterns. In other words: a revolutionary end may be achieved by reformist means, just as the reformer's utopia may have to be hastened by desperate, unavoidable abolitionist deeds. None of this, by itself, amounts to that new kind of total commitment which has characterized modern political passion.

By the vow I do not mean the mere acceptance of revolution as a method of social change in circumstances which are held to be patently hopeless without some recourse to immoderate and even violent measures. Nor do I mean the mere envisioning of an organically different social structure as the goal of social striving. I mean the coexistence of both the dream and the desperation in those men who are so intoxicated spiritually, so infatuated physically with either the violent means or the transcendent end, that one is unthinkable without the other. The vow is taken when the revolution is prized as the perfected method for the perfect result; it guarantees paradise at a stroke, for it combines the miracle of the means and the miracle of the ends. Thus, a new society comes to be impossible without a prior revolutionary commitment, and a revolution is only the true instrument to enforce the future when it destroys completely before building anew. Neither of these assumptions is true; both taken together have in the course of history proved tragic.

I will, for the moment, pass over the usual accompaniment of the familiar rodomontade. The following passage can do duty for a thousand other similar expressions of faith in the politics of paradise and the secret millennium.

It is now sufficiently evident that a great change is about to take place in the institutions of the civilized world. The crisis is arrived! the moral world is in a state of rapid transition; the reign of chicanery is about to close forever, and the black empire of church and state mystery will cease henceforward to terrify and enslave mankind ... god-like humanity proclaims aloud that a mighty moral revolution is necessary, and about to take place.[85]

This happens to be Bronterre O'Brien's trumpet call in 1831 on behalf of so-called Whole-Hog Chartism, and it is this raw appetite for going the whole hog which is the characteristic revolutionary instinct. Over the years, in its most sober formulation, it emerges as a persistent demand for nothing less than a total change in the System. But this has proved to be little else but a piece of symbolic action, the rhetorical gesture suited to the deep, if vague, longing for a sense of otherness. Usually, it implies nothing very specific, being ineffably complete in itself. Sometimes one outlandish detail is offered to indicate how total and how systematic a total change in the system might be.

Thus come the classic cries: one American revolutionary called for a new language in the New World (abolishing English and all European tongues in favor of some fresh and native means of communication, presumably an Indian tribal dialect); one French revolutionary proposed a radical change in the actual population (simply abolishing the excess by sloughing off the decadent and the useless); and one Russian revolutionary drafted a plan to destroy the entire living presence of the past (by burning all the art and razing the ancient buildings). Would anything less than this do? Obviously, no new system which followed in the wake of a completely authentic revolution representing "total change" could conceivably function within the traditional confines of old languages spoken by an old people, living among antiquated piles, surrounded by all the familiar objects of the past. The world is to be recreated, and man will be reborn.

The predilection for this special tone has, as I have already remarked, its counterpart in the medieval wrath of European religious insurgency.

Let us remind ourselves at this point how the precursors of utopia and revolution took their vows to act as the divine agents of terrestrial justice. Here, as illustrated in the *Reformatio Sigismundi* (ca. 1438),[86] perhaps the most famous and influential radical document on the eve of the Reformation, are the basic elements of the political commitment to change the world which we have been tracing from Dante and Joachim to Marx, Lassalle, and Bakunin:

1. The Final Crisis is Now

Obedience is dead. Justice is grievously abused. Nothing stands in its proper order.... But we ought to realize: matters cannot continue like this.... Our society has become sick and feeble.... Things have come to their final pass. There must be a new order.

2. A Time for Anger

A reformation cannot succeed in the empire unless it is imposed by force and with the pain of punishment.... An avenging judge is approaching, and he will come among us and judge us, and his judgments will be executed in a spirit of anger.... Weeds must be rooted out if fruits are to grow in the garden.

3. The Movement of the Just

... justice and goodness attract few followers, but in the end they overcome all adversity. The treasury of justice seems to be open to only the few and the lowly.... If all things were shared in the city, if people associated to own and do things in common, all these evils would disappear. If no man tried to injure the interest of his neighbor, if all men worked for the common good, there would be no struggling and no strife, and each would live in equality with his neighbor.... Let us rediscover our true interest and live by our conscience.... It is high time! ... When you see the approach of the just ones, enlist in their ranks, join them, and help destroy all those inequities and iniquities which now cause the whole world to be plunged into despair ... be in the vanguard of the campaign.

4. The Great Refusal

You may ask: How can this new order be introduced ... you must know that wrongdoing cannot forever prevail against the determination to set things right. Refuse to bow to their threats, reject their claims to be your judges, and they will become powerless. And the poor, the common folk, must show faith.... They will surely overcome.... You will see: one will arise who will establish the better order by means of force. Join him, one and all. The new order must come.... The time is near as you shall learn.

5. The Prophecy

In the fourth [apocryphal] book of Ezra we read: 'In the year 1439 there will arise a small consecrated man who will govern and punish the people. And he will rule from sea to sea. His feet shall suppress sin. All that are harmful shall be destroyed and burned. All people will be joyous. Justice will rise again!' This is not wrongly prophesied. We sense that the time is near . . . . The time of fulfillment is at hand.

All these elements were recombined and developed into an extraordinary communist manifesto by that astonishing Alsatian insurrectionist who goes only by the name of *der Oberrheinische Revolutionär*. The document of the so-called Upper Rhenish Revolutionary, rescued from the archives of Colmar, illuminates the character of the revolutionary vow as it issues from the apocalyptic commitment to a paradise on earth (in this case, evidently, in "beautiful Alsace"). He was convinced—and he argued the case with learned references and quotations—that the great and desired reform could neither be legal nor peaceful but would represent a violent renovation. He knew it would be a two-front struggle: against both the bishops and the monarchs, and he even suggests with a pre-Jacobinical insouciance, *"Man wird dem Kaiser ein Bauernhütlein aufsetzen und in das Elend schicken!,"* prefiguring the red bonnet which was to be placed on a crowned Bourbon head before dispatching him to limbo. "A Kaiser," he announced, "is made by the people; the people is not made by the Kaiser." He was preaching a holy war against evil and evildoers, especially the "blood-sucking enemies of the poor." How "miserable" it was, he cried, that "a wild animal should have more freedom than a man"! The times were out of joint; all coherence was gone. "The world is upside-down: truth is crushed, evil represses good, injustice reigns, law and loyalty are dead and love extinguished." He would organize a "Brotherhood of the Yellow Cross," and "with such a band of men I will challenge the world." What he was saying and what he proposed to be doing would be one, as in a unity of theory and practice: "Contend with words and fight with deeds!" As two of his aphorisms suggested, he was announcing the brotherhood of all men and proclaiming a reign of virtue (*"wir sind all gebrüder von Adam herkummen," "der heist nit edel, der nit in tugend lept"*).[87]

There is little sense in remarking, as so many historians do, that our man of the Rhine, like all the other social rebels of the Reformation era (Thomas Münzer, John Wyclif, Jan Hus), was essentially conservative or basically backward-looking, as if there were a proper compass or timepiece to determine such matters. All clocks in history tick forward. Every attempt to find one's direction calls for a new orientation. In his politics of paradise, the Rhine Revolutionary devised much that was original. His theory of government was a mixture of democratic constitutionalism and theocratic terror; his economics had a touch of both medieval and modern communism; his ideology, as in all radical temperments, veered between the certainties of a determined future and the individual opportunities for action now. He would have been at home in any of the subsequent centuries.

Insisting as he did on resistance to the established authorities, he appeared to be arguing on behalf of limitations to political power, for in the name of law and justice it would be possible to defy and even to remove a Pope or an Emperor. In fact he held to a doctrine of the self-determination of a sovereign people. All men were naturally free and noble ("*von Natur gleich frei und edel*"). But, insisting at the same time that the change in the human condition would come suddenly, dramatically, and all at once, he appeared to be moving irrepressibly into that visionary mysticism which, then as now, unites the revolution with the apocalypse. In his fantasy of the violent overturn, there would come "a man out of the people" who would inaugurate the epoch of "One Shepherd, One Flock, One Faith throughout the World." In his visions of the future, he glimpsed fire from the sky, torrential floods over the land, a rain of blood, a plague of hunger and disease. His astrology (he was known as an *astronomus*) kept his faith firm: for not only was the future in the stars, but the heavens could provide a sense of security and would indeed offer a frame of celestial inevitability. His messianism kept his rage at a constant boil: for not only would the leader come out of the mountain forest, but in his coming to Caesaropapist power there would be "murder, strangulation, burning, beheading, hanging ... " It is the moment of divine vengeance against the enemies of the people: "*Schlacht si all ze tot!* (Strike them all dead)."[88]

Were these rebels of the Rhine "revolutionaries"? Perhaps not. But then the rebels who actually came out of the Black Forest—no authentic sign of a messianic Friedrich was ever detected—were, recognizably and indisputably, reformers. A moment's exercise in comparative ideology reveals the profound bifurcation in language and temperament between the little men of small steps and the heroes who would bestride the world. I would contrast the *Reformatio Sigismundi* and the manifesto of the Alsatian paradise with one of the innumerable "practical and mundane" documents which historians have collected in assembling the literature of grievance and protest of that century. Consider the Articles of the Peasants of Stühlingen and Lupfen in the year 1525.[89] They set out, in the name of "fairness, reason, and common sense," exactly what it is that has outraged the people in the country and in the towns and precisely what has to be done to introduce a state of affairs more in accordance with divine and natural law. They petition redress for arbitrary imprisonment and wanton confiscations; they protest unwarranted exactions and exorbitant public costs (especially for lawyers and notaries); they insist on accountability for damages. Oppressive (and unpaid) personal services should be abolished, as should indiscriminate toll charges and illegal expropriations of land and farmhouses. The people should be allowed to live and work, marry and prosper, serve and be served, with due rights and responsibilities.

Over the course of the next centuries of European society, each of these reform demands was fulfilled—partially, then completely— slowly, and often with the prodding of renewed agitation from below, sometimes quickly with the help of hectic concessions from above (or, as a shrewd German statesman of the day observed, with "the measures that must be taken to keep the raging stream in its bed"). The oppressive social order of the time of the *Bundschuh* and *der arme Konrad* was unrecognizable by the time of Kant, Goethe, and Napoleon, as a society was transformed bit by bit, its institutions reconstructed and refashioned, its economic and legal bases replaced and indeed revolutionized. (Although history here can be mildly skeptical as to whether the new commonsensical reason and fairness that was awaited from objective commercial law, independent judiciary, impartial lawyers and notaries, and the like were ever quite fully consummated. All deprivation is relative to the passing contemporary objects of social grievance, although the cry of human pain and protest has a timeless ring.) The reformers, then, went quietly from strength to strength; many humane ambitions found fulfillment; even some of the most utopian dreams came true.[90]

Not so with the men of the apocalypse, waiting for the end with its final solution. When prophecy failed, they redefined past and future and held fast to a new expectation of present promise. The fire next time; but the great conflagration which would purify the world and the divine earthquake with its golden lava, these are yet to be seen.[91]

If the delusion of the revolutionary is in this vow for totality, the violence of his tragedy is that the revolutionary situation—that vaunted moment of transition which, ever since Joachim of Flora, holds such mighty promise—is not the low point of desperation. "Not hunger provokes revolutions," Nietzsche wrote, "but the people *en mangeant* acquiring an appetite . . . "[92] This is also Tocqueville's famous paradox.[93]

> For it is not always when things are going from bad to worse that revolutions break out. On the contrary, it oftener happens that when a people which has put up with an oppressive rule over a long period without protest suddenly finds the government relaxing its pressure, it takes up arms against it. Thus the social order overthrown by a revolution is almost always better than the one immediately preceding it, and experience teaches us that, generally speaking, the most perilous moment for a bad government is one when it seeks to mend its ways . . . . Patiently endured so long as it seemed beyond redress, a grievance comes to appear intolerable once the possibility of removing it crosses men's mind.

Our desperado arrives, then, when hope has begun again, when the possibility and prospects of change become suddenly real. Thus, the revolutionary is the wrong man at the wrong time. He comes too late—with too much. He calls for violent change when for the first time peaceful change seems possible. He insists on blood on the streets when ink on paper might well do. He is extreme and impassioned when, at long last, a moderate reasonableness can effectively be brought into play.

The tragedy is in the unnecessary explosion. The imbalance in the pressure derives from the excess in the active historical agent. Much crumbles, things fall apart. One thinks of 1789 and 1917, of Bonaparte and of Stalin, and one can only mourn for the sacrifice of generations. It is, alas, too high a price to pay for the revolutionary astigmatism which mistook the momentary scene and an accidental opportunity for the grand dramatic stage of history.

Yet who saw the scene clearly? And what was the drama that should more properly have been played out? Before I conclude with a brief consideration of these two questions, I want to take a last backward glance at the main current of revolutionary thought in the three European cultures which have mainly engaged us: England, France, and Russia. In one, where once in the past an old revolution had been made and thereafter no fundamental or violent change was ever considered necessary or proper, a new philosophy of gradual and peaceful reform was held to be not only adequate but celebrated as the glory of true political culture. In the second, where the fresh wounds of a new, modern, and grand revolution were never to cease smarting, the sense of a great national future was never envisioned without the prospect of an angry extension of basic innovation and renewal. In the third, the coming century-awaited revolution, no doubt both grand and glorious, was an underdeveloped dream: for some Utopian, for others Scientific, for almost all, a stern mission of catastrophic proportions which was destined to fulfill the highest moral and historical necessities.

What, then, is best—never to have made a revolution? to have made a revolution and forgotten it? to have made a revolution and to be forever engaged in remembering it, reviewing and renewing it?

At this point in my account, both reader and author should be hungering for a truthful simplicity, for a modest and adequate formulation, possibly even for a useful banality along the lines of: Reform if possible, Revolution if need be. But no. In one's own camp, any sign of compromise is a mark of weak-spirited hesitation on the way to betrayal. In the other camp, the stern spirit of devotion is taken to be only a variant of ruthless fanaticism. One's own cause calls for a militant and unwavering loyalty to basic principle; it is always the other man's crusade which demands tempering through the controlling virtues of moderation and prudence. Yet it should be obvious to all but doctrinaire meliorists that reform is not always historically possible. John Morley[94] was shrewd enough to note that Burke's prudence, for all its eloquence on behalf of moderation and gradualism, had historical limitations; he insisted on facing, as few liberals do, the problem of the tragic circumstances in which no trimming of branches but only going to the root of the matter will do.[95] Nor is this, as in Tocqueville, simply a matter of human will and temperament. There are also the structural reasons which Marx, sometimes mechanically, sometimes sensitively, recorded.[96] He once prophesied (in 1879, and we are fortunate enough to have the diary entry of Marx's luncheon partner in the London Devonshire Club):

> ... a great and not distant crash in Russia: thinks it will begin by reforms from above, which the old bad edifice will not be able to bear, and which will lead to its tumbling down altogether. As to what could take its place, he had evidently no clear idea, except that for a long time Russia would be unable to exercise any influence in Europe.[97]

Men believe they are making the history that history has made for them. The reformer, in the eyes of the militant, is the despicable betrayer of the true cause. He plasters and refuses to pull down. He tinkers and patches. He trims instead of cutting to the roots. He reconsiders when he should revolt. He compromises. He concedes. He hesitates and temporizes. He prefers prudence to passion, and caution to audacity. He feels safe with the old and uneasy with the new.

The revolutionary, in the eyes of the moderate, is the crazed subverter of a fragile social order. He comes to destroy. He adores the fire and longs for the ashes. He hears the sky thundering and the rumble of the earth. His demands can never be fulfilled, and he presses on ruthlessly for the next radical phase. There is never an end. His extremism is in permanence.

Here, in this dichotomy, is the temperamental disposition in political thought reduced to the barest psychic essentials, and on these foundations are erected thinking man's inescapable superstructures of social action and sentiment: Ideology, formula one and two: Reform and Revolution.

So it is that, between the late Burke and the early Lenin, a century of social idealism has been steamrollered, squeezed dry, imprisoned between the opposite poles of the same helpless narrow-mindedness.[98] Coleridge had an uncanny metaphorical insight into the political tragedy of Burke's extreme final period when (to keep within the central image) fighting fire with fire could only add to the conflagration. In the first number of *The Watchman* (1 March 1796), Coleridge noted: "At the flames which rise from the altar of freedom, he kindled that torch with which he since endeavoured to set fire to her temple ... " And he added, mordantly: "Peace be to his spirit, when it departs from us: this is the severest punishment I wish him—that he may be appointed under porter to St. Peter, and be obliged to open the gate of heaven to Brissot, Roland, Condorcet, Fayette, and Priestley!"[99] Coleridge was straining for some third solution to the tragic duality of the conflict, as had Hobbes before him. There is a paragraph in *Behemoth* in which Hobbes wearily comments on the great polemic between Salmasius and John Milton on the murder of kings; the battle of the two books had shaken opinion in England and the Continent:

> I have seen them both; they are very good [in] Latine both, and hardly to be judged which is better; and both very ill reasoning, and hardly to be judged which is worst; like two Declamations *Pro* and *Con*, for Exercise only in a Rhetorick School, by one and the same man: So like is a Presbyterian to an Independent . . . [100]

I am only adumbrating here another of the themes of the *politica perennis*: for the sense recurs again and again that *les extrêmes se touchent*, and there must be an ascent possible to some third camp above the warring positions, or to some high, safe, sovereign ground in between. There is this moment, too, in Burke, the early Burke, where he appears to reach for this same transcendence: an accommodating moment when he is both reformer and revolutionary, when he is that strange and ambivalent political animal, the utopian idealist and the radical realist. It occurs, significantly enough, in the time between the American and the French Revolutions. In 1776, we find him romantic enough to cry: "Nothing less than a convulsion that will shake the globe to its centre can ever restore the European nations to . . . liberty." In 1788, we find him prudent enough to argue that "a wise nation, when it has once made a revolution upon its own principles and for its own ends, rests there." For "the first step," he wrote, "is revolution, by which power is conferred; the next is good laws, good order, good institutions, to give that power stability . . . "

What Edmund Burke sensed in the immediate context of the Boston Tea Party (and before the storming of the Bastille), Friedrich Gentz tried to consolidate by a postmortem on the anatomy of the two recent revolutions. Gentz had translated Burke's *Reflections on the French Revolution*, and John Quincy Adams translated Gentz's *The French and American Revolutions Compared* and had it published in Philadelphia in 1800. What united them all—the Irish M.P., the Prussian "Secretary of Europe," and the U.S. President-to-be—was the reverential preference for the American model of hurly-burly. Following Burke, Gentz's verdict was based on a grateful appreciation of the ability of the American revolutionaries to gauge "how far they were to go and where they must stop."

. . . as their purpose was in no sort to create, but only to preserve, not to erect a new building, but to free the old one from an external, burdensome, straitening scaffolding, and as it never occurred to them, in the rigorous sense of the word, to reform, even their own country, much less the whole world, they escaped the most dangerous of all the rocks which in our times threaten the founders of any great revolution, the deadly passion for making political experiments with abstract theories and untried systems . . . [101]

Walter Bagehot was being quite the complete Burkean in echoing Gentz's concern about the deadly passion and the most dangerous rock. He wrote of the gift of "conservative innovation": the gift of matching new institutions to old, of controlling the "wild passion for instant action" and uniting "life with measure, spirit with reasonableness."[102] For him, what was essential was the subtle quality of "animated moderation."[103]

It is this philosophy that Hannah Arendt, if I understand her correctly, has tried to give a modern restatement in her book *On Revolution*. She refers to "this notion of a coincidence of foundation and preservation by virtue of augmentation"—but by that she only means that there is an interconnection between the revolutionary act of beginning "something entirely new" and "conservative care" to shield this new beginning.[104] Burke, hating as he did "the very sound of metaphysical distinctions," is somewhat more circumspect. "Nothing is more beautiful," he writes, "in the theory of parliaments than that principle of renovation, and the union of permanence and change, that are happily mixed in their constitution: that in all our changes we are never wholly old or wholly new." His standard of a statesman is "a disposition to preserve and an ability to improve, taken together." But was he, in fact, as well aware as he claimed to be that "power rarely reforms itself"?[105] We are back again to Thomas More's dilemma. Where can the utopian stand to move the world except at a point between reform and revolution? Nothing will move forward except under energy and pressure.

In the time of Cromwell, we find Lord Clarendon writing (in a letter of 1648):[106] "I do confess it is the office of wise men to find expedients to reform and reconcile the affections of distempered men." Such distempered men could always, surprisingly enough, find something appropriate in Burke, e.g., his remark on agitation—"I like a clamour where there is an abuse. The fire-bell at midnight disturbs your sleep, but it keeps you from being burned in your bed." In the agitated, riotous time of the great Reform Bill of 1832, we find James Mill and his friends shrewdly, artfully putting forth "images of revolution" in order to frighten the Establishment into granting liberal concessions. "No use now shying the word Revolution," one of them wrote, "they [the Cabinet] must make one or the People will." "We must frighten them," another confided, "we must pretend to be frightened ourselves."[107]

The theatrical elements in the art of revolution will be occupying us in a later chapter; for now I want only to note that the artful strategy of energy and pressure, with melodramatic tactics cued into the events of the day, actually worked. Bentham's strategy was based on what he called "this faculty on the part of many who suffer by abuses of creating uneasiness in the bosoms of those who profit by them," and on which, he felt, "rests the only chance of hope for the future ... "[108] Mill's tactics were "meant to bring concessions from men who feared the consequences of not conceding," from men who (as Peel admitted) looked "with anxiety for the alternatives by which civil strife may be honourably averted ... "[109]

But the honor of the matter is not so easily settled. There are gnawing personal problems here which must trouble the finicky liberal mind. Can anxious concessions, hectically granted, produce anything but poor and flimsy legislation? Giving way under pressure to one's angry opposition is surely a dishonorable course? And can one be certain that a first reform bill would not lead to a second and a third in a dangerous chain of consequences? Sydney Smith had made four valiant speeches on behalf of the Reform Bill of 1832; and, looking back, he was not above making this confession: "I was a sincere friend to Reform; I am so still. It was a great deal too violent—but the only justification is, that you cannot reform as you wish, by degrees; you must avail yourself of the few opportunities that present themselves." Alas, the greater part of human improvements are indeed made after war, tumult, bloodshed, and civil commotion. "Mankind seems to object to every species of gratuitous happiness, and to consider every advantage as too cheap, which is not purchased by some calamity." Smith, thus, tempered the Mill-Bentham strategy of reform politics with a sense of the ironic ruses of history. Gradualists cannot always operate by degrees, and constitutionalists must come to terms with extralegal excess. Working, as a minister frequently must, "in the midst of hatred, injustice, violence and the worst of human passions, his works are not the works of calm and unembarrassed wisdom—they are not the best that a dreamer of dreams can imagine. It is enough if they are the best plans which the passions, parties, and prejudices of the times in which he acts will permit."

Was it, then, "a great fear" which motivated the acceptance of lesser evils? Smith criticized the confounding of two sets of feelings: personal and political fear. There was certainly no tremble in his voice when he said:

... but I may rationally be afraid of producing great public agitation—

I may be honourably afraid of flinging people into secret clubs and conspiracies—I may be wisely afraid of making the aristocracy hateful to the great body of the people. This surely has no more to do with fear than a loose identity of name; it is in fact prudence of the highest order; the deliberate reflection of a wise man, who does not like what he is going to do, but likes still less the consequences of not doing it, and who of two evils chooses the least.[110]

All political classes fall into errors and misdemeanors; each effective institution tends to decay and corruption. Here, clearly, was the unique strength of the English ideology—that it was unashamed to fall short of utopia, and unembarrassed to touch the precincts of revolution.

Cant words creep in [Smith said in 1832] and affect quarrels; the changes are rung between Revolution and Reform; but, first, settle whether a wise government ought to attempt the measure—whether anything is wanted—whether less would do—and, having settled this, mere nomenclature becomes of very little consequence. But, after all, if it be Revolution, and not Reform, it will only induce me to receive an old political toast in a twofold meaning, and with twofold pleasure. When King William and the great and glorious Revolution are given, I shall think not only of escape from bigotry, but exemption from corruption.[111]

And here, by contrast, is the singular foible of the German ideology, at least in the apocalyptic sense which Rhine revolutionaries had given to the prospects of radical change. It was only a few years later that Engels, forsaking (as he wrote) "the dinner-parties, the port wine and champagne of the middle-classes," looked into English social conditions and made his estimate of what was likely to happen. It was, imminently and inevitably, to be Revolution: a real and majestic cataclysm which had nothing of Mill and Bentham's pretense,[112] or Smith's indifference to "mere nomenclature."

Prophesy [Engels concluded in his *Condition of the Working-Class in England*] is nowhere so easy as in England, where all the component elements of society are clearly defined and sharply separated. The revolution must come. It is already too late to bring about a peaceful solution ... too late for a peaceful outcome of the affair. The classes are divided more and more sharply, the spirit of resistance penetrates the workers, the bitterness intensifies, the guerrilla skirmishes become concentrated in more important battles, and soon a slight impulse will suffice to set the avalanche in motion. Then, indeed, will the war-cry resound through the land: "War to the palaces, peace to the cottages!"[113]

When Engels took his soundings of the coming avalanche, he was convinced (to the extent that it was an intellectual process) that "these are all inferences which may be drawn with the greatest certainty; conclusions, the premises for which are undeniable facts, partly of historical development, partly facts inherent in human nature ... " Almost a half-century later, he remained faithful (to the extent that it was a religious process) to his youthful prophetic spirit:

> I have taken care not to strike out of the text the many prophecies, amongst others that of an imminent social revolution in England, which my youthful ardour induced me to venture upon. The wonder is, not that a good many of them proved wrong, but that so many of them have proved right.[114]

What he meant by that was that if the prediction of violent revolution proved wildly beyond the mark, he had at least forecast the crisis in international trade; and this, in turn, would be putting the avalanche once again on the historical agenda.

The real wonder is that other observers assessed the balance between reform and revolution so much more accurately (and, had they been mistaken, would have been prepared to confess their error with rather more candor and consequence). Tocqueville, for example, was in London at the time, and he was impressed by the tumult and the shouting over the Reform Bill, but he was not at all taken in. He knew there would be no violent revolution, for "the English" (as he wrote in his notebooks) "are taking one small thing after another, and have not in any way conceived one of those general principles which announce the approach of the total subversion of the existing order ... " Some time later, Tocqueville made another entry, and it points up the miscalculation which sets in when a universalized notion of revolution neglects local contexts:

> The French wish not to have superiors. The English wish to have inferiors. The Frenchman constantly raises his eyes above him with anxiety. The Englishman lowers his beneath him with satisfaction. On both sides there is pride, but it is understood in a different way.[115]

This is, I submit, in the spirit of French profundity, but not so abstract as to escape the English comprehension completely. "There is a principle in human nature," as Hazlitt remarked, successfully rising to Gallic standards of insight, "not willing to endure the idea of a superior, a sour jacobinical disposition to wipe out the score of obligation, or efface the tinsel of external advantage."[116]

The pride of principle and of pragmatism was understood by Wellington in a somewhat different way when he remembered his battles with the French:

> The French planned their campaigns just as you might make a splen-

did set of harness. It looks very well, and answers very well, until it gets broken; and then you are done for. Now I made my campaigns of ropes. If anything went wrong, I tied a knot; and went on.[117]

Clearly, a common temperament was at work both in war and in peace. French history is littered with broken harnesses; the English story is knotted, but whole, all of one piece.

The abstract globalism of the revolutionary vow—its total commitment to *all* men and to change *everywhere*—is constantly vitiated by an assortment of local difficulties which persist in exposing the fragile nature of such ideological integrity. Nationalism wars against universalism; petty tribal prejudices militate against brotherly love. The French revolutionaries despise the English; the Germans have contempt for the Russians; the Americans are considered an "exceptional" and hence a hopeless case; and everywhere "the Jews" in the movement are darkly suspect. Political passions cannot by their very fissiparous nature be easily delivered whole to an enlisted cause; they drip, seep out, spill over, make a mess. There is a wildness to the invidious attitudes of a Marx to Lassalle "the Yid," Bakunin the Slav, and Weitling the autodidact; or of a Proudhon to a similar host of hateful enemies within and without. Ideas, images, and ideology never quite manage to be harnessed into a controllable troika. The specific case of Anglo-French contrasts may serve to illustrate the temperamental narrowness that can coexist with the large commitment to an enlightened world openness.

It was an exercise in revolutionary irony which dominated European opinion and rhetoric for centuries. It was pointless, Cromwell had argued (in September 1656) against anti-Puritan critics who looked across the channel, to take foolish France as an example: "Have they the gospel as we have? They have seen the sun but a little; we have great lights ... "[118] "It is useless," Robespierre said (in January 1794), "to speak to the English people"; from the point of view of moral enlightenment, they were "two hundred years behind."

But Gallic pride was checked by the spirit of universal revolutionism which, only a few days before, had celebrated the anniversary of Louis's execution by indicting "all kings," burning their portraits, and stamping the ashes underfoot. The English case was grievous, but surely not hopeless. "It does not follow," Robespierre assured himself and his followers (so enraged by the imbecile George, the corrupt Pitt, and an enemy which had dared to call them a "nation of cannibals"), "it does not follow that the English people will never have a revolution: they will, because they are oppressed and ruined." Still, the patriot (who had never been outside Paris and Artois) was having trouble with his internationalism.

As a Frenchman and as a representative of Frenchmen, I hereby declare that I hate the English people [applause], and that I shall do all I can to make my fellow-countrymen hate them more. Let them make what they can of it! ... Were they to destroy their government, perhaps we might yet be friends. Meanwhile, we shall see whether a nation of shopkeepers [*un peuple de marchands*], is as good as a nation of farmers [*un peuple agriculteur*], or their few ships as powerful as our fertile acres. There is one thing more despicable than a tyrant—it is a nation of slaves [applause].... There is an Opposition—good luck to it! When Parliament meets, we shall see what it can do. If it votes the Address, then the English people are not worth the trouble of governing; we need not concern ourselves any more with such a despicable race.... The best thing would be to plunge it again beneath the ocean from which it arose.[119]

Ten years later, when neither revolution nor the ocean sea had risen to its appointed function, some agonizing reappraisals were called for. Were the politics of the stubborn islanders so contemptible, and was the role of the Opposition so negligible? In 1804, Napoleon objects to the "echoes of the English constitution" in the claims put forward by the French Senate:

Nothing differs more from France than England. The Frenchman lives under a clear sky, drinks fiery and heady wines, and eats food which excites the activity of his senses. The Englishman, on the contrary, lives in a humid climate, under an almost frigid sun, drinks beer or porter, and consumes great quantities of dairy products. The blood of the two nations is not composed of the same elements, and thus their characters could not be the same either. The French are vain, light-hearted, daring, and above all, enamoured of equality. They have been observed, in all epochs of history, to make war on superiority of rank and fortune. The English are proud rather than vain, they are by nature grave and they direct their attacks not at frivolous distinctions, but at serious abuses. They are more eager to preserve their own rights than to usurp those of others. Englishmen are at once proud and humble, independent and obedient. It is unthinkable to give identical institutions to such dissimilar nations.

The Emperor of France viewed the matter with less elevation and equanimity as subsequent events pressed in on him. England became the clear counter-image of his own revolutionary dictatorship: there was the land of reform, welfare, and utopian dreams—all "English notions." "Go to England," he told the de Staëls, "there they love the Genevese, the quibblers and drawing-room politicians. Go to England ... "[120] Above all, it was the land where the parliamentary politicians never ceased quibbling about one intolerable thing, the rights of opposition.

[Conversation, 1803]

THE FIRST CONSUL (*in his bathtub*): An opposition, as in England, is that it? I haven't been able to understand yet what good there is in an opposition. Whatever it may be, its only result is to diminish the prestige of authority in the eyes of the people.

JOSEPH BONAPARTE: It's easy to see that you don't like it; you have taken good care of it.

THE FIRST CONSUL: Let another govern in my place, and if he doesn't, like me, make an effort to silence the talkers, he'll see what will happen to him. As for me, let me tell you that in order to govern well one needs absolute unity of power. I won't shout this from the roof tops, since I mustn't frighten a lot of people who would raise loud cries of despotism, if they were allowed to talk, and who would write about it, if they were allowed to write.[121]

Neither the revolutionary nor the nonrevolutionary mind has been quite able to cope with the intractable problem of the one and the many, unity and diversity, permanence and change, or the unique and the universal. In a recoil from the tensions between human ideals and social difficulties, psychic predispositions always seem to be determining the mix of monism and pluralism, the range of global ambition, the commingling of plenitude and austerity, the consistency of ethical motives and national methods. Could it be that it is always and unfailingly better to move in human affairs from the local to the large? Why does it prove so hard to translate profound principles into the provinces? How does one reconcile a passion for cosmic faith with a small and meticulous scruple for social skepticism and political doubt?

My last question in this chapter is this: Do the historical records of ideology reveal any such thing as a nonrevolutionary vow? I would suspect that they would, and that Edmund Burke took one in the faith-breaking year of 1789, making a singular English attempt to rewrite the peculiar lessons of one time and place into a reformer's general creed:

Prudence (in all things a virtue, in politics the first of virtues) will lead us rather to acquiesce in some qualified plan that does not come up to the full perfection of the abstract idea, than to push for the most perfect, which cannot be attained without tearing to pieces the whole contexture of the commonwealth . . . . In all changes in the state, moderation is a virtue, not only amiable, but powerful. It is a disposing, arranging, conciliating, cementing virtue . . . . Moderation (which times and situations will clearly distinguish from the counterfeits of pusillanimity and indecision) is the virtue only of superior minds. It requires deep courage, and full of reflection, to be temperate when the voice of multitudes (the specious mimic of fame and reputation) passes judgment against you. The impetuous desire of an unthinking public will endure no course, but what conducts to splendid and perilous extremes. Then to dare to be fearful, when all about you are full of presumption and confidence, and when those who are bold at the hazard of others would push your caution and disaffection, is to show a mind prepared for its trial; it discovers, in the midst of general levity, a self-possessing and collected character, which, sooner or later, bids to attract everything to it, as to a centre.[122]

Our quest remains to locate the true place of that center, the point between tactics and virtues, prudence and courage, reform and revolution. Because this territory is mapless and unchartered is not reason enough, and never has been, to leave it unexplored. It is, in any case, the ground ahead on which we must stand, in promise and in peril.

3

Every church is orthodox to itself; to others, erroneous or heretical.

—John Locke (1667)

To be in possession of an absolute truth is to have a net of familiarity spread over the whole of eternity. There are no surprises and no unknowns. All questions have already been answered, all decisions made, all eventualities foreseen. The true believer is without wonder and hesitation.

—Eric Hoffer (1951)

Every revolutionary ends by becoming either an oppressor or a heretic.

—Albert Camus (1951)

The art of free society consists first in the maintenance of the symbolic code; and secondly in fearlessness of revision . . . . Those societies which cannot combine reverence to their symbols with freedom of revision, must ultimately decay.

—A. N. Whitehead (1933)

The Heretic's
True Cause

1. The Company Words Keep
Bifurcation of Meaning and Linguistic Mischief—Science or Scientific—Doubt, Skepticism, Dogma—The Sino-Soviet Conflict: Insuring the Adoration of Theorems—A Sense of Danger and Error—Hating the Heretic—Eduard Bernstein's Uncertainties—Kautsky's Fury—Empiricism, Metaphysics, and "English Glasses"—Grasping Essentials of a Two-Sided Reality

2. Revising Left and Right
Weitling's Transatlantic Quest—A Revolutionary Redeemer: Half-Christ, Half-Bonaparte—A Quarrel with Marx (1846)—Revising to the Left—The Tactic of "Social Anarchy"—A Strategy of Urban Guerrilla Warfare (1849)—Weitling's Communia in Iowa—A New Road to Power: "Chinese Socialism," or Countryside Enclaves—Weitling's Bitter End in New York (1871)—Plekhanov between Lenin and Trotsky—Posadowsky's Question (1903)—Plekhanov's Fear of an "Oriental Despotism"—Who Liquidates Whom?—Maxim Gorky: the Shame and the Glory—"Maniacs of a Beautiful Idea"—Rosa Luxemburg vs. "Arthritic English Concepts"—"Noble Impatience"—How Free is Criticism?—Luxemburg's Dissent from Bolshevism—The Reflective Spirit of Heterodoxy

3. The Anatomy of Intellectual Courage
Martyrdom and the Mask of Madness—Secret Views (Sarpi, Campanella, More)—Erasmus and More (1535)—Erasmus and Luther (1519)—Holbein, Dürer, and the Personal Consequences—Calvin,

Castellio, and Michael Servetus's Death (1553)—Spinoza and Leibniz (1672)—Conscience, Compromise, and the Risks of Reprisal—Voltaire and Diderot (1758)—Lukacs and Merleau-Ponty (1956)—Ernst Bloch—The Difficulties of Changing One's Mind—Tensions between the Open and the Closed—Two Types of Revisionism—Hay, Djilas, and the Counterrevolution—The Return of Utopian Longing and Revolutionary Commitment—Voltaire as Exemplary—"The Craze for Domination"—Converting the Censor

4. Old Incantations and Primitive Word-Magic

Topical Philology—Malcolm X's Revolutionsim (1963–64)—Interchangeable Noises—Sukarno and the Full Delirium of a New-found Vocabulary (1964)—"Language is a mode of action, not an instrument of reflection" (Malinowski)—Proudhon as Rhetorical Model (1851)—Sartre, Fanon, O'Brien—A Poetry of the Blood—Verbal Magic and the Energy of Formulas—Régis Debray's Revolution within the Revolution (1967)—Castro and Guevera—New Revolutionary Virtues—The Sacred Mountain—The Heresy of "Mountain-Top-ism"—Hugo and Schiller—Chinese Doctrine

5. The Lost Metaphor

Recognizable Configurations—Reviving a New Left: "Politica Perennis"?—Formulas for Black Power—The Generation between Two World Wars—Necessary Cruelties and Destructive Elements—Bolshevik Vocabulary, Bohemian Sentiments—Disenthrallment in the 1930s—André Gide's Legend of the "Lost God" (1936)

6. A Noose of Words

A Discrimination of Disenchantments—The Linguistic Factor—Words and Things—Bacon, Sprat, Hobbes—The Dangers of "Mists and Uncertainties"—Springs of the Deviant Verbal Mechanism—Nietzsche's Eternal Linguistic Tragedy—On Slogans, Clichés, Abstractions—Verbal Villainy: Rabelais, Hooker, Dryden, North—Milton and the "Satanic Spell over Utopia" (1660)—Locke on Absurdity and Obscurity (1690)—Socialist Semantics from Proudhon to Sartre—Sacramental Words—Reforming or Revolutionizing All Languages—Robert South's "Mouth Granadoes"

7. The Bow and the Lyre

The Illusion of Revolutionary Omnipotence—The Myth of Definitive

Solutions—Persisting Conflicts and Piecemeal Change—The Complex Tension between Moral Ideals and Social Difficulties—Lenin's Hesitations: "The Exaggeration of Revolutionariness" (1921)—Radical Changes by "Small Doses" (Nietzsche)—Ideology and Utopia, Dogma and Revolution: Beyond the Pitfalls?—The Spiral of Reason and Passion— Evidence and Ambiguity—Tradition and Change—Bacon, Harrington, Hume—Günter Grass: Reason in Rage—The Simple and the Complicated—Leading Generations Astray—Bentham, Donne, Heraclitus—"A Harmony in the Bending Back"

1. The Company Words Keep

In the beginning—at the outset of both the first and second chapters—there was a word: a deleted word, and its omission served to blur the dual character of utopia; then an ambiguous word, and its several meanings distorted the true outlines of revolution and reform. Now, there is a mistranslated word, and its curious rendering has spelled out the difference between dogma and heresy. This is a case of what C. S. Lewis called the "bifurcation of meaning"; and there is linguistic mischief here, for "a word needs to be very careful about the phonetic company it keeps ... "[1]

Friedrich Engels's famous pamphlet, *Die Entwicklung des Sozialismus von der Utopie zur Wissenschaft* [The development of socialism from utopia to science], was first published as a series of articles in the Leipzig *Vorwärts* in 1877–78. I am struck by the fact that in most of the European translations the noun becomes an adjective—*Socialisme utopique et socialisme scientifique; Socialism: Utopian and Scientific; Il Socialismo utopico ed il Socialismo scientifico.* Thus began, in the grammar of politics, a series of subtle and significant variations on the authentic relationship between theory and practice, utopia and revolution, hope and principle. Surely, there is here an additional complication to the tone of Engels's thought. He appeared to be less concerned with the scientific qualities of method than with the systematic character of socialist philosophy. In his preface of 1882 he writes: "But scientific socialism is indeed essentially a German product and could only arise in that nation whose classical philosophy had kept alive the tradition of conscious dialectics: in Germany ... " Few students seem to have been aware of the verbal complexity. We have at least been cautioned that in Russian, for example, the words *nauka* and *nauchny* (like the German *Wissenschaft* and *wissenschaftlich*) have a considerably broader meaning than the English *science* and *scientific;* and when Russian Marxism came into being it hastened to conform to the nineteenth-century penchant for the epithet of "science." Another bilingual scholar has also been upset by the "difficult linguistic problem":

> The German word *Wissenschaft* is far more comprehensive a term than the word "science" which is generally used as its English equivalent. The German term refers to any discipline which attempts to establish system, generality, on some definite method. "Science," on the other hand, is largely limited to the natural sciences of physics, chemistry, etc., with their special methodology which stresses induction and empirical content. The difference between the two expressions is crucial.[2]

This, I submit, is another of our historic turning points. Words are great dividers. Loyalty to the adjective (*scientific*) tended to make for flexibility and open-mindedness; loyalty to the noun (*science*), for ponderous orthodoxy.

For what is scientific about science is its systematic sensitivity to error. Its hypotheses are tentatively held, always subject to revision in the light of evidence. This has been the great tradition of reason as well. "Only fools are certain and immovable," Montaigne wrote, and he quoted Dante from the *Inferno:* "It pleases me as much to doubt as to know." The contribution of scientific awareness, as Sir Peter Medawar has said, "is to have enlarged beyond all former bounds the evidence we must take account of before forming our opinions. Today's opinions may not be the same as yesterday's, because they are based on fuller or better evidence. We should quite often have occasion to say, 'I used to think that once, but now I've come to hold a rather different opinion.' People who never say as much are either ineffectual or dangerous ... "[3]

To what extent, then, have modern revolutionaries who, ever since Engels coined the phrase, have prided themselves on their "scientific socialism," been attached to the methods of logic and reason, the process of intelligence and critical reexamination? Or, put the other way, how deeply, how inextricably, have they been emotionally involved in the semireligious orthodoxy of articles of faith, in unshakable devotion to principles and policies which amount to an almost sacrosanct fundamentalism?

The problem of method is supremely important in itself. Every thoughtful socialist for a hundred years—or ever since Proudhon warned Marx against "tangling people up in doctrines," against establishing a new intolerant theology—must have faced the questions: What can one doubt? Dare one to be skeptical at all? A second theme emerges from the stormy controversies over revisionism: if dogma is the Scylla of the scientific attitude, failure is its Charybdis. Could it be that the apostles of revolution have been seriously mistaken? Is it conceivable that evil has become their good? For there are in history errors which are not only follies but crimes. Even Karl Marx differentiated himself from "those communists who were out to destroy personal liberty and who wanted to turn the world into one large barracks or into a gigantic workhouse."[4] To what extent, then, has there been among Marxists a sense of danger, of a possible wrong turning? Who has (in Shakespeare's phrase) given "warning to the world"?

These might have remained, as in the story of the utopians, matters of intellectual style and moral sensitivity. *"Trotz meinen Heresien,"* Peter Struve once wrote to Karl Kautsky, *"möchte ich gerne Sie besuchen* (In spite of my heresies, I should like to visit you)." *"Trotz meiner Dogmenfanatismus,"* Kautsky replied, *"freue ich mich, Sie wiederzusehen* (In spite of my dogmatic fanaticism, I should be pleased to see you again)."[5] The matter was still a humane one, still compatible with wit and civility; the time of grimness was yet to come.[6]

It could be, as Gustave Le Bon remarked, that doctrinal fluidity is common to and precedes the birth of any new belief, since dogmas do not harden until they have triumphed. Until the moment of victory, they remain mobile, and this mobility, he insisted, was the necessary condition of their success: it facilitated adaptations to a variety of circumstances and the satisfaction of diverse discontents.[7] Certainly, with the Bolshevik Revolution of October 1917 and the establishment of the Soviet Union, and now even more with the emergence of a Marxist, revolutionary China, questions of doctrinal orthodoxy and heresy have become life-and-death matters for individual thinkers. "To insure the adoration of a theorem for any length of time," Camus said, "faith is not enough; a police force is needed as well."[8] Yet two can adore the same theorem and the police mind may not deem it so. Doctrinal dispute now colors the substance of power politics between nation-states and their ruling parties. In November 1957, in one of the decisive opening rounds of the Sino-Soviet conflict, a twelve-party declaration in Moscow designated "revisionism" as the "main danger" to world communism. A Soviet spokesman argued (as early as 1960) that "revisionists are the agents of imperialism," with revisionism being defined (according to the Soviet *Political Dictionary*) as "a trend in the working-class movement that, for the benefit of the bourgeoisie, wants to debase, to emasculate, to destroy Marxism by means of a revision, *i.e.*, by way of reexamination, distortions, and negation of its basic tenets ... " A writer in the magazine *Moskva* declared: "Either we destroy revisionism or revisionism will destroy us. There is no third way." Yet, within a few years, the Russians themselves were "the revisionists," and the Chinese were sternly defending orthodoxy. In the impassioned polemics of the Sino-

Soviet dispute, the ideological guns were turned the other way. The Russians were "watering down," were "emasculating" the essential principles of Marxism-Leninism (and Marxism-Stalinism), and Khrushchev, now "the greatest revisionist in history," was even associated with Karl Kautsky. The Chinese were betraying the whole "scientific spirit of socialism" with their "dogmatism," and Mao was linked directly with Leon Trotsky. Mao Tse-tung, it was said, had become "an ultra-leftist, an ultra-dogmatist, indeed, a *left* revisionist." The Russians, almost exhausting all the possible phraseological permutations, have also called the Chinese "revisionist dogmatists"; they, in turn, as *"right* revisionists," would presumably be "dogmatic revisionists." By the 1970s, even more grave and indeed criminal charges were being preferred as the Russian Marxists claimed that the Chinese had actually published translations of Goebbels and Rosenberg and had thus moved Mao's communism into the precincts of Hitler's National Socialism. One should perhaps be grateful to Mao, in his turn, for having introduced a somewhat more poetic note of nineteenth-century imagery with his remark: "Revisionism is the opium of the people: it is a beguiling music for the consolation of slaves."[9]

Why should the heretic be so much more feared and hated than the unbeliever? There is ideological fury here, but also a dramatic irony. "The greatest revisionists in the history of Marxism," writes Professor Sidney Hook (himself a Marxian revisionist, of course),

> . . . were the Bolsheviks themselves. The very triumph of Bolshevism in the last forty-five years constitutes a refutation of Marx's theory of historical materialism in the form in which he expressed it. The mode of political decision determined the mode of economic production, not vice versa. . . . What is denounced as "revisionism" is not merely revisions of Marx's doctrines but revisions of Bolshevik revisionism . . .

It was a characteristic reminder from the so-called Father of Revisionism when old Eduard Bernstein said: "Let us not forget that Marx and Engels were, in their time, Revisionists too. Indeed, they were the greatest Revisionists in the history of Socialism."

The two original Marxists, at their best, could hardly be faulted on the grounds of intellectual inadequacy or moral insensitivity. Both had a sense of danger and a sense of error.[10] Marx, as I have just quoted, warned against false paths which would entail the destruction of "personal liberty." "There certainly are," he admitted,

> some communists who, with an easy conscience, refuse to countenance personal liberty and would like to shuffle it out of the world because they consider it a hindrance to complete harmony. But we have no desire to exchange freedom for equality.

This was published in London in 1847, and Marx said that he intended "to return to the matter in subsequent issues" of the *Communist Journal;* but he never did return, and the matter—namely, a socialist theory of political liberty—became one of the fatal lacunae of Marxist ideology. What he did get off, almost casually, was one clear mollifying sentence, extraordinary and almost forgotten; but for those who remember it, as for Camus, it "forever denies his triumphant disciples the greatness and the humanity which once were his," for "he never wanted (if indeed he predicted it) the additional degradation that has been imposed in his name." The sentence is this: "An end that requires unjust means is not a just end." As for Engels, he found rigidity and unrealism distasteful, and he could bring himself to confess (in an 1895 preface, reviewing events since 1848): "History showed that we were wrong, revealed that our views at that time were an illusion." After Marx's death in 1883, it was to Eduard Bernstein (like Marx, a German-Jewish intellectual) that Engels turned to as "literary executor." Bernstein spent five busy years in England with Engels, who preferred his "realism" to that of Karl Kautsky—who became in turn the guardian of orthodoxy against revisionism (although he, in time, was to be called "the renegade" by Lenin and his orthodoxists).[11]

"I began to doubt doctrines," Bernstein wrote. He was intellectually honest and courageous enough to admit his "uncertainties," to be puzzled by "objections," and to conclude that nothing could be held "incontrovertible" that did not square with facts and evidence: "The decisive influences on my thinking as a socialist were not of a doctrinaire kind, but facts, which forced me to correct the ideas underlying my beliefs." When his party rejected some of his views, he stood fast and, with typical dignity, said: "The vote of an assembly, however high its standing, cannot of course turn me from views I have gained from the examination of social phenomena."

Bernstein had realistically allowed in a footnote that the Social Democracy as a *Kampfpartei* could "within certain limits be dogmatic and even intolerant"; but he refused to compromise on the level of theory and analysis, especially when he was convinced that a valuable social science was being converted into a dangerous utopian dogmatism by those who "dreamt of a great leap forward [*einem jähen Sprunge*] into the perfectly complete communist society." He suggested that "we will have to get used to the idea of a partially collectivized economy," for "it would be a sad prospect if mankind were to face a future in which only one form of movement were possible." He saw, as he wrote in a prophetic dissent, "the realization of socialism not through the increasing miseries of the working classes, but rather from the rising curve of their cultural expectations [*von der zunehmenden Steigerung ihrer Culturansprüche*] ... " Would there be an "early collapse of capitalism"?

Could there be a "peaceful transition to socialism"? No doctrine was above criticism, and he proposed renaming his philosophy "Critical Socialism."

His own German critics were enraged—and at nothing more than this onset of skepticism and empiricism. Kautsky's fury led him to the charge that Bernstein had now ranged himself utterly against revolution, a word which he now understood "only as a policeman would." In fact, Bernstein had only suggested that "for the principled transformation of the social order the words social reconstruction [*sociale Umgestaltung*] will be used, thus leaving the question of the means [*i.e.*, legal or extralegal] quite open." The point of the distinction was "to prevent all misunderstandings and ambiguities"; and in this he surely failed. Kautsky, in a burst of mock-Ophelian despair, cried out, "O what a noble mind is here o'erthrown!" Bernstein took this bit of "psychiatry" as a literary and not a literal charge, and countered with the confession (again, in the Tieck-Schlegel rendering which has made Shakespeare so proverbial in Germany) that he was mad only by north-northwest and that by a south wind he could indeed tell a hawk from a handsaw.[12]

Rosa Luxemburg doubted it, and she accused him of seeing the world "through English glasses." Kautsky went even further: "You have decided to be an Englishman—take the consequences and become an Englishman.... Do not deceive yourself; you have completely lost touch with Germany.... Try to achieve a place in the English movement and to become a representative of English Socialism." It is one of the more splendid dialectical twists of our not unironic story that fifty years later, in a similar quarrel between two English socialists who for many years in the 1960s coexisted peacefully as ministers in Harold Wilson's Labour cabinet, Richard Crossman denounced the revisionism of Anthony Crosland as having "lost touch" and being "too German."[13] The people of Kantian metaphysics had turned empirical; the practical Benthamite reformers had become enamored of abstract principle.[14]

In a candid letter which Bernstein sent to August Bebel in 1898, he wrote:

> Up to two years ago I tried, by stretching Marxist teachings, to bring them into accord with practical realities.... I wanted to save Marx; I wanted to show that he had predicted everything that had and had not happened.

Bernstein was once asked "a few harmless questions," and when he answered "in the old manner" it "really finished me off."

> I said to myself—this cannot go on. It is idle to try to reconcile the

irreconcilable. What is necessary is to become clear just where Marx is right and where he is wrong.

In 1929, when he was almost eighty, Bernstein said in conversation (but he lowered his voice "as if afraid of being overheard"), "the Bolsheviks are not unjustified in claiming Marx as their own. Do you know, Marx had a strong Bolshevik streak in him . . . "[15]

What remains vivid and instructive in all this Marxological disputation is the matter of method and style. In these early quarrels over revisionism, there was much that was right and wrong on all sides. In a note scribbled on an envelope (later found among the Bernstein papers), Bernstein argued laconically: "Peasants do not sink; middle class does not disappear; crises do not grow ever larger; misery and serfdom do not increase." This, so far as it went, was true: capitalism, far from being "finished," had before it a surprising epoch of stability, democracy, prosperity. At the same time, Karl Kautsky, more orthodox, more pessimistic, was decrying the fantasy of peace and progress and predicting the coming of wars and catastrophes (*Krisen, Kriege, Katastrophen*). Who would deny that this awful vision, long before two world wars and a worldwide economic depression, had substance in it? They had each grasped essentials of a two-sided reality. Think of Bernstein's native Germany: he was right in 1904 (peace), but wrong in 1914 (war); he was wrong for 1933 (crisis), but right for 1973 (affluence).

In this spirit of transvaluation, even the conventional view of who is being truly "revolutionary"—the lonely radical dissenter or the conservative reaffirmer of orthodox militant traditions—needs to be revised. One historian of the period has ascribed the widely felt resentment against Bernstein's practical proposals to the fact that they departed from "the accepted comforts of revolution":

> It may seem strange to speak of a revolutionary doctrine as comfortable, but there is comfort in routine belief irrespective of *content*; Bernstein was proposing changes in outlook and policy which must radically alter many of the accepted notions on which the party's whole rhythm of life was based. To this extent Bernstein, with all his denial of violence and advocacy of reform, was the revolutionary, while the accepted doctrine provided the shelter of conservative tradition.[16]

2. Revising Left and Right

I have already referred, several times, to Wilhelm Weitling (1808–71),[17] and the relevance of his remarkable career as a heretical utopian and revolutionary revisionist is too sharp and central to be overlooked here.

Not unlike Dante's messianic medieval Emperor, Weitling's revolutionary redeemer was to lead the way to the "earthly paradise." His conception of that luminous figure, half-Christ and half-Bonaparte, was understandable. Weitling was born as the illegitimate son of a German servant-girl and one of Napoleon's officers. His manifesto of 1838, written for the League of the Just (which was later rechristened the Communist League), was entitled *Die Menschheit, wie sie ist und wie sie sein sollte* [Mankind as it is and as it ought to be]. In his *Gospel of a Poor Sinner* (1843), he described Jesus Christ as both a communist and an illegitimate child; and he was promptly convicted in Switzerland of blasphemy and condemned to jail. "This earnest and fearless German visionary," as Isaiah Berlin has observed,[18] "was the last and most eloquent descendant of the men who raised peasant revolts in the late Middle Ages ... " Perhaps the earliest and most important influence on the proletarianism of Marx and the anarchism of Bakunin, he had, for a brief historic moment, a foot in both camps.

No less than Marx, Bakunin was impressed by that "really remarkable book" of Weitling's, *Garantien der Harmonie und Freiheit;* and he copied out (for Arnold Ruge) a striking passage—"The perfect society has no government but only an administrator, no laws but only obligations, no punishments but means of correction." When they met in Zurich, Bakunin was pleased with his intelligence, energy, and—"above all"—his "undisciplined fanaticism." Weitling's difficulties with the police soon involved Bakunin. An official Swiss report led to a Tsarist decree depriving Bakunin of his noble rank and property, and to his banishment to Siberia.

If Weitling made Bakunin into a hunted exile, he had also made him into a professional revolutionary. As Bakunin's biographer writes:

> Hitherto revolution had been, in Bakunin's experience, a topic to be discussed by intellectuals to the sociable accompaniment of tea and tobacco. It was impossible to imagine any provocation which would have induced Ruge to abandon the pen for the sword; and Herwegh, though he loved to pose as a man of action, was fundamentally more interested in writing poems against tyranny than in overthrowing it. In the person of Weitling, revolution assumed the more practical form of a burning personal grievance.... He appears to have been the first to propose to "shoot without mercy all enemies of communism." Bakunin found in this blend of high-souled idealism and reckless brutality something congenial to his own turbulent nature.... The meeting with Weitling was one of the capital events of his life, completing his transformation from a speculative philosopher into a practical revolutionary. The Russian aristocrat became the servant of the international proletariat.[19]

As for Marx and Engels, they soon had their doubts as to how practical and how proletarian Weitling's influence truly was. Their admiration and cooperation was short-lived. Weitling became in their eyes a utopian *à la* Cabet and an insurrectionist *à la* Blanqui. Marx disliked both the dream and the desperation. For the first, he wanted to substitute the hope and confidence based on scientific analysis (and not primitive Christian longings for equality and brotherhood); and, for the second, a widely-based movement of the masses. Weitling, in turn, disliked the intellectualism of his new socialist rivals and predicted: "In the end they will devour one another."

The differences in tone and spirit between the philosopher and the journeyman tailor were clear and unbridgeable. At a dramatic meeting in Brussels (30 March 1846), Marx said that

it was a simple fraud to arouse the people without any sound and considered basis for their activity. The awakening of fantastic hopes ... would never lead to the salvation of those who suffered, but on the contrary to their undoing.... To go to the workers ... without strictly scientific ideas and concrete doctrine would mean an empty and unscrupulous playing with propaganda, which would inevitably involve, on the one hand, the setting-up of an inspired apostle and, on the other hand, simply asses who would listen to him with open mouth ...

This, he added, might be all very well in Russia; but for the rest one could not do without solid doctrine. (In a later quarrel, the German Communist leader Gottschalk echoed Weitling in his 1849 attack on the Marxists: "They are not in earnest about the salvation of the oppressed. The distress of the workers, the hunger of the poor, have only a scientific doctrinaire interest for them.")

The debate between Marx and Weitling ended with Marx in rage, pounding on the table, and leaping up with a shout, "Ignorance has never helped anybody yet!"[20]

Now Engels began to suspect that Weitling, once the author of "work of genius," had been plagiarizing from certain French and Russian sources; he reported to Marx his contempt for *Weitlingerei* (as for *Proudhonisterei*) and reassured him that after "the infamy of brother Weitling" the "little clique of tailors was about to be thrown out ... "[21] (Edmund Wilson refers to this as "the first Marxist party purge.") Weitling's response was one of bewildered indignation at the "slanderous" charge of being "a reactionary." He had rushed to return from the United States in 1848, but after the failure of the various European revolts and revolution he resumed his activity as a propagandist among the American oppressed.

What he left behind him was a revised third edition of his unique manifesto of both utopia and revolution, *Guarantees of Harmony and Freedom*, first published in 1842 and now reissued in 1849 with all his latest ideas and reconsiderations. The thoughtful utopian in the grips of restless reason tends to revise in the direction of inspired details and new rearrangements. The impassioned revolutionary under the hold of apocalyptic enthusiasm moves ever closer to his imagined final solution. Weitling revised to the left, not the right; and Marxological scholarship enables us to follow, almost line by line, the Promethean impetus of his last European interpolations.[22]

First, he attempted to clarify a number of misunderstandings. He had indeed cried, *"Es lebe die Revolution!"* but he had no illusions about the previous great events which had brought suffering humanity so little: it was the next one or, rather, the next "series of revolutions," that would make the ultimate difference. He had been called an anti-democrat, but he explained that complete democracy was to be found only in perfect communism. As for his antipathy to national and patriotic sentiments, could this "prison house" really be called a Fatherland and could this enslaved despised rabble be truly taken for a People? When the "old rotten house of the existing social order collapsed" (or was destroyed), there would be a Great Fire into which would be thrown all the paraphernalia of hateful capitalism: banknotes, tax forms, contracts, debtors' notes, the poor man's brass as well as the rich man's silver and gold. "Society will be born anew.... The earth will become a paradise and humankind one family."

Then he added a number of points from his experiences in the 1840s. An experienced inmate of Swiss and German jails, he now felt the need for an additional revolutionary demand: the liberation of all prisoners from all penitentiaries. An American impression of Negroes groaning under slavery led him to remark: "A lovely freedom, that! The devil take that freedom and that republic!" The experience in England of reading the London newspapers prompted him to say that "no freedom of the press at all would be better ... " In connection with his own outline of the new utopian society, he stood by his old statute, which called for the closing of the universities during harvest time so that all professors and students could work in the fields; and he reiterated his conception of an ideal lawlessness. No, police and judges and jails would not be required; theft is permitted only because by definition it is not possible; well, perhaps, a book could be stolen, he conceded, but that should only be taken as a kind of little joke at which one could laugh or not.[23]

One drastic new turn was taken by Weitling, who was leaving Europe for America in 1849, and it angered Marx and still distresses his Marxist editors today. He announced a great breakthrough in revolutionary theory, a new tactic of so-called *soziale Anarchie*. This went considerably beyond his previous insistence upon the constant sharpening of the social war between masses and classes, went indeed into the very precincts of brigandage and putschism. "He who robs the rich," he announced, "in order to help the poor with the booty, he is a noble righteous robber and a just thief . . . . He who meets his death in such a battle must be seen as a martyr in a holy cause." Yet he sensed that a Robin Hood ideal was not quite the proper casting for an insurrectionary drama in an increasingly industrial civilization. It was the masses who had to play the central role, and they had to be "electrified" with all their "ambitions and passions," and even their "prejudices." Only then would "our enemy find himself pressed to the extreme, and forced insistently to repression . . . "The original message was of Napoleonic, if not of messianic, proportions:

> Now one lesson must be preached which nobody has dared to utter till now—the lesson which demands that the bloody battlefield of the streets, in which the people are always at a disadvantage, be transformed into continuous guerrilla warfare . . . which the power of the soldiers, gendarmerie, and police will be unable to put down . . .
> But this lesson can only be taught effectively to the most desperate and poverty-stricken urban masses of our big cities. Once the word is out, it will be the signal for a new strategy with which our enemies will never be able to cope.[24]

It is no small part of the odd circular logic of the situation that, having formulated a strategy of urban guerrilla warfare for the metropolitan campaign, Weitling departed for the farmlands of the American Middle West.

On historical balance, Marx and Weitling appear to have scored one important point against each other. As the utopian tailor had surmised, revolutionary intellectuals with only doctrinaire interests in humane values did proceed to "devour one another." As the hardheaded scientific philosopher had argued, "emotional socialism" was neither sound nor stable enough on which to build an effective movement for systematic social change; and Weitling's career in the United States seemed to prove this.

This is not to suggest that Marx's socialism was any less rooted in personal emotions, stable or otherwise, or any less dependent on the "awakening of fantastic hopes." All things considered, it would seem that the illusions of the utopian socialists were only marginally greater than those of the scientific socialists. By and large, bourgeois society and its middle-class values remained untranscended; capitalism was not led to its collapse either way. Suffering humanity turned neither to the

social community of equal brothers nor to the political party of the revolutionary proletariat. The failure of the utopians, since the experimental
establishment of an actual community constituted a specific practical
test, was merely more dramatic and definitive; the failures of open-
ended predictions are harder to establish. "If all had followed me,"
Weitling was to confess in America, "as the children of Israel followed
Moses out of Egypt, I would have succeeded . . . " For the followers of
Weydemeyer (who had come to New York to defend the views of Marx
and Engels), this was only the "fog of fantasy." The great debate of
Brussels raged on.

Weitling's original revolutionary impetus distinguished his American
activities from those native and immigrant utopias which, in Marx's
indictment, sought for salvation "behind society's back." When he came
to Communia, Iowa, he said, "For the first time in my life I stand on the
sacred soil of a communal brotherhood." But he never intended to build
socialism in one farmland. He explained in the organ of his American
movement, *Die Republik der Arbeiter*, that his views were intended for a
whole state, indeed for the whole of human society. He lost sight of
neither power nor paradise. Communia, with its thousand acres and a
handful of brothers, was to be the beginning: when the communities
multiplied and the following grew, he could go on to build the Pacific
railroad, control the presidential elections, and establish the dream empire. Meanwhile, the *Bund*'s enrollment was planned to grow by a calculated geometrical progression, and its mounting capital resources, based
on a Proudhon-model People's Exchange Bank, were to undermine the
existing capitalist monopolies. "We shall come to power along this
road," he was confident, "if only the leaders will remain steadfast, and
the members will accept the leadership and not dissipate their strength
through internal factional controversies." (Weitling became interested in
the Orient and in something he called "Chinese socialism"; strangely
enough, the revolutionary road to power that he envisaged in America
was a curious pre-Maoist version of countryside enclaves enveloping the
urban class-enemy, that "babylon of capitalists, merchants, lawyers and
preachers [who live] by thievery, fraud, misrepresentation, and
hypocrisy . . . ")

Nor was his disillusionment unfamiliar. He knew that the English
would be most unlikely to resort to revolutionary methods, and now in
America he was tempted to wish for the old Paris proletariat, so uninhi-
bited by the Anglo-Saxon respect for legalities. Increasingly frustrated
and isolated, Weitling became tormented by the "impracticalities" of his
reforms and the recalcitrance of his human material: "Everywhere [he
wrote] I discover a desire to protect the individual." By the time of his
death in New York in 1871, he had withdrawn from both utopia and
revolution and confined himself mostly to patents for ingenious inven-

tions (he always felt the Singer Company had deprived him of his device for a better buttonhole) and to semantical studies for a new world language (which might "trample the monster of national hatreds underfeet"). The bitter irony of his last years was that the journeyman tailor whose fury had once inflamed the European Communist movement returned to his needle and thread, earning a meager living by making fancy white vests for such New Yorkers as Astor, Fisk, and Vanderbilt.[25]

One last point. In view of the close interest I will be giving in these pages to the connections between revolutionary language and astronomical imagery, I cannot help but note Weitling's attempt to "escape from this disgraceful earth" by turning to the mysteries of the heavens. He corresponded with Herschel, Humboldt, and Agassiz and submitted a paper to the Smithsonian Institution on "rotations and revolutions." Evidently his new system would restore the earth to the planetary center which it had occupied in Ptolemaic days. One of his sons had been named Tycho Brahe Edward, and another Gracchus Babeuf Robert, and this was indeed the last revolutionary ambivalence of his astonishing career.

No true prophet prophesies everything truly; nor are all false prophets without a touch of the truth. This axiom emerges from the records of the Russian Marxists no less than from those of the German Marxists. Lenin once argued against the notion, held at the time by Trotsky, that a proletarian dictatorship could be based on something less than "the enormous majority of the people," and he predicted: "Anyone who attempts to achieve socialism by any other route other than political democracy will inevitably arrive at absurd and reactionary conclusions, both economic and political." At another time, long before the 1917 Revolution (and the ultimate triumph of Stalin), the young Trotsky argued against Lenin's conception of a "conspiratorial revolutionary party": "The organization of the Party takes the place of the Party itself; the Central Committee takes the place of the organization; and finally the dictator takes the place of the Central Committee." Who was "revising" whom? Both were correctly revising each other.

Even the grand old Russian master of them both, George Plekhanov, defender of Marxist orthodoxy throughout a long militant life (1856–1918),[26] can be found looking in both directions. Let me recall an incident of the year 1903—Isaiah Berlin calls it "an event which marked the culmination of a process which has altered the history of our world."[27] A Russian socialist named Posadovsky posed a question. The scene was a Russian Social Democratic Congress in Brussels:

> Posadovsky inquired whether the emphasis laid by the "hard"
> socialists—Lenin and his friends—upon the need for the exercise of

absolute authority by the revolutionary nucleus of the Party might not prove incompatible with those fundamental liberties to whose realization Socialism, no less than liberalism, was officially dedicated. He asked whether the basic, minimum civil liberties—"the sacrosanctity of the person"—could be infringed and even violated if the Party leaders so decided.

It was Plekhanov who replied:

> *Salus revolutiae supreme lex*—certainly, if the revolution demanded it, everything—democracy, liberty, the rights of the individual—must be sacrificed to it.

He was not always so brutally confident. There was in him, as in so many Russian intellectuals, an echoing fear of a policy which (in the words of Shigalov in Dostoyevsky's *The Possessed*), "starting from unlimited liberty ends in unlimited despotism." He was afraid of a "dictatorship *over* the proletariat." He was plagued with doubts: "Did we not begin the propaganda of Marxism too early in backward semi-Asiatic Russia?" He warned against the "alchemists of revolution" (Lenin and his followers) and against the ideals of a "patriarchal and authoritarian communism with the only change [being] that a socialist caste would manage the national production instead of the Peruvian 'Sons of the Sun' . . . " He suspected the coming of a new "Oriental Despotism," and insisted: "And even if there came into being a state which—without giving you political rights—wanted to and could guarantee your material welfare, in that case you would be nothing more than 'satiated slaves, well-fed working cattle' . . . " He shuddered when his comrades uttered the word *liquidation* (and this, thirty years before the murder of Kirov and Stalin's ensuing purge):

> Imagine that the Central Committee recognized by us all possessed the still-debated right of "liquidation." Then this would happen. Since a congress is in the offing, the C.C. everywhere "liquidates" the elements with which it is dissatisfied, everywhere seats its own creatures and, filling all the committees with these creatures, guarantees itself without difficulty a fully submissive majority at the congress. The congress constituted of the creatures of the C.C. amiably cries "Hurrah!," approves all its successful and unsuccessful actions, and applauds all its plans and initiatives. Then in reality, there would be in the party neither a majority nor a minority, because we would then have realized the ideal of the Persian Shah.

In a spirit akin to that of Marx and even Bernstein, whom he had once said "must be destroyed," Plekhanov contended that a true revolution could only be a democratic one:

If socialism were imposed by force it will lead to a political deformation like that of the Chinese or Peruvian empires, a renewed Czarist despotism with a Communist lining.

Before he died (in Finland, in 1918), Plekhanov denounced Lenin's betrayal of all they had both fought for.[28] He recalled sardonically that the leader of the Austrian socialists, Viktor Adler, used to say to him reproachfully, "Lenin is *your* child"—and he used to answer, "But not a legitimate one ... "

The matters of legitimacy or illegitimacy, of orthodoxy or heresy, of loyalty or betrayal are rarely, if ever, as simple as the polemical protagonists make them out to be. The careers of revolutionaries, like that of revolution itself, constitute neither a circle, nor a line, nor a spiral. Revisionists may move to the left or to the right, from shame to glory or the reverse. There is this mixed duality in the intellectual biography of Maxim Gorky. Usually, in the West, we are confronted with the record of Gorky's famous *trahison*—how he returned from exile in Italy to become one of Stalin's abysmal "engineers of the soul." He took a high post and sang the song of Soviet success. In that dismal year of 1930, dark with starvation and the onset of purges, he grandiloquently announced that "Millions of eyes began to gleam with the same joyous flame.... " When he visited the Siberian corrective labor camps he found the inmates to be nothing less than "heroes" of socialist reconstruction, happily undergoing the soundest form of penal therapy. I remember as a boy reading his famous "humanist" address to the illustrious Paris Writers Congress of 1935 (Malraux and Pasternak were there). He was, for a brief moment, an effective persuader, as he apostrophized the birth of a New Man, "reading Shelley in the original." And when Stalin, in his wrath, turned on heretics and dissenters, Gorky argued in one of his stylish short sentences: "If the enemy does not surrender, he will be exterminated." (It could be that Gorky himself was, subsequently, exterminated; Richard Hare, in his biography, writes that "we still do not know for certain.")[29]

This was Maxim Gorky at his "orthodox" worst, and this much is notoriously certain. The spectacle of his "monstrous behaviour" recently moved one East European intellectual, full of personal bitterness at Gorky having been quoted at him in a GPU prison, to a cry of unforgiving outrage.[30] But there is, at least for the objective historian, the "other Gorky." I can recall once hearing Irakli Tseretelli, the gentle president of the Russian Duma during the 1917 Revolution, make the generous reminder (years later, in New York exile) that Gorky had tried to defend him against Bolshevik hooliganism. Boris Nicolaevsky, sometime

member of the Marx-Engels Institute in Moscow, in the same spirit
showed me the rare copies of *Novaya Zhizn,* Gorky's weekly paper during the Revolution, to which not even the complete Soviet bibliography
makes a reference, for it has to this day been completely consigned to
the Orwellian memory-hole. And Bertram D. Wolfe has located and
published that memorandum, prepared at Lenin's request by his wife,
Krupskaya, which outlined in 1923 the new Index of Forbidden Books
for Soviet libraries (it included the works of Plato, Kant, Schopenhauer,
Solovyiev, Taine, Ruskin, Nietzsche, and Tolstoy).[31] It was this which
horrified Gorky so much that he wrote angrily from Capri that he intended to renounce his Soviet citizenship.

To take cognizance of the full collection of Maxim Gorky's regular
articles in his "New Life" weekly during 1917–18 is to give him, at long
last, his moment of glory in the checkered history of the modern intelligentsia.[32] Gorky's paper did not last for long. He was permitted to write
as he pleased only for a single year of the Revolution. The first number
appeared in April 1917, and one of his first editorials announced: "We
strove for freedom of speech in order to be able to speak and write the
truth." The last numbers appeared in the summer of 1918; he was leading a campaign against "lies, slander and violence" when, on Lenin's
personal orders, the paper was shut down. But, taken together, the
fugitive documents manage to preserve for us an immensely valuable,
and indeed unforgettable, record of the spiritual crisis of a revolution—
as revealing in its way of the revolutionary ambivalence in 1917 on the
ideals of freedom, tolerance, and law, as Madison's papers are on 1776
or Condorcet's fragments on 1789.

For it clearly took no process of god-that-failed "disenchantment" for
Gorky to come to grips with truths and realities. From the beginning,
that is from the downfall of the Tsarist monarchy in February 1917, he
had few illusions about the difficulties and dangers facing the liberal
democratization and the cultural modernization of Russian society.
There was an old and obvious enemy on the Right—the forces of restoration, vindictive, anti-Semitic, autocratic, desperate. There was also, increasingly, a new enemy on the Left—the cold, ruthless, irresponsible
ideologues whom he called "the maniacs of a beautiful idea." We hear
little in the chronicles of *Novaya Zhizn* of the former; the paper speaks
mainly of the dramatic tension with the latter until it falls victim to that
not unfamiliar species of radical militance which fights for freedom but
never on behalf of those who think differently.

The conflict was, in a word, with the Bolsheviks (and how furiously
Gorky fought it one would never guess from reading, say, the historical
accounts by Leon Trotsky or Isaac Deutscher). Gorky saw the dangers of

a Leninist *putsch* early on; but at first he put things generally, even vaguely.

It is time [he writes on 23 April 1917, in no. 5 of *Novaya Zhizn*] to cultivate in ourselves a feeling of aversion to murder, a feeling of revulsion to it.... Is it possible that the memory of our vile past, the memory of how hundreds and thousands of us were shot at in the streets, has implanted in us, too, the calm attitude of the executioner toward the violent death of a man?

I cannot find harsh enough words to reproach those who try to prove something with bullets, bayonets, or a fist in the face. Were not these the arguments against which we protested, were not these the means of repressing our will, the means by which we were kept in shameful slavery?

He had hopes that things might become "more honest, kinder, more humane," but he could not avoid seeing that the knives and the revolvers were out on "the brutalized street." He heard the rumors of some "action by the Bolsheviks" during the summer, and he expressed his fear of "all the dark instincts of the crowd." Polemics were beginning to be mounted against him and his weekly, but he stood by his (call them utopian, revolutionary, or revisionist) principles: "I consider myself a heretic everywhere."

No matter in whose hands power rests, I retain my human right to be critical of it. And I am especially suspicious, especially distrustful, of a Russian when he gets power into his hands. Not long ago a slave, he becomes the most unbridled despot as soon as he has the chance to become his neighbor's master.

By November 7 he could no longer avoid naming names.

Lenin, Trotsky, and their companions have already become poisoned with the filthy venom of power, and this is evidenced by their shameful attitude toward freedom of speech, the individual, and the sum total of those rights for the triumph of which democracy struggled.

Blind fanatics and dishonest adventurers are rushing madly, supposedly along the road to "social revolution"; in reality this is the road to anarchy, to the destruction of the proletariat and of the revolution. On this road Lenin and his associates consider it possible to commit all kinds of crimes.... I ask: Does the Russian democracy remember the ideas for the triumph of which it struggled against the despotism of the monarchy? ... Does not Lenin's government, as the Romanov government did, seize and drag off to prison all those who think differently? ...

The only honest answer to these questions must be an immediate demand to free the ministers and other innocent people who were arrested, and also to restore freedom of speech in its entirety. Then the sensible elements of the democracy must draw further conclusions; they must decide: Is the road of conspirators and anarchists of Nechayev's type also their road?

The people's commissars had suppressed nine newspapers for publishing, without changes or editorial comments, the defunct Provisional Government's decree scheduling the meeting of the freely elected Constituent Assembly (in which the Bolsheviks were, of course, only a minority). Facing discontinuance, too, were the *Zemlya i Volya* (Land and Freedom) of the Socialist-Revolutionaries and the *Novy Luch* (New Ray) of the Mensheviks. Nor was Gorky's own independent paper without danger. In January 1918 a group of militants, objecting to his sharp criticism ("the demonstration was not conducted by you so it is not for you to criticize it"), threatened him with a sales boycott and warned him that "soon you will be prohibited." Gorky published their letter and warned darkly against a new "autocracy of political savages." Although at a later time he was to make his reconciliation with them, at the moment he was mincing no words.

Vladimir Lenin is introducing a socialist order in Russia by Nechayev's method—"full steam ahead through the swamp."
    Both Lenin and Trotsky and all the others who are accompanying them to their ruin in the quagmire of reality . . . cold-bloodedly dishonor the revolution and dishonor the working class by forcing it to organize bloody slaughter and by inciting it to outrages and the arresting of completely innocent people . . . . Imagining themselves to be Napoleons of socialism, the Leninists rant and rave, completing the destruction of Russia. The Russian people will pay for this with lakes of blood.
    Lenin himself, of course, is a man of exceptional strength. For 25 years he stood in the front rank of those who fought for the triumph of socialism. He is one of the most prominent and striking figures of international social democracy. A man of talent, he possesses all the qualities of a "leader" and also the lack of morality necessary for this role, as well as an utterly pitiless attitude, worthy of a nobleman, toward the lives of the popular masses . . . . Therefore he considers himself justified in performing with the Russian people a cruel experiment which is doomed to failure beforehand . . . .
    This inevitable tragedy does not disturb Lenin, the slave of dogma . . . . Life in all its complexity is unknown to Lenin, he does not know the popular masses, he has not lived with them. But he—from books—has learned how to raise these masses on their hind legs and how—easiest of all—to enrage their instincts. The working class is for a Lenin what ore is for a metal-worker. Is it possible, under all present

conditions, to mould a socialist state from this ore? Apparently it is impossible; however—why not try? What does Lenin risk if the experiment should fail?

Nobody could be blunter. Lenin was "leading the revolution to ruin"; and, as for Trotsky, "to frighten by terror and violence those who do not wish to participate in Mr. Trotsky's frenzied dance on the ruins of Russia is disgraceful and criminal."

The atmosphere grew more menacing. The young Stalin had got himself on the record with a characteristic dictum: "The revolution is not disposed either to pity or to bury its dead." One Red naval proclamation stated: "for every one of our murdered comrades we shall answer with the death of hundreds and thousands of the rich." *Pravda* reiterated, with only slightly more cautious arithmetic: "For each of our heads—a hundred of yours!" For Gorky this was the "arithmetic of madness": "to me—as, probably, to all those who have not yet completely lost their minds—the stern proclamation of the sailors represents not a cry for justice but the wild roar of unbridled and cowardly beasts!"

Where would it all end? By April 1918 Gorky detected the "readiness for mass-murder of unarmed and absolutely innocent people." "However they threaten me, I will always say that brutes are brutes and idiots are idiots, and that one cannot achieve the triumph of social justice by resorting to murder, violence, and similar methods." Gorky tried to speak of the old ideals of utopia and revolution: "of conscience, of justice, of respect for man," but the words choked him: "The Russian revolution is perishing."

> [According to the Bolsheviks] since the people were tortured, they also have the right to torture ... the right to avenge torture by torture, violence by violence. How can one get out of this circle?

The calamitous answer was, alas, that the circle was closed. Gorky's "serious, sensible people," devoted to a new democratic and progressive order for Russia, were "powerless in the turbulence of inflamed passions." He saw that now "Life is governed by people who are in a state of continuous 'excitability and irritability' .... " The "sectarians and fanatics and utopians" had taken over. They were, he wrote in June 1918, the representatives of only a "purely external, formal revolutionism," and in their cold asceticism they were "emasculating the creative power of the revolutionary idea." Worse than that, in their demagogic insistence on "deepening the revolution" they were only deepening the Russian national tragedy for generations to come.

> The [people] will have to pay for the mistakes and the crimes of their leaders—with thousands of lives and torrents of blood.... For the

welfare of the Russian people even a million persons could be killed. Why shouldn't they be killed? There are many people in Russia and there are plenty of murderers ...

It was a murderous vision, and might well have proved an intolerable burden for a Goya, a Shakespeare, a Nietzsche. How did Maxim Gorky in his years of Italian exile manage to survive it? Perhaps he should never have returned from Capri.

The straightforward issue of "reform or revolution" was often the great dividing line in the Marxist movement. *"Bernstein must be destroyed"*: few left-wingers attacked the "revisionist right" with the passion and brilliance of Rosa Luxemburg.[33] She felt that the theory of gradualism had become the excuse of conservative temperaments to do little and to do that slowly, that the Social Democracy's labor movement had settled down with "arthritic English concepts" to a tacit acceptance of the status quo. She had what Trotsky called (in a letter to Karl Kautsky in 1910) a "noble impatience"; and curiously enough it was intended, in part, as a critical comment. "I think that the governing tactical factor with Luxemburg is her noble impatience. This is a very fine quality, but to raise it to the leading principle of the [German] party would be nonsense. This is the typical Russian method ... " As far as the true apostles of patience, the British Fabians, were concerned, it was the typical Continental method. At an International Congress in 1886, the first to which the Fabian Society sent delegates, a Swabian delegate had said, "Comrades, we must now allow ourselves to be carried away by patience."[34]

I have already noted that the greater the sense of frustration the more romantic becomes the utopian longing, and the more intransigent the revolutionary commitment. "We are fighting for the gates of heaven," cried Liebknecht. Rosa Luxemburg, fancying herself at those very gates, announced that "the revolution will rise resoundingly tomorrow to its full height and, to your consternation, will announce with the sound of all its trumpets: I was, I am, I shall be."

There was a quieter aspect of Rosa Luxemburg which should not be overlooked. In her moving *Letters from Prison*, there are unforgettable passages, mostly about birds and trees: rare themes in the records of revolutionary sensibility. In 1917, a year before her murder, she wrote to the wife of Karl Liebknecht:

I suppose I must be out of sorts to feel everything so deeply. Sometimes, however, it seems to me that I am not really a human being at all, but like a bird or a beast in human form. I feel so much more at home even in a scrap of a garden like the one here, and still more in the meadows when the grass is humming with bees than—at one of our party congresses. I can say that to you, for you will not promptly suspect me of treason to socialism! You know that I really hope to die at my post, in a street fight or in prison.

And so she did die, at her post, for in her major militant mood she believed: "The revolution is magnificent, and everything else is bilge [*Quark*]."

How implicitly illiberal this absolute revolutionary commitment can be comes clearly through in the following passage (1899):

> As in every political party, freedom to criticize our way of life must have a definite limit. That which is the very basis of our existence, the class struggle, cannot be the subject of "free criticism." We cannot commit suicide in the name of freedom to criticize. Opportunism, as Bebel has said, breaks our backbone, nothing less.[35]

Would not her attempt to reconcile humanism with revolutionary ideology have the same "definite limit"? She wrote in 1918:

> Revolutionary determination, plus a deep feeling for humanity, these alone are the essence of socialism. A world must be overturned, but every tear that flows and might have been staunched is an accusation; and a man rushing to a great deed who crushes a worm underfeet out of brutal carelessness commits a crime.

But, once again, could the determined world-overturners risk being put off revolutionary course (a fate worse than suicide) by contrition over carelessly crushed worms? Wouldn't sentimentalism, like opportunism, tend to break their backbones? What revolutionary could ever afford to cry over tears? As a soul-searching thought, it was noble; as a program of action it was political pathos. A mortified socialist is like the self-conscious centipede; compunctions paralyze. No one can turn over worlds with remorse and regrets.

Yet even on this noisy embattled "Spartacus" left, the reflective spirit of heterodoxy held sway. If a revolution has ideals to realize, its implicit utopia can at least provide the critical standards by which to measure its own performance. Rosa Luxemburg opposed Lenin's "ruthless centralism" and a conspiratorial organization which could only call for "blind obedience" and "mechanical subordination." She fought for "the rule of the broad masses" but felt it to be "unthinkable ... without a free and uncensored press, without the untrammelled activity of associations and meetings." She wanted to have nothing to do with a socialism "decreed and imposed from above by a dozen intellectuals." She loathed the idea of "a regimented mass" and argued:

> To be sure, every democratic institution has its limits and shortcom-

ings, things which it doubtless shares with all other human institutions. But the remedy which Lenin and Trotsky have found, the elimination of democracy as such, is worse than the disease it is supposed to cure; for it stops up the very living source from which alone can come the correction of all the innate shortcomings of social institutions. That source is the active, untrammelled, energetic political life of the broadest masses of the people.

Here, once again, was a historic parting of the ways—this time, not between utopians and anti-utopians, or between revolutionaries and reformers, but between libertarian socialists and totalitarian socialists. In her book on *The Russian Revolution* (published in 1922, four years after her shameful murder, with Karl Liebknecht, by German militarists in Berlin), Rosa Luxemburg insisted:

Freedom only for the supporters of the government, only for the members of one party—however numerous they may be—that is not freedom. Freedom is always freedom for the man who thinks differently.

And here, too, is Marxism at its self-critical best, uncanny and tragic in its prophetic power:

With the suppression of political life in the whole country, the vitality of the Soviets too is bound to deteriorate progressively. Without general elections, without complete freedom of the press and of meetings, without freedom of discussion, life in every public institution becomes a sham in which bureaucracy alone remains active. Nothing can escape the working of this law. Public life gradually disappears; a few dozen extremely energetic and highly idealistic party leaders rule, and the élite of the working class is summoned to a meeting from time to time to applaud the speeches of the leaders and to adopt unanimously resolutions put to them. *Au fond* this is the rule of a clique—a dictatorship it is true, but not the dictatorship of the proletariat, but of a handful of politicians.

3. The Anatomy of Intellectual Courage

It is a mournful truth which emerges from the history of the intelligentsia that dissenters do not always have the moral courage of their intellectual convictions. "I wear a mask," said the great Venetian monk Fra Paolo Sarpi, concealing his Protestant sympathies, "but I am forced to do so, for no one can live safely in Italy without one." The mask of madness is often preferable to martyrdom, and even elementary cowardice sometimes wears an aspect of humanistic caution. "The world has gone mad," Campanella wrote, "and the wise, in order to cure it, have been compelled to speak, act, and live as if they themselves were mad, even though in secret they have other views." Secrecy also tempted Thomas More: he hesitated to publish, asked for more time to revise, and even confessed that his *Utopia* was a book which should "hide itself away forever in its own island ... "[36]

No one admired More more than his friend Erasmus ("What has Nature ever fashioned gentler or sweeter or happier than the character of Thomas More?"); but he was a man who knew his own weaknesses: "Not all have strength enough for martyrdom." When Erasmus heard the rumors of More's execution in the summer of 1535, he could only say, "Would that he had never embroiled himself in this perilous business and had left the theological cause to the theologians." And he went on to bemoan his own isolation from his friends "who now write nothing from fear ... as if under every stone there slept a scorpion." Erasmus had often been bitterly reproached for being "fearful"; in the case of Martin Luther, Ulrich von Hutten tried to dissuade him from suggesting that he was "altogether averse" to the cause of radical reform:

> Do not disown us. You know how triumphantly certain letters of yours are circulated, in which, to protect yourself from suspicion, you rather meanly fasten it on others.... If you are now afraid to incur a little hostility for *my* sake, concede me at least that you will not allow yourself, out of fear for another, to be tempted to renounce me; rather be silent about me.

But Erasmus was not, as his Dutch biographer reluctantly concedes, one of the heroes of history: "His character was not on a level with the elevation of his mind." In one of his own letters to Luther (30 May 1519), Erasmus tried to explain:

> I declared that you were quite unknown to me, that I had not yet read your books, and accordingly neither approved nor disapproved anything in them.... I keep myself as far as possible neutral, the better to assist the new flowering of good learning; and it seems to me that more can be done by unassuming courteousness than by violence. It was thus that Christ brought the world under His sway, and thus that Paul made away with the Jewish Law, by interpreting all things allegorically. It is wiser to cry out against the Popes themselves: and I think we should act in the same way with the Kings. As for the schools, we should not so much reject them as recall them to more reasonable studies.... We must everywhere take care never to speak or act arrogantly or in a party spirit.... Meanwhile we must preserve our minds from being seduced by anger, hatred, or ambition.

There was one last remark. "I am not advising you to do this," Erasmus hastened to add, "but only to continue doing what you are doing." He also said, in a vague note of limp encouragement, that he had "looked into" Luther's latest work and was "delighted" by it.[37] Doubtless, this was on the ingenuous side; for one scholar has established that the author of perhaps the boldest and most subtle anonymous pamphlet against the papal bull condemning Luther was none other than Erasmus.

If professional men of thought, regularly committed to pronouncing on the truth of things, proved reluctant to say an unequivocal yea or nay, would artists show themselves any less divided in spirit? Holbein appears to have shared Erasmus's attitude of public indecision toward Luther, and indeed privately saw in him "only his fearsomeness, his *atrocitas*, and not his vigorous faith." As for Albrecht Dürer: he was anguished and excitable, and far more susceptible to the temptations of "the martyr's crown." Dürer thought it only right and proper that "we must stand in disgrace and danger ... " Neither the danger nor the glory of martyrdom was very tempting for Erasmus. The pathos of Dürer's final appeal to him illustrates that moving moment in the early history of the intelligentsia when intellectual combatants begin to differ profoundly on the personal consequences of believing in a true cause.

> Oh Erasmus of Rotterdam, why dost thou not come forward? Look, what can the unjust tyranny of worldly force and the power of darkness avail? Hear, thou knight of Christ, ride forward by the side of the Lord Christ, protect truth, attain the martyr's crown. Thou art but an old little man; I have heard thee say that thou gives thyself two more years in which thou wilt be fit to accomplish something. Use these well.[38]

If some intellectuals could stand aside as mere spectators of the tragedy of their times, others were more murderously involved: as victims and sometimes as executioners. Michael Servetus, who had challenged the legitimacy of persecuting heretics, had been put to death; and Calvin, who had helped with the arrest and trial, objected only to the method (burning him alive). Sebastian Castellio, who had refused to dissimulate and broke with Calvin, was forced to support his wife and children as a common laborer. "To force conscience," Castellio explained, "is worse than cruelly to kill a man. For to deny one's convictions destroys the soul."[39]

It was Spinoza who voiced the most heroic principle of the age when he wrote (although under a fictitious foreign imprint and with the author's name suppressed):

> He that knows himself to be upright does not fear the death of a criminal, and shrinks from no punishment; his mind is not wrung with remorse for any disgraceful deed; he holds that death in a good cause is no punishment, but an honour, and that death for freedom is

He was convinced that "every man is by indefeasible natural right the master of his own thought," and that it followed that "men thinking in diverse and contradictory fashions cannot without disastrous results be compelled to speak only according to the dictates of the supreme power ... " He tried to hold out against inquisitors, policemen, informers, and hysterics, arguing that "everyone has inalienable right over his thoughts." But in his lifetime, and sometimes before his own eyes, he saw his friends, teachers, and colleagues butchered. The aged statesman Oldenbarneveldt was arrested, interrogated, and executed in Amsterdam; his old teacher Van dan Ende died on a gallows in France; the De Witt brothers were tortured, stabbed, clubbed, and hanged by their feet from a lamppost in the Hague. We have a vignette of Spinoza in anger and despair, recorded after the visit in 1672 by young Leibniz (who was later to warn against Spinoza, whose ideas "dispose all things to the general revolution threatening Europe" and whose followers would be capable of "setting on fire the four corners of the earth").

After dinner I spent several hours with Spinoza. He told me that on the day of the murder of the De Witts he felt impelled to go out in the evening and exhibit in the neighbourhood of the crime a poster with the words "Lowest Barbarians! [*Ultimi barbarorum!*]" But his landlord had locked the door to prevent his going out and incurring the risk of being torn to pieces.

What purpose, Spinoza could only cry, is served by the death of such men, what example proclaimed? "The cause for which they die is unknown to the idle and the foolish, hateful to the turbulent, loved by the upright." Yet there was a lesson, and Spinoza put it this way: "Flatter the persecutor, or else imitate the victim." Easier said than done? Doubtless. Small wonder that he himself was to choose silence as the way of prudence. He suppressed his *Ethics*, which was published only after his death and in which he had written:

Prop. LXIX. The virtue of a free man appears equally great in refusing to face difficulties as in overcoming them ...
    Therefore an equally great virtue or fortitude of mind is required to restrain daring as to restrain fear ...
    Corollary. Therefore a free man is led by the same fortitude of mind to take flight in time as to fight; or a free man chooses from the same courage or presence of mind to fight or to take flight.

Spinoza's biographer calls his last published treatise, the *Tractatus Theologico-Politicus*, "a farewell to Utopia." Wearily, the philosopher, before his death in 1677, wrote: "Such as persuade themselves, that the multitude or men distracted by politics can ever be induced to live according to the bare dictate of reason, must be dreaming of the poetic golden age, or of a stage-play." Philosophers, Spinoza explained (here exactly halfway between More and Marx), "have never conceived a theory of politics which could be turned to use"; and without one their doctrines could only be "chimera" and "Utopia."[40]

Clearly, then, it is not conscience that makes revisionists of us all. An intellectual's body of principles comes to revision as much out of the pressures of events and institutions as out of private bouts of lonely reconsideration. His mind is a function of changing perspectives, and he revises in response to the onset of new and attractive hopes and to old and overpowering dangers, sometimes moving toward heresy, sometimes toward apostasy. The course runs between fresh insights and familiar compromise: between freedom and necessity. Is it truth that makes free, or freedom that makes for truth? In any event, it is always an uneasy act of willful liberation from the internal demands of clear principle and coherent belief, and the external risks of isolation, reprisal, and worse. What courage there is needs to be shared out for both the mental dare and the moral decision. The intellectual's censor is both within and without, and it always takes two to make a martyr or a coward.

When the Paris censors decided to proscribe the new volumes of the *Encyclopédie*, Voltaire, safe enough from the Bastille at the distant Genevan frontier, decided to make no further contributions. Even Diderot, panicking in the face of a *lettre de cachet* for his imprisonment in the Tower of Vincennes, "confessed" to "the excesses that slipped out of me" and offered to reveal the names of the printers and publishers of his illicit works. "It is a real pity," Voltaire wrote to Diderot, "that we cannot tell the truth in anything touching metaphysics and even history . . . . We are compelled to lie, and then we are still persecuted for not having lied enough [*On est obligé de mentir, et encore est on persécuté, pour n'avoir pas menti assez*]."[41]

If duplicity is the understandable escape and refuge, even for men of the Enlightenment, how much more so must it be for men caught up in modern systems of coercive orthodoxy. I have already mentioned the case of George Lukacs, the suppression of his famous work of 1923 and his subsequent recantation. It is perhaps not surprising that he should have approved his own fate, feeling possibly with Hegel that what is, is right, and with Marx that out of evil comes good. He was, as we have seen, the anti-utopian revolutionary *par excellence*; like Marx, his revolutionary commitment was so true no idea of the future could intrude on it. The conflict between his ideas and his loyalties was more apparent than real. When the French philosopher Merleau-Ponty, in a book published some two decades later,[42] discussed some of the problems raised by the 1923 *History and Class Consciousness*, Lukacs replied with a furious protest. He called it "treachery and falsification" to return to a book "forgotten for good reason." To return to Lukacs's book today is to see the cunning of his good reason. Just as he once countered the dangers of moral revulsion by setting against it a dialectical theory of wickedness, so, too, he confronts the movement toward heretical dissent with a dialectical theory of scientific intransigence. "Let us assume," he says—but only "for the sake of argument"!—"that recent investigations had proved beyond doubt the factual incorrectness of every single assertion of Marx." Does that constitute a troublesome problem for him? It does not. All the new results could be unconditionally acknowledged, all of Marx's single theses could be abandoned—without having to give up Marxist orthodoxy "for a minute." This is the intellectual legerdemain that characterizes Lukacs's ingenious mind. Orthodox Marxism, he maintains, is *not* an uncritical recognition of the results of Marxist investigations. It does not mean, he insists, a "faith" in this or that thesis, nor is it the interpretation of a "sacred" text. For him, orthodoxy in questions of Marxism refers exclusively to method. It is, he says,

> the scientific conviction that dialectical Marxism is the correct method of investigation, that this method can be built up, continued, and deepened only in the sense of its founders. All attempts to overcome or "improve" it have led and will lead only to shallowness, triviality, and eclecticism.

Lukacs's heterodox admirers in the West were appalled. How and why could one hold fast to a method *if all predictions based upon it had proved false?* In the East, the official guardians of the orthodoxy had been no less outraged at his dangerous deviationism. For Bukharin, this was a "relapse into old Hegelianism," and for Zinoviev (speaking at the Fifth Congress of the Comintern in 1924), it was simply intolerable:

> We will not tolerate what our Hungarian comrade Lukacs is doing in the domain of philosophy and sociology.... If we get a few more of these professors spinning out their Marxist theories, we shall be lost. We cannot tolerate ... theoretical revisionism of this kind in our Communist International.[43]

Nor was Ernst Bloch, another professor spinning out Marxist theory, any more tolerable. He worked out his philosophy of a "humanist socialism" in Leipzig at East Germany's Karl Marx University, and in his book called *The Principle of Hope* he actually went so far as to write: "Seeing through things is not the only test of a sharp eye. Not regarding everything as being crystal clear is equally the sign of a penetrating vision...." Kautsky, in a similar spiritual break with intellectual pride and arrogance, had written sixty years earlier that "most of our people suffer from the delusion that one can find a solution to every problem, if only one is clever enough; but there are insoluble problems ... "

Ernst Bloch was, of course, arbitrarily retired from the university: the party said that "mystical philosophies of hope are irreconcilable with Marxism." Unlike many of his young followers, Bloch was not arrested or imprisoned, but the accusation remained: he had been "leading youth astray . . . " His friends were quick and proud to point out that this was literally the same charge that had been preferred against Socrates. In August 1961, after the erection of the Berlin Wall, the seventy-five-year-old philosopher who had meditated upon "the darkness of the lived moment" and had believed that "we have no confidence, we have only hope," chose to continue lecturing in Tübingen rather than return to what he had imagined for so many years could be "a true home for man."[44]

Sometimes it was a matter of mental style, as in the bristling marginalia which young Turgot scribbled on a friend's manuscript which did not strike him as elastic enough: *"true, but not always"*—*"perhaps?"*—*"some truth and some falsehood in the idea"*—*"depends on the circumstances."*[45] Sometimes it was a matter of the kind of resilient moral conviction which seeks to coexist with a questing skepticism, as in Thomas More's memorable letter to a friend who had changed his mind:[46]

> I easily foresaw that you would one day think otherwise than you then thought. But really that you would not only become wiser, but even in a most elaborate address testify that you had changed, and that so openly, genuinely, and categorically, this indeed went far beyond not only my expectation but also the hopes and almost prayers of all, for your action manifested incredible probity and utter self-restraint. For though nothing indeed is more usual than to change one's opinion about a matter, yet nothing is anywhere more rare than, after you have once declared your view and then confirmed it by assertion and then defended it with vehemence, after all that to reverse course upon realizing the truth and return once again to the harbor from which you sailed, as though your voyage had been in vain. Believe me, my dear Dorp, what you have done with such great humility, you would have asked in vain of those whom the world nowadays considers most humble . . . . Although you are so keen-witted, so learned and so eloquent that if you pleased to defend anything, even what appeared improbable or absolutely paradoxical, you could yet prove it to your readers, yet in your love of truth rather than shams you have preferred to declare to all men that you were once deceived, rather than go on deceiving.

Here, again, are the signs of that deep ambivalence we have been trying to trace in the utopian longing, the revolutionary commitment, and the passion for principle—the tension between the open and the closed, the humane and the perfect, the nonconformist and the faithful.

Clearly, revisionism has been more than a heretical sport with a few ideas by a few intellectuals. In both of its most important and vigorous periods—the first, round the turn of the last century (with Bernstein as its "Father"),[47] the second, in the 1950s and '60s in Eastern Europe (with the late and unlamented Stalin as its posthumous instigator)—it has been part of the significant historical drama of the time.

The early revisionism was associated with the emergence of a mass movement of the European left. The radicalism of impotence gave way to the reformism of growing power; societies which had appeared hopelessly evil now appeared capable of change and progress. In the day-to-day struggle against concrete maladjustments and for specific goals, the utopian longing lost its apocalyptic revolutionary edge. In a sense, this issue of reform or revolution represented a nervous conflict between the emotions and ethics of the radical élite. On the one hand, socialists were driven to an emotional withdrawal from an alienating society; on the other hand, they felt morally obliged to alter and amend it in every practicable way on behalf of the poor and downtrodden.

The Communist revisionists (who mushroomed in Eastern Europe after the death of Stalin in 1953) were involved in a variant of this utopian dilemma: the opposition between theory and reality. Once the crimes which had been committed in the name of the orthodox doctrine (and which had been so systematically, so dialectically explained away) were at long last officially confirmed, the hosts of the faithful were confronted with a series of painful questions. Could the excesses of a whole historic epoch, stretching a full quarter of a century from Stalin's purge of the peasantry (the collectivization program of 1929) to his last purge of the Party (1952–53), be simply ascribed to the pathological errors of a single accidental personality? Could historical materialists avert their eyes from the pattern of deeper social causation? Surely, if so much had gone so disastrously wrong, something was amiss in the body of received methods, principles, and values. In Warsaw, in Budapest, and even in Leningrad,[48] revolutionaries became skeptical and dared to doubt.

> The predictions of poetry are incorrect
> Everything happened differently.
> The fire in the poem was one thing
> A town in flames was another.[49]

A young East German rebel, Wolfgang Harich, who was a friend and follower of George Lukacs and Ernst Bloch, tried to formulate a new political platform. Marxist-Leninist theory, he felt, had to be "enhanced and enlarged through the perceptions of Trotsky and above all those of Bukharin"; he added "the thought of Rosa Luxemburg and, partially,

Karl Kautsky" and also took, as he called them, "worthwhile elements from the theories of Fritz Sternberg" and "aspects of the Yugoslav experience," as well as "those new elements which mark theoretical discussion in Poland and China ... "[50] The blind doctrinaire had become a one-eyed eclectic, and for his eclecticism he has recently completed a long-term prison sentence. Reinstated as an official intellectual of the Marxist régime, he now confines his innovations to an attempt to reconcile critics of the material scarcities of the poor environment by stripping revolutionary ideology of its optimistic dreams of peace and plenty and substituting a pessimism of austerity.

It is a most affecting paradox that it should be men whose training conditioned them so rigorously to the "class relativism" of truth who become such absolute devotees of truth-telling. "It should be our prerogative," Julius Hay, a lifelong Communist militant, said at the Petoefi Club in 1956 (and it became one of the revolutionary watchwords of the Hungarian rising),

> to tell the truth. To criticize anybody and anything. To be sad. To be in love. To think of death. Not to ponder whether light and shadow are in balance. To believe in the omnipotence of God. To deny the omnipotence of God. To doubt the correctness of certain figures in the Five Year Plan. To think in a non-Marxist manner. To think in a Marxist manner even if the created thought is not yet an official truth.

The same devotion to truthfulness against an orthodoxy enforced by the police has been exhibited by Milovan Djilas, recently released (for the second time) from prison in Tito's Yugoslavia. "The truth is breaking through," he wrote in one of his last books, "even if those who are fighting for it may disappear in the process." Could it be true, as the famous French socialist leader Jean Jaurès had hoped a half-century ago, that "Marxism itself contains the means by which it can be supplemented and revised"?

In the West, where the valid contributions of Marxism have been more or less incorporated into contemporary scientific study of man and society, such revisionists as there are have been more eccentric, more playful, less significant. It would be naïve to make a fetish of revisionism, although we have agreed that the scientific mind is revisionist in principle. It may be that some doctrines, like some societies, are incapable of reform and have to be cleared away to make way for the new. Certainly, it would be foolish to believe that all intellectual revisions are necessarily for the better. I am reminded of the unexpected revisions which John Stuart Mill made to the second edition of his *Political Economy*. Harriet Taylor had been deeply moved by the revolutions of

1848, and it was she who persuaded Mill to delete his criticisms of socialism and communism. The updating, his biographer says,[51] cost Mill "infinite pain and worry"; but he revised. In the first edition, schemes of communal ownership were described as being "almost too chimerical to be reasoned with"; in the second edition they were called "the most valuable elements of human improvement now existing." In something of the same hectic, inconsequential spirit, we have seen Marx linked to Freud, coupled with Heidegger and Jaspers and Sartre, even married to Zen Buddhism. Americans have tried to fuse Marxism with the philosophy of John Dewey, and Englishmen with the economics of John Maynard Keynes. These are interesting and amusing matters, but they cannot concern us now. What is directly relevant is that, in the context of the contemporary European social crisis, the death of orthodoxy has been leading to a rebirth of utopian longing and the renewal of old revolutionary commitment.

What happened in Hungary in 1956 remains one of the most extraordinary and instructive chapters in modern history.[52] I remember arguing for years in the East-West debates in postwar Berlin (with Bert Brecht, among many others); and I, for my own part, began to feel more and more that what had been called "bourgeois democracy" was *not* a thing of the past and that the Bolshevik Revolution did not represent (as we have been told) humanity's inevitable, progressive step forward. With the Berlin blockade and the evidence that the morale of the people had come under duress, it began to become clearer that freedom was not the forlorn ideal of a handful of intellectuals but a popular and dynamic force. With the rebellion in Eastern Germany in June 1953, one began to feel that it might even be justified to suspect that communism was a reactionary relic of the past and that the logic of events would one day pass *it* by. The people of Europe wanted liberty: and this was not a Western prejudice, nor a vestigial fragment of yesterday. The "masses" wanted individual rights, and longed for a more permissive way of life. In Eastern Berlin and Eastern Germany (on 16/17 June 1953), there had not really been a revolution, or even an uprising; millions of people had come out onto the streets of all the cities and towns in a spontaneous demonstration against the regime. But there was hardly a shot fired; there was no real fighting, and no violence (except in Russian reprisal). In Poland, except for the early flare-up in Poznan, what took place is referred to as "a thaw" or "a springtime." Under the leadership of Gomulka, a kind of Machiavellian palace intrigue had been effected, and, although some liberalization of political, economic, and cultural life did result, it was (and remains today) a precarious balance of contradictory forces which remain hidden and camouflaged.

In Hungary, the popular mass movement against the existing social order made a radical, open, historic break. Whether wisely or no, the people stormed out of their houses, full of anger, full of hope. Turbulent day-to-day events took on the classic pattern of a revolution which might have pleased Robespierre, and elated Engels. In fact, what no one had dared to believe had actually come to pass: a modern totalitarian régime had been overthrown—if only for a week—by a revolution out of the nineteenth century, with its rifles and barricades and singing masses marching with banners in narrow streets. I shall never forget watching the young Hungarian revolutionaries on captured tanks, waving their flags and crying out, "We have won! We have won! ... " Was this not that stormy popular rebellion of the poor and exploited of which the romantic Karl Marx had dreamed? But they had not won; they were promptly repressed by a Russian intervention; the revolution failed. Things in history, as Marx's famous phrase goes, happen for the first time as tragedy and the second time as farce. What can we call them when they happen for the third time? Perhaps that is, after all, the last time. For history knows many unhappy endings; yet causes which seem lost are often rewon in other ways, in other eras. On the historical agenda, revolution has given way to reform.

Here, associated with the current revival of utopianism, is the most spectacular of the turns and twists we have found ourselves caught up in: it is the full turn; we have come full circle. King Utopus, the Fabian, is among us again. The old dreams, as a romantic neo-Marxist has recently reminded us, "corresponded to the most elementary necessities of men, to the great hunger that had depressed human societies for thousands of years ... " But that time has passed: "Are not new needs arising," he asks, "and new dreams? Or are we to go on vegetating in the utopias of the last century and setting up idols in front of men who altogether repudiate them?" The answer is as simple and touching as a sentimental refrain:

> The best service and the sincerest homage that we can render to the memory of Marx is to deal with Marxism as he dealt with the systems of his age. That is: to challenge the social organization set up in his name, realizing that new dreams must be invented for a new world ... [53]

Our historical cycle has looped back on itself. We are again at our original point of departure: with Sir Thomas More, inventing a future so that "faults, enormities, and errors" may be amended. But how? Is it not still easier to wish than to have any hope? More placed no faith in the prospects of a "windfall" for a "hurly-burly" by those bold desperate spirits who have "nothing to lose." Nor did he have any illusions about beating new and strange counsels into those heads "whose minds be already prevented with clean contrary persuasions." What, then, are the proper means for the desirable ends? What challenge for what response? How should the matter be handled "wittily and handsomely for the purpose"? What are the prospects of the "indirect approach," of "crafty wile and subtle train"? More wrote in the first book of *Utopia* that "the most perplexing [and, as we have noted, the most perennial] question of all" is: "What is to be done?" A world waits to be moved, to be changed, and after centuries of visions and revisions we search again for the point at which to stand.

If, as I have been hinting, it seems all to have happened before, then the contemporary spectacle of the breakdown of orthodoxies violently enforced and the outbreak of heresy and tolerance may be illuminated by the so-called lessons of the past. The usefulness of the historian lies in his haunting sense of a *déjà vu*. A constitution of liberty has always been preceded by an intellectual revolt. And here, I should like, briefly, to take Voltaire as exemplary.[54]

We know that he never actually uttered those famous words attributed to him: "I do not agree with a word you say, but I will defend to the death your right to say it." But where he was, and remains, paradigmatic, is in the history of the modern intelligentsia. The Russians invented the word in the nineteenth century; the English created the thing—independent men of ideas, speaking their minds freely—in the seventeenth century; but the French in the eighteenth century fashioned the style. Here is the model of the modern intellectual: the man of letters as the witness to truth and justice. We have only to think of Voltaire, taking time off from the writing of masterpieces (and other pleasurable niceties), to engage himself in the passionate defense of the underdog, of victims of wrongdoing and intolerance, in that long and unprecedented series of crusades—on behalf of Desfontaines (saved from being burned alive, the penalty for homosexuality); on behalf of General Lally and of Admiral Byng (even the duc de Richelieu was persuaded to defend him); on behalf of the Sirven family and of de la Barre (who was burned together with a copy of Voltaire's *Philosophical Dictionary*, said to be the cause of his "irreverence"); and, most memorably, on behalf of Jean Calas (a Huguenot in the fanaticized city of Toulouse, whose innocence was ultimately established). In our own day of triumphant mendacity and persecution, we may, after all the intricate reevaluations of the Enlightenment and the *philosophes*, be feeling our way back to the simpler attitude of the revolutionaries of 1791 who removed Voltaire's coffin from his distant burial place and transported it in state to the Panthéon. It rumbled through the Paris streets in a hearse designed by the painter David—and it bore the inscription: "He taught us to be free."

In the teaching of freedom, the first lesson is surely that of tolerance. The word (and the thing) had been in circulation, in English, for a century and more, but the first time Voltaire used *"tolérance"* was in a letter from Paris in 1733, in which he expressed himself characteristically against intolerant believers: "I forgive them everything so long as they are not persecutors. I would like Calvin if he had not had Servet burned. I would be obedient to the Council of Constance but for the faggots of John Huss ... " Nor was the idea always so abstract and impersonal. Voltaire's age, like many another, was one of refugees. In his own period of long exile (after several terms in the Bastille), he was once absent from Paris for a quarter of a century; and in 1736 we find him writing, in a rare outburst into open and pathetic terms: "But what a frightful life! To be externally tormented by the fear of losing my liberty on the slightest pretext and without any process of law! I would prefer death."

In a letter to Diderot, Voltaire confessed (1749): "I despise the stupid barbarians who condemn what they do not understand and the wicked who associate themselves with fools to proscribe that by which they are enlightened."[55] When the authorities in Geneva burned Rousseau's *Contrat social* (along with his *Emile,* on 19 June 1762), Voltaire noted: "We burned this book.... There are things that a wise government should ignore. If this book was dangerous, it needed to be refuted. To burn a rational book is to say, 'We do not have enough intelligence to reply to it.'" Voltaire was, of course, not uncritical of Rousseau's ideas or of his way of life; but his principle was, "let us not consider his person, let us consider his cause." Rousseau, embittered both in his person and in his cause, renounced his Genevan citizenship, and his words of 1764 are the classic epigram of total disenchantment, with friends as well as countrymen: "They were silent when they should have spoken, they spoke when nothing remained but to be silent." Voltaire's position was clear: "Is there anything more tyrannical than to destroy the freedom of the press? And how can a nation call itself free when it is not permitted to think in writing? ... Whoever has power in his hands wants to be despotic: the craze for domination is an incurable disease [*la rage de la domination est une maladie incurable*]." To be free may be the "true and natural" life of man; but if it was the task of the intellectuals to be pathbreakers, their fate would be the most dramatically unnatural of all—"Compose odes in praise of Monseigneur Superbus Fadus, or madrigals to his mistress, dedicate a book of geography to his porter—and you will be well received. Try to enlighten men, and you will be crushed [*éclairez les hommes, vous serez écrasé*]." Voltaire had himself received enough blows from enough authorities to temper so-called optimism with a measure of irascibility:

The man of letters is without recourse. He resembles the flying fish—if he raises himself a little, the birds devour him; if he dives, the fish eat him up.*[56]

Nor were they merely blameless victims of the cruelties of the age. What in our own time has been called "the treason of the clerks" would seem to be an eternally recurrent turn in what we have called "the cycles of ideology." As Voltaire knew: "It is an old story of philosophers to be persecuted by fanatics: but it is possible for men of letters to get mixed up in this business, too, and often to sharpen the weapons that are used against their brethren and themselves. Miserable men of letters! Is it your job to turn informer? [*Malheureux gens de lettres! est-ce à vous d'être d'elateurs?*]." The names he mentions are unimportant today, but how well we know the feeling: "To be a hypocrite, how low! But to be a hypocrite and evil, how horrible! [*Etre hypocrite, quelle bassesse! mais être hypocrite et méchant, quelle horreur!*]."

It is, thus, nothing less than freedom of thought that Voltaire demands, and in his *Philosophical Dictionary*, under the entry *"liberté de penser,"* he sets out the following conversation, after drinks, between Lord Boldmind and a Portuguese count named Medroso (who had confessed that "I prefer the unhappiness of burning my neighbour to that of being roasted myself").[57]

BOLDMIND: All you have to do is to learn to think. You are born with a mind ... Dare to think for yourself.

MEDROSO: People say that if everybody thought for himself it would result in a strange confusion.

BOLDMIND: Quite the contrary. When people attend a play, they all freely speak their mind, and peace is not disturbed. But if some insolent protector of some bad poet wants to force all men of taste to find good what seems to them bad, then you would hear hissing, and the two parties would throw apples at each other's head, as once happened in London. The tyrants of the mind have caused part of the misfortunes in the world. We have been happy in England only since everyone has freely enjoyed the right of speaking his mind.

MEDROSO: In Lisbon, where nobody can speak his, we're very tranquil too.

BOLDMIND: You are tranquil, but you're not happy; it is the tranquillity of galley slaves who row in cadence and in silence.

MEDROSO: Do you believe, then, that my soul is in the galleys?

---

*L'homme de lettres est sans secours; il ressemble aux poissons volants: s'il s'éleve un peu, les oiseaux le dévorent; s'il plonge, les poissons le mangent."

BOLDMIND: Yes, and I would deliver it.

MEDROSO: But if I'm content in the galleys?

BOLDMIND: In that case you deserve to be there.

There is a final Voltairean irony (and it is closer to the specific point I will be making). Liberty did emerge out of the correlation of forces in which the authorities repressed from above, the intellectuals resisted from below, and the bureaucrats tried to liberalize from within. The one man (according to a scholarly biographer of Diderot) who "seems to have been about the only person in eighteenth-century France who desired real freedom of the press" was, in a paradox, the chief censor. He was an almost forgotten nobleman named Malesherbes (he has already been mentioned, briefly, in connection with Chateaubriand). Having to deal with books, he came to cherish them and, having to mix with men of letters, he found himself "led by unforeseen circumstances—and perhaps against my will—into a position to procure for them the liberty of writing that I had always seen them sigh for ... " He added: "I also considered this to be doing a service to the State, for this liberty has always seemed to me to have many more advantages than drawbacks." Possibly only Voltaire could have quite imagined the quixotic career of a censor thus cultivating his own garden. When Malesherbes once informed Diderot that the *Encyclopédie* was to be stopped again and that he would be giving the order the next day, the *philosophe* was desperate to find a way to save his manuscripts. "Send them all to me," said M. de Malesherbes. "No one will come here to look for them [*Envoyez-tous chez moi, l'on ne vierdra pas les y chercher*]." So Diderot sent half of his papers to the very man who was ordering the search for them![58]

This was, in the sense of our argument, the finest and most significant victory of the Voltairean spirit. "It is impossible to domineer over opinions," Malesherbes wrote, "and consequently unjust to suppress, garble, or correct books in which they are set forth." He had come to believe that "a man who had read only books that, when published, appeared with the express consent of the government the way the law prescribes, would be behind his contemporaries almost a century ... " Thus did the spirit of Voltaire convert the censor, and teach him to be not only modern but free.

4. Old Incantations and Primitive Word-Magic

Just as the Anglo-Saxons were once certain that westward moved the course of empire, the Slavs had been persuaded that eastward ran the course of revolution. Yet it was in the east that empire ran its ill-fated course; and it is in both the European east and west that the revolutionary faith has exhausted itself. "Time's noblest offspring" tend to have an erratic sense of direction. The storms of history bear little relation to the points of the compass. For Washington D.C., revolutionaries on the Asian and Latin American continents threaten to the west and the south; for Johannesburg, the Black Jacobins of Africa may be breaking through from the north. There is still, then, across a globally extended political arena, a future for the great dream of revolution. There are still prospects for the word, the idea, for the thing itself—even if the event sometimes happens without the idea and the idea often precedes the word. I remember once attending a meeting in Rangoon of a special Burmese literary committee which was engaged in modernizing the national language. Urgent attention was given to the new word for "revolution" since the old one, in its ancient meaning of *"impertinence in the court,"* was flagrantly inadequate. After much philological thought and a few sharp exchanges between local Buddhist monks and foreign Marxists, the decision was made in favor of the simple, unmistakable, and evidently meaningful homophone: *"revolutsia."*

Nor should there be any illusion about the capacity of these new signs and signals to sustain the kind of fire and force which marked the old European metaphor in the classic periods of revolutionary enthusiasm. They flash in Djakarta and ignite in Detroit. In his famous "Message to the Grass Roots" (Detroit, November 1963), Malcolm X intoned the leitmotif of the Black Power ideology:

> First, what is a revolution? Sometimes I'm inclined to believe that many of our people are using this word "revolution" loosely, without taking careful consideration of what this word actually means, and what its historic characteristics are. When you study the historic nature of revolutions, the motive of a revolution, the objective of a revolution, the result of a revolution, and the methods used in a revolution, you may change words.

But he refused to change words or to be distracted from a single element which he confidently took to be its true historic content:

> I'm telling you—you don't know what a revolution is. Because when you find out what it is, you'll get back in the alley, you'll get out of the way.... You haven't got a revolution that doesn't involve bloodshed. And you're afraid to bleed. I said, you're afraid to bleed....
> So I cite these various revolutions, brothers and sisters, to show you that you don't have a peaceful revolution. You don't have a turn-the-other-cheek revolution. There's no such thing as a nonviolent revolution ... Revolution is bloody, revolution is hostile, revolution

knows no compromise, revolution overturns and destroys everything that gets in its way.

Some time thereafter, Malcolm X took up the theme of "The Black Revolution" (in New York, April 1964) and reiterated, as if the single word constituted a whole vocabulary by itself:

> Revolution is never based on begging somebody for an integrated cup of coffee. Revolutions are never fought by turning the other cheek. Revolutions are never based upon love-your-enemy and pray-for-those-who-spitefully-use-you. And revolutions are never waged singing "We Shall Overcome." Revolutions are based upon bloodshed. Revolutions are never compromising. Revolutions are never based upon negotiations. Revolutions are never based upon any kind of tokenism whatsoever. Revolutions are never even based upon that which is begging a corrupt society or a corrupt system to accept us into it. Revolutions overturn systems.[59]

This revolutionism also emerged in the turbulent 1960s as a pattern for Afro-Asian ideological propensities, as national liberation movements came to dictatorial power. The same tones which died with old regimes (Nkrumahism in Ghana) reappeared in new regimes (Nyererism in Tanzania, Qaddafism in Libya). The latter presents, as I write, the most recent revival of the revolutionary absolute, a simple rhythmic version of the political idolatry and verbal superstition out of all the shadowy epochs of human history. Indeed, on most occasions "revolution" serves as the same all-purpose semantic signal for a traditionally authoritarian power structure that "King," "God," or "the State" served in other times. Loyalty to the Revolution, dying for King and Country, crusading for the Almighty, giving one's all to the State—in most ideological contexts the noises are interchangeable.[60]

Here is one great Southeast Asian dictator in the full delirium of his newfound vocabulary:

> Everytime I stand on this Podium of 17th August I not only hold a dialogue with the People of Indonesia who are carrying out the Revolution, but also hold a dialogue with the whole of Mankind who are also in the midst of Revolution. How is our Revolution going? How does the marching rhythm of our Revolution fit in with your step? . . . In brief, I always give the balance sheet of our Revolution— the rise and fall of its flow, the boom of progress and the growl of sufferings of our Revolution. . . . Yes! History marches on. Has history ever come to a stop? The Indonesian Revolution too marches on. . . . In Jogjakarta in 1948, under the flickering light of a candle I once wrote that the Indonesian Revolution is *"razende inspiratie van de Indonesische geschiendenis"*—the raving inspiration of Indonesian history—whoever

could put History to death, whoever could put the Indonesian Revolution to death, that raving inspiration of history? ... The thunder of Revolution, sometimes resounding as shouts of applause, sometimes voicing suffering and sorrow, as a whole we hear as a song, a symphony, a chorus, like the roar of the waves of the tumultuous ocean pounding on the shore which we hear as a mighty chorus to God.... This Revolution of constant movement proceeds via the path of strike and be struck, pound and be pounded, a rising flow and an ebbing flow, the way of cheering and the way of lament, the straight road and the winding road, the path that goes down and then goes up, down again, but later up, up, up! ... Once more I emphasize now: thus, Revolution calls for three absolute conditions: romanticism, dynamism, and dialecticalism.

He goes on to specify some of the laws of revolution:

First, a Revolution must have friends and foes, and the forces of the Revolution must know which are friends and which are foes.... Second, a Revolution which is a true Revolution is not a "palace revolution" or a "leaders revolution," but a People's Revolution.... Third, a Revolution is a symphony of destruction and construction, a symphony of uprooting and upbuilding, because destruction or uprooting alone without construction or upbuilding is the same as anarchy; on the other hand, construction or upbuilding only without destruction or uprooting means compromise or reformism ...

We must be on guard lest our Revolution die out. Therefore ... give it romanticism. Give it dynamism. Give it dialecticalism. Never allow it to stagnate. Let it march on ever forward! Let it keep on being Revolution! Let it continue to be *progressive*. Progressiveness is an absolute condition for a Modern Revolution in the twentieth century. Remember! Our Revolution is a Revolution of the twentieth century, not a Revolution of the seventeenth century! All that I, as a Great Leader of the Revolution, have done in leading the Revolution, is a reflection of the progressiveness of the Indonesian Revolution. There is not a single aspect in my leadership that is conservative in nature, not a single thing that is "stagnant," not a single thing that is unprogressive.

And, finally, his dithyrambic faith in the solution of all difficulties in a deathless revolution:

The Indonesian People have to be politics-conscious and revolution-conscious. Conscious! Yes, conscious! All the people! Everybody! ... Such is indeed the case with the Indonesian People! Their hearts are always on fire. Their minds forever active. Their spirit always "obsessed." Obsessed as if by angelic inspiration. Obsessed by ideals. Obsessed by an Idea. Obsessed by the objectives of the struggle. Obsessed by freedom. Obsessed by the idea of a just and pros-

perous society.... The life of a Revolution depends on the
Revolution-consciousness of the nation engaged in that Revolution.
Not on technology. Not on industry. Not on factories or airplanes or
asphalted roads ... Among the Western countries which are leaders
in the field of technology there is not a single one which now has
"Great-Men-in-making-Concepts" ... They had great men such as
Disraeli, Bismarck, and Gambetta ... such as Mussolini and Hitler.
Now, in this age of the "Universal Revolution of Man"—they have
nobody ...

Of course we are still facing and are still overcoming difficulties—
but really stupid is he who claims that Indonesia will collapse.... We
will never collapse! ... That's what the Revolution is for! That is precisely the task of the Revolution: to solve all difficulties, to sweep aside
all obstacles! ... Ours is a deathless Revolution.[61]

What begins in undifferentiated emotion ends in unlimited rhetoric, and
this mélange of enchanted volubility does not appear in the literature of
revolution to have changed substantially over the centuries. The rhetoric
grows in a prolix self-seeding process; the lucubrations have an auto-
intoxicatory quality. Here (to use Dr. Leavis's terminology)[62] are all the
favorite words of a fondled vocabulary, where critical intelligence is
switched off and poeticalities switched on. "In its primitive uses," as Dr.
Malinowski has written, "language functions as a link in concerted
human activity, as a piece of human behavior. It is a mode of action and
not an instrument of reflection."[63]

And here, on the level of incantatory rhetoric, I make no "Eur-Asian"
or "Afro-American" distinctions among the classical and contemporary
verbalizations of revolutionary delirium. A brief excerpt from
Proudhon's *General Idea of the Revolution in the Nineteenth Century* (1851)
should justify this identification of primitive word-magic in the world
politics of apocalyptic hope:

The Revolution stretches out her arms to you; save the people, save
yourselves, as did your fathers, through the Revolution.

Poor Revolution! Everybody throws a stone at it. They who do not
slander it distrust it, and strive to divert it.... But admit it or deny it
as you like, the Revolution is rushing upon you with a speed of a
million leagues a second....

Stop a revolution! Does not that seem a threat against Providence,
a challenge hurled at unbending Destiny, in a word, the greatest
absurdity imaginable? Stop matter from falling, flame from burning,
the sun from shining! ...

A revolution is a force against which no power, divine or human,
can prevail.... A revolution cannot be crushed, cannot be deceived,
cannot be perverted, all the more, cannot be conquered. The more you
repress it, the more you increase its rebound and render its action

irresistible.... Like the Nemesis of the ancients, whom neither prayers nor threats could move, the revolution advances, with sombre and fatal step, over the flowers cast by its friends, through the blood of its defenders, across the bodies of its enemies ...

The more the inevitable overthrow is put off, the more must be paid for the delay: that is as elementary in the working-out of revolutions as an axiom in geometry. The Revolution never lets go, for the simple reason that it is never in the wrong....

And now, reactionaries, ... you have sought blood and civil war. All this has produced as much effect on the Revolution as an arrow upon a rhinoceros.

And if the revolution was unconquerable, indefatigable, and inexorable, did it, then, not deserve to be loved, to be served, to command an immortal devotion?

The Revolution, I have just told you, has grown its teeth: the Reaction has been only a fit of teething sickness for it.... Are you willing then to serve this great cause; to devote yourselves, heart and soul, to the Revolution? ... Will you support the Revolution—yes or no? ...

Thus there is no middle way between Reaction and Revolution. But Reaction is mathematically impossible: we are not free to remain un-revolutionized; our only choice is how fast it shall occur. For myself, I prefer the locomotive.... My advice then is to clear the course at a single leap, and reach the goal without stopping by the way ...

If the trumpet of the last judgment should resound in our ears, which of us at that moment would refuse to make his confession? Let us make it then, for I vow the last hour is approaching for the ancient abuse. It is too late to talk of purgatory, of gradual penitence, of progressive reform. Eternity awaits you. There is no middle ground between heaven and hell. We must take the leap.... there is room for everybody in the sunlight of the revolution ...

The motto which I put at the head of my book on "Contradic-tions"—*Destruam et aedificabo*—I destroy and I will rebuild. This anti-thesis, taken from Deuteronomy, is nothing but the formula of the revolutionary law ... that every negation implies an affirmation, and that he only is the real rebuilder who is first a real destroyer ...

Revolutionize, I tell you.[64]

"Revolutionism," from Proudhon to Sukarno and Malcolm X, is poor fare, bare old bones from other feasts. But the political appetites of men have always had to feed themselves in an economy of semantic scarcity. There was little to go around, a handful of words, and those simple enough. For all the charm of occasional variations—and, to be sure, the emergence every now and then of some spectacular piece of mental or verbal originality—the student of comparative ideology cannot but be led to the conclusion that it has been an exercise in human limitation. It has been, for the most part, a brief sketch on an almost empty stage; a few melodramatized ideas, dressed in a patchquilt of colored metaphors, have been presented in one or two obvious temperamental moods, after a noisy fanfare of rousing cheers or mournful cries.

If there are still present-day prospects for the dream of revolution, it is sustained in a variety of ways and places—in the propaganda of delirious power (Sukarno), but also in the poetry of black violence (Frantz Fanon, Malcolm X, James Baldwin), in the ambitious *realpolitik* of Arab rivalry (Nasser, Qaddaffy), in the maxims of what the young Red Guards worship as "The Thought of Mao Tse-tung," in the Latin commentaries to Chinese guerrilla handbooks (Castro, Guevera), and sometimes in the overseas messages of long-distance ideological encouragement (Jean-Paul Sartre, C. Wright Mills, Conor Cruise O'Brien).

Aways, as in the desperate competition between rival religionists, there is the mortal concern about the challenge of reform to revolutionary movements, which Marx had so colorfully expressed to Engels on the successes of the Reform League: *"Die Reformbewegung hat uns beinahe killed."* Fidel Castro echoes, a century later, this same historic nervousness with his remark (in a newspaper interview): "These reformist leaders often delay revolutions longer than anything."[65] Just as Marx hastened to add his confidence that "soon *die Lauserei* of the reform movement would be recognized for what it is," so did Professor O'Brien feel compelled soberly to reassure the whole of Afro-Asia (and elsewhere) that

> revolutionary social and economic changes must occur throughout the whole of the underdeveloped—"non-aligned"—world, and further that such changes are not likely to be carried out except by disciplined, revolutionary, political movements, which are likely to be of communist type . . .

Sartre, in introducing Dr. Fanon's *Les Damnés de la terre*, strikes another, more metaphysical tone:

> Make no mistake about it; by this mad fury, by this bitterness and spleen, by their ever-present desire to kill us, by the permanent tensing of powerful muscles which are afraid to relax, they have become men. . . . Hatred, blind hatred which is as yet an abstraction, is their only wealth. . . . Violence is man re-creating himself.

Fanon, speaking for himself, makes a poetical, mystical unity out of these elements of revolutionary metaphysics and ideology. The path to what he calls (albeit, self-consciously, in quotation marks) "Utopia" is by means of "that co-ordinated effort on the part of two hundred and fifty million men to triumph over stupidity, hunger and inhumanity at one and the same time." This is "the upward thrust of the people." In that thrust, he tells us, "no one has clean hands; there are no innocents and no onlookers. We all have dirty hands.... Every onlooker is either a coward or a traitor." A familiar pattern is reemerging, and the haunting question returns: What, then, is to be done? "Since July 1954," Fanon writes, "the question which the colonised peoples have asked them-selves has been: 'What must be done to bring about another Dien Bien Phu? How can we manage it?'" The first answer is the recognition that "only violence pays." The enemy "will only yield when confronted with greater violence." And that violence itself is a "cleansing force." If this appears to be a subtle point, not readily comprehensible to all, Fanon explains that "there exists a brutality of thought and a mistrust of sub-tlety which is typical of revolutions." With a special sensitivity which he confidently contrasts to those who merely "bandy about in irresponsible fashion phrases that come straight out of European treatises on morals and political philosophy," he insists on a revolutionary destiny rooted in "an idea of man and the future of humanity" and (with equal unoriginal-ity) a government "by the people and for the people, for the outcasts and by the outcasts." With *Négritude*, it might be possible to discover that "there was nothing to be ashamed of in the past, but rather dignity, glory and solemnity"—but pride in the future belongs only to the "revo-lutionary terrorist brotherhood," for "violence alone, violence commit-ted by the people, violence organised and educated by its leaders, makes it possible for the masses to understand social truths and gives the key to them ... "[66]

What began in the cult of revolution as an image of the heavens ends here as a poetry of the blood. It has moved from the external fixities where man's changing fortunes were written to the internal coursing of the dark humors which determine man's rages. In either case, the great metaphor, repeated endlessly over three centuries, never fails to take on the verbal magic of traditional incantations.

For we are dealing here with the relics of a primitive word-magic. As the semanticists have instructed us:

> To classify things is to name them, and for magic the name of a thing or group of things is its soul; to know their names is to have power over their souls. Nothing, whether human or super-human, is beyond the power of words. Language itself is a duplicate, a shadow-soul, of the whole structure of reality.[67]

To which I should like to add the following profoundly pertinent obser-vation made by Karl Vossler in his analysis of the spirit of language:

> What is commonly called rhetorical emphasis, is merely a pale reflex-ion or echo of linguistic magic and incantations. We shall best under-

stand what emphasis really is if we imagine typical cases of its strongest, most glaring, and most condensed activity: fearful curses, terrible incantations, superstitious acts of baptism, the calling up of demons and gods, and not merely intellectual quotations from books.

The essential point for us is that the speaking magician, the man who is being emphatic, is completely shut in and, as it were, fused into the magic ring of the language community involved. In the instant of emphatic expression his relation to language is not that of an individual; it is not really he who is speaking, it is the word, it is language itself that is speaking. He does not talk, he does not speak, he says nothing that is his own—he is merely lending his voice to the formula. Anyone who knew the formula could do it just as well as he. The active principle, the energy of language, now lies in the word, in the formula, in language itself, not in the speaker. He functions merely as the accidental medium.... That abstract and dead things like words, syllables, parts of speech, formulae, should become concrete and living; that linguistic shells should be filled with supernatural powers, is only possible, indeed only thinkable, because a single will, a single sentiment, takes hold of all concerned, because all concerned allow it to take place.[68]

I have already suggested that, in what Kant called the great game of revolutions, the favorite spectator sport of the modern ideological class, there were just so many fixed pieces, so many limited moves. The revolutionary spark comes from the east or the west; from abroad or at home; from the weakest, most breakable link or the strongest chain cracking under great stress; from the forests where men are free or the villages which are greener; from the little hills where the air is clearer or the plains where men can roam; from the coastal shores where spirits are lively or the heartland where the sea offers no easy escape; from the city where urbanity stimulates or from the simple uncorrupted countryside.

It should, therefore, at this point, come to the reader with something less than astonishment that after pastoral utopians and rural revolts, urban uprisings and urbane rebels, we should at long last have a full-blown theory of the revolution that descends from the mountain, those "Delectable Mountains" (as Bunyan called them) which have always had for some dedicated men a deep ineluctable purpose: "The mountains also shall bring peace; and the little hills righteousness unto the people" (Ps. 72). I refer to the post-Marxist-Leninist myth of the *guerrillero*, as formulated in a book *Révolution dans la révolution?* by a young Paris intellectual who researched it in Cuba, published it in France, and was imprisoned for it in the hills of counterrevolutionary Bolivia.[69] "The city," Fidel Castro had proclaimed, "is the cemetery of revolutionaries," and Régis Debray, his Sartre-trained disciple, echoed with his own formula: "Abandon the city and go to the mountains." How did it come about that "it devolved on the Sierra to save the revolution"? Let us try and trace the course (and the sources) of this psycho-geographical mystification.

If Fidel had no compunctions about becoming "a heretic within the camp of Marxism-Leninism," neither would Debray: and he would dare what he called "the rigors of terrestrial dialectics" in which old forms "are born and die and are reborn ... " Was he a revisionist? No, for he had come, inevitably enough, not to revise but to "revolutionize revolutionary thought." Was his an orthodoxy? Not really, for he knew full well that "in a given historic situation there may be a thousand ways to speak of the revolution, but there must be one necessary concordance among all those who have resolved to make it." And it was a concordance with, above all, the future: for he had come "to free the present from the past," and to rid the "sacred" cause of those misguided utopian obstructions which stood in the way of "total war" and the ultimate peace of righteousness.

Régis Debray begins with a catechetical precept from Che Guevera, the hero of the Sierra Mestre whom he had sought out just before he was slain in a Bolivian guerrilla hideaway:

> What is decisive is the determination to struggle which is maturing daily, the awareness of the need for revolutionary change and the certainty of its possibility.

For himself, announcing "the death of a certain ideology," he adds:

> In the new context of struggle to the death, there is no place for spurious solutions, no place for the pursuit of an equilibrium.... Destroy them *en bloc* or accept them *en bloc:* there is no middle way.... To risk all means that, having risen in the mountains, the fighters must wage *a war to the death,* a war that does not admit of truces, retreats, or compromises. To conquer is to accept as a matter of principle that life, for the revolutionary, is not the supreme good .... It [the little group of guerrilleros] stakes everything. *Patria o muerte.* It will either die—physically—or conquer, saving the country and itself....
> "Our fight will culminate in death or in victory for the true revolution [Fidel Castro]."

It goes without saying for the reformists and all the other varieties of militants or radicals that "the revolution of which *they* speak is utopian" and that *their* "beautiful verbal approaches operate in reality like a trap." How weary Debray is of medieval and, even worse, ancient monotonies! "Prometheus struggling ceaselessly against a Zeus of a thousand disguises in order to steal from the fire of liberation and keep it burning." Here was a Prometheus who would come down from the mountain. The new Prometheans would at first suffer a clandestine ordeal of "absolute nomadism," but in the very freedom of their mobility "the Revolution is on the march."

What is decisive, according to Debray, is an end to "the old obsessions," the old formulas which represented only a "verbal-ideological relation to the revolution." All the traditional breeds of revolutionary, not to speak of the despicable reformers, are consigned to a new, extralarge dustbin of history:

> Let us try to understand: it is at bottom the same naive idealism that inspires those who are addicted to the electoral opium, for whom socialism will come on the day when one half plus one of the electorate vote for it.

Having proclaimed that there is "no exclusive ownership in the revolution," he goes on to deny the contemporary relevance (especially in the ripeness of Latin American struggle) of the theses of Marx, Lenin, Trotsky, Mao, and Ho Chi Minh. No, there can be no meaningful distinction between the political and the military, between the Army and the Party. Guerrilla warfare, as the lesson of the Sierra Mestre demonstrated, is "essentially political." There was no dichotomy; the old argument was (as Hegel liked to say) *aufgehoben;* all the old apostles of "hallowed principles" were totally in error:

> They live in a double world, genuinely dualist and—why not say it?—deriving from a strongly *idealist* tradition: politics on the one side, the military on the other. The people's war is considered to be a technique, practiced in the countryside and subordinated to the political line, which is conceived of as a super-technique, "purely" theoretical, "purely" political. Heaven governs the earth, the soul governs the body, the head governs the hand. The Word precedes the Act. The secular substitutes for the Word—talk, palaver, chatter— precede and regulate military activity, from the heavens above.

Now for the first time a new principle—one of "staggering novelty"— becomes clear: certainly clearer than it ever was in the Paris Commune, or in St. Petersburg in October , or on the Chinese Long March, or in the Asian jungles controlled by Vietminh and Vietcong: namely, "the essentially and totally political character of guerrilla warfare." Lenin and Trotsky, Mao and Chu Teh, Ho and Giap, were all "dual": but Castro and Guevera were "simultaneous." This was the dialectical transubstantiation of the century: two became one; and heaven was united with earth, the soul with the body, the head with the hand, the word with the act.

If this was the message from the mountain, it was not a simple piece of rhetoric, although it was also that. Proud as he was of revolutionary theory which was so "rich in metaphors," Debray's thesis was not one of rhetoric but of ruthlessness. As he writes:

> The destruction of a troop transport truck or the public execution of a police torturer is more effective propaganda for the local population than a hundred speeches. Such conduct convinces them of the essential: that the Revolution is on the march, that the enemy is no longer invulnerable.

Skilled deception is wedded to concentrated violence:

> To accept talks is already to waver.... We may speak of peace but only while making war. This is the only way that the slogan of peace can be turned against the oppressor rather than against the insurrection.

Finally, the spirit of old martyrdom leads desperately to a new technical efficiency. "In a limited and defined number of seconds, three men can now liquidate a troop transport truck carrying thirty soldiers."

These are the new virtues of revolutionary mountaineers who have turned their backs on "the jungle of the city." The city could only make one "infantile and bourgeois." But in "life in the mountains, in the seclusion of the so-called virgin forest," there is an end to the old vices of urban weakness. The city bourgeoisifies the proletarian; "the mountain proletarianizes the bourgeois and peasant elements" and inspires them to think "like a dispossessed class" (Guevera). The saving of the revolution by the Sierra is only in part a metaphor; it is also meant quite physiologically. For there is, as Debray confesses, "a close tie between biology and ideology." In the mountains, men become strong, at once resolute and responsible: and here, for a brief moment, the young Paris intellectual (who, fighting along in Guevera's little *foco* band in Bolivia took the guerrilla name of "Danton") becomes self-conscious: " ... The blasé will smile at this vision *à la* Rousseau. We need not point out here that it is not love of nature nor the pursuit of happiness which brought them to the mountain, but the awareness of a historic necessity." So it is that the necessary concordance remains inviolate, but not without the aid and protection of urbane abstractions about the certainties of history and the vague metaphorical richness of age-old devotions to the mountain.

For there has been, from time immemorial, the conception of (in Matthew Arnold's phrase) the "high mountain cradle": and it is in its holiness, as the biblical prophets proclaimed, both invulnerable and enchanting ("How beautiful upon the mountains ... " [Isa. 52:7]. John Milton's "Sweet liberty" was, it will be recalled, a "mountain nymph"; and Gerrard Winstanley's dream of "freedome for all mankinde" was of a "holy mountaine." As for the city, corrupt and enslaved enclave that it was, it could only be shunned as in Byron's *Childe Harolde:*

> I live not in myself, but I become
> Portion of that around me; and to me
> High mountains are a feeling, but the hum
> of human cities torture.

Whom does it surprise that the ideologist of modern crusaders from the mountain is convinced of the purity and power of the heights as were the hosts of romantical spirits (from Schiller to Hugo) before him.

> We are what suns and winds and waters make us;
> The mountains are our sponsors ...

This is from Walter Savage Landor's *Regeneration,* and here indeed is the true place of the world's renewal, because, as in Blake's vision (in his *Gnomic Verses*),

> Great things are done when men and mountains meet;
> This is not done by jostling in the street.

Obviously, it was ordained that only from on high could great transformations come, for if "the mountains divide us" (Scott) only "the mountains kiss high Heaven" (Shelley).

This note sounds through all romanticism like an echo in the valley. Shortly after his Alpine inspiration for *The Assassins* (1814)—where "a new and sacred fire was kindled in their hearts and sparkled in their eyes"—Shelley went on to claim,

> The wilderness has a mysterious tongue ...
> Thou hast a voice, great Mountain, to repeal
> Large codes of fraud and woe ... [70]

This cloud of eschatological mist and poetic haze has thrown its shadow over the mythology of the mountain *guerrillero,* that latter-day descendant of *La Montagne* of Robespierre and Danton; and it is a mixture of images and ideas which, I submit, can be easily located by a historian of metaphorics with access to European sources.[71]

As for the Chinese, sensitive as they have become to every form of bourgeois or even revolutionary deviation, they have now identified, classified, and denounced a new heresy which they have termed "mountain-top-ism."[72]

I can only speculate on the literary sources of a young Frenchman's revolutionary sensibility; but Hugo would seem to have as much to do with it as Havana. In Victor Hugo's *Quatrevingt-treize* (1874), there is an eloquent passage which formulates this version of the virtues of revolutionary mountaineers and the romantic persuasion of the purity and power of the heights.

> The Vendean rebellion failed. Other rebellions have succeeded, in Switzerland, for example. There is this difference between the mountain rebel, like the Swiss, and the forest rebel, like the Vendean: Nearly always—inevitable influence of the environment—the former fights for an ideal, the latter for prejudices. One soars, the other crawls. One fights for humanity, the other for solitude; one wants freedom, the other wants isolation; one defends the commune, the other defends the parish.... One deals with precipices, the other with bogs; one is a man of torrents and foam, the other is a man of stagnant pools from which fever rises; one has the blue sky over his head, the other has a thicket; one is on a peak, the other is in a shadow.
>
> What is taught by heights is different from what is taught by depths.
>
> A mountain is a citadel, a forest is an ambush; one inspires boldness, the other suggests traps. Antiquity placed the gods on peaks and satyrs in copses ... The configuration of the land suggests many of man's acts. It has a greater influence than is commonly believed ... one feels a secret provocation on the part of nature.*[73]

Hugo's historical romanticism is itself an echo of Schiller's youthful pathos about mountain revolutionaries: *"Auf den Bergen ist Freiheit! (Freedom is in the mountains!)"* And in a famous passage of his *Wilhelm Tell* (1804), one of his Alpine rebels cries:

> No, there is a limit to the tyrant's power. When the victim of oppression can find no legal remedy and the burden becomes intolerable, then he raises his hand with firm spirit to Heaven and grasps his eternal rights which dwell above, inalienable and indestructible as the stars themselves.†[74]

---

* "L'éducation n'est point la même, faite par les sommets ou par les bas-fonds. La montagne est une citadelle, la forêt est une embuscade; l'une inspire l'audace, l'autre le piège. L'antiquité plaçait les dieux sur les faites et les satyres dans les halliers ... La configuration du sol conseille à l'homme beaucoup d'actions. Elle est complice, plus qu'on ne croit ... on sent une sourde provocation de la nature."

  †Nein, eine Grenze hat Tyrannenmacht.
  Wenn der Gedrückte nirgends Recht kann finden,
  Wenn unerträglich wird die Last—greift er
  Hinauf getrosten Mutes in den Himmel
  Und holt herunter seine ew'gen Rechte,
  Die droben hangen unveräusserlich
  Und unzerbrechlich wie die Sterne selbst.

Nowhere has this congeries of image and symbol been expressed with greater contemporary clarity and mythic consistency than in "The Thought of Mao Tse-tung," which has now in Communist China been declared to be an ideology "of a higher order" than even the ideas of Marx, Engels, Lenin, and Stalin.[75] The simple Chinese theses have no less energizing force for being the most familiar strains in the history of utopian and revolutionary thought. They may be summarized (and illustrated) in the following way:

1. *In a time of tyranny and injustice, man must be a rebel.* "There may be thousands of principles of Marxism, but in the final analysis they can be summed up in one sentence: Rebellion is justified . . . " (Mao, 1939).

2. *The true and great struggle is itself a liberating good.* "What is correct always develops in the course of struggle with what is wrong. The true, the good, and the beautiful always exist in comparison with the false, the evil, and the ugly, and grow in struggle with the latter . . . "(Mao, 1957).

3. *Violence on behalf of the historic cause is both necessary and desirable.* "How can one say that, in the face of terror and atrocities, the peasants should not now rise and shoot one or two of them and bring about a small-scale terror in suppressing the counter-revolutionaries? . . . " (Mao, 1927).

4. *The revolution will begin all things anew, for its face is set toward the white shining blankness of the future.* "Poor people want change, want to do things, want revolution. A clean sheet of paper has no blotches, and so the newest and most beautiful words can be written on it, and newest and most beautiful pictures can be painted on it . . . " (Mao, 1958).

This ideological aspect of Maoism, as must be fairly obvious at this point, is neither original nor mysterious. It is traditional doctrine, made up of the essential links in the great chain of human hope: utopia and revolution. Like all ideologies of the past, be they of higher or lower orders, it carries within itself the seeds of its own dissent and diversion. As a manifesto of practical government, it produces social crises and contradictions; as a religious dogma, it entangles itself in fallacies and heresies; as a secular faith, it faces the inevitable trials of human disillusionment.

5. The Lost Metaphor

The largest and most dramatic movement of contemporary intellectual opinion in the West has been in the ideological rebirth of the so-called New Left and, more significantly, in the currents of impassioned ideas circulating about the "Negro Revolution" in America. What is new here and what is old? If the real substance of social issues is necessarily different, for history is always happening for the first time, what can we make of the familiar and recognizable configurations?

Let me put it another way. Given the century-old patterns which are traceable in the relationships between political temperament and intellectual climate, what would we expect to find in the symptoms of (in Burke's phrase) "the particular distemperature of our own air and season"? If we were to try to locate and identify the basic links in what I have called the great chain of human hope,[76] would they not emerge as the recurrent elements of utopian and revolutionary militance? We have here another full turn of the ideological cycle as the archetypes return: the high-minded quest for an ideal social order; an angry commitment to radical social change; an impatience with moderation and meliorism; a predisposition to violence as the morality and strategy of deep and genuine social reconstruction; a burning longing for the fires of redemption. And so the chain holds fast. One is tempted to think of it as a kind of *politica perennis*.

One radical New York intellectual, still holding out hope (the year is 1967) for the relevance of "Marx's messianic idea that to make the world right we have to make something new out of the old order," did sensitively go on to confess his troubled doubts:

> Is it possible that the distinction which I am trying to make between these opposing caricatures of Left and Right comes down at last not to a question of principle but to a way of feeling? Is it a flaw in me to be too quickly irritated by what may be perfectly correctable faults in the world if only I am patient? Is it their weakness to be complacent in the face of faults with which we have lived long enough? These are questions of nuance and shading.[77]

But there were precious few signs of nuance or of shading in the ideologized half-decade that followed.

Shortly after the tragic riots in the city of West Berlin in the summer of 1967, I spoke with a number of student and academic representatives of the Free University, which had suddenly become (in part under the direct inspiration of similar events and movements three years earlier in Berkeley, California) a center of youthful rebellion; and I was forcefully struck by the freshly cyclical enthusiasm for certain age-old basic principles of utopian and revolutionary sentiment.[78] 1. "We have a vision of a human personality and a social order which will for the first time in history be truly free, and for that vision we must sketch out a new and positive Utopia." 2. "Our own isolated attempts to set up an ideal community [i.e., the so-called *Studenten-Kommune*] cannot succeed, for it is the fault of society to present us only with distorted and crippled human material." 3. "The existing society cannot change itself in any fundamental or qualitative way from within, only from the outside in the name of totally different objectives and probably only by the necessary defensive use of extralegal violence." 4. "The new society would be a truly human social arrangement without war, poverty, injustice, hatred, and other present-day evils." 5. "The present task is to insist on the revolutionary negation, for what is urgent is not the detailed outline of the free house of the future but the destruction of the oppressive prisons of the present."

Not dissimilar notes were struck by a "Black Power" movement in Britain, especially after the visit (in July 1967) of the American Negro leader Stokely Carmichael, then *en route* from Havana to Hanoi. To be sure, the problem of the colored peoples (mostly recent emigrants from the new states of India, Pakistan, Africa, and the Caribbean, trying of their own free will to take advantage of opportunities in the United Kingdom) were significantly at variance with those in the United States. The obvious differences lay in how they came, why they came, what they came to (*i.e.*, ethnic and political origins, the nature of the British economy, the style of the English urban life). The sources of disaffection and the motives of protest may be, and indeed are, different for each restless minority in each historic case; but the limited resources of image and idea drive the rhetoric of dissident leadership into the traditional formulas of utopia and revolution. We are, once again, in a world populated by the ghosts of Winstanley and Saint-Just, Babeuf and Blanqui, Bazarev and Nechayev, again (to use the line of Shelley in *Prometheus Unbound*) among "the melancholy ruins of cancelled cycles."

Thus, in a pamphlet entitled *Black Power in Britain* (published in the name of a "Central Committee" by a Universal Coloured People's Association, September 1967), we have all the familiar central themes diffused from—or, if racial pride demands, running parallel to—the century-old longings for "white power."

1. The Cult of Destruction:

The only way the Black man can get real POWER is by smashing the system that incubates exploitation of the Black. If he cannot smash it from within, he must set in motion an international revolutionary force which will do the same job from without . . . . The Black man has no choice today. Either he smashes that system with active POWER or the system will take advantage of his passive powerlessness and smash him.

2. The True Revolutionary Commitment:

The White liberal believes in justice, equality and liberty for the Black man as long as this remains within the realm of abstraction. He believes in the fruits of revolution but disapproves of the revolution that brings them about. He cherishes the omelette but not the cracking of eggs. He wants chicken without slaughter, roses without gardening, rain-water without thunder and lightning.

3. The Semantic Dependence on Standard Metaphor (*blood and fire, thunder and storm, flood and quake*):

Black power is . . . a degree of anger which the oppressed Black man feels in his guts. It takes a single match-stick to burn London down. It takes one angry Black man to light that match. Black power is a revolutionary conspiracy of Black people . . . " Again: "The invisible Black leadership prefers to remain invisible. What use is press limelight when with a single cry of "Burn, baby, burn," you can set a whole city ablaze? . . . This is a new era. The era of BLACK POWER! . . . It is like water springing up from the bowels of the earth. It is like a well shattering open the surface of the earth. Before the water burst to the open, it doesn't know which course it is going to take. But once on top, there is only one way for it to go. The way to the south. Once on the move, there is only one course the water must run. The way to the sea. So it is with the Black revolution. It is now on the move. There is only one way for it to go. And that is the way to total liberation. All we can do is shorten the journey to the end. What we must do is slash open a revolutionary canal which will quicken our tidal move to liberation. Whether this will mean a swim through a tide of blood or not does no longer depend on us.[79]

But let us not, in the tempting topicality of all this, overlook one relevant and revealing historical parallel, and it is not in some long-vanished past. The student of comparative ideology cannot fail to remember that in the European West it was only the day before yesterday—I mean the generation between the two World Wars—that this rage for revolution was the poetry of the historical agenda:

> The blue eyes of the Revolution
> shine with a necessary cruelty.[80]

Or, as C. Day Lewis put it in 1935:

> Revolution, revolution,
> Is the one correct solution—
> We've found it and we know it's bound to win.
> Whatever's biting you, here's something will put life in you . . .

At that time W. H. Auden was writing—

> We shall build tomorrow
> A new clean town
> With no more sorrow
> Where lovely people walk up and down
> We shall all be strong
> We shall all be young

No more tearful days, fearful days
Or unhappy affairs
We shall all pull our weight
In the ship of state
Come out into the sun.

And Stephen Spender was convinced that "the way" was to immerse in "the destructive element."[81]

The revolution, as always, comes to destroy and renew. The younger postwar generation would find strength for new hopes; the older generation, exhausted and despairing, just managed apocalypse. "The world is plunging on to revolution," Lincoln Colcord wrote (in 1918, to William Bullitt), " ... it will be a tragic but a splendid time, lit by the lurid light of chaos." Even Colonel House, Woodrow Wilson's adviser (who had once written a utopian novel of a benevolent dictatorship), threatened to "turn socialist, even anarchist, overnight" and to "kick up a rumpus that will ring from end to end of the world ... " A new radicalism, as a recent historian suggests (not without some relish), was being made out of such "dreams of terror and utopia."[82]

For the first time in the history of the American mind, the rhetoric of revolution established itself: more deeply than in the rebellious time of Tom Paine, more systematically than in the abolitionist era of William Lloyd Garrison. In its conventional and humdrum form (in the 1920s and '30s, the period between the two great wars), it moved from a traditionally vague utopia of scientific socialism, with its imprecise and uneasy mélange of technological and humanist aspirations, toward the urgent seizure of state power by the true party of the proletariat in the name of all the masses. What gave this first great American outburst of revolutionary commitment special interest and distinction was the graphic trans-Atlantic emergence, in a classic land of pragmatism and reform, of the most extreme European archetypes.[83] The neo-deist vision, in Lincoln Steffens's words, was "of the resurrection and life of Man." The neo-Jeffersonian method was to abolish and dissolve; for, as Max Eastman insisted in *The Masses*, they had come not to make a reform but a revolution. One bard of that revolution chanted an ode "On Lenin's Birthday" in *The Liberator*:

... ye the axmen of truth, blasters of lies and wrong, Torch-bearers of the sun, incendiaries, petroleers, Marshallers of the storms, thinkers and pioneers, Hurlers of proclamations, bomb-throwers of song, Raisers of mobs and altars, knights of the mad crusade, Arise! Break from your chains, burst through your jails. Tear through the noose of the gibbets—the day of days has come!

Marxism was discovered, Leninism embraced. They were likened to the new worlds of Copernicus, Kepler, and Newton, only (as the young Max Eastman wrote in *The Masses*) "by revolution we do not mean the journey of the earth around the sun . . . " No, what was meant was the fire and the thunder of radical social upheaval. The Russian Bolsheviks of October 1917 had provided the spark:

> In them the fire leaps which may finally fuse us . . . beyond the curtain of fire, a little beyond the wall of battle-smoke, there stands waiting and radiant, Revolution. And in her arms is a little child: an inarticulate infant: the new Humanity.

An anarchist poet went on to give the assurance:

> . . . it is an earnest and living thing, a battle call, a shout of defiance, a blazing torch running madly through the night to set afire the powder magazines of the world . . .

I am not sure how "facetious" (as Daniel Aaron suspects) the young John Dos Passos was when he confessed in a letter:

> I've decided my only hope is in revolution—the wholesale assassination of all statesmen, capitalists, warmongers, jingoists, inventors, scientists—in the destruction of all the machinery of the industrial world, equally barren in destruction and construction.
>
> My only refuge from the deepest depression is in dreams of vengeful guillotines.

Or, again, when he wrote, " . . . God, I'm tired of wailing. I want to assassinate." How much was Nechayev, and how much Harvard lampoon? Nothing ever seems to get lost: it is almost as if there were some Goethean hidden law for the preservation of every ideological aberration.

In any case, for two American decades of agitated ideological commitment, it was never quite clear where the line between rhetoric and reality was drawn. His utopian dream, Floyd Dell once tried to explain, was "not Lenin's seven hundred million electric bulbs, but a houseboat and a happy family living in a state of moderately advanced and seminude savagery! . . . " Although the vocabulary was Bolshevik, the sentiment was often Bohemian. The scholarly chronicler of the American writers on the left imagines them living quite happily "in a utopia that combined the best features of the old Greenwich Village, Bellamy's twenty-first-century cities, a Bolshevik Soviet, a Fourier phalanstery, and a *Masses* editorial meeting . . . " All this was, as Professor Aaron has concluded,

> one more turn in the cycle of revolt . . . although each displays unique features, a recurring pattern seems to run through them all . . . for literary radicalism never seems to be sustained over a long period, and

the writer is gradually absorbed again into the society he had rejected. The aftermath of his revolt is sometimes tragic, sometimes pathetic or ludicrous. Often the disenthralled writer becomes embittered or ashamed after his adventure in nonconformity, or he becomes tired as his idealism flags and the prison-house of the world closes upon him.

But even as the old revolution is expiring, a new one is flickering into life and a new generation, equally brash, confident, or angry, will announce itself with the customary flourish.

We might well ask with Malcolm Cowley why a movement which started "with such purpose and dreams of a better society" ended so shabbily. Doubtless much of the degeneration was due to the deadening influence of a mechanical system of intellectual certainties, a jealous and monistic Marxism which was closed in its orthodoxy and savage in its intolerance; and much was due to the romantic illusions and sentimental self-deceptions about the toiling masses, so exploited in capitalist America and so free in the new paradisal Russia.

To be sure, the time was not without its premature heretics. John Chamberlain wrote his memorable *Fairwell to Reform* in the depths of the Depression; but if his personal alternative to "patching up the unpatch-able" was to try a brief career as a revolutionist, he remained unfashion-able enough to talk about his dislike of barricades and guillotines and the "tingling psychological thrill" to confess even his timorousness. "Yet there are revolutions *and* revolutions"; and Chamberlain's own undoctrinaire version was a kind of "revolution by indirection," or "a long, devious, often dramatic process ... "[84]

Still, starting out in the 1930s, as one contemporary American autobiographer records, "the fascination of the Revolution was still great, the wild hope of a totally new society.... " But disillusionment, as so often in the past, was to come to yet another literary generation. As Alfred Kazin (with rather undue haste and premature finality) concluded:

> What would never come back in this most political of ages—not even in Russia—was the faith in a wholly new society that had been implicit in the revolutionary ideal.... They would not be happy. The élan of their lives, revolutionary faith in the future, was missing.[85]

"Never" in the history of ideologies is never permissible. One generation's time for mourning is often followed by another's time for celebration, as it moves with innocent élan to rediscover old things which are taken to be new things. Ideology is a boomerang. But, in the 1930s, this particular generation of intellectuals did move back from the dead end of a rhetoric so disastrously and unpardonably out of touch with obvious realities: the stabilization and recovery of a capitalist economy under the

Rooseveltian New Deal; the brutalities of the Moscow Trials and the Hitler-Stalin pact; the urgencies of a united struggle against Nazi tyranny. There was for this generation a general return to older critical, pragmatic, and even national-patriotic habits. But what was left behind was a disenthrallment too deep and devastating for any simple readjustment. The Globe, in John Dryden's lines, was "dented inwards":

> ... I'm weary of my part.
> My Torch is out; and the World stands before me
> Like a black Desert, at th' approach of night.

The fire, in Andre Gide's retelling of the Homeric legend (apposite to his disenchanted return from the USSR in 1936), had to be abandoned. The naked child, placed secretly by the great goddess Demeter on a glowing bed of embers, endured the fiery charcoal and even gathered strength from the ordeal. (Gide imagined "the mighty Demeter bending maternally over the radiant nursling as over the future race of mankind.") But the goddess was thrust aside, and the bed of embers removed. The child was saved: the god was lost.[86]

A whole generation in the West went into grief over a lost metaphor.

6. A Noose of Words

Many who mourned or were saved, or who had become weary of their part, found themselves on the darker disillusioned turn of the ideological cycle. But here we must be careful to make (as A. O. Lovejoy would surely have demanded) a discrimination of disenchantments.[87] The life and death of different illusions has a variegated pattern, and part of the problem for the historian of mortal and short-lived ideas has, in an irascible passage, been remarked by C. S. Lewis:

> Men (and, still more, boys) like to call themselves disillusioned because the very form of the words suggests that they have had the illusions and emerged from them—have tried both worlds. The claim, however, is false in nine cases out of ten. The world is full of imposters who claim to be disenchanted and are really unenchanted: mere "natural" men who have never risen so high as to be in danger of the generous illusions they have claimed to escape from.... We need to be on guard against such people. They talk like sages who have passed through the half-truths of humanitarian benevolence, aristocratic honour, or romantic passions, while in fact they are clods who have never yet advanced so far.[88]

Whether disenchanted or merely unenchanted, there began yet again the search for some clue to what Lionel Trilling called "the code of excited humanitarianism." Could it be found in Benda's critique of the divinization of politics, or in George Orwell's "smelly orthodoxies," or Hoffer's fanaticism of the true believer? Joseph Freeman, in a wartime novel which summed up his own career as a utopian revolutionary, found the martyr symbol of the tragedy in Condorcet, the only *philosophe* who had participated in the Revolution and who continued to write his history of human progress as he hid from his Jacobin persecutors.[89] For my own part, I remember copying out into my notebook of the time the lines of John Donne on "the world's condition now."

> And new Philosophy calls all in doubt,
> The Element of Fire is quite put out;
> The Sun is lost, and th' earth, and no man's wit
> Can well direct him where to look for it.
> And freely men confess that this world's spent ... [90]

A few, indeed, had the wit which directed them to a rediscovery of the virtues of skepticism and revision; and, mustering the courage to take up new positions, some found mixed consolation in the words of Péguy:

> And yet, the life of an honest man must be an apostasy and a per-petual desertion. The honest man must be a perpetual renegade, the life of an honest man must be a perpetual infidelity. For the man who wishes to remain faithful to truth must make himself continually un-faithful to all the continual, successive, indefatigable renascent errors. And the man who wishes to remain faithful to justice must make himself continually unfaithful to inexhaustibly triumphant injustice.[91]

Yet could it be that there was as much fault in their stars as in them-selves? What was the meaning of these turnings of "fortune's Wheeles" which, as the seventeenth-century verse had it, possess the brain with "a strange Vertigo or delirium" while *"nothing but fine Utopian worlds i' the Moon are new form'd by Revolution"*? Is there not evidence here of a deeper helplessness of men and ideas, caught for centuries in such Copernican turnings? The cyclical variations we have been observing are consistently characterized by certain changing patterns of tone and rhythm, of sound and movement. How is it that what men were con-vinced to be the warmth of their hearts suddenly emerged as the fevers of their minds, that what were intellectually accepted as sovereign heights turned out to be vertiginous dangers? That these questions are put in the strained language of image and metaphor is, I admit, not to come with the solution but to remain part of the problem. There is a linguistic as well as an intellectual aspect to the disenchanting course of revolution and restoration which needs to be studied. At this stage of our analysis, I offer only two brief conjectures.[92]

What has determined the language of the utopian and the revolutionary is the very vocabulary of politics. Here some deep and complex process appears to be at work, a kind of rhetorical reification. The verbal mechanism tends to take on an independent life of its own. Malinowski has written persuasively of the role of primitive, magical attitudes in the general use and abuse of language and has emphasized "how deeply rooted is the belief that a word has some power over a thing, that it participates of the nature of the thing ... "

> The word gives power, allows one to exercise an influence over an object or an action.... The word acts on the thing and the thing releases the word in the human mind.[93]

It is a phenomenon which has in passing, if rarely systematically or historically, engaged many thinkers since Francis Bacon identified the so-called Idols of the Marketplace (*Novum organum*, 43), that besetment of men's minds in which discourse wars with reason and "words plainly force and over-rule the understanding, and throw all into confusion, and lead men away into numberless empty controversies and idle fancies...." It is what Sprat, in a characteristically Baconian outburst in his *History of the Royal-Society* (1667) termed a "trick of metaphors".

> ... in a few words, I dare say, that of all the Studies of men, nothing may be sooner obtain'd than this vicious abundance of Phrase, this trick of Metaphors, this volubility of Tongue which makes so great a noise in the World. But I spend words in vain; for the evil is now so inveterate, that it is hard to know whom to *blame* or where to begin to *reform*.[94]

We use words, and are used by words in turn.

Indeed, it is very much part of the rhythmic history of ideological cycles that the first generation which lived through a revolution should have devised the first theory of the linguistic sources of political tragedy and betrayal. The *locus classicus* is, of course, in Hobbes's *Leviathan*, published in 1651 just before the philosopher's return to Cromwellian England:

> The Light of humane minds is Perspicuous Words, but by exact definitions first snuffed and purged from ambiguity; *Reason* is the *pace*; Encrease of *Science*, the *Way*; and the Benefit of man-kind, the *end*. And on the contrary, Metaphors, and senseless and ambiguous words, are like *ignes fatui*; and reasoning upon them, is wandering amongst innumerable absurdities; and their end, contention, and sedition, or contempt.[95]

This is only the first in a long historical series of explanations of how the "foolish fires" of metaphorics were responsible for the ruin of the noblest human destiny. A devilish word had lost paradise, and corrupt utterance would destroy reason and science, too, and the benefit of mankind. A fanciful phrase, or an eloquent conceit, or an outlandish cry of enthusiasm, was inevitably held to be the sign of the fall from the true course. Even the slightest nuances of style could have dire social consequences—and did. "And what Pestilential Influences," a writer in the year 1666 remarks, "the Genius of Enthusiasme or opinionative Zeal has upon the Publick Peace, is so evident from Experience, that it needs not be prov'd ... " This sense of the dangers of deceit and delusion in the language of politics led to a verbal counterrevolution which, in poetry, was associated with the Restoration's neoclassicism and, in general, with an intellectual aversion to the exorbitance of prevailing forms of feeling and emotion. If words were so dangerous, then language itself was in need of purging and constant correction. Eloquence and rhetoric were held to be (as Sprat said, and he was speaking as the voice of the Royal Society's scientific avant-garde) "in open defiance against Reason" for "they give the mind a motion too changeable and bewitching." A dozen writers, all leading rebels in the so-called revolt against enthusiasm, developed a programatic appeal for a stylistic reformation in which "all the amplifications, digressions, and swellings of style" would be rejected, and there would be a "return back to the primitive purity" of "a close, naked, natural way of speaking ... "[96] Not unlike the later Wordsworthian appeal for a language of common men (then, in the ironies of cultural history, to be considered a romantic turn), here was an anti-romantic injunction against the kind of literary communication which only fosters "mists and uncertainties." "Preferring the language of Artizans, Countrymen, and Merchants" (in Sprat's words), it was a plea for "a native easiness" on behalf of the ideals of "shortness" and "plainness" which were closer to what was fancied to be sober and natural common practice.

What are the springs of the deviant verbal mechanism? On a literary level, writers have always sensed the process, as in Byron's lines in *Childe Harold:*

> I do believe,
> Though I have found them not, that there may be
> Words which are things ...

or in Lafcadio Hearn's remark:

> Words have colour, form character. They have faces, ports, manners, gesticulations: they have moods, humours, eccentricities: they have tints, tones, personalities. I write for beloved friends who can see colour in words, can smell the perfume of syllables in blossom, can be shocked with the fine elfish eccentricity of words. And in the eternal

order of things, words will eventually have their rights recognized by the people.

The French essayist Jean Paulhan has similarly observed that to understand a word or a sentence is not to have in mind the image of the real objects represented, but rather to feel in oneself "a vague stirring of all the tendencies which would be aroused by the actual seeing of the objects represented by the word ... "

Raising these kinds of insight to a higher level of philosophical abstraction, Ernst Cassirer has written:

> For it is the necessary destiny of culture that everything which it creates in its constant process of configuration and education removes us more and more from the originality of life. The more richly and energetically the human spirit engages in its formative activity, the farther this very activity seems to remove it from the primal source of its own being. More and more, it appears to be imprisoned in its own creations—in the words of language, in the images of myth or art, in the intellectual symbols of cognition, which cover it like a delicate and transparent, but unbreachable veil.[97]

Nietzsche is, perhaps, our most sensitive guide to these recurring signs of what he thought of as "decadence."

> ... life no longer resides in the whole. The word becomes sovereign and leaps out of the sentence, the sentence reaches out and obscures the meaning of the page, and the page comes to life at the expense of the whole—the whole is no longer a whole.[98]

In a passage entitled "Words block our way," he seemed to be going further and suggesting the pattern of an eternal linguistic tragedy:

> Wherever primitive man put up a word, he believed he had made a discovery. How utterly mistaken he really was! He had touched a problem, and while supposing he had solved it, he had created an obstacle to its solution. Now, with every new knowledge we stumble over flint-like and petrified words [*steinharte verewigte Worte*], and, in so doing, break a leg sooner than a word.[99]

Was there a way out of this leg-breaking tangle? If there was, it would appear to be in a form of semantic skepticism, in Nietzsche's radical critique of *"grosse Worte."*

> I am full of mistrust and malice towards what is called "ideal": this is my *Pessimism*, that I have recognized to what extent "sublime sentiments" [*höheren Gefühle*] are a source of evil—that is to say, a belittling and depreciating of man.
> Every time "progress" is expected to result from an ideal, disap-

pointment invariably follows; the triumph of an ideal has always been a *retrograde movement*.

Christianity, revolution, the abolition of slavery, equal rights, philanthropy, love of peace, justice, truth: all these big words are only valuable in a struggle, as banners: not as realities, but as show-words [*Prunkworte*] for something quite different (yea, even quite opposed to what they mean!).[100]

Thus, words (as one contemporary literary critic has perceived) tend to draw the mind into excessive rigor and destructive roles. Just as the personages of certain classic dramas literally talk themselves into irreconcilable hatreds, so do "words carry us forward toward ideological confrontations from which there is no retreat. This is the root tragedy of politics. Slogans, clichés, rhetorical abstractions, false antitheses come to possess the mind (the 'Thousand Year Reich,' 'Unconditional Surrender', the 'class war'). Political conduct is no longer spontaneous or responsive to reality. It freezes around a core of dead rhetoric. Instead of making politics dubious and provisional in the manner of Montaigne (who knew that principles are endurable only when they are tentative), language encloses politicians in the blindness of certainty or the illusion of justice. Instead of becoming masters of language, we become its servants. And that is the damnation of politics ... "[101] Thus does political rhetoric subvert humane reason, and in tragic turn become subverted itself.

At the root, then, of this contemporary onset of intellectual disenchantment—a continuation by other means of the ordeal which had in the past entangled Lilburne and Winstanley, Kant and Constant, Wordsworth and Shelley, Proudhon and Herzen, Victor Hugo and so many others—was the periodic disintegration of "eloquent unreason."

> CLOWN: ... To see this age! A sentence is but a cheveril glove to a good wit. How quickly the wrong side may be turned outward!
> VIOLA: ... They that dally nicely with words may quickly make them wanton.
> CLOWN: ... But indeed words are very rascals since bonds disgraced them .... words are grown as false, I am loath to prove reason with them.

> [*Twelfth Night*, 3:1]

Although the phenomenon of linguistic self-doubt is probably as ancient as language itself, the idea of the villainy of words has played an especially conspicuous role in the ideological cycles of utopia and revolution. The names of things have often been held to be devious, deceptive, and mysterious, and sometimes even worse, as in Rabelais's image: " ... and there I saw some Words that were very cutting; bloody

Words, which the Pilot told us sometimes returned to the Place from which they proceeded—but it was with their Throat cut; horrific words . . ."[102]

Philosophers have, in their periodic bouts of uncertainty, complained about the imprecision of language and "monstrous inexactitude in the use of words." Students of the meaning have called attention to the "possible treachery of words" which could "people the world with fictitious entities."[103] But what I am referring to here is a darker aspect than the mere general proposition that expressive discourse has pitfalls or that language is often the enemy of truth and the victim of logic. Words could do violence and in turn be violated. Words could betray, deceive, and seduce: could burn, kill, and destroy. Seventeenth-century English writers were familiar with "Bug Words," from the old Welsh association of *bugg* with specters and objects of terror, as in *bogey* and *bugbear*, as in *Timon's* "thou shalt not fright me with thye bugbeare words."[104] In Dryden, "Death is a bug-word"; and Hooker had already added a number of more general but equally demonized concepts when (in a manuscript note to his *Laws of Ecclesiastical Polity*, 1593) he warned that "there are certaine wordes, as Nature, Reason, Will, and such like, which wheresoever you find named, you suspect them presently as bugs wordes, because what they mean you do not indeed as you ought apprehend . . . " Nor was the realm of politics immune from the demon. "A Rebellion," wrote Roger North in his account of the Cromwellian era, "O no, that's a bug Word."[105]

Indeed, the most eloquent defenders of the principles of Cromwellian rebellion had repeatedly to face the charge, as one contemporary critic of John Milton's political pamphleteering put it, that "all your Politicks are derived from the Works of Declaimers." That the viewpoint of one's political opponent has gathered deceptive strength from the tricks of rhetoric and language is, of course, only a conventional strategem in the history of polemics.

> That it was all windy Foppery, from the Beginning to the End [the Rota critic of Milton went on], written to the Elevation of that Rabble, and meant to cheat the Ignorant. That you fight always with the Flat of your Hand like a Rhetorician, and never contract the Logical Fist. That you trade altogether in Universals, the Region of Deceits and Fallacy, but never come so near Particulars, as to let us know which, among divers things of the same Kind, you would be at.

But the suspicion had darker depths, as if indeed Milton was of the Devil's party ("that Party you call *We*" with its "fantastick Longing after imaginary Liberty"), and as if his ideology was a hellish sign of the Satanic spell which had been cast over the words of utopia and revolution.

> ... as all your Politics reach but the Outside and Circumstances of Things, and never touch at Realities, so you are very sollicitous about Words, as if they were charms, or had more in them than what they signify. For no Conjurer's Devil is more concerned in a Spell, than you are in a mere Word, but never regard the Things which it serves to express.
>
> ... all the Liberty you talk so much of, consists in nothing else but mere Words. For though you brag much of the People's managing their own Affairs, you allow them no more Share of that in your *Utopia*, as you have ordered it, than only to set up their throats to baul, instead of every three years, which they might have done before once in an Age.[106]

There were, after all, certain words which, as Locke had suspected, had "an evil sound . . . as though with some spectre." Still, quite apart from spectral mysteries, there were plainer and, doubtless, sounder reasons for this special species of linguistic trouble. Locke, the greatest theoretician of language in his day (and, in many ways, the forerunner of modern semantic analysis and even logical positivism), put the case in a paragraph of his philosophical masterpiece *An Essay Concerning Human Understanding* (1690), which summed up his thoughts on the use and abuse of words:

> ... there is no such way to gain admittance or give defence to strange and absurd doctrines as to guard them round about with legions of obscure, doubtful, and undefined words. Which yet make these retreats more like the dens of robbers or holes of foxes than the fortresses of fair warriors; which if it be hard to get them out of, it is not for the strength that is in them, but the briars and thorns and the obscurity of the thickets they are beset with. For untruth being unacceptable to the mind of man, there is no other defence left for absurdity but obscurity.[107]

There is, then, in every century a generation of men for whom things are no longer things and words no longer their names. This crisis belongs to what has been called "the symptomatology of language behavior," and the modern diagnosticians of "the devastating disease from which so much of the communicative activity of man suffers" argued the relevance of a distinction between word-dependence and freedom. Did adherence to special words "as though they had sovereign and talismanic virtue" necessarily betoken a crude and superstitious view of the relations of words to things?

> ... we have constantly to distinguish [Ogden and Richards write] between those who are unable to modify their vocabularies without

extensive disorganization of their references, and those who are free to vary their symbolism to suit the occasion. At all levels of intellectual performance there are persons to be found to whom any suggestion that they should change their symbols comes, and must come, as a suggestion that they should recant their beliefs. For such people to talk differently is to think differently, because their words are essential members of the contexts of their references. To those who are not so tied by their symbolism this inability to renounce for the moment favourite modes of expression usually appears as a peculiar localized stupidity.[108]

For some, I would go on to suggest, the linguistic disturbance is serious but corrigible; and, in the history of socialist revolutionaries from Proudhon to Sartre, we are continually met by the self-appointed protectors of the sacred vocabulary. "Everywhere," Proudhon complained, "comprehension of the Revolution has been extinguished by the very ones who were supposed to represent the Revolution." In a letter (1861) to a colleague Proudhon argued:

> We are the Revolution. It is annoying that this sacramental word should be misused, but it is for us to give it its true meaning. We are also democracy and socialism. We may at times laugh at both the names and the personnel, but what those words cover and what those people stand for belong to us also; we must be careful of them![109]

The impulse of semantic hygiene is even more drastic in Jean-Paul Sartre, who, less in existential anguish than in political optimism, holds that "if words are sick, it is up to us to cure them ... " Once one started to deplore the inadequacy of language to reality, one made oneself "an accomplice of the enemy"; the constructive task was to reestablish language in its dignity. Shining meanings had to be recovered: especially, for Sartre, the "key notions (*les notions-clés*)" in the nomenclature of political commitment, Socialism and Revolution.

> ... each party shoves words forward like Trojan horses, and we let them enter because they make the nineteenth-century meaning of the words shine before us. Once they are in place, they open up, and strange, astounding meanings spread out within us like armies; the fortress is taken before we are on guard.[110]

But was the fortress—strikingly enough, both Sartre and Locke speak in images of embattled positions (though each saw himself digging in on opposite sides)—truly defensible? Was it not an eternally lost cause to hope that from an old order so unredeemably evil anything could be salvaged, even a usable word? The young post-Sartre generation of revolutionary France disengaged itself from the linguistic sentimentalism which sustained itself on such reformist hopes of cure and recovery. As one young philosopher of the Sorbonne revolt of May 1968 argued, "no revolutionary movement can be really new so long as its aims are dreamt, programmed, in the vocabulary and grammar of the past. Old words carry an 'old future' in them. There will be no overthrow until language itself is made new, until speech as we now know it and use it ceases."[111] Locke was not fashionable enough in Paris for anyone to have recalled his old words, uttered centuries before (and then very new): "I am not so vain to think that anyone can pretend to attempt the perfect reforming of the languages of the world, no, not so much as of his own country, without rendering himself ridiculous."[112] Others, with larger vanities, would not hesitate to take the risk.

Thus, for some, a new rhetoric, grammar, and vocabulary were the radiant signs of a happy transformation. For others, the collapse of the traditional language was the collapse of the old world; and the dark power of a demonized discourse—with, in Robert South's phrase (1716), "the rabble-charming words which carry so much wild-fire wrapt up in them"—would appear to be irrevocably tragic. " . . . and all this tragic consuming flame generally kindled and blown up by the foul breath of some lying, tale-bearing wretch, throwing all into a combustion . . . "[113]

I have reverted to the semantic scene of several centuries ago for a special reason (and subsequent pages on Cromwell, Milton, and Halifax will be developing this theme). Among the first English generation of modern revolutionaries, there had emerged a new political vocabulary combined with the beginnings of a self-conscious use of activating phrases, an awareness of propaganda based on a feeling for mind-changing formulations. This vocabulary was, to be sure, never quite so conscious or so cunning as the counterrevolutionaries, enraged and embittered, were tempted to suspect. Yet, whether in victory or in defeat, there was revolution in the word. In that sermon of 1716 by the Reverend Robert South, one of the more impressive polemical talents of the post-Cromwell age, the text was Isaiah 5:20 ("Woe unto them that call evil good, and good evil"), and the point was to show "the first grand instance of the fatal influence of words and names falsely applied, in the late subversion of the church of England by the Calumnies of the fanatic party . . . " He knew how the people had been "worded out of their religion . . . by the worst and most plausible names applied to the very worst." He studied closely the language of the historic controversy ("popery," "true protestants," "reformation," "persecution," "moderation"), and could not help concluding that it was "the treacherous cant and misapplication of those words"—the "fanatics" were "no small artists at disguising things with names," thus: "to blow them up or burn them down"—that "put this poor church into such a flame as burnt it down to the ground ... " What he called "the spiritual artillery of the word" was brought to bear on other targets. For "the prime and most effectual engine to pull down any government is to alienate the minds of the subjects from it." In the "seditious coffee-house discourses," a new armory of "mouth granadoes" was prepared, a devious set of "words of art and malice" addressed to "the generality of mankind who are wholly governed by words and names." So did a villainous band of "moderation-mongers," in truth "restless demagogues and incendiaries," contrive to inflame minds and prepare a revolution:

> These four rattling words, I say, arbitrary power, evil counsellors, public spirits, liberty, property, and the rights of the subject, with several more of the like noise and nature ... are the great and powerful tools by which the faction hope to do their business upon the government once more ... what can be expected, if a company of bold, crafty, designing villains shall be incessantly buzzing into the rabble's ears, tyranny and arbitrary power ... ? I say, if the rout be still followed and plied by them with such mouth granadoes as these, can any thing be expected, but that those who look no further than words should take such incendiaries at their word, and thereupon kindle and flame out, and throw the whole frame of the government into tumult and confusion?

Two centuries later, another English writer, similarly preoccupied with "the meaning of meaning" and the tragic influence of language upon thought and action, related a little fable:

> And when Homo came to study the parts of speech, he wove himself a noose of Words. And he hearkened to himself, and bowed his head and made abstractions, hypostatizing and glorifying. Thus arose Church and State and Strife upon Earth; for oftentimes Homo caused Hominem to die for Abstractions hypostatized and glorified: and the children did after the manner of their fathers, for so had they been taught. And last of all Homo began also to eat his words.
> Now, after much time, there appeared Reason, which said, "Wherefore hast thou done this thing?"
> And Homo said, "Speech betrayed me."[114]

7. The Bow and the Lyre

One other decisive factor recurs. What always collapses is the illusion of revolutionary omnipotence. What was being abandoned yet again was the myth of definitive solutions. Did the disestablishment of the Church "solve the problem" for state secularism? The conflict persisted on a different level; the mutual give-and-take of deep institutional struggle went on. Did the abolition of serfdom and chattel slavery "eliminate the problem" of Russian peasants and American Negroes? Had there been no Emancipation Proclamation it would surely have been longed for as the only radical measure which could alone have given meaning and progressive purpose to the American Civil War. With it, we see that meanings are never complete, that historical purposes are never simply fulfilled. Human society cannot be artfully simulated by the theatrical device of arranging history in a drama of fundamental problems and final solutions. Nor can it be summed up, as much of modern social science pretends to do, in terms of situations of historic crises which are lucidly understood and historic results which can be correctly calculated.

All change is piecemeal. Even the most revolutionary acts are only a part of a longer historic process of gradualism. To liberate all the slaves at once by proclamation was, I am persuaded—both in nineteenth-century Russia and in America—radical, moral, and necessary; but the problem of freedom for poor men and black men was not thereby decisively resolved. An end was put to chattel bonds, and it was only the beginning of a long travail for peoples who were free in legal name only. Progress is often at its meliorative slowest when it appears to be most swift and final. Thus, reform is not an alternative to revolution; reconstruction can be both militant and minimal. Revolution is not an alternative to reform; even the most fundamental and violent of blows is part of a slow-moving pattern of social change and rearrangement. Great estates are broken up: peasants are given the land—where and when has this at long last solved what historians are pleased to call the agrarian problem? New nations break out, proudly and angrily, from imperial bondage—how substantially has this affected their poverty and essential helplessness? Industries are nationalized; the expropriators expropriated—when and where has this put an end to the crisis of political economy or human exploitation or class struggle? Whatever the merits of the changes involved—and in certain times and places they have indeed been both inevitable and sound, necessary and proper—their justification is in prideful error when it is set in the total and unconditional optimism of millennial hope and expectation. The fulfillment of human purposes is a complex tension between moral ideals and social difficulties. There has been no authentic sign yet of definitive solutions.

Revolution is not an alternative to reform—the heretical thought occurred to Lenin when, in 1921, he was hard pressed to justify "gradualist and cautiously devious methods of operation" at a time when the official ideology proclaimed that "the revolution as a whole is victoriously marching forward." It was a theoretical question which was giving rise to dangerous "perplexities and doubts." He tried to hold fast to the dogma:

Marxism alone precisely and correctly defines the relation between reform and revolution. . . . In principle the thing remains as before.

But, he added (with that fine casuistry which characterized his dialectical mind), "a change in form takes place which Marx could not foresee . . . " He acknowledged that the new economic policies were retreats to reformism.

> Compared with the previous revolutionary approach this is a reformist approach. (Revolution is a transformation which breaks the foundations and roots of the old and does not remodel it cautiously, slowly, gradually, trying to break as little as possible.)
> The question arises: if after having tried revolutionary methods you found them a failure and adopted reformist methods, does that not prove that you are declaring the whole revolution to have been a mistake? Does it not prove that the revolution should not have started at all, that you should have started with and confined yourself to, reforms?

The questions were blunt and discomfiting; but the answer was, of course, *no*: any other conclusion would only be sophistical, fraudulent, infantile. But he would concede this much (and this is the great culminating passage in which revolution appears to be following utopia into the limbo of untenable absolute commitments):

> The greatest danger, perhaps the only danger, that confronts a genuine revolutionary is exaggeration of revolutionariness, forgetting the limits and conditions in which revolutionary methods are appropriate and can be successfully employed. Genuine revolutionaries have most often broken their necks when they began to write "revolution" with a capital R, to elevate "revolution" to something almost divine, to lose their heads, to lose the ability in the coolest and most sober manner to reflect, weigh up and ascertain at what moment, under what circumstances and in which sphere of action it is necessary to act in a revolutionary manner, and when it is necessary to adopt reformist action.

The paper in which Lenin formulated this was entitled "The Importance of Gold . . . "[115] For now, he argued, it was necessary to save gold, sell it at the highest price, buy goods with it at the lowest price. But the old golden dream would not be repressed. Possibly, he went on, in "another decade or so" (that is, after the complete victory of socialism, "when we conquer on a world scale"), one could proceed to "use gold for the purpose of building public lavatories in the streets. . . . " King Utopus, who had decreed the use of precious metals for chamber pots (*Utopia*, Book 2), would have approved.

As for the paradox of radical change and piecemeal progress, it was touched upon by Nietzsche in aphorism 534 of *Die Morgenröte*:

The small doses.—If we wish a change to be as radical as possible, we have to apply the remedy in small doses, but unremittingly, for long periods. Can a great action be accomplished all at once? Let us therefore guard against precipitately and forcibly [*Hals über Kopf und unter Gewaltsamkeit*] exchanging the state of morals, with which we are familiar, for a new valuation—we even wish to continue to live in the former for many, many years to come—until probably, at some very remote period, we notice that the new valuation has become the predominant power within us, and that its small doses, with which in future we have to grow familiar, have imparted a new nature to us. We now begin even to understand this, that the last attempt of a great change of valuations, and that too with regard to political matters— the "great revolution"—was nothing more than a pathetic and bloody quackery, which, by means of sudden crises, knew how to fill credulous Europe with the hope of sudden recovery, and thereby has made all political invalids impatient and dangerous up to these very days.[116]

The whole idea of the entanglement of tradition with change is—in the wearisome refrain that no historian of ideas can avoid—very much older. For Aristotle had already put it this way:

And this chiefly happens when there has been any alteration in the government; for the people do not easily change, but love their ancient customs; and it is by small degrees only that one thing gains place from another; so that the ancient laws remain in force, while the power is with those who bring about a revolution in the state.[117]

If the record of the past is a graveyard of errors and illusion, is there a new intellectual spirit conceivable, beyond the pitfalls of ideology and utopia, dogma and revolution? And with what longing and purposeful sense of a true cause could this new spirit be associated? This is my very last consideration in this chapter. If in both East and West there is arising a new note of resolution among the intellectuals, what would they be likely to commit themselves to? Would they simply resolve to be "more intelligent," that is to say, to be more penetrating, incisive, coherent? Or would they feel that it is "more faith" that is needed and strongly resolve to be more civic, more enthusiastic, less cynical, more idealistic than ever before? We are, yet again, in the old spiral of Reason and Passion.

I suspect that it would only be a few elements in the world's intelligentsia who would resolve to commit themselves to a bit of both, in the spirit of Merleau-Ponty's maxim:[118] "The philosopher is marked by the distinguishing trait that he possesses *inseparably* the taste for evidence and the feeling for ambiguity." For there are today, and perhaps have always been, divided camps in what Hardy called "the meditative world." There are the men of mind and spirit who are involved in the life of reason; they want to be witnesses to the truth, however difficult and unpalatable; they are ceaselessly cerebral, and not infrequently at the expense of heart and warmth. And then there are the crusading men, armed with sharp pens and eloquent tongues, who dedicate themselves to grand and angry causes and struggle passionately for new and more hopeful societies. It would almost seem to be a natural division of labor, according to the basic temperaments of men—a division between head and heart, between (on the one hand) the reasonable and the cautious and the skeptical instincts and (on the other) the militant and impassioned and revolutionary. Are they, in point of fact, mutually exclusive or irreconcilable? "The Soul of Man," Harrington wrote in his *Oceana* (1656), following ancient maxims, "is the Mistris of two potent rivals, the one Reason, the other Passion, that are in continuall suit; and according as she gives up her will to these or either of them, is the felicity or misery which man partakes in this mortall life."[119]

It was a tradition that was often challenged over the centuries, notably by Hume who tried to argue (*Enquiry concerning Human Understanding*, II, 33): "In order to show the fallacy of all this philosophy, I shall endeavour to prove first, that reason alone can never be a motive to any action of the will; and secondly, that it can never oppose passion in the direction of the will." In our own time it was, I believe, Thomas Mann who was the author of the formulation: "Think as men of action, act as men of thought!" But, then, neither he, nor practically anybody else of his generation, actually lived up to the fullness of that contemporary maxim. The men of action, with very few exceptions, let themselves be guided by jejune ideas, ignorant prejudices, echoes of empty slogans. The men of thought were either too powerless (despite all those articles and all those books!) or too disinclined (see those scientists so busy in their laboratories) to participate in the reshaping of a world for too long trapped in a pattern of war and poverty and injustice. Still, I am reluctant to believe that we must all either be Hamlets or Harry Hotspurs—either "sicklied o'er with the pale cast of thought" or doing "the easy leap to pluck bright honour from the pale-faced moon ... " Thought need neither be pale nor sickly, and bright honor can be plucked without the deception of easy leaps.

But what would this mean in the context of the world as we know it today? Would it not imply a wholesale—dare we still say fundamental or revolutionary?—reorientation among the intellectuals? I would not be so foolish as to call for that, nor so visionary as to imagine its coming. What is required is—in spite of Halifax's "third opinion," de Staël's "third force"—much more modest. Let me offer a few examples, in the sense of Francis Bacon's aphorism in the *Novum organum*:

> It is the peculiar and perpetual error of human intellect to be more
> moved and excited by affirmatives than negatives; whereas it ought
> properly to hold itself indifferently disposed to both alike.[120]

Is it so difficult for a Western intellectual to recognize both the virtues
and vices of the European-American pattern of society in which he lives,
to think through its problems and processes and thus reach positions
from which he can both defend and criticize, preserve and create anew?
He need not be wedded to any narrow national shibboleths or vested
interests; he can defend prosperity and criticize its materialism; he can
stand up for liberty and still desperately want its extension to the oppressed and enslaved. He can believe in the achievements of what is
called Atlantic civilization, and know that no man is an island unto
himself and no culture an ocean to itself—there are always before us the
Indian Ocean and the Yellow Sea as symbols of a larger engagement.
Alas, this is too rarely the case. Western intellectuals are often either
defensists or defeatists. The one sees only virtues to be proud of; the
other detects only vices to be ashamed of. The one tends to be too
complacent, the other too alienated. Thus, the camps tend to remain
divided, and the intellectuals as a whole cut themselves off from the
proper exercise of mental and moral influence in their own societies and
in the world. One is almost moved to wish that Santayana's words,
describing the intellectual temper of another age, were still apt for our
own:

> Its wisdom consists in a certain contrite openness of mind; it floun-
> ders, but at least in floundering it has gained a sense of possible
> depths in all directions. Under these circumstances, some triviality
> and great confusion in its positive achievements are not unpromising
> things, nor even unamiable. These are the *Wanderjahre* of faith.[121]

Still, there are new voices, and signs of other times. The German
novelist Günter Grass has been the spokesman for a "new stand," based
on an indictment of a whole generation of his fellow writers and scholars
"to whom reality is repulsive and only utopias are sweet."[122]

> So they hammer out their reckless phrases and in their sheltered re-
> serves, according to demand, sing of intellectual freedom, the inde-
> pendence of the intellectuals, and their difficulties in writing the truth.
> Godlike, rope-walking, and dancing above the exhaust fumes of our
> society, they set out their seminar Marxism like fleecy clouds, worry
> about Indo-China and Persia, that is, about remote miseries which,
> thanks to their high vantage point, they can survey without an effort.
> Their pens would sooner bring off a long heroic epic hymning Fidel
> Castro and the sugarcane isle than a simple appeal in favor of Willy

Brandt that would take the wind out of the sails of liars in their own country. And who would expect this decorative cosmopolitan *élite* to get involved with our petit-bourgeois Social Democrats and their wearisome efforts for reform?

His final note is in Grass's characteristic trumpet tone of reason in rage:

> Oh, you narrow-chested radicals who find the pace of reforms too slow and too hesitant. You advocate revolutions that occurred and devoured themselves long ago, while the much-ridiculed reformists, if you were lucky enough to survive the revolutions on the Left and on the Right, continue undaunted to adapt their program to the changing times, making a small improvement here, hesitating there, but standing up for the right thing all the same, that is to say, moving on very slowly, restrained by compromises, under the name of Social Democracy.... They have my respect; their defeats are my defeats, and their failings I seek in my own self.

This would seem to suggest that the *Zeitgeist* may, here and there, be changing. Perhaps; but, for the rest, one is still reminded of Rebecca West's aphorism: "The trouble about man is two-fold. He cannot learn truths which are too complicated; he forgets truths which are too simple."

And what of the intellectuals of the Afro-Asian world? New nations have been created by the dozen; the ideals of "freedom" and "national independence" have been fought for, and a battle has been won. But will the intellectuals here, as elsewhere, in the coming years, recognize that the time for the old slogans is over? Some things have become very painfully clear: nationalism, however one defines it, will solve very few problems; the issue of larger areas of economic cooperation is on the agenda; statism, however well-meaning, is not likely to be the all-sufficient instrument for social progress; the issue of more subtle, more intelligent, more viable means of government and planning, far from the cant words of capitalism and communism, cannot for long be kept off the agenda. It is very tempting for men of action everywhere—and why not in Asia and Africa?—to want to live on in the simple and militant atmosphere of the great revolutionary struggles which plucked at "bright honor." "No one in our family," as Yevtushenko writes in his autobiography, "uttered the word 'Revolution' as if he were making a speech. It was uttered quietly, gently, a shade austerely. Revolution was the religion of our family ... "[123] The intellectual, however, must function irreligiously as "the gadfly of the state," where the state is old or new, underdeveloped or overdeveloped. I was impressed in my travels in both Africa and Asia—and this long before the ignominious collapse of what was called "Nkrumahism" and "Sukarnoism"—to meet so many thoughtful and public-spirited young minds devoting themselves to independent and courageous criticism: they knew the inadequacy of hoary sloganeering; they were beginning to rethink the problems of centralism and federalism, tribalism and modernism, civil liberties and authoritarianism, neutrality and internationalism, moderation and fanaticism. It was almost as if all of us together were catching up on the sad wisdom of Tocqueville, who more than a century ago had said, "A true but complicated idea has always less chance of succeeding than one which is false but simple."

Finally, what of the intelligentsia in that part of the world which coined the very phrase? There, in Russia (as we have seen) and in all the neighboring Communist countries behind the so-called Iron Curtain, very dramatic things have been happening. For the first time, tragic truths are being told: truths about crimes, brutalities, and innumerable human tragedies. The fictions of propaganda begin to crumble; the school of falsification is challenged. As one follows the revelations from Moscow, echoed clearly in Budapest and Warsaw and Prague, suppressed in Peking and Tirana, wrestled with excitedly in Paris, Lisbon, and Rome, one cannot help thinking of the remark by Alexander Herzen: "It is possible to lead astray an entire generation, to strike it blind, to drive it insane, to direct it towards a false goal. Napoleon proved this."[124] Stalin obviously proved it again in our own time. The intellectuals of the new generation are finding their way back, seeing again, directing themselves to saner, truer goals. This surely is the inner meaning of the turmoil.

And at the center of that inner meaning there is a dialectical tension of all the contraries and ambiguities we have been considering. "I have two minds," Bentham wrote in his last memorandum, "one of which is perpetually occupied in looking at and examining the other." For can the new dedication be to mere abstract truth without a loyal devotion to the ideal of truth-seeking and truth-telling? Should it be to mere abstract faith and a new enthusiasm without the witful clarity of honest intelligence? Of course it must be to *both*: just as we listen with both ears, speak with both lips, see with both eyes.

"What eye," John Donne once asked, "can fixe itselfe upon East and West at once?"[125] What eye indeed! What mind can embrace both passion and prudence? What philosophy can mediate between utopian longing and humane commitments? What heart can divide loyalties? Who, then, can keep his eye fixed at once on Burke and Mill, Milton and Locke, Voltaire and Tocqueville, Comenius and Bayle, Hegel and Herzen, Marx and More?

"People do not understand," Heraclitus observed, "how that which is at variance with itself agrees with itself. But as in the case of the bow and the lyre, there is a harmony in the bending back."[126]

Part 2

Images and Ideas

4

A hateful cure with hate to heal;
A bloody help with blood to save;
A foolish thing with fools to deal ...

—Sir Philip Sidney (1590)

Man's mind was suffocating in the close air of
a narrow prison house whence only dimly, and, as it
were, through chinks could he behold the far distant
stars.... Behold now, standing before you, the man who
has pierced the air and penetrated the sky, wended his
way amongst the stars and overpassed the margins of
the world.

—Giordano Bruno (1584)

Martyrs of Reason
and Passion

1. Sidney's "Arcadia" and the Circles of Imagination
The Contradictions of Arcadian Life—A Fiery Rebellion: Cunning
Rhetoric, Bloody Shirts—Fault-finding Young Men, "given to new-
fangleness of manners and apparel"—Portrait of a Tyrant—The Right
to Resist: Knox, Buchanan, Goodman

2. Overthrowing a Government in Arcadia
Portrait of an Insurgent—The Stages of Tumult and Violence—The
Difference between Dreamers and Utopians, Rebels and
Revolutionaries—Sir Philip Sidney and the Dutch Revolt against
Spain: "all on fire" (1574)—Fulke Greville on Sidney's Political Science

3. The Perils of Radical Flamboyance
Sidney's Cautious Revisions of a Manuscript—The "Sidney
Circle"—Dangers of "that zeale, wherein excesse only is the
meane"—Sidney's "Heroicall design" for America—Greville: "Why
are my revolutions strange ... "—Intellectual Commotion, and the
Missing Signal from God

4. The Widening Circle of Imagination
Extremities of "the People's Rage"—The "Skirmish betwixt Reason
and Passion"—Sidney's Warnings to Both Tyrants and Rebels

5. Bruno and the Margins of the World
Bruno in Oxford (1583)—"The Inanimate Messenger from Utopia"—

Cosmological Regeneration, or the Expulsion of the Beast—World Corruption and a General Reform—In the Tradition of Copernicus, Columbus, and More—"The Revolution of the Great Year of the World"

6. The Messianic Messenger
Towards Paradise—Firing the Human Will—Heroic Enthusiasts—A Brain of One's Own—Healing the World—The Consolation of the Future

7. The Great Purge in the Sky
Bruno's "Spaccio" (1584)—Jove and the Reform of Heaven—Voting on a Program of Radical Renovation—European Consequences: A New Intellectual Class?—Human Guidelines from the Jovian Revolution—Rejecting the "Idle Fantasies" of the "Postillions of Paradise"—Bruno and Ficino—Gods and Men, Heaven and Earth

8. The Revolution and the Circle
On "Upsetting a World that was Upside Down"—"There Are No Ends, Boundaries, Limits or Walls"—Doubts and Hesitations—The Dilemma of Finite Means, Infinite Ends—"A Dignified and Heroic Death": Bruno's Defiance of the Inquisition (1600)—Sky, Earth, and the Cosmological Revolution

1. Sidney's "Arcadia" and the Circles of Imagination

We must be wary of semantic anachronisms. Revolutionary movements that are not led by revolutionaries are a historic contradiction in terms, just as the yearning for political reform, social change, and basic civil liberties is something significantly less than the utopian longing for a good and possibly perfect society this side of paradise. Few documents of the European sixteenth century suggest this more dramatically than Sir Philip Sidney's allegorical fable of *Arcadia*.[1]

For there is in this Anglo-Grecian romance a profundity of political realism in those scenes of social convulsion which are interspersed with his stories of true Elizabethan love. Kings become murderous tyrants;

princes join violent rebellions; men's minds, even in Arcadia, turn to restless thoughts of justice and freedom, reprisal and renovation. Perhaps Sidney was, at bottom, thinking of England's troubles; he himself died at the age of thirty-two as a martyr to a just cause on a foreign battlefield (Zutphen, 1586). Still, whether inspired by imaginative powers or by the century's power politics, Sidney's Arcadian land was, for all its "sweetness," racked with conflict and disaffection.

Indeed, for all its fabled romance, Arcadia was a social order even less perfect and complete than More's Utopia. In the case of More, it was, as I have suggested, the aesthetic effort of a hard-pressed political spirit which produced a singularly loose-knit conception of felicitous social arrangements. With Sidney, the dramatic open contradictoriness of Arcadian life may well have been part of his governing intellectual intention: for he was persuaded that only a combination of pictorial harmonies with moral realism could provide the effective form for achieving what has been called the unity of heroic action in a book and a life. By playing the poet, the philosopher, and the historian (who, by his very closeness to the particular truth of things, added the elements of day-to-day conflict to the visions of love), Sidney produced an imaginary world of "complex and vivid combat." Perfect pictures required a contrary dimension which only the incorporation of practical experience could lend.[2] He aspired to avoid mere "wordish description" in order to "strike, pearce, and possesse" the soul.[3] In any event, Arcadia had, despite (or possibly because of) its imperfections, golden allures which would have tempted a Dante and seduced a Raphael Hythlodaye:

> This country Arcadia among all the provinces of Greece, hath ever been had in singular reputation; partly for the sweetness of the air and other natural benefits, but principally for the well-tempered minds of the people who (finding that the shining title of glory, so much affected by other nations, doth indeed, help little to the happiness of life) are the only people which, as by their justice and providence give neither cause nor hope to their neighbours to annoy, so are they not stirred with false praise to trouble others' quiet, thinking it a small reward for the wasting of their own lives in ravening, that their posterity should long after say they had done so. Even the muses seem to approve their good determination by choosing this country for their chief repairing place, and by bestowing their perfections so largely here that the very shepherds have their fancies lifted to so high conceits that the learned of other nations are content both to borrow their names and imitate their cunning.

Or so it was, and should have remained, under the reign of good King Basilius,

a prince of sufficient skill to govern so quiet a country, where the good
minds of the former princes had set down good laws, and the well-
bringing up of the people doth serve as a most sure bond to hold
them ...

But already in Book 1 there is the intrusion of unquiet problems from
abroad. We have to do with both invaders and rebels, "whetting their
courage with revenge, and grounding their resolution with despair," an
ill-tempered lot full of the most surprising strategems. In their deviousness they decided to "dress themselves like the poorest sort of the
people in Arcadia, having no banners, but bloody shirts hanged upon
long staves, with some bad bag-pipes instead of drum and fife ... "
Equally resourceful was the dispatch of "a cunning fellow (so much the
cunninger as that he could mask it under rudeness) who with such a
kind of rhetoric as weeded out all flowers of rhetoric" inflamed the
oppressed with desires of liberty. The rebellious Helots, we are told,
were "glad that their contagion had spread itself into Arcadia," for "it
was the best way to set fire in all the parts of Greece ... "

Thereafter, Sidney's *Arcadia* offers us a spectacle of "tumult upon
tumult arising." It is an extraordinary (and much neglected) source book
on the uses and abuses of government and opposition on the eve of that
great transformation which is our main theme in this section. With an
Athenian moderateness, which is to say, remarkably free from
theological conceits and prophetic Christian passions, Sidney records
the illnesses of an afflicted body politic. There was "grievous taxation to
serve vain purposes"; and there were "laws made rather to find faults
than to prevent faults." Add to these elements an unbridled licentiousness and factious disunity among the ruling great, and one moves
rapidly and inexorably to the prerevolutionary situation, classically formulated in the following:

> The dangerous division of men's minds, the ruinous renting of all
> estates, had now brought Arcadia to feel the pangs of uttermost peril,
> such convulsions never coming, but that the life of that government
> draws near his necessary period.[4]

The period represented not only the alienation between the powers and
the people but, within that division, a special generational estrangement
(an eternal theme which cries out for its universal historian):

> ... old men long nusled in corruption, scorning them that would seek
> reformation, young men were fault-finding, but very faulty, and so
> given to new-fangleness both of manners, apparel, and each thing
> else, by the custom of self-guilty evil, glad to change, though oft for
> worse ...

The monstrousness of a totally evil régime, documented as it has been from Suetonius to Svetlana Stalin, or from Haman to Hitler, may seem to us today almost a banality of historical experience. In Sir Philip Sidney's text, the outline of a Phrygian totalitarianism appears to have an outrageous freshness. Here (in Book 2) is

> a prince of a melancholy constitution both of body and mind; wickedly sad, ever musing of horrible matters, suspecting or rather condemning all men of evil, because his mind had no eye to spy goodness: and therefore accusing Sycophants, of all men, did best sort to his nature . . .

The portrait deserves to be extracted in full:

> . . . fearful, and never secure, while the fear he had figured in his own mind had any possibility of event. A toad-like retiredness, and closeness of mind; nature teaching the odiousness of poison, and the danger of odiousness. Yet while youth lasted in him, the exercises of that age, and his humour, not yet fully discovered, made him something the more frequentable, and less dangerous. But after that years began to come on with some, though more seldom, shows of a bloody nature. . . . Then gave he himself indeed to the full current of his disposition, especially after the war . . . and then thinking himself contemned (knowing no countermine against contempt, but terror) began to let nothing pass which might bear the colour of a fault without sharp punishment: and when he wanted faults, excellency grew to a fault! and it was sufficient to make one guilty, that he had power to be guilty. And as there is no humour, to which impudent poverty cannot make itself serviceable, so were there enough of those of desperate ambition, who could build their houses upon other's ruins, which after should fall by like practices. So as a servitude came mainly upon that poor people, whose deeds were not only punished, but words corrected, and even thoughts by some mean or other pulled out of them; while suspicion bred the mind of cruelty, and the effects of cruelty stirred up a new cause of suspicion.[5]

After such evil, what tranquillity? The catastrophe has its natural sequence from "the stormy mind of the tyrant" to the "popular inundation."

We have to do here not with a revolution but with a rebellion, a mutiny, perhaps even a restoration which would return men and institutions to a form of old, moderate, constitutional good order. Of the "great tumult" wherein some cried treason and the tyrant fled ("O the cowardise of a guiltie conscience"), Sidney writes:

> . . . wherewith certain young men of the bravest minds, cried with a loud voice, Liberty, and encouraging the other citizens to follow them,

set upon the guard and soldiers as chief instruments of tyranny: and quickly aided by the princes, they had left none of them alive, nor any other in the city, who they thought had in any sort set his hand to the work of their servitude, and, god knows, by the blindness of rage, killing many guiltless persons, either for affinity to the tyrant, or enmity to the tyrant-killers. But some of the wiser, seeing that a popular license is indeed the many-headed tyranny, prevailed with the rest to make Musidorus their chief.

The choice of a new chief put an end to the civil war; and, as Sidney muses, "fortune, I think smiling at her work therein, that a scaffold of execution should grow to a scaffold of coronation." But more than that:

... but with such conditions, and cautions of the conditions, as might assure the people, with as much assurance as worldly matters bear, that not only that governor, or whom indeed they looked for good, but the nature of the government, should be no way apt to decline to tyranny.

If this was the happy end of a sound alteration, a reform with limits and control, a rebellion on behalf of peaceful order, what of the very real perils of popular license or the advent of a new tyranny? Here is the profound (and, I suspect, insoluble) problem in political theory which the eloquent heretics and dissenters of the sixteenth century posed most insistently: in the pages of John Knox's *First Blast of the Trumpet* and the *Bekenntnis* of Magdeburg which proclaimed a divine right of resistance; in George Buchanan's *De jure regni* and Christopher Goodman's work on *Superior Powers*, "wherein they may lawfully by God's word be disobeyed and resisted"; in Francois Hotman's *Franco-Gallia* and the *Vindiciae contra tyrannos*, in which rebellion becomes both a right and a duty.[6]

Just as apocalyptists puzzled whether each prophet who came was a true one, just so were radical reformers troubled with the question of the false rebel and the true insurgent cause. How to keep a clear-eyed view of both when, as Sidney recognizes in one place, "some glosses of probabilitie might hide indeede the foulenes of treason, and from true commonplaces fetch down most false applications"? We are led here to the problem of the cunning and ambitious agitator, and to what Hobbes was to call the "perpetual and restless desire of power after power, that ceaseth only in death."[7]

2. Overthrowing a Government in Arcadia

When Sidney thought of "the picture of the age in which we live," he saw it as "an age that resembles a bow too long bent; it must be unstrung or it will break ... "[8] His genius lay in this sense he had of the tension of a great transitional time. Few political sensibilities in the century were more attuned to the subtleties of rhetoric and persuasion than the author of those remarkable studies in agitation and propaganda, the portraits of Clinias and Amphialus in the second and third books of *Arcadia*. According to Sidney's first description of him,

> This Clinias in his youth had been a scholar so far as to learn rather words than manners, and of words rather plenty than order; and often had used to be an actor in tragedies, where he had learned, besides a slidingness of language, acquaintance with many passions, and to frame his face to bear the figure of them.

Obviously, no movement in Arcadia whch enlisted such services could remain within the script of a sound political reformation; it would necessarily be a theater of excess. The question which Sidney makes Clinias confront, after the disasters of bloody altercations, is "how this frenzy had entered into the people." And Clinias, first dipping his hand in the blood of his own wounds, outlines the strategy and tactics of an Arcadian rebellion which takes us almost to the stage of the age-breaking revolutionary dramas which were yet to come.

The scene of the preliminary time of tensions and troubles, the prologue to violence and tumult, opens the sequential plot:

1. *Confounding Means and Ends.* In a "stir and debate" ("begot with thunder"), there grew "that barbarous opinion" which confounded means and ends: "to think with vice to do honour, and with activity in beastliness to show abundance of love."

2. *The Grudge of Discontent.* In the mounting discontent, established values were ruined: "Public affairs were mingled with private grudge: neither was any man thought of wit, that did not pretend some cause of mislike. Railing was counted the fruit of freedom."

3. *Fire in the Mind.* In the "proud talk" and "disdainful reproaches," a fiery sense of confidence emerged. It was a "never to be forgotten presumption" which issued from "the show of greatness in little minds ... till at length the very unbridled use of words having increased fire in their minds." And then they "began to say that your government was to be looked into; how the great treasures you had levied among them had been spent; why none but great men and gentlemen could be admitted into counsel, that the commons, forsooth, were too plainheaded to say their opinions; but yet their blood and sweat must maintain all."

4. *Our Country, Our Government.* In the new mood of sovereign demands, an extravagant claim was born. "Since the country was theirs, and the government an adherent to the country, why should they not consider of the one as well as inhabit the other?"

5. The Necessary Murder. Finally, there is the high climax of the invocation of the Glorious Name:

> To have said and heard so much was as dangerous as to have attempted: and to attempt they had the glorious name of liberty with them. Those words being spoken, like a furious storm, presently carried away their well inclined brains. What I, and some other of the honester sort could do was no more than if with a puff of breath, one should go about to make a sail go against a mighty wind, or, with one hand, stay the ruin of a mighty wall. So general grew this madness among them, there needed no drum, where each man cried, each spoke to other that spoke as fast to him, and the disagreeing sound of so many voices was the chief token of their unmeet agreement.... But as a drunken rage hath, besides his wickedness, that folly, that the more it seeks to hurt the less it considers how to be able to hurt: they never weighed how to arm themselves, but took up everything for a weapon that fury offered to their hands.... Thus armed, thus governed, forcing the unwilling, and heartening the willing, adding fury to fury, and increasing rage with running, they came headlong towards this lodge.

It was not the first, and certainly not the last, storming of a palace that would end with a purificatory violence what began as a loyal reform:

> ... so to their minds once passed the bounds of obedience, more and more wickedness opened itself, so that they, who first pretended to preserve you, then to reform you (I speak it in my conscience, and with a bleeding heart) now thought no safety for them, without murdering you ...[9]

If this was a revolution without revolutionaries, it was for the Arcadian insurgent—and, symbolically, for the new cadres who would bring to the cause of rebellion an art of fire and a science of storminess—a workshop for the refinement of certain political methods.

Firstly, the need for a broad and coherent front of popular forces. As Sidney tells us in Book 3 of *Arcadia*, Amphialus (evidently not uninfluenced by Clinias) would begin by dispatching

> private letters to all those principal lords and gentlemen of the country whom he thought either alliance, or friendship to himself might draw, with special motion from the general consideration of duty: not omitting all such, whom either youthful age, or youthlike minds did fill with unlimited desires: besides such whom any discontentment made hungry of change, or an overspended want, made want a civil war: to each ... conforming himself after their humours. To his friend, friendliness; to the ambitious, great expectations; to the displeased,

revenge; to the greedy, spoil; wrapping their hopes with such cunning that they rather seemed given over unto them as partakers, than promises sprung of necessity ...

Secondly, the importance of a larger sense of purpose and a firmer view of the relationship between means and ends.

For beginning in how much the duty which is owed to the country, goes beyond all other duties, since in itself it contains them all; and that for the respect thereof, not only all tender respects of kindred, or whatsoever other friendships, are to be laid aside, but that even long-held opinions (rather builded upon a secret of government than any ground of truth) are to be forsaken; he fell by degrees to show that since the end whereto anything is directed is ever to be of more noble reckoning, than the thing thereto directed, that therefore the weal-public was more to be regarded than any person or magistrate that thereunto was ordained.

Thirdly, the indispensability of a manifesto.

But because he knew how violently rumours do blow the sails of popular judgments, and how few there be that can discern between truth and truth likeness, between shows and substance, he caused a justification of this his action to be written, whereof were sowed abroad many copies.... They were to consider that new necessities required new remedies .... desiring all that either tendered the dangerous case of their country, or in their hearts loved justice, to defend him in this just action.... To this effect, amplified with arguments and examples, and painted with rhetorical colours, did he sow abroad many discources ...

Finally, the need to develop new techniques of manipulation and control.

But wherein he sharpened his wits to the piercingest point, was touching his men (knowing them to be the weapon of weapons, and master-spring as it were, which makes all the rest to stir: and that therefore in the art of man stood the quintessence and ruling skill of all prosperous government, either peaceable or military) ... [10]

I should like in a final illustration from *Arcadia* to take a summary look at the classical situation of crisis, with its traditional imbalance of social forces, which Sidney offers us in Book 4. It is a vivid glimpse of a historical disarray—"for alreadye was all the whole multitude fallne into confused and daungerous devisions"—which the modern movements of utopia and revolution, by the sheer force of ideas and organization, would so radically transform.

There was a notable example, how great dissipations monarchical
government is subject unto. For now their prince and guide had left
them, they had not experience to rule, and had not whom to obey.
Public matters had ever been privately governed, so that they had no
lively taste what was good for themselves. But everything was either
vehemently desireful, or extremely terrible. Neighbours' invasions,
civil dissention, cruelty of the coming prince, and whatsoever in
common sense carries a dreadful show, was in all men's heads, but in
few how to prevent: hearkening on every rumour, suspecting everything, condemning them whom before they had honoured, making
strange and impossible tales of the king's death, while they thought
themselves in danger, wishing nothing but safety; as soon as persuasion of safety took them, desiring farther benefits, as amendment of
fore-passed faults, which faults notwithstanding none could tell either
the grounds of, all agreeing in the universal names of liking or misliking, but of what in especial points, infinitely disagreeing. Altogether
like a falling steeple, the parts whereof, as windows, stones, and
pinacles were well, but the whole mass ruinous. And this was the
general cause of all, wherein notwithstanding was an extreme medly
of diversified thoughts, the great men looking to make themselves
strong by factions, the gentlemen some bending to them, some standing upon themselves, some desirous to overthrow those few which
they thought were over them; the soldiers desirous of trouble, as the
nurse of spoil, and not much unlike to them though in another way,
were all the needy sort, the rich fearful, the wise careful. This composition of conceits brought forth a dangerous tumult, which yet would
have been more dangerous, but that it had so many parts that nobody
well knew against whom chiefly to oppose themselves. For some
there were that cried to have the state altered, and governed no more
by a prince; marry, in the alteration, many would have the Lacedemo-
nian government of a few chosen senators, others the Athenian,
where the people's voice held the chief authority. But these were
rather the discoursing sort of men, than the active, being a matter
more in imagination than practice.[11]

The utopians were still, at best, "discoursing sort of men," dreamers
perhaps with solutions in the imagination, but clearly not practical or
practicing revolutionaries. And the revolutionaries (or, rather, the disorganized band of anti-tyrannical rebels), still motivated by the conventional passions of revenge and despair or by the classic ideals of liberty
and justice, were not utopians.

Many of these passages, I should note, have been ceaselessly
reexamined by philologists for contemporary allusion and political allegory; and from time to time, rummaging in a few tantalizingly ambivalent places, they seem to be able to detect those "pregnant Images of

life" which Sidney's friend and biographer (Fulke Greville) credited him with, traces of Kings and Queens and crumbling empires, or the shadows of Elizabeth and Mary, or Philip and Henri.[12] One would be prepared to accept some or even all of this, if it weren't for the pedantic implication that an idea or an image in itself was somehow less real and important than a possible reference to a passing reality.

In Sidney's own political career, of course, the historical details are unmistakable, and here we can indeed detect certain identities at work in both the Arcadian and Elizabethan temperament. There are places in allegorical achievement where the parallel lines must meet. Thus, at the time of the Dutch revolt against Spain, we find Sir Philip Sidney (who, like Ben Jonson, had gone abroad to bear arms for "the cause") writing to his Huguenot friend Languet:

> With respect to the Netherlands, truly I cannot see how it could have happened better: for though that beautiful country is all on fire, you must remember that the Spaniards cannot be driven from it without all this conflagration ... [5 April 1574]

Sidney himself, then, was not unlike one of his own Arcadians for whom "the glorious name of Liberty" served to "increase fire in their minds."

But, as so often in the history of political commitment, the burning temperament likes to wear the aspect of social studiousness. In his tribute to the heroic life and noble death of his friend, Fulke Greville almost conjures up a portrait of Sir Philip as political scientist:

> Now though I am not of their faith, who affirme wise men can governe the Starres; yet do I believe no Star-gazers can so well prognosticate the good, or ill of all Governments, as the providence of men trained up in publique affaires may doe. Whereby they differ from Prophets only in this; that Prophets by inspiration, and these by consequence, judge of things to come.
>
> Amongst which kind of Prophets, give me leave to reckon this Gentleman; who first having, out of the credible Almanach of History, registred the growth, health, disease, and periods of Governments: that is to say, when Monarchies grow ready for change, by over-relaxing or contracting, when the states of few, or many continue, or forsake to be the same: and in the constant course of these vicissitudes, having foreseen the easie satietie of mankinde with Religion, and Government, their naturall discontentment with the present, and aptnesse to welcome alteration: And againe, in the descent of each particular forme to her owne centre ... [13]

Here, possibly, is the beginning of a great tradition in the history of just causes: the exercise of the passions would always seek the legitimacy of reason and objective analysis; the activist longs to be at one with the theoretician.

But between the prophecy and the fulfillment, on the path from discontentment to alteration, there are the incalculable pitfalls of public affairs. At a moment when the rumblings of court dissent had reached dangerous proportions, Villiers, who was a secretary to the prince of Orange, begged his friends to refrain from further opposition:

> The way to pacify kings is not to oppose them, or to announce by writings, signatures, or remarks that one does not approve their doings, it is necessary to be humble, or at least to hold one's tongue . . . .
> [28 November 1579]

For others in Sidney's circle, this was a matter not of fixed principle but merely of flexible tactics. Thus, in a letter to Sidney, Hubert Languet (who, after all, was held to be the author of that radical Protestant manifesto *Vindiciae contra tyrannos*, and thus no mean authority on such matters) warned him of the dangers of his uncompromising tactics and the perils of his radical flamboyance.

> I admire your courage in freely admonishing the Queen and your countrymen of that which is to the state's advantage. But you must take care not to go so far that the unpopularity of your conduct be more than you can bear. Old men generally make an unfair estimate of the character of the young, because they think it a disgrace to be outdone by them in counsel. Reflect that you may possibly be deserted by most of those who now think with you. For I do not doubt there will be many who will run to the safe side of the vessel, when they find you are unsuccessful in resisting the Queen's will, or that she is seriously offended at your opposition.

His final admonition could not be more direct or sobering: "I advise you to give way to necessity, and reserve yourself for better times; for time itself will bring you occasions and means."

3. The Perils of Radical Flamboyance

The warnings may well have been needed. Sir Philip Sidney—grandson of the Duke of Northumberland, who perished at the block in 1553; nephew of Lord Guildford Dudley and Lady Jane Grey, executed the next year; and godson of King Philip of Spain—had gone as far as a court radical could go in his admonitions to the Queen against a proposed marriage to Alencon, the Duke of Anjou. Sidney sensed a plot of an illiberal, immoderate spirit. The sinister strategy (and he was bold enough to spell it out in a letter to Elizabeth) was to lift up Monarchie above her ancient legall Circles, by banishing all free spirits, and faithfull Patriots, with a kinde of shadowed Ostracisme, till the *Ideas* of native freedom should be utterly forgotten ...

No more than his Arcadian rebel would Sidney "suffer the realme to runne to manifeste ruine." The confusion, as Greville's biography records, would be "almost as fatall as the confusion of tongues," and it could only "bring the English people to the povertie of the French Peasants," that is, "when he had thus metamorphosed our moderate form of Monarchie into a precipitate absoluteness." Sidney would have none of it, even at the risk of falling from grace (as he promptly did). As far as he was concerned, it was nothing but an effort "to secure the old age of Tyranny from that which is never old: I mean, danger of popular inundations ... "[14]

To a number of literary as well as political necessities he certainly did give way, as his friend Hubert Languet had cautioned. In the original version of his *Arcadia,* Sidney revised those passages which might have exhibited in all too obvious allusiveness such dangerous thoughts. The final *Arcadia* manuscript indicated that the source of the discontent was not abroad but at home, and by a peculiar break in the narrative managed to leave unanswered the original question, "What raging motion was the beginning of this Tumulte?"

But "time itself," which in Languet's hope was to bring him other "occasions and means," brought him only to an early death (in 1586) from mustket-ball wounds on a Dutch battlefield. Biographers, critics, and scholars have since been obsessed with the puzzle of his true political views, and indeed whether his temperament, extraordinary in the agitated intellectual climate of his age, would have moved him "to the right" (there are some who contend that Sidney came to accept orthodox Tudor doctrine on the evils of civil insurrection), or, perhaps in a renewed outburst of the radical courage so much admired by his European contemporaries, "to the left."

Certainly, if the friends, colleagues, and advisers of the famous "Sidney Circle" played any shaping role on his mind and spirit, it would have been in the direction of an ideal order in which Arcadian virtues mixed with "Ideas of native freedom." There was Christopher Goodman, loyally befriended by the Sidney family, who was a rebel, a heretic, and an exile; who had twice been forced to recant before a Queen's commission; and whose work on *How Superior Powers Ought to be Obeyed* (1558) actually spelled out the compelling circumstances of how they should not. There was also Goodman's close friend, the recalcitrant Scotsman George Buchanan, "known to Europe as a political revolu-

tionary," who in his *De jure regni* (echoes of which can be found in
Sidney's *Arcadia*) propounded the most militant political theses of the
day—popular sovereignty, limited monarchy, the rule of law,
tyrannicide—and was much admired by readers in the Sidney Circle.[15]

Within Sidney himself, there was, for all his courtliness—*"Je l'estime,"*
the Queen had said, *"le plus accompli gentilhomme de l'Europe"*—a surging
adventurousness which had sources (to borrow a phrase from Greville's
biography) in "that zeale, wherein excesse only is the meane." It is
nothing if not characteristic that in this golden age of Discovery, of
Utopia, and the Transatlantic Quest, Sidney should have devoted himself to a plan to accompany Sir Francis Drake on a voyage to the New
World with a "Heroicall design of invading and possessing *America."* As
Greville records, "this first propounded voyage to America" came only
to "ashes," but for a moment what a flaming spirit of enterprise and
imagination it revealed!

> Wherein to incite those that tarried at home to adventure, he pro-
> pounded the hope of a sure, and rich, return. To Martiall men he
> opened wide the door of sea and land, for fame and conquest. To the
> nobly ambitious the far stage of *America*, to win honour in. To the Re-
> ligious divines, besides a new Apostolicall calling of the last heathen
> to the Christian faith, a large field of reducing poor Christians, mis-led
> by the Idolatry of Rome, to their mother *Primitive* Church. To the
> ingenuously industrious, variety of natural richesses, for new mys-
> teries, and manufactures to work upon. To the Merchant, with a sim-
> ple people, a fertile, and unexhausted earth. To the fortune-bound,
> liberty. To the curious, a fruitfull womb of innovation.[16]

Here indeed was a manifesto in the true Arcadian spirit of great expectations, filling "all youthlike minds with unlimited desires," appealing to a
broad spectrum of popular forces, each "after their humours." More
than that, here was a heroical design on behalf of liberty and innovations; and Sidney might well have gone on from there, as kindred spirits
were soon to do.

For had not Dante foreshadowed the divine adventure, with "that
unconquerable ardor to master the world's experience," when Ulysses'
ship reached the straits of Gibraltar

> Where Hercules assigned his landmarks
> to hinder man from venturing farther . . .

But Ulysses enjoined his men to sail onward:

> "O brothers!" I said, "who through a hundred thousand dangers
> have reached the West, deny not, to this the brief vigil of your senses
> that remains, experience of the unpeopled world behind the Sun.

Consider your origin: ye were not formed to live like brutes, but to follow virtue and knowledge."*[17]

And had not Giordano Bruno, in whose works Sidney figures more prominently than any other Elizabethan writer, tried to turn the poet's ambitions from low amorous versification to more divine themes and more heroic enthusiasms? In point of fact, Bruno dedicated his *Eroici furori*, which was written and published in England, to Sir Philip Sidney. I trust the reader will not find too fanciful the suggestion that there is real evidence of these temperamental affinities in the following verses by Fulke Greville, who was not only Sidney's friend and biographer but also a London companion of Bruno's.

> Day, Night, Houres, Arts, All God, or Men create,
> The world doth charge me, that I restlesse change;
> Suffer no being in a constant state:
> Alas! Why are my revolutions strange
>   Unto these Natures, made to fall, or clime,
>   With that sweet Genius, ever-moving Time?
>
> What Wearinesse; what lothsome Desolations
> Would plague these life and death-begetting Creatures?
> Nay what absurdity in my Creations
> Were it, if Time-borne had Eternall Features;
>   This nether Orbe, which is Corruptions Sphere,
>   Not being able long one shape to beare.
>
> Could Pleasures live? Could Worth have reverence?
> Lawes, Arts, or Sects (meere probabilities)
> Keepe up their reputation in Mans sense,
> If Noveltie did not renew his eyes;
>   Or Time take mildly from him what he knew,
>   Making both me, and mine, to each still new.[18]

Here, again, is a transitional expression of "restlesse change," of "revolutions strange" and "newness" in time. Things on earth could not be "eternall." Old shapes in "Lawes, Arts, or Sects" would give way to "Noveltie."

I do not want to be thought guilty of confounding poetry with politics, nor the sentiments of a character in a play (here Time's speech in *Mustapha*) with those of the author. I am calling attention to contexts, not

---

*"O frati," dissi, "che per cento milia / perigli siete giunti all' occidente, / a questa tanto picciola vigilia / de' nostri sense ch' é del rimanente, / non vogliate negar l'esperienza, / di retro al sol, del mondo sanza gente. / Considerate la vostra semenza: / fatti non foste a viver come bruti, / ma per seguir virtute e conoscenza."

convictions. Presumably, Greville would have gone along, rather, with Eternity's reply to Time:

> What meanes this New-borne childe of Planets motion?
> This finite Elfe of Mans vaine acts, and errors?
> Whose changing wheeles in all thoughts stirre commotion?[19]

A case can be made out for Sidney's conservatism and, rather more easily, for Greville's authoritarian orthodoxy. There is some understanding of, but no sympathy for, the efforts "to make the new" in Greville's *A Treatise of Monarchy:*

> Whereby these strengths which did before concurre
> To build, invent, examine, and conclude,
> Now turne disease, bringe question, and demurr,
> Oppose, dissolve, prevaricate, delude;
>   And with opinions give the state unrest,
>   To make the new, still undermine the best.[20]

Yet, surely, there was little political point to resisting the new and holding fast even to the best when the wheels of change were in constant and inexorable movement. How could there be examining without opposing, inventing without dissolving, or old conclusions without new questions? The shadow of social tragedy was inescapable once one recognized the strange revolutionary circles of human fortunes; and it found overwhelming expression in the *Chorus Sacerdotum* which concludes Greville's play about Mustapha's historic failure.

> Oh wearisome condition of Humanity!
> Borne under one Law, to another bound:
> Vainely begot, and yet forbidden vanity,
> Created sicke, commanded to be sound:
> What meaneth Nature by these diverse Lawes?
> Passion and Reason, selfe-division cause:
>
> Is it the marke, or Majesty of Power
> To make offences that it may forgive?
> Nature herself, doth her own selfe defloure,
> To hate those errors she and her selfe doth give.
> For how should man thinke that he may not doe
> If Nature did not faile, and punish too?
>
> Tyrant to others, to her self unjust,
> Onely commands things difficult and hard.
> Forbids us all things, which it knows is lust;
> Makes easie paines, unpossible reward.
> If Nature did not take delight in blood,
> She would have made more easie waies to good.[21]

There was, then, no easy way to the good, and mortal imperfection had a tragic periodicity of its own.

> Againe, whoe marke tymes revolutions, finde
> The constant health of Crownes doth not remaine
> In pow'r of man, but in the powres divine,
> Whoe fixe, change, ruyne, or build upp againe
> According to the period, wayne, or state
> Of good or evills seldome changing fate.[22]

We have here, again, the escape from the finite futility of man's vanities to the eternal confidence of a divine stability. But if, when sovereign state power should be abused and redress does not lie with man, there still remained an obvious and dangerous loophole in the orthodox argument that only God disposes. For would not Providence, apart from the direct intervention of miracles or plagues, deign to use a human instrumentality? Would we not find angry and pious men pressing to redress society's ills when they were seized by the persuasion that they were fulfilling God's purposes?

There is both a deficiency in dialectic and a failure of the imagination in this traditional reading of man's fate. "Fortune, art thou not forced sometimes to scorn, / That seest ambition strive to change our state?" Greville asks,[23] "As though ... wishes could procure themselves a fate!" Wishes could and would.

"I smile to see," Greville concludes, "desire is never wise, / But wars with change, which is her paradise." What would soon come to mark time's revolutions were precisely: change, desire, paradise. For it would be not mere men—vain, erratic, prideful—who would come to take their turn on the revolutionary cycle, but saints: long suffering saints whose fiery souls sensed a divine signal to pull down and build up anew.

This was yet to be: and not for a century. Cromwell was born fifteen years after Sidney's death, and he became a youthful convert to Puritanism in the year of Greville's murder. Still, the spirit of the Sidney Circle's language and the "pregnant Images of life" caught therein document their relevant place in a larger movement of the European temperament. We are well on our way toward the Faustian future. "Planets motion" is made to rhyme with intellectual "commotion," and this jingle will go far.

4. The Widening Circle of Imagination

The original question, then, of Arcadian restlessness—the source of the raging motion which was the beginning of the tumult—remained unanswered. This was in part caution and in part confusion: and both may be taken to attest to the political sense and intellectual integrity of the youthful heroic figure whom some thought would be "the savior of society." Sidney's only reply in the revised version of *Arcadia* appears in a restatement of the dilemma of Arcadian man, who is moved to resist tyrannical evils but is plagued by the disorderly prospect of rebellion in permanence (or, "what destroying fires have grown of such sparkles"). He tries at once to explain and to defend the position which Philanax took in protecting Timautus ("self-conceited"), that hasty ambitious rebel leader who had overlooked, in the politics of insurrection, that "factions are no longer to be trusted than the factions may be persuaded it is for their own good." Would—should—Timautus, then, have a bloody end?

> For Philanax, who hated his evil but not his person, and knew that a just punishment might by the manner be unjustly done, remembering withal that, although herein the people's rage might have hit right enough, yet if it were nourished in this, no man knew to what extremities it might extend itself, with earnest dealing and employing the uttermost of his authority, he did protect the trembling Timautus.

Thus, Sidney's ultimate, considered commitment was clear enough: neither a utopian nor a revolutionary by temperament, he refused to accept the simple polarities of authority or resistance, ancient values or modern-minded change, restoration or reformation. In the so-called "skirmish betwixt Reason and Passion," Sidney has the "seven appassionate shepherds" confront the seven reasonable shepherds, who sing out, "Thou rebel vile, come, to thy master yield," and are, in turn, answered, "No, tyrant, no; mine, mine shall be the field." For Sidney, this constituted in no sense a final and irreconcilable contest, although his personal quest for a higher harmony or a civilized solution was far from fulfillment. It was convenient but elusively vague for the shepherds to cease fighting, to embrace, and to proclaim together "Then let us both to heav'nly rules give place, / Which Passions kill, and Reason do deface."[24] After all, implicit in both More's Utopia and Sidney's Arcadia was the suggestion that there were no longer any operative "heav'nly rules" which could give order and purpose to European societies. No one in the century could as yet imagine the emergence of a new and secular third force, but Sidney sensed the dangerous futility of the two existing forces, trapped in traditional aspirations and locked in ruinous combat. Perhaps his warnings to the tyrants and to the rebels lacked more than just a little, in their modest and sober mixture of passion and reason, of that total tone of later times.

> But yet O man, rage not beyond thy neede:
> Deem it no glorie to swell in tyrannie.
> Thou art of blood; joy not to see things bleede:
> Thou fearest death; thinke they are lothe to die.
> A plaint of guiltless hurt doth pierce the skie.

He was a man neither of blood nor of fire; and neither of the camps impressed him as reliable defenders of human ideals.

> A hateful cure with hate to heal;
> A bloody help with blood to save;
> A foolish thing with fools to deal ...

He had his earnest political doubts, as in the following outburst (in the dialogue between Euarchus and Philanax, who, as Sidney pointedly tells us, was "not of the moderne mindes"):

> ... what assurance can I have of the people's will? which having so many circles of imaginations can hardly be enclosed in one point? Who knows a people that knows not sudden opinion makes them hope, which hope, if it be not answered, they fall into hate, choosing and refusing, erecting and overthrowing, according as the present-ness of any fancy carries them.[25]

The present fancies of Sir Philip Sidney's time were giving way to new and deeper compulsions. Other historic necessities were coming which would be yet greater than his. The future lay with an assured people's will, as unquestionable as a sacred commandment. A widening circle of imagination would include not only great refusals but terminal choices. Beyond the limits of Sidney's Aristotelian coolness, uncomplicated by the agitations of Judeo-Christian prophecy and as yet untouched by the coherence of systematic ideological simplifications, there was a new world of political intensity. If it recaptured and renewed a fancy for apocalyptic, it was only because mankind's hopes and hates appeared to be calling for an overthrowing and erecting on behalf of a reformulated human cause of hitherto undreamed powers.

5. Bruno and the Margins of the World

There is in this whole historical prologue to our theme—from, that is, Dante's challenge to the Roman Pope to, say, Marx's challenge to the Muscovite Tsar—a strange, almost mysterious concatenation of constitu-tent elements, and we shall never, in all that follows, lose sight of them: earthly reform and heavenly transformations, divine virtues and human will, utopian wonders and revolutionary motion. Thus, Giordano

Bruno, in presenting the heliocentric view of Copernicanism to an Oxford audience in 1583, disturbed some of his listeners with his suggestion of a new solar magic which could open up the possibilities of utopian miracles. (One of his young Oxford disciples proceeded to write a work called *The Inanimate Messenger from Utopia*.)[26] Bruno's astonishing idea was of an overwhelming reform beginning in the heavens with the rearranging or cleansing of the celestial images. This would lead ultimately to "a general reform of mankind," in which "we thus purge our habitations ... purify ourselves and make ourselves beautiful ... "; for man, the great miracle, could at last begin to exert his heroic enthusiasms toward a "universal sympathy" and a natural loving communion. All this derives in part from an ancient and lingering tradition, as Miss Frances Yates has reminded us,[27] which had once enjoined men:

> Unless you make yourself equal to God, you cannot understand God.... Make yourself grow to a greatness beyond measure.... Believe that nothing is impossible for you, think yourself immortal and capable of understanding all, all arts, all sciences, the nature of every living being. Mount higher than the highest height; descend lower than the lowest depth ... embrace in your thought all things at once, times, places, substances, qualities, quantities....

In a work, *Spaccio de la bestia trionfante* (the Expulsion of the Triumphant Beast), which he dedicated in 1584 to Sir Philip Sidney, Bruno outlines the cosmological regeneration which is envisioned:

> Truth, Being, Goodness drive out Deformity, Falsehood, and
> Defect ... Wisdom [*Sophia*] replaces Ignorance and Foolish
> Faith ... Natural and Human Law rises in place of Crime ... Justice
> replaces Iniquity ... Faith, Love and Sincerity drive out
> Fraud ... Union, Civility, Concord are found instead of Sect, Faction
> and Party ... Sincerity and Truth drive out Fraud and
> Treason ... Rapine and Falsehood [give way to] Magnanimity and
> Public Spirit ...

The laws which emerge from this "politico-religious message announced in the heavens" will shape human society: protecting the poor and weak, controlling tyrants, encouraging the arts and learning and science for communal benefit. An old order was to be destroyed, with its "false courts, porcine convents, seditious sects, confused ranks, disordered orders, deformed reforms, impure purities, filthy purifications ... " We have no picture from Bruno of his Utopia or his Arcadia, but in his mind's eye he did catch a glimpse of that great good place where, as he put it to Sir Philip Sidney, studious contemplation is not madness; where honor does not consist in avaricious possession, splendor in acts of gluttony, reputation in the multitude of servants, dignity in the best attire, greatness in possessing the most, truth in miracles, prudence in malice, astuteness in betrayal, prudence in deception, knowing how to live in dissembling, strength in fury, law in force, justice in tyranny, judgment in violence . . .

In one of the reports to the Venetian inquisitors about Bruno (in 1592), he is reported as having said that "soon the world would see a general reform of itself, for it was impossible that such corruptions should go on . . . "

Bruno, then, thought of himself as the true prophet (and philosopher) of the "Copernican liberation."[28] He strikes a new alliance between the universe and man, following new openings "from dark night into joyous light"; he is like a mountain between earth and stars; he becomes "a flaming Blaze"; he will be "the boundary between things above and below." In the Latin verses with which he introduced his *De la causa, principio et uno* (1584), Bruno wrote:

O erring stars, behold I also begin the circular course, associated
    with you, if you opened the way.
Your movement may grant me that the double door of sleep be opened
    wide, when I rush up through emptiness.
What lies hidden long, unfavorably in thick veil, let me draw from
    dark night, into joyous light . . .

These lines were "To the Principles of the Universe." In those "To My Own Spirit" which followed, he added:

Rootedly rests the mountain, deeply grown into one with the earth;
    But its head rises to the stars.
You are kindred to both, my Spirit,
    to Zeus as well as to Hades; and yet separated from both.
To Mind, a kindred mind calls you, from the height of things, that
    you should be the boundary between things above and below.
Do not sink, dumbly into Aneron's flow, low and heavy with
    dust.
No! Rather upward to heaven. There, search for your home.
For if a God touches you, you become a flaming Blaze.*[29]

"If in our times Columbus receives honour," he asks, rhetorically, "what then shall be said of him who has found a way to mount up to the

---

*"Nam, tangente Deo, fervidus ignis eris."

sky?"[30] At the least, as he put it, that such a man (namely, himself) had "released the human spirit and set knowledge at liberty." These self-confident words—whether "scientific," as the nineteenth-century liberal thinkers believed, or "talismanic," as modern scholars tend to suspect—remain the vivifying symptom of a radically new movement of men's minds.

Man's mind was suffocating in the close air of a narrow prison house whence only dimly, and, as it were, through chinks could he behold the far distant stars. His wings were clipped, so that he might not soar upwards through the cloudy veil to see what really lies beyond it and liberate himself from the foolish imaginations of those who—issuing from the miry caverns of earth as though they were Mercuries and Apollos descending from heaven—have with many kinds of deceit imposed brutal follies and vices upon the world in the guise of virtues, of divinity and discipline, quenching the light which rendered the souls of our fathers in antique times divine and heroic whilst confirming and approving the pitch dark ignorance of fools and sophists. Therefore during all this long while oppressed human reason, bewailing from time to time in her ludic intervals her base condition and turning herself to that divine prophetic mind whose voice murmurs always in her inner ear, cried out in words like these:

> Mistresse, who shall for me to heav'n up fly,
> To bring again from thence my wandring wit ...   [Ariosto]

Behold now, standing before you, the man who has pierced the air and penetrated the sky, wended his way amongst the stars and overpassed the margins of the world, who has broken down those imaginary divisions between spheres.... By the light of sense and reason, with the key of most diligent enquiry, he has thrown wide those doors of truth which it is within our power to open and stripped the veils and coverings from the face of nature. He has given eyes to blind moles.[31]

In this air-piercing, sky-penetrating tradition of Copernicus, Columbus, and More, who, each in his own way, had overpassed the margins of the world, now Bruno—"quello ch'ha varcato l'aria, penetrato il cielo, discorso le stelle, trapassato gli margini del mondo"—came to welcome a planetary earth that moved so that

> it may renewe itself [and] be born again ... And I say that the cause of its motion, not only its motion as a whole but the movement of all its parts, is in order that it may pass through vicissitudes, so that all may find itself in all places and by this means undergo all forms and dispositions ...

A wheel was turning, a change was coming—it would be "the revolution of the great year of the world."[32]

The revolution of the great year of the world is that space of time in which, through the most diverse customs and effects, and by the most opposite and contrary means, it returns to the same again . . . .
Therefore now that we have been in the dregs of the sciences, which have brought forth the dregs of opinions, which are the cause of the dregs of customs and of works, we may certainly expect to return to the better condition [*de ritornare a meglior stati*] . . . . And as in these days there is no evil nor injury to which we are not subject, so there is no good nor honour which we may not promise ourselves.

There would be an emergence out of the dregs; after evil and injury would come the turn of a better world. What else was Bruno offering but a visionary map of change, a magical picture of an America in the sky, an imagist poem of motion and infinity, an animated philosophy of vicissitude, fantasy, adventure, and reform? In revolution there was great human promise:

Whence philosophers are in some ways painters and poets; poets are painters and philosophers; painters are philosophers and poets. Whence true, true painters, and true philosophers choose one another out and admire one another.

What, as Frances Yates asks, "could the Oxford doctors have made of this man? What can anyone make of him? The megalomania of the magician is combined with a poetic enthusiasm of appalling intensity. The lunatic, the lover, and the poet were never all of imagination so compact as in Giordano Bruno . . . " But wait: we will find in the fantasies of the utopian and revolutionary imagination all of this magic and megalomania, enthusiasm, and intensity; lunacy, love, and poetry; and a bit more.

6. The Messianic Messenger

The stations of Bruno's tumultuous career trailed clouds of dissent and debate. Youthful heresies forced the Nolan out of Naples and Rome; he refused to make terms with Calvinist dogmatism in Geneva, and then fled from "Gallic tumults" in Toulouse and Paris (1581); he became unwelcome in Wittenberg,[33] only to be expelled from the University of Marburg and excommunicated in Helmstedt. Evidently more influenced by Jewish (and, some say, Moorish) conceptions than by orthodox Christian thought, he evinces an almost Old Testament joy and release in his prophetic cosmic invocations. Indeed, as one scholar has written, "there is little doubt that Bruno thought of himself as a Messiah, an illusion not uncommon in the Renaissance . . . " It could also be (as he himself suggests) that he was an earthly symbol of heavenly reform, having within him, "a Sun, or perhaps some greater luminary." He longed for "the day when man would walk like a new Adam in a world of new creation." In any event, his combination of Copernican astrology and Mosaic magic was helping to introduce into the European mind what Campanella was once moved to condemn as "Hebrew restlessness" and Calvin to denounce as "foolish Jewish fantasies." Whether old or new, the principle at work had vast and uncontrollable ramifications. As Bruno wrote in his *De immenso:*

> The individual is never completed; and among eternally pursuing individual forms, seeking eternally nevertheless those to pursue, resteth never content.... Thus is the infinity of All ever bringing forth anew, and even as infinite space is around us, so is infinite potentiality, capacity, reception, malleability, matter.[34]

How much of this can be taken to be cosmological theory, and how much social philosophy? But then, as Bruno argued, "All is in All." Many of the enigmatic emphases in the Brunian theory of celestial revolution have been directly (sometimes "emblematically," sometimes "anagogically") correlated with the politics of the day: Bruno's shifting hopes for Catholic reform (before the assassination of the liberal and tolerant monarch Henry III); his passing support for Lutheran, anti-Roman Protestantism; his late vague hope in a Papal revival ...

If I venture to select only a certain number of special aphoristic and analogical themes from a limited number of Bruno's books, this is not to overlook how complex, heterogeneous, and obscure Bruno's work is. "The more excellent the meaning," he warned us, "the less obvious it is." After centuries of neglect as (in Bayle's phrase) "a damnable doctrine of atheism," his writings burst again on the European consciousness with important, recorded influences on Goethe, Kant, and Hegel, as well as Schelling and Coleridge: all of which is well known in intellectual history. But it is, I feel, with especial good reason that we are reminded of the nineteenth-century romantic revolutionaries, and the parallel between Bruno and Shelley has sometimes been drawn. Bruno, who came to England to find his true voice, and Shelley, who went to Italy to see with fresh eyes, would have understood each other: both are inspired spirits of "heroic longing" (*l'aspirazione dell' eroico desio*), dazzled by glimpses of a new, true destiny for mankind and the universe. But let me extract a few of the dominant themes.

1. *Toward Paradise.* "The world cannot go on like this," Bruno cries. But what would save it? Faith and works? reason? love?

> One subject only I regard,
> One face alone my mind does fill,

> One beauty keeps me fixed and still;
> One arrow pierced my heart, and one
> The fire with which alone I burn,
> And towards one paradise I turn.[35]

2. *Firing the Human Will.* The hero of these lines is the *capitano*, who calls his warriors to arms at the trumpet's sound. "This captain," Bruno explains in *Gli eroici furori* (published in London, 1585), "is the human will [*la voluntade umana*], which dwells in the depths of the soul with the small helm of reason to govern and guide the interior powers against the wave of natural impulses." As for love, Bruno also explains why it is symbolized by fire:

> For many reasons, but at present let this one suffice thee: that as love converts the thing loved into the lover, so amongst the elements fire is active and potent to convert all the others, simple and composite into itself.

It is a fiery process of conversion whose varying activity and mounting potency we will be closely following in all the subsequent centuries; but for now let it suffice to note that Bruno was here indeed crossing great margins to a *novo nel mondo e raro:*

> Sweet is my pain: to this world new and rare.
> Eyes! Ye are the bow and torches of my lord!
> Double the flames and arrows in my breast,
> For languishing is sweet and burning best.
> [Poi ch'il languir m' e dolce e l'ardor caro.][36]

3. *The Heroic Enthusiast.* We are beginning to have to do with a new European protagonist: ardent in his commitments, extreme in his contradictions. Bruno tries to clarify how "this enthusiastic hero ... is different"—"not as virtue from vice, but as a vice which exists in a subject more divine or divinely, from a vice which exists in a subject more savage or savagely; so that the difference is according to different subjects and modes, and not according to the form of vice." In another passage, "the condition of that heroic enthusiast" is described as follows. He can meaningfully say

> "My hopes are ice and my desires are glowing," because he is not in the temperance of mediocrity, but, in the excess of contradictions, his soul is discordant, he shivers in his frozen hopes and burns in his glowing desires; in his eagerness he is clamorous, and he is mute from fear; his heart burns in its affections for others, and for compassion of himself he sheds tears from his eyes; dying in the laughter of others, he is alive in his lamentations; and like him who no longer belongs to himself, he loves others and hates himself.

In these prophetic flights of poetic genius, Bruno was adumbrating a whole modern era of revolutionary personality: or, as he phrased it, "the species of enthusiasm born from the light of reason" (*un' altra specie di furore, parturita da qualche lume di raggione*); and it was never to escape its original tensions of love and hate, compassion and dejection, hope and fear, affirmation and dissent, intellectualism and sensuality, limitation and limitlessness.

> He is now most dejected through meditating on the high intelligence, and the perceived feebleness of power, and most elated by the aspiration of heroic longing, which passes far beyond his limits, and is most exalted by the intellectual appetite; which has not for its fashion or aim to add number to number, is most dejected by the violence done to him by the sensual opposite which drags him down towards hell. So that, finding himself thus ascending and descending, he feels within his soul the greatest dissension that is possible to be felt, and he remains in a state of confusion through this rebellion of the senses, which urge him thither where reason restrains, and vice verse.[37]

4. *A Brain of One's Own.* In the first dialogue of *De la causa*, there is a striking exchange between two of the interlocutors, which sets Bruno, I venture to suggest, almost midway between Dante and Marx in the developing course of utopian and revolutionary ideas. It begins with a dramatic hint about the perils of taking intellectual liberties. Armesso asks to speak freely, for

> I don't want these discussions of yours to be turned into comedies, tragedies, laments, dialogues, or whatever name you prefer, like those that a short time ago, having come out into the open, obliged you to stay hidden and secluded at home.

A man of intellect, then, has to show his true face. But wasn't Bruno really only brilliantly and resourcefully playing with masks?

> I won't speak as a holy prophet, or an absent-minded soothsayer, or an apocalyptic visionary, or an angelic ass of Balaam. I shall not discourse as if inspired by Bacchus, or as swollen with wind by the prostituted muses of Parnassus, or as a Sibyl impregnated by Apollo, or as an oracular Cassandra, or as one infused from top to toe with Apollonian enthusiasm, or as a seer illuminated by the oracle or the Delphic tripod, or as an interrogated Oedipus faced with the Sphinx's riddles, or as a Solomon before the enigmas of the queen of Sheba, or as a Calchan interpreter of the Olympic Senate, or as a possessed Merlin, or as someone up out of the cave of Trophonius.[38]

Who was he, then? And on behalf of what fate or force would he dare to raise his lone voice in the universe? "No, I'll speak in the everyday and vulgar tongue," so runs his historic answer, " ... like a man who has no other brain than his own" (*Ma parlaro per l'ordinario e per volgare ... come uomo, dico, che non hol altro cervello ch'il mio*). We are in a new era of one man, one mind. Yet we must not be misled by Bruno's dialectic and rhetorical ingenuity, or by the demagogic flourish which protesteth too much. For, clearly, Bruno (from time to time) cast himself at least a little in most of these roles: Solomon, Merlin, Oedipus, and Cassandra: prophet, diviner, apocalyptic visionary, seer, and enthusiast.

5. *Healing the World.* It was not only a discovery of one's own brain and its public intellectual rights; Bruno also found an indomitable personal calling, private in its individuality yet cosmopolitan in its mission. It amounted to a sacred oath to heal the world.

> ARMESSO: It is said that one must not be a reformer in a foreign country.
> FILOTEO: And I assert two things: first, that one must not kill a foreign doctor, because he intends to perform those cures which those of this same country do not perform; and second, I declare that, to a true philosopher, every land is his fatherland.
> ARMESSO: And what if they do not accept you, neither as a philosopher, nor as a doctor, nor as a compatriot?
> FILOTEO: I will be so nevertheless.
> ARMESSO: Who assures you of that?
> FILOTEO: The gods, who have placed me here; I, who find myself here; and those who have eyes and see me here.
> ARMESSO: Your witnesses are few and not well known.
> FILOTEO: Real doctors are few, and little known; almost all are really ill. And I repeat that they have no right, the ones to cause, and the others to permit, that such treatment be given to those who offer such honorable merchandise; whether they are strangers or not.
> ARMESSO: There are very few who recognize that merchandise.
> FILOTEO: The gems are no less precious on that account; and we must with all our power defend them and make them defend, liberate them, and free them, from being trampled under the feet of the hogs.[39]

6. *The Consolation of the Future.* "As regards ourselves in all ordinary conditions whatever," Bruno writes, "the present afflicts more than the past, nor can these two together console, but only the future, which is always in hope and expectation...." He explains:

> Things of the past afflict by means of thoughts, but not so much as things of the present which actually torment, while the future ever promises something better [*ma sempre per l'avenire ne promettano meglio*] ...

More than this: oppressed minds, raising themselves to the contemplation of another, better state, cannot but "compare the two, and so
through the future despise the present" (*e per il futuro spreggiar il
presente*) ... This is, to be sure, an (if not *the*) idea of progress; but it
limits the linear aspect of improvement within the turn of the wheel of
fortune. There may not be "complete and perfected action," but there is
still *progresso all' infinito.* "As in these days there is no evil nor injury to
which we are not subject, so there is no good nor honor that we may not
promise ourselves." The upward turn would be from slavery to liberty,
from evil to good, from low estate to high, out of obscurity and into
splendor. "For this," Bruno concludes, "is the natural order of things;
outside of which order, if another should be found which destroys or
corrects it, I should believe it and not dispute it, for I reason with none
other than a natural spirit."[40] Whatever the researches of modern scholars may have proved,[41] here is the voice not of ancient necromancy but
of modern reasoning. And, indeed, a new "order" would be found
which would correct the simple cycle or pendulum swing of historic
events. A revised idea of progress—with Condorcet's "sweet hopes"
replacing Bruno's anguished expectations—would soon be coming to
confirm the promise of the future in permanence.

7. The Great Purge in the Sky

It is not quite clear how much pressure from below (or was it a moral
inspiration from on high?) led Jove to make his drastic political changes
in the celestial order of the gods. "Thundering Jove," we know, had led
a "reckless existence" and was now beginning to "break away" from
lascivious vices. One thing is clear: the old order was untenable, and all
would now discuss—the occasion being the celebration of Jove's great
victory over the Giants—openly and critically (and self-critically), where
the criminal irresponsibilities lay and what must be done. Heaven was to
be reformed; and as in all divine events, the earth, necessarily, was
deeply involved.

More than that, a godlike temperament is not one to put up with an
inert stability. In the very opening sentences of the first dialogue in
Bruno's *Spaccio,* the emphasis is, with almost Joachimite pride, on transition:

> that which satisfies us is the transit from one state to the other. In no
> present being do we find pleasure, if the past has not become weari-
> some to us.

The general theory of what is about to happen to the gods (and through them to mankind) posits a "coincidence of contraries"; and this is explained as "mutation from one extreme to the other through its participants, and motion from one contrary to the other."

> the beginning, the middle, and the end, the birth, the growth, and the perfection of all that we see, come from contraries, through contraries, into contraries, to contraries. And where there is contrariety, there is action and reaction, there is motion, there is diversity, there is number, there is order, there are degrees, there is succession, there is vicissitude.[42]

If this was to serve as the philosophical rationale for a heavenly revolution, it moved quickly into political "action"; for Bruno offers us these lines from Ariosto's *Orlando furioso,* and they are ominous. Heads will roll.

> The more depressed is man
> And the lower he is on the wheel,
> The closer he is to ascending,
> As with it round he turns.
> A man who but yesterday
> To the world gave laws,
> Now upon the block
> Has placed his head.

The danger to Jove's position remains, however, vague. It could be that he is growing "old," but then he may well be "maturing." If there should be a question of a "hereditary succession," would it or would it not be "like the preceding great mundane Revolution" (*grande mondana revoluzione*)? Hadn't Seneca told us that "each of us goes with uncertainty / Toward his own destiny"?[43]

The tension is short-lived. Jove takes command of the "great mundane Revolution," if that is what it is, in no uncertain terms. Albeit with a sigh and a touch of sadness and gloom, he calls for a convention of the grand council of gods of the round table ("that is to say, of all those gods who are not false"). Grave resolutions were to be pondered, "but it is necessary that the execution be winged, swift, and ready." Jove's report outlined a crisis that was irrepressible.

> For today we are worse in heaven than if we were not there, worse than we would have been had we been driven out of it.... The great reputation of our majesty, providence, and justice has been destroyed. What is worse, we do not have the faculty and strength to remedy our evil, to redress our shames; because Justice, by which Fate governs the rulers of the world, has completely deprived us of that authority and power which we so badly employed, our ignominies being revealed and laid bare before the eyes of mortals, and made

manifest to them; and it causes heaven itself, with such clear evidence, as the stars are clear and evident, to render us testimony of our misdeeds. For there are clearly seen the fruits, the relics, the reports, the rumors, the writings, the histories of our adulteries, incests, fornications, wraths, disdains, rapines, and other iniquities and crimes; and to reward ourselves for our transgressions, we have committed more transgressions, elevating to heaven the triumphs of vice and the seats of wickedness, leaving virtues and Justice banished, buried, and neglected in Hell.

He offered them a way out which was shocking, disagreeable, and arduous: a painful purge, a radical reformation.

Come now, come now, oh gods! Let there be expelled from the heaven these ghosts, statues, figures, images, portraits, recitations, and histories of our avarice, lusts, thefts, disdains, spites, and shames. May there pass, may there pass this black and gloomy night of our errors; for the enticing dawn of the new day of Justice invites us . . . . We must cleanse and make ourselves beautiful; it will be necessary that not only we but also our rooms and our roofs be spotless and clean. We must purify ourselves internally and externally.

Nothing and no one was to be spared: palaces were to be abandoned, gods and goddesses were to be banished not only from heaven but also from earth. They all had an ultimatum of three days to present a program to "change our customs," to "change our state."[44] In this great town meeting of the sky, each of the gods was to have a vote and to enjoy complete freedom of discussion.

If you think you can do better, declare so; if anything ought to be abolish'd, tell me your Opinion; if any thing ought to be added, let me hear it: for every one has full liberty to give his Vote [perché ognuno ha plenaria libertá di proferire il suo voto].

Jovean decisions were to be ratified by the consent of the governed.

If thus, oh gods, we shall have purged our dwelling place, if thus we shall have renewed our heaven, new will be the constellations and influences, new the impressions, new the fortunes; for upon this higher world everything depends . . . . [45]

And indeed, on that historic fourth day, there was a spirit of newness and renewal. It is, in its way, almost the very first political festival of Revolution:

Let, then, the day of our victory continue to be festive; but let what used to be said about the victory of the giants, be said about the victory of the gods, because on this day we have conquered ourselves. Besides let there be instituted as a festival day the present day on which heaven is being purged; and may it be more solemn for us than could ever have been the emigration of the leprous people for the Egyptians, and for the Hebrews, the passage from the Babylonian captivity. Today, disease, plague and leprosy are exiled from heaven into the deserts; today, broken is that chain of crimes and smashed are the shackles of errors that were binding us to eternal punishment.

The gods were touched, and the gods approved; and not without a responsible awareness that they were providing a revolutionary model—or, as Pallas put it, "in order that down on earth men may contemplate how things must be ordered among themselves."

Jove expressed hope in a future which, with "club and fire," would at long last "bring back the so-longed-for peace to wretched and unhappy Europe." Momus offered his view that such a heroic change would inevitably require an alternative intellectual class, which would be partisan, practical, and progressive. It would have nothing to do with that

idle sect of pedants who, without doing good ... consider themselves and want to be considered religious men pleasing to the gods, and say that to do good is good, and to do ill is wicked. But they say it is not by the good that is done, or by the evil that is not done, that one becomes worthy and pleasing to the gods, but rather it is by hoping and believing, according to their catechism.

A new class of men will prove to be "necessary to the republic"—this would comprise scientific experts and scholarly moralists imbued with a new commitment to society. The great task, whether for men alone or with the help of terrestrial gods, or demoted celestial demigods, as in the case of Hercules who would confront the evil forces and

turn them away, reform, expel, persecute, imprison, subdue, despoil, scatter, break, tear, shatter, abase, submerge, burn, destroy, kill, and annihilate them ...

was a formidable one of social transformation; and it would indeed have been recognized by Thomas More as authentically utopian. For it was nothing less than the fulfillment of the noble ideal of "the communion of men, civilized behavior."

... in order that the potent be sustained by the impotent, the weak be not oppressed by the stronger; that tyrants be deposed, just rulers and realms be constituted and strengthened, republics be favored; that violence not tread upon reason, ignorance not despise knowledge; that the poor be aided by the rich; that virtues and studies, useful and necessary to the commonwealth, be promoted, advanced and maintained, and that those be exalted and remunerated who profited from them; and that the indolent, the avaricious, and the owners of property be scorned and held in contempt.[46]

Was this not, then, a fancy for paradise, one of those (in Fulke Greville's phrase) "easie waies to good"? No, was Sophia's reassurance: "Although many things are possible which are not just, nothing is just which cannot be possible." The course of world history might well be— rather, could and should very well be—the immanent realization of the judgment of justice. From Dante to Hegel, the spirit of Bruno's high confidence would have been most congenial.

But we have not yet done with Jove's purge of the heavenly order. It was not always easy to decide who was to be exiled, and where. How guilty must one have been to be considered irredeemable? and must crime always be confounded with error? Jove appeared to be ambivalent.

> We want only good divinities in heaven and in these seats. Let those divinities who are wicked be driven away from here, both those who are more evil than good and those who are indifferently good and evil, among whom I believe you belong, you who are good with good people and very bad with wicked.

Jove was here addressing Wealth; but when Momus suggested that Wealth have neither a place on high or below, a prudent solution of compromise was adopted, enabling Wealth to play a role only in association with Justice, Truth, and Wisdom (and never with Violence, Avarice, and Ignorance).

Nor was the problem of Minerva uncomplicated, for it had been obvious that "those gods who are graduates in the sciences, in eloquence and laws," were not in point of fact more judicious, more eloquent, or wiser than the others.[47] Bruno did not make Jove's lot an easy one.

> ... for all that which is governed by the fate of mutation passes through the urn, through its revolution, and through the hand of your excellency ...

He had to temper himself, and lean "neither right nor left." He, too, had to remember the tragic schisms caused by overambitious striving. Bruno prompts him with classical cues. Had not Tasso warned against the perils of a dream of the Golden Age? And was there not a profound lesson in Tansillo's lines?

> Lasciate l'ombre, ed abbracciate il vero.
> Non cangiate il presente col futuro.

> Leave shadows and embrace the truth.
> Do not exchange the present for the future....
> For what reason do you seek paradise at so great a distance,
> If in yourselves you find it? ...
> So believing that you elevate yourselves, you go to the bottom,

And removing yourselves from pleasures, you sentence yourselves to
    sorrows,
And with endless deceit
Striving toward heaven, you remain in hell.[48]

Bruno does not hesitate to give the argument its dialectical counterpoint;
and even Momus, for a moment, joins in the critique of certain utopian
promises when he makes disdainful reference to

> the algebraists, the squarers of circles, the drawers of figures, the
> methodizers, the reformers of dialectics, the instaurators of orthog-
> raphies, the contemplators of life and death, the true postillions of
> paradise [*veri postiglioni del paradiso*]the new *condottieri* of eternal life
> recently corrected and reprinted with a great many useful additions,
> the good nuncios who promise butter, bread, meat, and wine . . .

But there was a proper distinction that had to be made, as Sophia
promptly argued. Those were only the "postillions of paradise" who
were offering empty figments, who

> want to convert all of the nobility and perfection of human life into
> mere idle beliefs and fantasies . . . .

What were on the practical agenda of the day were neither the excesses of passion nor the misshapen forms of reason; and perhaps Bruno
was now presenting precisely those "heavenly rules" which his friend
Sir Philip Sidney had hoped would transcend the limitations of Arcadia.

> You will not recklessly dare, nor rashly fear; you will not pursue
> pleasures, nor turn your back on sufferings. You will not be delighted
> by false praise and will not be awed by vituperation. You will not be
> exalted by prosperous times, nor give up because of adversities. The
> gravity of affliction will not weigh you down, and the wind of frivolity
> will not uplift you. Wealth will not inflate you, and Poverty will not
> confuse you. You shall scorn excess and shall have little consciousness
> of want. You shall turn away from lowly matters and shall always be
> intent upon high undertakings.

Was Jove's revolution, then, to be made without Wrath, Indignation,
Fury? How could Bruno reconcile the romance of heroic frenzy with the
cool classicism of civilized behavior? Mars earnestly entreated in behalf
of Wrath, surely a most necessary virtue; but Jove judged otherwise—
"Never allow her to approach heaven, unless Zeal goes before her with
the lantern of Reason." Above all others, Wisdom was needed to deal
with "things built on a most fragile foundation," with "things which in
themselves grow old, fall, are devoured and digested by time . . . "
Pallas underscored the heavenly rule on how the true revolution was to
confront the barbaric forces:

... we must resist and repel them in order that they do not destroy us through violent means before we reform them.[49]

But the dilemma remained, as both More's Utopians and Sidney's Arcadians had come to know it. Could a revolution effectively reform without violent means? Did not the very principles of resistance and the varying strategies of repulsion call for the heroic excesses which always accompany transports of enthusiasm and noble outrage? For, as must be abundantly clear by now, it was not a matter of a revolution in the heavens alone. Bruno makes reference to "the commonwealth of the world," and surely it was a set of "earthly rules" which were needed to direct the terrestrial drama. Nobody knew better than Bruno how the great globe itself was part of a universal motion; and the making of a new heaven and a new earth necessarily participated in the Oneness which determined the great revolutionary cycle.

It was a singular intellectual achievement, this conception of a primordial celestial revolution, this vision of a divine reformation involving both gods and men; and it was an unprecedented foreboding of topsy-turvy alterations that were to seize Western societies. Bruno sensed it, but it was also very much part of a developing European sensitivity; and the profound suspicion of it was already there when Marsilio Ficino, that Renaissance weather vane of European climates of opinion, wrote his *De vita coelitus comparanda* (1489) with its ambiguous suggestion of obtaining life from the heavens or instituting one's life celestially. In his *Theologia Platonica*, Ficino raised the questions to which the answers were soon in coming:

> Since man has observed the order of the heavens, when they move, whither they proceed and with what measures, and what they produce, who could deny that man possesses as it were almost the same genius as the Author of the heavens? And who could deny that man could somehow also make the heavens, could he only obtain the instruments and the heavenly material, since even now he makes them, though of a different material, but still with a very similar order?[50]

If men were ever to be like the gods, would they not first have to do like the gods?

8. The Revolution and the Circle

"I speak of revolution," Bruno proclaims in the Third Dialogue of his *De l'infinito universo et mondi*. It is the essence of his reply to the lament of

Burchio, "Where then is that beautiful order, that lovely scale of nature ... ?" "You would like to know where is this order?" runs Fracastoro's answer: "In the realm of dreams, fantasies, chimeras, delusions. For everything endowed with natural motion revolveth in a circle around either his own or some other centre. I speak of revolution ... "[51] But Burchio continued to speak of that faith and certainty which nothing would persuade him to abandon: for, as he confessed, "I would prefer ignorance in the great company of the illustrious and the learned than knowledge with a few sophists ... "

> BURCHIO: In this way, you would put the world upside down.
> FRACASTORO: Wouldst thou consider him to do ill who would upset a world that was upside down?
> BURCHIO: Would you then render vain all efforts, study and labours ... wherein so many great commentators, paraphrasers, glossers, compilers, epitomizers, scholiasts, translators, questioners and logicians have puzzled their brains? Whereon profound doctors, subtle, golden, exalted, inexpugnable, irrefragable, angelic, seraphic, cherubic and divine, have established their foundation?
> FRACASTORO: Add the stone-breakers, the rock-splitters, and horn-footed high-kickers [i.e., the donkeys]. Add also the deep seers, know-alls, the Olympians, the firmamenticians, celestial empirics, loud thunderers.
> BURCHIO: Should we cast them all at your suggestion into a cesspool? The world will indeed be ruled well if the speculations of so many and such worthy philosophers are to be cast aside and despised.

To this came only the ironic concession that "It were not well that we should deprive the asses of their fodder ... " This was almost too much. Was he saying that Plato was *"uno ignorante"* and Aristotle *"un asino"* and that all their followers were *"insensati, stupidi, e fanatichi"*? No, he was not saying that, explaining (with something of that polemical weariness which has characterized the exchanges between dogmatists and revisionists through all the ages),

> I do not say these are foals and those asses, these little monkeys and those great baboons, as you would have me do. As I told you from the first, I regard them as earth's heroes. But I do not wish to believe them without cause, nor to accept those propositions whose antitheses (as you must have understood if you are not both blind and deaf) are so compellingly true.
> Who then shall be the judge?
> Every well-regulated mind and alert judgment. Every discreet person who is not obstinate when he recognizeth himself convinced and unable either to defend their arguments or to resist ours.

With a touch of ironic and contemptuous detachment, Bruno recorded his own indictment. He was "a sophist" and a "presumptuous ass"; "a disturber of good letters" and "a murderer of talent"; "a lover of novelty" (*amatador delle novetadi*); and, most fateful of all, "an enemy of truth, suspect of heresy" (*nemico de la verita / sospetto d'eresia*).[52]

This putting of the world "upside down" (*sotto sopra il mondo rinversato*) was the greatest overturning of the age. It was the first and only permanent revolution, and it forced men, slowly and painstakingly deprived of old fantasies and chimeras, to search for a new relationship to the heavens. In place of ancient lovely certainties an infinite emptiness had come. If the skies no longer announced the glory of God, could they conceivably be taken to announce some new glory of what Copernicus had outlined in *De revolutionibus* and Bruno had thought of as "the revolution of the great year of the world"? If man and God's own earth were no longer at the center, and now an almost incomprehensible mechanical process controlled whirling planets and stars, could there possibly be some new active relationship between this lonely world and the vast revolutionary drama in the sky? Could a revolutionary drama on earth supply any kind of answer? An other-worldly scenario had failed. Could a this-worldly scenario serve frustrated human purposes and cast new, transcendentally heroic roles for mankind?

Let me put the question still another way. If, "in the constant change of all things" (as Bruno argues in the Fifth Dialogue of *De l'infinito*), "there are no ends, boundaries, limits or walls which can defraud or deprive us of the infinite multitude of things"—what then could man not achieve? The prospects were extravagant and scintillating. We are entering an era of new auspiciousness, and a band of heroic enthusiasts will be leading the way.[53]

Among the motley ranks of his heroic enthusiasts, Bruno makes a basic, extraordinary distinction. He himself is not so blinded as to overlook the defects of "irrational impetuosity" and a tendency toward "savage madness." His true protagonists were only those who,

> being skilful in contemplation and possessing innately a clear intellectual spirit [*e per aver innato un spirito lucido e intellettuale*], have an internal stimulus and natural fervour, excited by the love of the divine, of justice, of truth, of glory, and by the fire of desire and the breath of intention, sharpen their senses, and in the sulphur of the cogitative faculty, these kindle the rational light [*il lume razionale*], with which they see more than ordinarily; and they come in the end to speak and act, not as vessels and instruments, but as chief artificers and experts [*e questi non vegnono, al fine, a parlar ed operar come vasi e instrumenti, ma come principali artefici ed efficienti*].

Among such heroes, Bruno says, is to be seen "the excellency of humanity itself" (*l'eccellenza della propria umanitade*) . . . "⁵⁴

We can make out here the outlines of the modern intelligentsia, whose singular faith and special function were to be more fully developed in pre-Revolutionary France by the *philosophes*. Yet even here, clearly enough, we have the formation of that intellectual temperament and political predisposition which was to provide the essential bases for whole hosts of utopians and revolutionaries. I have been paying detailed attention to Bruno, for in this spiritual evolution he appears to be the "missing link" between Dante and Condorcet: between a medieval militancy on behalf of the earthly paradise and a modern passion for progress and political renovation. We do not have to wait for the Age of Reason with Voltaire and Diderot, or, indeed, for Shelley's romantic generation, to find the grand Promethean commitment to a godlike liberation of mankind.

These enthusiasms [Bruno insists] are but love of the beautiful and good, by means of which we are able to make ourselves perfect, by transforming and assimilating ourselves to it. It is not a precipitation, under the laws of a tyrannous fate, into the noose of animal affections, but a rational impulse, which follows the intellectual apprehension of the beautiful and good, which know whom it wishes to obey and to please, so that, by its nobility and light, it kindles and invests itself with qualities and conditions through which it appears illustrious and worthy. He [the enthusiast] becomes a god by intellectual contract with the divine object [*Doviene un dio dal contatto intellettuale di quel nume oggetto*] . . . he fears nothing . . . It is not a fury of black bile which sends him drifting . . . but it is a glow kindled by the intellectual sun in the soul [*Ma é un calor acceso dal sole intelligenziale ne l'anima*].

The enthusiast, according to Bruno in an especially striking passage, "beholds the flames, the arrows, and the chains." By this is meant that "he is moved by a most sensible and only too evident passion, which forces him to love that fire more than any coolness; more that wound than any wholeness; more those fetters than any liberty . . . Since this fire is the ardent desire of divine things, this arrow is the impression of the ray of the beauty of supernal light, these snares are the species of truth which unite our mind to the primal verity, and the species of good which unite and join to the primal and highest good."

Bruno's high confidence in that unification was more apparent than real. The metaphysician would have his doubts; the naturalist clung to his certainty.

In Nature is one revolution and one circle, by means of which, for the perfection and help of others, superior things lower themselves to things inferior, and, by their own excellence and felicity, inferior things raise themselves to superior ones.*

This natural movement of the Revolution and the Circle is reinforced—if only poetically—by a great flight into imagery in the final metaphor of the Third Dialogue.

Now these transmutations and conversions are symbolized in the wheel of metamorphosis, where man sits on the upper part, a beast lies at the bottom, a half-man half-beast descends from the left, and a half-beast half-man ascends from the right. This transmutation is shown where Jove, according to the diversity of the affections and behaviour of those towards inferior things, invests himself with diverse figures, entering into the form of the beasts; and so also the other gods transmigrate into base and alien forms. And, on the contrary, through the knowledge of their own nobility, they re-take their divine form; and the passionate hero [il furioso eroica], raising himself through conceived kinds of divine beauty and goodness, with the wings of the intellect and rational will, rises to the divinity, leaving the form of the lower subject. And therefore he said, "I become from subject viler still, a god. From an inferior thing change me to a god."†

Here serious difficulties begin, for Bruno has moved so speedily that he has broken out of his revoluzione e circolo without having effectively prepared the way. How much scope for final change and progress could there be on a wheel? Was not that eternal turning and whirling the source of all heroic torment? He assured himself that "the kingdom of Heaven is in us" and that "divinity dwells within and through the reformed intellect and will." But he also sensed the dangers of man's "constituting for himself a finality where no finality is." Could it be that, perhaps, neither perfection nor infinity was a meaningful concept for "the human intellect of this lower world"? It was a brilliant and formidable contest between heroic enthusiasm and philosophical doubt.

Up, up, oh my flying thoughts! Up, oh my rebel heart! Let live the sense of things that are felt, and the understanding of things intelligible.‡

---

*Nella natura é una revoluzione e un circolo, per cui, per l'altrui perfezione e soccorso, le cose superiori s'inchnano all' inferiori, e per propria eccellenza e felicitade le cose inferiori s'inalzano alle superiori."

†"Da suggetto piú vil dovegno un Dio. Mi cangio in Dio da cosa inferiore."

‡"Su, su, o miei fugaci pensieri, o mio rubella cuore; viva il sense di cose sensibili e l' intelletto de cose intelligibili."

But precisely that rebellious flight upward was held in check by the truest understanding. "Whence comes that spur," Cicada asks, "which urges the soul ever beyond that which it possesses?" The ensuing argument sets out Bruno's difficulties in moving with such sovereign rapidity from the margin to the center, from the finite to the infinite, from the particular to the universal, from limitation to limitlessness.

> T: From the beautiful that is understood, and consequently limited, and therefore beautiful through participation, the intellect proceeds towards that which is really beautiful, which has no margin, nor any boundaries.
> C: This progression appears to me useless.
> T: Not so. For it is not natural nor suitable that the infinite be restricted, nor give itself definitely, for it would not then be infinite. To be infinite, it must be infinitely pursued with that form of pursuit which is not incited physically, but metaphysically, and is not from imperfect to perfect, but goes circulating through the grades of perfection to arrive at that infinite centre which is not form, and is not formed.
> C: I should like to know how, by circumambulating, one is to arrive at the centre.
> T: I cannot know that.
> C: Why do you say it?
> T: I can say it, and leave it to you to consider . . .

The reply should not be taken for mere coyness. It is characteristic of a long historical tradition of ultimate evasiveness which extends, as we have been arguing, from the ancient apocalyptists who kept silent about their secret prophecies to the modern revolutionaries who refuse to disclose the shape of promised things to come. Bruno could proceed to perform feats of celestial prestidigitation; but the magician never explains his tricks.

Nor was the explanation offered to a related question any more satisfactory. "How can our finite intellect follow after the infinite ideal?" Bruno was to resolve the matter at hand only with as many open questions as Marx and Engels were subsequently to leave when they puzzled over the contradictions between dialectical continuity and historical finality. What finite state can be permanent when the process is infinite? Or the converse, as in Bruno's case: How can an infinite end ever be consummated with finite means?

> T: Through the infinite potency it possesses.
> C: This would be useless, if ever it came into effect.
> T: It would be useless, if it had to do with a finite action, where infinite potency would be wanting, but not with infinite action where infinite potency is positive perfection.

C: If the human intellect is finite in nature and in act, how can it have an infinite potency?

T: Because it is eternal, and in this ever has delight, so that it enjoys happiness without end or measure; and because, as it is finite in itself, so it may be infinite in the object.

C: What difference is there between the infinity of the object and the infinity of the potentiality?

T: This is finitely infinite, and that infinitely infinite.*

Now you see it, now you don't. How perspicacious of Bruno to speak of the "shadow beyond the limits of fantastic thought"! He knew the grief of overboldness and could only offer as a final counsel: "Fear not the utmost ruin, then ... [Non temer, respond'io, l'alta ruina ...]," and he prepared himself for a reconciliation with failure.

T: We, in this state, cannot desire nor obtain greater perfection than that in which we are, when our intellect, by means of some noble and intelligible conception, unites itself either to the substance of things hoped for, as those say, or to the divine mind, as it is the fashion to say of the Platonists ...

C: But what perfection or satisfaction can man find in that knowledge which is not perfect?

T: It will never be perfect [Non sará mai perfetta] ... Let it suffice that in this and other states there be present to him the divine beauty so far as the horizon of his vision extends [Basta ... per quanto s'estende l' orizonte della vista sua].

C: But all men cannot arrive at that ...

T: Let it suffice that all "run well," and that each does his utmost, for the failing worthily in the high undertaking, in which it shows the dignity of its spirit, than in succeeding to perfection in lower and less noble things [Basta che tutti corrano ...].

C: Truly a dignified and heroic death is better than a mean, low triumph.

This was, indeed, to be Bruno's fate, una degna ed eroica morte. He ran well, defying his Inquisitors at the point of fire, and turning his head away from their proferred cross. He had appropriated more than a few lines of poetry when he included these lines from a sonnet by Luigi Tansillo in his Eroici furori.

> I warm, I kindle, burn and blaze for ever,
> So ardent my desire,
> The object so supreme for which I burn;
> Glowing and unencumbered I behold,

---

*"Questa e finitamente infinita, quello infinitamente infinito ... "

And make my lightnings flash unto the stars.
No moment can I count in all the year
To change the inexorable cross I bear.*[55]

This was, uncannily enough, not the only time when Bruno seemed to be preparing his own epitaph. There are also these lines from *De monade:*

Much have I struggled. I thought I would be able to conquer ...
... However there was in me
Whatever I was able to do, which no future century
Will deny to be mine, that which a victor could have for his own;
Not to have feared to die, not to have yielded to any equal
In firmness of nature, and to have preferred a courageous death to
A noncombatant life.[56]

All great historic movements have been capable of producing martyrs for the faith; but it was clearly difficult in the sixteenth century to conceive of such fanatical stalwartness outside the orthodox frame of conventional religious conviction. One of Kepler's correspondents thought Bruno must have been insane, for if he denied God where could such fortitude come from?

Yet a faith in a new and true cosmic drama, turning on the discovery of revolution in the sky, led, I suggest, to a certain strengthening of temperament, character, and opinion as exemplified in Bruno's long years of suffering and ultimate martyrdom at the hands of the Inquisition. "Perchance," he told his judges who condemned him to be burned alive in the Piazza dei Fiori, "you who pronounce my sentence are in greater fear than I who receive it."

Sky and earth, in whatever cosmological conception, always appear to be mutually reinforcing. Now, with Bruno, there was an altered relationship of force, attraction, and example, as the Nolan associated a revolutionary and infinite motion in the heavenly system with heroic and enthusiastic changes in the earthly social order. To be sure, they would still be changes "from above". But it would not merely be a reformation based on expediency, as in Campanella, or on impersonal high principle, as in More, or on cool compromise, as in Sidney; it would be a universal movement on behalf of those "below," the injured multitude. The awakening giant (as Bruno tells the tale in *De immenso*) smashes the limits of the firmament by breaking the "painted ceilings" (*laqueria picta*),[57] discovers universes beyond the universe, and shouts joyously: "I am unfettered, I am free ... "

*"Mi scald', accend', ard', avvamp in eterno / Ho si caldo il desio / Che facilmente a remirar m' accendo / Quell' alt' oggetto, per cui tant' ardendo / Fo sfavillar agli astri il vamp mio. / Non han momento gli anni / Che vegga varlar miei sordi affani.

5

... and there I saw some Words that were very
cutting; bloody Words, which the Pilot told us
sometimes returned to the Place from which they
proceeded—but it was with their Throat cut; horrific words ...

—Rabelais (1535)

Wherever primitive man put up a word he believed
he had made a discovery. How utterly mistaken he
really was! He had touched a problem, and while
supposing he had solved it, he had created an
obstacle to its solution. Now, with every new
knowledge we stumble over flint-like and petrified
words and, in so doing, break a leg sooner than
a word.

—Nietzsche (1881)

In its primitive uses, language functions as a link
in concerted human activity, as a piece of human behaviour.... It is a mode of action and not an instrument of reflection.

—Malinowski (1929)

The Birth of a Metaphor: I

---

1. "Fine Utopian Worlds ... new form'd by Revolution"
The Realism of the Impossible—Enchanted Volubility—Delirium, Madness, and Tottering States—Milton's "New Models" and "Irrelevant Fantasies"—A Usable Utopia—The Absolute of Future Happiness

---

2. The Faustian Future
Bishop Hall and the "Dream of Utopical Perfection"—A Faction of Firebrands—King Charles and "that new Utopia of Religion and Government" (1642)—Lilburne's "Land of Promise" or "Utopian Paradise"—Turning the Great Wheel—Cowley's Images: Flood, Deviltry, Incendiarism, Destruction, Faustianism

---

3. Revolutionary Situations
From Queen Elizabeth (and Mary's "Revolution") to Cromwell—Misleading Translations—The Celestial Metaphor—Copernicus, Shakespeare, Kepler—Political Astronomy—"A Change of Masters"—Bruno and Greville

---

4. From Old Astrology to New Politics
Shakespearean Usages of a "Hard Word"—Hartlib's European Revolution—Rival Schools of Astronomy and Eschatology—"Foolish Jewish Fantasies"?—Winstanley and "Heaven here, and Heaven hereafter too ... "—Revolution, Reformation, Restoration

---

5. A New Manner of Newness
The Myth of Cyclical Nonchange—The Path of Christian Progress—
The Apocalypse's Promise of "a New Heaven, a New Earth"—Types
of Ambiguity—John Spencer's Contradictions—Novelty and
Innovation—Four Essential Archetypes: Resurrection, Reincarnation,
Redemption, Revolution—Elementary Forms of the Intellectual Life

1. "Fine Utopian Worlds ... new form'd by Revolution"

En route to *les événements* of Paris in that May of 1968, I chanced to have
an opportunity to listen to Herbert Marcuse, who was presenting, to the
thunderous applause of a European student audience, the following
proposition: "Utopia is the most *real* of all *real* possibilities! ... " Varying the spirit of the sentiment only a little (for he had been drinking at
the fount of young Wagner rather than old Hegel), the celebrated contemporary German composer Hans Werner Henze offered the ineluc-
ble corollary: "What the World needs today is not the making of Art nor
the making of Music, but the making of Revolution—everywhere in the
World." Already in the *Quartier Latin* the utopians were raising barricades on behalf of dreams; and, shortly thereafter, as I stood at Marble
Arch watching a "demo" of thousands of young English persons (some
carrying placards which read: BE A REALIST, DEMAND THE IMPOS-
SIBLE) marching past the historic spot where the Tyburn martyrs had
waited for the end, the full-throated cry suddenly went up, as in some
primitive chant of a warring tribe: "REV-*oh*-LOO-*shun*, REV-*oh*-LOO-
shun! ... "

In Africa men were pledging themselves to be "loyal forever to the
Revolution"; in Asia prison camps were crowded with "traitors to the
Revolution"; in Latin America small guerrilla bands struggled on, strong
in their faith that "a revolution could not be stopped ... diverted ...
defeated," that, like a "mighty storm ... fire ... earthquake ... flood,"
it would come to destroy so that revolutionary man with his utopian
dream could come to renew, rebuild, redeem.

Meanwhile, back at the British Museum, my antiquated dictionaries
and glossaries were still waiting for me: and the research I had been
fitfully conducting on the origins of utopia and revolution seemed to be
suggesting more insistently than ever before that, for the world's intellectual classes, in the beginning were always the words, that the slogans

of ideology were part litany and part liturgy, and indeed that the modern Europeanized temperament was inconceivable without this special political vocabulary of enchanted volubility.

How had this come about, and why should it be so?

The earliest literal association of the ideas of Utopia and Revolution that I have been able to locate occurs in some mid-seventeenth-century verses of a poet named Robert Heath. He begins with a few lines of doggerel about Copernicus's opinions, but he is clearly concerned less with the "Earth's Globe" and "Spherick motion" than with the social and political implications of the new "Delirium."

> Nor doth the State alone on fortune's Wheeles
> Run round; Alas, our Rock Religion reeles.
> We have sailed so far the Antipodian way
> That into darkness we have turn'd our day.
> Amidst these turnings, 'tis some comfort yet,
> Heaven doth not fly from us, though we from it.

Heath goes on, in lines that appear to have been widely quoted in his day:

> When Noah's flood had turn'd the Land to Sea
> And the Earth seem'd one floating Isle to be ...
> Yet true we find what was but Phansie then;
> (For the world if we but understand the Men
> that live therein;) For they alas turn round
> ... drunk with madness, with their poreblind eyes,
> Think States well-settled; totter tho they rise.
> A strange Vertigo or Delirium
> O' the Brain it is, that thus possesses 'um;
> Whilst like to fashions grown Orbicular
> Kingdoms thus turned, and over-turned are;
> Nothing but fine Utopian Worlds i' the Moon
> Must be new form'd by Revolution.[1]

This was the warning to the world: utopia was revolution, revolution was utopia, and that was all that men needed to know.

In John Milton's *Paradise Lost* (1667), the Angel admonishes Adam directly enough:

> Be lowly wise ...
> Dream not of other Worlds, what Creatures there
> Live, in what state, condition or degree.

Yet Adam's agreement is more apparent than real. He concedes the folly of "wandering thoughts and notions vain," but in effect preserves an opportunity for a dream of this world by exchanging abstract fancy for pragmatic hope, by descending from the "high pitch" to "a lower flight." What was objectionable was the idleness of philosophizing (after all, it was the occupation of the devils in Hell, discoursing vainly "of good and evil ... of happiness and final misery, passion and apathy, and glory and shame"); and he had no mind to abandon the imaginative adventurousness of human reason. "Our hearts are now more capacious," Milton writes in 1644, "our thoughts more erected to the search and expectation of greatest and exactest things." Milton was of Adam's party: and its vision was of "the highest that human capacity can soar to ... " So there remained a commitment to good and happiness, to passion and glory, if only it were a practicable, this-worldly proposition.

> But apt the Mind or Fancie is to roave
> Uncheck'd, and of her roaving is no end,
> Till, warn'd, or by experience taught, she learne
> That not to know at large of things remote
> From use, obscure and subtle, but to know
> That which before us lies in daily life,
> Is the prime Wisdom: what is more is fume,
> Or emptiness, or fond impertinence.

It was in this sense that Milton drew a line between himself and the fictions of More and Bacon. He approved of all those political petitions offering advice on behalf of "new models of a commonwealth" (for "it is a deed of highest charitie to help undeceive the people"); he despaired of irrelevant fantasies. The task—and he put the distinction with force and clarity some two centuries before Marx and Engels—was not "to sequester out of the world into Atlantick and Eutopian polities, which can nere be drawn into use; but to ordain wisely as in this world of evill ... " In yet another place, Milton praises

> that grave and noble invention which the greatest and sublimest wits in sundry ages, Plato in *Critias,* and our two famous countrymen, the one in his *Utopia,* the other in his *New Atlantis* chose ... a mighty Continent wherein to display the largeness of their spirits by teaching this our world better and exacter things, then were yet known, or us'd ...

(Something else again were those "petty prevaricators of America, the zanie of Columbus ... ").[2] In this our world, then, there were better things to come: a usable utopia which a "revolution of time" would bring.

This prescient foreshadowing of the modern conjunction of utopia and revolution is vividly suggested in Milton's brief account in his *Areopagitica* (1644) of his visits to Galileo, and especially of his sojourn among those foreigners who counted an Englishman "happy to be born in such a place of *Philosophic* freedom, as they suppos'd England was ... "

> There it was that I found and visited the famous Galileo grown old, a prisoner to the Inquisition, for thinking in Astronomy otherwise than the Franciscan and Dominican licensers thought. And though I knew that England then was groaning loudest under the Prelaticall yoak, nevertheless I took it as a pledge of her future happiness, that other Nations were so persuaded of her liberty.

It is this absolute of future happiness which, as I have been suggesting, is at the very heart of the modern revolutionary commitment; and for Milton it was indeed a pledge to "such a deliverance, as shall never be forgott'n by any revolution of time that this world hath to finish."[3]

2. The Faustian Future

As has so often been the case over all the centuries, the fine distinctions that utopians and revolutionaries tried to make among themselves were scarcely visible to the naked eye of the established opposition. Practical or fantastical, passionate or prudent, their dreams were deemed pernicious and their deeds most foul. Among Milton's Civil War antagonists, in this first generation of utopian revolutionism, there were those who rushed to judgment and (as with poor Cinna) saw only that there was conspiracy in the poetry. In a sermon preached in Whitehall in 1628 by Bishop Joseph Hall—an accomplished stylist, known in his day as "our English Seneca," and famous, of course, as one of Milton's great polemical targets—there were lavish strictures against those who would "dream hence of an Utopical perfection ... " He, and his Church, would have no part of either utopia or revolution.

> Here this then, ye Violent Spirits, that think there can be no piety that is not cruel; the Church is a Dove; not a Glead, not a Vulture, not a Falcon, not an Eagle, not any Bird of Prey or Rapine. Who ever saw the foot of the Dove armed with griping talons? Who ever saw the beak of the Dove bloody? Who ever saw that innocent bird pluming of her spoil, and tyring upon bones? ...
> Do you see any faction with knives in their hands, stained with massacres; with firebrands in their hands, ready to kindle the unjust stakes, yea woods of martyrdom; with pistols and poniards in their hands, ambitiously affecting a canonisation by the death of God's annointed; with matches in their hands, ready to give fire unto that powder, which shall blow up King, Prince, State, Church; with thunderbolts of censures, ready to strike down into hell whosoever refuses

to receive novel opinions into the Articles of Faith. If ye find these
dispositions and actions Dove-like, applaud them.

Oh, he was prepared to concede, "Liberty is a sweet word," and indeed
"the thing itself is much sweeter." But what had it in common with fire
and blood and thunderbolts? It was a quiet and truly practical thing, free
from obsessions with either a golden past or a utopian future. Hall's is
one of those voices on the eve of revolution whose eloquence waxes as
their world wanes.

There is a disloyal liberty of those rebellious spirits, which despise
government, and hold it a servitude to live within the range of wholesome lawes; there is no freedom with these unquiet dispositions, but
in the cold censures of authority, in the seditious calumniations of
superiours, and in their own utopical prescriptions. Everything is
good to these men save the present, and nothing save their own:
though all these are not so much liberties, as licentiousness.[4]

The King himself, with less eloquence but even more urgency, denounced the "Cabalists," who "broached new Doctrine" and would
"erect an upstart Authority without us." He argued against the Militia
Bill, which he contended was "but one Link of a great Chain, and but
the first Round of that Ladder, by which Our Just, Ancient Regal Power
is endeavor'd to be fetch'd down to the ground ... " Appealing to
Parliament (in 1642) to "declare against Tumults, and punish the Authors," Charles I was derisive about "some Persons who have now too
great an Influence even upon both Houses, [who] judg or seem to judg
for the publick Good, and as are agreable to that new Utopia of Religion
and Government into which they endeavour to transform this
Kingdom ... "[5]
What joy there was soon to be for those defenders of kings and
bishops when those dreamers of "Utopical perfection" began to encounter political difficulties in their efforts at the tumultuous transformation. In 1647, that bitter pamphleteer *Mercurius Anti-Pragmaticus* rejoices
at the dramatic falling out between moderates and radicals, at the new
hostility between *Pragmaticus* (his regular polemical enemy) and John
Lilburne, and at the defeat of the "Adjutators." Now, he could gleefully
retort, Colonel Harrison's regiment "having turned their refractorinesse
into submissiveness and their disobedience into penitence, with the rest
have promised a compliance and obedience in all things ... " What
course, then, would be left for Lilburne and his militant confederates—
"to guide them (no doubt) into the Land of Promise"? The critic is
triumphantly contemptuous. "But John and they are alike to wander
forty years, and to taste the bitter waters ... ere they arrive in their
Utopian Paradise." "And now," he concluded with satisfaction, "toles
out the Bell ... how is mighty fallen!"[6]

But if one utopia perishes in the power struggles of a revolutionary situation, another utopia is born in the compensatory dreams of restoration. Before the emergence of a clear, simple concept of linear progress, both utopianism and revolutionism took their turns on the wheel of fortune, now turning left with the firebrands of novel opinions, now turning right with the return of traditional balance.

In a remarkable passage in Cowley's "Vision Concerning the Government of Oliver Cromwell" (1661), the poet of royalist sympathies allows himself to be effectively accused as "an Utopian Dreamer" who stood for nothing but the "Golden Mediocrities" of "the Supreme place attained to by Virtues that must not stir out of the middle ... " Up to this point, Cowley had been relentlessly righteous in his indictment of the late Protector, or rather "the man who made himself to be called Protecteur." The charges were hurled furiously against "our blest Reformer ... Boldness ... Brutishness ... Rashness ... Phrensie ... There is no name can come up to it, and therefore we must leave it without one." For in the Cromwellian tyranny England had been plunged into chaos, confusion, Babel, and Bedlam.

> Ah, happy Isle, how art thou chang'd and
>   curst ... !
> Art thou the Country which didst hate
> And mock the French Inconstancy?
> And have we, have we seen of late
> Less change of Habits there, than Government
>   in thee?
> Unhappy Isle ! ...

His conviction was absolute: "no man can justify or approve the Actions of Cromwell." And yet:

> [Yet] many there are, even honest and well-meaning People, who, without wading into any Depth of Consideration in the Matter, and are purely deceived by Splendid Words, and the outward appearances of Vanity, are apt admire him as a great and eminent Person; which is a Fallacy that extraordinary, and especially successful, Villainies impose upon the World.

Cowley conceded too much (and too volubly) to his visionary antagonist:

> the general ground of your argumentation consists in this, that all men who are the effecters of extraordinary mutations in the world, must needs have extraordinary forces of Nature by which they are enabled to turn about, as they please, so great a Wheel ...

This was, he admitted, "a universal proposition, which seems so reasonable, and is so popular." But it was an inexcusable blindness to the true human and social disaster which accompanies "a total abolishment of the old". And in a torrent of image, metaphor, and analogy Cowley tried to make his antipathies clear.

1. *The Flood.* There are "Spring-Tides of publick affairs," when the "Deluge" comes and there is a "break-up of the Flood-gates," even a malicious opening of "all the Sluces"—"and all the art then and industry of mankind is not sufficient to raise up Dikes and Ramparts against it."

2. *Deviltry.* "Boldness" he conceded to Cromwell, but "so far from being a sign of manly courage," he held it to be "only a Demonstration of Brutish Madness or Diabolical Possession."

3. *Incendiarism.* "But did Cromwell think, like Nero, to set the City on fire, onley that he might have the honour of being founder of a new and more beautiful one? He could not have such a shadow of Virtue in his wickedness; he meant onley to rob more securely and more richly in midst of the combustion."

4. *Destruction.* "This man endeavoured to destroy the Building, before he could imagine in what manner, with what materials, by what workmen, or what Architect it was to be rebuilt."

5. *Faustianism:* " . . . since the *English* name was ever heard of, it never received so great and so infamous a blow as under the imprudent conduct of this unlucky *Faustus.*"

Surely not political partisanship but only poetical ambiguity could have allowed the spirit in Cowley's dream who was assigned to defend the heroic Cromwell to score a point or two so trenchantly. "You pretend extremely," he is allowed to say, "to the old obsolete rules of Virtue and Conscience." To be sure, this was obsolescence with classical honor, and perhaps Cowley came away equally well when the contest was formulated by the Cromwellian as being one between "Aristotle's Politiques" and the practice of "Machiavil." In situations of powerlessness, the militant political imagination is often generously permissive; it becomes large and embraces playful contradictions. Why else should the literary ideologue have portrayed himself as "a Pedant, and Platonical Statesman, a Theoretical Common-wealths-man, an Utopian Dreamer . . . "?[7]

For men of Cowley's persuasion, this particular utopian dream was soon to find its fulfillment in the revolution of 1688. For men of Lilburne's hope, no year was to bring them closer to the Promised Land; the idea of a special revolution all their own that would carry them forward to the utopian paradise was still to be conceived.

3. Revolutionary Situations

We have been moving toward this fanciful new imagery for at least a century now, and in a time when well-settled societies were tottering it seemed almost irrepressible. In the year 1571, the Bishop of Ross had written a curious letter to the English Duchess of Feria, and he hoped she would show it to the King of Spain.

> The life of the Queen of Scots had been in great danger.... A revolution in her favour might easily have been effected if the King of Spain had raised a finger, but he had given no sign.... If the persecutions continued, the spirit of the Catholics would be broken, and a revolution would then be impossible.

Again, the Spanish ambassador, in reporting to the King on the political crisis over Queen Elizabeth's possible marriage, noted:

> The people in general seem to threaten revolution about it [*y en general toda la gente amenaza revolución sobre esto*].

Here the usage of the term is approaching modern connotations, and it bears traces of both recent Machiavellian realism and older astrological fancy. Thus, in a similar Spanish report from a diplomat in London to the Duke of Alba, it was recorded:

> For the last five or six nights a terrible comet of immense size has been seen in the sky, and as these people are fond of speculation, a great deal of discourse is taking place about it, the general talk being that such a sign has never been seen here excepting when it has presaged a change of government.[8]

The revolution that was meant was, for the most part (and one has to be wary of English translations of foreign documents!),[9] still only the occasional celestial metaphor for a change in fortune or a circular return to "the original."

All the pregnant images of the transitional conception of heavenly commotion with earthly disorders were brilliantly caught, as might be expected, by Shakespeare, who, in a famous passage in *Lear* (1.2.107), describes in all but name what we have inescapably come to think of as a "revolutionary situation".

> These late eclipses in the sun and moon portend no good to us: though the wisdom of nature can reason it thus and thus, yet nature finds itself scourg'd by the sequent effects. Love cools, friendship falls off, brothers divide: in cities, mutinies; in countries, discord; in palaces, treason; and the bond crack'd twixt son and father.

This clearly echoes those contemporary news chronicles which reported "late and horrible obscurations, the frequent Ecclipsations of the fixed bodyes" and their dire consequences:

new Leagues, Traytrous Designements, Catching at Kingdomes, translation of Empyre, downefall of menn in Authority, aemulations, Ambition, Innovations, Factious Sects, Schisms and much disturbance and trobles in religion and matters of the Church, with many other thinges infallible in sequent such orbicall positions and Phaenomenes.[10]

Even Copernicus, before proceeding to the elaborate tables of mathematical calculations in his *De revolutionibus*, allowed himself a fine introductory trope about how "the Earth conceives by the Sun, and becomes pregnant with an annual rebirth ... " From Copernicus to Kepler, the association between earthly destiny and the "revolutionary" signs in the sky took on more dramatic significance as "new" and "unheard of" stars were discovered.[11]

This astral feeling of political mysticism, which linked local political events with universal signs, only deepened in the next half-century, especially after the onset of the English Civil War. In one of his "treatises of the late Revolutions," James Howell—who was, in 1661, appointed to be the Historiographer Royal—observed that "the European world is all in pieces"; and he suspected that since "that direful Comet of the year 1618 appear'd in the heavens, some malevolent and angry ill-aspected star hath had the predominance ever since, and by its maligne influxes, made strange unusuall impressions upon the humors of subjects, by inciting them to such insurrections, revolts, and tumults ... " This was, in so ambitious and learned a writer as James Howell, less political astrology than political astronomy. In his application for the post of "Historiographer Generall," he had outlined the intellectual promise of probing to "the depths of things":

1. This minister is presumed to be an Artist this way, who will disdain to make of his History, a meer Diary, by huddling together a confused heap of Materialls, but will take pains to polish and reare them up to a Structure with all its due proportions.
2. One who will observe the method of providence in the dispensation of his judgments, making researches into the causes of them which seldom com together, but many years & sometimes a whole Century with a long train of contingencies intervene twixt the Judgment & the Cause.

His researches, then, and the long view of the causes of what he referred to as "strange shocks and revolutions" led him to this persuasion:

That the Astronomers, who lay sentinel to watch the motion and aspect of that Comet, observ'd that the tail of it having pointed at diverse Climats, at last it seem'd to look directly on these North-west Islands, in which posture it spent itselfe, and so extinguished; as if thereby it meant to tell the world, that these Islands should be the Stage whereupon the last act of the Tragedie should be play'd.

Whether old astrology or new astronomy, from Copernicus to Cromwell the path of revolution was charted in the skies. The tragic fault may have been in the stars, but not exclusively so; Howell was too bitterly involved in mundane politics not to allow for revolutionary men and movements in the "Structure" of his analysis. Indeed, his familiarity with Italian events—and his sensitivity to words as a pioneering lexicographer—led him to one of the earliest associations of the word *revolution* with the dramatic meaning of "a change of Masters."[12]

We have already seen evidence that the strange new sounds of the turbulent Mediterranean vocabulary, especially Bruno's heroic and enthusiastic *revoluzione* of the spirit, had its echoes in the Elizabethan mind, *e.g.*, Fulke Greville's, "Why are my revolutions strange ... ?" (1609) and, again, in the lines of his sonnet:

> When all this All doth pass from age to age,
> And revolution in a circle turn,
> Then heavenly justice doth appear like rage,
> The caves do roar, the very seas do burn,
>   Glory grows dark, the sun becomes a night,
>   And makes this great world feel a greater might.[13]

Throughout the literature of this period a new word—and thing— hovers tantalizingly on the edge of modernity.

4. From Old Astrology to New Politics

If the language of men like John Florio, James Howell, and Samuel Hartlib, all of whom enjoyed more direct contact with Continental formulations, began to touch on something new and different, the usage of *revolution* in Shakespeare reflects older meanings. There are four references in Shakespearean texts and, with one possible (but unlikely) exception, they are unpolitical and have to do, generally, with the wheels of fortune, changes in circumstance, and related celestial implications:

ANTONY: ... the present pleasure,
        By revolution lowering, does become
        The opposite of itself.

[*Anthony and Cleopatra*, 1.2.126–29]

HAMLET: ... here's fine revolution an we
                         had the trick to see't!

                                                [*Hamlet*, 5.1.88–89]

HOLOFERNES: This is a gift that I have, simple, simple; a foolish
extravagant spirit, full of forms, figures, shapes, objects, ideas, apprehensions, motions, revolutions ...

                                          [*Love's Labour's Lost*, 4.2.66–68]

KING: O God! that one might read the
                            book of fate,
                         And see the revolution of the times
                         Make mountains level, and the
                            continent,
                         Weary of solid firmness, melt itself
                         In the sea! ...

                                          [*Henry IV, Part 2*, 3.1.45–49]

The word is only just beginning to take on new shape, idea, and
motion, even an "extravagant spirit." A writer in 1655 adds the word
revolution to an appended glossary in order to help "the explication of
some words not familiarly used."[14] But no seventeenth-century dictionary of exclusively English usage which I have consulted even hints at the
connotations to come. Only in the eighteenth century do lexicographers,
late as always, begin to record its political suggestiveness, and then
mostly in specifically historical terms of "the great Turn of Affairs after
the Abdication of King James, and the Admission of King William and
Queen Mary ... "[15]

When, in 1704, Clarendon's son dedicated the final volume of his
father's formidable *History of the Rebellion and Civil Wars* to the new
Queen, he offered her "the benefit of reviewing all the failings in those
times," for "now your majesty, who succeeds to a Revolution as well as
a Restoration, has the advantage of a retrospect on all these accidents ... "[16]

The lines of the semantic emergence of the political image of revolution (a theme to which I shall return in the second part of this chapter)
are foreshadowed again in two revealing references which I find in the
miscellany of the Thomason collection of pamphlets, brochures, and
broadsheets. The first is from the prefatory remarks by Samuel Harlib to
Clavis apocalyptica (1651), in which he considers "the end and issue of
this present Combustion and Continuance of Wars that are spread over
the face of Europe" and promises nothing less than this as a result of
prophetical analysis:

Farewel, (Wel-meaning Reader!) and bee patient for a short time, thou
shalt see the end of these distractions in great Revolutions both in
Church and State, within and without Europe.

The second is from an astrological calendar entitled *Now or Never* (1659), "wherein is Calculated and set forth The great Changes, Revolutions, and Turn of Times"; it called itself

The Princely Dismal Calendar:
Being
The Bloody Almanack, for the Year
of our Lord, 1660, Fore-telling the strange
Castastrophes, Changes, and *Revolutions*,
that will befall most Princes, States,
and *Commonwealths* throughout
Europe; And the Superlative
Actions, designed by the *Heavens*,
touching the *Crowns, Scepters,*
And *Royal Diadems*. [17]

We are, therefore, for the first time literally in a revolutionary century. A new astronomy linked forces with a new politics; but, in the usual admixture which history forces upon the elements of change, there were also the old astrology, the ancient religiosity, and the immemorial human hope for renewal and redemption. The Civil War, as some historians of Cromwell's movement have wittily formulated it, was fought between rival schools of astronomy, "between Parliamentarian heliocentrists and royalist Ptolemaics" (and Ptolemy perished with Charles I). But it was also fought between competing schools of eschatology, between protagonists of the lost and future Eden and critics of (in Calvin's words) foolish Jewish fantasies.

Inasmuch as this theme of the so-called Jewishness of utopianism will be recurring again and again, it might be useful to record here that in Calvin's own context he was actually referring to the Anabaptists of his day: culpable utopians for "foolishly imagining that perfection which can never be found in the common fellowship of men" and even more dangerous revolutionaries for being "madde and barbarous men who furiously go about to overthrow this order ... " In his own last, French edition of the *Institutio* (1541), he spoke of *"les phantastiques"* (which has been modernized in the recent Geneva edition to *"les frénétiques"*). The association of this frenetic fantasy of perfection with some suspected Jewish predisposition occurs in the following passage, which I cite from a seventeenth-century English translation of Calvin's Latin text.

They thinke that nothing shall bee safe, unlesse the whole world be reformed into a new fashion.... That is a Jewish vanitie [*Quum ergo Judaica illa sit vanitas*], to seek and inclose the kingdome of Christ under the elements of the world: let us rather (thinking, as the Scripture plainly teacheth, that it is a spirtuall fruit which is gathered of the benefit of Christ) remember to keepe within the bonds thereof this whole libertie which is promised and offered us.

As against the vociferous and boastful cries of "the phrenticke men that are delighted with unbridled licentiousnesse" (*Sic quidem fanatici, quos delectat effrenis licentia vociferantur ac iactant*), Calvin recommended an abstinent aloofness from troubled political affairs. For—except in special circumstances, when an abused people manages to find legitimate authority to champion its downtrodden cause—"the Magistrate cannot be resisted."

> under this obedience I containe moderation, which private men ought to binde themselves to keep in cases touching the publike state, that they doe not of their owne head intermedle in publike business, or rashly breake into the office of the Magistrate, and enterprise nothing publikely. If any thing shall be in a publike ordinance be behooved to bee amended, let not themselves raise uproares, nor put their hands to the doing of it ...
> But if thou thereupon conclude, that obedience ought to be rendered to none but just Governours, thou art a foolish sinner ... let us first call to minde the remembrance of our sinnes, which undoubtedly are chastised with such scourges of the Lord. Thereby our humility shall bridle our impatience.[18]

Another impatient generation of furious men, with its new fashion of world reform and its delighted promise of perfect liberty in common human fellowship, was not so easily dissuaded. England's enterprising, if self-appointed, saints still had "great works" to do—"the planting of a new heaven and a new earth among us."

"Why may not we have our Heaven here," Winstanley asked, "and Heaven hereafter too?" The teachings of Christ, "the greatest, first, and truest Leveller ever," were to be realized in the here and now. He who cruelly offered only the consolation of the hereafter was (in Winstanley's misquotations from Jude) "the filthy Dreamer, and the Cloud without rain ... " "Live not in darknesse any longer," Winstanley pleaded in his *Fire in the Bush*, "for the voyce is gone out, freedome, freedome, freedome ... " Yet it remained a providential liberation in which only Christ's coming would slay the Beast, destroy the Devil, and end all human oppression. In that "great battaile," he wrote, "Light fights against darkness, universall Love fights against selfish power, Life against death, True knowledge against imaginary thoughts." And the point of all "those pluckings up, shakings downe, tearing to pieces of all rule, power, and Authority" was to "bring mankinde back to that plaine hearted estate of simplicitie, in which the Devill found the man when he deceived him ... the state of a little child." What could resist "the fire of pure Light" and the "unquenchable flame"? Winstanley's forecast was "woe, woe, woe to the imaginary power that rules the world; he shall be shaken with terror, and fall, and burst asunder." Governments would crumble and tyrants be overturned in the time of what he called "that great reformation, and restauration."[19]

5. A New Manner of Newness

The first great revolution of the modern world was, as has been cleverly said by a young Marxist commentator (turning from a diet of Lenin and Trotsky to John Milton and John Knox), "a continuation of religious activity by military means."[20] Obviously, we are not yet at the point where revolution is a continuation of utopian longing by violent means; it has yet to find for itself its own secular language and this-worldly imagery. If this profound emergence will prove to be, in one sense, a revolution of the new, it is also a clear and familiar historical admixture of continuity and change, of a breakthrough of innovation trailing clouds of tradition.

Exactly how new is "the new"? We must be especially cautious here, for the intellectual impressionism of generations of conventional historians has often perpetrated naïve myths about how an old order of stability, stagnating in ancient conceptions of cyclical non-change, gives way to a modern social dynamic, linked to progress and its related idea of a linear forward movement of mankind. This is both unsubtle and aberrant in its uncomplicated simplicity. Just as the concept of revolution could imply both circularity and forwardness, so could the idea of progress and of the New manage to serve two masters. There was, after all, the immemorial path of Christian progress to the resurrection, as it transpired in the basic eschatological drama of sin and redemption, culminating with the final novelty of it all: a Paradise full of new creatures. Here, as throughout the story of utopia and revolution, one must never lose sight of the apocalyptic message in the book of Revelation after the fiery day of wrath with its blood and thunder and great earthquake: " . . . And I saw a new heaven and a new earth . . . And he that sat upon the throne said, Behold I make all things new . . . (Rev. 21: 1, 5). Here were the ingredients for a full sense of newness and futurity; and, although the eschatological perspective was significantly different from the modern evolutionary conception of a secular process in time (rather than a sacred drama which would dissolve all historical time into eternity), still it was "future-oriented" and had this in common with subsequent teleological world views. Long before the era of so-called secular progress, there was the transporting vision of a beckoning path forward, with all of mankind longing for the transforming event and ultimate climax, waiting for the divine end.

Historians, I suggest, have often failed to pay sufficient attention to the complexity of words, and to the structure of that complexity. No Empson is needed to discern the types of ambiguity that stare out at us from the relevant texts—for the meaning of "new" includes both the *old* New and the *new* New. Profound slogans are never simple colored banners which devotees blindly follow; the armies may clash at night but they are never as ignorant as all that. Men are not often dialectical, but they are rarely as uncomplicated as some intellectual historians make them out to be. They are often capable, consciously or unconsciously, of making fine distinctions and even more ingenious combinations, and have, throughout recorded experience, demonstrated a capacity for keeping two contradictory or conflicting ideas in play at the same time. One scientist of the day reveals an understandable eagerness to reconcile old and new, and even in the title of his work there is the sign of his hesitation and doubling back: *A New or, More Truly, a New-Ancient Explanation* ... [21]

A glance at that unique repository of seventeenth-century notions, John Spencer's anthology of *Things, New and Old*—"or a Store-house of Similies, Sentences, Allegories, Apophthegms, Adagies, Apologies, Divine, Morall, Politicall, &c. with their severall Applications"—provides evidence enough of this dialectical ambivalence and potential for contradiction. On the one hand, the breakthrough of newness, of innovation or what I have called the new New, is subversive of all true social and religious order; on the other hand, the old New is central to a faith in the transcendental meaning of the world. No one could have been stronger than Spencer in his reprobation of the "Affectation of Novelty." As he writes, with a mocking bitterness: "Thus some are for this Preacher, some for that; such doctrine as is begot in Thunder, full of Faction and Innovation, if it smell not of novelty, it shall not concern them." There was an explosive inconsistency here. The argumentation proceeded in a manner which was as learned as it was desperate, but divided against itself it could not stand; and the men of Spencer's persuasion saw the logic of their faith destroyed in their own lifetime. One of his apothegms reads: "INNOVATIONS IN CHURCH OR STATE, VERY DANGEROUS." Yet another claims: "REGENERATION, THE EXCELLENCY THEREOF," for "without this *new* Creation, there is no *Freedom* from damnation, no happinesse to be obtained ... " Nothing could have been more dangerously disorienting than the public effort to hold three obviously contradictory views at the same time—what was new was vicious; nothing was truly new but merely a version of the old; only the truly new could save.

"We look upon Guns and Printing as new inventions," Spencer observes skeptically, and begins a perfect circular argument.

Yet for all this, it is said that the Chinese had the use both of Guns and Printing long before we in these Western parts had any notice of them. Why then should Christians so eagerly hunt after *Novelties*, when Solomon by the Spirit of God sends a peremptory challenge to all Mankind, *Is there any thing where of it may be said, this is new*? Let every one labour to get spiritual eyes, to behold the beauty of the *new Creature*, the bravery of the *new* Jerusalem, get into Christ that he may be a *new Creature*, and so shall have a *new Name, a new Spirit, new Alliance, new attendance, new wayes,* and *new work, a new Commandment, a new way to Heaven* and new Mansions in heaven.

The headline to this passage enjoined "EVERY MAN TO LABOUR THAT HE MAY BE A NEW CREATURE," and this is soon followed by yet another: "DAILY AMENDMENT OF LIFE ENJOYNED TO THE MAKING UP OF THE NEW CREATURE." How could this ever have been felt to be invincible ground on which to combat a rival and revolutionary conception of newness?

For *old things* being put way, all things will become new; we shall be *new Men, new Creatures,* we shall have *new hearts,* and *new* songs in our mouthes, be made partakers of the *new* Covenant, and at last Inheritors of the *new Jerusalem.*

The more these articles of faith were reiterated, the more the weapons were being given to the hands of the enemy who could, and would, turn them the other way. We are confronted here with the spectacle of one of the great and fateful boomerangs in the history of European rhetoric; and in the end our traditional ideologist of *Things, New and Old* is left spluttering ineffectually in a final and hopeless round of irony, trying to prevent that which his apocalyptic doctrine had made possible.

Thus it is with us, We are all for invention, and new devices of Sin, altogether unknown to the Ages of our Forefathers; *New* Lords, *new* Laws; *new* lights, *new* doctrines; *new* fashions, *new* faces; nay almost *new* kinds of Men or Women ... *new* devices for gain, *new* wayes of cheating, *new* wayes of breaking; So that without all doubt, God is devising some new manner of Judgment.[22]

No, what was being devised was a new historic manner of newness.[23] In the words of a Florentine humanist to the king of Portugal, praising the progressive triumphs of his own pathbreaking era of secular adventure and exploration, this was a time of the "opening up [of] new lands, new seas, new worlds, even new constellations ... "

Nothing is as old as the longing for newness , and it is of its essence that it should itself always appear new, unique, and unprecedented. The recurrent passion for the new is the cry of the human animal spirit for rebirth, for energy, surprise, and adventure; it reasserts historical man's deep need for a sense of differentness and otherness, and his heartfelt hope of fresh purpose and fulfillment. It is here, at this point of its great modern recurrence, that another primary concept joins three traditional forms of essential archetypes—to *resurrection, reincarnation,* and *redemption* comes *revolution,* with its related promise of a splendored newness and another golden chance for mankind. It represents, with Utopia (and Paradise, or Nirvana, before it), one of the elementary forms of the intellectual life, experienced at the high-pitched transcendental level where the cosmic drama of imagined human destinies unfolds. The "Golden Age" was projected forward and Arcadia given temporal realism and topical relevance, as men of determined will, armed with knowledge and inflamed by benevolent moralities, tried to reshape this world into more perfect molds.

Utopia was the revolutionary concept in the new realm of social aspiration. Revolution, even in the sense of Copernicus's *De revolutionibus*— "And why not admit that the appearance of daily revolution belongs to the heavens but the reality belongs to the Earth?"[*24]—was a utopian glimpse of new worlds, new perspectives. Both began by shattering an existing given conception of this time and place with a new and hitherto inconceivable other world. Thomas More's Utopia on a faraway island and John Milton's revolutionary battlecry for "a mutual bond of amity and brotherhood between man and man over all the world" would prove to be the twin stars of both the political and moral imagination of modern man. He could now imagine that (in Milton's phrase, as he put it in the title of his very last political pamphlet) there was always another *"readie and easie way."* One more revolution and the earth itself would turn, at long last, to that fine and newly form'd utopian world.

*" . . . neque fateamur ipsius quotidianae revolutionis in caelo apparentiam esse, et in terra veritatem?"

6

... there is no such way to gain admittance or
give defence to strange and absurd doctrines as
to guard them round about with legions of obscure,
doubtful, and undefined words. Which yet make
these retreats more like the dens of robbers or
holes of foxes than the fortresses of fair
warriors; which if it be hard to get them out of,
it is not for the strength that is in them, but
the briars and thorns and the obscurity of the
thickets they are beset with. For untruth being
unacceptable to the mind of man, there is no
other defence left for absurdity, but obscurity.

—John Locke (1690)

The Birth of a
Metaphor: II

6. The Missing Word
Regress, Progress, and Restoration—A "Turning Backe to its first place"—The Language of Reformers—Milton and "the reforming of Reformation itself"—A Dramatic Bifurcation of Meaning

7. The Coming of Masaniello
Historical Etymology—Villani, Guicciardini, Machiavelli, Montaigne—John Florio and the Italian Connection—James Howell's Translation of Giraffi (1650–52)—Images of Neapolitan Revolt—Metaphorical Imperatives: Spark and Fire, River and Torrent, Storm and Whirlwind, Volcano and Earthquake

8. Toward a New Vocabulary
Milton on Linguistic Conservatism—1648: the Rhetoric and the Wrath—Henry More on Enthusiasm, Fluency, and "Poeticall Fits"—Thomas Sprat on War, Language, and "New Thoughts, New Expressions"—Thomas Blount on Metaphor—Classical Usages—Anachronistic Slips of Modern Translators—From Polybius to Copernicus and Hobbes—From Circularity to Linear Progress

9. Milton, Nedham, Locke
Milton's "Revolutions of Time"—"The Writings of Zealous Incendiaries"—An Ideological Coinage—Nedham as the First Revolutionary Ideologue—Locke on "New Notions, New Terms"—Locke's Anti-Prometheanism—Words, Deceptions, and Aphasia

10. Between Pragmatism and Romance

Elements of a Modern Ideology—Utopian Hope, a Will to Systematic Change, a Penchant for the Painful Extreme—John Pym's Pragmatic Warning—Harrington, "Gothick Politicians," and "Blowing Up"— The Romance of Domestic Revolutions

11. The Mythological Scenario

Copernican   Capabilities—The   Victory   of   Astronomy   over Astrology—Anthropological Suggestions—The Indians and the World Renewal Cycle—Ritual Songs and Ghost Dances—The Meaning of the Masked Words—The Structure of a Semantic Framework—A Primordial Tradition: Celestial Archetypes for Terrestrial Realities—The "Sacred Horror"—Apocalyptic Revolution—Victor Hugo's Avalanche and "a Voice on a Mountainside"—Planetary Certainties

6. The Missing Word

Revolution in the seventeenth century rarely went under its own name; and when it did, it suggested, at least in England, regress rather than progress, a restoration, a "turning backe to its first place." It is perhaps a sign of the genius of the English language and character that revolution, even at a time of violence and rebellion, should have gone by the name of reform. In a sermon preached before the House of Commons in 1641, the exhortation was:

> Reformation must be Universall . . . . I beseech you, reform all places, all persons and callings; reform the Benches of Judgment, the inferiour Magistrates . . . . Reform the Church . . . . Reform the Universities, reform the Cities, reform the Countries, reform the inferiour Schools of Learning; reform the Sabbath, reform the Ordinances, the worship of God.

"You have more work to do than I can speak," the preacher (Thomas Case) concluded. "Every plant which my heavenly father hath not planted shall be rooted up":

> Not broken off, then it may grow, and sprout again; but pull'd up by the very roots. If it be not a plant of God's planting, what do's it in the Garden? Out with it, root and branch, every plant, and every whit of every plant.

Although this is the most familiar garden-variety of revolutionary metaphor, it is not at all the usual language of reformers; they do not generally identify themselves with uprooting, nor with "a great Reformation" which would be "zealous ... resolute ... speedy ... " But this was a rare and unusual historic occasion: as John Milton sensed, the time was now "to begin some new and great period," and, as he phrased the extreme prospect, "even to the reforming of Reformation itself."[1]

Was it merely that the word—revolution—was missing or, rather, that it was not readily available for political usage? There was to be in this vocabulary of dramatic historical change a fateful transvaluation of values. The word REFORMATION was to lose its general political pointedness and become confined to a technical term for a religious alteration; while REVOLUTION would slowly begin to arrogate to itself an unprecedented range of drastic human sentiments. The dramatic bifurcation of meaning can be detected in the plosive phrase with which Clarendon's son introduced the first edition of his father's great work on *The Rebellion and Civil Wars:* this was, he wrote (in 1702), "an age when a revolution hath been thought necessary to make a reformation ... "[2] The new word will, in point of fact, be henceforth recurring with such astronomical regularity and inevitability that its extraordinary historical debut must be looked at more closely.

7. The Coming of Masaniello

It has been claimed by one student of historical etymology that "among the first, if not *the* first" to employ the word in its modern political connotation was Montaigne (in one of his essays, 1595); and he claims, too, that an Italian historian, writing of the Neapolitan revolt against the Spaniards, popularized the notion of *rivolutioni*.[3] Other research, however, has antedated this by several centuries. Matteo Villani, chronicling a popular revolt in Siena, used the word *revoluzione* in 1355.

It was often used by a number of other Italian historians (including Guicciardini) in their reports of Florentine unrest in the fifteenth and sixteenth centuries.[4] I also note the following in Savonarola:

> Believe me, Florence, that much blood was to have been shed in this revolution [*revoluzione*], but God tempered his hand.[5]

Apparently the term is rarely employed by Machiavelli, although many modern translators use it anachronistically as a rendering of *mutazione di stato*. Indeed, in the Anglo-Italian dictionary which John Florio prepared (*A World of Wordes*, 1598), there is this entry:

Rivolgiménto, a revolving, a revolution, a turning and tossing up and downe. Also a winding or cranking in and out. Also a cunning tricke or winding shift. Also a revolt, a revolting or rebellion.

The function of the modern revolutionary concept was patently carried out by the use of *Ribellione*—"rebellion, rising against authoritie, or right, law and Prince." The word *Riformatione* is defined as: "a reformation, a repairing, a renewing of anything to its old state again" (although a second edition adds, "Also a law or ordinance made by the people without the Senate"). And the word *Riuolatione* appears as "a revolution, a revolving, a turning backe to the first place or point, a revolution of celestial bodies or spheres." It is of special interest that among the names of the authors and books that Florio lists as having consulted for his dictionary there are the London works of Giordano Bruno, as well as writings by Machiavelli, Tansillo, and Guicciardini.[6] In any event, it would seem to be clear that *revolution* came to Northern Europe from Italian political turbulence, and not—as R. G. Collingwood once tried to maintain—from seventeenth-century French literary criticism.[7]

English writers may well have been peculiarly slow to adapt to a political vocabulary which for at least two centuries had marked the pages of various Italian chroniclers of rebels and their insurrectionary efforts. The brilliant Howell translations into English of contemporary Italian historical accounts are, in my view, the central texts to be considered; and the Naples revolts of 1647–48—led in their extraordinary first episodes by Masaniello, a young, barefooted fisherman in blue shirt and red bonnet, who seized power with the support of enthusiastic Neapolitan masses—are the major linking event between the Mediterranean and the modern ideological idiom. For European minds to whom revolution was essentially a concept still associated with the Copernican paths of planetary progress, a dimension of different destiny was about to be added. We have reached that decisive moment in Western history and thought when the old politics of paradise takes to itself a new secular abstraction, original and powerful enough to be capable of translating heavenly hope into celestial certitude and of relating the movement of the skies into a great and special human drama. This is the moment which was registered by James Howell and which makes him so important for us.

"Now in this prodigious Revolution," Howell writes in his preface to *Parthenopoeia* (1654), a history of the Kingdom of Naples which paid pointed attention to Masaniello's great uprising, "there were many things of extraordinary remark that are considerable ... " He noted "the heat of the Air" and "the sulphurous quality and heat" of the Italian soil which caused "Incendiums and Earthquakes," and he went on to correlate the geology with the politics. "Indeed the Napolitan, according to the quality of the Soyl," he supposed, "is of a fiery boyling Nature, which makes the Spaniard ride him with a Bitt and a Martingall; he hath as many Whirlwinds in his Brain and quicksands in his Breast, as the *French* or any other Nation." Hence their "sundry Innovations," and more than that: for "I have not read of any Politicall Instrument so often out of tune, having had forty popular *Revolutions* in less than four hundred years." The most recent of these, and Howell knew it well from his translation of Giraffi's historical narrative, was Masaniello's rebellious explosion against Spanish exploitation and injustice.

> Touching this last Revolution in the year 1647, it was the violent'st of *all*, it was like a Candle burning at both ends, the common people were all as mad as they had bin hit by a worse thing then the *Tarantola*: In which Revolution there were so many prodigious things happened, that were they not *recent*, and done as it were but t'other day, they would be held for meer *Romances* ... that this Tumult from a small spark should come to be so huge a fire, from a little source should come to be such a rapid Torrent, that from a weak blast it should so suddenly come to such an impetuous Whirlwind ... [8]

Thus: Revolution was born in metaphor, and the literary marks of its birth have been ineradicable. Indeed, its whole political evolution as one of mankind's archetypal concepts and mythological symbols has, through changing circumstances over turbulent centuries, been dominated by what we may think of as a metaphorical imperative. It has, now as then, always been close to the spark and the fire, the river and the torrent, the storm and the whirlwind, the volcano and the earthquake, and above all the circles of time and the progressions of the very heavens.

8. Toward a New Vocabulary

How long would it be before yet another language would absorb the new terminology? John Milton underscored the stylistic caution and verbal restraint of English linguistic conservatism when he wrote:

> if in dealing with an outlandish name they thought it best not to screw the English mouth to a harsh forreigne termination, so they kept the radicall word, they did no more than the elegantest Authors among the Greeks, Romans, and at this day the Italians in scorne of such a servility use to do. Remember how they mangle our British names abroad; what trespasse were it, if wee in requitall should as much neglect theirs. [9]

Words struggle, language resists.

But the times were especially propitious for a new vocabulary, as the year 1648 marked the outbreak all over Europe of social conflict, political hope, and the inflamed enthusiasms of rebellious men. The rhetoric and the wrath advanced together. A contemporary student of words and language—Henry More, one of the most admired philosophers of the age—sketched the "strong temptation" which overtakes the enthusiastic spirit:

> He feels a storm of devotion or zeal come upon him like a mighty wind, his heart being full of affection, his head pregnant with clear and sensible representations, and his mouth flowing and streaming with fit and powerful expressions, such as would astonish an ordinary Auditorie to hear.

Henry More, to be sure, was critical, and he considered "all that excesse of zeal and affection and fluencie of words" to be "a kind of *naturall inebriation*." Although his remarks were intended essentially to describe the "Poeticall fits" of the "more highly pretending Enthusiasts," they apply with equal cogency to the political fits of the great first wave of revolutionary enthusiasm which we will be describing. Dr. More's perspicacious critique of eloquence may well be taken to illuminate the very emergence of the word *revolution*, around which so many recurring outbursts of human enthusiasm would cluster in the next centuries: " ... the imagination is so extravagant that it is farre easier for her to ramble abroad and fetch in some odde skue conceit from a remote obscure corner, than to think of what is nearer and more ordinarily intelligible."[10] This explains much, but it cannot explain away that "mighty wind" which swept up so many of his contemporaries. What was "nearer" and most extraordinary was the storm, the convulsion, the earthquake. Young Thomas Sprat, only a boy when the land was rocked with civil war and rebellion, followed on with a somewhat cooler correlation of language and politics:

> In the [Civil] Wars themselves (which is a time, wherein all Languages use, if ever, to increase by extraordinary degrees; for in such busie, and active times, there arise more new thoughts of men, which must be signifi'd, and varied by new expressions) then I say, it receiv'd many fantastical terms, which were introduced by our *Religious Sects*; and many outlandish phrases, which several *Writers* and *Translators*, in that great hurry, brought in, and made free as they pleas'd, with all it was enlarg'd by many sounds, and necessary Forms, and Idioms, which it before wanted.[11]

Revolution was such a varied new expression, a difficult word being refashioned in busy, active, warring times, to signify that men were beginning to consider a wanting new thought.

This element of contemporary self-consciousness—a remarkable awareness of the whole process by which words and things, or names for realities, are formed and re-formed—is as surprising as it is systematic. Thomas Blount, who, with Milton's nephew Edward Phillips, and James Howell, was one of the outstanding lexicographers of the day, exhibits an uncanny insight into the historic emergence we are trying to trace. "A Metaphor," Blount writes in his *Academie of Eloquence* (1653),

> is the friendly and neighbourly borrowing of a word, to express a thing with more light and better note, though not so directly and properly as the naturall name of the thing meant, would signifie....
> The rule of a Metaphor is, that it be not too bold nor too far fetch'd; and though all Metaphors go beyond the true signification of things, yet are they requisite to express the roving fancies of men's minds.

In his illustrative material he outlines the literary techniques of "amplification" by the accumulation of synonymous words. The example is "a Sedition":

> ... a sedition; tumults; mutinies, uproars, desperate conspiracies, wicked confederacies, furious commotions, trayterous rebellions, associations in villany, distractions from allegiance, bloody garboyles, intestine Massacres of Citizens.[12]

One amplifying synonym is conspicuous by its absence; the roving fancy of men's minds had still a little way to go.

To describe a sudden and radical political change, Hobbes—like Bacon, Coke, Greville, Selden—was content to use such words as *revolt, rebellion,* and *overturning.* Others indeed preferred *tumult, sedition, civil war.* Here the classical usages of the ancient writers were being followed, for, if revolutions can be found in the pages of Herodotus, Thucydides, Plato, and Aristotle, there was no single Greek word for them. One Latin lexicon has this entry:

> *Revolution:* conversio ... mutatio ... vicissitudo ... res novae ... rerum mutatio.

A French lexicographer, with a special national feeling for the echoes of 1789, notes:

> *Changement brusquement et violent dans un Etat:* rerum mutatio ou commutatio permutatio civilis (Cic.), magna rerum perturbatione;
> *Faire une révolution:* res commutare (Suet.), turbata respublica ... seditiosus ... turbulentus.

Finally, a glossary of later Latin records:

> *Conversio:* revolution (of the heavens), turning of sinful man in repentance, conversion ...
> *Revolutio:* rolling back, return, revolution (of Time ...)[13]

It is indeed with these lingering implications of change and sin, revolt and repentance, and the vicissitudes of violent mutations that John Milton refers in his Latin writings to the great Cromwellian overturnings; and it is, for the most part, only the anachronistic slips of modern translators which have him appear to speak of social revolution at all.[14]

What also persisted was Polybius's notion of the cyclical change of "Fortune's wheel":

> Such is the cycle of political revolution, the course appointed by nature in which constitutions change, disappear and finally return to the point from which they started....[*History*, 6.5.1]

And, in point of fact, in Cotgrave's *Dictionarie* of 1611, the following definition was given:

> *Revolution:* f. a revolution; a full compassing; rounding, turning backe to its first place or point, the accomplishment of a circular course.[15]

This was part Polybius, part Copernicus. Not until after the "glorious Revolution" did English lexicographers (*e.g.*, Samuel Johnson's *Dictionary*, 1755) assign the term a new political meaning.

That it was being used increasingly in a general context of both history and politics has become abundantly clear. After the trial and execution of Charles I, Matthew Wren wrote a study of "those strange revolutions we have seen"; and Anthony Ascham's Civil War pamphlet (1649) was entitled *Of the Confusions and Revolutions of Governments*. In each of King Charles II's basic messages to General Monk, to the Lord Mayor of London, and to the House of Peers and the Commons, dispatched from the court at Breda just before his return to the throne, there was a reference to "these great revolutions which of late have happened ... "[16] In *Oceana*, James Harrington spoke of "Natural Revolution" (which "happens from within") and "Violent Revolution" (which "happens from without"). I would in general agree with Dr. Hatto's surmise that the events of 1848–49 failed to be given the definitive name of revolution in their own epoch because they were not a return to a previous régime. A revolution was an aspect of the principal of circularity, not of linear progress; and this was forcefully illustrated by Hobbes, writing rather gleefully on the last page of his *Behemoth*:

> I have seen in this Revolution a circular motion of the Sovereign Power, through two Usurpers, from the late King, to this his Son; for ... it moved from King Charles the First, to the Long-Parliament, from thence to the Rump, from the Rump to Oliver Cromwell, and then back again from Richard Cromwell to the Rump, thence to the

Long-Parliament, and thence to King Charles the Second, where long may it remain.[17]

9. Milton, Nedham, Locke

Nowhere, so far as I can make out, in the historical and political texts of either John Milton or John Locke—and both were deeply involved in the revolutionary upsets of the century—is there any distinctively modern usage. From Milton's English works and, in places, from the contemporary translations of his Latin writings, there still emerges the earlier Shakespearean atmosphere of "forms, figures, shapes, ideas, apprehensions, motions, revolutions ... " It is curious that Milton's nephew Edward Phillips made in 1694 an English version of his uncle's State Papers and that in one of them (a 1659 letter to the King of Denmark) the phrase "a Revolution of this government" is used; curious, since in Phillips's own dictionary of about the same time (*The New World of Words*, 1696) no such association is registered. Another seventeenth-century translation documents the imaginative expansion of the revolutionary metaphor into general historical (and even sociological) denotation. Thus, a passage in Milton's *Declaration against Spain* reads very much in the spirit of latter-day interpretive language: "The Reformation of Religion and the Discovery of the West Indies, which two great Revolutions [*conversiones*], happening near about the same time, did very much alter the State of Affairs in the World."[18] But in this respect Milton's vocabulary was essentially traditional, if in places transitional. So very much like the writings of the historians who were to come, there is "revolution" on the first and on the last page of Milton's *History of Britain* (1670).[19] He opens with a speculation on the fate of nations: " ... were it the violence of barbarous inundations, or they themselves at certain revolutions of time, fatally decaying, and degenerating into Sloth and Ignorance ... " And he closes with the remark: "If these were the Causes of such misery and thraldom to those our Ancestors, with what better close can be concluded, then here in fit season to remember this Age in the midst of her security, to fear from like Vices without amendment the Revolution of like Calamities."

But, for all its large philosophical implications (and subsequent theoretical pretensions), the term *revolution* needs to be sought less in such high and abstract efforts to come to grips with events than in the low texts, in the agit-prop of the day, where it begins to find its own proper future. In Marchamont Nedham's pamphlets, which were often semi-official in their polemical thrust (many had first been originally licensed by John Milton on behalf of the Cromwellian regime), I find the word employed more often than in any other single place. As the political concept of revolution bursts for the first time into the events of the 1650s, a conservative like James Howell, who could almost be said to have coined its ideological usage in English, employs it continuously in terms of a monstrous calamity; a radical like Nedham responds to the verbal opportunity with dozens of usages, all glowingly positive. As one hostile critic remarked of Nedham's Cromwellian writings: "It is incredible what influence they had upon numbers of unconsidering persons who have a strange presumption that all must needs be true that is in print." Then the revolution was indeed true, for Nedham had put the new proposition more originally than it had ever been put and with greater clarity than it was to have for almost another century, a historic achievement for which both American and French revolutionaries were to be suitably grateful. *The Excellencie of a Free State* (1656) was Nedham's most considerable work, and in it he emerged as literally the first "revolutionary" ideologue.[20]

> Necessity and Extremity opening the people's Eyes so that (as the only Remedy) they dislodged the Power out of those hands, putting it into their own, and placing it in a constant orderly Revolution of persons Elective by the Community.

Again, in an even more drastic formulation (and one that demonstrably shaped the spirit of '76 and '89), he announced that

> a revolution of Government in the Peoples hands hath ever been the only means to make Governours accountable, and prevent the inconveniences of Tyranny, Distraction, and Misery ...

One can sense why John Adams resented Nedham's influence on the radicals in the American colonial rebellion, and why Condorcet saluted his memory during the Revolution in France.

Some of this literature was known to John Locke, but we can only guess how much of it the young scholar of Westminster School and Christ Church, Oxford, had been exposed to in the early years of his intellectual development, so marked by conservative, monarchist and Hobbesian views. We know that he had read "Mr. Ascham's book" on *Revolutions of Government* (1649), and I have seen a copy of a work entitled *Notable Revolutions* (1653) which had been in the Earl of Shaftesbury's collection (of which Locke had been librarian for many years). Yet Locke was evidently taken neither by the word nor the concept, not even as he made his ideologue's progress from the conservative right to the liberal left. Was it because he was a sensitve and finicky stylist who had an aversion to the "evil sounds" of certain words, "as though with some spectre"?[21]

In his theory of language Locke allowed, of course, for the emergence of what he called "mixed modes"—"He that hath new notions will, perhaps, venture sometimes on the coining new terms to express them." Yet he remained very wary of alterations in the significations of words. There was enough absurd wrangling as it was, as "men fill one another's heads with noise and sounds." Given the inevitability of men's *"inconstancy"* in the use of words, it is (as Locke sharply warns) "plain cheat and abuse when I make them stand sometimes for one thing and sometimes for another, the wilful doing whereof can be imputed to nothing but great folly or greater dishonesty ... " Worst of all was the danger of *"affected obscurity"*—as a consequence of "either applying old words to new and unusual significations, or introducing new and ambiguous terms without defining either, or else putting them so together as may confound their ordinary meaning ... " For Locke, the ordinary meaning of the word *revolution*, as it appears in his philosophical pages on time and duration, was a precisely astronomical reference to "the annual revolutions of the sun," the "regular and apparently equidistant revolutions" in the universe, etc., etc.[22]

Once, in a youthful political tract, he uses the word in a conventional reference to "all those tragical revolutions which have exercised Christendom these many years," and the usage has more in common with the general sense of mutability in Shakespeare and Milton than with the agitated new political formulations of Howell and Nedham. In the major work of his mature period, the *Two Treatises of Government* (1690), there are in all only two additional places where the term occurs, and both are to be found in the final chapter treating "Of the Dissolution of Government." For the philosopher who for so long has been taken to be the exemplary defender of the right of revolution, neither is especially revolutionary. The first appears to describe the political cycle in which a people returns, or is "brought back again," to a previous point of departure: the "many Revolutions," Locke observes, "never carried the People so far, as to place it in another Line." The second emphasizes the rare seriousness of an ill-treated people arousing itself, justifiably, against "a long train of Abuses, Prevarications, and Artifices": "such Revolutions happen," Locke notes, in order to "put the rule into such hands, which may secure to them the ends for which Government was at first erected."[23]

"He was never a candid man," Locke's biographer has written. "He had an almost Gothic fondness of mystery for the sake of mystery: he used all kinds of little cyphers, he modified a shorthand system for the purposes of concealment, and on at least one occasion he employed invisible ink." Perhaps this vignette by Professor Cranston goes part of the way toward an explanation of the curious spectacle of a radical philosophy in which sudden and violent political change was not even presented with assured confidence as rebellion. No, ran the devious argument, it could not truly be called rebellion, for was it not rather the best defense against rebellion? Was not the tyrant the real rebel? A revolution, presumably, only takes society back to the original point of the constitutional cycle. Whatever its increasingly diverse political connotations—and it could now mean everything from providential destiny to terrestrial mutiny, from dynastic displacement to social transformation—it signified for most contemporaries some form of a completed circular movement.

Locke, incidentally, owned in his library several copies of seventeenth-century editions of More's *Utopia*, and a remark in the first *Treatise* (sect. 147) suggests that he saw in utopian thinking—to "make out what Model of an Eutopia will best suit with his Fancy or Interest"—a novel solvent of the empire of authority and government. It is characteristic and indicative that although he began in his Paris journals of the 1670s to make notes for an "Atlantis," the desultory remarks were never worked up to a full and final picture of his ideal society. Both utopia and revolution appear to be a shade too drastic—too total and too uncontrollable—for Locke's cautious disposition. Even as a young man, as he confessed in a letter to his father, he felt little but antipathy for those who had preached "nothing but fire, sword and ruin." The incendiary image is worth underscoring here again: for it has been one of my main themes throughout these pages that the metaphors of fire in all its Promethean ramifications prove to be among the most reliable and revealing indicators of the utopian revolutionary temperament. Over a long literary life, Locke argued the case against the enthusiasm of perfection through violent change, and his language as well as his logic offers decisive evidence of his true temper.

> And if perchance there is in us a small flame of divine origin, yet by that flickering and restless motion whereby it strives perpetually towards its original dwelling place, it gives us more trouble and anxiety than light, and it bestows on this clay of ours merely the awareness that is ablaze and is both consumed and tormented with the silent torture of an imprisoned fire. Hence Prometheus' theft must be deplored by us no less than by him who committed it.

Breathes there a revolutionary with soul so dead as not to be inflamed by a Promethean inspiration? One may well ask. The fiery rebels of subsequent American and French revolt took great heart from the so-called philosopher of England's Glorious Revolution whose ideas seemed to offer such powerful sanction for a new world of reason and reform. "But is there not a danger," as Dr. Snow has written (rephrasing Locke's argument in somewhat anachronistic modern terms),

> that rebels will become enamoured of political novelties and that a revolt will open Pandora's box of political evils? On the contrary, claims, Locke, a revolution does just the opposite. A revolution is a reactionary movement, a backward-looking movement in which the people revert to previous experience to reconstruct a government along traditional lines for future generations ... There is little need to fear that they will turn to Utopian schemes.[24]

How can this be? Can utopia be both revolutionary and counter-revolutionary? There is a point at which historical etymology can confuse as well as clarify. In this particular case the confusion may well be constructive, for it can lead to a more self-conscious awareness of the deceptive relationship between word, metaphor, and reality. There are times, as C. S. Lewis used to say,[25] when even a momentary aphasia is to be welcomed.

10. Between Pragmatism and Romance

The word, then, in major areas of political discourse, was to all intents and purposes missing. But the substance was there. It was surely in a mood of recognizably revolutionary assurance that the House of Commons was told (by John Arrowsmith in 1643), "I am confident you never dreamt of reforming a church and state with ease...." Whatever the dream was, it undoubtedly had elements of what was effectively constituting itself into a modern ideology.

1. *Utopian Hope.* "Paradise is our native country" (Richard Greenham).

2. *A Will to Systematic Change.* "Take heed of building upon an old frame, that must be all plucked down to the ground, take heed of plastering when you should be pulling down ... " (Henry Wilkinson in the Commons, 1643).

3. *A Penchant for the Painful Extreme.* "You are physicians to the state and these are purging times; let all malignant humours be purged out of the ecclesiastical and political body ... " (Francis Cheynell in the Commons, 1643).

Small wonder, then, that Marxist historians, ever since Eduard Bernstein and Karl Kautsky, have been feeling increasingly at home in the English seventeenth century.[26] Christopher Hill reads Sir Francis Bacon in terms of Marx and Lenin, and although he concedes that the complexity of the tasks these prophets were setting for humanity was always underestimated, he insists (with rather more sincerity than logic) that "in all three cases the apocalyptic vision acted as a stimulant to action which was its own justification." Michael Walzer, studying "the origins of radical politics" in *The Revolution of the Saints*, is captivated by that moment in the historic process "when large numbers of men, suddenly masterless, seek a rigid self-control; when they discover new purposes, dream of a new order, organise their lives for disciplined and methodical activity ... " These men, he feels, are "prospective saints and citizens; for them Puritanism, Jacobinism, and Bolshevism are appropriate options ... "

Yet what I have already risked referring to as a more characteristic English note was always there. The temper of those men whom John Knox had denounced as "neither hot nor cold" was to prevail; they were not persuaded, as he had been, that "all which our adversaries do is diabolical"; nor did they find gratification in the prospect of "fearful shakings and desolations."

> There must be a leisurely and advised proceeding in every alteration. Nature hath left us a pattern ... we must let it grow by degrees. [Edward Forset, 1606]

> Now all stirring changes are dangerous, especially when the body of the commonwealth is full of diseases. [Calybute Downing, 1634]

John Pym himself, rebel and libertarian, pointed out in a famous speech of 1628:

> If this mutual relation and intercourse be broken, the whole frame will quickly be dissolved and fall in pieces, and instead of this concord and interchange of support, whilst one part seeks to uphold the old form of government, and the other part to introduce a new, they will miserably consume and devour one another. Histories are full of the calamities of whole states and nations in such cases. It is true that time must needs bring some alterations, and every alteration is a step and a degree towards a dissolution ... therefore it is observed by the best writers on this subject, that those commonwealths have been most durable and perpetual which have often reformed and recomposed themselves according to their first institution and ordinance; for by this means they repair the breaches and counterwork the ordinary and natural effects of time.[27]

Here, then, were the beginnings of that pragmatism in social affairs which practitioners of English politics over several centuries were to elevate into an absolute principle of history. Revolutionary ideology was to be left to others, or so the reigning fancy of Anglo-Saxon attitudes liked to have it. And in point of fact, except for relatively minor episodes in the general course of English political thought, the vast possibilities and tempting opportunities of utopian revolutionism were to be harmlessly bypassed.

In none of this have I been asking (or answering) which came first, the word or the thing. Each historical episode begins somewhere in the middle of another, and either point of departure can be taken to record the sinuous course of political rhetoric. Men and events produce images, and the images fashioned out of old words and new conceits begin to interanimate each other and often to emancipate themselves from their social and semantic origins. Noting the "peculiarities of imagery and sense," F. R. Leavis observes "a general tendency of the images to forget the status of metaphor or simile that introduced them and to assume an autonomy and a right to propagate, so that we lose in confused generations and perspectives the perception or thought that was the ostensible *raison d'être* of imagery ... "[28] But a loss of clarity or vitality is not necessarily involved. Vague concepts take on vivid content and aging metaphors recover a fresh lease of life; the course can run from confusion and casualness to a heightened relevance. Thus, it is only an antique Promethean inspiration which makes Sir Philip Sidney, with "fire in the mind," greet the flames of Dutch rebellion: for "without all this conflagration" there could be no triumphant liberation. Harrington, who dedicated his *Oceana* to General Cromwell, a living engineer of victory, gave the conceit a melodramatic updating which marked the transition of the metaphor to a new context of more modern violence. When Oceana mourned the passing of Lord Archon, *"Pater Patriae ... Inviolable in his Faith ... The Happiest of Legislators,"* it was recorded that it was he "Who setting the Kingdoms of the Earth at Liberty, Tooke the Kingdome of the Heav'ns by Violence." In a striking passage which Sidney would have recognized (to use his own phrase) as a new composition of conceits, Harrington writes:

Your Gothick Politicians seem unto me to have invented some ammunition, or Gunpowder, in their King and Parliament (*duo fulmina belli*) then Government. For what is become of the Princes (a kind of people) in Germany? blown up. Where are the Estates, or the Power of the people in France? blown up. Where is that of the people in Aragon, and the rest of the Spanish Kingdoms? blown up. On the other side, where is the King of Spain's power in Holland? blown up. Where is that of the Austrian Princes in Switz? blown up. This perpetual peevishnesse and jealousie, under the alternate Empire of the Prince and of the People, is obnoxious [liable] unto every Spark. Nor shall any man shew a reason that will be holding in prudence, why the people of Oceana have blown up their King, but that their Kings did not first blow up them: The rest is discourse for Ladies. Wherefore

your Parliaments are not henceforth to come out of the bag of Aeolus
["He did enfold . . . all th' airy blasts that were of stormy kinds,"
Homer, *Odyssey* X, tr. Chapman], but by your Gallaxy's, to be per-
petual food of the fire of Vesta.

Given this special interest in the movement from storm to fire, or from
spark to explosion on the "Gothick" scene of European political conflict,
Harrington could only dissociate himself from those "Historians, whose
custome it hath been of old, to be as diligent Observers of Forraigne
Actions, as carelesse of those Domestique Revolutions, which (lesse
pleasant it may be, as not partaking so much of the Romance) are unto
Statesmen of far greater profit; and this fault if it is not mine, is so much
more frequent with Modern Writers, as hath caused me to undertake
this work . . . "[29]

More modern writers would avoid the fault: the romance of domestic
revolutions was yet to come.

11. The Mythological Scenario

I can only wonder what students of Lovejoy's "philosophical
semantics"—or of what Ernst Robert Curtius used to call
Metaphorik[30]—will make of such explorations into the origins of Europe's
new political imagery.

As we have already noted in Locke and the literature of 1688, revolution was at first synonymous with restoration. Both were celestial references and could be taken to signify the movement of change and balance; but the Copernican metaphor was capable of so much more.
Open, secular, and outward looking, it could assimilate the new vitali-
ties of the idea of science and, later, the prospect of progress. As
Rudolf Bultmann has pointed out, the usage of the Greek word
apokatastasis ("restoration") referred in astrological literature to

> the periodical return of a star to its starting-point, and consequently
> the Stoic philosophers use the word for the return of the Cosmos at
> the end of a world-year to the origin from which a new world-year
> starts. But in the Acts of the Apostles (iii. 21) and in later Christian
> language, following Origen, *apokatastasis* became a technical term of
> eschatology.[31]

In this sense, the revolutionary metaphor represents a victory of astronomy over astrology.

Its fundamental themes are like the governing lines of force which
Mircea Eliade has discovered in the earliest history of man's beliefs, and
what he has called *"archétypes et répétition"*[32] will be abundantly disclos-
ing itself in these pages. I do not wish to press the cyclical thesis, al-

though I realize that I may already be well beyond my original intention, which was only historical illustration rather than philosophical demonstration. Yet the point is a persistent intruder, and both author and reader may well be plagued at this stage by puzzling questions. For my own part, I have often been tempted to search for a measure of deeper satisfaction in the scope of anthropology (even with the Parisian playfulness of one contemporary master, Lévi-Strauss, who has told us that if there are questions to which there are no answers, there are also answers for which there are no questions).[33]

The trouble with the anthropologists has been their studied indifference to the comparative peculiarities of European customs and mores and their tidy preference for aboriginal forms which are always held to be purer and more self-sufficient than the real course of interfused historical events allows. In many peripheral sectors of the Western experience, it has been precisely the special Christian note of eschatological drama which has added a unique element to older modes of human hope and social despair. All too often this is disguised, overlooked, or underplayed: as in the analysis of the millennial outburst among the American Indians, in the last days of their tragic decline.

The desperate outbreaks of tribal revolt and the fervent and often crazed belief in an impending millennial event—accompanied by storms, whirlwinds, and earthquakes—were based on a mélange of traditional Indian views of a World Renewal Cycle and an added doctrinal element deriving from their fitful exposure to Judeo-Christian notions.[34] One contemporary chronicler of the so-called Ghost Dance religion and the Sioux Outbreak of 1890 noted the deep changes in tribal ritual and mythic belief; he was elated by the surprising turn to a new ethic (as exemplified in the words of one messianic message to the Prairie tribes: "You must not hurt anybody or do harm to anyone. You must not fight. Do right always."), and he was moved to observe: "It is such a revolution as comes but once in the life of a race." But it was a "revolution" which recapitulated both the activism and the passivism of ambivalent Christian attitudes—could one *do something* for the regeneration of the earth, or should one *wait* for the imminent end and the establishment, amid universal peace, of the good and free and supremely happy life?

Some Indians fought, some Indians danced. All felt certain that the messiah was en route, for they sensed that a great wheel was turning. The glorious promise was of a final release from death, disease, and misery. Warriors went into battle as if invulnerable, and cataleptic prophets led their dancing flock (now with the participation, for the first time, of the women and children) in a new circular Ghost Dance movement, away from the old stationary up-and-down rhythms. "Give us back our arrows!" some chanted. Others sang of the prophet who had

said, "I bring the whirlwind with me.... It is I who make the loud
thunder as I circle about.... Look! the earth is about to move."

> The father will descend.
> The earth will tremble.
> Everybody will arise.

A sacred message had come down from the mountains: the white
enemies would be exterminated by a great flood or by "a wall of fire"—
the buffalo would return—the dead braves would live again—the aboriginal people would reign supreme—and the whole earth would become
new.

As the Indian messiah Wovoka said, touching upon so many of the
central conceits of the revolutionary imagination: " ... the earth was
getting old and worn out and the people getting bad.... I was to renew
everything as it used to be and make it better." It would be a time of
fraternal justice for the injured and the oppressed:

> Because I am poor,
> I pray for every living creature ...
> In my poverty I hold out my hands towards him and cry.

And as the ritual songs in the various Arapaho, Shoshoni, Paiute,
Cheyenne, and Sioux dances had it:

> There is a dust from the whirlwind,
> The whirlwind on the mountains ...
> > The mountain,
> > The mountain,
> > It is circling around,
> > It is circling around ...
> The sun's yellow rays are running out....
> > Lightning! Lightning!
> > Whirlwind! Whirlwind!
> I circle around
> The boundaries of the earth ... [35]

To recall the Indian millennial experience reminds us that there are
indeed open issues which the impression of historical human experience
among the Prometheans, the Doomsday metaphysicians, and the Sweet
Dreamers (which I will be trying to record in subsequent chapters) does
raise most insistently. What is the meaning of the masked words, or the
patterns of the communicated symbols? Can we make out the hard
outline of the semantic framework, or a universal formula for the permutations and combinations? Is there an explanation for the reappearance
of the same or similar motifs, and are these all fragments of a meaningful
whole? Are we, in Lévi-Strauss's sense, involved here with some kind of

structure, ruled by an internal cohesiveness, or perhaps some pattern of transformation in which the similar properties in apparently different systems are brought to light? In the absence of inaccessible factual truths, can we arrive at "a truth of reason"? Lévi-Strauss, hard-pressed by puzzlement, turned to a poet:

> All forms are similar, and none are the same,
> So that the chorus points the way to a hidden law.

For now, let us, similarly, leave the tentative answer here with Goethe.

To be sure, the way will often be pointed even if the hidden laws are never found. Of course, no one can authentically know whether society follows certain basic structures or prove whether history does or does not truly move in cycles (or indeed in any other form of pattern). I am only suggesting that men's beliefs about such cycles seem themselves to have such cyclical turns. As the scholarly translator of the Dead Sea Scriptures has recorded, the ancient writers of the scrolls and the men of Qumran were inspired by

> a widespread and well-attested contemporary belief that the great cycle of the ages was about to complete its revolution. This belief was based on a conception, which can in fact be traced to remote Indian antiquity, that existence consists not in linear progressive development—that is, in "history"—but in a constant cyclic repetition of primordial and archetypal events. When major upheavals occurred, it was promptly supposed that the cycle was nearing its end, that the Great Year was at hand, and that the cosmos was about to revert to chaos. The primal elements, restrained and regulated at the beginning of the world, would again be unleashed; all things would dissolve in an overwhelming deluge or be burned in that everlasting fire which rages in the depths of the earth. Then the cycle would begin again: a new world would be brought to birth . . . [36]

More than that: the tentacular hold of the metaphor of revolution over the imagination of modern man raises far-reaching questions about its deep mythic character. To what extent does it have its basic roots in the great primitive tradition of celestial archetypes for terrestrial realities? Surely, it is tantalizing that no other word for radical social change—rebellion, uprising, overturn—has so captivated, so dominated the modern vocabulary. Born in the mysteries and certitudes of the heavens, only the astronomical *revolution* could, as a figure of speech and a figure of thought, satisfy in a special, sanctifying way.

> When I behold this goodly frame, this World,
> Of Heaven and Earth consisting, and compute
> Their Magnitudes—this Earth, a spot, a grain,
> An atom, with the firmament compared
> And all her numbered stars, that seem to roll

> Spaces incomprehensible (for such
> Their distance argues, and their swift return
> Diurnal) . . . and on their orbs impose
> Such restless revolution day by day.
> [*Paradise Lost*, 8. 15–31]

In the more political context of modern revolutionary history ("those climacteric catastrophes which devastate and revivify civilizations"), Victor Hugo—writing, shortly after the Paris Commune of 1871, of the climacteric year 1793—puzzled over

> those vertiginous words which sometimes, unknown even to the man who has uttered them, have the fateful accent of revolutions, and after which material facts suddenly seem to have a kind of dissatisfaction and passion, as though they had taken umbrage at the things that have just been heard; what happens seems angered by what is said; catastrophes occur, furious and as though exasperated by the words of men. Thus a voice on a mountainside is enough to set off an avalanche. One word too many may be followed by a landslide.

When Hugo contemplated the greatness of the revolutionary Convention, he conceded that "everything that is great has a sacred horror," and he reminded himself of the president's place above the rostrum, underneath a black-framed copy of the Declaration of the Rights of Man, surrounded by colossal statues of Lycurgus and Solon, Plato and Montaigne, the chair itself round and gilded and the table supported by four one-foot winged monsters who "looked as though they might have come out of the Apocalypse to witness the Revolution." His sense of the *horreur sacrée* was acute:

> Revolutions have two slopes, ascending and descending, and on these slopes they bear all seasons, from ice to flowers. Each segment of these slopes produces men adapted to its climate, from those who live in sunlight to those who live in lightning.*[37]

Sacred mountains, as Mircea Eliade has often pointed out,[38] had ideal prototypes in the sky; temples and cities had divine or extraterrestrial counterparts in the constellations. Nothing less would serve. Thus revolution, on this kind of anthropological reading, might be taken as an episode in the ancient and familiar sacred dramas of the cosmos, as a part of an inescapable ritualistic process of legitimizing human acts through an extra-human model. The sky sets the scene, with its old

---

*"Les révolutions ont deux versants, montée et descente, et portent étagées sur ces versants toutes les saisons, depuis la glace jusqu'aux fleurs. Chaque zone de ces versants produit les hommes qui conviennent à son climat, depuis ceux qui vivent dans le soleil jusqu'à ceux qui vivent dans la foudre . . . "

dwelling places of the gods and its world-shaking signs of thunder, lightning, and storm.

> At certain revolutions all the damn'd
> Are brought, and feel by turns the bitter change
> Of fierce extreams, extreams by change more fierce,
> From Beds of raging fire to starve in Ice
> Their soft Ethereal warmth, and there to pine
> Immovable, infixed, and frozen round
> Periods of time, thence hurried back to fire.
>
> [*Paradise Lost*, 2. 597–603]

In this great mythological scenario, with its ritual role for hostilities, its states of sacred fury, its hopes of human redemption, its planetary certainty, and the coming of the Great and Golden Time, revolution belongs in its way to the paradigmatic gestures of archaic humanity, to the archetypes of the primordial world.

7

The days of the old order are numbered. When
capitalism goes under, it will go in a crash. We
must rise up and help destroy the power structure
root and branch. For the first time in history
mankind is capable of living free, without the
chains of repression or alienation. The present
oppression, this totally evil system of war,
poverty, and exploitation, is doomed. The revolution
that is coming will transform all life and culture
as we have hitherto known it.

—Student Representative to the Conference
  of Revolutionary Youth in London,
    June 1968

The Metaphysics
of Doomsday

1. **John Rogers, Fifth Monarchy Man**
   Dreams of Raining Fire—"Teetering and Tumbling Affairs"—Father
   and Son—Millenarian Optimism

2. **The Millennial Moment**
   "The Revolution of the Times"—Paradise Seekers—Wrath, Vengeance, Destruction

3. **Words and Swords**
   The Confrontation between John Rogers and Oliver Cromwell
   (1654)—Troubled Warriors and Embittered Comrades—The Falling
   Out of Factions—The Limits of Freedom and the Rights of
   Resistance—Preaching, Praying, or Fighting?—Men of Ideology v.
   Men of Power

4. **Rebellion in Permanence**
   "Overturning, overturning, overturning"—Nedham's Critique of
   Boundlessness—Milton: "License they mean when they cry
   libertie"—Cromwell's Formula for "a true Reformation"—Agitators
   and Reformadoes—The Arrest of John Rogers and the Fifth Monarchist Leaders

5. **The Dustbin of History**
   Adapting Texts and Revising Doctrines—Apocalyptic Certainty and

the Imminent Destruction of the Beast—The Signal for Revolt—"Begin the Earthquake"

6. The Great Chain of Human Hope
Venner's Insurrections (1657, 1661)—"An Incredible Impulse of Infatuation"—Rogers's Flight, Harrison's Execution—The Eternal Temptation of Audacity—Basic Elements in the World of the Radical Temper

1. John Rogers, Fifth Monarchy Man

Some years ago (and I have already mentioned the text) H. R. Trevor-Roper published an ironical study of "Three Foreigners and the Philosophy of the English Revolution." If we are to believe the historian's scholarly exercise in paradox, none of "the real philosophers, and only philosophers," whose "wild, bloodshot mysticism" had made vivid for the gentry of seventeenth-century England a vision of society which they hoped somehow to attain, were English. Samuel Hartlib, who hoped for "the reformation of the whole world," was a Prussian, from Polish Prussia; he wrote his utopian sketch of *Macaria* after the "pattern" of More and Bacon ("shewing its excellent government, wherein the Inhabitants live in great Prosperity, Health and Happiness ... Vice punished and virtue rewarded. An example to other Nations"); and he dedicated it in 1641 to Parliament, which he thought would "lay the cornerstone of the world's happiness." John Dury, an indefatigable idealist and crusader who even succeeded in bringing Cromwell together with Rabbi Menasseh ben Israel (Spinoza's teacher), came from Elbing on the Baltic Sea. And the famous Comenius, a Bohemian Brother, arrived from Poland (on Hartlib's invitation) to help realize Bacon's New Atlantis in England; only when events proved too turbulent did he depart for Sweden, promising John Pym, who had been his (and Hartlib's, and Dury's) constant supporter, to return "when affairs in England were more tranquil." Comenius never returned, but he was to write:

> We are all fellow citizens of one world, all of one blood, all of us human beings. Who shall prevent us from uniting in one republic? Before our eyes there is only one aim: the good of humanity, and we will put aside all considerations of self, of nationality, of sectarianism.

The more representative English mind was, presumably, exempt from what Trevor-Roper calls this kind of "peculiar metaphysics."[1]

Yet, peculiar or not, a vocal, conspicuous, and very English part of this Cromwellian generation of warriors and revolutionaries—the so-called Fifth Monarchy Men[2]—was rooted firmly on native ground with their devotion to abstract principle. The evil kingdoms of the world (the first four being, according to cryptic hints in the Book of Daniel, the Babylonian-Assyrian, the Mede-Persian, the Greek, and the Roman) were symbolized as monstrous beasts with horns, and their destruction would inaugurate the reign of the just in a fifth and final monarchy.

If the apocalyptics were basically pessimistic characters (for what hope of real improvement could there be before the end of the world?), the millenarians appeared to be stronger in this-worldly hope. There would indeed be a reign of saints on earth before the end of all things. One modern historian, in an effort to calculate "the extent of the millenarian wave," has examined statistically the seventeenth-century pamphlet collection of the London bookseller George Thomason. During the period of 1640–43, the greatest years of the movement, he estimates that 70 percent of the hundreds of published works can be identified as millenarian: "they believed in an imminent kingdom of glory on earth, either a literal thousand years' reign, or (often in the case of Presbyterians) a period of 'latter-day glory,' and often explained the civil war as its precursor."

> Here you must look for fight [John Spencer wrote in 1642] if ever you would come to heaven . . . . The Lord hath told you, *in the last days there should be terrible times* . . . . do you not already perceive the very drops of blood begin to fall?

> If this British Northern nation bee the people chosen of God to accomplish the last wonders of the world [Christopher Syms asked in 1644], was it not necessary the nation itself be first purged?

> The Sword of the Lord will be sheathed in the sides of all Kingdoms by a Civill War [Thomas Banaster prophesied in his *Alarm to the World*, 1649]. *England*, thou hast begun to drink blood, and thou shalt yet drink one draught more to all the world, and they shall pledge thee round in a bowl of blood again.

These were the revolutionary watchwords: blood and purge, terrible times, the overthrow of rotten structures, a flood tide of change. "This is the age wherein all men's souls are in a kind of fermentation," a chronicler recorded: "Methinks I see how all the old rubbish must be thrown away, and the rotten building overthrown and carried away with so powerful an inundation."[3]

Here were tumultuous men for a time of tumult. They were called

"Fanatiques"; they were angry men and, some thought, demented. As young John Rogers, later a leader among the Fifth Monarchists, recalled, his converter to the cause was

> full of zeal, stirring about and thundring and beating the pulpit . . . I was amazed and thought he was mad; I wondred what he meant, and whilest I was gazing upon him I was struck, and saw it was we that were mad, which made him so; O sayes he! you knotty, rugged, proud piece of flesh! you stony, rocky, flinty, hard heart! what wilt thou doe when thou art roaring in Hell amongst the damned?

This led, he confessed, to his own "raging fits" (in which "every thunder and lightning I look'd upon as my fate . . . ") and to fearful dreams of raining fire.[4] Presumably, it also led to that stormy eloquence with which he tried to impress on Oliver Cromwell and his generals the nearness of the millennium, and "all the teetering and tumbling affairs on Earth now . . . "

The Rogers family itself presents an instructive picture in generational conflict which anticipates more modern versions of the deep temperamental diversity of fathers and sons. Both Nehemiah and John Rogers were preachers, Protestants, and pamphleteers. "Unlike his son," their biographer has noted,

> Nehemiah Rogers was of a gentle and peaceful disposition, and of moderate opinions; unlike his son, he had the art of conciliating those with whom he was brought in contact; and unlike his son, he loved to dwell not on political, but on practical religion, not on the iniquity of his adversaries, but on the kindness of his friends.

Not only did the two Rogerses appear to be inhabiting two different spiritual worlds in which God spoke with opposing voices: it was as if they were living in two different societies where what was virtuous progress for the father was abhorrent perdition for the son. Two pairs of eyes beheld two nations, neither recognizable in the vision of the other. The following passage is from a sermon which Nehemiah Rogers published in *The Fast Friend* (1658) about six weeks before the death of Oliver Cromwell:

> Let us look backward, and then take forward. How can we, in the first place, but lament and bewail our horrible ingratitude and unkind dealing with so bountiful and liberal a master. Marvellous hath been God's dealings towards this land and nation. Never any nation under Heaven that tasted more of the riches of God's bounty, nor stood more bound to God than this for his liberality. What peace! what plenty! what deliverances! What brightness of heavenly light for fourscore years did we enjoy! Whilst our neighbour nations were

wearied with bloody wars, and scarce received any other dew than the blood of the inhabitants, we sat under our vines and fig-trees, having peace within our walls and plenteousness within our palaces. We slept when they bled, we abounded when they wanted, we surfeited when they starved. Our sun did shine out gloriously whilst theirs was set. We had magistrates, ministers, schools, churches, laws, trade, all of the best, whilst they would have been glad of the worst, being deprived of them all. Ask Bohemia, ask Germany, what they thought of us. Would they not say, Happy art thou, O England! who is like unto thee ...

Surely whilst we should have been recounting mercies we were finding faults and spying flaws in our state and government. The civil was tyrannical, the ecclesiastical papistical, etc. Nothing pleased, not the hedge, not the wine-press, not the watch-tower, not the watchmen. These we trample down with our own feet, pluck down with our own hands.... Thank we unthankfulness for what we have lost.

No such liberal optimism could touch John Rogers, no such national pride or kindly gratitude. He was a young man of fits and rages, holding fast to his boyhood dreams of fire. Even in his worst moments, suffering extremely under the "inhuman tyranny" (especially the fierce prison regime of a Major Bull), he could find dark resources of special consolation. "O it is good," he confesses, "it is good to be beaten into more good rather than be without it, for these blows do make my head ring with the music of Heaven." And then he added the following remarkable conceit (I will subsequently be calling attention to this unusual image as found in Dante):[5]

It is said that *Domitian* his mother, when she was of child of him, dreamed that she had a wolf in her, flaming with fire out of his mouth. Such a flame came out of thy mouth, O fierce Bull, as shall be sure to burn thee up.

All was certain to come right in the final conflagration.

2. The Millennial Moment

Revolution in the seventeenth century, as I have already pointed out, rarely went under its own name; and when it did, it suggested (at least in England) regress rather than progress, a restoration, an astronomical "turning backe to its first place." But if the word was missing the disposition was there, full of Copernican certainties about the great universal event which would happen "when the *Times* are turned and *States* are changed." Rogers's texts almost cry out for the expressive modern political metaphor which alone could integrate all the superlatives and imperatives: "The loud and longing expectations of the People. . . . This worke is the greatest. . . . This worke must be done." Rogers came close enough: as he wrote in an open letter to Oliver Cromwell (20 April 1653), " . . . in the revolution of the times the changes will run their round out, and then the Lord will come to reign." Men could be of diverse minds as to the precise time, "yet all concur in the nighnesse and swiftnesse of its coming upon us."

In Rogers's own calculations, the "revolutionary" work would by 1660 get "as farre as Rome" and, by 1666, would "be visible in all the earth." Its mysterious entrance would be at once gradual and sudden ("O terrible Doomes-Day"), accompanied by the "shakings of all Nations," and would finally redeem the people from all bondage, corruption, slavery, and "bloody base, unjust, accursed, tyrannical Laws." He was only slightly embarrassed that it had been "a Heathen" who had once said, *Fiat justitia, perat mundus,* for he could record that "Jehovah saith now, *Justice shall be done though the world perish for it.*" He associated himself with the prophecies of Joachim of Flora (as had Dante and Columbus before him, paradise-seekers on other terrains); and he made Paracelsus's vision his own, "a terrible Eclipse of the Sun, together with great inundations . . . and after that will be divers tumults, seditions, battels, burnings, and bloodsheddings."

> O! then enters the great change, which shall be called the happy
> Reformation that followes, which is without deceit, arts, subtleties;
> but in plaine, naked innocent Laws.

The message was quickly despatched to the established powers. In yet another letter to Cromwell (21 December 1653), Rogers warned of the furious fall that was coming unless "the old State principles of carnal policy" were abandoned. Once Sir Philip Sidney had thought of state policy basing itself not on prophetic star-gazing but on experienced analysis of public affairs; for a John Rogers, such a turn to humanist reason represented only an additional sign of the anti-Christ.[6] "Let them give you counsel," he proposed to the Lord Protector,

> that are conversant with the secrets of God and the visions of these
> days. . . . When you find, my Lord, all the wise men of the world to
> fail you in the visions of these times and seasons by their liberal arts
> and sciences, philosophical notions or rules, then send for the
> *Daniels.*

This Daniel was already waiting. The secret vision and the apocalyptic prophecy were all. The liberal changes which the father had welcomed were matters almost of indifference to the son; after the revolution, the millennium.

Indeed, "in these overturning, overturning, overturning days," it was not simply a matter of building the Fifth Monarchy in one country: it would, to be sure, "begin at home" (according to John Spittlehouse's advice to Cromwell in 1653), but it would soon be extended "to the uttermost parts of the earth." The saints would "proclaim liberty to the captives and oppressed ones of other Nations." This was a program for a world overturning; and on one of his own pamphlets Rogers put the subtitle:

> or, Doomes-day drawing nigh,
> With Thunder and Lightening to Lawyers,
> In an Alarum
> For New Laws, and the Peoples Liberties from
> the Norman and Babylonian Yokes
> Making Discoverie
> Of the present ungodly Laws and Lawyers of the
> Fourth Monarchy
> and of the approach of the Fifth ...

Revolutionaries are rarely modest in their geographical ambitions. Paradise in a single park or land is taken to be anomalous, or short-sighted, and even a betrayal of the universal mission. Not only the Fifth Monarchy enthusiasts but the Cromwellian propagandists as well had sought a planetary dimension. England, according to Spittlehouse's reading of the great drama, was only "a Theater to act a precedent of what he [God] intends to do to all the Nations ... " Hugh Peter had spelled out the scenario[7] in 1648 when he announced to the Commons his conviction that "*This Army must root up Monarchy, not only here but in France, and other kingdoms round about . . . . This Army is that Corner stone cut out of the Mountain, which must dash the powers of the earth to pieces.*" John Rogers knew it with equal certainty: all the established powers would collapse "over all the *World* ere long, till not one be left."[8]

All this world revolutionism, for a time, was put by the Fifth Monarch-ists in a cautionary and almost respectful tone. The local charges against them of having stirred up the people to "risings, tumults, or carnal warfare" were denied as false. The Fifth Monarchy's appeal[9] was in-tended to be moral and religious. "Where is the spirit of old?" Rogers asked (he was then all of twenty-six), in a pamphlet which he had secretly and anonymously printed,

> yea, the spirit, and faith, and courage that we ourselves had some ten, twelve, or fourteen years ago, among the good old Puritans? Yea, the spirit of Englishmen and rational men among us. O! what a change it is! What sheepishness, what sleepiness, what deadness,

what darkness, what timorousness, and what tameness is now seized upon us!

As the despair and the nostalgia mounted, Rogers's language grew increasingly intemperate (and, for the constabulary, less ambiguous). "Rout Babylon," he would cry, "and destroy the Beast's dominion root and branch ... "

Once, earlier in the century, it had seemed to be a matter of magic or mysticism, as in Ben Jonson's *Alchemist* (1613) wherein the would-be master, a worldly knight named Sir Epicure Mammon,

> *Of a fifth monarchy talk'd I would erect,*
> *With the Philosopher's Stone....*

[4.3]

But now, for Rogers, it was less a matter of philosophy than of politics. Heroic past and future promise seemed to be concentrating themselves into the one present moment which is the supreme release for millennial martyrs: " ... for it is no time to dally; the danger is great, the day is come, and we are engaged (there is no going off); live or die, stand or fall, fight or flight, is at hand." The voices of the Fifth Monarchy sounded less and less like otherworldly trumpet calls. Wrath, vengeance, destruction, "blood cryeth unto blood"—how much was rhetoric, and how much rebellion?

Cromwell himself was not sure: nor, probably, was John Rogers. But it did seem to be one thing to borrow an ancient image of "the earthquake that shall rend them up by the roots," and quite another to announce that the wondrous remnant of Witnesses "shall assault the great city, and climb up the wall like men of war ... " If the end remained the inauguration of the Fifth and Final Monarchy, were the means still only faith and prayer and the prospect of miracles? A police report quoted this verse which Rogers composed and publicly sang:

> For God begins to honour us,
> The saints are marching on
> The sword is sharp, the arrows swift,
> To destroy Babylon:
> Against the kingdom of the Beast
> We witnesses do rise, &c.

The soul of the movement hovered between natural impulse and supernatural hope.

3. Words and Swords

On a day in February 1654, there was a most extraordinary confronta-tion[10] between Oliver Cromwell and John Rogers.[11] The Fifth Monarch-ist leader, released from Lambeth prison for the interview, led a delega-tion of twelve—because twelve was "the Lamb's number against the Beast, and the root and square number of the hundred and forty-four thousand in *Rev.* xiv"—and they all presented themselves, each with Bible in hand, at Whitehall.

They had been wickedly lied about by paid informers, arbitrarily de-tained in prison without legal justification, maltreated by constables and jailers in brutal fashion. And now they would, at long last, speak their piece: with "plainness, foolishness and simplicity . . . without any poli-tic, studied, or artificial frame of words or expressions after the wisdom of the world or the princes of the world." They were not evil-doers but sufferers for conscience. It was not a distinction that the guards at Whitehall had in mind—and, before they found their way in to see "the Great Man," they had been roughly handled by swords, halberds, and rude abuse. Rogers and several others were finally admitted into the chamber, crowded with "Machiavellian sycophants"; Cromwell was at the window (where, they noted, "a pistol lay prepared").

"You might have had patience in your words," Cromwell opened. "Now you have liberty to speak . . . but do not abuse your liberty." He reiterated his own viewpoint: that they were suffering for the evildoing of seditious transgression, and not for conscience. "But some words are *actions*, and words are conjugall with *actions*, for actions and *words* are as sharp as swords, and such things I charge you with."

"I desire to know," Rogers began, "in what capacity I stand before you—as a Prisoner, or as a Freeman; as a Christian to a Christian, with equal freedom that others have, or as a slave?" With Cromwell's assur-ance that "a Prisoner is a Freeman," Rogers was encouraged (if he really needed it) to go on to challenge the indictment.

> But your words are not proofs, my Lord. But yet, seeing my way is more clear now, I shall say somewhat more; there is no law of God nor yet of man that makes me such an offender but yours, which is worse than the Roman law and tyranny, that makes a man a Traitor for words.

The exchanges were quick and furious. "Who calls you a Traitor? I call you not." "But who made you the judge of Scriptures, my Lord?" "Why, who will hinder your preaching the Gospel of Christ—yea, His Personal Reign?" "I know, my Lord, that you are a Sophister. And so it seems, for a part of the truth we may preach, but not the whole, not ... against the crying sins of men in power or out of power; for that seems to strike at your interest too much." "Why, what interest is mine?" "A worldly interest, which God will destroy." "Ha!—And do you judge me?" "Yea," Rogers replied, "by the word of the Lord."

What Rogers looked forward to, as an uncompromising Puritan radical, was either "a fair trial, or a Christian debate." He was to have only a very little of both. What the Lord Protector lacked in theological subtleties he more than made up in a robust sense of the statecraft necessary to defend his own power. He was satisfied that the evidence which had been accumulated proved a case of dangerous subversion. Rogers dismissed all the proffered documentation as the work of informers, as illegal as they were dishonest. "Nor will I be tried," he added, "in hugger-mugger, but if I have offended, it is fit I have open justice." Cromwell, again, found himself in a corner, on the defensive (if, that is, we can have implicit faith in this *Faithfull Narrative*). "Who tries you? and who says it is a charge? Who calls it a charge? I say not so; and see! before you hear them you call them spurious." Rogers felt himself to be above such a legalistic quibble.

> O, my Lord, I cannot but mourn for you and your condition, which is sad and to be bewailed.... I think my condition, through Grace, though a poor prisoner, a great deal better than yours; I would not change with you.

Apparently Cromwell began to lose his temper. "Well, well, you are known well enough, and what spirit you are of." He meant blasphemy, and called it so. (The marginal comment of the Fifth Monarchy pamphlet notes: "Mr. Rogers, amazed at such language, again lifted up his hand and eyes towards heaven, appealing to God to judge righteously.") But anger led only to abuse.

> Yea, I say Blasphemy again, for all your lifting up of your eyes, and I tell you, yea, that in a good box of ointment a little thing—a dead fly—may spoil all, yea, a little fly.

Quickly recovering his composure, Cromwell indulged in a revealing burst of sentimentalism, so often the refuge of troubled warriors and embittered comrades. "Well you know," he told Rogers, "that the time was there was no great difference betwixt you and me. I had you in my eye, and did think of you for employment (and preferment); you know it well enough."

> True, my Lord; and then you could say to me you thought no man in England so fit, but since the case is altered indeed; but I pray consider who it is is changed.

Old rebels betray; young rebels sit in judgment. The pathos of the falling out of factions stains the history of all revolutionary movements.

Cromwell was to lose one or two more rounds of the argument before proceeding ruthlessly to win the battle. "Look you to your conscience," was his disengaging cry, "and I will look to mine." It was a safe retreat, for his conscience[12] was proving impervious to all the considerations of logic, law, politics, and theology which the quick-witted dialecticians tried to insinuate.

> ROGERS: ... as I said before, the privative or negative part of the Testimony you cannot bear.
> CROMWELL: Pish! here is a great deal of positive and private to show you are a Scholar, and 'tis well known that you are. And where do you find that distinction?
> ROGERS: In logic.
> CROMWELL: Ha!

Legalistic Latin was even less agreeable than logic.

> ROGERS: Those you call Fifth-Monarchy-Men are driven by your sword to love one another.
> CROMWELL: Why, I tell you there be Anabaptists (*pointing at Mr. Kiffin*) and they would cut forms; so would the Presbyterians cut the throats of them that are not of their forms, and so would you Fifth-Monarchy-Men. It is fit to keep all these forms out of the Power.
> ROGERS: Who made you, my Lord, a judge of our principles? You speak evil of you know not what. For that Fifth-Monarchy principle, as you call it, is of such a latitude as takes in all Saints, all such as are sanctified in Christ Jesus, without respect of what form or judgment he is. But "*Judicium sit secundum vim intellectualis luminis.*" (*He was interrupted.*)
> CROMWELL: What do you tell us of your Latin?
> ROGERS: Why, my Lord, you are Chancellor of Oxford, and can you not bear that language?

Whoever edited the transcript could not resist the temptation to add for marginal printing his own remark, "An Ignoramus ... " Indeed, the cut and thrust of the colloquy comes with such speed and dramatic byplay that one is forcibly reminded how little the style of political dialectics must have changed over the centuries; and, more poignantly, one is impressed with what intrepid élan and bravura a few political prisoners in every age have dared to hurl their peremptory challenge at the highest authorities.

At one turbulent point in the debate, the Fifth Monarchists came as close to a confession of some ambivalent revolutionary commitment as they ever had the clarity, or courage, to do. The issue was first joined

with the angry demand, "Then, my Lord, let us have Liberty of Conscience. Will you not give us so much liberty as the Parliament gave?" In
his usual exculpatory manner of answering a question with a question,
Cromwell countered: "I tell you there was never such Liberty of Conscience, no, never such liberty since the days of Antichrist as is now—for
may not men preach and pray what they will? and have not men their
liberty of all opinions?"[13] (Our marginalist added drily, "no wonder the
Prisons are so full of precious saints.")

This could not but lead to the explosive problem of the limits of freedom and the rights of resistance. For, according to Rogers, if absolute
power issued in slavery, then "it was no resisting of magistracy to side
with just principles ... " Cromwell evidently exploded. "And who?
Hear me: who?—who, I say, hath broken that? Where is an arbitrary or
absolute power? (nay, hear me): where is such a power?" Rogers's reply
was pointed and specific enough.

> Is not the Long-sword such? By what law or power are we put into
> prison, my brother *Feake* above these twelve months, I above
> twenty-eight weeks, and several others of our brethren, and we
> know not for what to this day? which I say again is worse, yea worse
> than the Roman law. And is not this Arbitrary? And is not your
> power with the armies Absolute, to break up Parliaments and do
> what you will? But, if you please, let me instance in others. (But they
> would not suffer him.)

The interruption came from an army officer in the chamber (presumably
Lieutenant Colonel Worsley, of Cromwell's own regiment): "but I pray
by what rule do you resist Powers set up of God?" It was too late in the
day, indeed too late in the century, for such threadbare theology. "Sir,
you are mistaken," Rogers replied, "we do not resist such as are set up
of God, but we resist sin in all men." Cromwell's colonel was to be
pressed even harder by another intervention:

> That gentleman asked by what rule we resist Powers. We desire,
> then, to be satisfied by what rule you resisted the King, and warred
> against him and his adherents, and destroyed the Government be-
> fore, seeing they were accounted too a lawful authority.

Cromwell insisted on replying himself; it was conventional, lame, and
almost irrelevant. The King's absolute power; the people's grievances;
the defensive war—yes, but does not that which begins in justified
rebellion end in permanent revolution? As the day follows the night, as
the moon orbits the earth, new generations of men come to renew old
and good causes. Rogers was quick to seize the opportunity for a magniloquent sermon, a flight of political rhetoric which carried him further
than he had yet been prepared to go.

Yea, my Lord ... our controversy is decided, and this case is plain on our side, and seems so now more than ever; for do not the poor people of God feel a Prerogative Interest now Up? As the old Non-conformists, or the good old Puritans were persecuted, imprisoned, reproached, and denied protection from men, and therefore were forced to fly to God by faith and prayer and tears day and night, not ceasing till the Vial of Wrath was poured out upon the heads of the King and his Prelates; so I say the new Non-conformists are abused, disowned, and denied protection, persecuted, imprisoned, banished, and forced day and night (yea thousands of them in city and country) to their faith, tears, prayers, and appeals which are the "Bombarda Christianorum," and will prevail, as sure as God is in Heaven, to bring down the next hot, scorching Vial of His Wrath upon these new enemies and Persecutors....

Now, my Lord, let the loud cries of the blood, shed against these things you have set up, be heard, and make restitution of that blood, those lives, tears, bowels, faith, prayer, limbs, and skulls of us and our relations left in the fields and laid out against this kind of Government, whether in Civil or Ecclesiastical; or else let us have what they were laid out for; otherwise we must and will, with the Lord's help, side with those just principles that have been so sealed to and owned by the Lord. And this will be a most apparent defensive war as ever was in the world.

He was, he concluded, ready for the call to side with just principles, "whether it be '*praedicando, precando,* or *proeliando,*' by preaching, praying, or fighting." There was an astonished question from one of Cromwell's men: "Said you not '*proeliando*'?" Rogers did not hesitate; he affirmed it. "For the case," he said, "was never so clear as now it is, in the state of the controversy."

It was clearer and more fateful than he knew. The turn of the case not only sealed the doom of the Fifth Monarchists; in the long historical perspective, a premature revolutionary commitment served to end forever the fiery prospects of the apocalypse in England. For a brief historic moment, the millenarians were in high and irresistible gear. There was no holding them back. What could prevail against the triumph of the Final Overturning? An unshakable confidence, half zealotry and half dogmatics, prefigured all the supreme moral contempt which men of ideology would for centuries be able to muster against men of power.

"Your condition is very desperate," Rogers had told Cromwell, "for the next Vial which is to be poured out is the scorching hot one.... And look to it, it is like to fall heavy upon your heads and those that are about you." And again,

ROGERS: For the controversy is not now between man and man,

one Government of the world and another Government of the world, or King and People, but it is now between Christ and you, my Lord, Christ's Government and yours; and which of these two are the higher Powers for us to side with and be obedient unto, judge ye.... For I beseech you, my Lord, to consider how near it is to the end of the Beast's dominion, the 42 months, and what time of day it is with us now. [*But* Mr. Ro. *was interrupted.*]

CROMWELL: Talk not of that, for I must tell you plainly they are things I understand not.

And finally, as "the Great Man" was going out, scoffing at the liberty they would fight for, he was yet again reminded that he must be judged, for the Day was near. The swords that were now drawn against them would be "cut in pieces." Doomsday was upon him; couldn't the Lord Protector sense it? This was too metaphysical and quite beyond him. And they had laughed.

4. Rebellion in Permanence

Cromwell's disquieted concern was for the precarious stability of a new and not quite legitimate regime which had gone through the period of "turnings and tossings" but had not yet had time for "healing and settling." As he told Parliament in 1654, there were "many honest people, whose hearts are sincere, and the evil that hath deceived them is the mistaken notion of the Fifth Monarchy." He conceded that it was "a thing pretending more spirituality than anything else ... " But he could not overlook the grave challenge to state power implicit in their presumption that "they are the only men to rule kingdoms, govern nations, and give laws to people; to determine of property and liberty, and everything else."

How long could one risk tolerating the intolerable? "If these were but notions," Cromwell explains, "if I say they were but notions, they were to be let alone. Notions will hurt none but them that have them. But when they come to such practices ... this is worthy every magistrate's consideration, especially where every stone is turned to bring confusion." How clear and present, then, was the danger? Cromwell was able to offer Parliament only an alarming picture of the hurly-burly:

> ... the nation rent and torn in spirit and principle from one end to another after this sort of manner I have now told you,—family against family, husband against wife, parents against children, and nothing in the hearts of men but overturning, overturning, overturning, a Scripture very much abused and applied to justify unpeaceable practices by all men of discontented spirits ...

From Ireland, too, where his son had been sent to investigate the opposition to the Protectorate, the reports were dispiriting:

> I heare of some strange passages of your Anabaptists of Dublin to the greife and offence of lord Henry Cromwell.... There is a cer-, taine generation amongst us are of a muddie and disturbed temper; and if they cannot get into government and greatnesse, as the Hebrews did into Canaan through Jordan, they will ... attempt it by the way of Munster. Captain Vernon (the church's emissary) has ben abroade.... Confident I am, that somewhat is in agitation and secretly managed, which speakes it the more dangerous and to be reguarded.... What their consultations have ben is yet darke: however it concernes you to have a special care.... Remember Leyden. Though the same principle doe not allwaies produce the very same effect in circumstance, yet give it time, and but a conniving encouragement, and in substance it will.[14]

Two years after his first alarm, Cromwell could almost speak of all this in the past tense: "how the Fifth-Monarchy men and others did endeavour to roll us into blood ... " The first round with the assassins had been won: "for they must cut throats beyond human consideration before they had been able to effect their design." But now there were apparent regroupings:[15] the Levellers with the Commonwealth men, the Baptists with the Fifth Monarchists, and always the hidden Cavalier (and Papist) hand fomenting new discontentments. He enjoined Parliament "to see and discern that which is obvious," namely, that "we shall sink and the house will fall about our ears upon such sordid attempts as these are."

What the triumphant rebel had to deal with was the spirit of rebellion in permanence. Every revolution produces a faction which cries out for its further and even continuous extension: a truer and deeper fulfilment always awaits. For some, what was happening was mere prelude, and the grand climax was yet to come (and very soon); for others, there was a suspicion of a diversion or an obstruction in the way of the otherwise irresistible path of human events. Men in the provinces tended to be a shade naïve, and radical petitioners from Kent and Devon felt confident that "the day of the accomplishment of the Promises ... is dawned." Yet the Blackfriar preachers in London, closer to the realities of the established Cromwellian power, were worried about the "obstructors of Reformation" and referred to the moderate members of Parliament as "unsainted" and indeed as "condemned into the Fourth Monarchy." John Rogers, keen-eyed revolutionary tactician that he was, offered the necessary explanation of the difference between making mere reforms and establishing the final order of things.

It is not enough to change some of these *Lawes*, and so to *reforme* them (as is intended by most of you).... O no: that will be to poore *purpose*, and it is not *your worke* now, which is to provide for the *Fifth* [Monarchy] ... by bringing in the *Lawes* of God given by Moses for *Re-publique Lawes.*[16]

Rogers and his friends were all evidently united in the hope that the struggle would go on, that the revolution would take yet another, more purposeful turn.

As one of John Milton's political critics wrote (somewhat unjustly so far as the actual politics of Cromwell's Secretary was concerned),

a Commonwealth is like a great Top, that must be kept up by being whipped round, and held in perpetual Circulation, for if you discontinue the Rotation, and suffer the Senate to settle, and stand still, down it falls immediately ...

But how, then, to stop the spin?

Pamphleteer Marchamont Nedham—a friend of Milton's, from whom he had received his weekly editor's license and who was often taken to be the author of Nedham's leading articles—sensed this danger to the "new Establishment" most acutely in the following argument. (It is a striking adumbration of the challenge of permanent revolution some three centuries before the theoretical formulations of the idea by Parvus and Trotsky, not to mention the restless cultural conception of Chairman Mao.)

... it were a thing to be wished, that Popular Consent might alwaies, and at all times, have the sole influence in the Institution of Governments; but when an Establishment is once procured, after the many shakings and rents of civil Divisions, and Contestings for Liberty, as here now in England, doubtless we have the greater reason to value it, being purchased at the price of our bloud, out of the claws of Tyranny; and we conceive it highly concerns us, to put in some pure *Proviso*, to prevent a razing of those Foundations of Freedom that have been but newly laid; especially in such an Age as this, wherein men are very apt to be rooting and striking at Fundamentals, and to be running out of one Form into another.... Which being considered, it was high time, some Power should pass a Decree upon the wavering humours of the People, and say to this Nation, as the Almighty himself said to the unruly Sea: *Here shall be thy Bounds, hitherto shalt thou come, and no further* ...

Unless, he says, "unless we would alwaies be altering and shifting of Settlements, and so live for ever in Distraction." This stabilization of the new establishment of the People's Liberties through, namely, the defense of the rule of law, was "the only course to keep up wandring any more in the maze of our own Contentions ... "[17]

In a similar spirit, but with rather sterner practical consequences, the Lord Protector himself avowed that there was "a generation of men in this nation that cry up nothing but righteousness, and justice, and liberty." For some, with their "poor and low conceits," he had simple contempt. He preferred to think of the notions of the Fifth Monarchy men as "more seraphical."[18] But even their "very seraphical notions," once allied to other forces of subversion, could only "end in blood and confusion." Indeed, the warrant that was issued for the arrest and imprisonment in the Tower of John Rogers and others charged them with "attempting to disaffect and exasperate the hearts and spirits of the people, so that thereby they might bring the nation again into blood."

The best general formula for protection that Cromwell could devise was "doing all things that ought to be done in order to reformation." But it had to be "a true reformation." There was so much that had to be improved. "I would say in my very conscience, and as before Almighty God I speak it, I think your reformation, if it be honest, and thorough, and just, it will be your best security." More specifically, there would be a new program of vigilance on behalf of the public safety, and he called it "a little inspection upon the people." According to the published instructions to the Major Generals who were each to command a Commonwealth district,

> They are to endeavour the suppressing of all Tumults, Insurrections, Rebellion, as also Invasion. . . . They are to see that all Papists are disarmed; they are to make highways and roads safe for travellers. . . . They are to have a strict eye upon the Conservation and Carriage of all Disaffected persons within the several Counties . . . as also that no Horse-races, Cock-fightings, Bear-baitings, Stage-plays, or any unlawful Assemblies be permitted within their Counties. Forasmuch as Treason and Rebellion is usually hatched and contrived against the State upon such occasions, and much Evil and Wickedness committed.

Would this put an end to the troubles which began with *Agitators* and *Reformadoes*?[19] How much faith did the Lord Protector put into his little schemes of political and spiritual repression? "The mind is the man," he had declared in his impressive opening speech to Parliament in September 1656: "If that be kept pure, a man signifies somewhat; if not, I would very fain see what difference there is betwixt him and a beast. He hath only some activity to do some more mischief."

But weren't the saints being beastly, or at least mischievous, when from a dozen pulpits and pamphlets they were shouting at him that the handwriting was on the wall and that it augured the end of "wounds and woe . . . anguish, tribulation . . . sighing, sobbing, weeping, wailing, crying, imprisoning, hanging, murthering . . ."? Things were going too far when "laws are to be abrogated, indeed subverted." When his patience was exhausted, and he sensed that the "pulling down of Babylon" and the "burning of the whore's flesh with fire" had now become signals for the onset of force and insurrection, most of the Fifth Monarchist leaders were hunted down and kept under arrest.

5. The Dustbin of History

The saints remained impenitent. The system of oppression had to be totally overturned, and for that "smiting work" there was no way for a soul to appear except in "a military posture." Cromwell had disdained to convoke a "Jewish Sanhedrin" or Parliament of Saints, and the so-called Barebones Parliament was short-lived. Fifth Monarchist spokesmen were soon reviling the newly proclaimed Lord Protector as the "dissemblingst perjured villaine in the whole world."

The beast would be destroyed with all its horns; the millennium was coming. Scriptural arithmetic calculated the end of the beast's reign some 1,260 years after the death of paganism in A.D. 396. Suffering saints became fighting saints, and their "quiet dreams" gave way to desperate schemes for armed revolt. As Chaplain Sedgwick tried to remind General Fairfax (who had taken the surrender of the King's forces at Oxford in June 1646), "You must remember my sermon to you at Windsor ... Overturn, overturn, overturn; 'tis Scripture still, and that word [Ezek. 21:27] lives in and upon you."

Having adapted texts and revised doctrines in order to prophesy with apocalyptic and strictly mathematical certainty[20] that their rule was imminent, the saints were growing wildly impatient. As Chaplain Erbury wrote, "The best of us fancy a reign of Christ for a thousand years, and the Saints to reign with him." They would try, if in vain (for they were incapable of making allies of the popular forces), to follow Chaplain Dell's preaching that "the power is in you the people: keep it, part not with it." They were convinced of the argument (even if John Lilburne and his Levellers had some political differences with it) put in a sermon by Chaplain Peters: "Yee talk of Laws, Laws; the Kingdom is not to be maintained by Lawes, but by perfect men." And this was clearly enough understood by a hostile pamphleteer who wrote in his *Confusion Confounded* (1654): "the Statute Book (the long experience and caution of our wise ancestors) shall be thrown out of doors, and men shall come into a Senate to consult of Politick Emergencies with Bibles in their hands ... "[21]

What could be worse than this time and this place? "We are under,"

Rogers wrote, "as barbarous a spirit of the Beast as at this day exercised in any part of the world, and as miserable a servitude as among the Turks." Although the provocation was great, he warned "not to stir untimely ... to some rising or action of defence"; he called for unity among Fifth Monarchists and Commonwealth Men "which may easily be obtained, and then, March, for the signs are upon us, and the trumpets sound, Horse, horse, and away!"

Was this the signal to revolt? Not quite.

Yea they pretend plots, and do this lest there should be any rising, when indeed by their insupportable oppressions, persecutions, and provocations, they do all they can to stir us up, whether we will or no, unto it, for the necessary preservation of our lives, liberties, relations, religion, and consciences, from their so monstrous inhumanity and persecution in hypocrisy.

But if not now, when? Rogers himself had been in the "old Butcher's shop and shambles of the Saints," where Wycliffe's chains were still on the walls, where martyrs like Cranmer, Ridley, and Latimer had suffered. He, too, like his brethren, had "passed through prisons, reproaches, tumults, beatings and buffetings often, throwings headlong, banishment and spitting upon, yea spoiling of my goods ... and in plunderings often, and in perils of life, sickness, fevers, storms, cold, snow, and tempests, without bed, without bread, in sore travels and several other trials ... " And he dared (thinking of his jailer, Major Bull) to cite Jeremiah 50:27: "Slay all their Bulls, let them go down to the slaughter." He would even venture "a little further":

From what I foresee and may easily gather, I dare affirm ... That either extraordinary sufferings or extraordinary actings, in either of which we must carry our lives in our hands to offer up, are at the door of England. But the last rather I look for.

Was this only a forecast? Scarcely. "Awake, awake, yea rouse up, O Saints," Rogers called,

and shake yourselves from your prison dust ... for it is high time; yea, the time is now come to start up like Lions (too stout for sufferings as before) ... Appoint the day, appropriate the duty, and to it. Yea, do it with such a shout too as may make the ears of the enemies ring; yea, begin the earthquake, and rend up by the very roots the foundations ... yea, till there be such a trembling, shaking, and consternation, yea a *metathesis*, translation, overturning, and total amotion of them, that the Beast's government may never have a being more in England.... But our Cause cannot miscarry, my friends; it cannot fail us, who are heirs of the promise.

The great transformation would mean also a very special personal release.

> ... for I tell thee through thy cruelty I am set upon a Mount so high, as I see thee and all the Kings of the Earth to boot, as proud as they be ... but like ants about a molehill, which I laugh at when I see them most busy about their nests, which in one crush will be destroyed, kicked down, and dispersed like the dust on the floor ... [22]

The history of revolutions appears to circle around a gaping and omnivorous dustbin.

6. The Great Chain of Human Hope

The good old cause had been betrayed. The Fifth Monarchists were now "thoroughly convinced of the Apostacy, Hypocrisie, Murders and Treason of Oliver Cromwell"; and, when "our principle to the world" was published, it was to establish "a Standard for all ... that hunger after the Truth, that wait for Justice and Righteousnesse ... " In 1657, when we find Rogers in outrage against "the present Wickednesses, Hypocrisies, Blasphemies, Persecutions and Cruelties of the Serpent Power," one diarist referred to the Fifth Monarchy men as "Enthusiasts and desperate Zealots, pretending to set up the Kingdome of Christ with the Sword: to this passe was this age arrvd ... " Another chronicler, fearing a turn to the "fire and sword," confessed that "we daily expect a massacre"; and from Blackfriars a visitor wrote, "I heard one prayer and two sermons; but good God! what cruel, and abominable, and most horrid trumpets of fire, murther and flame." An ironically bitter item in the *Bibliotheca fanatica* warned: "The Saints shall possess the Earth; proving, That it is lawful for the brethren to stab, cut the throats of, or any way make an end of the Wicked of this World, if so be there will therby any profit accrued to themselves." But one report to the government observed more generously, "Men variously impoverished by the long troubles, full of discontents, and tired by long expectation of amendment must needs have great propensions to hearken to those that proclaim times of refreshing—a golden age—at hand."[23]

It was not for long a time for refreshing, nor was the golden age close at hand. Old militants succumbed to despair and worse; new enthusiasts arrived to rejuvenate hope. Rogers himself noted the defections among the saints: "Coldness, Cowardliness, and Carelessness is (almost) *incredible* ... " Perhaps there would be no millennium, or the calculations were far off the mark, or the theater of events would be in another place, possibly Germany. At various crises in the 1650s, the movement seemed on the verge of breakup and disintegration, and it seemed to many only right to change course.

There appeared to be four conventional options. Some found refuge in political purism—and even refused to petition for the release of Feake and other prisoners, for the abolition of tithes, for the disbanding of the army, all on the grounds that a petition implied recognition of the evil governmental establishment. Some others turned in the opposite direction, began to advocate moderation, and even argued that Fifth Monarchists might hold office under the Fourth Monarchy, if they discharged it in a godly manner. Still others turned quietly inward, to the mysticism of the Kingdom Within. A hard core of the movement took the final option of ultra-militant desperation: as one favored Swan Alley text from Deuteronomy 32:42 had it, "I will make mine arrowes drunk with blood ... " Were they still capable of bringing "terrour to them that do evil"? Could they still hold high *"a light amidst a crooked generation"*? Surely the prophetic visions of danger and safety—of *the black panther*, who by stealth could overcome the world, and *the red lion* who had the saving strength of the Tribe of Judah—had remained viable symbols for the imagination of men? Was it still not desirable that "peace and safety, plenty and prosperity should overflow the Land"? Whatever cynics like Thurloe might say about their "great words" and "large promises," was it not a compelling millenarian ideal to look forward to the time when (in Bunyan's phrase) it would be "always summer, always sunshine, always pleasant, green, fruitful, and beautiful"? The death of Oliver Cromwell, and the fall of his son Richard, gave renewed hope to the desperadoes: the new situation *"strengthens me in my former opinion, viz. That the Earth-quake* is begun."[24]

Thomas Venner was the last of these desperate leaders to commit the remnant of the faithful to direct action. He was the angry incorruptible among the saints, undaunted in his conviction that God would be acting through him as revealed in Jeremiah 51:20: "Thou art my battle-axe and weapons of war: for with thee I will break in pieces the nations ... " The first of Thomas Venner's two attempts at insurrection occurred in the year 1657, which one of the Fifth Monarchist pamphleteers (prefaced by Rogers and Feake) had called *The Time of the End*. It was supported mainly by the lower ranks of the movement; apparently General Harrison, Rogers, and others of the leadership withheld their approval, doubting whether the exactly and properly calculated time (two and forty months after the reign of the Beast) had yet come.

Venner, a winecooper who had re-emigrated from Salem in New England, had always had trouble with dissident factions as he tried to give militant leadership to the Fifth Monarchist movement. Marchamont

Nedham attended one of his Blackfriars meetings as a governmental observer (he was then John Milton's leading Cromwellian propagandist), and he recorded this unruly incident after a speech of Vavasor Powell's:

> Thus Mr. Powell having done, one seated at a corner began to speak, and would have gone on to oppose somewhat that [which] had been spoken; which the man pressed, and strained his voice with utmost violence to overcome the out-cries; but after half an hour's tumult, Mr. Cokain getting into the pulpit, they cried down the other.

In a subsequent pamphlet, Nedham went on to attack the principles of those men "captive by a deluded phancie," which "led them violently on to attempt and promote many things, the consequence whereof (however it might not be intended by the generality of them) would have been *A Subverting the Fundamental Laws of the Land* ... " For Nedham, one utopian revolution, realistically conceived and practically executed, was enough. To go on in permanence was only a mad exercise in destructive passion. " ... In truth, their principles led them to a pulling down all, and establishing nothing ... they were running out into meer Anarchy and confusion." So, inevitably, would end "the dreams of an imaginary Paradise."[25]

In Venner's own journal of the day (since deciphered by historians), there is continuous reference to agitated discussion and debate, to "dissenting brethren," and especially to one brother Spencer who was later suspected of betraying the group's insurrectionary plans to the police.

> [Spencer] did stirr up much strife ... it was wonderfull we were not all broken. We begg'd and besought him to leave it; he told us he knew our designe; we told him we much layed the breach of the meeting at his doare; he sayd he thought it was a good worke to breake the meeting.

Venner was not to be deterred, and he dispatched such faithful followers as he had "to view and espie out townes and countrey," to make notes on troop locations and possible places of rendezvous, and to collect all maps "for discovering all bridges, woods, and high wayes ... "

The disagreements mounted as Fifth Monarchists like General Harrison and John Rogers, for some theological and tactical reason (they often came to the same), objected to Venner's plans. As Venner recorded in his journal, " ... and Mr. Rogers had given out to one from whose mouth we had it, i.e. our Sister Hardye, that he would be hanged before he would goe out with this spiritt ... and that if we should goe out, he would submit to the mercy of the adversary before he would follow us ... " If the timing of the rising was not calculated just right, they would be destroyed.

At this time also John Jones did very much revile us behind our backs and did affirme to some of us, that we had not the Spirit of God, and that we shall be blasted, because first the ancient wise Christians are not with us, as Mr. Harrison, Carew, Mr. Rogers; secondly because this time is not come by two months. Mr. Rogers also doth now much reproach us to our friends.

Venner's resolution remained undaunted, and he did resolve to make the following modest start, offered obviously in a spirit of strategic compromise:

> That we appoynt a place of rendezvous, and being there ready appoynted and fitted in order, a number of brethren may be sent forth well horsed and armed to publish and proclaime our Declaration in some great market towne, at and on the markett day, and that done to invite all to stand up for Christ and their owne liberties, and so to dispose and disperse the Declarations among the countrey people, who will carry and spread them abroad, so that it will be as a seed sowne, and see without doing violence to any returne, save in case of opposition.

Some of the brethren found this pretense of a peaceful propagandistic beginning in Epping Forest nothing less than "a deceipt, a lye, a hipocrisy." This time the treason to the cause was not without but within, and Venner's critics denounced him for departing from "our professions and principles." They doubted that he was "qualified for this worke." Venner has obliged us by recording all the objections: " . . . if we went out in that spiritt we did then manifest (Mr. Chapman said) he was confident we should stumble, and that we should serve the common enemy, give them advantage, and bury the cause." There is no more grievous charge in any revolutionary movement than the sin of "objectively" working for the enemy. The defectors demanded that their names be "blotted out" of the membership list, "and so they went off from us."[26]

As it happened, the London authorities were very well informed, Secretary Thurloe having had somehow several hours' notice; and the uprising was frustrated by the capture of the conspirators' "pistols and holsters, powder, shot, and match proportionable . . . " There had only been a small nucleus of armed men on horse and on foot: the plan had been to disarm by surprise isolated regular detachments, to swell their own ranks by welcoming common soldiers from the opposing forces, and to fill the military chest with spoils (to help pay wages and relieve families). All was in readiness: the bundles of manifestos for distribution, the taffeta standard bearing the red lion of the Tribe of Judah (with the words: *"Who shall rouse him up?"*). But it was not to be. They were trapped in their Shoreditch headquarters, "armed, booted, and spurred," and their cache in Swan Alley was confiscated.

Venner had courage enough to try again in 1661. The fiery remnant of the movement would either "bury the cause" (as the pessimists had predicted) or bring it at long last to holy triumph in England and everywhere.

> And when we consider the great opinions of this year, the wonderful effects it is like to produce, the sweet harmony and agreement of the prophecies, the visibility of those things herein foretold to fall in the time of the witnesses death, the great likelihood of the witnesses resurrection, the great New Covenant-promises of the Spirit made to this work, the wonderfull, undeniable signs of the times, and how miraculously we have been cut out, and preserved for this work ... we are mightily awakened and stirred up, and that fire that has been hid under our ashes will break out into flames, and that fountain of the rivers of living waters into streams, as the bubbling springs that searcheth the ground, and finding entrance gusheth out. Our lives, and everything that is dear unto us upon a worldly account, we despise as a mean thing ... untill *Rome* be in ashes, and *Babylon* become a hissing and a curse ... and when we shall in a holy triumph, have led our captivity captive, to sit down under our vines and fig-trees, but to go on to *France, Spain, Germany*, and *Rome*, to destroy the Beast and Whore, to burn her flesh with fire, to throw her down with violence as a mil-stone into the sea ... [27]

This time the final contest took place; and this time Venner's men, as was reported, "fought with an incredible infatuation, as making themselves to believe that one should chase a thousand and no weapon formed against them should prosper." But how far could even the most indestructible faith of a handful of fifty or so saints move the events of the day? This is Pepys's diary entry for 9 January 1661:

> Waked up in the morning about six o'clock, by people running up and down in Mr. Davis's house, talking that the Fanatiques were up in armes in the City. And so I rose and went forth; where in the street I found everybody in armes at the doors. So I returned (though with no good courage at all, but that I might not seem to be afeared), and got my sword and pistol, which, however, I had no powder to charge; and went to the door, where I found Sir R. Ford, and with him I walked up and down as far as the Exchange, and there I left him. In our way, the streets full of train-bands, and great stories. What mischief these rogues have done! And I think near a dozen had been killed this morning on both sides.... The shops shut, and all things in trouble.[28]

Most of the insurgents were trapped between Highgate and Hampstead. Thomas Venner, wounded nineteen times, was captured. They had all fought, as one record of the defeat observes, "with a courage more brutish and develish than was ever seen in men, and if their numbers had been equal to their spirits they would have overturned the city, and the nation, and the world ... "

The leadership of the Fifth Monarchy movement was decimated. Sir Henry Vane and John Carew were executed. Vasavor Powell now thought that "it is a great piece of prudence in an evil time to be silent ... " Christopher Feake went into hiding in Dorking. John Rogers, now thirty-three, fled to Holland; and when he returned he dedicated ("hypocritically", says one historian) a book on medicine to the Earl of Clarendon (who, after all, had predicted to the King that the Fifth Monarchists "like to make madde worke, and will be the first who must begin the worke" of creating a back-lash in favor of a Restoration).[29] In October, Major General Thomas Harrison had been hanged, drawn, and quartered; and now, in January, the heads of Venner and Hodgkin were put on top of poles on London Bridge. When General Harrison was being taken to the gallows at Charing Cross, someone shouted, "And now—where is your good old cause?" He replied, pointing to his breast, "Here it is! And I am going to seal it with my blood."

The seal was set upon a heavenly ideal "here on earth." A devout commitment to "a well-ordered Commonwealth, ruled by the best of men, of sound principles, of known integrity" had called for revolutionary action "to take off all yoaks and oppressions both of a civil and spiritual nature from the necks of the poor people." The audacity may have been premature, but for those who would follow there would always remain (in the titular phrase of the Fifth Monarchy program) *A Door of Hope*.

How could they, the fighting and suffering saints, ever doubt that there would be reward and recognition for their steadfastness? "We in our preachings and writings may to the present age seem audacious men, thus to meddle with dark prophecies, yet the succeeding generations shall bless the Lord for raising up some before their times." The confidence in the future of a meddling prophetic darkness was to prove to be misplaced; but if "their times" were never to come, their audacity was to be an eternal temptation. Even for historians. Of two twentieth-century students of the Fifth Monarchists,[30] one has contended: "The slow pragmatic process of change is more in accordance with the English national temperament than a sudden transformation imposed by force." The other, however, has written: "They held an ideal which for purity and splendour is, when compared with those for which our generation gives its strength, as a Matterhorn among molehills!"

Thunder and lightning ... overturning days ... teetering and tumbling affairs ... blood will have blood ... doomes-day drawing nigh ... the rule of the

*just ... a true reformation ... a flood tide of change ... audacious men and
dark prophecies ... words are actions ... the minds of men ... purge the
nation ... overthrow rotten structures ... the holy destruction of the evil of
oppression and injustice ... the golden age is at hand ... the fire and the
sword.*

For three centuries these accents, with a few historic variations, would
remain the basic elements in the world of the radical temper. They are
the constant links in the great chain of human hope. A modern cycle of
revolution would begin with its saints and would end with its scientists.
But there is a meeting point—and it is, as we shall see again and again,[31]
an emotive as well as a semantic convergence—between the new radical
who would dream of secular solutions in terms of religious forms or
phrases and the old rebel who envisioned an eschatological end to his
this-worldly struggle for the good cause. One man's metaphor was always another man's reality.

8

Perhaps it will be otherwise. Perhaps the
intellectual will lose interest in politics
as soon as he discovers its limitations. Let
us accept joyfully this uncertain promise.
Indifference will not harm us. Men, unfortunately,
have not yet reached the point where they have
no further occasion or motive for killing one
another. If tolerance is born of doubt, let us
teach everyone to doubt all the models and
utopias, to challenge all the prophets of
redemption and the heralds of catastrophe.

  If they alone can abolish fanaticism, let
us pray for the advent of the sceptics.

—Raymond Aron (1953)

The Novelty
of Revolution

1. James Howell and "a New Kind of Metaphysicks"
A Historian's Credo—"Policy Science"—"History is the Great Looking-Glass"—The Unprotected Intellectual—Howell's Arrest—Expedience, and the Art of Self-Censorship—"Worthy Champions of the Utopian Cause"

2. The Rotation of Fortune's Wheel
Circularity and Linear Motion—"A Totall Eclipse of Reason"—Grand Reformers and Fiery Dogmatists—"Pragmaticall" Mischief—"A Change of Masters"

3. Consequences of Poverty and Affluence
The Role of Innovations and Novelties—Philo-Semitism and Anti-Semitism—Dangerous Ideas—Whitehead's Seventh Wave—Hebraical Influences and the "White Jew"—"Tenderness of Conscience"

4. Stereotypes of Political Imagery
Howell's Masaniello, or the Revolutionary as Hero—The Mediterannean Link—Warrior and Saint, Ancient Prophet and Renaissance Virtuoso—Masaniello's Victory in Naples—Stability, Inertia, and Immobilism

5. A King's Theory of Concessions
Strategy of Change, or Diversionary Tactic?—The Illusion of Secret Strength—"Golden Bait"—Shakespeare's "Traitorous Innovator" and

the Shape of "Hurly-Burly Innovation"—The Fatal Either/or : to Concede or Not to Concede

---

6. The Unstable Center
The Polarization of Forces in Conflict—The Excluded Middle—Prometheans and Epimetheans—On Knowing in Advance, or Learning Too Late—Montesquieu on Change and Revolution—Hobbes's Dogma of Changelessness—Compromising the Principle of Compromise—Clarendon's Suggestion—Reform between Reaction and Revolution—Howell and the Fall of "Celestial Man"

---

1. James Howell and "a New Kind of Metaphysicks"

In all catastrophic episodes in history there is a mixed contemporary sense of something old and something new in the tragedy. James Howell—Royalist and admirer of Charles I; Commonwealthsman and admirer of Oliver Cromwell; loyalist and Historiographer Royal to Charles II; and, not least, that master of seventeenth-century English prose who was so admired by Thackeray—is perhaps our most sensitive and interesting witness, in this epoch of the so-called Puritan revolution, to the ambivalence of the historical sense, confounded by events for which the record of the past seems to offer parallels and even a general sense of reassurance but no sure guide through the poignant immediacy of the confusions.

"The European world is all in pieces," Howell wrote: "The World is turned topsey-turvey." Would the "revolution of the time" turn back to its old point of origin, or would it bring "a change of masters"? Could the "worthy champions of the Utopian cause," armed with so much zealous cunning, so much seductive fantasy, and indeed "a new kind of Metaphysics," reverse all the known maxims of history?

Men caught in history as it is happening look to history as it was. For there were, Howell was convinced, lessons of European experience which "have brought *policy* to be a *Science* which consists of certitudes." His own conclusions were, he averred, the result of "research" into the story of mankind, and his counsels were always confirmed "by my researches." The human past was an oracle; and, for all the minor obscurities, the major message was clear and triumphant. The revolution would fail; the counter-revolution was under providential guidance. It was "the common fate of all Rebellions" to end in doubts, dissidence, and disintegration; as for the rebels, in the outcome of their "Utopian plots" they would only "find a Tomb in their own ruines ... "

It was an intellectual confidence that only a worshipful believer in the lessons of the human past could muster. Here is the overmastering historical credo:

> Now, among those sundry advantages which accrue to a Reader of History, one is, that no modern Accident can seem strange to him, much less astonish him. He will leave off wondring at anything, in regard he may remember to have read of the same, or much like the same, that happen'd in former times; therefore he doth not stand staring like a Child at every unusual spectacle, like that simple American, who, the first time he saw a Spaniard on horse-back, thought the Man and the Beast to be but one Creature ...
>
> Now, indeed, not to be an Historian, that is, not to know what foreign Nations and our Forefathers did ... this is still to be a Child who gazeth at everything. Whence may be inferr'd, there is no Knowledge that ripen·eth the Judgment, and puts one out of his non-age, sooner than History ...
>
> Hence may be inferr'd, That History is the great Lookingglass thro' which we may behold with ancestral eyes, not only the various Actions of Ages past, and the odd Accidents that attend time, but also discern the different humours of Men, and feel the pulse of former times.[1]

Certainly the pulse of his own times beats audibly through his writings and the excitements of his literary career. He has been called one of the earliest instances of a man of letters successfully maintaining himself with "the fruits of his pen," and he escaped none of the besetting perils of an unprotected intellectual. In one of his letters Howell described the circumstances of his arrest which (according to an entry in the Commons Journals for 14 November 1642) committed him to the Fleet Prison, "there to remain during the Pleasure of the House."

> I was lately come to London upon some occasions of mine own, and I had been divers times in Westminster-hall, where I convers'd with many Parliament-men of my Acquaintance; but one morning betimes there rush'd into my chamber five armed Men with Swords, Pistols, and Bills, and told me they had a Warrant from the Parliament for me: I desir'd to see their Warrant, they deny'd it: I desir'd to see the date of it, they deny'd it: I desir'd to see my name in the Warrant, they deny'd all. At last one of them pull'd a greasy Paper out of his Pocket, and shew'd me only three or four Names subscrib'd, and no more: So they rush'd presently into my Closet, and seiz'd on all my Papers and Letters, and anything that was Manuscript; and many printed Books they took also, and hurl'd all into a great hair Trunk, which they carry'd away with them ...[2]

The displeasure lasted eight years, although he was able to write much of his best prose in prison and to revise, with much longing for his itinerant days as a student abroad of politics and language, his memorable *Instructions for Forreine Travell* (1642).

> And by these various wandrings true I found,
> Earth is our common Mother, ev'ry ground
> May be one's Countrey: for by birth each Man
> Is in this World a *Cosmopolitan,*
> A free-borne Burgesse . . .[3]

Howell came under the amnesty of 1650 and was released; he remained "under bayle" for seven years more, during which, as he later complained, he was "three times plundered." Yet somehow he came to terms with his political predicament and even paid his respects to the new Establishment. One of his books was dedicated to Parliament and another to Oliver Cromwell. To be sure, not all who changed their color or turned their coats were cynical opportunists; it was a turbulent age, and in the tumult and shouting many a man's opinions were sincerely changed and changed again. One can only wonder about the element of expedient calculation in Howell's career. Once he had dedicated a first collection of his Letters to the King and probably wrote those verses which constituted an epitaph in the *Eikon Basilike* ("Great Charles, thou earthly god, celestial man"); yet now he could speak coolly of the royal martyrdom which cured the country of the "King's evil." One sympathetic biographer was driven to this defense of intellectual makeshift:

> Altogether it is clear that we have not to deal in Howell's case with any Athanasian rigidity of conviction on the politics of his day. Nor need we apply any lofty ethic norm to adjudge of his vacillations. He belonged to the class, so numerous in our days, only just coming into existence in his, whose function in political matters is to express, excite, and simulate conviction, not necessarily to feel it. If we do not too harshly condemn the journalist who votes Radical and writes Tory, we need not waste our denunciations on James Howell for changing his published opinion on politics according to his personal needs or the changes of public opinion around him.[4]

Our own concern here is even less with the moralities of political vacillation than with the light which these agitated movements can shed on the temperament of utopian revolutionaries who, under similar stress, were trying to make their way toward a new rigidity of political conviction.

For, if the essence of the revolutionary disposition turns on a unique attitude toward futurity and pastness, it is inevitable that its fundamentalist vision of both prospect and retrospect should have words, images, and gestures which serve to make up the outward signs of a new orthodoxy of its own. Thus, as the political concept of "revolution" bursts for the first time into the events of the 1650s, a radical like Marchamont Nedham responds to the verbal opportunity with dozens of usages, all positive; whereas a conservative like James Howell, who could almost be said to have coined its ideological usage in English, employs it continuously in terms of a monstrous calamity. But there is, in Howell's case, at least one significant exception. For reasons which we can surmise but never know—they are a compound of personal opportunism and genuine political relief at Cromwell's dissolution of the Long Parliament—Howell dedicated one of his works "to His Highness the Lord Protector," whom he suddenly felt was a "Hercules-like" figure worthy of praise for a "multitude of Mighty achievements." The dedication deserves to be quoted: indeed one might say that the whole checkered political history of the post-Gutenberg intelligentsia could almost be written in terms of dedicatory epistles, acknowledged or unacknowledged.

> There is a memorable saying of Charles Martell in that mighty Revolution in France, when he introduc'd the second race of Kings. That in the poursuit of all his actions he used to say, that He followed not the Ambition of his Heart, so much as the Inspirations of his Soul, and the designs of Providence. This may be applyed to your Highnes in the conduct of your great affairs and admirable successes . . . I rest, in the lowliest posture of obedience,
>   *At your Highnes command*
>
>   J. H.

This was written in 1655; and some five years later, when the fourth edition appeared, the "revolutionary" dedication to Cromwell had disappeared. The missing page of the piece did not escape the attention of his colleagues in the royal camp who had never indulged in this form of useful, untroubled revisionism. Howell, not unsuccessfully, tried to convince them that in all his pieces "there is never a Line, Word, or Syllable therein but breathes out of the spirit of a perfect Cavalier . . . " Yet at least one critic (Roger L'Estrange) had the pertinacious acerbity to note:

> We will allow the Gentleman to be a perfect Cavalier, a perfect Republican (if he pleases), a perfect Protectorian, a perfect Anything, rather than disagree about his Perfection, but I would he had not appealed to his *Pieces* . . .[5]

Not unlike latter-day Kremlinologists with their fine eye for deviations and impurities, Cavalier and Roundhead ideologists sought the telling detail, for they knew how small fundamentalist formalities could deter-

mine personal fates. Sir Roger L'Estrange was horrified at some of the
new royal appointments and could not bear to forgive Howell for what
we today call "making it." But if anybody in this onbreaking age of
revolutionary ideology understood the demands of the printed word, it
was James Howell; he was not the official historian of the realm for
nothing. Pages were cut, pages restored. In 1662, Howell put out a new
English edition of John Selden's *Mare Clausum*. This valuable study of
"The Right and Dominion of the Sea" had been translated by Marchamont Nedham, no unskilled hand himself at the accommodation of old
texts to new regimes. Nedham's "epistle dedicatorie" was "to the Supreme Autorite of the Nation, the Parliament to the Commonwealth of
England." In his own prefatory remarks, Nedham wrote:

> let me have leave here (without Flatterie or Vanitie) to say, though in
> other things I may injure the eminent Author, yet in this he will be a
> Gainer, that his Book is now fallen under a more noble Patronage, in
> the tuition of such heroick Patriots, who, observing the errors and
> defects of former Rulers, are resolved to see our Sea-Territorie as
> bravely maintained by the Sword as it is by his Learned Pen. It is a
> gallant sight to see the *Sword* and *Pen* in victorious Equipage to-
> gether ... Men are never raised to so high a pitch of action as when
> they are persuaded that they engage in a righteous cause.

Howell put an end to all that, and (in his edition of 1662) restored the
true royal tradition of "the Imperialist." Nothing was changed in the
translation, only "what treasonable Comments and false glosses there
were" in the editing. Nedham had been guilty of "impudent impiety" in
giving himself "the license to foist [it] in the name of a Commonwealth,
instead of the Kings of England (besides the suppression of the Epistle
Dedicatory to his Majesty now restored as the Ornament of this
Work) ... " Selden's book (first published in 1635) now reemerged in
the proper spirit—"To the Most Serene and Mighty Prince Charles, by
the Grace of God, King of Great Britain, France, and Ireland, Defender
of the Faith ... "[6] Here was, following the spirit of the age, a little
revolution of its own, in the pristine and perhaps truest meaning of the
word, as Howell himself had approved it in one of his dictionaries:[7] "a
full compassing ... turning back to its place ... the accomplishment of
a circular course." We are only a turn away from the imminent "Glorious Revolution," and the final round.

2. The Rotation of Fortune's Wheel

If the troubles of the time were old and familiar, nothing could be more
reassuring than the traditional philosophy of history with its simple,

powerful images of celestial order and the inescapable wheel of fortune. Howell had pondered the story of rebellions and "odd Insurrections," the "popular puffs ... of the pesants and mechanicks," the uprisings of Jack Straw, Wat Tyler, Jack Cade, even the French *Jacquerie*, and he remained persuaded that "there is a periodical fate hangs over all Kingdoms after such a revolution of time and rotation of furtune's wheele ... " There was a sermon in every stereotype. "For out of this fatal black Cloud which now ore-sets this poor Island," Howell wrote, "there will break a glorious Sunshine of peace and Happiness ... " Again, "to put a period to all these fearful confusions is to put the great Masterwheel in order, and in its due place again ... " The revolution was inevitable. The enemy—and he had an unusual respect for the "worthy Champions of the Utopian cause"—could not but go under.

> Let them beat their brains, scrue up their witts, and put all the policy they have upon the tenderhooks as farre as possibly they can, yet they will never be able to establish a durable standing Government otherwise. They do but dance in a circle all this while, for the Government will turn at last to the same point it was before, *viz.* to *Monarchy*, and this King will be restored ...

This was the true revolution of time, the balancing of the wheel, the full circle of restoration. "This must be your course," he advised his friends, "by a gentle retrogradation to come into the King's high road again ... " Success would crown their politics and their patience, for although Britain "had four or five Revolutions and changes of Masters" the circular course had never failed.[8]

If, however, the troubles were new and different, then all manner of startling and unprecedented things might become historically conceivable: a linear motion forward rather than an orderly stable circularity, even a revolution of progression instead of a revolution of retrogradation. There are important signs in Howell of puzzlement, of uncertainty, of a sense of the deeper incoherence of the epoch. "But it seems God Almighty hath a quarrel of late years with all earthly Potentats," Howell wrote, on the eve of those outbreaks of a more fundamental radicalism which (in 1648, as in 1848) was to upset half of Europe: "there never happen'd such strange shocks and revolutions ... " What was happening so to turn the world "topsey-turvey" and leave the European scene "all in pieces"? Why were men now "transported by Eccentric motions" and "roving at random to treat of universals"? How did "a new kind of Metaphysicks" come to play such an overturning role?

One detects in Howell traces of both confusion and pessimism. He resented "the calamities of the time" and, with a grimness which Hobbes would have appreciated, registered the onset of what he called "pure Lycanthropy," a wolfish disposition among his countrymen to tear one another apart. "If ever the old saying was verify'd," he wailed, "it is now"—*Homo homini lupus*.

> They err who write, no Wolves in England range,
> Here Men are all turn'd Wolves; O monstrous change!

Howell has one of his foreign observers say this in a general indictment of the designs of the "Grand Reformers":

> I am afraid the English have seen their best dayes; for I find a general kind of infatuation, a totall Eclipse of reason amongst most of them; and commonly a generall infatuation precedes the perdition of a people.[9]

What, then, were the sources of the infatuation and the ferocity, and where had the metaphysics come from, and why had traditional order given way to eccentricity and randomness, and how could one be sure that *your* revolution would not become *their* revolution?

"A strange race of people," Howell tried to argue, had sprung up amongst them, and a little theology went a long way toward explaining the calamity. They were "fiery Dogmatists," and the badges of their nature were "black irreconcilable malice and desire of revenge." They claimed to be infallible oracles, "as if these Zealots were above the common condition of mankind to whom errour is as hereditary as any other infirmity." They were the spokesmen for "this Monster of Reformation (which is like an infernal Spirit clad in white, and hath a cloven head as well as feet) . . . " Howell had come to fear, hate, and despise them, but his contempt was occasionally tempered by a qualification and even a perverse note of admiration.[10]

> True it is, there is a kind of *zeal* that burns in them (and I could wish there were so much piety) but this *zeal* burns with too much violence and presumption, which is no good symptom of *spirituall* health, it being a rule, that as the natural heat, so the spirituall should be moderate, else it commonly turns to a frenzy, and that is the thing which causeth such a giddinesse and distraction in their braines. This (proceeding from the suggestions of an ill spirit) puffs them up with so much spirituall pride for the Devill is so cunning a Wrastler, that he oftentimes lifts men up to give them the greater fall . . .

Curious, that such a black, white, giddy, frenzied, and distracted pack should have proved so formidable in the field and the forum. Howell's researches, if not his policy science, led him to concede another point:

> It may be said that *Mischief* in one particular hath something of *Vertue* in it, which is, That the Contrivers and Instruments thereof are still

stirring and watchful. They are commonly more pragmaticall and fuller of Devices than those sober-minded men, who while they go on still in the plaine road of *Reason*, having the King and knowne Laws to justifie and protect them, hold themselfs secure enough, and so think no hurt ... The Members of Westminster were men of the first gang, for their Mischievous braines were always at work how to compasse their ends.[11]

Here, then, was a practical purposefulness which helped to equalize the confrontation between the insurgent party of the "first gang" and the established party of the second gang. Their proud self-confidence made the zealots an awesome opposition, for "they make it nothing to interpret every tittle of the Apocalypse ... They think they are of the Cabinet-Council of God, and not only know his Attributes but his Essence ... "[12] Neither the religious nor the secular government had remained safe. They had brought the Church to the bar, and (more than that, and this was decisive) went so far as to "prie into the *Arcana Imperii*." They had challenged both pillars of the Establishment and, with the strength of the Old Testament giant, had brought both down.

A revolution of time had come and there had been a change of masters. Not only had new men taken over the "intern Counsell of State," but these worthy champions of the utopian cause were now also the "Divines" who, "according to the Etymologie of the word, use to be still conversant in the exercise of speculation of holy and heavenly things." Both heavenly and earthly things were in other hands now.

3. Consequences of Poverty and Affluence

Howell understood that calamitous causes went deeper than even the most dramatic differences of temper and personality. He comprehended the role of social distress as a factor in political revolt, but the factor of social well-being seemed almost too paradoxical. How could both general poverty and general affluence produce revolutionary turns? Thinking of Naples and its "pernicious popular Rebellion," with its "civil combustions" raging "in lesse than the revolution of a year" (he knew the tale so well from his work on Giraffi's manuscripts about Masaniello), Howell pointed to "a Fate that hangs over most rich popular places that swim in luxe and plenty." This was the ancient social war of classes and masses, but it was evidently too conventional a pattern to explain something so unique as his own national tragedy in his very own time.

... this Island was reputed few years since to have bin in the completest condition of happiness of any part on earth, insomuch that she was repin'd at for her prosperity and peace by all her neighbours who were plung'd in war round about her, but now she is fallen into as deep a gulf of misery and servitude as she was in a height of felicity & freedom before. Touching the ground of this change, I cannot impute it to any other then to a surfet of happiness; *now, there is no surfet so dangerous as that of happiness* ... There is a monstrous kind of wild liberty here that ever was upon earth.

Scarcely a viable theory of social change—but, considering that this is probably the first exploration of the social psychology of "revolution," it is surely worth noting both theses which link misery with insurrection as well as happiness with rebellion. Revolution is thus associated with an explosive relationship between affluence and poverty wherein the fight for material justice can alternate with the flight from felicity or from freedom as a prime mover of turbulent men.

Perhaps it was Howell's cosmopolitan penchant for the paradoxes of national character which led him on to contrast English, French, and Italian movements of social rebellion. In a cautionary sketch of France, Howell once wrote:

I never saw so many poor people in my life; I encountered a Pesan, and asked him what the reason was, that there should be so much *poverty* in a Country where there was so much *plenty*. Sir, they keep the Commonalty poor in pure policy here, for being a people, as the world observes us to be, that are more humerous than others, and that love variety and change, if we were suffered to be pamper'd with wealth, we would ever and anon rise up in tumults, and so this Kingdom should never be quiet, but subject to intestine broils ...

The Italian passion derived from poverty; the French tumult from a fancy for variety and change; and the British unrest was a species of perverse petulance.

Overseas irony gave way to local bitterness in this vignette of the English scene in which Howell refers to

the discrepant and wavering fancies of mens braines, specially that of the common people, who (if not restrained) are subject to so many crochets and chymeras, with extravagant wanton desires, and gaping after innovations. Insulary peeple are observed to be more transported with this instability then those of the Continent, and the Inhabitants of this Ile more then others, being a well-fed spriteful peeple; In so much, that it is grown a Proverb abroad, that *The Englishman doth not know when he is well.*

Howell's emphasis on innovations and novelties as both material and psychic factors in revolutionary enthusiasm was to be echoed two centuries later by Tocqueville; and, like the French observer who studied in

depth the institutional factors which made for the collapse of the *ancien
régime* and who still returned to his obsession with "the first of a new
race of men" (namely, "revolutionaries of a hitherto unknown
breed ... who balked at no innovation"), so too was Howell impressed
by the revolutionary mentality and its qualities of apocalyptic devotion
and radical discipline.

In one of his London letters, Howell reports of a preacher in Fleet
Street "who spoke of nothing but of the fire and flames of Hell ... his
mouth methought did fume with the Lake of Brimstone, with the infernal Torments and the thundrings of the Law—he had also hot and fiery
incitements to War, and to swim in blood for the Cause." This is, perhaps, only the conventional *argumentum ad hominem* of a polemicist in
combat; yet he sensed the strength of character behind the fire and the
blood. In another place he was shrewd and fair enough to explain:

> you know there is nothing so agreeable to the nature of man as
> *novelty*; and in the conduct of humane affairs, it is always seen that
> when any new design or faction is afoot, the Projectors are com-
> monly more pragmaticall and sedulous upon the world; they lie cen-
> tinell to watch all advantages, the Sand of their brains is always run-
> ning. This hath caused this upstart Faction, to stick still close to-
> gether, and continue marvellously constant to their ends; they have
> bin used to tyre and out-fast, to weary and out-watch the moderate
> and well-minded Gentlemen; sometimes till after midnight by clancu-
> lar and nocturnall sittings.

And when he thought long and hard about "the two Sectaries which
sway most," namely, the Presbyterians and the Independents, he became convinced that "the Presbyterian is a spawn of the Puritan and the
Independent a spawn of the Presbyterian." More than that:
" ... there's but one hop 'twixt the first and a Jew, and but half a hop
'twixt the other and an Infidell."

> ... and one of the fruits of this blessed Parlement, and of these two
> Sectaries is, that they have made more Jewes and Atheists then I
> think there is in all Europe besides ... these two Sectaries, I mean
> the Presbyterian and Independent who were the fire-brands that put
> this poor Island first in a flame ... [13]

This Jewish element in the ideology of European political conflict is a
dark and recurring note throughout the whole history of utopia and
revolution; and it cannot be overlooked here, although in this indirect
form it has only a very limited affinity to the modern versions of anti-
Semitism.[14] Indeed, the matter needs at times to be considered out of
the miserable context of sinister prejudice and human pain. For my own

part, I find it one of the more regaling curiosities of utopian literature that it should have been a wise and learned Jewish "Merchant of Bensalem" who supplied Francis Bacon with so much of his information about New Atlantis.[15] Joabin of Bensalem was evidently a member of New Atlantis's happily assimilated Jewry, for there was in him (we are told) no "secret inbred rancour against the people amongst whom they live." Still, he seems—even in New Atlantis!—to be full of what Bacon refers to as "Jewish dreams," which suggests that there are utopians even in Utopia, dreamers within the dream. So history does not end: there is still something to come. The Wandering Jew is, in this sense, the permanent revolutionary.

A philosophical reading of ancient traditions reinforces this. Reflecting with undisguised pleasure on the nature of the Judeo-Greek tradition, Alfred North Whitehead has observed:[16] "Between them, the Hebrews and the Greeks provided a program for discontent. But the value of their discontent lies in the hope which never deserted their glimpse of perfection." A general idea, Whitehead goes on to say,

> is always a danger to the existing order. The whole bundle of its conceivable special embodiments in various usages of society constitutes a program of reform. At any moment the smouldering unhappiness of mankind may seize on some such program and initiate a period of rapid change guided by the light of its doctrines.

Again:

> a great idea in the background of dim consciousness is like a phantom ocean beating upon the shores of human life in successive waves of specialization. A whole succession of such waves are as dreams slowly doing their work of sapping the base of some cliff of habit; but the seventh wave is a revolution ...

Thus, all "dreams of an unrealized world" must spread "the infection of an uneasy spirit ... "

To be overwhelmed by the seventh wave is, for some, to drown in oceanic despair. Clarendon records an incident in which the King, passing through London in January 1642, was humiliated by the popular antagonism, expressed in one instance by the rude chant *"Privilege of Parliament, Privilege of Parliament!"* and in another by an especially intemperate fellow pressing very close to the royal coach crying *"To your Tents, O Israel."* It was, of course, a battle cry taken from 1 Kings 12:16 and from the title of one of the more seditious pamphlets of the day. What might the King have thought of these democratic and Hebraical challenges from the smoldering folk? Clarendon only notes that "the King, though much mortified continued his resolution, taking little notice of the distempers ... "[17]

The conflict of views between Puritanism and Royalism extended, for a complex variety of reasons, deep into the contemporary attitude toward the Jews. Philo-Semitism was a natural by-product of the enthusiasm with which the Puritan generation returned to the old books of the Bible for inspired guidance. As early as 1614, one Baptist writer deemed it logical that toleration be extended even to the Jews; others looked with sympathy on the formal movement for Jewish readmission to England, since it could only facilitate their conversion and thus hasten the high climax of the Christian eschatological promise. For some Jews, too, there was an element of messianic necessity in the return to England, for then the prophesied universal dispersion would be complete and the final deliverance could begin; it was a factor which impressed Menasseh ben Israel in his eagerness to open negotiations with Cromwell.

Conversely, the anti-Puritan opposition was marked by a suspicion and even hatred of the Jews. "And touching Judaism," as James Howell wrote from London to a friend in Amsterdam, "some corners of our City smell as rank of it as yours doth there." Royalist propagandists put it about that the City of London might be sold to the Jews, that there had been offers to purchase St. Paul's for a synagogue, etc. Nevertheless, it was (ironically enough) Charles II who finally issued in 1664 written instructions which authorized the residence of Jews in England. It was a practical arrangement, magnificently humdrum. By that time, exotic considerations of ideology and theology had become remote.[18]

Yet, if power sometimes wearies of the burden of passionate abstractions, intellectuals remain indefatigable. There was, in Howell's view, a Jewish element in the distemper of the uneasy radical spirit. It was, under the circumstances, more of a symbolic suspicion than a literal one; it is unlikely that he had ever met a Jew; this was only a subject which he had researched: "the present condition of the Jews, once an Elect People, but now grown contemptible, and strangely squandered up and down the World ... " Yet he also found a familiar property in them; they were "light and giddy-headed"; and this he judged as "much symbolising in spirit with our Apocalyptical Zealots and fiery interpreters of Daniel and other Prophets ... "[19] Indeed, when he thought of those irrefragable zealots who were "the causes of all civil commotions and distempers in State," who "call every Crotchet of the brain, *tenderness of conscience*," and who believe that "they are the only Elect whose souls work according to the motion of the Spirit, that they are the true Children of promise, whose faces alone look towards Heaven," then he concluded that "they symbolise with the Jew." Again, he writes that "they are nearest to the nature of the Jew as any people upon earth"; and, finally, when from Fleet prison he sent his *Sober and Seasonable Memorandum* (1644) to the Earl of Pembroke warning him against the adviser "who hath infused such pernicious principles into you," he referred to him as "the *White Jew*."[20]

4. Stereotypes of Political Imagery

Such easy and colorful (or, from another point of view, dismal and invidious) animadversions on the hidden sources of revolutionary power served only to blur a consistent view of the true nature of the new ideological phenomenon. When Howell contemplated the stormy Scottish fanaticism from that "Northern Nation that brought cataracts of mischiefs upon us," he quoted a dour couplet:

> Out of the North,
> All ill comes forth.

Evidently, it was less painful to believe that the whole time of troubles was a simple matter of eccentric religiosity or of geographical latitude. But the strange revolutionaries were new men seizing at power in the center, not figures from the periphery or antique protagonists from other dramas. The beginnings of a new kind of revolution were being played out on the stage of the century, and Howell's importance for us is that he knew the name of the game even if its strange new rules confused him. Revolutionary man was emerging, and from time to time Howell caught a glimpse of his shadow and substance.

"Now in this prodigious Revolution," Howell writes in his preface to a history of the Kingdom of Naples which paid pointed attention to Masaniello's great uprising,[21] "there were many things of extraordinary remark that are considerable ... " He noted "the heat of the Air" and "the sulphurous quality and heat" of the Italian soil which caused "Incendiums and Earthquakes," and he went on to correlate the geology with the politics. "Indeed the Napolitan according to the quality of the Soyl," he supposed, "is of a fiery boyling Nature, which makes the Spaniard ride him with a Bitt and a Martingall; he hath so many Whirlwinds in his Brain and quicksands in his Breast, as the *French* or any other Nation ... " Hence their "sundry Innovations," and more than that: for "I have not read of any Political Instrument so often out of tune, having had forty popular *Revolutions* in less than four hundred years ... " The most recent of these, and Howell knew it well from his translation of Giraffi's historical narrative, was Masaniello's rebellious explosion against Spanish exploitation and injustice.

Apparently, in the clearer, more distant Italian light, things were seen more sharply; and in the historical account of Masaniello which Howell translated into English he has preserved for us an unforgettable portrait of a revolutionary.[22] It probably was not easy to accept the realization that in the turbulent hurly-burly of a revolution as well as in the traditional excitements of official wars there was (as we well know in the story from Aristonicus to Trotsky and Guevara) a historic opportunity for human achievement, for performances of unusual panache. Here, in a long memorable passage worth rescuing from the archives, is an almost unprecedented recognition of the heroic proportions of the revolutionary personality in its most majestic moments.

> Masaniello, although but young, and of a very low birth, but having the empty gale of popular applause blowing upon him, and of such a huge masse of people as are in Naples, obtain'd the truncheon of generall command over them. But the wonder is greater that so base a creature (I will not say a Fisherman, but a Fishermans boy, nor a complete man, but a youth in manner) should draw after him such swarms of people, and the second day to be attended by the civillest and discrete of men; the third to make himself the absolute Commander o're them, and the charge of Generalissimo, ev'ry one shewing obedience to his commands accordingly: the fourth and fifth day by his sagacious orders, ready dispatches, and opportune expedients; and above all, by his spiritfulness, efficacy and capacity in negotiating businesses of so great importance. He was held to be of such wisdome and counsell, that he rais'd a kind of admiration in all men, and particularly in the mind of the Arch-bishop, who more than any other had occasion to try his capacity and treat with him, and by the rigorous justice from the first day of his reign to the last of his usurped dominion which he exercis'd, as also for his precipitated barbarismes, as we shall touch anon, the ugly horrors and astonishments he struck into the whole City. He had with an unspeakable boldness which seem'd wonderfull to the present, and will seem incredible to the absent, not as a Plebean or some abject fellow, but like a kind of great martiall Commander, having threats in his looks, terrors in his gestures, and revenge in his countenance, subjugated all Naples.

The mutant emergence of the revolutionary as hero—wise and resourceful, fearsome and overwhelming—combines the generic virtues of mythical warrior and blessed saint, of ancient prophet and Renaissance virtuoso.

> This Naples, though having six hundred thousand souls in her, saw herself commanded by a poor abject vile Fisherboy, who rais'd a numerous Army amounting in a few hours to one hundred and fifty thousand men. He made trenches, set sentinells, laid spies, gave signes, chastised the Banditi, condemned the guilty, viewed the

Squadrons, rank'd the Files, comforted the fearfull, confirm'd the
stout, incouraged the bold, promised rewards, threatened the suspected, reproach'd the coward, applauded the valiant, and marvel-
lously incited the minds of men, by many degrees his superiors, to
battell, to burnings, to plunder, to spoile, to blood and to death. The
whole City, yea the Spaniards themselfs stood astonished, that in so
great and so confus'd a multitude of infinite numbers of armed
people, he could proceed so regular in his orders, and that they were
so exactly observed, that there was never seen nor known the
like ... That among such a world of tempting rich goods which
there were burnt up and down, he would not suffer the value of a
pin to be converted to private use.[23]

The end of the story—and it had the kind of unhappy end which could
only have encouraged Howell and his faithful readers—shall be left to
another place.[24]

But for now what must be asked is whether in the sight of so "unparal-
leled" a revolutionary force, let loose to shake the European established
order, any new political insight or principle of statesmanship emerged.
We are here in the earliest stages of the modern formulations of the
strategies of reform and revolution. Did the revolutionaries succeed because the reformists failed? The issue was not quite understood in that
differentiated way; a modern left, right, and center had not yet taken
their fixed ideological places; utopianism and revolutionism were too
new to be seen steadily or whole. Yet Howell tried to grope his way
erratically to the English tactics which might preserve a political establishment, indeed a whole social order, from the onset of mortal danger.

Howell's indictment of the men who would reform everything, who
would (in Milton's phrase) even "reform reformation itself," was the
conventional one, set out in the stereotyped imagery of a limited political vocabulary.

To mend a thing by demolishing it, is as curing a sick body by knocking him in the head ... It was easier far to pull down, then build up;
one may batter to pieces in one houre that which cannot be built in
an age.

They were bad carpenters, incompetent doctors, and even worse sailors.

'Tis true there were a few small leakes sprung in the great vessel of
the State (and what vessel was ever so tite but was subject to leakes?)
but these wise-akers in stopping of one have made a hundred ...

But if there were only "a few small leakes," then surely the new repairs
could be easily attended to; there are even a few simple cures for some

sick bodies. What stood in the way, however, was an absolutist principle of traditionalism which sought stability in inertia and permanent safety in established fixities. No motion or new impetus could be introduced into the system to disturb an ancient immobilism.

> Innovations are of dangerous consequence in all things, specially in a settled well tempered ancient State; therefore there should be great heed taken before any ancient Court of Judicature, erected as a Pillar to support Justice by the wisdom of our Progenitors, be quite put down; for it may shake the whole Frame of Government, and intro- duce a change; and changes in Government are commonly fatall, for seldom comes a better ...

And yet things did move; and when the unforeseen tumblings and shakings proceeded to upset the existing form of things, a hectic attempt was made to introduce some give-and-take into the inflexible frame. Old imagery was revised, and familiar metaphors redeployed. Howell's ad- vice now was "moderation":

> I would have you to keep as neer as you can between the Tropiques and temperate Zones. I would have things reduced to their true Principles, would have things *reformed*, not *ruin'd* ...

The prudent traveler, presumably, could now coolly find his bearings, as the gardener would wisely try different methods.

> I well hoped, that in regard they pretended to *reform* things only, they would not have quite extirpated, but *regulated* only ... to have lopp'd and prun'd, not to have destroyed root and branch of that ancient tree.[25]

To prune and not to uproot—we have met this formula before, and we will meet it again most dramatically in the late Leveller ideology of a chastened Lilburne and Walwyn. The extremes came to touch; coming confusedly from opposite directions, they met for a fleeting moment, lost and desperate, in a moderate middle.

5. A King's Theory of Concessions

But revolutionary events did not quite vouchsafe such privileged insight to the central tragic figure of the epoch.

"I resolved to reform what I should," King Charles wrote in the *Eikon Basilike*, copies of which were already in circulation on the day of his execution in Whitehall (30 January 1649).[26] His sacred duty had been "to preserve," but (as it became posthumously known, with much retro- spective poignancy) at least I looked for such moderate desires of due reformation of what was indeed amiss in church and state as might still preserve the foundation and essentials of government in both, not shake and quite overthrow either of them without any regard to the laws in force ...

These royal concessions were too little and too tragically late; he was not to be the only ill-starred monarch who seized at the prospect of liberalization when events had already outrun the opportunities for expedient compromise. Nor was it, I suspect, that there was here a serious change of mind or heart about the principle of social amelioration. There was, rather, a shrewd and sensitive shift in verbal tactics, and Dr. John Gauden, ghostwriting here for the King,[27] turned with much stylistic élan to that basic semantic strategy of every establishment under radical attack: We are all reformers now. "I had formerly declared to sober and moderate minds," Dr. Gauden has the King say,

> how desirous I was to give all just content when I agreed to so many bills, which had been enough to secure and satisfy all, if some men's hydropic insatiableness had not learned to thirst the more by how much more they drank, whom no fountain of royal bounty was able to overcome, so resolved they seemed either utterly to exhaust it or barbarously to obstruct it ...

Indeed this is the eternal illusion of rulers destroyed by revolutionary extremism: that they had offered enough, and even more than enough.

> No man can be more forward than myself to carry on all due reformations with mature judgment and a good conscience in what things I shall, after impartial advice, be by God's word and right reason convinced to be amiss. I have offered more than ever the fullest, freest and wisest Parliaments did desire.

Where he failed in the actual political crises of the day, whether by default and deviousness or by disastrous policy, he now tried to make good in reminiscence. History was past politics, rewritten. The differences among the embattled factions may have been great, but "I was willing to condescend as far as reason, honour, and conscience would give me leave ... "

> I was willing to condescend so far to the settling of them as might have given fair satisfaction to all men whom faction, covetousness, or superstition had not engaged more than any true zeal, charity, or love of reformation.

It is difficult to tell how much was genuine royal conviction and how much a propagandist's excess. In the shadow of death, the ruler dramatically emerges as a proud reformer, a convinced instrument of glorious change and progress: it is almost too much. "No glory is more to be envied," according to the *Eikon Basilike*, "than that of due reforming either church or state, when deformities are such that the perturbation and novelty are not likely to exceed the benefit of reforming ... " The King adds: "I should be glad to see it done ... " And he confesses that he was "well pleased with this Parliament's first intentions to reform what the indulgence of times and corruption of manners might have depraved ... "

He appeared to be talking hard politics here, but he also seemed to sense the unrealism of it all when he confessed: "I may seem less of a politician to men ... " He was a ruler of almost absolute power, and yet he thought he could find his greatest strength in the secret resources of what he poetically called "the empire of my soul." He was the commander of great state forces, and still he liked to think he could fall back on the argument that "they confess their known weakness as to truth and justice who choose rather to contend by armies than by arguments ... "

For, if it was indeed a debate, then he would not win. He was setting certain finite rules and regulations for the contest, and these would not withstand what he knew to be "the infinite activity of those men." He preferred to make his appeal to the white clarities of reason, argument, and principle: and how should these hold out against the "black arts" which were raising up "the raging of the sea and the madness of the people," "popular inundations" which could (and would) "overbear all the banks of loyalty, modesty, laws, justice, and religion?" Did he really see through, as he proudly claimed, the "odious disguises of levity, schism, heresy, novelty, cruelty and disloyalty"? And how would he finally face up to a crisis of confrontation and polarization? For he had an acute sense of how the struggle of contending forces might "by enormous actions ... widen differences and exasperate all sides to such distances as may make all reconciliation desperate." Very late in the day, he put in a claim for the high central ground of the political battlefield— for "the special notion," as he called it, of "keeping the middle way between the pomp of superstitious tyranny and the meanness of fantastic anarchy." It was a middling posture that failed to convince.

Even within his own terms of power and principle, he appeared to be deeply divided in himself, a division which affected (and was, in turn, affected by) the social conflicts, political divergences, psychological disorientation, and linguistic ambiguities abroad in the land. He no longer could muster a clear and unequivocal view of his own authority and the way in which it should be naturally exercised in the realm. "Force must crown in what reason will not lead." But by this he meant not his own forceful philosophy of divine monarchical leadership, but only the dastardly tactic of "the chief demagogues and patrons of tumults."

But was he quite beyond demagogy himself? He wavered disastrously between points of high principle and pleas for shrewd strategy. If he was no horrid innovator, he was at least (or so he tried to claim) a prudent reformer.

> ... at least, I looked for such moderate desires of due reformation of what was indeed amiss in church and state as might still preserve the foundation and essentials of government in both, not shake and quite overthrow either of them without any regard to the laws in force, the wisdom and piety of former Parliaments, the ancient and universal practice of Christian churches, the rights and privileges of particular men; nor yet anything offered in lieu or in the room of what must be destroyed, which might at once reach the good end of the other's institution and also supply its pretended defects, reform its abuses, and satisfy sober and wise men, not with soft and spe-ious words, pretending zeal and special piety; but with pregnant and solid reasons, both divine and human, which might justify the abruptness and necessity of such vast alterations.

This was intended to be taken as the voice of a national consensus, with only a bemused handful to be reckoned among the forces of dissent. He no longer wondered "at the variety and horrible novelty of some propo-sitions, there being nothing so monstrous which some fancies are not prone to long for ... " This was the evildoing of a small and sordid minority who "kindled and blew up into those horrid flames the sparks of discontent." They had resolved "to destroy, root and branch ... " They were extreme men of a desperate obstinacy, afflicted with "the itch of novelty and the leprosy of disloyalty."

Epigrams of no little psychological insight stud the polemical text of the *Eikon Basilike*.[28]

> ... some kind of zeal counts all meriful moderation luke-warmness; and had rather be cruel than counted cold ...

> What hinders that any sects, schisms, or heresies, if they can get but numbers, strength, and opportunity, may not according to his opin-ion and pattern set up their ways by the like methods of violence?

> And yet such is the inconstancy that attends all minds engaged in violent motion that whom some of them one while earnestly invite to come to their assistance, others of them soon after are weary of and with nauseating cast them out.

> As liars need have good memories, so malicious persons need good inventions, that their calumnies may fit every man's fancy.

To repair, not to ruin: this was the formula which (at least in retrospect) Charles Stuart thought he had offered; he would be a restorer, not an oppressor.

> A little moderation might have prevented great mischiefs ... Discretion without passion might easily reform whatever the rust of times, or indulgence of laws, or corruption of manners have brought upon it.

> Freedom, moderation, impartiality are sure the best tempers of reforming counsels and endeavours; what is acted by factions cannot but offend more than it pleaseth.

He was for moderation, peaceableness, quiet (he disliked especially "the noise of a thorough reformation"). He was against passion, zeal, hot tempers.

> ... good ends cannot justify evil means ... nor will evil beginnings ever bring forth good conclusions.

He knew how serious the coming struggle might be:

> ... no flames of civil dissensions are more dangerous than these which make religious pretensions the grounds of factions.

But, worse than that, "some men thought that the government of this church and state, fixed by so many laws and long customs, would not run into their new molds till they had first melted it in the fire of a civil war ... " Still, he chose to discuss the mounting hatefulness with a certain lofty air, and he did not even deign to mention his antagonists by name (there are no references in the *Eikon Basilike* at all to Pym or Fairfax or Cromwell). They were merely subjected to the standard charge of personal hypocrisy, and to the usual injunction to change their own selves first before experimenting on the institutions of society:

> Public reformers had need first act in private and practice that on their hearts which they purpose to try on others; for deformities within will soon betray the pretenders of public reformations to such private designs as must needs hinder the public good.

It will not do to think of this as only a rhetorical ploy against an opposition of conspicuous idealism; it was certainly also a principle of Charles's own Christian piety. For Charles Stuart surely believed that "our greatest deformities are within," and he would want to include himself among those who would make the effort to become "the severest censurers and first reformers of our own souls." He could bring himself, at times, to be self-critical and almost brutally frank; he candidly went about trying to prove the fallacy of an old maxim which he quoted as: "Better the man perish, though unjustly, than the people be displeased or destroyed." But he did not intend himself to be the martyr to a popular revolution.

Yet he seemed to be obsessed, and not infrequently blinded, by the horrid vision of a great conflagration, the spectacle of a natural catastrophe, the premonition of a feverish and possibly fatal disease.

> What flames of discontent this spark (though I sought by all speedy and possible means to quench it) soon kindled, all the world is witness.

> Those tumults ... were ... like an earthquake, shaking the very foundations of all, than which nothing in the world hath more of horror.

> Nor was this a short fit or two of shaking, as an ague, but a quotidian fever, always increasing to higher inflammations, impatient of any mitigation, restraints, or remission.

> But as it is no strange thing for the sea to rage when strong winds blow upon it, so neither for multitudes to become insolent when they have men of some reputation for parts and piety to set them on.

> For I look upon this now done in England as another act of the same tragedy, which was lately begun in Scotland; the brands of that fire, being ill-quenched, have kindled the like flames here.

The language speaks dramatically for itself. The limited number of familiar images take their turn, again and again: *fire, fever, earthquake, storm.* And these will, in turn again, figure centrally in the imagery of the other camp; for the revolutionaries no less than the counter-revolutionaries were prisoners of the metaphorical imperative.

But where one saw in the dreaded sign of disaster the end of an ideal order, the other saw in it a dark and desperate stroke of great good fortune which would transform destiny itself and fulfill the highest human hopes. So it is that utopian revolutionaries, in their longing and their fury, came to welcome that which the social defenders found appalling. How perverse it must have seemed to some that men's hearts could leap with joy at the prospect of natural catastrophes which in normal responses on land and sea caused men to shudder in mortal fear! This unnatural aspect of the language and imagery of political ideology will continue to occupy us throughout these pages.

Here, only one formula in the debate between the Old and the New must detain us; for its analysis will call attention to a dramatic change in the conception of the politics of innovation, today the hallmark of a progressive modern temper, yet once the dreaded outbreak of the blackest forces.

The demands of the seventeenth-century reformers reeked—at least in the nostrils of the established guardians of the social order—of *novelty*, and of something ever worse, *innovation*. As the King, with a proper traditional horror, pointed out, "for many of them savor very strong of that old leaven of innovations, masked under the name of reformation ... " The distinction is an important one, and it has been embodied in the language of politics from Shakespeare to Burke (who argued precisely that "to innovate is not to reform"). Its horrific implications in the minds of the traditionalists of power and authority derived from the word's early use as a precursor of the word *revolution*: to be an innovator was to be a revolutionary.

This was not without its aspect of deep complication, for, after all, the Latin root simply denoted renewal, alteration, making new. And it was undeniable, as Christian writers rarely failed to point out, that "theology teaches that this world shall either be abolished by annihilation, or be innovated, and, as it were, transfigured ... " This familiar thesis, coming as it did from the pen of Robert Boyle, suggested that not only theology welcomed (in its appropriate, final time) innovation but also that innovative change was the essence of scientific pursuit. Francis Bacon even gave the word an early deviant note of social liberalism when he insisted: "He that will not apply new remedies must expect new evils; for time is the greatest innovator ... "[29] In the context of seventeenth-century politics, however, there is scarcely an overt trace of this inner ambivalence. Writers record the "feare of sedition and innovations," point out that "A desire to innovate all things moveth troublesome men," warn against the dangers of "innovative violence," and argue that "It is the duty of private men to obey, and not to make innovation of states after their own will."[30]

A number of Shakespeare's remarks document this conservative attitude in even richer formulation. There is a reference in *Coriolanus* (3.1.175) to *"a traitorous innovator / a foe to the public weal."* In *Henry IV, Part 1*, the King speaks of the fine-colored "garment of rebellion"

> that may please the eye
> Of fickle changelings and poor discontents,
> Which gape and rub the elbow at the news
> Of hurlyburly innovation;
> And never yet did insurrection want
> Such water-colours to impaint his cause,
> Nor moody beggars starving for a time
> Of pellmell havoc and confusion.

[5.1.74–82]

These lines are again echoed in the passage which Shakespeare presumably added to *The Booke of Sir Thomas More* when he faced the task of underscoring the consequences of "hiddious violence" in the much-censored insurrection scene. The revised Elizabethan text had set the original scene of "dangerous ... troublous ... bloody tymes"; and Shakespeare went on to scribble in (or so the paleographical evidence of the miniscules and majuscules appears to suggest)[31] the following:

> ... and that you sitt as kings in your desyres
> aucthorye quite silent by your brawl
> and you in ruff of your opynions clothd
> what had you gott; Ile tell you, you had taught
> how insolence and strong hand should prevayle
> how ordere should be quelled, and by this patterne
> not one of you should live an aged man
> for other ruffians as their fancies wrought
> with self same hand self reasons and self right
> would shark on you and men like ravenous fishes
> would feed on one another ...
>   ... if you will marke
> you shall perceive howe horrible a shape
> your innovation beares ...

Recoiling, then, from the "horrible shape" of "hurlyburly innovation," from Howell's "novelty of revolution," the King belatedly tried to put the case for readjustment and reform. It would be decisive in any definitive historical evaluation to match his words against the actual happenings of those pell-mell years: once again, how much of the defense was reasonable and how much rationalization? I can only content myself here with something less than ultimate judgment on the mélange of fact and fiction, and confine the analysis to those constituent psychological and semantic elements which make up the framework of every ideological apologia. It is a structure of sentiment and language which, alas, holds together coherently, irrespective of its relationship to factors of truth and sincerity. Historians will always differ about the complicated realities and whether the Civil War and the Puritan revolution were inevitable and justified or not.[32] The patterns of ideological explanation would appear to be of a simpler nature. The true believer in things as they are either goes down to defeat in defiance or, with some courage and much casuistry, revises his principles in order to survive. Charles Stuart understood the dilemma. In one of the most revealing sentences in the *Eikon Basilike*, the King confessed: "It is some skill in play to know when a game is lost; better fairly to go over than to contest in vain." From the point of view of the essential principles of conservatism and liberalism, or of reform and revolution, the King here was "going over." And there is an additional measure of melancholic profundity in the fact that it was a posthumous movement.

So various are all human affairs and so necessitous may the state of princes be that their greatest danger may be in their supposed safety and their safety in their supposed danger.

As it happened, Charles's supposed danger was also his real danger; there was no safety anywhere, surely not in belated exercises in tactical rhetoric; and doubtless he knew this all too bitterly. "Some remedies are worse than the disease and some comforters more miserable than misery itself ... "

In the end (and it was literally the end), neither the King's personal desperation nor Dr. Gauden's literary strategy could prevent the simple essence of traditional power politics from burning through. Charles had known early on how dangerous and incompatible were those dissenting zealots who claimed to speak in the name of the public good and happiness and sought to transform the kingdom into a "new Utopia of Religion and Government." This awareness was closer to the true political illumination of his life: " ... the devil of rebellion doth commonly turn himself into an angel of reformation and the old serpent can pretend new lights ... " All the rest was tactics and casuistry; and there is a touch of personal sadness and spiritual confusion about the final spectacle in which the "necessitous" danger forced a Divine Monarch himself into such a devilish and serpentine pretense of new lights ...

> Let nothing seem little or despicable to you in matters which concern religion and the church's peace, so as to neglect a speedy reforming and effectual suppressing errors and schisms: which seem at first but as a handbreadth, by seditious spirits as by strong winds, are soon made to cover and darken the whole heaven.

Where, then, was the "glory" of reform? Wasn't it all "condescension"? Clearly we are dealing here not with a strategy of change but with a diversionary tactic (and an ineffectual one at that) for the preservation and consolidation of the existing order. In telling support of this, there is Clarendon's frank comment about the King's "concessions": " ... which his late majesty yielded unto with much less cheerfulness than he walked to the scaffold, and upon the promise of many powerful men then in the Parliament that he should not be obliged to accomplish that agreement ... "[33]

The personal politics of royal tragedy in history is always marked by such dissembling conceptions of promises and obligation, coupled with an almost suicidal obliviousness to the contours of unfamiliar and very dangerous terrain. Of an early set of proposals from the parliamentary commissioners, the King had said curtly: "They that principally contrived and penned them had no thought of peace in their hearts, but to make things worse and worse ... " Such in the usual blur of an astigmatic power-holder who is unable or unwilling to make elementary distinctions among the hordes of seditionists he seems himself resisting. Some radical reformers, convinced as they were that things could not become better before they became much worse, were indeed set on a course of destruction; but others, clearly, were practical meliorists who wanted to make things better.

Not to see this was for the monarch an easy, convenient strategem for haughtily ignoring all possibilities for accommodation or compromise. Henry Ireton, a general in Cromwell's command (and Oliver's son-in-law), was astonished at being subjected to "very tart and bitter discourse" when he and his political friends called on the King to discuss another set of proposals.

"You cannot be without me," Charles repeated, again and again, "You will fall to ruin if I do not sustain you." The comment which one of the King's advisers ventured to whisper in the royal ear has the ring of funereal wit about it: "Sir, your Majesty speaks as if you had some secret strength and power that I do not know of, and since your Majesty hath concealed it from me I wish you had concealed it from these men too."

Indulging in an understandable exaggeration of the royal strategical cunning, Ireton soon denounced the King for offering "that glorious golden Bait which the people, wearied with war, are most apt to catch at," for presenting himself as "the Restorer of their beloved Peace, Ease, and Freedom—the Restorer of their Trade and Plenty," and for coming "to make a war against the poor deceived people for that which is really their own cause ... " The tactic, as Ireton sought polemically to unmask it, was "exquisite" (and he certainly saw more fine method in it than was there): "by making use of all interests to set up his own above all—have you not found him at this play all along?"

At any rate, the play had not long to run. Abandoning all efforts to reach a compromise solution with the King, the army leaders concluded that "we can see no further hope of settlement or security that way ... " It was *he* who could not be without *them*, and it was he who fell to ruin, once they decided no longer to sustain him: in Cromwell's final, fatal judgment on the royal person, "he was so great a dissembler and so false a man, that he was not to be trusted ... " John Milton was quite right when in his *Eikonoklastes*, that formidable and relentless polemic against the *Eikon Basilike*, he called attention to that element of double-dealing which hovered in the Royalist mind between ambiguity and hypocrisy.

> He [Charles Stuart] *hoped by his freedom, and their moderation, to prevent misunderstandings.* And wherefore not by their freedom and his moderation? But freedom he thought too high a word for them; and

moderation too mean a word for himself: this was not the way to prevent misunderstandings.[34]

The authority and power of a sacred establishment had been effectively challenged by the insolent forces of utopia and revolution. To reform as quickly, and as little, as possible might conceivably have been to divert. But to resist, holding on to a petulant inflexibility in order to fulfill some haphazard sense of duty, honor, and necessity, was to take on an untenable posture, always in the shadow of an elemental fear that to extend a hand is to endanger a royal crown: to give a finger would be to lose an arm, and more.

6. The Unstable Center

It was as if there were in the high crises of political history a law of the excluded middle, operating inexorably to drive men and events into the extremes.

What is it that so polarizes great forces in conflict? Why do such historic issues get resolved in so drastic a fashion and make all the middling saving efforts of hosts of prudent peacemakers another exercise in futility, another lost cause? It is not only that the forms of power in an ancient regime turn sclerotic; it is also that the ideological atmosphere in which the old establishment attempts its struggle for existence serves to reinforce the vitality of its enemies while debilitating its own. This will be happening so often in the next centuries, crowded with so-called revolutionary situations, that it would be useful for the sake of historical perspective to anticipate the two basic schools of modern thought and their steady patterns of ideological response which will consolidate themselves around certain identifiably fixed points at the left and in the center.

There is a dualism of temperament here which, in a sense, can already be read in the ancient mythological characterizations of the brothers Prometheus and Epimetheus, the one who knew what was to come (for he was the intrepid friend of mortal men and he would liberate all mankind), and the other who always learned too late (it was no accident that he found himself mated with Pandora and her vessel of troubles).[35]

The Prometheans—and we can recognize the profile among Levellers, Jacobins, Bolsheviks: eloquent in victory, defiant in defeat—cannot but believe that the true lessons of world-shaking events become increasingly vivid and urgent, that there is a cumulative interpretive grasp, a final intellectual insight into the nature of the titanic struggle, especially the fated irreconcilability of the conflict, which encourages the taking at long last of certain fundamental decisions.

The Epimetheans—and we know them by their modest silences in victory and their pathos in defeat—slowly come to be persuaded that in protracted human struggle there is a natural onset of unnatural attitudes, a sheer degeneration of viewpoint and behavior from the sanities, decencies, and simple practicalities of ordinary life into the more primitive components of anger and aggression, as an uncontrollably elemental violence begins to dominate the course of events.

In France, the generation which was to witness the Promethean days of the *grande Révolution* knew well that passage in Montesquieu which has often been taken as the epitaph of the Bourbon regime:

> It is a capital maxim, that the manners and customs of a despotic empire ought never to be changed; for nothing would more speedily produce a revolution. The reason is, that in these states there are no laws, that is, none that can be properly called so; there are only manners and customs; and if you overturn these you overturn all.*[36]

This was a fatal either/or: to change is to inaugurate ruin, but not to change at all is to be condemned to wait helplessly for the end. Ideology only deepened the cruel dilemma, for if the Promethean revolutionary holds that the end is inevitable and reforms are either impossible or unavailing, the Epimethean counter-revolutionary is convinced that utter and total immobilism is the essence of his safety and the stability of all things.

In England, the dogma of the inert sovereign absolute was formulated with characteristic extremism by Thomas Hobbes in his *Leviathan* (1651):

> And to descend to particulars, the people are to be taught, first, that they ought not to be in love with any form of government they see in their neighbouring nations, more than with their own, nor, whatsoever present prosperity they behold in nations that are otherwise governed than they, to desire change. For the prosperity of a people ruled by an aristocrat, or democratical assembly, cometh not from aristocracy, nor from democracy, but from the obedience and concord of the subjects: nor do the people flourish in a monarchy because one man has the right to rule them, but because they obey them. Take away in any kind of state, the obedience, and consequently the concord of the people, and they shall not only not flourish, but in short time be dissolved. And they that go about by

---

*"C'est une maxime capitale, qu'il ne faut jamais changer les moeurs et les manières dans l'état despotique; rien ne seroit plus promptement suivi d'une révolution. C'est que dans ces Etats il n'y a point de loix, pour ainsi dire; il n'y a que des moeurs et des manières et si vous renversez cela, vous renversez tout.... "

disobedience, to do no more than reform the commonwealth, shall find they do thereby destroy it; like the foolish daughters of Peleus, in the fable; which desiring to renew the youth of their decrepit father, did by the counsel of Medes, cut him in pieces, and boil him, together with strange herbs, but made not of him a new man. This desire of change is like the breach of the first of God's commandments ...

There were those, among the contemporary readers of Hobbes's *Leviathan*, who thought this tended to reflect the loyalism of the scholarly monarchist who was for many years part of the Stuart court in French exile. There were also those who suspected that it was an opportunistic justification for the aggrandized power of the Lord General, the political price in fact (as Clarendon charged, recalling Hobbes's remark: "I have a mind to go home") for his unmolested return to England. Or did he have two masters in mind when he wrote:

> how great a fault it is, to speak evil of the sovereign representative whether one man, or an assembly of men; or to argue and dispute his power; or any way to use his name irreverently, whereby he may be brought into contempt with his people, and their obedience, in which the safety of the commonwealth consisteth, slackened.

Constitutionalists could not but think him a reactionary apologist for arbitrary, changeless, and decrepit tyranny; yet his abstract theories, so rigorously reasoned and still so full of "Utopian fancy," were considered by orthodox royalists to be a dangerous piece of intellectual subversion.

In times when a social order is in a process of bewildering change, any incursion of innovating ideology, from whichever militant quarter, is taken to be a species of radical incendiarism. One of Hobbes's contemporary readers felt that such artificial theorems of government would only "put all to fire and flame." In a striking epigram that would suit all the ages of utopia and revolution, a seventeenth-century critic wrote: *"New statesmen promise golden mountains."* Old statesmen feared even worse: for what was being upset was not only the social but the cosmic order itself; Hobbes was "positive for Copernicus" and in his views of time and earthly motion "would have the earth itself turned upside down in nature ... " Unmoved and uncompromising, Hobbes ranged himself loftily against all those doubters who objected that there could be no "principles of reason" to support such an adventurous exercise in absolute theory:

> Wherein they argue as ill, as if the savage people of America, should deny there were any grounds, or principles of reason, so to build a house, as to last as long as the materials, because they never yet saw any so well built ... so, long time after men have begun to constitute commonwealths, imperfect and apt to relapse into disorder,

there may principles of reason be found out, by industrious meditation, to make their constitution, excepting by external violence, everlasting.

America? Perhaps it was there that one could find "a fit place" for the
experiment in everlasting political perfection, and his ironical adversary
could not leave off recommending that Hobbes "should have the sole
privilege of setting up his form of government in America, as being
calculated and fitted for that Meridian . . . . And if it prosper there, then
have the liberty to transplant it hither; who knoweth (if there could but
be some means devised to make them understand his language),
whether the Americans might not chuse him for their sovereign?"

For the time being, however, some of Hobbes's less spirited critics
held up to him an alternative of moderate improvements, even if "insensibly and little by little." Flourishing the pragmatical superiority of
the working politician for the political theorist, Clarendon suggested
that Hobbes try to learn a few real things by turning from his "solitary
cogitations" and taking a practical place in Parliament. There he could
learn, slowly, like some mason's apprentice, to build with his hands;
and here we are back again to the language of homely similes. What
could have been more galling for the linguistic philosopher who (not
being above a fiery analogy himself) considered metaphors to be like
"ignes fatui" and had relegated them curtly to the realm of "senseless
and ambiguous words"? "Reasoning upon them," Hobbes said, "is
wandering amongst innumerable absurdities . . . " Perhaps Clarendon
knew what he was doing when he offered him an old trusty of an
architectural metaphor:

> It is a very hard matter for an architect in state and policy, who doth
> despise all precedents, and will not observe any rules of practice, to
> make such a model of government as will be in any degree pleasant
> to the governor or the governed, or secure for either.[37]

In any event, the spirit of Hobbes's principle of authoritarian inflexibility, whomever it tended to serve, could only discourage the frame of
mind in which change and reform would ever be taken to be timely,
practical, or believable. Somewhere in the panic and disarray of the
Stuart circle, among the moves and moods of Clarendon and Hobbes
and even the King himself, that ancient benevolent maxim of "condes-
cent by grace"—by which rulers constantly improved the condition of
their subjects, thus making for prosperity and contentment through
harmonious rearrangements—was scuttled. The one principle which it
was death to compromise was, namely, the principle of compromise.

There is a perennial drama here in the temperamental human conflict over the evaluation of the cues of basic self-interest and personal *amour-propre*, and the timing of prudent conciliation or principled steadfastness; and it will never be played out in any one version deemed to be wise, sound, correct, and supported by the putative maxims of experience or the alleged lessons of the past. Reform between reaction and revolution resides at an inevitably unstable center, at which point—even if it could hold—the tragic pressures of "passionate intensity" from the combined extremes of the best and the worst are inescapable.

In one of the King's final prayers—the lines were actually Sir Philip Sidney's, taken (as Milton wickedly pointed out) from the pagan *Arcadia*—there is the last, vain hope: "Let calamity be the exercise, but not the overthrow, of my virtue. O let not their prevailing power be to my destruction ... " In Howell's royal epitaph, there remained only the grave, pious, mid-revolutionary regret:

> So falls that stately cedar, while it stood
> That was the only glory of the wood.
> Great Charles, thou earthly god, celestial man ...[38]

9

The same theory which serves as a weapon
against error, may sometimes do a disservice
to the cause of truth.

I began to know, during the siege of Vienna,
how greatly I was mistaken in fancying mankind
were quite cured with regard to those chimerical
hopes that are so often grounded on visions. I
met everywhere with people, who spoke of nothing
but ... the truth of which they seemed perfectly
persuaded; and who built so many castles in the
air, that they were to destroy Babylon in an
instant.

The world is too unteachable to profit by
the follies of past ages. Every age behaves as
if it were the first.... The worst is, men do not
profit by what is past; every generation betrays
the same symptoms.

—Pierre Bayle (1697)

The Great
Intelligencers: I

1. A Progressive Mentality

"Dreaming Rabbis"—The Forms of Human Mentality and the Reforms of Men's Affairs—The Two Camps—Illusions of Imminence—"At the Verge, within the Whirle"—The Euphoric Transition—The Prospects of "Great Revolution": "Successful Beginnings, Further Advances"—The Usefulness of Foreign Ideas—"And thus will every generation thrust out the other ... "

2. Three Foreigners: Hartlib, Dury, Comenius

Cosmopolitan European Wanderers—"All countries are now allmost alike ... "—Hartlib's Thirty English Years—Scholars, Strangers, Refugees—Dury's "Peace" Program for Gustavus Adolphus—Pacifying the Intellectual Habits of True Believers—Toward a Cool, Calm Weighing of Arguments—Emergent Watchwords—A New Temper of Neutrality: "An indifferent spectator of the strife of Tongues"—A Triple Alliance (1642)

3. Andreae's German Utopia

The Lost Paradise and Its Restoration—Bacon's Triad—Unifying Theory and Practice—A Shipwreck Motif—The Temperamental Class Struggle—"This very drama may be played again in our own day"

4. Hartlib, "the Great Intelligencer of Europe"

The Dream of Peace, Plenty, and Universal Happiness—Toward Political Conversion—Heavenly-Mindedness and the "As-If" Paradise—

Difficulties in the Calculation of Millennial Salvation—Macaria in One Country and in the World—"Piece-Meale . . . or All at Once"—"The Known Untowardness of the People"—The "Office of Address" as a Model of a Welfare State—Loving the Public Good

---

5. **The Utopian International**
Between Reason and Imagination—Petty v. Descartes on Facts and Fantasy—Natural Propensities: Utopia and Science, Revolution and Social Science—Robert Boyle and the Invisible College: "They take the whole body of mankind for their care"—Exact Intelligence from Utopia—Still No Macaria to be Charged

---

1. A Progressive Mentality

Most revolutions only take place in countries of the mind. They are myths and dreams, plans and powerful hopes, made out of images and ideas, phrases and volatile emotions; and for most of modern history, except for those occasional instances when certain basic elements in science, or industry, or government are overturned, displaced, transformed, they run a mental course quite apart from the precincts of power and real effectiveness in society. They have more to do with the forms of human mentality than with the reforms of men's affairs. They constitute brilliant, excited episodes in the history of each generation as a coterie of enthusiasts exhausts itself between eloquence and invective, sacrifice and suspicion, visceral energy and psychic strain. The true story of the revolutionary mind[1] is itself a utopian tale, marred only by its propensity to confound the suspense engendered by its simple fictions and imaginative figments with the dramatic tensions of complex historical change.

A ringing epithet—"dreaming rabbis"—which Marchamont Nedham used in a slanging match between the estranged revolutionary camps, suggests the great divide between the two types of revolutionary mentality increasingly in conflict during the convulsive European epoch we have been considering.

In the one camp: men who are not unmindful (as in Nedham's own case) of large matters of principle and even philosophy, but who still attempt to keep their eye on the main chances of political power, its devious opportunities and promising compromises. In soldiers of power, like Cromwell, or among intellectuals in office, like Milton, there is a precarious effort to balance an original ideological passion with so-called practical politics.

In the other camp: men who are not oblivious to the temptations to seize for themselves the levers of real authority, yet who are driven to remain true to the word from which they had their inspired beginning, unflagging, uncompromising, unreal to the very end of their energies. In figures of prophetic anger, like John Rogers and Thomas Venner, or in men of the noblest dreams, like Comenius and Samuel Hartlib, there is a devotion to the irrepressible human myth that faith can move mountains, indeed that faith is itself a sacred mountain.

A reading of the political literature of the Puritan period alerts us constantly to the ease with which impatient men in crises slip into a chronic form of self-deception: the illusion of imminence. Day is breaking, the dawn is here, all things will soon be bright. Throughout the 1640s and well into the 1650s, hopes ran high for the children of light who were holding out against the forces of darkness. The images of hope were as extravagant as the expectations; its semantics were as excited as its psychology. One great English preacher of the day gave his audience melodramatic cues as to the adventurous roles they were about to play. For we "live now in the Extremity of Times, where Motions and Alterations being so near the Centre, become quickest and speediest ... " The following two phrases must have been quite as effective: "we are at the Verge, and as it were, within the Whirle ... " Hartlib's way of putting it was a shade less florid but equally euphoric:

> Yet now behold we live, and instead of desolation, the breaches of the old are repaired, instead of confusion, the foundations are laid for many Generations to build upon, and instead of fears, a great doore is opened to us, that we shall be firmly and fully settled in all abundance of peace and truth.

Indeed, it was at the onset of this mood that Hartlib had originally written to Comenius to come and share with him days that would shake the world: "Come, come, come: it is for the glory of God: deliberate no longer with flesh and blood!"[2]

Such watchwords of euphoric transition—whether they have to do with a furious central motion and a quick, speedy alteration at the verge and within the whirl, or with an earthier process of laying new foundations for a new time of firmness and fullness—are the reliable indicators of an apocalyptic atmosphere. This, then, was the way our protagonists lived now as both paradise and utopia seemed to beckon from on high and the grand prospect of reformation and revolution appeared imminent and overwhelming. All stood, erect and eager, before a great door of hope. John Dury supported the Cromwellian overturnings and confidently explained his acquiescence in "this revolution of government" (especially since, in his cheerful view, "it has been effected quietly and easily"). And, in the London preface to Dury's *Clavis Apocalyptica*, Hartlib (as the reader may recall) admonished his reader: "bee patient for a short time, thou shalt see the end of these distractions in great Revolutions both in Church and State, within and without Europe ... "[3]

Would the vaunted change, although beneficent, prove to be cataclysmic? Some were eager and impatient, and even lusted after the catastrophe; others vacillated between mystical urgency and quiet expectation; but not a few managed a measure of equanimity in the face of all the social and spiritual turmoil. If the eschatology promised long-term certainty, the more modest ethics of humanism suggested slow but vivifying progress. A remark of Comenius's indicates with what firmness the European mind had taken on the shape of a new progressive mentality. "For unless," he writes (in a work characteristically dedicated to help "spread the light of wisdom throughout the human race"), "we wish to remain stationary or to lose ground, we must take care that our successful beginnings lead on to further advances ... "[4] But evidently, in the struggle to spread wisdom, much depended on the presence of wise men; and when both Comenius and Dury decided to return to foreign parts (in 1642), there was a mood of dejection among Hartlib's English friends. How could they maintain their resolve to consummate the beautiful work? Would "action and motion" still go forward?

> In truthe the goinge away of those [two] good men hath and dothe yet muche weaken that springe and strength of resolution that was in me, not but that (me thinkes) I see some beauty in the worke, but not the same possibility of the end; and without possibility of that, all action and motion ceases.

Only a few years later, the momentary dejection had been displaced by resurgent joy that "the democraticall-growing spirits ... have taken such roots in this nation."

> ... and thus will every generation thrust out the other; and as we come nearer the center of Spirituall and Civill truth soe will the motion be quicker and the day (in any one place or kinde of governments) will be shorter.[5]

Hartlib's own English contemporaries may have found (as Trevor-Roper has suggested) the peculiar metaphysicians foreign but, for all that, deeply congenial. In the prefatory words of praise to Hartlib which accompanied his essay on education, John Milton expressed his "esteem of a person sent hither by some good providence from a far country to be the occasion and incitement of great good to this island." Cromwell's secretary continued: "And as I hear, you have obtained the same repute with men of most approved wisdom, and some of highest authority among us ... " Not unlike Matthew Arnold's subsequent appeal some two centuries later to redress unphilosophical English provincialism with a cosmopolitan spirit, Milton welcomed ideas from far countries:

> For the sun, which we want, ripens wits as well as fruits; and as wine and oil are imported to us from abroad, so must ripe understanding, and many civil virtues, be imported into our minds from foreign writings, and examples of best ages: we shall else miscarry still, and come short in the attempts of any great enterprise.[6]

In a ripening, revolutionary time, one generation would indeed thrust out another. For a new generation was coming forward which (in Hartlib's words) would not be "wedded to things, because they are Customary and received" and which would want to displace the old established figures who "are either so far engaged unto the Road way, that they will not think of any better Course to be taken; or suspect all New Designes as light Projects of unsetled braines ... " Old "rubbish" had to be cleared, and antiquated systems disestablished.

> Although the Designes of this Age [Hartlib wrote to the Speaker of Parliament in 1654] do tend, as I am verily persuaded, to a thorough Reformation, yet hitherto we cannot see much more than the Overthrow and Deformation of former Establishments: partly, because there is much rubbish to be removed; partly, because it is not possible to build a new House where an old one is standing, till the old one be pulled down. Yet no wise man will lay his old habitation waste, till he know what to erect instead thereof: Hence it is, that a New Modell is commonly first prepared before the old one be removed.[7]

2. Three Foreigners: Hartlib, Dury, Comenius

That the greatest intellectual entrepreneur of the age should have come from the bleaker regions of the ancient German *Reich* was not to be taken as a cheerless augur. The leading intellectuals of the day formed a marvelously cosmopolitan group, a free-floating cultural vanguard capable of being produced only by a century which had not yet lost its old Latin internationality nor yet hardened into national spiritual provinces. In an earlier generation, Giordano Bruno, expelled and excommunicated from Continental centers of learning, came to London to mix with Sidney, Greville, and Florio and to write several of his finest works. Comenius, too, moved (and sometimes ran) from land to land, publishing all the way. Dury served as the minister of the French church in Cologne and found himself, as an "English preacher" in Poland, invited to emigrate to America. "All countries are now allmost alike," wrote one of Hartlib's correspondents from Amsterdam (in 1644), "and it mattereth not much where a bodie have or make his abode ... "

Little, alas, is known about Samuel Hartlib's early movements: how, and why, and when, did he transplant himself to England? One can establish little more than the fact that there he was in the late 1620s at the University of Cambridge, presumably after a period of study at Königsberg (and possibly Heidelberg), and already beginning to earn a reputation as the most extraordinary German refugee of the century, certainly the most indefatigable; and it is understandable that his German biographer takes familiar national pride in recording his inexhaustible diligence (*"denn unthätig konnte er einmal nicht sein"*).[8]

Hartlib himself has left us an illuminating, if fragmentary, autobiographical account which for various reasons (tone, language, social nuance) is best resumed in his own words:

> my Father was a Merchant, but no ordinary one, being the King of Poland his merchant, who hath founded a church at Posnania in Poland, and when the Jesuits prevayled in that kingdom, he was fain to remove hims. into Prussia, where he came to Elbing, where not any house of credit was yett built, but he with another Patrituis of Breslaw in Silesia built two stately houses, which are yett standing at Elbing, being the principall houses of that towne the building whereof cost my father many thousands of Rix-dollars in those cheap dayes ... My father had married before 2 Polonian gentlewomen of noble extraction, both of them being ladyes according to the fashions in those countries, in regard of which he obtained the sooner his third wife my own mother.

For some odd reason, he does not mention that his mother was English, the daughter of a wealthy English merchant of Danzig, with many well-placed relations in her father's home country. Of the ten Hartlib brothers who remained in Central Europe, in one form of service or another in the "German Empire," we are told that "some of them have been Privy Councellours to the Emperour, some to other inferiour Princes, some syndics of Augspurg and Norimberg. But they passed afterwards not so strictly *für edelleute* in the Empire when some turned merchants, which you know is derogatory to the German nobility." There remain large and important gaps in this exceptional autobiographical document ("I have been upbraided for my too much neglicence of my pedigree"). Obviously this whole exercise in personal history was discomfiting for him; and his explanation, so much of a piece with his entire life and career, is thoughtful and creditable:

> And truely I may speak it with a safe conscience that I never all the days of my life reflected seriously upon my pedigree; but if I had I believe I should have made an other kinde of hystory, preferring my heavenly birth above all such vanities, and afterwards studying more to this very day to be useful to Gods creatures, and serviceable to his church, then to be rich or honourable.

He confines himself to a few passing remarks on his wide circle of friends and acquaintances, from archbishops and merchants and "Professors of both Universities" to "all sorts of learned or in any kind usefull men," and on the honors bestowed upon him, of which he makes a special point to mention only the recommendations of Parliament and the books dedicated to him. "I could fill whole sheets in what love and reputation I have lived these 30 years in England ... But I grow weary to pursue such vanities."[9]

Over those thirty English years, Hartlib did indeed fill whole sheets, and his own books and letters are full of topical, even sensational delights. Could Dury convince Gustavus Adolphus of the advantages of peace and tolerance? Would Comenius agree to Winthrop's offer to become president of Harvard? Could Hartlib, through his friends Milton and Dury, be instrumental in getting approval of Rabbi Menassah's petition to Cromwell for the return of the Jews? There is political news, literary gossip, and incidental intelligence: and the items range from the latest about the Fifth Monarchists (and the millenarian support now commanded by "Rabbi" John Rogers) to the location of long-lost manuscripts of Flavius Josephus in the Cambridge library. He records in his *Ephemerides* current information about Milton's literary plans (and indeed he plays something of a direct editorial role himself when he in turn tells a nervously pugnacious Milton that Salmasius is about to publish a polemical reply). He suggests a public library in London, and proceeds to concern himself with the disposition of good private collections (i.e., before the London "hugster" gets to the most valuable books). Still, when he was praised by his admirers it was not so much for his local civic service, although this was always felt to be the practical test for noble ideals, as for his universality; and, when he argued on behalf of "universal education," he appears to have meant it globally and was, in fact, involved in projects for the schooling of Indians in the New World. Most affecting of all is his persistent dedication over the years to programs of assistance to refugees from wars and persecutions, especially to foreign scholars and students. He could wear no finer

badge of distinction than the simple and unadorned recognition that he
was "the constant friend of distressed strangers."

Of the major themes in Hartlib's life—science, liberty, and utopia—
the extravagant preoccupation with the largest vision of a free and
happy mankind began very early, and such biographical data as we have
throws some light on the contexts of youthful inspiration and the general intellectual currents of the day. Here the influence of certain Continental masters was to be as formative on his political metaphysics as his
adopted English environment was later to be on his social pragmatism.
A brief glance at the attitudes and activities of John Dury and of John
Valentin Andreae is necessary to illustrate the sources of the utopian's
cumulative concern with the problems of reform and revolution.

In November 1631, Dury traveled across a continent still being rav-
aged by the Thirty Years' War to Würzburg, where he took the risk of
confronting the Emperor Gustavus Adolphus. "I stood in the King his
way," he writes in his account to Hartlib,[10] "when hee went from his
chamber to supper; who seeing me to bee a stranger looked very earnestly upon me and went slowly, which gave me boldnesse and leisure
to draw neere." The Emperor recalled one of Dury's manifestos for
ecclesiastical peace, "then turning about to those that stood by, hee said
smiling, this man doth intend to agree us all together in Religion: doe
you think it possible? no bodie answering ... " On a subsequent occasion a few days later, Dury had opportunity enough to give his own
answers. "Hee came to the matter of pacification wherin hee insisted
with me a large houre and one halfe drawing from me by continuall
questions a full information of the whole worke, and some tymes objecting and proposing difficulties which I was to answer ... " Was Dury
acting alone or on behalf of others? what was the nature of the agreement sought? what means would be used to bring about a new unity?
and, finally, "what then would you have me to doe?"

I need not stress that our interest in this fascinating colloquium is less
in its possible historical consequences ("pacification" was still a decade
away) than in its ideological atmosphere. Dury's theses were that peace
and tolerance were both desirable and possible: "at least a mutual toleration without bitter condemnation of one another, if not a full agreement
and brotherly conionction ... " The Emperor took the point, if with a
measure of skepticism; and he promised that he "would doe every thing
tending to moderation of mens bitter affections and contentious-
nesse ... " He could not resist adding that these vices "proceeded for
the most part from the pride and covetousnesse of Clergie men, which
(smiling hee said) if I could take away hee would soone make them
peacable ... " The men of Hartlib's circle could not agree more, per-

suaded as they were that the price of social peace and progress was a certain pacification of the intellectual habits of all true believers. In a statement which Dury prepared at Hartlib's prompting, the task was set out in these words:

> ... to heale up that breach and reconcile that deadly fude and malice. There was not greater reasons for controversies and writing before then now for peace and reconcilement. This way at first had not bin so seasonable, nor so hopeful. It was fitt men should try the power of arguments and throughly debate the questions, say what they could for the truth. Now that is done men have tryed their strength; they see how little they prevayle by force; the fire is more kindled and both sides exasperated, now let them sitt downe and coole and in the calme there will be more equall wayghing all arguments and yealding it is likely. Againe wee have warred as long as it is safe for us both, the common adversary will now devoure all if wee joyne not in amity.

The principle of "coole" was, later, also to have its English moment of triumph when Locke and Halifax celebrated the "revolutionary" achievement of a moderate and tolerant flexibility. Here, as in so many other instances, ideology recapitulates theology.

We are witnessing the progressive emergence of some of the great watchwords of the next centuries: *peace and plenty, the public interest, unity and harmony, tolerance, men of good will, community and solidarity, liberty and happiness, mutual help.* What was "wanting," a correspondent writes to Hartlib, is "some universal and common spirit, such as Unity and Harmony"; and this needed new "temper" found one of its most explicit formulations in another letter by Dury (again to Hartlib):

> ... when things are not cleare unto me, I love to be indifferent, abhorring to choose a side ... In like manner when things controverted though with much heate, seeme not to me to very materiall into edification or necessary unto salvation, then alsoe I love to refraine from disputes and partiality, either for or against him that is not consenting with me; because I know the danger of mans vainglorious humor in disputing about needles matters, when it cloaketh it selfe with the faire pretence of maintayning truth in Theory, whiles all Truth in matter of practize and sincerity of godly love is neglected by the one disputant towards the other. This is my disposition which makes me either a newtrall in some things now in agitation, or an indifferent spectator of the strife of Tongues. Newtrall I say as being different in judgment from both opposites in somethings and alsoe I say indifferent in looking on those that strive too violently as being voide of heate and intemperancy for things not material.[11]

United in so many shared tenets of religion and politics, but above all in this disposition toward a new and enlightened ethics of controversy, Dury and Hartlib, together with their mentor Comenius, joined in a remarkable triple alliance (*Foederis fraterni ad mutuam in publico* ... 1642).

But there was to be nothing neutral or indifferent about their pact to define "the publique good, now perverted to private ends ... " Referring to the "knot" which tied them together, Dury wrote: "I meane Master *Comenius*, Mr. *Hartlib*, and my selfe: For though our taskes be different, yet we are all three in a knot sharers of one anothers labours, and can hardly bee without one anothers helpe and assistance ... "[12] The three men, later to be reinforced by several others, entered into a formal agreement of mutual material and intellectual support, to promote peace and education and reform. They constituted in point of fact a small central committee of a far-flung utopian international,[13] dedicated to the "rules of reformation"—"methodizing" (in their phrase) the guidelines for that happy accomplishment of a longed-for revolution in the affairs of men.

3. Andreae's German Utopia

Johann Valentin Andrae's contribution to the inspiration of the Hartlib circle was rather of a different order. He was a prophet of "light in darkness" and the herald of "the blessed dawn" that would soon appear. These and similar phrases are to be found in his earliest writings, and the *Fame Fraternitatis* (which circulated in manuscript for years before its publication in Strasbourg in 1614) captivated with its notion, so consoling when a continent was on the brink of a disastrous war, that small bodies of men would band together to institute a general reformation *divini et humani*. His vision of an ideal state, *Reipublicae Christianopolitanae Descriptio*,[14] went to print in 1619, during the opening battles of the Thirty Years' War; and if it had a chiliastic note it was a subdued one: "Let us lament the lost paradise and long for its restoration ... "[15]

This so-called German utopia of Andreae, influenced as it was by Thomas More and influencing in turn Francis Bacon, completes in a strikingly circular way the first century of European utopianism. Christianopolis was conspicuously more religious in its essential spiritual conception than the regime of King Utopus, but both were equally involved in the dilemmas and complexities of the utopian political impulse. The private hope of imaginative escape is balanced by the ethical injunction to help transform an evil world; the motives of hate and anger against glaring iniquities are mixed with the tenderest feelings for all mankind; the patient promise of gentle progress is overshadowed by a prophetic rage for action this day. These are all themes which begin to dominate the revolutionary temperament as early as the seventeenth century, and there are notable pages in Andreae's work which document the shaping of attitudes among a generation's representative minds.

There is, in the first place, a new semi-secular rhythm to the utopian movement which tends more and more to displace the simpler older swing from the lostness of paradise to its restoration. Bacon caught it most perceptively when he referred to the three essentials in his *New Atlantis*: (1) "the knowledge of causes and secret motions of things"; (2) "the enlarging of the bounds of human empire"; and (3) "the effecting of all things possible." We shall be considering many of the variations on this triadic structure in a later place, but it may be useful to suggest here its relevance to the forms of the utopian and revolutionary imagination. In Marxism the triad becomes: (1) historical materialism; (2) the class struggle and the proletarian movement; (3) the coming of the kingdom of Freedom. And in Hartlib's circle it became: (1) science; (2) educational and social reform; (3) a utopian (variously called "Macarian" or "Antillian") model of liberty, peace, and plenty.

In this perspective, Andreae can be seen to have transcended some of the traditional limitations of Christian prophets of paradise and to have placed himself in the ranks of a new intellectual movement which tried to put the divine apocalypse at the service of human progress and refused to allow its nostalgia for a past Eden to preclude its present commitment to a better future.

Nor were the various new intellectual fancies of his day satisfactory enough for his serious political purposes. In a lighthearted piece on Campanella, Andreae makes fun of the ingenious Italian's conception of a kind of automatic political machine (*automa monarchicum*) in which nations turned to and from the imperial greatness of world power like Archimedean "wheels within wheels." In another short piece in a late work, Andreae goes on to link what he presented as sound utopian doctrine with two principles of which we will never again be allowed to lose sight. *Practice*, he argues, must never be divorced from preaching; eloquence, wisdom, and understanding must all be associated with *successful action*. More than that, the protagonists of this new hoped-for unity of theory and practice will be utopian heroes drawn not from the old ruling classes but from the ranks of the dispossessed. Much in this dialogue is at once traditional and transitional, as Christian and Greco-Roman commonplaces are mixed with a groping for a new politics; but this radical exchange is of special interest:

A: For knowledge and inactivity, activity without knowledge are to be seen all over, but both knowledge and activity combined are to be found almost nowhere.

B: Unhappy separation! How rightly do the inhabitants of Utopia sweat to unite the two!

A: What is this Utopia you mention?

B: That colony which is inhabited by such rare settlers.

A:You have been given the task, then, of collecting them?

B: As you see, but what progress I have made this document will inform you. Look at the list.

A: There is plenty of paper, but where are the names?

B: Turn the pages.

A: There is nothing to be seen.

B: Turn over, and over again.

A: I am baffled.

B: Turn to the end.

A: Ah, here are some, at the very end, and from the lowest class of mankind.

B: That's right: for those of higher station all refused to make the journey.

A: Do please add me too, I beg you, if for no other reason, at least because I am low and base in the eyes of all, and everyone despises me . . .

B: There is no need to hurry yourself, for we are not sailing today or tomorrow.

A: Well, if there are no other worthy persons to join the party, we will make the voyage to Utopia not in a ship but in a rowboat or even on a plank.[16]

When Andreae's utopian journey is finally launched, the narrative begins with a familiar shipwreck motif. A voyage of expedition is endangered; a storm batters a helpless vessel against the rocks; a blessed island offers fortunate refuge for a saved remnant. As Andreae's survivors report, "We soon saw destruction before our eyes and stood in readiness for death." One thing is clear: shipwreck goeth before utopia in the same pattern of paired extremes which links chaos and creation, the dark and the dawn, apocalypse and paradise. "You are ours," are the opening words of welcome to the happy few; for they had been "washed clean." As shipwreck comes en route to the Blessed Isle, so does despair precede happiness, storm herald transformation, revolution lead to utopia. These are the rhythmic changes which man's mind rings on the profound image-idea of "a violent casting ashore." It is perhaps the metaphor of man's physical birth, and in man's beginning are all his means and ends.

On a more mundane political level, Andreae's work—although, as he himself conceded, it was less "clever and serious" than More's, and is markedly inferior to the classifical utopian texts as a piece of imaginative literature—carried forward in its ambivalent way certain central preoccupations of the utopian mind and gave them a topical relevance in a time of European war and upheaval. "The world is not so sure of its affairs as it would like to seem," he wrote, "nor is it so steadfast in its views that it cannot be turned aside." The very instability of things provided the real social foundations for utopian change; and for his own part Andreae was prepared to face the barrage of "all the words, 'fanatic,' 'turbulent,' and 'a danger to literature' . . . " that would be flung at him. The ineluctable intellectual task was to continue questioning an immoral and unreasonable world.

> What utterly absurd things are done in a republic because the WHY is neither known nor tolerated. The world has faith in the unbelieving, follows the blind, is mortally afraid of the weak, raises the lazy, and admits Heaven knows what absurdities. It ought not, then, take offense when someone laughs at it; it should rather appreciate the talkative ones who keep asking it with importunity why it does and suffers this or that. The world will never regret having been urged from darkness into light, from servitude into freedom.[17]

How, then, would the talkative ones turn an absurd world aside? Could words alone urge the world forward into freedom?

To the extent that we can, in Andreae's case, speak of a theory of strategy and tactics, it was based on a simple, somewhat mechanical rule-of-thumb conception of a political class struggle which takes place in society between two opposing temperaments—between (in our later labels) the forces of change and the status quo, between conservatives and liberals. In a passage of considerable psychological perspicacity, Andreae observed:

> I see two classes of men in the commonwealth. A class of those who do not so much approve of those things over which they are set or under which they are placed, as they admire them and defend them to the teeth. The other class, men who endure human affairs, but in such a way, it is true, that they do not hesitate to wish for better things and to obey moderate changes. But as the latter class never readily causes disturbance, because of backwardness and sense, but rather as far as possible gives way, is silent and tolerant; so also the former, because of blind madness and lack of self-control, attacks, torments, and not rarely drags those into conflict who merely grumble at them though they may not at all desire it.

Given the historical tensions of this uneasy and contradictory relationship, it was surely not utopian to expect a revolutionary situation sooner or later. This might be regrettable, and the guilty responsibilities for it could not be facilely apportioned; nevertheless, the dramatic moment of breakdown represented a collapse of certain illusions as to what "can be

done with moderate and tolerable means." Here, in the briefest of encounters, we meet the moderate in rage, the reformer turned radical, the
seventeenth-century utopian as revolutionary.

> It was thus that our hero Doctor Luther proceeded; when men would
> not heed his prayers and tears, he began to breathe threats out of the
> Word of God. Accomplishing nothing by submissiveness, he began
> to rise up. When he had carried on siege for a long time, he began to
> storm the opposing power, and with such success, that WE REJOICE
> though they gnash their teeth. I am rather inclined to think that this
> very drama may be played again in our own day.[18]

With these lines, and their resounding echoes of storm and siege and a
rising to come, the scene was set for the contemporary theater of revolution, and on its stage men like Hartlib and Milton, Lilburne and Walwyn, Howell and Nedham (among so many others) would all be playing
their extraordinary roles.

4. Hartlib, "the Great Intelligencer of Europe"

Hartlib's most literary attempt to incite (as Milton put it) the greatest
good was a brief excursion into the utopian genre, with "a Fiction"
which he freely admitted had as its model both Thomas More and Francis Bacon.[19] But its intention was no less topical, urgent, and politically
targeted.

"Composed by way of Novel," the little treatise was "designed to
intimate a new Model of Government ... as the properest Means to
reconcile the destructive Breach ... " We are on the eve of an incomparable hurly-burly, and Hartlib's Traveller from "over the Sea" is especially eager to give his news, for he has heard that England's Parliament
is "generally bent to make a good Reformation." This being so, Macaria
and the Macarians[20] have a lesson to teach, for there "the People do live
in great Plenty, Prosperity, Health, Peace, and Happiness, and have not
half so much Trouble as they have in these European Countries ... "
The land has been improved; highways have been built and rivers
spanned with bridges; well-regulated fisheries yield immense riches;
there is a free health service with everything from medicines to surgery
"at the publick Charge"; above all, life is lived in a state of permanent
peace. Here was news, then, of paradise found—"the whole Kingdom is
become like to a fruitful Garden."

These Macarian virtues were not intended to be merely vague utopian
promises. Hartlib's was a pioneering scientific spirit, and his practical
schemes for agriculture and industry were widely esteemed; indeed,
they had so impressed Governor Winthrop of New England that he had

called him "the Great Intelligencer of Europe." In fact Hartlib thought, with a rare largeness of horizon, in transatlantic terms; and he was concerned as much with the New World's ideal material prospects as with its immediate imperial fate. "I count it my duty," he wrote to Winthrop in 1661, "to let you know that I heare the Court are upon sending a Governor into New England, and that there are some Private Agitations on foot concerning that Countrey . . . " To be sure, his various incursions into politics and scientific innovation were not often rewarded with the instantaneous successes he hoped for. Impatient spirits in every generation persuade themselves that they are, at last, the appointed witnesses of the new day: and that they would see, as Hartlib rashly predicted, "the end of these distractions in great Revolutions both in Church and State, within and without Europe." The world revolution was unaccountably delayed, and we find him bemoaning (again to Winthrop) all the "Publique Miseries": "For the times of such a Publique and Universal Happiness seems not yet to bee at hand."[21] These were the real social complications that overtake any movement on behalf of abstract and perfect human ideals, and if fictional far-away Macaria was rather different and could be unencumbered in its imaginative abandon, still it had evident difficulties of its own.

The English Scholar whom Hartlib's overseas Traveller is rapidly converting to his faith in a practicable paradise is, nevertheless, a trifle puzzled by the report from Macaria that there is "no Diversity of Opinions amongst them."

SCHOLAR: How can that be?

TRAVELLER: Very easily; for they have a Law, that, if any Divine shall publish a new Opinion to the common People, he shall be accounted a Disturber of the publick Peace, and shall suffer Death for it.

SCHOLAR: But that is the Way to keep them in Error perpetually, if they be once in it.

TRAVELLER: You are deceived; for, if any one hath conceived a new Opinion, he is allowed every Year freely to dispute it before the great Council; if he overcome his Adversaries, or such as are appointed to be Opponents, then it is generally received for Truth; if he be overcome, then it is declared to be false.

One wonders whether a nonfictional English scholar would have been altogether convinced by this Macarian form of what would later come to be called democratic centralism. Still, Hartlib has his own spokesman make a clear endorsement of this novel program for general happiness.

SCHOLAR: I have read over Sir Thomas More's *Utopia*, and my Lord Bacon's *New Atlantis*, which he called so in Imitation of Plato's old one; but none of them giveth me Satisfaction, how the Kingdom of

England may be happy, so much as this Discourse, which is brief and pithy, and easy to be effected, if all Men be willing.

Even at this stage of the argument, when all that remained was really the question of what was to be done, Hartlib took pains to emphasize that the utopian fiction, his "Novel," was not intended merely to amuse. "It is no Laughing matter." In France, Spain, Germany, and elsewhere, there was the earnest news of "Combustions." How could a house divided against itself stand? All the inhabitants of England had to join, "with one Consent," to make the country "like Macaria" and thus to make it "rich" and "invincible." On, then, to agitation and propaganda—"None but Fools or Madmen will be against it," says the Scholar. "You have changed my mind ... and I will change as many Minds as I can ... " The first thing to do was to arrange for the printing of the proceedings of their conference.

And yet a lingering doubt appeared troublesome: namely, the general opinion that "no such Reformation, as we would have, shall come before the Day of Judgment." Was it truly conceivable that such ultimate felicity could come to man in this life?

Hartlib, although he took an easy way out, was aware of the vast complexities of this theological issue. No prophet of paradise could evade the calculations of terrestrial or of supernatural fulfillment. Some, like Gerrard Winstanley, counted on both; others, like John Norris, blurred the distinction in a general infatuation with "heavenlymindedness." What was at once imminent and imperative was to be "admitted to that intimate and naked Vision of that Mysterious and Incomprehensible Excellence ... to meditate upon the blessed Society of Saints and Angels ... the City of God ... that ravishing Harmony of Divine Love and intellectual sympathy ... " And, as Norris emphasized,

> to contemplate all this not coldly or indifferently as a thing that is a great way off, or an uncertain Reversion, or imaginary Utopia, but as a state that will shortly and certainly be, and with that Faith and Assurance which is the substance of Things hoped for, and the evidence of things not seen; to Dwell, Converse, and have our Civil Life in Heaven ... as if we were already Inhabitants of that Blessed Place, and actual Members of the sacred Policy and Community.[22]

Hartlib's Macaria was just such an "as-if" paradise, a utopia between imagination and reality. He contemplated civil excellence and would move heaven and earth for its revolutionary installation.

But the intricacies of the question of Christian eschatological promise were not so easily resolved by so simple an association of theory and practice. Hartlib knew better, for he had been intimately involved in much of the theological controversy which, in the age of the Puritan exegetes, had such decisive political (and "revolutionary") implications. No less an authority than the famous Dr. Joseph Mede, Milton's tutor at Cambridge, patiently explained it all to him in a notable document. Dated 16 April 1638, it is "Mr. Mede's Letter to Mr. Hartlib, concerning the Number 25, the Root of the Beast's Number, *viz.* 666, with his judgment of an Analytical Table of the Apocalyps which was sent him; his differing from the Author thereof in four particulars." In outlining to Hartlib his differences with the views of a Mr. Potter, Mede stated that "the Golden Number" (namely, 1666) "I have known long, but never had any fancy to … " Further,

> I hold but one Millennium, and that to begin at the destruction of the Beast. He [Potter] holds two, one beginning at Constantine, another at the destruction of the Beast … I take the Resurrection, both of them, First and Second, to be proper and real; he Metaphorical. 'Tis not safe to deprive the Church of those Texts whereon her faith of the Resurrection is builded. For this interpretation will necessarily rob us of that of *Daniel* Chap. 12, also, whereon I believe the Church of the Old Testament built her faith of that Article…. He seems to appropriate the Second Millennium (which I think the only) to the glory of the Jews only. I extend it to the whole Catholick Church of the Gentiles, when the Jew shall come into the fold; and that the *Apocalyps* is properly and primarily the Gentiles Prophecy, I mean of the Church of the Gentiles, and of the Jews but by accident and coincidence only. The *Jews* have prophecies enough of their own in the Old Testament.[23]

I trust it will not be considered premature or fanciful to suggest, at this point of our inquiry, that the nineteenth- and twentieth-century exegetists of the so-called secular apocalypse, the millenarians of the social revolution, incorporated similar patterns of controversy in their polemical commentaries on the end of a "beastly" epoch and the coming of a "golden" day. When would the evil system be destroyed? How imminent is the end? When it comes, will it bring millennial salvation only to advanced industrial countries, "ripe" for the change, as in Marxian prophecy, or will it be a world revolution, a universal resurrection including all the world's backward communities? And, lastly, do the scientific and prophetic texts indicate that the end will transpire in one stage (with the victory of socialism), or will there be (before the ultimate victory of communism) a second and final stage when all will have "come into the fold"?[24]

Dispensing curtly with the burdensome dialectical baggage, Hartlib takes a Macarian shortcut as his Traveller reassures the Scholar—"but I can shew a hundred Texts of Scripture, which do plainly prove, that such a Reformation shall come before the Day of Judgment." If this was so, nothing now stood in the way of their both being "good Instruments in this Work of Reformation." On, then, with Gutenberg!

> TRAVELLER: These be natural Causes also to further it; for the *Art of Printing* will so spread Knowledge, that the Common People, knowing their own Rights and Liberties, will not be governed by Way of Oppression; and so, by little and little, all Kingdoms will be like *Macaria*.
>
> SCHOLAR: That will be a good Change, when as well Superiors as Inferiors shall be more happy; Well, I am imparadised in my Mind, in thinking that *England* may be happy, with such Expedition and Facility.

All that now remained was for all men to be "imparadised" in society, in the here and now, with a new and happier earthly order of things. It was certain to come, although (as Hartlib, a peculiar metaphysical foreigner, was sensitive to surmise) high and exciting social drama seemed little suited to the local insular temperament. Hartlib's Scholar ends on a note of quiet English optimism.

> ... and, though our neighbour Countries are pleased to *call the English a dull Nation*, yet the major Part are sensible of their own Good, and the Good of their Posterity, and those will sway the rest; so we and our Posterity shall be all happy.

The blessed future of a happy mankind, or the prosperity of posterity: these were his deep utopian impulses and the source of his enthusiastic public devotion to good causes; and I find the radical modernity of his mind conspicuously in evidence in all his intellectual preoccupations. He argued glowingly on behalf of "the Peoples Rights" and insisted that they take priority over intolerant churchly squabbles—"Different religions, nor irreligion, quit not humanitie and justice." He had an open, enlightened and sympathetically nonsectarian approach to men of the widest variety of views, although the personal generosity was mixed with cunning tactics when a man like James Howell, so antipathetic in essential public attitudes, could be considered as the possible first president of the Academy. "Excellent use may be made of him," as a report to Hartlib (on the mission of "gleaning together great and honest spirits") explains, "as a man, though of deprav'd opinions yet of a generous and high soul ... "[25] Hartlib's quick-wittedness, too, had the celerity of an ideological dialectician, and his advice to his embattled comrades was shrewd: "We are politickly called Fomenters of Warre; we must be wise and not feare words, we must *foment* (if *foment* they call it), that is, we must stir up and second defensively, against such offenders, who would surprise us, by preventing resistance ... " This was, in the year 1648, very much in the useful spirit of a doctrine of defensive revolutionary initiative. Nor was he under any illusions about the ease with which a mood of popular militance could be maintained; he knew how forgetful people are, and how bouts of public amnesia erase yesterday's political memories. "Each one forgets what the King did, so [they forget] what they are freed from,—being only taken up with their present sufferings, of which they are most sensible ... "

The specter of Macarian felicity was haunting not only England but Europe and the whole of humanity as well. If all now (Hartlib wrote in 1647)[26] had "occasion to be Instrumentall towards ... the perfect wayes of such a desired Reformation," then "in due time," he added, it would "ferment the rest of the world." The great change might come slowly, falteringly: but perhaps, who knows, even "all at once."

> I know that elsewhere the Matters here mentioned, have been practiced piece-meale, and therefore there is no reason why they may not be all at once jointly made use of amongst Us ... But I am somewhat in doubt of the Season, Whether the Spirits of this Age bee not too much as yet (to say no more) discomposed and scattered to entertain such Overtures. But let Men be as they will, such seeds as these must be sown in their hearts, and presented to their thoughts. Who knoweth what they may worke?

This skeptical, almost quizzical note of hope—for all his resources of theological faith and secular benevolence—is characteristic of the humane and practical utopian who is too restlessly busy to have time for abstract fanaticism. Who but a revolutionary reformer and an inveterate meliorist would speak of sowing seeds in men's minds and hearts (and not, say, of destroying and uprooting)? Such a fateful distinction was (and remains) fundamental to the rhetoric of politics, and it was never very far from Hartlib's mind. "For if,"as he wrote in a manuscript of 1653 which has only recently been published, "we pull downe and scatter, before we know what to set up, and how to order things in a better way than they were before we shall proove onely skillfull in destroying and not in building ... " Sound progress would come "by degrees, and without any hindrance to that which is of some use in the present way."[27]

Hartlib's paternalistic panaceas always promised much, but they pretended to no infallibility or finality. Their most solid foundation was to be a transformed economic base, not the least important feature of which was to be the achievement of full employment.

> And although these things may perhaps seem to some of no great moment, yet if they be lookt into duly, they will be found such as

have an influence upon the Fundamentalls of the Settlement of
Common-wealths. For if Husbandry and Trade at home and abroad
be well-regulated, all hands may be Employed, and where all hands
are at work there the whole strength of a Nation doth put forth its
endeavours.

Nor was he naïve enough to entertain simple-minded illusions as to the
ease and speed with which this could be accomplished. Sometimes he
had qualms about the readiness of mankind to embrace the proferred
cornucopia, especially "in respect of the known untowardness of the
major part of the people, who being wonderfully wedded to old cus-
tomes, are not easily wonne to any new course, though never so much
to their own profit ... " Sometimes he even had his doubts about his
self-appointed role as the champion of "the Publike Good," confessing
that "for the most part it proves a thankless office, and the more abundantly one is found to love the Publike, the less he is loved ... "[28]
     In his very self-questioning, often wry and resilient, lay his strength.
Unlike many other unquiet spirits who devoted themselves to the
world's happiness, Hartlib's energy found release in the variety of practical human challenges and not merely in the totality of a blinding vision. He was constantly discovering and inventing, and one "Engine"
(as he called it) was the central piece of social machinery which would
help solve most of the nation's grievous problems. He thought of it as an
"Office of Addresse," and it amounted to an early model of a welfare
state. Following as it would "the word of God and clear Principles of
Reason," it was in part a philanthropic foundation, a data bank, a labor
exchange, and an institute of advanced studies, all contributing to "the
Publick Good of All" by the "redresse of Publick Evils." Through the
Office, men would obtain employment, improve their agriculture, learn
the latest bits of science, help the poor and ailing, and even find spiritual
solace. It was on this last point that a distressed Dury almost defected; he
thought the emphasis on the "Material Engine" tended to exclude
spiritual affairs. Dury was also concerned about the untoward consequences of developing models of alternative educational institutions,
fearing that with the possible adoption of such ambitious proposals "all
universities and eminent places of learning might subtilly be undermined and made useless ... "[29]
     Men of power were being advised by men of imagination to create
new institutions which would be "instrumentall in our owne Felicity."
This is indeed the basic instrumentalism of utopia and revolution; as
Hartlib puts it,

Such an Office will be the onley proper Remedy and Help to that
disorderly and confused condition of Life wherein we may lye for

want of profitable Contrivements begetting sociable encounters and communications ... This Office will be a Center of all Mens satisfactions to gaine their Interest in each other for mutuall help.

Untold excellences dangled tantalizingly before mankind: news of the latest books from all the world's major librarians, Comenius's methods of teaching in all the schools, bulletins of progressive developments everywhere, even a "Committee for Rules of Reformation." The Macarian Manifesto was more than a dream; it might well yield a science of politics and social reconstruction. "For the Supreme Magistracy in all purposes of State, but chiefly in that of a healthful Reformation," Hartlib explains reassuringly, "it may be in his hand (if he will make use of it) an Engine to reduce all into some Order which is confused ... " If some of the mechanical contrivances by which a felicitous society of mutual help and harmony were new (or at least given new names from an enriched vocabulary), the essential visionary injunction was ancient; and it is characteristic that Hartlib closes his pamphlet to Parliament with lines from Philippians (4:8):

Whatsoever things are true, whatsoever things are honest, whatsoever things are just, whatsoever things are lovely, whatsoever things are of good report; if there be any Vertue, and if there be any praise, thinke on these things.[30]

5. The Utopian International

Hartlib was not alone in thinking on these things. He was close to the center of one of the most extraordinary intellectual sets to leave an important mark on early modern European history. From his London base, he was in constant touch with both Europeans and Americans, warning New Englanders against imperial strategems, encouraging Dury in his interview with Gustavus Adolphus to press for peace and tolerance, instigating Robert Boyle to take up correspondence with Descartes, arranging English refuge for exiled Continental scholars, facilitating a freer flow of manuscripts and translations among intellectuals in a dozen lands, popularizing schemes for both social reform and scientific advance, hoping against hope finally to arrange for the establishment (on the Rhine, or perhaps in Florida or Virginia) of a sound utopian community. Samuel Hartlib was, as I have suggested, the first founder of a utopian international. In his own time, thought of as "the Great Intelligencer of Europe," he was also called "a person soe eminent among the Ingenios" (Christopher Wren), "the greatest Instrument of publicke edification" (Dury), "the great Genius which animates and conducts this present Age" (John Hall). The admiration of Hartlib by Milton, Comenius, and Boyle was shared by Parliament, and he was distinguished by a special designation[31] as "an Agent for the Advancement of Universal Learning and the Publick Good."

He was, then, a man of reason and revolution (and I do not mean this description to serve as an anachronistic projection of modern catchphrases onto earlier intellectual sentiments). For Hartlib, it was obvious that reason was revolutionary, and that the revolution of the age would be reasonable. He was the propagandist for the new forces of European Enlightenment, taking on in intellectual combat the encrusted elements of ignorance and irrationality; he wanted to demonstrate "the universall method of ordering the thoughts, to finde out by our own industry any truth as yet unknown, and to resolve any question which may be proposed in nature, as the object of a rationall meditation . . . " Nor would the new adventurous inquiry fail to embrace the questions of society and world history. He referred to these as "the superstructure," and in it was included "the Chiefest Revolutions and Changes which are befallen . . . " Both error and vice were the targets, for it was these "which bring forth the miseries, under which all the Societies of Mankind doe groane at this day." Clearly, he was (if a century too soon, and in another land) a *philosophe* and an *encyclopédiste*.

> For the Encyclopedia of Sciences must answer the wheel of humane faculties, and this wheel must answer the Circle of the Creatures whence man is to supply his defects. As then in a watch, one wheel rightly set doth with its teeth take hold of another, and sets that awork toward a third, and so all move one by another, when they are in their right places for the end for which the watch is made; so is it with the Faculties of the humane nature.[32]

To be sure, Hartlib was no scientist himself, and he was little more than a dabbler in advanced experimental pursuits. Yet the variety of his own technical work and the warmth of his own personal relationships with so many of the keenest scientific minds of the day support the general impression of his central place in the dynamic new world of scientific learning. The one biographer who has examined the mass of Hartlib papers—and they teem with proposals for agricultural improvements, animal husbandry, mechanical innovation, and ingenious invention (from air conditioning to nautical bombs, from better ways of making bread to machines for setting crops)—has testified that it would take "several volumes" to give an exhaustive account of them. Some of his scientific correspondents went diligently ahead in order to obtain the private profit that would accrue to themselves (and, in prospering England, often did); others were devoted to the purer love of truth and knowledge. As for Hartlib, I think we can accept Professor Turnbull's point that the scientific commitment here was essentially *social*. How could the new knowledge assist the universal reformation? How could it be put at the service of the health and wealth of mankind? This public concern was at the heart of his religious mission: to enlist science for (in Bacon's phrase) the relief of man's estate. Far from being troubled by the apparent ambivalence of Hartlib's dedication to both science and society (it did upset one old-fashioned biographer), we find it to be the very basis of his importance in the history of those utopian and revolutionary spirits who wanted nothing more than to lay cornerstones for the world's happiness.

One memorable letter written to Hartlib by Sir William Petty illustrates something of the cunning historical ambiguity which may have united as well as divided these two pioneering spirits.

> Meethinks it would make a dog laugh to see men that do not know the things they talke and dispute soe much about, when they see them, to thinke themselves better philosophers than such as experimentally know them and their operations one upon another, that are daily conversant in the works of nature, that doe diligently observe, compare and apply them ...

Petty was thinking mainly of Descartes when he criticized those who "were employed in spinning cobwebs and out of principles, which though they may bee true, yet are too remote, abstracted and general."

> In the mean tyme they doe but hinder one another in wrangling each against the others figments, whilst nothing certayne is produced by them all either to theory or practice ... [as they] scribble whole reames about frivolous conjectures and imaginations with controversies for and against them. But lett men doe as they please.... [I] never knew any man who had once tasted the sweetness of experimental knowledge that ever afterward lusted after the vaporous garlick and onions of phantasmaticall seeming philosophy.[33]

What Petty was talking about, of course, were problems and experiments in the natural sciences. But I find the polemical passion seductive, and perhaps to good purpose. If we apply his words to the social questions which have dominated utopian thinking from More to Robert Owen and Saint-Simon, we find ourselves with a remarkably sharp foreshadowing of Marx and Engels's critique of the cobweb spinners of their own day, and of their plea for diligent sociological observation instead of abstract philosophical disputes about remote generalities. The essential thrust of both excessively disputatious polemical outbursts was the demand for a new empirical era of theory and practice, free of frivolity and imaginative conjectures, of the vaporous figments of fantasy. We

are dealing here with central intellectual issues in the impassioned
ideology of science and social science.

What I am suggesting is that an important aspect of Hartlib's
achievement was to document the early efforts of a European mind to
hold to the high and middle ground between reason and imagination, or
between facts and fantasy. His life and work, it seems to me, illustrate
a historic bridge connecting science and society—associating, that is,
the new knowledge of men with the new dream for men. Science, and
not merely ethical aspiration, would be the foundation of a felicitous
social order of happiness and plenty. In the eloquent final words of the
first history of the Royal Society,

> . . . while this Halcyon Knowledge is breeding [Sprat writes], all
> *Tempests* will cease; the Oppositions and Contentious Wranglings of
> *Science,* falsely so call'd, will soon vanish away; the peaceable calm-
> ness of Mens *Judgments* will have admirable influence on their *Man-*
> *ners;* the sincerity of their *Understandings* will appear in their *Actions;*
> their *Opinions* will be less violent and dogmatical, but more certain;
> they will only be *Gods* one to another, and not *Wolves;* the value of
> their *Arts* will be esteem'd by the *great Things* they perform, and not
> by those they speak. . . . While the Old could only bestow on us
> some barren Terms and Notions, the New shall impart to us the Uses
> of all the *Creatures,* and shall enrich us with all the Benefits of *Fruit-*
> *fulness* and *Plenty.*[34]

Hartlib's seventeenth-century utopianism hoped to link science and society; Marx's nineteenth-century break with utopianism hoped to link
revolution with a science of society. Although we have already seen
traces of a beginning of "policy science" (hinted at by Philip Sidney,
formulated by James Howell), the full and authentic sociological dimension was still to come. In a word: utopia's natural propensity was for
science, revolution's for social science.

Hartlib's singularly "utopian" relationship with one contemporary
scientist may be taken to illustrate the onset of scientific utopianism.
Young Robert Boyle, then only twenty, and at the outset of his career in
physics, chemistry, and medicine, came to London, was bewildered by
"such a labyrinth," but, taking up Hartlib's invitations to join the special
circle, found one great and redeeming virtue.

> The best on't is, that the corner-stones of the *invisible,* or (as they
> term themselves) the *philosophical college,* do now and then honour
> me with their company, which makes me as sorry for those pressing
> occasions that urge my departure, as I am other times angry with
> that solicitous idleness that I am necessitated to during my stay; men
> of so capacious and searching spirits, that school-philosophy is but

the lowest region of their knowledge; and yet, though ambitious to lead the way to any generous design, of so humble and teachable a genius, as they disdain not to be directed to the meanest, so he can but plead reason for his opinion; persons that endeavour to put narrow-mindedness out of countenance, by the practice of so extensive a charity, that it reaches unto every thing called man, and nothing less than an universal good will can content it . . . they take the whole body of mankind for their care.[35]

In another letter of that same year (1647), Boyle reports to Hartlib of his enthusiasm for certain utopian texts he has just been reading—he refers to Campanella's *Civitas solis* and Andreae's *Respublicae Christianopolitanae*[36]—and the young utopian convert confesses that "my expectations will be none of the smallest . . . " Great literary expectations were linked to real and earnest political prospects. He held "those commonwealths (as the Hollanders and the Venetian) to be the most happy and the most flourishing, where ingenuity is courted with the greatest encouragements." Consequently, as he then tells Hartlib, "we shall endeavour to freight our letters with many *Utopian* intelligences, to express at least this way the very good will with which we bear towards all manner of ingenuities . . . "[37] And so they did.

The Invisible College prepared the way for the establishment in England of the Royal Society; of the twenty-one members of the council named by Royal Charter in 1663 and therefore the original Fellows of the Society, Hartlib had known most (including Boyle, John Wilkins, Theodore Hask, Christopher Wren, John Evelyn, Elias Ashmole, John Aubrey, John Pell, et al.).[38] When Hartlib outlined his revolutionary proposals for a more modern educational system which would, among other things, break the "Grammatical Tyranny of Teaching Tongues," he proposed a list of commissioners which included a fine selection of contemporary tyrannophobes: John Dury, John Pell, Marchamont Nedham, John Milton.[39]

This was the superb moment of a European intellectual enlightenment which accompanied a great social reformation, just as a century later the age of *les lumières* was to be the brilliant prologue to *la grande révolution*. "You interest yourself so much in the Invisible College," Boyle writes to Hartlib, "and that whole society is so highly concerned in all the accidents of your life, that you can send me no intelligence of your own affairs, that does not (at least rationally) assume the nature of *Utopian*." Years later, he is still acknowledging and thanking him "for the exact intelligence you are pleased to oblige me with from Utopia . . . " And, in another letter, he modestly explains that he doesn't want to bother him with requests for bits of news ("of which a whole sheet may be had for a penny")—"No, I will stint my requests to your *Utopian* intelligence ... " What the letters lacked in circulation they made up for in dramatic personal impact and influence.

> I thank you [Hartlib to Boyle, 9 May 1648] for your new discoveries in anatomy and enquiries of other useful and ingenious knowledges. I shewed Mr. Hobbes your letter, who liked it so well that he desired me to lend it to him, which I did.

In moments like these, when a scrawled letter passed from hand to hand, the aching difference between the present inadequacies and future plans became almost too painful to bear—oh, how much more could be accomplished for the progress of mankind if only, as in his happy fictional island, the art and science of Gutenberg were a handy ally.

"My soul is crying out," Hartlib writes; there was so much to do and so little wherewithal; debts were overwhelming him; "the truth is, I design all such and the like works or tracts be printed upon the charges of *Macaria*, whose scope it is most professedly ... to endeavour the reformation of the whole world."[40]

But, as yet, there was still no Macaria to be charged.

10

For no human wit can refute, nor no
human force or power oppose this work of
innovating the world, nor no humane goodness
able to wish better things to mankind . . . . see
that ye delay not to assist the sacred fire
with your sparks, nay, rather with your torches
and with your fans.

—Comenius (1670)

For the times of such a Publique and
Universal Happiness seems not yet to bee at
hand . . . . the smoke is over, but the fire is not
altogether extinct. It may be it will flame
in due time.

—Samuel Hartlib (1661)

So easie is the passage from one extreme to
another; and so *hard* it is, to stop in that little
point, wherein the right does consist.

—Thomas Sprat (1667)

The Great
Intelligencers: II

6. The Onset of Scientific Utopianism
Sprat's Revolution of "Hand and Brain" Aiming at "the Greatest Things"—The New Garden of Plenty—An "American" Revolution?—Prudent Scientists and Generous Spirits—Sprat's "Impetuous Men"—Science and Salvation—War, Tyranny, and Reform—"The Passage from One Extreme to Another"—Between Zealotry and Enthusiasm—Basic Science and Political Error—The Romantic Rebel—"Consequences of a Rational Age"

7. Comenius and the Apocalyptic Revolution
Prophecies of Light in Darkness—Kotterus, Poniatovia, Nicholas Drabicius—Bayle on "the Imposture of Extatic Grimaces"—Erratic Prophets and the Blame for Failure—Comenius's Machiavellian Millennium—An Inconsistent Plea for Tolerance—"Wildfire, catching from Country to Country"—Drabicius and Henry More

8. Pierre Bayle's Critique of Comenius
The Paradoxes of Truth and Error—The Danger of the "Fumo Chiliastico"—When Prophecy Fails—Evasions, Subterfuges, Indulgences—"The Engine for Bringing about Great Revolutions"—The Tragedy of the Man in the Middle—The Historical Amnesia of Each New Generation

9. Hartlib's Experiments, Novelties, and New Things
The Consolations of Practicable Fantasy—Hartlib's Histrionic

Contemporaries—"We seem to overact some well-contrived Romance"—Sprat, Worthington, Boyle—"Affrighting Signs" in the Air—"That happy Island where huge lemons grow"—A Desirable Society and the Pretense of Wonders—Macaria, Antilia, and Mystical Names—Worthington Breaks with Hartlib—The Prosperity of Posterity—A Last Utopian Testament: "The smoke is over, but the fire is not altogether extinct ... "

---

10. Reading, Writing, and Revolution
John Evelyn's Impression—Ants, Bees, and Human Industriousness—Secrets and Conspiracies—Hartlib and Central European Plotters—"He was in himself a kind of imaginary institution"—"Midwife and Nurse" to the Birth of the New

---

6. The Onset of Scientific Utopianism

Thomas Sprat was a youthful amateur in scientific circles when he prepared his *History* for the Royal Society, and his enthusiasm as a propagandist and literary talents as a polemicist cast him happily in the role of the first English ideologist of the new European movement of experimental science. Bacon had only managed to set up what Glanville called a "Romantick Modell." Now one would have the real thing, a genuine manifesto of scientific utopianism, based on the irresistible forces of intellectual and social change, and announcing the practical stages of a profound transformation. It would be the prophecy to the world of "the help of an *Universal Light*, which seems to overspread this *Age* ... "

Sprat came to praise famous men, to honor the new "free way" of a host of unprecedentedly "Inquisitive Minds."

I will take permission to say in general of them that in all *past* and *present* times, I am confident there can never be shewn so great a Number of *Contemporaries* in so narrow a space of the World, that lov'd truth so zealously; sought it so constantly; and upon whose labours, mankind might so freely rely.

Devoted as they all were to "an inviolable correspondence between the hand and the brain," they heralded the end of an old era of the "glorious Pomp of Words." The new time would be triumphantly different, with "a Philosophy of Mankind," issuing in "real Productions." The unity of all protagonists of hand and brain would mark the progress of the scientific revolution, and its genius would be the "Instrument whereby Mankind may obtain a Dominion over *Things*."

> It was said of *Civil Government* by *Plato*, that then the World will be best rul'd, when either *Philosophers* shall be chosen *Kings*, or *Kings* shall have *Philosophical* Minds. And I will affirm the like of *Philosophy*; it will then attain the perfection, when either the *Mechanic Laborers* shall have *Philosophical* heads, or the *Philosophers* shall have *Mechanical hands* ... [1]

This is, as I see it, the link between the first and last great utopian impulses, the utopia from above and the utopia from below; it is the half-way house between the ancient formula of the happy few and the more modern versions of the discontented mass—as in Marx and, later, Veblen—wherein the "mechanical hands" (of workers, or engineers, or scientific technocrats, or self-sufficient participators) take over the philosophical task of determining the perfect arrangements of men in society.

The vision of the scientific utopia expanded by great leaps and bounds, as if the new notion of the future was itself some magical cornucopia. Never before had the human ideal of plenitude been so rich and varied in its promise of earthly plenty and spiritual prowess. "Whoever aims not at the *greatest* Things," Sprat avows, "will seldom proceed much farther than the *least* ... " His fervor continued to feed hungrily on itself. "We may well ghess," he speculated, abandoning all of his skeptical caution about the habits of prophetic fantasy, "that the absolute perfection of the *True Philosophy*, is not now far off ... " The moment was drawing near for a great coming, and in such a tremulous prospect what was science but a high road to paradise? The attractive shape of things to come had a very special and intimate promise about it, and the fulfillment it offered would be personal and complete. "The Beautiful Bosom of *Nature*," Sprat tells us, "will be Expos'd to our view." Even better (if at all possible), "we shall enter its Garden, and taste of its *Fruits*, and satisfy our selves with its *plenty* ... "

If the technical achievements of men's ingenious minds were dizzying, the perspective of infinite progress was even more so. Indeed, the new world of experimental thought was not unconnected with the implications of the recent explorations in transatlantic lands. Sprat is a shade embarrassed whenever he assumes the "vain prophetic spirit" but goes on anyway to foretell the discovery of worlds beyond worlds. "America," as both an idea and a reality, was in alliance with the great hopeful forces of the age, and he is led to the conclusion that "if ever that vast Tract of *Ground* shall come to be more familiar to Europe, either by a free Trade, or by Conquest, or by any other *Revolution* in its Civil Affairs, *America* will appear quite a new *Thing* to us."[2] Thus, very early on, some kind of American Revolution became part of the utopian dream. In a sense we are at a historic point at which the grandest utopian conceptions we have been considering, from Dante and Columbus and Bruno to More, Sidney, and Milton, appear to be combining in an enriched imaginative fulfillment.

Yet, in this context, the utopian was still in an uneasy alliance with the revolutionary. Although I have not been speaking narrowly of the political imagination here, nevertheless the accretion of an element of scientism to the utopian temperament is not without its consequences for the mode of future political action. What happens to the modest skeptical ideal of reasonable prudence when the human vision of hope and transformation becomes so cosmic and extravagant? The ingredients of political apology and literary excess in every ideology prove to be a very unstable basis for intellectual consistency or viability. Original ideals become inevitably, if unwillingly, subjected to qualifications, revisions, and exceptions, and sometimes they get turned by some recurring and perverse human dialectic into their very opposite. The excesses of others may well be a species of vicious immoderation, but can one think of one's own excesses as anything but a spillover of heroic aspiration? Can the greatest of human achievements be conceived without boldness, and restlessness, and perhaps even the intrusion of violent irregularities?

It is thus that Sprat faces this fundamental and ubiquitous dilemma, and gets classically caught in its cruel toils. In his portrait of the new culture heroes of the age, praising "the *Generosity* of their *Spirits*," he writes:

> *Invention* is an *Heroic* thing, and plac'd above the reach of a low and vulgar *Genius*. It requires an active, a bold, a nimble, a restless *Mind:* a thousand difficulties must be contemn'd, with which a mean heart would be broken: many *attempts* must be made to no purpose: much *Treasure* must sometimes be scatter'd without any return: much violence, and vigor of thoughts must attend it: some irregularities, and excesses must be granted it, that would hardly be pardon'd by the severe *Rules of Prudence.*

"All which may persuade us," he concludes, that only "a large and unbounded Mind is likely to be the Author of greater *Productions.*" This, as I have been arguing throughout, is a conflict between basic temperamental principles, a tension between boundaries and limitlessness which will remain permanently unresolved in the European mind. Utopia and revolution, taking inspiration as they do from both reason and passion, longing for both order and change, embracing classical hopes as well as romantic ambitions, carry constantly and inexpungably within themselves the seeds of conflict and contradiction.

In one half of his mind the historian of the scientific revolutionaries thrilled to the excitement of the unexpected and the rapture of the break-through. In point of fact he pleaded for a necessary "mingling of Tempers," including the "violent and fiery ... the Impetuous men."[3] Yet, in another half of his awareness, he was able to persuade himself to believe that the new scientists had given an "assurance of eternal quietness and moderation in their experimental progress." One part of Thomas Sprat would have no fat, the other would have no lean. He piously hoped that the new spirit would "moderate and reform by abolishing or restraining the Fury of *Enthusiasm*." He worried about "the difficulty of ordering the very Motions of senseless and irrational things" and knew "how much harder it is to rule the restless Minds of Men." He thought with a shudder of the direct consequences which might issue from "the violence of *spiritual madness*," from some divine turning away from grace; he called it "a revolution which cannot be thought on without horror," for "the subversion of all Europe would attend it." Fearing as he did the charges of his contemporaries that the scientific movement for which he was the spokesman might well lead to the baleful undermining of all things, he tried to divert the hostility on to quite other (and allegedly unrelated) intellectual tendencies.

> The *Science* that is acquir'd by *Disputation* teaches men to cavil well, and to find fault with accurate subtility; it gives them a fearless confidence of their own judgments; it leads them from contending in sport, to oppositions in earnest; it makes them believe that every thing is to be handled for, and against, in the *State*, as well as in the *Schools*.

That was the blameworthy faction, and there were the culpable fellows!

This was disingenuous, and unconvincing. Sprat heard no end of rebuttals from his assailants (not least among them Dr. Henry Stubbe and Robert South), who expressed more than mild astonishment at the thesis that the new innovating philosophy was so prudent, and quiet, and politically innocuous. Some of Sprat's inconsistency, of course, had its cause in the argumentative swordplay of a polemical apologist, trying to thrust and parry as best he could in a hard-pressed situation. But it also had a deeper source in the almost universal temptation of the age to take on millennial accents. One of Sprat's modern editors has gone so far as to charge that Sprat was capable of arguing "as fervently as the wildest apocalyptic."[4] He was not the first or last intellectual who spoke science and meant salvation. Even men of reason could be led into the euphoric passions of rage and hope. Out of the most careful tentative experimentalism often came carefree prophetic spirits who, in their impatience with so much old, intractably encrusted reality, jumped at the prospect of "an utter *Destruction, Root* and *Branch* ... " No amount of scientific discipline could entirely repress the kind of romantic longing which aspires to the greatest achievements of transformation and perfection: when men would indeed "be Gods one to another."

That this excursion into ambivalence had to do not merely with the vagaries of the personal style of scientific activity but also with the wider attitude toward political change and social progress emerges with striking clarity when Sprat details the expansion of "traffic and business" and explains the various underlying reasons for the profound alterations of his turbulent time. Among the prime causes he mentions "the Civil War itself." This, he says—in one of the most trenchant formulations of the uncertain potential for good or evil of revolutionary violence—"'is always wont to be the cruellest *Tyrant,* or the best *Reformer;* either utterly to lay waste, or to civilize, and beautify, and ripen the Arts of all Countries." Again, the dualism was simple, convenient, and arbitrary. For now the either/or appeared to be a necessary dichotomy. More romantic and violent spirits would entertain the conception that the utter laying-waste of the old was the very price that human society had to pay for civilizing beautification, and that only by means of a necessarily destructive tyranny could the end of reform be served.

Part of Thomas Sprat's ingenuity was doubtless his ability to hold to the high central ground while occupying both flanks at the same time. He was by turns a champion of heroic adventurousness, even to the extremes of enthusiasm and romantic prophesy; a reassuring advocate of a prudence so moderate it could promise "eternal quietness"; and a man of the middle who reveled in the "varieties of opinions" and in the elevated scientific role as "Umpire of them all."

There were supreme moments when he clearly identified the errors which are so "very natural to men's minds" (not, of course, excluding his own): "they love not a long and a tedious doubting, though it bring them at last to a real certainty: but they choose rather to conclude presently, than to be long in suspence, though to better purpose ... " Call it haste or imprudence or instability, Sprat recognized "the universal inclination of mankind to be mis-led by themselves." Presumption, weariness, and negligence were all involved as philosophers erected "superstructures" of "sudden confidence of the certainty of their knowledge." A chastened ideologist of science, now both cautious and critical, Sprat was full of verve in his search for both frontiers and limits. His touch of melancholy can be seen in other rhetorical attempts to hold to the high middle ground: Winstanley, Bayle, Kant, Mackintosh, Mme de Staël, Camus, among others. "So easie is the passage from one extreme to another," Sprat wrote, "and so *hard* it is, to stop in that little point, wherein the right does consist." Seen from "that little point" in the center, it was always a majestic justification of truth and reason to acknowledge the outbreak of a war on two fronts.

> While some over-zealous *Divines* do reprobate Natural Philosophy as a carnal knowledge, and a too much minding worldly things: the men of the World, and business on the other side, esteem it meerly as an idle matter of Fancy, as that which disables us from taking right measures in humane affairs. Thus by one party it is censur'd for stooping too low; by the other, for soaring too high: so that methinks, it is a good ground to conclude, that it is guilty of neither of these faults, feeling it is alike condemn'd by both the extreams.

Issues in the struggle changed, but the topography of the battle remained the same: the high central ground in the middle had to be held against the flanks. The rash modern rationalists on the one side, the fanatical theological sects on the other—both shared in the same pernicious immoderation. Why should it be true that "nothing can be well-done in new *Discoveries* unless all the *Ancient Arts* be first rejected, and their Nurseries abolish'd"? Those extremists, Sprat argued, "have come as furiously to the purging of *Philosophy,* as our *Modern Zealots* did to the *reformation* of *Religion.* And the one Party is as justly to be condemn'd, as the other."

> Nothing will suffice either of them, but an utter *Destruction, Root* and *Branch,* of whatever has the face of Antiquity. But as the *Universities* have withstood the fierceness of the ones zeal without knowledge; so there is no doubt, but they will also prevail against the violence of the others pretences to *knowledge* without *prudence.*

This is, in many ways, one of the most formidable attempts in this early modern era to formulate a strategy of resistance to the recurrent polarization of intellectual forces. If, as in Sprat's case, the effort went erratically awry, the failure can only be ascribed to that contradiction within impassioned reason itself which upsets rhetorical balance and temperamental control.

Thus, with much valiance, and no little elegance to disguise his essential ambiguities, Sprat plodded on, avoiding any direct reply to critics, but still trying to meet their points.

> The common Accusations against *Learning* are such as these; That it inclines man to be unsettled, and *contentious; . . .* That it makes them *Romantic,* and subject to more perfect images of things, than the things themselves will bear.

Here, in a context of seventeenth-century anti-intellectualism, is an early sign of the fear of the romantic rebel, his subversiveness in the name of high ideals, and especially his utopian dream of an impracticable perfection. Could it be that there was something in the nature of scientific utopianism that "makes our Minds too *Lofty* and *Romantic,* and inclines them to form more perfect Imaginations of the Matters we practise, than the Matters themselves will bear"?[5]

If it was the kind of self-critical doubt that could (and did) trouble men like Thomas More and Samuel Hartlib, it left little trace of a shadow on Sprat's mind. The new experiments would bring both profit and delight, and he confidently affirmed that "by the pleasure of their *Discoveries* they will wear off the roughness, and sweeten the humourous peevishness of mind, whereby many are sowr'd into Rebellion ... " Basic science would be the corrective to political error. For were not he and his friends closer than any other generation of men had ever been to the earthiest realities of Nature? The open and proud defense of the romantic imagination would be left for yet another generation; Sprat shrewdly preferred to counterattack. He was armed—and, as the course of history would have it, invincibly so—with a buoyant and energizing sense of the true causes of all happenings, and like a headstrong marauder he belabored the antiquated empires of untruth.

> It is indeed a Disgrace to the Reason and Honour of Mankind, that every fantastical *Humorist* should presume to interpret all the *secret Ordinances of Heaven;* and to expound the Times, and Seasons, and Fates of Empires, though he be never so ignorant of the very common *Works* of *Nature,* that lye under his Feet.... This weakens the Constancy of human actions. This affects men with fears, doubts, irresolutions, and terrors. It is usually observ'd, that such *Presaging,* and *Prophetical Times,* do commonly fore-run great *destructions,* and *revolutions* of human affairs. And that it should be so is natural enough, though the *Presages* and *Prodigies* themselves did signify no such events. For this *melancholy,* this *frightful,* this *Astrological* humor disarms mens hearts, it breaks their courage; it confounds their Councils; it makes them help to bring such *calamities* on themselves ...

Thus, the ambience of the new scientific thinking has brought us decisively closer to the emergence of the distinctively modern form of utopian revolutionary: a man of fearlessness and resolution, romantic if you wish, imaginative in his conception of perfect ideals, armed with heart and courage for the fulfillment of human actions. This, surely, was one (and not the least important) result of what Sprat referred to as "the consequences of a *Rational Age* ... amidst all the improvements of *Knowledge,* and the subversion of old Opinions about Nature, and introduction of new ways of Reasoning thereon."[6] It was—in a word he insisted upon—a "Reformation" of old habits of mind and action.

For all his efforts to accommodate the new science to the restored establishments of church and state, Sprat seemed to be especially pleased to be able to credit the recent era of revolutionary turbulence openly with one singular achievement:

> The late times of *Civil War*, and *confusion*, to make recompense for their infinite calamities, brought this advantage with them, that they stirr'd up mens minds from long ease, and a lazy rest, and made them *active, industrious* and *inquisitive*: it being the usual benefit that follows upon *Tempests*, and *Thunders* in the *State*, as well as in the *Skie*, that they purifie, and clear the *Air*, which they disturb.[7]

How characteristic for the florid spokesman of plain language against "tricks of metaphor" to turn to the metaphorical milieu of natural upset, to images of thunder and storm! It was the kind of simile in which such ambivalent apocalyptic spirits always take deep satisfaction. The conceits of terrestrial catastrophe constitute the essential imagery in which romantic scientists—not unlike their kindred spirits among the utopians and revolutionaries—find their most vivid justification.

7. Comenius and the Apocalyptic Revolution

The men in Hartlib's circle bore "very good will" (in Boyle's phrase) "towards all manner of ingenuities." But if this included the novel dream of utopian advance, did it also embrace a revolutionary prospect of apocalyptic change? Unlike so many of their visionary contemporaries, they rarely, if ever, gave the impression of holding their breath for the impending fulfillment of eschatological promise.

"If ever"? Here the historian of climates of opinion must shrink back from the dangers of impressionism and enter a caution. Inasmuch as this is a point almost impossible to quantify, short of computing every literary reference to apocalyptic themes in a thousand texts, it should really be qualified. For most intellectual spirits of an age which was still deeply Christian in thought and feeling, the sense of a dramatic terrestrial end (as in the books of Daniel and Revelation) was a real, earnest, and constant personal factor, although it took on a fiery intensity among the mystics and became almost a casual article of faith among the rationalists. Just as even the greatest of seventeenth-century scientific minds often entertained anomalous notions about alchemy and witchcraft, so also do we find the social thought of sober and moderate men often veering wildly in the direction of the catastrophic denouément which doctrinal religion held to be the sign of divine and final felicity. This can be observed in the work of even such admirable exponents of right reason as Comenius and Henry More.

In the various editions of his *Lux e tenebris* (between 1657 and 1665—some critics have pointed meaningfully to the change in title from the earlier *Lux in tenebris*), Comenius made an extraordinary collection of mystical prophecies of the approaching ruin of the House of Austria as well as the imminent downfall of the Pope. Like a revolutionary in despair, responding eagerly to the hopeful flickerings of light in darkness, he culled the predictions from the works of three sensational prophets of the day—Kotterus, Poniatovia, and Nicholas Drabicius—and the books were illustrated with glowing prints of their visions. The popularity of the work was more than matched by its critical and even outraged reception in European intellectual circles, where important spokesmen refused to accept any backsliding from the standards of the new values of skeptical reason.

Pierre Bayle's sharpness in pronouncing Comenius to be "inexcusable" was only representative of the counterattack which raged forty years in Paris, Amsterdam, London, and elsewhere in a European world seriously disoriented by large competing demands on men's minds and faith. This much Bayle, in the course of a withering critique, was generous enough to concede to Comenius:

> He was a man of parts and learning; he argued very sensibly on other matters, and in these like a man of wit; and there was nothing in his person that appeared like an enthusiast. This made people conclude that he did not believe the things he uttered. There may be, and sometimes is, imposture in extatic grimaces; I am willing to have it thought that Comenius did not harbour any sinister design.[8]

Even after three centuries, there remains a bewildering note about Comenius's turn to the apocalypse,[9] although we are no longer tempted by explanations of satanism or insincerity; or, indeed, by those subsequent criticisms in the age of Enlightenment from rationalistic historians of chiliasm who saw in the whole episode only more evidence of "childish gullibility."[10] But in its mélange of mysticism, politics, and desperation, Comenius's zealous and determined apologia for millennial prophecy is of more than passing interest precisely because of its subtle complexity—and in ways that are especially pertinent to our main theme.

Bayle has recorded that Comenius's work "in a few years was continued and forgot; but was prodigiously sought after when the Turks besieged Vienna in 1683." Apparently, those who had lodged copies of it in garrets, gathering dust, took them out and sold them at high prices. "Had Vienna been taken," Bayle remarks drily, "Drabicius would have been more talked of than the Grand Vizier." There is even a poignant note to the sarcasm.

I began to know [Bayle concludes], during the siege of Vienna, how greatly I was mistaken in fancying mankind were quite cured with regard to those chimerical hopes that are so often grounded on visions. I met everywhere with people, who spoke of nothing but Drabicius' prophecies, of the truth of which they seemed perfectly persuaded; and who built so many castles in the air, that they were to destroy Babylon in an instant.

Who is to say that the faith in instantaneous liberation has substantially declined over the years?

Comenius himself was far too keen-witted to remain completely untroubled in his surprising and unwonted role as the defender of political chiliasm. In one of his letters to Drabicius, he was evidently "filled with great bitterness" when he wrote:

If you, Friend, are so certain of God's speaking to you, your certainty will serve for yourself, but not those whom the contrariety of events renders uncertain. And we see continual examples of such as have embraced errors for truth, have been willing to lay down their lives for them, as for the very most truth, being persuaded nothing else in the sight of God than that they had believed, taught and wrought things most true. And yet therefore, did not Error cease to be Error . . .

He begged the Moravian prophet who had become a subject of wonder and dispute all over Europe to confirm his integrity "by not concealing that some of those things which are so manifestly false, have been additaments of your own conjecture." He pleaded with him "to deal sincerely with me."[11]

And yet the defense, despite marginal doubts, was wholehearted. Comenius took pains to refute "the Objection of things not coming to pass accordingly." He tried to argue that all "Prophetick predictions are conditional," that "there is a possibility of fulfilling most still . . . For Prophets are subject to Error, Passions, Affections, &c. which the spirit of Prophecy does not always take away . . . . All Prophecy is a Riddle and obscure." He was convinced that "that which is not fulfilled today, may be tomorrow," a thesis which hardly strained any one's credulity, although its inevitable corollary has long been a source of annoyance in such apologies as: "If, lastly, events don't answer, blame man as some way faulty . . . " For the true chiliast is never in a position to abandon either the prophet or the prophecy; the blame for failure always lies elsewhere. No, he would not turn his back on the "great Revolutions" that were foretold in the prophecies of Christina Poniatova to the Poles (against Wallenstein), of Kotterus to the Germans (for the destruction of the Papacy), and of Drabicius to the Hungarians (against the House of Austria).

> And Machiavil himself was not such an Atheist and Infidel, but that he acknowledged God's usual manner of foretelling all great Revolutions. I beseech you, O Divines! ... let not Politicians exceed you in attention to the Words and Works of God; Machiavil, comparing former times with present, as he easily confesses, He knows not the cause; so he also sayes it ought to be acknowledged out of all Ancient and Modern Examples: That all great Motions whatsoever, that have happened either to a City, or a Country, have been wont to be foretold, by either Guessers and Conjecturers, or some Revelation, or Prodigies, or Signs in the Heavens ...

This ingenious recruitment of the Italian master of political strategy was not an accidental rhetorical maneuver; for clearly the "great Revolution" which Comenius had in mind would be both millennial and Machiavellian. It was, in part, the vision of the traditional eschatological fulfillment and, in part, the radical rearrangement of European power relations.

> But behold in our times the words of all the Prophecies old and new are consummated, which the universal commotion of Nations, which you seen, and the universal change of thing, which you shall shortly see, do witness. Ho! therefore take again unto you your power, and leave not your scepters any longer in a strange and wrong hand: I have commanded you, O Kings and Princes, that you your selves Govern ...
> But what must you do when you take unto you your power, O Kings? That very thing which the King of Kings (whose Ministers you are at this time) require of you. TO REFORM THE WORLD AND ALL THINGS IN IT, THROUGH ALL NATIONS.[12]

The clear injunction was to "make all things new," to begin "this glorious Renovation." The "Messianic" task was to cease the persecutions of men, end all wars, and proclaim a lasting peace. As Comenius observed in a plain if indirect warning, "The present commotion of the World, and so many unlooked for Mutations, do not signifie nothing."[13]

Was this the same cool and reasonable reformer, armed only with his noble plans for schools and scholarship, who had come on Hartlib's invitation to London in the 1640s and had found the English scene too turbulent and dangerous?[14] Obviously, it was no longer a time to interpret the world, or even to improve it, but a time to change it—totally. The message now was: " ... either a Total Reformation, or a Total Destruction, one of the two ... " Things in their Babylonian corruption needed "to be reformed from the very foundation, or to be rooted up from the very foundation ... "[15]

As for the book itself, a wild and fearful manifesto of revolution which doubtless must still be capable of moving rebellious spirits, Comenius asks its readers "not to pass rash Judgment, or over-hasty Execution," by which he intended essentially a plea not to have it consigned "to the fire."

> I beseech you, O Theologers! ... O Modern Councils, Synods, Consistories, Universities ... Desist to prohibit this Book. For no human wit can refute, nor no human force or power oppose this work of innovating the world, nor no humane goodness able to wish better things to mankind.

The argument for tolerance was more in Comenius's characteristic tone and style, although the plea must surely have been beneath the invincible dignity of a tract which presented itself as so irrefutable and irresistible. How anomalous it is for a humanist to be requesting a polite hearing for the apocalypse! And, after all, what we have here is an open and frank declaration of apocalyptic mission—"This Book is the Trumpet to Wars ... "[16] But it is not the first, nor will it be the last, occasion in which inconsistent men of great revolutions, eager to rally support for the inevitable, insist upon rights which their theory dismisses as either meaningless or unnecessary.

The London edition which in 1670 presented these Central European views "for the Common Use and Information of the English" set them in a historical context which was remarkable for its sensitivity to the new properties of the concept of revolution. It grasped with some acuity, although not necessarily with sympathy, that revolutions could be systematic, and contagious, and indeed permanent. Noting the new spirit everywhere, "even in New-England," the author is obviously struck by the principle of perpetual commotion at work. "Strange," he says, "that Reformation should be always doing, and never done"—

> As if Religion were intended,
> For nothing else, but to be mended ...

He offers a comprehensive chronicle of "the late *grand Revolutions* of *Europe*": with special attention to "the Revolutions of the Low-Countries, of France, of England, of Bohemia," to "the Revolutions of the Empire," and to "the Foundation and Revolutions of the present Turkish Empire," and he comes to this conclusion:

> Thus have we seen in this last and worst age of the World, all Christendom all on a flame of Wars and Confusions like *Wildfire* everywhere, catching from Country to Country, and then taking its course round. Neither has any Nation escaped scot-free from Stupendous Revolutions both Ecclesiastical and Civil.

The attitude expressed here toward the various subversions and depositions, the "civil wars, Broyls, Commotions and Factions," is too troubled
to entertain any notion that, even with the confident promise of Comenius's apocalyptic prophets, the state of affairs in this world was conceivably likely to improve. No, the revolution was not yet progressive (at
least to this English mind), but it was already seen to be the mightiest
and most breathtaking historical force in contemporary politics.

> ... the marvellous and unheard of Alterations and Troubles; The
> terrible and bloody Wars, and most wonderful Revolutions even of
> all *Asia* and *Africa*, in this present Age likewise; but especially of the
> mighty ancient and most flourishing Empire of *China*; have been no
> less astonishing and stupendous, than the European.[17]

Thus, it was also a world revolution.

Before I return to my point of departure—to Pierre Bayle, and to the
men of Hartlib's circle and their own confrontation of the problem of
reason and revolution—let me cite at least one passage from Drabicius[18]
as an illustration of the prophetical style which Comenius, for one desperate reason or another, found inspiring. I also intend it as a way of
establishing a useful contrast with the English apocalyptic strain as
examplified in the work of Dr. Henry More. Here is Drabicius in a fine
frenzy.

> Howl, O howl, thou cursed House of Austria; weep and lament; for
> behold, the arrows of my wrath are flying over to thee, which I have
> poured forth from my throne to revenge thy iniquities, and thy
> tyranny which thou hast exercised over the nations committed to thy
> charge, and over the people who have upheld thee and maintained
> thee. Thou, O House of Austria, hast made thyself drunk with the
> blood of many excellent illuminated persons, who have served thee
> and given thee good counsel; but thou hast enforced them from the
> land and inheritance of their fathers, raging in thy cruelty until the
> day and hour of thy ruin, which I have appointed for thee: for thou
> didst ride upon the beast, and the beast on thee, commanding thee
> to murder thy subjects, pull down their cities, and lay waste their
> countries, without any fear of God, or compassion of man: therefore,
> now the time is come of thy lamentation, for I have heard the cry of
> the souls of the slain for my word, crying under the altar. Fly,
> therefore, ye nations of the world, and assemble yourselves together
> to the supper of my anger.[19]

Pressed by critics who charged that his revelations were mere figments
of his brain and even satanical delusions, Drabicius took a solemn oath,
denying that he had been offering "strange fire out of the forge of my

own brain." If it were not the Manifest Word, then in the just zeal of God "the fire may go forth ... and devour and burn me in the midst of my Brethren ... *Amen!*"

This outburst from the heart of the European continent is, as I have hinted, worlds apart in both rhetoric and wrath from those tepid English verses of Dr. Henry More (whose insular, and insulating, influence helped to domesticate Hartlib's Continental spirit):

> These be our times ...
> A three-branch'd Flame shall soon sweep clean the Stage
> Of this old dirty Dross; and all wax Young.
> My Words into this frozen Air I throw,
> Will then prove Vocal at that general Thaw.[20]

The very mildness of the visionary formulation, its note of almost casual catastrophism, may be taken as a sign of how much English progress was being made toward the taming of the apocalypse.

8. Pierre Bayle's Critique of Comenius

Few disputes of the century were carried on with more modern political remorselessness than the critique which Pierre Bayle launched in 1695 against Comenius's astonishing defense of the three Central European prophets and their vision of a political apocalypse. It is difficult to make out which more outraged the French skeptic (then a refugee in Rotterdam)—the betrayal of an intellectual style which he considered the shared heritage of humane, reasonable men; or the obliviousness to disastrous social consequences which in a time of illiberal persecution and violent conflict bordered on pernicious irresponsibility.

How could any burned child of the age not shy away from the fire? Bayle himself was the son of a Protestant minister in the heart of old Albigensian France; he became, in turn, a Catholic convert and Jesuit scholar, a relapsed heretic who returned to reformed religion, and finally, as an impassioned defender of reason, the encyclopedist of the errors and follies of mankind. He scoured the annals of history, theology, and politics in the relentless pursuit of mistakes, superstitions, and fallacies. No bit of intellectual nonsense was too recondite to be ignored in his *Dictionnaire*, and a wealth of disputatious references swelled his footnotes until they quite crowded out the text on the folio pages. If his critics thought his work to be superficial and ostentatious scholarship, his admirers were not ashamed to hail it as a superb achievement of European letters, perhaps even the first intellectual classic of high journalism. "I recognize quite plainly," Bayle once confessed in a letter which could be taken as one of the charter documents of a new literary estate, "that my insatiable craving for news is one of those inveterate diseases that set all treatment at defiance. It's dropsy; that's what it is. The more you give it, the more it wants."[21] His correspondents at all Europeans centers kept him supplied with all the data he needed to take on Comenius and, especially, Drabicius; and he warmed to the task.

Still, for all their single-mindedness, his strictures were free of the fanaticism of the one-eyed polemicist; Bayle's mixed career and varied training had given his mind a skeptical cast which made it too dialectical for simplism and too sensitive not to respond to paradox and ambiguity. "The same theory which serves as a weapon against error, may sometimes do a disservice to the cause of truth." Bayle was convinced that the one thing you will always find if you look long enough is antinomy, contradiction. More than that: man was in such a *"mauvaise situation"* because "the light which enables him to avoid one evil leads him into another ... "[22] Bayle went even further than this in his attempt to plot the sinuous course of intellectual effort—and it was a spiral twist and turn that later warriors against unreason were naïvely to ignore.

There is no perversion of the truth, however absurd it be, that is not passed on from book to book, from generation to generation. Lie with a bold face, we may say to the sorriest mountebank in Europe, print what outrageous extravagance you will, you will find plenty of people to copy your tales, and, if you are extinguished now, the day will come, circumstances will arise, when it will be in someone's interest to bring you back to life again.[23]

One other moral and methodological principle informed Bayle's work; and it prompted Ernst Cassirer to declare him the originator of the ideal of historical accuracy.

All those who know the laws of history, will agree that a historian who wishes to fulfill his tasks faithfully must free himself of the spirit of flattery and slander. He must, as far as possible, adopt the state of mind of the Stoic who is moved by no passion. Impervious to all else, he must heed solely the interests of the truth, to which he must sacrifice resentment aroused by an injustice as well as recollection of favors—and even his love of country. He must forget that he belongs to any particular country, that he was brought up in any particular faith, that he is indebted to this person or that, and that he has these or those parents and friends. A historian in these respects is like Melchizedech, without father, without mother, and without genealogy. If he is asked: "Whence art thou?" he must reply: "I am neither a Frenchman nor a German, neither an Englishman nor a Spaniard, etc.; I am a citizen of the world; I am not in the service of the Emperor, nor in that of the King of France, but only in the service of Truth. She is my queen; to her alone have I sworn the oath of obedience.[24]

Flourishing, then, both the weapons of analytical reason and a sage if somewhat aloof cosmopolitan attitude toward intellectual folly, Bayle made his way in the various volumes of his *Dictionnaire* from Aaron and Abelard to Zoroaster (with an appendix offering afterthoughts on Obscenity); and we pause to consider the substance of his trenchant and almost forgotten counter-statement as exemplified in his three pieces on Kotterus, Drabicius, and Comenius himself.[25] Most historians, mindful of the formidable contributions of Comenius to modern education and humane letters, have been inclined to disparage the unfairness of Bayle's hostility to a noble and urbane pioneer; in so doing they have missed the importance of Bayle's great and penetrating dissent from the developing ideology of utopian revolutionism. For what Bayle detected in the contemporary chiliastic movement—and the so-called secular religions of the future were to share the same characteristics—were the psychological vulnerability of its enthusiasts, the social explosiveness of its programmatic extremism, and the dark tragic potential of its totalistic commitment to a future prospect which promised felicity through purificatory violence. Prometheanism tends to bedazzle and blind: and in the fascination with the fire one gets inured to the smoke. "Ye men of learning," Comenius had cried out (and the appeal has not failed to rouse fine spirits in all times),[26] "see that ye delay not to assist the sacred fire with your sparks, nay, rather with your torches and with your fans." Bayle, for his part, tried rather to alarm Europe to the burning danger of the *fumo chiliastico*.

This last phrase was borrowed from one of Comenius's most prolific critics, Maresius, of the University at Groningen, who indeed provided the keynote for Bayle's own commentaries: "*Sed praefertim est Comenius Fanaticus, Visionarius, et Enthusiasta in solio ...* "* The case against visionary enthusiastic fanaticism was built up argument by argument.

1. *Events prove prophets wrong.* Bayle diligently assembled all the relevant historical data and took the trouble to provide even his footnotes with footnotes. What, if anything, could be said on behalf of the large predictions of ruin and renovation? Which powers perished, and when were reforms and changes actually instituted? The record appeared to him to be incontrovertible and devastating:

---

*"But especially Comenius is a Fanatic, a Visonary Creature, and an Enthusiast of the first class ... "

No false prophets ever met with such cruel affronts as those which the prophecies published by Comenius received ...

His conclusion contained a two-fold warning: first, against the dialectical wrigglings which would attempt to explain away enormous error; and, second, against the illiberal threats which fanaticized emotion is apt to produce in the course of heated argument. *"Voilà de nos gens,"* he says of Drabicius and his defenders, "they never are at a loss if they have but time to adjust their affairs ... * Still further:

Take warning by these confusions of Comenius' false prophets, all you who had presumed to menace, with the book of revelations, all those who are not agreeable to you ... †

Thus, after a general proposition about the faulty nature of prophetic predictions, a corollary about the erratic character of the visionary prophets readily presented itself.

2. *The prophetic temperament remains irreconcilable even in failure and defeat.* This was, for Bayle, the most hopeless and depressing property of the phenomenon of enthusiasm. A "bigotted" effect was inevitable when, as with Comenius, "he filled his brain with Prophecies, Revolutions, the ruining of Anti-Christ, the Millennium, and such like ideas of a dangerous enthusiasm ... "‡. But when prophecy fails,[27] would not a process of disenchantment set in? How is it that neither shame, nor confusion, nor disgrace contribute to a soberer appreciation of facts and realities? What factors serve the continual self-renewal of chiliastic self-confidence? Nobody before Bayle had faced such intricate questions of political psychology with such a modern combination of analytical subtlety and ideological passion. Busying himself with the latest news from everywhere, he could wryly note that "Comenius was always attentive to the events which happened in Europe in order to reconcile them with the system of his Chimeras [*au Système de ses Visions*]!" He observed that "It is the custom of such persons (as has been seen by late instances) to square and adjust some part of their predictions to the articles of the News-Papers [*selon les nouvelles de la Gazette*]." But, after all, he had read the same papers following the same events, and he recorded both the mounting exasperation and the deviousness of the Comenian prophet.

---

*" ... ils ne demeurent jamais court, pourvu qu'on leur donne le loisir d'ajuster leurs flûtues ... "

† ... l'audace de manacer de l'Apocalypse ceux qui ne vous plaisent pas ... "

‡"il se coiffa encore plus de Prophéties, de Révolutions, de ruïnes de l'Antechrist, de Regne de mille ans, & de semblables morceaux d'un dangereux Fanatisme ... "

No other expedient was necessary in order to make him the object of ridicule, but to oppose his own arguments one against the other. This exasperated him to the highest degree. And such is the fate of obstinacy and self conceit; and of those who become fanaticks, by imbibing too eager a fondness for certain opinions. Their first works destroy their last; and if any man presume to reproach them with their contradictions, they immediately fly into a great passion.

"Consider this well," Bayle admonishes us, as he draws his portraits of arrant intellectual self-indulgence:

> they never lack evasions; there is always some clause, which they did not take notice of; and thus they always reserve for themselves a back-door, and a resource in order to begin their Prophecies afresh ... Comenius was more subtle than we imagine, when he tacked his three seers together [*quand il compila son triolet*]. We find more subterfuges in three Prophets than in one.

If this seemed a shade too personal in its indictment, Bayle qualified it with a recognition of the cultural context and, indeed, the social or popular responsibility of widespread political delusion and ignorance.

> These Gentlemen are of an excellent temper; nothing can ruffle them, or put them out of countenance; and they appear as boldly in company after the expiration of the period as before; they do not fear either the jokes or the serious reproaches to which they must be exposed. They are ever ready to begin again; in a word, they are proof against the most justly grounded mortifications. We must not ascribe this wholly to the odd cast of their minds and affections; the public is more to be blamed than they, because of their too extreme indulgence to such people ... so true it is, that people love to be imposed upon in certain things [*tant il est vrai qu'on se plaît à être trompé sur certains articles*].

In the individual case of Comenius (how well he knew himself, when he said he was "a man of longing"), Bayle thought he understood—perhaps because he, too, had shared the uprooted lot of a refugee and exile—what it was that drove him onward in his devotion to the "Great Revolution." How else but through a total reformation and a total destruction could he ever escape the cruel labyrinth of European power politics and find his way home again? Bayle, with a measure of skepticism and cold irony, offered him instead only what Comenius himself had called "the paradise of the heart."

> It would have been more laudable in him, had he turned his eyes inward, and applied his whole thoughts to his salvation, during his exile, rather than to busy himself so much about the transactions of

Europe, in order to discover, in the interests of Princes, in their wars, alliances, &c. wherewithal to sooth the hopes he entertained of being restored to his country, as well as revenged of his enemies: it was this that threw him into enthusiasm.

It was an alternative which, with as much justness and irrelevance, might well have been presented to Dante and Bruno and all the other European protagonists of national nostalgia and heroic longing. For the ultimate revolutionary commitment was a matter of both deep personal romanticism and a wider historical process.

3. *The making of a revolution requires a prophetic vision, a utopian compound of enthusiasm, certainty, and apocalyptic drama.* To the extent that Bayle argued this point he can, in a sense, be taken to be the father of the sociology of revolution (and the founder, if I may say so, of such studies in comparative ideology as this). As he tersely observed, "in all ages and countries, Prophecies have been forged in order to excite people to Rebellion ... "* Yet it would be altogether simple-minded to believe that in the course of a violent and complex struggle for new power, the utopian cause and the revolutionary effect may not be divided, diverted, tragically or cynically disengaged. Prophecies are too important to be left to the prophets. "It is very possible," Bayle shrewdly remarks, "that a Prince of sagacity enough to despise these chimeras, may form schemes and great designs agreably to the visions of these people ... " He concluded with what must surely be one of the most percipient—and, ironically enough, prophetic as well—thoughts of the whole first century of classic utopian revolutionism: " ... for it is a very powerful engine for bringing about great revolutions, to prepare the people by explications of the Apocalypse, uttered with an air of inspiration and enthusiasm."† The irony runs deeper, and we will be forced to return to the paradox of how a skeptical, non-Utopian, and anti-revolutionary spirit like Bayle became the father of the *philosophes* and was seized upon by the enraged political generation of 1789 as an ally of *la grande révolution*. Angry men with inspired dreams of perfection were strange company indeed for the prudent and moderate critic who had written:

> Let a man do the best he can, let him build better systems than Plato's *Republic*, More's *Utopia*, or Campanella's *Commonwealth of the Sun*, &c. All these fine ideas will be found short and deficient when they come to be reduced to practice. The passions of men, that arise

---

*"de tous temps & en tout païs, on a supposé des Prophéties pour porter les peuples à la révolte ... "
†"Car c'est une trés-puissante machine pour amener sur la scène les grandes Révolutions, que d'y préparer les peuples par des explications apocalyptiques, débitées avec des airs d'inspiration & d'enthousiasme."

from one another in a prodigious variety, would presently ruin the hopes we had conceived from these fine systems.[28]

"See what happens," he admonishes, when "the finest things imaginable" are "found defective when applyed to that matter which exists out of our minds, that is, to hard and impenetrable matter ... " There was, alas, no convenient bridge—and certainly not "Revolution"—between "the speculations of a man who forms a notion of a perfect government" and what Bayle set out as the real "image of human passions." Perhaps this much, at least, should be suggested here: just as Robespierre despised the too-cool and critical spirit of Voltaire, Condorcet, and the other *philosophes* (and refused to allow them into the Jacobin Pantheon— "the virtuous Rousseau" was preferred), so too would Bayle, whose *Dictionnaire* was about to be republished in 1790, have been found wanting in the proper fire with which to destroy an old world and build anew a golden age for man. But this is not the place to explore the serious historical confusion which went into the making of such absurd cases of mistaken identity.

In brief, the utopian revolutionaries chose to believe that what held true for men of religion could only be utterly irrelevant to men of reason and secular hope; they could never accept that both types of total commitment shared the same forms of political imagination. As modern utopianism developed, the apocalypse no more belonged to ancient theological dogma than revolution belonged to medieval astrological fancy: both were part and parcel of what must be seen (as I have been arguing) as the elementary forms of the ideological life, shaped in point of fact by the same imperious images of language and vagarious turns of temperament which had been detected by Bayle in Comenius, Harrington in Milton, Walwyn in Winstanley, Worthington in Hartlib, Howell in Masaniello, and before them by Sir Philip Sidney in his Arcadian rebels.

What is overpowering in Bayle—one is almost tempted also to call it premature—are these remarkable and prescient double-focused insights into the dual pattern of modern absolutist aspiration. Utopian revolutionary was but apocalyptic enthusiast writ different. After such knowledge, what remained of hope and purposefulness? Bayle grasped more poignantly than any other intellectual of his epoch the distressing implications of a position which deprived itself so candidly of all the easy supports of optimism and certitude. There is indeed in some of his troubled asides a foreshadowing of two profound themes which will plague the subsequent career of the European intelligentsia for centuries. They can, I think, be put and illustrated in the following way.

1. *The tragedy of the man in the middle.* Of one contemporary effort to hold to a reasonably neutral balance, Bayle wrote these memorable lines:

... it was in vain that he hoped to stand upon the shore, a quiet spectator of the boisterousness of that sea. He found himself more exposed to the storm than if he had been in either of the fleets. This is the inevitable fate of those who pretend to keep a neutrality. They are exposed to the insults of both parties at once, and they obtain enemies without procuring themselves friends. Whereas, by espousing with zeal either of the two causes, they have friends as well as enemies. A deplorable destiny of man, a manifest vanity of philosophic reason! It makes us look upon the tranquility of the soul and the calmness of the passions as the end of all our labors, and the most precious fruit of our most painful meditations. And yet experience shows that as to the world there is no condition more unfortunate than that of friends who will not devote themselves to the waves of faction ....

Such men as howl with the wolves have the advantage of not knowing they are in the wrong, for no men are capable of seeing the faults of their faction and the good that may be found in the other party than those who are controlled by a fiery zeal and a quick resentment, and who are under the power of strong prejudice. Such men ... are miserable. They will not be a hammer, and, therefore, they are an anvil upon which both sides beat continually.[29]

From Bayle to Mme de Staël to Albert Camus, it is this "deplorable destiny" between hammer and anvil that the intellectual historian has to confront: the struggle to hold out against the boisterous sea, to resist the waves of faction, to escape the howling wolves, to rise above the controlling powers of zeal, resentment, and prejudice *à droite et à gauche*. Its splendors and miseries will be as mixed as these metaphors.

Bayle knew, then, the "inconveniences of moderation," the tormenting implications of a reluctance "to adhere either to those who maintained the abuses, or to those who opposed them": for he thought "both too violent" and said, with Tully, *"quem fugiamo habeo, quem sequar non habeo"* ("I know whom to avoid, but not whom to follow").[30] Yet why is it that this effort of "philosophic reason" to transcend the two warring causes should be felt to be condemned to an "inevitable fate"? Bayle's work pointed to a simple theorem which from time to time tempts the historian of ideas but rarely finds expression with so much grim, elemental candor.

2. *The historical amnesia of each new generation.* Was this, then, the original sin of the European spirit? What of progress, and cumulative wisdom, and the lessons of the past? "No!" Bayle cries out, more in sorrow than in skepticism, "The world is too unteachable to profit by the follies of past ages. Every age behaves as if it were the first." He thought, with no little bitterness, that the historical spectacle of "a thousand dark passions" ought at least to produce in men "a salutary and mortifying

humiliation"—but no: "The worst is, men do not profit by what is past; every generation betrays the same symptoms."[31]

9. Hartlib's Experiments, Novelties, and New Things

Pierre Bayle's critique of the apocalyptic mentality was, of course, shared by other contemporaries who also subjected Comenius's *Lux in tenebris* to withering commentary. Even Samuel Hartlib, who was after all the great popular advocate of Comenius in England, coolly puts some distance between himself and the cause of visionary frenzy by quoting to Dr. Worthington the following unsympathetic remark of one of his friends: "When I first heard of Drabicius, this I made my chief enquiry, but withal I suspected in him that which I soon found, that he was an ecstatick. I am confident, that God will not send a person, infamous amongst good men for falsehood, on his embassy. And the suffrage of good men is a kind of foundation to our faith."[32]

There is, then, this pregnant English difference which begins to divide utopia from revolution and both from the apocalypse. John Evelyn once expressed the hope (in a letter to Boyle)[33] that they would "in a short time ... be possessed of the most blessed life that virtuous persons could wish or aspire to in this miserable and uncertain pilgrimage, whether considered as to the present revolutions, or what may happen for the future in all human probability ... " But he was merely pleading support for a piecemeal improvement of the English academic scene— the establishment of a proposed new college "in some healthy place" outside London (and he submitted, of course, a detailed budget and schedule). Here is the mien and manner of the utopian reformer: "Now, sir, in what instances and how far is this practicable permit me to give you an account of, by the calculatings which I have deduced for our little foundation ... "

For if the revolutionary has the consolation of the apocalypse, the reformer has the consolations of practicable fantasy. The distress of the one is alleviated by accountable, calculable detail; the miseries of the other by ineffable certainties. In the life of politics and society these temperamental predispositions are put to stress and test, and we can observe how they turn soft and hard, hot and cold, become optimistic or pessimistic, change course and character. Revolutionaries may, in disenchantment, turn to piecemeal reform; reformers, in anger, turn to revolution. That there was a theatrical element in the self-casting of roles was clear to many of the players. But if Andreae's vehement outburst of impatience with the ineffectuality of "moderate and tolerable means" led him to applaud the "drama [that] may be played," the Macarians' dramaturgical sense of the real political consequences prompted another and more critical attitude to the stormy events on stage. Mixing his metaphors but not his meaning, John Hall recorded in 1647:

> Jealousie dayly heighten, new parties appeare, and new interests are discovered, that we seeme to . . . act some wel contrived Romance. In which, every page begets a new and handsome impossibility. Such sicknesses have now seazed on the body politicke, that is nothing but crampes, convulsions and fearfull dreames.

These were times when military victory and defeat hung in the balance, and he proclaimed "these two safe Maxims": "That it is the safest way in a civil war to be seized of the Metropolis: and the other, That people are never so forward, nor so daring, as to preserve or regaine their Liberties." He went on to announce a number of other general conclusions which recapture the ideological ambience of the moderate Hartlib circle:

> It is a great argument of weaknesse in a State, when parties subdivide into such fractions, and every small party able to hold it selfe and become terrible, while the greatest party is unable to move.
> Violent alterations, and taking away of one government, before they be certaine of another, are extreame dangerous . . .
> If things had beene carried by the Parliaments party with moderation, things had beene in a calmer condition then now . . .
> Learning hath incomparably suffered by these times, and twere good to cherish it lest the next age feele a decay.
> It were a good way to mollifie peoples minds to suffer Play-houses againe, and it would be a considerable addition to the education of the Gentry.[34]

This last recommendation was perhaps only a poet's imaginative strategem by which the play would be the thing to catch the conscience of his histrionic contemporaries.

Yet all the elements in this intellectual movement, balancing as best it could the old and the new, appeared to have one thing in common: an aversion to excess. It was a temperamental factor of moderation which united theologians with poets and scientists, and nothing could be more mistaken than the all too simple distinction which is often drawn between the traditional religious mind and the innovating experimental spirit.[35] This is not the way the dividing line ran. True, the men of science alone were capable of an unequivocal commitment to the new, for it was the very essence of their quest for knowledge: and Sprat, in his defense of the Royal Society against its social critics, could not avoid putting the dangerous case plainly.

> That it will probably be the Original of many *new things*, I am so far from denying, that I chearfully acknowledge it. Nor am I frighted at

that, which is wont to be objected in this Case, the hazard of *altera-tion* and *Novelty*. For if all things that are *new* be *destructive*, all the several means and degrees by which Mankind has risen to this per-fection of *Arts* were to be condemn'd. If to be the *Author* of *new things* be a crime; how will the first Civilizers of *Men*, and makers of *Laws*, and Founders of Governments escape? Whatever now delights us in the Works of *Nature*, that excells the rudeness of the first Creation, is *New*. Whatever we see in Cities, or Houses, above the first wildness of Fields, and meaness of Cottages, and nakedness of Men, had its time when this imputation of *Novelty* might as well have bin laid to its charge. It is not therefore an offence to profess the introduction of *New things*, unless that which is introduced prove pernicious in it self; or cannot be brought in, without the extirpation of others, that are better.

In this sense, science itself, in a purer manner than either political or religious reformation, represented the true revolution of the new. But the psychological line of division we are trying to clarify ran conspicu-ously through the center of all the camps; each of them, in their groping efforts for some novel alteration, soon came to take a measure of their own destructive and constructive elements. Inevitably, if sometimes slowly and painfully, came a dawning recognition of the moderates and the extremists among them, and an ultimate falling out between the men of prudence and the men of violent zealotry. Sprat, to cite him once again, understood the true order of battle between the warring temper-aments when he wrote:

I confess there have not been wanting some forward *Assertors* of *new Phylosophy*, who have not us'd any kind of *Moderation* ... But have presently concluded, that nothing can be well-done in *new Discov-eries*, unless all the *Ancient Arts* be first rejected, and their Nurseries abolish'd. But the rashness of these mens proceedings, has rather prejudic'd, than advanc'd, what they make to shew promote. They have come as furiously to the purging of *Philosophy*, as our *Modern Zealots* did to the *Reformation* of *Religion*. And the one Party is as justly to be condemned as the other. Nothing will suffice either of them, but an utter *Destruction, Root* and *Branch*, of whatever has the face of Antiquity. But as the *Universities* have withstood the fierce-ness of the one's Zeal without Knowledge; so there is no doubt, but they will also prevail against the Violence of the other's pretences to Knowledge without *Prudence*.[36]

In the case of Robert Boyle, who was often accused of having a defi-cient religiosity, the Macarian disposition finds its characteristic level at a line of unexcitable sobriety: the reasonable temperament of a scientist immune to the temptations of mysticism or zealotry. He was susceptible to romantic inspiration, but on specific issues tended to a cautious skepticism (as when, in a letter to Hartlib, he registers his momentary neutrality among the "Tychonians, Copernicans and the other novelists"). In the turbulent year of the Putney debates, when radical and moderate tempers began to divide and clash, Boyle wrote to Dury about "our upstart sectaries" and compared them to "mushrooms of last night's springing up." An alarmed and exasperated Boyle seemed to think that "instead of lighting them into the right way with the candle" one should be "flinging the candlestick at their heads." They were "smitten at the root with the work of their own irrationality," and he ventured to predict that they "will be as sudden in their decay, as they were hasty in their growth." "Indeed," he concludes, "perhaps the safest way to destroy them is rather to let them die, than attempt to kill them."[37]

A dozen years later, as the Cromwellian commonwealth begins to show chronic signs of political disintegration, there is rather less confidence about finding safe ways to hold to a central position against irrational extremes. Hartlib was moved to justify the dissolution of Parliament to his various correspondents. To John Pell, a Cromwellian diplomat in Switzerland, he reports that "we are still troubled with the old royal political toads," as well as with croakings from quite other quarters.

> Believe it, it was of that necessity that, if their session had continued but two or three days longer, all had been in blood, both in city and country, upon Charles Stuart's account ... Besides, there was another petition set on foot in the city for a commonwealth, which would have gathered like a snow-ball; but by the resolute sudden dissolving of the parliament, both these dangerous designs were mercifully prevented ... [38]

To Boyle, he permits himself an astronomical aside on "the fear of a universal insurrection," as if to suggest in weary despair that the fault lay not in themselves but in their stars. "The several differences are not yet composed; and the agitators, with the common soldiers, are worst of all. Thursday night were observed some affrighting signs in the air, about ten o'clock at night a blazing star with a great tail in the form of a rod, and afterwards of a sword, appearing over Whitehall and towards Westminster."[39]

These last years of Hartlib's life (he died in 1662) were filled with troubled inner uncertainties. Indeed, one editor of Hartlib's writings reports that the whole period from 1654 to 1660 was one of "relentless disappointment for the Hartlib circle." A less effervescent Parliament was ignoring, and in fact opposing, imaginative schemes which might upset the established arrangements even more; and "even the minor

advantages gained at the inception of the republic were slowly lost ... "
Challenges of romantic innovation were no longer taken up, and the
radical reform movement lost its momentum. Historians have wondered
at the neglect Hartlib suffered during this period and long after: the
studied indifference of his friends and acquaintances, the unnoticed
event of his death, the almost complete disappearance of his fame and
memory. Perhaps his associations did evoke "too many memories of the
puritan revolution". In the view of Professor Webster, who has studied
Hartlib's unpublished papers:

> His carefully preserved correspondence contained embarrassing in-
> formation, at a time when few intellectuals wished to draw attention
> to their careers under the protectorate. Thus Hartlib's voluminous
> papers, petitions and reform tracts were consigned to oblivion, along
> with the evidence relating to other reform movements, such as the
> Leveller tracts and the works of Winstanley. They were regarded as
> expressions of a transient and unfortunate experiment.[40]

Like Thomas More before him, Hartlib was a utopian in politics whose
qualities of balance and "tender-heartedness" (as one of his admirers
once put it) were under dreadful and relentless attack by onrushing
everyday events. Not all of his old companions in the Invisible College
were afflicted with such an excess of conscience and sensitivity. Some,
like Sir William Petty, could when the opportunity presented itself manage a convenient turn of temperament and twist of allegiance (after all,
he hadn't been an assistant to Hobbes in Paris for nothing). In the year
of the Stuart Restoration, one of Hartlib's correspondents reported to
him that Petty "wrote me lately that we now had a Philosophicall and
Mathematico-Mechanical King ... indeed under such a virtuoso why
may not something rare and extraordinarie be expected ... " This must
have appeared to Hartlib as an unthinkable political eccentricity on the
part of a scientist not sufficiently, consistently, or earnestly engaged in
public affairs.

He began to detect "affrighting signs" everywhere. In his general
distress (and he also suffered physically from "the stone," for which
none of his medical friends could offer him effective relief), he took
quick offense at criticism and at even the vaguest hint of satire. "But
have you seen," he writes with some annoyance to Dr. Worthington
(vice-chancellor of Cambridge University) "a certain anonymous book in
[quarto] called *Olbia*? I confess I was not well pleased, seeing the book
directed to my name as it is. They say it reflects upon me as if I were a
refined Quaker, or a fanatick; insomuch that I was almost resolved to
give public notice of my dissatisfaction, as for the addressing of it; for I
never heard a word of it before, nor could I guess at the author of the

said book."[41] When Hartlib did read this book, he satisfied himself that it was not at all a satiric thrust against him. On the contrary, it was by an old friend (John Sadler, who had helped the Jews to build a synagogue for themselves in London) for whom he had affection.[42] The work itself was a wild and incoherent exercise in apocalyptic mysticism (the number of the beast, 1666 and all that), and yet another sign of utopian desperation.[43]

"I am still of my former opinion," Hartlib writes in June 1660. "If Macaria were but once extant or acting ... " But in August the mood had passed, presumably for the last time. "We are wont to call the desirable Society by the name Antilia, and sometimes by the name of Macaria: but name and thing is as good as vanished." But, wait!—he has heard of the offer of the Count de Worth to give both lands and protection on his territories near Cologne. Others, he goes on to record, "are much in love with the country of the Bermudas, as the fittest receptacle for the gallantest spirits to make up a real Macaria." His estimate is that two thousand pounds would buy out the present Company of Merchant Adventurers. *Dahin! dahin* ...[44]

The alternation of old hope and new despair now came in shorter bursts. Hartlib was faced with what will become over the centuries a familiar pattern of despairing alternatives—the abandonment of vanished ideals; a last desperate grasp at some exotic prospect; or a return to square one of utopian theory. "I suppose you have heard," he writes, "of a Nova Atlantis in print, by way of Supplement to that of Lord Verulam ... " The new Baconian work in question took up many of Hartlib's favorite ideas—"a pleasant intermixture of diverse rare Inventions, and wholesome Customs, fit to be introduced into all Kingdoms, States, and Commonwealths"—and, although he could not help noting that it was "far inferior" to previous "grave and judicious contrivances," he gave it his approbation. "Yet such as it is would make a noble alteration, if it were practiced in all human affairs ... " Again he mourns for his very own lost dream: "if Macaria had discovered themselves ... "[45]

These careless little flights of romantic fancy were given a rude jolt by a formidable letter from John Worthington which must have been as painful as it was frank. It represents perhaps the most archetypal confrontation of the century between the native English temperament and the transplanted European spirit, a conflict between the local practical meliorist and the cosmopolitan utopian reformer. It was possibly not the most auspicious moment for a polemic of principles and predispositions of such gravity; for it was a nerve-racking time of panic and disarray, with Harrington heading for the tower, Nedham changing his line, Milton retiring to his poetry, John Rogers in full flight. But Hartlib's sentimental and uncritical musings were apparently too great a provocation. I do not know, Worthington begins,

> why in your later letters the name Antilia was given to that nothing, as it now proves: And so indeed a friend of ours always suspected that it would appear to be but words. For my part the design did pretend to such high things and stupendous effects (and yet the causes were so hidden, and appeared so little) that I could never much build upon it, or expect an issue agreeable on its pretensions. Nothing kept me in any measure of supposing some reality, but the discourse of a worthy friend; who if he had conversed immediately (and not per internuntios) would in his sagacity have smelled it out. Therefore the internuntii have the greater sin.

This was but a small concession, and for all its personal kindness hardly balanced the severity of his final conclusion:

> The best things, such as are of greatest use and importance, and those who would promote them in the world, are more modest, more distant from pretending from affecting the praise and stupid admiration of men. *Mediocria firma. Moderata durant ...*

The stormy debates about utopia and revolution never move very far from this ubiquitous theme of the temper of judiciousness and moderation. Worthington himself remained hopeful "of a society more desirable (and less pretending to wonders) which in good time may find place in the earth"; but it would, he avowed, "attract and unite such modest souls in whom there is no guile." Absolutist motives were morally suspect.

A fortnight later came Hartlib's reply from London to what, given his generally low spirits after almost half a century's singleminded devotion to the cause of "universal reformation," must have been one of the unkindest cuts of all. Worthington had asked that his letter be kept confidential ("I write freely, and therefore what I say is not fit to be communicated to all; and when communicated the writer needs not to be mentioned"). Hartlib reassures him: "I have been faithful to you in not dispersing your letter," and I imagine that in this instance the greatest communicator of the day was pleased to hold the message private. His explanation was defensive and had just that touch of lameness about it which characterizes most attempts to bridge the historical experiences of different generations. "The word Antilia I used because of a former society, that was really begun almost to the same purpose a little before the Bohemian wars. It was as it were a tessera [watchword] of that society ... It was interrupted and destroyed by the following Bohemian and German wars." It was all a long time ago; events were cruel, and the movement was weak; and besides it was in another country. The argument over the Antilian past was a quarrel in part over a name—a numinous utopian name which had become (as it always would) a "mystical word"—and, in part, over the unworthiness of certain apparent allies. Hartlib points to the "cheats of the Fraternity of the Holy Cross" and their "infinite disguises and subterfuges." Distracted by the ailments of the last years of his life, Hartlib (now over sixty) omits meeting most of the disagreeable issues and contents himself with a promise that "we shall therefore take heed for the time to come," and that he would be writing to Comenius again about it all.

The altercation has within it all the symptoms of what in the subsequent history of utopian movements develops feverishly into a rage of splits, denunciations, and expulsions. Worthington was under more quiet control.

> It seems [he replies to Hartlib] that Antilia was a secret tessera used by that society. Macaria (the word we used in our letters) is too good a word for this late pretending company ... the pretenders usually covering their designs with specious shows and expressions of religion and love to mankind. It seem'd always too big for my faith.

He offered the counsel of a safer and more prudent course. Good words, like the utopian and revolutionary things they represent, are always in danger of being betrayed.

There is in the last letters of Hartlib to Worthington something of the pathos of the strangled cry, but it is muffled by the still-confident sounds which a utopian can legitimately allow himself in a pre-revolutionary engagement. He had not (at least, not systematically) confounded his future hopes with any present realities; and there were no clear and overwhelming lessons of the past to be learned from recent historical experience. Unlike some of the dissident Puritans who, as we shall shortly see, had nobly wept that they had lost their way ("How have our hopes been blasted! how have our expectations been disappointed! how have our ends been frustrated!"), there was no evident political or spiritual need for Hartlib to proclaim that the dream had become a nightmare; or, like an embittered Milton, to announce that the nation had become "the common Laughter of Europe," the reformation having merely opened the door "for new Slavery." True, Hartlib's friend Culpeper had warned him a long time before about a weakening of "the springs and strength of resolution," of the danger that when the "possibility of the end" recedes "all action and motion ceases ... " One obstacle or another had appeared insuperable; and Culpeper had been afraid, as he wrote Hartlib in 1646, that "in this (as in the reste of your life) you wrestle not onely without but againste hope ... "

Yet, for all the setbacks of a long career, Hartlib retained a direct, if occasionally slender, hold on his optimism and purposefulness. In a curious (and unsuccessful) appeal to the restored King for his state pension, Hartlib chronicles his services "for the benefit of this Age, and of Posterity ... for the Good of Mankind in all respects ... "[46] Writing to Worthington again about Antilia, he makes the gentle plea: "be not offended if I continue to use this mystical word ... " He busies himself with some of the implications of Giordano Bruno (and his relations with Sir Philip Sidney): and he tries in his own spirit to remain true to the historic role which a new breed of European intellectuals—"persons of publick spirit and good will towards men," utopian philosophers of "capacious and searching spirits" who took "the whole body of mankind for their care"—had created for themselves. "Now I confess," Hartlib writes in the last year of his life, "that I am so surprised with wonder at the present advancement, and I dare promise our posterity that knowledge shall in this following age abound in very great perfection, and to the best of noble operations."[47]

As for his own most noble operation, it has only been delayed and diverted. To Governor Winthrop of New England, in that same year, Hartlib explains: "the designed Society, which I sent you, is not put in practise, the Principal Leaders judging Europe no ways worthy of it. They intend to erect the said foundation in some other part of the World.... For the times of such a Publique and Universal Happiness seems not yet to bee at hand ... "[48] There are, after all, only two possibilities: a revolution in the affairs of men begins either at home or abroad. If the center fails, there still remains hope from the periphery; and this, from Hartlib to Marx to Sartre, has been the simple pendulum swing of the prophetic prospects of progress. In one colorful—and quite inevitable—burst of imagery, Samuel Hartlib summed up his last utopian testament (26 June 1661): "Of the Antilian Society the smoke is over, but the fire is not altogether extinct. It may be it will flame in due time, though not in Europe."[49]

10. Reading, Writing, and Revolution

There is a vivid glimpse of Hartlib in John Evelyn's *Diary* for 27 November 1655, when he went

> to visite honest & learned Mr. Hartlib, a Publique spirited and ingenious person who had promulgated many Useful things & arts: ... Told me of the Castles which they set for ornament on their stoves in Germanie ... of an Inke that would give a dozen Copies, moist Sheetes of Paper being pressed upon it, & remaine perfect ... This Gentleman was Master of innumerable Curiosities, & very communicative.[50]

This sounds deceptively eccentric, but these interests were all coherently involved in the new ethos of a modernizing society. Hartlib's emphasis on "industry" and on "profits and riches" can be easily misinter-
preted to fit him into some narrow and dogmatic category of a class
spokesman, a representative (as it is oddly put by students of sociological levitation) of the so-called rising bourgeoisie.[51] This kind of
pigeonholing is unhelpful and unilluminating. His was the broadest
idealism of the energetic adventurer—seeking, in the great utopian tradition, a lost Eden, a new world, a widening circle of the imagination.
He dared to discover; and he was as inventive with schemes for animal
husbandry as he was for educational reform and political amendment.
He advertised his book on *The Reformed Common-wealth of Bees* as "con-
taining Many Excellent and Choice Secrets, Experiments, and Discoveries for attaining of National and Private Profits and Riches." Hartlib's
concern for "Industry" was primarily an insistence on sheer human
industriousness, the qualities of which now seem so blurred when we
use the word—strangely blown off course by the influence of Saint-
Simonian French—to denote the systematic enterprise of trade and
manufacture. Its semantic association was with the later *industria*, "a
vertue comprehendynge bothe study and diligence" (according to
Elyot's dictionary of 1538), and its historical milieu was that of an energetic society in motion which placed special emphases on skill, effort,
ingenuity, assiduity. Inevitably, in this context of social endeavor, the
ant was taken to be a vivifying model of purposefulness. That these
enterprising traits of the ants and the bees should find their best expression in a "Reformed Commonwealth" was for a man of Hartlib's public
commitment only the natural analogy of the age. The previous, most
authoritative handbook on the subject (published in 1634) suggests the
dramatic span of social and ideological development in two decades. It
was a work on the same species of bees "shewing their admirable nature
and properties; their generation and colonies; their Government, Loyalty, Art, Industry; Enemies, Wars, Magnanimity"; and it was entitled,
as befitted other times, *The Feminine Monarchy*. So do metaphors have
their little revolutions; even figures of speech suffer through innovating
hurly-burly; language too has its wheels within wheels of fortune.[52]

Neither Evelyn's impression of eccentricity nor the learned gentleman's quick-tongued communicativeness measures up to the full portrait. For, in some other matters, more serious than ornamental German
stoves and inked copying paper, this ingenious person was apparently
very discreet and effectively secretive. There seems to be evidence that
in his later "Hungarian period" Comenius had organized, together with
Dury, Hartlib, and some others (Peter Filgus, Comenius's son-in-law,

and a Baron Sadovsky) "a secret Evangelical association with the ambitious objective of overthrowing Austrian rule." This, his biographer admits,[53] "sounds fantastic," but he finds numerous intimations in letters which point to such a revolutionary organization. Hartlib had delivered an appeal to Cromwell, "written in the name of all our exiled nation," imploring him to take up the cause of the oppressed Protestants of Bohemia, Moravia, Silesia, and Austria; the Lord Protector disappointed him with an offer only of some lands for the Protestant exiles in Ireland.[54] To Hartlib himself, Comenius had written to counsel the most extreme caution. Evidently, a high Hungarian official had revealed that "we hear there are three sworn enemies of the Emperor—a certain Dury, J. A. Comenius, and a third whose name I have not been able to learn ... "

In this light, the description of Hartlib in Dircks's *Memoir* is almost that of a modern portrait of the intellectual as utopian revolutionary.

> He does not appear to have had any immediate business, or professional or public engagements; but seems to have wholly devoted his time to making himself acquainted with the literary, scientific, theological, and political information of his day; by which means he became the centre, as it were, of a large and mixed society, for whom he fulfilled duties approaching, in many respects, that of a general agent or secretary. He was in himself a kind of imaginary institution, of which he represented the proprietors, council, and all the officers; the funds too, being wholly his own.[55]

Hartlib was thus one of the first in a long gallery of European intellectuals who found London[56] a congenial center for reading, writing, and revolution. When Hartlib is encouraged by Boyle[57] to think of himself as being "the midwife and nurse" of a historic movement, we are—metaphorically—halfway (or thereabouts) to Marx and the birthpangs of the new from the womb of the old.

Part 3

Ideologies

11

... in some things to be overcome is more honest
and laudable than to conquer.

—John Milton (1649)

... a revolution of Government in the Peoples
hands hath ever been the only means to make
Governours accountable, and prevent the
inconveniencies of Tyranny, Distraction, and
Misery ...

—Marchamont Nedham (1656)

Happiness. Happiness is a continuation of
content without any molestation. Very imperfect
in this world. No body happy here certain. May
be perfect in an other world possible probable.

—John Locke (MS note, ca. 1660)

And he gathered them together into a place
called in the Hebrew tongue Armageddon.... And there
were voices, and thunders, and lightnings; and
there was a great earthquake, such as was not
since men were upon the earth, so mighty an
earthquake, and so great.

—Revelation 16:16, 18

To Armageddon
and Back

1. The Miltonic Frontier
John Milton and Revolutionary Utopianism—"Wild Vast Notions"
and "Boundless Consequences"—The Rota Critique (1660)—A Faith
"Invincible" to Reconsideration or Recantation—Milton and Bruno—
Stars, Earth, Sea, Winds, Tempests: "Mother Nature Herself"—
Heroic Wisdom and Public Faith—The Return of the "Unforeseen or
Fortuitous"—Doubleness, Ambiguity, Delusion—Fury and Bewitch-
ment in the *Eikonoklastes* (1649)—The High Road to Armageddon—
Apologia for Violence—Destroying and Creating—"Two Bugbears,
Novelty and Perturbation"—Milton's Last Pamphlet: "The Readie and
Easie Way" (1660)—The Reformation Betrayed?—Invincible Loyalty to
the Good Old Cause—Retreat from the Promised Land

2. Nedham's Full Circle
The Latest Dispatches from Somewhere in Utopia (1657)—The Impor-
tance of Never Being Earnest—"Perfect Liberty: none obey, all
command"—The Expediency of all Government—"Knacks to Govern
the World"—Collaborating with Milton—Marchamont Nedham as
Posthumous Spokesman of the American and French Revolutions—
The Gynecological Analogy—"A Revolution of Government in the
People's Hands"—Defending Power against a "nasty, lousy, beaten
generation"—Loyal Submissiveness to the New Establishment—
Nedham's Two Warnings against Revolutionary Extremism—The
Doctrinaire Arrogance of an Exclusive Elite—The Shadow of Unifor-
mity in a New Absolutism—Nedham's Exile, Return, and Post-
Revolutionary Astigmatism—The Hero of the People's Revolution:
"All Zeal, No Knowledge; All Purity, No Humility"—Disenchantment
in "Joco-Serio" Doggerel

3. Locke and the Similes of Strength

Spokesmen for Different Generations—Locke's "Impatient Scepticism"—"Where is that great Diana of the world Reason?"—Failure of "Glorious Promises"—Quenching Fire with Blood: "Zealous Mistakes and Religious Furies"—Illusions of Future-Directed Hope—Locke's "One Furious Thought" (1659)—The Banners of Liberty and Conscience—"Watchwords of Wonderful Effect"—Locke's "Oracles of the Nursery"—Sources of Original Error and Permanent Distortion—Between Old Gehenna and New Jerusalem—Liberators and the "Zeal to be Executioners"—Ambitious Thoughts and Discontented Minds—Breaking Out of the Dualism of Extremist Politics—"We do indeed lack that liberty which we think we lack"—Locke as an "Enemy to the Scribbling of this Age"—The Cycle of Revolutions: Utopian Departures, Authoritarian Returns—Locke Moves from Right to Left Center—Stripping the Metaphor

1. The Miltonic Frontier

Properly qualified and understood (and I have already suggested some of the political, theological, and semantic distinctions that need to be made), John Milton could arguably be said to be the commanding figure in the early emergence of revolutionary utopianism. True, his ideological vocabulary was as yet old-fashioned and only half-secularized, and his practical political feelings often ran against abstract flights of social fantasy. Yet, when one of Milton's traditionalist contemporaries in the moderate camp spoke with fear and trembling of the "boundless and endless consequences" that were opening up, he drew with rough accuracy the line of the new Miltonic frontier which the ideological imagination had crossed. New and absolute decisions were to be made on behalf of human justice and happiness; a holy community of saintliness and general excellence was to be reconstructed out of the fragments of imperfect, evil, and intolerable states. The truest and only indestructible commitment or "engagement" (in the phrase of that day, and of ours) was between man and liberty, between godly conscience and thoroughgoing reformation, between human will and the earthly paradise.

And therefore [General Ireton argued, in the Putney debates of 1647], when I hear men speak of laying aside all engagements to

consider only that wild or vast notion of what in every man's conception is just or unjust, I am afraid and do tremble at the boundless
and endless consequences of it.[1]

This was, once again, a voice not of "the Revolution" but of the conservative and moderate center within the Puritan insurgency; hesitations
and negations are often clearer in their self-consciousness than affirma-
tions. A wild and vast notion was abroad in the land, and for bounds
and ends an infinity of worldly progress and hope was beginning to be
substituted. Where indeed would things end? Thomas Case, for one,
worried about the totalism of liberty and the permanence of its challenge. Sectarians who would be awarded tolerance and freedom, Case
feared,

> may in good time come to know also (there be them that are instruct-
> ing them in these principles too) that it is their birthright to be freed
> from the power of parliaments and from the power of kings, and to
> take up arms against both where they shall not vote and set accord-
> ing to their humours. Liberty of conscience, falsely so called, may in
> good time improve itself into liberty of estates, and liberty of houses,
> and liberty of wives, and in a word, liberty of perdition of souls and
> bodies.[2]

Only a half-dozen years earlier, Case had been the root-and-branch
spokesman we have already cited as the very apostle of zealous and
resolute reformation!

The emergence of utopian revolution on what we call today the extreme left alarmed the Commonwealth center, and not least because of
the common elements of language and sentiment which in the beginning had appeared to unite them indissolubly in a good cause. Thus,
Milton was often censured for being a fellow fanatic; his rhetoric was
impassioned enough to sound zealous and his hopes high enough to
seem apocalyptic; and, whatever the political setbacks and renewed social difficulties, there was always in the simple urgencies of his mind "a
readie and easie way." As the Rota critic put it, the only differences
among the extremists were those of terminology not principle: "This is
the way you go, which will never fail you, as long as there are Fools and
Madmen to carry on the Work." The Rota critique associated Milton
with the radical saints, with "the Fifth Monarchy Men, who would have
been admirable for your Purpose, if they had but dreamed of a Fifth
Free-state . . . "[3] The indictment was of the collective guilt of all the
utopians and revolutionaries, whatever their debates over tactics or
theoretical niceties. It pointed accusingly at "that Party you call *We*" and
their "fantastick Longing after imaginary Liberty."

Once there had been an untroubled vision of the future and the tasks which it enjoined on men; in the great year of 1648, Milton found these words for the translation of Psalm 82:

> Regard the weak and fatherless
>   Despatch the poor man's cause,
> And raise the man in deep distress
>   By just and equal laws.
> Defend the poor and desolate,
>   And rescue from the hands
> Of wicked men the low estate
>   Of him that help demands.

Nor did the murder of the King appear then to darken the bright path ahead.

> There can be slain
> No sacrifice to God more acceptable
> Than an unjust and wicked king.[4]

A spurious divine right had given way to an authentically divine justice, and the means had been a human instrumentality: the political passion of a people who had abjured "to sequester out of the world into *Atlantick* and *Eutopian* polities, which can never be drawn into use, will not mend our condition ... " The menders of the human condition—put more meanly, "our long-sword State menders," in Nedham's sardonic phrase—had been possessed by the profoundest concern for man's fate. The signal may have been God's, but the call to every human heart was within. If men could be masters, then men could also be gods.

> ... the spirit of man, no longer confined within this dark prison-
> house, will reach out far and wide, till it fills the whole world and
> the space far beyond with the expansion of its divine greatness. Then
> at last most of the chances and changes of the world will be so
> quickly perceived that to him who holds this stronghold of wisdom
> hardly anything can happen in his life which is unforeseen or fortui-
> tous. He will indeed seem to be one whose rule and dominion the
> stars obey, to whose command earth and sea hearken, and whom
> winds and tempests serve; to whom, lastly, Mother Nature herself
> has surrendered, as if indeed some god had abdicated the throne of
> the world and entrusted its rights, laws, and administration to him.[5]

Like Bruno, whose mind had also been "suffocating in the close air of a narrow prison house" and who would dare as a heroic enthusiast to penetrate the sky and overpass "the margins of the world," Milton was resolute in his devotion to the godlike mission as it unfolded in the Great Revolution of the Year. In another context, he had called it "that Faith which ought to be kept as Sacred and Inviolable as any thing holy, *The*

Publick Faith," and it was, in his mind, invariably associated with a "Heroick Wisdom."[6]

"So great a longing in the human mind" (as he put it in a *Prolusion*) could not be denied. The age of longing was now coming to its highest climax as his countrymen, "with pre-eminent virtue and a nobility and steadfastness surpassing all the glory of their ancestors," went about accomplishing nothing less than "the most heroic and exemplary achievements since the foundation of the world ... " He was convinced that "Justice, in her very essence, is all strength and activity, and hath a Sword put into her hand, to use against all violence and oppression on the earth." If the deed could only be done with violence, then the blood was purificatory and the fire a true sign of the ultimate liberation. If men would create, then men must destroy. "Why should we not acknowledge with the prophet Daniel," Milton argued, "that God changeth times, sets up one kingdom, and pulls down another? Certainly—yet it is by means of men."[7]

And yet the new order of men by and for men appeared to be in danger of being pulled down in turn. Why had not the stars obeyed and the earth and sea hearkened to the commands? How was it that the winds and tempests proved to be so unserviceable? What had determined the insidious return of the "unforeseen or fortuitous"? In the dark and fearful corners of the revolutionary mind there always skulk enemies, new and old. In his sonnet "To the Lord General Cromwell," Milton warned that

> new foes arise
> Threatening to bind our souls with secular chains ...[8]

What, then, had Milton misread or misunderstood in the signs of the times? They had been on the high road to Armageddon, and now there was to be a turning back? Had the "signal to ascend" been mistaken? I have previously spoken of the complex role of ambiguity and "doubleness" in the sinuous simplifications of utopian revolutionaries. And indeed Milton himself writes of the "sharp and double edge" of liberty;[9] and in other matters, too, he sensed the source of tragic wrong turnings.

> But what have been thy answers, what but dark
> Ambiguous and with double sense deluding,
> Which they who asked have seldom understood,
> And not well understood as good not known?[10]

But the dualism which obtained in Miltonic politics was of quite another character and exhibited other properties. It was the special European compound which we have examined in its various admixtures since Dante and Joachim, Bruno and Philip Sidney, Comenius and

Thomas More. Its basic elements were fury and bewitchment—the fury comprising an all-encompassing indictment of the evil of the old ways of living and believing, the bewitchment amounting to a transporting vision of the politics of paradise which would issue in society's salvation. Both were structures of thought and passion that proved solid enough to sustain a holy public faith "invincible" to onslaught or betrayal. What Milton called the "double sense deluding" was the affliction of his enemies; for him, even if in the end he was to stand almost alone in a crumbling Commonwealth, it was a double sense sustaining. This should, I believe, emerge with dramatic clarity after an examination of the first and last great pamphlets of the Cromwellian decade, Milton's remorseless critique of the Stuart *Eikon Basilike* (1649), which he rushed into print in the same year, and his last offer of a "ready and easy way" (1660) full of a high confidence which could be managed by no other spirit in the land.

First, the *Eikonoklastes:* and on the very title page there were joined together two mottoes from Proverbs which might well have troubled a true believer with lesser dialectical skill. For 28:15 reinforced a revolutionary temperament: "As a roaring Lion, and a raging Bear, so is a Wicked Ruler over the poor People." But 28:17, in the year of the royal execution (and after almost a decade of bloody civil war), might well have given a moment's pause to prophets of peace and good conscience: "A man that doth violence to the blood of *any* person, shall fly to the pit, let no man stay him." How, then, was it possible for Milton to (in his own phrase) "reconcile contradictions"?[11]

No political philosophy or party strategy which has ever promised or planned a revolutionary fulfillment has yet been able to maintain itself intact in the complicated stress of insurrectionary events; and its desperate attempt to conserve an organic semblance of consistency and validity has usually left a disaffecting impression of cynicism, Machiavellianism, hypocrisy, or dialectical cunning. There are always good and sufficient reasons for tactical zigzag which can somehow reconcile theory and practice; but the original innocence, shining in its confident unity of words and deeds, is lost in the process as slogans deceive, men disappoint, decisions divert, and consequences mix with conceptions in bitter unease.

In the whole rhythm of his ideological performance, Milton, whom one anatomist of revolution has properly classified, with Paine, Robespierre, and Lenin among the great revolutionaries,[12] is characteristic of this hectic quest to find an assured balance between utopian principles and revolutionary acts. But he remains singular among that resolute few who never were tempted either by the intellectual lures of reconsideration or the psychic (and other) attractions of recantation. His confidence was to the end invincible, and I use the word advisedly, for it was a quality and a posture which Milton admired in his own righteous cause and decried in the camp of the enemy.

> *But he* [Charles Stuart] *had a soule invincible.* What praise is that? The stomach of a Child is ofttimes invincible to all correction. The unteachable man hath a soule to all reasons and good advice invincible; and he who is intractable, he whom nothing can perswade, may boast himself invincible whenas in some things to be overcome is more honest and laudable than to conquer.[13]

There was indeed something intractable in Milton's holy public faith, something invincible to all doubt and correction. What could have persuaded him that all creatures were not sighing to be renewed, that not all of the accomplishments of the decade were heroic, exemplary, and suffused with preeminent virtue?

The most viable basis for ideological emotion is usually an unflagging sense of outrage at the evil, taken to be total and irreparable, of the existing order of things. The forces are being marshalled for the final conflict, like the angry hosts at Armageddon,[14] "the battle of that great day of God Almighty" (Rev. 16:14). So it is that local events, in a given time and place, of greater or lesser constitutional importance in the continuing political history of human society, are universalized and absolutized into the ultimate drama. In the perspective of the centuries, what was happening was that an old authoritarian monarchy was being (temporarily) subverted and a new, more mixed state of duties and liberties was being established on a small, European offshore island. The ideological imagination, full of "wholesome heat," serves to convert this into "such a deliverance, as shall never be forgott'n by any revolution of time that this world hath to finish."

It may seem odd that such an "incomparable deliverance" which takes man across the frontiers into the Promised Land should have, as its initial impetus and motivation, a protective and merely defensive spirit. Milton goes to great pains to pin the responsibility for the blood and violence of the day on "one miserable man." He was "the first beginner"; he started it all. The people, persecuted and desperate, had no choice but to resort to a militant defense of "the civil Liberties of a Nation." The King was the aggressor:

> He never reck'ns those violent and merciless obtrusions which for almost twenty years he had been forcing upon tender consciences by all sorts of Persecution; till through the multitude of them that were to suffer, it could no more be call'd a Persecution, but a plain Warr.

Men of peace and liberty had to protect themselves; and this was no mere rhetorical rationalization, for the very logic of social causation gives a deep moral rationale to insurrectionary forces of resistance. "Those Tumults," Milton argues, "were but the milde effects of an evil and injurious reign; not signes of mischiefs to come, but seeking relief for mischiefs past."[15]

"For besides that," Milton goes on, "in good Governments they happ'n seldomest, and rise not without cause." Moreover, "if they prove extreme and pernicious," then it was only because "extremes one with another are at most Antipathy." Was, then, the "revolution of time" a phenomenon of extremism, or did that little "if" represent only a momentary verbal tactic? What of those "men of iron" whom Milton called for "by one . . . or by a thousand"? Was he trying to "justifie what enormities the Vulgar may committ in the rudeness of their zeal," "the infirmities of best men, and the scandals of mixt hypocrites in all times of reforming"? No, but "Neither can the evil doings of some be the excuse of our delaying and deserting."[16]

Milton comes to his conclusion—"These therefore are not to deter us"—along four different routes. The first, as we have seen, takes the course of simple argumentativeness: the "first beginners" started it, the enemy is at fault, the bloodshed was defensive violence. The second is that "in all times of reforming" there were excesses, as a good cause gets involved in a "false fraternity" with "a sort of moodie, hot-brain'd, and always unedify'd consciences, apt to engage their leaders into great and dangerous affairs . . . and then, upon a sudden qualm and swimming of their conscience, to betray them basely in the midst of what was chiefly undertak'n for their sakes . . . " Thirdly, all violence is only an aspect of an innovative revolution, and he would have no part of the obsessive "fear [of] all change." Tumultuous overturnings are the usual accompaniment of great innovations. He conceded the theoretical point that "Tis true that the *method of reforming* may well subsist without *perturbation of the State*." But, he contended, "it falls out otherwise for the most part," and he referred to "the plaine Text of Scripture" in which Christ says: "The Kingdom of Heaven suffereth violence, and the violent take it by force" (Matt. 11:12).[17]

Finally, how could a true "revolution of time" ever be immoderate? The reformation which was on the human agenda was by definition a course of authentic virtue fully and invariably justified. He begged to differ with those who "look'd for moderate desires of due Reformation"—"as if," Milton comments (with something less than impeccable logic, for he was arguing by definition in a circle) "any such desires could be immoderate." For after the darkness of the eclipse, would not the Reformation be "our true Sun light"? The Stuart King wanted to "be tak'n for our sun itself," but it was not only here that the

Stuart astronomy erred with a faulty reading of the stars and the planets. King James had considered himself to be the *primum mobile*, and from his throne of power he would maintain a "steady and ever constant course to govern all other changeable and uncertain motions of the inferior planets ... " And his son Charles thought his enemies were behaving with "a motion eccentric and irregular," which "allusion from the Celestial bodies" Milton refused to allow. His argument was less Copernican than casuistical, for was it not obvious to all that "irregular motions may be necessary on earth sometimes, as well as constantly in Heav'n"?[18] In other words, the plea on behalf of violence as a factor in the triumph of the good cause was that it was only used in self-defense; it was peripheral; and inevitable; and indeed in the final accounting of things not truly violence at all.

Thus, reinforced by astronomy and history, by scriptures and other plain texts of moral and political philosophy, Milton's faith remained "undeterred." The defense of liberty and the progress of the sacred deliverance was all; no argument could come between him and his appointed task. What if a tyranny could produce (as James Howell and Nehemiah Rogers and others had contended) a state of prosperity? Small matter, "For wealth and plenty in a land where Justice reigns not, is no argument of a flourishing State, but of a nearness rather to ruin or commotion." The economics of the human condition was of subsidiary importance, and he hastened to make clear in the second edition (1650) the priority of liberty.

> And not to have in ourselves, though vaunting to be free-born, the power of our own freedom, and the public safety, is a degree [of enslavement] lower than not to have the property of our own goods. For liberty of person and the right of self-preservation is much nearer, much more natural, and more worth to all men, than the propriety of their goods and wealth.[19]

The sweet dream of a vast and boundless liberty, when coupled with an angry dedication to destroy tyrannous evil, gave Milton's revolutionary ideology a peculiar protection against the onslaught of events and the inroads of doubt, against what he called "our delaying and deserting." No man of the century was cut more to the spirit of that famous "root and branch" phrase of the 1640 petition. He was no trimmer, and would have no part of "a stupid Reconcilement." He knew the traps of compromise and warned that "what he [the King] granted for the present out of fear, he might as soon repeal by force, watching his time ... " The old regime at its best was only "like a rotten building newly trimm'd over." The rot in the body politic had gone too deep, and he coined a word for it, *dyscrasy* (which a Milton editor defines with "the

literal meaning of its two Greek elements ... an evil or morbid mixture
of the four humours of the body to produce bad health of a kind very
hard to cure."). Could it be treated, doctored, healed? No: "we shall
disagree to the world's end." No mediating proposal or strategem could
find his approval, for they were only "the old circulating dance
of ... shifts and evasions."[20]

Nor was the danger past when the old order had passed away and
new men had come to power. Every revolution needs a theory of its own
permanence, for even in its finest moments of triumphant consolidation
it is besieged by its own niggling fears that this too might pass away,
that its own watchwords of mutability and change could be turned
against itself. Although the rumblings among the military and among
the extremist political factions were at times an obvious cause for alarm,
Milton dismissed the "irrational" proposition that revolutions must
needs come full circle as "a Game at Ticktack with words; *Tumults and
Armies, Armies and Tumults* ... " But it was a game that was to be played
out earnestly in his lifetime, and he could not repress the premonition of
(in our words) counterrevolution, or even a revolution within the revolution; of (in his words) being put "back to a second wandering over that
horrid Wilderness of distraction and civil slaughter" once the frontiers of
the Promised Land had already been reached. He was concerned about
"the worthless approbation of an inconstant, irrational, and Image-
doting rabble" and about backsliding in general. It was not quite within
even Milton's resources of faith and certainty to scotch the possibility
that the people might

> show themselves to be by nature slaves, and arrant beasts: not fit for
> that liberty which they cri'd out and bellow'd for, but fitter to be led
> back again into their old servitude, like a sort of clamouring and
> fighting brutes, broke loose, that know not how to use or possess the
> liberty they fought for ...

But to compensate for the inconstancy or irresolution of the many there
would be the unwavering devotion of that loyal elect—like Justice, "all
strength and activity"—who would refuse to be "frustrated, disappointed, deny'd and repuls'd."[21]

More than that, for Justice did not stand alone: she had allies. "Truth
and Justice are all one, for Truth is but Justice in our knowledge, and
Justice is but Truth in our practice ... " How, then, could true theory
disappoint and just practice fail? Milton was warmed in his mind by the
notion of "the wholesome heat of well governing" (as distinct from the
"feverous rage of tyrannizing"). Perhaps the spirit of the century most
susceptible to metaphorical imperatives, he sensed that all the forces of
nature herself—the elements, fair or foul; the heavens, regular or
eccentric—would help defend what he once prophesied (in 1641) as "a

good time, our time of Parliament, the very jubilee and resurrection of the state ... " For had they not already proved their green hand not by accepting "only the excresciencies of evil prun'd away for the present" but by "striking at the root"?[22]

In the twentieth chapter of the *Eikonoklastes*, Milton takes umbrage at the hostile presentation of "an Antimasque of two bugbeares, *Noveltie* and *Perturbation*," fearing that "the ill looks and noise of those two may ... drive off all endeavours of a Reformation." He might well have used the two synonyms coming into vogue, namely utopia and revolution, which had within themselves more music and a pleasing aspect. But, as so often in Milton's political works, strained images had to do heavy duty for the easier words which all subsequent ideologues would have at their disposal. Nothing would stop "the Common-wealth steering under full sail to a Reformation," certainly not those "little pests of the Sea" (Pliny's *remora*, fish that were supposed, according to the *Natural History*, to hinder ships by fastening themselves to the keels).[23]

Ten years later, other ships were at sea, preparing to steer under full sail, unpestered and undelayed, to land a force which would destroy the last remnants of Milton's Commonwealth forever. Milton's final pamphlet,[24] his farewell to revolutionary politics, was published in 1660 when he was fifty-one, about to run for his life from those who were suggesting he be "condemned to travel to Tyburn in a cart." Only three copies appear to have survived. It was in every sense a dangerous and courageous deed to have done, characteristic of the man and, equally revealing, representative of the mind. But surely by this time it was not only old-line Royalist sympathizers but also disaffected friends who would have recognized the force of the withering critique to which the pamphlet was subjected:

> No conjurer's devil is more concerned in a spell than you are in a mere word, but never regard the things which it serves to express.
> You fight always with the flat of your hand like a rhetorician, and never contract the logical fist.
> You trade altogether in universals, the region of deceits and fallacy, but never come so near particulars as to let us know which among diverse things of the same kind you would be at.
> All your politics reach but the outside and circumstance of things, and never touch at realities.
> All your politics are derived from the works of declaimers.
> Your stiff, formal eloquence ... you arm ... with anything that lies in your way, right or wrong, not only begging but stealing questions, and taking everything for granted that will serve your turn.[25]

When (in October 1659) Parliament had been surrounded by troops,

Milton called the military move "illegal, scandalous, barbarous"; and
when General Monk assumed power, John Aubrey (who has left us an
account of the Rota Club discussions dominated by the views of Harrington and Milton) observed that "upon the unexpected turn . . . all
these airy models vanished." One airy model remained—Milton's
"readie and easie way" to solve all the urgent political problems of a
nation sick unto desperation with conflict and chaos.

Now the old premonitions were taking on alarming shapes. There was
a real fear of "returning to old bondage." The nation was about "to fall
back, or rather to creep back, so poorly as it seems the multitude would,
to their once abjur'd and detested thralldom of kingship." What an
"ingratefull backsliding" this was! "Where," Milton asks bitterly, "is
this goodly tower of a Common-wealth which the English boasted they
would build to overshadow king and be another *Rome* in the West?" He
could not help but register the "treading back again with lost labour all
our happie steps in the progress of reformation." He was almost prepared to mourn the loss of "the noblest, the manliest, the equallest, the
justest government."

Where, then, had the "strange, degenerate corruption" come from,
and why had the "contagion suddenly spread among us"? There was
hardly time for elaborate exercises of revolutionary self-criticism or for a
searching inquiry into the causes of the reformation betrayed. These
were, perhaps, "the last words of our expiring liberty." Still, this much
he thought important to set down about the errors of the past; and it was
a lesson that was to be learned and unlearned, time and again, over the
centuries.

> When monarchy was dissolved, the form of a Commonwealth
> should have forthwith been framed, and the practice thereof im-
> mediately begun, that the people might have soon been satisfied and
> delighted with the decent order, ease, and benefit thereof. We had
> been then by this time firmly rooted, past fear of commotions or
> mutations, and now flourishing. This case of timely settling a new
> government instead of the old, too much neglected, hath been our
> mischief.

Yet since when had care for settling a "decent order," with "ease and
benefit" immediately to delight the people, been the prime object of the
revolutionary deliverance? Even now, Milton carelessly proceeded to
hurl promises and assurances which could hardly be fulfilled in the most
auspicious of times.

Was it too late? Not at all, for "now is the opportunitie, now the very
season wherein we may obtain a free Commonwealth, and establish it
forever in the land, without difficulty or much delay . . . " He modified

a few ingenious schemes for electoral reform, "so we be still going on by degrees to perfection." He deleted a long passage on freedom of conscience, perhaps in order to argue all the more easily that "the way propounded is plain, easy and open before us; without intracacies, without the introducement of new or obsolete forms, or terms, or exotic models ... " Any assurance would do to try and head off "our zealous backsliders" who

> after ten or twelve years prosperous war and contestation with tyranny, basely and besottedly run their necks again into the yoke which they have broken, and prostrate all the fruits of their victories for nothing at the feet of the vanquished.

When he spoke of "war and contestation," he was indeed speaking "the language of (that which is not call'd amiss) the good old cause." But it was surely his last illusion to think that those words could now fall on receptive ears, and one suspects that he realized that much himself; it might well be that he was speaking

> only to trees and stone, and had none to cry to, but with the Prophet's *O earth earth earth.*

The final resting place of all the Miltonic eloquence was in a refuge of miracles. Only there could he have found his "children of reviving libertie," and only there could he persist in believing that he had "shewn with what ease we may now obtain a free Commonwealth, and by it with as much ease all the freedom, peace, justice, plentie that we can desire ... " He was beginning to betray symptoms of serious difficulties with the promises of so much ease. "I have no more to say at present: few words will save us, well considered; few and easie things, now seasonably done ... a few main matters now put speedily into execution, will suffice to recover us, and set all right." But only a page or two after his resignation to say no more—except, perhaps, for those few saving words—he took flight into a remarkable outburst, and it suggests that the fear of counterrevolution can inspire as much significant stylistic confusion as the hopes for the revolutionary coming. This was the jumble he committed as he appealed to the mass of his countrymen:

> ... to bethink themselves a little and consider whither they are rushing; to exhort this torrent also of the people, not to be so impetuous, but to keep their due channell; and at length recovering and uniting their better resolutions, now that they see alreadie how open and unbounded the insolence and rage is of our common enemies to give a stay to those ruinous proceedings, justly and timely fearing to what a precipice of destruction the deluge of this epidemic madness would hurrie us through to this general defection of a misguided and abus'd multitude ...

Commenting on this passage, David Masson has shrewdly pointed out:

> To exhort a torrent! The very mixture and hurry of the metaphors in
> Milton's mind are a reflex of the facts around him. Current, torrent,
> rush, rapid, avalanche, deluge hurrying to a precipice: mix and jum-
> ble such figures as we may, we but express more accurately the mad
> haste which London and all England were making the end of April
> 1660 to bring Charles over from the Continent.[26]

The final critique, and the unkindest cut of all, occurred in a work of
the same year entitled *The Spirit of the Phanatiques Dissected*, in which
Milton was told, in effect, to go back where he came from: namely,
Utopia. It was asked, with undisguised contempt, "whether his new
frame of a Commonwealth ... together with that fool Harrington's,
ought not to be sent to *terra incognita* or Sir Thomas More's Utopia,
together with the authors themselves, to frame a free state there?"[27] He
who had declined to "sequester out of the world into Eutopian polities,"
who had wanted to purge the world's condition and was convinced he
had reached the battlefields of Armageddon, was now to be consigned
to intellectual exile and a spiritual diaspora. The good cause—new for
More, old for Milton—was, after a first century of utopian revolution,
rudely returned to square one.

2. Nedham's Full Circle

At least one writer of the day was able to free himself from the humor-
less certainties and confusions with which valiant men of swords and
well-meaning men of dogma went about rearranging the life of society.
He contributed what in the perspective of history can only be taken as a
small joke, but it was one which the first century of utopia and revolution sorely needed. In the spring of 1657, Marchamont Nedham, the
brilliant and unpredictable editor of the Cromwellian *Mercurius Politicus*
(he had once been the Royalist editor of *Mercurius Pragmaticus*), contributed a series of five articles, each purporting to be the latest dispatches
from somewhere in Utopia.[28]

   The first item of faraway news hinted at trouble (slightly relieved by
the happy incident of a reported landing by "a Jolly crew of the Inhabitants of the Island of Oceana, in company of the learned Author himself"). The utopians had been "sorely afflicted with an infectious Itch of
scribbling political discourses ... The world hath run a madding here in
disputes about Government." This was especially serious because it
broke a fundamental law of Utopia—"by daring to be earnest." Apparently the tragedy of the utopian founding father (i.e., Thomas More's

fate on the block) had induced the original setting down of "a sure Maxim of State, to live in Jest, and never to be in Earnest, except it be in order to die."

The second report announced the orders for a new Utopian Assembly which was "to consult about the waies and means of reducing this Commonwealth to a happy Establishment.... But still all must be taken jovially, according to the Law of Utopia." The third report seemed to be conceding the importance of being earnest.

> Sir, Sorry I am that so many of your Countrimen have been searching the Map and can not tell in what part of it to find out our *Utopia*. But the truth is, they are the more to be excused, because we ourselves, with all the learned in Geographie, as yet know not in what Longitude or Latitude to describe it; though I may tell you, we had some heretofore that travel'd for it at least a dozen years together, and like Sir Francis Drake, went round and round the world, and so went home again. Why then should anyone be angry, that in all the voyages made through the *Terra Incognita* of Three Forms of Government, and the Four Monarchies of the world, no safe footing should be found, nor any like to be but by landing in a Fifth? Indeed (Sir) all that we have learn't by travelling is this, now to live at home and be quiet, having gained so much of experience, as to know there is a necessity of a settlement, and that it matters not what the Form is, so we attain the ends of Government.

Evidently Utopia had been troubled by revolutionary utopians!

> They thought we ought to have been as boundless as the Sea, as common as the Earth, as free as the Aire, and as wild as the Fire, that by combustion, like rare Chymists, we might extract more fine than ever was known to our Predecessors. Thus we might have been reduced to our primitive freedom.

"This only is perfect liberty," the reporter from Utopia remarks, with authorized irony, "where none obey, all command, and every one doth what he list."

Thus change and innovation came to Utopia: now an even happier Establishment was conceivable and reform would itself be reformed.

" ... for all this, we had no Free State then, save that the People were free to feed themselves with Phantsies, and were told that they were the supreme Power, and should come to use it in a Revolution or Rotation of their Assemblies, the consideration whereof made their Worships giddy ... "

It was, in a sense, a historic plea against revolutionary giddiness. Although Nedham was at times on the conservative right, with the Royalists, and on the radical left, with the Independents, his formulation of "Utopian Resolve"—in its emphasis on trial and experiment, change and contingency, and most of all on the practical consequences of social models and political forms—would have given small comfort to either camp.

> *That there is no everlasting Principle in Government, as to any one Particular Form.* For, the Rules and Reasons of Government cannot be always the same, it depending upon future Contingents; and therefore must be alterable according to the variety of emergent Circumstances and Accidents; so that no certain Form can be prescribed at all times, seeing that which may be most commendable at one time, may be most condemnable at another, and that is ever best which best fits the present State and Temper of Affairs and is most conducible to the end of Government: and so a Free State may be no less, and many times much more, in that which Men call Monarchy, then in any other Form. 'Tis not the name of a Free State or Commonwealth that makes it be so indeed, but that it is a free State in every form, where Men are put into the way of a free enjoyment and security of their Rights and Properties. Which being so, it is a fundamentall Article of our State-Creed in *Utopia,* That he who cals his brother an Apostate for moving, according to Reason, with the great Wheel of Government, may himself, if he happen to suffer for his obstinacy, be justly esteemed his own Martyr, not the Publick.

"But more another time," the utopian report concludes, "at present I fear I have been too serious ... "

Marchamont Nedham was too canny a political theoretician[29] to risk losing an important point in an excess of spirited journalism. There was, perhaps, a third way "between Dreaming and Disputation," for there was "a secret that we had great Experience and use in our Utopia." The essence of the problem, as he saw it, was how "to Correct all that presume to Print or Dispute about Models of Government," so that "the little Wits of the City, being duly Lasht, are kept from Lashing Out," and thus to help the Laws "escape the Torments they are put to by every small Faction." The new insight was this:

> This our Utopians now generally understand, and begin to see, That all Forms of Government are but temporary Expedients, to be taken upon Tryal, a necessity and right Reason of State enjoins in order to the publick safety; and that as 'tis madness to contend for any Form, when the Reason of it is gone, so 'tis neither dishonour nor scandal, by following right Reason, to shift through every Form, and after all other Experiments made in vain, when the ends of Government cannot otherwise be conserved, to revert upon the old bottom and Foundation.

"Til the next," the fourth letter ends, "I rest, *Joco-Serio* ... "

But the next and final dispatch is not from *Utopia* at all, but now from *Oceana*. There was, conceivably, too much seriousness in the jocularity, and it might have been safer to change the political venue. "I desire you would not foul your fingers any more with your foolish Correspondent of *Utopia* ... " It was best to "have done with ... all the Builders of Castles in the aire," and evidently it was not hard to find (or purchase) "a better Island than *Utopia*." *Oceana* was presumably better; and here the new correspondent loses himself in the details of the organization of "Urns, Balls, and Balloting Boxes" for ten thousand parishes and fifty tribes (and their fifty pavilions) with wages for surveyors and Surveyors General. These were, after all, the "Knacks to Govern the World."

Perhaps only a figure with so checkered a career could have arrived at such a mixed principle of political reasonableness, mixed in color, pattern, and movement.[30] For Nedham had been a young Royalist sympathizer who had been jailed for casting aspersions on the monarch, and subsequently jailed again for railing against the new government. He received a pardon in both cases, was deeply influenced by John Milton's views (and blandishments), and was allowed to edit and publish a weekly entitled *Mercurius Politicus* (for which Milton obtained the license and served as editorial controller). He was often cynical and opportunistic, as his theories and fortunes changed over forty turbulent years. "Perhaps thou art of an opinion contrary to what is here written," Nedham addressed the reader in one of his later pamphlets (1661); "I confess that for a time my mind was wandring too till some Causes made me reflect." His satire could verge on the scurrilous, and his unpredictability hovered on the edges of suspicious coat-turning. But his was at its best a clear, cultivated and powerful mind; and on many of his pages there ring through the magniloquent simplicities of an *idéologue* before the age of ideology, which has led to his recent recognition as "one of the master propagandists."

In point of fact, great events which were still to come would give him yet another career as the posthumous spokesman of the American and the French Revolutions. Nedham's *Excellencie of a Free-State* (in its edition of 1767) was well known among the American revolutionaries in the colonies and had (as John Adams unhappily noted)[31] "many partisans" among them.[32] There was also a French translation, entitled *De la souveraineté du peuple;* and dressed up by his Paris editor with long passages from Montesquieu, Voltaire, and Rousseau it was published in Paris in the first year of the French Revolution.[33]

Marchamont Nedham is thus, for the student of comparative ideology, that rare historical thing, a meaningful "missing link" in the ideological evolution of three revolutions.

Like all ideologues under pressure in a revolutionary time, the inconsistencies in his views (and perhaps also in his character) can only be
reconciled by reference to the temptations and terrors of new political
power. He had learned from Machiavelli that only the "armed prophet"
would prevail, and thus violence in the name of a people's revolution
had both its sacred and profane justification. "If this be not obvious
enough out of profane histories," he argued, "take a view of those in
Holy Writ where you shall find the sword the only disposer of titles to
commonweals and kingdome." He had read somewhere in Plutarch of
how popular tumults were "like the pangs of a woman in travail" (it was
to become the standard gynecological analogy in revolutionary literature), and he went on from there to explain the clinical rationale of the
painful transition: "The late commotions and contests betwixt King and
Parliament were as so many sharp fits and feverish distempers which,
by a kind of antiperistasis, are ever most violent in old age upon the
approaching instants of dissolution." He had pondered the relations
between means and ends ("*Qui vult media ad finem, vult etiam & ipsum
finem*"), and concluded that—as Aristotle had taught—one necessarily
justified the other. For nothing less than a utopian revolution in the
affairs of men was at stake, and "a revolution of Government in the
Peoples hands hath ever been the only means to make Governours
accountable, and prevent the inconveniencies of Tyranny, Distraction,
and Misery . . . " Nor was this mere theory. With the triumph of what
he called "the national revolution of government," namely the Cromwellian regime (from which he received favors via his good friend John
Milton), it was a matter no longer of propagating a noble ideal but of
defending a real established power. "For, we are bold to say (weighing
all circumstances together) that this Nation was never really Free, nor in
a way of enjoying its Freedom so fully as now."[34]

If this were the case, then ideology could no longer function as a
utopian dissolvent of social order but had to be enlisted in the service of
a new revolutionary Establishment and its stability.

> O how comely it is and how reviving
> To the spirits of just men long oppressed
> When God into the hands of their deliverer
> Puts invincible might
> To quell the mighty of the Earth, the oppressor . . .
>   [*Samson Agonistes*, 1268–72]

Nedham, like Milton, saw the dangers coming. "Those brave men, who
glorified themselves in laying the foundation of a Commonwealth, well
knew that in a short Revolution, others of a less publick Spirit would
arise in their places, and gape again after a Kingdom." It was therefore

imperative to "imprint such principles in men's minds, as might activate them with an irreconcilable enmity to the former Power"—or indeed to a future Power, proferred by those who felt that the revolution must be kept rotating, that it had not yet made its full turn. The dangers lurked on both left and right, and neither "Royalist or Presbyterian" was justified in "denying a submission to the present government," not to mention employing violent means to achieve his own political ends. Nedham had learned from Guiccardini of the perils of the extremist momentum: "many times when a people have got loose from the yoke of a tyranny or kingly government out of a desire of liberty, they proceed from one extreme to another." For the moment, the Royalist extreme appeared to be posing no urgent problem. It represented, in Nedham's contemptuous words, a "nasty, lousy, beaten generation." The actual and fearful threat was at the other extreme; the danger came from the revolution within the revolution. The enemies were among them.[35]

Were they, as he sometimes thought, "mere anarchists"? Were they only, as he said of the Fifth Monarchists, "poor deluded souls"? or, like the Diggers and Levellers, fiery factionalists dedicated to "pulling down all and establishing nothing"? Whatever they were, and in whatsoever combination they might emerge (the men of Putney and Blackfriars aided and abetted by Stuart plotters), the challenge to the Commonwealth represented a subversive force which was endangering the first and most inviolate rule of this (or any other) revolution: its own inviolability. Nedham repeated with emphasis that "the power of the sword ever hath been the foundation of titles to government"; and hence, presumably, no sword dare ever be raised again. He preached to all peoples "a patient submission . . . under their various revolutions."[36]

> Whosoever therefore shall refuse submission to an established government upon pretense of conscience in regard of former allegiances, oaths, and covenants, or upon supposition that it is by the sword unlawfully erected, deserves none but the character of peevish, and a man obstinate against the reason and custom of the whole world. Let his pretense be what it will, resistance, in the eye of the law of nations, is treason; and if he will needs perish in the flames of his own phrenetic zeal, he can at best be reckoned but the madman's saint and the fool's martyr.

Thus it was that in the very first century of utopia and revolution the fresh and audacious right to resist became the ancient and hoary duty to submit. But it was with this profound and unprecedented difference: that now the people's obedience to the powers-that-be represented, according to a new ideological casuistry, a loyalty to their very own power, their "fuller freedom" in a grand revolutionary design. Nedham waxed positively Miltonic (and there are scholars who feel that the poet had his hand in some of these formulations) in his fury against "the whipsters." This was no time for utopian fun and games on some imaginary island—fanatics were offering "Chimaeras of Liberty, as might fit their own Ends and Phantasies ... They sought not Liberty, but Licentiousnesse."[37]

Two charges of historic gravity were raised in this indictment of the revolutionaries within the revolution, and both deepened Nedham's argument that utopia must have a stop and a revolution must know its own proper limits.

1. *The Doctrinaire Arrogance of an Exclusive Elite.* The new factions, "bold and impudent," were taking upon themselves, "Dictator-like, to define what is *Liberty*, and what not, and how it ought to be established; as if Themselves alone were infallible, and the only Champions of Universall Freedom." Worse than that, these "restless spirits" were set on a "violent course."[38]

2. *The Shadow of Uniformity under a New Absolutism.* In place of the *latitudo prudentalis*, that "prudential latitude" without which no people could live and breathe freely, they would "proceed to introduce an *absolute Community*." Nedham's standpoint here was unambiguously in favor of a social tolerance and an intellectual diversity.

> And since it is of unavoidable necessity, that (while the world stands) there will be divisions of Opinion, certainly such a Course must needs be most rationell, which shall provide ways of remedy against such Inconveniences as may follow them, rather than Inventions of Torture and Torment to thwart and stifle them; because the *understandings* of men can no more be compelled than their *Wills*, to approve what they like not.

But now onto the scene came the new men of darkness, "those high imperious *Uniformity-mongers* that would have men take measure of all Opinions by their own." They seemed to him "of the same humour as the tyrant Mezentius, who, if his Guests were too long for his Bed, cut them shorter, and if they happened to be too short, he had Engines of Torture to stretch them longer; being resolved to fit them all to his own measure and humour ... "[39]

Looking back on the decade of the Miltonic fifties, after his exile abroad and his final political disenchantment, Nedham found it easy to see, in a familiar blur of post-revolutionary astigmatism, all Commonwealthsmen, moderates as well as militants, prudent liberals as well as apocalyptic enthusiasts, in this dark and horrific light. It meant yet another parting of the ways for old friends, among whom were not a few "Hot-Spurs" and "Fire-brands."

I know the high Talkers, the lighter and censorious part of people, will shoot many a bitter Arrow to wound my reputation, and charge me with levity and inconstancy, because I am not obstinate like themselves.... Did they not (like fire too close besieged with Clouds) sally out in Thunder and Lightning, to the Terrour and destruction of all that stood in the way? ... [40]

He made his peace with the royal restoration, and thought he saw his true political enemies more clearly now. The vaunted hero of the People's Revolution now appeared to him a man of "all Zeal, no Knowledge; all Purity, no Humility; all Simplicity, no honesty: and if you never trust him, he will never deceive you."[41]

Some years before his death in 1678, Nedham composed in verse *A Short History of the English Rebellion*, and although his old friend John Milton would scarcely have recognized the sentiments or the style, a few of the doggerel stanzas are worth quoting; for they do, in a *"Joco-Serio"* way, serve to silhouette some of the main themes we have been trying to isolate in the developing political culture of the century, from Copernicus and the full circle of revolution to the pangs of Promethean failure to establish the earthly paradise. Of course, Copernicus is invoked:

> *Copernicus,* thy learned skill
> We praise, since we have found
> The truth; for now doth Heav'n stand still
> Whilst that the Earth turns round.
> See how the Wheel of Providence
> Back old Confusion brings!

And the vain pride of those saintly seekers of "an *Earthly Paradise*" is scored:

> A *Heav'n on Earth* they hope to gain,
> But we do know full well,
> Could they their glorious ends attain,
> This Kingdom must be *Hell.*

Nor has Nedham forgotten all those debates in a theologized politics with those "Rabbies" versed in every phrase of Revelation:

> Texts are tormented one by one.
> Like Votes, now here, now there:
> Thus *Hocus-Pocus* is out done
> By them at Westminster.

As for the actual course of events, and this was supposed to be a "history":

> *Rebellion* makes our Nation bleed
> With fresh Alarm (we see):

> But yet it is not well agreed
> Who must the Rebel be.

> The Round-head first the Rebel was,
> (If Truth be in the Laws)
> Till Treason did for Gospel pass,
> To bolster up the Cause.

This, accordingly, was Nedham's sentimental farewell not only to rebellion but to reform:

> *Reforming* is a dull Device,
> Dreads nought but strife and rage:
> Thou putt'st us into Paradice,
> And bring'st the Golden Age.

> Thou art Religion, God, and all
> That we may call Divine:
> Thy Temple is Westminster-Hall,
> And all our Priests are thine . . . .

> Hell now is thought an idle Dream
> To fright Men from their Crimes:
> Religion but a crafty Theam,
> Made to Bug-Bear the Times . . . .

> They banish all men in their Wits,
> Vote King, Lords, all *Offenders;*
> And authorize the phrentic Fits
> Of our long-sword *State-menders.*

Two last bits of a jingle or two, and Marchamont Nedham is also done with revolution:

> . . . and things must pass away,
> And so shall all your new . . . .

> 'Tis a damn'd Cause, that damns the Laws,
> And turns all up-side down.[42]

3. Locke and the Similes of Strength

The year 1660 was dramatic enough, yet for the intellectual historian it takes on added excitement as newly discovered documents throw a sharp and different light on the historic exits and entrances of the famous men who were spokesmen for different generations. We now know—the texts were only recently published for the first time, with a delay of some three hundred years—that at the time when John Milton was publishing his last political pamphlet John Locke was writing the manuscript of his first political tract. Locke was not quite thirty; Milton was past fifty. Blind, harassed by suggestions that he might be "condemned to travel to Tyburn in a cart," stunned by the defeat of all his hopes for the Commonwealth and now living "in perpetual terror of being assassinated," Milton—like Harrington and Nedham—went into hiding. A whole Cromwellian generation of embattled radicals was fast disappearing. For the young (Locke received his Oxford M.A. in June 1658) who had their fill of "giddy folly," the end of one revolution of time and the beginning of another was coming none too soon.[43]

The intellectual sources of the impatience are in a conservative reaction against an age which for two hectic decades had with enthusiasm and certainty raised great questions and offered ultimate solutions, and which even at the bitter end was capable of announcing yet another "readie and easie way." As Locke asked sharply in one of his letters, "Where is that great Diana of the world Reason ... there is not a man but thinks he alone hath this light within and all besides stumble in the dark." And in one of his manuscript notes, there is this characteristic bit of post-revolutionary skepticism from a political philosopher who would in the years to come get around to offering a few confident answers of his own:

> Happiness. Happiness is a continuation of content without any molestation. Very imperfect in this world. No body happy here certain. May be perfect in an other world possible probable.[44]

Whatever else was possible or probable, one thing seemed murderously certain: that "all those glorious promises" which had dominated this age of longing led but to death and destruction. Why had there been a failure of "all those tragical revolutions which have exercised Christendom these many years"? What had happened "to pervert the doctrine of peace and charity into a perpetual foundation of war and contention"? And who had kindled "all those flames that have made such havoc and desolation in Europe, and have not been quenched but with the blood of so many millions"?

The young Locke's replies amounted to one of the earliest indictments of the new seventeenth-century ideology, a bill of charges so formidable and comprehensive indeed that had it been available to be read and pondered its author might never have come to enjoy his luminous reputation as a mentor of European (and American) revolution. Perhaps he was cleverer than he knew when he suppressed these texts. Which men of '76 and '89 would still have gone into battle under a Lockean banner of liberal democracy if they had been instructed that "a liberty for tender consciences was the first inlet to all those confusions and unheard of and destructive opinions that overspread this nation," and if they had been

warned that "the same hearts are still in men as liable to zealous mistakes and religious furies, there wants but leave for crafty men to inspirit
and fire them with such doctrines ... "? Locke's own doctrine, in its
earliest phase, was doleful and dispiriting.

> ... however much happiness nature may promise, what she in fact
> offers is little and trifling, as can be seen well enough from the com-
> plaints of the whole of mankind, and from the hopes, vain and di-
> rected always to the future, whereby the mind, as if set on a rack, is
> continually stretched but never satisfied.[45]

Who indeed would have been inspired to pursue liberty and happiness
if, as in Locke's view of the law of nature, a "powerless and pitiable"
mankind dragged itself on "from pain to pain" leaving no point at all to
the restless Promethean quest for felicitous improvement?

Yet men of tender conscience or of dissatisfied future-directed hope
always knew that in the struggle for "a better life" it might be necessary
to destroy, to do unheard-of things, to burn with a new faith. Thirty
years on, a maturer Locke—no longer "showing only the black side of
the cloud"—would take a somewhat different view of the spirit of rebellion, and certainly a more generous attitude to the necessity of enlightened tolerance, especially when he himself sails back to England
from Dutch exile under the Orange flag of the "Glorious Revolution."

But for now an angry young man, with an "indelible memory of our
late miseries," could not be contained. As he once explained, "I no
sooner perceived myself in the world but I found myself in a storm."
The storm wasn't the worst of it. Others (he wrote to his father in 1659)
were dreaming of "nothing but fire, sword and ruin."[46] He, for his own
part, was dreaming of *felicitas* and *tranquillitas*, and he tried (with more
zest than his prudent temper should properly have allowed) to persuade
himself that "The world itself and all its frippery are scarce worth one
furious thought; he that pays down any part of his quiet and content for
it hath a hard bargain." Yet this one furious thought had to be put down
on paper, even if it was never given to the printers.

> Indeed [I have] observed that almost all those tragical revolutions
> which have exercised Christendom these many years have turned
> upon this hinge, that there hath been no design so wicked which
> hath not worn the vizor of religion, nor rebellion which hath not
> been so kind to itself as to assume the specious name of reformation,
> proclaiming a design either to supply the defects or correct the errors
> of religion, that none ever went about to ruin the *state* but with the
> pretence to build the *temple*, all those disturbers of public quiet being
> wise enough to lay hold on religion as a shield which if it could not
> defend their cause was best like to secure their credit, men finding

no cause that can so rationally draw them to hazard this life, or compound for the dangers of a war as that which promises them a better.

What was darkly involved here was no mere meliorism: for, obviously, "liberty, country, relations, glory being to be enjoyed only in this life can give but small encouragement to a man to endanger that." What is it that drives men to such a tragic paradox—that in order "to improve their present enjoyments a little" they are prepared to "run themselves into the danger of an irreparable loss of all"?

Locke was pointing his accusing finger at what we today call ideology—that body of ideas, notions, labels, and pretenses which serves to defend as a visor and a shield as well as to give credit to a revolution which dares to risk all to build the temple of a new and better life. Even more, its great watchwords function as the inspiring flags of a totally committed new force.

> . . . all things sacred as well as profane are held as nothing and so long as they march under the banners of liberty and conscience, those two watchwords of wonderful effect in winning support, they assert that each may do what he will. And certainly the overheated zeal of those who know how to arm the rash folly of the ignorant and the passionate multitude with the authority of conscience often kindles a blaze among the populace capable of consuming everything.

Some commentators have been apt, shortsightedly, to classify such insights under one or another variety of a conspiracy theory of social causation. True, Locke does ascribe the doctrinal perversions to "the cunning and malice of men" and often, as in a letter to his father at about the same time (the spring of 1660), offers the familiar explanations of the day in the limiting terms of "violent factions" and their "pernicious designs." Yet any reader who is unblinkered can profitably note the deeper sense of society, and its interconnecting processes, that was always with Locke, even too much so.

The delusions of ideology were ultimately attributable, according to Locke, to the social forces of custom and interest which shape the lives of all men. Their knowledge and their judgments are, he argues, "nothing but opinion moulded up between custom and interest, the two great luminaries of the world, the only lights they walk by." If this adds to the problem of aberrant opinions an extra dimension of substantial and even more serious social significance, it does not follow that the "watchwords of wonderful effect" were any more authentic, in the sense of truly corresponding to real human needs. For all his subsequent devotion to the cause of intellectual liberties—"Men must think and know for themselves," was his resounding cry—Locke began with a low, and occasionally cynical, view of the possibilities of man's mental life. He was impressed by the traveler's story of the blockaded Chinese city which finally surrendered to the Tartars; the gates were thrown open, and all were freely delivered to the victor: wealth, liberty, family; but when the vanquished were ordered to cut from their heads their traditional hair plait, they took up their arms again and fought fiercely until, to a man, all were killed. An ancestral custom, "the slightest of things," was preferred to life itself. Nor did this seem to Locke to be particularly exotic or remote. "Certainly," he concluded, "whoever cares to contemplate our own civil commotions will confess that perhaps even among us war has at times been waged by some with equal barbarity and similar bitterness over issues of no greater weight." All men, his own countrymen included, were passing strange. And this tough-minded young observer was beginning to learn, as he confessed, "not to rely on men, these bubbles however swollen and glittering, soft and inviting are not fit to be leaned on and whoever shall make them his support shall find them nothing but a little gilded air ... "

His pessimism about the general human condition did not release him from specific intellectual obligations in accounting for the phenomena of "tragical revolutions." Beyond the psychological level of personal cunning and political malice, then, lay an anthropological dimension of arbitrary and absurd cultural custom: a pattern of "men's necessities, passions, vices and mistaken interests, which turn their thoughts ... " How could human thoughts so turned prove to be anything but "shortsighted" and altogether defective? As Dr. Abrams has succinctly put Locke's view, "Partiality remains the distinctive feature of the collective predicament of man." Locke's distinctive faith in the possibility of mastering partiality through the exercise of critical reason was to come later. For now, Locke leaves us on the verge of a theory of "false consciousness," with its dismaying view of original error and permanent distortion plaguing the lives and minds of men in society. Could anybody be certain of anything? The young Locke, who was to become the philosopher of liberty, appeared to be sure at least of one thing, and it was an oddly disturbing thought that did not deserve to lie hidden for centuries—that everything was "so bound up with the opinion of everyone else ... it may be taken as certain that we do indeed lack that liberty which we *think we lack*."*[47]

Man's tenuous grasp of social and political realities, as arbitrary and erratic as it was conventional (and, above all, indifferent to genuine moral values), had yet another ground of explanation. It is appropriate

*"ut certum sit eam vere nobis libertatem deesse, quam nos non habere putamus."

to cite the following oft-quoted passage here, although it was formulated much later, since it completes the effort of a contemporary mind to confront what James Howell, similarly troubled by the advent of utopian revolutionism, called the "strange new Metaphysicks." In its notion of "the Oracles of the Nursery," it links Locke's early version of a theory of false consciousness with an equally remarkable approach to the infantile in man.

> Who is there almost that has not opinions planted in him by educa-tion time out of mind ... which must not be questioned, but are then looked on with reverence, as the standards of right and wrong, truth and falsehood; where perhaps these sacred opinions were but the oracles of the Nursery, or the tradition and grave talk of those who pretend to inform our childhood, who receive them from hand to hand without ever examining them? By these and perhaps other means opinions came to be settled and fixed in men's minds, which, whether true or false, there they remain in reputation as substantial material truths; ... and if they happen to be false, as in most men the greatest part must necessarily be, they put a man quite out of the way in the whole course of his studies. Men take up prejudice to truth without being aware of it, and afterwards feed only on those things that suit with and increase the vicious humour.[48]

So this is what they had been reduced to, those heroic figures of the 1640s and '50s who had come to "lay the cornerstone of the world's happiness"! Men of "sacred opinions" which were settled and fixed in their minds but amounted to nothing but unexamined prejudices; men of revered standards, as false as they were childish; men of a "vicious humour"—how outraged John Milton would have been at all this, if he had only known! How bitterly unfair a young and somewhat lost gener-ation can be to its ideological predecessors! Yet what else is to be ex-pected from a new and representative spokesman who senses only the "disorder and darkness" of an epoch, and none of the radiance which had inspired Milton to announce that "Our hearts are now more capaci-ous, our thoughts more erected to the search and expectation of greatest and exactest things"? Milton had joyously outlined new models of commonwealth in enthusiastic visions of "the highest that human capac-ity can soar to"; Locke coolly preferred Hobbes and echoed him in remarking the consequences: "no peace, no security, no enjoyment, enmity with all men and safe possession of nothing, and those stinging swarms of misery which attend anarchy and rebellion ... " Between old Gehenna and New Jerusalem no treaty was negotiable.

For no ideology comes to a natural end; it is murdered in its sleep. Young Locke went about his business efficiently. He hacked away at the

ideals of a previous generation, its compromised hopes and its violent
aberrations, its philosophical presuppositions and its political trickeries.
He thought he knew them well, those men of "passionate zeal," and he
hated above all their "zeal to be executioners." He saw through their
pretensions of love for the public good when society was "open to be
torn and rent in pieces by everyone that could but pretend to conscience
and draw a sword ... " He disdained the incendiaries of the age with
their fiery images, and deplored the whole tradition of Prometheanism.
He appeared to have an antipathy to the very word revolution, used it
only rarely (in fact, as we have seen, only twice), and was deeply suspicious of the "affected obscurity" of new terms coined to express noisy
and ill-defined notions. He raised the awkward question, so perennially
embarrassing to freedom fighters, of whether there should be liberty for
the enemies of liberty, or peace for the warriors against peace.

> Were offences arguments against anything, I know not who might
> not clap on a tender conscience and therewith sufficiently arm him-
> self against all the injunctions of the magistrate, and no law could lay
> hold on him without encroaching on this law of charity and his just
> freedom. How far we ought to part with our own liberty to gratify
> another's scruple is a question full of niceness and difficulty. But this
> I dare say, that of what value soever the inward and private peace of
> a Christian be, it ought not to be purchased at the settled and public
> peace of the commonwealth, especially where it will not remove the
> offence and only cast the scandal on the other side and disturb the
> peace of the contrary persuasion, since some men will be as much
> offended at the magistrate's forebearance as others at his injunc-
> tions.[49]

No, he was on to "the subtlety of malicious men," and on to their ways of
frightening "the weak and scrupulous" (the technique was simple: "to
clap disgraceful appellations upon innocent actions to deter men from
them"). He grasped how they "search out those arguments and spin
those consequences," all leading to that dreadful revolutionary ultimatum to the magistrate: "if he will not reform what they think amiss,"
then there was nothing left but "to carve out a reformation with the
sword ... " He saw them as pilots who would not "guide the ship into
harbour [but] on to the rocks ... " He was taken in neither by their
private strategies nor by their public philosophy. Had not Hooker accurately identified the danger of those fanatics who would "overturn the
world and make every man his own commander"? Locke, here again
echoing old masters, spelled out the anarchichal prospect:

> ... discipline will be everywhere at an end, all law will collapse, all
> authority will vanish from the earth and, the seemly order of affairs

being convulsed and the frame of government dissolved, each would be his own Lawmaker and his own God.[50]

This, then, was the "furious thought" that would put an end to a weary and threadbare ideology. "Exhausted as we are," Locke writes in 1660, "by so bitter a clash of opinions and of arms, we ought to rest content with our liberty and quiet." This was understandable, but naïve; and Locke sensed the intellectual inadequacy of the sentiment. What would happen when the exhaustion passed and social energies returned, and a restless discontent began to afflict men who believed, yet again, that they lacked that liberty and happiness they thought they lacked? It is at this point that we find our young conservative beginning to move from his youthfully excited position on the right to his more characteristic place at the prudent and moderate liberal center. He attempts his first breakout from the cursed dualism of extremist politics in the following passage:

> I confess . . . men should fly from *oppression*, but *disorder* will give them but an incommodious sanctuary. 'Tis not without reason that *tyranny* and *anarchy* are judged the smartest scourges can fall upon mankind, the plea of *authority* usually backing the one and of *liberty* the other: and between these two it is, that human affairs are perpetually kept tumbling. Nor is it to be hoped that the prudence of man should provide against these, beyond any fear of their return, so long as men have either *ambitious thoughts* or *discontented minds*, or till the greatest part of men are well satisfied in their own *condition*.[51]

Until then (if ever), history would offer a cycle of revolutions and counter-revolutions, spinning the consequences of utopian departures and authoritarian returns. It would be a class struggle of the extremes of aspiration and disaffection. Conceivably, conciliatory measures of increasing toleration would help to mediate the harshness of the conflict. It was an old and noble recipe, and Locke reminded his readers of Juvenal's pertinent lines in the fifteenth satire: "Each party is filled with fury against the other because each hates its neighbour's gods, believing that none can be holy but those it worships itself." How comforting it must have been to find ancient literary allies to enlist for the cause: the present scene was so desolate, and Locke thought of himself as a lonely and isolated figure. Which of the writers now alive had not dipped their pens in blood? Had not men of letters all betrayed?

> [I have] always professed myself an enemy to the scribbling of this age and often accused the *pens* of Englishmen of as much guilt as their *swords* judging that the issue of *blood* from whence such an inundation hath flowed had scarce been opened . . . [If only] men been more sparing of their ink and that these Furies, War, Cruelty,

Rapine, Confusion, etc., which have so wearied and wasted this
poor nation have been conjured up in private studies and from
thence sent abroad to disturb the quiet we enjoyed.

The reader will recall that these lines were first published in 1967 and
will forgive, under the circumstances, their unavoidably topical association with ideas of a *trahison des clercs*. It is a common trope, and the
young Locke would have shown himself to be something less than the
stalwart son of a new generation had he not concluded his "furious
thought" with a sweeping indictment of the older intelligentsia as the
architects of social ruin. It was they who were responsible for fashioning
"that temper that this age is scarcely blessed with . . . "

> *truth* is seldom allowed a fair hearing, and the generality of men
> conducted either by *chance* or *advantage* take to themselves their opin-
> ions as they do their wives, which when they have once *espoused*
> them think themselves concerned to maintain, though for no other
> reason but because they are theirs, being as tender of the credit of
> one as of the other, and if 'twere left to their own choice, 'tis not
> improbable that this would be the more difficult divorce.[52]

Although much was revised and much newly conceived in Locke's
political philosophy over the next decades (until his death in 1704, at the
age of seventy-two), the witty bite and the polemical fury of his thoughts
on the subject of certain intellectual tendencies remained fairly (and
unfairly) constant. He hated the manner of enthusiasm, and despised its
pretenses of righteousness. He rejected "any truth that gets not possession of our minds by the irresistible light of self-evidence or by the force
of demonstration."

> The strength of our persuasions are no evidence at all of their own
> rectitude: crooked things may be as stiff and inflexible as straight,
> and men may be as positive and peremptory in error as in truth.
> How come else the intractable zealots in different and opposite par-
> ties?

This, he said, "is the way of talking of these men":

> they are sure because they are sure, and their persuasions are right
> only because they are strong in them. For, when what they say is
> stripped of the metaphor of seeing and feeling, this is all it amounts
> to; and yet these similes so impose on them that they serve them for
> certainty in themselves and demonstration to others.[53]

But the metaphors—as Locke suspected—would not be so easily
stripped, and the similes would go on imposing themselves for a long
time to come.

12

How have our hopes been blasted! how have
our expectations been disappointed! how
have our ends been frustrated! ... how are
they withered in a night! how are they
vanished, and come to nothing! ... We have
sown the wind, and we have reaped a
whirlwind; we have sown faction, and we have
reaped confusion; we have sown folly, and
we have reaped deceit; when we looked for
liberty, behold slavery! when we expressed
righteousness, behold oppression! when we
sought for justice, behold a cry, a great
and lamentable cry throughout the nation!

—Leveller Letter (1658)

The Politics of Paradise

1. The Divine Tryout
Utopia in the very world—"Among the Bowers of Paradise itself"
(Wordsworth)—Not Graves Burst Opened, but Institutions Broken
Down—Hope for Human Salvation in History—Gradualism or Catas-
trophe, Possibility or Inevitability, Progress or Decay—Temper,
Temperament, Temperature—Turning Away from "Opinionative
Zeal"—The Aspiration "to be like Gods"—The "Laodicean Temper of
neither hot nor cold"—Cool Spirits, Worthy Souls, and Sterling
Guardians of "that signal and last revolution"

2. Knowledge to Cure, Power to Mend
Bernstein's Humility (1895): "How old political wisdom is"—The
Levellers and "Fanatick Moderation"—Fears of Extreme Con-
frontation—The Practice of Abstractions—Cromwell v. Lil-
burne—The Leveller Appeal to Charles Stuart (1658)—A Godliness
that Failed—"How have our hopes been blasted!"—Forgetful
Generations—Cycles of Public Exhilaration and Private Despair—
Winstanley's Lament—Self-Deception about Absolute Triumphs—
The Intoxication of the Abstract—Walwyn's Political Confession—
Roots

3. The Third Opinion
"It looks like a Revolution" (John Evelyn, 1688)—From Divine Kings
to Revolutionary Monarchs—"The Divine Right of the Revolution"
(1706)—Meteorological Changes—"A wise Mean, between the barbarous Extreams"—Words as Weapons—From Halifax to

Wordsworth—A Victory over the Apocalypse—Alternatives in the Bowers of Paradise: A Force that Uproots, or a Careful Hand that Trims

4. Dryden's Uneasy Course

"Blind by-paths to Paradise"—Between Personal Thorniness and Anodyne Caution—"Those ungodly Man-killers, whom we Poets when we flatter them, call Heroes"—Confronting Poetical Metaphors with Prosaic Realities—Dryden's "Shakespearean" Usages of Revolution—From Cromwell to William of Orange—Between Conformity and Nonconformism—The Revolution "purges" Dryden— "The Mad World" and "Occasions of Laughter"—Intellectual Transplants—Pleasure Principles

5. Burnet's Defense of a Revolutionary Establishment

The Critique of M. Varillas's *Histoire des Révolutions* (1686)— Revolutions as Singular Acts of Reformation—The Dangers of Permanent Habits of Restless Upheaval—"Hearts Prone to Tumults and Disturbances"—Need Anybody ever be a Revolutionary again?— Secularization of Thought-forms, and Eschatologization—Burnet as "Theologue"—Burnet and Halifax—Burnet Translates More's *Utopia*—The Special English Discount

6. The Wordsworthian Recoil

In the Tradition of the Paradise-Seekers—The Bishop of Landaff's "Cries of Modish Lamentation" (1793)—The Tradition of Apologetics—"Necessities" (from Milton to Auden)—Two Tactics in the Struggle for a more Humane Democracy—Sacred Incendiaries, or Profane Arsonists—To Forgive and Relent?— Poetical Politics—The Infallible Results of Precise Rules and Theories—"I wish, fret, burn, and struggle"—Disenchantment and Disarray: "I recoil from the bare idea . . . "—Alien Frenzy—Wordsworth's *Convention of Cintra* (1809)—Frenchified Minds and Jacobinal Pathos—Strong Causes, Weak Men—Just Wars, Transcendental Battles, Inspired Prophecies—Futurity, Perfection, and the People's Happy End— Coleridge on Wordsworth's "Hot Tints"—"The Changeful Winds of an anxious Author's Second Thoughts"—Inward Passions, Outward Arrangements—"Changes, Commotions, Revolutions"—Paradise: Institutionalized or Internalized?

1. The Divine Tryout

For more than another century, English thought and its climate of opinion would still be caught up in the problem of what one theologian referred to as "the Period and Accomplishment of certain great Revolutions" (Samuel Clarke, 1705). At the risk of appearing to make of history a ballet of twisting metaphors, I will continue to argue that as the idea of revolution moved from astronomy to sociology, the idea of the true place of felicity descended from theology to politics. Or, put another way, as the millennium lost its transcendence and became part of this world, the faraway utopian refuge (which from its inception was always somehow, somewhere part of this world) lost its escapist character and became the whole of this world.

> Not favoured spots alone, but the whole earth,
> The beauty wore of promise, that which sets
> (As at some moment might not be unfelt
> Among the bowers of paradise itself)
> The budding rose above the rose full blown.
>
> [Wordsworth]

Revolution—for some a hope, for others an inexorability; for some a drama, for others a process—had become the new name for the consummation of the golden end. The modern point that had to be reached, and from which there could no longer be felt to be any theological or secular return, was intuitively grasped by Wordsworth in these final lines from his French Revolution: As It appeared to Enthusiasts at its Commencement:

> Not in Utopia, subterranean fields,
> Or some secreted island, Heaven knows where!
> But in the very world, which is the world
> Of all of us,—the place where in the end
> We find our happiness, or not at all![1]

Thus Dr. Joseph Mede (1586–1638), the eminent biblical scholar at Cambridge who was Milton's tutor, turns to pondering "that signal and last revolution which makes way for the new Heavens and the new Earth"; and William Worthington writes of "Revolutions" in connection with "the final Renovation of all Things" (1773). What was happening was (as Mark Schorer has phrased it) that the millennium was being conceived anew in terms "not of graves burst open but of institutions broken down ... " If the millennium could be taken to be a temporal and not a transcendental state, then "all fulnesse of all temporall blessings, as peace, safety, riches, health, long life, and whatsoever else was enjoyed ... can be had in this world" (Henry Archer, 1642).

Human progress toward a holy utopia would be in the here and now. Would it begin "secretly," as some thought? Or could one discern the pattern of man's progressive redemption from all kinds of evil in some "large and comprehensive plan for the recovery of the whole creation from this complicated malady under which it all groans together"? And would it be a gradual change toward happiness for mankind (as John Edwards argued)? Or would it involve some catastrophic inaugural (as John Burnet believed)?[2]

Thus, before one made what we have referred to as the move from More to Marx, there was a divine tryout. All the themes of reform or revolution, of gradualism or catastrophe, of possibility or inevitability, of progress or decay—even the dispute over the legitimacy of leadership by a small learned elect, offering only easy and seductive allegories to the vulgar generality of men—were to be rehearsed on the theological plane before the transfer to the secular. E. L. Tuveson's study of *Millennium and Utopia* has made it clear that the seventeenth- and eighteenth-century divines argued through all the counterparts to the dialectical faction fights of the nineteenth- and twentieth-century revolutionaries. So far as the English scene was concerned, it would appear that with the triumph of the idea of progress as a hope for human salvation in history the school of gradual melioration began its domination over the English mind.

Temper, temperament, temperature—all were involved in the historic turning away from burning certainties and zealous commitments. But few things in history are as sudden as we dramatically suppose, and this revolt against enthusiasm was a half-century in the making. "Fancies are but the *Dreams* of Men *awake*." This was the keynote of the influential indictment of *Enthusiasmus* which the authoritative Dr. Henry More published in 1656. What More's martyred namesake had once offered as an inspired effort of the political imagination—and it had decisively molded several generations of utopians—was now felt to be an obnoxious and peremptory delusion. The affliction of the age was held to be "an unusual kind of popular Eloquence, a Rapsodie of slight and soft words, or rowling and streaming Tautologies . . . " What was it but "a full but false persuasion in a man that he is inspired"? The ingredients that went into this heady brew were clearly identified: Vehemence, Fervour, Zeal, Fluency, Rhetorick, Fury, Wildness, Wrath, and Indignation. All operated in a most vicious fashion to undermine the calm and cautious insinuations of free reason. Henry More was thinking not merely of the mystic and ecstatic visionaries of his time but also of the political enthusiasts, both abroad ("the tumultous Anabaptists in Germany") and at home (the Fifth Monarchists, among others). That such excesses in political as well as religious[3] life were intended in the early polemics against enthusiasm was more plainly indicated a decade later by another Civil War contemporary, who, in somewhat safer circumstances, could note: "And what Pestilential Influences the Genius of *Enthusiasme* or opinionative Zeal has upon the Public Peace, is so evident from Experience, that it needs not be prov'd from Reason."[4]

Perhaps only the controlled enthusiasm of the cooler scientific temperament could provide an outlet for so many dashed hopes. Critical though he was of dreams, visions, chimeras, fictions, and sundry other romances, Joseph Glanvill still refused to join forces with those who "start and boggle at every *unusual* appearance, and cannot endure the sight of the *bug-bear, Novelty* ... " As he reassured the scientists of his day, "Solomons House in the *New Atlantis* was a Prophetick Scheam of the *Royal Society* ... " This was the profoundly important, although not fully and openly recognized, exception to the indictment of enthusiasm as "the grand deceit" and of fanciful opinions as "the grand delusions of our Age." It left a path open along which utopianism could be renewed at the price of a sober alliance between social hope and scientific methods. But this is an aspect which belongs, in that felicitous and historic phrase which Glanvill seems to have coined, to other *"Climates of Opinion."* In the present climate we are describing, it was clear enough that the public miseries of state affairs were connected with what Glanvill referred to as "the Aspires to be *Like Gods."* There was a tragic element in "the *Image* of Prime *perfection,"* and the thought and the language are not far from Pascal's famous aphorism[5] when Glanvill considers the whole curiously cursed spectacle of beastliness and human aspiration and points to "A proud affecting to be like *Gods* having made us unlike *Men* ... "[6]

To be sure, some intellectual elements of the impassioned old guard tried to hold fast to their original anger, especially their pristine hostility (as one writer of the day put it) to "the Laodicean Temper of neither hot nor cold, luke-warmness and neutrality in zeal and affection: a thing loathed of God, and detestable to all good men ... "[7]

But soon even millennarians became convinced that "the happiness of the Millennial State shall take place in the world without that Disorder and Confusion which some men have extravagantly imagined." As Dr. Mede's seventeenth-century biographer writes of that remarkable theologian's works (which some contemporaries associated with the revolutionism of subsequent Commonwealth violence):[8] "Not one clause, not a syllable that naturally tends to blow men up into such furious heats as threaten publick Disquietness and Embroilments, is to be found therein ... " No, here was "a man *of a cool spirit,"* and "so likewise is his Notion and representation of the Millennium cool and calm and moderate, not ministring to Faction and Sedition, to Tumults and subversion of all Degrees ... " What needed to be avoided at all costs were "carnal conceits and intolerable fancies."

> Nor shall those *tempora refrigerii* ... those *times of cool refreshing*, ever be brought in by hot fanatic Zelots, *men set on fire* ... and ready also to *set on fire the Course of Nature* ... such as are skilful only to destroy and overturn; *Destruction and wasting are in their ways* (they are good at making the World a miserable, uncomfortable, and uninhabitable place), *but the way of peace they have not known* ... And therefore the temper and Quality of those Better times, they are thereby rendered incapable either of furthering and hasting the Felicities of the New Heaven and Earth, or of enjoying them ...

The men who would lead that "signal and last revolution" which Dr. Mede had heralded would be revolutionaries of very special character, with hallowed minds and consciences, and ancient sobriety and innocence.[9] As his biographer (John Worthington) went on to explain:

> For the primary Character of that Future State being universal righteousness and good will, piety, and peace, it naturally follows that they who are men of embittered passions and of a destroying Spirit, altogether devoid of civility, gentleness, and moderation, kindness and benignity towards men, and altogether unacquainted with what is lovely, decorous, venerable, praiseworthy, equitable, and just, can have *no part nor lot in this matter*; so gross and coarse a constitution of spirit as theirs is, speaks them unqualified for the Happiness of this Better State ...

The English revolutionaries who were to usher in the New Jerusalem would be worthy: their souls would have to be free of self-love and warring lusts, of pride, envy, wrath, and bitterness. The future state of better times required guardians of sterling, if not saintly, character. It was a characteristic English longing which united a hundred millennial dreamers from Mede to Wordsworth.

2. Knowledge to Cure, Power to Mend

Nor was this English longing, on certain touching occasions, entirely uncongenial to foreign revolutionary spirits, hard-pressed to excommunicate their own angry prophets of doom and destruction. How pleased Eduard Bernstein was to be when, in his pioneering researches into the Leveller literature, he discovered that the journal of the most extreme political party of the period bore the singular title of *The Moderate* (and he reassured himself, in a polemical aside with the older Disraeli, that it was not meant ironically or hypocritically).[10]

One passage in *The Moderate* especially elated the old German Social Democrat. It was in a number for September 1649; and trying as he was to explore the relations between "Socialism and Democracy in the Great English Revolution," he found in it "a line of argument which sounds very modern."

> Wars are not only ever clothed with the most specious of all pretences, *viz.*, Reformation of Religion, The Laws of the Land, Liberty of the Subject, etc., though the effects thereof have proved most destructive to them, and ruinous to every Nation.... But Pride, Covetousness, and Self-Interest ... and many being tempted to Swim in this Golden Ocean, the Burthen and Oppressions of the people are thereby not onley continued but increased, and no end thereof to be imagined. At this the people (who cannot now be deluded, will be eased, and not onley stiled, but really be the original of all Lawful Authority) begin to rage, and cry out for a lawful Representative, and such other wholesome Laws as will make them truly happy. These not granted, and some old Sparks being blown up with the Gales of new Dissentions, the fire breaks out, the wind rises, and if the fewel be dry and some speedy remedy be not taken for prevention, the damage thereby may be great to some, but the benefit conceived greater to all others.

By their metaphors shall ye know them? Not quite. For all the rage for happiness, with its sparks of fire and winds of gale, this was essentially a plea for speedy preventive remedies. And it was surely this note which moved Bernstein to write, "The world moves but slowly, and it gives a feeling of humility to realize how old political wisdom is."

Yet, in point of fact, even the Levellers were not without their immoderate outbursts. If they were moderates, they were also exemplars of what was called in a tantalizing seventeenth-century paradox "Fanatick Moderation."[11] As Richard Overton put it in 1647, "extream danger driveth to extreme means." These rare instances of English extremism are worth studying, all the more so because they were so short-lived: for the Levellers lacked, except for brief moments of visionary vagueness and radical impatience, both the emotional absolutism and ideological consistency which characterizes the central tradition of utopia and revolution. Still, they were capable of these sparks.[12]

1. *The Dedication to the Death*. "I am sorry," John Lilburne told the Speaker of the House of Commons in 1649, "I have but one life to lose in maintaining the Truth, Justice, and Righteousnesse of so gallant a piece." Again, as Overton wrote, "And if I have been a little too sharp in my advice and admonishment, impute it I pray you to the heat of my zeal and ardent affections to the promotion of that Cause; for truly to me it is as the life of my life; without it I'm nothing, with it I live."[13]

2. *The Monolithic Unity of Single-minded Action.* "I can no longer forebeare," Lilburne writes: "rise up in Armes as one man, and destroy all the aforesaid conspirators without mercy or compassion ... " A similar exhortation to the faithful is given by Overton in his *Appeals from the Degenerate Representative Body of the Commons of England Assembled at Westminster* (1647). "As one man," he cries, "rise up in the cause of the Army."

3. *The Turn to Force and Violence.* At first reluctantly: according to what Overton called the "Defensive principle of resistance." Then defiantly, for (in Lilburne's words) "this poore and distracted Kingdome ... have no other course to take but to remonstrate and ... by force of Armes to root up and destroy these tyrants."

4. *The Fury against a Revolution Betrayed.* What had come of "our endeavours for the advancement of a communitive Happinesse"? Only a land "new fettered in chaines." In *A Manifestation* (1649), composed in the Tower "in the grand year of hypocritical and abominable dissimulation"—signed by Lilburne and Overton, and probably written by Walwyn—the imprisoned Leveller leadership cried out plaintively that the only changes that had been wrought were "Notionall, Nominall, Circumstantiall, whilst the reall Burdens, Grievances, and Bondages be continued, even when the Monarchy is changed into a Republike ... "[14]

Nevertheless, from Bernstein onward, historians of the Leveller movement have correctly ascribed its political ideas and opinions to another tradition. On general balance, these have been taken to be part of the inescapable English ideology: a sentimental system of peaceableness and practicality. I am unprepared to go as far as one recent scholar who, assessing the Levellers' "major contribution to the history of modern ideas," argues that: "When examined from the vantage point of these three centuries, this contribution can be broken down into four constituent elements, which, though overlapping and interlinked, can be labeled optimism, secularism, rationalism, and pragmatism."[15] A sensitive analysis of the relationship between political temperament and climate of opinion would suggest something more complex and ambivalent. In fact, what also contributed to make these singular figures what they were, were some of the very opposite elements: a touch of irrational theory, a note of religious melancholy. They were transitional men. They had lost their unconquerable faith in the supernatural triumph of the righteous cause and had not yet acquired the firm hope that would come only with the new dogmas of progress and science. Only a belief in perfection and in inevitability could have saved their original high spirits: but they were too clear-eyed for the one and too honest for the other. They were tragic men of the middle, their spirits slowly crushed by an either/or polarization which they were helpless to prevent.

What could be said or done to avoid such a fearful and extreme confrontation? Their explanations and clarifications came to nothing, for critics and enemies who were defending power as well as principles refused to allow the "natural truth and lustre" of their cause. So aglow with their own humdrum sobriety, the Levellers were still charged (by Marchamont Nedham) with framing "such comments and chimaeras of liberty as might fit their own ends and fantasies." Another hostile pamphleteer saw as the horrid consequence of the democràtic insistence on immediate free elections "an utopian anarchy of the promiscuous multitude." They were accused of constituting a "Utopian party" in yet another sense: for obviously only their official version comprehended social reality true and whole—yet "where are those famishing babes? and where are those pining carkasses? Why are they not brought forth to the view of some pitiful eye . . . . Where are those faces black with sorrow and famine?" The final and most telling argument against Lilburne's ideals was less rhetorical and demogogic; indeed it remains an authentic expression of the immemorial conflict between two basic political temperaments.

> The dispute is not now of what is absolutely best if all were new, but of what is perfectly just as things now stand: it is not the Parliament's work to set up an Utopian Commonwealth, or to force the people to practice abstractions, but to make them as happy as the present frame will bear.[16]

In the eyes of the temperamental critic and the political enemy, if not in their own, the Levellers were utopians and, even worse, revolutionaries. "Truly my Lord General's intended government of this commonwealth for the future," a Cromwellian observer noted, "and Lilburne's turbulent restless spirit, seem to be altogether incompatible." It was Clarendon's opinion that Lilburne would either hang Cromwell, or Cromwell hang him. "Ruin, or be ruined," as a remark in a state paper had it. And indeed Lilburne's anger was unbounded ("the blood ran up and down in my veins . . . being scarce able to contain myself") when— just before being taken off to the Tower—he overheard Cromwell shouting and thumping his fist on the council table, "I tell you, you have no other way to deal with these men, but to break them in pieces . . . if you do not break them, they will break you . . . I tell you again, you are necessitated to break them."

In this extreme and violent confrontation there were a number of startling reversals of alliances. An extraordinary appeal for support and solidarity from a group of harassed Levellers and others (among them, that wild and irrepressible republican conspirator, John Wildman)[17] reached Charles Stuart, in 1658 still in royal exile but with hopes for a restoration rising. The King was encouraged by the implacable hatred that had grown up between Cromwell and his left wing, the Independents, Anabaptists, Quakers, indeed "the whole body of sectaries." But surely he did not need them to convince him of (as they put it) "the strange and strong convulsions of State, the various and violent motions and commotions of the people, the many changings, turnings and overturnings of governors and governments, which in the revolutions of a few years have been produced in this land ... " Yet, beyond what Clarendon refers to as their "wild propositions," how striking must this document have been! If to the advisers of the court it seemed to signalize a welcome relapse from a state of blackest sinfulness, it appears in the long perspective of post-revolutionary utopianism to be one of the first spirals in all the twisted endings of ideology.

In the personal cover letter which accompanied the Leveller address, the pious conclusion was ventured that "the series of affairs, and the revolution of a few years, would convince this blinded generation of their errors." It was a personal, painful confession to make, for

> liberty, religion, and reformation (the wonted engines of politicians) are but deceitful baits, by which the easily deluded multitude are tempted to a greedy pursuit of their own ruin. In the unhappy number of these fools, I must confess myself to have been one; who have nothing more now to boast of, but only that, as I was not the first was cheated, so I was not the last was undeceived.

All the other parties to the collective document, appear to have shared this sense of a godliness that failed.

> Like poor wildered travellers, perceiving that we have lost our way, we are necessitated (though with tired and irksome steps) thus to walk the same ground over again, that we may discover where it was that we first turned aside, and may institute a more prosperous course in the progress of our journey ....
>
> We know not, we know not, whether we have juster matter of shame or sorrow administered to us, when we take a reflexed view of our past actions, and consider into the commission of what crimes, impieties, wickednesses, and unheard of villainies, we have been led, cheated, cozened, and betrayed, by that grand impostor, that loathesome hypocrite, that detestable traitor, that prodigy of nature, that opprobrium of mankind, that landscape of iniquity, that sink of sin, and that compendium of baseness, who now calls himself our Protector.

A whole world of faith and dedication had collapsed, and Zion "lay in the dust."

> In all the rest of our motions, ever since to this very day, we must confess we have been wandering, deviating, and roving up and

down, this way and that way, through all the dangerous, uncouth, and untrodden paths of fanatic and enthusiastic notions, till now at last, but too late, we find ourselves intricated and involved in so many windings, labyrinths, and meanders of knavery, that nothing but a divine clue of thread handed to us from heaven can be sufficient to extricate and restore us.

What, then, could possibly have gone wrong? Where was the source of the error, betrayal, or deviation? The formulation of the "clue" was terse and illuminating:

We were sometimes wise to pull down, but we (now) want to build; we were ingenious to pluck up, but we have no skill to plant; we were strong to destroy, but we are weak to restore.

Still, the clue of political insight seemed at the moment to matter less than the liberating emotional outburst, the confession of lost illusions, the ideological catharsis.

How have our hopes been blasted! how have our expectations been disappointed! how have our ends been frustrated! All those pleasant gourds under which we were sometimes solacing and caressing ourselves, how are they perished in a moment! how are they withered in a night! how are they vanished, and come to nothing! Righteous is the Lord, and righteous are all his judgments. We have sown the wind, and we have reaped a whirlwind; we have sown faction, and we have reaped confusion; we have sown folly, and we have reaped deceit: when we looked for liberty, behold slavery! when we expressed righteousness, behold oppression! when we sought for justice, behold a cry, a great and lamentable cry throughout the nation![18]

We are witnessing here some of the earliest beginnings of a new genre of political literature, the literature of (in John Strachey's phrase) "the strangled cry";[19] and were not history a recurrent struggle with human amnesia, its piercing echo should have been heard through all the modern centuries. But the clear sounds of the past often constituted only an interfering field of noise for the fresh efforts of each succeeding generation. There are central social and intellectual experiences which have to be fancied as if they were happening for the very first time. What is past is not so much prologue as discomfiting reminder that most human ambitions have been essayed at least once before, and that the bounds of originality and virginal newness are very limited. Who would ever long to fall in love when burdened wth a thousand classic tales of aching romantic unhappiness, or who would rush to risk his life adventurously if the details of danger and death were ever-present in his mind's eye? There appear to be deep psychic reasons for the forgetfulness which overtakes most of man's ideological initiatives. Certain forms of passion, enthusiasm, and certitude thrive only on the sense that no such personal and intellectual engagement has ever before been made in such a way, with so much personal desperation and historic hope, and so little danger of error or failure. *Now* is the time, as never before in human history; *this* is the true cause, unique in the annals of human aspiration. Casually to overlook or simply to forget (or, perhaps, deeply to repress) man's long record of the cycles of public exhilaration and private despair is one of the temperamental conditions of the periodical renewal of ideology. Who, in a rubbish heap of broken doctrines, could rise to true belief? and who would manage to muster fine faith for a noble struggle under the dispiriting shadow of ages of remembered failure?

In this whole seventeenth-century world of half-utopianism and near-revolutionism, those haunting lines of the poem which Winstanley had put at the end of his final work, *The Law of Freedom* (1652), could serve as a shared lament:

> Truth appears in Light, Falsehood rules in Power;
> To see these things to be, is cause of grief each hour.
> Knowledg, why didst thou come, to wound, and not to cure?
> I sent not for thee, thou didst me inlure.
> Where knowledge does increase, there sorrow multiply,
> To see the great deceit which in the World doth lie.
> Man saying one thing now, unsaying it anon,
> Breaking all's Engagements, when deed for him are done.
> O power where are thou, that must mend things amiss? ...[20]

In such a mood, no apocalyptic vision could redeem practical political defeat, and no dream of fiery renovation could redress the wounds of despair. What the Levellers (or, at least, most of their leaders) had hoped for was neither paradise nor utopia; their most insistent programmatic demands were always involved in realistic detail for specific political and social reforms (popular franchise, health services and pensions, land ownership, fairer wages and taxation, legality and justice, free education, etc.). As it was trenchantly put in the final *Agreement of the Free People*, " The life of all things is in the right use and application, which is not our worke only, but every mans conscience must look to it selfe, and not dreame out more reasons and opportunities ... "[21] Or, as Walwyn wrote in his pamphlet *A whisper in the eare*: "I abandon all niceties and uselesse things.... My manner is to enquire what is the use: and if I find it not very materiall, I abandon it."

They were forced to abandon much. They distrusted violence as a desirable instrument of social change, and their leaders usually warned against raising any "tumult or uproare." Sound permanent alterations had to take place democratically and constitutionally. They often denied they were "levellers" and defended democratized property relations. They had a prescient and uncanny awareness of the dangers of abstract causes and the tragedy of needless martyrdom. As Walwyn wrote in *The Bloody Project* (1648),[22] "But especially let men pretending conscience take heed how they either engage themselves or perswade others to engage to fight and kill men for a cause not rightly stated or not thoroughly understood to be just." Walwyn goes further:

> Or was it sufficient thinke you now, that the Parliament invited you at first upon generall termes to fight for the maintenance of the true Protestant Religion, the Libertyes of the People, and Priviledges of Parliament; when neither themselves knew, for ought is yet seen, nor you, nor any body else, what they meant by the true Protestant Religion, or what the Liberties of the People were, or what those Priviledges of Parliament were, for which yet nevertheless thousands of men have been slain, and thousands of Familyes destroyed!

There was a foreshadowing here of some of the classic nineteenth-century warnings against the intoxication of abstract political ideas and the self-deception about an absolute social triumph. Walwyn is anticipating, as we shall see, the chastened European insights of Coleridge, Kant, Constant, Proudhon, and Herzen.

> ... all the quarrel we have at this day in the Kingdome is no other than a quarrel of Interests, and Partyes, a pulling down of one Tyrant to set up another, and instead of Liberty, heaping upon our selves a greater slavery then that we fought against.

More than that, we can detect those other interlinking constituent elements which Eduard Bernstein was to think of as realism (Kautsky would name it opportunism) and as wisdom (Lenin would call it cynicism).

1. *The Balancing of Freedom.*

> I look upon the King as an evill man [Lilburne told a meeting in 1648]. But the Army has couzened us the last year, and fallen from all their Promises and Declarations, and therefore could not rationally any more be trusted by us without good cautions and security: In which regard, although we should judge the King as Arrant a Tyrant as they supposed him ... and the Parliament as bad as they could make them; yet there being no other balancing power in the Kingdome against the Army but the King and Parliament, it was our interest to keep up one Tyrant to balance another, till we certainly knew what the Tyrant that pretended fairest would give us as our freedoms.[23]

2. A Choice of Evils.

That we are for Government and against Popular Confusion [Wal-wyn wrote], we conceive all our actions declare ... our aim having bin all along to reduce it as near as might be to perfection, and cer-tainly we know very well the pravity and corruption of mans heart is such that there could be no living without it; and though Tyranny is so excessively bad, yet of the two extreames, Confusion is the worst: Tis somewhat a strange consequence to infer that because we have laboured so earnestly for a good Government, therefore we have none at all ... [24]

3. Moderation v. Fanaticism.

Lilburne had been so taken by some re-marks of John Milton (*Defensio pro Populo Anglicano*, 1651)—'if haveing bin valiant in warr, you shall in time of peace prove base and unworthy"—that he made a free translation from the Latin and inserted the quotation in his *As You Were* (1652). Thus, "Mr. Milton's excellent and faithful advice" now (in Lilburne's words) included:

to shew forth as much Justice, Temperance and Moderation in the preservation of your Liberties as ever you have manifested courage in casting the yoake of bondage from your necks; ... to evince that you are none of those public Enemies, Traitors, Thieves, Murderers, Parricides, Fantastic Enthusiasts [*fanaticos*] ... that you have not, moved with ambition or a desire to invade anothers right, nor pricked and spurred on with sedition, any base lusts, madnes or fury, murdered a King; but that you have, being inflamed with the love of liberty, religion, justice, common honesty and your native Country, punished a tyrant.[25]

4. The Hazard of Defection.

We confesse indeed [the Leveller leaders admitted in their final *Mani-festation*], that the experimentall defections of so many men as have succeeded in Authority, and the exceeding difference we have hitherto found in the same men in low and in an exalted condition, make us even mistrust our own hearts, and hardly beleeve our own Resolutions of the contrary. And therefore we have proposed such an Establishment, as supposing men to be too flexible and yeelding to worldly Temptations, they should not yet have a means or oppor-tunity either to injure particulars, or prejudice the Publick, without extreme hazard and apparent danger to themselves ... [26]

5. The Hearts of Men.

We aim not at power in our selves, our Principles and Desires being in no measure of self-concernment: nor do we relie for obtaining the same upon strength, or a forcible obstruction; but solely upon that inbred and perswasive power that is in all good and just things to make their own way in the hearts of men, and so to procure their own Establishment.[27]

Both Lilburne and Walwyn were outraged by the charge that they had been advocating a program of "Utopian anarchy," but neither cared to indulge in the hypocrisy that the notion was completely far-fetched. They had made a choice of comrades, and as Walwyn loyally wrote in one of the most candid political confessions of the revolutionary century,

> though I am not in fellowship with those good people you call sectaries, yet I joyn heart and hand with them in anything that I judge to be right: and tending to the publike good: and love them as heartily as those that are at one with me in judgment. Sometimes I contest with them somewhat vehemently in arguing, but it is as I conceive for Truth, and for their good: and they take it so, and bear with me as I with them: and we meet and part in love....
> There are plain useful doctrines sufficient to give peace to my mind: direction and comfort to my life: and to draw all men to a consideration of things evidently useful, hath been a special cause that I have applied myselfe in a friendly manner unto all: but hence it is that some have said I am a great Annabaptist, others (upon as good ground) a great Antinomian: and you a seeker. Mistake me not, I do not esteem these as names of reproach, no more than to be called Presbyterian or Independent; nor do I take upon me peremptorily to determine what is truth, and what is error, amongst any of them. All have a possibility of error: I judge all Consciencious.

"A friendly manner unto all"—this might even be taken for a weak and defensive gentleness, did it not take its place among the toughest and most durable qualities of the English pragmatic radical in the long span from Walwyn to George Orwell. Few testaments in the annals of European political polemic can match the nobility of this humane commitment of Walwyn to "the cause I loved".

> I am one that do truly and heartily love all mankind, it being the unfeigned desire of my soul, that all men might be saved and come to the knowledge of the truth.... It is my extreance grief that any man is afflicted, molested, or punished, and cannot but most earnestly wish, that all occasion were taken away. There is no man weake, but I would strengthen; nor ignorant, but I would informe: not erronious, but I would rectifie, nor vicious, but I would reclaim, nor cruel, but I would moderate and reduce to clemency. I am as much grieved as any man should be so unhappy as to be cruel or unjust, as that any man should suffer by cruelty or injustice: and if I could I would preserve from both, and however I am mistaken, it is from this disposition in me, that I have engaged my self in any pub-

lick affairs, and from no other . . . . I never proposed any man for my enemy, but injustice, oppression, innovation, arbitrary power, and cruelty, wherever I found them. I ever opposed my self against them; but so, as to destroy the evil, but to preserve the person. And therefore all the war I have made . . . hath been to get victory on the understandings of men: accompting it a more worthy and profitable labour to beget friends to the cause I loved rather then to molest mens persons . . .[28]

One vivid image remains. The Levellers had been hard-pressed by the argument of one critic: "He that out of a desire to repair his house, shall move all the foundations, will sooner be *buried* in the ruines of the *old*, then *live* to see the erection of a *new* structure . . . " After so many fearful shakings and desolations, they had come to see the point. No, they were not set on moving all the foundations and making ruins of the old. They were for repair and renovation. Or, as they preferred to put it, they would have "the dead and exorbitant Branches pruned" and not "pluck the Tree up by the roots."[29] Certainly by this metaphor shall we know them. It is a heritage which historians can record even if history forgets.

3. The Third Opinion

The principle that was to triumph, after an epoch of divine and secular trials, was symbolized by that historic piece of semantic ingenuity which, as we have seen, called a conservative restoration a glorious revolution. To be sure, it looked and sounded and *felt* like an act out of a genuine revolutionary drama. "Universal Consternation," John Evelyn recorded in his diary for 2 December 1688, "it lookes like a Revolution." It announced itself with the wonted fearfulness, and when it passed there were always those who congratulated themselves on having survived. Observing his sixty-eighth birthday in that year, Evelyn confided this private prayer into his notebook: "O Blessed Lord . . . Be thou my protector this following year, and preserve me and mine from these dangers and greate confusions, which threaten a sad revolution to this sinfull Nation." On his sixty-ninth birthday he could register, in the kind of post-revolutionary sigh of relief which the Abbé Sieyès was to make proverbial (*J'ai vécu*), his gratitude to the providential fortune which had "prolonged my years to this greate Age, and given me to see so greate and wonderfull Revolutions, (&) preserved me amidst them, to this moment."[30]

For all that, it was a profoundly ingenious misnomer; and it served to confound the radical spirit for three centuries and, in England at least, to divert it from finding its great new modern ally, the longing for utopia. It is one of the most meaningful incongruities of modern European history that this first revolution was simply not revolutionary. As the historian Trevelyan has written, "the slight change that was effected in the order of succession at the expense of James and his son, although it was the most revolutionary aspect of the Revolution, was in fact the necessary condition of its otherwise conservative character."[31] It was a paradoxical complication in which a historic revolution was taken to be sensible, peaceful, constitutional, practical, quiet: a conciliatory live-and-let-live arrangement, without fanaticism or vindictiveness or intolerance or even enthusiasm; indeed, it was anything but an immoderate adventure in new and arbitrary ideas of violent social reorganization. The men of 1688 spoke of the "Revolution Settlement," with "Revolution Governments" (for Scotland and Ireland) and "Revolution finance," all on "a Revolution basis." Not the least of its confusions was the semantic complexity by which even the careers of the most Tory (or Cavalier, as they once were) representatives of the existing establishment could be summed up in terms of "Revolution politicks" and "Revolution principles."[32]

Where was rebellion, and what was revolution now? Rebels were reprehensible subversives, and revolutionaries now constituted a new noble establishment. One pamphleteer, reporting from Scotland to a friend in London, wrote:

> I will show you how the *Scotch* are a Company of Rebels against our Constitution, and run down the *Revolution,* and call it no better than a Rebellion against God and the King; and that all that had a Hand in bringing it about, and maintaining it, deserve to be hang'd.[33]

We have moved breathtakingly far from divine kings to revolutionary monarchs. Nothing could suggest more graphically the undulating movement of English ideology over this century of turbulence than the title which a loyal, royal writer—denying vigorously, by the way, any intellectual fraternity with Algernon Sidney or John Locke ("I never read ten Sentences in the former, nor ten pages in the latter")—could give his conservative manifesto: *The Divine Right of the Revolution.*[34]

As a consequence, both political metaphysics and the apocalyptic sense of fiery renovation were never to be without the persistent elemental harassment by what was emerging as a characteristically English climate of opinion. Winstanley becomes a Quaker quietist and is heard of no more; the Leveller leaders, except for Lilburne, retire or otherwise disappear from the public scene (and even Lilburne, in the end, declares that he has "become dead" to his "former bustlings and actings in the world");[35] that restless radical conspirator, John Wildman, is knighted by King William for his sterling services as postmaster general; John Rogers

abandons agitation and hurly-burly for a career in medicine and dedicates a treatise, inconceivable as it seems, to Clarendon, whom an entire
generation would once have considered the very sign of the Beast.

A large meteorological change had transformed the atmosphere. "Our
climate," as Halifax explained in 1688, is

> between that part of the World where men are Roasted, and the
> other part where they are Frozen.... between the Phrenzy of
> Platonick Visions and the Lethargic Ignorance of Popish Dreams
> ... between the Excess of unbounded Power, and the Extrava-
> gance of Liberty not enough restrained. True virtue hath ... its
> dwelling in the middle between the two Extremes.

Balance was the image of a secure state and a tolerable society. "If Men
are together in a Boat," Halifax tells us, "and one part of the Company
would weight it down on one side, another would make it lean as much
to the contrary; it happeneth there is a third Opinion of those, who
conceive it would do as well, if the Boat went even, without endangering the Passengers ... " What guaranteed survival was "going even";
the men of the third opinion had prevailed, and it was a victory less of
an ideology than of a temperamental predisposition and a metaphorical
imperative. Chiliasm had been routed. The absolutists of hope and the
metaphysicians of doomsday had enough difficulty maintaining themselves in helpless isolation, much less uniting for any discernible radical
social action. Even the zealous men of conservative recalcitrance felt
themselves drawn to a center, and an arch-Tory like Nottingham could
console himself by "remembering the house of commons proverb that
half a loaf is better than no bread," for he was "as deep as anybody in all
the new methods of moderation."[36] Weary extremist generations who
had already known what it was to be hot and cold, violent and fanatical,
enthusiastic and despairing, had no other choice but "going even".

One incident in the first decades of the "Glorious Revolution" is illuminating. In the impeachment of Dr. Henry Sacheverell (who faced
charges calling for a sentence to the Tower and the burning of all his
writings), the Whig motive was apparently the vindication of the legitimacy of "Revolution principles." Sacheverell, in Burnet's view, was
guilty of "inveighing against the Revolution," and his vote was cast with
the unforgiving majority. Yet, even from the farthest reaches of the
opposition, there were no tones which could be taken to be reactionary
or counterrevolutionary. In fact, the dissenters in Parliament (among
whom were Nottingham, Rockingham, and a dozen other Lords) made
a special point of explaining their defense of the so-called treasonable
sermons of Sacheverell, "because we humbly conceive, there are no
Reflections therein contained on the Memory of the late King William,

nor the Revolution; and that there is no Offence charged therein upon Doctor Sacheverell against any known Law of the Land ... " Holding fast to a concept of revolutionary legality, the Tories argued: "For the People's only Guide is the Law, and they can never be guided by what they can never be informed of."[37] The final sentence of the court was, for all the excitement, significantly mild. All the political forces of the day could be seen trying to huddle together on the high and safe middle ground.

Halifax, again, had captured the whole historic mood in the recurrent metaphor—"to be neither all in Flame, nor quite cold ... "[38]

Thus, at the end of a century which had teetered on the brink of certain modern formulations of revolutionary utopianism and secular political apocalypse, a number of sober conclusions impressed themselves on a representative English mind. Let me specify these as formulated in the writings of Halifax.

1. *Deep social alterations are thinkable but undesirable.* "It would be well," Halifax wrote, "if Hopes carried Men only to the top of the Hill, without throwing them afterwards down the Precipice." He was neither cynical nor defeatist, but distrusted the great leap forward of revolutionary action. "Hope is generally a wrong Guide, though it is very good Company by the way. It brusheth through Hedge and Ditch till it cometh to a great Leap, and there is apt to fall and break its Bones." He believed that the *salus populi* was "the greatest of all fundamentals" but felt that "the angry Buzz of a Multitude is one of the bloodiest Noises in the World."

2. *Governmental change is usually superficial.* With a sharp eye on the glorious readjustments of his day, Halifax noted: "After a Revolution, You see the same Men in the Drawing-room, and within a Week the same Flatterers."

3. *A messianic ideology of perfection is a poor counselor.* Halifax recognized the constant struggle over freedom between rulers and radicals and observed: "Power is so apt to be insolent, and Liberty to be saucy, that they are very seldom upon good Terms." But he was moderately optimistic about the prospects of liberal effort. "There may be fresh Gales of asserting Liberty, without turning into such storms of Hurricane, as that the State should run any hazard of being Cast away by them; these strugglings which are natural to all mixed Governments, while they are kept from growing into Convulsions, do by a mutual agitation from the several parts, rather support and strengthen, than weaken or maim the Constitution." And yet, "when all is done, those who look for Perfection in this World, may look as the Jews have for their Messias ... "

4. *Revolutions are betrayed.* "When the People contend for their Liberty, they seldom get any thing by their Victory but new Masters."

Halifax sensed the shadow which fell between means and ends: "That which looketh *bold* is a great Object that the People can discern; But that which is *wise* is not so easily seen: It is one part of it that it is not seen, but at the *End* of a Design. Those who are disposed to be wise too late, are apt to be valiant too early." He recommended "a wise Mean, between the barbarous Extreams."

5. *Political power corrupts.* "There is a wantonness in great Power that Men are generally too apt to be corrupted with . . . " It leads to violence, to "fear and terrour," unless checked by the principles of consent and respect; "for power without love hath a terrifying aspect" and "all force is a kind of foul-Play . . . "

6. *Words are weapons.* Halifax, much abused in his day and much distressed by fashionable frenzies, had a notable sensitivity to "a murdering Word, that carrieth Injustice, and no Sense." Men's words, he wrote (mixing metaphors peaceably as he went along), "are Bullets that their Enemies take up and make use of against them . . . and the same word which at first maketh the Company merry, groweth in time to a Military Signal to cut one anothers Throats." Halifax would appear to be one of the founders of modern semantical interest. "The World hath of late years," he observed in *The Anatomy of an Equivalent*, published in the year of the Glorious Revolution, "never been without some extraordinary *Word* to furnish the Coffee-Houses and fill the Pamphlets. Sometimes it is a *new* one invented, and sometimes an *old* one revived. They are usually fitted to some present purpose, with intentions as differing as the various designs several parties may have, either to delude the People, or to expose their Adversaries: They are not of long continuance, but after they have passed a little while, and that they are grown nauseous by being so often repeated, they give place to something that is newer . . . " It was an uncanny adumbration of the role that what he called "fashionable words" would play in the modern history of ideology and propaganda. " 'Tis hard," he concluded, "that Men will not only invent ill Names, but they will wrest and misinterpet good ones; so afraid some are even of a reconciling sound, that they raise another noise to keep it from being heard, lest it should set up and encourage a dangerous sort of Men, who prefer Peace and Agreement, before Violence and Confusion."

A century and a half later, if I may leap from Halifax to Wordsworth, these linked sentiments were holding fast as in a chain. In lines characteristically dedicated to "Liberty and Order," similar connections (though with another epoch's accretion of passion and despair) were made by the nineteenth-century poet trying to look back on another post-revolutionary period:

Ah why deceive ourselves! by no mere fit
Of sudden passion roused shall men attain
True freedom where for ages they have lain
Bound in a dark abominable pit....
What, is there then no space for golden mean
And gradual progress? ...
Thought that should teach the zealot to forego
Rash schemes, to abjure all selfish agitation,
And seek through noiseless pains and moderation
The unblemished good they only can bestow.[39]

I believe it would be true to say that by the time of Adam Ferguson's *Essay on the History of Civil Society* (1767), with its sober devotion to "plausible proposals" for "plans of improvement," a famous English victory over the apocalypse had been all but won. It needed only to be properly celebrated. In Dryden's line, "Our temperate isle will no extremes sustain ... "[40]

The beginnings of the classic European ideologies of revolution and reform were, then, accompanied by an efflorescence of image and idea, metaphor and didactic analogy, which through all the subsequent epochs of social and economic transformation was never to subside. These were the words and pictures in which essential realities were thought to be identified and great life decisions justified. "The terminology and formulae," as Professor Bredvold has written in his study of Dryden's intellectual milieu, "vary from age to age: but the insights and realities behind these transient formulae continue from age to age and reappear in many guises."[41] Classes would struggle and human temperaments collide; political factions would maneuver erratically for power and its various rewards; developing material forces would constantly mix with changing collective ambitions; other philosophers and poets would come to ponder the different patterns of "the way we live now." And yet: the ideological forms in which the first great revolutionary experience and its aftermath had molded the modern political mind were never to be broken, or discarded, or even significantly reshaped.

Certain fixed positions had been established on a map: one knew now where to locate the two extremes and a middle in between. Certain basic temperature readings were taken, and the excited tempers of both hopeful enthusiast and outraged traditionalist were registered against an agreed and acceptable scale of committed coolness. A measuring rod came into use which illustrated the graphic possibilities, large and small, which obtained between all and nothing.

If men of the first revolution had dreamed of giving power to the utopian imagination, to images of paradise and perfect human happiness, the post-revolutionary men of power never for a moment imagined that power could or should be trusted in association with anything but prudence, moderation, balance. To guide society and guarantee the civilized advance of mankind, one needed a careful hand that trims, never a force that uproots: one had to take the course that "went even" and under no circumstances follow a captain who dared to make adventurously for the winds and the storms.

4. Dryden's Uneasy Course

The new course was not easy. Combat veterans of the two major warring schools of opinion could not lightly turn away from the memories of the long tempestuous years. For some at least, the "third opinion" was scarcely feasible. Consider the case of John Dryden, poet laureate and historiographer royal. He had moved from the *Heroique Stanzas, Consecrated to the Glorious Memory of his most Serene and Renowned Highnesse OLIVER Late Lord Protector of this Common-Wealth* (1659) to a defense of the Roman Church and a justification of his Catholic conversion in *The Hind and the Panther* (1687). In the former, the heroic Cromwellian achievement left the eulogizing poet almost speechless:

> How shall I then begin, or where conclude
> To draw a *Fame* so truly *Circular*?
> For in a round what order can be shew'd,
> Where all the parts so *equall perfect* are?

And now, in a confessional mood of near Wordsworthian volubility, he looks back in self-criticism to the prelude of the old, false path:

> My thoughtless youth was wing'd with vain desires,
> My manhood, long misled by wandring fires,
> Follow'd false lights; and when their glimpse was gone,
> My pride struck out new sparkles of her own.

These lines are from *The Hind and the Panther*, and Dryden knew how disputatious the expression of his new views would be. "The Nation is in too high a Ferment," he wrote, "for me to expect either fair War, or even so much as fair Quarter from a Reader of the opposite Party." Little wonder, for he was now announcing that *"doctrine turns the reformation round / And all the rest are false reformers found,"* and that *"More liberty begets desire of more, / The hunger still encreases with the store."* He had come to suspect that the false and doctrinaire reformers *"each has a blind by-path to Paradise,"* indeed that *"fallacies in Universals live."* He would no longer be *"Drawn to the dreggs of a Democracy."* If, as he said, *"a down-hill Reformation rolls apace,"* then it was time to jump off; and if he seemed to be suggesting that that state was *"least deform'd because reform'd the least,"* then the new path surely lay uphill on the opposite side.

When the Revolution came, Dryden was deprived of (among other things) his laureateship, although many of his finest and most characteristic sounds almost matched the new conventional noises of the day.

> And though the Clymate, vex't with various Winds,
> Works through our yielding Bodies, on our Minds,
> The wholesome Tempest purges what it breeds;
> To recommend the Calmness that succeeds.

Perhaps his famous "satyre against Sedition," addressed pointedly to the Whigs, was still a shade too polemical in its old-style thrust against the type of rebel who

> Maintains the Multitude can never err;
> And sets the People in the Papal Chair ...
> The pow'r is always theirs, and pow'r is ever wise.
> Almighty Crowd, thou shorten'st all dispute;
> Pow'r is thy Essence; Wit thy Attribute! ...
> The Most have right, the wrong is in the Few.
> Such impious Axioms foolishly they show ...[42]

Even if his politics (and his religion) opted for the extreme, his verse seemed to vote for the middle. *"But Common quiet is Mankind's concern."* Dryden, with this line, might almost have been the keynoter of the age. But perhaps it was the divergence between the thorniness of the radical reactionary personality and the anodyne caution of the conservative intellectual that caused the man and the message to be so clearly at odds.

> In Lusts we wallow, and with Pride we swell,
> And Injuries, with Injuries repell;
> Prompt to Revenge, not daring to forgive,
> Our Lives unteach the Doctrine we believe ...

The life of the poet was still full of mid-revolutionary passions; but his doctrinal temper had already made its peace with post-revolutionary reasons. A weary generation, exhausted by profound historical excitements, tried to reach a point when enough was enough.

> Enough of our Ills our dire Rebellion wrought,
> When, to the Dregs, we drank the bitter draught.

Yet the disposition could not always or completely control the doctrine, and this mood breaks through old ideological maxims only on uncontrollable occasions when Dryden seems to grasp the indictment of the

"third opinion" against the proud, unforgiving views of vindictive con-
troversialists.

> Add long prescription of establish'd laws,
> And picque of honour to maintain a cause,
> And shame of change, and fear of future ill,
> And Zeal, the blind conductor of the will;
> And chief among the still mistaking crowd,
> The fame of teachers obstinate and proud,
> And more than all, the private Judge allow'd.
> Disdain of Fathers which the daunce began,
> And last, uncertain who's the narrower span,
> The clown unread, and half-read gentleman.

One senses that there was here somewhat less an intellectual inclination
to rise above "the narrow span" than a concern to escape its personal
dangers. After so many revolutions of time, who could with any optimism hope for a turn for the better? " 'Tis to be feared," Dryden wrote,
"That as a Fire the former House o'rethrew, Machines and Tempests will
destroy the new." More than mere political arrangements might perish,
and it was only understandable—and prescient, for this is the year
1687—for the poet to entertain a private worry.

> You hinted fears of future change in state,
> Pray heav'n you did not prophesie your fate;
> Perhaps you think your time of triumph near,
> But may mistake the season of the year.

No, he could not, as he confesses, *"conclude all fiery Trials past."*

> For Heav'n will exercise us to the last;
> Sometimes will check us in our full carreer,
> With doubtful blessings, and with mingled fear.[43]

These lines are from *Britannia Rediviva*, "a Poem on the Birth of the
Prince" written in 1688; and when in that year it turned out that he had
indeed mistaken the season, it was inevitable that he would be among
the first victims of the new forces of so-called Revolution. He liked to
think that he was preaching "Ballance," but he was more deeply drawn
in his person to the drama of what he called "sacred adversity." This
was the psychological root of the trouble. He was a committed and
embattled poet and could not help believing that *"Opposition makes a
Heroe Great."* But would it not have been truer to say that opposition, in
its zealous excess, was also a doubtful blessing and could in fact make a
hero greatly unbalanced? He quite conceded as much when in a later
mood of chastened bitterness, he spoke of "those ungodly Man-killers,
whom we Poets, when we flatter them, call Heroes; a race of Men who

can never enjoy quiet in themselves 'till they have taken it from all the World ... "[44]

In earlier days, fairly secure in the time of a stable Stuart Restoration, Dryden had made his commitment unequivocally clear, and it was to prove a fateful association of power and propaganda. In the dedication of his *All for Love* (1678) to Danby, the Lord Treasurer, Dryden wrote:

> There is somewhat of a tie in Nature betwixt those who are born for Worthy Actions, and those who can transmit them to Posterity; and though ours be much the inferior part, it comes at least within the Verge of an Alliance.... It is indeed their Interest, who endeavour the Subversion of Governments, to discourage Poets and Historians; for the best which can happen to them is, to be forgotten ...[45]

Dryden erred here: was it so inconceivable (and in the age of Milton!) that there could be a poetry of subversion or a historical chronicle of revolutions? Too narrow a span restricted his political imagination, but then intellectual generosity is a rare virtue in any ideologue, and Dryden was at this time possessed by the factious spirit.

> And yet there are not wanting malcontents amongst us, who, surfeiting themselves on too much happiness, would persuade the people that they might be happier by a change. It was indeed the policy of their old forefather, when himself was fallen from the station of glory, to deduce mankind into the same rebellion with him, by telling him that he might yet be freer than he was.... We have already all the liberty which free-born subjects can enjoy, and all beyond it is license ...
>
> [It is not] enough for them to answer, that they only intend a reformation of the government, but not the subversion of it: on such pretence all insurrections have been founded; it is striking at the root of power, which is obedience. Every remonstrance of private men has the seed of treason in it; and discourses which are couched in ambiguous terms, are therefore the more dangerous, because they do all the mischief of open seditions, yet are safe from the punishment of the laws.

All this was unambiguous enough: unlike Milton (in whom he apparently only saw "majesty" and "loftiness of thought"),[46] Dryden could never for a paradoxical moment be taken to be of the Devil's party. That satanic "old forefather" was a seducer into license, an insurrectionary rebel, irredeemably and forever guilty of seditious treason. Call it revolutionary zeal (as Milton and his friend Nedham would have), or counterrevolutionary passion (as Howell might have), what the two warring temperaments shared was a related quality of frenetic indignation and the self-indulgent habit of instantaneous rage. It is this persistent intellectual—or, if you will, ideologized—imbalance that tipped the scales against the would-be prophet of the temperate isle in its epochs of common quiet and the calmness that succeeds. Dryden remained trapped in what he had himself called the narrow span. In a word, Dryden did not come with peace: he was still part of the commotion.

But his verse, as I have been arguing, manages to speak with another, almost independent voice. A more conciliatory note of transcendent sobriety struggles to come through. Thus, in a revealing and surprising scene in his drama of *The Indian Emperour* ("or, the Conquest of Mexico by the Spaniards"), Dryden can scarcely refrain from allowing the Christian spokesman to be upstaged by Montezuma.

> MONTEZUMA: ... to mankind
> One equal way to bliss is not designed;
> For though some more may know, and
>   some know less,
> Yet all must know enough for happiness.
> CHRISTIAN PRIEST: If in this middle way you still pretend
> To stay, your journey never will have end.
> MONTEZUMA: Howe'er, 'tis better in the midst to stay,
> Than wander farther in uncertain way.[47]

Evidently Dryden himself could not hold to the course of this journey of the middle way. He wandered farther, thoroughly out of step with the deliberate centrism of his own constitutional advice, which had been to fasten onto the virtues of "moderation" and "steadiness of temper" and therewith to "stand like an isthmus betwixt the two encroaching seas of arbitrary power and lawless anarchy ... " The nautical trope was fanciful; and the political impulse, although very real, was equally improbable. In an aside which betrayed that the poet was not very long for this Canute-like role of holding back tidal waters, Dryden added that "the undertaking would be difficult to any but an extraordinary genius, to stand at the line, and to divide the limits ... "[48]

As it turned out, Dryden was among those whom "the Tempest purged." He was, as Sir Walter Scott wrote, "deprived by the Revolution of present possession and future hope." Yet his poetry was like a mercurial barometer in its sure forecast of the climate of calmness that was to prevail.

> For, in some Soyles Republiques will not grow:
> Our Temp'rate Isle will no extremes sustain,
> Of pop'lar Sway, or Arbitrary Reign:
> But slides between them both in the best;
> Secure in freedom ...[49]

Whole new generations of his countrymen were now ready and eager to make just that slide between the extremes. Others would even come to try and make a fair job of standing at the line and dividing the limits.

If the essential difficulty of political discourse is its intellectual tendency to confound poetical metaphors with prosaic realities, then we must be equally wary not to confuse the analysis of even the most eventful ideological outbursts (and all the other "pregnant images") with the basic historical happenings themselves.

Workaday men in an active society, naturally agitated by change and growth and conflict, usually make their decisions about war and politics (if theirs is the decision to make) without pedantic reference to the formulations of poets and philosophers. To suggest that the intelligentsia, in its phraseology and moral palpitations, often brings to "self-consciousness" the problem of an epoch, is not to say that the word is the thing. A generation wearies of the storm and stress, the fire and blood of a revolutionary epoch, not because of an aesthetic impatience with a cliché (although that is always a sure semantic symptom) but because years of violent unrest have imposed too much suffering felt to be unnecessary and too many sacrifices sensed to be futile. Reduced to its simplest terms: farmers wanted peace to farm, traders wanted unmolested opportunities to transact their business, families wanted surcease to be *en famille*, a whole society longed for "quiet" rather than "overturning" or "uprooting." Yet the life and death of an idea or an image can often serve as a soft analogical reference to the hard state of social forces that dominate a historical epoch.[50]

Metaphors in politics are the imaginative symbols of social realities but they serve not infrequently as escape mechanisms: for images can illuminate or darken, and analogues turn easily into a species of false literary consciousness in which the sunniest of similes can conceal more than it reveals. In the history of political thought and sentiment, where so much has been couched in the opulent vocabulary of color and fancy, the price of intellectual probity is ceaseless linguistic awareness. Dryden's genius as a poet need not blind us to his metaphorical self-deceptions; indeed his very power with words makes his weaknesses (and through them the ideological distortions of the age) brilliantly obvious. In his masterpiece of political versification, Dryden offers us this vision, something less than persuasive, of the "glorious prize" held out to men by cosmic fate and public fortune:

> Heav'n, has to all allotted, soon or late,
> Some lucky Revolution of their Fate:
> Whose Motions, if we watch and guide with Skill,

(For humane Good depends on humane Will,)
Our Fortune rolls, as from a smooth Descent;
And, from the first Impression, takes the Bent:
But, if unseiz'd, she glides away like wind;
And leaves repenting Folly far behind.
Now, now she meets you, with a glorious prize,
And spreads her Locks before her as she flies.[51]

Lucky revolution? This is a private whimsical conceit, shored up from the fragments of old notions of astrological chance and determinism, theological predestination and personal free will, curiously unmarked by all the latter-day preoccupations with social change and political upset. Dryden's language here evinces a significant ideological lag. Given the poet's deep immersion in contemporary public affairs, this concept of "revolution" was already a historical anachronism; it is, in essence, an image of a personal yearning for an ancient constellation of forces. All of Dryden's usages are "Shakespearean" in their traditional non-political contexts: viz., "I never thought to see / Strange Revolution for my Farm and me," or "Let their first revolution / Bestow a bride upon his darling son," or "What Revolution can appear so strange, / As such a Lecher, such a Life to change?"[52] Can it be without significance that Dryden nowhere in his vast body of verse uses revolution in the new political sense? It occurs, oddly enough, only in the couplet put into Dryden's mouth by Thomas Shadwell, the poet and playwright who displaced Dryden as poet laureate:

Has this stupendious Revolution past
A Change so quick, and I not turn as fast?[53]

No, the quick revolutionary turn was not for Dryden; not even the stupendous word (at least in his poetry). In the perspective of the work of writers like Howell (a predecessor as Historiographer Royal) and Nedham, this abstinence can only strike one as quirky, capricious, idiosyncratic; but even as such it has its special pertinence for our analysis.

I have already noted that Dryden flirted, as a young man, with a passion for the Lord Protector (and it was a Cromwellian episode which his enemies never ceased to taunt him for, maliciously reprinting those early verses again and again). But his was a mind that was finely impervious to the metaphysical charms of utopia and revolution; he was thoroughly immune to the temptations of millennial aspiration or what he once referred to as "the windy satisfactions of the brain." The word utopia is never used in his poetry, and the thing itself is consistently repudiated; for *"thoughts of what may be, destroys what is."* Not even when certain public urgencies seemed to call for destructive political change could he (in contast to the "utopianism" of a Cowley) bring himself to be reconciled with notions of innovation, novelty, and perfect theorems of social amelioration. *"Poor human kind must wander in the dark ... "* If in its political reading his systematic indifference to large human hope seems cynical, philosophically it was part of an achieved Stoicism. *"Rest then, my soul"* (he wrote in his *Religio Laici*), *"from endless anguish freed ... "* His slow self-liberation emancipated him from even the most workaday political expectations.

In the first years of the Revolution, Dryden made a number of hesitant and tentative efforts toward accommodation. He dedicates his *King Arthur* to the Marquis of Halifax, who had once been Charles II's favorite Minister and now was the powerful new kingmaker in the land.[54] Refraining, as he candidly admits, from commenting on "Invidious Topicks," he appears only to be recommending "wholesome counsels, which wisely administered, and as well executed, were the Means of preventing a Civil War, and of extinguishing a growing Fire which was just ready to have broken forth among us ... " He speaks of his own "Ruin" as a champion of "a lost Cause" and places his hopes with "the more reasonable sort of my Countrymen."

It was only a mild, unspectacular form of personal accommodation which he attempted "since this wonderful Revolution" (and I take wonderful here to mean astonishing rather than admirable).[55] Dryden's career at this point raises again the role of inconstancy in the political allegiances of the literary intelligentsia; and we must be wary of conventional attitudes which prompt only admiration for the lone rebel and his splendid defiance, or strictures for the men who compromise, concede, or (in the operative word of that day) "trim." The whole century was one long field day for moralizing polemic against the oppositionist who, in his strength or weakness, was either a knave or a fool, a cynic or an opportunist, always on the verge of recanting or turning his coat. Intellectuals in politics have rarely been taken seriously: out of power, they are seen as possessed fanatics; in power, they are held to be mercenary hirelings; and to change one's views is usually considered an unfailing sign of mental or moral corruption. Dryden had more than his share of brass rings on this carousel. He was "a hired Libeller" with a "prostituted Muse"; and Shadwell went on in those embittered years of the early 1680s to say:

> Now he recants, and on that beating thrives:
> Thus Poet Laureats, and Russian Wives,
> Do strangely upon beating mend their Lives.

For Shadwell, it was a self-proclaimed heroic feat to have held out

against an age of wretched conformity, and he did not hesitate to give
voice to his own pride. "I never could recant in the worst of times," he
writes, "when my ruin was designed, and my life was sought ... "

> No wonder common-sense was all cried down,
> And noise and nonsense swaggered through the town.
> Our author, then oppresst, would have you know it,
> Was silenced for a nonconformist poet.

With the coming of the Revolution, there was a transposition of roles;
but the simpleminded alliance of power and the pen remained. Shadwell took Dryden's place, and the new poet laureate began with lines to
the conquering Prince as liberator, a "Glorious Deliv'rer of Mankind"
who *"Invaded us with Force to make us free ... "*

> Inspir'd by Heav'n, thus the great Orange said,
> Let there be Liberty, and was obey'd.

How wrong Dryden had been when he thought that the subversion of
governments would have no need of poets or historians: Shadwell ver-
sified the revolution in accents which, at other times and in Dryden's
other moods, might well have been congenial.

> The quickening Mass moves now in ev'ry part,
> And does the Plastick Faculties exert,
> The jarring Attomes move into peace,
> And all Confusion and Disorders cease:
> The ugly undigested Lump became
> The perfect, glorious, and well order'd Frame.[56]

Surely the modern critic can, in the long perspective of the history of
the intelligentsia, sometimes permit himself the liberty of being less
involved in the rounds of pathos and pity. For intellectuals appear to
bend toward power like plants in a tropism toward the sun. A few, with
different roots and forms of response to outside stimuli, exhibit other
growth curvatures. None appears to be free to make his own choice; and
the historian, like the gardener, need not always fly into rage or rapture.
Like it or not, the garden has its own rules and determinations. That the
spectacle of this pitiless process is determined by natural necessities
does not, to be sure, preclude the element of ethical meaning; a garden
is beautiful and useful, a swamp is not. But, of course, men are not
plants; and the human species cannot be narrowly and arbitrarily
classified as flower or weed.

No one will ever call Dryden's withdrawal from the agitations of public affairs heroic, but it had a certain dignity of its own and, in the larger
inquiry we are making, a paradigmatic importance. The times were not
unreasonable, nor was the Revolution proving to be inconsistent with an

ethos of political culture. Or, as Sir Walter Scott puts the point in his edition of Dryden's work:

> when is it that a government, erected by a party successful in civil dissension, does not far exceed their just, and even their original pretensions? The parties had each founded their plea and pretensions upon sacred and integral parts of the constitution, as the contending factions of the Jews occupied, the one the temple, and the other the palace of Jerusalem. In a civil war, one bulwark or the other must have fallen with the party which it sheltered; and it was only the Revolution of 1688, which, leaving both Whig and Tory in full strength, compelled them mutually to respect the Constitutional vantage-ground assumed by each other.[57]

Thus, the "purging" of Dryden by the Revolution was not quite as sinister as it sounds today; it was a poetic piece of hyperbole. Dryden was not at the mercy of unread clowns and half-read gentlemen. On the contrary, he could turn to countrymen

> who, though they are of a contrary Opinion themselves, yet blame not me for adhering to a lost Cause ... so long as I am a patient Sufferer, and no disturber of the Government. Which, if it be a severe Penance, as a great Wit has told the world, 'tis at least enjoyn'd by me by my self: And Sancho Panza, as much a Fool as I, was observed to discipline his Body, no farther he could endure the smart. I suffer no more than I can easily undergo; and so long as I enjoy my Liberty, which is the Birth-right of an English Man, the rest shall never go near my Heart. The Merry Philosopher is more to my Humour than the Melancholick; and I find no disposition in my self to Cry, while the mad World is daily supplying me with such Occasions of Laughter ... [58]

Four years after the onset of so-called Revolution Politics, Dryden permitted himself (in the dedication of *Examen Poeticum*, 1693) an almost quixotic outburst. "No Government has ever been, or ever can be, wherein Time-servers and Blockheads will not be uppermost. The Persons are only chang'd, but the same jugglings in State, the same Hypocrisie in Religion, the same Self-Interest and Mis-management, will remain for ever." This impatience went far beyond mere out-of-office Tory despair, and in the following passage the dispirited farewell to politics was presaged by a more stoical formulation:

> In wishing nothing, we enjoy still most;
> For even our wish is, in possession, lost:
> Restless we wander to a new desire,
> And burn ourselves by blowing up the fire:
> We toss and turn about our fev'rish will,
> When all our ease must come by lying still:

> For all the happiness mankir.d can gain,
> Is not in pleasure, but in rest from pain.

It is almost as if Dryden's mind rejected the intellectual transplants of the new European tradition which we have been trying to follow over the post-medieval centuries from Dante and Joachim through More and Bruno and Sidney to Milton, Hartlib, and Nedham. He detected a pleasure principle in the movement of the spirit toward utopia and revolution, and he attempted austerely to keep free of the fevers of paradise and the lures of a desiring will. He could sense the shape of things to come but could not, or would not, become part of them.

> 'Tis well an old age is out:
> And time to begin a new.

These elegiac lines are from his last written work, *The Secular Masque*, which was performed within a few days of his death in May 1700. The revolution, in both its literal and literary senses, simply passed him by.

I have said that the new course was not easy, and that for some "the third opinion" was not feasible. Others, however, less burdened with classical tradition and authoritarian loyalties (and one must, with respect, add: with erratic unmanageable literary genius), found the ideological transition easier to make.

5. Burnet's Defense of a Revolutionary Establishment

There may well be, as I say, a certain larger significance in the very technical relationship that Dryden had to the new words of the emerging ideological vocabulary. In 1686 Dryden, then still laureate and royal historiographer and not unsympathetic to the views of the court (his conversion to James II's faith was soon to follow), began a translation of a famous French manifesto of the day. This was Varillas's disputatious account, *Histoire des révolutions arrivées dans l'Europe* . . . , in which, as the prefatory note to the King of France makes clear, European revolutions were understood to be a series of heresies, conspiracies, democracies, and rebellions. For one reason or another, Dryden never went on with the work. But other spirits, more committed and with a clearer—which under the circumstances, also meant more consistent and militant— involvement in revolutionary (and counterrevolutionary) politics, took up the famous battle of the books. Gilbert Burnet, that formidable Scottish ideologue among English churchmen, responded to the challenge first with his *Reflections on Mr. Varillas' History of Revolutions* . . . and then with a further reply to Varillas's own defense of himself. It was, once again, a grand debate in the spirit of Nedham versus Howell, a continuing contest between the yea-sayers and the nay-sayers of revolution, now broadening out onto a wider European scale.

> ... as in *England* at present, so in *France* too, the same person that is Historiographer, is also Laureat: Hence it might be, that *Monsieur Varillas* in his Revolutions, tâkes all the liberties of a Poet, and Mr. Dr—— in his Conference between the *Hind and Panther*, tho in Verse, has aim'd at all the plainness and gravity of an Historian.

Burnet was pleased to think that his critique of Varillas had earned him Dryden's malice; he had spoiled the poet's three months' labor of translation; it was now, presumably, a useless project, for Varillas had been discredited and the principles of European revolution rehabilitated.[59]

A number of years later, after Burnet had been appointed to be the Bishop of Salisbury, he went on to write a pamphlet entitled—and the two captivating nouns are associated here in a modern sense for possibly the very first time—*The Revolution and the Present Establishment Vindicated* (1697). "The Temper of the Nation," he wrote, was "Universal Moderation." A historical writer of much originality and power, fortified now by the triumphant self-confidence of a world that had won, he was the formal and perhaps the best expositor of the nature and destiny of the English Revolution. To justify "the Progress of the Whole Revolution," he had only to recall that "this Nation had become a Scene of Fire and Blood ... " To explain "the True Causes of the Revolution," he called practical attention to defensive strategical necessity: "It was the late King's open throwing off the Restraint of Law, and his setting about a total Subversion of the Constitution, that drove the Nation to extream Courses."

The extremism was temporary, tactical, therapeutic; not only was it felt to be perfectly justified but it was taken to be a force of conservative preservation. There is, however, a small hint of apprehension, if not of alarm, at the prospect of "Revolutions that may happen hereafter." Burnet tried to draw the line firmly: revolutions were not permanent but singular acts of unique reformation.

> A Revolution so brought about, carries in it no Precedent against the Security of Government, or the Peace of Mankind. That which an Absolute Necessity enforced at one Time, can be no Warrant for irregular Proceedings at any other Time; unless it be where the like Necessity shall require the Remedies.[60]

Was it truly inconceivable that this formula could indeed serve as a regular precedent for irregular proceedings? Ideological idealism prefers to see only those realities to which it chooses to keep its eyes open. Wasn't the genie now out of the bottle?

One of Burnet's critics, in a rebuttal which was obviously moderate out of caution rather than principle, warned against the whole vague and erratic ideological superstructure that was being imposed on recent constitutional events. "I humbly beg of you," Sewell wrote in mild irony to Burnet (who had implied that there were forces working toward the "undermining of Revolution"), "in the Name of many of us the Ignorant People of Great Britain, that you will be pleased to give us *an entire and compleat* Set of *Revolution-Principles* that we may be better informed what they are; as also to direct us in the Use of them . . . " Even so, as he hastened to make clear, the difference between them lay "not in the Revolution itself, but in the Consequences of that Revolution." It was a shrewd if somewhat demagogic distinction; and it represented in general a deep movement to disengage the so-called Revolution from those excessive political passions which only a few ideologues like Burnet had contrived to give it. One of Burnet's biographers has caught this variance between the wonted moderation of the new Establishment and the excitable devotion to the Revolution. Here is the vivid sense of one of the bishop's sermons in Fleet Street:

> At this dramatic moment Burnet's apprehensions reached their climax . . . . The political situation alone claims heart and mind and tongue. The sins of the nation crowd on the preacher's remembrance; a profanity almost universal—satiric cruelty at its height—the pamphlet war, whereof the ink "may soon turn to blood—and party spirit "our plague as well as sin." . . . Calamity hangs suspended by a single frail thread . . .
> To those who actually heard, this outburst must have been strangely impressive; a prophet, as of the Hebrews, appeals to the age of Anne. The absent of course ridiculed his fervent vaticinations; and Sewell, more particularly, sneered in his usual brilliant vein. Burnet is the Quixote of the day; and with Blood, Fire, Popery, on the brain tilts on at political windmills.[61]

Each revolution goes through a phase when, beginning to doubt its political purity and sheer physical momentum, it raises the cry for yet another revolution, moral or economic or cultural, which would carry it authentically forward to safety and final glory. In the perspective of less fiery spirits, the danger of such ideological excess at this point is not merely that it agitates unnecessarily the cool and sober victory of a revolutionary establishment, but that it could tend to inculcate permanent habits of restless upheaval.

"Because there was once a *Revolution both just and necessary*," Sewell writes to Burnet, "*and we were forced* (according to your Confession) *to depart a little* from our Constitution, must we therefore be continually insisting on that? Must we be still magnifying an Act of *Necessity*, and crying it up as the very Basis and Foundation of the Government?" The answer was yes, if one operated under an ideological imperative; the answer was no, if one felt nothing but classical distaste for what Harrington had once called the "romance of domestic revolutions." Not least among the disagreeable ideological consequences was precisely the crying danger of having set a revolutionary precedent, and Sewell counseled against the magnified use of romantic arguments which might "enflame the Hearts of a People too prone to Tumults and Disturbances ... "[62] Here are all the withdrawal symptoms of a revolutionary generation trying to make the adjustment from incendiary pressures and excitements to the cool and quiet of an established political consensus.

In formulating what amounts to the official ideology of (in his phrase) "the English Revolution," Burnet managed a moment of admirable calm in which to associate the highest authority with a passably pragmatic version:

> His Majesty does not apprehend any thing from the Intimation given in the Memorial [from King James], of Revolutions that may happen hereafter. There is no great Reason to think, that these Nations which have been in all past Times so careful to preserve their Laws and Liberties, should at any Time hereafter come to lose all Regard to them so entirely, as not to maintain a Revolution which has secured them from imminent Ruin, and has given their Constitution such a Confirmation, and such Explanations, as the Injustice and Violence of the former Reign had made necessary.[63]

In effect, the message came to this: We are all revolutionaries now, and nobody need ever be a revolutionary again. This is a unique episode in the history of European ideology, and a supreme English moment of political assurance and intellectual paradox.

It would be a difficult if not futile undertaking to attempt an analysis of how much was theology and how much ideology in Burnet's philosophy of Revolution Politicks. So much should be clear and acceptable: that we are in the first great transitional period of a two-stage process in the history of utopian and revolutionary attitudes. There is, at the outset, a secularization of the basic thought-forms of political life as images and ideas emancipate themselves from old religious contexts; and there follows then an eschatologization of the new ideologies which never, in any case, freed themselves from implicit human predispositions to temperamental absolutes of hope and transformation.

Burnet was, in Dryden's epithet, "a theologue," and within the framework of his fiery Reformation faith a full, if still provisional, ideological conception of the Revolution had developed. He talked old theology and meant new politics. When he sermonized on some current topic of national debate, it was fresh factious ideology with ancient divine blessings; or, as his biographer puts it, "a Hebrew prophet—a hermit of the Crusades—a zealot of the Covenant might thus have urged his hearers against the Foes of God." But not all those in earshot of this fierce, vital, and enthusiastic man who has been called the most moving rhetorician of the day were persuaded or even responsive. Although Burnet had been rewarded by an appointment as a royal chaplain, King William had his understandable aversions to a garrulous propagandist with so much officious zeal; in fact he thought him a "dangerous man" and, according to a Dutch source, actually called him *"een rechte Tartuffe"* (or, as his English biographer translates it, "a regular Pecksniff").[64] We know, too, that Lord Halifax, though ostensibly amicable, looked on him with some contempt; indeed it is said that Halifax, on his deathbed, declined Burnet's last ministrations, lest the theologue should use him to the last and "triumph over him after his death."[65] The difficulties ran deeper than the antipathies of personality and politics. It is clear that the King considered himself, with Halifax, "a Trimmer," which is to say that he wanted to transcend parties and unite all factions in a grand national coalition. If this was to be the glory of the Revolution, then Burnet was too robust and rabid by half; he was nervous, forceful, strenuous, overwhelming; and, as such, readily identifiable in those lines of *The Hind and the Panther*:

> Prompt to assail and careless of defence,
> Invulnerable in his Impudence,
> He dares the World, and eager of a name,
> He thrusts about, and justles into fame.

Dryden's portrait of "the noble Buzzard" was almost aloof compared to Swift's ferocious satiric thrusts against Burnet's "party madness"; and a parodist of the day, hearing the glad news of a fire in the bishop's study, rushed to distribute these lines:

> . . . he meant to bless the age
> With flagrant Prefaces of party rage
> O'erwrought with passion and the subjects' weight,
> Lolling he nodded in his elbow seat
> Down fell the candle; grease and zeal conspire,
> Heat meets with heat, and pamphlets burn their fire,
> Here crawls a Preface on its half-burned maggots,
> And there, an Introduction brings its faggots;
> Then roars the prophet of the Northern Nation,
> Scorched by a flaming speech on moderation.

Yet there was an essential unfairness in the polemical acrimony, and the witty last line only underscores it. Burnet was an enthusiast but not a doctrinaire; he was an energetic tactician, not an inflexible and fanatical campaigner.

I must note, finally, with what unperturbed equanimity Burnet presents to his readers his own translation of Thomas More's *Utopia*, which (as he says in his preface) "seemed to me to contain so many fine and well-digested notions." Yet Burnet's relationship to utopia was as special and differentiated as his relationship to revolution. The virtues of both were not absolute but relative and limited; one accepted them and, on balance, approved them with a measure of reasonably controlled enthusiasm. Thus, not a few of *Utopia*'s political methods and social objectives, especially its economic communism, were considered by Burnet to be "wild and immoral" and "a piece of rough and fierce philosophy." That such regrettable lapses did not prove to be overly bothersome may be attributed to the new pragmatic atmosphere, wherein an eclecticism of give and take, and even a certain experimentalism of trial and error, conditioned men's minds to resilience. For all his doctrinal differences with the text (and, doubtless, with the Catholic author), he accepted the work as "writ by one of the greatest Men this Island has produced." Burnet was convinced that More "only intended to set many Notions in his Reader's way"; and a few obstacles in the path only improved the course. So it was that the fixed values of a utopia were reduced to an expedient tentativeness, just as the high global drama of a revolution was compressed into a useful local scenario. Both utopia and revolution are still with us in Burnet's world, but they are to be had only at this very special English discount.[66]

6. The Wordsworthian Recoil

I have already referred to Wordsworth's utopianism, and in this respect he stands in the direct line of such European paradise-seekers as Dante and Joachim, Columbus and Bruno, Milton and Comenius. The poet is himself the best witness for a political faith in an all-consuming quest for total human happiness "in the very world." From this point on, it was but a small step to grand hopes for revolutionary renovation:

> Rise up, thou monstrous ant-hill on the plain
> Of a too busy world! . . .

The poet found himself captivated by a new "faith" which tossed him about "in whirlwinds." For a brief historic moment, as he was later to confess, he was deceived by "volcanic burst, earthquake, and hurricane" to "lend an eager hand / To social havoc." But for the generation

of 1776 and 1789 and for a young romantic poet, this appeared to be a
time of "wondrous revolution," of hope and joy, of dawn and bliss, of
heavenly youthfulness; and he could convince himself that

> ... good men would not long
> Pay fruitless worship to humanity,
> And this most rotten branch of human shame,
> Object, so seemed it, of superfluous pains,
> Would fall together with its parent tree.
>
> [*Prelude*, 10. 258–62]

It was a rare and passing burst of English impetuosity: yet in its essence
a true revolutionary commitment, and as such associated inevitably not
only with stormy uprooting but also (as we have seen again and again)
with the sense of a youthful destruction of the old.

> Not in my single self alone I found,
> But in the mind of all ingenuous Youth,
> Change and subversion from that hour. No shock
> Given to my moral nature had I known
> Down to that very moment; neither lapse
> Nor turn of sentiment that might be named
> A revolution, save at this one time.
>
> [ll. 266–72][67]

At that one time his youthful enthusiasm carried him into the first of
two exercises in political pamphleteering which will occupy us in the
next pages. Wordsworth was twenty-three, and the French Revolution
was then in its fourth year. It was perhaps a little late in the day for a
pure utopian apologia, but all pleas on behalf of ongoing revolutionary
events must necessarily depart from a defense of the dream to a
rationalization of real events. The Bishop of Landaff's "strictures" had
angered young Wordsworth, brimming with the impressions of his two
visits to France. The guillotining of the King? "Sorrow for the death of
Louis" would be "irrational and weak," and he refused to join the "cry
of modish lamentation."

> What! have you so little knowledge of the nature of man as to be
> ignorant that a time of revolution is not the season of true Liberty?
> Alas, the obstinacy and perversion of man is such that he is too often
> obliged to borrow the very arms of Despotism to overthrow him,
> and, in order to reign in peace, must establish herself by violence.
> She deplores such stern necessity, but the safety of the people, her
> supreme law, is her consolation.

He recognized an "apparent contradiction" between the principles of
liberty and "the march of revolutions," and he did not avert his eyes

from the anguishing aspects of the "war between the oppressors and the oppressed." Still, his revolutionary faith survived untroubled.

> Political virtues are developed at the expense of moral ones; and the sweet emotions of compassion, evidently dangerous when traitors are to be punished, are too often altogether smothered. But is this a sufficient reason to reprobate a convulsion from which is to spring a fairer order of things?[68]

No discernible reason at all. The convulsive means were certain to lead to benign ends, and for these he was prepared to accept "a necessary suspension of the mild and social virtues." From Milton's "acceptable sacrifice" to Wordsworth's "necessary suspension" to Auden's "necessary murder," there is a constant ideological note in a great European tradition of apologetics.

But the argument, as it is so often among the sympathizers and censors of faraway revolutions, was less about foreign affairs than about home troubles. Young Wordsworth was also concerned with an English struggle against "oppressive principles." He objected to "the extremes of poverty and riches," and to "the overwhelming corruption of the present day." His concern was for the poor and society's lamentable tendency "to dishonour labour." He favored an important (perhaps even what might be called a fundamental) change in the existing system of property relations, such as that which would be entailed by "wise and salutary regulations counteracting that inequality among mankind which proceeds from the present *fixed* disproportion of their possessions ... " His local indignation reinforced his cross-channel loyalties; so much so, indeed, that a slight touch of fanaticism emerged behind the high tone of sweet reasonableness. He went so far as to suggest that "the friends of Liberty congratulate themselves upon the odium under which they are at present labouring ... " Backsliders like Lafayette and Mirabeau had proved themselves to be dangerous and insidious, and he was grateful for such "desertions" from the cause. No modish lamentation either for "an enemy lurking in our ranks"! In the drama of "political convulsions," these words and deeds were all "necessities" which were "attached to a struggle for Liberty."

It is difficult to see why the Bishop of Landaff's remarks had elicited this extraordinary outburst (which was only published after Wordsworth's death in 1850, and he seemed to have long forgotten it). The bishop himself had been an early sympathizer of 1789, and his bromidic sermon, far from being an "extraordinary avowal of political principles," was essentially only a restatement of certain traditional English attitudes which we have already identified as the emerging English ideology.

> I am far from insinuating [Bishop Landaff wrote] that the science of politics is involved in mystery; or that men of plain understandings should be debarred from examining the principles of the government to which they yield obedience. All that I contend for is this—that the foundations of our government ought not to be overturned, nor the edifice erected thereon tumbled into ruins because an acute politician may pretend that he has discovered a flaw in the building, or that he could have laid the foundation after a better model.
>   What would you say to a stranger who should desire you to pull down your house, because, forsooth, he had built one in France or America, after what he thought a better plan?[69]

This was a mood of English caution which Wordsworth had great difficulties in sharing completely. His political temperament was unpredictable in its outbursts of enthusiasm, and his preoccupation with political strategy in the national arena was serious and absorbing. He was heavily involved in the complexities of militance and moderation, and in a letter of 1809 (to Daniel Stuart, editor of the *Morning Post*) he made a remarkable effort to work out the two tactics in the struggle for a more humane democracy.

> If we, who work for temperate reform, are utterly to reject all assistance from all those who do not think exactly as we do, how is it to be attained? For my part I see no party with whom in regard to this measure I could act with entire approbation of their views, but I should be glad to receive assistance from any. If I have a hill to climb and cannot do it without a walking-stick, better have a dirty one than none at all. I do not think the reform will ever be effected unless the people take it up; and if the people do stir, it can only be by public meetings, and it is natural that in meetings of this kind the most violent men should be the most applauded, but I do not see that it necessarily follows that their works will be realized in action. The misfortune of this question of reform is that the one party sees nothing in it but dangers, the other nothing but hopes and promises. For my part, I think the dangers and difficulties great, but not unsurmountable, whereas, if there be not a reform the destruction of the Liberties of the Country is inevitable ... [70]

In the same year he had worked out a related strategical principle in *Cintra* (a pamphlet to which we will shortly be returning), and it reveals the interrelationship between tactics and temperament which has been one of our main themes, from Dante's ardent politics of the two paradises onward.

> Hatred and love, and each in its intensity, and pride (passions which, existing in the heart of a Nation, are inseparable from hope)—these elements being in constant preparation—enthusiasm will break out from them, or coalesce with them, upon the summons

of a moment. And these passions are scarcely less than extinguishable.... The difficulty lies—not in kindling, feeding, or fanning the flame; but in continuing so to regulate the relations of things—that the fanning breeze and the feeding fuel shall come from no unworthy quarter, and shall neither of them be wanting in appropriate consecration.[71]

But was it so easy, when burning with a Promethean fury, to keep apart the sacred incendiaries from the profane arsonists? Wordsworth was obliged to defend his return to extremist simplicities in letters to Coleridge, De Quincey, and others:

Now the reason which induced me to use this language was not intemperate indignation, but a deep conviction of the importance of keeping—in some cases of this kind—as close a connection as possible in the minds of men between disapprobation or hatred of vice and of the vicious person, of crime and the criminal.

What he was trying to do was to make a distinction between private vices and public virtues that was sharp enough to excuse and explain the language of unrelenting indignation in politics. In matters of personal pique or injury, it might be well "to encourage relenting and forgiving dispositions." But

in public offences, under settled Governments, there is no feeling more to be dreaded than this disposition to forgive and to relent; it approaches the mind under the mask of charity and humanity and so forth; and in fact it is at the bottom nothing but remissness, indolence, weakness and cowardice; an inability to keep the mind steadfastly on its object; the sensations wound up to their proper tone. Accordingly duties which it would be laborious to discharge, and difficulties which it would be hard to overcome, are all gotten rid of at once with this flattering promise that the future will make amends and set all things right of itself.[72]

The Wordsworthian problems are clear, the Brechtian answers less so: for they seem to be lost somewhere in the no-man's-land between the art and morality of political action, between the strategy and the psychology of the public deed. What is effective is often unethical; what is wrong often fails for quite other reasons. How is one ever to measure the quality of enthusiasm so as to exclude that which is unworthy? How to regulate the kindling, fanning, and feeding of the flames? How "dirty" can an acceptable walking stick be before dry rot sets in? Let, at least, this much be said at this point. I suspect that the questions of principle and compromise, of ends and means, will one day have to be rudely removed from the contexts of imagery and metaphor before the signs of any new wisdom can ever emerge.

For, at bottom, this species of intellectual devotion to the public inter-

458IDEOLOGIES

est is a form of poetical politics, and it is inseparable from the language of very literary men. In these lines from *The Recluse* (written in 1800), Wordsworth moves between treacherous simplicities and confident complications.

> Hundreds of curves and circlets, to and fro,
> Upwards and downwards, progress intricate
> Yet unperplexed, as if one spirit swayed
> Their indefatigable flight.

It is, admittedly, the magic of "romantic hope" which turns the trick.

> In every quarter something visible,
> Half-seen or wholly, lost and found again,
> Alternate progress and impediment,
> And yet a growing prospect in the main.

Indeed, he very much belonged to those who strove to conquer "the random chaos of futurity" and who maintained

> We now have rules and theories so precise
> That by the inspection of unwearied eyes
> We can secure infallible results.

Even when he was retreating from "*all Arcadian dreams, / All golden fancies of the golden Age,*" even as he was saying "*farewell to the Warrior's schemes*"

> . . . and farewell
> That other hope, long mine, the hope to fill
> The heroic trumpet with the Muse's breath!

he confessed how he was still drawn to the spectacles of danger, courage, resolution, and even glory.

> Yea to this hour I cannot read a tale
> of two brave Vessels matched in deadly fight,
> And fighting to the death, but I am pleased
> More than a wise man ought to be. I wish,
> Fret, burn, and struggle, and in soul am there.[73]

Here we find Wordsworth in the direct heritage of the *eroici furori*, the Heroic Enthusiasts, announced centuries earlier by Giordano Bruno, who also wished, fretted, burned, and struggled to keep his soul (and his body) at the point where inward luster and outward fellowship joined in a life-and-death purpose. The poet is trying to cling somehow to the central aspiration of the utopian and revolutionary tradition:

> . . . foes
> To wrestle with, and victory to complete,
> Bounds to be leapt, darkness to be explored,

All that inflamed thy infant heart, the love,
The longing, the contempt, the undaunted quest,
All shall survive—though changed their office, all
Shall live,—it is not in their power to die.

And yet, a small inner voice admonished:

Be mild and cleave to gentle things . . .

Wordsworth's disenchantment, at least in the context of his poetry, is too well-known a story to be recapitulated here at any length.[74] "Wild theories were afloat," as he knew, and he came piteously to recognize the consequent "wild varieties of joy and grief" in the disarray of the politics of an earthly paradise. There had once been more than a glimpse of utopia in his mind's eye.

Paradise, and groves
Elysian, Fortunate Fields—like those of old
Sought in the Atlantic Main—why should they be
A history only of departed things,
Of a mere fiction of what never was?
For the discerning intellect of Man,
When wedded to this goodly universe
In love and holy passion, shall find these
A simple produce of the common day.[75]

Far beyond the specific good causes which he supported for "the progress of human improvement," there had been the vision of a revolutionary enthusiast: "I conceive that a more excellent system of civil policy might be established among us . . . " But quite apart from the French experience there were special English hesitations. As he writes in a letter of June 1794, "Yet, in my ardour to attain the goal, I do not forget the nature of the ground where the race is to be run."[76] On these native grounds, could a revolution be the grand path to utopian excellence? Evidently not. "The destruction of those Institutions which I condemn appears to me to be hastening on too rapidly. I recoil from the bare idea of a Revolution."

Perhaps, as he suggested later in *The Excursion* (4.324–327), one was powerless against "those revolutions of disturbances" which roll in "the heart of man"; but an anxious sense of social havoc was very much with him. Indeed, if the "dreadful event" was to be averted, "a writer who has the welfare of mankind at heart should call forth his best exertions to convince the people . . . " Society could be preserved from convulsion only by "a gradual and constant reform of those abuses which, if left to themselves, may grow to such a height as to render even a Revolution desirable." He was convinced, as "a determined enemy to every species of violence," that there were general principles of social order which were applicable to all times and places; and these included the principle of political justice ("from which the further any government deviates the more effectually must it defeat the object for which government was ordained"). The rules taken together would constitute, he hoped,

> an entire preservative from despotism. They will guide the hand of Reform, and if a revolution must afflict us, they alone can mitigate its horrors and establish freedom with tranquility.

Ultimately he would bring himself to the point of seeking

> from God defence
> Against far heavier ill, the pestilence
> Of revolution, impiously unbound! . . .

He was thus driven to plead that "long-favoured England" not be mis-led "by monstrous theories of alien growth," nor be seized by "alien frenzy." Even foreigners were not beyond the pale of wiser counsel. On the occasion of insurrections in Bologna (1837), he tried to caution the "jarring fractions":

> . . . thy rights approve
> To thy own conscience gradually renewed;
> Learn to make Time the father of wise Hope . . .

But some two decades earlier, or halfway between the wild bliss of wondrous revolution and the tranquility of wise hope, Wordsworth wrote his incomparable and overwhelming indictment of *The Convention of Cintra* (1809).[77]

The earthquake had struck again. "The tidings of this event did not spread with the commotion of a storm which sweeps visibly over our heads," as he observed, "but like an earthquake which rocks the ground under our feet." The poet was shaken enough to pen a furious pamphlet against the betrayal of the cause of liberty in Spain and Portugal by British military expediencies; and it was indeed into such a halfway house that Wordsworth moved his waning political passions. "We are all here cut to the heart" (by the conduct of Wellington's strategists in allowing the escape of the enemy armies): "we are here all in a rage about the Convention in Portugal." The composition of his polemical manifesto "occupied all his thoughts," Dorothy noted; and he sent off the white-hot pages to young Thomas De Quincey in London, who would help put the pamphlet through the presses, expecting "not a farthing from it" for it was all for "Truth's sake and Liberty's."

Given the fact that he was so "agitated and afflicted," it was very curious that he should have thought of what he had produced as a cool exercise in social science. "In my mind," he wrote (26 March 1809), Cintra was "an action dwelt upon only for the sake of illustrating principles, with a view to promote liberty and good policy; in the manner in which an anatomist illustrates the laws of organic life from a human subject placed before him and his audience . . . " Quite other laws were being illustrated; *Cintra* the poem, not Cintra the conspiracy, deserves to be anatomized for its own sake: as an exercise in utopia and revolution. For the revolutionary ideals and the utopian rhetoric which had come to grief in the form of internal social conflict were now displaced onto an external war of national liberation. This was the difference between the dreadfulness of Jacobin France and the nobility of insurgent Iberia, or so he claimed. "Taught by the reverses of the French revolution," he wrote, "we looked upon these [Spanish] dispositions as more human—more social—and therefore as wiser, and of better omen than if they had stood forth the zealots of abstract principles, drawn out of the laboratory of unfeeling philosophists . . . "

It was a complex and magnificent self-deception. He thought he was turning his back on "the pestilential philosophism of France," and he persuaded himself that "the paradoxical reveries of Rousseau and the flippancies of Voltaire are plants which will not naturalize in the country of Calderon and Cervantes." But, in the country of his own mind, crowded with abstractions and absolutes, still governed by the principle of "the superiority of radical feelings," there reigned a devotion to Freedom and the People which would have greatly pleased the ideologues of Paris and Geneva. "Our duty is,—our aim ought to be," Wordsworth insists, "to employ the true means of liberty and virtue for the ends of liberty and virtue." It was the good old cause and the grand historic mission.[78] For "the cause of Spain is the most righteous cause in which, since the opposition of the Greek Republics to the Persian Invader at Thermopylae and Marathon, sword was ever drawn!"

And when the sword drew blood? For a determined enemy to every species of violence, he was strangely "delighted" that "the people have done summary justice upon the traitorous governor of Cadiz," and added: "A little more of this, and the cause will go swing; these traitors must be purged off . . . " Lost in this manner in the rhetoric of a Saint-Just, Wordsworth was right to suspect that his views might "create me a world of enemies, and call forth the old yell of Jacobinism." And all the while he kept up his contempt for "foolish fellows" with "Frenchified minds."[79]

How did Wordsworth manage to intoxicate himself with such French magniloquence, to blind himself to those abhorrent "french delusions"? Coleridge admired *Cintra*'s oracular and impassioned tone of "high dogmatic Eloquence," even as he found fault with an enthusiasm for

foreign masses "somewhat too much *idealized*."[80] But, in the middle of
his journey, Wordsworth felt compelled to hold fast to a mood of ideali-
zation from which few utopians or revolutionaries ever contrived a quick
or easy escape. In those middle years, his political sensibility, never
strong on distinctions, tried to feel its way along to a separation of "the
pathos of humanity" from "jacobinical pathos."[81] But what theoretical
differences there appeared to be between that which remained sacred
and that which had been profaned were lost in an impassioned blur
which was to prove troublesome for long periods in his intellectual career. (And let us not overlook that he had, as the poet himself once estimated, "given twelve hours thought to the conditions and prospects of
society, for one to poetry.") More than once would he be seduced by the
philanthropic universal and betrayed by the political particular. Was it
that causes were strong and men were weak? Could it be that ideals
were noble but men and movements always decayed? Whatever the
case, Wordsworth struggled to maintain his own faith in the original
goodness of the revolution, despite its deplorable course. Indeed, he
insisted that Napoleonic France, the scourge of Europe,

> with all the terrible features which it has gradually assumed, is a
> child of noble parents—Liberty and Philanthropic Love. Perverted as
> the creature in which it has grown up to (rather, into which it has
> passed),—from no inferior stock could it have issued. It is the Fallen
> Spirit, triumphant in misdeeds, which was formerly a blessed Angel.

The poet persisted in his involvement with blessed angels and once
again found himself listening to the music of the spheres. In fact, *The
Convention of Cintra* has been called "perhaps the greatest trumpet blast
sounded by English lips upon that often equivocal instrument since
Milton."[82] As such, it should take its place in our recording of utopian
and revolutionary sounds as the very model of the tone of time, for this
is a score with all the classical themes and modern rhythms. Change
only a note here and there and you have the overpowering music that
was to be made on a hundred other resounding European occasions.

1. *The Most Just War.* "But let us now hear them, as 'a whole people is
more powerful than disciplined armies . . . must triumph over tyranny . . . will inevitably conquer, in a cause the most just that has ever
raised the deadly weapon of war; for she fights, not for the concerns of a
day, but for the security and happiness of ages; not for an insulated
privilege, but for the rights of human nature; not for temporal blessings,
but for eternal happiness; not for the benefit of one nation, but for all
mankind.'"

2. *The Transcendental Battle.* "It was not for the soil, or for the cities,
and the forts . . . but for the human feeling that was there; for the rights

of human nature which might be there conspicuously asserted; for a triumph over justice and oppression there to be achieved, which could neither be concealed or disguised, and which should penetrate the darkest corner of the dark Continent by its splendour. We combated for victory in the empire of reason, for strongholds in the imagination."

3. *The True and Inspired Prophecy.* "Bitter was the sorrow of the people ... overwhelming was their astonishment, tormenting their shame; their indignation was tumultuous; and the burthen of the past would have been insupportable, if it had not involved in its very nature a sustaining hope for the future.... This was the feeling of the people; an awful feeling: and it is from these oracles that rulers are to learn wisdom. For, when the people speaks loudly it is from being strongly possessed either by the God-head or the Demon; and he, who cannot discover the true spirit from the false, hath no ear for profitable communion.... The voice ... had the unquestionable sound of inspiration. If the gentle passions of pity, love, and gratitude, be the porches of the temple; if the sentiments of admiration and rivalry be pillars upon which the structure is sustained; if, lastly, hatred, and anger, and vengeance, be steps which, by a mystery of nature, lead to the House of Sanctity;—then was it manifest to what power the edifice was consecrated; and that the voice within was of Holiness and Truth."

4. *Futurity and a Limitless Forgetting.* "Deliverance and safety were but intermediate objects;—regeneration and liberty were the end, and the means by which the end was to be attained ... She had risen—not merely to be free; but, in the act and process of acquiring that freedom, to recompense herself, as it were in a moment, for all which she had suffered through ages ... They had been trampled upon, tormented, wronged—bitterly, wantonly wronged, if ever a people on the earth was wronged—Riddance, mere riddance—safety, mere safety—are objects too defined, too inert and passive in their own nature, to have ability either to rouze or to sustain. They win not the mind by any attraction of grandeur or sublime delight, either in effort or in endurance.... All courage is a projection from ourselves; however short-lived, it is a motion of hope. But these thoughts bind too closely to something inward,—to the present and to the past,—that is, to the self which is or has been. Whereas the vigour of the human soul is from without and from futurity,—in breaking down limit, and losing and forgetting herself in the sensation and image of Country and of the human race..."

5. *The Perfection of Humanity.* "These are times of strong appeal—of deep-searching visitation; when the best abstractions of the prudential understanding give way, and are included and absorbed in a supreme comprehensiveness of intellect and passion; which is the perfection and the very being of humanity ... There is no middle course ... Was there

ever—since the earliest actions of men which have been transmitted by affectionate tradition or recorded by faithful history, or sung to the impassioned harp of poetry—was there ever a people who presented themselves to the reason and the imagination, as under more holy influences ... as a mass fluctuating with one motion under the breath of a mightier wind ... "

6. *The Fiery Rising.* "Let the fire, which is never wholly to be extinguished, break out afresh; let but the human creature be rouzed; whether he have lain heedless and torpid in religious or civil slavery—have languished under a thraldom, domestic or foreign, or under both these alternatively—or have drifted about a helpless member of a clan of disjointed and feeble barbarians; let him rise and act ... the fire ... is reanimated in him ... Then does intense passion, consecrated by a sudden revelation of justice, give birth to those higher and better wonders ... and exhibit true miracles to the eyes of men, and the noblest which can be seen."

7. *A Voice for Mankind.* "The theme is justice; and my voice is raised for mankind; for us who are alive, and for all posterity:—justice and passion; clear-sighted and aspiring justice, and passion sacred as vehement."

8. *A Golden Opportunity.* "[Events] have attested the efficacy of the passions which we have been contemplating—that the will of good men is not a vain impulse, heroic desires a delusive prop;—have proved that there are golden opportunities when the dictates of justice may be unrelentingly enforced, and the beauty of the inner mind substantiated in the outward act."

9. *The People's Happy End.* "The events of the last year, gloriously destroying many frail fears, have placed—in the rank of serene and immortal truths—a proposition which, as an object of belief, hath in all ages been fondly cherished: namely,—that a numerous Nation, determined to be free, may effect its purpose in despite of the mightiest power which a foreign Invader can bring against it. These events also have pointed out how, in the ways of Nature and under the guidance of Society, this happy end is to be attained: in other words they have shown that the cause of the People ... is safe while it remains not only in the bosom but in the hands of the People; or (what amounts to the same thing) in those of a government which, being truly *from* the People, is faithfully *for* them ... "[83]

This was Wordsworth's last political vision: as well-meaning as More's, as dedicated as Winstanley's, as ardent as Rousseau's. But it was a burst of prophecy and apocalyptic that disappeared in a welter of ironies and contradictions.

In the first place, Wordsworth's manuscript came too late for the turbulent events; Coleridge dreaded the book's "dying." By the time it was published, in an edition of five hundred by Longman, badly and slowly proofread by young De Quincey, who was mostly concerned to experiment with his new system of punctuation, there were few sales and copies had to be disposed of as waste (many going to trunkmakers for paper linings). In June, Wordsworth had hopes for a second printing; in August, Dorothy noted, "Many are astonished with the wisdom of it—but nobody buys!!" "If I were superstitious," the author wrote to his publisher, "I should deem that there was a fatality attending this, my first[84] essay in politics ... "

Cintra belongs, then, not to history but to the history of rhetoric and personal opinion. As such, it represents a dramatic illustration of the break in the English romantic mind between politics and poetry, art and experience, between the world outside and the inward dream. There was a deep and irrepressible conflict here between the local immediacy of experienced social arrangements and the transcendental devotion to aesthetic absolutes. Ideology had less and less to do with the stuff of realities and became the mere vehicle of perishable enthusiasms and the categorical beauties of the inner mind.

The break in *Cintra* almost tears the pamphlet in two. Ineluctably there came a difficult moment which Wordsworth refers to in *The Prelude* (14.137–38) as involving *"lapse and hesitating choice, / And backward wanderings along thorny ways."* After all the vehemence and zealous fury—it was (in Coleridge's words) "all in hot tints ... positive, violent, and 'in a mad passion'"—Wordsworth is compelled to confront the practical political issue: What is to be done? And now, as in a broken spell, he tries to find his bearings among the real constitutional questions of British policy. These, he confesses, are "delicate" and "ought not to be lightly or transiently touched." How then would the wrong be righted? The poet had come in with the roar of a biblical prophet and would go out like an English lamb. "No *immediate* effect can be expected," he was forced to admit, "from the soundest and most unexceptionable doctrines which might be laid down for the correcting of this evil." He consoled himself with the thought that perhaps there was "some result of *immediate* good by a direct application to the mind," that is, by increasing the stock of "appropriate and indispensable knowledge"—but, given an unsold edition, there was hardly even that. Subsequently, he was mildly encouraged by a report that Canning had conceded that the author of *Cintra* has spoken with "the bone of truth." He went on to claim some portion of "the gift of prescience"; even more, he tried foolishly to argue that "in fact, everything that has been done in Spain, right or wrong, is a comment upon the principles I have laid down." So indeed, generously interpreted, is the next century and a half of European history.

The English plague of what Coleridge liked to call "political empirics" began its counterattack. "We as well as my Brother," Dorothy wrote when the pamphlet was done, "could not help regretting that he had not more time to reconsider it." Was not all enthusiasm of a "perishable nature"? Was there not "danger in being a zealot in any cause—not excepting that of humanity"? And how had the problem of the corruptions of power been overlooked?[85]

> ... whatever may be the cause, the fact is certain—that there is an unconquerable tendency in all power, save that of knowledge acting by and through knowledge, to injure the mind of him who exercises that power; so much so, that best natures cannot escape the evil of such alliance.

The mournful notes of *Cintra*'s closing pages are unmistakable. "The true sorrow of humanity consists in this," Wordsworth writes: "not that the mind of man fails; but that the course and demands of action and life so rarely corresponds with the dignity and intensity of human desires ... "

But all these possible reconsiderations, "blown about by the changeful winds of an anxious author's second thoughts" (Coleridge), were as nothing compared to one astonishing remark which illuminates so much in the history of intellectual commitments to just causes: "The things with which we are primarily and mainly concerned are inward passions and not outward arrangements ... "

It was, of course, a tenet of romantic politics that a social order was to be judged ultimately not by the structure of its institutions but by the spirit of its associated minds and souls. Utopia was personal culture: feelings, knowledge, tranquillity, joy, love. The difficulty for this species of political temperament sets in when the tenuous sense of a connection between the inward and the outward, between the public and the private realities, comes under the radical stress of an agitated climate of opinion. Outward arrangements become less and less decisive (or even relevant), not only for the idealized future but for the burdensome present. Inward passion is all. Peace becomes psychological, and warfare too. The battle is indeed a transcendental one: a combat for strongholds in the imagination, for victories in the empire of reason. What Wordsworth felt to be the sweetness of futurity was a dream of the breaking down of outward limits through a losing and a forgetting in sensations and images. How could there be a middle course which compromised with sorrowful realities, those same dismal alienating realities where "the splendour of the Imagination has been fading" and all was coming under "a shadow calling itself Good Sense"?

> ... calculations of presumptuous Expediency—groping its way

among partial and temporary consequences—have been substituted for the dictates of paramount and infallible Conscience, the supreme embracer of consequences: lifeless and circumspect Decencies have banished the graceful negligence and unsuspicious dignity of Virtue.

The return to poetry was an embracing of aesthetical absolutes and an abandonment of any need to mix human desires with the demands of action. The mind of man would not fail: but only if it could turn away from anything that might throw a shadow over paramount infallibilities. *Cintra* seemed to Coleridge "almost a self-robbery from some great philosophical poem," and perhaps its fatality can best be understood in the light of a letter which Wordsworth wrote to Coleridge touching precisely upon the changing nature of a new reasoning comprehensiveness.

> ... this is the time when a man of genius may honourably take a station upon different ground. If he is to be a Dramatist, let him crowd his scene with gross and visible action; but if a narrative Poet, if the Poet is to be predominant over the Dramatist,—then let him see if there are no victories in the world of the spirit, no changes, no commotions, no revolutions there, no fluxes and refluxes of the thoughts which may be made interesting by modest combination with the stiller actions of the bodily frame, or with the gentler movements and milder appearances of society and social intercourse, or the still more mild and gentle solicitations of irrational and inanimate nature.[86]

Both utopia and revolution were in the gentler process of becoming inward arrangements in the milder world of the spirit. It was no longer a matter of the institutionalization of Paradise—of the spirit of those Fortunate Islands which was to become part of "common day"—but a matter of its internalization.

Many years later Wordsworth recognized the "considerable mistake" he had made in *Cintra* about the nature of his heroic band of liberating rebels, that is, "the degree in which men who might compose it would be liable to french delusions ... "[87] By that time, Wordsworth had put behind him both storm and passion, and especially the infatuation with the once and future goodness, so characteristic of "impetuous minds" with that *"restless oblique eye / That looks for evil like a treacherous spy."*

> Alas! with most, who weigh futurity
> Against time present, passion holds the scales:
> Hence equal ignorance of both prevails,
> And nations sink; or, struggling to be free,
> Are doomed to flounder on, like wounded whales
> Tossed on the bosom of a stormy sea.

In these lines, published in 1842 in the last decade of his life (he was then seventy-two), Wordsworth made his final political commitment to

> Thought that should teach the zealot to forego
> Rash schemes, to abjure all selfish agitation,
> And seek through noiseless pains and moderation
> The unblemished good they only can bestow.

If politics there had to be, and it was at best a partial art of outward arrangements, then the English genius would be to embrace the golden mean of gradual progress ("perilous is sweeping change"). It would abandon any alien devotion to the tempestuous breaking of chains or "the terror of redress." Thus Revolution, that fiery image torn from the astronomical heavens, came to be restored to a natural rhythm of moderate change under an orderly sky.

> Twilight leads to day,
> And, even within the burning zones of earth,
> The hastiest sunrise yields a temperate ray;
> The softest breeze to fairest flowers gives birth:
> Think not that Prudence dwells in dark abodes,
> She scans the future with the eye of gods.[88]

13

We are not in a riot but in a revolution.
All the established institutions must be
destroyed.

—Student leader, at a Berlin
demonstration (April 1968)

One thing we must, at the cost of our
souls, stay away from—the bonfire. It is an
obscenity.

—Günter Grass, in Frankfurt, to
young demonstrators setting
newspapers and magazines alight
(September 1967)

Réforme non, Révolution oui!

—Cry of Daniel Cohn-Bendit, at the
Sorbonne demonstrations (1968–69)

The Prometheans

1. Phlogiston in the Heart

Bazarov's Nihilism—The Difference of Generations—Bakunin's Creative Passion—Michelet and the "Regenerating Sap"—Blake's "Porches of the Sun"—The Fascination in the Redness—Coleridge and the "Ebullience of Schematism"

2. The Fire of All Time

The Recurrent Ritual—The Flaming River to Paradise—Fiery Words—The Warrior's Fire—The Ideology of Heat—A Torch for a World Aflame—The Burning Enthusiast—The Inextinguishable Blaze—Revolution through Conflagration—The Red Cloud—A Passion Kindled

3. The Metaphorical Imperative

Napoleon and the Obstacles of the Elements—Bakunin and Herzen—Blok's Scythians—From Winstanley to Wordsworth—Baldwin's Incendiary Cliché—The Kantian Doomsday

4. Saints, Martyrs, Rebels

Heraclitus on Motion and Flux—The Double Image: Blood and Fire—Lassalle between Heraclitus and Faust—George Brandes—Zeus and the "Net of Ruin"—Campanella, Marx, and the Caucasian Chains

5. The New World of Man

Byron's Poet: "The new Prometheus of new men" (1819)—Shelley and

the Romantic Protagonist—"Hurling up Insurrection"—Earth made
"like Heaven"—The Defiance of Power—Adventurous Thoughts

6. The Ultra-living Element
Bachelard's Psychoanalysis of Fire—Norman O. Brown and the Pro-
methean Platitude—Incendiarism's Paradoxical Spiral—Arson in
Paradise—Frazer's   Two   Theories—The   Flood   and   the
Conflagration—Freud on Urethral Erotism—Adam, Eve, and Revolu-
tionary Priorities—Dr. Frankenstein's Failure—The Dream of a Social
Parturition—From other Wombs, after other Throes

1. Phlogiston in the Heart

Given the fiery and ferocious topicality of the mottoes which serve as my
point of departure for this chapter, the place at which, I feel, one must
inevitably begin is in those pages of Turgenev's *Father and Sons* (1862)
where the nihilism of "complete and unqualified destruction" is given a
nineteenth-century classic presentation.[1] It is part of our journey, not
merely "to the Finland Station," but onward to the Paris barricades.

Bazarov observes: "We act by virtue of what we recognise as beneficial. At the present time, negation is the most beneficial of all—and we
deny—"

"Everything?"

"Everything!"

"What, not only art and poetry ... but even ... horrible to say ... "

"Everything," repeated Bazarov, with indescribable composure. Pavel
Petrovitch stares at him; he had not expected this. Arkady fairly blushed
with delight.

"Allow me, though," began Nikolai Petrovitch. "You deny everything; or, speaking more precisely, you destroy everything.... But one
must construct too, you know."

"That's not our business now.... The ground wants clearing first."

Pavel Petrovitch registers an objection: "The Russian people is not
what you imagine it." Bazarov does not dispute that; he is even ready to
agree that he is right, but that "proves nothing." "How does it prove
nothing?" mutters Pavel Petrovitch, astounded. "You must be going
against the people then?" "And what if we are?" shouted Bazarov.

The argument goes on. Bazarov explains the source of his nihilism
("we saw that our leading men, so-called advance people and reformers,

are no good"), justifies confining himself to abuse, and then cuts things short. "I shall be quite ready to agree with you," he adds, getting up, "when you bring forward a single institution in our present mode of life which does not call for complete and unqualified destruction." Pavel's cry—"I will bring forward millions of such institutions, millions!"—is to no avail. There was no point; it was, in those fateful Russian words, a difference of generations.

"So that's what our young men of this generation are! They are like that—our successors!"
"Of course, you can't understand me. We belong to two different generations. . . . Our turn has come. Our successors can say to us, 'You are not of our generation; swallow your pill.' "

I would not want to leave any narrow, invidious, national impression. The pill is not peculiarly Russian; it has been swallowed, earlier and later, by other generations in other lands. A leading member of the French revolutionary assembly—M. Rabaut de St. Etienne, who was to be chosen president (and the election did not fail to horrify Burke)—was the Bazarov of his own day:

All the established institutions of France only crown the misery of the people; to make the people happy it is necessary to renovate, to change the ideas, the laws, the morals . . . to change the men, the things, the words . . . to destroy everything, yes everything; for everything must be started anew.

Out of each conflict of generations, between fathers and sons, comes a Bazarov: a nihilist, an angry dreamer, a utopian destroyer. Indeed, the history of revolutionary enthusiasm appears almost as a series of variations on Michael Bakunin's maxim: "The passion for destruction is a creative passion." But it is not without its interesting and subtle turns on the ideological cycle.

When Radischev looks out of his cab window at the state of eighteenth-century Russia, at the miseries of the exploited peasantry, he writes in his *Journal from St. Petersburg to Moscow* (promptly to be suppressed by Catherine, and its author exiled): "Oh, if the slaves raging in their despair would, with the iron that bars their freedom, crush our heads, the heads of the inhuman masters, and redden their fields with our blood!" In the next, more militant century, it was always *their* heads, *their* blood. Chateaubriand was witty but perhaps not serious enough when he remarked: "Contagion is a wonderful thing in France, and a man would cry 'Off with my head!' if he heard his neighbour cry the same."[2] The contagion afflicted enemies as well as neighbors, and the cry always became, "Off with *his* head!"

A Paris radical (Michel de Bourges) stood with Georges Sand beside the Seine, looking across the Tuileries, and told her that "in order that society should be renewed, the river must flow with blood and the palace must be reduced to ashes."[3] There was an eternal fascination in the redness: in Blake's wondrous "red clouds," in the barbaric power of the "vital heat" (Michelet), in "the red fool-fury of the Seine" (Tennyson), in the rosy hope of an "affirming flame" (Auden). As Michelet explained himself, "Often in these days, the rise and progress of the people are compared to the invasion of the Barbarians. The expression pleases me; I accept it. *Barbarians!* Yes, that is to say, full of new, living, regenerating sap.... We other Barbarians have a natural advantage; if the upper classes have culture, we have much more vital heat [*nous avons bien plus de chaleur vitale*]."[4]

As for Blake, who was said to have paraded in London wearing the red cockade, his uncompleted poem on the French Revolution argued "Fear not dreams, fear not visions,"

> For the Commons convene in the Hall of the
>   Nation, like spirits of fire in the beautiful
> Porches of the Sun, to plant beauty in the desert
>   craving abyss, they gleam
> On the anxious city . . .

In the same spirit of these Jacobinical 1790s, the twenty-two-year-old Coleridge (exchanging letters with the youthful Robert Southey) went to the combustible essence of the principle of fire: within, that is, the metaphorical (and scientific) limits of the day. "Your undeviating Simplicity of Rectitude," Coleridge wrote, "has made you too rapid in decision—having never erred, you feel more *indignation* at Error, than *Pity* for it. There is Phlogiston in your heart." Indeed there was, and the twenty-one-year-old Southey refused to turn away (at least not yet) from phlogistic emotions and general inflammability. "God forbid! that the *Ebullience of Schematism* should be over. It is the Promethean Fire that animates my soul—and when *that* is gone, all *will be Darkness*."[5] But there were already shadows across the beautiful Porches of the Sun.

2. The Fire of All Time

In another place I want to consider the problem of the wider anthropological context of this recurrent spectacle of fire: for, whether we turn from the modern secular faith to ancient mythology or to primitive religions or to Christianity, we are dramatically confronted by an ineluctable imaginative engagement with the forces of external nature and the elements of human biology.

Is there any other human concept which can vie with the resilience of the idea of revolution in its capacity to combine elemental instincts and organized politics, planetary certainty and animal vigor? The history of the very word *revolution* has within it, as we have seen, the association of the fire of the cosmos with the blood of man's fate. In its very first appearance in the English language as a peculiarly modern sign of political violence, it makes its historic debut in the following unforgettable scene in *Le Rivolutioni di Napoli* (1647, and brilliantly translated by James Howell in London three years later), in which a young barefooted fisherman, clad in a blue shirt and a red bonnet, leads an aroused mass of tens of thousands in a great uprising.

"The hour of your redemption draws near," Masaniello had promised them, and now the cry went up *muora il mal governo*! "God gives plenty, and ill government a dearth." The revolutionary manifesto explained what had become necessary in the course of events: "This most faithfull people hath been constrained to have recourse to the natural remedy for their own preservation, and having no hopes otherwise of quietnesse, or that the royall Ministers would perform what they promis'd so often." The government, then, would be destroyed in a spectacular holocaust. "Words inflam'd marvelously the minds of the people," but what pride there was that there was not a man who looted—nothing was expropriated as everything in sight (furniture and food, jewelry and money, and the great castles) was fed day and night into the ritual fires of revolution.

All should be dedicated to the fire, being the quintessence, as it was said, of their blood. Therefore they would not have a jot of anything preserved from the fury of the fire. The people taking hereby more and more boldnesse and courage because they found no resistance or obstacle, and the number still increasing to the number of about 10,000 ... The cry still continued more louder than ever ... *let the ill government perish.*

This transpired on the very first *giorno della rivolutione*, and nothing was spared in the great purificatory outburst.

... all which were brought to the Market-place, and hurld into a great fire, where they were all burnt to cinders, with huge out-cries of the people round about, who said, *These goods are our blouds, and as these burn, so the Souls of the dogs who own them* deserve to fry in hell fire ... They threw bottles of oile into the fire to make it flame with more violence ... Though it was in the night time, yet every corner of the street was as clear as if it had been noon day.

So did "this first act of the fiery tragedy" conclude. "The face of things," as Giraffi observed, "look'd as if the Day of Judgment had come ... "[6]

The usage of *revolution* here is, as I have already pointed out, transitional and ambivalent. It is modern in the sense that it refers not to vague dramatic change but to the violent overthrow of a political regime. This was, to be sure, done not in the name of new principles of social organization (as more modern revolutionaries would come to insist) but under the aegis of traditional loyalties which were still felt to be consistent with the rectification of intolerable abuses. Masaniello (a contraction of Tomas Aniello) and his followers—the so-called *Lazzari* and *Scalzi*, the "unshod" urban poor—were still cast from the old mold of popular rebels. The slogans they shouted—"*Viva Dio ... viva il Papa ... viv' il Re d'Spagna ... e muora, muora il mal governo*"–indicated that their hopes lay in the restoration of the people's ancient liberties and privileges. It was a nostalgia for the past, not yet a longing for the future. But the future was in their bones. Within the year, that fateful 1648 which featured six contemporaneous revolutions,[7] their horizons had expanded and their perspectives deepened. "*Viva la Republica, Viva il Popolo*" was now the cry. As Giraffi notes, "the people thought they had all the justice of the world on their side"; and there were here, too, the beginnings of a world revolutionary consciousness. Merchants had brought the news of events in England, "therefore oftentimes they cry out, *Viva il Parlamento d'Inghilterra* ... " Commotions continued to flare up, "some crying up *Spain*, others *France*, some *The Parliament of England*, and others the *Republique*: So that every one began to Arm."

Howell's comment on this point was acute. "Now in this prodigious Revolution," he writes, "there were many things of extraordinary remark that are considerable ... " He goes on to observe sensitively both the parallelism and the diffusion of the revolutionary impulse, connecting the events in Naples with the revolts elsewhere in Europe (Sicily, Portugal, Catalonia, Flanders, discretely for the moment omitting his own native land). It was as if "by a miraculous suddenness ... as if it had bin done by intercourse of Spirits, and the news thereof transported by a supernaturall way; insomuch that this Commotion may be sayd to be like a great Pond frozen over, where if the Ice break in one place it will commonly crack all over."[8]

I have already dealt with the fate of Masaniello and the tragic course of revolutionary drama. But I can scarcely refrain from making, as I write, the association over three centuries between two youthful firebrands,[9] between the revolutionary tumults of Masaniello and of Daniel Cohn-Bendit, between the old Neapolitan and new Parisian incendiarism. For the burning of the palaces, as Howell has written, "became sacrifices to Vulcan by the fury of the People, which was more raging than the flames of the Fire ... " Is it, one cannot help wondering, only the names of the gods that change in the recurrent fire ritual?

Several thousand students [in May 1968] armed with axe handles, wooden clubs and iron bars, stormed the Bourse gates chanting *"Temple d'Or, temple d'or!"* ... The Bourse was alight. It was a small fire at first which suddenly bellowed and seemed to have caught hold. The reflection of the flames could be seen on the buildings opposite, and the rapidly diminishing group of young anarchists who had begun to run away from the entrance like small boys knowing they have done something naughty, danced only a few moments around what they hoped was to be the funeral pyre of capitalism.[10]

My present concern is, in any case, to offer some historical glimpses of the larger metaphorical milieu.

1. *The Flaming River to Paradise.* In the collection of ancient Greek texts known as the Sibylline Oracles, which has preserved for us the visions of the early Judeo-Christian apocalyptists, fire is graphically associated with both the end and the new beginning of terrestrial things.[11] The great wrath will cause the forces of evil

> ... to approach
> The pillar, where around a circle flows
> The river inexhaustible of fire.
> Then will the angels of the immortal God,
> Who ever liveth, direly punish them
> With flaming scourges and with fiery flames,
> Bound from above with ever-during bonds.
> Then in Gehenna, in the midnight bloom,
> Will they be to Tartarean monsters cast,
> Many and fierce, where darkness is supreme.
>   But when all punishments have been entailed
> On all whose hearts were evil, then straightway
> From the great river will a fiery wheel
> Circle them round ...

Only a few lines later we are led to the prospect of the earthly paradise, for the just and the pious will be carried

> thro' the flaming River, into a place of Light, and into a Life without Cares, where the immortal Path of the great God is, and where three Fountains of Wine, Honey and Milk flow. And the Earth shall be equal to all, not divided by Walls or Partitions, but shall bear much Fruit spontaneously: All shall live in common, and their Wealth shall be undivided; neither Poor nor Rich shall be there, nor Tyrant, nor Servant, nor one greater or less than the other: No King nor Leader, all shall enjoy all Things in common; and none will say the Night is come, nor to Morrow or Yesterday is past; and no Care shall be for many Days: there shall be no Spring nor Summer, no Winter nor

Autumn, nor Marriage, nor Death, nor buying or selling, nor setting and rising of the Sun, for there shall be a long Day.

2. *Fiery Words*. So also in the prophetic books of the Old Testament (and I cite only one of the innumerable examples) where, as in Jeremiah (20:9, 5:14), the word remained in his heart "like a burning fire" and, moreover, "Because ye speak this word, behold, I will make my words in thy mouth fire, and this people wood, and it shall devour them."

3. *The Warrior's Fire*. The Romans themselves had a conception of fury as a fire burning in the head or brain; and this (we are told) explains the strange passage in the *Aeneid* where Turnus, raging for battle, "is stirred by these furies and from all his face, as he burns, leap sparks, and from his fierce eyes darts fire ... " Indeed, "the Chimaera on his head flames more fiercely in proportion to the fierceness of his warfare."[12]

4. *The Ideology of Heat*. What has been called "the ideology of 'inner heat' " appears to be central to many archaic tribal conceptions of magic, sorcery, and religious power. For the Indian Mohammedans, a man in communication with God is "burning"; among the Hindus, powerful divinities enjoy the possession of fire; Australian medicine men are held to be "fire-walkers." According to Eliade, at the center of the ideology is the mastery of fire, its exaltation, and its association with a celestial destiny.[13]

5. *A Torch for a World Aflame*. Nor are these aboriginal or exotic aberrations, for this relationship between fire, power, and prophecy obtains as well in other cultural traditions. In canto 12 of Dante's *Paradise*, there is the tribute by St. Bonaventura, the Franciscan, to St. Dominic (just as in the previous canto St. Thomas, the Dominican, had undertaken the encomium of St. Francis). As the last words fall from *"la benedetta fiamma"* and the high great festival of song and flashing light ceases, a voice rises from "out of the heart of a new fire" to extol the saint, sweet and faithful, who was "kind to his friends and ruthless to his foes":[14]

> A soul created so pre-eminent
> In living might, that a prophetic power
> From her womb's burden through his mother went.*

Dante scholars have referred these lines to an explanatory passage about Dominic in the Roman Breviarium: "His mother when pregnant dreamed that she had in her womb a dog-whelp [*Domini canes*, "the dogs of the lord"], with a torch in his mouth, whereby to set the world aflame when he should come into the light." The text (under 4 August in "The Proper Office of the Saints") goes on: "By this dream was figured that

---

*"E come fu creata, fur repleta / si la sua mente di viva virtute, / che, nella madre, lei fece profeta ... "

burning and shining light of holiness of life and power of doctrine, whereby he should enkindle godliness throughout whole nations. The end proved the truth of the image."[15]

6. *The Burning Enthusiast*. In his epochal work on the *Eroici furori* (1585), Giordano Bruno carefully distinguishes the various stages which his new European hero has to endure as the fire of his spirit "warms, kindles, burns, blazes or inflames ... " His enthusiasm becomes "absorbed in profound thought, stricken with urgent cares, kindled with fervent desires, excited by frequent crises." He cries, "I burn with fervid head [*Infinito mi scaldo*]." Bruno's heroic enthusiasm "becomes agitated, and fluctuates amid the waves of hope, fear, doubt, ardor, conscience, remorse, determination, repentance, and other scourges which are the bellows, the coals, the hammer and the anvil ... " Out of "a condition of infinite aspiration," he records the lines:

> If anguish infinite your fears should rouse
> Make space, give way, oh peoples!
> Beware of my fierce penetrating fire,
> For if it should invade and touch you, ye
> Would feel and know the fires of hell
> To be like winter's cold.*[16]

7. *The Inextinguishable Blaze*. There were, of course, infernal moments when the fiery image was something less than the clear signal of divine power and the undisputed instrument of pure purposes. I have already cited young John Rogers's furious dream of revenge against his enemy, a brutal political prison warden named Bull, from whose mouth would come a fire "as shall be sure to burn thee up ... " The Dantesque burning torch which was the saintly symbol of the "shining light of holiness of life" could, dramatically enough, emerge even from the most Satanic mouths. In a brief chapter in his description of the utopian *Christianopolis* (1619) entitled "The Tongue", Johann Valentin Andreae warned good men against the nature of an evil enemy—"the carnal-minded carry around burning torches in their mouth with which they set God, men, the world, and themselves afire so that finally they blaze in inextinguishable flame."[17]

8. *Renovation through Conflagration*. Confident and untroubled theologians, early in the seventeenth century, constantly associated (and not without a sense of tumultuous political implication) the "renovation of the world" with the "world's conflagration." Trying to explain "how the Destruction of the World by Fire is to be understood" (and his

---

*"Se d'infinite male / Avete orror, datemi piazza, o gente; / Guardatevi dal mio fuoco cuccente; / Che, se contagion di quel v'assale / Crederate che inverno / Sia ritrovarsi al fucco de l'inferno."

friends subsequently argued that the Puritan extremists had misunderstood him), Dr. Mede wrote:

> the *Beatum Millennium* is to begin in flaming fire ... whereof the World that now is shall be *refined*, and delivered from the bondage of corruption ... This conceit sure had its ground from that of Paul, 1 Cor. 3.13, *The day* (*viz.* of Judgment) *shall declare* (what is combustible in our works) *because it shall be revealed by fire; and the fire shall try every man's work*, of what sort it is ... Yet did they, at least some of them, expect *another fire* at the end of the thousand years for the destruction of Gog and Magog.

Later, on the Continent, in a time of violent religious conflict and imperial domination, we find the same theological spirit; but in Comenius's revolutionary appeal for a "total reformation" of the European scene, for example—"Ye men of learning ... see that ye delay not to assist the sacred fire with your sparks, nay, rather with your torches and with your fans"—it is allied with a more agitated apocalyptic immediacy.[18]

9. *The Red Cloud*. Nor were the non-theological eighteenth-century achievements of enlightened reason and rebellion ever very far from this ancient metaphorical center. In his tribute (half-hearted though it was) to Rousseau as the true burning spirit of *la lumière* and *la révolution*, Proudhon wrote: "He put the flame to the power that during the preceding two centuries French men of letters had amassed. It is something to have kindled in the souls of men such conflagration. It is in this that the force and vitality of Rousseau consists."[19] As for the souls of the Americans, kindled in a not unrelated outburst of vital force, William Blake was entranced by the prospect that "Empire is no more, and now the Lion and Wolf shall cease," and by the sight of "Washington, Franklin, Paine ... "

> Red rose the clouds from the Atlantic in vast wheels of blood,
> And in the red clouds rose a Wonder o'er the Atlantic sea,
> Intense! naked! a Human fire, fierce glowing, as the
>   wedge of iron heated in the furnace.[20]

10. *A Passion Kindled*. Taking his cue from Jesus' own description of his mission (Luke 12:49: "I am come to send fire on the earth"), Kierkegaard argued that

> Christianity was a fire kindled by Christ which should be kept burning ... a setting of men on fire by kindling a passion ... a setting on fire which was to bring conflict between father and son, daughter and mother ... a setting on fire intended to tear "kindred" apart in order to make single persons of them, which is God's will.... If you want to have Christianity bursting forth again, as a fire ... then by

this token the word is, "Away, away with abstractions ... " for every work of this kind is treachery to the fire.[21]

3. The Metaphorical Imperative

Thus it may not be wholly surprising that throughout the entire modern complex of utopian and revolutionary incantations the controlling imagery of iron and fire and blood persisted. The politics of paradise are dominated by the metaphorical imperative. Every "living fruit of human progress," Bakunin declared, has been "watered with human blood." He spoke with enthusiasm of the "childish almost demoniac delight of the Russian people in fire"; he was thinking, of course, of the Moscow flames which singed Napoleon, and similar thoughts burned bitterly through Napoleon's mind. On a torn scrap of paper in his own hand (said to have been found after his death), Napoleon wrote: "A new Prometheus, I am nailed to a rock to be gnawed by a vulture. Yes, I have stolen the fire of Heaven and made a gift of it to France. The fire has returned to its source, and I am here!"

There had been a time, to be sure, when he was certain that the fire was a Bonapartist weapon. "A revolution can be neither made nor stopped ... the revolutionary fire smoulders under the ashes, and sooner or later the conflagration flares up again with new vigor and devours all obstacles." It was Nature, or the very gods, that had turned the weapons the other way.

> There never was a vaster project conceived in the interests of civilisation with more generous intent or one that came closer to realisation. And here is the remarkable thing: the obstacles that made me fail did not come from men; they all came from the elements. In the south, the sea has been my undoing; in the north, the burning of Moscow and the cold of winter. Thus water, air, and fire, all of Nature, nothing but Nature—these have been the enemies of a universal regeneration which Nature herself demanded! The problems of Providence are insoluble.
>
> [*Conversation with Las Cases*, 1816][22]

Minds addicted to the incendiary motif never appear to be able to command the historical perspective which would enable them to understand how old and recurrent, indeed immemorial, the record of political pyromania actually is. They must discover the fire for themselves, sometimes with an infantile audacity, sometimes like prehistoric men in a cave making out for the first exhilarating time the origin and meaning of the flickering shadows. Young Alexander Herzen, observing a certain jubilation at the spectacle of Russian political arson (in the 1830s), noted how "fire, 'the red cock,' is in general a very national means of revenge among us," and he concluded that "A fire has something revolutionary about it; it laughs at property and levels ranks."[23]

Bakunin, naïve and inexperienced in the ways of ideology and power, never lost his innocence, never learned that one could burn, and be burned. Herzen relates that Bakunin, on the way from Paris to Prague, met some German peasants shouting and demonstrating around a baron's castle. He alighted from his carriage, showed them what to do, and, as he drove away, saw to his satisfaction that the whole castle was in flames. He was perfectly prepared to imagine "the whole of Europe, with St. Petersburg, Paris, and London, transformed into a vast rubbish heap ... " A contemporary novel attributes to Bakunin a characteristic definition of democracy: "Democracy is a temple of fire wherein the human race must be purged from the dross of slavery."

In Trotsky's Marxist lexicography, this was rather the definition of revolution itself, and in March 1905 he wrote in *Iskra* (whose subtitle on the masthead commemorated the pledge of a Decembrist poet, "OUT OF THIS SPARK WILL COME A CONFLAGRATION"): "Peasants, let this fire burst all over Russia at one and the same time, and no force will put it out. Such a nation-wide fire is called revolution."[24] Once, in warning Marx against the arbitrariness of revolutionary force, Proudhon confessed that he "would prefer to burn Property by a slow fire" rather than "make a St. Bartholomew's night ... "[25] It was a finicky distinction which had little to recommend it, as Alexander Blok pointed out with irony and contempt in "The Intelligentsia and the Revolution": "With voluptuous malice we stuck firewood, shavings, dry logs into a heap of timber damp from the snows and the rains; but when the sudden flame flares up to the sky (like a banner), we run around, crying 'Oh, ah, we're on fire!' " Blok's Scythians knew better, for they had not *"forgotten of a love / That burns like fire and like fire lays waste."*[26] "Let the fire," cried Wordsworth who had been disenchanted by revolution in France but re-inflamed by the uprising in Spain, "let the fire break out afresh; let but the human creature be roused ... "[27] Finally, in an interview (with a French journalist, in 1966), Che Guevara said: "The Revolution must be a deed beyond all measure, burning all things before it.... If mankind is ever to escape from its misery, there is only one method: the destruction of everything in fire and blood.... There is no other way, no other hope."[28]

I have collected a hundred similar passages: from the seventeenth-century vision (in Winstanley's *The Fire in the Bush*) of the end of oppression with "the Spirit burning, not consuming, but purging Mankinde" to the twentieth-century manifestos of Black Power revolutionaries. It was always (in the phrase popularized by a contemporary American Negro pamphlet) the fire next time.[29] It is the fire of all time, the great incendiary cliché, the paramount Promethean stereotype of man's political temperament.

All this was once referred to by Kant as "the terroristic manner of representing human history": " . . . now things cannot grow worse. Doomsday is at our door-step, and the pious enthusiast is already dreaming of the restoration of all things and a renovated world after the time that this one will have perished in flames."[30]

4. Saints, Martyrs, Rebels

Nothing could be more superficial than the notion that all this has to do with some arsonist's simple pyromania ("Burn, Baby, Burn"). As I have already indicated, the incendiarism goes deeper. Both in legend and in philosophy, the fateful association of fire with politics and power has ancient roots, as in the fragment of Heraclitus: "In its advance the Fire will seize, judge, and execute everything."[31] One historian of ideas, confronting the question of what brought Heraclitus to the notion of universal change and why he chose fire as its symbol, suggests that it was "terrifying personal suffering brought about by revolutionary social and political upheaval."

> Heraclitus' philosophy of change arose out of personal experiences which were themselves terrifying: heir to the royal family of the priest-kings of Ephesus, he lived in a time of social revolution; there was an upsurge of new democratic forces and to these forces the Greek tribal aristocrats were beginning to yield. Heraclitus witnessed their yielding, and out of the suffering of this social experience was born the idea of the transitoriness of all things; everything is in continual motion and flux. . . . He saw in fire something we experience as a thing and which is yet a process having its own law of motion. . . . Everything, therefore, could be seen as a transformation of fire.[32]

Earlier commentators had compared Heraclitus's discovery with that of "an earthquake in which everything seems to sway", and Karl Popper has a similar view. "I do not doubt," Popper writes, "that this discovery was impressed upon Heraclitus by terrifying personal experiences suffered as a result of the social and political disturbances of his day . . . . [a] reaction to the social revolution which he witnessed." Fire thus became the symbol of transmutation from one stage to another. There are even traditional reports of Heraclitus's belief in a *periodical conflagration*—just as revolutionaries came to believe in periodical rebellions in which the blood of martyrs watered the tree of liberty. The constant double image of revolution has been: blood and fire.

In one of his memorable bursts of ironical eloquence, that turbulent German revolutionary Ferdinand Lassalle exclaimed:

> What! Can anybody have struggled, like Faust, with firm and serious tenacity through the philosophy of the Greeks and the system of Roman law, through the various departments of historical science, as far as modern political economy and statistics, and can you seriously believe that the conclusion of this long course of development is to place the incendiary's torch in the hands of the proletariat?

Of course it was seriously believable: wasn't that Faustian struggle for the incendiary's torch recognizably his own? The book which established Lassalle's reputation as a scholarly writer, in the years before he devoted himself to agitating for social democracy, was a long study of *The Philosophy of Heraclitus the Obscure* (published in 1858). It served for him as the discovery of "absolute motion," for Heraclitus had "banished all peace and quietness from the world." He was strongly drawn to the philosophical hero of fire, motion, and struggle; and he registered with deep satisfaction that "Heraclitus was far removed from that apathy which inspired the ethical-political arguments of the Stoics with such profound monotony. His nature was one of storm [*Es war Sturm in dieser Natur!*]." The turbulence was classical; and Lassalle, whose look was once described as "defiance incarnate," often pondered a favorite line from Virgil: *Flectere si nequeo superos, Acheronta movebo* ("If I cannot bend the will of heaven, I will cause turmoil in hell").

Something of this fiery nature was caught by George Meredith in his portrait of Lassalle as Alvan, the passionate lover in the *The Tragic Comedians* (1880). But perhaps only George Brandes, with his special antennae for the sights and sounds of the European personality in the nineteenth century, could have sensed the true revolutionary vibrance.

> The old Greek thinker Heraclitus, whom Lassalle made the subject of long research, was in the habit of using various symbolical expressions to denote the primary force of existence—Fire, Stream, Justice, War, Invisible Harmony, Bow and Lyre; these expressions rise involuntarily in the mind if we seek some symbol to represent the dominant principle of Ferdinand Lassalle's life. Somewhere, in one of his letters, which is full of impatient outbursts against the tardiness with which events develop, Lassalle uses the phrase, "my ardent soul." Thousands use the expression as the mere figure of speech which it has become. Lassalle, perhaps, alone could use it without exaggeration, for his innermost being concealed some force akin to fire. His burning love for knowledge and science, his thirst

for righteousness and truth, his enthusiasm, his unrestrained self-confidence, his deep self-conceit, his courage, his delight in power—these were characteristics which all found expression in the same fiery and devouring manner. He was a bearer of light and fire to the world; a bearer of light, bold and defiant as Lucifer himself; a torch-bearer who delighted to stand in the full glare of the torch with which he brought enlightenment—*grand oseur et grand poseur*.[33]

If the idea of fire emerged in defiance and despair, the thing itself was born in mythological hope.[34] Prometheus is riveted to the rock because of his pity and feeling of fellowship for mankind: without fire and the arts of civilization the human race could never take on godlike powers. Worse than that, had not Zeus planned genocide?

> As for long suffering men, he took no care at all;
> indeed his plan was to make the whole of their race
> extinct and then to form another race instead.
> Except for me no one opposed his purpose.

Zeus was adamant, and an eagle feasted all day long on Prometheus's liver, gnawing it black; but Prometheus remained hopeful:

> My lot
> Is to win freedom only after countless pains.
> ... Zeus cannot fly from fate.

All our themes are there in the spectacle of Prometheus, the opponent of genocide, the savior of mankind, the lonely rebel, the uncompromising avenger.

> But he will never win me over
> with honeyed spell of soft, persuading words,
> nor will I ever cower beneath his threats ...
> First he must free me from this savage prison
> and pay for all my pain.

In the fragmentary *Prometheus Unbound*, Heracles tries to save Prometheus when Zeus decides to "let moderation prevail," and the Prometheans have to take Hermes' criticism:

> ... your own want of good sense
> has tangled you in the net of ruin, past
> all hope of rescue.

Here, again, we have the ancient primordial association of fire with freedom, with kindly pity for oppressed man, with civilization and its progress, and the dark shadow of a "net of ruin." Whatever may have happened in the lost plays, *Prometheus the Fire Bringer* and *Prometheus*

Unbound, it is small wonder that the image of the Suffering Champion captured the imagination of Blake, Hölderlin, Goethe, Byron, Shelley, and indeed Rimbaud, whose poet becomes "the thief of fire, charged with the government of humanity ... " Campanella, languishing year after year in frightful Spanish dungeons and dreaming of the warmth and love of a Sun State, cried that he was like Prometheus chained to the Caucasus (*ego tanquam Prometheus in Caucaso detineor*, 1 June 1607).

Similarly, Marx avows (in Aeschylus's words) "I shall never exchange my fetters for slavish servility. 'Tis better to be chained to the rock than bound to the service of Zeus."[35] For the young Marx, who began his philosophical career with a doctoral dissertation on aspects of ancient Greek thought, Prometheus was, as he confessed in his preface, "the grandest saint and martyr in the philosopher's almanac ... " Both Marxist philosophy and revolutionary politics were to bear the traces of this Promethean point of departure. "Just as Prometheus, having stolen fire from heaven, begins to build houses and to establish himself on earth, so philosophy, having embraced the whole world, revolts against the world of phenomena [*wendet sich gegen die erscheinende Welt*] ... " Or, in that memorable phrase of transcendental exultation: "*Was innerliches Licht war, wird zur verzehrenden Flamme, die sich nach aussen wendet*[36] [That which was an inner light becomes a consuming flame, turned outward]."

5. The New World of Man

In a sense Shelley concluded what Byron began: by rewriting the cosmic drama in which a new protagonist was to dominate the whole world's stage. Like Bruno's heroic enthusiast before him, Byron's poetic hero was to burn and blaze in the firmament on behalf of an earthly plan of astronomical proportions. An interfused literary and political culture was to produce that long-awaited new class of men—poets of intellect and men of action—of whom it could be said that they "*compressed / The god within them, and rejoined the stars* ... " They were the divine, if still necessarily tragic, missionaries of life, and this was to be their fate: to aim

> At an external life beyond our fate,
>   And be the new Prometheus of new men,
>   Bestowing fire from heaven, and then, too late,
> Finding the pleasure given repaid with pain,
>   And vultures to the heart of the bestower,
>   Who, having lavished his high gift in vain,
> Lies chained to his lone rock by the sea-shore ...[37]

It was Shelley who ended the sainthood and martyrdom of Prometheus by converting him into the triumphant hero of utopian revolution. He refused to be tempted by traditional practice and merely restore the lost dramas of Aeschylus. In his preface to *Prometheus Unbound* (1820), Shelley explains his aversion from "a catastrophe so feeble as that of reconciling the Champion with the Oppressor of mankind." No, Prometheus was to be a romantic protagonist of his own time: "the type of the highest perfection of moral and intellectual nature, impelled by the purest and the truest motives to the best and noblest ends."[38]

> We will take our plan
> From the new world of man,
> And our work shall be called the Promethean.
>
> [4.156–58]

As for his own personal plan, it was to make an alliance with "the great writers of our own age," those "companions and forerunners of some unimagined change in our social condition or the opinions which cement it." The time was now. "The cloud of mind is discharging its collected lightning ... "

So does the drama begin with images of an overwhelming catastrophe.

> Hark! the rushing snow!
> The sun-awakened avalanche! whose mass,
> Thrice sifted by the storm, had gathered there
> Flake after flake, in heaven-defying minds
> As thought by thought is piled, till some great truth
> Is loosened, and the nations echo round,
> Shaken to their roots, as do the mountains now.
>
> [2.3.23–42]

If heaven itself was being defied, Jupiter was under no illusions about the onset of immortal danger.

> ... alone
> The soul of man, like unextinguished fire,
> Yet burns towards heaven with fierce reproach, and doubt,
> And lamentation, and reluctant prayer,
> Hurling up insurrection, which might make
> Our antique empire insecure ...
>
> [3.1.4–9]

This time there would be no pity, no release, no respite; the thunder and the fiery wheels were grinding the winds; there could be no refuge, no appeal. "Like a cloud," Jupiter groans, "mine enemy above darkens my fall with victory ... " And when the thunder "mingled with clear echoes," Prometheus, as the captain of the victorious insurrection, took

the happy morning report from the "Spirit of the Hour," who had just
returned from the terrestrial fronts.

> ... I floated to the earth:
> It was, as it is still, the pain of bliss
> To move, to breathe, to be; I wandering went
> Among the haunts and dwellings of mankind,
> And first was disappointed not to see
> Such mighty change as I had felt within
> Expressed in outward things; but soon I looked,
> And behold, thrones were kingless, and men walked
> One with the other even as spirits do,
> None fawned, none trampled; hate, disdain, or fear,
> Self-love, or self-contempt, on human brows
> No more inscribed, as o'er the gate of hell,
> "All hope abandon ye who enter here";
> None frowned, none trembled, none with eager fear
> Gazed on another's eye of cold command ...
> None wrought his lips in truth-entangling lines
> Which smiled the lie his tongue disdained to speak; ...
>
> [3.4.124–43]

Who now could doubt it? Earth had been made "like heaven." No revolution was ever so triumphant, no utopia so fulfilled.

> The loathsome mask has fallen, the man remains
> Sceptreless, free, uncircumscribed, but man
> Equal, unclassed, tribeless, and nationless,
> Exempt from awe, worship, degree, the king
> Over himself; just, gentle, wise ...
>
> [ll. 193–97]

The lesson, in Shelley's final lines, was there for all the world's despairing rebels to read and, perhaps, to go and do likewise on behalf of "a
new world that rights the disaster of this."

> To suffer woes which Hope thinks infinite;
> To forgive wrongs darker than death or night;
>   To defy power, which seems omnipotent;
> To love, and bear; to hope till Hope creates
> From its own wreck the thing it contemplates;
>   Neither to change, nor falter, nor repent;
> This, like thy glory, Titan, is to be
> Good, great and joyous, beautiful and free;
> That is alone Life, Joy, Empire, and Victory.
>
> [4.570–78]

I should note that Shelley had warned that didactic poetry was an
abhorrence to him and that "it is a mistake to suppose that I dedicate my

poetical compositions solely to the direct enforcement of reform." No one would be reluctant to concede that there was here both the purity of poetry and the partisanship of politics (although, elsewhere, there were contradictions between the writer and the radical). In that same year of 1820, when he learned of the rising in Spain which forced the abolition of the Inquisition, he also composed his *Ode to Liberty*, and with the same motive of apocalyptic trance. It opened with a line from Byron on the banner of freedom streaming "like a thunder-storm against the wind"; and among Shelley's so-called relics this cancelled passage was found:

> Within a cavern of man's trackless spirit
>   Is throned an Image, so intensely fair
> That the adventurous thoughts that wander near it
>   Worship, and as they kneel, tremble and wear
> The splendour of its presence, and the light
>   Penetrates their dreamless frame
> Till they become charged with the strength of flame.[39]

6. The Ultra-living Element

Where we have come to is this: in the great blaze of revolutionary imagery, full of adventurous thoughts from heaven-defying minds, fire is the process of change and the pattern of hope and liberating struggle. It is the eternal human dream of light and power, as well as a recurring nightmare of death and destruction. As Gaston Bachelard has written:

> Fire suggests the desire to change, to speed up the passage of time, to bring all of life to its conclusion, to its hereafter. In these circumstances the reverie by the fireside becomes truly fascinating and dramatic; it magnifies human destiny; it links the small to the great, the hearth to the volcano, the life of a log to the life of a world. The fascinated individual hears the call of the funeral pyre. For him destruction is more than a change, it is a renewal.

Thus, fire emerges as one of the principles of universal explanation:

> If all that changes slowly may be explained by life, all that changes quickly is explained by fire. Fire is the ultra-living element. It is intimate and it is universal. It lives in our heart. It lives in the sky. It rises from the depths of the substance and offers itself with the warmth of love. Or it can go back down into the substance and hide there, latent and pent-up like hate and vengeance. Among all phenomena, it is really the only one to which there can be so definitely attributed the opposing values of good and evil. It shines in Paradise. It burns in Hell. It is gentleness and torture. It is cookery

and it is apocalypse . . . It is a tutelary and a terrible divinity, both good and bad. It can contradict itself.[40]

To move, in recent fire imagism, from Bachelard to Brown is to move from the poetry of the spark to the poeticality of the embers, almost as if to suggest the historic exhaustion of an immemorial metaphor. In Gaston Bachelard's *Psychanalyse du feu*, the imagery is still set meaningfully in a spirited version of a general historical psychology; in Norman O. Brown's neo-Nietzschean context, a manner of contradictory epigrammatism reduces it grimly to the zero point of meaninglessness and incoherence. For Brown, who contends that metaphor is "the original mistake in every sentence"—that "metaphor consists in giving the thing a name that belongs to something else" and that "metaphor is a mistake or impropriety; a *faux pas,* or slip of the tongue; a little madness, *petit mal*; a little seizure or inspiration"—there can remain only this sententious last parody of Prometheanism:

The real prayer is to see this world go up in flames.
The true sacrifice is total, holocaust. *Consummatum est.* The one is united with the all, in a consuming fire . . . .
The final conflagration; or apocalypse. The unity of life and death as fire . . . . The fire next time. The revolution, or second coming . . . . A fiery consummation . . . . Learn to love the fire. The alchemical fire of transmutation: *Wolle die Wandlung. O sei für die Flamme begeistert.* To be content in the purgatorial fire . . . . The apocalyptic fire . . . this world always was and is and shall be ever-living fire . . . .
The resolution of the antinomy between liberation and repression: fire . . . . To be aflame at every point. To be alive is to be burning.
Fire is freedom. Spontaneous combustion. Spontaneity is ardour . . . . Love is violence . . . . Birth is bursting, the shell burst . . . . Peace lies in finding the true war. The reconciliation of opposites, the making of friendship, takes place on the battlefield.
Find the true fire . . . . Fight fire with fire . . . . Save us from the literal fire . . . . The final judgment, the everlasting bonfire, is here now. Truth is error burned up.
Freedom is fire, overcoming this world by reducing it to a fluctuating chaos, as in schizophrenia; the chaos which is the eternal ground of creation . . . . Thank God the world cannot be made safe, for democracy or anything else.[41]

Apocalyptic has been reduced to a *pointe;* and Prometheus has become a platitude. Old troupers are trotted out onto the stage, forced to taking their vaudeville turns in an antiquated repertory of noise and gesture.

To dream thus is to destroy, and for all the fine Promethean good-will there is no fire without ashes. Among those cinders and charred fragments, man has always fancied a useful ember which could also warm, perhaps a spark which could renew or a spirit that could rise reborn: and so the cosmic drama begins again. Is there any way out of this fiery labyrinth in which the human spirit seems to have been condemned to wander?

The historic path of incendiarism moves in paradoxical spirals; like Dante's burning torch in the mouth, it is liberating and immolating. This is also suggested analogically by the following story told by a contemporary philosopher who has been similarly troubled by the problem of mankind's motivations in the light of changing internal sanctions. It is a story originally told about a monk (by Marie Jean Guyau, in his *Esquisse d'une morale sans obligation ni sanction*, 1884).[42]

One day Brother Yves saw an old woman in Damascus who was carrying a bowl of fire in her right hand and a phial of water in her left. Yves asked her what she planned to do with these things. She answered that she wanted to burn paradise with the fire and to quench hell with the water. Yves asked, "And why do you want to do that?" The woman replied, "Because I do not wish that anyone do good in order to gain the reward of paradise, nor for fear of hell, but simply for the love of God!"

Once again, we are confronted with the conjunction of absolutist ends and terroristic means, and once again we have a profound instance of the vicious fiery circle of man's cosmic aspiration. There are, as I have said, dreamers within the dream; history goes on. There are utopians in utopia, and incendiaries survive after all pyromania is spent. Neither time nor human temperament has a stop, and there is arson even in paradise. Even paradise—for the final coming of which whole millennia longed to brave (and, sometimes, to raise) the great conflagration—even paradise could be burned down.

Two final references, for I cannot of course make any systematic attempt here to look into the direct relevance of the vast anthropological and psychoanalytical literature, from Frazer and Freud onward, to this theme. Sir James Frazer's classic study, *The Golden Bough*, is naturally enough rich in suggestiveness: fire as a charm to rekindle the sun, the sacred fires, the fire festivals of Europe, fire as a protection against witchcraft, fire and the burning of human effigies, etc. As in the metaphor of flaming revolution, which comes both to destroy and to renew, there is a striking dualism exemplified in Frazer's summary of the two theories for the explanation of the fire festivals.

On the one hand it has been held [the solar theory] that they are sun-charms or magical ceremonies intended, on the principle of imitative magic, to ensure a needful supply of sunshine for men, animals and plants by kindling fires which mimic on earth the great source of light and heat in the sky . . . .

On the other hand it has been maintained [the purificatory theory] that the ceremonial fires have no necessary reference to the sun but are simply purificatory in intention, being designed to burn up and destroy all harmful influences, whether these are conceived in a personal form as witches, demons, and monsters, or in an impersonal form as a sort of pervading taint or corruption of the air . . . .

On the one view, the fire, like sunshine in our latitude, is a genial creative power which fosters the growth of plants and the development of all that makes for health and happiness; on the other view, the fire is a fierce destructive power which blasts and consumes all the noxious elements, whether spiritual or material, that menace the life of men, of animals, and of plants. According to the one theory the fire is a stimulant, according to the other it is a disinfectant; on the one view its virtue is positive, on the other it is negative.

The two explanations, Frazer suggests, "are perhaps not wholly irreconcilable."[43]

Indeed, sunlike fires, like tidal waters, are the essential sources of earthly purification: what won't wash clean will be burned.[44] The hygiene may be humdrum, but in its ultimate form it is the flood and the conflagration, those great and inescapable metaphors of that cosmic revolution which will turn the earth—after the deluge, or out of the ashes—to new life.[45]

Freud too—and he was not uninfluenced by his reading in 1911 of Frazer's Golden Bough[46]—speculated on the role of fire in human history. His paper on "The Acqusition of Power over Fire" (1932) considers both Prometheus and the phoenix in the context of a psychoanalytic interpretation of fire myths.[47] Freud's point of departure was his own footnote in Civilization and Its Discontents, in which he wrote:

Psycho-analytic material, as yet incomplete and not capable of unequivocal interpretation, nevertheless admits of a surmise—which sounds fantastic enough—about the origin of this human feat [the acquisition of power over fire]. It is as if primitive man had had the impulse, when he came in contact with fire, to gratify an infinite pleasure in respect of it and put it out with a stream of urine. The legends that we possess leave no doubt that flames shooting upwards like tongues were originally felt to have a phallic sense. Putting out fire by urinating—which is also introduced in the later fables of Gulliver in Lilliput and Rabelais' Gargantua—therefore represented a sexual act with a man, an enjoyment of masculine potency in homosexual rivalry. Whoever was the first to deny himself this pleasure and spare the fire was able to take it with him and break it in his own service. By curbing the fire of his own sexual passion he was able to tame fire as a force of nature. This great cultural victory was thus a reward for refraining from gratification of an instinct. Further, it is as if man had placed woman by the hearth as the guardian of the fire he had taken captive, because her anatomy makes it impossible for her to yield to such a temptation. It is remarkable how regularly analytic findings testify to the close connection between the ideas of ambition, fire and urethral erotism.[48]

If there is a possible meeting point between Frazer and Freud, it could, I imagine, be located on the island, east of New Guinea, where a Melanesian myth recorded by an anthropologist ascribes the origin of fire to "the vagina of an old woman." Mircea Eliade adds the comment that this "seems to indicate that the feminine magic is earlier than the masculine sorcery ... "[49] If true, this would only add to the recent consternation in Freudian circles over the whole reversal (based mostly on current endocrinological research) of the Adam-and-Eve relationship.[50] Has the whole history of civilization and culture been a conspiratorial male exploitation of basic femininity? One can almost hear the crack of the thunder and the lightning. The spectacle of Eve resuming her original priority over Adam could be the most revolutionary restoration of all time.

For, in a sense, the whole historical movement for woman's liberation has been in one form or another, a claim for a distaff Prometheanism. From Mary Shelley to Kate Millett, there is an insistence, tacit or open, on Eve rather than Adam as the protagonist of the earthly drama, as the hero—or, rather, the heroine—of history. The leadership of men, indeed every male initiative, is suspect. Mary Shelley's *Frankenstein*—her novel is subtitled: *the Modern Prometheus*—sounds the dark, tragic note of male Prometheanism: its pseudo-creativity, its false and monstrous galvanism. Dr. Frankenstein's failure is only the symbol of mankind, meant literally, trying in vain to create new life, to fashion a new man.[51]

Perhaps it is because it is woman alone, in her private self, who becomes great with child, that it has always been man who, in his public collective aspirations ("pregnant," in Sir Philip Sidney's phrase, "with Images of Life"), has dreamt of a social parturition. A truly unique event in history, unprecedented in all annals, it would constitute a "re-birth of Man." Small wonder that all of nature, even the whole of the universe, would have to be in such uproar. It represented a faith in a miraculous conception. A wholly new and different creature was destined to emerge—as in Karl Marx's favorite images—from other wombs, after other throes.

14

"Ancient institutions and modern improvements,
I suppose, Mr. Tadpole?"
"Ameliorations is the better word;
ameliorations. Nobody knows exactly what it
means."
—Benjamin Disraeli (1844)

The duty of governments is to be first
of all practical. I am for makeshifts and
expediency. I would like to make the people
who live on this world at the same time as I do
better fed and happier generally. If incidentally
I benefit posterity—so much the better—but I
would not sacrifice my own generation to a
principle however high or a truth however great.
—Winston S. Churchill (1896)

Our alternative Cabinets, though belonging
to different Parties, have never differed about
the foundations of society. And it is evident
that our whole political machinery presupposes
a people so fundamentally at one that they can
safely afford to bicker; and so sure of their
own moderation that they are not dangerously
disturbed by the never-ending din of political
conflict. May it always be so.
—A. J. Balfour (1928)

The English Ideology: I

1. The Popular Cause

Rediscovering "the People" and Heroic Masses—The Generation of '89—Enthusiasts for Liberty: Major John Cartwright, Reverend Christopher Wyvill, Dr. Richard Price—Revolution, 1688–1788: a Century of the Glorious Word—The Anglo-French Ideological Fraternity—On the Left Bank: Englishmen in Paris—Henry Yorke, Revolutionary of "Three Revolutions"

2. Elements of the Special Tone

"Lady Defender of the Revolution," Mrs. Anna Laetitia Barbauld (1790)—The Doom of an Established System—The Force of Nature—Sudden Flash of the Times—The Destructive Element—Unity of Theory and Practice—A System of Principle—Hour of Natural Birth—Cry for Perfect Government—Government of and for the People—Beyond Oppression to Peace and Plenty—Our Law and Theirs

3. Enthusiastic Affinities

A Peculiar Cross-Channel Fog—English Circularity and French Linearity—Holcroft and Tooke on "the Meaning of Words"—Faction Fights about Linguistic Tactics—Convention or Meeting?—Thomas Muir and the "Scrutiny of Every Syllable"—The Metaphors of a Revolutionary Temperament—Cobbett on "Figures of Speech"—Dr. Priestley, Dr. Price, Mary Wollstonecraft—The Natural Conceits of an Island People—The Blackmail of Revolutionary Pretenders—Burke

and Paine: "Opposite Extremes of Madness"—Cobbett's Critique of
Radical Absolutism, Globalism, Dogmatism

---

4. Retreat to the Center
Pitt, Mackintosh, and the Conciliation of Differences—New Watchwords: Moderation, Accommodation, Compromise—Holding a Middle Course—Tooke, Cartwright, and the Idea of "Fellow-
Travellers"—Getting Off "the Stage-Coach of History"

---

1. The Popular Cause

One of the essential preconditions of the establishment, or in some cases
the reactivation, of a revolutionary tradition and its associated components of utopian hope and militant temper is the creation of "The
People" as a political factor. Its capitalization bears witness to a large and
dramatic discovery of elemental social forces, to a moral and emotional
alliance with a grand and ultimately decisive abstraction; indeed, fraternity with the virtuous and heroic masses,[1] downtrodden for so long but
now at last risen to a giant's strength, has obvious physical and
metaphysical attractions. As Sir George Savile pointed out to a handful
of radical friends, when the English mind was on the eve of one of its
rare but grandiose flirtations with utopia and revolution: "In the present
acceptation of the term People, it may be hard to define; but, if they are
pleased to apply their hands to the work, *the People* will not be an
abstract or metaphysical idea . . . . "[2]

Such work as was not purely literary or ideological had always to do
with the grubby realities of reform. Desperate issues—political evils,
social distortions, economic malpractices—were long at hand; although,
as Savile again pointed out in the early 1780s with an apt metaphor, it
was of little use to be thrusting with poles till the tide should begin to
flow again and lift the grounded ship of its own accord. English feelings
ran strong on the subject of the corrupt system of parliamentary representation, on the restrictions of tolerance for Catholics and Dissenters,
on the immoralities of slave trading. Only yesterday, men had rejoiced
in the establishment of a free society, with unprecedented liberties and
privileges. Now, all too clearly, the liberties seemed partial and the
privileges restricted; and the whole framework of freedom appeared to
be an as-yet-unfinished social construction. Each political generation

rediscovers, with a mixture of rage and betrayal, this sense of failure and shortcoming and relives the onset of a conscience-stricken dedication to new and final tasks.

The English generation with which we will be mainly concerned in these pages appeared to be doubly blessed; the dawn of 1776 became the high noon of 1789, as promise moved dramatically to fulfillment. In April of 1776, Dr. Richard Price was anything but optimistic: " . . . nor have I much hope that any great reformation will take place in this country until some calamity comes that shall make us feel more, and awaken us more to reflection."[3] Some men, then, would wait for Price's calamity or for Savile's buoyant tide; the coming of great, dramatic, earnest, and even desperate events would determine the timetable of reformation. Others, according to principle or predisposition, preferred voluntarism to determinism. Who would deny that mankind could shape its own destiny? Human will, fired by the intensity of moral ideals, could alter the course of history and mold society closer to the heart's desire. It is an ancient alternative, this central crossroad of the passive and the active, between the path of those who decide to wait confidently and those who choose to do desperately.

In this first great century of modern revolutions, there is an additional element, namely, the emergence of a new type of radical, a revolutionary personality, a complex hybrid of prophet, Prometheus, and politico. In England in these years his profile was best sketched by Major John Cartwright. He intended it as "a general answer to those who endeavour to discourage all great attempts against the current of public vices and fashionable habits." The injunction was to turn away from fashion and to have no fear of resisting the current. He considered the conformist doctrine of "swim with the stream" vicious and dissipated. He would stand alone not merely because he could do no other, but also because, standing there, even in his loneliness, he might well be at exactly the point at which to move the world! After all, it had happened before to heroes of great reformations. "Luther, in his day, was treated as a visionary, a washer of blackamoors white, a madman; but it is to Luther we owe our religious liberty." In the lean years of political frustration, "those who act on right principles" need have no cause to despair.

> Seeing themselves neglected or ridiculed, finding themselves foiled in all their attempts, and feeling the sacrifices they make to their duty, they are yet happy in themselves; they enjoy the tranquility within, and they taste the supreme of all earthly delights, the love and esteem of the virtuous.[4]

And at the first sign of a change in the historic current it would no longer be a matter of the happy, tranquil few, lonely in their virtuousness. There was, after all, a more supreme political delight than the passive, patient saintliness of the reformer in isolation: finally the visionary of right principles would be given the historic opportunity to participate in the popular struggle for the cause of liberty. The People were only waiting for leadership.

Yet timing was all. As Christopher Wyvill explained, "they will wait in silent expectation till the altered sentiments of their fellow-citizens shall have rendered it expedient ... to renew the struggle to destroy the System ... " Recalling the dour decades of the 1770s and '80s, he underscored that "it would have been disadvantageous to the cause of Liberty to have wearied the friends of political Reformation with hopeless exertions. It was evident that the nation, at that time, was not ripe for Reformation." Finally, writing in April 1792,[5] he now beheld "with pleasure the increasing zeal of our countrymen in the cause of Reformation ... "

No, the lines were being drawn for a political struggle which, as the flights of rhetoric took wing, would inevitably assume the absolutized battle formations of ancient, sacred, and mythical contests. Dr. Richard Price warned the despots: "You cannot hold the world in darkness ..., " and he rallied his friends with the grand spectacle of peoples "starting from sleep, breaking their fetters, and claiming justice from their oppressors ... "[6] A piece of universal salvation had been staked out, and the vision was as individual as the political commitment was personal.

When the Bastille fell, Horace Walpole made haste to send his congratulations to Hannah More as if she and her friends were the stormers from the Invalides themselves: "I congratulate you on the demolition of the Bastille .... I always hated to drive by it, knowing the miseries it contained." But this was about as far as an old-fashioned English spirit would go; the conventional wisdom of his own strong-minded political tradition led him on to a certain distant, skeptical coolness.

> The destruction of it was silly, and agreeable to the ideas of a mob, who do not know stones and bars and bolts from a *lettre de cachet* .... If despotism recovers, the Bastille will rise from its ashes—recover, I fear, it will. The *Etats* cannot remain a mob of kings, and will prefer a single one to a larger mob of kings and greater tyrants. The nobility, the clergy, and people of property will wait, till by address and money they can divide the people; or, whoever gets the larger or more victorious army into his hands will be a Cromwell or a Monk. In short, a revolution procured by a national vertigo does not promise a crop of legislators. It is time that composes a good constitution:

it formed ours. . . . The Revolution was temperate, and has lasted; and, though it might have been improved, we know that with all its moderation it disgusted half the nation who would have brought back the old sores.[7]

Nothing could be more characteristic of a gulf between temperaments than this attitude toward the harsh futilities of violent power struggles, as against the advantage of temperate change based on a constitution of improved legislation. But, as once before, the men of moderated calm underestimated the force of heat and passion in excited times: the infectiousness of *enthusiasm*.

Let not the word be condemned [Major Cartwright wrote to Wyvill]. You, my dear Sir, are an enthusiast; without enthusiasm, who ever excelled? Who ever became illustrious by great achievements, without this heavenly spark? Who ever toiled in the cause of truth or virtue or public freedom?

Enthusiasm is the ardent spirit in the composition of the mind, without which it neither resists corruption, nor is influenced by a genuine love of liberty.[8]

It followed, therefore, that the very first task of the new movement of reform was, in a phrase of one of the radical reformers, "not to prevail with the deputies but to animate the people." There was a growing sense that change was not really possible through the normal channels of protest and legislative amendment: an extra-parliamentary force was needed.

I am persuaded [John Jebb said] that a reform, when effected, must take place in consequence of the active energy of the people.[9]

Such an appeal to new resources of heart and mind—energy, animation, anger, conscience, steadfastness, principle—always endangers the emotional configuration which had triumphed after the subsiding of the last historic outburst of storm and impatience. Once again, the hard-won virtues of yesterday had become encrusted vices. Prudence paled, as the spirit of compromise—once felt to be the guarantor of all the basic political and social achievements of a peaceful post-revolutionary England—became a vile and shameful thing, held in contempt by all men who would fight for the People's truest interests. These new organ-tones emerged ever more vigorously in the circles of the various English clubs which grew up in the 1780s—the Constitutional Society and the Revolution Society, above all. Major John Cartwright—who had magnificently ruined his prospects by refusing to serve in the military repression of the American Revolution, and who has been called "the pure essence of Radical spirit as it existed on the eve of the French Revolution"—is the author of the classic formulation of this mood: *"Moderation in principle is criminal."* John Jebb was not far behind in succinctness; when he and his Radical friends were pressed to make concessions, his answer was clear: *"In my opinion, the spirit of accommodation will ruin all."* Years later Cartwright recalled: "As my old friend John Jebb used to say, *'Don't tell me of a moderate man, he is always a rascal.'"*[10]

Between 1776 and 1789, certain philosophical absolutes, enunciated with passion and sincerity (although with a consistency which only a later generation would, in turn, find tinged with hypocrisy), served to create a deep ideological gap between what was and what ought to be. If all men were created equal, who would dare to be a moderator between freedom and enslavement? And, if tolerance was (or, at least, should be) a pure and total virtue, then who could accommodate himself to restrictions, proscriptions, and censors?

Nor was enthusiasm the only word that had now to be rescued from the vocabulary of the condemned. The very idea of revolution was to be revivified, and indeed the glorious old word itself had to take on a new lease of life. Let us then, pleaded Sir Brooke Boothby in 1790,

> teach it diligently to our children, let us talk of it when we sit in our houses, and we walk by the way; when we lie down and when we rise up; let us bind it for a sign upon our hands and as a frontier between our eyes; let us write it upon the posts of our house and on our gates.

In another thundering pamphlet replying to Burke, Boothby tried to take up the challenge to think through the "theory" of revolutionary change. As he put it to Burke directly, "You have made it necessary for us *now* to examine when and how, under what pressure of evil and under what sanction of right, a revolution may ever again at any future period be recurred to in this country." If, presumably, it was to be an English revolution, then certain special distinctions had to be made. "In the loose analogies of declamation," Boothby warned, "it is not difficult to confound revolution with rebellion, reformation with irreligion, resistance with revolt.... they have all some features in common, and by presenting the resemblance and artfully concealing the difference [they] might in the jumble be mistaken for each other."[11] In fact, in one of his many declamatory moods Dr. Priestley had resolved the matter too facily.

> ... every successful revolt is termed a revolution, and every unsuccessful one a rebellion.[12]

How, then, to be successful? What would be the most "propitious conjuncture" for a "strong effort in favour of liberty"? Boothby wrote:

The people as I have observed before must feel the actual pressure of the evil and feel it pretty strongly too before they can be made to move. They will not hazard present good for contingent advantage; and in this I think their gross good sense directs them perfectly well; for premature resistance instead of serving the cause of liberty, has generally ended in most effectually playing the game into the hands of power. . . . I would endeavour to provide for the future by turning the thoughts and attention of men to the past; the GLORIOUS REVOLUTION should be perpetually recalled to their remembrance, and the immortal decree of the Convention Parliament continually impressed upon their minds. . . . If this is the object of the Revolution Society . . . I should be proud to see my humble name upon its rolls.

For the moment, accordingly, until the popular forces were in motion and the conjuncture of events propitious, the enthusiasts were necessarily confined to words, not deeds; but there was a power of hope in that great "word of fear."

Revolution should resound through the palaces of Kings and the levee-rooms of Ministers. Far from endeavouring to hide—

> *"This word of fear,*
> Unpleasing to a royal ear,"

in the tawdry rags of sophistry, I would present it to them in large and legible characters, that he that runneth might read. I would write it upon the wall at the feast of Balshazzar; I would force them to look up to it, like the "bow in the cloud, as the token of a covenant for perpetual generations."

For Brooke Boothby, in a moment of a propagandist's inspiration, here was the great watchword of the day, to be broadcast to friends and enemies alike:

I would find them where they lay asleep and hollow in their ear REVOLUTION.[13]

Indeed, the "friends of the Great and Glorious Revolution of 1688" who had established themselves as a Revolution Society to commemorate a centenary found less antiquarian work on their hands in the very first year. The French events of 1789 proved the renewed relevance of their "Revolution Principles." They were elated by "the glorious success of the French Revolution," and they hastened to express their "ardent wishes that the influence of so glorious an example may be felt by all Mankind, until Tyranny and Despotism shall be swept from the face of the globe, and Universal Liberty and Happiness prevail . . . " All reformers appeared to be revolutionaries now, and as "Men, Britons, and Citizens of the World" they cheered a new revolution which was (in Lord Stanhope's words)

> ... to introduce a general reformation in the governments of Europe, and to make the World free and happy.

The messages which were exchanged between the Revolution Society in London and the National Assembly in Paris intensified cross-channel emotions and enhanced the poetical prose.

> Pourquoi craindrions-nous de l'avouer, Messieurs, la Révolution qui s'opère aujourd'hui dans notre patrie, est due surtout à l'exemple que l'Angleterre nous a donné depuis un siècle? ... Tandis que de toutes parts, les tyrans s'efforcaient d'éteindre le feu sacré de la Liberté, nos voisins veillaient avec un soin courageux, à l'entretenir toujours dans leurs seins. Nous en avons recueilli des étincelles bienfaisantes; et ce feu embrassant toutes les âmes, va, dans l'Europe entière, réduire pour jamais en cendres les liens dont le despotisme accablait les Nations.*[14]

Both the English spirit and the French pen seemed to be at one.

Nowhere was the Anglo-French fraternity of radical ideologies more direct—and as personally ill-fated in proportion to its political intimacy—than in the capital city of the Revolution itself. There was a large British colony in Paris, and the *sympathisants* constituted a strange and impressive lot of idealists, romantics, adventurers, eccentrics, heroic fools, and self-sacrificing humanitarians. They revered the Englishmen upon whom French citizenship had been conferred, among them Dr. Priestley, Thomas Paine, Jeremy Bentham, William Wilberforce, and James Mackintosh. They toasted, at the British Revolutionary Club's meetings, "the Lady Defenders of the Revolution," including Mrs. Anna Laetitia Barbauld. Carlyle caught them all in a phrase: "They came with hot unutterabilities in their heart, as pilgrims towards a miraculous shrine."[15]

One brought with him from Manchester a bust of the martyred Algernon Sidney. Another was supposed to have fallen in love with Théroigne de Méricourt, the Paris courtesan turned Bastille stormer.[16] A

---

*The following is the official translation made by the Revolution Society in London:

"Why should we be ashamed, Gentlemen, to acknowledge that the Revolution which is now establishing itself in our country, is owing to the example given by England a century ago? ... Whilst on all sides Tyrants were attempting to extinguish the sacred flame of Liberty, our Neighbours with intrepid watchfulness and care cherished it in their bosoms. We have caught some of these salutary sparks; and this fire, enflaming every mind, is extending itself over all Europe, for ever to reduce to ashes those shackles with which Despotism has oppressed mankind."

third (Benjamin Vaughan, a wealthy M.P., who died in America and bequeathed a fine library to Harvard University) alternated between a work on Benjamin Franklin and, having been "smitten with the craze of Revolution," a treatise on how the Book of Daniel was being fulfilled. (The nineteenth-century historian of *Englishmen in the French Revolution* observes, with theological dryness: "A Unitarian should have escaped the prophecy interpretation mania,[17] but the Revolution upheaval turned merchants into fanatics and rationalists into mystics ... ")

All were enthusiastic and purposeful, and each had an idea of his own on how to help the grand cause. Bentham sent a copy of his book on prisons to the Paris revolutionaries, suggesting that he come over and establish a prison based on his own system (even offering to stay on as keeper); but the revolutionary prisons were to be run on other principles. John Oswald, a young Edinburgh poet, became a member of the Jacobin Club, was appointed commandant of a battalion of pikemen, found time to translate Collot d'Herbois, established a political magazine called *Chronique de mois*, and dispensed with cravat and wig to wear his hair *à la Titus*. He was less consistent in his vegetarianism (a Brahmin influence from his year in India), for although he thought it cruel to take an innocent animal's life he argued that bloodshed was necessary to the success of the Revolution. In fact, one drastic suggestion of his achieved some notoriety, namely, the revolutionary effectiveness of putting to death every suspected man in France. To which Thomas Paine cuttingly replied, "Oswald, you have lived so long without tasting flesh that you have a most voracious appetite for blood."[18]

Some, like George Grieve (the younger brother of the high sheriff of Northumberland), enjoyed necessarily abrupt careers as terrorists. Grieve became famous as the hunter of Madame Du Barry, and he boasted of having brought at least seventeen persons to the guillotine. He liked to sign himself: "Man of Letters, *officieux* defender of the brave *sans-culottes* of Louveciennes, friend of Franklin and Marat, factious [*factieux*] and anarchist of the first water, and disorganizer of despotism for twenty years in both hemispheres ... " He quarreled with Jacques Roux, the Jacobin ex-priest, and denounced him as Charlotte Corday's accomplice. No less proficient in denunciations was J. J. (John James, which became Jean-Jacques in admiration for Rousseau) Arthur who, as a close collaborator of Robespierre in the Paris Commune, was on the list of witnesses against Danton; he fell during Thermidor, guillotined at the age of thirty-three.

Visiting revolutionaries, not unlike the native breed, appear to maintain a spirit of fraternity or even a semblance of organizational unity for only the briefest of periods. A committee of forty-nine met at the Hotel

d'Angleterre on Sunday, 18 November 1792, to draft and sign a manifesto of common faith. Its second meeting, some weeks later, was also
its last. Not even the august presence of Thomas Paine could keep the
quarrelsome factions from splitting and seceding. The not altogether
unfamiliar lines of the split would seem to indicate some basic structural
weakness in the edifice of ideologies—there is a crack between the loyalty to revolution in one country and an outgoing devotion to the cause
of international liberation.

Can a revolution be made permanent in only a single country, or is not
the very essence of the historic mission (and indeed even the national
security of the first new regime) a larger worldwide matter beyond all
formal frontiers? Had not Paine admonished that only when France
was "surrounded with revolutions" would she "be in peace and safety"?
Was it not recorded that even More's utopians had assisted in the fraternal deliverance of their less fortunate neighbors?

A special resolution was introduced at the Hotel d'Angleterre on that
Sunday in 1792 calling for the emancipation of oppressed England, even
suggesting a French invasion to "rescue England from slavery." Henry
Redhead Yorke led the vociferous opposition but lost by a majority of
one; whereupon he and his friends walked out. Oswald, in a rage, told
Yorke he was not fit to live in a civilized society; Robert Rayment (an
economist who had offered his expertise on national income and expenditure to his French followers) proceeded to denounce Yorke to the Paris
authorities as an English spy whose real name was Redhead. A warrant
for his arrest was issued, and his effects were seized; but Yorke, one of a
new breed of wandering revolutionaries, had already departed (and we
shall be picking up his story later).[19]

The chronicler of the British colony in Paris during these years has
done some painstaking research on the vicissitudes which befell members of the Revolutionary Club. Six had violent deaths. One took poison
to avoid the gallows; another was killed resisting arrest; two brothers
were executed; Oswald fell in a Vendée battle ("probably through
treachery"); another perished on the scaffold. Ten suffered imprisonment in Paris (including, of course, Paine, and Yorke's enemy, Rayment).

If we pause for a moment to inquire more pertinently who in all this
galère preached, beyond the "hot unutterabilities," a significant doctrine
of utopia and revolution,[20] then it would appear that, apart from Paine,
whose views are well-known enough, there were only two: Joel Barlow
and Henry Yorke. Both were "foreigners," even in the British colony in
Paris.

Even Paine, it should be recalled, appeared to be a man without a country, and in the valiant efforts to liberate him from Luxembourg prison it was difficult to determine whether he was still an Englishman by birth, an American by naturalization, or a Frenchman by virtue of honorary citizenship. Barlow was an American who came to England in 1791, left London as a representative of the Corresponding Societies, and was to die in the retreat from Moscow while on a United States mission to Napoleon. "Doubtless," he announced, "a great revolution in the management of the affairs of the nations is soon to be expected through all Europe ... " In 1792, we find him straddling the warring revolutionary factions by arguing that the French Revolution was essentially a model, by which he meant that it was only its inspiration (and perhaps its insurrectionary strategy and tactics as well) that was for export. "After the example which France has given," he wrote in a formal message from Paris to London, "the science of revolutions will be rendered easy, and the progress of rising liberty rapid." Soon thereafter, Barlow transmitted a further French message with his latest reflections on "the science of revolutions," namely, that one would not be enough inasmuch as "the second revolution is only the completion of the first ... "[21] Confident in the two-stage process of scientific revolutionism, he ventured to predict that addresses of felicitation would shortly be crossing the sea to a National Convention in England.[22]

Henry Yorke, who had actually crossed the sea to attend personally to the rising of liberty, was not quite certain that progress would be so easy; but he was not a man lightly deterred. He recognized that "People are not so easily got out of their old forms, as some are apt to suggest.... such revolutions happen not upon every little mismanagement in public affairs." Still, as he was once quoted[23] as saying with his characteristic bravura,

> ... you behold before you, young as I am, about 22 years of age, a man who has been concerned in three revolutions already; who, though late, assisted in the revolution in America; who so essentially contributed to that in Holland; who has materially assisted in that of France; and who will still continue to cause revolutions all over the world.[24]

"Yorke" was indeed only an alias. He was born in the West Indies as Henry Redhead and, if his biographical details are to tally at all, he must have begun his international career at a very tender age. Certain revolutionary personalities appear to function with a special panache when, uprooted from somewhere else, they change their names and take on a new and extravagant identity. As we know from so many other careers in the revolutionary ranks, there is some private purposive power in such men which is evidently released when they plunge themselves into public activities under a strange name and in an alien place. In this sense, Henry Redhead Yorke is one of the first flamboyant figures among modern "world revolutionaries."

Sixteen eighty-nine may have had its bit of old Orange glory, but it was not enough; more was needed. "If the Revolution were not a Revolution for the people, it was no Revolution at all, but a conspiracy of a few ennobled oppressors against the liberty and happiness of the many."[25] He was, as he confessed, "madly in love with ideal Liberty," and the true romance of his life would be to spark revolutions, to embrace the fiery cause of utopia and "the whole part we have to act on this stage of the world ... "

> We desire to see wisdom demanding of miserable millions their wants, and humanity at hand to supply them. We desire to see the sanctuary of virtue erected, and the standard of Liberty planted in our land, around which the people may rally as to a Holy of Holies. In short, we desire to see the altar of Equality blazing in Britain, whose streams of fire, whilst they shock, convulse, and tear down the rotten pillars of prejudices; whilst they shall consume tyrants, and terrify public delinquents; shall pierce into the hearts of the whole hearts of the whole people, and confirm the wide empire of morals on the wreck of superstition and vice ... Let revolution of sentiment precede reformation in government and manners.[26]

Whereupon (the speech was made on Castle Hill in Sheffield in April of 1794) he was acclaimed by thousands, and his carriage was pulled through the town in a triumphal procession. This was Henry Yorke's greatest day, the high—and final—climax to his youthful career as a revolutionary rhetorician. The Sheffield text, in all its eloquence and rhodomontade, was reprinted again and again in the various transcripts of the state trials of the 1790s; and Thomas Erskine himself, so cool and formidable in his successful defense of Thomas Hardy (in part a defense of his client against the linguistic excesses of Yorke's fulminatory manner), was moved to note that "this extraordinary performance" still read so well that "every man in the court was affected by it."[27]

Henry Redhead Yorke was never more English than in that self-deprecatory moment when he reflected on his early days in Paris and remarked that "no subject of the British Crown, who entered into the views of the French, returned from France without importing with him much of the ferocity of the French character, and much of the bombast of their style ... "[28]

2. Elements of the Special Tone

Looking back on heroic times that only enthusiasm can suffuse and vivify, one tends to react to the lost unity of public and private concerns with a note of melancholy. When revolutionaries weary and revolutions fail, or fail to take place, one sorely misses "the feverish excitement of public emotion" (in the phrase of Lamartine, the poet of romantic politics). Coleridge's daughter Sara once recalled "how gravely and earnestly used Samuel Taylor Coleridge and William Wordsworth, and my Uncle Southey also, to discuss the affairs of the nation, as if it all came home to their business and bosoms, as if it were their private concern!" But now, she had to concede: "Men do not canvass these matters nowadays, I think, quite in the same tone."

We are dealing here with the public ideas and private passions of an English generation with a special tone, and one which appears—at least on first reading—to be tinged with all the special characteristics of revolutionary ideology. It was a "triple forg'd" ideology, and that sensitive ideologue, Dr. Richard Price, felt it most personally. "After sharing in the benefits of one Revolution, I have been spared to be a witness to two other Revolutions, both glorious." The "bliss" and "very Heaven" that Wordsworth experienced was matched by an intellectual joy at the prospect—in words to be found in one of the first numbers of the newly published *Analytical Review* (its enthusiastic editor just back from revolutionary Paris)—of "advancing to a great era in the history of human affairs."[29]

We can, conveniently, make a compact summary of some of the essential ingredients of that special tone by quoting from an address made in 1790 by one of the enthusiasts of the day, Mrs. Anna Laetitia Barbauld, who was toasted in Paris as one of the noble "Lady Defenders of the Revolution."[30]

1. *The Doom of an Established System.*

All the power and policy of man cannot continue a system long after its truth has ceased to be acknowledged, or an establishment long after it has ceased to contribute to utility. It is equally vain to expect to preserve a tree whose roots are cut away. It may look as green and flourishing as before for a short time; but its sentence is passed, its principle of life is gone, and death is already within it.

2. *The Force of Nature.*

We appeal to the certain, sure operation of increasing light and knowledge, which it is no more in your power to stop, than to repel the tide with your naked hand, or to wither with your breath the genial influence of vegetation.

3. The Sudden Flash of the Times.

The spread of that light is in general gradual and imperceptible; but there are periods when its progress is accelerated, when it seems with a sudden flash to open the firmament, and pour in day at once. Can ye not discern the signs of the times? The minds of men are in movement.... The genius of Philosophy is walking abroad, and with the touch of Ithuriel's spear is trying the establishments of the earth.

4. The Destructive Element.

Whatever is loose must be shaken, whatever is corrupted must be lopt away; whatever is not built on the broad basis of public utility, must be thrown to the ground.... Obscure murmurs gather, and swell into a tempest.

5. The Unity of Theory and Practice.

Man, as man, becomes an object of respect. Tenets are transferred from theory to practice. The glowing sentiment and the lofty speculation no longer serve 'but to adorn the pages of a book'; they are brought home to men's business and bosoms; and, what some centuries ago it was daring but to think, and dangerous to express, is now realised, and carried into effect.

6. A Sytem of Principle.

Systems are analysed into their first principles and principles are fairly pursued to their legitimate consequences.

7. The Hour of Natural Birth.

The enemies of reformation, who palliate what they cannot defend, and defer what they dare not refuse; who, with Festus, put off to a more convenient season what, only because it is the present season is inconvenient, stand aghast; and find they have no power to put back the important hour, when nature is labouring with the birth of great events. Can ye not discern?—But you do discern these signs; you discern them well, and your alarm is apparent. You see a mighty empire breaking from bondage, and exerting the energies of recovered freedoms ...

The careful student of comparative ideology will perhaps be aware of the incompleteness of this new English version of the "triple forg'd" revolutionary consciousness. Where is the Cromwellian sense of an insurrectionary rising, the American sense of the just struggle, the French sense of perfection? But these too can be found, if not in great or coherent formulations, then sometimes in satirical and farcical texts.

8. The Cry for Perfect Government.

JACK: What paper have you got there? What dost look so glum for?

Tom (*looking on the paper*): Cause enough. Why, the news here tells
me that I am very unhappy, and very miserable, which I never
should have known hadn't I the luck to light on this paper? Jack:
What is the matter? Tom: Matter? Why, I want liberty.... I want a
general reform. Jack: I'll tell you a story.

> When our Squire married his lady, who is out of the way fine and
> likes to do everything like the French, she begged him to pull
> down the old house, and build it up in her frippery way. "What!"
> says the Squire, "shall I pull down this fine old house, which has
> stood firm these many years,—this house in which my fathers
> have lived comfortable for ages past,—this house too, which has
> weathered many a stormy war, and only underwent a little need-
> ful repair in the Revolution that took place years ago,—this house
> too, which all my neighbours take pattern by, shall I pull it all
> down, because may be, there's a bad passage here, and a dark
> closet there, and an awkward room or two in it? Our forefathers
> took time for what they did. They understood foundation-work;
> none of your lath-and-plaster buildings, which are up in a day and
> down in a night, for me!" My lady mumpt and grumbled, but the
> old house was let stand, and a glorious one it is; though there may
> be a little fault or two in it, and though a few decays want stop-
> ping; so now and then they mend a little thing, and they'll go on
> mending, I dare say, as they have leisure to the end of the chapter,
> if they are but let alone. But no pull-me-down works.

Jack: What is it you are crying out for, Tom? Tom: Why for a perfect
government.[31]

Did, then, perfect government imply popular government? This was,
as we have seen, rarely the case. The subversive saints were theocratic;
but the secular revolutionaries tended toward democracy. And even if,
several years after the enthusiasm of the manifesto quoted above, Mrs.
Barbauld seemed to be cooling her populism, the ideological ingredient
in her writings still evinced a new sense of social class, of involving a
silent and neglected majority of the poor and the exploited, now ripe for
self-determination, in a new participatory task.

9. Government of and for the People.

Government is the art of managing a community. Our community
consists of nearly twelve millions, of whom I suppose about nine
millions maintain themselves by some kind of manual labour. If,
therefore, you of the lower classes have nothing to do with Government, three millions are allowed to manage as they please the affairs
of nine millions. Government is not the art of managing the affairs of
the moon, but your own affairs. It is not true therefore that you have
nothing to do with it. Ask those who tell you that Government is
nothing to you, whether it is nothing to you how much of your

wages and hard earnings are taken from you in taxes—how much of your corn you may put in your own barns, and how much you must put into the barns of other people—for what things you may be put in prison, and for what things your life may be taken away—by what means you may obtain redress if you have suffered wrong from any one—to which of your children your little property will go after you are dead or whether to any of them?—on what occasions you may be obliged to go into other countries to fight and kill people whom you never quarrelled with, or perhaps to be killed yourselves. I think you will hardly say, that these things are nothing to you; yet all these things belong to Government, and are determined by it.[32]

Blood and violence seem far away—even in the following London placard the bloodthirsty element is all too obviously qualified by the wit in the ink. It announces at the Federation Theater, in Equality Square, a new and entertaining farce, called *La Guillotine, or George's Head in the Basket*. Among the cast are: "Banditti, Assassins, Cut Throats, and Wholesale Dealers in Blood, by the Empress of Ruffians, the Emperor of Harm-Any, Thing of Prussia, Prince of S. Cash-Hell, &c." When the government produced this placard as evidence in one of the great state trials of 1794, it was angrily challenged by Thomas Erskine (defense counsel in the trials of Tom Paine and John Horne Tooke) as being "fabricated by the spies who support the prosecution . . . "

More serious and more authentic was a militant sense of outrage and anger that was abroad in the land. However, as I have already suggested, moods of high complacency and deep dissatisfaction alternate in historic succession and often in opposing camps. Usually they can be found coexisting, as in some simultaneous performance of both *Prometheus Bound* and *Prometheus Unbound*. Thus, it was perfectly in character for Lord Justice Braxfield, in good voice and eloquence, to address the jury with this version of the state of the nation (and it required, as he candidly said, "no proof"):

> . . . the British constitution is the best in the world:—for the truth of this, gentlemen, I need only appeal to your own feelings. Is not every man secure in his life, liberty, and property? Is not happiness in the power of every man, except those perhaps, who, from disappointment in their schemes of advancement are discontented? Does not every man enjoy unmolested the fruits of his industry? And does not every man sit safely under his own vine and his own fig-tree, and none shall make him afraid?

At roughly the same time, in the same land, came an anonymous "Address to the Poor" (it figured in another state trial of 1794) which, in its contrasting color and comment, rivals the contradictory seventeenth-century depositions of Nehemiah and John Rogers which I have previously cited. One sees only the good, happily achieved; the other sees only the evil, painfully endured.

Social conditions become transformed over centuries, and although the real terms of both prosperity and poverty, of individual well-being and misery, take on new and different levels—there would be no social and economic history to record, were it otherwise—the recorder of ideologies seems only to be able to register an important element of literary constancy, an almost static psychological component. The ration of hypocrisy and of self-pity may well be fixed for men and classes in organized society; and although the piteous cry must always command more human sympathy and attention than the complacent boast, neither the voice of gloom or doom nor the voice of the turtle is a reliable guide to the historical truth of things. But the witness must be heard:

> Great God! What spectacle so affecting to a reflecting mind as Great Britain in her present state! On the one hand, we see the impudent nobles advertising their *"Grand Dinners,"* in the very face of the hungry poor, whom they have ruined!! On the other hand, widows, orphans, and others are weeping, and often dying for want of bread! What can be more odious in the sight of heaven, than feast and famine in the same nation? Yet this is literally the case in this kingdom, at this moment, and not only in the nation, but in every town, in every street, yea, often under the very same roof!
>
> Open your eyes, O ye poor of the land!—in vain are your hands and your mouths open! Do you not see how you are cajoled and degraded, by the paltry subscriptions made for you, at different times and in various parts of the nation; which serve only to make your slavery more servile, and your misery of longer duration? ...Ye poor, take a further look into your rights, and you will see, that, upon the principles of reason and justice, every peaceable and useful person has a right, yea, a *"Divine Right"* to be satisfied with the good of the land!

For Lord Justice Braxfield, here was only another "grumbletonian," seeking to bring about reforms "by force of arms" and taking the country to "the very brink of destruction." The fact that there were indeed such "grumbletonians," hovering between bouts of anger and despair and visions of a new and better world, was almost incidental to the mechanical certainties of an arrogant noble to whom sedition was always an infernal mixture of faith and folly. He knew what the puritans of demagogy were up to, whether they were up to it or not; and, as it happened, a few were. As the "Friend to the Poor" concluded his address, he offered a tenth ingredient of the special tone we are examining:

10. Beyond Oppression to Peace and Plenty.

Hearken! O ye poor of the land! ... Awake! Arise! arm your-

selves—with truth, justice and reason—lay siege to corruption; and
your unity and invincibility shall teach your oppressors terrible
things! Purge the Representation of your Country ... choose a representative ... from among the lower order of men, and he will
know how to sympathise with you, and represent you in character.
Then, and not till then, shall you experience universal Peace and
incessant Plenty.

At a general meeting of the London Corresponding Society, held at
the Globe Tavern in the Strand in the same month of January 1794, an
address was read (and agreed to) which provides us with a final ingredient. For there can be no making of a revolutionary ideology without
the daring thesis that extra-legal insurgency is justified, without the
brute confidence that the rising of just and desperate men is entitled to
fashion a law unto themselves.

11. *Our Law and Theirs.*

... it is both our duty and our interest to stand and fall together ... We must now choose at once either liberty or slavery for
ourselves and our posterity.... You may ask perhaps, by what
means shall we seek redress? We answer, that men in a state of
civilised society are bound to seek redress of the grievances from the
laws; as long as any redress can be obtained by the laws. But our
common Master whom we serve (whose law is a law of liberty, and
whose service is perfect freedom) has taught us not to expect to
gather grapes from thorns, nor figs from thistles. We must have
redress from our own laws and not from the laws of our plunderers,
enemies, and oppressors.[33]

3. Enthusiastic Affinities

To what extent can any of these ardent spirits, all touched by the
heavenly spark of enthusiasm, be called revolutionaries? What happens
to the various ingredients of the special tone?

Most of the essential characteristics, so clear in the crisper air of the
Continent, appear to get slowly lost in a peculiar English fog. Language
deviates, tone is transformed, and differences in temperament disrupt
apparent unities of political principle. It is one thing to be a radical who
is devoted to the fulfillment of some utopian dream,[34] but, for the true
revolutionary, the English reformer, no matter how nobly persistent in
his militancy, was never sufficiently logical, thorough, and inflexible. He
was never extreme enough, for with the rarest of exceptions he never
felt at ease in the largeness of either theory or rhetoric. In the Puritanism
of the seventeenth century, there was the homely comfort of Christian

theology and biblical language, without which such English revolutionaries as flourished could hardly have fully stretched themselves. Both the accents and the framework were substantially different in the eighteenth century.

When the eighteenth-century English reformers spoke of revolution, it was with the last lingering echoes of its earlier meaning: a restoration, a return to the fullness and purity of original principles. Old inflections do not disappear easily from the scene. But here old English circularity had to compete directly and dramatically with new French linearity, as a great revolutionary coup d'état announced itself boldly as a forward step of progress toward the new and the unprecedented. The English reformers, to the extent that they accepted the foreign vocabulary, necessarily found themselves on strange and different grounds. Words are worlds, and the two political languages were separated by more than a channel; they were indeed worlds apart.

No doubt the French revolutionary intellectual had it easier. In the development of the national public mind, the powerful elements of reason and dialectic, of rhetoric and philosophical abstraction, proved to be armaments for one side. The *ancien régime* had never been able to work out a system of ideas, an ideological argument, for the defense of its own established interests; in this sense it was taken to be "the stupid party." In England, however, there were very substantial traditions by the time of the French Revolution—ranging from the preoccupation with Anglo-Saxon constitutionality, the post-Cromwellian ideal of moderation, and at least a century of subservience to pragmatic slogans. The debate between the old and the new took place in a different atmosphere.

Listen, for example, to the defense of an English radical against charges of being a "Jacobin, Leveller, and perhaps Traitor." Thomas Holcroft was a member of the Society for Constitutional Information, and a friend of William Godwin. After the government had abandoned the attempt to try him for high treason, he proceeded to castigate the "political superstitions" of the age, arguing "how necessary it is for men to inquire accurately what they mean," for "philosophers themselves have erected many an imaginary being, each as their idol ... "[35]

Holcroft warned against the dangers of a political language that overused systematic terms of classification; "abstract words and phrases denoting arrangement and relative ideas, have been personified." What do the superstitions of the raging controversy really mean? For him, all "language [was] incomprehensible and absolute as its perfections." He would have none of it—the imaginative creation of idols, the absolutization of the relative, the personification of ideas—and his was a characteristic and symptomatic refusal. As he pleaded, "Only suffer those, who are not thus amused by words, to inquire into facts."

I make no apology for yet another semantical interruption. A historian does well to pay attention to the uses of words in the course of great events; and this for various reasons, not least being the striking fact that in heightened moments of historic action the actors themselves become very aware of words and their special consequences. This is especially true of the self-consciousness to which I have called attention among English ideologists from their initial seventeenth-century concern with the "word of God" and the "Devil's rhetoric" onward. It is a factor which, we are increasingly persuaded, has had fateful consequences for the vocabulary of revolution. As John Horne Tooke (who had stood with Thomas Holcroft in the dock at the Old Bailey on charges of treasonable subversion) wrote in his remarkable book on language:

> *F.*: Must we always be seeking after the meaning of words?
> *H.*: Of important words we must, if we wish to avoid important error. The meaning of these words especially is of the greatest consequence to mankind; and seems to have been strangely neglected by those who have made the most use of them.[36]

A revolutionary, thus handicapped, is hopelessly tongue-tied. The English radical, proud of his linguistics, his maturity, and his common-sensical sobriety, found himself being consistently cut off from those extravagant resources of spontaneity and youthful, if sometimes infantile, energy. "Exert your faculties, Sir; think but a little," Holcroft affirms, "and you will find, that, when we thus amuse ourselves with words, we act like children." Once deprived of the weapons of phraseology, the English radical found himself helpless before the withering contempt of his equally word-wary opponents. In a speech in the House of Commons, the dramatist Richard Brinsley Sheridan put it strongly: "As to the phrases Convention, Citizen, &c. in which they had affected an imitation of the proceedings of the French, the worst that could be said of them was, that they were contemptibly foolish."

There were even faction fights about linguistic tactics, about the propriety of proud and orthodox terminology and the necessity of holding to native and persuasive phraseology. Various local partisans could agree neither on the wording of their resolutions nor even on the word to be used for their national conclave—convention or meeting. The quarrel was actually about the choice of etymological roots: *meeting* deriving from Old English, and *convention* from the Latin *conventio*. It was felt by some that the latter, now tinged with Paris politics, "might give offence to weak minds ... Upon which the Latin word was put out and the Saxon word stood."

In Scotland, sturdier souls even dared to use at least one dangerous word, as they called delegates from the societies of the Friends of the

People to a first general convention in Edinburgh. To judge from the published minutes of the meeting (11–13 December 1792),[37] a good deal of the time was taken up by subsequent differences over words and phrases. A *Convention* it was, in true reverence for the French model; but could it accept, without taking on the risk of treason, a resolution which went so far as to say: "Not by a *calm* contented secret wish for reform, but by openly, actively, and urgently *willing* it, with the unity and energy of an embodied nation"?

Thomas Muir argued that "our great business is to reform, not to alter." A critic went further and, objecting to *restore*, proposed the word *establish*. Muir objected to *strike at the root of*, which might be another clause to be construed as treason. Skirving wanted to omit *restore* and insert *obtain*. A country delegate suggested the word *remove* instead of *strike at the root of*. But he was countered by a proposal to use *sweep away* instead of *remove*.

The issue began to narrow down to a conflict between the protagonists of the progressive future and those of the once-glorious past. A strong faction insisted on *obtain*, which at least smacked of something new, rather than *restore*, which suggested an ancient purity that probably never was. An equally adamant group contended "that no word in the English language was so proper as 'restore'; that if any other word such as 'obtain' or 'establish' was adopted, we might justly be accused of *innovation* ... "

Was there no reformer about who would dare the revolution of the new—the idea of it, the word for it? What had happened to the old radical Puritan temperament which had so naturally opted for "root-and-branch" changes? Who was there to argue, as uncompromising fundamentalist spirits had in the previous century, for a new man in a new world? Was there no task, in any sense of the word, that was *fundamental*?

> Mr. Muir said that he was not willing to dispute about words, or to spend the time of the Convention in mere verbal criticism, although the metaphor of "removing a source" did not quite please him. But gentlemen would do well to attend to the inferences that might be drawn from such a mode of expression. "What is the source of these abuses?—The royal influence. What! Are you going to remove the King?"

In the end Muir congratulated all for having "entered into the *minutiae* of everything, and scrutinised every syllable before they gave it their consent." After so much care, so much prudence, they allowed themselves one carefree moment at the finale, when all took the French oath, *To live free or die* ...

The whole Convention as one man rose, and, holding up their right hands, took the oath. (Reiterated plaudits.)

At bottom, the failure of the revolutionary ideology to cross the channel safely was associated with the inability of the English public mind to make welcome (in a prescient phrase used in a parliamentary debate in 1790) "the strange mixture of metaphysics with politics, which we are witnessing in the neighbouring country ... "[38]

No revolutionary temperament can thrive without such metaphysics, or without its great sustaining imagery. In England, the natural metaphors—whose emergence in the European imagination I have tried to chronicle—now appeared to be (except to a handful of romantic poets) unnatural and antipathetic. Radicals, liberals, and reformers alike turned away from the conceits which everywhere else were to remain the distinctive signs of the revolutionary's metaphorical imperatives. No one put it more succinctly than William Cobbett in an issue of his *Political Register*:

We have so often been told about the earthquake, the volcano, the burning lava of the French revolution, that some of us seem, at last, to have taken this figure of speech in its literal meaning.[39]

Would, then, the earth not shake and a great storm come to herald the purifying fire? What would become of a revolutionary faith when it could not draw strength from a sense of being allied to the beneficent course of nature herself, and especially to her catastrophes?

The vision of the English revolution, such as it was, had to make do with more humdrum imaginative materials. "A partial change, no doubt will be preferable," Dr. Priestley concedes, "to a total one, if a partial change will be sufficient for the purpose." However, under some circumstances, it might conceivably be "more advisable to pull down an old and inconvenient house, and build another from the foundation, rather than lay out money in repairs ... " Another defender of revolutionary solutions admits that he would not have objected if Burke had only confined himself to "exposing the hollow and shapeless phantoms existing ... in the brains of a few senseless enthusiasts." He is also troubled by the dire temptations of corrupting power with which the men of a successful revolution would be confronted: "They have not only the passions and interests of their adverse parties but, what is much more dangerous, their own to contend with. Power is the strongest of all tests of human virtue, an ordeal almost too severe for the infirmity of our nature." A member of the Revolution Society concedes that Dr. Price "had stepped far beyond the line of prudence and propriety." Neither zeal nor eloquence would drive him to consider a revolution as anything but "a last resource." And Mary Wollstonecraft is prepared to go so far as to "allow that Dr. Price's zeal may have carried him further than sound reason can justify," that "his political opinions are Utopian reveries," and that all political revolutions are dangerous "till we can see the remote consequences of things ... "[40]

Like Cocteau's mirror, the English revolutionary mind was reflecting too much before sending forth its images. The glory of a great change was still attractive, but if it *was* to be another revolution, then let it be partial, fearful of power, within the proper limits of prudence, without the vagueness of utopian illusions, with a certain sense of consequences, and then only as a last resort. A hundred years of hardheaded and keen-witted political analysis, from Locke and Halifax to David Hume, had proved to be a stern taskmaster for the English mind. It was as if in the century since the Glorious Revolution, it had been thoroughly debriefed.

Looked at very closely, the English radicals could not conceivably be taken for the "new race of men" that Tocqueville had discovered in France—"Revolutionaries of a hitherto unknown breed ... men who carried audacity to the point of sheer insanity; who balked at no innovation and, unchecked by any scruples, acted with an unprecedented ruthlessness."[41] If the Anglo-Saxons were revolutionaries at all, they were a known breed of scrupulous men: sane, circumspect, and, ultimately, reluctant. How could the putative promise of an earthquake evoke anything but appalling images of a Lisbon disaster? And what sense could there be, for a seafaring folk whose genius lay in the discovery of the safest ocean routes, in offering the vaunted oceanic prospect of a great world-shaking storm? The language of the English ideology tended to reflect the temper and the natural conceits of an island people[42] soberly preoccupied with its struggle against the elements. The English gardener wanted to prune; the English mechanic to tinker; the English carpenter to repair. The English merchant liked to bargain and adjust, and the English sailor preferred his charted seas and safe harbors. And the English revolutionary? Driving himself to ruthless lengths of imaginative audacity, he offers only this dry Newtonian conceit on behalf of a cause whose true believers would always be prepared to make supreme sacrifices.

> The very regulation of time [Brooke Boothby writes] by which every thing else is regulated has been found subject to errour and requiring change. To the Julian has succeeded the Gregorian system, and to that another must succeed if the world should so long endure. Our

poor little institutions like our watches require to be periodically
wound up and frequently repaired. They all contain in their very
essence and original concoction latent principles of destruction. It is
the best office of the collective wisdom of the times to mark the
decay and to retard its progress, and when the day comes, as come it
must sooner or later, that the machine ceases entirely to answer the
purposes for which it was constructed, to direct the formation of a
new one if possible on a better principle and of more durable materials.[43]

A time bomb, rather than a timepiece, might have been a more relevant
offering to a new race of audacious men.

If the calling of revolution figured at all in the radical reform movement, it did so as a matter of what almost all of its proponents felt to be
practical politics. So far from being an apocalypse and a path to paradise,
it was a fateful and ruinous event that had best be avoided: and it could
only be avoided by powerful concessions to the powerless. Revolution,
or the threat thereof, was a political stratagem, calculated to instill fear or
uncertainty or, in any event, a sufficient readiness in the ruling establishments to give as a desperate alternative what they had not been
prepared to give in argument and persuasion. It was an obvious ploy
and hence a favored one; and there were few, if any, among all the
Christian theologians enlisted in the cause who felt qualms about this
new form of making evil (and they held it to be such) their good. But the
trouble with blackmail is that, if the bluff should fail, one may be forced
to assume a role for which one was essentially unprepared. Beyond the
first opening rounds of threat and counterbluff lay consequences whose
repugnance could not be quite justified by their uncontrollability or assumed inevitability.

The English reformers were not the revolutionaries they appeared to
be pretending to be. Neither their ideas nor their emotions—I have
already indicated that their language and their temperaments imposed
similar limitations—could be fully extended to cover a revolutionary
mission. To the extent that, for a brief historical moment, they sounded
or even behaved as if they were anything but meliorists, additional
pressures were placed on an already unstable ideological personality to
render it even more contradictory, untenable, and transitory.

There was an incident at the very first anniversary celebration of the
French Revolution which foreshadowed the divergences and the defections to come. It was held at the Crown and Anchor in London, on 14
July 1790, and the Earl of Stanhope was in the chair. There was a spirit of
"rejoicing" at the meeting, upset only after a resolution had been introduced which seemed to some to be "an unqualified motion and appro-

bation of the French revolution ... " John Horne Tooke, for one, thought "it might produce an ill effect out of doors." He recognized that "the form of government in France [was] so foul and decayed, that no repair merely could save it from destruction"; but that the English constitution, with important and necessary reforms, was quite serviceable. The effect was tumultuous; the disapprobation was rude and disorderly. A friend of Tooke's tried to qualify the qualification, but Tooke in turn (as he quipped) "moderated the moderator." The Earl of Stanhope managed to restore order, and later recalled the scene:

> ... he [John Horne Tooke] proposed, as an amendment, that something should be added about our own constitution, and he spoke something about ships and timbers ... I recollect an expression he used, which was that "all our timbers were sound," and he was very much hissed and hooted indeed for it .... It was with some difficulty I could procure Mr. Tooke a hearing, for they seemed very angry ... I don't know whether I could have got him a hearing if I had not done something disrespectful ...

The chairman suggested that they hear him first and hiss him afterward. " ... and then they did hear him ... and the substance of it was, that we did not want a revolution in this country ... "[44]

It would be a mistake to think that such cross-channel enthusiasm as flowered for the Revolution was an exclusive emotion of England's revolutionary pretenders. It was a widely shared sentiment among many in England who would have thought of themselves as moderate reformers but, given the high drama of the events (and their not inconvenient venue in a foreign land), made for a moment common cause with those whom one historian has called the doctrinaires of "the Clean Sweep." Thus, good liberal English doctrine managed to accommodate itself, and eloquently, to the French climacteric of the new spirit abroad in Europe. For Charles James Fox, too, the capture of the Bastille was a historical denouement: "How much the greatest event it is that ever happened in the world; and how much the best!"[45]

That claim covered, by any reckoning, a great many world happenings, not a few of which would on the calculations of a soberer day be accorded no small moral worth. But the affinity between enthusiasm and the superlative is not to be denied. What is new is quickly taken to be unique; what is hopeful or meliorative, in the modest way of complex human affairs, is greeted as a sign of final things; and what may be good or important or encouraging must needs be elevated to a place in some cosmic scenario.

From young Wordsworth to old Godwin, the infatuation was never at a loss for words. When Dr. Joseph Priestley took his turn among the dozens of radicals who rushed to refute Edmund Burke's polemic against the enthusiasts of French Revolution, he conveniently discovered that some of the rhetoric of both extremes was handily interchangeable.

> These great events, in many respects unparalleled in all history, make a totally new, a most wonderful, and important, era in the history of mankind. It is, to adopt your own [i.e., Burke's] rhetorical style, a change from darkness to light, from superstition to sound knowledge, and from a most debasing servitude to a state of the most exalted freedom. It is a liberating of all the powers of man from that variety of fetters, by which they have hitherto been held. So that, in comparison with what has been, now only can we expect to see what men really are, and what they can do.[46]

And here are the even more lurid words of William Hazlitt's with which, in describing the *idée maîtresse* of his generation, he almost (but not quite) entranced himself:

> A new world was opening to the astonished sight. Scenes, lovely as hope can paint, dawned on the imagination; visions of unsullied bliss lulled the senses, and hid the darkness of surrounding objects, rising in bright succession and endless gradations, like the steps of that ladder which was once set upon the earth, and whose top reached to heaven. Nothing was too mighty for this new-begotten hope; and the path that led to human happiness seemed as plain as the pictures in the *Pilgrim's Progress* leading to Paradise.[47]

The imaginative extension of political ideas and their embellishment by myth and metaphor induce an ideological atmosphere in which men, beginning with more ordinary and even humdrum social concerns, come to think of their activities in terms of the life-and-death purposes of mission and destiny. Symbolic deeds become seductive, and the whole movement takes on a compulsive human solidarity which a more sober choice of comrades would have avoided. One English committee, with a curious combination of utopianism and revolutionism, established itself to gather funds for the construction of a large mill in Nottinghamshire; it is the year 1788, and the mill was to stand as the symbol of the centenary of the English Revolution of 1688: indeed it was to be called "the Revolution-mill." Alas, it failed miserably. Even more permanently troublesome is the problem of political alliance and personal association which I have referred to by using Ignazio Silone's phrase about "the choice of comrades."

Two prevailing attitudes emerge and, in turn, come to dominate the intellectual scene. In the beginning there are only a few who can bear to secede from enthusiasm long enough to examine their own ranks. When they do—as we shall soon see—they tend to withdraw from the simpler notions of good versus evil and from an uncritical confidence that all who would strike a blow against old tyranny are necessarily stalwarts of an authentic new freedom. An Anglo-French exchange on the subject of the debate between Burke and Paine may be used to illustrate this briefly. Sir Samuel Romilly, in the spring of 1791, reported to his liberal correspondents in Paris of the stir being made by Thomas Paine's *Common Sense*. This latest polemic against Burke was "full of spirit and energy, and likely to produce a very great effect ... " In fact, it had done so already, having gone through three editions in a fortnight, and indeed had "made converts of many persons who were before enemies to the revolution ... " In a striking reply, the French correspondent offered the following dry comment:

> "*Nous avons lu l'ouvrage de M. Paine en réponse à M. Burke; c'est la folie inverse* [We have read Mr. Paine's work in answer to Mr. Burke; it is the opposite extreme of madness]."[48]

I have already referred to this interchangeable polarity of the extremes, and it appears to be a lurking suspicion among many contemporaries. "Since you could not be one of the grand movers," Mary Wollstonecraft wrote to Edmund Burke, "the next *best* thing that dazzled your imagination was to be a conspicuous opposer." Perhaps she was only trying to score a debater's point, but she went on to speculate: "had you been a Frenchman, you would have been ... a violent revolutionist ... Your imagination would have taken fire."[49]

One other turning point in the fiery debate needs to be mentioned. In the decline of Anglo-French ideological affinities, there developed a deep political and intellectual suspiciousness of the viability of "a system," a distrust of the idea and a dislike for the word. The young William Cobbett, from his transatlantic vantage point in Philadelphia (he had been traveling from London to Paris when the turbulence of French events forced him to turn back, board a sailing ship in Le Havre, and land in America in October 1792), expressed it with characteristic vigor and perception. In 1794, he published some observations on Dr. Joseph Priestley's own "emigration," which amounted to a furious critique of an English Jacobin for his "systematic" revolutionary views and for his utopian indictment of "the [old] System."

> System-mongers are an unreasonable species of mortals: time, place, climate, nature itself, must give way. They must have the same government in every quarter of the globe; when perhaps there are not two countries which can possibly admit of the same form of government at the same time. A thousand hidden causes, a thousand circumstances and unforeseen events, conspire to the forming of a gov-

ernment. It is always done little by little. When completed, it presents nothing like a *system*; nothing like a thing composed, and written in a book.[50]

To the charges of absolutism and globalism, Cobbett added a third which derived from his own impassioned libertarian critique of the French Revolution. With the authors of both *The Rights of Man* (Thomas Paine) and *The Rights of Women* (Mary Wollstonecraft) in Paris dungeons, he begged to be forgiven for dwelling on the wrongs rather than the rights that accompany a violent transformation of society. The repressive intolerance—indeed the guillotine itself, whose latest victims were Mmes Roland and Hebert, the "goddesses of liberty"—had given the lie to Dr. Priestley's promise of a new, harmonious, and virtuous system.

> Either he foresaw the consequences of the French revolution, or he did not foresee them: if he did not, he must confess that his penetration was far inferior to that of his antagonists, and even to that of the multitude of his countrymen; for they all foresaw them. If he did foresee them, he ought to blush at being called the "friend of human happiness"; for, to foresee such dreadful calamities, and to form a deliberate plan for bringing them upon his country, he must have a disposition truly diabolical. If he did not foresee them, he must have an understanding little superior to that of an idiot; if he did, he must have the heart of a *Marat*. Let him choose.

Cobbett did not need to wait for Priestley's choice; he was confident he knew what it would be: "No: the French revolution is his system, and sooner than not see it established, I much question if he would not with pleasure see the massacre of all the human race."

Returning, however, from such flights of polemical rhetoric, Cobbett put forward the more sober point of democratic choice and consent: for it is on this issue that populistic dogmas are severely tested.

> Even suppose his intended plan of improvement had been the best in the world, instead of the worst, the people of England had certainly a right to reject it. He claims as an indubitable right, the right of thinking for *others*, and yet he will not permit the people of England to think for *themselves*. Paine says, "What a nation *wills*, it has a right *to do*." Consequently, what a whole nation does *not will*, it has a right *not to do*.

Whether or not the right of revolution could be so easily coupled in democratic theory with the right of counter-revolution, it was obvious that so long as the right of reply existed the counterattack would grow in force and intensity. Had not the utopian dream shown itself to be only a "visionary delusion"? If "A man of all countries is a man of no country," was the cosmopolitanism of the new enlightenment anything but "political cant"? Cobbett's questions were calculated to upset every troubled English friend of revolution—"Would he really prefer the proceedings of a *revolutionary tribunal* to those of a court of justice in England?"[51]

4. Retreat to the Center

When the liberal moderates had recovered their equanimity, always at the expense of their enthusiasm and their fraternity, they would manage to find their way to a new position which would try to hold to a center without either Burke or Paine, embracing neither "extreme of madness." This position at the center which a whole generation hoped that William Pitt would hold was a very English one. Pitt's "apostacy" from liberalizing principles was felt to be unconscionable, and his identification of French revolutionism with English reform was held to be even worse. If the noisy cheerleading from the ranks of the English Jacobinical sympathizers had helped to give that impression in 1789, by 1793 hasty attempts were being made on many sides to divorce the historical phenomena in foreign parts from the political urgencies of one's native land. Nobody less than James Mackintosh (although the pamphlet was signed only "By an Honest Man," the young radical hero of the debate with Burke was known to be the author) tried to clarify the point in an open letter to Pitt:

> These attempts to obtain Reform disclaim all alliance with the magnificent principles, or the perilous speculations, by when men, according to their various prepossessions, will suppose our neighbours to have been nobly animated or fatally deluded.

The disclaimer suffered for its coming so late and so ambivalently. The polarization had already gone too far for Pitt's forces to be convinced that the Reformers were basing themselves on "notions of liberty purely English ... " The original delight in the spectacles of Paris had doubtless touched, beyond all obvious political sensitivities, on a deep nerve of tribal loyalties. Of course, important issues of principle—and of property and power—divided the disputants; an extra element of outraged Englishness in the national argument only reinforced the factor of extremism in the mutual response. Mackintosh deluded himself if he thought that he could beat an easy or convincing retreat and try to rejoin the issue on other, higher ground.

> Every passion and every frailty, in the ardour of dispute, seduced men into extremes. Many honest men were driven into Toryism by their fears. Many sober men were betrayed into Republicanism by their enthusiasm.

Would Pitt now be prepared to "mitigate extremes, conciliate differences"? Or would he continue to "paint moderation as the virtue of
cowards, and compromise as the policy of knaves, to the stormy and
intolerant enthusiasm of faction"?

The same harassed, desperately concerned note was struck two years
later by William Godwin, trying his best to head off a final polarization
of forces, even at the price of criticizing his own friends on the extreme
reformist left: "The London Corresponding Society has been
thoughtlessly pursuing a conduct, which was calculated sooner or later
to bring on scenes of confusion." He remained confident that "reform
must come, it is a resistless tide," but precautions must be taken.

> In order to maintain the peace and tranquility of society, it is neces-
> sary to temporise. We must both accommodate ourselves to the em-
> pire of old prejudices, and to the strong and decisive influx of new
> opinions . . . . We must not stretch the strings of our instrument so
> far, as to put them in instant danger to snap.

Something was indeed in danger of snapping, when no forces were
there "to hold the balance even." Alarm on the right had led to a broiling
irritability, to folly, to a call for blood, to "an unscrupulous and sanguinary spirit." Godwin was horrified by the prospect of the new legislation
proposed in this atmosphere by Lord Grenville and William Pitt.

> The present bills force men into the extremest state of hostility; they
> leave no opening for treaty; they inculcate an obstinate and imprac-
> ticable temper upon both parties. At a time when conciliation is most
> necessary, they most deeply inspire into us sentiments of animosity.

Sir Philip Francis, who had unimpeachable radical credentials as the
chief instigator of the trial of Warren Hastings and as a founder of the
Friends of the People, tried to put the retreat to the center in another,
more positive way:

> At first sight, it looks like bravery to run into extremes; but I am sure
> that to keep the middle path, and to be ready to encounter the vio-
> lence of either side, or of both, when they unite, as they very often
> do, is the surest proof of political courage, as well as of public vir-
> tue.[52]

From this quarter came what were indeed new watchwords: conciliation, moderation, accommodation, compromise. It surprised no one that
they were to be taken not as matters of principle but only as desperate
tactics. And yet in that turbulent decade of the 1790s, when great European events greatly changed men's minds, the desperation was not
unconnected with sincerity. For more than a decade now, Christopher
Wyvill had been conducting his correspondence with Pitt in public, and

by 1796 he had few enough hopes that another letter would help win back the apostate. Yet he, like Mackintosh and Godwin, felt it imperative to win new space for the Reformers by blocking out a central area between "the wild projects of Paine" and "the wild counsels of Burke." Pitt was lost, Pitt had failed:

> Sound policy required him to hold a middle course between the two dangerous extremes of Paine and Burke.... Instead of shunning each of these inflammatory men, he flew from the turbulent Republican to embrace the factious Enthusiast of the Aristocracy. To the wildest flights of Burke's maddening imagination he nods approbation....

The sharper sense of his own lost cause and the growing feeling of failure had some maddening effect on Wyvill's own imagination, and a year later in the next exchange with Pitt (it was, alas, all one-sided) there was a reversion to the earlier formula of reform or revolution. A decade earlier, this stratagem had appeared to be—and would again appear so for the generation of 1832!—a legitimate and hopeful kind of blackmail: liberal concessions were to be wrested from a reactionary ruling class under threat of the direst catastrophe. Now it seemed at best a poignant cry for living space in a time of repression. In any event, it issued from such confused minds and battered hearts that only something like this emerged—the characteristically mixed metaphor of the day:

> It is but too evident that the fortress of our Constitution is in a delapidated state, and ready to overwhelm us beneath its ruins. It behoves us to repair with speed the venerable pile; to labour in this work of Love with unwearied assiduity; and with the wise counsel and assistance of those *Master Builders* in political architecture, to whom we are already so deeply indebted, to fortify and complete the spacious Tower of the Constitution, in which we and our Posterity may then rest securely protected against every foe, and safe from those storms and tempests, which, in the course of ages, may assail us.[53]

But in the early and high period of a radical movement's ingathering, when men are being rallied to the white light of a principle, the tone and the language and the whole militant thrust are, as we have seen, profoundly different. There is little concern with middle courses when the storm and tempest are themselves the natural agencies for good and true safety. Men of mitigation seem to be either cowards or knaves, and all worthy souls have no doubts about the choice between the noble animation of magnificent principles or the so-called fatal delusions of perilous speculations. And there is indeed little enough sensitivity to the darker elements of "madness," or of badness.

In the great political trial of John Horne Tooke in 1794, the attorney-general forced Major Cartwright as a defense witness to confront just this point: namely, "what persons he would take to his assistance in compassing the end he had in view." More specifically, the question was whether the Tookes and the Cartwrights and the Wyvills would work together "with people of different political principles, whatever their principles were." Cartwright's answer indicated his rigorous lack of concern over this calculated feeler toward some form of guilt by association: "I would take the assistance of any man whose end I thought right." He went on to be even more candid, realizing that his reply could be misunderstood as a defense only of the movement of right- and like-minded.

> I have signed many petitions for a reform in parliament, in company with men whom I have thought very bad men indeed; but there is no man so bad with whom I could not sign a petition and concur for obtaining that object.

In a word: there could, by definition, be no enemies in his own ranks or among his own allies. The comment by Chief Justice Eyre scored a point with which Major Cartwright never came to grips:

> That may be a very sincere declaration, but it is not a prudent one; because, in connecting yourself with bad men, you can never be sure that you may not be carried beyond your own purpose.

Prudence, however, was not a virtue to which, at the moment, persuasive appeal could be made. When purposes become redefined in the vague affinities of metaphorical language, one is no longer quite aware of exactly how far one is being carried along in a historic movement.

Here the metaphor was one of *fellow travelers* (and we will never hereafter be able to lose sight of this old horse-and-buggy of an image). John Horne Tooke stated that his object "did not go as far as Mr. Paine's." He spoke of "persons travelling in the same stage-coach, and getting out at different places ... " But getting off the moving stage-coach of reform would obviously present the same kind of dangers as (in the later trope) "jumping off the locomotive of history." For Cartwright, these were perils that were necessary and, in any case, unavoidable: for, as he insisted (his language, a contemporary noted, was one of "bold, nervous, animated eloquence"), he was a man not of prudence but of truth.

> As the matter originated in my having been asked if I would get into the stage-coach of reform, without regarding the company that might happen to be in the coach, or to that effect, I must also remark that he who has a necessary journey to take, and no means but by stage-coach, has not the choice of his company.

As his niece has written in her biographical memoir, "This opinion he never changed, and to the end of his life he never refused to join in any political act, which he himself approved, with any persons whom he believed to be travelling the same road."[54] But what happens when stage-coaches break down or, as occurs rather more often, fellow-travelers fall out among themselves?

There is still a final act in this drama of English ideology, a climax of doubt and disenchantment but also (as ideological cycles go) of "resurrection"; and it is these themes which will be dealt with in the next chapter.

15

Filled with enthusiasm, in very early youth,
by the promise of a better order of society, I
most unwarily ventured on publication, when my
judgment and taste were equally immature.... The
revolution continued so much to occupy my
thoughts, that I could not help consistently
exercising my judgment on it. I could not
forget it, nor shut my eyes on its events....

My changes were slow, and were still more
slowly avowed.... Like most other men, I was not
very fond of owning that I had been mistaken, or
of contradicting the opinion of those with whom
I lived, or of adopting any part of the doctrines
of those whom I had been accustomed to oppose....
I often reproached myself for being prevented
from speaking, as I thought, by false honour
and false shame. I sometime lamented the
peculiarities of my condition which seemed to
make concealment a virtue....

I can easily see that I rebounded from my
original opinions too far towards the opposite
extreme. I was carried too far by anxiety to
atone for my former errors. In opposing
revolutionary principles, the natural heat of
controversy led to excess....

I therefore take it upon me to rejudge my
past judgments.

—Sir James Mackintosh (1804)

The English Ideology: II

5. On the Stage of History
Melodramatic Conceptions—Theatricality and the Forms of Intellectual Life—Samuel Romilly in Paris—Barère and David: Anglo-French Stages (1792)—Tooke and the Pretense of Power—Rousseau's Theory of Theater and Politics—Machiavellian *Fantasia*—Henry Yorke: "Acting a Part on this Stage of the World"—Man the Dramatist—Anthropology and Dramaturgy—Marx on Tragedy and Farce—Huizinga's "Play and Nonplay"—William Cowper: "A French Tragedy on the State of England"?—David Hume and English Antipathies

6. Doubt and Disenchantment
The Short-Lived Consolations of Samuel Romilly, Arthur Young, William Cowper—John Horne Tooke and the "Fashion of Political Principles"—Mrs. Barbauld on the Treason of the Intellectuals (1793)—James Mackintosh and the End of an Ideology—Burke on "the Semblance of Public Happiness"—"Robbers of the Revolution"—Mackintosh and Godwin—A Napoleonic Misunderstanding—Ideologues and the Fear of Apostasy, Defection, and Renegadism—Mackintosh's Journey to a "Middle Position" (1800–32)

7. The Recantation of Henry Redhead Yorke
Reconsidering the "Just Cause"—Thomas Muir and Thomas Erskine—Yorke's Pamphlet on Release from Prison (1798)—A "Fatal Misapprehension"—Exotic Liberty or Rational Freedom?—Wandering in "the Boundless Regions of Chimaera"—A Personal Farewell to

Utopia and Revolution—Repentance and Confession—Yorke in the Louvre—From Darkness to Dawn: A Promethean's Stations of the Way—Shifting from Right to Left to Right again—Robespierre and Montesquieu—Calling on Théroigne de Méricourt (1793)—Paine and the Failed "Revolution of the World"—The Politics of Melancholy—Interviewing Jacques-Louis David, Unrepentant and Unreconstructed (1802)—Generous Minds, Moral Excess, and Political Atrocities—The Fatality of "the Revolutionary Whirlpool"

---

8. Disenchantment and Resurrection
The Half-life of Zealotry—A Backlash against the Cause of Reform—Selkirk's Explanation to Major Cartwright—The Dilemma of "Ultra-democratic Demagogy" and "the Evils of Plutocracy"—Polarizing Left and Right—Hazlitt and "the Trance of Theory"—The Once-kindled Spark and "Still It Burns" (1816)—The Central Axes of the Ideological Cycle—Center or Extreme, Stability or Chaos, Movement or Balance, Progress or Moderation—From Bentham to Mill—"The Revolution . . . is not English"—From Passion to Inertia—The Need for Menders in the World: Tooke, Cartwright, Wilberforce—Southey, Shelley, and the "Ghost" of the Youthful Past (1794–1812)

---

5. On the Stage of History

If there is a note of the melodramatic in James Mackintosh's self-confrontation it is (as I have had occasion to suggest) a consequence of the very theatricality which metaphor necessarily introduces into the forms of intellectual life. Just as fine phrases may be taken to act out a meaning, so do political rhetoricians appear to be performing on a special stage with lighting and sound effects that contrast dramatically with the play of events in ordinary relationships and discourse. So far as the theater of revolution is concerned, the English sensed the melodrama in the French, and the French sensed it in themselves. Samuel Romilly, after the first exciting events of 1789, "could not resist the desire of being a near spectator of them"; and his perceptive observations may be offered as representative of that dawning suspicion which overtakes the civic temperament when confronted with the ambiguous realities of a revolutionary romance.

Romilly went to Paris with a letter to Necker; he made the acquaintance of Mirabeau, the Abbé Sièyes, and the Bishop of Chartres; he heard

Robespierre ("but he was then so obscure, and spoke with so little talent or success, that I have not the least recollection of his person"). His shrewd and incisive summing up of his impression of that season when it was bliss to be alive is worth quoting, and not least because it reminds us that Tocqueville's and Flaubert's later development of this theme was not simply an exercise in national self-criticism.

> What struck me as most remarkable in the dispositions of the people that I saw, was the great desire that everybody had to act a great part, and the jealousy which in consequence of this was entertained of those who were really eminent. It seemed as if all persons from the highest to the lowest, whether deputies themselves, declaimers in the Palais Royal, orators in the coffee-houses, spectators in the galleries or the populace about the door, looked upon themselves individually as of great consequence in the revolution. The man who kept the hotel at which I lodged at Paris, a certain M. Villars, was a private in the National Guard. Upon my returning home on the day of the benediction of their colours at Notre Dame, and telling him that I had been present at the ceremony, he said, "You saw me, Sir?" I was obliged to say that I really had not. He said, "Is that possible, Sir? You did not see me! Why I was in one of the first ranks—all Paris saw me." I have often since thought of my host's childish vanity. What he spoke was felt by thousands. The most important transactions were as nothing, but as they had relation to the figure which each little self-conceited hero acted in them. To attract the attention of all Paris, or of all France, was often the motive of conduct in matters which were attended with most momentous consequences.[1]

Perhaps, in the theater of revolution, Romilly's impressions touch on only one small aspect of a walk-on role, giving us merely a minor English glimpse of a French extra. But even Bertrand Barère, once chairman of the Revolution's Committee of Public Safety, professed himself (at least in his recollections) to have been upset by the sheer role-taking effrontery of all the participants on the political stage. In the wonted tribal prejudice of the day, however, such histrionics were felt to be not a French failing but a foreign—more precisely, an English—vice. Barère tells how a band of Paris petitioners arrived to demand the death of King Louis XVI. They were, mostly, "women and children holding and waving in their hands torn garments and strips of shirts and cloth covered with blood." Before their case was put to the Assembly (it is the year 1792), they went through "hideous preparations [which] were well calculated to grip the imagination." There was "a tumultuous movement in the galleries" as they exhibited "attitudes of grief, misery, and despair." Finally came their spokesman, an orator of stentorian voice (Barère writes here as if he himself had not been one of the Revolution's most ferocious orators).

> His speech was full of that revolutionary energy and of that popular style which is calculated to inflame people's minds, especially when joined to the dangerous effects produced by that species of dramatic representation and by that spectacle of rags and blood-stained garments.

Barère's mind is cast back to the spectacle of Antony waving the blood-stained robe of Caesar in the Forum; and then he records that "The galleries cheered this petition with a violent unanimity which was terrifying." He claims that he tried, with calming words of his own, to work on the "pitch of agitation and public effervescence"; but to little avail.

> The Assembly seemed terrified and indignant, so revolting were these proceedings, which were suitable rather to the *English stage*.[2]

This was, of course, disingenuous on Barère's part; he was a close collaborator of his Jacobin colleague, the painter Jacques-Louis David, who had been brilliantly arranging the French stage in the new form of public political pageantry on behalf of the Revolution.

> David provided his multitude of actors with costumes, stage properties and emblems; he had them appear in gigantic ballets replete with evolutions, gestures and music; and he coordinated every detail of the program with the skill of a master stage manager. He presented each scene of his drama on a different open air stage—one of the public squares, quais or bridges of Paris. To assist him, David built up a team of specialists which included playwrights, theatrical directors, actors, choreographers and dancers as well as painters, sculptors and architects . . . . David's programs for the various *fêtes révolutionnaires* were the painter's most significant contribution to history.[3]

How far, then, from even the bottommost rungs of Hazlitt's ladder to Paradise—or from Romilly's theater of revolution and its democratization of all roles on the stage of history, or from Barère's notion of stage-struck English habits—were those poor English souls who assembled as the Society of Friends of the People and tried to give assurances that reform was to be not innovation but restoration, that (quoting Bacon) "Time is the greatest innovator"! The watchword of these parliamentary liberals was "temperate reform," and it was shared, as one historian records, by the flower of the young Foxite Whigs. But in the book of Jacobinical sympathizers it was only cowardly to deny that France was proving to be the model and the leader, and intolerable to turn away not merely from the passions of Paris but the politics of Paine. The author of *The French Revolution in English History* manages the conventional contempt: "The position of the moderate man, anxious to wash but not to get wet, was more than usually pathetic." (When Burke was to get cholerically into the argument, the watery metaphor would be matched by more colorful tropes: for was it not a matter of washing in blood?)

Another reformist club, the London Corresponding Society, seeking to expand its influence among working men, reinforced the moderate cause by its disavowal of "tumult and violence." As their adopted resolution had it: "Reason and firmness, and unanimity, are the only aims they themselves will employ, or persuade their fellow-citizens to exact, against abuse of power." They were convinced that an honest Parliament, representing the people at large, could remove all the chief grievances of the common man. Thousands of members held meetings, distributed pamphlets, paid dues.[4] If they appeared to be more influential than in all probability they actually were, it might be because they were shrewdly following that classic precept which *agit-prop* missionaries, sooner or later, come to formulate. Here it was, in the artful words of John Horne Tooke to the Friends of the People: " ... if you wish to be powerful, pretend to be powerful."[5]

This kind of artfulness—and wherever it took place: on the English stage, in a French town square, or in a Geneva theater—was precisely what Jean-Jacques Rousseau (ironically enough, when one considers his place in the Pantheon) had wanted to exclude from the new politics of Reality as against the theatrical politics of Appearance. In his famous letter of the *Citoyen de Genève* to d'Alembert in 1758, Rousseau abjured the aesthetics of deception and demanded above all authenticity and sincerity, consequently (for the good of the community) renouncing Molière as Plato had renounced Homer.

> What is the talent of an actor? It is the art of counterfeiting himself, of putting on another character than his own, of appearing different than he is, of becoming passionate in cold blood, of saying what he does not think as naturally as if he really did think it.[6]

Yet, when subsequently in *The Social Contract* (1762), he had to confront, at least in the form of social theory, the real political dilemmas of a free community as it involved itself in problems of legislation, oratory, and public persuasion, he found himself forced to recommend something less than transparency; indeed, a strategy of unnatural prudence and even a tactic of cool dissimulation seemed to be the only available means to the end of great and good government. His precepts as drama critic yielded to the exigencies of the political act. Here, too, Rousseau's spirit cast its troubled shadow over events to come.[7]

For the theatrical temper will out. Rousseau's first plan to ban the play of dramatic instincts in its entirety proved to be shortsighted. The same deep impulses which drove men into the fictional world of stage and story would also, despite any formal attempts at cultural censorship, contribute on very special occasions to making a spectacle of their public civic life. There was little to be faulted in Rousseau's view of the social function of the drama; what he appeared to be overlooking was the dramatic function of society. I am not seeking to play with words; the relationship is in fact a dialectical one. Rousseau deplored the politics of the theater, but he had to give way to the theater of politics. He objected to the factors of hypocrisy and social passivity in the classic apologies for the performing art: catharsis, the purging of emotions, and the ultimate residue of heightened human values (pity, love, justice).

> In giving our tears to these fictions, we have satisfied all the rights of humanity without having to give anything more of ourselves;
> whereas unfortunate people in person would require attention from us, relief, consolation, and work, which would involve us in their pains and would require at least the sacrifice of our indolence, from all of which we are quite content to be exempt.

But what happens in history when the rights of humanity have to be satisfied in a nonfictional situation? when men in social crises are actually impelled to offer attention, relief, consolation, and work? when pain and not pleasure is the order of the day, and restless energy displaces all indolence?

The spirit of such a happening is fully caught in the following passage, from the testimony of the state trial in 1795 in which Henry Redhead Yorke defended his revolutionary role in the dramatic events of French and English politics:

> A man feels an energy about him when embarked in a just
> cause ... that which is engendered by virtue, that which enables a man to kindle in the common blaze of liberty, and impels him in a time of danger, from an enlightened love of country, to be foremost, and to share its various fate, whether of destruction or of glory ....
> The public safety is not injured by those who assemble in public squares and meetings, and advance doctrines, couched in the spirit of error, but from those who never show their faces among the people, who never publicly avow any opinions, who temporize always between truths and falsehoods, or who undulate from one side to the other, as the tempest of opinions blow them ....
> It may be replied that these observations have a direct tendency to ferment the public mind, and to promote sedition; but to have right thoughts of things, and to communicate those thoughts to others, is the whole part we have to act on this stage of the world.[8]

Here we are dealing with theatricality and politics. In an essay of that title, Kenneth Minogue has offered a subtle and stimulating interpretation of Machiavelli's concept of *fantasia*: and it is precisely in the operations of *fantasia* that Minogue tries to locate the perennial source of political drama.[9] Politics, he writes, is "in a deep sense an exercise in theatricality.... Machiavelli is a dramatist.... His account of political skill is primarily an account of how to play upon the passions of an audience, the first condition of whose existence is that their attention must primarily be focused upon the stage of public affairs."

What Rousseau seems to have missed, therefore, is that the politics of the theater was only a special form of society's general involvement in the theater of politics. For some observers this notion functions merely as a trope, a familiar analogy: if all the world's a stage, then a politician is *like* an actor, a riot *resembles* a mass scene with thousands of extras, a governmental crisis moves from climax to climax *as if* it were a drama's denouément. For others, it is rather something more and different: and I share with them the suspicion that the virtues and vices of *homo theatricus*, of Man the Dramatist, antedate his particular activities on any formal stage. He plays, accepts roles, gives and takes cues, accommodates himself to changing casts and a mixed repertoire, shouts and whispers and gesticulates—because he is necessarily a player. Lights and curtains and a proscenium arch can, on occasion, help to provide special effects; but the live show would go on without them. It remains for the historians to reinforce this critical claim with a full documentation of human behavior—of man's actual, literal theatricality—in the "dramatic" situations of the recorded past.

One historian of the English seventeenth century quotes the following letter, written in 1643 by a Parliamentary commander in the civil war to his Royalist counterpart:

> ... hostility itself [writes Sir William Waller to Sir Ralph Hopton] cannot violate my friendship to your person, but I must be true to the cause wherein I serve ... with what a sad sense I go upon this service and with what a perfect hatred I detest this war without an enemy ... We are both upon the stage and must act the parts ... assigned us in this tragedy: let us do it in a way of honour and without personal animosities.[10]

Yet one could collect a thousand such suggestive documents and still not be quite sure, in the last analysis, whether one was dealing with simile or substance. That is to say, it is not so easy to tell whether men in history obey some deep theatrical imperative which recurrently gives a dramatic form to their so-called normal or natural behavior (anthropology would then be a form of dramaturgy); or whether man only acts as if his actions were being played out on the world's stage. This may well be a matter for epistemologists, philosophers of history, and metaphysicians of game theory. In any case, historians who do not confront, at the very least, the element of play in great historical events display a mistaken seriousness.[11]

The whole theme, one must be prepared to concede, is subject to the limiting and distorting influences of trends and fashions. "Theatricality" often becomes an *ad hominem* term to differentiate *my* reality from *your* illusion, my seriousness from your staginess. But then, dramatic conceits have always served as a function of polemic. Recall Marx's oft-quoted epigram from the opening paragraph of *The 18th Brumaire of Louis Bonaparte* to the effect that great events and personages happen for the first time as "tragedy" and the second time as "farce." This was a well-turned phrase, a testy put-down of Napoleon's nephew; but as an adaptation of Hegel it was essentially meaningless. It merely indicated that Marx, the drama critic of history, knew what he liked—if a historic event merited his applause, it was an authentic drama; if he was contemptuous, then it was simply ridiculous. My performance is Shakespearean, yours is a Punch-and-Judy show. Surely a tragedy, should it repeat itself, would still be tragedy (e.g., the First and Second World Wars). Surely there are some events in history which happen for the first time as farce and for the second time as tragedy (e.g., Hitler's *Putsch* first in Munich and then again, ten years later, in Berlin).

Nevertheless, the very usage of such terms underscores the link between the historian's presentation of past events and his sense that there was an aspect of dramatic representation in the original unfolding. "Civilisation today is no longer played," Huizinga wrote in *Homo Ludens*, "and even where it still seems to play it is false play—I had almost said, it plays false, so that it becomes increasingly difficult to tell where play ends and non-play begins. This is particularly true of politics." But, once again, in the absence of the clearest and mutually binding definitions of what is authentically playful (or tragic, comic, farcical), then my play is true and yours is not. We may be caught here in a maze without exit, until historical research presents us with a *wertfreie* dramaturgy.

Rousseau fulfilled his own role as drama critic only in the theater, and not in the marketplace. As a spectator (and he knew the dramatic repertory in both Paris and Geneva), he was concerned with the sociology of the formal stage and not with the psychology of the informal political spectacle such as was to take place in France, and elsewhere in Europe, not too long after his death.

In the final accounting, when a man has gone to admire fine actions in stories and to cry for imaginary miseries, what more can be asked of him? Is he not satisfied with himself? Does he not applaud his fine soul? Has he not acquitted himself of all that he owes to virtue by the homage which he has just rendered it? What more could one want of him? That he practice it himself? He has no role to play; he is not actor.[12]

This was by no means a final accounting. As we have seen, much more can be asked of a man. Dissatisfied with himself and even more with the world around him, driven on by the rage in his untranquil soul, he devotes himself to rendering homage to virtue in an unprecedented public commitment. What more could one want of him? To comprehend the dramaturgy of the great revolutions of his time; to find a new role to play; to be an actor.

But this was not an easy show in which to cast an Englishman. He would, again and again, find himself repelled by the extremism of sensibility and its "rude and boisterous" unpredictability. Just as David Hume came to find his friend Rousseau more and more intolerable (for he was "a monster," black, atrocious, frenzied),[13] so did a deep English antipathy to the exhibitionism of the theatrical personality, and to its habit of public overstatement, come to militate against ideological dramatics. It was a prejudice that was writing itself large in the national character.

6. Doubt and Disenchantment

As the course of the Revolution in France hurtled on, as faction displaced faction, with each claiming to be the only defenders of the pure and true revolutionary message and "the blade of the law" taking its toll of those heads that nodded wrongly, the ranks of English moderation began to swell. To those who had been prematurely skeptical came those who were belatedly disenchanted. Except for an obdurately sentimental handful who were permanently addicted to Hazlitt's paradisiacal visions, the visionary glory lasted only a summer or two, or (for a few) a short season longer. The news of massacres and invasions was dispiriting, and gods seemed once again to be failing. In May of 1794, Samuel Romilly, the law reformer, still appeared to be holding his ground, for the Revolution was, in spite of everything, "the most glorious event, and the happiest for mankind that has ever taken place since human affairs have been recorded ... " He was not oblivious to the degenerate aspects of these revolutionary years, but, in a distinction which would have been understood (and approved) by kindred spirits from John Milton to Leon Trotsky, he sought to save his faith in the principle or the theory from his doubts about the practice.

... and though I lament sincerely the miseries which have happened, and which still are to happen, I console myself with thinking
that the evils of the revolution are transitory, and all the good of it
permanent.

The consolation was short-lived. By September, his lamentation had
reached uncontrollable proportions: "How could we ever be so deceived ... !" He now saw only the vicious spectacle of victims and
executioners, and he bitterly concluded: "One might as well think of
establishing a republic of tigers in some forest of Africa as of maintaining
a free government among such monsters."[14] Thereafter the glory had
fled.

For others, the disenchantment had come a season earlier. Arthur
Young, whose *Travels in France* is one of the great documents of the end
of the *ancien régime* and the onset of the Revolution, recognized the
intellectual difficulties and the political dangers of having to change
one's mind. In *The Example of France a Warning to Britain* (1793), he confessed: "In attempting to give expressions adequate to the indignation
every one must feel at the horrible events now passing in France, I am
sensible that I may be reproached with changing my politics, my 'principles,' as it has been expressed." But day had turned into darkness.

> The Revolution before the 19th of August, was as different from the
> Revolution after that day as light from darkness; as clearly distinct in
> principle and practice as liberty and slavery; for the same man to
> approve therefore of both, he must either be uncandid or change-
> able; uncandid in his approbation before that period—changeable in
> his approbation after it.[15]

As yet another liberal spokesman put it, perturbed as he was that "we
have many spirits in the country eager to revolt, and act a French
tragedy on the stage of England,"

> I will tell you what the French have done. They have made me weep
> for a king of France, which I never thought to do, and they have
> made me sick of the very name of liberty, which I never thought to
> be. Oh, how I detest them! Coxcombs, as they are, on this occasion,
> as they ever are on all. Apes of the Spartan and Roman character,
> with neither the virtue nor the good sense that belonged to it. Is this
> treason ... ? I hope not. If it is, I must be a traitor.[16]

John Horne Tooke had also come a long way from his first impression
(as early as 1782) that "we were on the eve of a peaceful revolution, more
important than any which has happened since the settlement of our
Saxon ancestors in this country; and which will convey down to endless
posterity all the blessings of which political society is capable ... "

Slowly but surely, he foreshortened the perspective of endlessness and was prepared to settle for considerably less than "all" the blessings. At a tumultuous meeting of the Revolution Society in 1790, it was he who insisted on qualifying the enthusiastic messages of the extremists. England was not France, and Horne Tooke argued that "the English nation had only to maintain and improve the constitution which their ancestors have transmitted to them ... " To *maintain* and to *improve* were hardly the proper watchwords of even a peaceful revolutionary, but as he tried to explain—in a resolution which was ultimately accepted, although at first opposed "with tumult and vehemence"—each nation may well have a separate road forward and the English "have not so arduous a task to perform as the French ... " Still, it was a compelling task, and it would not be without its dramatic difficulties, although the drama appeared to be more in the words than in the deeds. His biographer and friend recalls of Horne Tooke that "no one was ever more ready to exclaim" these lines from *Hamlet*:

> ... Let it work,
> For 'tis the sport, to have the engineer
> Hoist with his own petard: and it shall go hard;
> But I will delve one yard below their mines,
> And blow them to the moon!
>
> [3.4.206–10]

More than that, as the biographer goes on to record, "it was always a maxim with Mr. Tooke, in the war of politics, to turn the *enemy's cannon on themselves* ... " One doubts whether very many—quite apart from the authorities, who were misled into fright and hysteria and put him on trial for sedition (he was acquitted)—ever took very literally this pre-Leninist counsel to turn the guns the other way.

But there was a continuing element of "sport," and the games that revolutionaries are led to play are sometimes fraught with unsporting consequences. In the years before his great state trial in 1794, Horne Tooke was closely watched. Spies reported on him, and he did not mind talking with the reporters ("a new name, first used about this period, to diminish the odium attached to the word spy"). One such reporter received from him alarming and terrifying confidences—and was duped with tales of political melodrama.

Mr. Tooke began by dropping remote hints, relative to the strength and zeal of the popular party, taking care to magnify the numbers, praise their unanimity, and commend their resolution. By degrees he descended to particulars, and at length communicated confidentially, and under most solemn promises of secrecy, the alarming intelligence, that some of the guards were gained; that an armed force was organized; and that the nation was actually on the eve of a revolution.[17]

Had the Revolution, then, already become a piece of fiction, a fable for fools, a tale signifying nothing?

The sport went on; others played the game: and it was Horne Tooke who was almost "hoist with his own petard." The following letter, written to him by a member of the Constitutional Society (and the tutor to the Earl of Stanhope's children), was intercepted, and absurdly enough it was taken by the uneasy government to confirm the worst fears of an imminent insurrection.

> DEAR CITIZEN,
> This morning, at six o'clock, citizen Hardy was taken away, by order from the secretary of state's office: they seized everything they could lay hand on.—Query, is it possible to get ready by Thursday?
> Yours,
> J. Joyce

The Joyce/Hardy affair led to a warrant, and Horne Tooke was arrested in Wimbledon early in the morning of 16 May 1794 and conducted to a prison cell in the Tower to await his trial for treason. (Among the others: Thomas Hardy, Thomas Holcroft, John Thelwall. All were found not guilty and were released to the cheers of a crowd outside the Old Bailey.)

The bit of cryptic prose from J. Joyce was found to mean something else altogether (something to do with "selecting from the court-calendar a list of all the places held by the Grenvilles, by way of throwing an odium on Mr. Pitt, his family and his abettors"). The so-called treasury of the insurrection was discovered to have a total revenue of about sixty guineas. Even Thomas Hardy's favorite tune was not found to be very incriminating.

> Plant, plant the tree, fair freedom's tree,
>   Midst dangers, wounds, and slaughter,
> Each patriot's breast, its soil shall be,
>   And tyrant's blood, its water.[18]

Playful and high-spiritied as ever, Horne Tooke offered to sing the song to the court just in case the treason might be lurking in the music. It could be that more humorlessness is required of a genuine revolutionary.

Even more resources of confidence and constant optimism were demanded than the most sanguine of reformers could steadily muster. Tooke, in rising to the defense of his lifelong unswerving devotion to his original political principles, declaimed: "I might have quitted them, as

Mr. Secretary [William Pitt] has done, and have received the reward of my treachery. But my politics will never be changed, nor be kept back on any occasion: and whilst I have my life, it will neither be embittered by any regret for the past, nor fear for the future."[19] In the chronicle of ideology, we have here a curious and perhaps inevitable human specta- cle: steadfastness allows for bravura, flexibility has a suggestion of shame and even personal defeat. It is worth noting that in this case, as in not a few others, the grand flourish of consistent inflexibility was made on the very eve of certain long-repressed changes of mood, attitude, and political principle.

Hope for change gave way to hope for a change in atmosphere in which hope for change could thrive again. In a dialogue which John Horne Tooke recorded in 1802, the new and somewhat saddened long- ing was clearly less for reform or revolution than for a reversal of the general trend, indeed for a new turn in "fashion."

> *F.:* Well, well. I did not mean to touch that string which vibrates with you so strongly.... Your political principles at present are as much out of fashion as your clothes.
> *H.:* I know it. I have good reason to know it. But the fashion must one day return, or the nation be undone. For without these princi- ples, it is impossible that the individuals of any country should long be happy, or any society prosperous.[20]

The string, as is its nature, did not vibrate so strongly for long. The principles which were to guarantee both happiness and welfare were in part attenuated, in part transformed. An aging John Horne Tooke went on to take his place as a Member of Parliament, disclosed to a perhaps surprised Commons that "I hate *innovation* in all things," argued his devotion to "established government" (although with an aside to his reforming friends, "*DO* but establish"), and saw no real inconsistencies with his past—for had he not always rejected "Paine Principles" and denounced those "ignorant men, far better calculated to pull down than build up governments"? Shortly before he died in 1812, at the age of seventy-seven, he drew up the text for his tombstone. It read: "CONTENT AND GRATEFUL."[21]

Our enthusiast of 1790, Anna Laetitia Barbauld, who provided us at the outset with many of the major ingredients of a revolutionary rhetoric, had also within a few years clearly changed her tone, once so pure and untroubled. She was now more obviously preoccupied with the an- guished problem of keeping "our hands clean"—for "ours is the blame, when the hurricane is abroad in the world, and doing its work of mis- chief ... " A beneficent storm had turned into a mischievous hurricane, but this clearly represented a change of mind and not merely of metaphor.

Mrs. Barbauld seemed to be groping tentatively, in her second thoughts of 1793, toward a critique of the political intellectual, his psychology and social function. Is there not a dangerous and irresponsible arrogance when the radical ideologue blithely assumes that he does in fact speak and act in the name of the People? Can it indeed be his true and viable role both to speak and to act, to unite theory and practice? And what of his penchant for revolutionary violence, for an impatient attempt when all seems desperate to force men to be free? She tried to explain.

> Reformers, conceiving of themselves as of a more enlightened class than the bulk of mankind, are likewise apt to forget the deference due to them. Stimulated by newly discovered truth, of which they feel the full force, they are not willing to wait for the gradual spread of knowledge, the subsiding of passion, and the undermining of prejudices. They too condemn a *swinish multitude*, and aim at an aristocracy of talents. It is indeed their business to attack the prejudices, and to rectify, if they can, the systems of their countrymen, but, in the mean time, to acquiesce in them. It is their business to sow the seed ... to prepare, not to bring about revolutions.

It was a striking adumbration of a later century's preoccupation with the chronic political failings of the intelligentsia, with the spectacle of what would come to be known as *la trahison des clercs*. Mrs. Barbauld did not hesitate to choose the people as against their self-appointed and ruinous representatives.

> The public is not always in the wrong for not giving in to their views, even where they have the appearance of reason; for their plans are often crude and premature, their ideas too refined for real life, and influenced by their own particular cast of thinking: they want people to be happy their way; whereas every one must be happy his own way. Freedom is a good thing; but if a nation is not disposed to accept of it, it is not to be presented to them on the point of a bayonet.[22]

With the passing of time, and the agitations of even more tumultuous events, Mrs. Barbauld made her withdrawal not merely from political action but even from public concernment. In a letter of 1814 she wrote: "I do not know what we can gather from the contemplation of all these revolutions, but this; that the concern and destinies of all the world are too high for us; that we must wait the winding up of the drama, and be satisfied in promoting and enjoying the happiness of our own little circle."[23] This mood is, as we have already seen (and will see again), part of the general atmosphere of ideological disintegration, which is almost always accompanied by a scaling down of dedication, and not infrequently by a complete collapse of high commitment.

Tooke, Mrs. Barbauld, and now James Mackintosh: there are three distinct patterns here. If the first represents an aging, fatigued reconciliation with the establishment of the day, and the second a world-weary, if sagacious, withdrawal from spurious ideological decison-making, the third is a remarkable effort to hold fast to a revised political commitment. We are almost at the end of an aberrant ideology. And, like so many post-ideological observers who, for one reason or another, find themselves withdrawing from the action and the passion, Mackintosh took his intellectual refuge in the "lessons of history."

> Of all the lessons of history, there is none more evident in itself, and more uniformly neglected by governments, than that persecutions, disabilities, exclusions—all systematic wrong to great bodies of citizens—are sooner or later punished; though the punishment often falls on individuals, who are not only innocent, but who may have had the merit of labouring to repair the wrong.

There was a touch of melancholy and of pathos here, but no more; it was a strikingly detached substitute for the fury and outrage of yesteryear.

> The French Revolution has strongly confirmed the lesson taught by the history of all ages, that while political divisions excite the activity of genius, and teach honour in enmity, as well as fidelity in attachment, the excess of civil confusion and convulsion produces diametrically opposite effects—subjects society to force, instead of mind— renders its distinctions the prey of boldness and atrocity, instead of being the prize of talent—and concentrates the thoughts and feelings of every individual upon himself—his own sufferings and fears.[24]

Perhaps these insights into the nature of utopian revolutionism strike us so forcefully (more so, indeed, than the related remarks of Burke) because they reflect more directly the "sufferings and fears" of a generation which had known its genius and honor, its fidelity and distinction and talent and mind. When it came to know its atrocity, there could only follow a great ideological disintegration, and we have already seen its multifarious fragments.

Almost alone among all the disenchanted, James Mackintosh had the political self-consciousness and personal self-control to maintain a certain special dignified posture in the wreckage. He tried, if fitfully, to stand erect in a place (to use his own phrase) on "the democratic side of the centre." His enlightened liberal efforts in India and his active role in putting through the Reform Bill of 1832 fulfilled his later years with (as Burke had predicted) "a great deal of service."

Eclectic reforms, sociology and psychology, and, especially, philosophical meditations on the lessons of history may seem to some committed critics to be taking the easier path ahead. In all of this journey, Mackintosh would appear, from the point of view of ideology—i.e., from the partisanship of an agitated, impassioned political moralism—to be escaping from fidelities and attachments. This may be true, but only in the sense that he had withdrawn himself from the stage of history and the theater of revolution, from the scene-stealing and false histrionics which always accompany the playing out of such melodramatic conceptions. He tried his best to put this point quietly.

> ... frequent changes of government, however arising, promote a disposition to acquiesce in change. No people can long preserve the enthusiasm, which first impels them to take an active part in change. Its frequency at last teaches them patiently to bear it. They become indifferent to governments and sovereigns. They are spectators of revolutions, instead of actors in them.

He now preferred another scenario. "Such revolutions, as those of England and America," he argued, only slightly troubled by the paradox of it all, were conducted with "a regard for moderation and humanity" and even with a "respect for established authorities and institutions." This, then, was the true way:

> The example of reverence for justice—of caution in touching ancient institutions—of not innovating, beyond the necessities of the case, even in a season of violence and anger ... [25]

But it had not been easy to put that violent and angry season behind him. Mackintosh had been only a young man of twenty-six when he won fame as the author of *Vindiciae Gallicae* (1791), generally held by his contemporaries to be the most effective reply to Edmund Burke (and still, in my view, the ablest ideological defense of the French Revolution ever written). In Aberdeen, he had been a schoolboy enthusiast of 1776; in Edinburgh, he had been influenced by Adam Smith, David Hume, Dr. Robertson, Adam Ferguson; in London, he immediately found himself at home in the radical circle of Horne Tooke. No, the break would not be easy when, as his own son was later to put it, "a day-dream of liberty became darkly overcast ... " In a letter which he finally brought himself to write to Burke in 1796, he still shows himself to be hesitant and of two minds.

> For a time, indeed, seduced by the love of what I thought liberty, I ventured to oppose, without ever ceasing to venerate, that writer who had nourished my understanding with the most wholesome principles of political wisdom. I speak to state facts, not to flatter: you are above flattery; and, permit me to say, I am too proud to flatter even you.

Since that time a melancholy experience has undeceived me on many subjects in which I was then the dupe of my own enthusiasm. I cannot say (and you would despise me if I dissembled) that I can even now assent to all your opinions on the present politics of Europe.

Burke replied to Mackintosh, not without some obvious satisfaction (but not without a bit of dissembling on his own part):

The view of a vigourous mind subduing by its own constitutional force the maladies, which that very force of constitution had produced, is in itself a spectacle very pleasing and very instructive. It is not proper to say anything more about myself, who *have been*,* but rather to turn to you who *are*, and who probably will be, and from whom the world is yet to expect a great deal of instruction and a great deal of service. You have begun your opposition by obtaining a great victory over yourself; and it shows how much your sagacity, operating on your own experience, is capable of adding to your own extraordinary talents, and to your early erudition. It was the show of virtue, and the semblance of public happiness, that could alone mislead a mind like yours. . . . As it is on all hands allowed that you were the most able advocate of the cause which you supported, your sacrifice to truth and mature reflection adds much to your glory.[26]

It was in a rather different mood that Burke tried frankly to evaluate how far his eloquent adversary had come along the road to "conversion." In a letter to a friend, he wrote this:

I forgot to speak to you about Mackintosh's supposed conversion. I suspect, by his letter, that it does not extend beyond the interior politics of this island; but that with regard to France and many other countries he remains as frank a Jacobin as ever. This conversion is none at all; but we must nurse up these nothings, and think these negative advantages as we can have them; such as he is, I shall not be displeased if you bring him down.[27]

Mackintosh was brought down to Beaconsfield, and a personal reconciliation between two great antagonists was sealed. But the "conversion" was still far from complete. Mackintosh was not yet there when he began thinking about a new political and philosophical work, as is clear from this letter from a friend who had been with him in the Friends of the People:

Jemmy, I will look at my old musty folios in the library; I will look out the passage in Aristotle, and will do any thing you wish, you dog. I have something to tell you about the simplification of principles, or rather the simpleton-jargon about R-r-r-eason, and you let us

---

*Burke was very ill, and was to die in 1797.

do the business well. I don't mean us, but you; and, you dog, nobody can do it better; nobody, I say—not Hume, not Adam Smith, not Burke, not Dugald Stuart; and the only exception I can think of is Lord Bacon. Yet, you dog, I hate you, for you want decision. . . . Oh! Jemmy! feel your own powers; assert your dignity: out upon vanity.[28]

The Bonapartist turn of events in France pushed him, finally, to a personal decision. With the "robbers of the revolution" at work, would "this accursed revolution be destined to be permanent"? He wrote to his friend George Moore to express his admiration for his honesty "in openly professing your conversion . . . "

> I think I shall have the courage to imitate you. I have too long submitted to mean and evasive compromises. It is my intention, in this winter's lectures, to profess publicly and unequivocally, that I abhor, abjure, and for ever renounce the French revolution, with all its sanguinary history, its abominable principles, and for ever execrable leaders. I hope I shall be able to wipe off the disgrace of having been once betrayed into an approbation of that conspiracy against God and man, the greatest scourge of the world, and the chief stain upon human annals. But I feel that I am transported by my subject to the borders of rant.[29]

How much was momentary rant and how much was mature reflection I shall leave to another place (for I mean to return to the intellectual career of Mackintosh more fully). Suffice it to record here that the lectures were delivered in London at Lincoln's Inn Hall during the winter of 1800, and, as Hazlitt reported,

> the effect was electrical and instantaneous . . . Dazzling others with the brilliancy of his acquirements, dazzled himself by the admiration they excited, he lost fear as well as prudence—dared everything— carried everything before him. . . . The havoc was amazing, the desolation was complete. As to our visionary . . . Utopian philosophers, they stood no chance with our lecturer; he did not 'carve them as a dish fit for the gods', but hewed them as a carcass fit for hounds.[30]

Hazlitt also noted that William Godwin himself had come to hear what new light had broken in upon his old friend. "Poor Godwin . . . was obliged to quit the field, and slunk away after an exulting taunt thrown out at 'such fanciful chimeras as a golden mountain or a perfect man.'"

There were moments during his years in faraway India when Mackintosh seemed to be deeply reluctant, even nervously so, to think back to the great French themes, to his own vision of a golden mountain and a perfect man.

A diary item for March 1811 (Bombay) has only this brief remark: "It is now about twenty years since I published my answer to Burke. It was not a brilliant dawn, but it promised a better day; we are now in the afternoon." The rather infelicitous, and in any case banal, analogy appeared to be sufficient political reconsideration for the moment. And, when a contemporary of his, Thomas Green, published in his own *Diary* an account of Mackintosh's conversations, there was positive annoyance. Nor did he hide the reasons for his being "more dissatisfied than flattered." He feared that this would constitute "one more proof of the various states of political feeling successively produced in my mind by the French revolution. This will be regarded as a new proof of my inconsistency in the judgment of the vulgar." After his public confession of conversion in London in 1800, how is it that he was still reluctant to display such candor? Again, in England a few years later, he noted taciturnly that in a number of the *Yellow Dwarf* ("a democratical weekly paper, printed at two pence"), he found "strong quotations from the *Vindiciae Gallicae*, and many compliments to my former talents, contrasted with my present opinions and powers." He was, perhaps, not yet prepared to surrender that glowing image of the angry young man of the 1790s.[31]

Although in its way the publication of the *Vindiciae Gallicae* was the greatest single moment in his life, the work had slowly with the years become something of an albatross. What reply could Mackintosh have mustered up for Napoleon Bonaparte when the First Consul, as he then was, asked to see him in Paris? Would it have been, "Sire, I am no longer a defender of your faith"? For Napoleon had intended to pay him "many compliments upon his reputation as a writer, and particularly as the author of *Vindiciae Gallicae* ... " But, as it happened, in a crowded room, Napoleon confused the various introductions to his English guests and the ambivalent compliments were paid to the wrong man; Mackintosh was spared both the praise and the embarrassment. There was something symbolic about the confusion in this encounter between the French revolutionary and the English ideologue, the one proud of principles he no longer truly represented, the other ashamed of principles he could no longer maintain.[32]

All ideologues have a mortal fear of the dreadful charge of inconsistency—of apostasy, defection, and renegadism—that lurks implicit in any attempt to reconsider a strong state of political feeling or to revise a basic tenet of doctrinal belief. Is it possible, even if it were desirable, always to persevere? What secret, seductive human merit is there in the spectacle of a sage of firm, changeless convictions? Does God's angry man, in standing there and doing no other, suggest some steadfast perfection in an otherwise mutable and corrupting world?

Both aspiration and anxiety are involved in this aspect of the ideological psyche. The factor of hope—the deep longing for firm, undeviating, even inert rectitude—is associated with a related component of fear: the fear of betrayal, weakness, of selling out. Here we can detect traces of the trauma that afflicts all spirits in Christendom, the Judas syndrome: going over to the other side, to the oppressors and crucifiers, or (in later, more secular dramas) to the aristocrats and the class enemy. Given the fact that a revolutionary ideology always aspires to a total coherence which is held together emotionally by an inner frame of high confidence and enthusiasm, each little doubt and passing mood of hesitation becomes devious and dangerous.[33]

Thus, Holcroft is upset to the point of painful consternation when he hears in 1798 of Mackintosh's plans for his series of London lectures. We must recall that for men of Holcroft's and Godwin's indestructible faith in progress, these were the years in which the utopia of perfectibility had seemed very imminent indeed. Godwin's notion of a harmonious "law-less society" appeared practical, desirable, and around the corner. Holcroft finds a passage in Boswell's *Life of Johnson* which, as he records in his diary, leaves him "highly gratified"—it referred to a possible condition of human life, to "a state of reciprocal benignity in which laws shall be no longer necessary ... " It can therefore be imagined with what shock the signs of Mackintosh's apparent defection would be observed. The alarm is sounded about a possible apostate, as in this passage in Holcroft's diary:

> I learn *Mackintosh* intends to read lectures on law; in which political government is to be introduced, and the established systems of this country highly praised. Expressed the pain I felt, that a man of such superior powers should act so false a part, and so contrary to his convictions, of which I must, in all human probability, be able to form a tolerably accurate opinion, from the many conversations I have had with him. His judgment was (and doubtless, still is, for his faculties are in their full vigour) so clear, his perceptions so penetrating, and his opinions so decided, that I can conceive no possibility of their being so totally changed.[34]

This general problem and poignant ordeal—of changing one's opinions, mixing praise and dispraise of a so-called system, playing a true part—kept gnawing away at Mackintosh's intellectual equanimity.

> A degree of wisdom is certainly conceivable, which would have reached principles and habits of feeling so comprehensive as to have adapted themselves to every succeeding convulsion without change, and of course without excess; but probably no man in Europe had attained this exalted perfection. The consistency of the far greater

number arose either from ignorance, from obstinate party spirit, from blind enthusiasm, from fear of the shame of inconstancy, and from motives of policy still more sordid. In the three former it was irrational, in the two latter it was insincere.

"If I had," Mackintosh concludes modestly, and thus nicely postponing the matter for another day, "Lord Bacon's power of illustration I could make clear my own middle position between the sage and the multitude."[35] We will be hearing more from him and his contemporaries about this middle position.

7. The Recantation of Henry Redhead Yorke

There came a time when Henry Redhead Yorke had only tears for the drama and apologies for his part "on this stage of the world." Had the expenditure of all that energy truly been on behalf of a just cause? If his doctrine had been "couched in the spirit of error" (this was, at the time, only a rhetorical concession to the jury trying him), would not any slight bit of temporizing between truth and falsehood, between one side and the other, have served the public interest better? How could he ever have been so outraged, so "insulted" in fact, by what he once felt in that earlier period to be an *abject* idea to "distrust the powers which nature has given us"; the *passive* notion to "acquiesce in institutions which, though injurious, may be preferable to those that may be endured by others"; the *foolish* attitude to "balance between tolerable vices and positive good, between unnatural systems and novel untried but just maxims"? Were not these the very ideas, notions, and attitudes that increasingly appeared to him to be the better part of political wisdom? What seductive pride had impelled him to want to be "foremost," to kindle in a "blaze of liberty," to seek to share in the glory of man's fate even at the risk of "destruction"?[36]

The jury at the York assizes had found him guilty of "unlawful combination and conspiracy," and the judge had given him a sentence of two years. Some of the dissenters of the day had been acquitted, some convicted. Thomas Muir in Edinburgh had declined Thomas Erskine's legal services because he insisted on determining for himself the conduct of the case; he was, frankly, less interested in "getting off" than in promoting the cause. Like Muir, Henry Yorke rather mismanaged his own defense—[37] although the Yorkshire legal atmosphere was mild in comparison to the illiberal fury which reigned in Lord Braxfield's Scottish courts and which sent radicals like Muir and Maurice Margarot to Botany Bay for fourteen years.

Yorke—who later was admitted to the Inner Temple as a barrister and also achieved a reputation as a scholar—had read much and reflected deeply in his prison cell. He emerged in 1798, after his years of confinement in Dorchester, with the manuscript of *A Letter to the Reformers*, which he promptly rushed into print.[38]

Yorke's pamphlet was addressed to those "who have been egregiously misled by the artifices of demogogues," or—he was candid enough to add—"by the fatal misapprehension and enthusiasm of men like myself." A strange extremism had been at fault: " ... the exotic plant of French liberty (and I call it so, in contradistinction to rational freedom) was admired and received by us, neither with sobriety nor prudence." It had all been a "foolish intoxication." Once he had been certain: "The human mind is progressive; so is the social mind." Now he saw complexities in the progressive faith.

Henry Yorke was reverting to the traditional vocabulary of older English ideologists: to sobriety, prudence, caution, care. These, he now discovered, had been most admirable features of the English past: "our forefathers at the time of the revolution," whether they were "new-modelling" or restoring, "affected no visionary schemes of speculative perfection." The intellectual differences, as he distinguished them, between exotic libertarianism and the movement for rational freedom were that the one offered chimerical visions and the other faced real historical dilemmas.

> What is just or unjust? What constitutes the happiness or misery of nations? What in their various situations is favourable or adverse to their good qualities? What is the highest point of felicity to which communities may aspire?—are all questions of the greatest importance, and are to be derived from the materials with which we are furnished by the lights of history. The love of novelty and system has, notwithstanding, prompted ardent imaginations to reject his mode of reasoning, and to wander in the boundless regions of chimaera.

He was, for all the elevated tone of argument, making a personal farewell to both utopia and revolution. He was breaking with his former life as a "Utopian artist" and as a political pilgrim to some new "Holy of Holies."

> ... in the universal uproar which succeeds the reign of laws, the abettors of such a system, awaken from their delirium, and retire with affright from the monster which they have raised. But the repentance of the Utopian artists comes too late; the tumult of the passions are not so easily asswaged; and they are doomed to be mortified spectators, perhaps victims, of a howling storm, which they

perceive it is easier to set in motion, than to appease. I speak feelingly.

This felt note of repentance gives a confessional character to the whole text, although Yorke attempted to explain how revolution degenerates into imperialism, why the rage of innovation had become "too general and too violent," why even his old guiding lights (Pym, Sidney, Locke) were less relevant than his old friend Condorcet's plea for gradualism in the struggle to "obtain a freedom more effectual, more substantial." The inner essence of his recantation was reserved for his last two pages.

I have now done. By thus openly declaring my sentiments, I may incur blame or excite malevolence. . . . My principles, religious and political, are certainly different from what they were when I entered the prison. I am prepared, if it be necessary, to explain the causes of that change. I solemnly declare that I have nothing to hope from any party; from ministers or from opposition. I am totally unconnected with either. Altho' I have deeply and severely suffered from long imprisonment, both in fortune and domestic happiness, and altho' I have been invited to repair the mischiefs by entering again on political engagements, yet I will not sacrifice my future tranquillity to temporary advantages, nor my opinions to interest. If through me, the country have been wounded, I implore its forgiveness, and sincerely pray that the evils which may arise from any misconduct of mine, may light on my head, and not on Great Britain; and that in charity to the failings of human nature, it may be ascribed to the levity and inconsiderateness of youth . . . . * If for such opinions, I am destined in an ill-fated hour of my country to be led to the scaffold, I shall willingly resign my life, in testimony of a constitution, the beneficent effects of which I have felt even in the melancholy solitude of a prison.

Some years later, when he had recovered from these lingering traces of his old penchant for melodramatic self-presentation, he found himself tranquilly calling on the painter David in his apartment in the Louvre. He astonished himself, as he recorded in one of his published letters from France, by calmly "sitting down under the roof of a man who actually signed a warrant for my arrest some years ago."[39] But it was all in another country, and besides the revolution was dead. "But in this capital these things are of course, and quite as natural as if in the year 1793 I had dined with him, and in the evening he had sent me to prison, and two days after to the guillotine." Here indeed was ideology recollected in tranquillity.

*Yorke's footnote: "I was only *twenty-two* years of age when I was first imprisoned, and have remained nearly four years in custody."

It would be useful to remind ourselves of the stations on the untranquil way Henry Redhead Yorke had come. The decade had been an ebullient one, beginning with the excitement on the streets of Paris (in 1792) as he wandered among "a nation of Gods." For him, the high climax came with his fiery Yorkshire pamphlets of 1793–94 on behalf of reason and revolution[40] and his wildly acclaimed speech in Sheffield on 4 April 1794. It moved to a dramatic and unexpected denouement with his confession and recantation after his release from jail (in 1798) and his final summing up of the splendors and miseries of his career as a utopian revolutionary (in a posthumous work, written in 1802 and published in 1814, entitled *Travels in France*). In a period of ten years, he encompassed one of the basic cyclical patterns of revolutionary ideology. Let us recall the ringing phraseology with which the young man had first committed himself.

Dazzled by the prospect of a new dawn after all the darkness and filled with a detestation of established evils, prepared for a career of plotting and scheming and conspiring in order to break all chains and to make a clean sweep, ready to apologize in advance for any chaos and anarchy that might be part of a necessarily wild transitional phase (indeed it might even be necessary, in the fury and the agony, to sacrifice a whole generation), he was invincibly armed with the certainty that all power would be seized by the poor and the oppressed, that it was, after all, the final conflict, that universal emancipation, peace on earth, and the world brotherhood of man were the sweet prizes of the future.

This is the way these principles, passions, and prejudices emerged in one ideologue's historic eloquence. Or: how a young Promethean committed himself to that generous zeal which (as he would later observe of himself and other "Utopian artists") inspired nothing but "holy insurrections against established authority" and led to the exterminating fury of revolutionary inhumanity, to that boundless permissiveness in which *"any thing* may be done."

1. Darkness before Dawn.

Gaiety, joy, hilarity, are banished from our island; a fixed gloom and melancholy have seized us; the heart is no longer glad; and every man suspects an enemy in a friend . . . . Men think little, say nothing, and are afraid of reasoning; they are even alarmed at their own ideas. Mistrust and terror form the basis of the general manners. The citizens live separate from each other, and the whole nation becomes melancholy, pusillanimous, stupid, and silent. Such is the scale of misfortune and degradation to which Despotism or Inequality would reduce the human race. But observe the celestial walk of sweet EQUALITY.[41]

2. Detest and Destroy.

COMRADES! We are at length arrived to the period of emphatic distress.... Party leaders of all kinds are unmasked, and proved to be conspirators against the People.... The *Ins* and *Outs* are alike your common enemies. The *Ins* wish to keep their places, the *Outs* wish to get *in* them. *Men*, and not *Principles*, are the object of the contest; *Power*, and not Freedom, the cause. *You* are to be the reward and spoil of the conquering party....

But the merchants of the Exchange, and the politicians of St. James's, should reflect that the happiness of a people is not to be estimated by the abundance of wealth and the extent of territories; both of which are capable of sapping the foundations of national freedom....

Citizens! the day of account and retribution is at hand. Then will the people be called upon to exert all the severe energy of Justice.... A vast majority of the people are excluded from their lawful rights, and consequently there must always be a strong party who hate and detest the government, and who must at different periods acquire strength, and trouble, convulse, or finally destroy it.[42]

3. Break the Chains.

The contest is between principles opposed to errors, Man opposed to his Oppressors; it must therefore be great and terrible. A system rooted in the soil of a country, and deriving a sacredness from prescription, appears to be a powerful obstacle to the efforts of the oppressed. But if men would analyse governments, they would discover that they are excessively weak, and are upheld only by those chains of prejudices and circumstances, by which they hold mankind in awe. Break but these chains, and the whole scaffolding of authority falls to the ground. The trumpet of political salvation has been sounded in triumph through Britain.[43]

4. The Clean Sweep.

Nor ought a people ... labouring under oppression, to await the operation of some unexpected vicissitude, which may happen in the slow revolution of ages, to effect a sudden transition to happiness from the extremity of miseries.... When corruptions have mounted to their climax, then it is that unskilful legislators are for applying temporary repairs, instead of prudently sweeping the whole away, and beginning afresh.[44]

5. Three Great Revolutions.

The ever memorable revolution of America promoted a spirit of enquiry and discussion, that soon made men long after Freedom. At this period Reason, with her offspring Liberty, were recalled from their long exile, into the cabinets of Philosophers, and the strangers were welcomed into the homely mansions of Poverty. Like the periodical overflowings of the Nile, their return has excited an universal joy . . . . Overlapping a vast chaos of prejudices and abuses, the French nation rushed at once into Liberty, and exhibits a brilliant Aurora to an astonished world. She is now moving in magnificent splendour towards her meridian, from whence she will scorch and consume the Tyrants of the Universe . . . . It has only enlarged the sphere of enquiry, which pervades the [British] nation with the swiftness of wildfire, and will, though at present taking a subterranean passage, in despite of every effort to prevent it, BURST FORTH WITH A TERRIBLE EXPLOSION, WHEN AND WHERE IT IS LEAST EXPECTED![45]

6. All Power to the Powerless.

During all ages, the repose of the world has been distributed by the agitation of one great, though simple question—not whether there be power, nor whence it came, but *who should have it* . . . . In the general poverty and wretchedness of the people, we can easily discover for whom Government was made. On all sides, there is a conspiracy of the Great to oppress the poor; and laws, instead of opposing, have sanctioned this guilty league, by conferring on the one both power and influence, and by reducing the other to the extremity of wretchedness and ignorance . . . . And as a law of coercion prevails everywhere, as Truth itself cannot be whispered without danger, and personal security is at the mercy of hired and miscreant informers, and a worse than Spanish Inquisition established throughout our country, in contempt of its Constitution and Laws, I think it is high time that we come to a speedy and definitive settlement with our Rulers.[46]

7. Plotting and Scheming.

It is oppression alone that ferments the public mind, and animates men to conspire the overthrow of a rotten Government, a wicked Minister, or a despotic King . . . . By an electric and general resurrection of Reason, the palsied faculties of man are put into motion . . . . And now that I mention [Algernon] Sidney, I feel my heart glow with a patriotic fervour, and I glory to hold up his life, writings, courage, and even his death to the imitation of Englishmen. He was ever plotting and scheming the subversion of a cruel and iniquitous system of oppression.[47]

8. The Sacrifice of a Generation.

Almost all the revolutions that have happened were turbulent, bloody, and unprincipled; but surely no good man will think that a revolution giving happiness to the present age, and transmitting a rich bequest to future generations, leaving to their discretion the liberty to correct, improve, pawn or annul that inheritance in favour of a better, no one will think that such a revolution is dearly earned, altho' a whole generation perish in the contest.[48]

9. A Time of Wildness.

For, believe me, I would rather live in the world, when it is run wildest, than tamely breathe under a Government which is nothing but disorder, and which destroys all those affections that would flourish, unsullied, even in a disorganized state of society ... Encouraged by that liquid fire that sweeps prejudice from the earth, the people may prefer for a time society without a government, rather than tolerate a government that breaks the harmony and peace of society, and affords to a band of despots a perpetual scramble for power.... It is a common remark in China, that at the eve of a revolution, there is always a great increase of rigorous punishments.[49]

10. The Afro-Asian Fury.

I call every man a tyrant who holds another in chains. Relinquish your colonies.... But it is not the Slave Trade only, that ought to be abolished; you should strike at the root of the evil, and exterminate SLAVERY itself. Throughout every nation of the earth, let the oppressed awaken from their drunken sleep;—let the African, the Asiatic, the European, burst asunder their chains, and raise a pious war against tyranny. Should tyrants, sensible of the indignant temper of the oppressed, refuse to expiate their crimes by a voluntary renunciation; should they wrestle with Freedom, let the PEOPLE roll on them in a tempest of fury, and compel them to expire in agonies![50]

11. Peace or War.

War can never benefit the PEOPLE, because their happiness consists in order, plenty and liberty, and as it discomposes all these, they must be plunged sooner or later into an abyss of misery. It is commonly proclaimed in haste, and always conducted in cruelty (for what is honourable war, but honourable butchery?) and its most inevitable consequence, is, the loss of some portion or other of public liberty.... THEY declare wars at random—it is the wretched lot of the PEOPLE to wage them.... Happy had it been for the sons of the earth, if their crowned and mitred Tyrants, instead of delivering up to massacre, millions of useful beings, to avenge their quarrels, and those of their harlots, had erected a public Theatre, and with poignards in their hands, exhibited to the world the utility and glory of war. One generous example would have curbed the unbridled fury of future heroes, the lives of millions have been saved, and the world been this day in peace. But the times are at length accomplished:—a mighty change has taken place in the reasoning of man, and tyrants know it—and tremble. The political world begins to move, and the awful voice of the people is heard. The hand of oppressed nations is about to dwell heavy on the oppressor, and Europe may congratulate itself that War is on the wane, and that a final and terrible blow will be given to those ferocious and unjust plans of murder, which have for ages past, desolated the fairest portions of the earth.[51]

12. The Final Conflict.

There never was, nor ever will be again, a war like the present. It is the last of Europe. It is a war of twenty-eight million of human beings, contending for everything that is dear to man, against a few kings vainly attempting to subjugate them.[52]

13. World Brotherhood.

Benevolence is of no country, but embraces within the wide circle of her arms, from Lake Huron to the wall of China, the brotherhood of the human race.[53]

14. Living in the Universal Future.

Doubtless the moment of universal emancipation is far off; but the contemplative man, who is a friend to the human race, lives much beyond his own age, and becomes the contemporary of distant times. Future generations occupy his care, their sorrows afflict him as sensibly as those of the present age; he feels an interest in the universal happiness of the world, and lives for ever with all nations.[54]

Taken together, all this amounted to a rare and extraordinary ideological configuration, almost unrivaled in its range of revolutionary imagery and ethico-rhetorical richness till the age of Marxism and the apocalyptic Left. But within ten years it was in a shambles. Events forced second thoughts, as Henry Yorke reconsidered his "utopian artistry" in a Dorchester Castle cell.

Nor was it the first time that his beliefs had been undermined. For all the momentary fanaticism of his powerful convictions, Henry Yorke was not temperamentally averse to changing his mind. He had done so once before, at the very outset of his political career; "having ardently espoused the cause of Despotism," he subsequently admitted embracing "a contrary mode of thinking," thus initiating one of the first of the great modern intellectual moves from right to left and then back again. Coming from the West Indies, he had made a defense of Negro slavery and the economic advantages of a colonial empire. This left him with a strong sense of guilt, but also with a lively eagerness to cope with it openly. "I have injured the wretched Negro, by formerly denying him his rights. In the sincerity of my heart, I spoke not what I thought, but what I believed I thought. The only retribution I can make, is to see him righted." In the previous century, such ideological conversions were less public; and he would have been labeled a "turn-coat," not unlike Marchamont Nedham, whom in many ways he resembled. Now the political confession was becoming a new literary genre. "I am not ashamed publickly to avow that I am that changeling, and apostate."[55]

Henry Yorke's quarrel with the Revolution—less abstract than James

Mackintosh's, more far-reaching than Thomas Paine's—brought him into a state of even profounder apostasy. The differences, at once personal and political, had accumulated over the years; and they had actually begun in his turbulent time in Paris when there had been the elements of both factional rancor and personal danger, usually a potent recipe for ideological estrangement and ultimate defection. I have already noted the incident of his falling out with his Jacobin comrades, his denunciation and near-arrest as he fled for his life. This could not have been an altogether unexpected turn of events. Yorke recalls a conversation with Robespierre in which the Jacobin leader had given him an "awful rebuke" for extolling *The Spirit of the Laws*—no, Montesquieu had a weak, dogmatic, prejudiced mind and was nothing but *un parlementaire*, not at all *un bon républicain*. "I need not here tell you the effect," Yorke writes, "which this stroke of criticism wrought upon me, for when I heard that Montesquieu would have been less by a head, had he fallen into Robespierre's hands, I felt such an unpleasant tickling in my neck, that the argument *convinced* me in a moment." Perhaps it was here, on the spot, that the suspicion began to dawn on him that the vaunted violence of profound social change might be less metaphor than murder. For the moment, the public safety of the Revolution commanded his political approval; but it could not have personally escaped him that this did not necessarily entail the private safety of any revolutionary.

Yorke also recalls his meetings in Paris with Théroigne de Méricourt, whom he found "young, handsome, humane, well-informed" but also "wild, savage, and ferocious."

> One day she invited me to breakfast with her, and on my entering her apartment, the first objects that struck my sight were a pike, a dagger, a broad sword, a brace of pistols, and the *bonnet rouge* suspended over her chimney-piece; scattered about the floor lay about a hundred volumes and pamphlets, on her bed the Paris Journals, and on her table, *L'Ami du Peuple* by Marat. On my inquiring "why a lady of her charms"—(I was going to say, kept such dreadful instruments in her room)—
>
> "No compliment, Citizen, society is undergoing a grand reorganization, and women are about to resume their rights. We shall no more be flattered in order to be enslaved; those arms have dethroned the tyrant, and conquered freedom. Sit down and take your chocolate."
>
> The countenance, tone, and manner in which this chastisement was conveyed, left no room for reply; I obeyed her mandate, and was submissive during the rest of the morning.

Yorke's fellow radical in Paris, John Sheares, had evidently fallen in love with Théroigne, and in the hope of giving up politics and retiring into private life he had proposed marriage. "When he tendered his proposals, she pulled a pistol from her pocket, and threatened to shoot him if he uttered another syllable upon the subject." The end of the story, as Yorke bitterly records, was that Sheares was hanged as a rebel in Dublin a few years later, and Théroigne went slowly mad and was committed to a Paris asylum.[56]

I mention these anecdotal details because it is in the context of this remembrance of things past that Henry Yorke finally tried to make a serious reckoning, larger and more reflective in scope but still (unlike that of Sir James Mackintosh, as we have seen) never very far removed from the aching personal experience of revolutionary events. When he returned to Paris in 1802, he revisited the hotel in the Rue Coqueron where he had resided in 1792–93; he looked in at the Convention hall where he had been present at the trial of King Louis; he sought out his old friend Thomas Paine and found him living despondently in a bookseller's apartment in the Rue du Théâtre Français ("Republic! do you call this a Republic? Why, they are worse off than the slaves of Constantinople."). Yorke had known many of the leading French political figures, and he now almost lost himself in the memories of "death and devastation."

> Why am I not blessed with the faculty of forgetfulness? Why cannot I forget myself? . . . I will drop a tear on this part of my history, and endeavour to blot it out for ever from my mind.

This was not so easily done, especially after his extraordinary confrontations with Thomas Paine and Jacques-Louis David—the one disillusioned and disenchanted, the other unrepentant and unreconstructed[57]—which gave him, at long last, the personal, face-to-face points of departure for his rather reluctant and much-postponed attempt to reflect on the revolutionary personality.

There are some superb passages in Henry Yorke's account of his elegiac interview with Paine, and the whole of it should one day be reprinted.[58]

> After I had waited a short time, Mr. Paine came down stairs, and entered the room, dressed in a long flannel gown. I was forcibly struck with his altered appearance. Time seemed to have made dreadful ravages over his whole frame, and a settled melancholy was visible on his countenance. He desired me to be seated, and although he did not recollect me for a considerable time, he conversed with his usual affability. I confess I felt extremely surprised that he should have forgotten me; but I resolved not to make myself known to him, as long as it could be avoided with propriety.

When they did finally get to conversing about the old fraternal days, it was in the spirit of the traditional English coolness toward French political culture and character which has been a recurrent theme in these pages.

> They have shed blood enough for liberty, and now [Paine remarked ironically to Yorke] they have it in perfection. This is not a country for an honest man to live in; they do not understand any thing at all of the principles of free government, and the best way is, to leave them to themselves. You see they have conquered all Europe, only to make it more miserable than it was before.

Yorke was shown some of Paine's manuscripts, and he took the trouble to copy out one passage, underlining every word.

> As for myself [Paine wrote], I used to find some relief by walking alone in the garden after it was dark, and cursing with hearty good will the authors of that terrible system that had turned the character of the Revolution I had been proud to defend.
>
> I went but little to the Convention, and then only to make my appearance; because I found it impossible for me to join in their decrees, and useless and dangerous to oppose them. My having voted and spoken extensively, more so than any other member, against the execution of the King, had already fixed a mark upon me: neither dared any of my associates in the Convention to translate, and speak in French for me any thing I might have dared to have written.[59]

Young Englishmen of Yorke's generation were being constantly surprised by the disjunction between English preconceptions and the French scene, by the shadow which fell

> Between the conception
> And the creation
> Between the emotion
> And the response ...
> Between the desire
> And the spasm
> Between the potency
> And the existence
> Between the essence
> And the descent ...[60]

Outraged by the course of what Paine had hoped would be (as he put it in his famous London Tavern toast of November 1791) "the Revolution of the World," he was, especially after his own imprisonment, as good, as experienced and instructive, a guide to the falling shadow as could be had. Once, at a Paris dinner, a youthful visitor from London noted with some puzzlement how well-known political enemies of the 1790s could still meet and talk, and Paine took the trouble to explain: " ... Paine smiled, and said, that in the course of the Revolution persons dined together for the purpose of making each other talk, and then denounced the conversation to the Committee of General Safety."[61]

Perhaps more than any other single factor, it was this immoral "spirit of denunciation" which Paine felt to be the cause of the internecine fratricidal warfare among the revolutionaries and thus of the ignoble descent of the noble cause. Yet Paine had no other ethical alternative but to offer punishment for the men of punitive violence, to turn the charges of treason the other way.

> If every individual is to indulge his private malignancy or his private ambition, to denounce at random and without any kind of proof, all confidence will be undermined and all authority be destroyed. Calumny is a species of treachery that ought to be punished as well as any other kind of treachery. It is a private vice productive of public evils; because it is possible to irritate men into disaffection by continual calumny who never intended to be disaffected.[62]

Obviously, Paine himself was one of those so disaffected. It is always late in the day when revolutionaries come to realize the missing elements in a boundless commitment of total enthusiasm, namely, the bounds and limits which give meaning and definition to a theory of liberty and justice. Is there anything which a revolutionary may not do? Was it desirable for the plea of historical necessity always to amount to a limitless license? And who was there—or what was there, in the absence of an effective constitution of liberty—to draw a line, somewhere, anywhere?

Even the best of friends could evidently think of no way to avoid escalating differences of political opinion into grave suspicions of treason. Barère was one of Paine's closest colleagues in the Convention, but it was Barère who delivered the speech leading to Paine's confinement to a cell in Luxembourg Prison. (Barère later apologized to Paine "by saying he felt himself in danger and was obliged to do it ... ")[63] It was Vadier, then president of the Convention which had conferred honorary citizenship on the heroic figure of the American Revolution, who signed the paper for Paine's arrest; and Vadier in his turn felt himself justified because

> [Paine's] mind has not perceived the nature of the Revolution which has regenerated France; he has conceived the system only in the light of the delusions with which the false friends of our revolution have surrounded it ... [64]

Once again, we have men preaching reason but meaning dogma, secular prophets who were religious casuists. Indeed here was the authentic spirit of excommunication as inspired by the theology of a true revolutionary faith which finds heresy, sin, and evil lurking in the slightest deviation. The very fact of holding power as the representatives of history means that they alone possess true consciousness and are thus entitled (nay, compelled) to combat ruthlessly any and all illusory opinions of the system, the old one or the new one, and if necessary to exterminate the dangerous minds caught in something so devilish as delusion. In point of fact, Paine's cell had been marked for the executioner, and only an accident saved him from the guillotine.

> . . . the door of our room was marked, unobserved by us, with that number in chalk; but it happened, if happening is the proper word, that the mark was put on when the door was open and flat against the wall, and thereby came on the inside when we shut it at night; and the destroying angel passed by it.[65]

Paine sensed the problem of corruption even in the Incorruptible Robespierre (among whose papers, after his death, there was found a memorandum preparing a decree of accusation against Paine); and perhaps he was indeed the very image of the "destroying angel" incarnate. How could there be intellectual liberty or personal safety for the man of opinion *par excellence* when all opinions had to meet the measure of an official doctrinal truth? Paine (as he said) put his faith in the pen, and not in the guillotine; revolutionary politics was to be a conflict of viewpoints, not of knives to the death. But (as Robespierre replied) "that method might do with such a country as America, but could avail nothing in one highly corrupted like France." "To disagree in opinion," an observer noted, "with a mind so heated, was to incur all the resentment it contained."[66] Yet surely it was less the heatedness of the mind than the coolness of the spirit which rendered him calm and confident in the incorruptibility of his own powerfulness: his might was right. At an Anglo-French breakfast in Paris (among the guests: Paine, Holcroft, Goldsmith, Tallien, Santerre, and Merlin de Thionville), the French argued classically in defense of the doctrine, Caesaro-Roman rather than Socratic Greek, that the most legitimate right which exists is that of the strongest.

> Mr. Holcroft attempted to say something against this doctrine, but Paine desired him to hold his tongue, as he might as well talk of honour to a gang of thieves as to contradict revolutionary Frenchmen in their notion of right and wrong.[67]

Paine's bitterness extended from these table-talk ironies to a large disenchantment with France as a primary carrier of the revolutionary idea; a people, a nation had failed, not the idea. Between the desire and the spasm or the potency and the descent, there was no permanent shadow; for in theory, as Paine still believed (and Yorke and Mackintosh no longer did), other historic forces would come to make some more effectively moral beginning to his "Revolution of the World."

Hopes may have been momentarily dashed, but not—as we know from Paine onward to Ernst Bloch—hope in the principle of hope. As Paine wrote to Thomas Jefferson (20 April 1793),

> Had this revolution been conducted consistently with its principles, there was once a good prospect of extending liberty through the greatest part of Europe; but I now relinquish that hope.... As the prospect of a general freedom is much shortened, I begin to contemplate returning home. I shall await the event of the proposed Constitution, and then take my final leave of Europe.

To Danton, a few weeks later, he again made it clear that his despairing mood had little to do with the essential "character of the Revolution," only with its excesses and misconduct, with what a young English disciple of Paine's had termed "the triumph of imbecility and inhumanity over talent and virtue."

> I now despair of seeing the great object of European liberty accomplished, and my despair arises ... from the tumultuous misconduct with which the internal affairs of the present revolution is conducted ...

And the future revolution? "Under that impenetrable veil, futurity, we know not what is concealed, and the day to arrive is hidden from us." It would seem that, by leaving corrupted France and its "murderous system" for a still innocent, more moral America, he was returning to the bosom of what he called, in a phrase that seemed most curious coming from him, "the mother church of government."

> Painful as the want of liberty may be, it is a consolation to me to believe that my imprisonment proves to the world that I had no share in the murderous system that then reigned. That I was an enemy to it, both morally and politically, is known to all who had any knowledge of me: and could I have written French as well as I can English, I would publicly have exposed its wickedness and shown the ruin with which it was pregnant.... Imprisonment with preservation of character, is preferable to liberty with disgrace.[68]

The pregnant ruin, then, was conceived not in the principles of revolution, of violent regeneration and total change, but only in aberrant revolutionary misconduct; it was villainous, venomous factionalism that had betrayed the revolution.

The politics of melancholy turned to polemical pique during Henry

Yorke's meeting with Jacques-Louis David in his apartment in the Louvre.[69] He put forward a somewhat embarrassing question—could David recollect having signed the warrant for Yorke's arrest, and what were the charges that were to be preferred against him in that terrifying winter of 1792–93? David replied that it was simply impossible for him to recall all the warrants of arrest which he had issued when he was a member of the Committee of General Safety. After all, hundreds were sometimes signed in one day. Often, "in the hurry of business," he had put his name to warrants on the basis of some colleague's report. But, no doubt, every arrest was based on some previous information.

But then, "in the hurry of business," was not much injustice done? Yes, but "what could we do? . . . surrounded by traitors at home . . .was it always possible to discriminate?"

There was good reason for Yorke to suspect that once his name had been put on some list, on the basis of some vague or inaccurate or malicious information, then he might well have been liquidated by David's Committee. As Dr. John Moore, a fellow countryman of his, wrote in his Paris journal at that time:

> A groundless suspicion, or a calumny invented and propagated by an enemy, may kindle the fury of a few fanatics, and the head of the person who is the object of it may be fixed on a pike before the magistrate can assemble force to protect him. His innocence is made apparent when it is too late; everybody laments his fate; the murderers however are excused, because they were misled (*égaré* is the palliative word used on such occasions) by the noblest of all errors, too much zeal for their country's good; and tranquillity is restored only till fresh suspicions and calumnies excite new murders.[70]

Yorke grew increasingly incensed with David's extenuation of the guilt of the atrocities, not least perhaps because something atrocious had almost been done to him; he listened impatiently to David's sentimentalities about the days of revolutionary glory.

> . . . and after a flourish on the civil wars and massacres attendant on the acquisition of our English freedom, he challenged me to produce an instance of the establishment of a Republic, without wading through seas of blood.

Yorke's comment on this echoes Paine but irascibly goes further:

> M. David, like every other Frenchman (and here I do not make a single exception of any one with whom I have been in company) is utterly ignorant of the nature of the liberty we enjoy, and of all our institutions. They have not a conception of the possibility of freedom existing in any state with a monarch at its head; with them, there is not a vestige of liberty among any people who have not high-sounding Roman titles. In the same manner they cannot com-

prehend the being of that middle class of society which constitutes
the bulwark of our Isle.

David recognizes no freedom that is not open to holy insurrections
against established authority. Wherever the shrieks of murder and
the notes of the trumpet are not heard, there can be no liberty.

In the last analysis, then, this brilliant artist whose paintings had so
impressed him was "a monster."

To begin a sentence with expressions of humanity, and to end it with
a climax of blood, is his chief delight. . . . The prospect of a bleeding
world [is] the darling theme of his atrocious imagination.[71]

It is fortunate that his raging rejection of the Frenchman of 1802 did
not drive Henry Yorke completely into *ad hominem* argumentativeness.
True, he despised the Paris intelligentsia, "that secondary swarm of
literati, whose existence like that of reptiles, depends on depredation
and injury," and, especially, "those political writers and orators who
affect a great deal of information when they possess none." For centuries we have had this tone in the cross-channel cultural conflict: "No
people upon earth possess greater facility than the French in setting
themselves off to the greatest advantage, especially in persuading the
world they know everything, when, in fact, they know very little or
nothing."

But surely the question of revolution was not identical with the problem of a single national character? Yorke tried, in the end, to pose the
issues of political violence and revolutionary ideology in a more general
way. His preoccupation still remained: character and ethics, means and
ends, their morals and ours. He still found it incredible that men of
sensitive natures, "who were so humane they *would not kill a fly*," proved
themselves to be "when immersed in the revolutionary whirlpool, the
most cruel and inexorable devils incarnate . . . " Whence, then, the exterminating fury in the revolutionary character? How explain the
"vortex of excesses"? Why is it that "so many excellent men [became] converted into butchers"? What is the "fatal quality" of this "political pestilence"? Yorke's notable answer includes an element of psychological
insight which gives a striking modern tone to the patterns of revolutionary ambivalence I have been trying to analyze.

. . . as the cause of Liberty naturally invites the zeal of generous
minds, atrocities are committed from which, as spectators, their
minds would revolt with horror. But as agents, they conceive that
any thing may be done for freedom; they gradually become callous to
every feeling beyond their own sphere of action, till at length, the
moral sense being extinguished in their breasts, they are open to
every crime. The impetuosity of the torrent on which they are borne,

is so great, that there is no retrocession, no time even for reflection; but forward they rush spreading desolation in their progress, unmoved by pity or compunction, and encouraging each other with the contemplation of their numbers, and the apparent grandeur of their cause. If any among them should by any fortuitous occurrence be snatched from their columns, and reach once more the bank of safety, he becomes confounded with the immensity of his dangers. Looking fore and aft, he trembles at what he has passed, and is petrified with the idea of what he had to go through. Eternal sorrow and repentance cloud the remainder of his days.

Clearly, the alternating outbursts of melancholy and of resentment, rooted in his need for retribution and his longing to forget, continued to hold Henry Yorke back from rising to a higher level of abstraction, to a historical dimension of comparative ideology, or to a philosophical idea of the tragic sense of the revolutionary life. His own autobiography was too much with him, understandably enough; and he was convinced that the truth lay in the details, more details. He wanted history, not metaphysics.

This much he would concede: that "this disease of the human understanding, this rapid transit from humanity to fierceness, merits the most serious investigation ... " Yet where should one begin if not with the personal drama itself?

Metaphysicians may write whole volumes in attempting to account for it, but unless they had been actors in some of the scenes, they cannot develop them with fidelity. It is an undertaking that belongs exclusively to experience, and I am happy to add that such a work will soon appear.

He does not say from whom; nor do we know when or whether it ever appeared. One can only wonder if it would have deeply altered the story as we already know it, from a generation of English ideologists for whom ideology was exclusively the politics of experience—erratic, instructive, and avoidable.

8. Disenchantment and Resurrection

The consequences of liberal disenchantment, in terms of practical politics, were disastrous. This was clear to all except the unfortunate French, for revolutionaries hear (and need to hear) only those voices that keep their spirits high and persist in magnifying the faintest echoes of lingering encouragement. In Paris, they were convinced that England was soon to follow along the trail they had blazed. Imprisoned in their own optimism, they misread all the signs from across the channel. The French ambassador (or perhaps it was his secretary, Talleyrand) warned the optimists: "They curiously deceive themselves who regard England on the eve of a revolution ... " No, England was on the eve of reaction, and the English liberal ranks were left in disarray by a combination of their own confusion and Pitt's effective campaign against them as "wicked advocates of subversion." In October 1794, Romilly reported from London to a correspondent in France his estimate of the bitter balance:

> There are indeed many persons here who wish a total overthrow of our constitution, and many more who desire great changes in it; but the great majority of the nation, and particularly the armed part of it (which is at present a very large portion, for volunteer regiments have been raised in every county), are most ardent zealots for maintaining our constitution as it is, and disposed to think that the reform of the most palpable abuse, which has been of long continuance, as a species of sacrilege.

Zealotry in any ideological camp appears to have only a half-life; it tends to complete its brief, intense run by making a zigzag shift from one side to the other. The liberal and radical reformers, themselves once full of ardor, were overwhelmed by what another age would come to call a "backlash" (only a new word for an old phenomenon of rhythm in political tension). Romilly, taking another reading a few years later of the prospects for humane changes which once seemed so hopeful, registered an English spirit of conservatism which now bordered on savage reaction:

> If any person be desirous of having an adequate idea of the mischievous effects which have been produced in this country by the French Revolution and all its attendant horrors, he should attempt some legislative reform, of humane and liberal principles. He will then find, not only what a stupid dread of innovation, but what a savage spirit it has infused into the minds of many of his countrymen.[72]

The backlash left the cause of reform dead.

The indomitable optimism of a handful of last-ditch radical spirits received blow after blow. In 1809, the Earl of Selkirk tried to explain to Major Cartwright, with whom he had been associated in so many struggles, why this time he had to turn down the request for him to join together with the Friends of Parliamentary Reform. One thing he underscored again and again and tried to make unquestionably clear: he had not changed his humane principles nor abandoned his critical sense of society's shortcomings.

... I am very far from thinking that there is nothing which requires reform in our government. I am well convinced, that there are many corruptions of most pernicious tendency, which may and ought to be eradicated.[73]

But the times were no longer propitious, and a whole generation may well have lost the historic opportunity which had once seemed so bright.

But we have to consider how that object is to be effected, without endangering benefits of still greater importance. The advocates of a radical and entire Reform, have not perhaps fairly considered the extreme difficulty of guarding every avenue to abuse, and how often the measures which are taken for repressing it in one quarter, serve only to open it for some new channel still more pernicious.

How could one, then, move forward without risking the achievements of previous efforts? There was much corruption and many hardships, but the struggle for "public happiness" had issued in no little victories on behalf of "the personal liberty of the subject," of justice and security.

Let the value of that which we possess be fairly appreciated; and then let us consider coolly, whether the blemishes of our government are of such magnitude, as to warrant the application of remedies, which, if they do not cure, may kill.

Selkirk was, of course, referrring to the heritage of a revolution in France which had gone astray. The foundations of "a gradual improvement" had been established, but "slow progress, however, did not suit the ideas of the ardent friends of liberty." They sought an "immediate and complete regeneration ... in pursuit of a phantom of ideal perfection." But this was, by now, an old story. Selkirk was a sophisticated liberal and tried to keep away from the familiar debate ("I shall not repeat the hackneyed topics to which the French Revolution has given occasion.")

Yet behind the caution, hesitation, and coolness which he was recommending was the hardening English fear of ideology.

Though I do not suppose that the English Reformers would imitate the mad fury of the French Revolutionists, their principles have the same tendency, and their efforts may have in a great measure the same effect. Popular ferment is a two-edged weapon, which most frequently inflicts the wound where it was not aimed. Often it has ruined the cause of liberty, and seldom contributed to improve the condition of mankind! Before we risk the infinite mischief, which may be dreaded from the use of such an engine, let us weigh well the value of the object.

Yet no scales were available (nor are they today) to measure accurately all the factors that had to be weighed, to do a balanced social accounting of the costs of political and economic change. Selkirk's recourse was the classical one of trying to chart an ancient course between Scylla and Charybdis. For the issue, as he saw it, was between *the vices of an ultra-democratic demagogy* ("power into the hands of men, whose only merit consists in being masters of stage effect, and the tricks of popular delusion") and *the evils of plutocracy* ("the undue influence of wealth"). He and Cartwright were still of one mind and heart about the abuses to be eradicated; and these included economic as well as political vices. But the times, as I hope to have made abundantly clear, had induced a failure of nerve. Selkirk would soon leave to cross the Atlantic and make a new and adventurous career for himself in the Canadian Northwest; but this was his message to his contemporaries who were still caught in the old toils of English post-revolutionary public affairs:

> A struggle for Parliamentary Reform would come at the present moment most seasonably to the aid of the Anti-jacobin hypocrites, who are trembling for their ill-gotten gains . . . . I would entreat the advocates of Parliamentary Reform, to reflect how many men there are who, though prepared to support every substantial oecumenical Reform, would tremble at the idea of Constitutional changes, to which they see no termination. If the notions of a radical and entire change are pursued with violence, moderate men will again be forced to believe, that there is no alternative between measures of a Revolutionary tendency, and a resistance to every reformation whatever.

It was a confrontation between revolution and counter-revolution that he sought at all odds to avoid, the polarization between left and right, between the old and the new.

> Many sincere friends of oecumenical Reform may thus be driven to a cooperation with men, who have no principle but to support every established abuse.
> Anxiously do I hope, that those who wish honestly to pursue the good of the country, may not again be forced to make their option between Jacobin and Anti-jacobin. I am no Alarmist; but as I firmly believe, that amidst violent changes, there is more probability of making our government worse than better, I deprecate the discussion to which you wish me to lend my name, as calculated to divide the friends of substantial reformation, and to defeat every valuable, safe, and attainable improvement in the management of our public affairs.

I have already referred to Hazlitt's entrancing vision of a paradisaical human happiness; but, unlike so many of his contemporaries, he needed no prodding from events to recognize (with sobriety and without bitterness) how it would end.

The love of truth and virtue which seems at all times natural to liberal-minded youth, was at this time carried to a pitch of enthusiasm, as well by the extraordinary events that had taken place, as by the romantic prospects of ideal excellence which were pictured in the writings of philosophers and poets.

Alas, neither youth nor philosophy nor poetry prevailed. Imagination could not take power, for, as Hazlitt wrote, "Imagination was unable to keep pace with the gigantic strides of reason, and the strongest faith fell short of the supposed reality." Yet his balance sheet of the spirit of the age was not one-sided. Ideals, even when they fail or are betrayed or in some perverse manner pervert the idealists themselves, have a certain historic merit.

This anticipation of what men were to become, could not but have an influence on what they were. The standard of morality was raised high; and this circumstance must excite an ardent emulation in the minds of many persons to set an example of true and disinterested virtue, unshackled by the prejudices or interests of those around them.

Yet if, in the moral accounting, the idealism of a revolutionary epoch might "add new force to the practice of virtue in the liberal and well-disposed mind," in the actual course of events it was the practice of vice in illiberal and ill-disposed minds which made for the political tragedy.

The curb of prudence was taken off; nor was it thought that zeal for what was right could be carried to an excess. There is no doubt that this system would be taken advantage of by the selfish and the hypocritical to further their own views at the expense of others.

For Hazlitt's generation, as for so many others before and after him who have lived through (in the Chinese phrase) "interesting times," the moments of both illusion and disillusion seemed to be, each in their own bright and dark way, permanent. But the historian, trapped in his own mental forms, can only record, again and again, the transitoriness of the hope and the despair.

Kind feelings and generous actions [Hazlitt wrote in 1816] there always have been and there always will be, while the intercourse of mankind shall endure: but the hope, that such feelings and such actions might become universal, rose and set with the French Revolution. That light seems to have been extinguished for ever in this respect. The French Revolution was the only match that ever took place between philosophy and experience: and waking from the trance of theory to the sense of reality, we hear the words, *truth, reason, virtue, liberty*, with the same indffference or contempt, that

the cynic who has married a jilt or a termagant, listens to the rhap-
sodies of lovers.[74]

As we know, the words will return, and the loving rhapsody will recur.
There are a whole series of matches between philosophy and experience
which are still to come, for few "lights" in history are extinguished "for
ever." Between the trance of theory and the sense of reality there will be
many a human awakening, yet again.

Or, to remix the metaphor (and this cannot be helped in a history of
ideology), here is the sense of inextinguishable hope as it was put by a
group of Scottish radicals in 1816:

> A mental revolution has taken place which the *ratio regum*, the logic
> of legitimacy, the point of the bayonet cannot counteract ... A spark
> was kindled at the French Revolution which the enemies of freedom
> think they have extinguished, but still it burns, and every fresh oc-
> currence fans the flame.[75]

E pur si muove, and still it moves; and still it burns.

The central axes along which the ideological cycle can be observed are,
usually, *location* and *motion*. In its late phase, the main points to be
plotted are: center or extreme, stability or chaos. But, in its early phase, a
reading of the cycle includes: movement or static balance, radical
progress or immobile moderation.

On both counts, Jeremy Bentham's pamphlet of 1817 on "the necessity of radical, and the inadequacy of moderate, reform" represents a
prophetic foreshadowing of the turning point of 1832, which can be
taken as ending the late phase of post-Revolutionary centrism and moderation and renewing the mood of action, hope, and militance.

The first point is disposed of by Bentham in the following vigorous
paragraph:

> Talk of *balance:* never will it do: leave that to Mother Goose and
> Mother Blackstone. Balance! balance! Politicians upon roses—to
> whom, to save the toil of thinking—on questions most wide in ex-
> tent, and high in importance—an allusion—an emblem—an
> anything—so as it has been accepted by others, is accepted as con-
> clusive evidence—what mean ye by this your *balance?* Know yet not,
> that in a machine of any kind, when forces *balance* each other, the
> machine is at a stand? Well and in the machine of government,
> immobility—the perpetual absence of all motion—is that the thing
> which is wanted? Know ye not that—since an emblem you must
> have—since you can neither talk, nor attempt to think, but in
> hieroglyphics—know you not that, as in the case of the body *natural*,
> so in the case of the body *politic*, when motion ceases, the body dies?

Once again, it was a case of one man's high principles being another man's hieroglyphics. An ideological debate, for all its allusiveness, is never merely about "emblems"; as in Bentham's own work, it now raged around real social values, privileges of power and property, democratic rights and liberties. But the imperious choice of words and metaphors is, as we have seen, no less real; language is a necessary comfort, and the properly congenial vocabulary serves as a source of strength and enhanced faith.

Movement was progress; *balance* was stagnation. (Conversely: motion tended to a wildness which disrupted and ruined delicate social arrangements; only at the center could things be held together.) *Radicalism* was effective; *moderation* was inadequate. (Or: a radical uprooting or subversion of faulty institutions does, "on balance," more harm than good; decent and lasting changes are effected only "little by little.")

Bentham's own temperamental predisposition was clear and confident:

> ... what is required is—from all the several arrangements in question, to show—this having been the result of the inquiry—that while, by *radical* reform, a remedy, and that an adequate one, would be applied—by *moderate* reform, no remedy would be applied, or next to none.

Still, this represented in the radical English mind of the next generation (from Bentham to John Stuart Mill) something rather less than a full return to a revolutionary commitment. Bentham, in one of his unpublished manuscripts, had hastened to draw a line of caution where the men of 1789 had rushed into the excesses of Jacobinical enthusiasm. *Radicalism Not Dangerous* was the title of his proposed pamphlet. But only a revolutionary revels in the danger; for the risk is only a historic sign that something great, necessary, fundamental, and audacious is being undertaken.[76]

We are dealing here with the profound distinction between English radicalism and European revolutionism which came to mark utopian thinking ever since the brief, ill-starred flirtation with ideology on the part of the generation of '89. It was a distinction which was nowhere better and more succinctly formulated than in a letter John Stuart Mill had written after the Paris Commune of 1871. It was addressed to a working-class militant from Nottingham, Thomas Smith, who was a member of Marx's First International and a defender of the recent "mighty Convulsions in the Martyr City of Liberty." Smith had sent Mill a copy of his pamphlet entitled *The Law of the Revolution*, and I quote Mill's critique not least because one of the central themes of these pages—Anglo-French differences and the character of English thought, the ideological role of "vague words" and "unreal abstractions" under the banner of "the Revolution"—can be taken by the reader as little more than a historical explication of this fine passage.

Mill found, generously enough, little to dissent from and much to approve in the radical principles of the International. He was especially pleased with the "full and thoroughgoing recognition . . . of the claims of women to equal rights in every respect with man" and also "of minorities, proportionally to their numbers, with majorities." But one thing troubled him: the "generality" with which all the principles were laid down, so that it was impossible for him to say "to what extent I should concur in the political measures which the Association would propose in order to bring the principles into operation." Two may say the same things yet mean something different; like Milton and Harrington, Hartlib and Worthington, Comenius and Bayle, Rogers and Cromwell, or like Burke and Mackintosh, Cartwright and Horne Tooke, Southey and Shelley, two who may appear to be traveling the same high road can soon come to a parting of the ways, and for reasons which were at the outset barely discernible and almost inconceivable. Mill was rightly disturbed by the "phraseology."

> What advantage is there in designating the doctrines of the Associa-
> tion by such a title as "the principles of the political and social Revo-
> lution"? "The Revolution" as a name for any sort of principles or
> opinions, is not English. A Revolution is a change of government
> effected by force, whether it be by popular revolt or by military
> usurpation. And as "the man" in English always means some par-
> ticular man, so "the Revolution" means some particular revolution,
> such as the French Revolution, or the English Revolution of 1688.

Mill began with semantical objections but went on to a fuller dissent:

> The meaning intended to be conveyed by "the principles of the
> Revolution" can only be guessed at from a knowledge of French, in
> which language it seems to mean the political ideal of any persons of
> democratic opinions who happens to be using it. I cannot think it is
> good to adopt this mode of speech from the French. It proceeds from
> an infirmity of the French mind, which has been one main cause of
> the miscarriages of the French nation in its pursuit of liberty and
> progress; that of being led away by phrases, and treating abstractions
> as if they were realities which have a will and exert active power.
> Hitherto the character of English thought has been different; it has
> required propositions, not vague words, which only seem to have a
> meaning. There is no real thing called "the Revolution," nor any
> "principles of the Revolution." There are maxims which your As-
> sociation, in my opinion, rightly consider to be essential to just gov-
> ernment, and there is a tendency increasing as mankind advances in

intelligence and education towards the adoption of the doctrines of just government. Those are all the facts there are in the case, and the more clearly and unambiguously these, and nothing but these, are stated, the better people will understand one another, and the more distinctly they will see what they are disputing about, and what they are concerned to prove. When instead of this men range themselves under banners as friends and enemies of "the Revolution," the only important question which is just and useful is kept out of sight, and measures are judged not by their real worth but by the analogy they seem to have to an irrelevant abstraction.

Mill was not making a point so peculiarly English that it would have been lost on France's own critics of abstract revolutionism: on, say, Constant or Tocqueville. Indeed, Mill was very pleased with the "very salutary intercourse" which had grown up across the channel (especially "between portions of the English and the French working classes"). But he was afraid that it would be "dearly paid for if it causes the advanced politicians of this country to abandon one of the best characteristics of the English mind, and replace it by one of the worst of the French."[77]

Great social movements in history are rarely explained by the ideas, sound or illusory, with which they are associated; and their defeats or failures can scarcely be attributed in any simple manner to their emotional naïveté, their temperamental self-indulgence, or their ideological contradictions. I am merely calling attention to the persistence of these factors in the agitated chronicles of utopians and revolutionaries.

We almost seem to know, as if the study of history were providing us with cues, what is going to happen. The historian can neither wish it nor deplore it, as if in any case he could rewrite what once has been writ. But surely some measure of understanding history is in the sense of confirmed expectation which haunts the historian as he searches for an order of meanings in the new and old debris of great events. In the debris of the revolutionary interlude in the liberal English mind which I have been trying to summarize, we can discern a familiar pattern of post-ideological sadness: a melancholy complex made up of guilt, self-criticism, withdrawal, and escape. Reformers and radicals abused themselves for their own inadequacies; Thalwall regretted that they had wasted so much of their efforts in "wrangling." They vaguely sensed that perhaps the very romantic extravagance of their hopes and emotions had led to a cyclical turn to inertia and despair. As Sir Philip Francis, a good observer, informed that old militant, Major Cartwright, "As far as I can judge, the mass of the English population is inert. The country has lost its passions and is not fit for action." Nobody less than that heroic radical spirit of the 1790s, John Horne Tooke, confirmed the collapse of hope: "I think the cause of reform is dead and buried." But in the margin of this letter John Cartwright penned a characteristically irreverent dissent: "But J. C. is a believer in the resurrection."[78]

That this "resurrection" of the cause of reform would in fact come; that the passions were not lost forever, and this inertia too would pass, is another matter, indeed a matter for another chapter. In the long run, the wheel of fortune would turn again; but in the long run this genera-tion, so grandiloquent in its aspirations and so chastened by murderous events, would be dead. A few knew in their bones, held by some to be no bad repository for human hope, that a time would come again. When, in the spring of 1801, Major Cartwright met his friend Dr. Wilber-force in a London street and exchanged a few words of greeting and encouragement, Wilberforce said he "hoped we should meet in a better world ... " Whereupon (as Cartwright wrote to his wife, italicizing his articles of faith), "I answered, that 'I hope we should first mend the world we were in.' "[79]

The world has need of its menders, and the menders no less a need of faith in mission and purpose. That it sometimes requires a whole new generation to recover the nerve for utopian revolution seems to them only another reason for steadfast patience. That the new utopians and revolutionaries, eyes fixed on another glorious vision of the future and the daring deeds which would accomplish them, never have the histori-cal sense to look backward, would seem to us to be only another reason to tell yet again another familiar story. For as Southey confessed, when he looked at Shelley as at the ghost of his own youth, "He is just what I was in 1794."[80]

Almost a quarter of a century had passed since the first English en-thusiasts had greeted the destruction of the Bastille, and in those years sensitive ardent spirits of two full English generations had been touched by "visions of human perfectibility, and of a golden age of equality and innocence and joy." In Shelley, as a biographer records of the year 1812, Southey fancied that he beheld the image of his own revolutionary youth revived from the past. "At present," Southey observed (with only the slightest trace of irony), "he has got to the Pantheistic state of philosophy." He expected that his young friend would shortly become a Berkeleyan, "for I have put him upon a course of Berkeley." Southey assured Shelley that he understood him perfectly and justly, that "all the difference between us is that he is nineteen and I am thirty-seven ... "

The sympathies of the generations touched for a moment. Shelley was taken with Southey's great eloquence and candor; Southey was kind to Shelley, helpful with money and with books. But the perfect under-standing was short-lived. Shelley turned from Southey ("Now he is corrupted by the world, contaminated by custom") to a purer source of revolutionary vitality, to Godwin; and it was to Godwin that he announced: "I have but just entered on the scene of human operations . . . . I am young: I am ardent in the cause of philanthropy and truth." Southey was never more perceptive than when he saw in the youthful Shelley the image of his own early utopianism. "God help us!" he wrote: "The world wants mending, though he did not get about it exactly in the right way."

It was indeed an uncanny insight into the ideological gap between generations. "Here is a man who acts upon me as my own ghost would do. He is just what I was in 1794."

16

The mind of the philosopher rests with
satisfaction on a small number of objects;
but the spectacle of stupidity, slavery,
extravagance, barbarity, afflicts him still
more often; and the friend of humanity can
enjoy unmixed pleasure only by surrendering
to the sweet hopes of the future [*aux douces
espérances de l'avenir*].

—Condorcet (1795)

. . . from such crooked wood as man is made of,
nothing perfectly straight can be built.

—Kant (1798)

The Sweet Dream

1. Condorcet's Ambiguity
Stereotypes of National Character—Mill and Tocqueville—
Condorcet's Plaintive Cry: "Who ever talked of destroying everything
at once?"—Transient Evils—Condorcet's Death in the Cell (1794)—
Who were the "Political Charlatans"?—Heretical Doubts and
Revisions—Revolution as the Dangerous Moment of a Reforma-
tion—A Suspect Word—Robespierre Purges the Ideological
Forebears—Whose Martyr?

2. The Kantian Dilemma
Kant as a Friend of Revolutions—Fantasy, Enthusiasm, Philanthropy—"The Sweet Feeling of Benevolence"—A Philosopher between Reform and Revolution—Gradualism or Upheaval—The Devotion to Stout Principle

3. Of Passion and Prudence
Kant, Moderation, and "Stern Measures"—Despotizing Moralists and
Moralizing Politicians—The Middle Ground—Reason and
Perfection—"Dying of Improvement"—The Love of Mankind and the
Love of Men—The Straight and the Crooked—From Top to Bottom, or
Bottom to Top

4. From More to Marx
Daydreams and Tyranny—More, Luther, and Tyndale—"Turning
Honey into Poison"—Burning One's Own Books (More, 1532)—The

Utopian's Self-critical Tradition—Marx, the Dreamers and the Philistines (1877)—The Ideal and the Real—The Kantian "Compass of Reason"—Kant's "Game of Great Revolutions"

---

5. **Of Truth and Sincerity**
"The Stain of Injustice in the Means Applied"—Means and Ends—More's Caution, Erasmus's Fearfulness, Spinoza's Silence—Kant and the King of Prussia (1794)—On Inner Convictions—Subtle Distinctions between Sincerity and Candor—Imagination and the Political Artist

---

6. **The War of the Temperaments**
Dr. Arendt's "Conservative Care"—Hobbes and Mme de Staël—Pierre Bayle and the Burning Danger of "the Fumo Chiliastico" —"A Trail of Equivalent Symbols"—from Mme de Staël to Albert Camus—Men in the Noble Middle—"The Primary Color"—Sartre, Mme de Beauvoir, Raymond Aron—An Anonymous Future in the name of Invented but Undisclosed Values—The Sweet Dream as Inviolate Dogma—The Revolution Remains their Utopia

---

1. Condorcet's Ambiguity

A dramatic nineteenth-century sense of the historic divergence between England and France led Walter Bagehot to formulate a more general notion of national character. "All nations have a character," he was convinced, "and that character when once taken is, I do not say unchangeable—religion modifies it, catastrophe annihilates it—but the least changeable thing in this ever-varying and changeable world." Certainly he was in no doubt of the national characteristics of the French—"clever ... versatile ... intellectual ... dogmatic ... excitable ... volatile ... superficial ... over-logical ... uncompromising ... " All this amounted to "some lurking quality, or want of quality, in the national character of the French nation which renders them but poorly adaptable for the form and freedom and constitution which they have so often, with such zeal and so vainly, attempted to establish." Bagehot's handy epigram was that they were "too clever to be practical, and not dull enough to be free." As for the English, here too there was no puzzlement, although he could not refrain from putting the rhetorical question: "Why are we free and they slaves? we praetors and they barbers? Why do stupid people always win?" He gave the answer away. "What we opprobriously call stupidity, though not an enlivening quality in common society, is Nature's favourite resource for preserving steadiness of conduct and consistency of opinion." He found it consoling that "in real sound stupidity the English are unrivalled"; they learned, slowly, only what they must, and they did their duty because they knew of nothing else to do. Yet, beyond the irony, was there no glimmer of wisdom here? Was it only dullness and slowness that saved his countrymen from that "superfluous energy which flows over into philosophy, and has worked into big systems what should have been left as little suggestions"?

> Old things need not be therefore true,
> O brother men, nor yet the new;
> Ah, still awhile the old thought retain,
> And yet consider it again.[1]

There is a grotesque and exasperating moment when in the shadow of the stereotypes of national character there is suddenly a hint in the course of actual events that this indeed may be the way things truly are. Once, when a serious clash seemed to impend between London workingmen and the police whom the Tory government had mobilized, John Stuart Mill, true son of his radical father (who had pondered so long over "the art of revolution"), went out into Hyde Park to advise the militant workers: "I told them that a proceeding which would certainly produce a collision with the military could only be justifiable on two conditions; if the position of affairs had become such that a revolution was desirable, and if they thought themselves able to accomplish one. To this argument, after considerable discussion, they at last yielded."[2] How far we are from desperate Russia, tortured France! What would those others have said? Would they have taken thought, sketched out conditions, calculated the chances, left open the possibilities of reconsideration?

Small wonder that Tocqueville, in Paris, lost patience with his countrymen's penchant for "wholesale destruction," never reforming, always transforming; and lost himself in thoughts of what might have happened in France had a monarch of Frederick the Great's temperament been on the throne. Was there a conceivable constitutional remedy, or was it only a narrow choice "between meekly accepting everything or destroying the whole system"?[3]

The issue of a third choice was actually faced by the revolutionaries, but almost always too late and usually in the shadow of the guillotine. A keen European observer, writing to James Madison from Paris, thought that "if they do not aim at too much they may begin a good constitution." He also warned Condorcet that "it was not possible to destroy everything at once." Condorcet's reply is one of the great plaintive cries in the history of revolution: "Who ever talked of destroying everything at once?"[4]

Condorcet was possibly the first in a long line of revolutionary French intellectuals who were, in the final analysis, ambivalent about the nature and degree of their political commitment. Had they taken an absolute vow, or was an impure alternative of slower reform and piecemeal reconstruction acceptable under some historical circumstances? Condorcet was the only *philosophe* of the Voltaire-Diderot generation who participated in the French Revolution; he helped to depose the King (although he voted against execution), and in June 1793 he was still a member with Robespierre of the Committee of Public Safety. While hiding from his Jacobin persecutors in 1793–94, he outlined his *Historical Picture of the Human Mind*, that masterful summary of eighteenth-century liberalism, and in the "ninth epoch" we find him writing:

> . . . a great revolution was inevitable, and there were only two ways in which it could come about: either the people themselves would establish the reasonable and natural principles that philosophy had taught them to admire, or governments would hasten to anticipate them and carry out what was required by public opinion. If the revolution should come about in the former way, it would be swifter and more thorough, but more violent; if in the former way, then freedom and happiness would be purchased at the price of transient evils; if in the latter, then these evils would be avoided but, it might be, at the price of long delaying the harvest of the fruits that the revolution must, nevertheless, bear. The ignorance and corruption of the governments of the time saw that it came about in the former way, and the human race was avenged by the swift triumph of liberty and reason.[5]

But if, despite the undesirable violence, the evils were only transient, and if the result was indeed *"le triomphe rapide de la raison et de la liberté,"* then who could fail to opt for revolution rather than reform?

In the subsequent "tenth epoch," the perspective has shifted a little toward a reconsideration (like Marx's, later) of revolution in the double vision of here a peaceful and there a violent transition from the old to the new.

> As we move from nation to nation, we can see in each what special obstacles impede this revolution, and what attitudes of mind favor it. We can distinguish the nations where we may expect it to be

introduced gently [*doucement*] by the perhaps belated wisdom of their government, and those nations where its violence intensified by their resistance must involve all alike in a swift and terrible convulsion [*dans ses mouvements terribles et rapides*].[6]

But Condorcet still fell significantly short of formulating the problem of the "third choice" as it was to be faced by Mme de Staël, Tocqueville, J. S. Mill, Herzen, and others. Perhaps the general excitement was too great; there was scarcely time for the "snow-capped volcano" (as d'Alembert had called him) to cool off; the events raged. After leaving the house of refuge where he had written his last pages, Condorcet failed to find another asylum; he was identified and imprisoned. He was found dead in his cell the next day.[7]

Was there anywhere a dawn of a doubt about "the swift triumph of liberty and reason" which was so cruelly and needlessly to destroy him and so many others? In 1793, in his *Journal d'instruction sociale* (which he had established with Sièyes), Condorcet wrote this suggestive passage:

> Societies which are not enlightened by philosophers [*éclairée par des philosophes*] are cheated by charlatans. Now we only have yet another species to combat: the political charlatans. Not all of them are Caesars or Cromwells; it is enough for these types to be of mediocre talent and often of very little interest in order to cause great evil. They all follow the same path, wanting to be the favorites of the people before becoming their tyrants . . . . To demonstrate to the people the trap in which these men would ensnare them—this is one of the primary obligations of writers who are devoted to the cause of truth and country . . .

One can very well understand one liberal French historian's temptation to believe that here were the beginnings of a "journal of opposition" which would expose the political charlatans, namely, Robespierre and his friends. But he had to admit, on the contrary, his astonishment that Condorcet fully approved the actions of the Convention and of the Committee of Public Safety. He sanctioned "the suspension for a time of certain liberties," and the various laws on émigrés, passports, etc. As Condorcet explained in his article *Sur le sens du mot révolutionnaire* (a sensitive flight into semantics, characteristic of writers in a revolutionary time):

> Let us make revolutionary laws, but only in order to hasten the time when we will no longer have any need for them. Let us adopt revolutionary measures, not to prolong or to bloody the revolution, but to complete it and to end it.[8]

So it was that, although he bemoaned the spirit which would destroy everything at once (and he wept when he learned of the fate of the

Girondins), Condorcet did not come to understand the nature of the destructiveness, where it came from or how far it would go.

Yet his old faith did resiliently make space for heretical doubts. Perhaps it was because he had made no fetish of the abstraction of the People, but rather mediated his democratic enthusiasm through distinctions betweeen *peuple* and *populace* and kept a self-critical awareness of the extremes and the excess to which unlimited ideals could slide. It could also be that his very devotion to the utopian ideal of progress reinforced in his intellectual temperament a clear-eyed sense of what fell short of being truly progressive in the struggle for enlightened values in society. He warned against *"l'ivresse du pouvoir,"* and praised "moderation in the exercise of power" as the deep historic distinction between "European" and "Asiatic" principles of authority.

In any case, he was driven in his last years to indulge a certain spirit of revisionism. The revolution was not singular but plural, and he tried to divide its Oneness into the many-sided complexities of a revolutionary's responsibilities. *"Les choses vont mal,"* he noted as he began to worry about the next waves in an increasingly stormy course of events. Were they only *"les orages inséparable d'une révolution"*? Or would they manage to destroy *"l'espoir de notre révolution"* (a revolution which after all had been "decisively made" if not yet "concluded")? How, then, to end it? In September 1792, we find him calling for *"la cessation du mouvement révolutionnaire,"* for it now appeared clear to him that it was only *"un principe de destruction."* A fundamental reform of the state had been the objective, and this had been achieved. To go on, and on, would rob the revolution of its reasonable content and compound the mounting illegalities and disorders. The true national will resided not in the chaos of anarchic multitudes but in the people's representatives and their mandate to establish sound and stable institutions. But if it turned out that it was precisely those representatives who, in their enthusiasm or fanaticism or corruption, were inspiring the violence in permanence, then he would be impelled to find a way to defend an alternate theory which now put the virtues of *le peuple* before the vices of *les chefs*. The revolution neither "from above" nor "from below" seemed reliable enough to offer safety and security. Condorcet began to sense, in the phrase he used in the National Convention (in late 1791), that the *révolution* was indeed *"le moment dangereux de la réformation ... "*[9]

The very word itself began to be a little suspect, and in some of his manuscripts (only recently examined by scholars) one finds *révolution* crossed through and *changement* substituted. Here the new-found political legitimacy of the great metaphor seems to be wavering. It had not been so long ago that it had won its first great triumphs in the French vocabulary. In 1720, Vertot had altered the title of his *Conjuration de*

Portugal into a *Histoire des révolutions;* and in 1753 Voltaire, rewriting history in the spirit of the times, argued that Charlemagne had not been guilty of a *"révolte"* or *"sédition"* but rather that the *Translatio imperii* to the European West had constituted *"une révolution excusable par la nécessité, et respectable par le succès ... "* For half a century, the eloquent *philosophes*, by constant repetition, had made one fine phrase fashionable: *une heureuse révolution.* Condorcet's troubled spirits on the eve of his death raised great doubts about whether the revolution was, or could ever be, at once happy, necessary, respectable, successful, and excusable.

Some find it just—others, passing strange—that the Convention in the Year III was persuaded to adopt unanimously a project whereby three thousand copies of Condorcet's posthumous *Esquisse* were to be acquired. As Daunou, who proposed the decree, observed,

> Condorcet wrote this work in such forgetfulness of himself and of his own misfortunes that nothing in it reminds us of the disastrous conditions under which he wrote. He speaks of the Revolution with nothing but enthusiasm. We see that he considered his own proscription only as one of those personal mishaps nearly inevitable in the midst of a great movement productive of general happiness.

This was prophetically close to the latter-day notion (Adlai Stevenson's, I believe) that "you can't make an omelette without breaking eggheads ... " In any case, the moving *Avertissement* to the 1795 edition of the *Esquisse* was not without a quiet, dissenting note of irony and protest:

> May this death, which will in no small degree contribute in the pages of history to characterise the era in which it has taken place, inspire a firm and dauntless attachment to the rights of which it was a violation! Such is the only homage worthy of the sage who, the fatal sword suspended over his head, could meditate in peace the melioration and happiness of his fellow-creatures; such the only consolation those can experience who have been the objects of his affection, and have known all the extent of his virtue.

Is there a recurring pattern of revolutionary psychology at work here? In 1795, after Condorcet's body was found mysteriously in a prison cell, a Jacobin in the Convention was moved to buy thousands of copies of an edition of Condorcet's last manuscript: for the *philosophe* had presumably remained loyal to the Revolution and considered his proscription only a "personal mishap." But, when the posthumous edition was printed, a prefatory note managed to express the hope that the author's death would "inspire a firm and dauntless attachment to the rights of which it was a violation!" In every revolution, the friends of the executioner try to justify the necessary murder, and the friends of the victim gather to keep alive the tragic memory of a martyr. If the revolution must devour its children, it is manifestly desirable that at least one obliging child should come to understand that, after all, the revolution was hungry. Most of the devoured ones prove to be less obliging. Still, once a body is in the grave, the spirit can go marching on, invoked by the forces of both camps.

Did Condorcet sense who, in the Revolution, his friends and his enemies were? I have already referred to the ambiguous vagueness (possibly intentional, possibly not) of his announced campaign against "the political charlatans." Who were they? Still only the men of the old regime, whose religion and politics and greed he had continued to unmask in the spirit of Voltaire and Diderot? Or could they now be located among the zealous citizens of the new regime whose sweet hopes for the future he had always shared? If he had heard the debate between Brissot and Robespierre at the Jacobin Club in April 1792, he would surely have been led to look to his left, to those who believed in a boundless commitment to unlimited politics and who, in demanding all power for the Revolution, left no space for rights (or a sense of their violation) even for themselves.

> At the very moment [Brissot said] when the worthy patriot is fighting illness and still trying stoutly to complete the plans for Public Instruction, the very moment when he is teaching the foreign powers to respect a free people, just at this very moment you choose to slander this great man!
> Do you think that if the burning genius of these great men—Condorcet, Voltaire, d'Alembert—had not slowly but surely inflamed our souls that the tribune would be ringing today with your speeches on liberty? You hack away at Condorcet although his life as a revolutionary has been nothing but sacrifices for the people. As a philosopher, he became a politician; an *académicien* became a journalist; a nobleman became a Jacobin . . . . He is being accused of coolness because he works quietly, of being an enemy of the people because he does not hang around the people's tribune.

Robespierre's sharp reply clarified the intellectual past and hinted at the political future. It was, again, "a choice of comrades"—Condorcet or Rousseau.

> If our intellectual masters [*nos maîtres à penser*] are supposed to be the academic friends of d'Alembert, I have only one answer to give: the reputations of the new régime cannot be based on the old reputations. If d'Alembert and his friends ridiculed the priests they sometimes flattered the great and the powerful [*les grands et les rois*]. I have but one objection: that all these great philosophers persecuted with

such tenacity the virtue, genius, and liberty of Jean-Jacques Rousseau, that virtuous and sensitive philosopher, the only one who in
my view deserves *les honneurs de l'apothéose*, otherwise squandered in
intrigues on behalf of political charlatans and despicable flatterers.[10]

As we have seen, Barère initiated the move which (but for an accident)
would have sent his Convention colleague Thomas Paine along to the
guillotine; and Robespierre, who once openly remarked that a weak,
prejudiced dogmatist like Montesquieu would have been "less by a
head," was evidently in the grips of an ideologized anger which would
surely have purged Condorcet, that last of the illustrious pre-
Revolutionary generation of *philosophes*.

"*Citoyens!*" Robespierre had thundered, "*vouliez-vous une révolution
sans révolution?*"[11] How could there be such a thing? It was a contradiction in terms. There was only one categorical imperative, and revolution
was its name. The blood of martyrs waters the soil of ideology.

2. The Kantian Dilemma

From this moment onward, this was, inescapably, the issue that would
try men's minds—whether (and if yes, how; and if not, why not) a new
breed of men, the committed revolutionary intellectuals, was to proceed
to a total and immediate destruction in the name of a complete and
permanent renewal. Kant, who had spoken most favorably of the
French Revolution (and of the American rebellion too) and who was
convinced that without "fantasy" and "enthusiasm" nothing great had
ever been achieved in the world, thought incessantly about this problem
and finally issued a historic warning about the relationship between
moral and political ideals and social realities. He who had known what it
was to give oneself up to "the sweet feeling of benevolence [*dem süssen
Gefühl des Wohltuns*]" and who had "dreamed the sweet dream," argued
that the idea of the highest political good (e.g., perpetual peace) must
not be "taken in a revolutionary sense and made the basis of a sudden
change through violent overthrow of a previously existing wrong condition." Rather, it must be "sought for and realised by gradual reform in
the light of firm principles ... " There were not inconsiderable difficulties here. How could he reconcile firmness with gradualism, principles with the slow process of "an endlessly progressive approximation
[*eine ins Unendliche fortschreitende Annäherung*]"?[12]

The revolutionary Kant wrestled with Kant the reformer. When he
militantly insisted that "the rights of man must be held sacred," he
could not help but go on to say, "One cannot compromise here and seek
the middle course of a pragmatic conditional law between the morally

right and the expedient. All politics must bend its knee before the right."
Fiat justitia, pereat mundus—a "true maxim" whose meaning, *zu deutsch*,
he spelled out as "Let justice reign even if all the rascals in the world
should perish from it"—was for him "a stout principle of right." But,
when he thought of abstractions as the motive force of human action, he
had his hesitations. "Very few people act from principles, and that is
good; the more general the principles are and the most steadfastly a
person adheres to them, the more damage is done." More than that,
there was on occasion a distinct tone of aversion in his attitude toward
"general philanthropy." "Love of mankind as a whole contains the
largest volume but the lowest intensity. If I am interested in the well-
being of a particular man in proportion to my love of mankind, my
interest will be small." With such a small interest, what prospect could
there be for the fulfillment of the duty to respect one's neighbor and
"never to use him merely as a means for my purposes but to honor his
dignity"? Surely only a dim hope.[13]

For clearly, as Kant came to fear, it was not only rascals who perished
in an uncompromising, unpragmatic reign of justice. Inasmuch as the
revolutionary upheaval produced its effects "tempestuously and violently," it could hardly be "ushered in according to plan without damage to freedom." How indeed could its mistakes be expunged except
through yet another "new (and at any time dangerous) revolution"?
And if, in fact, a revolution accomplished "the fall of personal despotism
or of avaricious or tyrannical oppression," would this constitute a real
victory for enlightenment and "a true reform in ways of thinking"? For
would not "new prejudices serve as well as old ones to harness the great
unthinking masses"? No, the transition to a new progressive order of
affairs could only be effected through "gradually advancing reform."

Yet was not the price of Kantian progress often the crude and painful
excesses of just such a Kantian devotion to stout principle?

> I grant that I cannot really reconcile myself to the following expres-
> sions made use of even by clever men. "A certain people (engaged in
> a struggle for civil freedom) is not yet ripe for freedom." "The
> bondmen of a landed proprietor are not yet ready for freedom." And
> hence, likewise, "Mankind in general is not yet ripe for freedom of
> belief." For according to such a presupposition, freedom will never
> arrive, since we cannot *ripen* to this freedom if we are not first of all
> placed therein. (We must be free in order to be able to make purpo-
> sive use of our powers in freedom.) The first attempts will indeed be
> crude and usually will be attended by a more painful and more
> dangerous state than that in which we are still under the orders and
> also the care of others. Yet we never ripen with respect to reason
> except through *our own* efforts (which we can make only when we
> are free).

Kant's dilemma deepened. There was always a small strain of the Jacobin in him, and one wonders whether he had ever heard the rumor that he had accepted an invitation from Sièyes to come to Paris as his adviser. How would he have survived? (Even the Marquis de Sade, who just before his liberation had been rousing the revolutionary crowd from his cell window in the Bastille and was given his freedom as a victim of the old regime, found himself resentenced to prison by the Revolution for the political crime of *"modérantisme."*)[14]

3. Of Passion and Prudence

The root of the dilemma was in an uneasy association between the revolutionary category of the perfect and the political imperative of reason. Kant had only contempt for what he thought of as mindless empiricism and practicality. "Moderation," or "steering a mid-course," left him cold—"its medicine is like the 'Venetian treacle' wherein so many good things have been mixed that it is good for nothing." Confronted with the ills and miseries of a defective social order, he put an urgent question: "How can they be remedied as soon as possible?" Reconciliation might have been a duty of man, but he was quick to insist that it not be confused with "the weak toleration of wrongs which renounces stern measures."[15]

Yet here, too, a tension recurred in him between passion and prudence, between principle and practice (as if, indeed, there were in him a touch both of Burke and Bakunin).

It would be absurd to demand that every defect be immediately and impetuously changed [*sofort und mit Ungestüm*].... But it can be demanded that at least the maxim of the necessity of such a change should be taken to heart by those in power, so that they may continuously approach the goal of the constitution that is best under laws of right.

Still, were there not situations (and he had to admit that there were) which were "ripe for complete transformation [*zur völligen Umwälzung*]"? And how would he finally feel about "a violent revolution, engendered by a bad constitution, introducing by illegal means a more legal constitution"? These issues troubled Kant; but his ultimate disposition was toward the kind of prudence embodied in such maxims as: If you bend the reed too much you break it, and: He who attempts too much attempts nothing. He opted for "peacable means," for he feared "the anarchic condition which would result from precipitate reform." Above all (and this in the time of the Jacobin terror),

... even when nature herself produces revolutions, political wisdom will not employ them to legitimise still greater oppression. On the contrary, it will use them as a call of nature for fundamental reforms to produce a lawful constitution founded upon principles of freedom, for only such a constitution is durable.

Thus Kant set himself in a great critical tradition, estranged from both "despotising moralists" and "moralising politicians," alarmed at the imprudent precipitateness of the one and contemptuous of the unprincipled practical tinkering of the other.

In a famous work of 1793, he can still be seen wavering between a cautious course which bordered on unattractive middling principles of moderation and the perfect path of human transformation which could only be the revolutionary apocalypse. How is man ever to become a truly human, moral, and virtuous creature? Such a heroic state of earthly affairs, he argues in one place, "cannot be brought about through gradual reformation [allmähliche Reform] ... but must be effected through a revolution in man's disposition.... He can become a new man only by a kind of rebirth, as it were a new creation." Yet, in another place, he is forced to reject those simple-minded propositions from Seneca to Rousseau against which "the history of all times cries out," disengaging himself from the sharp disjunctions of "rigorists" and "latitudinarians," and even going so far as to content himself with the unexciting observation that "Experience actually seems to substantiate the middle ground between the two extremes."

Here Kant openly confesses his inner reluctance to go to such equivocating liberal lengths. Mitteldinge had to be rigorously resisted; for, after all, "it is of great consequence to ethics in general to avoid admitting, so long as it is possible, of anything morally intermediate ... for with such ambiguity all maxims are in danger of forfeiting their precision and stability." That he might also be called upon to offer a stable contribution which could make precise just this troublesome principle of ambiguity was not his momentary concern. It was enough that he was being driven on to intellectual revisions; and when ideal possibilities and real consequences came into increasingly open conflict, a sense of new dangers replaced some of Kant's old fears of intermediacy.[16]

It is not fully clear how Kant intended to occupy the middle ground, free from the strains of the extremes. Writing of "a glorious ideal" in his study of Education,[17] Kant argued that

it matters little if we are not able to realise it at once. Only we must not look upon the idea as chimerical, nor decry it as a beautiful dream, notwithstanding the difficulties that stand in the way of its realisation. An idea is nothing else than the conception of a perfection which has not yet been experienced. For instance, the idea of a perfect republic governed by principles of justice—is such an idea impossible because it has not yet been experienced?

That such an idea might become "dangerous" and the drastic actions which it promoted "culpable"—these suspicions overtook Kant in the 1790s when he contemplated the course of the French Revolution.

The revolution of a gifted people which we have seen unfolding in our day may succeed or miscarry; it may be filled with misery and atrocities to the point that a sensible man, were he boldly to hope to execute it successfully the second time, would never resolve to make the experiment at such cost—this revolution, I say, nonetheless finds in the hearts of all spectators (who are not engaged in this game themselves) a wishful participation that borders closely on enthusiasm, the very expression of which is fraught with danger.[18]

There are still traces here of Kant's two minds on the subject. If, as has been said by a recent critic,[19] there is "a fundamental ambiguity" in Kant's thought, it is an ambiguity which illuminates more meanings than do most fundamental clarities.

Kant, for all his sedentary Königsberg life, lived very much in the intellectual climate of the day, and his political temperament was ceaselessly engaged in the onrushing European events. Agitated by the developments of the Revolution in France ("the topic of every conversation around here"), a Berlin correspondent raised with Kant the relevance of his views to the new questions being argued and offered a humble suggestion to the *Meister*: "I believe that there are many interesting things to be said about the rationality of the basic principles on which the French Republic bases itself, if only it were prudent to write about such things." One of Kant's friends has recorded that political matters were not to be mentioned in his study—only at table could they be discussed; then from his table, as another friend reported, "a cosmopolitan and free-thinking philosopher watched the experiment which was to realise the idea of a perfect constitution demanded by reason with the same pleasure as a scientist has in looking upon an experiment which is to corroborate an important hypothesis."[20] With whatever wisdom he extracted from the lessons of experience, he sought to disengage social ideals from utopian chimeras, to salvage a faith in the perfect from the dismal failures of brave human effort, and to maintain his optimism about progress in the face of the snail's pace of destiny.

Kant's metaphysical ingenuity saved him, but humor helped too. His intellectual rigor was not above allowing an old joke—he tells it in the conclusion to his *Streit der Facultäten* (1798), and perhaps then it was new—about the doctor who constantly reported an improving pulse, respiration, and stool, and the ailing patient who replied, "How's my illness? How should it be? I'm dying of improvement, pure and simple! [*Ich sterbe vor lauter Besserung!*]" Kant, the philosopher of the *Aufklärung*, could not bring himself to blame those who had begun to despair of the ideals of the Enlightenment. The utopians loved mankind too much, and the revolutionaries loved men too little.

Kant tried to resolve his difficulties by revising his utopian longing and reducing his revolutionary commitment. He made a distinction between millennium and utopia. He defended the reasonable dreams of More, Plato, and Harrington but separated himself from the pious enthusiasm for "a renovated world after this one will have perished in flames." He vindicated the devotion to "distant aims" and, indeed, "the conscious expectation of the future" as the decisive mark of humanity; but he disdained the confounding of man's true hope with an uncultured and instinct-ridden wish for some form of paradise. Thomas More would have understood. Kant made sure to point out that, in the achievement of a universal civic order "with the greatest freedom," what would emerge would be a society "in which there is mutual opposition among the members." More than that, any "complete solution" is impossible, for "from such crooked wood as man is made of, nothing perfectly straight can be built [*Aus so krummen Holze, als woraus der Mensch gemacht ist, kann nichts ganz Gerades gezimmert werden*]."[21]

These were sensitive and subtle revisions. But, like Spinoza before him, who had concluded that doctrines could only be "chimaera" and "utopia" if philosophers could not conceive "a theory of politics which could be turned to use," Kant came no further toward a usable strategy of political action. Progress must come, but it would be slow and devious; glorious ideals must be dreamed, but they might prompt pernicious passions. He could not return to a confidence in an enlightened King Utopus, for he sensed that any philosopher-king would founder on the corruption of reason which power inevitably brings. What remained of his notions of utopia and revolution was a cautious hope that social reform would somehow go forward "from above," i.e., "not from bottom to top, but from top to bottom." This was not, of course, reason enough to abandon hope. On the contrary, the evolutionary perspective confirmed his optimism about the future: "evolution instead of revolution." But this was less political philosophy than the metaphysics of history.

4. From More to Marx

In this context of essential temperament, the sharp contrasts in the ultimate messages of those three European masters of political metaphysics, More, Kant, and Marx, emerge most forcefully. More preferred utopia to revolution (or what he called "hurly-burly"); Marx preferred revolution to utopia. And Kant, increasingly suspicious of the ruinous violence of the total overturn as well as the perfect absolutism of the millennial fantasy, tried to overcome his peculiar penchant for both.

This may or may not be the tragic contradiction of that utopian state of mind which, as writers like Friedrich Hayek and J. L. Talmon have insisted, "always" starts with daydreams and ends with tyranny.[22] I am not eager to press polemically either side of this argument, especially since the utopian founding father himself would appear to have been in real uncertainty. The troubled passage I am referring to occurs in Sir Thomas More's *Confutation of Tyndale's Answer* (1532). This work was written in a bitter and intolerant mood against "Luthers pestylent heresyes," which led him to a justification of the banning of the English Bible. These were days, he notes (and here I modernize some spelling), "in which Tyndale hath (God amend him!) with the infection of his contagious heresies, so sore poisoned malicious and new-fangled folks"; hence the decision "for the while to prohibit the scripture of God to be suffered in English tongue among the people's hands, lest evil folke by false drawing of every good thing they read in to the colour and maintenance of their own fond fantasies, and turning all honey into poison, might both do deadly hurt unto themself, and spread also that infection farther abroad."

At this point, More is overtaken by a personal sense of troubled self-consciousness: what of his own works? Here he makes his historic retreat, an intellectual withdrawal which has left a disfiguring question mark on the whole story of simple utopian innocence.[23]

> I say therefore, in these days in which men by their own default misconstrue and take harm of the very scripture of God, until men better amend, if any man would now translate [Erasmus's] *Moria* into English, or some works either that I have myself written ere this, albeit there be no harm therein, folke yet being (as they be) given to take harm of that which is good, I would not only my darling's books [i.e., Erasmus's] but mine own also, help to burn them both with mine own hands, rather than folke should (though through their own fault) take any harm of them, seeing that I see them likely in these days so to do.

If More himself is quite prepared to burn his own book to avoid the deadly hurt of utopian fantasies, one would be hard put to deny the critic's equation of literary virtue and political vice. More might well have agreed with Tocqueville that "what is a merit in the writer may well be a vice in the statesman and the very qualities which go to make great literature can lead to catastrophic revolutions." Nor would he conceivably have disputed those nineteenth-century words which Robert Southey put into his mouth in an imaginary colloquy in his *More* book:

> If in the latter part of my mortal existence I had misgivings concerning any of my writings, they were of the single one, which is still a living work, and which will continue so to be. I feared that speculative opinions which had been intended for the possible but remote benefit of mankind, might, by unhappy circumstances be rendered instrumental to great and immediate evil.[24]

However, this great (and surprising) self-critical tradition of the utopian's own fear of utopianism is not my present concern.

What I have been trying to suggest is that the utopian detail makes possible a critical focus between the real and the ideal. In dreams begin responsibilities. If the primary aspiration of all history is held to be a genuine community of human beings, then the utopian prophecy becomes the usable measure of all things. It is precisely this prophetic tradition that Marx, as an anti-utopian revolutionary, abjured. Revolutionary man tends either to be a connoisseur of the apocalypse or a visionary of the terrestrial paradise. Prophetic utopians like Saint-Simon, Fourier, Robert Owen, were cursorily dismissed: "Those new social systems were from the outset doomed to be utopias; the more their details were elaborated, the more they necessarily receded into pure fantasy."

It is only fair to reiterate that this was not done without some mixed feelings, for Marx and Engels had defended the "dreamers" against the "philistines": "We, on the contrary, delight in the inspired ideas and germs of ideas which everywhere emerge through their covering of fantasy." But then these solutions were only "produced out of their heads [*aus dem Kopfe erzeugt*]." The prophetic utopians may have "anticipated with genius countless truths," but it was only when Marxism came along that "the validity of these truths could be proved scientifically." Marx was infatuated and Engels intoxicated with the scientific aspect of their sociological inquiries; and they recovered soon enough from the early ambivalence of their attitude toward the prophets. Utopia could not realize itself without the abolition of romantic longing and political escapism; and these could not be abolished without the recognition of historical revolutionary necessity. Utopia will not come because it is desirable; it will come because it is necessary and inevitable. The others may have seen a vision, but they had been privileged to hear the crack of the thunder. And suddenly "the task was no longer to manufacture a system of society as perfect as possible, but to investigate the historical economic process from which these classes and their antagonisms had of necessity sprung and to discover in the economic position thus created the means for solving the conflict." The others, possessing only their vision, were mere dreamers; they, with the logic of history at their command, had won the prize of certitude. Today, with a century of hindsight at our command, it would only appear that one man's logic is another man's fantasy.

"I am working like mad all through the nights," Marx wrote to Engels in December 1857, "so that I may at least have the outlines clear before the *déluge* comes."[25] They did not pause, impatiently waiting for the apocalypse, to ask themselves: Was there truly a contradiction between the ethical projection of the ideal and the critical analysis of the real? Were these two moral and intellectual tasks mutually exclusive? It is clear, as can be seen from the political career of Thomas More, that utopian vision without a social base is politically helpless; but a political movement without utopian vision is morally blind.

This was the sense of Kant's last words on behalf of what he called the "sweet dream." More's *Utopia*, like Plato's *Republic* and Harrington's *Oceana*, "have never so much as been tried (Cromwell's abortive monster of a despotic republic excepted)." True, in the bitterness Kant had come to feel about the costly revolutionary experiment of his own day, he became persuaded that it was "rash" to propose dreams and, indeed, "culpable to abolish what presently exists." He who had confidently announced that "the ultimate destiny of the human race was the greatest moral perfection" now felt that "we must not hope too much from men in their progress towards the better ... " He was reluctant to face the mockery of politicians who took "the hopes of man as the dreamings of distraught minds."

Yet, as he wrote, "it is sweet, however, to imagine constitutions corresponding to the requirements of reason." Utopian ideals were not "empty chimaerae"; and the perpetual approaches to their consummation were not only thinkable but obligatory. What was to remain throughout as his constant personal guide was, in a happy phrase, "the compass of reason." A whole chastened conception of the hazardous relationship between heroic human ideals and historic social difficulties was summed up in this passage from one of his letters:

To dash with hasty, enterprising steps toward a far away goal has always been injurious to a thorough insight. He who shows us the cliffs has not necessarily set them up, and even if someone maintains

that it is impossible to pass through them *with full sails* (of dogmatism), he has not on that account denied *every* possibility of getting through. I think that you will not find the compass of reason to
be unnecessary or misleading in this venture.[26]

When, then, is a utopian an anti-utopian? When his extravagant concern for the ideal future drives him back to a renewed involvement in the
real present. Second thoughts forced More to a self-destructive critique
of irresponsible social fantasy; and Marx to an uncontrollable rage
against all dreamers and their "rotten spirit," which "plays with fancy
pictures of the future structure of society . . . silly, stale, and basically
reactionary." In the case of Kant, the tension of a utopian's anti-
utopianism issued in a mild, reasonable revision of "sweet dreams."

That the *Zeitgeist* was not pleased will surprise no student of ideology.
Young Schiller was outraged and now found Kant's views *"empörend"*;
Goethe, similarly upset at the promulgation of Kant's concept of a "radical evil" (*das radikale Böse*) in human affairs, could hardly contain his horror (in a letter to Herder) at this "wanton and shameful spot" on the
revered philosopher's record. It is understandable that such unorthodox
departures on the part of the philosopher of "the German theory of the
French Revolution" (as Marx, following Heine, was to call him) should
have proved so alarming for so many of his faithful readers. In a sense,
Kant's doubts and deviations from the contemporary revolutionary
ideology cast him in the role of the first German revisionist.[27]

There is a passage in the *Streit der Facultäten* (1798) which, touching
upon utopia and the future, astronomy and revolution, progress, reform
and the mixture of good and evil, moves suggestively through many of
our main themes.

Kant begins by puzzling over the question: "What have we to expect
of the future? Continual progress or continual regress?" He was tempted
to see only the farcical aspect of "all the doings on our globe." The global
reference led him directly to an astronomical standpoint: for the planets
themselves, as seen from the earth, seemed to go "now forward, now
backward, and now to stand still." However, according to the Copernican hypothesis (and even the tangle of Tycho Brahe's cycles and epicy-
cles), there would appear to be some "regular course." The astronomical
references led Kant onward to the problem of revolution, which he had
once previously associated with the systematic structure of the cosmos,
albeit with very little hope of fixing its short path in the context of
human affairs. Yet how sturdy was the astronomical analogue, and how
long could it survive a reasonable critique? What if the revolution as it
actually happens in society does not conform to either Copernicus's

principle of circularity or Condorcet's principle of linear progress? Was there ever, in historical events, a "full compassing" or a complete, original turn? Was not what men were pleased to call "revolution" only an ingenious metaphor which made up in beguiling echoes of celestial certitude and heavenly promise for what it lacked in sober meaningful content? And, even if it came to command human enthusiasm and sympathy, political zeal and even moral greatness, Kant was convinced—both by "reading the signs of the day" and by facing "the mixture of good and evil in man's predisposition"—that mankind's progress in the course of history would proceed "gradually, not by revolution but by evolution ... "

All this might well have been what Kant himself referred to as "simply the mode of thinking of the spectators which reveals itself publicly in this game of great revolutions ... "*

It is a game, evidently, with only so many fixed pieces, just so many limited moves. Contemplating the record of post-revolutionary reconsiderations from, say, Kant to Koestler, one cannot help reinforcing Professor A. O. Lovejoy's suspicion (in that masterful study in intellectual history, *The Great Chain of Being*) that each age seems to evolve new species of reasonings and conclusions, although upon the same old problems, " ... the truth is that the number of essentially distinct philosophical ideas or dialectical motives is—as the number of really distinct jokes is said to be—decidedly limited."

Kant himself once noted the two most maniacal elements in the *Schwärmerei* that had been gaining ground in a Europe badly befuddled by "loquacious ignorance" and "airy possibilities": namely, faddish French omniscience and systematic German fanaticism. He felt that perhaps for the moment "disdainful silence" would be "more appropriate toward such madness." Movements of this kind, he reassured one of his worried students (in a letter which was surely too ironical for real comfort), "have but a short duration before they make way for new follies."[28]

5. Of Truth and Sincerity

A number of important considerations remained for a philosophy which sought belatedly to qualify in this singular fashion the new imperatives of utopian ideals and revolutionary methods—e.g., the reciprocity of

---

*" ... bloss die Denkungsart der Zuschauer, welche sich bei diesem Spiele grosser Umwandlungen öffentlich verrät ... "

means and ends, the role of the independent intellectual, and the relationship between ideals and ideology.

In October 1793, a Berlin editor had written to Kant about the "disgusting" turn taken by the French Revolution, "as all true freedom and morality as well as all art of government and legislation is trodden under foot . . . " He went on to say: "Of course, the cutting off of heads is easy, especially if one has it done by others." And he expressed his relief that in the September issue of the *Berliner Monatsschrift* Kant had evidently clarified his political position in an article which reconsidered "empty ideals and philosophical dreams—in short, that what sounds all right in theory has no value in practice." The argument was rather more complex than his correspondent had sensed, for Kant had in point of fact declined to abandon the ideas of a Rousseau or an Abbé de Saint-Pierre, or, indeed, the kind of general theory which outlines what *ought to be* and which, by recommending the earthly powers to act as if this were possible, "by this very action makes it possible." He felt certain that "after many failures Reason will emerge as victorious"; he still counted on "human nature," for he could not and would not believe it to be "so swallowed up in evil that all respect for rights and duties should be quite extinguished in it." Yet the horror of the violent purge remained; and he was later to write:

> No pretended good intention can wipe off the stain of injustice in the means applied. And if it is argued that the whole earth would still be in a lawless condition if those who introduced laws had shied from using violence, this is still no excuse. Nor is it an excuse for political revolutionaries [*Staatsrevolutionisten*] that when constitutions have degenerated, the people must be allowed to reform them by force and to be unjust once and for all in order to establish justice later more safely.

Could a philosopher, even if he wanted to change the world, do any more under the circumstances than interpret it and criticize it? Kant was under no simple-minded illusions about the delimited intellectual task.

> That kings should philosophise or philosophers become kings is not to be expected. Nor is it to be wished, since the possession of power inevitably corrupts the untrammelled judgment of reason. But kings or king-like peoples which rule themselves under laws of equality should not suffer the class of philosophers to disappear or to be silent, but should let them speak openly. This is indispensable to the enlightenment of the business of government.

It was but a modest proposal (More had asked a bit less, Mill would ask for a good bit more); and Kant coupled it with an assurance that philosophers should not be confounded with plotters, propagandists, or lobbyists.[29]

But men of power, then as now, were not so easily persuaded of the virtues of tolerance and the usefulness of reason and philosophy for the enlightened business of government. To "speak openly" was often to invite personal disaster. The lessons of More's caution, Erasmus's fearfulness, and Spinoza's silence were not lost upon Immanuel Kant. His philosophical attempts to "stray beyond the limits" ran similarly afoul of royal Prussian edicts on orthodoxy and censorship.

The courageous effort to revise the conventional interpretations of existing doctrine in the light of reason earned only the "great displeasure" of Frederick William, who, in 1794, wrote sternly from Berlin to "Our Most Worthy and Erudite Professor and Dear Loyal Kant, Königsberg in Prussia." It was an "abuse of philosophy" to distort and debase "certain fundamental doctrines of Holy Scripture and Christianity." The King was disappointed: "We should have expected better things from you.... You must youself realise how irresponsibly you behave against your duty as a teacher of youth and against Our well-known sovereign intentions." The royal admonition was ominously straightforward: "In case of continued insubordination, you must unfailingly expect unpleasant consequences." Indeed, the King was pressing his officials to institute proceedings against Kant, and (in a letter to Wöllner) he expressed his dissatisfaction with the mildness and the slowness of the censorship. "At Frankfurt there is Steinbart who must be driven out; at Königsberg, Hasse who is a chief radical; of such things as well as of the disgraceful writings of Kant there must be an end.... There must be an absolute stop to this disorder."

Kant responded, as he admitted, "most submissively." He gave promises of "obedience" and of "not becoming guilty again," as befitted a "most faithful subject." He was then in his seventy-first year, but survival was all. "I shall in future completely desist from all public lectures or papers concerning religion, be it natural or revealed." As he later explained, he was choosing his phrases "most carefully"—"so that I should not be deprived of my freedom of judgment in religious matters *for ever*, but only so long as His Majesty was alive" (and, in point of fact, the philosopher survived the king by some seven years).

Years before (in a letter to Moses Mendelssohn, in April 1766), Kant had tried to work out, in the face of so many difficulties in truth-telling, a personal principle of compromise:

The loss of self-respect, which arises from the consciousness of an insincere mind, would be the greatest evil that could ever befall me, but it is quite certain that it will never happen. . . . It is indeed true that I think many things with the clearest conviction and to my great satisfaction, which I never have the courage to say. But I will never say anything which I do not think.

And in Kant's unpublished papers there is the following remark of ultimate explanation:

> To revoke and deny one's inner conviction is vicious and cannot be demanded of any person, but to remain silent in a case like this is a subject's duty, and while everything a person says must be true, it is not his duty to proclaim publicly all that is true.[30]

The temporizing philosopher's self-justification has often been subjected to censure. Even in his own day (viz., the attitude of the Berlin publisher, Nicolai), Kant's accommodating conduct apparently gave offense. His Berlin editor, Biester, put it to him as gently as he could when he reported that "everyone" regretted the voluntary promise, for it could only mean "a great triumph for the enemies of the Enlightenment," and "the good cause suffers a great loss." It seemed to him that "you did not need to make this promise." Kant should have continued to write on the dangerous topics in question. "Granted, you would then perhaps have had to defend yourself again on specific points. Or you could even have remained silent for the rest of your life but without giving these people the satisfaction of being released from the fear of your words."

One's attitude depends on a judgment as to whether or not the subtle distinction between sincerity (*Aufrichtigkeit*) and candor (*Offenherzigkeit*) is viable. "I can admit, though it is much to be deplored," Kant observed in one of his censored books, "that candor (in speaking the *whole* truth which one knows) is not to be found in human nature. But we must be able to demand *sincerity* (that *all that one says* be said with truthfulness), and indeed if there were in our nature no predisposition to sincerity, whose cultivation merely is neglected, the human race must needs be, in its own eyes, an object of the deepest contempt."[31]

Among those of his recent critics who have not refrained from a note of contempt is an American commentator who has written:

> I share with Nietzsche the feeling that Kant is an old Tartuffe. Thus, where others stress Kant's sweetness of character and nobility of purpose, I see the added hues of a petulant dogmatist, annoyed at public indifference to his great work; of a thin-blooded recluse, whose knowledge of human nature lacks depth and subtlety of insight. Others stress Kant's enlightened political views; I see also the half-hearted courage and the conformity to authority of a careful old man.[32]

There is a nobler tone in the older tradition of Kant criticism. As a nineteenth-century German biographer puts it:

It cannot be denied that more discretion than courage is manifested in this solemnly imposed duty of silence. The old man of seventy might have calmly awaited the "unpleasant consequences" threatened by the order. The Berlin authorities could scarcely have done more than to prohibit his writings and perhaps to withdraw the increase of his salary. Nevertheless, Kant was not of the stuff of which martyrs are made. And he might comfort himself with the thought that he had already said all that was most essential. So he chose what was in accord with his nature, silence and peace. Of course, if he had declared, like the seventy-year-old Socrates in a similar position, that he had a higher mission in the world than the professorship which had been entrusted to him by the Royal Prussian Commission, that to this mission of teaching truth and combating error and lies he would not and could not become untrue, then a page of his life history, and a page of the history of German philosophy, would have been more splendidly distinguished than is now the case.[33]

How deeply might Kant have objected? I should like to think that he would have felt not only the personal wound but also the ethical force of the argument. In a fragment found among Kant's *"lose Blätter,"* there is an indirect political comment on this moral dilemma of personal safety and civic obligation: *"Die beste Regierungsform ist nicht die worin es am bequemsten ist zu leben, sondern worin dem Bürger sein Recht am meisten gesichert ist."*[*][34]

Here, then, was a revolutionary and a reformer, a utopian and a gradualist, a militant and yet a moderate, an endlessly critical philosopher who knew the temptations of ideology and who, even in the bitterness of its deceptions, retained a feeling of fellowship for those who wanted to associate imagination with power, for those who "dreamed the sweet dream."

A political artist can rule the world by the power of imagination: for example, when he declaims in the English parliament about the freedom of the people, or in the French Convention about the equality of all classes, as if they really existed. Yet it is better even to have the pretence of the good things which ennoble mankind than to be palpably deprived of them.[†][35]

---

[*]"The best form of government is not that in which it is most comfortable to live, but rather than in which the rights of the citizen are most secure."

[†]"Aber es ist doch besser, auch nur den Schein von dem Besitz dieses die Menschheit Veredelnden Guts für sich zu haben, als sich desselben handgreiflich beraubt zu fühlen."

6. The War of the Temperaments

This high-minded message from Königsberg might not have found its proper relevance in the Paris under the shadow of the guillotine. The pretense of good things? It was an outrageous "as-if" compensation for the palpable deprivations of a grand revolution gone berserk. Was there no more seasonable counsel for a noble generation trapped in an ignoble course of events?

In her philosophical study of revolution, Dr. Hannah Arendt refers to the "notion of a coincidence of foundation and preservation by virtue of augmentation"—but by that she only means that there is an interconnection between the revolutionary act of beginning "something entirely new" and "conservative care" to shield this new beginning.[36]

This "care" was termed by Mme de Staël, more old-fashionedly, "moderation": and in full flight from the Terror she did not underestimate the difficulty of holding fast to it.

> The more odious the old government, the more agreement there was to overthrow it, and the more difficult it is to distinguish among the various opinions separating those who, united for destruction, are divided in rebuilding . . . .
>
> During a revolution the party that holds moderate opinions needs, more than any other, courage of soul and breadth of mind. It has two struggles to carry on, two kinds of argument to refute, two dangers to avoid . . . .
>
> Some people heap ridicule upon opinions that are removed equally from two conflicting extremes. It is understandable that the two extreme parties should agree in attacking this common enemy. But it is by no means understandable that anyone should dare to call this way of thinking weak and indecisive. People have the knack of reducing everything to extremes in the belief that these are certain to be preferred. Opinions do exist that we must adopt without modification. But are we to allow every lunatic who discovers a new madness to erect a new barrier to the truth?

Clearly, she was too involved in the moral and strategic urgencies of the struggle to confront realistically the deeper psycho-mechanisms at work.

Hobbes, in fact, with characteristic tough-mindedness, suggested a form of permanent class war of the extremes versus the moderates. And he cast a cold eye on the perfervid efforts of the men of his own generation to maintain themselves against the obnoxious "Force of Others," not excepting the belated calls of the Lilburnes and the Miltons "to shew forth Temperance and Moderation."

> Considering the great difference there is in Men [Hobbes wrote], from the Diversity of the Passions, how some are vainly Glorious

and hope for precedencie and superiority above their Fellows, not only when they are equall in Power but also when they are Inferiour; we must needs acknowledge that it must necessarily follow, that those men who are moderate, and look for no more but Equality of Nature, shall be obnoxious to the Force of Others, that will attempt to subdue them. And from hence shall proceed a general dissidence in Mankind, and mutuall fear one of another.[37]

It was not a peculiarly English insight, although when Pierre Bayle made a similar point, with (as I have already illustrated) even more pungency, he was an exile from France and conducting his magisterial argument against apocalyptic visionaries and their extremist passions from the more congenial intellectual atmosphere of Rotterdam. In fact, it was in his article on Hobbes (in his *Dictionnaire*, begun in 1695) that Bayle most clearly indicated his disassociation—for all the subsequent misinterpretations of the *philosophes* and their Jacobin followers—from the mind-set of utopian revolution, and the burning danger of the *fumo chiliastico*.

We are here, at the end of our chronicle of utopians and revolutionaries and their ideological cycles, faced at every turn by the spectacle of the long war of the temperaments and the follies of forgetfulness. It may well be, in the suggestive phrase of one political philosopher (himself echoing so many others), the one constant in history, "the constancy of a process that leaves a trail of equivalent symbols in time and space...."[38]

I return to my point of departure, to Mme de Staël, not because she offered any unforgettable solution but because she is, memory for memory, so much part of the problem: the symptomology of recurrent bouts of historical amnesia. Recall her desperate mid-revolutionary plea on behalf of the moderate party and the men in the noble middle:

Far from rallying to itself feeble and timid souls, this party needs more than any other the courage that braves all kinds of distrust and danger. It must impress by the boldness of its character those whom it heartens by the wisdom of its opinions. It must be itself and not some absurd mixture or an irrelevant alternative to opposed extremes. It must, in short, demonstrate to all that reason is not a shade of meaning between extremes, but the primary colour.[39]

In language and in sentiment, this is the true and, alas, forlorn French longing. A century earlier Pierre Bayle had deplored the tragedy of the man in the middle, handicapped by the manifest vanity of philosophic reason and balance, valiantly trying to hold out against zeal and faction *à droite et à gauche*. A century and a half later, Albert Camus, pressed by his great radical antagonist Jean-Paul Sartre, was still dreaming of the

third choice, of the moderate party, and went back for refuge to Heraclitus, "the inventor of the constant change of things who nevertheless
set a limit to this perpetual process," and even further, to Nemesis, "the
goddess of moderation and the implacable enemy of the immoderate."
For it was against Sartre, unnamed and overwhelming, that Camus had
written his manifesto on behalf of *l'homme révolté:* a curious title this,
comprehensible only in the intimate context of French intellectual
polemic. The passage which first formulated for Camus (I had always
suspected as much, and he once confirmed it to me) the deep difference
between him and Sartre, between the rebel and the revolutionary, is a
passing paragraph in Sartre's little book on *Baudelaire*. Let me give our
last great committed revolutionary intellectual his due by citing it.[40]

> The revolutionary [says Sartre, speaking for himself and, no doubt,
> Mme de Beauvoir] wants to change the world; he transcends it and
> moves towards the future, towards an order of values which he him-
> self invents. The rebel is careful to preserve the abuses from which
> he suffers so that he can go on rebelling against them. He always
> shows signs of a bad conscience and of something resembling a feel-
> ing of guilt. He does not want to destroy or transcend the existing
> order; he simply wants to rise up against it. The more he attacks it,
> the more he secretly respects it. In the depths of his heart he pre-
> serves the rights which he challenges in public. If they disappeared,
> his own *raison d'être* would disappear with them. He would suddenly
> find himself plunged into a gratuitousness which frightens him.

Nothing, I trust, could be clearer: except, possibly, that characteristic
and revealing remark in the second volume of Simone de Beauvoir's
autobiography where, speaking for herself and, no doubt, Sartre, she
refers to their friend, Raymond Aron, as a "despised" moderate, and
goes on to explain: "We were temperamentally opposed to the idea of
reform: society, we felt, could change only as a result of sudden cataclysmic upheaval on a global scale."[41]

The intellectuals of utopia and revolution—clever, versatile, excitable,
volatile, never reforming, always transforming—have come full turn. In
their end is their beginning. The King is on his way to the scaffold. The
cataclysm is upon us, the globe is in upheaval. All present things will be
destroyed at once. Guiltless and without conscience, they embrace an
anonymous future in the name of invented but undisclosed values. The
sweet dream has become inviolate dogma. The revolution remains their
utopia.

Notes

Preface

1. Spinoza, in his *Tractatus Politicus* (1677; tr. Elwes, 1951), pp. 288–89:
   I have looked upon passions, such as love, hatred, anger, envy, ambition, pity, and other perturbations of the mind, not in the light of vices of human nature, but as properties just as pertinent to it, as are heat, cold, storm, thunder, and the like to the nature of the atmosphere, which phenomena, though inconvenient, are yet necessary, and have fixed causes, by means of which we endeavour to understand their nature, and the mind has just as much pleasure in viewing them aright, as in knowing such things as flatter the senses.

2. I am grateful to Dr. Harry Gideonse, chancellor of the New School of Social Research, for the opportunity to present some of this new material in a series of lectures in New York in March 1968. I am especially grateful to Mr. McGeorge Bundy, president of the Ford Foundation, for a research grant which made possible a thousand forays into the St. James Square stacks of the London Library and the reading room of the British Museum.

3. In the revolutionary hysteria of these days, the word Revolution has become a kind of magical formula. Revolution is the fashion. If you want to keep up with the times, if you don't want to be left behind, then the word Revolution must come trippingly off the tongue. [*Frankfurter Allgemeine Zeitung*, 6 November 1968, p. 1]

   A half-dozen years later, when six leading American members (mostly white, middle-class, and under thirty) of the so-called Symbionese Liberation Army were killed in Los Angeles in a gun fight with the local police, the magniloquent word was still resounding on the streets. As the *New York Times* reported (19 May 1974), p. 30:
   Even before the gunfire ended, some black youths on the block were already singing the praises of the defenders of the yellow stucco house. "You can kill our brothers," shouted one black teenager, "but you can't kill the revolution. You and all your guns can't kill that."

4. A. O. Lovejoy enjoined the historian of ideas—"if he means to take cognizance of the genuinely operative factors in the larger movements of thought"—to work at something he called "philosophical semantics," which he defined as
   a study of the sacred words and phrases of a period or a movement, with a view to a clearing up of their ambiguities, a listing of their various shades of meaning, and an examination of the way in which confused associations of ideas arising from these ambiguities have influenced the development of doctrines, or accelerated the insensible transformation of one fashion of thought into another, perhaps its very opposite. It is largely because of their ambiguities that mere words are capable of this independent action as forces in history ... [Arthur O. Lovejoy, *The Great Chain of Being: A Study in the History of An Idea* (1936), p. 14]
   In the preface to his *Essays in the History of Ideas* (1948), pp. xiv–xvi, Professor Lovejoy

specified a number of assumptions and procedures underlying the study of philosophical semantics with which, as will become obvious, I should like modestly to associate myself:

1. The presence and influence of the same presuppositions or other operative "ideas" in very diverse provinces of thought and in different periods ...

2. The role of semantic transitions and confusions, of shifts and of ambiguities in the meanings of terms, in the history of thought and of taste ...

3. The internal tensions or waverings in the mind of almost every individual writer—sometimes discernible even in a single writing or on a single page—arising from conflicting ideas or incongruous propensities of feeling or taste, to which, so to say, he is susceptible ...

But he hesitated to explore one fundamental consideration—so central to our own inquiry into the relationships between political temperament and intellectual climate. "It may, indeed, be suggested, with some plausibility, that these ideas are but the expression of some constant propensities of human nature, which became, for some reason, peculiarly potent at this time ... " The general issue raised by such a suggestion—

the question how far men's philosophies are generated, not by the logical, or supposedly logical, working out of accepted premises, but by emotional cravings, by idiosyncrasies of personal temperament, or by the social and other practical problems of a particular historic conjuncture [*The Great Chain of Being*, p. 298]

—he did not attempt to discuss and, so far as I am aware, he left the question unanswered.

5. He that hawks at larks and sparrows, has no less sport, though a much less considerable quarry, than he that flies at nobler game.... [His] searches after truth are a sort of hawking and hunting, wherein the very pursuit makes a great part of the pleasure. [John Locke, "Epistle to the Reader," in *An Essay Concerning Human Understanding* (1690–1706; ed. Yolton, 1964]

6. Stephen Vincent Benet, *John Brown's Body* (1928), p. 192.

7. William Butler Yeats, "Vacillation," in *Collected Poems* (1950), p. 282.

Chapter 1

1. Aylmer Maude, *The Life of Tolstoy: First Fifty Years* (1908), pp. 18–19.

2. *Phaedo*, 81C–D, 82. Plato, *The Last Days of Socrates* (tr. Tredennick, 1959), pp. 134–35; *The Works of Plato* (tr. Jowett, 1928), p. 143; *Five Dialogues* (ed. Lindsay, tr. Cary, 1938), pp. 166–67.

3. John Milton, *The Ready and Easy Way to Establish a Free Commonwealth* (1660; ed. Clark, 1915), pp. 18, 94–95. Thomas Hobbes, *Leviathan, or the Matter, Forme and Power of a Commonwealth Ecclesiastical and Civil* (1651; ed. Oakeshott, 1946), p. 111.

4. Bismarck's little-known remark can be found in Sidney Whitman, *German Memories* (1913), pp. 153–54; Nkrumah's, in *Ghana, the Autobiography of Kwame Nkrumah* (1959), p. 185.

5. B. F. Skinner, *Walden Two* (1962), p. 253. Writing in the embittered mood of the anti-totalitarian 1950s, Albert Camus remarked in *L'Homme révolté* (1951), p. 294; *The Rebel* (tr. Bower, 1953): "*La cité qui se voulait fraternelle devient une fourmilière d'hommes seuls*" ("The city that planned to be the city of fraternity becomes an ant-heap of solitary men").

In the 1960s, this attitude was clearly part of the general liberal awareness in the West, as suggested by the conventional passage in President Lyndon Johnson's Inaugural Address (*New York Times*, 21 January 1965): "I do not believe the Great Society is the ordered, changeless, and sterile battalion of the ants. It is the excitement of becoming, trying, probing, falling, resting, and trying again."

6. Fyodor Dostoyevsky, *Summer Impressions* (tr. Fitzlyon, 1955), pp. 85–86.

7. There are, of course, almost endless variations in the exploitation of the ant in political and social imagery.

The German Dominican Johannes Nider wrote the first popular essay on the horrible depravity of witches and witchcraft, and published it (in 1437) as the fifth and culminating book of his *Formicarius* [Anthill]. The French Protestant Pierre Viret, in his sixteenth-century attempt to justify the chastening of tyrants by popular uprisings (*par mutinations populaires*), warned secular rulers of what could happen if they continued to oppress their people—and he quoted an old adage, "Even the ants have their wrath and anger . . . " See Roland Bainton, *G. L. Burr, His Life and Writings* (1943), p. 177. Robert D. Linder, "Pierre Viret and the Sixteenth-Century French Protestant Revolutionary Tradition," *Journal of Modern History* (June 1966), p. 131.

One literary historian (Fussell) has referred to Alexander Pope's "exquisite manipulation of the insect image as an emblem of humanistic contempt for that which is below man and towards which, alas, man's depraved nature perpetually urges him." In Pope's *Verses on Gulliver's Travels* (1727), there is the contemptuous reference to "Beetles, Britons, Bugs and Butterflies" and also (following the remark: *"Fond of his Hillock Isle, his narrow Mind / Thinks Worth, Wit, Learning, to that Spot confin'd"*):

> Thus Ants, who for a Grain employ their Cares,
> Think all the Business of the Earth is theirs.
> Thus Honey-combs seem Palaces to Bees;
> And Mites imagine all the World a Cheese.

We have, thus, in our own little gallery: the ant as Wise One (Proverbs), as Good Citizen (Plato), as Witch (Nider), as Rebel (Viret), as Commonwealthsman (Milton), as Narrow Mind (Pope), as Brother (Tolstoy), as Prussian (Bismarck), as Spartan (Toynbee), as Utopian (Belt), as Collectivist (McCook), as Internationalist (Forel), as Christian Socialist (Maeterlinck), as Party Worker (Nkrumah), as Scientific Engineer (Skinner), and as Enemy of the Great Society (L.B.J.).

For a similar exploration in changing symbolism, see J. W. Johnson's brief paper, "That Neo-Classical Bee," *Journal of the History of Ideas* (April–June 1961), pp. 262–66; and the study of insect figures as an "index or touchstone of 18th-century humanism," in Paul Fussell, *The Rhetorical World of Augustan Humanism: Ethics and Imagery from Swift to Burke* (1965), pp. 233–61.

For a sober exercise in scientific description, see T. C. Schneirla and Gerald Piel, "The Army Ant," *Scientific American* (June 1948), pp. 17–22. The authors are wittily aware of the unsophisticated errors of traditional anthropomorphism; but evidently the lure of metaphor and analogy is too strong. Reporting on the "suicide mill" in which army ants, under some special conditions, are "literally fated to organize themselves in a circular column and march themselves to death," they are irresistibly led to remark that this calamity "may be described as tragic, in the classic meaning of the Greek drama. It arises, like Nemesis, out of the very aspects of the ant's nature which most plainly characterize its otherwise successful behavior." Add, then, to our gallery: the ant as Greek Tragedian.

8. Maurice Maeterlinck, *The Life of the Ant* (1930), pp. 17, 34–35, 104, 171, 175.

9. Henry C. McCook, *Ant Communities and How They Are Governed: A Study in Natural Civics* (1909), p. 304. Auguste Forel, *The Social World of the Ants* (1928), 2:350. Thomas Belt, *The Naturalist in Nicaragua* (1874), pp. 28–29.

10. *An Essay on Man* (1734), *The Poems of Alexander Pope* (ed. Butt, 1963), p. 531.

11. "Insect Societies and Human Utopias," Arnold J. Toynbee, *A Study of History* (1934), 3:88–90. For the contrary view, i.e., utopias as the spur to upward and progressive movements of society, see the two-volume work by Fred L. Polak, *The Image of the Future* (1961); an angry critique of Toynbee ("here is a piling up of error upon error") can be found in 1:391–401.

12. Walter Bagehot, *Physics and Politics* (1872), ch. 2. Lewis Mumford, "Utopia, The City and the Machine," *Daedalus* (Spring 1965), p. 278; repr. in *Utopias and Utopian Thought* (ed. Manuel, 1966).

13. Friedrich Schiller, *Sämtliche Gedichte* (dtv. ed., 1965), 1:175.

14. Translations of Campanella's *Civitas solis* (1623) can be found in *Famous Utopias of the Renaissance* (ed. White, 1946), pp. 155–204, and in Marie-Louise Berneri, *Journey through Utopia* (1950), pp. 88–102.

15. Johann Valentin Andreae, *Reipublicae Christianopolitanae Descriptio* (1619); *Christianopolis: An Ideal State of the Seventeenth Century* (tr. Held, 1916), p. 27.

16. Thomas More, *Selected Letters* (ed. Rogers, 1961), p. 85. J. H. Hexter, *More's Utopia: The Biography of an Idea* (1952), p. 109. Berneri, *Journey*, p. 4.

17. Andreae, *Christianopolis*, p. 140.

18. Andreae, who admitted that his work was not "as serious or as clever" as More's, nevertheless managed to introduce some more interesting chromatic variations. Writing of the dress among his own utopians, he noted: "The color appropriate for religion is white, that of statesmanship red, of scholarship blue, of the working class green" (*Christianopolis*, pp. 141, 253).

19. A strong emphasis on "open-endedness" is made by Father Edward Surtz, S.J., in the Yale edition of More's *Selected Works*, introduction to *Utopia* (tr. Richards), pp. xxvi, xxix.

> Is the success of *Utopia* due to dialogue? After all, dialogue is symbolic of open-mindedness, humility, and inquiry ... It is no accident that *Utopia* ends with challenges ... The *Utopia* therefore is an open-ended work—or, better, a dialogue with an indeterminate close.

Again:

> In the great common prayer ... each Utopian asks God to let him know whether there is a state better and happier and more pleasing to Him: he is ready to accept and adopt it. Each Utopian is thereby admonished to keep an open mind—which prevents a closed system ...

20. The "mythologized version" (he would call it a formal model or an ideal type) of utopian thought can be found in a provocative essay by Dr. Ralf Dahrendorf, "Out of Utopia: Toward a Reorientation of Sociological Analysis," *American Journal of Sociology* (September 1958). His objections, surely applicable to *some* utopias but not *all*, are not new; he knows that Socrates made them long before him; and he acknowledges the passage in Plato's *Timaios*:

> Then I may now proceed to tell you how I feel about the society we have just described. My feelings are much like those of a man who has beheld superb animals in a drawing, or, it may be, in real life, but at rest, and finds himself longing to behold them in motion, executing some feat commensurate with their physique. That is just how I feel about the city we have described ...

21. Thomas More, *Responsio ad Lutherum* (1523), in *Complete Works* (ed. Headley, tr. Mandeville, 1969), 5, pt. 1:119, 277, 383; pt. 2:754, 938, 959, 981.

22. More, *Utopia* (tr. Robinson, 1910), p. 18.

23. J. H. Hexter, *More's Utopia: The Biography of an Idea;* "The Loom of Language and the Fabric of Imperatives: the Case of *Il Principe* and *Utopia*," *American Historical Review* (July 1964), pp. 945–68; and the Introduction, pt. 1, to *The Complete Works of St. Thomas More* (ed. Surtz and Hexter), vol. 4 (1965), *Utopia*, especially pp. cv–cxxiv.

24. Writing of More and Erasmus, Hexter observes (*Utopia*, p. 125):

> Such men must come to terms with the fact that although unattached intellectuals are often quite free to propose innovations, they rarely get a hearing from the men who have the power to put their proposals into execution. If the unattached intellectual remains an innovator, his only alternative to coming to terms with the above sad fact is to change his situation, to cease to be an unattached intellectual, and to become either a revolutionary or a bureaucrat.... Their only real alternative to detachment was entrance into public office where they might seek to win a hearing for their views ... Whatever may be the ultimate source of conscious

peaceful social innovation, its main and normal channel runs through the governing body . . .

25. Plotinus (like Plato, before him, in Dion's Syracuse) almost succeeded in uniting theory and practice, fulfilling a utopian inspiration for actual social change; but the margin of failure was historic. The utopian project was Platonopolis, to be built in an ancient ruin; the means was the enlightened goodwill of the Emperor Gallienus (253–268 A.D.), who had issued—possibly under the influence of Plotinus—the first edict of toleration for the Christians. According to Porphyry's *Life of Plotinus* (cf. Ernest Barker, *From Alexander to Constantine* [1956], p. 334),

> The Emperor Gallienus and his wife Salonina greatly honoured and venerated Plotinus. He made use of their friendly feeling towards him to beg for the restoration of a city of philosophers which had once stood, as tradition had it, in Campania, but had now fallen into ruins. He also asked that the surrounding country should be granted to the city when it was refounded, that its inhabitants should follow the laws of Plato, and that its name should be Platonopolis; and he promised that, if this were done, he would retire there with his associates. The philosopher's wish could very easily have been carried into execution, if some of the emperor's courtiers, instigated by envy or spite or some such evil passion, had not opposed the scheme.

Alternative explanations have been offered. In his study of *The Philosophy of Plotinus* (1929), 1:116–17, W. R. Inge suggested that "the site was probably malarious, and the project would have certainly ended in a fiasco, had not the emperor withdrawn his consent, probably in order to save his friend from so great a blunder . . . " The chief interest of the story for Dean Inge was in the light which it threw on the utopian character of Plotinus:

> He is frequently reprimanded for building a philosophy in the clouds and leaving the Empire to its fate. But it is plain that he had his plans for the reconstruction of society, and courage to carry them out. The scheme was, after all, no wilder than some modern attempts to found socialistic communities.

26. Barker, *From Alexander to Constantine*, pp. 61–62.

27. Montaigne, *Essays* (tr. Cohen, 1958), p. 119. The *Discourse on the Cannibals* (1580) is included in White, *Famous Utopias*, pp. 141–50.

28. The phrase, curiously enough, crops up in four contexts: More, *Utopia* (Surtz-Hexter ed.), p. 89; Edmund Burke, *Thoughts on the French Revolution* (1791; Everyman ed., 1910), p. 330; Robert Owen, *The Revolution in the Mind and Practice of the Human Race* (1849), p. 151; and in V. I. Lenin's pamphlet of 1902, *What Is to be Done?* (in turn borrowed from Chernyshevsky's 1866 novel of the same name).

29. "Aristotle was summoned to Pella, the capital of Macedonia, by Philip of Macedon, and here for some six years (342–336) he acted as the tutor of Philip's son . . . " (Ernest Barker, *The Politics of Aristotle* [1946], p. xvii).

How deep was his political influence on Alexander (who, on his expeditions in the East, always made sure to send back biological specimens to his old teacher)? In his exhortation "On Colonies," Aristotle advised Alexander to distinguish between Greek and barbarian, to deal with the former as a leader or *hegemon* and with the latter as a master or *despotes*. Apparently, Alexander did the opposite. He was advised by others not "to agree with those who divided all mankind into Greeks and barbarians," and that "it was better to divide men simply into the good and the bad."

A second exhortation, "On Kingship," inverted the famous dictum of Plato (that states would never prosper until kings became philosophers, or philosophers became kings), by arguing that "for kings to be philosophers was so far from being a necessity, that it was rather a hindrance: what was really necessary was that they should be willing to hear, and ready to accept, the advice of genuine philosophers" (Barker, *Politics of Aristotle*, pp. iix, 386, 388).

According to W. W. Tarn (*Cambridge Ancient History*, 6:353), Aristotle's influence on Alexander was one of "a philosopher who taught that moderation alone could hold a state together ... "

30. "Politik als Beruf," in *From Max Weber* (1918; tr. Gerth and Mills, 1947), as "Politics as a Vocation," has these concluding words (p. 128):

> Only he has the calling for politics who is sure that he shall not crumble when the world from his point of view is too stupid or base for what he wants to offer. Only he who in the face of all this can say "In spite of all!" [*dennoch!*] has the calling for politics.

31. Letter to John Fisher, chancellor of Cambridge (ca. 1517–18), in *Selected Letters*, p. 94.

32. More, *Utopia* (Robinson ed.), pp. 41–42; (rev. ed., 1951), pp. 47–48; (Yale ed.), pp. 99–101.

33. Mendieta is a fascinating, important, and much neglected figure. For, if the seventeenth and eighteenth centuries (in the eras of Cromwell and Winstanley, Robespierre and Babeuf) were to inaugurate the modern age of utopia and revolution, the sixteenth century in its high ideological moments (More and Montaigne, Bruno and Campanella, Münzer and Savonarola: but also Las Casas, Quiroga, and Mendieta) was but a short step away. Where motives were secular, militance was still underdeveloped; where radicalism raged, motives were still religious. The transposition was coming. As John Leddy Phelan observes in his penetrating study of the writings of Geronimo de Mendieta, *The Millennial Kingdom of the Franciscans in the New World* (1956), p. 71:

> Mendieta's terrestrial paradise contained germs of the utopian idea. In fact, Mendieta was more Utopian ... than Thomas More himself [whose] utopia was located in a space and time of his own imagination. In contrast with Münzer and Mendieta, More was utterly pessimistic about concrete materialization. Münzer and Mendieta placed their utopias in a particular space and time—Münzer in Germany and Mendieta in New Spain. Mendieta's terrestrial paradise was an attempt to transcend the whole Spanish colonial order. In his thinking there is a fusion of the Messianic-apocalyptical vision of the millennial kingdom on earth with the active demands of an oppressed stratum of society. The final step which would have committed Mendieta to social revolution was never taken. Münzer urged the exploited groups to participate actively in vindicating their rights by violence. Mendieta wanted the leadership to come from the top—from the Messiah–World Ruler. The Indians were to take no part in their own liberation. In his yearning for the Messiah-Emperor Mendieta belonged to the Joachimite tradition; but his notion that the Messiah was to break the chains of economic exploitation of a particular class, so that the Indians might achieve "the most perfect and healthy Christianity that the world had ever known," was a step removed from the Joachimites in the direction of the utopian mentality of Münzer.

34. Ernst Kantorowicz, *Frederick the Second* (1931), pp. 259, 350–51; and see, generally, Lynn Thorndike, *Michael Scot* (1965). John Armstrong, *The Paradise Myth* (1969), p. 3.

35. "Letter to the Nurse of the Prince Don John" (1500), in *Memorials of Columbus* (1823), p. 224. "Journal of the First Voyage" (1492) and "Letter of Columbus Describing His Fourth Voyage," in *The Voyages of Christopher Columbus* (ed. Jane, 1930), pp. 110, 142, 157, 304–7. See also Samuel Eliot Morison, *Christopher Columbus, Mariner* (1955), pp. 43, 115, 121; S. de Madariaga, *Christopher Columbus* (1939), pp. 325, 352, 362, 380; Henri Baudet, *Paradise on Earth: Some Thoughts on European Images of Non-European Man* (1965), ch. 2; Charles L. Sanford, *The Quest for Paradise* (1961), pp. 40–41, 60–61.

36. In his Fourth Voyage letter from Jamaica (7 July 1503), Columbus wrote: "Gold is most excellent. Gold constitutes treasure, and he who possesses it may do what he will in the world, and may so attain as to bring souls to Paradise [*el oro es excelentissimo; del oro se hace tesoro, i con él, quien lo tiene, hace quanto quiere en el mundo, i ilega á que echa las ánimas al Paraíso*] ... " (*Voyages of Christopher Columbus*, p. 304).

Historians have, of course, been of many minds about the relationship of the mystical and the mercenary elements in Columbus's makeup. Some, like Ramón Iglesia, have made out a case for the hardheaded merchant adventurer with a keen eye for profits. At the other extreme, there is Don Salvador de Madariaga's intriguing thesis of Columbus's Jewish ancestry: which would have made him (as a *converso*) doubly heir to the most intense Judeo-Christian religiosity.

In his brilliant study of *The Millennial Kingdom*, pp. 21–22, 120–23, Phelan tries to strike an intricate balance, but with an arresting emphasis on the factors of Franciscan mysticism and apocalyptic Joachimism in Columbus's mind. He doubts whether Columbus, as sometimes has been held, was a member of the Franciscan order, despite his appearance in the streets of Seville in the mendicant habit and his deathbed sackcloth. But he argues his close connections with the mystical temperament of the Spiritual Franciscans, who, like Columbus, were strongly influenced by the various Joachimite commentaries on their two most popular Old Testament prophets, Isaiah and Jeremiah. This psychic affiliation is clear from Columbus's own unfinished *Book of Prophecies* and from the biblical citations he asked Friar Gaspar Gorritio, an old Italian friend, to assemble on the subject of the liberation of Mount Zion (and among which frequent references to the Abbot Joachim of Flora occur). Phelan writes

> Columbus regarded his voyages as the "opening of the door of the Western sea," through which the missionaries could rush in order to reach all the remaining Gentiles of the world. The global note in Columbus' apocalyptical universalism ought to be stressed. As far as he was concerned he had reached Asia, the continent which contained the largest number of pagans. In the scriptural passages that Gorritio collected there are countless references to the salvation that is to include all men and all peoples. The Admiral of the Ocean Sea was dazzled by the vision that Christianity, which had always been dogmatically universal, could now become geographically world-wide. Little wonder that he was obsessed by the image of himself as the instrument of Divine Providence. . . . The god of the Indies, which Columbus described as the richest dominion in the world, would be consecrated and hallowed by rebuilding the temple of Sion. Columbus convinced himself that the district of Veragua (in Panama) was the region from which David and Solomon had extracted precious stones with which to build the temple described in the Old Testament. Columbus dreamed of rebuilding the temple in Jerusalem with the precious stones extracted from what he mistakenly thought were Solomon's mines. Never was the popular image of the gold of the Indies more mystically spiritualized than on this occasion. . . . The discovery and the conquest of America, among many other things, was the last crusade. If Columbus had had his way, this would have been literally so.

37. I repeat here that I should not like the reader to be misled into believing that these remarks on the movement from Dante's Paradise to More's Utopia—via Joachim of Flora, Christopher Columbus, and Amerigo Vespucci—are anything but a shorthand transcription of very complex problems in the history of ideas. Yet, the pattern seems to me at once interesting, relevant, and true.

In his study of "The American Utopia of the 16th Century," Silvio Zavala has made a related point (*Huntington Library Quarterly* [1947], 10:338–39):

> As a vast continent full of unknown natural resources, peopled by men whose civilization was strange to the Occidental, it was bound to stir the imagination of the Utopians. An accident of geography offered them a material opportunity to try and fulfill their longings, not entirely satisfied with the chimerical past of the Golden Age or the opportunity to adapt the conventions of humanism to the spent and sophisticated atmosphere of Europe.

And, in his exploration of "the emotions and expectations which agitated the conquerors of the New World," Leonardo Olschki traces how the old complex of myths and marvels moved westward ("Ponce de Leon's Fountain of Youth: History of a Geographical Myth," *Hispanic American Historical Review* [August 1941], pp. 361–85). He emphasizes

Columbus's influence on Ponce (who had sailed with him on the second voyage) and others, transmitting moods and convictions,

> stimulating their spirit of enterprise and their imagination beyond their habitual greed of gain, conquest, and power. The curiosity for this world believed to lie *"extra Gangem"* was still haunting the most intelligent and educated among the conquerors of the Columbian era, and the discovery of strange things known only from legend or hearsay was considered an element of geographical identification no less important than astronomical calculations or nautical observations for finding one's way through unchartered waters.

Thus it was that

> a legend crossed the Ocean with Columbus' companions, together with the myths of the Earthly Paradise, of the Amazons, of St. Thomas' wonder-working tomb, of the Ten Tribes of Israel, of God and Magog, and of the monsters into which Columbus inquired after his landing at Expañola. The Fountain of Youth is an inevitable element in this traditional imagery of the wonders of Asia.

38. Herbert Grundmann's study is a masterful inquiry into this point: "Dante and Joachim von Fiore: *Paradiso* X–XII," *Deutsches Dante-Jahrbuch* (1932), 14:210–56.

39. Americo Vespucio, *El Nuevo Mundo* (ed. Levillier, 1951), "Letter of 18th July 1504 to Lorenzo di Medici," pp. 102, 274. Germán Arciniegas, *Amerigo and the New World* (1955), pp. 161–62, 183–86. R. W. Chambers, *Thomas More* (1935), pp. 123, 138, 143.

40. *Paradiso*, 12:139–41; the translation is Lawrence Binyon's in *Dante* (ed. Milano, 1972), p. 431. A more spirited rendering is in Dorothy Sayers's edition (1962), p. 161: " ... here, and last in view, / Calabria's abbot ends where I begin; / Joachim, spirit-fired, and prophet true."

41. The most complete scholarly account in English is Marjorie Reeves, *The Influence of Prophecy in the Later Middle Ages: A Study in Joachimism* (1969).

42. Henry Bett, *Joachim of Flora* (1931), p. 9.

43. Inasmuch as I will be dealing repeatedly with the problem of the historic apartness of "Anglo-Saxon attitudes," it would be useful to note here that one historian, studying "Joachism and the English Apocalypse," has observed an "aloofness which remains impervious to Joachist ideas." English artists and English theologians were the weakest link in the great chain of late medieval fanaticism. "Roger Bacon conceived the singular idea of organizing the sciences and promoting studies (*naturae et artis*) with a view to the defeat of the coming Antichrist. This very insular recourse to practical measures in a situation of despair may well be seen as a parallel to the temperate response of the English Apocalypse to the revolutionary stimulus of Joachim" (R. Freyhan, "Joachism and the English Apocalypse," in *Journal of the Warburg & Courtauld Institutes* [1955], 18:228–29).

The response was temperate, practical, and humdrum. Very early on the English climate of opinion began to insure itself against the ingenuity which saves the prophet when the prophecy fails. Joachim's crucial dates have been bypassed, and what could be worse than not to get one's sums right? A fifteenth-century English chronicler expressed his disgust at the failed prophet: "He erred in many things ... he failed foule and erred in his counting" (Marjorie Reeves, *The Influence of Prophecy in the Later Middle Ages: A Study in Joachimism* [1969], p. 70).

44. It is also given as "third realm" or "third status," but: "Third Reich" is undoubtedly the best translation of *tertius status*. Ruth Kestenberg-Gladstein, "The 'Third Reich': A 15th-Century Polemic against Joachism," *Journal of the Warburg and Courtauld Institutes* (1955), 18:283.

45. *Psalterium decem cordarum* (1527), in Frank Manuel, "Augustine and Joachim," *Shapes of Philosophical History* (1965), p. 40.

46. *Expositio in Apocalypsim* (1527), in Gordon Leff, *Heresy in the Later Middle Ages* (1967), 1:72.

47. *Expositio*, in Reeves, *Influence of Prophecy*, p. 265.

48. Reeves, *Influence of Prophecy*, p. 62.

49. Freyhan, "Joachism and the English Apocalypse," 18:226. Reeves, *Influence of Prophecy*, p. 175.

50. *Liber concordie novi et veteris Testamenti* (1519), in Manuel, *Shapes of Philosophical History*, p. 40. Kestenberg-Gladstein, "The Third Reich," pp. 246, 283.

51. *Liber concordie*, in Reeves, *Influence of Prophecy*, p. 292. See, generally, the works of the great German scholar Herbert Grundmann, from whose research I have benefited: *Studien über Joachim von Floris* (1927; reissued 1966), and *Neue Forschungen über Joachim von Floris* (1950). Among the most interesting contemporary evaluations of Joachimism in Western thought are Karl Löwith, *Meaning in History* (1949), ch. 8; Erich Voegelin, *The New Science of Politics* (1952), and *Science, Politics, and Gnosticism* (1968).

52. *Dantis Alagherii Epistolae* (ed. Paget Toynbee, 1920), pp. 177, 201: "... *a principio horribilis et foetida est, quia Infernus; in fine prospera, desiderabilis et grata, quia Paradisus ...* " *A Translation of the Latin Works of Dante Alighieri* (tr. Howell and Wicksteed, 1904), pp. 349–50. More, *Utopia* (Surtz-Hexter ed.), p. cxxxviii.

53. My quotations are from the translations in Dante, *Monarchy, and Three Political Letters* (tr. Nicholl and Hardie, 1954), pp. 3–4, 18–19, 97. For an earlier translation, see R. W. Church, *Dante and De Monarchia* (1879). The original Latin text (ca. 1309–13) is in Dante, *De monarchia* (ed. Moore and Reade, 1916) and the letters, in *Dantis Alagherii Epistolae*.

54. Etienne Gilson, *Dante the Philosopher* (1948), p. 179; and A. P. d'Entreves, *Dante as a Political Thinker* (1952), pp. 46–48.

55. Dante, *Monarchy and Letters*, pp. 113, 26–27, 106, 14.

56. *Dantis Alagherii Epistolae*, pp. 61, 76. The original phrase in Letter 5 (p. 54) reads: "*Evigilate igitur omnes, et assurgite regi vestro ...* "

57. Dante, *Monarchy and Letters*, p. 92; *De monarchia*, p. 375.

58. Dante, *Monarchy and Letters*, p. 93; *De monarchia*, p. 376.

59. *De vulgari eloquentia*(ca. 1304–6), in Dante, *Selected Works* (ed. Milano, 1972), p. 633; d'Entreves, *Dante*, p. 11.

60. F. Scott Fitzgerald, *The Great Gatsby* (1925), p. 317.

61. Several important studies which I have not yet been able to consult are Silvio A. Zavala's *La Utopia de Tomás Moro en la Nueva España, y otros estudios* (1937), and his *Ideario de Vasco de Quiroga* (1941); also, Jose Antonio Maravall, "La Utopiá Politíco-religiosa de los Franciscanos en Nueva España," *Estudios Americanos* (January 1949), 1:197–227.

In his study of the sixteenth-century American utopia, which I have already cited, Zavala refers to Quiroga's "humanistic program based upon More's *Utopia* which, in his judgment, should serve as the Magna Charta of European civilization in the New World ... " Evidently, Quiroga was also influenced by Lucian's account of the Saturnalia, which he quotes from the version translated by Erasmus and Thomas More. He combined the idea of a Golden Age, at once old and new, with the hope of "a renascent Church," for this was to be (unlike More's) a Christian utopia in which he would "place and plant righteously the kind of Christians as in the primitive Church ... "

With a bit of touching sentimentality that even the most rigorous of historians occasionally permits himself, Zavala writes:

> The ordinances, according to the words of Don Vasco, set forth on various occasions, faithfully transmitted the theory of More, but translated it from the atmosphere of theoretical speculation to immediate application. Undoubtedly the Chancellor of England would have been interested to know how the Indians of Mexico City and Michoacan were faring in their life based upon his *Utopia*. But on the 5th of July, 1535, the day after Quiroga wrote his opinion, More was beheaded by the executioner of Henry VIII of England.

62. Zavala, "The American Utopia of the 16th Century," 10:337–47. Howard Mumford Jones, *O Strange New World* (1964), p. 36. Lewis Hanke, *The Spanish Struggle for Justice in the Conquest of America* (1949), p. 56.

63. In the volumes of his *Historia eclesiastica indiana* (which had for centuries been consigned to oblivion—an edition was first published in 1870), Mendieta went through all the phases of optimism and pessimism, collective hope and personal gloom, fanatical exultation and final disenchantment, that so often characterize the turns of the ideological cycle. The political temperament may vary and the intellectual climate may be different, but the relationship is (as we shall see, again and again) essentially the same. A number of passages from Mendieta's *Historia* and his letters (quoted in Phelan, *The Millennial Kingdom*), are worth noting.

1. *Universal Destruction and Final Conversion*
I am firmly convinced that as those Catholic Monarchs (Ferdinand and Isabella) were granted the mission of beginning to extirpate these three diabolical squadrons: "perfidious" Judaism, "false" Mohammedanism and "blind" idolatry, along with the fourth squadron of the heretics whose remedy and medicine is the Holy Inquisition: in like manner the business of completing this task has been reserved for their royal successors; so that as Ferdinand and Isabella cleansed Spain of these wicked sects, in like manner their royal descendants will accomplish the universal destruction of these sects throughout the world and the final conversion of all the peoples of the earth to the bosom of the church . . . [P. 13]

2. *The Greatest Earthly Happiness*
[The Indians] are the best in the world. Their disposition is so good . . . that I, a poor useless good-for-nothing . . . could rule with little help from associates a province of fifty-thousand Indians organized and arranged in such good Christianity that it seemed as if the whole province were a monastery. And it was just like the island of Antillia of the Ancients, which some say is enchanted and which is located not far from Madeira. In our own times it has been seen from afar, but it disappears upon approaching it. In Antillia there is an abundance of all temporal goods, and the people spend their time marching in processions and praising God with hymns and spiritual canticles . . . The Indians [should] be organized and distributed in islands like those of Antillia; for they then would live virtuously and peacefully serving God, as in a terrestrial paradise. At the end of their lives, they would go to heaven, and thus they would avoid all those temptations for which many of us go to hell . . . They [would] possess the greatest happiness that one can desire upon this earth. [P. 66]

3. *The End of Wickedness*
[The Indians] are a defenseless and helpless people whose only protection against the countless cruelties and ill-treatment that insolent and wicked Christians have sought to inflict upon them is that defense which is provided for them by a far-away king. . . . O false servants and wicked flatterers, you who deceive kings under the pretext of serving them, you with your diabolical plots to increase the royal revenues, are only concerned with your own interests and advantages even at the cost of destroying kingdoms and vassals! May God destroy your intrigues! . . . In our times God has placed Spain above all the kingdoms of the earth. Be not the cause of her ruin and her fall because you followed your personal interests and the mere temporal interests of the King . . . Our Lord did not have this world of the Indies discovered, nor did He place it in the hands of our kings, merely that gold and silver might be shipped from here to Spain. God gave the Indies to Spain in order that she might cultivate and profit from the mines of so many Indian souls. . . . In no part of the world [does] avarice and lying reign more supreme than among the laymen and the secular clergy of the Indies. [Pp. 78–81]

4. *The Confrontation of Conscience and Chaos*
The chaos is so great and the evils so many that have ensued . . . that I believe it would have been safer for the conscience of His Majesty to have left these natives . . . without justice or anyone to administer it than to have given them the judicial system that they now have. It is obvious to anyone who compares these two regimes that their condition, society and old way of life, with the religion and the sacraments that they had, were preferable to the situation that prevails today. . . .

Once the Indians are exterminated, I do not know what is going to happen in this land except that the Spaniards will then rob and kill each other.... What they really seek is to continue a situation in which they can fatten and enlarge themselves in order that they can have more for their vanities and superfluities at the cost of the sweat and blood of the Indians. They wish to keep the natives in perpetual captivity, for they do not take into account the future. They only seek to profit as much as possible from the present.... [Pp. 85–96]

  5. *The Choice between the Beast and Man's Hope*
Not only can I not conclude my history with a psalm of praise, but on the contrary ... this is indeed the right time for me to sit down with Jeremiah, and to relate and bewail the miserable fall and the catastrophes of our Indian Church with tears, sighs, and laments that would reach to heaven itself (as Jeremiah did over the destruction of the city of Jerusalem) ... Great evil, evil of evils, which are numberless and one cannot describe them. And all this proceeds from having allowed the wild beast of avarice, who like the beast of the Apocalypse has made himself adored as the lord of the whole world, to ravish and destroy the vineyard. The beast had blinded all men by making them put hope and happiness in black money, as if there were no other God in whom men could trust and hope ... [Pp. 99–101]

The themes change, the counterpoint remains.
  64. Phelan's work, *The Millennial Kingdom*, presents a detailed study of Mendieta's writings.
  65. More, *Utopia* (Surtz-Hexter ed.), p. 301.
  66. *Timon, a Play* (1600; ed. Dyce, 1842), 3.3.35.
  67. Hans Baron, *The Crisis of the Early Italian Renaissance: Civic Humanism and Republican Liberty in an Age of Classicism and Tyranny* (rev. ed., 1966).
  68. In his essay on "Utopia and Violence," in *Conjectures and Refutations* (1962), Karl Popper also, and memorably, writes (p. 361):

Wherein, then, lies the difference between those benevolent Utopian plans to which I object because they lead to violence, and those other important and far-reaching political reforms which I feel inclined to recommend? If I were to give a simple form or recipe for distinguishing between what I consider to be admissible plans for social reform and inadmissible Utopian blueprints, I might say: Work for the elimination of concrete evils rather than for the realisation of abstract goods. Do not aim at establishing happiness by political means. Rather, aim at the elimination of concrete miseries. Or, in more practical terms: fight for the elimination of poverty by direct means—for example, by making sure that everybody has a minimum income. Or fight against epidemics and disease by erecting hospitals and schools of medicine. Fight illiteracy as you fight criminality. But do all this by direct means. Choose what you consider the most urgent evil of the society in which you live, and try patiently to convince people that we can get rid of it. But do not try to realize these aims indirectly by designing and working for a distant ideal of a society which is wholly good. However deeply you may feel obliged to work for its realisation, or that it is your mission to open the eyes of others to its beauty, do not allow your dreams of a beautiful world to lure you away from the claims of men who suffer here and now. Our fellow men have a claim to our help; no generation must be sacrificed for the sake of future generations, for the sake of an ideal of happiness that may never be realised. In brief, it is my thesis that human misery is the most urgent problem of a rational public policy and that happiness is not such a problem. The attainment of happiness should be left to our private endeavours.

This is eloquent and almost entirely convincing. But I have some difficulties with the thesis: (1) the correlation of utopia and violence, of *all* "benevolent utopian plans" with totalitarian *Gleichschaltung*, seems to me to be based more on fears than on facts; (2) even the admissible plans for improvements would require, if they were not to slip into technocratic tinkering, a larger sense of the ideal good, a fuller notion of the general ethical impetus; (3) there are, clearly, virtuous aspects to the quest for "public happiness": the pleasure of the citizen in just and reasonable institutions, the joys (as Jefferson conceived of them) of "a participator in the government of affairs."

In his *Utopian Essays and Practical Proposals* (1962), Paul Goodman remarks (pp. 17–19):

We have come to the very antithesis of pragmatism. In this new climate, where experts plan in terms of an unchangeable structure, a pragmatic expediency that still wants to take the social structure as plastic and changeable comes to be thought of as "utopian." And meantime, of course, the structure is really changing with violent rapidity—impractically.... In the context of a pragmatic social science, utopian thinking may be practical hypotheses, that is, expedients for pilot experimentation....

The following paragraph from *Cacotopias and Utopias*, Center for the Study of Democratic Institutions [1965], pp. 14–15, is also worth noting:

Machines are moving so much faster than we are able to comprehend them that they stand as a great unused natural resource because we don't know what to put into them; we can't program them because our minds aren't quick enough. It seems to me that we must accelerate our minds to think about these new problems ... We need new myths about the possibilities in a society oriented toward leisure, toward abundance ... It is not just an idle spectator sport or occupation to construct new Utopias; it is an absolute necessity to find workable ideas to replace the myths that have now been outrun by technology and world conditions ...

69. "Utopia and Violence," in Popper, *Conjectures and Refutations*, pp. 355–63. See, generally, his two-volume *The Open Society and Its Enemies* (4th ed., rev., 1962).

70. On the central issue of tolerance in Utopia, there was more than a touch of Mill in More. King Utopus, he explains in Book 2 of *Utopia* (Surtz, pp. 133–34),

did not venture rashly to dogmatise ... even if it should be the case that one single religion is true and all the rest are false, he foresaw that, provided the matter was handled reasonably and moderately, truth by its own natural force would finally emerge sooner or later and stand forth conspicuously. But if the struggle were decided by arms and riots, since the worst men are always the most unyielding, the best and holiest religion would be overwhelmed because of the conflicting false religions, like grain choked by thorns and underbrush. So he made the whole matter of religion an open question and left each one free to choose what he should believe.

Compare John Stuart Mill, *On Liberty* (1859):

If all mankind minus one were of one opinion, and only one person were of the contrary opinion, mankind would be no more justified in silencing that one person, than he, if he had the power, would be justified in silencing mankind.... If the opinion is right, they are deprived of the opportunity of exchanging error for truth; if wrong, they lose, what is almost as great a benefit, the clearer perception and livelier impression of truth, produced by its collision with error.... We can never be sure that the opinion we are endeavouring to stifle is a false opinion; and were we sure, stifling it would be an evil still.

71. David Hume, *Theory of Politics* (ed. Watkins, 1951), pp. 228–29.

72. There is in *Roper's Life of More* (1626; 1950) a touching glimpse of the dissembling, disenchanted intellectual at the court of King Henry, repressing even his vivid and high spirits (pp. 19–20):

And because he was of a pleasant disposition, it pleased the King and Queen after the Council had supped, at the time of their supper, for their pleasure commonly to call for him to be merry with them. Whom when he perceived so much in talk to delight that he could not once in a month get leave to go home to his wife and children, whose company he most desired, and to be absent from the Court two days together but that he should be thither sent for again—he much misliking this restraint of his liberty began thereupon somewhat to dissemble his nature; and so little by little from his former accustomed mirth to disuse himself, that he was of them from thenceforth at such seasons no more so ordinarily sent for ...

73. More, *Selected Letters*, p. 145.

74. On this relationship between abstraction and political ideas, the most suggestive formulation is that of F. W. Maitland, as prompted by Coleridge (quoted by Crane Brinton, *The Anatomy of Revolution* [1952], p. 176):

> ... Coleridge has remarked how, in times of great political excitement, the terms in which political theories are expressed become, not more and more practical, but more and more abstract and impractical. It is in such times that men clothe their theories in universal terms ... The absolute spirit is abroad. Relative or partial goods seems a poor ideal. It is not of these, or those men that we speak, of this nation or that age, but of Man.

Erasmus sensed another aspect of this process—the iron law of controversy—when, in 1523, he cautioned the excited polemicists of his day (Roland Bainton, *Hunted Heretic: The Life and Death of Michael Servetus 1511–1553* [1960], p. 34):

> ... define as little as possible, and in many things leave each one free to follow his own judgement, because there is great obscurity in many matters, and man suffers from this almost congenital disease that he will not give in when once a controversy is started, and after he is heated he regards as absolutely true that which he began to sponsor quite casually.

75. John Milton, *Reformation in England* (1641), and *Animadversions upon the Remonstrants Defense* (1641), in *Works* (ed. Patterson, 1931), 3:78, 112, 148.

76. *Common Sense*, in *The Complete Writings of Thomas Paine* (ed. Foner, 1945), 1:45.

77. Albert Camus, *L'Homme révolté*, p. 149: *"Nous avons atteint le milieu des temps. Les tyrans sont murs"* (Fauchet).

78. This point about the revolution being itself utopia was shrewdly sensed, in a somewhat different context, by the Russian socialist Peter Struve. In his article on "Die Marxische Theorie der sozialen Entwicklung," *Archive für soziale Gesetzgebung und Statistik* (1899), vol. 14, Struve was arguing against the idea of revolution and in favor of a continuous process, an evolutionary socialism. He rejected the concept of "absolute conflict" and offered instead the notion of "continuous partial collisions and adjustments." He was especially sensitive to the confusions of Marx's figurative language. In all this—Struve's article is discussed in Richard Kindersley, *The First Russian Revisionists* (1962), pp. 131–40—he was striking at the heart of orthodox Marxism, and was naturally eager to throw back the familiar epithet of "utopianism." In order to "prove" the inevitability of socialism, the orthodox Marxists (according to Struve) were calling in "a passionately desired but impossible social miracle," *i.e.*, the partisans of social revolution were, in fact, utopians.

In my own context, I am, of course, less concerned with the prospect of the passionate desire than with its nature. What I am trying to follow is how, in the movement from utopian longing to revolutionary commitment, the miracle of the end became the miracle of the means.

In a brilliant and unjustly forgotten essay of 1896, Eduard Bernstein also noted the emergence of this new revolutionary belief in social miracles. (See "Utopismus and Eklekticismus" [1896], *Zur Geschichte und Theorie des Socialismus* [1901], pp. 171–79.) He traced it, similarly, to the curious onset of a late form of utopianism. Bernstein did not disguise his Marxian pride in the classic transcendence of old-fashioned *Zukunftsstaatsmodelei*, picture-making of happy futures for suffering mankind. He conceded the usefulness of some futuristic sketches, the importance of predictions, and even the value of fantasy; but "recipes for tomorrow's restaurants" were "finished."

Still, there was (Bernstein was alarmed to note) another type of utopianism at the other extreme. "One avoids anxiously every concern with the future organization of society, but one substitutes for it a great leap forward [*einen jähen Sprung*], from capitalism into socialism." Could any such sharp line be drawn between the two social orders? "The most scientific theory can lead to utopianism if the results are taken dogmatically." And what else was the catastrophic conception of revolution, with its idea of a precipitate jump into a new society, but utopian? *"Ohne an Wunder zu glauben, unterstellt man Wunder."* No one believes in miracles, but miracles are assumed ...

79. There are two recent translations, and none is (perhaps inevitably so, with such a subtle and intricate text) quite satisfactory. Friedrich Schiller, "Seventh Letter," in *On the Aesthetic Education of Man* (tr. Snell, 1954), p. 53; (tr. Wilkinson and Willoughby, 1967), p. 59. Schiller, *"Über die ästhetische Erziehung des Menschen"* (1793–93), in *Werke* (dtv ed., 1966), 19:28:

> Dringend spricht das Unglück seiner Gattung zu dem fühlenden Menschen, dringender ihre Entwürdigung, der Enthusiasmus entflammt sich, und das glühende Verlangen strebt in kraftvollen Seelen ungeduldig zur Tat. . . . Der reine moralische Trieb ist aufs Unbedingte gerichtet, für ihn gibt es keine Zeit, und die Zukunft wird ihm zur Gegenwart. . . . Vor einer Vernunft ohne Schranken ist die Richtung zugleich die Vollendung, und der Weg ist zurückgelegt, sobald er einge-schlangen ist.

80. J. M. Thompson, *Leaders of the French Revolution* (1929), pp. 196, 231. Martin Buber, *Paths in Utopia* (1949), p. 88. Robert Tucker, *Philosophy and Myth in Karl Marx* (1961), p. 78. Marx/Engels, *Historisch-Kritische Gesamtausgabe* (ed. Rjazonov, 1927), vol. 1, pt. 1, p. 131: "Was innerliches Licht war, wird zur verzehrenden Flamme, die sich nach aussen wendet . . . "

81. See, in the Loeb Classical Library editions, *Diodorus of Sicily* (ed. Oldfather, 1935), 2:69–71; and *Philo* (ed. Colson, 1935), 6:201–11. I have used, with minor additions, the translations in Barker's anthology, *From Alexander to Constantine*, pp. 62, 161–63.

Chapter 2

1. The U.S. Department of Defense announced on 8 July 1965 that it was cancelling its $4,000,000 "Project Camelot." No formal work on the project had yet begun abroad, but some $300,000 had been spent on "preliminary research." *The New York Times* noted (9 July 1965):

> While the American sponsors apparently treated the project as a routine experiment in the behavioral sciences, it was promptly seized by leftist newspapers (mainly in Latin America) as proof of a "Pentagon plot" against constitutional governments.

In "Project Camelot: An Autopsy," in *The Public Interest* (Fall 1966), pp. 45–69, Professor Robert A. Nisbet wrote:

> Project Camelot may well have been the worst single scientific project since King Canute dealt with the tides: the worst conceived, worst advised, worst designed, and worst executed. But this much has to be said for it. Never has one project in the social sciences aroused interest so broad, so diverse, and in such high places of the national government. More important, never has one project produced, or at least stimulated, results so momentous (and possibly beneficial) in the long run to gov-ernment policy with respect to the social sciences.

2. Norman Cohn, *The Pursuit of the Millennium* (1957; rev. ed., 1970), p. 209. H. G. Koenigsberger, "The Organization of Revolutionary Parties in France and the Netherlands during the Sixteenth Century," *Journal of Modern History* (December 1955), pp. 335–51.

3. Alexis de Tocqueville, *The Old Regime and the French Revolution* (1856; tr. Gilbert, 1955), pp. 141, 157. Antoine Nicolas de Condorcet, *Esquisse d'un tableau historique des progrès de l'esprit humain* (1795, tr. Barraclough, 1955), pp. 366, 384; *Oeuvres* (1847), 12:516.

4. Marx/Engels, *Werke* (East Berlin ed., 1964), 17:343, 557; *Selected Works* (ed. Adoratsky, 1951), 2:504.

5. Letter to Domela Nieuwenhuis, 22 February 1881, in Marx-Engels, *Selected Corre-spondence* (1942), p. 387.

6. Philippe Buonarroti, *Conspiration pour l'égalité dite de Babeuf* (1828; ed. 1957), 1:78–79.

Buonarroti's *History of Babeuf's Conspiracy for Equality* (1836; tr. Bronterre, 1965), p. 66. See, generally, Alfred Plummer, *Bronterre: A Political Biography of Bronterre O'Brien* (1971).

7. See, of course, the classic study in sociological (and political) theory by Karl Mannheim, *Ideology and Utopia* (1936). "A state of mind is utopian," he writes (p. 173), "when it is incongruous with the state of reality within which it occurs." But he confines it only to "that type of orientation which transcends reality and which at the same time breaks the bonds of the existing order." Ideology, on the other hand, is nonrevolutionary: "One can orient himself to objects that are alien to reality and which transcend actual existence—and nevertheless still be effective in the realisation and the maintenance of the existing order of things."

The formal distinction is clear and easy. But if an "incongruent orientation" becomes utopian only when it also "tends to burst the bonds of the existing order," the historical critic must ask: When? how soon? where? An ideology in France becomes a utopia in Russia; a fond German daydream becomes a bond-breaking radicalism in Italy, etc. Mannheim does concede (p. 176): "To determine concretely, however, what in a given case is ideological and what utopian is extremely difficult . . . "

8. Friedrich Nietzsche, *Die Morgenröte* (1881), in *Werke* (ed. Schlechta, 1954), aphorisms 147 and 551, 1:1116, 1271; *The Dawn of Day* (tr. Volz, 1903), pp. 149, 374–75.

9. *The Mind of Napoleon* (ed. Herold, 1955), pp. 68, 251–66.

10. Marx to Engels, 8 December 1857, *Briefwechsel* (1949 ed.), 2:314. Marx to Sorge, 19 October 1877, *Selected Correspondence*, p. 350. *Karl Marx: Selected Writings* (Penguin ed., 1963, ed. Bottomore and Rubel), p. 250. *Economic and Philosophic Manuscripts of 1844* (ed. Struik, tr. Milligan, 1964), p. 135. Marx/Engels, Werke (E. Berlin ed., 1968), 1:536: "Er [der Kommunismus] ist das aufgelöste Rätsel der Geschichte und weiss sich als diese Lösung."

Marx's riddlesome maxim (from the *Economic and Philosophical Manuscripts of 1844*) is in *Karl Marx: Selected Writings*, p. 250:

> Communism as a complete naturalism is humanism, and as a complete humanism is naturalism. It is the *definitive* resolution of the antagonism between man and Nature, and between man and man. It is the true solution of the conflict between existence and essence, between objectification and self-affirmation, between freedom and necessity, between individual and species. It is the solution of the riddle of history and knows itself to be this solution.

11. Proudhon to Marx, 17 May 1846, in Proudhon, *Les Confessions d'un révolutionnaire* (1849; ed. Riviere, 1929), pp. 435–36.

12. Marx/Engels, *Historisch-kritische Gesamtausgabe* (ed. Ryazanov, 1927), 1:42.

13. Martin Buber, *Paths in Utopia* (1949); chs. 7 and 9 contain a close reading of both Marx and Lenin. Robert Tucker, *Philosophy and Myth in Karl Marx* (1961), p. 75. James Joll, *The Anarchists* (1964), ch. 3. George Woodcock, *Pierre-Joseph Proudhon* (1956), pp. 92–93.

14. Ronald A. Knox, *Enthusiasm: A Chapter in the History of Religion* (1950), p. 265.

15. Martin Buber, *The Prophetic Faith* (tr. Witton-Davies, 1960), pp. 175–79.

16. H. H. Rowley, *The Relevance of Apocalyptic* (1944), p. 14.

17. Buber, *Paths in Utopia*, p. 44.

18. On this point of the vague hints, Marx's own utopia, Tucker writes (*Philosophy and Myth*, p. 201):

> Only on one occasion did he himself attempt to say something concrete about the future order. This was in *The Civil War in France*, written in 1871 . . . In one passage he allowed that communism would be a system under which "united co-operative societies are to regulate the national production under a common plan." In the very next breath, however, he lapsed back into his usual antipathy toward any discussion of communism as a social system. Speaking of the working class, he said: "They have no ideals to realise, but to set free the elements of the new society with which the old collapsing bourgeois society is pregnant" . . .

19. Marx/Engels, *The German Ideology* (ed. Pascal, 1947), p. 22; (Moscow ed., 1964, pp. 44–45). *Die deutsche Ideologie* (1846; E. Berlin ed., 1969), 3:33:

> ...während in der kommunistichen Gesellschaft, wo Jeder nicht einen aus-schliesslichen Kreis der Tätigkeit hat, sondern sich in jedem beliebigen Zweige ausbilden kann ... heute dies, morgen jenes zu tun, morgens zu jagen, nachmit-tags zu fischen, abends Viehzucht zu treiben, nach dem Essen zu kritizisieren, wie ich gerade Lust habe, ohne je Jäger, Fischer, Hirt oder Kritiker zu werden.

Curiously enough, in the margin of the manuscript pages of this section, Marx has sketched the figure of a young swashbuckling hero who appears to be neither hunter (or fisherman) nor shepherd (or critic), but presumably the author himself flourishing a sword!

20. Plato, *The Republic* (tr. Lindsay, 1935), pp. 253–58; (tr. Lee, 1955), p. 333.

21. Roderick MacFarquhar, "Mao's Last Revolution," *Foreign Affairs* (October 1966), p. 121.

22. V. I. Lenin, *Selected Works* (1937), 9:397, 474.

23. If Marx was called by Proudhon (in a diary entry) "the tapeworm of socialism," Proudhon has been seen by his critics as its sour apple. J. Salwyn Schapiro calls him, in his *Liberalism and the Challenge of Fascism* (1949), p. 365, "a harbinger of fascist ideas" (a "re-evaluation" which betrays the fact that the book was written during the Second World War). Joll's view is more generous and conventional, calling him "the first and most important anarchist philosopher," as befits the prophet with this utopian vision (*The Anarchists*, p. 79):

> Humanity will do as in Genesis, it will concern itself with the tilling and caring for the soil which will provide it with a life of delights—as recommended by the philosopher Martin in *Candide*, man will cultivate his garden. Agriculture, once the lot of the slave, will be one of the first of the fine arts, and human life will be passed in innocence, freed of all the seduction of the ideal ...

Just before their breach (17 May 1840), Proudhon wrote to Marx (*La révolution sociale*, in *Oeuvres complètes* [1938], p. 292):

> We must not suppose the *revolutionary* action is the means of social reform, because this so-called means would simply be an appeal to force, arbitrariness, in short a contradiction.

After the revolution of 1848, he wrote (*Oeuvres complètes*, 18:6):

> And then the Revolution, the Republic, and socialism, one supporting the other, came with a bound. I saw them; I felt them; and I fled before this democratic and social monster ... An inexpressible terror froze my soul, obliterating my very thoughts. I denounced still more the revolutionists whom I beheld pulling up the foundations of society with incredible fury ... No one understood me.

24. Michael Hamburger, *Reason and Energy* (1957), p. 6.

25. It is fairly obvious, even to sociologists, that the important problem of "generations" needs to be studied not in its theoretical abstract but in its specific historical detail. As Professor Trevor-Roper has remarked in an article in *Encounter* (February 1960), p. 6:

> For if we are able to understand changes in human history and human philosophy, we must always remember the importance of single generations. One generation of men may be bound together by common experiences from which its fathers and sons are exempt; and if those experiences have been signal, terrible, inspiring, they will give to that generation a character distinctive to itself, incommunicable to other men. How can we, who lived through the 1930s, whose minds and attitudes were formed by the terrible events of those days, understand or be understood by men to whom those events are mere history, reduced to the anodyne prose of text-books? Of course not every generation has common experiences sufficient to mark it out in this way; the experiences, if they are to have this effect, must be powerful, formida-ble, inspiring. But if they are inspiring, then there are such generations. Spaniards, in their history, talk of "the generation of '98" as an enormous, significant fact which alone gives meaning to a part of its course. In Europe the generation of the

1930s may well prove similar. And in seventeenth-century Europe, and particularly protestant Europe, the generation of the 1620s was the same. ["Three Foreigners and the Philosophy of the English Revolution," repr. in H. R. Trevor-Roper, *Religion, the Reformation, and Social Change* (1967), pp. 245–46]

26. Albert Camus, *L'Homme révolté* (1951); *The Rebel* (tr. Bower, 1956), p. 8; (1951), p. 19: " . . . *et dans la solitude cependant, les armes à la main et la gorge serrée.*"

27. It was no hyperbole to speak of "an irony of fate." When Pobedonostsev—the procurator of the Holy Synod and the "Tsar's Eye" himself—searched in vain for a copy of Carlyle's *French Revolution* but found copies of Marx's *Capital*, he complained to the chief director of press affairs:

> All Carlyle's words ought to be allowed—they are steeped in moral principle to the point of severity! And imagine it: Marx's *Capital*, one of the most inflammatory books there are, has been published in a Russian translation. [*The First Russian Revisionists* (1962), pp. 73–78]

Was the censor asleep? Sometimes he was; and Marxists watched his personal habits closely. A work by Plekhanov, under a finely camouflaged title, was submitted on 20 December 1894 and went on approved sale in about a week's time. "The gamble," Kindersley writes, "on the censor's Christmas holidays was justified . . . "

Yet Article 94 of the Censorship Statute (1828) forbade "audacious and insolent subtleties, directed against faith and true wisdom." And Article 95 forbade publications which "expound the harmful doctrines of Socialism and Communism, and tend to shake the existing order, to stir up class hatred and to establish anarchy." Wasn't Marx, then, considered dangerous? He was. His name is included in 1884 in the Minister of Interior's list of banned authors (which also included Bagehot, Huxley, Lassalle, Lecky, Louis Blanc, Mill, Réclus, Adam Smith, and Herbert Spencer). Still, the first volume of *Capital* had been passed—"on the grounds that it was an obscure and abstract treatise, without relevance to Russian conditions . . . " In December 1885, the St. Petersburg Censorship Committee passed the second volume of *Capital* with the comment that it was a "serious piece of economic research . . . comprehensible only to specialists."

Only a decade later did the censor become alarmed by the books which were creating "a sort of cult of Marx." By 1894, both volumes of *Capital* were forbidden to be issued in public libraries and reading rooms, and their reprinting was prohibited. But the three volumes in German, although they were not to be "allowed in circulation," could be issued "upon written application to those who require them by the nature of their scholastic work, or who merit confidence by their social and professional position."

Marx would have been amused by the irony of the Russian censorship's devotion to the principle of an economic interpretation of intellectual influence. The fear was not so much of ideas as of their possible popular appeal. Russian imperfections could be criticized in "special learned discourses," in books of more than ten printed sheets, and in reviews with an annual subscription of not less than seven rubles! This was the Achilles heel of traditional premodern censorship. The coming of the cheap leaflet, pamphlet, and paperback put the ideas of revolution within the reach of every man's pocket.

If the Russians did not quite understand this until too late, it was plain enough quite early in England and in France (Joll, *The Anarchists*, p. 38; Peter Gay, *The Party of Humanity: Studies in the French Enlightenment* (1959, p. 36). William Pitt, unworried about Godwin's *Enquiry Concerning Political Justice* (1793), remarked: "A three-guinea book could never do much harm among those who had not three shillings to spare . . . " And Voltaire had written to Alembert in 1766: "Twenty folio volumes will never make a revolution: it's the small portable books at thirty sous that are dangerous. If the gospel had cost 1,200 sesterces, the Christian religion would never have been established . . . "

28. Karl Marx, *Briefe an Kugelmann* (1952 ed.), pp. 71–72.

29. Robert C. Tucker, *Philosophy and Myth in Karl Marx* (1961).

30. Marx to Engels, 7 December 1867, *Briefwechsel,* 3:547.

31. Franz Borkenau, *World Communism* (1962), pp. 172–73. *Thomas Manns Briefe: 1937–1947* (1963), p. 579. Thomas Mann, *The Magic Mountain* (tr. Lowe-Porter, 1945), pp. 402–4. M. J. Lasky, "Georg Lukacs," *New York Times Book Review* (10 May 1964). Karl Kerenyi, "Zauberberg-Figuren," in *Tessiner Schreibtisch* (1963), pp. 125–41.

See also Isaac Deutscher, "Georg Lukacs and 'Critical Realism,' " *The Listener* (3 November 1966), pp. 659–62; George Steiner, "Georg Lukacs and His Devil's Pact," *Kenyon Review* (Winter 1960), pp. 1–18; T. W. Adorno, "Erpresste Versöhnung," *Der Monat* (November 1958), pp. 37–49; George Lichtheim, "An Intellectual Disaster," *Encounter* (May 1963), pp. 74–80, and *Lukacs* (Modern Masters ed., 1970).

32. In noting the absence of philosophical audacity, I am referring here to the official worldwide Marxist movement. To be sure, in heretical and independent circles there have been a number of adventurous attempts to reassociate the idea of revolution with a tragic sense of life. But few of them appear to be entirely free from the suspicion that the ulterior motive is less philosophical amplification than political apologia. For a recent such effort from an East German Marxist critic, see the arguments for a "socialism of austerity" in Wolfgang Harich, *Kommunismus ohne Wachstum? Babeuf und der "Club of Rome"* (1975).

It is clear that Raymond Williams, in his *Culture and Society* (1958) and *The Long Revolution* (1961), has been deeply troubled about his revolutionary commitment. "I know," he confesses in his book *Modern Tragedy* (1966), pp. 61–83, "that the revolutionary societies have been tragic societies, at a depth and on a scale that go beyond any ordinary pity and fear." He has forced himself to recognize that revolutionary regimes have acted, "repeatedly and brutally, against every kind of human freedom and dignity." These he calls "real complexities." Worse than that. "We see the struggle to end alienation producing its own new kinds of alienation ... " And he even concedes that "it is undoubtedly true that a commitment to revolution can produce a kind of hardening which even ends by negating the revolutionary purpose."

But if his faith is shaken, his loyalty is not. "To see revolution in this tragic perspective," he argues, "is the only way to maintain it." To abandon it would be to desert to "a familiar kind of North Atlantic thinking" or to what he refers to as "the received ideology of tragedy." This unattractive prospect entails (1) "the old tragic lesson, that man cannot change his condition, but can only drown his world in blood in the vain attempt"; and (2) "the contemporary reflex, that the taking of rational control over our social destiny is defeated or at best deeply stained by our inevitable irrationality, and by the violence and cruelty that are so quickly released when habitual forms break down." He wants no part of these—or of utopianism, or reformism, or evolution, or, indeed, of any reconsideration which suggests that "any absolute purpose is delusion and folly." It certainly comes as no surprise when he reveals that "what we learn in suffering is again revolution ... " To be sure, it is "a long revolution," involving "a new struggle against the new alienation." It is "the authentic activity reborn and newly lived." But it remains "absolute reform" and (with Marx) "its absolute aim is the 'total redemption of humanity' ... " So does the true believer come full circle: the complexities could not have been as real as all that.

As Professor Frank Kermode has put it (*Encounter* [August 1966], p. 85),

> Thus the cost of an understanding of modern tragedy is an understanding of modern revolution. This, one gathers, had better be Pasternak's than Stalin's, but the implication seems to be that Stalin's was better than anything we can manage ...

Lucien Goldmann's philosophical audacity is on an altogether different level of intricacy and radical confrontation. In his important study of *The Hidden God* (1964), he breaks with the official traditions of optimistic simplicities and makes a devious attempt to return to the Marx of "the tragic vision," via Pascal, Racine, Kant, Goethe, and Hegel:

> Tragic vision marks a transitional phase between rationalism and the dialectic ...
> The appearance of the tragic vision marks the reappearance of good and evil as

genuine realities which determine a man's existence ... Evil still remains totally opposed to goodness, but the two are now inseparably linked together ... The theme reappears with the dialectical vision, with Goethe, Hegel, and Marx. Initially, they see the problem in the same terms as the tragic thinkers do, and recognize that, for the individual, good and evil are at one and the same time both real, in conflict, and inseparable. However, they all admit that the "ruse of reason," the March of History, will transform individual evil into the very vehicle of a progress which will bring about the good as a whole.

For if in Pascal and Kant goodness remains the opposite of evil (while, and herein lies the essence of tragedy, remaining inseparable from it) in Goethe, as in Hegel and Marx, evil becomes the only path that leads to goodness.... From Hegel and Marx onwards, both the finite goods and even the evil of terrestial life—Goethe's Devil—will receive a meaning inside the framework of faith and of hope in the future. [*The Hidden God*, pp. 175–76 n, 301–2]

Lucien Goldmann is, naturally enough, strongly taken by the early Lukacs—and just as Naphta (Lukacs in Thomas Mann's portrait) is both Jesuit and Jew, Marx emerges as both Faust and Mephisto. Once again: how much of this philosophical revaluation is metaphysics and how much ideology and apologia is as yet unclear. As Pascal said, too much clarity darkens.

If one accepts the categories employed by George Steiner in his *Death of Tragedy* (1961), this whole effort would appear to be futile. "Marx repudiated the entire concept of tragedy," he argues (p. 4). "The Marxist world view, even more explicitly than the Christian, admits of error, anguish, and temporary defeat, but not of ultimate tragedy." Despair is a mortal sin; and a Communist society (as Lunacharski, the first Soviet commissar of education, said) could have no tragic drama of its own. "The Marxist creed is immensely, perhaps naively optimistic ... even the grimmest setback gives no ground for tragic despair. The march forward continues, for it has behind it the inexorable laws of history; final victory is as certain as the coming of dawn ... " (pp. 342–43). Curiously enough, Steiner makes an exception for Bert Brecht, making him stand "midway between the world of Oedipus and that of Marx"; and he also appears to be able to discern the new beginnings of authentic tragedy in certain "rites of defiance" in Communist China.

33. The anti-utopianism of both Marx and Brecht are astutely linked by Martin Esslin (*Brecht: A Choice of Evils* [1959], pp. 232–33), and I would only qualify his analysis with the suggestion that the failure was in Marx essentially one of theory and imagination, in Brecht one of character and ethics:

Brecht, too, has nothing concrete to offer when it comes to showing how a better system would work. The very violence of his demand for a change, his recurrent assertion that things cannot, must not, go on as they are at present, springs from this failure. In fact, if we extract the meaning contained in his plays ... the result belies the facile optimism of Brecht's professed, and monotonously asserted, eschatological hope of a Marxist earthly paradise. For he constantly shows the weakness of man, his inability to deal with his problems according to his insight into what would be rational, his subjection to instinct and blind passion ... The system must be changed. But, in Brecht's view, it simply cannot be changed slowly and gradually: only violence can bring about a really fundamental change. But violence is wicked. And wicked methods, Brecht shows again and again, make wicked people ... He is unable to suggest a way of breaking this vicious circle:

"Would you deny that the use of force debases him who resorts to it?"

"No, I do not deny that ... " [*Die Tage der Kommune*]

Brecht's work thus fails, as the Communists rightly felt, in conveying the message of hope in man's redemption by a radical change in the social order,. which he so earnestly and persistently sought to put into it.

34. Esslin, *Brecht*, pp. 133, 151 n, 206. Herbert Luethy, "Of Poor Bert Brecht," *Encounter* (July 1956). Bertolt Brecht, *Die Massnahme*, in *Versuche* 4 (1930), *Lehrstücke* (1966), and the *Colorado Review* (Winter 1957–58; tr. Bentley).

35. The incident in Berlin occurred in April 1955. *Vespers,* in *W. H. Auden* (Penguin ed., 1958), pp. 189–91.

Hannah Arendt prefaces her long and incisive profile of Brecht in the *New Yorker* (5 November 1966), p. 68; repr. in *Men in Dark Times* (1973), p. 204, with the following lines by Auden:

> You hope, yes,
> your books will excuse you,
> save you from hell:
> nevertheless,
> without looking sad,
> without in any way
> seeming to blame ...
> God may reduce you
> on Judgment Day
> to tears of shame,
> reciting by heart
> the poems you would
> have written, had
> your life been good.

It may be journalistically apt to tie these lines to Brecht, but they are taken from Auden's autobiographical poems in *About the House* (1966), p. 23, and actually refer not to Brecht but rather to Auden himself.

36. *The Mind of Napoleon,* p. 86.

37. *A Kierkegaard Anthology* (ed. Bretall, 1946), p. 434.

38. J. W. Goethe, *Maximen und Reflexionen* (definitive ed., 1963), 21:15: "Eine falsche Lehre lässt sich nicht widerlegen, denn sie ruht ja auf der Überzeugung, dass das Falsche wahr sei."

39. Sören Kierkegaard, *Journals: 1834–1854* (ed. Dru, 1958), p. 29.

40. P. J. Proudhon, *La Justice poursuivie par l'église* (1858), vol. 1, no. 3; Henri de Lubac, *Proudhon: The Un-Marxian Socialist* (1948), p. 231.

41. Mircea Eliade, *The Sacred and the Profane* (1961), pp. 205–7. See also Alastair MacIntyre, *Marxism: An Interpretation* (1953), ch. 7, and *Marxism and Christianity* (1968), pp. 103–16; and Rudolph Bultmann, *History and Eschatology* (1962), pp. 68–70.

42. Reinhold Niebuhr, *Faith and History* (1949), pp. 210–11.

43. Karl Löwith, *Meaning in History* (1949), p. 46.

44. See the work of the Polish Marxist philosopher Adam Schaff: *A Philosophy of Man* (1963), and *Marxismus und das menschliche Individuum* (1965). Also, Raymond Williams, "Tragedy and Revolution," pp. 61–83; and the recent essays by Leszek Kolakowski, especially *Can the Devil Be Saved?—A Marxist Answer* (1974).

45. Rowley, *The Relevance of Apocalyptic* (1944; rev. ed., 1963), pp. 13–105. Martin Buber, *The Prophetic Faith,* p. 172.

46. J. M. Thompson, *Robespierre* (1936), 2:211, 224.

47. *The Mind of Napoleon,* pp. 66–67. *Journal of the Private Life and Conversations of the Emperor Napoleon at Saint Helena by the Count de las Cases* (8 vols., 1823), 2, pt. 3:29; *Le Mémorial de Sainte-Hélène* (ed. Pleiade, 1935), 1:470–71:

> ...les grandes principes de notre Révolution ... elles seront la foi, la religion, la morale de tous les peuples.... j'ai fait briller le flambeau, consacre les principes, et aujourd'hui la persécution achève de m'en rendre le Messie. [9–10 April 1816]

48. Henry More, *Enthusiasmus Triumphatus; or a Brief Discourse of the Nature, Causes, Kinds, and Cure of Enthusiasme* (1656), in *A Collection of Several Philosophical Writings of Dr. Henry More* (1712), p. 22.

49. Friedrich Meinecke, "Campanella," in *Die Idee der Staatsräson* (1924), pp. 113–46; *Machiavellism* (tr. Scott, 1957), pp. 110, 115.

50. Wilhelm Weitling, *Garantien der Harmonie und Freiheit* (1842; ed. Kaufhold, 1955), pp. 281, 366:

> Und einen neuen Messias sehe ich mit dem Schwerte kommen, durch seinen Mut an die Spitze der revolutionären Armee gestellt werden, wird mit ihr den morschen Bau der alten gesellschaftlichen Ordnung zertrümmern, die Tränenquellen in das Meer der Vergessenheit leiten und die Erde in ein Paradies verwandeln.

51. Karl Kautsky, *The Dictatorship of the Proletariat* (1918; 1964), pp. 17–18; Bertram D. Wolfe, *Marxism* (1965), pp. 163, 243–44; Edmund Wilson, *To the Finland Station* (1940), p. 167. J. L. H. Keep, *The Rise of Social Democracy in Russia* (1963), p. 20.

52. Michael Gold, *Jews without Money* (1930), a novel by a once prominent American Communist, p. 309.

53. *Ferdinand Lassalles Tagebuch* (ed. Lindau, 1891), pp. 85–86, 189–90, 258.

54. This *"Kriegsmanifest gegen die Welt,"* written by Lassalle in September 1845 and addressed (*"Triumviri!"*) to three youthful friends, is an extraordinary document, and deserves more attention than the intellectual historians of the main currents of nineteenth-century thought have given it. "In it," Schirokauer remarks, "we have the declaration of an Isaiah who has adopted the gestures of Robespierre [the handle of L.'s famous walking stick was a model of the Bastille, fashioned in gold, generally believed to have belonged to the Jacobin] and the words of Hegel ... " It is also strikingly "pre-Nietzschean." I quote one passage in greater fullness:

> I am servant and master of the idea, priest of the god I myself am ... Whatever I do, I know to be the moral demand of the idea. I brandish the weapon of Zeus, the lightning of knowledge [*ich schwinge die Waffe des Zeus, den Blitz des Wissens*] ... I have overcome the defiance of my body. I have made an end of the difference between it and my will, I have deprived it of its own entity and independent physiognomy so that it has been compelled unresistingly to accommodate itself and to accept the stamp of my thought. I have compelled it to be the reflex of my will. I have become an actor. The tremulous tones of my voice and the flashings of my eyes [*Ich—wurde Schauspieler, plastischer Künstler ... der zitternde Ton meiner Stimme und der leuchtende Glanz meines Auges*], every one of my gestures, must slavishly reproduce the passion which I desire at that precise moment to vivify me and illumine me. From head to foot I am nothing but will ... I have made it true of myself that being is only the being of thought ... I have the will to destroy, and I have the means of spreading woe and disaster over those on whom I breathe [*Ich habe den Willen zur Vernichtung und die Mittel dazu, Weh zu verbreiten und Unheil über die Menschen, die mein Atem berührt*] ...

Two other remarks, outlining the stormy course of Lassalle's proclaimed *Religions-Krieg*, are of special interest here:

> Power is only in me, for I am its living apex. Through me it sustains its negative violence. Now, on to the battle! As I make my decision, committing myself to the struggle, the earth trembles in its foundations and the whole structure of the intellectual world rumbles in its depths ...
>
> The major reason why my victory is certain is that my struggle is conscious and purposeful. Over the chaotic state of robbery which is the world, there is a pretence of moral regulations, of a moral community [*Es schlingt sich um diesen verwirrten Räuberzustand der Welt ein Schein sittlicher Bestimmungen sittlicher Zusammenlebens*] ... the illusion of a morally ordered world. And when in the individual struggle there is a conflict with one of these moral rules—the substance is no longer there, but appearances still serve—timidity grows, and respect, and there is no daring consciously and systematically to transgress. So the struggle goes on—with tied hands.... For me it is a life-and-death struggle and must be fought with full strength. Yes, the contradiction is total ... Consequently, I am paramount and boundless [*übermächtig, ungebunden*]. To me all means are equal, and nothing is so sacred that I would spare it. I have achieved the right of the tiger, to tear right apart [*Gleich vor mir sind alle Mittel, nichts ist so heilig, dass ich es schonte, und ich habe errungen das Recht des Tigers, das Recht zu zerreissen*].

The full text is in *Briefe von und an Lassalle bis 1848,* of Gustav Mayer's edition of *Nachgelassene Briefe und Schriften* (1921), 1:213–34.

Here, indeed, is the spectacle, as Professor Hermann Oncken has observed, of a robust twenty-year-old trying to justify with cold intellectuality his self-proclaimed role as an *Übermensch:* that which "escaped Nietzsche" in the last sickly stages of his most morbid intensity. See Hermann Oncken, *Lassalle zwischen Marx und Bismarck* (rev. ed. Hirsch, 1966), p. 57.

55. *Heinrich Heines Briefwechsel* (ed. Hirth, 1917), 2:567; *The Poetry and Prose of Heinrich Heine* (ed. Ewen, 1948), p. 446. *Nachgelassene Briefe* (1925), 6:410. G. Brandes, *Lassalle* (1911), p. 193.

As for Lassalle as "the Messiah," two of the contemporary reactions to Lassalle's untimely death in a duel at the age of thirty-nine may represent the century's wild uncertainty as to whether the messianic spirit would come as a man of peace or as a man with the sword. "For eighteen centuries," remarked his erstwhile revolutionary colleague, Karl Vogt, "we have been worshipping a crucified Jew. Now we are going to make a Jew who has been shot into a second redeemer!" But his loyal followers in the Breslau churchyard where he was buried sang less critically, more modestly, *"Dort schlummert der Eine, der Schwerter uns gab."*

Eduard Bernstein emphasizes the distinction, trying as always to refine and reduce the total psychic investment in the great rational cause:

> The Social Democracy has no legends, and needs none; it regards its champions not as saints but as men. . . . The time for victory was not yet, but in order to conquer, the workers must first learn to fight. And to have trained them for the fight, to have, as the song says, given them swords, this remains the great, the undying merit of Ferdinand Lassalle.

See: Arno Schirokauer, *Lassalle: The Power of Illusion and the Illusion of Power* (tr. Eden and Cedar Paul, 1931), p. 301; Oncken, *Lassalle zwischen Marx und Bismarck,* p. 390; E. Bernstein, *Ferdinand Lassalle as a Social Reformer* (tr. Aveling, 1893), p. 192.

56. Lassalle, *Arbeiter-Programm* (1862), in *Gesammelte Reden und Schriften* (ed. Bernstein, 1919), 2:200. See, generally, Bernstein, *Ferdinand Lassalle as a Social Reformer* and Oncken, *Lassalle zwischen Marx und Bismarck.*

57. Cesare Pavese, *The Business of Living: Diary, 1935–50* (tr. Murch, 1961), p. 227; *Il Mestiere di Vivere* (1960), p. 316: "Un discorso di comizio ha la natura del rito religioso. Si ascolta per sentire cio che gia si pensara, per esaltarsi nelle comune fede e confessione."

58. E. A. Olssen, "Marx and the Resurrection," *Journal of the History of Ideas* (January–March 1968), pp. 131–40.

59. Erich Fromm, *Marx's Concept of Man* (1961), pp. 64, 68.

60. Friedrich Engels, "Zur Geschichte des Urchristentums," *Die Neue Zeit* (1894–95), Marx/Engels, *Werke* (East Berlin ed.), 22:449; *On Religion* (ed. Moscow, 1955), p. 316. In a curious commentary on the Book of Revelation ("Das Buch der Offenbarung," 1883), Engels quotes this from Ernst Renan:

> When you want to get a distinct idea of what the first Christian communities were, do not compare them to the parish congregations of our day; they were rather like local sections of the International Working Men's Associations . . .

And Engels adds: "And this is correct. Christianity got hold of the masses, exactly as modern socialism does . . . "

61. *Der Spiegel,* 25 July 1968, p. 62.

62. Marx/Engels, *Werke* (East Berlin ed., 1969), 21:9. *On Religion,* pp. 205–6.

63. Engels to Vera Zasulich (23 April 1885), *Selected Correspondence,* pp. 437–38. Melville, *Billy Budd* (1961 ed.), p. 7. William Butler Yeats, *Collected Poems* (1950), p. 358. Pascal, *Pensées* (ed. Trotter, 1932), p. 99.

64. Joseph Conrad, *Under Western Eyes* (1911), pp. 134–35.

65. Nor is the Bonapartist touch in the Marxist psyche absent from contemporary revolutionary figures. In his biography of *Mao Tse-tung* (1966), p. 25 n, Stuart Schram notes:
His schoolboy's admiration for Napoleon has survived down to the present day; in 1964, Mao told a French parliamentary delegation that while Robespierre was a great revolutionary, he was personally more impressed by Napoleon.

66. *The Revolt of Islam* (1818) an original draft of which was subtitled "The Revolution of the Golden City: A Vision of the Nineteenth Century," in Shelley, *Poetical Works* (ed. Hutchinson, 1967), pp. 122–23.

67. My various quotations are from the following: R. R. Palmer, *Twelve Who Ruled* (1941), p. 129; *The Mind of Napoleon*, p. 64; Carl Wittke's biography of Weitling, *The Utopian Communist* (1950), pp. 54, 102; Marx, *The Eighteenth Brumaire of Louis Bonaparte* (ed. 1948), p. 93; *Der Achtzehnte Brumaire* (ed. Reclam, 1967), p. 80: *"die glühende Lava der Revolution,"* and *"A Memoir of Guevara,"* in *Der Spiegel* (Hamburg), 29 July 1968, p. 62; and E. H. Carr, *Michael Bakunin* (1937; 1961), p. 452.

68. With reference to the phenomenon of political mixed metaphors, the fear of counterrevolution can inspire as much significant stylistic confusion as the hopes for the revolutionary coming. Thus, John Milton, writing hectically in 1660 as general opinion finally swung back from the Cromwellian Commonwealth men to the Stuart Royalists, committed this jumble; as he appealed to the mass of Englishmen
... to bethink themselves a little and consider whither they are rushing; to exhort this torrent also of the people, not to be so impetuous, but to keep their due channell; and at length recovering and uniting their better resolutions, now that they see alreadie how open and unbounded the insolence and rage is of our common enemies to give a stay to these ruinous proceedings justly and timely fearing to what a precipice of destruction the deluge of this epidemic madness would hurrie us through to this general defection of a misguided and abus'd multitude ... [John Milton, *The Ready and Easy Way to Establish a Free Commonwealth* (1660; ed. Clark, 1915), p. 41]
Commenting on this passage, the great Milton biographer David Masson has shrewdly pointed out (*The Life of John Milton* [1877], 5:688):
To exhort a torrent! The very mixture and hurry of the metaphors in Milton's mind are a reflex of the facts around him. Current, torrent, rush, rapid, avalanche, deluge hurrying to a precipice: mix and jumble such figures as we may, we but express more accurately the mad haste which London and all England were making the end of April 1660 to bring Charles over from the Continent.

69. S. H. Baron, *Plekhanov: The Father of Russian Marxism* (1963), p. 93.

70. Alexander Blok, "The Intelligentsia and the Revolution" (1918), in *Russian Intellectual History, an Anthology* (ed. Raeff, 1966), pp. 366–67.

71. Samuel Taylor Coleridge, *Zapolya* (1817), in *Complete Poetical Works* (ed. E. H. Coleridge, 1912), 2:895.

72. *The Memoirs of Chateaubriand* (1848; tr. Baldick, 1961), p. 98.

73. "Letters on the French Coup d'État of 1851," in *Bagehot's Historical Essays* (ed. St. John Stevas, 1965), p. 386.

74. J. S. Mill, *On Liberty* (1859), in *Utilitarianism, Liberty and Representative Government* (ed. A. D. Lindsay; Everyman's ed. 1910, repr. 1962), p. 117. Boris Pasternak, *Dr. Zhivago* (1958), pp. 378, 384. Ernest Renan, *History of the People of Israel* (1896), 3:416. Miriam Beard, *A History of the Businessman* (1938), p. 465. Eric Hoffer, *The True Believer* (1950), p. 131. *The Political Philosophy of Bakunin* (ed. Maximoff, 1953), p. 380.

75. Nathaniel Hawthorne, *The Blithedale Romance* (1852; Sears ed.), ch. 9, pp. 67–68.

76. Carr, *Michael Bakunin*, pp. 395, 457. See also Bakunin's long letter to Nechayev (2 June 1870), in *Encounter* (July/August 1972), and in Professor Michael Confino's edition, *Daughter of a Revolutionary: Natalie Herzen and the Bakunin/Nechayev Circle* (1974), pp. 238–80.

77. Friedrich Nietzsche, "Der Fall Wagner" (1888), in *Werke*, 2:910–11.

78. Richard Wagner, *Prose Works* (tr. Ellis, 1895), 8:232–38; *Wagner on Music and Drama* (ed. Goldman and Sprinchorn, 1964), pp. 67–74.

79. Wilson, *To the Finland Station*, pp. 274, 386. *Letters of Richard Wagner* (ed. Burke, 1950), p. 233. David Thomson, *The Babeuf Plot* (1947), p. 30. Carr, *Bakunin*, pp. 196–202.

80. On the sentiments of Gustave Landauer, see the chapter on him in Buber, *Paths in Utopia* (1949), pp. 46–57. Landauer's outbursts of realism only accentuated his romantic revolutionism. He did discern the "feverish" uncontrollability of the revolutionary personality; and in fact went on to warn against "the forces of negation and destruction": " . . . fanaticism and passion turn to distrust and soon to bloodthirstiness, or at least to an indifference to the added terrors of killing; and before long terror by killing becomes the sole possible means for the rulers of the day to keep themselves provisionally in power." Yet, for all his humane dissent, he remained (as in his book *Die Revolution* of 1907) a revolutionary loyalist, enchanted by "the fire, the ecstasy, the brotherliness," indeed "the love" which he found in the militant movements. In a letter of 1911 he came close to expressing, in a very few sentences, the essence of utopian revolutionism, namely its populist longing for a wholeness beyond the realm of possibility. "Do we want to retreat into happiness? Do we want our lives for ourselves? Do we not rather want to do everything possible for the people, and long for the impossible? Do we not want the whole thing—Revolution?"

Karl Mannheim, *Ideology and Utopia*, p. 203. H. W. Thoreau, *Walden* (Modern Library ed.), p. 69. Thompson, *Leaders of the French Revolution* (1929), p. 180. Thomson, *The Babeuf Plot*, p. 20.

81. Carr, *Bakunin*, pp. 1, 24–25.

82. Frank Manuel, *The New World of Henri Saint-Simon* (1956), pp. 54, 90–91, 117. G. D. H. Cole, *The Life of Robert Owen* (1925), and Cole's introduction to Owen's *A New View of Society* (1927 ed.), p. xviii: "Perhaps the easiest answer to the riddle of his personality is that he was a little mad." Also, P. J. Proudhon, *De la justice dans la révolution et dans l'église* (1870), 6:164.

See, generally, the writings of Erik H. Erikson, especially *Childhood and Society* (1963), *Young Man Luther* (1958), and his revealing "Autobiographic Notes on the Identity Crisis," in *Daedalus* (Fall 1970), pp. 730–59.

See also, Frank Manuel, "The Use and Abuse of Psychology in History," in *Freedom from History* (1971), pp. 23–52; E. Victor Wolfenstein's "psycho-sexual" study of Lenin, Trotsky, and Gandhi, entitled *The Revolutionary Personality* (1967); *Psychoanalysis and History* (ed. Mazlish, 1963); *Psychoanalysis and Social Science* (ed. Ruitenbeek, 1962); and Harold D. Lasswell, *World Politics and Personal Insecurity* (1934).

83. Michael Walzer, *The Revolution of the Saints* (1965), pp. 315–20. J.-P. Nettl, *Rosa Luxemburg* (2 vols., 1966), 2:477. J. L. H. Keep, *The Rise of Social Democracy in Russia*, p. 65.

84. Bert Brecht, *Me-Ti: Buch der Wendungen* (1965), p. 58:
> Damit das Grosse erreicht wird, bedarf es grosser Änderungen.
> Die kleinen Änderungen sind die Feinde der grossen Änderungen.

85. Plummer, *Bronterre*, p. 35.

86. "Reformatio Sigismundi" (ca. 1438), in *Manifestations of Discontent in Germany on the Eve of the Reformation* (ed. and tr. Strauss, 1971), pp. 3–31. The original is in *Reformation Kaiser Siegmunds*, vol. 4 of *Monumenta Germaniae Historica: Staatsschriften des späteren Mittelalters* (ed. Koller, 1964). See, generally, Lothar Graf zu Dohna, *Reformatio Sigismundi: Beiträge zum Verständnis einer Reformschrift des fünfzehnten Jahrhunderts* (1960).

87. I have used mainly the account by Dr. Hellmut Haupt who discovered the document: "Ein oberrheinischer Revolutionäär aus dem Zeitalter Maximilians I," in *Westdeutsche Zeitschrift für Geschichte und Kunst* (1893), pp. 79–228. There is a brief translation in *Manifestations of Discontent* (ed. Strauss), pp. 233–47; these are excerpts from the complete edition, *Das Buch der Hundert Kapitel und der Vierzig Statuten des sogenannten*

Oberrheinischen Revolutionärs (ed. Zschäbitz and Franke, 1967). See also Haupt, "Ein oberrheinischer Revolutionär," pp. 236, 246.

88. Haupt, "Ein oberrheinischer Revolutionär," pp. 159, 169, 195–98, 201–12. *Oberrheinischer Revolutionär* (ed. Zschäbitz), pp. 107, 226. *Manifestations* (ed. Strauss), p. 244: "Great changes always occur at times of great conjunctions...." Zschäbitz suggests (*Oberrheinischer Revolutionär*, p. 39) that the "astronomer" was probably a maker of calendars.

89. *Manifestations*, pp. 153–66.

90. Franz von Sickingen, that noble crusading knight, could hardly imagine that his cry for "honest laws to lighten the burden of the people" could ever have a serious echo in this earthly vale of tears. Had not Sebastian Franck seemed to have had the better of the argument of the late medieval day when he insisted on nonresistance to evil, on "silence and patience," on waiting for a providential alleviation in good time from the hand of God? See *Dialogus* (1523), "Franz von Sickingen at the Gates of Heaven", Sebastian Franck on "The Great Peasant Rebellion" (1531), in *Manifestations*, pp. 166–69, 170–79.

91. In the case of the Rhine revolutionary, his eschatological scheme was regularly revised and updated. In the years 1503–7 he announced the final judgment for the year 1509; later he changed it to 1511 (although a friend later indicated he meant 1521); and in the last texts he was waiting for 1515. *Oberrheinischer Revolutionär*, p. 93.

See, generally, G. H. Williams, *The Radical Reformation* (1962); Howard Kaminsky, *A History of the Hussite Revolution* (1967), and his "Wyclifism as Ideology of Revolution," in *Church History* (1963), 32:57–74; Claus-Peter Clasen, *Anabaptism: A Social History, 1525–1618* (1972); and Wilhelm E. Mühlmann, *Chiliasmus und Nativismus* (1964). I would also recommend that formidable and penetrating work by Leszek Kolakowski, *Chrétiens sans Eglise: La Conscience religieuse et le lien confessionel au XVIIe siècle* (tr. Posner, 1969).

92. Nietzsche, *Aus dem Nachlass*, in *Werke*, 3:637: "Nicht der Hunger erzeugt Revolutionen, sondem dass das Volk en mangeant Appetit bekommen hat ... "

93. Tocqueville, *The Old Regime*, pp. 176–77. I apologize for quoting this well-worn passage, but it is a *locus classicus* and indeed one that is, for some peculiar reason, generally accepted and on the grounds so often deemed sufficient that it appears to be so plausible and true. Yet it has always alternated with the converse thesis, namely, poverty and despair as the basic ground of revolutionary extremism; and no one has yet thought it necessary to investigate empirically how many of the determinable explosions of recorded history can be ascribed to one or the other of these two eternally persuasive explanations. Once again, in the absence of overwhelming evidence (and sometimes even then), the ideological temperament predisposes men's minds to a self-serving view of social causation.

94. In his perceptive critique of Taine—"France in the Eighteenth Century," in *Critical Miscellanies* (1888), 3:261–89—John Morley conceded that "both Rousseau and Diderot were conscious literary revolutionists, before they were used as half-conscious social revolutionists." But, he argues, "it was not a literary aptitude in the nation for *raison raisonnante* which developed the political theories of Rousseau, the moral and psychological theories of Diderot, the anti-ecclesiastical theories of Voltaire and Holbach. It was the profound disorganization of institutions that suggested and stimulated the speculative agitation." And these same disorganized institutions, with the men and classes that served them, constituted the force which limited historical alternatives:

"*Si on avait été sage!*" those cry who consider the Revolution as a futile mutiny. If people had only been prudent, all would have been accomplished that has been accomplished since, and without the sanguinary memories, the interpolations of despotism, the waste of generous lives and noble purpose. And this is true. But then prudence itself was impossible. The court and the courtiers were smitten through the working of long tradition by judicial blindness. If Lewis XVI had been a Frederick, or Marie Antoinette had been a Catherine of Russia, or the nobles had even been stout-hearted gentlemen like our Cavaliers, the great transformation might then have been gradually effected without disorder. But they were none of these, and it was their characters that made the fate and doom of the situation . . . . In measuring the force of the various antecedents of the Revolution [M. Taine] has assigned to books and philosophical ideas a place in the scale of dissolvent conditions that belongs more rightly to decayed institutions, to incompetent and incorrigible castes, to economic incongruities that could only be dealt with trenchantly . . .

95. John Morley, *Critical Miscellanies*, 3:281–82.

96. This remarkable and little-known passage deserves to be quoted in its entirety. The entry for 31 January 1879 in the fourteen-volume *Notes From a Diary* (1898) by Sir Mountstuart E. Grant Duff begins (pp. 103–6):

Lunched at the Devonshire Club, with Leonard Montefiore, to meet Karl Marx. I embodied my impressions of him in a letter to a friend on the Continent, which I subjoin with some omissions . . .

His talk was that of a well informed, nay, learned man, much interested in comparative grammar, which had led him into the old Slavonic and other out-of-the-way studies, and was varied by many quaint turns and little bits of dry humour, as when speaking of Hezechiel's *Life of Prince Bismarck* he always referred to it, by way of contrast to Dr. Busch's book, as the Old Testament. It was all very *positif*, slightly cynical, without any appearance of enthusiasm, interesting and often, as I thought, showing very correct ideas, when he was conversing of the past or the present, but vague and unsatisfactory when he turned to the future.

He looks, not unreasonably, for a great and not distant crash in Russia: thinks it will begin by reforms from above, which the old bad edifice will not be able to bear, and which will lead to its tumbling down altogether. As to what would take its place, he had evidently no clear idea, except that for a long time Russia would be unable to exercise any influence in Europe.

Next, he thinks that the movement will spread to Germany, taking there the form of a revolt against the existing military system. To my question, "But how can you expect the army to rise against its commanders?" he replied: "You forget that in Germany, now, the army and the nation are nearly identical. These socialists you hear about are trained soldiers, like anybody else. You must not think of the standing army only. You must think of the Landwehr. And even in the standing army there is much discontent. Never was there an army in which the severity of the discipline led to so many suicides. The step from shooting oneself to shooting one's officer is not long; and an example of the kind once set is soon followed.

"But supposing," I said, "the rulers of Europe come to an understanding amongst themselves for a reduction of armaments, which might greatly relieve the burden of the people, what would become of the revolution which you expect that burden one day to bring about?"

"Ah!" was his answer, "they can't do that. All sorts of fears and jealousies will make it impossible. The burden will grow worse and worse as science advances, for the improvements in the art of destruction will keep pace with its advance, and every year more and more will have to be devoted to costly engines of war. It is a vicious circle. There is no escape from it."

"But," I said, "you have never yet had a serious popular rising unless there was really great misery."

"You have no idea," he rejoined, "how terrible has been the crisis through which Germany has been passing in these last five years."

"Well," I said, "supposing that your revolution has taken place, and that you have your republican form of government, it is still a long, long way to the realization of the special ideas of yourself and your friends."

"Doubtless," he answered, "but all great movements are slow. It would merely be a step to better things, as your revolution of 1688 was only a stage on the road."

The "friend on the Continent" to whom Sir Mountstuart dispatched this portrait of Marx was, melodramatically enough, the Empress Frederick: eldest daughter of Queen Victoria and mother of Kaiser Wilhelm II, the last of the Hohenzollern monarchs. "The above," his personal letter continued,

... will give Your Imperial Highness a fair idea of the kind of ideas about the near future of Europe which are working in his mind. They are too dreamy to be dangerous, except just in so far as the situation with its mad expenditure on armaments is obviously and undoubtedly dangerous. If, however, within the next decade the rulers of Europe have not found means of dealing with this evil without any warning from attempted revolution I for one shall despair of the future of humanity at least on this continent.

The ironies of history are too bold to need any special italicization:
In the course of conversation Karl Marx spoke several times both of Your Imperial Highness and of the Crown Prince and invariably with due respect and propriety. Even in the case of eminent individuals of whom he by no means spoke with respect there was no trace of bitterness or savagery—plenty acrid and dissolvent criticism but nothing of the Marat tone.... Altogether my impression of Marx, allowing for his being at the opposite pole of opinion from oneself, was not all unfavourable, and I would gladly meet him again. It will not be he, who whether he wishes it or not, will turn the world upside down.

This invaluable letter, which was brought back from Germany to the British Royal Archives by the Librarian at Windsor Castle in 1945, has been published in *The Times Literary Supplement*, 15 July 1949, p. 464.

97. Entry for 31 January 1879, in Duff, *Notes from a Diary: 1873–1881*, p. 104.

98. Writing from Paris in 1830, a Prussian historian, Friedrich von Raumer, observed:
For liberals, the word "revolutionary" signifies the suppression of a decrepit and obsolete social order, pernicious and ignominious, while "counter-revolution" is in their eyes equivalent to a leading toward injustice and an outworn order. On the contrary, their opponents, the conservatives, understand by the word "revolution" the aggregate of all follies and delinquencies; while the word "counter-revolution" is for them a synonym for order, authority and religion.

Roberto Michels quotes this—in his *First Lectures in Political Sociology* (1927; rev. ed., 1965), p. 151—and finds it "sensible," for after all "from the purely logical point of view" the terms *revolution* and *counterrevolution* were equivalent, both implying only a fundamental change of a legal order. "It is, then, a question of words that express only sentiments and evaluations, perhaps quite appreciable but entirely personal and arbitrary. Political science should not countenance such kinds of terminology."

99. Samuel Taylor Coleridge, *Essays on His Own Time* (1850), 1:118–19; John Colmer, *Coleridge: Critic of Society* (1959), p. 48.

100. Thomas Hobbes, *Behemoth: or an Epitome of the Civil Wars of England, from 1640 to 1660* (1679), p. 172; *The Life Records of John Milton* (ed. French, 1956), 4:441–42.

101. Friedrich Gentz, "The French and American Revolutions Compared" (1800), in *Three Revolutions* (ed. Possony, 1959), pp. 69–70.

102. Walter Bagehot, *Physics and Politics* (1867), ch. 5.

103. "Animated moderation," "conservative innovation," etc.: these characteristic maxims of English liberal reformism would appear to be true and nationally acceptable even today; but their relevance is confined to where England needs them least—on the level of abstraction. They sound like pragmatic precepts, but are they? Pragmatism, too, has its unpractical ideology. As Mr. Tadpole pointed out to Mr. Taper as long ago as 1844 (in Benjamin Disraeli's *Coningsby* [1962 ed.], p. 122):
"Ancient institutions and modern improvements I suppose, Mr. Tadpole?"
"Ameliorations is the better word; ameliorations. Nobody knows exactly what it means."

Contemporary political observers, curiously perplexed by the conservatism of a British Labour government, have been turned to Bagehot's analysis of "the quirks" of the British character and parliamentary system. See Alan Watkins, "Labour in Power," in *The Left* (ed. Kaufman, 1966), pp. 179–80. A. J. Balfour, writing an introduction to Bagehot's *English Constitution* (1928 ed.) offered a very English explanation of this English puzzle:

> Our alternating Cabinets, though belonging to different Parties, have never differed about the foundations of society. And it is evident that our whole political machinery presupposes a people so fundamentally at one that they can safely afford to bicker; and so sure of their own moderation that they are not dangerously disturbed by the never-ending din of political conflict. May it always be so.

And the then Prime Minister Wilson (as Alan Watkins assumed) "would say a quiet 'hear hear' to that."

The Labour left, in its disquiet, might be heard to say quite other things. Writing in the third year of the era of Wilsonian pragmatism, the perspicacious political correspondent of the *Times* (London), 2 December 1966, recorded:

> The pledges come to nothing. The reality falls far, far short of the ideal. So it happens with all parties when they come into government, but when it does happen the trauma on the Labour side is always harder to bear than on the Conservative side. For Labour, unlike Conservatives, do not enjoy power for its own sake. For Labour power means the opportunity to live in a Britain, or even a world, made ideal, and pragmatism is a euphemism for the betrayal of principle. It will be a long, long day before the ordinary member of the Labour rank and file learns what every Tory knows as soon as he is out of the cradle—that politics is the art of the possible. But you only have to promote a Labour man from the rank and file to the Cabinet for the truism to burst upon him in a blinding flash.

But the flash passes, usually with power. Writing in the third year of the successor government (Prime Minister Edward Heath's Tory administration), the late R. H. S. Crossman, who was one of the leading Ministerial figures of the Labour Party in office, made one of his periodic turns to other temperamental values.

> Whenever I am lectured on the virtues of moderation in Labour politics I feel as Hermann Goering did about culture and reach for my revolver. Westminster is a place where moderation thrives and vigour is steadily sapped. [Richard Crossman, "The Curse of Moderation on Labour," in the *Times* (London), 15 November 1972, p. 16.]

True to the truism, as befits the conservative temperament, remain certain reliable Tory ideologues. Quintin Hogg (or Lord Hailsham, as he previously was) put it succinctly in a warning to the right-wing extremism of Mr. Enoch Powell:

> Let me remind him of one principle that has come to us from ancient times: a gem of perennial wisdom uttered by the Greeks before the coming of the Christian hope— 'do not become an extremist,' *meden agan*. Moderation in all things [applause]. Moderation is the hallmark of our country and the guerdon of our Conservative faith. [*Times* (London), 11 October 1968, p. 4]

The ideological element here lies precisely in the absolutization of a prescript which, moderately applied, is reasonably unimpeachable. Lord Hailsham (as he is again) has in his own career amply demonstrated that he holds for moderation only in some things, in many things, but surely not in all, for there were always those special extreme occasions on which forceful outbursts of political audacity, personal passion, and even proper violence, appeared necessary and justifiable.

104. Hannah Arendt, *On Revolution* (1963), p. 203.

105. *The Philosophy of Edmund Burke* (ed. Bredvold and Ross, 1960), pp. 157, 166, 216. Arendt, *On Revolution*, pp. 113, 203.

106. B. H. G. Wormald, *Clarendon* (1964), pp. 218–19.

107. See, generally, Joseph Hamburger, *Intellectuals in Politics: John Stuart Mill and the Philosophic Radicals* (1965), and his *James Mill and the Art of Revolution* (1963).

108. Jeremy Bentham, *The Handbook of Political Fallacies* (1824; ed. 1962), p. 198.

109. Hamburger, *Intellectuals in Politics*.

110. Sydney Smith, *Selected Writings* (ed. Auden, 1957), pp. 325–34.

111. Smith, *Writings*, p. 341.

112. It is curious that the young Trotsky, as yet Leon Bronstein, should have been taken

with the writings of Bentham and John Stuart Mill. He described himself as a "staunch Benthamist," and it was in this period that he once stood up, raised his glass, and cried out (December 1896): "A curse upon all Marxists, and upon all those who want to bring dryness and hardness into all the relations of life!" (Leon Trotsky, *My Life* [1931], p. 99; Isaac Deutscher, *Trotsky: The Prophet Armed (1879–1921)* [1965], 1:25–28).

He also once confessed that at dinner and at tea and during his walks he kept repeating this sentence: "As to the geographical location of paradise precise directions are lacking." Sir Thomas More had pointed out as much in his *Utopia* in almost identical words more than three centuries earlier. There is, indeed, more than a touch of More, especially the utopian sense of the future, in the writings of the young Trotsky (*The Prophet Armed*, pp. 54–55):

> As long as I breathe, I shall fight for the future, that radiant future in which man, strong and beautiful, will become master of the drifting stream of his history and will direct it towards the boundless horizon of beauty, joy and happiness! ...
>
> Death to Utopia! Death to faith! Death to love! Death to hope! thunders the twentieth century in salvoes of fire and in the rumbling of guns.
>
> Surrender, you pathetic dreamer. Here I am, your long awaited twentieth century, your "future."
>
> No, replies the unhumbled optimist: You—you are only the *present*.

Of course, as Trotsky moved leftward to Menshevism and Bolshevism, science replaced utopia as the basis of his unhumbled optimism (p. 92):

> They were Utopians; we aspire to express the objective trend. They were idealists ... we are materialists ... they were rationalists, we are dialecticians ...

113. Friedrich Engels, *The Condition of the Working Class in England* (1845), in Marx/Engels, *On Britain* (ed. Moscow, 1962), pp. 334–36. *Die Lage der arbeitenden Klasse in England*, in Marx/Engels, *Werke* (East Berlin ed., 1962), 2:505–6. The critical edition translated and edited by Henderson and Chaloner (1971) is especially useful.

114. Engels's preface to the English edition of 1892, in *On Britain*, p. 23; Marx/Engels, *Werke* (East Berlin ed.), 2:642:

> Ich habe mir nicht einfallen lassen, aus dem Text die vielen Prophezeiungen zu streichen, namentlich nicht die einer nahe bevorstehenden sozialen Revolution in England, wie meine jugendliche Hitze sie mir damals eingab. Ich habe keinen Anlass, meine Arbeit und mich selbst besser darzustellen, als wir beide damals waren. Das wunderbare ist, nicht dass so viele dieser Prophezeiungen fehlgingen, sondern dass so viele eingetroffen sind.

The Moscow edition, as I have quoted it above, curiously omits the second sentence, possibly because it introduced a shade too much unorthodox modesty.

115. Alexis de Tocqueville, *Journeys to England and Ireland* (1958), pp. 68–69, 75.

116. William Hazlitt, *Table Talk* (1821–22; ed. Maclean, 1960), p. 309.

117. Sir William Fraser, *Words on Wellington* (1889), p. 37.

118. *Speeches of Oliver Cromwell* (ed. Stainer, 1901), p. 254.

119. J. M. Thompson, *Robespierre* (1936), 2:134–36.

120. Chauvinistic factors, no doubt, played an important role in the choice of favorites: Napoleon chose France, Burke and Bagehot chose England. But the intense power of ideas and ideals often gave ideology a victory over simple patriotism and narrow national prejudice. Thus, an English philosopher could favor "universalizing" French traditions against Anglo-Saxon insularity; and a philosophizing U.S. president, who looked to Burke and Bagehot, could excommunicate even an American founding father for being "too French."

In Woodrow Wilson's fantasy of U.S. political history, "there was nothing revolutionary" in the "truly organic growth" of American institutions. But he was painfully aware that American revolutionaries would hardly have agreed. Thus Thomas Jefferson was read out of the national pantheon: "We must pronounce him, though a great man, not a great American." Wilson thought he was being a proper Burkean and a sound Darwinian when he wrote:

> In politics nothing radically novel may be attempted. No result of value can ever be reached ... except through slow and gradual development, the careful adaptations and nice modifications of growth.

Neither Burke nor Darwin would have agreed. All of his "father images," as Freud suggested in his study (with Ambassador Bullitt) of Wilson's psychology, were spectacular exercises in distortion. (See Sigmund Freud and William C. Bullitt, *Thomas Woodrow Wilson: A Psychological Study* (1967); and Richard Hofstadter, *The American Political Tradition* (1948), pp. 238–39.

Writing of the Age of Reason and the Rights of Man, A. N. Whitehead—in his *Adventures of Ideas* (1933), ch. 2—argued that "this great French age of thought has remade the presuppositions of the civilized world, in speculation, in science, and in sociological premises ... the English modes always retained the note of insularity. The French broadened, clarified, and universalized. They thus made world wide, ideas which such a man as Edmund Burke could only grasp in their application to one race, and even at times to one island."

Whitehead erred here. A truth, as it emerges locally in one time and place, may well be more apposite in a worldwide context than all the abstract universalisms inconsequentially related to any piece of reality anywhere.

121. *The Mind of Napoleon*, pp. 78, 84, 251, 268.

122. Letter to M. Dupont, October 1789, in Burke, *Correspondence*, 3:118–20.

Chapter 3

1. C. S. Lewis, *Studies in Words* (1960), pp. 135–41.

2. Richard Kindersley, *The First Russian Revisionists* (1962), pp. 110–11 n. Peter Gay, *The Dilemma of Democratic Socialism* (1952), p. 127 n.

3. Montaigne, *Essays* (tr. Cohen, 1958), p. 56. Sir Peter Medawar, "Science and the Sanctity of Life," in his *The Hope of Progress* (1972), pp. 199.

4. *Communist Journal* (London), September 1847, appendix to the Ryazanov edition of *The Communist Manifesto* (1930), p. 292.

5. Kindersley, *The First Russian Revisionists*, p. 188 n.

6. On the matter of wit, civility, and grimness, I should note that some of the post-Jacobin, pre-Bolshevik wit was closer to grim *Galgenhumor* than to innocent civility. At a German Socialist conference in 1905, Rosa Luxemburg had said, in a characteristically impassioned speech:

> Surely we can see in history that all revolutions have been paid for with the blood of the people. The only difference is that up till now this blood had been spilled for and on behalf of the ruling classes, and now when we are within sight of the possibility that they might shed their blood for their own class interests, at once there appear cautious so-called Social Democrats who say no, that blood is too precious ... When will you finally learn from the Russian revolution?

Was this only—as J. P. Nettl suggests (*Rosa Luxemburg* [1962], 1:309–10)—"an excess perhaps of revolutionary excietement"? August Bebel made a "half humorous" reply:

> The debate has taken a somewhat unusual turn ... I have attended every congress except during those years when I was the guest of the government, but a debate with so much talk of blood and revolution I have never listened to. [laughter] Listening to all this I cannot help glancing occasionally at my boots to see if these weren't in fact already wading in blood. [Much laughter] ... In my harmless way I certainly never intended this (with my mass-strike revolution) ... Nonetheless I must confess that Comrade Luxemburg made a good and properly revolutionary speech.

To which Comrade Luxemburg replied (in a private letter):

> August accused me (though in a perfectly friendly manner) of ultra radicalism and shouted: "Probably when the revolution in Germany comes Rosa will no doubt be on the Left and I no doubt on the Right," to which he added jokingly, "but we will hang her, we will not allow her to spit in our soup." To which I replied calmly, "It is too early to tell who will hang whom."

In Bolshevik humor it was never to early to tell. In 1907, Lenin had been asked by a follower what would happen when the revolution came (cf. Adam Ulam, *The Bolsheviks,* 1966, p. 201). Lenin "answered jocularly that people would be asked whether they were for or against the revolution. If against they would be stood up against a wall and shot ... " (Lenin's wife is said to have entered an objection: she didn't find this funny.)

But *Galgenhumor* is a complex matter, and no one can pretend to know where to draw the line between the gag and the gallows. Herzen recalled the days in 1848 when Caussidière, trying to organize the Paris barricades, worried about getting rid of the tirelessly eloquent Bakunin: "*Quel homme! quel homme!* On the first day of the revolution he is simply a treasure, but on the day after he ought to be shot!" Herzen could not help going him one better. " 'Tell Caussidière,' I said in jest to his friends, 'that the difference between Bakunin and him is that Caussidière, too, is a splendid fellow, but it would be better to shoot him the day before the revolution.' " (Alexander Herzen, *Memoirs* [tr. Garnett, 1926], p. 134).

In England, the levity was of purer, untroubled vintage. Bernard Shaw—in the 1948 Jubilee Edition of the *Fabian Essays*—described the occasion when

> H. H. Champion delivered a blamelessly reasoned and documented lecture to a crowded audience. Suddenly he declared that if the entire capitalist class had only one throat, he would cut it without a minute's hesitation. While we were gasping ... he rushed to the edge of the platform and, pointing down at the Press table, shouted: "Look! They are all scribbling as hard as they can, though. And when Cunninghame Graham returned from a spell of hard labor at Pentonville Prison Lord Salisbury asked him—in the House of Commons—"Well, Mr. Graham, are you thinking where to put your guillotine?" (Ann Fremantle, *This Little Band of Prophets: the British Fabians* [1959], p. 78).

7. Gustave Le Bon, *The Psychology of Peoples* (1898); *The Crowd* (1896; ed. Merton, 1960); *The Psychology of Revolution* (1913). Fremantle, *This Little Band of Prophets,* ch. 3.

8. Albert Camus, *L'Homme révolté* (1951), p. 92; *The Rebel* (tr. Bower, 1953).

9. See, generally, *Revisionism: Essays on the History of Marxist Ideas* (ed. Labedz, 1962). Edward Crankshaw, *The New Cold War: Moscow v. Pekin* (1963), p. 107. Klaus Mehnert, *Peking and Moscow* (1963), p. 445; *Peking Review* (15 March 1963); *New Statesman* (11 January 1963); *Süddeutsche Zeitung* (Munich), 9 August 1974. See, also, Donald S. Zagoria, *Sino-Soviet Conflict, 1956–61* (1962), and William Griffiths, *Sino-Soviet Relations, 1964–65* (1967).

10. The quotation from Karl Marx against "those communists who were out to destroy personal liberty and who wished to turn the world into one large barracks or into a gigantic workhouse" is in striking contrast with Lenin's remark, in *State and Revolution*: "The whole of society will have become a single office and a single factory, with equality of labour and equality of pay." See Sidney Hook, *Marx and the Marxists* (1952), p. 32.

The full passage, which is taken from the *Communist Journal* (London), September 1847, can be found in the valuable appendixes in the Ryazanov edition of *The Communist Manifesto,* p. 292:

> We are not among those communists who are out to destroy personal liberty, who wish to turn the world into one huge barrack or into a gigantic work-house. There certainly are some communists who, with an easy conscience, refuse to countenance personal liberty and would like to shuffle it out of the world because they consider that it is a hinderance to complete harmony. But we have no desire to exchange freedom for equality. We are convinced, and we intend to return to the matter in subsequent issues, that in no social order will personal freedom be so assured as in a society based upon communal ownership.

11. Eduard Bernstein, *Aus den Jahren meines Exils* (1917); *Entwicklungsgang eines Sozialisten* (1930); and, in translation, *Evolutionary Socialism* (1909), and *Cromwell and Communism* (tr. Stenning, 1930). See also the excellent studies by Peter Gay, *The Dilemma of Democratic Socialism: Eduard Bernstein's Challenge to Marx* (1952), and Carl Schorske, *German Social Democracy: 1905–1917* (1955).

12. Eduard Bernstein, "Utopismus und Eklekticismus" (1896) and "Das realistische und das ideologische Moment in Socialismus" (1898), in *Zur Geschichte und Theorie des Socialismus* (1901), pp. 171–79, 262–86.

13. R. H. S. Crossman, *Planning for Freedom* (1965), pp. 113–22; C. A. R. Crosland, *The Conservative Enemy* (1962), pp. 132–42.

14. Any number can play this game, and if the English were now "too German" and the Germans had become "too English," what of the French? Well, France and Germany were partners in the Common Market but neither Kant nor Descartes prevailed. As a leading Paris technocrat remarked of the new French spirit: *"On n'est plus dans le pays de Descartes, on est plus près du pragmatisme des Anglais ... "* (PEP Pamphlet, 14 August 1961, "Economic Planning in France," p. 228). Six years later, in Paris, a British Prime Minister (Mr. Harold Wilson, in the *Times*, 25 January 1967) confirmed the startling Gallic takeover of Anglo-Saxon attitudes: "We have observed the pragmatism with which France has given a new shape to Europe ... " He added, a little lamely, "We are ourselves pragmatists."

15. Gay, *Dilemma of Democratic Socialism*, p. 73. Sidney Hook, *Towards the Understanding of Karl Marx* (1933), p. 43 n.

16. Nettl, *Rosa Luxemburg* (1966), 1:150.

17. Wilhelm Weitling, *Garantien der Harmonie und Freiheit* (1842; ed. Kaufhold, 1955); *Evangelium eines armen Sünders* (1843), in *Der Frühsozialismus* (ed. Ramm, 1956). The *Evangelium* has been reprinted as a rororo "classic text of Socialism and Anarchism" (ed. Schäfer, 1971) together with *Die Menschheit, wie sie ist und wie sie sein sollte;* the former has also been translated as a "Christian text" by Sheed and Ward as *The Poor Sinner's Gospel* (tr. Livingstone, 1969).

Carl Wittke, *The Utopian Communist* (1950); A. Barnikol, *Wilhelm Weitling* (1929). There are accounts, wtih varying degrees of sympathy and hostility, in the following: Franz Mehring, *Karl Marx* (1935); G. D. H. Cole, *A History of Socialist Thought: The Forerunners*, vol. 1 (1953); Leopold Schwarzchild, *The Red Prussian* (1948); Bertram D. Wolfe, *Marxism* (1965); and Edmund Wilson, *To the Finland Station* (1940).

18. Isaiah Berlin, *Karl Marx* (1939), p. 109.

19. E. H. Carr, *Michael Bakunin* (1937; 1961), p. 128.

20. P. V. Annenkov, *The Extraordinary Decade: Literary Memoirs* (1880; ed. Mendel, 1968), pp. 168–170. See also the accounts in Edmund Wilson, *To the Finland Station* (1940; 1971), pp. 193–96. David McLellan, *Karl Marx: His Life & Thought* (1973), pp. 155–57, and (in a German rendering of Annenkov's original Russian account) *Gespräche mit Marx und Engels* (ed. Enzensberger, 1973), pp. 58–63.

21. Marx/Engels, *Briefwechsel* (1949), 1:56, 62, 108.

22. Weitling, *Garantien der Harmonie und Freiheit* (Kaufhold, ed.)—a valuable East German edition which includes all emendations.

23. Weitling did go on (p. 361) to specify rules for firing squads: certain enemies just had to be eliminated in the new order. His tenderness for humanity did not go so far as to include the abolition of capital punishment for political offenders.

24. Weitling, *Garantien*, pp. xliv, 259–60, 355.

25. See Carl Wittke's invaluable biography, *The Utopian Communist*, p. 310 and passim. For Karl Kautsky's objections to "Messianism" and "the dicatorship of a single person," see his critique of Weitling, Blanqui, and the Bolsheviks in *The Dictatorship of the Proletariat*

(1918; 1964), pp. 17–18 and passim. For criticisms of Weitling's American career (apparently he outraged American abolitionist radicals by not paying sufficient attention to their burning moral issue, i.e., Negro slavery), see Philip S. Foner, *History of the Labor Movement in the United States* (1947), pp. 228–30, and especially, Herman Schlüter, *Lincoln, Labor and Slavery* (1913), pp. 73–74.

26. George Plekhanov, *In Defense of Materialism* (1948); *The Role of the Individual in History* (1946); *Essays in the History of Materialism* (1934). Samuel Baron, "Between Marx and Lenin: George Plekhanov," in *Revisionism*, pp. 42–54; "Plekhanov," the *Russian Review* (January 1954); "Plekhanov on Russian Capitalism," *American Slavic and East European Review* (December 1953); "Plekhanov's Russia," *Journal of the History of Ideas* (June 1958).

27. Isaiah Berlin, "Political Ideas in the Twentieth Century," *Foreign Affairs* (April 1950); "The Father of Russian Marxism," *The Listener* (27 December 1956); Daniel Bell, "On the Trail of Posadovsky," the *New Leader* (27 November 1950).

28. E. H. Carr, *Studies in Revolution* (1950) describes the scene:
> When over-zealous Red Guards ransacked the house in Tsarkoe Selo where Plekhanov lay sick, his friends protested to Lenin; and an order was issued . . . "to protect the person and property of citizen Plekhanov." The material guarantee was thus accompanied by a verbal insult. Plekhanov was no longer a socialist "comrade" but a bourgeois "citizen" . . .

Carr remarks further (p. 119): "He is perhaps the only man who, having crossed swords with Lenin in bitter controversy, is to-day quoted with respect in the Soviet Union . . . "

29. See, generally, Richard Hare, *Maxim Gorky: Romantic Realist and Conservative Revolutionary* (1962), and the *Letters of Gorky and L. Andreyev* (1958). The reference to Gorky's possible poisoning is in the foreword to Hare's biography; see also A. Orlov, *Secret History of Stalin's Crimes* (1953) and the novelistic treatment of Gorky's last years in Igor Gouzenko, *The Fall of a Titan* (1954).

30. The late Tibor Szamuely, in *The Spectator* (14 August 1971).

31. Bertram, D. Wolfe, "Krupskaya Purges the People's Libraries," in *Survey* no. 72 (Summer 1969), pp. 141–55.

32. All my quotations from Gorky's *Novaya Zhizn* are taken from Herman Ermolaev's edition of Maxim Gorky, *Untimely Thoughts: Essays on Revolution, Culture, and the Bolsheviks* (1971).

33. Rosa Luxemburg, *The Russian Revolution and Leninism or Marxism?* (1961 ed.); *Letters from Prison* (1946); *The Accumulation of Capital* (1951); *Reform or Revolution* (1937); *Letters to Karl and Luise Kautsky* (ed. Lochner, 1952). Paul Fröhlich, *Rosa Luxemburg: Her Life and Works* (1940). J. P. Nettl, *Rosa Luxemburg* (2 vols., 1966); George Lichtheim, "Rosa Luxemburg," *Encounter* (June 1966), pp. 55–60; F. L. Carsten, "Freedom and Revolution: Rosa Luxemburg," in *Revisionism*, pp. 55–66.

34. Nettl, *Luxemburg*, 1:433; Fremantle, *This Little Band of Prophets*, p. 40.

35. Nettl, *Luxemburg*, 1:235, 364.

36. Eugenio Garin, *Italian Humanism: Philosophy and Civic Life in the Renaissance* (1966), p. 215. Thomas More, *Selected Letters* (ed. Rogers, 1961), p. 90. Friedrich Meinecke, *Die Idee der Staatsraison* (1924), pp. 119–20; *Machiavellism* (tr. Scott, 1957), pp. 94–95.

37. J. Huizinga, *Erasmus of Rotterdam* (1952), pp. 128, 159, 162, 200, 230–31, 252.

38. Fritz Saxl, "Dürer and the Reformation," and "Holbein and the Reformation," in *A Heritage of Images* (ed. Gombrich, Honour, and Fleming, 1970), pp. 113, 114–15, 126–27.

39. Francois Wendel, *Calvin* (1963), pp. 93–97; Erwin Panofsky, *Meaning in the Visual Arts* (1955), p. 346; Roland H. Bainton, *Hunted Heretic: The Life and Death of Michael Servetus, 1511–1553* (1960), pp. 169, 207.

40. Spinoza, *Ethics* (Everyman ed., 1910), p. 188; *Tractatus Theologico-Politicus* (1919), pp. 287–89; and, generally, Lewis S. Feuer, *Spinoza and the Rise of Liberalism* (1958).

41. Voltaire to Diderot (26 June 1758), in *Correspondence* (ed. Besterman, 1953–), 33: 278; to Bertrand (21 March 1759), 35:212–13, 20. Arthur M. Wilson, *Diderot: The Testing Years* (1957), pp. 108, 337. Peter Gay, *The Party of Humanity: Studies in the French Enlightenment* (1964), p. 47.

42. Maurice Merleau-Ponty, *Mes Aventures de l'anti-Marxism* (1956), pp. 158–59.

43. Georg Lukacs, *Geschichte und Klassenbewusstsein* (1923), p. 13; Morris Watnick, "George Lukacs: An Intellectual Biography," in *Soviet Survey* (London), 1958–59, nos. 23–25 and 27.

44. Ernst Bloch, *Das Prinzip Hoffnung* (2 vols., 1959); Jurgen Rühle, "Ernst Bloch," *Der Monat* (Berlin), September 1958; George Steiner, "The Principle of Hope," *Times Literary Supplement* (London), 31 March 1961.

45. Frank E. Manuel, *The Prophets of Paris* (1962), p. 300.

46. More, *Selected Letters*, pp. 112–13.

47. For a sharp-witted analysis of the various orthodox and heterodox elements in Marxist thought, the reader should turn to the late George Lichtheim's excellent study of *Marxism: An Historical and Critical Study* (1961), especially the chapters on "Kautsky," "The Revisionists," "The Radicals," and "Lenin." On the Kautsky-Bernstein controversy, Lichtheim writes:

> Where Kautsky in 1891 had envisaged a bleak future of mounting class tensions, increasing centralisation, and "for the proletariat and the submerging middle strata," the certainty of "growing insecurity, misery, oppression, enslavement, debasement, exploitation," Bernstein in 1899 saw evidence of increasing order, security, tranquillity, prosperity, and more equitable distribution of wealth ... [Both] were looking at the same set of facts through differently colored glasses.

In general, however, Lichtheim tended to admire the "intellectual boldness and ingenuity" of radical pessimism:

> Events did not in the end shape themselves quite in accordance with the forecast, but after two world wars the picture has certainly come a good deal closer to the revolutionary prospectus ... than to the rather more commonplace expectations of the moderate school ...

But he is aware that "Kautsky's fatalistic doctrines tended to confirm the party leadership in its traditional do-nothing policy ... " Practical political demands, the fulfillment of which so encouraged the moderate socialists in their dream of progress, tended to distract the radical temperament. Programs for social legislation and extended franchise were almost afterthoughts. At the time of the completed Erfurt Program, Engels wrote to Kautsky:

> At any rate the theoretical part of the programme can hold its own; the chief thing is that it should contain nothing objectionable from the theoretical viewpoint, and that has in the main been secured ...

All of these lurid strands were, thus, intertwined: optimism v. pessimism, fatalism v. activism, theoretical purity v. practical compromise. Can one, then, ever say definitively what the great revisionist debate was really all about? According to Lichtheim (pp. 283–84):

> ... it concerned the adaptation of Marxism to the modern world of industrialism and democracy, as it presented itself in Western Europe and North America around 1900 ... The explanation, if there is one, lies in the tension which Marxism set up in the minds of people who had to adjust to a new situation, but did not wish to let go of certain fundamentals they had come to accept ...

There was at times in Lichtheim, too, an unbearable tension between fundamentalism and adjustment. Why was the gloom of the pessimists any less commonplace than the hopefulness of the moderates? In his later work on *Marxism in Modern France* (1966), Lichtheim appeared rather more openly sympathetic to "a diluted Marxism," to "the efflorescence of an undogmatic, or—if one prefers it—eclectic socialist doctrine and practice." He noted that

the collapse of 1940 and the Resistance had broken down ancient barriers against foreign, specifically German, influences which now came pouring in: Hegel, Kierkegaard, Marx, Freud, Weber, Husserl, Heidegger . . .
and he concluded (p. 50):

> What this nation-wide discussion in the 1960s signified was that the prewar dispute over reformism had finally been overtaken by a drive for *structural changes democratically controlled:* a mental innovation of great significance, since it cut the ground from under the stale controversy over ministerialism. The question was no longer—as it had been from 1900 to 1940, *i.e.* from Jaurès and Millerand to Léon Blum—whether Socialists might participate in a bourgeois government, and on what terms, but rather, how they could promote social changes which were anyhow leading away from liberalism, but which might, if left unguarded, lead to an uncontrolled technocracy, or to a kind of corporate régime. In this perspective, socialism had ceased to be a distant utopia, without therefore becoming "politics" in the pejorative sense of the term. It was now seen as a possible answer to the problems of a mature and literate democracy: something quite different from the forced-draft modernization of backward countries, which was what socialism had come to signify in Eastern Europe or in the *tiers monde.*

These were issues which George Lichtheim and I debated in London, Berlin, and New York for almost twenty years: until the shocking suicide (in January 1972) of this most stimulating Marxist spirit since Karl Marx.

48. Leopold Labedz argues in his introduction to *Revisionism* (1962), that diversities within the Communist states are making for a new distribution of power among them, but that this "polycentrism" does not mean the diffusion of political power *within* the individual communist states:

> This and this alone could promise a more pluralistic society pressing for a greater degree of freedom. The diffusion of political power remains the decisive criterion of democratic development and its necessary condition. Without it open revisionism cannot reappear, the shackles of orthodoxy cannot be removed, and the problem of the freedom of thought in general cannot be posed . . .

49. Zbigniew Herbert, in *Polish and Hungarian Poetry: 1945–1956* (ed., Gömöri, 1966), p. 244.

50. "Die Politische Platform Harich," in *SBZ* Archiv (Cologne, 1957); tr. Haffner in the *Observer* (London), 17 March 1957. Wolfgang Harich, *Kommunismus ohne Wachstum? Babeuf und der "Club of Rome"* (1975).

51. Michael St. John Packe, *The Life of John Stuart Mill* (1954), pp. 313–14.

52. Paul E. Zinner, *Revolution in Hungary* (1962). Paul Kecskemeti, *The Unexpected Revolution* (1961). Terence A. Váli, *Rift and Revolt in Hungary* (1961). Tibor Meray, *Thirteen Days That Shook the Kremlin* (1959). Hannah Arendt, "Totalitarian Imperialism: Reflections on the Hungarian Revolution," *Journal of Politics* (February 1958), Melvin J. Lasky (ed.), *The Hungarian Revolution* (1957).

53. Jean Duvignaud, "France: The Neo-Marxists," in *Revisionism*, p. 323.

54. See, generally, Peter Gay, *Voltaire's Politics: The Poet as Realist* (1959); *The Party of Humanity* (1964); and *The Enlightenment: An Interpretation* (1966).

55. *Selected Letters of Voltaire* (tr. Besterman, 1963), pp. 37–39, tp, 103; *Correspondence* (ed. Besterman, 1953–):

> je passe tout aux hommes, pourvu qu'ils ne soient pas persécuteurs; j'aimerais Calvin, s'il n'avait pas fait brûler Servet; je serais serviteur du concile de Constance, sans les fagots de Jean Huss . . .
>
> [3:138]
>
> Mais quelle vie affreuse! etre éternellement bourrelé par la crainte de perdre, sans forme de procès, sa liberté sur le moindre rapport! J'ammerais mieux la mort . . .
>
> [5:351]

je méprise les barbares stupides qui condamnent ce quils n'entendent point, et les méchants qui se joignent aux imbéciles pour proscrire ce qui les éclaire ...
[17:86–87]
I have used, wherever available, the translations by Besterman and Gay.

56. Voltaire, *Idées républicaines* (1762), in *Oeuvres complètes* (ed. Moland, 1879), 24:424. J.-J. Rousseau, *Oeuvres complètes* (ed. Pleiade, 1964), 3:687, 1578. The remark occurs twice, in *Lettres écrites de la montagne* (1764) and in a letter of September 1763: "On n'avait rien dit quand il fallait parler: on parla quand il ne restait qu' à se taire ... " (Voltaire, *Correspondence*, 19:127; *Oeuvres*, 19:576–77; *Philosophical Dictionary* (tr. Gay, 1962), 2:348–49.

57. *Oeuvres*, 19:583–86; 20:199; *Philosophical Dictionary*, 2:353–55, 423–24.

58. Denis Diderot, *Oeuvres complètes* (ed. Assezat, 1875); *"Memoires"* by his daughter Mme de Vandeul, 1:xlv. Arthur M. Wilson, *Diderot: The Testing Years* (1957), pp. 162–64, 337–40. There are some complications to this magnificent incident, for even historians have continued to confound the various members of the Malesherbes family participating in eighteenth-century literary controls. See L. G. Krakeur, "The Problem of Malesherbes' Intervention," in *Modern Language Quarterly* (1941), 2:551–58; Pierre Grosclaude, "Malesherbes et l'*Encyclopédie*," in *Revue des Sciences Humaines* (1958), pp. 351–80; E. P. Shaw, *Problems and Policies of Malesherbes as Directeur de la Librairie* (1966); and Jacques Proust, *Diderot et l'Encyclopédie* (1962).

59. *Malcolm X Speaks* (ed. Breitman, 1966), pp. 9, 50.

60. There are many relevant and illuminating passages in Emile Durkheim's *Elementary Forms of the Religious Life* (tr. Swain, 1954), pp. 228–29.

Collective representations very frequently attribute to the things to which they are attached qualities which do not exist under any form or to any degree ... Yet the powers which are thus conferred, though purely ideal, act as though they were real; they determine the conduct of men with the same degree of necessity as physical forces.... This is all because social thought, owing to the imperative authority that is in it, has an efficacy that individual thought could never have; by the power which it has over our minds, it can make us see things in whatever light it pleases; it adds to reality or deducts from it according to the circumstances.... The idea is the reality ... The object serving as support for the idea is not much in comparison with the ideal superstructure, beneath which it disappears, and also, it counts for nothing in the superstructure. This is what that pseudo-delirium consists in, which we find at the bottom of so many collective representations.

61. *"A Year of Living Dangerously." Independence Day Message by President Sukarno, Supreme Commander of the Armed Forces, Great Leader of the Revolution* (Djakarta, 17 August 1964), pp. 1–20. See, generally, Robert Shaplen, *Time out of Hand: Revolution and Reaction in Southeast Asia* (1969). Writing of the fall of Sukarno and the bloodbath that followed attempts at a coup, Shaplen notes (p. 189) that in the cautious New Order of Sukarno's successor General Suharto, the use of the word *revolution* has been banned—because of its "Marxist connotation" it was no longer applicable.

62. F. R. Leavis, *Revaluation: Tradition and Development in English Poetry* (1949), pp. 203–32.

63. B. Malinowski, "The Problem of Meaning in Primitive Languages," in C. K. Ogden and I. A. Richards, *The Meaning of Meaning* (1949 ed.), p. 312.

64. P. J. Proudhon, *Idée générale de la Révolution au XIXe siecle* (1851); *General Idea of the Revolution in the Nineteenth Century* (tr. Robinson, 1923), pp. 8, 9, 13, 15, 16, 31–32, 39, 187, 194, 224, 239, 285.

65. Marx to Engels, 6 April 1866, *Briefwechsel* (1949), 3:387; the *New York Times*, 3 November 1965, p. 1.

66. Frantz Fanon, *The Damned* (ed. Présence Africaine, 1963), preface by J.-P. Sartre. Gamal Abdel Nasser, *The Philosophy of the Revolution* (1959); Fidel Castro, *Discours de la Révolution* (ed. Glucksmann, 1966); C. Wright Mills, *Listen Yankee!* (1960) and *The Marxists* (1965), and "Illusions and Realities," in *Non-Alignment* (1966), pp. 134–35.

67. C. K. Ogden and I. A. Richards, *The Meaning of Meaning*, p. 31.

68. Karl Vossler, *The Spirit of Language in Civilization* (tr. Oeser, 1932), pp. 190–91.

69. Régis Debray, *Révolution dans la révolution?* (1967); *Revolution in the Revolution* (tr. Ortiz, 1967). See also *Che's Guerilla War* (tr. Sheed, 1975).

70. Shelley, *The Assassins* (1814), in *Prose Works*, 2:153; *Mont Blanc* (1816), in *Poetical Works* (ed. Hutchinson), p. 553.

71. My own references are mainly borrowed from the *Oxford Dictionary of Quotations* (1953), perhaps a more innocent form of dependence on plagiarism than that dictated by the secret affinities of apocalyptic and romantic temperaments.

72. "Mountain-top-ism" is a notion devised by Mme Mao Tse-tung (Chiang Ching), in her speech of 5 September 1967 in Anhwei Province. In addition to this phrase used by Mme Mao (it is a literal rendering from the Chinese *Shan T'ou Chu'yi*), there is also the usage of "mountain-stronghold mentality."

"Mountain-stronghold mentality" is a form of exaggerated individualism. The advocates of this kind of mentality consider their own organisations as an independent kingdom. They crave for personal fame and interest. They care nothing about the overall situation, far less about other people, and are totally lacking in communist spirit.

"Mountain-stronghold mentality" is a form of sectarianism. Its advocates consider themselves most revolutionised and most correct. They see the faults only of others but not of themselves. They fail to realise that in dealing with other organisations they have the duty to cooperate, but not the right to attack.

"Mountain-stronghold mentality" is a form of feudalist and bourgeois thought reflected into the ranks of the revolutionaries. It has a strong disruptive and corrosive influence on unity and is an extremely dangerous phenomenon. At present, the class enemy is trying in every way to disrupt the unity of the proletarian revolutionaries and the revolutionary great alliance; "mountain-stronghold mentality" can be most easily exploited by the class enemy. Whatever the enemy opposes we will support; whatever the enemy supports we will oppose. The class enemy likes "mountain-stronghold mentality," so we must strike it down.

73. Victor Hugo, *Quatrevingt-treize* (ed. Flammarion, 1965), p. 193; *Ninety-Three* (tr. Bair, 1962), p. 163.

74. Friedrich Schiller, *Gesamtausgabe* (dtv. ed., 1966), 8:85: *Die Braut von Messina*, 4.7e–2585; 8:133: *Wilhelm Tell*, 2.2e–1274; tr. Garland, *Schiller* (1949), p. 247.

75. See, generally, Stuart Schram, *The Political Thought of Mao Tse-tung* (1964); *Mao Tse-tung: An Anthology of his Writings* (ed. Fremantle, 1962). Jerome Ch'en, *Mao and the Chinese Revolution* (1965). "Thoughts on Mao Tse-tung," *Times* (London), 31 October 1966, with quotations from the booklets carried by the Red Guards in the riots and demonstrations of that year which (according to a report in *Newsweek*, 9 October 1967) were ended by a dictum from Mme Mao: "Last year was the time to kindle the flames of revolution. To go out into the streets now is precisely the wrong thing to do."

76. With "the great chain of human hope," I am deliberately echoing here that most fascinating and famous phrase in the history of Occidental philosophy which Arthur O. Lovejoy subjected to such masterful analysis in his *The Great Chain of Being: A Study in the History of an Idea* (1936). This "persistent dynamic factor in the history of thought" has not, to my knowledge, been identified (even in the wealth of Lovejoy's illustrative passages) in a more strictly political context.

In his sketch of "the Temporalizing of the Chain of Being" (ch. 4), Lovejoy carries his account of the transformations of an ancient idea forward to the general eighteenth-century frontiers of social philosophy. Here, clearly, there was a dramatic mixing of the abstract notions of progress, change, revolution, perfection, and even (in his predating of Goethe's Faustian longing) the interminable pursuit of unattainable goals. Leibniz argued (in his *Principles of Nature and Grace* [1718]):

Our happiness will never consist, and ought not to consist, in a full enjoyment in which there is nothing more to desire, and which would make our minds dull, but in a perpetual progress to new pleasures and new perfections . . .

In a note to his *Poem on the Lisbon Disaster* (1755), Voltaire observed:

The chain is not an absolute plenum. It is demonstrated that the heavenly bodies perform their revolutions in a non-resistant space. Not all space is filled. There is not, therefore a series [*suite*] of bodies from an atom to the most remote of stars; there can therefore be immense intervals between sensible beings as well as between insensible ones. We cannot, then, be sure that man is necessarily placed in one of the links which are attached one to another in an unbroken sequence.

And there are Edward Young's lines (*Night Thoughts*, 1742–44):

> From obscure to bright
> By due gradation, nature's sacred law ...
> Nature delights in progress; in advance
> From worse to better....
> O be a man! and thou shalt be a god!
> And half self-made! Ambition how divine!

Yet none of this is as specifically political as the idea of "the great chain of human hope" would imply. I wonder if Arthur Lovejoy had marked in his copy of Condorcet (he does not quote him in *The Great Chain of Being*) the following two relevant and suggestive passages from the *Esquisse d'un tableau historique des profils de l'esprit humain* (1795), pp. 366, 384; (tr. 1955), pp. 193, 201):

In short, will not the general welfare that results from the progress of the useful arts once they are grounded on solid theory, or from the progress of legislation once it is rooted in the truths of political science, incline mankind to humanity, benevolence and justice? In other words, do not all these observations which I propose to develop in my book, show that the moral goodness of man, the necessary consequence of his constitution, is capable of indefinite perfection like all his other faculties, and that nature has linked together in an unbreakable chain truth, happiness, and virtue [*la nature lie, par une chaîne indissoluble, la vérité, le bonheur et la vertu*] . . .

How consoling for the philosopher who laments the errors, the crimes, the injustices which still pollute the earth and of which he is often the victim is this view of the human race, emancipated from its shackles, released from the empire of fate and from that of the enemies of its progress, advancing with a firm and sure step along the path of truth, virtue and happiness! It is the contemplation of this prospect that rewards him for all his efforts to assist the progress of reason and the defence of liberty. He dares to regard these strivings as part of the eternal chain of human destiny [*Il ose alors les lier à la chaîne éternelle des destinées humaines*] . . .

Lovejoy would also, I imagine, have been much taken by a "chain" passage in Lenin, here concerned (as always) more with tactics than principles (or, perhaps, with the principles of tactics):

It is not sufficient to be a revolutionary and an adherent of Socialism or a Communist in general. One must be able at each particular moment to find that special link in the chain which one must grasp with all one's might in order to hold the whole chain, and to make lasting preparations for the transition to the next link; the order of the links, their form, the manner in which they are linked together, their difference from each other in the historical chain of events, are not as simple and not as senseless as those in an ordinary chain made by a smith. [V. I. Lenin, *Selected Works*, (1937), 7:347]

77. Jason Epstein in the *New York Review of Books*, 20 April 1967, pp. 19–21.

78. See, also, the long accounts of the views of Professor Herbert Marcuse (who lectured as "the prophet of the student revolution" at the university during those turbulent days), and of Herr Rudi Dutschke (the leader of the student rebels) in *Der Spiegel* (Hamburg), 10 July 1967, pp. 129–33, and 21 August 1967, pp. 112–18.

79. *Black Power in Britain: A Special Statement*, published by the Universal Coloured Peoples Association (London), September 1967, pp. 1–14. See also Colin MacInnes,

"Michael and the Cloak of Colour," *Encounter*, December 1965, pp. 8–15. It was no doubt inevitable that a commentator for the *Observer* (London), 10 September 1967, p. 17 should have attempted a very white, very liberal, and very English conclusion:

> For a growing handful, the Black Power slogan "Burn, baby, burn!" is already a rallying cry. But in Britain it seldom, if ever, stands for violence: it is an emotional way of saying that things must start to change and soon . . .

So far as Michael X was concerned, this proved to be very Pollyannish; for a grim documentary account of the next years, see V. S. Naipaul, "The Killings in Trinidad," *Sunday Times Magazine* (London, 12 and 19 May 1974); and the fictionalized version in his novel, *Guerrillas* (1975).

80. Louis Aragon, "The Red Front," (tr. Cummings), in David Caute, *Communism and the French Intellectuals* (1964), p. 110.

81. Neal Wood, *Communism and British Intellectuals* (1959), pp. 108–19. See, especially, the reevaluation in George Watson, "Were the Intellectuals Duped?," *Encounter* (December 1973), pp. 20–30; and in David Caute, *The Fellow-Travellers* (1973).

82. Christopher Lasch, *The New Radicalism in America: 1889–1963* (1966), pp. 242–50.

83. See, generally, Daniel Aaron's documented account of *Writers on the Left* (1961).

84. John Chamberlain, *Farewell to Reform* (1932), pp. 191, 309, 323.

85. Alfred Kazin, *Starting Out in the Thirties* (1965), pp. 70, 157–59.

86. André Gide, *Return from the U.S.S.R.* (1937), p. vii. See also his chapter (along with those of Arthur Koestler, Ignazio Silone, Stephen Spender, and Louis Fischer) in *The God that Failed* (ed. Crossman, 1948).

87. A. O. Lovejoy, "On the Discriminations of Romanticisms," in *Essays in the History of Ideas* (1948), pp. 228–53:

> It is not any large *complexes* of ideas . . . but rather certain simpler, diversely combinable, intellectual and emotional components of such complexes, that are the true elemental and dynamic factors in the history of thought and of art; and it is with the genesis, the vicissitudes, the manifold and often dramatic interactions of these, that it is the task of the historian of ideas in literature to become acquainted.

88. C. S. Lewis, *Rehabilitations and Other Essays* (1959), p. 17.

89. Joseph Freeman, *Never Call Retreat* (1943), pp. 515, 552–53.

90. John Donne, *An Anatomy of the World* (1611) in *Poems* (ed. Fausset, 1931), p. 182.

91. Charles Péguy, *Basic Verities* (1943), pp. 50–51; Aaron, *Writers on the Left*, p. 387.

92. There is, conceivably, a third decisive factor at work here in "the disenchanting course", and I have listened to Paul Tillich put it most persuasively. If I mention it tardily only in this place it is because it is, as he would have admitted, a meta-historical consideration. In the unforgettable lectures which I heard in Berlin in 1951—*Politische Bedeutung der Utopie im Leben der Völker*—he began by arguing that *"Menschsein heisst: Utopie Haben,"* by affirming the human truth, necessity, and fruitfulness of a utopian sense of the future. But he then proceeded to demonstrate its untruth (because "it forgets the finitude and estrangement of man"), its unfruitfulness (because "it describes impossibilities as real possibilities"), and its impotence (because "its negative content of untruth and unfruitfulness leads inevitably to disillusionment"). This latter is *"eine metaphysische Enttäuschung,"* and he explained:

> The disillusionment must be discussed metaphysically, not psychologically. It is a disillusionment experienced again and again, and in such a profound way it disrupts man in the deepest levels of his being. Such disillusionment is an inevitable consequence of confusing the ambiguous preliminary with the unambiguous ultimate . . . If we commit ourselves idolatrously [*götzendienerisch*], then metaphysical disillusionment is inevitable . . .

One must note that after much brilliant theological dialectics Professor Tillich found a transcendent solution to the "tensions" he had set up. Beyond both the sterility of mindless passivity and the fanaticism of terrorizing absolutes, there remain in *"die Idee"* real and radical human purposes. His conclusion: "It is the spirit of utopia that conquers utopia."

A partial translation has been included as a chapter in *Utopias and Utopian Thought* (ed. Manuel, 1966), pp. 296–309. The full text of this important and moving document was published at the time as a brochure for the Hochschule für Politik by Gebrüder Weiss (Berlin, 1951).

93. Malinowski, in Ogden and Richards, *The Meaning of Meaning*, pp. 322–23.

94. Thomas Sprat, *History of the Royal-Society of London* (1667), p. 112.

95. Hobbes, *Leviathan, or the Matter, Forme and Power of a Commonwealth Ecclesiastical and Civil* (1651; ed. Oakeshott, 1946), pp. 29–30.

96. Samuel Parker, *A Free and Impartial Censure of the Platonick Philosophie* (1666), pp. 72–73. Sprat, *History of the Royal-Society*, pp. 111–13.

97. Ogden and Richards, *The Meaning of Meaning*, pp. 45, 235–36. *Theories of Society* (ed. Parsons and Shils, 1961), 2:1014; Ernst Cassirer, *The Philosophy of Symbolic Forms* (trans. Manheim, 1953), p. 113. See also, generally, Kenneth Burke's essays in *The Philosophy of Literary Form* (1941) and in *Language as Symbolic Action* (1966).

98. Friedrich Nietzsche, *Der Fall Wagner* (1888), in *Werke* (ed. Schlechta, 1954–56), 2:917; Walter Kaufmann, *Nietzsche* (1956), p. 61 (and p. 372, where he notes that this is a paraphrase of a passage from Paul Bourget).

99. *Die Morgenröte* (1881), in *Werke*, 1:1045; *The Dawn of Day* (tr. Volz, 1903), p. 43.

100. *Der Wille zur Macht*, in *Werke* (Leipzig ed., 1922), 15:200; in Karl Schlechta's new edition, the aphorisms of this posthumous work have been left untitled and unnumbered, 3:668; *The Will to Power* (ed. Levy, tr. Ludovici, 1910), pp. 67–68.

101. See George Steiner, *Death of Tragedy* (1961), pp. 56–58.

102. Rabelais, *The Five Books and Minor Writings* (tr. Smith, 1893), 2:228; *Gargantus and Pantagruel* (tr. Cohen, 1955), p. 569. *Oeuvres complètes* (ed. Pleiade, 1955), p. 693:

> Et y veids des parolles bien picquantes, des parolles sanglantes, les quelles le pillot nous disoit quelques foys retourner on lieu duquel estoient proferées, mais c'estoit la guorge couppée; des parolles horrificques . . .

103. *Dialogues of Alfred North Whitehead* (ed. Price, 1956), pp. 264–65; Ogden and Richards, *The Meaning of Meaning*, p. 206.

104. There is also a sixteenth-century usage by John Heywood (1562): "But all be bugs woords that I speake to spare . . . " (*Proverbs, Epigrams and Miscellanies of John Heywood* [ed. Farmer, 1966], pp. 66, 336). Heywood, who married a niece of Sir Thomas More's, is the author of an allegorical poem *The Spider and the Flie*, in which the symbols stand for Protestants and Roman Catholics. Still, the *O.E.D.*'s references (1:1159–61) would seem to suggest that the identification of Bug and Insect was a somewhat later issue, and presumably because insects were as terrifying as specters and not vice versa. Thus, Coverdale's Psalm, "Thou shalt not nede to be afrayed for any bugges at night" (1535) became, in the King James version (1611), "Thou shalt not be afraid for the terror by night" (91:5). Shakespeare, similarly, uses this synonymous meaning in *Henry VI*: "Warwick was a Bugge that fear'd us all"; and in *Winter's Tale*: "The bug which you would fright me with . . . " See John Phin, *The Shakespeare Cyclopedia and New Glossary* (1902), p. 64: "The use of the word bug to signify insect is comparatively recent"; and B. and C. Evans, *Dictionary of American Usage* (1957), pp. 73–74.

One other lexigraphical reference is relevant to our trail of verbal superstitions. "Such bugbear thoughts," John Locke wrote, "once got into the tender minds of children, sink deep, so as not easily, if ever, to be got out again . . . " Samuel Johnson, *A Dictionary of the English Language* (1830 ed.), p. 151.

The interested reader is also referred to the related entries in the *O.E.D.* (8:1563–64). For example,

> *puck* . . . an evil, malicious or mischievous spirit or demon . . . identified with the biblical devil . . . puck-bug, a bug-bear, a malignant spectre . . .

The *Timon* quoted is not Shakespeare's, but the so-called academic *Timon*, presumably an earlier anon. source: *Timon, a Play* (1600; ed. Dyce, 1842), p. 6.

105. Richard Hooker, *Of the Laws of Ecclesiastic Polity* (1597, ed. Morris, 1954), 1:171–72 n. Roger North, *Examen: or, an Enquiry into the Credit and Veracity of a Pretended Complete History* (1740), p. 87. North—in his attempt to "vindicate the Honor of the late King Charles II and his Happy Reign from the Aspersions of the Foul Pen"—also refers to "the most horrible and bug-bear Denunciations."

106. *The Censure of the Rota upon Mr. Milton's Book Entitled The Ready and Easy Way to Establish a Free Comonwealth* (1660), repr. in the *Harleian Miscellany* (ed. Park, 1809), 4:179–86.

107. John Locke, *Two Tracts on Government* (ed. Abrams, 1967), p. 235; Maurice Cranston, *John Locke: A Biography* (1957), pp. 270–74; *An Essay Concerning Human Understanding* (1690–1706 Yolton, 1964), 2:94.

108. Ogden and Richards, *The Meaning of Meaning,* pp. 216–17.

109. P. J. Proudhon, *Correspondence* (1874), 5:376; 11:209; Lubac, *Proudhon,* pp. 29–30.

110. Jean-Paul Sartre, *Qu'est-ce que la litterature?* (1948), pp. 338–42; *What Is Literature?* (tr. Frechtman, 1950), pp. 208–10.

111. Raoul Vaneigem, *Traité de savoir-vivre à l'usage des jeunes générations* (1968), as reported in the *Sunday Times* (London), 21 July 1968.

112. Locke, *An Essay Concerning Human Understanding,* 2:106.

113. These and the subsequent quotations from the Rev. South are in: Robert South, *Sermons Preached upon Several Occasions* (1727; 1823 ed.), 4:203–287.

114. Ogden and Richards, *The Meaning of Meaning,* pp. 294–95.

Similarly troubled by the tragic influence of language upon thought and action, students of the new science of "psycholinguistics" have introduced a clinical and presumably disinterested note to the historic pleas for some form of semantic revolution against the tyranny of words. One psycholinguist has recently added his warning against the "contagious magic" and "incantations" of those "noises and squiggles" which result (as he put it) from that "very remarkable relation between these physical manifestations called signs and certain processes in language-users called meanings." He went on to quote Einstein to the effect that "a new manner of thinking about our world will first require a revolution in how we talk about it." This would imply, in the present context of our discussion, a "revolution against 'Revolution'", and a most utopian thought indeed. See the articles by Charles Osgood, Professor of Psycholinguistics and Communications Research at the University of. Illinois, in *The Listener* (London): "The Words of Power" (5 October 1967) and "Radical Sentences" (19 October 1967).

115. V. I. Lenin, Selected Works (1937), 9:295–302.

116. Nietzsche, *Werke* (Schlechta ed.), 1:1257–58; *The Dawn of Day* (Volz tr.), pp. 355–56.

117. Aristotle, *Politics,* 4.5.1292 b (tr. Ellis, 1853), p. 139.

118. Maurice Merleau-Ponty, *In Praise of Philosophy* (1963), p. 4.

119. James Harrington, *Oceana* (1656; ed. Liljegren, 1924), pp. 21, 244–45.

120. Aphorism 46, in *The English Philosophers: From Bacon to Mill* (ed. Burtt, 1939), p. 36.

121. George Santayana, *Winds of Doctrine* (1913), p. 23.

122. Günter Grass, *Rede über das Selbstverständliche* (1965).

123. Yevgeny Yevtushenko, *A Precocious Autobiography* (1963), p. 11.

124. Alexander Herzen, *From the Other Shore* (1855; tr. 1956), p. 157.

125. Sermon VII, St. Paul's, Christmas Day 1629, in John Donne, *Complete Poetry and Selected Prose* (Nonesuch ed.), p. 593.

126. Philip Wheelright, *Heraclitus* (1959), Fragment 117, p. 102.

Chapter 4

1. *The Complete Works of Sir Philip Sidney* (ed. Feuillerat); the text of *The Countesse of Pembrokes Arcadia* (1590) is in vol. 1 (1912) and vol. 2 (1922). The text of the original, unrevised, so-called *Old Arcadia* is in vol. 4 (1926); and in a new, more accurate edition (ed. Robertson, 1973). I have, with exceptions that are obvious, quoted from the nineteenth-century editions which modernized spelling and punctuation (Friswell ed., 1867; Baker ed., 1907).

2. One scholarly student of Philip Sidney has made much of the fact that "the center of *Arcadia*'s world is a cave exemplifying the ambiguity of reality and man's soul rather than the usual temple or shrine," i.e., "the ambivalence rather than the innocence of the human condition." As he concludes in his study of the *Map of Arcadia:*

> This tenor of Sidney's romance sets it apart from all previous ones. Innocence is a state that one achieves rather than inherits, and the state of original justice which the romance posited implicitly for its end can be reached only through trial. Sidney's microcosmic pastoral retreat has more astringency than its models, for it contains temptations as well as guideposts; his action is more realistic, for he knew that purification comes about by suffering, not by some tender-hearted mortal gift. As that other great English humanist, Platonist, and Calvinist, Milton, wrote, "Assuredly we bring not innocence into the world, we bring impurity much rather; that which purifies us is trial, and trial is by what is contrary." [Walter R. Davis, *A Map of Arcadia: Sidney's Romance in Its Tradition,* in W. R. Davis and R. A. Lanham, *Sidney's Arcadia* (1965), pp. 178–79]

This is, as I have been trying to suggest, one of the lost chords in the developing history of utopian thought. Tender hearts tend to drive out tough minds. Utopian harmony silences the strong noises of a contrary humanity.

3. *Defense of Poesie* (1595), in *Complete Works,* 3:14. See, generally, Davis and Lanham, *Sidney's Arcadia.*

4. *Arcadia* (Baker ed.), 5:577; (Feuillerat ed.), 2:145; (Robertson ed.), p. 351.

5. *Arcadia* (Baker ed.), 2:162–63; (Feuillerat ed.), 1:196–97.

6. See, generally, J. W. Allen, *A History of Political Thought in the Sixteenth Century* (1957).

7. *Arcadia* (Baker ed.), 2:166–67; (Feuillerat ed.), 1:200–201. Thomas Hobbes, *Leviathan* (1651; ed. Oakeshott, 1946), p. 65.

8. *The Correspondence of Philip Sidney and Hubert Languet* (ed. Bradley, 1912), p. 40.

9. *Arcadia* (Baker ed.), 2:261–65; (Feuillerat ed.), pp. 319–24.

10. *Arcadia* (Baker ed.), 3:312–15; (Feuillerat ed.), 1:371–73.

11. *Arcadia* (Baker ed.), 4:564–65; (Feuillerat ed.), 2:130–31.

12. E. A. Greenlaw, "Sidney's *Arcadia* as an Example of Elizabethan Allegory," *Kittredge Anniversary Papers* (1913), pp. 327–37; "The Captivity Episode in Sidney's *Arcadia,*" Manly Anniversary Studies (1923), pp. 54–63; W. D. Briggs, "Political Ideas in Sidney's *Arcadia,*" *Studies in Philology* (April 1931), 28:137–61; "Sidney's Political Ideas" (October 1932), 29:534–42; W. G. Zeeveld, "The Uprising of the Commons in Sidney's *Arcadia,*" *Modern Language Notes* (April 1933), 48:209–17. See, generally, R. W. Zandvoort, *Sidney's Arcadia, a Comparison between the Two Versions* (1929), and M. S. Goldman, *Sir Philip Sidney and the Arcadia* (1934).

13. Sir Fulke Greville, *Life of Sir Philip Sidney* (1652; ed. Nowell Smith, 1907), pp. 141–42.

14. *The Correspondence of Philip Sidney and Hubert Languet,* pp. 187–88. J. Huizinga, *Sir Philip Sidney* (an address, 1957), p. 11; and Hubert Languet (or, perhaps, Philippe de Mornay), *A Defense of Liberty against Tyrants* (ed. Laski, 1924). See also Malcolm Wallace, *Life of Sir Philip Sidney* (1915), p. 12; and Greville, *Sidney,* pp. 53–54.

15. James E. Phillips, "George Buchanan and the Sidney Circle," *Huntington Library Quarterly* (November 1948), 12, no. 1:23–55. W. H. Bond, "A Letter of Languet about Sidney," *Harvard Library Bulletin* (1955), 9:105–9; J. A. van Dorsten, "Sidney and Languet,"

Huntington Library Quarterly (May 1966), 29, no. 3:215–22; Irving Ribner, "Machiavelli and Sidney," *Studies in Philology* (April 1950), 47, no. 2:152–72; "Sir Philip Sidney on Civil Insurrection," *Journal of the History of Ideas* (April 1952), 13, no. 2:257–65. See, generally, John Buxton, *Sir Philip Sidney and the English Renaissance* (1954); and Roger Howell, *Sir Philip*

16. Greville, *Sidney*, pp. 77, 119.

17. Dante Alighieri, *Inferno*, canto 26, ll. 97–120, in *The Divine Comedy* (tr. Carlyle and Wicksteed, 1934), pp. 149–51.

18. *Mustapha* (1609), in *Poems and Dramas of Fulke Greville, First Lord Brook* (ed. Bullough, 1939), 2:105; F. B. Newman, "Sir Fulke Greville and Giordano Bruno," *Philological Quarterly* (October 1950), 29, no. 4:367–74; A. M. Pellegrini, "Bruno, Sidney, and Spenser," *Studies in Philology* (April 1943), 40, no. 2:128–44.

19. *Poems and Dramas of Greville*, 2:107.

20. Sir Fulke Greville, *The Remains: Being Poems of Monarchy and Religion* (ed. Wilkes, 1965), p. 52.

21. *Poems and Dramas of Greville*, 2:136.

22. Greville, *The Remains*, p. 63.

23. Sir Fulke Greville, *Caelica* (ed. Ellis-Fermor, 1936), p. 97.

24. *Arcadia* (Robertson ed.), pp. 354–55, 136–36.

25. *Arcadia* (Feuillerat ed.), 2:77–78, 156; (Baker ed.), p. 586; (Robertson ed.), pp. 132, 362–63.

26. Dorothy Waley Singer, *Giordano Bruno, His Life and Thought, with Annotated Translation of His Work "On the Infinite Universe and Worlds"* (1950), pp. 183–84. On this English occasion, as so often in his academic career (at university centers in France and Germany), Bruno's natural argumentativeness was too ebulliently in evidence and caused a rupture with Oxford University; this proved to a special embarrassment since (Bruno himself noted this) there was in the audience a distinguished Polish nobleman, a Prince Laski.

27. I am following here suggestions to be found in the adventurous works of Frances A. Yates, *Giordano Bruno and the Hermetic Tradition* (1964), and D. P. Walker, *Spiritual and Demonic Magic from Ficino to Campanella* (1958). The tradition of which Miss Yates writes is from Hermes Trismegistus, the father of the *prisca magia*, as given in Marsilio Ficino's *De vita coelitus comparanda* (1489), of which Walker writes (p. 3): "This title might mean either 'on obtaining life from the heavens,' or 'on instituting one's life celestially'; in view of Ficino's fondness for puns, it probably means both."

28. Paul Oskar Kristeller, "Bruno," in *Eight Philosophers of the Italian Renaissance* (1965), pp. 127–44.

29. Bruno, *Opere italiane* (ed. Gentile, 1908), 1:139. I am using the translation in Sidney Greenberg, *The Infinite in Giordano Bruno, with a translation of his Dialogue "Concerning the Cause, Principle, and One"* (1950), p. 88; there is also a translation of this text by Jack Lindsay, *Cause, Principle and Unity* (1962).

30. The feelings of "honor" for Columbus were not shared by Bruno. "To mount up to the sky" was obviously a greater achievement than merely sailing out across an ocean. On the page of *La cena* where Columbus is referred to as the idol of the century (*si nostri tempi vien magnificato il Colombo*), he expresses his skepticism about the benefits of universal commerce and insists that the audacious navigators in reality only

> disturbed the peace of others ... merged together that which a foreseeing nature had kept apart, increased the vices of nations, spread fresh follies by violence, introduced unheard-of ones where they never existed ... taught men a new art and new means of tyranny and assassination amongst themselves.

See Paul Henri Michel, *La Cosmologie de Giordano Bruno* (1962); *The Cosmology of Giordano Bruno* (tr. Maddison, 1973), p. 236.

31. *La cena de le ceneri* (1584), as translated in Yeats, *Bruno*, pp. 236–37. See also Hans

Blumenberg's penetrating introduction to the German translation: Bruno, *Das Ascher-mittwochsmahl* (tr. Fellman, 1969); and, generally, his *Die kopernikanische Wende* (1965).

32. The original reads: *"La revoluzion dunque, ed anno grande del mondo . . ."* Giordano Bruno, *Dialoghi Italiani* (ed. Gentile and Aquilecchia, 1958), p. 1073. I shall be returning, below (see chs. 5 and 6, "The Birth of a Metaphor") to the often neglected problem of the early astronomical and political usages of the word *revolution.* See also *Opere italiane*, 2:402, translated as *The Heroic Enthusiasts* (tr. Williams, 1887–89), 2:2.

33. Bruno departed when friendly Lutherans gave way to more factional (and more anti-Copernican) Calvinist influences in Wittenberg. In his *Oratio valedictoria* (1588) he had words of praise for Martin Luther. Despite his caustic remarks about gluttony and inebriety in Germany, Bruno assigned the Germans a special destiny: "The day the Germans fully evaluate the power of their genius and apply it in higher studies, they would no longer be men but gods."

34. *Causa* (tr. Lindsay), p. 8; Singer, *Bruno: His Life and Thought*, pp. 59, 75; Yates, *Bruno*, p. 339.

35. *Gli eroici furori* (1585), in Bruno, *Opere italiane*, 2:963. I am using the nineteenth-century translation by Williams: *The Heroic Enthusiasts*, 1:43. There is also a more recent translation: *The Heroic Frenzies* (tr. Memmo, 1966), with a useful introduction and notes. I have inserted phrases and sentences from the original Italian where it appeared to me to be suggestive or necessary.

36. Bruno, *Opere italiane*, 2:966; *Heroic Enthusiasts*, 1:46.

37. *Opere italiane*, 2:978–80; *Heroic Enthusiasts*, 1:59–62.

38. *De la causa, principio et uno*, in *Opere italiane*, 1:144–45; (Greenberg tr.), pp. 91–92; (Lindsay tr.), pp. 58–59.

39. *Opere italiane*, 1:149–50; *De la causa* (Greenberg tr.), pp. 95–96.

40. *Opere italiene*, 2:362, 402–4; *Heroic Enthusiasts*, 1:113; 2:2–4.

41. With the kind of reading of medieval and Renaissance ideas that recasts the conventional notions of magic and modernity, Campanella's *City of the Sun* can be associated with this same mystical tradition of a *magia divina*. As Miss Yates writes: "The work is entirely misunderstood if it is viewed as a blue-print for a well-governed state in any modern sense. The City is arranged so as to be right with the stars, and thence flows all its happiness, health, and virtue" (*Bruno*, pp. 369–70).

To the extent that our modernity is conceived in narrow scientific and rationalistic terms, this is an important and welcome correction. But my impression of Miss Yates's stimulating work is that she is so infatuated with her necromantical theses that she overlooks the possibility that Campanella, and indeed Bruno, were at once "magical" and "pragmatic," and that what brilliant sense and nonsense they offered are beyond the simple tags of restrictive historical periodization. There is no little magic and superstition in even the most modern of intellectual movements; there is much modernity in ancient and medieval ideas and attitudes. There is small point, except for redressing a one-sided balance, to swing along on this old pendulum.

42. *Spaccio de la bestia trionfante* (1584), in *Opere italiene*, vol. 2. There is an anonymous eighteenth-century translation: *The Expulsion of the Triumphant Beast* (1713); but I have used, mainly, Arthur D. Imerti's valuable edition (1964). The *Spaccio* was the only work of Bruno's to be singled out by the Inquisition at his trial in Rome.

43. Bruno, *Expulsion* (Imerti tr.), pp. 89–93.

44. Bruno, *Expulsion* (Imerti tr.), pp. 103–16; *Opere italiene*, 2:26.

45. Bruno, *Expulsion* (1713 tr.), pp. 49–50; *Opere italiene*, 2:54.

46. Bruno, *Expulsion* (Imerti tr.), pp. 119–29, 144–45.

47. Not the least of Jove's problems, as Bruno would have it, was the need for a fairly drastic university reform. Libra, or the Scales, was to be conscripted for this assignment:

Let the Scales roam through the academies and universities where they may examine whether those who teach are of correct weight, whether they are too light or tip the scales, and whether they who presume to teach from their chair and writings need to listen and study. And by balancing their intellect, let them [the Scales] see whether that intellect gives those who teach wings or weighs them down. Let them see whether it has the nature of the sheep or rather of the shepherd, and whether it is fit for the feeding of pigs and asses, or rather, of creatures capable of reason. [Bruno, *Expulsion* (Imerti tr.), p. 232]

48. Bruno, *Expulsion* (Imerti tr.), pp. 156, 177–180, 203–4; (1713 tr.), p. 176; *Opere italiene,* 2:141.

49. Bruno, *Expulsion* (Imerti tr.), pp. 213–14, 180, 227, 258; (1713 tr.), pp. 190–91; *Opere italiene,* 2:152.

50. Marsilio Ficino, *Platonic Theology* (tr. Burroughs), in S. J. Greenblatt, *Sir Walter Raleigh: The Renaissance Man and his Roles* (1973), p. 45.

51. Bruno, *On the Infinite Universe and Worlds* (tr. Singer), pp. 314–25; *Opere italiene,* 1:346–59. ("Revolution" is Mrs. Singer's somewhat misleading rendering of *circolare.*)

52. Bruno, *On the Infinite Universe and Worlds,* p. 325; *Opere italiane,* 1:360.

53. In addition to the new Bruno translations cited above, such as those of Memmo (*The Heroic Frenzies*) and Imerti (*Expulsion*), see also generally, Alexander Koyré, *From the Closed World to the Infinite Universe* (1958); F. R. Johnson, *Astronomical Thought in Renaissance England* (1937); and Paul Henri Michel, *The Cosmology of Giordano Bruno* (tr. Maddison, 1973).

54. Bruno, *Opere italiene,* 2:332–33; *Heroic Enthusiasts,* pp. 69–72. I have used the nineteenth-century translation of Williams throughout, and have (again) added parenthetically the original, necessarily richer and more suggestive Italian, where useful.

55. *Opere italiene,* 2:381; *Heroic Enthusiasts,* 1:141; *Heroic Frenzies,* p. 158. Bruno often borrowed verses from Luigi Tansillo (1510–68), often without acknowledgment; Tansillo, whose name was on the Papal Index for most of his literary life, appears as a character in several of Bruno's works.

56. Bruno, *Expulsion* (Imerti tr.), p. 64.

57. A further word about the breaking of the "painted ceilings". In a sensitive passage of much insight, Paul Henri Michel has called attention to the aesthetic implications of Bruno's "revolution," as men began to see the firmament with other eyes, "and painters gave witness to this new vision which they were the first to interpret." In his *Cosmology of Bruno* (pp. 227–28), Michel notes:

The geometrical skies of Romanesque paintings, symbolically decorated with circular orbits against golden Byzantine or Gothic backgrounds, gave place to less abstract skies.... These gave place in ever increasing numbers to animated skies, deep and gaping, which disturb more than they reassure, and certain of which fill with terror: the chaos from which St. Michael breaks free, by Tintoretto in the Dresden Museum; the sky of the Trinity, by Bassan at the Church of Angerano, in which the mantle of the Eternal Father rises in a spiral as though caught up in an immense void; the impetuous whirlwinds in the Assumptions by Malosso; chasms of brilliance from which the Holy Spirit of Pentecost falls in a rain of fire.

These are the new "revolutionary" images which we will be following from Milton to Sartre: chasms and gaping depths, terror and chaos, spirals and whirlwinds and rains of fire.

Chapter 5

1. Robert Heath, *Clarastella* (1650), in John Booker, *Telescopium Arcanicum* (1661), cited by Marjorie Nicolson, "English Almanacs and the 'New Astronomy,'" *Annals of Science* (1939), 4:20–21. See also "Kepler, the *Somnium,* and John Donne," in Marjorie Nicolson,

Science and Imagination (1956), chs. 3 and 4; and Christopher Hill, *Intellectual Origins of the English Revolution* (1965), p. 110.

2. John Milton, *Paradise Lost* (1667), in *Works* (ed. Patterson, 1931), 2:173–76, 188–89; 2:562–65, xxx, 242. *Considerations Touching the Likeliest Means to remove Hirelings out of the Church* (1659), 2:44–45. *An Apology against a Pamphlet call'd a Modest Confutation* (1642), 3, pt. 1:294.

3. *Areopagitica* (1644), in *Works*, 4:318, 329–30, 345.

4. *The Works of Joseph Hall* (1837 ed.), 5:237–38. Joseph Hall, *The Shaking of the Olive-Tree: The Remaining Works of Joseph Hall* (1660), pp. 19–20. See, generally, T. F. Kinloch, *The Life and Works of Joseph Hall, 1574–1656* (1951).

5. John Rushworth, *Historical Collections* (1692), 1:iii, 725–35.

6. *Mercurius Anti-Pragmaticus, communicating Intelligence from all parts Touching Affairs, Designes, Humours, and Conditions, throughout the Kingdome* (November 1647), nos. 6, 18–25, pp. 1–8.

7. "A Discourse By Way of Vision, Concerning the Government of Oliver Cromwell" (1661), in Abraham Cowley, *Essays, Plays and Sundry Verses* (ed. Waller, 1906), pp. 342–76.

8. The letter from the Bishop of Ross is in J. A. Froude, *History of England from the Fall of Wolsey to the Defeat of the Spanish Armada* (1870), 10:151. On the Bishop of Ross, see "John Leslie (1527–1591)," *Dictionary of National Biography* (ed. Lee, 1909), 11:972–78; and D. M. Lockie, "The Political Career of the Bishop of Ross," *University of Birmingham Historical Journal* (1954), pp. 98–137.

9. Thus, I now find in the original transcript of the Bishop of Ross's letter—which in Froude's rendering refers twice to "revolution"—no trace of this usage. It is, once again, a case of misleading translation, for Froude was rather fond of "revolutionary" formulations. See his handwritten copy in James Anthony Froude, *Transcripts from the Archives at Simancas Relating to English Affairs, A.D. 1567–1575* (British Museum Add. MS. 26,056 B, fol. 166).

10. Shakespeare, *King Lear* (Arden ed., 1963), pp. xxi, 30, 252–53. Critics have also suggested that Shakespeare is here also echoing notions in Florio's translation of Montaigne, where "the power and domination" of the stars ("Not onely upon our lives, and condition of our fortune . . ." but also over our dispositions and inclinations, our discourses and wils, which they rule") is propounded.

11. At the same time as Kepler's famous study of the new star of 1604, *De stella nova* (1606), another work was published, and I cite its title as illustrative of the connection between "revolution" and current astronomical (and astrological) conceptions: Elias Molerius, *De sydere novo seu de nova stella quae ab 8 die Octobris anni domini 1604 inter astra Sagittarii videri coepit ac annuae revolutionis 1605 periodo proxima extincta avenuit enarratio apodeictica* (1606). Copernicus, *De revolutionibus orbium caelestium* (1543; tr. Dobson and Brodetsky, 1947), p. xx.

12. James Howell, *Twelve/Several Treatises of the Late Revolutions in these Three Kingdomes: Deducting the Causes thereof from Their Originals* (1661), pp. 4–7, 320, 409. James Howell, *Epistolae Ho-Elianae: The Familiar Letters* (ed. Jacobs, 1892), 2:687.

13. *Poems and Dramas of Fulke Greville, First Lord Brook* (ed. Bullogh, 1939), 2:105, *Caelica* (ed. Ellis-Fermor, 1936), p. 80.

14. William Bagwell, *The Mystery of Astronomy, Made plain to the meanest Capacity, by an Arithmetical Description of the Terrestrial and Celestial Globes. Briefly shewing (by way of Question and Answer) the wonderful works of God, from the earth his footstool, to his Throne of heaven* (1655).

15. Robert Cawdrey, *A Table Alphabetical, contayning and teaching the true writing and understanding of hard usuall English words* (1613); John Bulloker, *An English Expositor* (1616). Henry Cockeram, *The English Dictionarie* (1623); Thomas Blount, *Glossographia, or a Dictionary Interpreting the Hard Words of Whatsoever Language, now used in our refined English Tongue*

(1674); Elisha Coles, *An English Dictionarie* (1676); E. Phillips, *The New World of Words* (1696); N. Bailey, *Dictionarium Britannicum* (1730); Samuel Johnson, *A Dictionary of the English Language* (1755).

In Nathan Bailey's *New Universal Etymological English Dictionary* (rev. ed., 1772), the following is recorded:

> RÉVOLUTION, Fr. (*revoluzione,* It. *revolucion,* Sp. of *revolutio,* Lat.).
> 1. The act of rolling or turning round, rotation in general, returning motion.
> 2. (In politics) a great turn or change of government in a country or state.
> 3. (In geometry) the motion of any figure, round a fixed line, as an axis.
> 4. (In astronomy) the period of a star, planet, comet, or other phaenomenon; or its course from any of the zodiac points till it return to the same.

16. Edward, Earl of Clarendon, *The History of the Rebellion and Civil Wars in England* (1702–4; ed. Macray, 1888), 1:xlvii. This edition includes the original prefaces by Laurence Hyde, Earl of Rochester, to the first publication of the Clarendon manuscript. King Charles II's brother James had married Lord Chancellor Clarendon's daughter; both Queen Anne and the late Queen Mary were Hydes and thus the editor's nieces. This was "revolution from above," indeed!

17. *Clavis Apocalyptica* (1651) and *Now or Never . . . A Bloody Almanack* (1659) are both in the British Museum's seventeenth-century collection (British Museum, E. 1260, E. 999).

18. Jean Calvin, *Institution de la religion Chrétienne* (1541; ed. Lefranc, 1911), pp. 6, 753; *Institutio Christiane religionis* (ed. 1846), p. 476; *The Institution of Christian Religion* (trans. Norton, 1634), 4.20.47, 732.

19. *Works of Gerrard Winstanley* (ed. Sabine, 1941), pp. 409, 447–80; *Complete Prose Works of John Milton* (ed. Wolfe, 1966), 4, pt. 1:25–26.

20. Michael Walzer, *The Revolution of the Saints* (1965), p. 110.

21. L. Savet, *Nova seu verius nova-antiqua de causis colorum sententia* (1609), in Lynn Thorndike, "Newness and Craving for Novelty in 17th-century Science and Medicine," *Journal of the History of Ideas* (October 1951), 12:598.

22. John Spencer, *Things, New and Old* (1658), pp. 313, 382, 453, 591, 611. Still, apparently, of some intellectual relevance two centuries later, this work was reprinted, in a modern two-volume edition, in 1867.

23. For the general intellectual background, see Lynn Thorndike's invaluable *History of Magic and Experimental Science* (6 vols., 1923–41). In Professor Thorndike's essay on "Newness and Craving for Novelty in 17th-century Science and Medicine," pp. 584–98, he calls special attention to "a remarkable feature" of both scientific and pseudo-scientific works of the seventeenth century, namely, the frequency with which such words as *new* and *unheard of* appear in their titles. It is true, he concedes, that this nomenclature was not unknown in previous periods of history; in the thirteenth century alone, we have the *Poetria nova,* the *Rethorica novissima,* not to mention Dante's *Vita Nuova* and the *Dolce stil nuovo.* Yet the preference for the antique rather than the new which characterized the Italian Renaissance gives way, he feels, with the realization of a *novus orbis* following the voyages of Columbus and Vespucci. In this presentation, the analysis is, in my view, neither broad nor complex enough. By ignoring the intellectual content of the "new" texts, the whole dimension of *Weltanschauung*—usually of controversial religious philosophy, but not infrequently also of political metaphysics—has been lost. For all the interest of his excellent researches, Professor Thorndike omits in his catalog of "Newness" the distinctions which I have tried to make between the *old* New and the *new* New. His concern for book titles is, alas, too narrow.

> With the appearance of new stars from 1572 on, a new heaven as well as a new earth began to gain recognition. But the idea of newness was already present in other fields of knowledge than geography and astronomy. . . . With the next century the employment of such titles became more widespread and numerous, more habitual, repetitious, and even stereotyped. . . . Treatises on the new star of 1604 almost

inevitably had the word "new" in their titles.... The titles of books on machines almost invariably laid claim to a novelty which their actual contents seldom corroborate ... The progress of anatomical investigation in the sixteenth century and its continuation in the 17th century made it natural enough to employ the term "new" in that field ... Assertions of new methods and departures, advances and discoveries, occur more often in the titles of medical works in the 17th century than anywhere else.... Some titles oppose rather than profess novelty.... The titles of other works indicate an aim to reconcile old and new.... In any case, the new was very much in the consciousness of the men of the seventeenth century.

The evidence offered is undeniably fascinating: Kepler's son-in-law's work on a planetarium entitled *Aspects Old and New;* Bacon's *Novum organum;* Galileo's *Two New Sciences;* Pascal's *Expériences nouvelles;* Boyle's *New Experiements Touching the Spring of the Air;* Wilkins' *Discovery of a New World in the Moon;* not to mention a work of 1685 entitled *A New and Useful Method of Curing Apoplexy.*

But, unfortunately, the mere use of *new,* or its frequency, is less revealing than the contexts in which it appears and from which it takes on deeper meaning. This could be theological, or ideological, or (last but not always least) simply a conventional everyday reference to something different or original or surprising. There has been in much of modern scholarship a sudden oversensitivity to words and metaphors. Not every image or turn of phrase is fraught with significance. This is, essentially, the error of Stanley Edgar Hyman's very challenging study, *The Tangled Bank* (1959), in which he relentlessly assigns "imaginative" value to every last bit of verbal or mental playfulness in the writings of Darwin, Marx, Frazer, and Freud.

Just as Professor Hyman finds "poetry" everywhere, so does Professor Thorndike detect some kind of dramatic historical significance in each and every appearance of the word *new,* whether in some revision of an old medical textbook or in various technical additions to the studies of gravity, algebra, and botanical gardens. This has, as I say, a certain interest, but its large interpretive thrust is seriously off the mark. Each text and context has to be examined with some careful attention to what I have called the metaphorical milieu. Is the physicist aflame with a new principle which would displace all the old cosmologies? And is the enthusiastic mathematician trying to establish a new formula which would demonstrate the traditional Christian faith in providential order? As for the botanist, could it be that his interest extends only to the surprising differences noted in flowers now accurately examined and sketched for the first time? The difference in each case for the historian is profound; and it is regrettable that this difference has so often been overlooked in the academic rush to apply literary critical methods to the records of historical experience. Thus, in Professor Hyman's *Tangled Bank,* much ingenious effort is wasted in studying Marx by assigning some deeper poetic significance to all his innumerable classical allusions; most of them have no more importance than to illustrate the fact that Marx had a very good grounding in Latin and Greek at the University of Berlin.

24. Nicolaus Copernicus, *On the Revolution of the Heavenly Spheres* (tr. Wallis, 1952), p. 519; *Des Revolutions des orbes celestes* (tr. Koyre, 1934), p. 92. See, generally, Thomas S. Kuhn, *The Copernican Revolution* (1957).

Chapter 6

1. Thomas Case, *Two Sermons Lately Preached at Westminster, before Sundry of Honourable House of Commons* (1641), pp. 4–22. John Milton, *Areopagitica* (1644) in *Works* (ed. Patterson, 1931), 4:340.

2. Edward, Earl of Clarendon, *The History of the Rebellion and Civil Wars in England* (1702–4; ed. Macray, with original prefaces by Laurence Hyde, Earl of Rochester, 1888), 1:xxvi.

3. Alessandro Giraffi, *Le Rivolutioni di Napoli* (1647). In contrast to James Howell's invaluable translation of this work (1650–52), the five-act drama written and published in the same year by an English "Gentleman who was an eyewitnes where this was really Acted upon that bloudy Stage, the streets of Naples" is of little historical or literary interest: *The Rebellion of Naples, or the Tragedy of Massaniello (commonly so called: But Rightly Tomaso Aniello di Malfa, Generall of the Neopolitans)* (1647; in the British Museum's Thomason Collection, E. 1358). The anonymous playwright does, however, manage in places to rise above his conventional authoritarian hostility and to give his protagonist credit for more than the low vices of an "incendiary." It may have been only "madnesse," but the rebel leader did want to strike a blow for "a brave world" (p. 45); he did seek "to be like one of these thundering gods" and to "begin a new world" (p. 68); he longed for "the golden age the Poets prophesied of" (p. 73). There is, incidentally, no mention of "revolution," only of "Tumults . . . stirs . . . discontents . . . commotions . . . insurrections."

4. Vernon F. Snow, "The Concept of Revolution in Seventeenth-Century England," *Historical Journal* (1962, no. 2) pp. 167–74. Arthur Hatto, "'Revolution': An Enquiry into the Usefulness of an Historical Term," *Mind* (1949), pp. 495–517.

5. Roberto Ridolfi, *Vita di Girolano Savonarola* (1952), p. 129; (tr. 1959), p. 86.

6. John Florio, *A World of Wordes, or Most copious and exact Dictionary in Italian and English* (1598); *New World of Words* (rev. ed., 1611).

In connection with Florio's early English references to "revolution . . . revolt . . . rebellion," and the usages I have already cited in the writings of Bruno, Sir Philip Sidney, and Fulke Greville, it may possibly be more than amusing to note the following curiosity. At the celebrated London supper party which was supposed to have taken place at Fulke Greville's house in 1584—the Ash Wesnesday dinner which Giordano Bruno describes in his book *Cena della Ceneri*—Sir Philip Sidney "was at the head of the table, and at the opposite end was John Florio, with Greville on his right and Bruno on his left." Small world! . . . See F. E. Halliday, *A Shakespeare Companion* (1964), pp. 168, 321; Howell, *Sidney*, p. 111.

As Richard David points out in his Arden edition of *Love's Labour's Lost*(1951, p. 83 n.), "Holofernes" in the play has often been identified with John Florio; Florio and Shakespeare may have been friends (through their common patron, Lord Southampton). In any case, Shakespeare knew Florio's translation of Montaigne's essays (echoed so vividly by Gonzalo in *The Tempest*), a copy of which exists in the British Museum bearing the (possibly valid) signature "Wllm Shakspere."

Florio's influence made itself felt not only through his rendering of Montaigne but more directly through his lexicographical work. Some Shakespeare scholars find it undeniable that "Montaigne had a substantial influence on the thought of *King Lear*" and have registered innumerable echoes of passages as well as dozens of words which can only be attributed to Florio's usage and, in some cases, coinage. The list of words which is said to establish the extent of Florio's influence on Shakespeare's vocabulary (especially in *Lear*)—includes *affectionate, bellyful, contentious, curiosity, depraved, evasion, frustrate, impetuous, incestuous, intelligent, jovial, monopoly, reciprocal, ripeness, sophisticated, sterility, waywardness*. I am struck by the following, which, in our special context, may well be relevant: *. . . catastrophe . . . disaster . . . mutation . . . planetary.* See: G. C. Taylor, *Shakespeare's Debt to Montaigne* (1925), and the discussion by Professor Kenneth Muir in his Arden edition of *King Lear* (1963), pp. 249–51. See also Frances A. Yates, *John Florio: the Life of an Italian in Shakespeare's England* (1934).

7. R. G. Collingwood, *The New Leviathan* (1942), pp. 199–201. See also Perez Zagorin's introductory remarks to *The Court and the Country: The Beginning of the English Revolution* (1969).

8. James Howell, *Parthenopoeia, or the History of the Most Noble and Renowned Kingdom of*

Naples (1654). The first part is "by that Famous Antiquary Scipio Mazzella," and the second part, which takes "the Thread of the Story to these present Times," was compiled by Howell.

9. *Animadversions upon the Remonstrants Defense* (1641), in Milton, *Works*, 3:110–11.

10. Henry More, *Enthusiasmus Triumphatus, or a Brief Discourse of the Nature, Causes, Kinds, and Cure of Enthusiasme* (1656), in *A Collection of Several Philosophical Writings of Dr. Henry More* (1712), pp. 16, 57.

11. Thomas Sprat, *History of the Royal-Society of London* (1667), p. 42.

12. Thomas Blount, *Academie of Eloquence* (1653), pp. 1–2, 19. On the usage of the word *garboyle*, the *O.E.D.* registers: "*Garboil* (*obs. exc. arch.*) . . . confusion, disturbance, tumult . . . a brawl, hubbub, hurlyburly . . . 1548: 'When ye shal heare all the worlde to bee in a garboile of sedicions' . . . 1600: 'The citie of Lisbon, as also all the rest, were in great garboile' . . . 1610: 'Whiles Commodus was Emperour, Britannie was all of a Garboile' . . . " *Oxford English Dictionary* (1933), 4:52.

13. C. D. Yonge, *An English-Greek Lexicon* (1869), p. 423, entries on *revolution* and *to revolutionise*; and also his *Phraseological English-Latin Dictionary* (1855), p. 383. L. Quicherat, *Dictionnaire Français-Latin* (1891), p. 1255. *Glossary of Later Latin* (ed. Souter, 1949), pp. 78, 335.

14. See the various renderings by S. L. Wolff, George Burnett, Moses Hadas, among others, in the Columbia edition of *The Works of John Milton* (1931–38): 7:40–41, 248–49, 398–99; 9:172–73; 13:468–9. Thus, in such phrases as *our revolution* and *this revolution in England* Milton had actually written *conversione* and *Anglos mutatione*, etc. *Revolution* is rendered occasionally by Milton's seventeenth-century translators; and he himself, of course, used the term a number of times in the general Shakespearean sense, e.g., "the sad and ceasles revolution of our swift and thick-coming sorrowes" (3:77), "a new and fatal revolution of calamity on this Land" (10:187).

15. Polybius, *The Histories* (tr. Paton, 1923), 3:289. Randle Cotgrave, *A Dictionarie of the French and English Tongues* (1611). The word *Rebellion* is given as: " . . . a publike revolt; resistance of a lawful authoritie; stubborness, disobedience, willfulnesse."

16. Clarendon, *History of the Rebellion*, pp. 203–9.

17. Thomas Hobbes, *Behemoth: or an Epitome of the Civil Wars of England, from 1640 to 1660* (1679), p. 214.

18. Milton, *Works* (1937), 13:516–17.

19. *Works* (1933), 10:1, 316.

20. Marchamont Nedham, *The Excellencie of a Free-State: or, the Right Constitution of a Common-Wealth. Wherein All Objections are answered, and the best way to secure the Peoples Liberties, discovered: With Some Errors of Government, and Rules of Policie. Published by a Well-wisher to Posterity* (1656), pp. 80, 154.

The attack on Nedham (also spelled Needham) is in *A Rope for Pol.* [*i.e.,* "Politicus"], *or, A Hue and Cry after Marchemont Nedham* (1660). This monarchist critique is a curious collection of the "scurrilous News-writer's . . . horrid Blasphemies and Revilings," and the editor apologizes for their republication, for "they deserve rather to be burn'd than read." It is a moot question, however, who is more culpable: Nedham or Gutenberg. Nedham was "the Goliath of the Philistines," and "had the Devil himself (the Father of Lies) been in this man's office, he could not have exceeded him."

Yet the fault apparently was less in him than in "the mischief occasioned by the Invention of Typography." The indictment was of Journalism. For if the old regime had been "traduc'd and profan'd by the Writings of zealous Incendiaries . . . Fanaticks and Enthusiasts," it was all "the issue of trayterous and pestilent minds . . . brought into the world and propagated by the existence of the Presse."

21. John Locke, *Two Tracts on Government* (ed. Abrams, 1967), pp. 235, 248. Lion

Aitzema, *Notable Revolutions: Being a True Relation of what Hap'ned in the United Provinces of the Netherlands* (1653); at Quaritch's in London. See, generally, *The Library of John Locke* (ed. Harrison and Laslett, 1965).

22. Locke, *An Essay Concerning Human Understanding* (1690–1706; ed. Yolton, 1965), 1:155–58; 2:71–92.

23. Locke, *Two Tracts,* p. 160. Locke, *Two Treatises of Government* (1689; rev. ed. Laslett, 1965), pp. 462–64.

24. Maurice Cranston, *Locke* (1961), p. 17, and, generally, his *John Locke: a Biography* (1957). *Two Treatises,* p. 289. *Two Tracts,* p. 53. Locke, "Oratio Censoria Funebris" (1664), in *Essays on the Law of Nature* (ed. von Leyden, 1954), p. 221. Snow, "The Concept of Revolution," p. 174. *Library of Locke,* p. 142. Locke's notes are in the British Museum (Add. MS. 15,642) and in the Bodleian Library; I am grateful to Professors W. von Leyden and John Lough for help in the location of these still unpublished fragments.

25. C. S. Lewis, *Studies in Words* (1960), p. 6: "Prolonged thought *about* the words which we ordinarily use to think *with* can produce a momentary aphasia. I think it is to be welcomed. It is well we should become aware of what we are doing when we speak, of the ancient, fragile and (well used) immensely potent instrument that words are."

26. Eduard Bernstein and Karl Kautsky, *Die Geschichte des Sozialismus* (1895), vol. 1. Eduard Bernstein, *Cromwell and Communism* (1895; tr. Stenning, 1930). Karl Kautsky, *Thomas More and his Utopia* (tr. Stenning, 1959).

27. Michael Walzer, *The Revolution of the Saints* (1966), pp. 10–12, 21, 130, 175–77, 315. Christopher Hill, *Intellectual Origins of the English Revolution* (1965), pp. 111, 202. *The Good Old Cause* (ed. Hill and Dell, 1949), p. 259.

28. F. R. Leavis, *Revaluation: Tradition and Development in English Poetry* (1936), p. 206.

29. James Harrington, *Oceana* (1656; ed. Liljegren, 1924), pp. 124–25, 223–24, 226, 322.

30. E. R. Curtius, *Europäische Literatur und Lateinisches Mittelalter* (1948), ch. 7; rendered as *metaphorics* in Willard Trask's translation, *European Literature and the Latin Middle Ages* (1953), p. 128.

31. Rudolf Bultmann, *History and Eschatology* (1957), p. 26.

32. Mircea Eliade, *Le Mythe de l'éternel retour: archétypes et répétition* (1949).

33. Claude Lévi-Strauss, *The Scope of Anthropology* (tr. Paul, 1967), pp. 27–37: "It is not contradictory that a history of symbols and signs engenders unforeseeable developments, even though it brings into play a limited number of structural combinations. In a kaleidoscope, each recombination of identical elements yields new results."

34. Kenelm Burridge, *New Heaven, New Earth: A Study of Millenarian Activities* (1969), pp. 76–83. Robert H. Lowie, *Indians of the Plains* (1963), pp. 199–204. Philip Drucker, *Indians of the Northwest Coast* (1963), p. 169.

35. James Mooney, *The Ghost-Dance Religion and the Sioux Outbreak of 1890* (1896; ed. Wallace 1965), pp. 23–28, 181, 201 ff.

36. Theodore H. Gaster, *The Dead Sea Scriptures* (1956), p. 98. For a recent discussion of linear and cyclical theories, see Frank E. Manuel, *Shapes of Philosophical History* (1965).

37. Victor Hugo, *Ninety-Three* (tr. Bair, 1962), pp. 121–39; *Quatrevingt-treize* (1874; ed. Flammarion, 1965), p. 163.

38. Mircea Eliade, *The Myth of the Eternal Return* (1954), pp. ix–x, 6–7, 27; *The Sacred and the Profane* (1961), pp. 59–60, 121. See, also, his *Myths, Dreams and Mysteries* (1960) and *Images and Symbols* (1961).

Chapter 7

1. *Encounter,* February 1960, reprinted in H. R. Trevor-Roper, *Religion, the Reformation, and Social Change* (1967), pp. 237–93. H. Dircks, *A Biographical Memoir of Samuel Hartlib*

(1865), pp. 17, 55–56. Christopher Hill, *Intellectual Origins of the English Revolution* (1965), pp. 128–129 n.

2. P. G. Rogers, *The Fifth Monarchy Men* (1966). C. H. Simpkinson, *Thomas Harrison, Regicide and Major-General* (1905). S. R. Gardiner, *History of the Commonwealth and Protectorate: 1649–1660* (1901), 3:114–15. C. H. Firth, *The Last Years of the Protectorate* (1909), 1:207–19. See, generally, D. W. Petegorsky, *Left Wing Democracy in the English Civil War* (1940), and Perez Zagorin, *A History of Political Thought in the English Revolution* (1954, 1965). The most recent scholarly study (it includes the statistical analysis I refer to) is especially valuable: B. S. Capp, *The Fifth Monarchy Men: A Study in 17th-Century English Millenarianism* (1972).

3. H. H. Rowley, *Darius the Mede and the Four World Empires in the Book of Daniel* (1935). Capp, *Fifth Monarchy Men*, pp. 36–38, 53.

4. Capp has called attention to the psychological factors in the conversion of the Fifth Monarchists, as against the simpler political explanations. He challenges, for example, Perez Zagorin's conventional ideological notion that the Fifth Monarchist ranks swelled when the disillusion with Leveller militancy set in (*i.e.*, that the rise of Fifth Monarchism was the "inevitable product of the failure of the left-democratic revolution). In each case there was, early on, both a radical temper and a series of social demands, although it is quite clear that the Levellers were an "egalitarian" movement and the Fifth Monarchists were "élitist." Perhaps it could be said that one movement drew its strength from minds and hearts that needed a dream of a final social solution, and the other from the longing for spiritual salvation at last (with, to be sure, an associated secular dividend).

> The fear of hell and damnation, implanted deliberately by the preachers, increased anxiety over salvation, and was described in vivid terms by many of the [Fifth Monarchist] saints. Terrified at the age of ten by preachers "thundring" on the agonies of the damned, John Rogers expected every night to be seized by the devil, brooded on the *"endlesse, easlesse* and *remedilesse"* torments in store, cursed "that ever I was born," and thought he "heard the *damned* roaring and *raving,* and saw them ... *roasting,* and their frisking and frying in everlasting torments." Before long he lost his reason. Edward Wayman dreamed that he was seized and torn by a great black dog (the devil). One woman was terrified when her dog jumped on her bed one night, thinking the devil has come to take her away. A girl of eleven dreamed of "fire ... shreeking and a "burning lake," and saw the "Devill with his chaines" waiting for her. Sarah Barnwell related how a preacher used an outbreak of plague in Dublin to dwell "on the sad condition of some (even *Professors*) that were in *Hell* howling! Oh! this sad doctrine struck deep to the heart." Nine members of these two churches were tempted or did attempt to commit suicide, to end at least the torments of this life. Rogers tried to kill himself several times. One small girl tried to choke herself by swallowing feathers from her pillow. [Vavasor] Powell had once tried to take his life. [Capp, *Fifth Monarchy Men,* pp. 95–96]

5. Edward Rogers, *Some Account of the Life and Opinions of a Fifth-Monarchy-Man: chiefly extracted from the Writings of John Rogers, Preacher* (1867), pp. 3–6, 268–69. For Dante, see above, ch. 13, "The Prometheans."

6. The difference between the men of reason and the men of unreason did not derive from the elements of either political militance or fiery temperament; these, as in the cases of Philip Sidney and John Rogers, were shared. After all, Sidney himself died at the age of thirty-two as a martyr to a just cause on a foreign battlefield. As he wrote at the time of the Dutch revolt against Spain to his Huguenot friend Languet (15 April 1574): "With respect to the Netherlands, truly I cannot see how it could have happened better: for though that beautiful country is all on fire, you must remember that the Spaniards cannot be driven from it without all this conflagration." Sidney was very much like one of his own Arcadians, for whom "the glorious name of Liberty" served to "increase fire in their minds."

Yet, for all the fire there was a Greek, an Aristotelian coolness to Philip Sidney's mind, uncomplicated by the agitations of Judeo-Christian prophecy and as yet untouched by the coherence of systematic ideological simplifications. Rogers and the other saints regarded reason as ungodly. Feake's hope was expressed in the phrase: "a glorious, Evangelical inquisition." Spittlehouse denounced the universities and independent scholarship: "What are the Authors which their Libraries are stuffed withal other than Heathenish and Antichristian?" There was much attraction to magic, alchemy, and astrology in the radical politics of the day. (See: Capp, *Fifth Monarchy Men*, pp. 187–89.)

In sharp contrast, Sir Philip Sidney's burning temperament had an aspect of social studiousness (see above, pp. 187–88). I have already considered the place of Philip Sidney in the history of utopians and revolutionaries; but it may still be useful to suggest now that here, possibly, is the beginning of a great liberal tradition in the history of just causes: the exercise of the passions would always seek the legitimacy of reason and objective analysis; practical work requires a larger framework of ideas, and the activist longs to be at one with the theoretician.

7. I use the word *scenario* advisedly, and this will emerge more clearly in the fuller examination of theatricality and politics contained in ch. 15, "On the Stage of History." There was, of course, drama enough in the Reverend Hugh Peter's life. He has been called "the army's most political preacher," and one historian has written of his role in 1648–49: "Only Peter exulted openly in the grisly progress of a monarch to the scaffold. During the king's trial he harangued the assembled troops outside Westminster Hall and led them, like a cheer-leader in a sports stadium, in a thunderous chanting of 'Justice, Justice,' and 'Execution, Execution,' to drown any expressions of protest or dissent." See: *In God's Name: Examples of Preaching in England, 1534–1662* (ed. Chandos, 1971), pp. 425, 442.

But my special point, and I will be documenting it throughout, is that the historical actors in a revolution appear to sense the element of drama in the events as they unfold. One contemporary critic of Hugh Peter, who hated him as "a Fire-brand" and rejected his "absurd and ridiculous Expressions," went on to make the point: "His Sermons were like Stage-Plays ... " (*Rebels No Saints* [1661], p. 84).

The play ended badly. Six months after the return of Charles II, he was apprehended by Royalist troops, taken by force (he insisted all the while that his real name was Thompson) to the Tower of London. He was condemned to be hanged, drawn, and quartered; and on 13 October 1660 "the sentence was carried out with even more than usual barbarity."

8. John Spittelhouse, *The First Addresses to the Lord General* (1653), p. 5; R. P. Stearns, *The Strenuous Puritan: Hugh Peter, 1598–1660* (1954), p. 330; John Rogers, *Ohel or Beth-shemesh* (1653), p. 23; Capp, *Fifth Monarchy Men*, p. 53.

9. The radicalism of the Fifth Monarchist movement derived more from the fanatical messianism of a small theocratic élite than from any militant sense of democratic political rights or social equalitarianism. Even in their own day, the Fifth Monarchists were felt to be rather anomalous allies in the struggle against "Tyranny and Oppression." In his sharp indictment of "Political Enthusiasm," Dr. Henry More, the famous Cambridge Platonist, went so far as to suggest an aspect of melancholy "Villany" in those "false *Messiases*" who, despite the virtues of sincere religious feeling and humane compassion, deluded themselves and others with the obnoxiously eloquent promises of a deliverance that was not to be. He has left us a vignette of one radical's undemocratic ways which is fair and telling:

> [One political enthusiast] I had the hap to meet withal, whose discourse was not only rational, but pious, and he seemed to have his wits very well about him; nor could I discover the least intimation to the contrary, only he had this flaw, that he conceited that he was by God appointed to be that fifth Monarch, of which there is so much noise in this age; which imagination had so possessed him, that he would sometime have his Servant to serve him all in plate and upon the knee ... [Henry More, *Enthusiasmus Triumphatus, or a Brief Discourse of the Nature, Causes, Kinds, and Cure of Enthusiasm* (1656), p. 22, in *A Collection of Several Philosophical Writings of Dr. Henry More* (1712)]

This suggests an important distinction in the historical movements of the so-called left-democratic revolution between those who, in practice or in theory, were democrats only "in part," i.e., only within their own center and circle, and those rarer creatures whose democratic ideal meant a "whole" equalitarianism involving *all* men.

> The Fifth Monarchists were an élitist movement, seeing the saints as God's aristocracy and therefore justified in ruling over the reprobate. Divine grace ignored existing social distinctions, and the saints believed that it necessitated a social revolution. But within the ranks of the saints, it made them egalitarian. A journeyman, apprentice or labourer might possess the grace of God, and persons of these social degrees were accepted as equal saints, able to hold office in the congregation. [Capp, *Fifth Monarchy Men*, p. 230]

10. Of this meeting between John Rogers and Cromwell, Professor Wilbur Cortez Abbott remarks in his formidable edition of *The Writings and Speeches of Oliver Cromwell* (1945), 3:607:

> ... and there ensued one of the longest, the most entertaining and illuminating conversations of which we have any record in this period, marred only by the fact that the greater part of the talking was done by the voluble and inconsecutive Rogers, perhaps the most notorious man of his time for excessive verbiage and irresponsible utterance.

This is unnecessarily pejorative. From Cromwell we have enough utterance; the historian should be grateful for the recorded volubility which illuminates so much of the utopian mind and revolutionary temperament. Professor Abbott's insensitivity on this score leads him, in my view, to a misjudgment of the real course of the contest between the brilliance of a seraphical dissenter and the stolidity of an impatient man of power. He is quite unconvincing when he writes:

> ... according to his custom, Cromwell was as eager to meet his opponents in the field of dialectical theology as on the field of battle, trusting, not without reason, on the skill he had developed through the years since his earliest experiences in Puritan conventicles, to confound them out of their own mouths and out of the Scripture in which he was no less gifted than they ...

Apart from this bias in favor of his heroic protagonist, Professor Abbott's conclusions are worth noting (p. 616).

> [1] ... there could be no common meeting-ground for two men and two schools of thought so widely separated as those of the Fifth Monarchists and the Cromwellians—nor, in fact, could any school of thought, or emotion, contend with the verbose and inconsequential pertinacity of men who, with all their virtues, strove for an ideal impossible of realization in an imperfect world, and were prepared to overthrow any power which stood in the way of the rule of the Saints.
>
> [2] ... it is evident that Cromwell found himself in a difficult position in regard to them. He had used that spirit of enthusiasm to the limit in his rise to power; he had believed that he could control it by persuasion; but he now found that there was no remedy but the sword; and it is obvious that he realized the impossibility of conciliation and was prepared to take the consequences, even at the cost of losing some of his most ardent supporters. It was not the first time, nor the last, that a revolutionary leader has found himself in the position of being compelled to repudiate the more extreme of his followers.

11. Dissatisfied with the brief and partisan account that had been published in the Government's newspaper, the Fifth Monarchy men rushed into print with a version of their own: *The Faithfull Narrative of The Late Testimony and Demand made to Oliver Cromwell, and his Powers, on the Behalf of the Lords Prisoners ... to prevent mistakes, and misreports thereupon* (1654). Both texts are in Rogers, *Life and Opinions of a Fifth-Monarchy-Man*, pp. 172–214. There is a convenient summary in *The Writings and Speeches of Oliver Cromwell* (ed. Abbott, 1945), 3:607–16.

12. As Cromwell memorably put it, in 1655: "Is there not yet a strange itch upon the spirit of men? Nothing will satisfy them unless they can press their finger upon their

brethren's conscience to pinch them there ... " (Charles Firth, *Oliver Cromwell* [1900], p. 368).

13. Not a few historians have tended to support Cromwell's claim. "It was true, Cromwell's was the most tolerant government which had existed in England since the reformation. In practice, he was more lenient than the laws, and more liberal indeed than most of his advisers" (Firth, *Cromwell*, pp. 367–68).

14. 4 September 1654 and 17 September 1656, *Speeches of Oliver Cromwell* (ed. Stainer, 1901), pp. 127–46, 211–55. Louise Fargo Brown, *The Political Activities of the Baptists and Fifth Monarchy Men in England during the Interregnum* (1912), pp. 154–55.

15. In his study of *English Democratic Ideas in the Seventeenth Century*, G. P. Gooch called attention to the close connections during this period between the Baptists and the Fifth Monarchists and to the fact that "many conversions from one party to the other" were recorded. Professor Perez Zagorin, as was noted above, has offered the explanation in his *History of Political Thought in the English Revolution* that millenarianism emerged only after the failure of the movement for "political and secular solutions." He speculates that "it is probable that this would have remained a negligible phenomenon if the Leveller's objectives had been achieved." Making too sharp and simple a distinction between what is secular and what is millenarian in this-worldly politics, and overlooking the common elements of ideological temperament, Zagorin thinks of the rise of the Fifth Monarchists as the result of some kind of massive switch. "Fifth-monarchism, therefore, was the moan of the distressed creature lamenting the cruelty and heartlessness of the world. In an age still religious, it was an inevitable product of the failure of the left-democratic revolution to consummate itself." This formula is dismissed as too pat, too mechanical, and too unempirical by Capp in his history of *The Fifth Monarchy Men:*

> The Fifth Monarchists' wish for the tyrannical rule of the elect over the ungodly was diametrically opposed to the Levellers' egalitarian tendencies. Nevertheless, some of the rank and file of the Leveller supporters may have drifted into Fifth Monarchism because the saints shared many of the objectives of the other contemporary radical movements. They called for legal reforms, lower rents and the abolition of feudal relics. They attacked monopolies, condemned tithes, and sought to relieve the plight of the poor. The existence of a body of shared objectives may have facilitated movement between the fringe members of the radical groups, but there is no evidence that the Fifth Monarchists owed their rise to the defeat of the Levellers, or that their ideas were derived from the Levellers.

See: G. P. Gooch, *English Democratic Ideas in the Seventeenth Century* (1898; ed. Laski, 1927), p. 227. Zagorin, *History of Political Thought in the English Revolution*, p. 105. Capp, *Fifth Monarchy Men*, pp. 89, 230.

16. Capp, *Fifth Monarchy Men*, pp. 74–75, 162; John Rogers, *Sagrir, or Doomes-day drawing nigh, with Thunder and Lightening to the Lawyers* ... (1653).

17. *The Censure of the Rota upon Mr. Milton's Book* (1660), p. 15. Marchamont Nedham, *A True State of the Case of the Commonwealth* (1654), p. 34.

I should mention that Milton's Rota critic associated him—as have many modern Milton scholars—with the radical saints, "the Fifth-Monarchy-Men, who would have been admirable for your Purpose, if they had but dreamed of a fifth free-State ... " But Milton himself, fairly loyal Cromwellian that he was, was clearly out of sympathy with the fanatically radical sects, perhaps most angrily so when he wrote in Sonnet XII, against those

> That bawle for fredom in their senseless mood,
> And still revolt when truth would set them free.
> License they mean when they cry libertie.

18. "*Seraphic, seraphical* ... allusively applied in the sense of zealot ... rapturous, ecstatically devout.... In the 17th c. often ironical, applied to fanatical religionists or to impassioned orators ... " *Oxford English Dictionary* (1933), 9:489–90.

19. When the New Model Army was established in 1645, the disbanded soldiers (they became a political problem) were referred to as *"Reformadoes."* The chosen representatives the various regiments were known as *"Agitators"* (often misspelt and held to be a form of "Adjutators"), or official military agents: *agitate*, to do the actual work of, to manage.That it had a subversive connotation is clear from Marchamont Nedham's little playlet, *The Levellers levelled* (1647), in which the main persons are "Five Ajutators, or Levellers," namely "Apostasie, Conspiracie, Treacherie, Democracie, Impietie." But its consistent modern usage apparently dates only from the time of Burke, a century later. See *O.E.D.*, 1:184; S. R. Gardiner, *History of the Great Civil War* (1891), 3:60; and Staines, *Speeches of Cromwell*, pp. 6–9, 412–13.

20. Apocalyptic prophets long for mathematical certainty, but when prophecies fail, revisionism is inevitable. If some spirits waver in confidence and find their hopes dashed in disappointment, others go back and do their sums all over again. There never was, in any case, general agreement about the exact date of the Great Day or Golden Year or the methods of its precise calculation. Among the dates mentioned in the literature of the period are: 1641, 1645, 1648, 1649, 1650, 1655–57, and 1660. By the time the dark favorite of the apocalyptics had dawned—1666—militant hope had given way to quietist acceptance; nothing much happened, or was made to happen. It was obvious that even the calculations from the Number of the Beast—which was 666 (Rev. 13:18)—had gone awry. In 1672, Henry Danvers tried to explain that it was really quite impossible to specify exact years.

But, when the Glorious Revolution of 1688 took place, there were some millenarians who reexamined the sacred texts and conveniently proved that what the prophecies were really referring to was 1688–89. For a few, even the Restored King, Charles II, could be taken to be the true Fifth Monarch. See: Capp, *Fifth Monarchy Men*, pp. 193–94.

21. Leo F. Solt, *Saints in Arms: Puritanism and Democracy in Cromwell's Army* (1959); and "The Fifth Monarchy Men: Politics and the Millennium," *Church History* (September 1961), 30:314–24.

22. *Jegar-Sahadutha* (1657), in Rogers, *Life and Opinions of a Fifth-Monarchy-Man*, pp. 225–304.

23. *The Diary of John Evelyn*, 6 August 1657 (ed. de Beer, 1955), 3:196. P. G. Rogers, *Fifth Monarchy Men*, p. 97. Brown, *Political Activities of Baptists and Fifth Monarchy Men*, p. 27 n. Solt, "Politics and the Millennium," p. 321. *Bibliotheca fanatica* (1660), p. 7. Capp, *Fifth Monarchy Men*, p. 125.

24. Rogers, *Jegar-Sahadutha*, pp. 3, 37; William Aspinwall, *The Legislative Power* (1656), pp. 36–37; Capp, *Fifth Monarchy Men*, pp. 111–18, 140–56.

25. Marchamont Nedham, *A True State of the Case of the Commonwealth*, pp. 3, 13–14. Champlin Burrage, "The Fifth Monarchy Insurrections," *English Historical Review* (October 1910), p. 723.

26. Extensive excerpts from the deciphered manuscript of Thomas Venner's journal are printed in Burrage, "The Fifth Monarchy Insurrections," pp. 722–47.

27. *A Door of Hope. Or, A Call and Declaration for the gathering together of the first ripe Fruits unto the Standard* ... (1661), pp. 2–3.

28. Samuel Pepys, *Diary* (ed. Wheatley, 1907), 1:298; Rogers, *Life and Opinions of a Fifth-Monarchy-Man*, pp. 327–28.

29. On the so-called back-lash, Capp quotes the confident political prediction of the Earl of Clarendon from Edward Hyde's manuscripts, a letter to King Charles II, 24 May/3 June 1657. In his meticulously careful history of *The Fifth Monarchy Men* (pp. 126–30), he tends to agree with the basic formula as we have come to know it, that the extremism of an ultra-left creates an opportunity for the right to swing back into power:

> Charles II was proclaimed on 8 May (1660), and entered London on 29 May. The saints, of course, were not solely responsible for the Restoration. But their vociferous demands for political, social and religious revolution discredited the republican

governments which proved unable to contain them. In 1653 they had been partly responsible for the conservative reaction which led to the Protectorate. Their activities, and the rumours of imminent massacres and spoliation, helped to lead in 1660 to the general belief that there could be no settled order until the king returned.

30. P. G. Rogers, *Fifth Monarchy Men*, pp. 155–56.

31. "The number of possible political ideas is very limited and, once they have been adumbrated, the greatest political philosopher can only make new permutations and combinations." Christopher Morris, *Political Thought in England: Tyndale to Hooker* (1953), p. 151.

Chapter 8

1. James Howell, *Twelve / Several Treatises of the Late Revolutions* (1661), pp. 4, 75, 195, 225–30, 294, 409; *Epistolae Ho-Elianae: The Familiar Letters* (ed. Jacobs, 1892), 1:371.

2. Howell, *Epistolae*, 1:xiii, 335; 2:576, 667.

3. *The Vote, or A Poeme Royall* (1642), p. 5; *Epistolae*, 1:8. In his *Instructions for Forreine Travell* (1642; ed. Arber, 1868), Howell observed (p. 54): "For as Kingdomes and States with all other Sublunary things are subject to a tossing and tumbling, to periods and changes, as also all Naturall bodies corrupt inwardly and insensibly of themselves, so Languages are not exempt from this Fate, from those accidents, and revolutions that attend Time."

4. Joseph Jacobs, in his edition of Howell's *Epistolae Ho-Elianae*, 1:xli–xlii.

5. Howell, *Some Sober Inspections* (1655); Philanglus, *Some Sober Inspections* (1660); Roger L'Estrange, *A Modest Plea* (1662).

6. John Selden, *Mare Clausum* (1635); *Of the Dominion, or, Ownership of the Sea* (tr. Marchamont Nedham, 1652); *The Right and Dominion of the Sea* (ed. Howell, 1662).

7. I refer here to Howell's 1660 edition of Cotgrave's *Dictionarie*. Neither here nor in Howell's impressive *Lexicon Tetraglotton* (1660) is there any suggestion of a political meaning, although he himself had been using *revolution* in this new sense for years. This is no doubt attributable to the conventional lexicographical lag.

8. James Howell, *The Sway of the Sword* (1645); *An Italian Perspective* (1647); *Advice Sent from the Prime Statesmen of Florence* (1659); *A Vindication of His Majesty* (1661), all in *Twelve/ Several Treatises of the Late Revolutions*, pp. 251, 259, 294, 312, 401, 407–9.

9. Howell, *Epistolae*, 1:371. *Several Treatises*, p. 78.

10. *Several Treatises*, pp. 229–30, 328–30.

11. Howell, *His Late Majesties Royal Declaration or Manifesto* (1661), in *Several Treatises*, p. 145.

The usage of "pragmaticall' here is in the sense of the older meaning which the *Oxford English Dictionary* (1933) 8:1224, gives as "Busy, active; esp. officiously busy in other people's affairs; interfering, meddling, intrusive"—as in Ben Jonson ("I love to hit these pragmaticke young men at their own weapons," 1616), or Bishop Hall ("the absurd prag- maticall impudence of the present Pope," 1624), or John Milton ("these matters are not for pragmatics or folkmooters to babble in," 1645). It has also meant, as etymological irony would have it, "opinionated, dictatorial, dogmatic." Still, its opposite connotation— popularized in the use of *pragmatisch* by Kant and in the "practical" philosophy of pragmatism by William James—can also be found in earlier centuries (viz., "theirs was not a curious and idle knowledge but a pragmaticall knowledge, full of labour and business," 1597).

12. Howell, *Epistolae*, 2:634–35.

13. *Epistolae*, vol. 2, p. 604. *Several Treatises*, pp. 102, 298–99.

14. See, especially, the courageous study by J. L. Talmon, "Jews between Revolution and Counter-Revolution," in *Israel among the Nations* (1970), pp. 1–87; George Lichtheim, "Socialism and the Jews," in *Dissent* (July-August 1968), pp. 314–42; and W. H. Chaloner and W. D. Henderson, "Marx/Engels and Racism," *Encounter* (July 1975), pp. 18–23.

15. *Famous Utopias of the Renaissance* (ed. White, 1946), pp. 234–35.

16. A. N. Whitehead, *Adventures of Ideas* (1964), pp. 19–27.

17. Edward, Earl of Clarendon, *History of the Rebellion and Civil Wars in England* (1702–4; ed. Macray, with original prefaces by Laurence Hyde, Earl of Rochester (1888), 1:486; 2:10–11, 100.

18. Cecil Roth, *A History of the Jews in England* (3d ed., 1964), pp. 149–72, 285. Lucien Roth, "Cromwell's Jewish Intelligencers," in *Essays in Jewish History* (1934), pp. 93–114. Howell, *Epistolae,* 2:617.

19. Howell, *Epistolae,* 1:313–15.

20. *Casual Discourses* (1643), *A Sober and Seasonable Memorandum* (1644), in *Several Treatises,* pp. 10–13, 141.

21. James Howell, *Parthenopoeia, or the History of the Most Noble and Renowned Kingdom of Naples* (1654).

22. In a letter to his friend Samuel Bonnell in Old Jewry Street, Howell wrote: "I also highly thank you for the Italian Manuscript you sent me of the late Revolutions in Naples." He was referring to the text of Alessandro Giraffi's, *Le Rivolutioni di Napoli,* published in Venice in 1647. Howell's translation appeared in 1650: *An Exact Historie of the Late Revolutions in Naples; and of their Monstrous Successes, Not to be parallel'd by any Ancient or Modern History.* A final installment was published in 1652: *The Second Part of Masaniello . . . A Continuation of the Tumult.*

23. This is from the 5th day *della rivolutione,* 11 July 1647, *An Exact Historie of the Revolutions in Naples,* pp. 102–5.

On the semantic aspects, see: V. F. Snow, "The Concept of Revolution in Seventeenth-century England," *Historical Journal* (1962, no. 2), pp. 167–74. Arthur Hatto, " 'Revolution': an Enquiry into the Usefulness of an Historical Term," *Mind* (1949), pp. 495–517. J. M. Goulemot, "Le Mot révolution et la formation du concept de révolution politique (fin XVIIe siècle)," *Annales historiques de la Révolution française,* no. 190 (October–December 1967), pp. 417–44.

24. I also leave to a subsequent page the curious role that the figure of Masaniello played in the history of nineteenth-century revolution, viz., in the Belgian revolution against Holland which was sparked by the riots that followed a tumultous performance of Auber's opera about Masaniello (*La Muette de Portici*) in Brussels's Royal Theater; in the attitudes of Goethe to these revolts of 1830, after a local performance of *Masaniello* in Weimar; in the radicalization of Richard Wagner in the Paris of the 1840s, when he admired Auber's "Masaniello masterpiece" and took inspiration for his manifestos on behalf of "Utopia" and "Revolution"; in the striking comment of Russia's Tsar Nicholas on Bakunin's adventurous proposals for a Pan-Slav uprising throughout Europe; and in the oddity of even Tocqueville, while in Amalfi, turning to thoughts of Masaniello.

This aura of uncanny fascination already attached itself to the figure of Masaniello in his own day. John Locke pondered the nature of political sovereignty from Adam to Cromwell and Masaniello. And there was among Spinoza's papers (found after his death in 1677) an astonishing self-portrait in which the philosopher, out of some complex impulse (Leon Roth warns us against "oversimplifying" the point), pictures himself as Masaniello; and Spinoza can be seen wearing the young fisherman's attire as in the first stormy days of the Neapolitan *rivoluzione!* . . . John Locke, *Two Treatises of Government* (1689; rev. ed. Laslett, 1965), par. 79. Johann Colero, *Das Leben des Bened. von Spinoza* (1733), pp. 37–38. Léon Roth, *Spinoza* (1929), p. 11. Benedetto Croce, *Storia del regno di Napoli* (1925), p. 36.

25. James Howell, *Apologs, or Fables Mythologized* (1643). *An Italian Perspective* (1647), *A Nocturnal Progress* (1645), in *Several Treatises,* pp. 174, 191–92, 295, 330–31.

26. *Eikon Basilike: The Portraiture of His Sacred Majesty in His Solitudes and Sufferings* (1649; ed. Knachel, 1966). All my quotations are from the edition published for the Folger

Shakespeare Library. See also: Francis F. Madan, *A New Bibliography of the Eikon Basilike* (1950), and H. R. Trevor-Roper, "Eikon Basilike: The Problem of the King's Book," in *Historical Essays* (1957), pp. 211–20.

27. The authorship of the *Eikon Basilike* is a problem to which vast scholarly attention has been paid, ever since John Milton charged (with, at the time, almost no evidence) that the work attributed to the late King was a "forgery." The consensus of specialist opinion today, as summed up by Philip A. Knachel of the Folger Library (*Eikon Basilike*, p. xxxii), is: " ... *Eikon Basilike*, though actually written by Dr. John Gauden, was based on a core of material which the King had himself composed—and Gauden's manuscript was read and corrected by the King before going to press."

28. John Milton, remorselessly pursuing every phrase and argument in the *Eikon Basilike*, refers rather grudgingly to "flashes" (*OED:* "Superficial brilliancy, ostentation"). It is almost a backhanded tribute when he refers to the King's style as "a garb somewhat more Poetical than [befits] a Statist." The passage has its special ironies when Milton, the literary man of politics par excellence, goes on to damn with faint praise: " ... and hearing him reported a more diligent reader of Poets, than of Politicians, I begun to think that the whole Book might perhaps be intended a piece of Poetrie. The words are good, the fiction smooth and cleanly; there wanted only Rime, and that, they say, is bestow'd upon it lately." John Milton, "Eikonoklastes" (1649), in *Complete Prose Works* (ed. Hughes, 1962), 3:478, 406.

29. Francis Bacon, Essay on Innovations.

30. *O.E.D.*, 5:314. Here, again, we can note the parallelism of psychological forms on two extremes: i.e., between dogmatic principles both in secular political religion and in theology. Both have a mortal fear of the chain reaction of change, causing a permanent deviationism. "Avoid the novelties in your discourse," as Bossuet quotes Chrysostom, "for matters will not rest there: one novelty produces another; and we deviate without end, once we have begun to deviate." See the chapter on Bossuet and Voltaire in Eric Voegelin, *From Enlightenment to Revolution* (ed. Hallowell, 1975), pp. 3–34. Jacques Benigne Bossuet, *Histoire des Variations des Eglises Protestantes* (1688), 1:4 (the Preface): "Evitez lez nouveautez dans vos discours, car les choses n'en demeureront pas là: une nouveauté en produit une autre, & on s'égare sans fin quand on a une fois commencé à s'égarer."

31. R. C. Bald, "*The Booke of Sir Thomas More* and Its Problems," in *Shakespeare Survey 2* (1949), pp. 44–65.

32. Thus, against the historical version which sees in the "Puritan revolution" a necessary and decisive stage of capitalism, "the rise of the bourgeoisie," and general modernization, Professor Trevor-Roper has argued:

> Socially, as politically, the Revolution had been a failure, and the history of England after 1660 was a continuation of its history before 1640. The Interregnum was merely an untidy interruption. The only permanent changes were a few constitutional changes that could have been, and sometimes had been, achieved by peaceful legislation, and certainly did not require civil war, revolution and military dictatorship ... [H. R. Trevor-Roper, "The Social Causes of the Great Rebellion," in *Historical Essays*, p. 204]

For a sharp critique of the errors and contradictions of Christopher Hill's efforts at a Marxian interpretation, see also Charles Wilson, "Economics and Politics in the 17th Century," in *Economic History and the Historian* (1969), pp. 1–21.

33. Clarendon, *History of the Rebellion*, 6:180.

34. John Rushworth, *Historical Collections* (1659–1701), 7:958–62. R. W. Ramsey, *Henry Ireton* (1949), pp. 13, 75, 101–19. *The Memoirs of Edward Ludlow* (ed. Firth, 1894), pp. 159–60; *Memoirs of Sir John Berkeley* (1699), pp. 34–35. *Writings and Speeches of Oliver Cromwell* (ed. Abbott, 1937), 1:575; Clarendon, *History of the Rebellion*, 4:281. John Milton, "Eikonoklastes" (1649), in *Collected Prose Works*, 3:356.

35. Karl Kerenyi, *Die Mythologie der Griechen* (1966), 1:164–75; and, generally, his *Prometheus* (1946).

36. Montesquieu, *The Spirit of the Laws* (tr. Nugent, 1966), p. 297. *De l'esprit des loix* (rev. ed., 1757), 2:198; *Oeuvres complètes* (ed. Laboulaye, 1877), 4:318.

37. Hobbes, *Leviathan* (1651; ed. Oakeshott, 1946), pp. 28–30, 220–22. John Bowle, *Hobbes and His Critics* (1951), pp. 90–98, 120, 169, 185.

38. *Eikon Basilike*, pp. 184, 195.

Chapter 9

1. I have tried, on various occasions, to collect contemporary evidence on the varieties of revolutionary personality; see, especially, three topical articles in *Encounter:* "Ulrike Meinhof & the Baader-Meinhof Gang" (June 1975), pp. 9–23; "Revolution Diary" (August 1968), pp. 81–92; and "Lady on the Barricades" (July 1972), pp. 16–31. One brief passage from the latter is relevant here, for it may help to lengthen the historical perspective of the personal viewpoint being elaborated.

> Rebellion is the bitter work of the poor; revolution is a privilege of the middle classes. The rebel comes from the poor, from the workers and the peasants, from the *lumpen* or the déclassé, from the injured and the oppressed. In intolerable times of trial and impatience they proceed to make revolts, overturnings, uprisings, riots, jacqueries, coups and putsches. Their violence is sometimes vindictive and their momentary hope extravagantly high; but, basically, theirs is a practical and authentic struggle for extra rights, liberties, and decencies.
>
> The revolutionary, coming almost always from the well-to-do, is a creature of fantasy. He has the leisure to cultivate his utopian imagination, and he has the educated nimbleness to work out all manner of theory and practice, strategy and tactics, ideology and dogma. He rarely comes to power, for he is never—except in his own fine rhetoric—an authentic Man (or Woman) of the People, and is invariably seen by the people not to be one. The most powerful class struggle in modern political history—say, from Robespierre to Lenin, and Rakosi, and Novotny—has been between the Revolutionary, seizing power in the name of Others and exercising that power with narrow, priestly dogmatism and cruel, vain and selfish bureaucratic self-indulgence . . . and, on the other hand, precisely those Others who feel cheated, betrayed, and often even more oppressed than before. Revolution is the conspiracy of an élite and is, thus, the enemy of genuine popular reform. The revolutionary élite is the only new class that emerges from the blood-letting free and fulfilled. For what is Revolution but the apocalyptic longing to create Paradise at a stroke? When has it ever been the proposal of men of reason and realism? Who can claim that it offers a serious considered reconstruction of a defective social-order? Does it not, rather, appear to be an affliction of the modern mind—a faith in ideal means for ideal ends, a fantasy of the perfect act to inaugurate the perfect society, a fevered dream of a storm and an earthquake that were never seen on land or sea?

2. Thomas Goodwin, *Works* (1683), vol. 2, "An Exposition upon the Revelation", p. 190. *Samuel Hartlib and the Advancement of Learning* (ed. Webster, 1970), pp. 33–34, 92. Hartlib, *England's Thankfulnesse, or An Humble Remembrance presented to the Committee for Religion in the High Court of Parliament* (1642), p. 2; R. F. Young, *Comenius in England: The Visit of Jan Amos Komensky (Comenius) to London in 1641–1642* (1932), pp. 38–39.

3. G. H. Turnbull, *Hartlib, Dury and Comenius: Gleanings from Hartlib's Papers* (1947), pp. 187, 272, 314. John Dury, *Clavis Apocalyptics* (1651), pref. by Hartlib. See also: H. R. Trevor-Roper, "Three Foreigners: The Philosophers of the Puritan Revolution," in *Religion, the Reformation, and Social Change* (1967), pp. 237–93; and H. Dircks, *A Biographical Memoir of Samuel Hartlib* (1865).

4. Comenius, *Opera Didactica Omnia* (1657), chs. xxxi, sec. 15; *The Great Didactic* (tr. Keatinge, 1910), p. 285.

5. Letter of Culpeper to Hartlib, 13 July 1642 and 11 March 1645/6, quoted from the Hartlib Papers in the Sheffield University Library, by Charles Webster in his valuable edition of *Samuel Hartlib and the Advancement of Learning,* pp. 38–41.

6. John Milton, *Of Education: To Master Samuel Hartlib* (1644), in *Works* (ed. Patterson, 1951), 4:275–76.

7. *Hartlib and the Advancement of Learning,* pp. 193–94.

8. Turnbull, *Hartlib, Dury and Comenius,* p. 241 n. Friedrich Althaus, *Samuel Hartlib: Ein deutch-englisches Charakterbild* (1884), p. 262.

9. Letter to Worthington, 3 August 1660, in Turnbull, *Hartlib, Dury and Comenius,* pp. 110–11.

10. Letter of Dury to Hartlib, November 1631, in Turnbull, *Hartlib, Dury and Comenius,* pp. 323–25.

11. Turnbull, *Hartlib, Dury and Comenius,* pp. 136, 331–32.

12. John Dury, *A Motion tending to the Publick Good of this Age* (1642), in *Hartlib and the Advancement of Learning,* pp. 107–9.

13. For a somewhat different interpretation of the achievements of this "utopian international," see Frank Manuel's "Pansophia, a 17th-Century Dream of Science," in his *Freedom from History* (1971), pp. 89–113. But he does emphasize the "shared ideals in a broad spectrum of writers" (among them: Bruno, Campanella, Bacon, Andreae, Leibniz, as well as Comenius, Dury, and Hartlib), and an "essence that is the same in the visions of the men from Moravia, Tübingen, London, Paris, Elbing, Nola, and Calabria . . . bearers of the 17th-century utopia."

14. Johann Valentin Andreae, *Reipublicae Christianopolitanae Descriptio* (1619); *Reise nach der Insul Caphar Salams* (tr. Georgi, 1741); *Christianopolis: An Ideal State of the Seventeenth Century* (1619; tr. Held, 1916). See, generally, a number of useful German biographies and translations: J. P. Glökler, *Johann Valentin Andreä, Ein Lebenshild* (1886); Harald Scholtz, *Evangelischer Utopismus* (1957); *Selbstbiographie* (tr. Seybold, 1799); *Dichtungen zur Beherzigung unsers Zeitalters* (pref. by J. G. Herder, 1786); *Entlarvter APAP (Papa) und Hahnenruf* (ed. Pabst, 1827).

15. What a remarkable figure Andreae was, and how regrettable it is that so little of his work is remembered! To read even the few fragments of his writings that are accessible is to understand how J. G. Herder could carry on so admiringly about "the man who flowered in his century like a rose among thorns [*der Mann, der in seinem Jahrhundert wie eine Rose unter Dornen blühte*] . . . " The dialogue of forty Latin lines which he wrote on the subject of Machiavelli in his *Menippus* constitutes a little gem of concentrated wit and political insight, and is only one of a dozen memorable set pieces which are quite outstanding in the European literature of the day.

In a parable of Judgment Day, written with much charm and aphoristic power, Andreae seems to be reveling (as elsewhere in his *Mythologiae Christianae*) in the new critical independence of his radical humanism. In what almost amounts to a total sociological countdown, he allows all the peoples, classes, and forces of the age to pass under review—from the monarchs of the world (trying to defend themselves with the help of Machiavelli, their attorney) to the poets (led by blind Homer); from the Jews, Christians, heretics, and heathens to the various nations of Europe, Asia, Africa, and America ("groaning over the cruelty of the conquerors"). He is tempted to add the particulars of his own bitter indictment; but, having heard that the day of liberation is approaching (*sed quia imminere audio liberationii nostrae diem*), he is prepared to overlook a few things—the tyranny of the great, the pride of the aristocracy, the ruthlessness of the troops, the hypocrisy of the priests, the murderousness of the doctors, the swindles of the philosophers, the incompetence of the artists, the affectation of the poets, the fables of the historians, the trash of the booksellers, the sycophancy of the politicians, and—if this were not enough to send a utopian dashing off on a fanciful voyage—the transformation of

Asia, the degeneracy of Europe, the distress of Africa, the foolishness of America (& *Asiae metamorphosin, & Europae libidinem, & Africae dolos, & Americae stuporem*) . . .

In another political parable, presented as a narrative of the year 2040, Andreae relates the following. One knows that our era explored that which was sought in previous centuries with so much vain expense of men and treasure. The lands of the North and South Poles have been discovered. From the reports of our Columbus it is well known what barbarism reigned 'there. Religion, morality, politics, all were different from ours. Europe had the greatest sympathy for the unhappy plight of so many millions. All the aids of culture and civilization were rushed to them and they were taught their usages. The more powerful elements in the nations soon made the most encouraging signs of progress toward enlightenment. The best evidence for this was their behavior toward the people, whom they previously had served as selected leaders; now they became their tyrannical despots. Everything was at their whim: to believe or to obey, to eat or to hunger, to live or to die. Resistance to them became all the more difficult the later one realized that it had become necessary. The power of the people had long become extremely weakened. But effort and intelligence raised them up again. They finally took to battle against their oppressors and were victorious. The yoke had been broken, and the people were free again as once they were. Now they wanted to thank the teachers of their old rulers. So it was that they sent a painting across to Europe, and it portrayed the following scenes: a wolf taking the sheep to pasture; a fox preaching to the geese; a stork leading the frogs; a cat judging between two mice; a hound guiding the hares. Its title read: CIVILIZATION.

See: Johann Valentin Andreae, *Dichtungen zur Beherzigung unsers Zeitalters*, pp. iii, 97–99, 179–80. *Mythologiae Christianae* (1619), pp. 102–3. *Menippus, sive dialogorum, satyricorum centuria* . . . (1673), pp. 13–14.

16. Andreae, *Mythologiae Christianae*, p. 10. *Menippus, sive dialogorum satyricorum centuria*, pp. 125–26. I am grateful to Dr. Jennifer Hall (of the Classics Dept., Westfield College, University of London) for sending me her annotated translations of these Latin passages. One should also note that much in Andreae's work was inspired by Campanella's *Civitas solis*, which had in fact been circulated in manuscript form and then published by Andreae's friend Tobias Adami in 1623. Webster, *Hartlib and the Advancement of Learning*, p. 30 n.

17. Andreae, *Christianopolis*, pp. 138–39, 185.

18. Andreae, *Christianopolis*, pp. 133–34.

19. Samuel Hartlib, *A Description of the Famous Kingdome of Macaria* (1641); also reprinted several times in the *Harleian Miscellany* (1744), 1:564–69; (1808), 1:580–5. John Milton, "Of Education: to Master Samuel Hartlib" (1644), in *Works* (1931), 4:275–76.

20. "Macaria," from *makarios*, blessed or happy. Thomas More describes the "Macarians" in his *Utopia* as neighbors of the Utopians.

The problem of the authorship of *Macaria* has recently been raised by Charles Webster after further investigation of the voluminous Hartlib papers in the Sheffield University library. He now believes that it was basically drafted by a young Hartlib protégé, Gabriel Plattes (he died a few years later, in 1644). Although, as he feels, "there is no reason to doubt this authorship of the utopian tract previously ascribed to Hartlib," Webster goes on to conclude: "Hartlib's precise part in the composition of *Macaria* must remain conjectural, but it is almost certain that he was active at some stage. Plattes confessed to having little education. This impression is supported by his writings, which indicate unfamiliarity with classical languages. It is also probable that he would have been ignorant of the extensive continental utopian literature. Consequently Hartlib may have played a more than usually active part in framing the text." See "The Authorship and Significance of *Macaria*," *Past & Present*, no. 56 (1972), pp. 34–48; also another paper, which he was kind enough to send me, Charles Webster, "Marcaria: Samuel Hartlib and the Great Reformation," *Acta Comeniana* (Prague, 1970), xxvi, pp. 147–64.

21. *Correspondence of Hartlib ... with Governor [John] Winthrop of Connecticut, 1661–1672* (ed. Winthrop, 1878), pp. 4, 12–13.

22. John Norris, "A Discourse concerning Heavenly-Mindedness," in *Practical Discourses* (1691), pp. 176–78.

23. *The Works of Joseph Mede* (ed. Worthington, 1672), p. 880.

24. On the whole question of the politics of the millennium, see: *Millennial Dreams in Action: Essays in Comparative History* (ed. Thrupp, 1962); and Wilhelm E. Mühlmann, *Chiliasmus und Nativismus: Studien zur Psychologie, Soziologie und historischen Kasuistik der Umsturzbewegungen* (1964).

25. G. H. Turnbull, "John Hall's Letters to Samuel Hartlib," in *Review of English Studies* (July 1953), 4:232.

26. Samuel Hartlib, *Considerations tending to the Happy Accomplishment of Englands Reformation in Church and State, Humbly presented to the Piety and Wisdome of the High and Honourable Court of Parliament* (1647), preface.

27. *Some Proposalls towards the Advancement of Learning* (MS., 1653), in *Hartlib and the Advancement of Learning*, pp. 188–90.

28. Samuel Hartlib, *A Discoverie ... with a Philosophical Query concerning the Cause of Fruitfulness* (1653); *His Legacie* (1651–53); *A Design for Plentie* (1652); *Cornu Copia* (1652).

29. John Dury, *The Reformed School* (1651), p. 1. *Hartlib and the Advancement of Learning*, p. 57.

30. Hartlib, *Considerations*, pp. 41, 45, 59.

31. The parliamentary distinction is recorded in Hartlib's preface to *Clavis Apocalyptica: or a Prophetical Key* (1651).

32. *Hartlib and the Advancement of Learning*, pp. 105, 152, 160, 169.

33. Turnbull, *Hartlib, Dury, Comenius*, p. 68. The Petty letter is in G. H. Turnbull, "Samuel Hartlib's Influence on the Early History of the Royal Society," *Notes and Records of the Royal Society of London* (1933), 10: pp. 120–21.

34. Thomas Sprat, *The History of the Royal-Society* (1667), pp. 437–38.

35. Robert Boyle, *Works* (ed. Birch, 1772), 6:xxxiv.

36. Hartlib busied himself, not with complete success, in making arrangements for the English translations of both Campanella and Andreae. The poet John Hall managed to submit to Hartlib only two smaller related works of Andreae: *Christianae Societatis Imago* and *Christiani Amoris Dextera Porrecta* (1620). These were printed and "dedicated to Mr. S. Hartlib" as *Model of Christian Society* (1647) and *The Right Hand of Christian Love*, in John Hall's *Of the Advantageous Reading of History* (1657). An English translation of Andreae's "utopia" had to wait centuries, until F. E. Held's edition of 1916 (the edition I have been citing).

A recent scholar doubts whether Comenius knew Bacon's *New Atlantis* but records that when Campanella's *Civitas Solis* was published in 1623 Comenius read it with "incredible delight." See John Edward Sadler, *J. A. Comenius and the Concept of Universal Education* (1966), p. 71.

In any event, as Sadler summarizes his views (using perhaps a little too much of the vocabulary of modern sociology and current Czech commentary), Comenius occupied himself with speculation and plans for a Utopian society which he associated with the prospect of "a complete change in social structure." As an ardent chiliast and mystical millenarian, it was his hope that "there would be a sudden and dramatic change in the human situation which would immediately solve all the political, social and economic problems.... There were, indeed, times when Comenius' belief in the millennium or, at least, his acceptance of prophecies about it, caused him to engage in political intrigue or to raise false hopes in his friends." Sadler suggests that it was John Valentine Andreae's allegory of a city of God ("Christianopolis") which became for Comenius "a blue-print of the Utopian society"; it was to be a bridge between what he had called "the Labyrinth of the World and the Paradise of the Heart." Or as he put it (soberly, politically, without benefit of mystical metaphor), what had to be found was a philosophy ("Pansophy") through which "men, seeing in a clear light the ends of all things, and the means to those ends, and the correct use of those means, might be able to direct all that they have to good ends" (*Via Lucis*). His was an "insuperable optimism concerning human affairs": human corruption was only superficial. As Comenius once remarked, when troubles had so greatly increased as to give reason to some to abandon the cause—"Far from it! While the disease continues, measures for cure must continue. We must redouble our labours and vary our processes . . . ." If only the case for Universal Reform could be put clearly enough "nobody who had a healthy reason could refuse it" until "nothing would remain without reform . . . " (*Panorthosia*).

It should not be surprising that Czechoslovak socialists and communists, in the dramatic and desperate reformist period of 1968, should have turned to Comenius. His basic political categories belonged to what I have called the elementary forms of the ideological life, and they have (as I have been arguing throughout) a pattern of persistence and recurrence. Thus, three hundred years after Comenius published his *Via Lucis* ("The Way of Light"), the Czechoslovak Academy found this uncannily appropriate text to quote on a poignant New Year's card dispatched to thousands in East and West, following the post-Soviet-invasion course of events.

> The more powerful people then betook themselves to another method of assuaging the strife of men: they sought by attacking whole nations and subduing and reducing them to subjection, to establish whether in the state or in the realm of religion a single order or rule which should embrace them all; but always, as unvarying experience proves, rather with the effect of making things worse than with any good result. For there is inborn in human nature a love of liberty—for liberty man's mind is convinced that it was made—and this love can by no means be driven out: so that, wherever and by whatever means it feels that it is being hemmed in and impeded, it cannot but seek a way out and declare its own liberty. Inevitably resistance, opposition, rebellion follow whenever force becomes an element in the government of men [*The Guardian*, London, 7 January 1969, p. 9].

37. Boyle, *Works*, 6:xxxix, xl.

38. For somewhat differing historical accounts, see two articles in *Notes and Records of the Royal Society of London*: R. H. Syfret, "The Origins of the Royal Society" (1948), 5:75–137; and G. H. Trumbull, "Samuel Hartlib's Influence on the Early History of the Royal Society" (1933), 10:101–30. See also *The Royal Society, Its Origins and Founders* (ed. Hartley, 1960). For the more general background (and, especially, the French influence on English initiatives), see: Martha Ornstein, *The Role of Scientific Societies in the Seventeenth Century* (1938), and Harcourt Brown, *Scientific Organizations in Seventeenth Century France* (1934).

39. *Hartlib and the Advancement of Learning*, pp. 21, 58.

40. Boyle, *Works*, 6:xlvi, lxxxi, 77, 131–32.

Chapter 10

1. Thomas Sprat, *History of the Royal-Society of London* (1667), pp. 60–81, 397.

In his *Scepsis Scientifica* (1665), Joseph Glanville noted that Francis Bacon's "Salomon's House in the *New Atlantis* was a Prophetick Scheam of the Royal Society," and in his *Plus Ultra* (1668) he remarked: " . . . the Great Man desired, and form'd a *Society* of Experimenters in a Romantick Modell; but could do no more: His time was not ripe . . . " See the valuable annotations in the modern reprint of Sprat (ed. Cope and Jones, 1959).

2. Sprat, *History of the Royal-Society*, pp. 29, 124, 382–84.

3. The essential form for the "mingling of Tempers," of the impetuous and the judicious, would be "*joyning* them into *Committees*." This is of some special interest, for Sprat is obliged to add: "if we may use that work in a Philosophical sense, and so in some measure

purge it from the ill sound, which it formerly had . . . " He was probably referring to its role in the recent parliamentary challenge to the monarchy, in which the word had subversive associations. Cromwell was known as "the chief Committee man," and one contemporary records that the word was even associated with a personal rebel style: "They mostly had short hair, which at the time was commonly called the Committee cut." Sprat, *History of the Royal-Society*, p. 85. *Oxford English Dictionary* (1933), 2:684–85.

4. Sprat, *History of the Royal Society* (Cope and Jones ed.), p. xxxii.

5. Sprat, *History of the Royal-Society*, pp. 331–34, 407.

6. Sprat, pp. 364–71.

7. Sprat, p. 152.

8. Pierre Bayle, *Dictionnaire historique et critique* (1697; rev. ed., 1740), 3:204; *A General Dictionary, Historical and Critical* (1738), 6:569–70.

9. The psychological complications of this extraordinary man's intellectual history still await a satisfactory analysis. The best that one modern biographer can offer on these aspects of Comenius's apocalyptic political mysticism is that they constitute "a phase of his life which bears a convincing testimony to the truth that even the wisest of men are subject to occasional aberrations." This kind of nonexplanation will not do, not merely because of its banality but also because the sources of the wisdom and the aberration were often common ones. Liberal and humane modern historians, like their rationalistic enlightened predecessors, find themselves in the grip of a curious spiritual paralysis when confronted with the contradictions of ideal and noble aspirations in impassioned politics.

Some small improvements can, however, be registered. Older commentators like Corrodi and Amelung were altogether one-sided in their utter outrage at Comenius's departures from the simple precepts of the *Aufklärung*. In his "History of Human Folly," J. C. Amelung gave Comenius a prominent place among the ranks of magicians, alchemists, and soothsayers—"a truly humiliating position for the father of modern education," as one professor of modern education has justly remarked. Corrodi at least found it surprising that a European, who was otherwise as serviceable and upright as Comenius should have been carried away by such *Schwärmerey* that he allowed himself to speak on behalf of patent lies and the prospect of hideous violence and atrocious wars. *"Diese Verblendung,"* according to his stern judgment, *"lässt sich beynahe mit mit gar nichts entschuldigen."* On the other hand, a late nineteenth-century scholarly biography (Kvacsala's, in German) exercises so much objective academic restraint on this much argued point as to be completely noncommittal.

One looks forward with some curiosity to new turns of contemporary attitudinizing (although they are hardly likely to be more than variations on these themes) as the great new Prague edition of Comenius's works progresses. Older Czech liberals, for all their pieties of patriotism and cultural pride, could not look away from what was for them the distasteful spectacle of a noble humanist's "mystical belief in the millennium." As Jakubec remarks in his essay on Comenius (which has the placet of a foreword by Thomas G. Masaryk, then President of the Republic), "that belief may be described as the mental disease of the age . . . " Marxian formalists of a later Prague regime took a necessarily different view of Comenius's defense of the apocalyptic prophets, and with just a little dialectical canniness even established its progressiveness—for "he wanted to use them as weapons which might change the course of the world for the better." Here once again, we have a familiar duel of metaphors wherein one man's debility is another man's strength.

See: Mathew Spinka, *John Amos Comenius: The Incomparable Moravian* (1944), p. 139. Comenius, *The Great Didactic* (ed. Keatinge, 1910), p. 100. J. C. Amelung, *Geschichte der menschliche Narrheit, oder Lebenschreibungen berühmter Schwarzkünstler, Goldmacher, Teufelsbanner, Zeichen- und Liniendeuter, Schwärmer, Wahrsager, und anderer philosophischen Unholden* (1785). H. H. Corrodi, *Kritische Geschichte des Chiliasmus* (1781), 2, pt. 3:109–10. Johann Kvacsala, *Comenius, Sein Leben und Seine Schriften* (1892), p. 477. Jan Jakubec, *Johanes*

Amos Comenius (1928), p. 57. Frantisek Kozik, *The Sorrowful and Heroic Life of John Amos Comenius* (1958), p. 163.

I trust that my own emphasis on the "darker" Comenius has nothing in common with the *idées fixes* of these antiquated intellectual traditions; we are just beginning to understand a little more about the phenomenon of the apocalyptic temperament in politics and the vagaries of revolutionary reason and utopian passion. It may, therefore, be useful for the reader to be reminded, at least in this belated place, of the "lighter" Comenius: the gentle and tender-minded reformer, the magnificent humanist. The following passages are taken from the edition of *Selections* (1957), published by UNESCO and introduced by Jean Piaget (pp. 157, 167, 170).

> Consider by what means peace and tranquility could be preserved through out all human society without the use of violent means, as far as possible; without prisons, swords, nooses, gallows, etc.
>
> Teach and force all men to live together in a humane fashion, and that rather by preventing than by punishing offences, troubles and damage done ... Teach and admonish the people not to lower their human dignity by starting hatred and litigation for material things. For it is fitting for man to act according to reason, or if a matter of doubt arises, to try and judge, but not to act in passion or in anger, with force or arms; that is akin to the animals and cannot be tolerated any longer ...
>
> The saying of Cicero is admirable: "It is unworthy of the dignity of a wise man to believe what is false or to defend without hesitation anything accepted without due investigation ... "

Finally (and more pertinently than Comenius could ever have known),

> Publishers must be requested and urged not to multiply pages, but wisdom; not taking as their goal the lucre of money bags, but the enlightening of minds; that they may be true ministers of the light and not slaves of Pluto, creators of darkness and confusion.

10. H. H. Corrodi, *Kritische Geschichte des Chiliasmus* (1781), 2, pt. 3:79–118. A noted nineteenth-century Czech historian, mixing national pride with embarrassed liberal sensitivities, confessed that he could record Comenius's "fatal credulity which induced him to study the 'prophecies' of Kotterus, Poniatovia and Drabik" (those "fatal influences on the mind of Komensky [Comenius], always inclined to mysticism") only with a feeling of "pity and shame." Count von Lutzow, *Bohemia, an Historical Sketch* (1896), p. 396, and *A History of Bohemian Literature* (1899), pp. 250–72; see also the Note in his edition of Comenius, *The Labyrinth of the World and the Paradise of the Heart* (1623; tr. Lutzow, 1901), pp. 265–306.

11. My quotations are taken from a contemporary English summary of *Lux in tenebris*, of which the full title is: *A Generall Table of Europe, Representing the Present and Future State thereof: viz. the Present Governments, Languages, Religions, Foundations, and Revolutions, both of Governments and Religions, the Future Mutations, Revolutions, Government, and Religion of Christendom and of the World, &c. From the Prophecies of the three late German Prophets, Kotterus, Christian, and Drabicius, all Collected out of the Originals, for the Common Use and Information of the English* (1670).

12. *A Generall Table of Europe*, pp. 184, 193, 204.

13. *A Generall Table of Europe*, pp. 211–12, 220.

14. R. F. Young, *Comenius in England: The Visit of Jan Amos Komensky (Comenius) to London in 1641–1642* (1932), p. 44.

15. *A Generall Table of Europe*, pp. 224, 233.

16. *A Generall Table of Europe*, pp. 220–38: "Believe it ... nothing like to this Book, has the World had since the Apostles times ... I say, That here is the Revelation of Saint John, which hath distracted so many Commentators, differing among themselves ... Therefore this Book is a new commentary upon the old Revelations of St. John ... "

17. *A Generall Table of Europe*, pp. 108, 160, and Appendix, p. 1.

18. For students interested in the fascinating aftermath of "when prophecy fails,"

Crossley mentions several aspects of Drabicius's career that are worth noting (*Diary and Correspondence of Dr. John Worthington* (1847):

1. He continued his predictions from 1638 to 1666, "altering the period fixed for their accomplishment from one year to another, with the usual unblushing effrontery of his tribe."

2. "The worst still remains to be said—after all his invectives and predictions against the Roman Catholic Church, he ultimately embraced it!" (The maneuver failed to alleviate his plight.)

3. "To crown all, the unhappy prophet himself, who had predicted that he should die peaceably in his bed, with all manner of comfort, fell into the hands of the furious imperialists, who brought him to trial and sentenced him to death, as a rebel and disturber of the public peace in 1671 . . . . His execution was by decapitation, his right hand being first severed from his body, and his tongue afterwards cut out."

A copy of Comenius's book *Lux in tenebris* was burned in the flames which reduced Drabicius's body to ashes. Centuries later, historical memories were still apparently fresh and still fanning European enmities. In 1892, the schools in Bohemia were forbidden by the Austrians to celebrate the tercentenary of Comenius's birth; the order came from Emperor Franz Josef, who had been shown a copy of Comenius's book with its offending passages underscored.

See: *Diary and Correspondence of Worthington*, pp. 357–60. Spinka, *Comenius*, pp. 139–40. *Locke's Travels in France 1675–1679* (ed. Lough, 1953), p. 190.

John Locke was evidently interested in Drabicius; and in Paris, in April 1678, he wrote a paragraph in his journal noting Comenius's book and summarizing some of the political prophecies. Apparently, he had been given (and a copy of it is in the Lovelace Collection of Locke's papers) a thirteen-and-a-half page letter in French, addressed to Louis XIV, appealing to him to direct French policy in accordance with Drabicius's predictions.

19. *The Prophecies of Christopher Kotterus, Christiana Poniatovia, Nicholas Drabicius, foretelling, many years ago, the present Invasion of the Turks into the Empire of Germany, and the events that will ensue; as, also, predictions concerning the Pope and the King of France, with the sudden destruction of the papal power, and the miraculous conversion of the Turks, &c.; presaging also, the uniting of all Religions into one visible Church* . . . (tr. Codrington, 1664), p. 108.

20. Richard Ward, *The Life of the Learned and Pious Dr. Henry More* (1710; ed. Howard, 1911), p. 111.

21. Paul Hazard, *La Crise de la conscience européenne* (1935), 1:133; *The European Mind, 1680–1715* (tr. May, 1953), p. 100. Bayle to Minutoli, 27 February 1673: "Je vois bien que mon insatiabilité de nouvelles est une de ces maladies opiniâtres contre lesquelles tous les remèdes blanchissent; c'est une hydropsie toute pure; plus on lui fournit, plus elle demande."

22. Hazard, *La Crise*, p. 144: "Le même principe qui sert quelquefois contre le mensonge rend quelquefois de mauvais offices à la verité . . . . En un mot, le sort de l'homme est dans une si mauvaise situation que les lumieres que le délivrent d'un mal le précipitent dans un autre." The English edition (p. 108) has jumbled these texts; see "Takkidin," in Bayle, *Dictionnaire*, 4:2688.

23. Hazard, *La Crise*, p. 142; *European Mind*, p. 107. Bayle, *Dictionnaire* 4:398:

Il n'y a point de mensonge, pour si absurde qu'il soit, qui ne passe de livre en livre et de siècle en siècle. *Mentez hardiment, imprimez toutes sortes d'extravagances,* peut-on dire au plus misérable lardoniste de l'Europe, *vous trouverez assez de gens qui copieront vos contes, et, si l'on vous rebute dans un certain temps, il naîtra des conjonctures où l'on aura intérêt de vous faire ressusciter.*

24. Ernst Cassirer, *The Philosophy of the Enlightenment* (tr. Koelln and Pettegrove, 1951), pp. 206–9. *General Dictionary*, 5:531. *Dictionnaire*, 4:486: "Si on lui démande, D'où êtes-vous? il faut qu'il répond, je ne suis ni Francais, ni Allemand, ni Anglois, ni Espagnol, &c.,

je suis habitant du monde ... seulement au service de la Verité; c'est ma seule Reine, je n'ai prêté qu'elle le serment d'obeïssance."

25. Bayle, *Dictionnaire* (5th ed., 1740), 2:202–5, 306–9; 3:20–22. *A General Dictionary, Historical and Critical* (tr. 1736), 4:418–20, 644–48; 6:567–72. The subsequent quotations from these three articles on Kotterus, Drabicius, and Comenius, in French and English, are taken from the pages listed. See, generally, Howard Robinson, *Bayle the Sceptic* (1931); L. P. Courtines, *Bayle's Relations with England* (1938), and his "Notes on the Dissemination of Bayle's Thought in Europe," *Revue de littérature comparée* (1937), 68:700–5; Daniel Mornet, *La Penseé franqise au dix-huitième siècle* (1926).

26. The passage is cited by Dorothy Waley Singer in her eloquent contribution for the wartime anti-Hitler tribute to Comenius: *The Teacher of Nations* (ed. Needham, 1942), p. 73.

27. The seventeenth-century discussion of prophecy and prophets was, needless to say, an argument within a religious context; but the forms and categories of theological dispute have more in common with subsequent secular phenomena than modern historians (reacting against Carl Becker's brilliant thesis in his *Heavenly City of the 18th-Century Philosophers*, 1932) are usually willing to concede. As I have been suggesting, it is impossible to comprehend the rise of utopian revolutionism in what might be called the secular city of the seventeenth-century theologues without recognizing the shared constituent elements which characterize both early and late versions of the modern European debate on the nature and destiny of man in society.

Thus, Hobbes sensed as percipiently as any latter-day student of *futuribles*, the problem of, say, self-fulfilling prophecies. I refer the futurologists to the following passage from *Behemoth: or an Epitome of the Civil Wars of England from 1640 to 1660* (1679), p. 197:

> B. I understand now how the Dreams and Prognostications of madmen (for such I take to be all those that foretel future contingencies) can be of any great disadvantage to the Common-Wealth.
> A. Yes, yet: know there is nothing that renders Humans Councils difficult, but the uncertainty of future time, nor that so well directs men in their deliberations, as the fore-sight of the sequels of their Actions. Prophesie being many times the principal Cause of the Even foretold.

28. Bayle, *General Dictionary*, 3:469. This passage occurs in the article on Hobbes, and is included, along with the entries on Molière, Spinoza, and others, in a brief volume of excerpts, *Selections from Bayle's Dictionary* (ed. Beller and Lee, 1952). *Dictionnaire* (ed. 1820), 8:164:

> Qu'on fasse ce qu'on voudra, qu'on bâtisse des systèmes meilleurs que la République de Platon, que l'Utopie de Morus, que la République du soleil de Campanella etc.: toutes ces belles idées se trouveraient courtes et défecteuses, dès qu'on les voudroit réduire en pratique. Les passions des hommes, qui naissent les unes des autres dans une variété prodigieuse, réuineraient bientôt les espérances qu'on aurait conçues de ces beaux systèmes ...

29. Robinson, *Bayle the Sceptic*, pp. 177–78. *General Dictionary*, 5:74. *Dictionnaire* (ed. 1820), 6:214–15:

> Mais ce fut en vain qu'il éspéra de se tenir sur le rivage, spectateur tranquil des émotions de cette mer. Il se trouva plus exposé à l'orage que s'il eût été sur l'une des flottes. C'est là le destin inévitable de ceux qui veulent garder la neutralité pendant les guerres civiles, soit d'état, soit de religion. Ils sont exposés à l'insulte des deux partis tout à la fois; ils se font des ennemis sans se faire des amis au lieu qu'en épousant avec chaleur l'une des deux causes, ils auraient eu des amis et des ennemis. Sort déplorable de l'homme, vanité manifeste de la raison philosophique! Elle nous fait regarder la tranquillité de l'âme et le calme des passions comme le but de tous nos travaux, et le fruit le plus précieux de nos plus pénibles méditations; et cependant l'expérience fait voir que, selon le monde il n'est point de condition plus disgraciée que celle des âmes qui ne veulent point s'abandonner aux flots des factions; ni de conditions moins incommode que celle des hommes qui hurlent avec

les loups, et qui suivent le torrent des passions les plus agitées. Ils ont entre autres avantages celui de ne pas connaître qui'ils ont tort; car il n'y a point de gens plus incapable de connaître les défauts de leur faction, et le bien qui se peut trouver dans l'autre parti, que ceux qui sont transportés d'un zèle ardent et d'une vive colère, et sous les liens d'une forte préoccupation. . . . ils sont misérable: ils ne veulent point être marteau, et cela fait que continuellement ils sont enclume à droite et à gauche.

This article on Eppendorf, a German Reformation figure, is also included in another recent edition of translated selections: Bayle, *Historical and Critical Dictionary* (ed. Popkin, 1965), pp. 75–77.

30. I follow here the eighteenth-century English text, *General Dictionary*, p. 74; Tully was, of course, the then-common Anglicization of Marcus Tullius Cicero. I have corrected the Latin; cf. the Loeb Classical Library edition of Cicero's *Letters to Atticus* (tr. Winstedt, 1913), 8.7.120–21: "Yes, I have a foe to flee from, but no friend to follow."

31. Robinson, *Bayle the Sceptic*, p. 179. *General Dictionary*, 1:63, 623. *Dictionnaire*, 1:22, 184: "Non . . . le monde est trop indisciplinable pour profiter des maladies des Siècles passez. Chaque Siècle se comporte comme s'il étoit le premier venu. . . . Le pis est qu'on ne profite pas due passé: chaque génération fournit les memes symptômes."

32. *Diary and Correspondence of Dr. John Worthington*, 1:357–59.

33. Robert Boyle, *Works* (ed. Birch, 1772), 5:397.

34. John Hall, *A True Account and Character of the Times, Historically and Politically Drawn* (1647), pp. 1–8.

35. There is another aspect to the complex of science, religion, and ideology, and the way in which certain psychological factors intermingled in these wars of the temperament. Professor Frank Manuel makes the point boldly in his description of "Newton as Autocrat of Science," in his *Freedom from History* (1971), p. 184.

In order to secure itself, the science of Isaac Newton used certain of the mechanisms of a conquering new religion or political ideology. It triumphed, a truth in its day, but it seems to have availed itself of the same apparatus as any other kind of movement. Followers were assembled and bound to an apotheosized leader with ties of great strength. An internal institutional structure was fortified. The word was propagated by chosen disciples. Since the doctrine was rooted in a national society, its relations with the government gave it special privileges and emoluments. It became the second spiritual establishment of the realm, and at least in its origins presented no threat to the primary religious establishment that it was destined to undermine and, perhaps, ultimately to replace. As in many militant doctrinal movements, the truth was not allowed to fend for itself, and on occasion the sacred lie and the pious fraud became means to a higher end.

36. Sprat, *History of the Royal-Society*, pp. 321–22, 328–29.

37. Boyle, *Works*, 6:xxxix, xl.

38. The letters of Hartlib to John Pell are included in *The Protectorate of Oliver Cromwell* (ed. Vaughan, 1838), 2:442, 11 February 1658.

39. Boyle, *Works*, 6:127–28.

40. *Samuel Hartlib and the Advancement of Learning* (ed. Webster, 1970), pp. 61–64.

41. John Sadler, *Olbia, the new island lately discovered; with its religion and rites of worship; laws, customs and government; characters and language; with education of their children in their sciences, arts, and manufactures; with other things remarkable . . . For Samuel Hartlib . . .* (1660).

42. *Diary and Correspondence of Worthington*, 1:251–53.

43. John Sadler's *Olbia* has been called "one of the strangest of strange books." The author, who was a friend of Hartlib, had an interesting career, which included being Town Clerk of London, Master of Magdalene College in Cambridge, and a Member of Parliament who was looked on with favor by Cromwell.

44. My Goethean emphasis (from *Kennst du das Land wo die Zitronen blühn*) is deliberate. The poet Waller had taken refuge in the Bermudas during the Civil War and celebrated its beauties in his "Battell of the Summer Islands" (*Poems* [ed. Dury, 1893]):

Bermuda, wall'd with rocks,—who does not know
That happy island where huge lemons grow . . .

It was, of course, also to Bermuda that the philosopher Berkeley wanted to set westward sail in 1728 in order to realize his dream of establishing an ideal college (G. J. Warnock, *Berkeley* [1969], pp. 216–18).

45. *Diary and Correspondence of Worthington*, 194–95, 211–14. I have consulted a transcript of these Hartlib-Worthington letters in the British Museum, Add. MS. 32,498.

46. Culpeper to Hartlib (1646), "To the Kings most Excellent Majesty. The Humble Petition of Samuel Hartlib Senior" (1660), in *Hartlib and the Advancement of Learning*, pp. 5–6, 44.

47. *Diary and Correspondence of Worthington*, 238–46, 372–73.

48. *Correspondence of Hartlib . . . with Governor [John] Winthrop of Connecticut, 1661–1672* (ed. Winthrop, 1878), pp. 10–12.

49. *Diary and Correspondence of Worthington*, 1:342.

50. *The Diary of John Evelyn* (ed. de Beer, 1955), 3:162–63. Letters between Evelyn and Hartlib are in the British Museum, Add. MS. 15,948.

51. Superficial economic interpreters of history have been tempted on occasions to seize upon such mid-seventeenth century references as some kind of semantic evidence for the narrowly "bourgeois" character of the so-called Puritan Revolution. A more careful attention to contextual meanings might well disabuse them of this habit. When Thomas Sprat wrote in 1667, "The first thing that ought to be improved in the *English Nation*, is their *Industry* . . . , " he was not referring primarily to economic activity and certainly not referring to anything which corresponds to our notion of factory enterprise. Like Hartlib, Sprat was concerned with the development of personal habits of diligence and a social ethos of effort and improvement.

"If our *Labourers* had been as diligent as our *Law-givers* [Sprat writes in his *History of the Royal-Society* (pp. 421–23)] we had prov'd the most laborious Nation under *Heaven*. But the true Method of increasing *Industry*, is by that Course which the *Royal Society* has begun in Philosophy, by *Works* and *Endeavors*, not by the prescriptions of *Words*, or *Paper Commands*.

What tempted such prophets of industry was not the mean motives of personal and class aggrandizement but, rather, the elimination of idleness, infirmity, vagabondage, and general poverty and unemployment. "Industry" represented the transcendence of laziness (Holland was the attractive example). "The true Concernment of England," Sprat argued, was to "advance its Industry in peaceful *Arts;* to increase its People; to improve its Manufactures . . . " etc. He recommended "true Labours and industrious Virtue" and held out the hope of a people "rouzing themselves from Lethargy . . . by Action, by Trials, by Working." Diligence would then become at once a necessity and a pleasure. This may well be what Max Weber called in his famous book "the Protestant Ethic," although there have been many workaday societies that are non-Protestant and indeed non-Christian. It is what R. H. Tawney, in his own sequel to Weber, thought of as "the spirit of capitalism," but only if we take it in the largest possible sense of the working spirit of any capital-creating community (whether bourgeois, or Bolshevik, or Buddhist for that matter).

The changing pattern of meanings can be easily traced in the various references given in the *O.E.D.*, 5:236–37. The older Shakespearean context (as in *Cymbeline*, 3.6.31: "The sweat of industry would dry . . . ") is still relevant, even for the usages of Adam Smith in the *Wealth of Nations* ("The funds destined for the maintenance of industry . . . "), especially if we recall that so-called Colleges of Industry in the seventeenth century were workhouses for the teaching of various useful occupations (as in Bellers' book of 1696, *Proposals for raising a College of Industry for all useful Trades and Husbandry*). The world moves to its modern connotation of factory technology in the nineteenth century in such references as "The rights and properties of our national industries" (Disraeli, *Coningsby*), and "The

Leaders of Industry are virtually the Captains of the World ... " (Carlyle, *Past and Present*).

For the French influence I have referred to, see *The New World of Henri Saint-Simon* (1956), where Professor Frank Manuel writes (p. 189): "There were controversies over who actually coined the nouns *industriel* and *industrialisme*, neologisms which Saint-Simon thought he had invented, problems in historical semantics which cannot be resolved with absolute certainty and which have limited significance ... "

In any event, nothing is gained by making historical words mean anything but what they were intended to mean. At least when Humpty-Dumpty insisted on his own "master meanings," he reassured Alice: "When I make a word do a lot of work like that, I always pay it extra."

52. Samuel Hartlib, *The Reformed Common-Wealth of Bees* (1655). Charles Butler, *The Feminine Monarchy, or the History of the Bees* (1634).

53. Spinka, *Comenius*, p. 127.

54. James Harrington, *Oceana* (1656; ed. Liljegren, 1924), pp. 11, 234. The "slotheful, depopulated" Irish island was also suggested by Harrington as a place of refuge and return for Jewish exiles, expelled from England since the time of King Edward I centuries before.

55. H. Dircks, *A Biographical Memoir of Samuel Hartlib* (1865), p. 000.

56. Hartlib, who was always interested in library reform, was tempted by an Oxford offer of the post as Bodley's librarian. But his friends beseeched him not to accept, not to be "buried in Oxforde"; for any move from London "takes you from that stage which is most proper for that publique trade of ingenuity, which you desire to put into motion" (Letter in Hartlib Papers, *Hartlib and the Advancement of Learning*, p. 205).

57. Boyle, *Works*, 1:xi, xlvi.

Chapter 11

1. A. S. P. Woodhouse, *Puritanism and Liberty* (1938), p. 27; Arthur E. Barker, *Milton and the Puritan Dilemma* (1942), p. 151. *The Clarke Papers* (ed. Firth, 1891; repr. 1965), 1:264.

2. Barker, *Milton*, p. 142.

3. *The Censure of the Rota upon Mr. Milton's Book Entitled the Ready and Easy Way to Establish a Free Commonwealth* (1660), repr. in *Harleian Miscellany* (ed. Park, 1809), 4:188–95.

4. *The Poems of John Milton* (ed. Carey and Fowler, 1968), pp. 312, 323 (the last three quoted lines are Milton's translation from Seneca).

5. Milton, *Complete Prose Works* (ed. Hughes, 1962), 2:526; 1:296.

6. Milton, *Digression* (1671) to the *History of Britain* in *Complete Prose Works* (ed. Fogle, 1971), 5, pt. 1:444–45.

7. *Defensio Secunda* (1654), in *Complete Prose Works* (tr. North, ed. Wolfe and Roberts, 1966), 4:548–49. *Eikonoklastes* (1649), *Complete Prose Works* (ed. Hughes, 1962), 3:584. *First Defence* (1651), in *Works* (ed. Patterson, 1931), 7:83, 199.

8. *Poems* (ed. Carey and Fowler), p. 327.

9. *Digression, History of Britain,* in *Works*, 10:324; *Complete Prose Works*, 5, p. 1:448–9.

10. *Paradise Regained* (1671), Bk. 1; ll. 434–47, in *Poems*, p. 1094.

11. *Eikonoklastes* (1649–50), in *Complete Prose Works* (ed. Hughes), 3:558. All my quotations are from this Yale University Press edition. (I have modernized some of the spelling and punctuation.)

12. Crane Brinton, *The Anatomy of Revolution* (1938), p. 116. See also Merritt Y. Hughes, "Milton as a Revolutionary," in *Ten Perspectives on Milton* (1965), pp. 240–75.

13. John Milton, *Eikonoklastes* (1649), in *Complete Prose Works*, p. 434.

14. "And he gathered them together into a place called in the Hebrew tongue Armageddon ... And there were voices, and thunders, and lightnings; and there was a great

earthquake, such as was not since men were upon the earth, so mighty an earthquake, and so great" (Rev. 16:16, 18). See: T. F. Glasson, *Commentary on the Revelation of John* (1965), p. 94; and R. H. Charles, *A Critical and Exegetical Commentary on the Revelation of St. John* (2 vols., 1920), 2:50–51.

There is evidently no satisfactory explanation of the origins of *Armageddon*. It is usually connected with Megiddo, where many decisive battles took place and Josiah was defeated by Pharaoh (2 Kings 23:29). Some suspect it to be a possible corruption of "glorious holy mountain" (Mt. Zion?), or even "the desirable city" (Jerusalem), which was to be the scene of the last great struggle; others have found in the mysterious phrase "a survival of some ancient myth . . . which associated the final conflict of the gods with some ancient mountain."

There is also the view that *Harmagedon* (the transliteration of a Hebrew word into Greek) was intended to "convey a secret message," a dangerous and treasonable suggestion that the city of the seven hills at the heart of the evil Empire, namely Rome, was to be utterly destroyed, thus fulfilling John's eschatological scheme (Martin Kiddle, *The Revelation of St. John* [1940], pp. 329–31).

15. *Eikonoklastes,* pp. 447, 412, 457, 389.

16. *Eikonoklastes,* pp. 388–90, 535–36.

17. *Eikonoklastes,* pp. 534, 599–600, 503, 536.

18. *Eikonoklastes,* pp. 464, 455, 561–62.

19. *Eikonoklastes,* pp. 438, 454.

20. *Eikonoklastes,* pp. 536, 542, 404, 374, 547.

21. *Eiknooklastes,* pp. 564–65, 601, 579–81.

22. *Eikonoklastes,* pp. 583, 498, 464; "Animadversions" (1641), in *Works,* 3:112, 148.

23. *Eikonoklastes,* pp. 409, 501.

24. [John Milton], *The Readie and Easie Way to establish a free Commonwealth; and the Excellence thereof Compared with the Inconveniences and Dangers of Readmitting Kingship in this Nation* (1660). My quotations are from the edition edited by E. M. Clark (1915).

25. William Riley Parker, *Milton: A Biography* (2 vols., 1968), 1:549, 559. According to Parker (2:1074), the only located copies are in the Bibliothèque Nationale in Paris, the Royal Library in Copenhagen, and at Harvard. *The Censure of the Rota upon Mr. Milton's Book* . . . (1660), was often ascribed to James Harrington, who was one of the mainstays of the Rota Club's discussions, along with William Petty, John Wildman, Thomas Venner, et al.

26. David Masson, *The Life of John Milton* (1877), 5:688.

27. William Colline, *The Spirit of the Phanatiques Dissected* (1660), pp. 7–8. Parker, *Milton, A Biography,* 1:549.

28. *Mercurius Politicus, comprising the sum of Forein Intelligence, with the Affairs now on foot . . . For the Information of the People* (March-April 1657), nos. 352–56.

29. It is regrettable that so little of Nedham's writings have been reprinted in three centuries. Some of his pamphlets remain most remarkable contributions to the history of democratic thought and opinion. See, especially, *The Excellencie of a Free-State: or, the Right Constitution of a Common-Wealth. Wherein All Objections are answered, and the best way to secure the Peoples Liberties, discovered: With Some Errors of Government, and Rules of Policie. Published by a Well-wisher to Posterity* (1656). "Necessity and Extremity opening the people's Eyes," he wrote (p. 154), thus emerging in this neglected work as literally the first "revolutionary" ideologue, "so that (as the only Remedy) they dislodged the Power out of those hands, putting it into their own, and placing it in a constant orderly Revolution of persons Elective by the Community."

30. On Nedham, see Charles Firth's entry on "Needham or Nedham, Marchamount (1620–1678)," in *Dictionary of National Biography* (ed. Sidney Lee, 1894), 40:159–64. Anthony

à Wood, *Athenae Oxoniense: The History of Oxford Writers* (1691), 1:465–71. Perez Zagorin, *A History of English Political Thought in the English Revolution* (1954), pp. 121–27. See also Philip A. Knachel's valuable introduction to the Folger Shakespeare Library edition (1969) of Nedham's *The Case of the Commonwealth of England, Stated* (1650). There is a biographical work in progress by Professor Joseph Frank of Amherst College.

31. John Adams's antipathy to the radicalizing effect of Nedham's revolutionary pamphlets developed with the years into a weary resignation with all such political philosophy. But it did not appear to be as total as Thomas Jefferson's. When Adams sent Jefferson a new book published in London (1795) on the Revolution in France (and in Geneva), Jefferson replied:

> I consider all Reasoning upon French affairs of little moment. The Fates must determine hereafter as they have done heretofore. Reasoning has been all lost. Passion, Prejudice, Interest, Necessity has governed and will govern and a Century must roll away before any permanent and quiet System will be established. An Amelioration of human affairs I hope and believe will be the result, but You and I must look down from the Battlements of Heaven if We ever have the Pleasure of seeing it.

He thanked Adams for the book with a curious apology: "But it is on politics, a subject I never loved, and now hate. I will not promise to read it thoroughly . . . " (28 February 1796).

Some sixteen years later, in another letter which commented on some public affairs of the day, Jefferson wrote: "But whither is senile garrulity leading me? Into politics, of which I have taken final leave. I think little of them, and say less. I have given up newspapers in exchange for Tacitus and Thucydides, for Newton and Euclid; and I find myself much the happier . . . " (3 February 1812).

Nedham figured again in Adams's reply: "What an Exchange have you made? Of Newspapers for Newton! Rising from the lower deep of the lowest deep of Dulness and Bathos to the Contemplation of the Heavens and the heavens of Heavens. Oh that I had devoted to Newton and his Fellows that time which I fear has been wasted on Plato and Aristotle, · Bacon . . . Bolingbroke . . . Harrington, Sidney, Hobbes . . . Marchamont Nedham . . . " (*The Adams-Jefferson Letters* [ed. Cappon, 1959], 1:259–60; 2:291–95).

32. *The Works of John Adams* (ed. C. F. Adams, 1851), 6:6. *The Adams-Jefferson Letters* (ed. Cappon, 1959), 1:261 n; 2:294–95. *Diary and Autobiography of John Adams* (ed. Butterfield, 1961), 3:358–59.

In a letter to Thomas Jefferson (6 April 1796), Adams wrote:

> This is indeed as you say the Age of Experiments in Government. One Tryal has been fairly made in America and France of Nedhams perfect Commonwealth, and at length given up. Holland is trying it again and if Britain should have a Revolution she will try it too. An hundred thousand Dutchmen guillotined or beknifed will convince Holland as soon as five hundred thousand Frenchmen and Women have convinced France. How many Hecatombs must be slaughtered to convince John Bull I cannot calculate . . . .

33. Marchamont Nedham, *De la souveraineté du peuple et de l'excellence d'un état libre* (tr. Mandar, 1790, 2 vols.), with notes by Rousseau, Mably, Bossuet, Condillac, Montesquieu, Raynel, etc. The French editor considered it *"une étude profonde,"* and ranked it with *L'Esprit des loix* and the *Contrat social*. Only Milton, and perhaps Algernon Sydney, seemed to mean as much to the French revolutionary spirits. Also appended to the Nedham translation was the "Declaration of the Rights of Man."

34. Marchamont Nedham, *The Case of the Commonwealth of England, Stated* (1650). My quotations are largely from the Knachel edition, pp. 35, 17, 101, 13, 91; and from *A True State of the Case of the Commonwealth* (1654), p. 47, and *The Excellencie of a Free-State*, p. 80.

35. Marchamont Nedham, *The Excellencie of a Free-State*, pp. 13–14. *The Case of the Commonwealth*, pp. 50, 100, 59.

36. *The Case of the Commonwealth*, pp. 27–28. *A True State*, p. 4 (I am following here Professor Michael Fixler's attribution of this pamphlet to Nedham: see his *Milton and the Kingdoms of God* [1964], pp. 197, 280).

37. *The Case of the Commonwealth*, pp. 28–29, 43, 96; (1650 ed.), p. 69. J. Milton French, "Milton, Needham, and *Mercurius Politicus*," *Studies in Philology* (1936), 33:236–52; and H. S. Anthony, "*Mercurius Politicus* under Milton," *Journal of the History of Ideas* (1966), 27:593–609.

38. *The Case of the Commonwealth* (1650 ed.), p. 70; (Knachel ed.), p. 97.

39. *The Case of the Commonwealth* (1650 ed.), pp. 79, 91; (Knachel ed.), pp. 43, 125.

40. For an attack on Nedham's "inconstancy," see: *A Rope for Pol., or A Hue and Cry after Marchemont Nedham, the late Scurrulous News-writer* (1660), in which a royalist writer also pays this grudging tribute to Nedham:

> ... 'tis incredible what influence they had upon numbers of unconsidering persons, who have a strange presumption that all must needs be true that is in Print. This was the Goliath of the Philistines, the great Champion of the late Usurper, whose Pen was in comparison of others like a Weavers beam ... Had the Devil himself (the Father of Lies) ... been in this man's office, he could not have exceeded him.

See, also, *Mercurius Politicus: A Private Conference Between Scot and Needham, Concerning the Present Affairs of the Nation* (1660).

41. Marchamont Nedham, *The True Character of a Rigid Presbyter: with a Narrative of the Dangerous Designes of the English and Scottish Covenanters* (1661), prefaces and pp. 11, 34.

42. Marchamont Nedham, *A Short History of the English Rebellion, Compiled in Verse* (1680), pp. 1–37.

43. Locke's two untitled papers (one in English, one in Latin) are in the Lovelace Collection of Locke manuscripts in the Bodleian Library, Oxford. Unpublished for three centuries, they were edited (and translated) for the first time by Philip Abrams in 1967. All my quotations from these manuscripts are from Dr. Abrams's excellent edition: John Locke, *Two Tracts on Government*. Parker, *Milton: A Biography*, 1:562–69; 2:1075. Maurice Cranston, *Locke: A Biography* (1957), pp. 43, 61.

44. *Two Tracts*, p. 6. John Dunn, *The Political Thought of John Locke* (1969), p. 1.

45. Locke, *Oratio Censoria Funebris* (1664), in *Essays on the Law of Nature* (ed. von Leyden, 1954), p. 221.

46. *Two Tracts*, pp. 53, 119, 125.

47. Locke, *Two Tracts*, pp. 96, 196, 225.

48. Lord King, *The Life of John Locke with Extracts from his Correspondence, Journals and Commonplace Books* (1830), 1:188.

49. Locke, *Two Tracts*, pp. 162, 166–67.

50. Locke, *Two Tracts*, p. 227; Richard Hooker, *Of the Laws of Ecclesiastical Polity* (1597; ed. Morris, 1954), 2:363.

51. Locke, *Two Tracts*, p. 119.

52. Locke, *Two Tracts*, pp. 117–18.

53. Locke, *An Essay Concerning Human Understanding* (1690–1706; ed. Yolton, 1964), 2:288–93.

Chapter 12

1. William Wordsworth, *Poetical Works* (ed. Hutchinson and de Selincourt, 1966), p. 166, ll.13–17, 36–40; and the almost identical lines in *The Prelude*, ll.140–44, p. 571.

2. Ernest Lee Tuveson, *Millennium and Utopia: A Study in the Background of the Idea of Progress* (1949). Mark Schorer, *William Blake: The Politics of Vision* (1946), p. 42. Don M.

Wolfe, *Milton and the Puritan Revolution* (1941), p. 2. Samuel Clarke, *A Discourse concerning the Being and Attributes of God* (sermons of 1704–5, 8th ed., 1732), p. 264.

3. In addition to the political and the religious elements in the excess, there is a third element here, and I do not mean to minimize it: namely, the literary. One historian of literature who has studied "The Restoration Revolt against Enthusiasm" has made this admirable summary of the point:

> The revolt against Enthusiasm will not explain every phase of style during the third quarter of the seventeenth-century, but it will do much to explain the change of temper out of which the neo-classical style developed. The revolt against Enthusiasm, which is the immediate cause of this change of temper is itself the culmination of the thought of the first half of the century, however its manifestation may vary in religious, scientific and literary style.... Here we have one of the major problems of the seventeenth century, one which only grew more pressing after the emotional explosion of the Civil Wars, and one which eventually told against emotion and imagination. Here we are at the heart of the belief which led into neo-classicism. It was always a part of seventeenth-century thought, but it required the tergiversation of Enthusiasm to transform it into dogma. Feeling and emotion in literature are altered, and may even be diminished, by whatever an age believes to be real or true. And that is why the revolt against Enthusiasm seems to me so important, so necessary to an understanding of the altered feeling, the modified tension of the emotions, the tempered imagination, the dominance of the plain style, and other features of the literature of the Restoration. [George Williamson, "The Restoration Revolt Against Enthusiasm," *Studies in Philology* (October 1933), 30, no. 4:571–603]

The essential references here are, to be sure, to the imaginative literature of the age; but most literary scholars have understood the importance of the political context and have been aware of the social consequences. In my own remarks, I have emphasized the transformations in the world of the political imagination. No suggestion is made of priority or essential causation. All three elements were aspects of psychological changes rooted in both the material and mental experiences of men in a changing society. It makes little difference if Bacon, Hobbes, Sprat, More, Dryden, et al., meant poetry or theology or politics when they made their large pronouncements on the nature of truth and style; their spirits were shaped by the lives they lived in both the quiet library and the noisy marketplace. And the consequences of their own words shaped in turn both the literature and the politics of the next generation of readers and rebels.

4. Henry More, *Enthusiasmus Triumphatus, or a Brief Discourse of the Nature, Causes, Kinds, and Cure of Enthusiasme* (1656), in *A Collection of Several Philosophical Writings of Dr. Henry More* (1712), pp. 1–22. Samuel Parker, *A Free and Impartial Censure of the Platonick Philosophie* (1666), pp. 72–73.

5. *Pascal's Pensées* (1672; ed. Stewart, 1950), pp. 90–91: "*L'homme n'est ni ange ni bête, et le malheur veut que qui fait l'ange fait la bête.* (Man is neither angel nor beast, and the mischief is that he who would play the angel plays the beast.)"

6. Joseph Glanvill, *Scepsis Scientifica: or, Confest Ignorance, The Way to Science; in an Essay of the Vanity of Dogmatizing, and Confident Opinion* (1665; ed. Owen, 1885), pp. lxv, 2–6, 12, 110, 196.

7. William Bagwell, *The Mystery of Astronomy* (1655), preface.

8. *The Works of Joseph Mede* (ed. Worthington, 1672), p. xii. Worthington, in his "Author's Life" (p. xxviii), refers to the various conflicting interpretations by quoting one of Mede's own sayings: "That in the revolution of about twenty years by-past he had by the self-same persons been look'd upon, and accordingly reported of, as Popish, Protestant, and Puritane ... " The nineteenth-century biographer in the *Dictionary of National Biography* (ed. Lee, 1894), 37:180, notes that "Inferences opposed to his own principles were drawn by others for his apocalyptic writings; there is extant on this subject, from the pen of an

anonymous admirer, 'An Apologie, or a Defence of Joseph Mede against the Puritans' ... " See, also, Brook's *Lives of the Puritans* (1813), 2:429 ff.; and Robert Southey, *Sir Thomas More: or, Colloquies on the Progress and Prospects of Society* (1829), 1:32–38; 2:368–69.

9. "Mede's ideas," as Professor Tuveson has written, "received a great access of importance and influence from the apocalyptic stirrings during the period of the Commonwealth ... it is no accident that Mede was an important source for the crowd of millennial enthusiasts who later attempted to interpret the course of the Puritan Revolution in terms of the sacred Book, and to find in it programs for action" (Tuveson, *Millennium and Utopia*, pp. 77–85).

Robert Southey had been a close reader of Worthington's edition of Mede's writings; and the seventeenth-century millenarian texts (see the quotations, 2:368–69) prompted him to an imaginary nineteenth-century exchange on the general subject of apocalyptic revolution between "Sir Thomas More" and "Montesinos." The following deserves to be recorded from this long-forgotten work "on the progress and prospects of society."

More challenges the school of optimism: "You hold then that the human race will one day attain the utmost degree of general virtue, and thereby general happiness, of which humanity is capable." Montesinos finds this too argumentatively broad and tries to put the proposition in a less disputable form.

> A happier condition of society is possible than that in which any nation is existing at this time, or has at any time existed. The sum both of moral and physical evil may be greatly diminished by good laws, good institutions, and good governments ... Surely this belief rests upon a reasonable foundation, and is supported by that general improvement (always going on if it be regarded upon the great scale) to which all history bears witness.

He has, however, to concede the widespread presence of pernicious principles, whereupon More forces the question:

> Is there not a danger that these principles bear down every thing before them? and is not that danger obvious ... palpable ... imminent? Is there a considerate man who can look at the signs of the times without apprehension, or a scoundrel connected with what is called the public press, who does not speculate upon them, and join with the anarchists as the strongest party? Deceive not yourself by the fallacious notion that truth is mightier than falsehood, and that good must prevail over evil! Good principles enable men to suffer, rather than to act.... Remember too how rapidly the plague of diseased opinions is communicated, and if it once gain head, it is as difficult to be stopt as a conflagration or a flood. The prevailing opinions of this age go to the destruction of every thing which has hitherto been held sacred. They tend to arm the poor against the rich; the many against the few: worse than this ... for it will also be a war of hope and enterprise against timidity, of youth against age.

Here Southey was deliberately ignoring the real More's sympathy for the poor in the class struggle against the exploitative ruling class, as expressed in a famous passage in the *Utopia*; in another place, Southey skillfully went on to argue More's subsequent disenchantment with his own utopianism, as suggested by a less-known passage in the *Confutation against Tyndale*.

Montesinos found this to be "dreadful alarmism," especially on the part of a ghost. The ghost pressed on:

> I admit that such an improved condition of society as you contemplate is possible, and that it ought always to be kept in view: but the error of supposing it too near, of fancying that there is a short road to it, is, of all the errors of these times, the most pernicious, because it seduces the young and generous, and betrays them imperceptibly into an alliance with whatever is flagitious and detestable.... You need not be told in what manner revolutions in opinion bring about the fate of empires; and upon this ground you ought to regard the state of the world, both at home and abroad, with fear, rather than with hope.

Whereupon Montesinos took flight with a neat burst of political cosmology, or what he called speculations about "what is hidden in the darkness of time and eternity." He explained: "I have sometimes thought that the moral and physical order of the world may be so appointed as to coincide; and that the revolutions of this planet may correspond with the condition of its inhabitants; so that the convulsions and changes whereto it is destined should occur ... "—i.e., downward to corruption, upward to regeneration. "Our globe may have gone through many such revolutions. We know the history of the last; the measure of its wickedness was then filled up. For the future we are taught to expect a happier consummation."

More refused to accept either the the suggestion of a Revolutionary Cycle or the prospect of Apocalyptic Hope.

> Remember that the Evangelists in predicting that kingdom, announce a dreadful Advent! ... wars, persecutions, and calamities of every kind, the triumph of evil, and the coming of Antichrist are to be looked for, before the promises made by the Prophets shall be fulfilled. Consider this also, that the speedy fulfilment of those promises has been the ruling fancy of the most dangerous of all madmen, from John of Leyden and his frantic followers, down to the Saints of Cromwell's army, Venner and his Fifth-Monarchy men, the fanatics of the Cevennes, and the blockheads of your own days, who beheld with complacency the crimes of the French Revolutionists, and the progress of Buonaparte towards the subjugation of Europe, as events tending to bring about the prophecies.... But you surely do not expect that the Millennium is to be brought about by the triumph of what are called liberal opinions; nor by enabling the whole of the lower classes to read the incentives to vice, impiety, and rebellion, which are prepared for them by an unlicensed press ... methinks the thought of that consummation for which you look, might serve rather for consolation under the prospect of impending evils, than for a hope upon which the mind can rest in security with a calm and contented delight.

Montesinos hurried to put distance between himself and the visions of the apocalypse and the coming of Antichrist ("no longer a received opinion in those days"). The liberal faith was rather more up-to-date and therefore unperturbed by this conservative polemical onslaught.

> Your reasoning applies to the enthusiastic Millenarians who discover the number of the Beast, and calculate the year when a Vial is to be poured out, with as much precision as the day and hour of an eclipse. But it leaves my hope unshaken and untouched. I know that the world has improved; I see that it is improving; and I believe that it will continue to improve in natural and certain progress. Good and evil principles are widely at work; a crisis is evidently approaching; it may be dreadful, but I can have no doubts concerning the result. Black and ominous as the aspects may appear, I regard them without dismay.

He remained loyal to the cause of the poor, the helpless, and the oppressed.

Southey, as was only to be expected, gives "Sir Thomas More" the last word in this colloquy of 1829.

> We have come however to some conclusion in our discourse. Your notion of the improvement of the world has appeared to be a mere speculation, altogether inapplicable in practice; and as dangerous to weak heads and heated imaginations as it is congenial to benevolent hearts. Perhaps that improvement is neither so general, nor so certain as you suppose. Perhaps, even in this country there may be more knowledge than there was in former times, and less wisdom ... more wealth and less happiness ... more display and less virtue. This must be the subject of future conversation. I will only remind you now, that the French had persuaded themselves this was the most enlightened age of the world, and they the most enlightened people in it ... the politest, the most amiable, the most humane of nations ... and that a new era of philosophy, philanthropy, and peace was about to commence under their auspicies ... when they were upon the event of a revolution which, for its complicated monstrosities, absurdities, and horrors, is more

disgraceful to human nature than any other series of events in history. Chew the cud upon this, and farewell! [Southey, *Sir Thomas More*, 1:29–38]

10. Eduard Bernstein, *Cromwell and Communism* (1895; tr. Stenning, 1930), pp. 165–66.

11. In a "Catalogue of Pamphlets," the following title is listed: *Fanatick Moderation; exemplified in Bishop Hall's "Hard Measure," as it was written by himself. To which is annex'd a Specimen of the unparralleld Behaviour of the Sectaries towards some others of that Sacred Order; as likewise a List of the London Clergy, who were Sequestered, Plundered, and Harrassed, during the Havock of the Grand Rebellion. Price 6 d.* This is appended to the third edition of *Old Stories, Which were the Fore-runners of the Revolution, in Eighty-eight* (1702).

12. *Leveller Manifestoes of the Puritan Revolution* (ed. Wolfe, 1944). *The Leveller Tracts, 1647–1653* (ed. Haller and Davies, 1944). See, generally, M.A. Gibb, *John Lilburne The Leveller, A Christian Democrat* (1947); M. H. Ashley, *John Wildman, Plotter and Postmaster* (1947); G. P. Gooch, *English Democratic Ideas in the Seventeenth Century* (1927); J. W. Allen, *English Political Thought, 1603–1660* (1938); T. C. Pease, *The Leveller Movement* (1916); and, especially, Joseph Frank, *The Levellers, A History of the Writings of Three Seventeenth-Century Social Democrats: John Lilburne, Richard Overton, William Walwyn* (1955).

13. "Englands New Chains Discovered" (1649), *Leveller Tracts*, p. 169; Frank, *The Levellers*, p. 215.

14. "A Manifestation," published in *The Moderate* for 10–17 April 1649; *Leveller Tracts*, pp. 276–84.

15. Frank, *The Levellers*, p. 245.

16. *A Declaration of Some Proceedings of Lieutenant-Colonel John Lilburne and his associates, with some Examinations and Animadversions upon papers lately printed and scattered abroad* (1648), in Gibb, *Lilburne*, pp. 222–30.

17. Ashley, *John Wildman*, pp. 7–8, 104–6. Of Wildman—that "dark and restless spirit" (Hallam's phrase) who plotted, with varying degrees of success, against the regimes of Charles I, Cromwell, Charles II, James II, and William III—Carlyle once remarked that he was "the noisiest man in England," and Disraeli went so far as to say that "he was the soul of English politics in the most eventful period of this kingdom." In any case, as Ashley notes, Wildman "conspired for fifty years and through five reigns . . . "

18. Clarendon (*Rebellion*, 6:70–75) refers to the author, William Howard, as "an Anabaptist"; for an account of the zig-zag career of the third Lord Howard of Escrick (1624–1694), marked by fiery sermons and republican plots, see the *Dictionary of National Biography* (ed. Lee, 1891), 28: 83.

19. John Strachey, *The Strangled Cry* (1962).

20. *The Works of Gerrard Winstanley* (ed. Sabine, 1941), p. 600.

21. "An Agreement of the Free People of England" (1649), *Leveller Tracts*, p. 319.

22. *Leveller Tracts*, pp. 135–46.

23. "The Legall Fundamentall Liberties of the People of England" (1649), *Leveller Tracts*, pp. 415–16.

24. *Leveller Tracts*, pp. 280–82.

25. *The Life Records of John Milton* (ed. French, 1954), 3:217–19. Milton, *Works*, 7:552. Wolfe, *Milton in the Puritan Revolution*, pp. 460, 478.

26. *Leveller Tracts*, p. 282.

27. *Leveller Tracts*, p. 282.

28. William Walwyn, *A Whisper in the Eare* (1646), pp. 3–10. John Lilburne, *The Oppressed Mans Oppressions declared* (1646), pp. 23–28.

29. *Leveller Manifestoes*, pp. 262, 391.

30. *The Diary of John Evelyn* (ed. de Beer, 1955), 4:603, 609, 650.

31. George Macaulay Trevelyan, *The English Revolution: 1688–1689* (1938), pp. 130–31.

32. *Revolution Politicks: Being a Compleat Collection of all the Reports, Lives, and Stories, which were the Fore-runners of the Great Revolution in 1688* (1733). See also, Henry Horwitz, *Revolu-*

tion Politicks (1968), a biography of Daniel Finch, Second Earl of Nottingham (1647–1730), pp. viii, 219.

33. *Old Stories, Which were the Fore-runners of the Revolution, in Eighty-Eight* (3d ed., 1702), p. 66.

34. Robert Fleming, *The Divine Right of the Revolution* (1706).

35. Gibb, *Lilburne*, p. 340.

36. Horwitz, *Revolution Politicks*, pp. 183, 189.

37. T. E. S. Clarke and H. C. Foxcroft, *A Life of Gilbert Burnet, Bishop of Salisbury* (1907), p. 443. *Journals of the House of Lords* (1709), 19:109, 113. See, generally, Geoffrey Holmes, *The Trial of Doctor Sacheverell* (1973).

38. "Political Thoughts and Reflections" (ca. 1695), in *The Complete Works of George Savile, First Marquess of Halifax* (ed. Raleigh, 1912), p. 219. See, generally, the biography of Halifax by H. C. Foxcroft, *A Character of a Trimmer* (1946), a revision of her book *Life and Letters*, written of a half-century earlier.

39. Wordsworth, *Poetical Works*, pp. 403–4.

40. Dryden, *The Medal*, in Ashley, *John Wildman*, p. 268.

41. Louis I. Bredvold, *The Intellectual Milieu of John Dryden* (1956), p. 150.

42. *Heroique Stanzas* (1659), *The Medall, a Satyre against Sedition* (1682), *The Hind and the Panther* (1687), in *The Poems of John Dryden* (ed. Kinsley, 1958), 1:7, 255–60; 2:467–537.

43. *Britannia Rediviva* (1688), in *Poems*, 2:542–49.

44. Dedication to *Examen Poeticum* (1693), in *Poems*, 2:790.

45. *The Works of John Dryden* (ed. Scott, 1808), 5:298–303.

46. *Lines on Milton* (1688), in *Poems*, 2:540.

47. *The Indian Emperour* (1665), in *The Works of John Dryden* (ed. Loftis, 1966), 9:100.

48. *Works* (Scott ed.), 5:300.

49. *Poems*, 1:260.

50. See, for a rather different interpretation, Christopher Hill, *Antichrist in Seventeenth-Century England* (1971). "The evolution of the theology," Hill argues (p. 176), "must also be related to the economic and social history of these centuries." This is impeccable so long as the "relationship" is not taken too narrowly or mechanically. Images disappear for Hill only in connection with the inevitable failure of the "bourgeois revolution," conveniently leaving a more viable imagery (i.e., Marx's) for truer fulfillment another day.

51. *Absalom and Achitophel* (1681), in *Poems*, 1:223.

52. *Poems*, 2:697, 906; 4:1804.

53. *The Address of John Dryden, Laureat, to His Highness the Prince of Orange* (1689), in Thomas Shadwell, *Complete Works* (ed. Summers, 1927), 5:352.

54. *King Arthur: or, the British Worthy* (1691), in Dryden, *Works* (ed. Scott and Saintsbury, 1884), 8:131.

55. The *O.E.D.* also offers under "wonder . . . wonderful—an object of astonishment . . . an extraordinary natural occurrence . . . shameful actions . . . something novel and unexpected, or inexplicable . . . astonishment mingled with perplexity or bewildered curiosity . . . *Milton* (1667): 'Satan looks down with Wonder' . . . Lithgow (1632): 'They made a wonderful massacre of poore afflicted Christians' . . . " (*Oxford English Dictionary* [1933] 12:252–55).

56. *The Medal of John Baynes: A Satyr against Folly and Knavery* (1682) and *A Congratulatory Poem on His Highness the Prince of Orange, His Coming into England*, in Shadwell, *Complete Works*, 5:245–62, 335–40.

57. Dryden, *Works* (Scott and Saintsbury ed.), 8:130.

58. *Amphitryon* (1690), in Dryden, *Works* (Scott and Saintsbury ed.), 8:6–8.

59. Antoine Varillas, *Histoire des révolutions arrivées dans l'Europe en matière de Religion* (1686), and *Réponse de Mr. Varillas à le critique de Mr. Burnet* (1687). Gilbert Burnet, *Reflec-*

tions that Have Happened in Europe (1686), and *A Defense of the Reflections* (1687). Dryden, *Poems*, 4:1988; Charles E. Ward, *The Life of John Dryden* (1961), p. 233.

60. Gilbert Burnet, *The Revolution and the Present Establishment Vindicated. In a Memorial Drawn by King William's Special Direction . . . Justifying the Revolution, and the Course of his Government* (1715), pp. 1–18; and *A Short History and Vindication of the Revolution* (1716), p. 6. See, generally, *Bishop Burnet's History of His Own Times* (1724), and T. E. S. Clarke and H. C. Foxcroft, *A Life of Gilbert Burnet, Bishop of Salisbury* (1907).

61. Clarke and Foxcroft, *Burnet*, pp. 465–66.

62. George Sewell, *A Second Letter to the Bishop of Salisbury* (1715), pp. 4–7.

63. Burnet, *The Revolution and the Present Establishment Vindicated*, p. 17.

64. Clarke and Foxcroft, *Burnet*, pp. 266, 271, 425.

65. My suggestion of the profound ideological difference between Halifax and Burnet should not be taken to imply that it was, as all too often in other post-revolutionary times, part of a disastrous personal enmity. Macaulay has given us a finely etched portrait of the two figures:

> Halifax and Burnet had long been on terms of friendship. No two men, indeed, could resemble each other less. Burnet was utterly destitute of delicacy and tact. Halifax's taste was fastidious, and his sense of the ludicrous morbidly quick. Burnet viewed every act and every character through a medium distorted by party spirit. The tendency of Halifax's mind was always to see the faults of his allies more strongly than the faults of his opponents. Burnet was, with all his infirmities, and through all the vicissitudes of a life passed in circumstances not very favourable to piety, a sincerely pious man. The sceptical and sarcastic Halifax lay under the imputation of infidelity . . . Halifax therefore incurred Burnet's indignant censure; and Burnet was often the butt of Halifax's keen and polished pleasantry. Yet they were drawn to each other by a mutual attraction, liked each other's conversations, appreciated each other's abilities, interchanged opinions freely, and interchanged also good offices in perilous times. [Lord Thomas Macaulay, *The History of England* (1858), 2:534–35]

See, also, the portrait of Burnet in W. E. H. Lecky, *A History of England* (1877; ed. 1925), 1:100–4.

66. Sir Thomas More, *Utopia* (tr. Burnet, 1684), preface.

67. Wordsworth, *Poetical Works*, pp. 165–66, 402, 539, 565; Wordsworth, *The Prelude* (text of 1805, Hutchinson-de Selincourt ed.), p. 183.

68. William Wordsworth, *Prose Works* (ed. Grosart, 1876), 1:3–23: "A Letter to the Bishop of Landaff on the Extraordinary Avowal of his Political Principles, contained in the Appendix to his late Sermon: By a Republican" (1793).

69. The Bishop of Landaff's "Appendix to Bishop Watson's Sermon" (1793), in Wordsworth, *Prose Works*, 1:28–29.

70. *The Letters of William and Dorothy Wordsworth* (ed. de Selincourt, 1937), 1:314–15 (25 May 1809).

71. Wordsworth, *Prose Works*, 1:149–50.

72. *Letters of Wordsworth*, 1:305–6.

73. *The Recluse* (1800), in *The Poetical Works of William Wordsworth* (ed. de Selincourt and Darbishire, 1949), 5:321–37, 345.

74. F. M. Todd, *Politics and the Poet: A Study of Wordsworth* (1957). See, generally, C. Cestro, *La Révolution française et les poètes anglais* (1906); Crane Brinton, *The Political Ideas of the English Romanticists* (1926), and Amanda M. Ellis, *Rebels and Conservatives: Dorothy and William Wordsworth and Their Circle* (1967).

75. Preface (1814) to *The Excursion*, in *Poetical Works*, p. 590.

76. *The Letters of William and Dorothy Wordsworth: The Early Years, 1787–1805* (rev. ed. de Selincourt and Shaver, 1967), pp. 123–24; *Letters of William Wordsworth* (ed. Wayne, 1954), pp. 16–18.

77. Wordsworth, *Prose Works*, 1:31–174; *Concerning the Relations of Great Britain, Spain, and Portugal, to Each Other, and to the Common Enemy, at this Crisis; and specifically as affected by The Convention of Cintra: the Whole brought to the Test of those Principles, by which alone the Independence and Freedom of Nations can be preserved or recovered* (1809). Two later editions are: *The Convention of Cintra* (ed. Dicey, 1915), and, somewhat abridged, in: *Political Tracts of Wordsworth, Coleridge, and Shelley* (ed. White, 1953), pp. 117–93. See, also, J. E. Wells, "The Story of Wordsworth's 'Cintra,'" *Studies in Philology* (January 1921), pp. 15–76.

78. Wordsworth's century-old pamphlet was rushed into print again in 1915, for its editor, A. V. Dicey—and he was not alone—found in *Cintra* a characterization of the cause of the Great War and a "rich treasury of lessons." As one writer noted in 1921,

> Of the vital importance for the Great War of Wordsworth's political writings in prose and verse composed during the struggle of England with Napoleon, there has been a growing recognition since the autumn of 1914. In them, and notably in the tract on the Convention of Cintra, are enunciated with no less power than nobility the essential principles of moral and political truth that have inspired and supported the associated peoples against Germany, and that are today, more clearly than ever before, realized to be the bases of any enduring formula for a rightly constituted world. [J. E. Wells, "The Story of Wordsworth's 'Cintra,'" *Studies in Philology* (January 1921), p. 15]

To paraphrase Marx's epigram about tragedy and farce in historical repetitions: what happens for the first time as rhetoric, happens for the second time as propaganda. Thus, a century after, Wordsworth's "high dogmatic Eloquence" has a useful reassuring patina for another militant generation. For his own contemporaries, *Cintra* appeared somewhat less inspiring. Southey, for example, was convinced that "Wordsworth's pamphlet will fail of producing any general effect." He found almost everything wrong with it: the sentences were too long and the punctuation unusual, the Miltonic involutions made worse by the bad habit of dictating ("if he were his own scribe his eye would tell him where to stop"). Most of all, Wordsworth was too *complicated* for timely and direct communication to embattled partisans. In Southey's version, the betrayal of the cause had amounted to "degrading into a common and petty war between soldier and soldier, that which is the struggle of a nation against a foreign usurper, a business of natural life and death, a war of virtue against vice, light against darkness, the good principle against the evil one . . . " (*Robert Southey, Life and Correspondence* [ed. C. C. Southey, 1850], 3:176, 246–47).

This lower form of verbal strategy also proves serviceable, and it echoes through the years as part of the so-called rich treasury of enduring formulas. All the conventional functions of human memory—the lessons of history, the record of experience, the quest for a "usable past"—merge into a kind of vast lending library of well-worn slogans which can be borrowed for all suitably pressing occasions. This is, in the immemorial manner of *les terribles simplificateurs*, that primordial tradition of ideological simplification which has always been more a function of internal spiritual needs than of knowledge of the external world.

79. *Political Tracts*, pp. 173, 187–88, 191. *Letters* (de Selincourt-Shaver ed.), 1:273–74, 285, 290.

80. *Collected Letters of Samuel Taylor Coleridge* (ed. Griggs, 1959), 3:214–16 (13 June, 22 June 1809).

81. *Letters* (de Selincourt-Shaver ed.), 1:325.

82. Todd, *Politics and the Poet*, p. 11. *Political Tracts*, pp. xxviii, 287.

83. *Political Tracts*, pp. 139, 149–50, 156–61, 161–63, 163–64, 165, 166, 166–67, 179.

84. His first essay in politics? Had Wordsworth already repressed the memory of the pamphlet against the Bishop of Landaff?

85. On the problem of power, explaining to a friend a point of disagreement with Robert Southey, Wordsworth wrote (22 June 1817):

> We have repeatedly conversed upon the state of the country with little difference of opinion; except that in his vivid perception of the danger to be apprehended from the disaffected urging on the Rabble, and the consequent necessity of government being empowered to keep them down, he does not seem sufficiently jealous of the Power whose protection we all feel to be necessary . . .

He referred to the maxim laid down in *Cintra,* in fact quoted it in its entirety, as "this law of our infirm nature," *Letters* (ed. de Selincourt, 1937) 2:793.

86. *Collected Letters,* 2:198; *Letters,* pp. 100–101 (19 April 1808).

87. *Letters* (ed. de Selincourt, 1937), 2:711 (25 February 1816).

88. "Sonnets Dedicated to Liberty and Order," *Poetical Works,* pp. 401–4.

Chapter 13

1. I am using here Constance Garnett's translation of *Fathers and Sons* (1910), ch. 10, pp. 74–94; see also the rendering of these passages in the translations of George Reavey (1950), pp. 50–64, and Richard Hare (1947), pp. 42–51. See, generally, David Magarshack's biography, *Turgenev* (1954), and for a recent discussion of "Turgenev and the liberal predicament," Sir Isaiah Berlin's Romanes lecture, *Fathers and Children* (1972).

2. *The Philosophy of Edmund Burke* (ed. Bredvold-Ross, 1960), p. 161. Allen McConnell, *A Russian Philosophe: Alexander Radischev, 1749–1802* (1964), p. 60. *The Memoirs of Chateaubriand* (1965 ed.), p. 302.

3. Douglas Johnson, *Guizot: Aspects of French History 1777–1874* (1963), p. 440.

There is a fuller account of this incident along the Seine in Curtis Cate's biography of *George Sand* (1975), p. 367.

> "Civilization!" cried Michel de Bourges, striking his cane against the bridge's stone balustrade. "Ah yes, the big word with artists! Civilization! Well, I'll tell you that to rejuvenate and renew your corrupt society, this fine river will have to turn red with blood, this accursed palace be reduced to ashes, and this vast city turned into a wilderness over which the poor man's family will steer the plow and build its cottage!" George Sand listened in silent awe to these apocalyptic fulminations, and when the breathless Michel finally paused to ask her opinion on the matter, she encouraged him to continue, saying that this apologia for universal death and destruction reminded her pleasantly of Dante "just returned from hell. I'm beginning to enjoy your pastoral symphony: why interrupt it so soon?" Michel de Bourges was now beside himself with fury. "All that interests you is my poor eloquence, my phrases, words and images! As though you were listening to a poem or an orchestra!" And with that he launched into another, even more vehement diatribe against society and its corruptions, finally breaking his cane against the stone rampart of the Louvre.

4. *In Memoriam* (cxxvii), *The Works of Alfred Lord Tennyson* (1926), p. 289. *September 1, 1939,* in *The Collected Poetry of W. H. Auden* (1945), p. 59. Jules Michelet, *Le Peuple* (1841; 1956), p. xxxv.

5. *The French Revolution* (1791), in Blake, *Complete Writings* (1966), p. 136. *Collected Letters of Samuel Taylor Coleridge* (ed. Griggs), vol. 1:1785–1800 (1966), pp. 106, 164.

6. Alessandro Giraffi, *Le Rivolutioni di Napoli* (1647); *An Exact Historie of the Late Revolutions in Naples* (tr. Howell, 1650), pp. 21–51; *The Second Part of Massaniello . . . a Continuation of the Tumult* (1653), pp. 30, 114, 181–83.

7. See R. B. Merriman, *Six Contemporaneous Revolutions* (1938), for an account of the revolts in Italy, Spain, Portugal, England, France, and Holland: and Philip A. Knachel, *England and the Fronde: the Impact of the English Civil War and Revolution on France* (1967).

8. James Howell, "Epistle to the Reader" in *Parthenopoeia, or the History of the Most Noble and Renowned Kingdom of Naples* (1654).

9. The association over three centuries between the two youthful fire-brands, between Masaniello and M. Daniel Cohn-Bendit, the Sorbonne rebel, is not fanciful; or, rather, it

only appears so in the absence of adequate historical accounts of the role of students, and youth generally, in the revolutionary explosions of Europe. In *The Second Part of Massaniello*, Alessandro Giraffi preserves for us this not unfamiliar scene (pp. 24–25):

> The Students of Naples would have a share also in these Revolutions, therefore they went all in a body and presented a Petition to the Viceroy, the effect whereof was, That they should pay no more Fees for their Degrees then was used to be paid in the time of Charles the Emperour. The Viceroy gave them no positive answer for the time, which they imputed to some ill offices that the Prince of Avellino had done; thereupon they attempted at their return to burn his house, but it was prevented by some means the Viceroy wrought; and the next day he caused divers of the Students to be imprisoned, who were the chief ring-leaders.

Writing at about the same time, Thomas Hobbes was even more deeply concerned about discontented young men predisposed to "rebellious actions."

> And because Opinions which are gotten by Education, and in length of time, are made Habitual, cannot be taken away by force, and upon the sudden; they must therefore be taken away also by Time and Education. And seeing the said Opinions have proceeded from private and publick Teaching, and those Teachers have received them from Grounds and Principles, which they have learned in the Universities, from the Doctrine of Aristotle and others, who have delivered nothing concerning Morality and Policy demonstratively, but being passionately addicted to Popular Government have insinuated their Opinions by eloquent Sophistry. There is no doubt, if the true Doctrine concerning the Law of Nature and the Properties of a Body Politick, and the Nature of Law in general were perspicuously set down and taught in the Universities, but that Young men, who come thither void of prejudice, and whose minds are as white paper, capable of any Instruction, would more easily receive the same, and afterward teach it to the people, both in Books and otherwise, then now they do the contrary. [Thomas Hobbes, *De Corpore politico* (1650), pp. 184–85]

10. *Sunday Times* (London), 26 May 1968, p. 13.

11. *The Sibylline Oracles* (tr. Terry, 1890), p. 65; (tr. Floyer, 1713), pp. 30–31.

12. R. B. Onians, *The Origins of European Thought* (1951), p. 147.

13. Mircea Eliade, *Shamanism* (tr. Trask, 1964), pp. 474–77.

14. Dante, *Paradiso* (ed. Wicksteed, 1899), canto 12 ll. 58–60, pp. 146–47. *Paradise* (tr. Sayers and Reynolds, 1962), pp. 158–63; *The Divine Comedy* (tr. Carlyle and Wicksteed; ed. Grandgent, 1932), pp. 476, 479.

15. *The Roman Breviary* (tr. Bute, 1879), 2:1194. In his *Readings on the Paradiso of Dante* (1901), 1:404, W. W. Vernon remarks that the whelp was said to have been black and white, "hence the habit assumed by the order ... " A. J. Butler, in his edition of the *Paradise* (1885), p. 157 n, adds that "the play on *Dominicani, Domini canes*, will be familiar to all who have seen the fresco of Simon Memmi in Santa Maria Novella at Florence" (whereon the wolves, symbolizing the heretics, are being mangled by black-and-white "dogs of the Lord").

16. Bruno, *Opere italiane* (ed. Gentile, 1908), 2:370–88, 466; *The Heroic Enthusiasts* (tr. Williams, 1887–89), 1:142–54; 2:97.

17. Edward Rogers, *Some Account of the Life and Opinions of a Fifth-Monarchy Man: chiefly extracted from the Writings of John Rogers, Preacher* (1867), pp. 268–69. Johann Valentin Andreae, *Reipublicae Christianopolitanae Descriptio* (1619); *Christianopolis: An Ideal State of the Seventeenth Century* (tr. Held, 1916), p. 190.

18. *The Works of Joseph Mede* (ed. Worthington, 1672), pp. 618–19. Comenius, *Teacher of Nations* (ed. Needham, 1942), p. 73.

19. P. J. Proudhon, *De la justice dans la révolution et dans l'église* (1870), 4:169: "Il mit de feu aux poudres que depuis deux siècles avaient amassées les lettres français. C'est quelque chose d'avoir allumé dans les âmes un tel embrasement: en cela consiste la force et la virilité de Rousseau."

20. William Blake, *America* (1793), in *Complete Writings* (1966), p. 197. On the political imagery in this poem and in related pieces (*The French Revolution*, 1791, and *Europe*, 1794), see John Beer, *Blake's Humanism* (1968), especially ch. 5, "The Genius of Revolution," pp. 95–138.

21. Sören Kierkegaard, *The Last Years: Journals 1853–1855* (ed. Smith, 1965), pp. 291–92, 294.

22. *The Mind of Napoleon* (ed. Herold, 1955), pp. 64, 192–93, 281.

23. Alexander Herzen, *My Past and Thoughts* (tr. Garnett, 1924), 1:201, 225; (rev. ed. Higgins, 1967), 1:162, 181.

24. Herzen, *My Past and Thoughts* (Garnett ed.), 5:134. E. H. Carr, *Bakunin* (1937; 1961), pp. 187–88. Isaac Deutscher, *The Prophet Armed, Trotsky: 1879–1921* (1965), p. 123.

25. Aaron Noland, "Proudhon and Rousseau," *Journal of the History of Ideas* (January-March 1967), pp. 33–54. George Woodcock, *Pierre-Joseph Proudhon* (1956), p. 93. Proudhon to Marx (17 May 1846), in *Les Confessions d'un révolutionnaire* (1849, ed. Riviere, 1929), pp. 435–36: "je préfère donc faire brûler la Propriété à petit feu, plutôt que de lui donner une nouvelle force, en faisant une Saint-Barthélemy des propriétaires ... "

26. Alexander Blok, "The Intelligentsia and the Revolution" (1918), in *Russian Intellectual History, an Anthology* (ed. Raeff, 1966), p. 371. *The Scythians* (1918), in *A Treasury of Russian Verse* (ed. Yarmolinsky, 1949), p. 168.

27. William Wordsworth, *Concerning the Convention of Cintra* (1809), in *Political Tracts of Wordsworth, Coleridge, and Shelley* (ed. White, 1953), p. 165.

28. "Che Guevara: Erlöser aus dem Dschungel," Interview with Jean Marcilly, in *Der Spiegel*, 29 July 1968, p. 62.

29. *The Works of Gerrard Winstanley* (ed. Sabine, 1941), p. 451; James Baldwin, *The Fire Next Time* (1963).

30. Immanuel Kant, *On History* (ed. Beck, 1963), pp. 139–40; *Werke* (ed. Weischedel, 1964), 6:353: "Von der terroristischen Vorstellungsart der Menschengeschichte ... nun kann es nicht mehr ärger werden: der jüngste Tag ist vor der Tür, und der fromme Schwärmer träumt nun schon von der Wiederbringung aller Dinge, und einer erneuerten Welt, nachdem diese im Feuer untergegangen ist."

31. Like so much in these ancient and cryptic maxims, this version of the fragment of Heraclitus has been much disputed. Karl Popper uses it in *The Open Society and Its Enemies* (4th ed., rev., 1962), 1:15, and employs a variant of it in his notes (p. 206): "In its advance, the fire will judge and convict everything." It derives from the basic renderings of the great German scholar Hermann Diels, in his *Heraklitis von Ephesos* (1909), p. 33: "Denn alles, sagt er, wird das Feuer, das heranrücken wird, richten und verdammen." A similar spirit informs Bruno Snell's translation (1940), p. 23: "Denn das Feuer wird kommen, allen zu richten und zu verdammen."

But in his *Heraklit* (1959), Heinrich Quiring has registered the interesting objection (p. 106 n) that these versions are "teleological" and have a "strange Christian colouring." He offers: "Denn alles wird das herangekommene Feuer sondern (zerlegen) und erfassen." This harks back to the older Bywater edition of G. T. W. Patrick's translation, *The Fragments of Heraclitus of Ephesus* (1889), p. 90: "Fire coming upon all things, will sift and seize them." Philip Wheelwright, in his *Heraclitus* (1959), p. 68, suggests: "Fire in its advance will judge and overtake all things."

Thus, much depends on whether one is predisposed to make of the ancient philosopher a poet, a mystic, a scientist, or an ideologue.

32. C. I. Smith, "Heraclitus and Fire," *Journal of the History of Ideas* (January-March 1966), pp. 125–27. Karl R. Popper, *The Open Society*, 1:11–17, and especially the notes, pp. 204–8.

33. Ferdinand Lassalle, *Die Philosophie Herakleitos des Dunklen von Ephesos* (1858), in *Gesammelte Reden und Schriften* (ed. Bernstein, 1920), 7:114; 8:656–57. George Brandes, *Lassalle* (1877; tr. 1911), p. 7.

34. Aeschylus, *Prometheus Bound* (tr. Warner, 1947); H. P. Parkes, *Gods and Men* (1960), pp. 210–11; and, especially, Michael Grant, *Myths of the Greeks and Romans* (1964), pp. 178–89, and Karl Kerenyi, *Prometheus* (1946).

35. Friedrich Meinecke, "Campanella," in *Die Idee der Staatsräson* (1924), p. 118; *Machiavellism* (tr. Scott, 1957), p. 194. Marx/Engels, *On Religion* (Moscow ed., 1957), p. 15. *Marx/Engels Werke* (East Berlin ed., 1968), 1:263.

36. Marx/Engels, *Historisch-Kritische Gesamtausgabe* (ed. Rjazonov, 1927), 1, pt. 1:10, 64, 131. This edition reproduces as its frontispiece a contemporary "allegorical" print inspired by the prohibition of Marx's *Rheinische Zeitung* in 1843; for those interested in iconographical evidence, it is a sketch of *Der gefesselte Prometheus:* presumably the young Marx, chained to a printing press and attacked by a royal (Prussian) eagle.

37. *The Prophecy of Dante* (1819), in *Byron's Verse* (ed. Dunn, 1974), pp. 33–34.

38. Shelley, *Prometheus Unbound*, in *Poetical Works* (ed. Hutchinson, 1967), p. 205.

39. Shelley, *Poems Published in 1820* (ed. Hughes, 1963), pp. 9, 146–56, 224.

40. Gaston Bachelard, *La Psychanalyse du feu* (1938), pp. 19–20, 35; *The Psychoanalysis of Fire* (tr. Ross, 1964), pp. 7, 16.

41. Norman O. Brown, *Love's Body* (1968), pp. 177–83, 248.

42. Hans Barth, *Die Idee der Ordnung* (1958), p. 195; *The Idea of Order* (tr. Hankamer and Nowell, 1960), p. 159.

43. J. G. Frazer, *The Golden Bough* (1940), p. 642.

44. Purification, or washing clean, is part of the revolutionary complex. As John Tanner, G. B. Shaw's revolutionary anarchist in *Man and Superman* (1903; Penguin ed., 1946, p. 218), argues: " . . . hot water is the revolutionist's element. You clean men as you clean milk-pails, by scalding them."

45. In these remarks on the flood and the conflagration, I have been emphasizing here only the context of idealistic hope in which these paradoxically optimistic metaphors usually appear. But surely their dark power and persuasiveness derives from an essential ambivalence: they are also symbols—and realities—of deep mortal fear and anxiety.

Jonathan Swift sensed this when he had Lemuel Gulliver impeached in Lilliput for having urinated on the Imperial Palace. True, what Gulliver had done was to extinguish a fire and thus preserve from destruction "that noble Pile, which had cost so many Ages in erecting . . . " But he had earned no gratitude. The Empress "conceiving the great Abhorrence of what I had done . . . could not forbear vowing Revenge." And, in the Articles of Impeachment drawn up against "the Man-Mountain," there were charges of treason, heresy, and worse. "Under Colour of extinguishing the Fire kindled in the Apartment of his Majesty's most dear Imperial Consort, did maliciously, traitorously, and devilishly, by discharge of his Urine, put out the said Fire . . . " Not only that it was an "infamous and illegal Method": it represented an intolerable danger, for it "might, at another time, raise an Inundation by the same Means . . . " (Jonathan Swift, *Gulliver's Travels* [1728; ed. Quennell, 1953], pp. 70–72, 83–87).

Freud saw in this scene not so much political anxiety as essential masculinity in determining civilization (the role of "fire and urethral erotism"). It is, like so much that is ingenious in imaginative literature, capable of both macro- and micro-interpretation.

"Jonathan Swift was recalling with bitterness the ingratitude of Queen Anne, who long ago had put the prim niceties of her court above his spirited writings," Jacob Bronowski writes. But Dr. Bronowski does not leave it there; he also goes on to find in the flood and the conflagration symbols of a deep disquiet at the human condition.

> Thus Gulliver pissing on the flames of the miniature palace perpetuates in giant form an age-old gesture of revolt. When the Gordon rioters burned Newgate prison in 1780, it was noticed that they climbed recklessly along roofs and ledges in order to stand high above the flames and piss into them. Today small boys still celebrate the end of a camp-fire evening by happily standing in a circle and putting out the primitive fire . . . [J. Bronowski, *The Face of Violence* (rev. ed., 1969), pp. 56–57]

Yet, in noting the element of personal disquiet and the gesture of revolt, one should not lose sight of the profound quiet and primeval peace which characterizes the revivifying religious role of water in the symbolism. As Mircea Eliade has written on this point:

> Immersion is the equivalent, at the human level, of death at the cosmic level, of the cataclysm (the Flood) which periodically dissolves the world into the primeval ocean. Breaking up all forms, doing away with the past, water possesses this power of purifying, of regenerating, of giving new birth . . . . Water purifies and regenerates because it nullifies the past, and restores—even if only for a moment—the integrity of the dawn of things. [Eliade, *Patterns in Comparative Religion* (1958), p. 194]

Thus, in the profusion of dialectical commentary, Prometheanism and "Gulliverism" emerge as ambiguous as the Flood and the Conflagration. The fire purifies and destroys, the water protects and inundates.

46. Ernest Jones, *Freud* (1957), 3:350.

47. Sigmund Freud, *Collected Papers* (1950), 5:288–89.

48. Sigmund Freud, *Civilization and Its Discontents* (ed. Jones, tr. Riviere, 1930), pp. 50–In.

49. R. F. Fortune, *Sorcerers of Dobu* (1932), pp. 296–97; Eliade, *Shamanism,* p. 363 n.

50. See the stimulating paper by Dr. Mary Jane Sherfey, "The Evolution and Nature of Female Sexuality in Relation to Psychoanalytic Theory," in *Journal of the American Psychoanalytic Association* (January 1966), pp. 28–128. It has, naturally enough, become a basic text in the popular literature of the Women's Liberation movement; see, for example, *Psychoanalysis and Women* (1973, ed. Miller), an anthology, pp. 135–53; and Dr. Sherfey's own further work, *The Nature and Evolution of Female Sexuality* (1972).

51. Mary Wollstonecraft Shelley (née Godwin), *Frankenstein, or the Modern Prometheus* (1818; ed. Joseph, 1969). Kate Millett, *Sexual Politics* (1971).

Chapter 14

1. The idea of the heroic masses, of the People as Hero, or the whole nation as the collective protagonist of the revolutionary drama, became widespread in France (where it was supplemented by the self-serving notion that the new leaders could also take on heroic mold) and also in England (where it had to serve as a substitute for the immemorial stature of traditional heroes). "The present appears to me," the poet William Cowper wrote in 1789, "a wonderful period in the history of mankind." But he was also candid enough to observe, as he looked up from the manuscripts of his translation of the *Iliad* and the *Odyssey,*

> Though to say the truth, I am much better qualified to write an essay on the siege of Troy than to descant on any of these modern revolutions. I question if, in either of the countries just mentioned [i.e., France and the Austrian Netherlands], full of bustle and tumult as they are, there be a single character whom Homer, were he living, would deign to make his hero. The populace are the heroes now, and the stuff of which gentlemen heroes are made seems to be all expended.

When Cowper subsequently vented his outrage and disgust at the violent deeds of the modern French heroes (as if no blood ever flowed in Homeric action), he remarked:

> I cannot tell you the joy I feel at the disappointment of the French [quarrels among the Girondians and Jacobins, the defeat of Dumouriez and the retreat from Holland]; pitiful mimics of Spartan and Roman virtue, without a grain of it in their whole character. [*The Correspondence of William Cowper* (ed. Wright, 1904), 3:408–11; 4:391]

In these lines from a poem entitled *Heroism,* he went on to praise more humdrum native virtues (*Cowper's Poems* [ed. Fausset, 1931], p. 66):

> Oh, place me in some heav'n-protected isle,
> Where peace, and equity, and freedom smile;
> Where no volcano pours his fiery flood,
> No crested warrior dips his plume in blood;
> Where pow'r secures what industry has won;
> Where to succeed is not to be undone;
> A land that distant tyrants hate in vain,
> In Britain's isle, beneath a George's reign!

Ultimately, it would appear, Cowper turned against the very notion of heroes, old or new, all with their "puny hands . . . and baby minds":

> Great princes have great playthings. Some have play'd
> At hewing mountains into men, and some
> At building human wonders mountain-high . . .
> Some seek diversion in the tented field,
> And make the sorrows of mankind their sport.
> But war's a game, which, were their subjects wise,
> Kings would not play at. Nations would do well
> T'extort their truncheons from the puny hands
> Of heroes, whose infirm and baby minds
> Are gratified with mischief; and who spoil,
> Because men suffer it, their toy the world.

> [*The Task*, p. 387]

2. P. A. Brown, *The French Revolution in English History* (1918; 1965), pp. 15–16. See, generally: Edward Dowden, *The French Revolution and English Literature* (1897); Allene Gregory, *The French Revolution and the English Novel* (1915; 1966); A. E. Hancock, *The French Revolution and the English Poets* (1899).

3. *Life and Correspondence of Major Cartwright* (ed. F. D. Cartwright, 1826), 1:95.

4. *Life and Correspondence of Cartwright*, 1:102.

5. Christopher Wyvill, *A Defence of Dr. Price and the Reformers of England* (1792), pp. iv–vi.

6. Brown, *French Revolution in English History*, p. 31.

7. Walpole to Hannah More (September 1789), in *The Letters of Horace Walpole* (ed. Toynbee, 1905), 14:208.

8. *Life and Correspondence of Cartwright*, 1:296–97.

9. Brown, *French Revolution in History*, p. 19.

10. Cartwright, *Life and Correspondence*, 1:352. Brown, *French Revolution*, pp. 17, 25–26 (italics added).

11. Sir Brooke Boothby, *A Letter to Edmund Burke* (1791), pp. 102–3, 77, 57.

12. Dr. Joseph Priestley, *Letters to Edmund Burke* (1791), p. vii.

13. Boothby, *Letter to Edmund Burke*, pp. 101–4.

14. *The Correspondence of the Revolution Society in London, with the National Assembly, and with various Societies of the Friends of Liberty in France and England* (1792), pp. 1–3, 12–15.

15. John G. Alger, *Englishmen in the French Revolution* (1889).

16. For a brief portrait of Théroigne, see my "Ladies on the Barricades," in *Encounter* (July 1972), pp. 22–27.

17. The Book of Daniel was usually associated with the "prophecy interpretation mania"; and an Edinburgh editor has left us with another example of the mixture of religious drama, theological mysticism, and, in this case, a kind of childish sense of the occult which can accompany the high moments of an ideological crisis. Writing in his *Tait's Magazine* of the famous trial of the young Scottish radical Thomas Muir in August 1793, William Tait has recorded the following:

> A friend of ours, then a child, and bred among the most noted of the Reformers of the period, gives a lively idea of the general state of feeling in Edinburgh, by recording his own notions. The day of the trial, or of the sentence, was thundery

and exceedingly dark, and the rain fell in torrents. There was but one topic, one interest—Muir, and the trial; and every one had gone to witness it. A Trial was beyond the comprehension of our friend; but, gazing through the window, he felt that some awful thing was acting by wicked men; that some terrible catastrophe was impending, like the Crucifixion or the Judgment Day, to which the dismal weather bore token, and in which the fate of Muir was somehow involved. Our young friend was only reassured by the sensible reflection, that this could not be the Day of Judgment, as the Jews, for whose conversion his Puritan grandfather regularly petitioned in his family prayers, were not yet converted and "brought in with the fulness of the Gentile nations." [*Memoirs and Trials of the Political Martyrs of Scotland, Persecuted during the Years 1793 and 1794, viz. Thomas Muir ... Maurice Margarot* (1837), p. 9 n]

18. "John Oswald," in the *Dictionary of National Biography* (ed. Lee, 1909), 14:1221–22; Henry Redhead Yorke, *Travels in France* (2 vols., 1814), 1:162.

19. John G. Alger, "The British Colony in Paris: 1792–93," in *English Historical Review* (October 1898), pp. 672–94.

20. There was, I am suggesting, very little significant doctrine of utopia and revolution. Accordingly, I should like to underline, with a few additional details, the distinction between the occasional English outbursts of radical impatience and romantic fury and the steady consistent efforts of the English ideologists to remain on a course of reform and not revolution.

Thus, a reformer of extremist temperament like John Thelwall could boast that he belonged to "the only avowed Sans Culottes in the metropolis" and could feel pride that they "fear me as much as they hate." To one of his correspondents he made the chiding remark: "I fear you are somewhat short of the true Sans Culotte liberty .... you have too much veneration for property, too much religion, and too much law" (*Trial of Thomas Hardy for High Treason*, in *A Complete Collection of State Trials* [ed. Howell, 1818], 24:377).

If Thelwall was to the left of his correspondents, most of the other London leaders tried to restrain what they considered to be unfortunate and thoughtless outbursts of extremism. Some of it was only rhetorical. Thus Hardy kept on receiving letters from enthusiasts who would conclude: "Farewell, hoping that the hydra of tyranny and imposition shall soon fall under the guillotine of truth and reason ... " This brought them under the suspicion—among fellow reformers as well as government observers—of preparing their cadres to be Jacobinical keepers of the public safety ("the safety of the People is the Supreme, and in cases of necessity the only law"), indeed that they would only be substituting the Royal hangman's rope for a republican blade. (*The Proceedings at large on the Trial of John Horne Tooke for High Treason at the Sessions House in the Old Bailey* [ed. Blanchard, 1795], 1:294–95; *Hardy Trial*, pp. 366–77).

Again, a correspondent writes to Thomas Hardy (17 September 1792): "Would not all the evil be done away at once by the people assembled in convention?" (*Tooke Trial*, p. 220) Why must changes be slow and gradual? Why couldn't there be one clean sweep? A Norwich radical group, puzzled by the discrete or timid ambiguities of the "moderate reform" program—"covered with a sort of obscurity in its language"—inquired of Thomas Hardy (11 November 1793) whether the London groups would really "rest satisfied with the Duke of Richmond's plan only; or whether it is their private design to rip up monarchy by the roots, and place democracy in its stead ... " They also indicated that they wanted to adopt the old name of "the Revolution Society" (*Hardy Trial*, p. 393).

Maurice Margarot hastened to reply on behalf of the London Corresponding Society. Titles were of little moment; it was "a matter of small importance whatever name you choose to adopt." More important was that if they divided themselves in cellular fashion, "into small societies, each of which [was] to choose a delegate," that at the end a representative committee should emerge. But this was the central message and warning:

> But, above all ... let no dispute be carried to excess; leave monarchy, democracy, and even religion, entirely aside; never dispute on these topics ... The committee offer you every assistance in their power, but request that your questions may relate chiefly to the methods of obtaining a reform in parliament. Like yourselves, they are friends to peace [*i.e.* opponents of the war against France] ... and well-wishers to the rights of man; yet not so sanguine in their expectations as to imagine those rights will be restored by the spontaneous consent of those who have so long been deprived of them. [*Hardy Trial*, p. 394]

This was the characteristic caution of skeptical liberal reformers who knew the simple-minded optimism of the militance they had to encounter. Thomas Erskine made much of Margarot's reply to the Norwich query, and he reformulated it in his historic peroration for the defense so unambiguously that it certainly must have helped sway the jury to acquit Thomas Hardy (as it would John Horne Tooke, for much the same reasons):

> The Attorney General says, this is lamely expressed. —I, on the other hand, say, that it is not only not lamely expressed, but anxiously worded to put an end to dangerous speculations.—Leave all theories undiscussed;—do not perplex your-selves with abstract questions of government;—endeavour practically to get honest representatives,—and if they deceive you—then, what?—bring on a revolution?—No!—Choose others in their stead. [*Hardy Trial*, p. 934]

This formula for reform was, as we have been arguing, on its way to becoming a central article of faith in the English ideology.

21. The notion of a second revolution as the completion of the first was less a concept of social or political theory (as it was later, under Marxian intellectual influence, to become) than a slogan of the time, a standard formula, a dramatic cliché of the day (and understood to be such at the time). As Dr. John Moore wrote in his journal of 1792:

> The influence of theatrical entertainments on the public mind is too powerful to be neglected on the present occasion: the music, the pantomime, and the new pieces brought forth, all are calculated to inspire sentiments and passions favourable to the second *Revolution*, for the affair of the 10th (August) is already dignified with that name.
>
> I am much mistaken, however, if there was not a considerable risk of its terminat-ing so as that, instead of a revolution, it would have been called a rebellion; in which case we should have heard a very different language from the same mouths at the theatres. [John Moore, *A Journal During a Residence in France* (1793), 1:109]

22. *Tooke Trial*, 1:203, 207. *Hardy Trial*, p. 510.

23. I have taken the liberty in my account of quoting certain disputed passages, although Henry Redhead Yorke—supported by friendly and loyal witnesses during his trial at the York assizes—attempted to deny them. I feel justified in so doing. The fact of the matter was that the official pamphlet of the great Sheffield speech had been printed by Yorke's close friends, who had asked him to give them a text for publication and distribution. It was this published version which had been submitted in evidence. In his efforts to chal-lenge its validity—he denied saying such things and none of his friends could recall having heard such things—the one point which would have been decisive was the charge that the pamphlet had been tampered with, that someone had inserted passages from another hand, that (in a word) a fake had been concocted, presumably by the authorities in order to "frame" an otherwise impeccable radical reformer on charges of revolutionary incen-diarism. This charge could not be established, nor was it even properly made.

In his own cross-examination of his defense witnesses, Yorke was too clever—and too rhetorical—by half. For he had been arguing that the extreme passages in question ("fire," "explosion," "burying despotism," and the like) were not only his own, but were after all only "a jumble of metaphors." One of the great young orators of the day, he thought that he could with irony deny that he had "bewitched" anybody with "my eloquence and sublime metaphors." He protested too eloquently. The judge and the jury must have raised their eyebrows at his courtroom flights of oratory, and they presumably concluded that Yorke's language, as charged and as heard, was all of a metaphorical piece. Consider this exchange:

"You have generally heard that I was a man-butcher fond of blood and slaughter? ... "

"I have often heard you say in private, that no one but a knave or a madman would think of bringing about a revolution in this country."

There were too many published texts which elaborated Yorke's revolutionism for this "private" assurance to have counted for much.

"What do you think was the general tendency of my speech upon Castle-hill?"

"I conceive it was to advise the people to be very orderly in their conduct, to endeavour to disseminate political information, and that your ideas extended to no greater degree than that, and by that means they would become sensible of any abuses in the mode of election or representation."

"Then you thought the political knowledge I wished them to acquire, was the knowledge of their own country; not to teach them revolutionary doctrines, or the doctrine of the holy and immaculate guillotine? ... "

If the jury could believe that, they could believe anything; and that last characteristic turn of phrase didn't help (*Proceedings on the Trial of Henry Redhead, otherwise Henry Yorke*, in *State Trials*, 25:1130–35).

A good deal of the exaggerated and contrived quotations which government informers had offered to the court were effectively brought into doubt; yet even these do not seem to be very much out of character, except possibly for the trite imputation of drunkenness ("he appeared to me rather in liquor," "he did not appear to be so sober a man as he generally is"). One witness put it more fairly, and probably more accurately, when he characterized Yorke as a man who "used to get a little warm in conversation now and then" (*Hardy Trial*, pp. 654, 662). Some quotations, then, should be used with caution; but then so must Yorke's denials. The following, which I quote only for purposes of giving the atmosphere of the courtroom charges, is from one Henry Alexander whom Thomas Erskine had convincingly demolished as a paid government informer. It is a garbled and probably untrustworthy report, but nevertheless of interest. The meeting was supposed to have taken place some time toward the end of 1793 at Robinson's Coffee-house in Shire-lane, London.

"On the last night that he was at the society, he took leave of them by a long speech—he said he was going to Bel-gi-um—Bel-gi-na."

"Did he say for what purpose he was going there?"

"Yes; that he was going to head the French army, and should be back by Christmas; that he had received a letter from a friend of his in Bel-gi-um, where they were going; that they would be ripe by Christmas—he was going at the head of them.

"Ripe for what?"—"For a revolution."

"Did he say whether he meant to return into England again?" "He did."

"What did he say to you in that speech—the substance of it?"

"The substance of it was as I informed you before—that he had received a letter to go over; that he had an offer of being a member of the National Convention in France; and that he was in hopes that he should have the pleasure of coming here either by Christmas; or the beginning of the year, at the head of them; and that he should find them all ready to join him; and that he was in hopes that Mr. Pitt, with the different ministers he mentioned, and the king's head, would be upon Temple-bar ... "

"Did he say anything about the Sans Culottes?"—"He said a great deal about them, that they were a set of brave fellows ... "

"What did he say about bloodshed?"

"He said, that there would be no good done without some bloodshed ... "

"Where was the blood to be shed?"

"He did not say."

[*Hardy Trial*, p. 640]

It is, of course, impossible to untangle truth and falsehood here, how much was made up, exaggerated and elaborated (or simply misunderstood), and how much represented a kernel of truth about the personality and activities of this most flamboyant English radical on the European scene.

24. "Henry Redhead Yorke (1772–1813)," *Dictionary of National Biography*, 2:1258–59; *Yorke Trial*, p. 1046.

25. *Tooke Trial*, 1:311.

26. *Tooke Trial*, 1:326–27. *Yorke Trial*, p. 1085.

27. *Hardy Trial*, pp. 614 ff., 924.

28. *Memoirs and Correspondence of Castlereagh* (ed. Vane, 1848), 1:258.

29. Frank Hamel, *A Woman of the Revolution* (1912), p. 312. *The Debate on the French Revolution* (ed. Cobban, 1950), pp. 42, 64, 55.

30. Anna Laetitia Barbauld, *Works* (ed. Aikin, 1825), 2:355–77; *Debate on the French Revolution*, pp. 49–50.

31. *Debate on the French Revolution*, pp. 281–82, quoting Hannah More's *Modern Politicians, a Word to the Working Classes of Great Britain*.

32. Anna Laetitia Barbauld, *Civic Sermons to the People* (no. 1, 1792), p. 11.

33. *State Trials*, 25:640–44. *Tooke Trial*, 2:340–43.

A resolution of 10 January 1794, by invoking the fate of George Jeffreys (1645–89), who had delivered the harsh sentences on Titus Oates, Algernon Sidney, and others, went even further in suggesting the violence implicit in political fury:

> "Resolved, That law ceases to be an object of obedience, whenever it becomes an instrument of oppression.
>
> "Resolved, That we recal to mind, with the deepest satisfaction, the merited fate of the infamous Jefferies, once Lord Chief Justice of England, who, at the era of the glorious Revolution, for the many iniquituous sentences which he had passed, was torn to pieces by a brave and injured people.
>
> "Resolved, That those who imitate his example deserve his fate."

It was subsequently explained that the violence was only "metaphorical." Jeffreys had not, in fact, been "torn to pieces." After the flight of King James II, Jeffreys attempted his own escape, but was recognized and arrested, narrowly avoiding death at the hands of an angry tavern crowd. He was imprisoned in the Tower and died there, awaiting trial. See: H. M. Hyde, *Judge Jeffreys* (1940); and *Tooke Trial*, 1:247.

34. If (as I have tried to maintain) the radical reformers were in no sense genuine revolutionaries, this is not to say that they were not visionaries or (to use Henry Yorke's phrase) men of "Utopian artistry." One passage, written by Maurice Margarot and Thomas Hardy (6 August 1792), is worth rescuing from the volumes of the *State Trials* as an example of how even so sober an institution as representative government, so humdrum in its ideological appeal for centuries now, once had the charm of a parliamentary utopia.

> Too visible are the numerous encroachments on our rights, too common the insolence of office, the venality of magistracy, the perversion of the laws, the letting loose the military on every occasion, and those occasions eagerly sought. The subject's complaints derided—the one part of the nation turned into spies and informers against the other—the—but wherefore more? Is here not enough to prove beyond a doubt, that while we boast the best constitution, the mildest laws, the freest government, we are in fact slaves!
>
> Yet, fellow-citizens! Numerous as are our grievances, and close rivetted and weighty to the shackles on our freedom; reform one alone, and the others will all disappear ...
>
> Soon then should we see our liberties restored, the press free, the laws simplified, judges unbiassed, juries independent, needless places and pensions retrenched, immoderate salaries reduced, the public better served, taxes diminished, and the necessaries of life more within the reach of the poor, youth better educated, prisons less crowded, old age better provided for, and sumptuous feasts at the expense of

the starving poor less frequent. Look not upon this, dear countrymen, as an enthusiastic vision; but rather let us together take a calm and reasonable review of such an honest parliament assembled. [*Hardy Trial*, p. 385]

The vision, then, was not of a good and perfect society but of a better social order; the utopia was, if you will, calm and reasonable rather than total and ecstatic. Indeed, after almost two hundred years, during which time social and economic conditions have been vastly transformed, this program could be repeated and put out as the relevant manifesto for most reforming political parties in the West at the present day! The forms of hope—or, perhaps, the structure of what we have called the utopian longing—would appear to have remained a constant among all the vaunted changes and progress of European-American civilization.

35. Thomas Holcroft, *A Letter to the Rt. Hon. William Windham, on the Intemperance and Dangerous Tendency on his Public Conduct* (1795), pp. 23–27; quoted in *The Debate on the French Revolution,* pp. 325–26.

36. John Horne Tooke, *Diversions of Purley* (rev. ed., 1829), 2:3.

37. Henry W. Meikle, *Scotland and the French Revolution* (1912), pp. 239–73, Appendix A.

38. *Debate on the French Revolution,* pp. 324, 106. *Tooke Trial,* 1:418; 2:142–43.

39. *Political Register,* November 1804, in *Cobbett's Political Works* (ed. Cobbett, 1836), 1:483.

40. Priestley, *Letters to Edmund Burke,* p. 3; Boothby, *A Letter to Edmund Burke,* pp. 37, 76; Anon., *A Letter to Edmund Burke, in Reply* (1790), p. 2; Mary Wollstonecraft, *A Vindication of the Rights of Men, in a Letter to Edmund Burke* (1790), pp. 33–34.

41. Alexis de Tocqueville, *The Old Regime and the French Revolution* (1856; tr. Gilbert, 1955), p. 157.

42. The natural conceits of an island people reinforced the English ideology; but the stormier spirits on the French side of the channel could not be so quietly contained, as if the Continental landmass were so far removed from nautical realities. As Lamartine once suggested, his countrymen had combined radical politics with "the philosophy of the tempest." And this, as I have contended, had nothing to do with the imagery which the English spirit had come to find congenial.

Two passages from the verse of William Cowper (1731–1800) would appear to reinforce this point (*Cowper's Poems,* pp. 258, 220):

> But shipwreck, earthquake, battle, fire, and flood,
> Are mighty mischiefs, not to be withstood;
> And honest merit stands on slipp'ry ground,
> Where covert guile and artifice abound.
> Let just restraint, for public peace design'd,
> Chain up the wolves and tigers of mankind.

And again, making the metaphorical point more generally:

> Man, on the dubious waves of error toss'd,
> His ship half founder'd, and his compass lost,
> Sees, far as human optics may command,
> A sleeping fog, and fancies it dry land:
> Spreads all his canvas, ev'ry sinew plies;
> Pants for 't, aims at it, enters it, and dies!
> Then farewell all self-satisfying schemes,
> His well-built systems, philosophic dreams;
> Deceitful views of future bliss, farewell!
> He reads his sentence at the flames of hell.

43. Boothby, *A Letter to Edmund Burke,* pp. 78–79.

44. *Tooke Trial,* 2:83–85.

45. Christopher Hobhouse, *Fox* (1934; ed. Nicolson, 1964), p. 188; *Memorials of Fox* (ed. Russell, 1800), 2:361; Brown, *French Revolution in English History,* p. 38.

46. Priestley, *Letters to Edmund Burke,* pp. 140–41.

47. William Hazlitt, *Memoirs of Holcroft* (1816), 2:195; *The Life of Thomas Holcroft* (ed. Colby, 1925), 2:92.

48. *Memoirs of the Life of Sir Samuel Romilly* (1840), 1:415–18.

49. Mary Wollstonecraft, *A Vindication of the Rights of Men,* pp. 108–9.

50. William Cobbett, *Observations on Priestley's Emigration* (1794), in *Cobbett's Political Works,* 1:25. A more complete text is in William Cobbett, *Peter Porcupine's Works* (12 vols, 1801), 1:147–220. See also: Anne Holt, *A Life of Joseph Priestley* (1931); Asa Briggs, *William Cobbett* (1967).

51. Cobbett, *Peter Porcupine's Works,* 1:168–69.

52. *A Letter to the Rt. Hon. William Pitt on his Apostacy from the Cause of Parliamentary Reform.* By an Honest Man (1793), pp. 29, 38, 43; *Debate on the French Revolution,* pp. 327–28; Letter to the Rev. Christopher Wyvill (20 January 1795), in Wyvill, *Political Papers* (1800), 5:280–81. *Debate on the French Revolution,* p. 142.

53. Christopher Wyvill, *The Correspondence of the Rev. C. Wyvill with the Rt. Hon William Pitt* (1797), p. vii. Correspondence with Pitt (1796), pt. 1, pp. 74–75.

54. Cartwright, *Life and Correspondence,* 1:218–21.

Chapter 15

1. *Memoirs of the Life of Sir Samuel Romilly* (1840), 1:106–7.

2. Bertrand Barère, *Memoirs* (tr. Payen-Payne, 1896), 2:55–56 (Barère's italics). This, I may note in passing, is not the last we will hear of this curious Paris intellectual habit of displacing a French affair onto a foreign stage. In its way, Jean-Paul Sartre's famous play *Kean* (1954) is an illustration of this, as it sets the dawn of French existentialist philosophy into the acting milieu of eighteenth-century London theater.

3. David L. Dowd, "Art and the Theater during the French Revolution: The Role of Louis David," in *Art Quarterly* (Spring 1960), 23:9. Dowd goes on to suggest (p. 16), almost too tentatively, that "David's inclination for the theater—his taste for the dramatic phrase, the melodramatic gesticulation, and perhaps an inner compulsion to assume the heroic grandeur of a tragic role—may have influenced his political attitude during the Revolution."

4. One English historian contends: "The English societies were not copies from French models; the Jacobins, in fact, are sometimes supposed to have been founded in imitation of the London Revolution Society ... " P. A. Brown, *The French Revolution in English History* (1918; 1965), p. 68. On the London Revolution Society, see G. S. Veitch, *Genesis of Parliamentary Reform* (1913), ch. 6, and generally, W. P. Hall, *English Radicalism 1791–1797* (1912).

5. Coleridge's *Table Talk* (1 May 1832), in Brown, *French Revolution in English History,* p. 59.

6. J.-J. Rousseau, *Politics and the Arts: Letter to d'Alembert on the Theatre* (1758; tr. Bloom, 1960), p. 79.

7. See, especially, Maurice Cranston, "Ethics and Politics," in *The Mask of Politics* (1973); and his introduction to the Penguin edition of *The Social Contract* (1762; tr. Cranston, 1968).

8. *Proceedings on the Trial of Henry Redhead, otherwise Henry Yorke,* in *A Complete Collection of State Trials* [ed. Howell, 1818], 25:1083–85.

9. Kenneth Minogue, "Theatricality and Politics," in *The Morality of Politics* (ed. Parekh and Berki, 1972), pp. 148–62. Allen Gilbert, in his edition of *The Letters of Machiavelli* (1961), translates *fantasia* as "imagination" (p. 97).

10. Perez Zagorin, *The Court and the Country: The Beginning of the English Revolution* (1969), p. 341.

11. See, especially, J. Huizinga, *Homo Ludens: A Study of the Play Element in Culture* (1938; tr. 1950); Roger Caillois, *Man, Play, and Games* (tr. Barash, 1961); and Ervin Goffman, *The Presentation of Self in Everyday Life* (1959). For topical recent works, see Robert Brustein, *Revolution as Theatre: Essays in Radical Style* (1971), and Ferdinand Mount, *The Theatre of Politics* (1972).

12. Rousseau, *Letter to M. d'Alembert*, p. 25.

13. Hume wrote of Rousseau, after the breakup of their friendship in London:

> He has read very little during the Course of his Life, and has now totally re-nounced all Reading: He has seen very little, and has no manner of Curiosity to see or remark: He has reflected, properly speaking, and study'd very little; and has not indeed much Knowledge: He has only felt, during the whole Course of his Life; and in this Respect his Sensibility rises to a Pitch beyond what I have seen any example of: But it still gives him a more acute Feeling of Pain than of Pleasure. He is like a Man who were stript not only of his Cloaths but of his Skin, and turn'd out in that Situation to combat with the rude and boisterous Elements, such as perpetually disturb this lower World.

In another letter, Hume added: "Was ever anything in the world so unaccountable? For the purposes of life and conduct, and society, a little good sense is surely better than all this genius, and a little good humour than this extreme sensibility" (E. C. Mossner, *The Forgotten Hume* [1934], pp. 152–55).

14. *Memoirs of Romilly*, 2:2–5.

15. *The Debate on the French Revolution* (ed. Cobban, 1950), p. 365.

16. Brown, *French Revolution in English History*, p. 89; William Cowper to William Hayley, 29 January 1793, *The Correspondence of William Cowper* (ed. Wright, 1904), 4:363–64.

17. Alexander Stephens, *Memoirs of John Horne Tooke* (1813), 2:112–18.

18. Stephens, *Horne Tooke*, 2:119, 152–53.

19. John Horne Tooke, *Diversions of Purley* (rev. ed., 1829), 1:218–19 n.

20. Tooke, *Diversions of Purley*, 2:17.

21. Stephens, *Memoirs of Tooke*, 2:243, 312 n, 323, 384. Tooke, *Diversions of Purley*, 2:486.

22. Anna Laetitia Barbauld, *Works* (ed. Aikin, 1825), 2:411–12.

23. Barbauld, *Works*, 2:140.

24. "On the State of France in 1815," *Monthly Review* (vol. 34), in Sir James Mackintosh, *Miscellaneous Works* (1846), 3:193, 201.

25. Mackintosh, *Miscellaneous Works*, 3:201–2.

26. *Memoirs of the Life of Sir James Mackintosh* (ed. R. J. Mackintosh, 1836), 1:87–89. There are some minor differences in the versions of this exchange of letters (December 1796) in *The Correspondence of Edmund Burke* (ed. McDowell and Woods, 1970), 9:192–95.

27. *Memoirs of Mackintosh*, 1:89 n; *Correspondence of Burke*, 9:204–5.

28. Letter from Dr. S. Parr (1799), in *Memoirs of Mackintosh*, 1:105–6.

29. Letter to Moore (1800), in *Memoirs of Mackintosh*, 1:124–25.

30. William Hazlitt, *The Spirit of the Age* (1825; ed. Mackerness, 1969), pp. 155–56.

31. Mackintosh was much encouraged by the European-wide scope of the process of ideological disenchantment. In a letter from Bombay in December 1804, he wrote:

> I have lately read the lives, and private correspondence of some of the most memor-able men in different countries of Europe who are lately dead. Klopstock, Kant, Lavater, Alfieri—they were all filled with joy and hope by the French revolution—they clung to it for a longer or a shorter time—they were all compelled to relinquish their illusions. The disappointment of all was bitter, but showed itself in various modes, according to the variety of their characters. [*Memoirs of Macintosh*, 1:129]

As I have indicated, I will be returning in a sequel to a fuller analysis of Mackintosh and "comparative ideology"; for he represents, in my view, the first self-conscious protagonist in the modern drama of disenchantment from utopia and revolution. There were, as he notes, "various modes"; but in his own personal case the intensity and the incisiveness of his introspection make him a notable pioneering spirit. Not until the confessional literature of hope and bitterness in connection with the Russian Revolution has there been so subtle and valuable a delination of the role of moral faith and intellectual self-deception in the maintenance of ideological illusions.

32. *Memoirs of Mackintosh*, 2:95, 148–49, 287, 238. Thomas Green, *Extracts from The Diary of a Lover of Literature* (1810), pp. 139–40.

33. There may well also be a deep anthropological element here. In her analysis of the primitive concepts of pollution and taboo, Dr. Mary Douglas has reminded us: "Purity is the enemy of change, of ambiguity and compromise. Most of us indeed would feel safer if our experience could be hard-set and fixed in form . . . of course the yearning for rigidity is in us all. It is part of our human condition to long for hard lines and clear concepts" (Mary Douglas, *Purity and Danger* [1966], p. 162).

34. William Hazlitt, *The Life of Thomas Holcroft* (1816; ed. Colby, 1925), 2:235–36.

35. *Memoirs of Mackintosh*, 2:149.

There is a vivid impression of Mackintosh in Thomas Carlyle's *Journal*. It was the last year of Mackintosh's life (1832), and Carlyle saw him and heard him—they never spoke—at a party in London.

> On Saturday saw Sir James Mackintosh (at Jeffrey's), and looked at and listened to him, though without speech. A broadish, middle-sized, grey-headed man, well-dressed, and with a plain courteous bearing; grey intelligent (unhealthy yellow-whited) eyes, in which plays a dash of cautious vivacity (uncertain whether fear or latent ire), triangular unmeaning nose, business mouth and chin; on the whole, a sensible official air, not without a due spicing of hypocrisy and something of pedanty, both no doubt involuntary. The man is a Whig philosopher and politician, such as the time yields, our best of that sort, which will soon be extinct. He was talking mysteriously with other "Hon. Members" about "what was to be done"—something *à la* Dogberry the thing looked to me, though I deny not that it is a serious conjunction . . . only believe that change has some chance to be for the better, and so see it all with composure. [James Anthony Froude, *Thomas Carlyle* (1882), 2:205, 282]

So even Carlyle, in his complex cantankerous way, could lend a sympathetic ear to Mackintosh's campaign for reform and be persuaded of both its urgency and hopefulness. Remarkably enough, Mackintosh had succeeded in his vow, of thirty years earlier, to avoid rebounding from his disillusionment with revolution "towards the opposite extreme," indeed to maintain a position "on the democratic side of the centre."

36. Yorke's phrases are from his Sheffield speech, quoted in *The Proccedings at large on the Trial of John Horne Tooke for High Treason at the Sessions House in the Old Bailey* (ed. Blanchard, 1795), 1:321.

37. A few further remarks on Henry Yorke's mismanaged defense. It was perhaps understandable why, in the case of the trial of Thomas Muir in Edinburgh, the services of Thomas Erskine were declined. Muir was evidently intent on a confrontation with the so-called justice usually meted out by Scotland's harsh chief judge, Lord Braxfield; and his victimization might well serve "the cause." The strategy of Henry Yorke in conducting his own defense is less clear. It could be that Yorke had taken umbrage at the lengths to which Erskine would go in the courtroom to obtain an acquittal, as he had in the cases of Hardy and Tooke. The Tooke trial took place on 17–22 November 1794, some eight months before the Yorke trial in July 1795. At the Tooke trial, Erskine had made a special point of differentiating among the various strands of radical thought. He was especially concerned to identify Yorke's "extremism" as inapplicable to an understanding of John Horne Tooke's "moderation." He wanted the jury to dismiss as irrelevant "all that trash and farrago which has been making everybody sick for these three last days . . . " He was making a reasonable plea for a reasonable man. "I am not here defending all the papers which you have heard read, many of them are indecent, many are rash, and many of them

Notes to Pages 550–53

are absurd; but that is not the question; here the question is, What were the objects of this man?" *(Tooke Trial,* pp. 378, 386). The result was a memorable victory for freedom of speech and dissenting expression.

Yorke marshaled much legalistic lore and studded his remarks with learned references to Hume and Burke, Locke and Beccaria, Blackstone and Sir George Savile. But he had been ill-advised to attempt to deny the undeniable—that his views could be more properly subsumed under revolutionary theory than reformist moderation. He still might have defended his "fiery metaphors" as forms of free speech which were not intended to, nor did they in point of fact, lead to conspiracies or seditious combinations. The government's case about arms and weapons ("long knives," "pike blades to be fluted like a bayonet," "night-cats" against cavalry charges) proved to be very thin indeed. Yorke was simply too rhetorical to be able to defend his rhetoric on sober legal grounds. It might well have succeeded. In his summing up, Sir Giles Rooke (the Justice of His Majesty's Court of Common Pleas at the York assizes) said this:

> ... you should be apprized of what I consider to be the right of every man in this country; namely, that he has a right to discourse upon speculative plans of reform, with this proviso, that he shall not endanger the peace of his country ... if the conduct of the defendant had been merely a speculation of his own, it would have been different thing. [*Yorke Trial,* pp. 1149–52]

He reassured the jury that if Yorke, and his friends, had been merely "honest speculators," then the verdict would have to be *not guilty.* But beyond political speculation there was the danger of "tumult and disaffection." The jury returned within twenty minutes with a verdict of guilty. Yorke was fined and sentenced for two years in prison, although he actually was to serve closer to four in a Dorchester Castle cell. One would have thought that by a modern standard of the legal limits of free speech and expression, namely, the necessity of proving "a clear and present danger," there was little evidence indeed that this English revolutionary rhetorician had been the instigator of deep disaffection, not to mention actual tumult.

38. H. R. Yorke, Esq., *A Letter to the Reformers* (1798).

39. Henry Redhead Yorke, *Letters from France* (2 vols., 1814), 1:299.

As one historian has written of Jacques-Louis David's role as "artist-policeman," he was

> closely associated with the levers of power during the so-called "Reign of Terror." As a member of the Committee of General Security he ranked with a dozen other top police officials at the very summit of the political hierarchy of the First Republic. This supreme national security organization, co-partner of the better-known Committee of Public Safety, performed functions similar to those of the Cheka in the Russian Revolution. The central police authority, armed with sweeping powers, was informed and obeyed by a complicated network of agents and auxiliaries throughout France. Contrary to the traditional view, David was an active, responsible and conscientious member of the Committee. During this period of office (15 September 1793 through 26 July 1794) he regularly attended its sessions.... In general he was an active participant in the daily business of the police authority and he signed almost as many decrees as Robespierre did during the same period. [David L. Dowd, "Jacobinism and the Fine Arts: *The Revolutionary Careers of Bouquier, Sergent, and David,*" in *Art Quarterly* (Autumn 1953), 16:207–8]

40. Henry Redhead Yorke, *These Are the Times that Try Men's Souls! A Letter to John Frost, a prisoner in Newgate* (1793). *Thoughts on Civil Government: Addressed to the Disfranchised Citizens of Sheffield* (1794).

41. Yorke, *These Are the Times,* p. 37; *Thoughts on Civil Government,* p. 75.

42. Yorke, *Thoughts on Civil Government,* pp. 5–7; *These Are the Times,* pp. 22, 62.

43. Yorke, *These Are the Times,* p. 24.

44. Yorke, *These Are the Times,* pp. 30–33,

45. Henry Redhead Yorke, *Reason Urged against Precedent in a Letter to the People of Derby* (1793), pp. 40, 51.

46. Yorke, *Reason Urged against Precedent*, pp. 7, 10, 23.

47. Yorke, *Reason Urged against Precedent*, p. 52; *These Are the Times*, p. 51.

48. Yorke, *These Are the Times*, pp. 29–30.

49. Yorke, *Thoughts on Civil Government*, p. 57; *These Are the Times*, pp. 53, 56.

50. Yorke, *Reason Urged against Precedent*, pp. 34–35.

51. Yorke, *Reason Urged against Precedent*, pp. 26–30.

52. Yorke, *These Are the Times*, p. 74.

53. Yorke, *These Are the Times*, p. 45.

54. Yorke, *Reason Urged against Precedent*, p. 36.

55. Yorke, *Reason Urged against Precedent*, pp. 4–5, 36–37. The *Dictionary of National Biography* (ed. Lee, 1909), mentions the matter (21:1258); see also the obituary in the *Gentlemen's Magazine* (March 1813), 83:283–84.

56. Yorke, *Letters from France*, 1:273–76, 142. There is a shortened version of this work, edited by J. A. C. Sykes, under the title *France in Eighteen Hundred and Two* (1906), which is not very useful.

57. One revolutionary repents, the other remains (after a fashion) unrepentant and unreconstructed. Henry Yorke had wondered, when he met David in 1802, how the painter had ever escaped after "Retributive justice at length overtook some of these monsters, and David, with others of the homicidal crew, were committed to prison, in order to take their trials for their lives ... " (*Letters from France*, 1:325).

As a matter of fact, David had, in one of the great melodramatic outbursts of the Terror, vowed to take his stand with Robespierre to the very death. At midnight on 8 Thermidor (26 July 1794), on the eve of Robespierre's fall, those present at an agitated meeting of the Jacobin Club—"in the gloom of the vaulted chapel of the Old Dominican monastery of the Rue Saint-Honoré"—were treated to the following spectacle.

ROBESPIERRE (*concluding the reading of what is to be the last political speech of his life*): Friends and brothers, the speech that you have just heard is my last will and testament. My enemies, or rather those of the Republic, are so many and so strong that I cannot hope to escape their blows for long.... Now is the moment to prove your courage.... If you support me, the new traitors will share the fate of the old. If you forsake me, you will see how calmly I shall drink the hemlock.

DAVID (*rising excitedly, rushed to the front, shouts*): I will drink it with you!

But the next morning David was absent from the Convention floor when Robespierre was shouted down, arrested, and sent to the guillotine with his brother Augustin, Saint-Just, and Couthon. David survived both Robespierre and Marat whom he had defended (on 12 April 1793) with the cry, "Strike here—I demand my own assassination; I, too, am a virtuous man! Liberty will triumph!" See: David L. Dowd, *Pageant-Master of the Republic: Jacques-Louis David and the French Revolution* (1948), p. 86; and also his "Art and the Theater during the French Revolution," pp. 16–17.

During his subsequent, brief imprisonment, David wrote a statement which was at once an apology for and a defense of his revolutionary career. Evidently he now believed, as Barère had suggested to him, that Robespierre was somehow linked to a British spy! Insisting that he had "never had other desires or other thoughts than to live and die for the cause of the People and of liberty," he also went on to concede that his accusers could "only reproach me with an exaltation of ideas which deluded me as to the character of a man whom many of my colleagues, more enlightened than I, regarded as a mariner's compass of patriotism ... " As Dowd remarks: "like so many others, David denied Robespierre in order to save his own skin and claimed that he simply had been deceived by a clever but unscrupulous imposter. He may have bitterly regretted his cowardice but he lived to paint again ... " (Dowd, "Jacobinism and the Fine Arts," pp. 209–10).

No bitter regrets overshadowed his ideology, or impeded his career. Napoleon offered him a seat in the Senate and the title of baron (David declined); Metternich appointed him to the Fine Arts Academy in Vienna; the King of Prussia proposed to make him his minister of fine arts at Berlin; and even Louis XVIII continued to purchase the paintings of the exiled artist (he died in Brussels in 1825, at the age of seventy-five).

Yet Henry Yorke's portrait of him as an unrepentant and unreconstructed revolutionary would appear to be quite accurate. Apparently only the Bourbons never forgot, and the Royalist officials in Paris continued to regard David as a dangerous revolutionary, even refusing to give permission for his burial in France (for fear of political demonstrations). As his biographer has written, "friends and foes agreed that David was a partisan of the Revolution from first to last ... " And, in the curious way that biographers have of identifying themselves with their protagonists, Professor Dowd (to whom we are indebted for so much excellent research) proves himself to be a partisan of the partisan of Revolution from first to last.

The apologia is pertinent and instructive. It is conceded that David served during the Terror as an efficient, conscientious, and enthusiastic policeman. He controlled the movements of his fellow-deputies to the Convention and censored the work of his fellow-artists. He signed some 406 orders "to question, search, detain, arrest, imprison, release, or turn over to the Revolutionary Tribunal for trial ... " Yet none of this, we are told, should be considered immoral or culpable, disreputable or monstrous; and only malevolent critics could make such odious imputations. On the contrary, the impression from Professor Dowd's various accounts of David's career is one of a public-spirited artistic genius, warm in his love of the people, devoted to the ideals of liberty and progress, conscientious and selfless in his execution of his duties. How can this pious, uncritical, half-hagiographical view be reconciled with the historian's recognition (the words are also Dowd's) that the Committee of General Safety—"the central police authority, armed with sweeping powers, informed and obeyed by a complicated network of agents and auxiliaries throughout France"—did in point of fact "perform functions similar to those of the Cheka in the Russian Revolution"? (Dowd, *Art Quarterly* [Autumn 1953], 16:208).

Here is the extraordinary defense mechanism for the exculpation of utopian blindness and revolutionary excess. If a critic (Gérard Walther, and he meant well) claims that David was "a bad policeman," then the biographer hurries to point out that during his active police career (1793–94) he attended 131 (or 42%) of the 315 meetings; and of the 4,737 decrees promulgated "not less than 406 (approximately 9%) bear the signature of David." He was, thus, a very good secret policeman. If the guillotining of Lavoisier, the great chemist (and David had painted a magnificent portrait of him), is deemed a tragedy, then the biographer is relieved to find that it was not David's signature that had dispatched the man to his death. If the playwright Marie-Joseph de Chénier is forced to confess his errors and to burn the manuscripts of his work (David *did* sign the certificate testifying to this), then the biographer, ever alert to incriminating evidence, states that "there is no indication that David was personally responsible for the suppression" (although indeed "Chénier never forgave the painter"). Thus, in an Orwellian use of the adverb *merely*, David was "merely guilty" of "extreme rigor."

Professor Dowd will not be budged; he refused to turn his back on his chosen hero in history. If "the only valid criticism that could be made of David's conduct was that he was relatively inflexible," then to have maintained anything but "an attitude of complete impartiality" would indeed have been "immoral and illegal." The guilty and the innocent were impartially condemned. He forgave no errors and urged no clemency. Thus, on balance, "David's rigorous non-intervention is actually admirable." More than that, "his austere disinterestedness was, according to contemporary standards of conduct, a mark of virtue." Professor Dowd finds it "commendable" that there was no corruption or private enrichment (curious, the logic of this morality: for the taking of a few francs might have saved a few innocent lives!). He even finds it "refreshing to learn" that "the political police of the Revolution usually observed the legal safeguards and amenities of arrest, and did not engage in sadistic brutalities such as extracting information by means of torture ... " What a regaling revolutionary example—that even an artistic genius "did not neglect his more sinister duties as a security agent for the First French Republic ... " (All my references here are to: David L. Dowd, "Jacques-Louis David, Artist Member of the Committee of General Security," *American Historical Review* [1952], 57:871–92.)

This species of contradiction-ridden apologia may be taken as characteristic of the attempt to evaluate a revolutionary personality within the terms of his own utopian aspirations, and at the expense of the moral ambiguities and tragic personal consequences to be discerned in the full historical context. The "contemporary standards of conduct" to which Professor Dowd makes his abstract appeal were in fact more varied, more complex, more realistic. An architect, who was to be a witness in the trial of Danton and associates, observed David and other members of the Committee of General Security sitting at the Tribunal, and recorded: "They were unrecognisable from anger, pallor and fright, so much did they seem to fear they would see the victims escape death." See Alphonse Dunoyer's biography of Fouquier-Tinville, *The Public Prosecutor of the Terror* (tr. Evans, 1914), p. 196.

One last brief citation to suggest that it was not only French participants who saw the vice in the putative virtue; foreign observers especially could manage to be relatively free from what Henry Yorke called the "ferocity and bombast" of the local revolutionary style. Perhaps the most perceptive in his detachment was the Scottish doctor and man of letters (biographer of Smollett), and author of a novel (which inspired Byron) who kept a valuable record of everything he saw and heard. See: John Moore, *A Journal During a Residence in France* (2 vols., 1793); also "John Moore, M.D. (1729–1802), *Dictionary of National Biography*, 13:810–12, and Robert Anderson, *Life of John Moore* (1820). Offering slightly higher standards of political conduct than historians often give the age credit for, Dr. Moore wrote the following (*Journal*, 2:449–50, 490):

> The most deplorable circumstance which distinguishes this Revolution from others is, that when its original object was in a great measure obtained, order, tranquillity, and submission to law did not return. One revolution has been grafted on another; new alterations have been imagined, and executed by men more violent, and means more bloody, than the former; the populace, stimulated by unprincipled leaders, have committed all the excesses of revolted negroes, or of slaves who have burst from the galleys. At this moment, four years after the first insurrection, instead of the blessings of freedom, the unhappy people of France, under the name of a Republic, suffer more intolerable oppression than they ever did under the most despotic of their monarchs; and are at the same time exposed to the attacks of external enemies, whose number is daily increasing by the imprudent conduct of their new governors.
>
> Of all the evils which have attended this extraordinary Revolution, the most important to mankind in general, perhaps, is that it weakens the indignation which every liberal mind naturally feels for despotism, and inclines them to submit to the awful tranquillity of methodified oppression, rather than risk such scenes of anarchy and carnage as have been of late exhibited in this country ....
>
> And with regard to the inhabitants of this country, it must be acknowledged that the revolution has been hitherto so wretchedly managed, as to render the higher orders of society miserable, without making the lower happy.

58. See Audrey Williamson, *Thomas Paine, His Life, Work and Times* (1973), pp. 254 ff., A. O. Aldridge, *Man of Reason: Life of Thomas Paine* (1959), pp. 267–70, and M. D. Conway, *Life of Paine* (1892), 2:300–304, all of which include excerpts.

59. Yorke, *Letters from France* (1814), 2:354; Thomas Paine, *Complete Writings* (ed. Foner, 1945), 2:1124.

60. T. S. Eliot, *The Hollow Men* (1925), in *Collected Poems* (1963), p. 89.

61. From Lewis Goldsmith's memoir, *Antigallican Monitor*, 27 September, 1 November 1812, and 6–13 February 1814; in A. O. Aldridge, *Man of Reason: The Life of Thomas Paine* (1959), p. 266.

62. Aldridge, *Man of Reason*, p. 201.

63. Aldridge, *Man of Reason*, pp. 204, 336; Conway, *Paine*, 2:131.

64. Aldridge, *Man of Reason*, p. 210; Conway, *Paine*, 2:109–10.

65. Conway, *Paine*, 2:132; Aldridge, *Man of Reason*, p. 217.

66. Aldridge, *Man of Reason*, p. 205; Conway, *Paine*, 2:79.

67. Aldridge, *Man of Reason*, p. 267.

68. Conway, *Paine*, 2:48, 52–53; Paine, *Complete Writings*, 2:1331–32, 1335; Conway, *Paine*, 2:144–46; Paine, *Complete Writings*, 2:1126.

69. On David and the relationship between revolutionary art and politics, see: Dowd, *David and the French Revolution*; Louis Hautecoeur, *Louis David* (1954); and Robert L. Herbert, *David, Brutus and the French Revolution: an Essay in Art and Politics* (1972).

David was rather less ferocious as a commissar of revolutionary art than as a zealous Jacobin policeman. Few artists of the day (and so many were Royalists) were "purged": a few were imprisoned, none was guillotined. David actually protected Vien, the director of the old Academy, as well as the rococo master, Fragonard. One historian, in an odd phrase, refers to David's "admirable lack of vindictiveness." However, the new political guidelines for artists, supposedly now liberated from automatic manipulation, were single-minded and severe. David's pupils were, of course, in all the central jury posts, and they were relentless defenders of ideology and propaganda in the required new art. One (Topino-Lebrun) bemoaned that few of the paintings revealed sufficient revolutionary fervor; another (Fleuriot-Lescot) found the sculpture, especially the low reliefs, lacking in true and useful revolutionary spirit. A third (Wicar), in denouncing French artists who remained abroad, proposed that a painting in the Academy by Xavier Fabre be dragged to the Tree of Liberty, mutilated by every faithful revolutionary artist, and then burned amid cries of *"Vive la République!"* Small wonder that, after a few terrifying years, a leading revolutionary aesthetician, looking at the pictures exhibited at the Salon of 1795 by timid, frightened, a-political artists, could cry: "O! mes belles espérances, comme vous avez été déçues!" [James A. Leith, *The Idea of Art as Propaganda in France 1750–1799* (1965), pp. 113–17, 150–55]

70. John Moore, *A Journal During a Residence in France* (1793), 2:137–38.

71. Yorke, *Travels in France*, 1:320–25. Nor was Yorke alone in his harsh judgment of Jacques-Louis David. Sir Walter Scott met him and thought him "a bloodthirsty terrorist." A dinner in Paris in 1815 was "thoroughly poisoned" for him by David's presence (J. G. Lockhart, *The Life of Sir Walter Scott* [1902], v:79):

> The poet, on entering the saloon, was presented to a stranger, whose physiognomy struck him as the most hideous he had ever seen; nor was his disgust lessened when he found, a few minutes afterwards, that he had undergone the *accolade* of David "of the blood-stained brush."

For Carlyle, too, there was a fastidious dislike of the person and the politics.

> The swoln cheek, choking his words in the birth, totally disqualified him as an orator; but his pencil, his head, his gross hot heart, with genius in a state of convulsion, will be there. A man bodily and mentally, swoln-cheeked, disproportionate; flabby-large, instead of great; weak withal, as in a state of convulsion, not strong in a state of composure . . . " [Thomas Carlyle, *The French Revolution* (Belloc ed., 1906), 2:169]

Even Lamartine, in the course of defending the Girondins, expresses his distaste of the Jacobin painter and politician, especially for his role in the Terror beginning with the murder of the King:

One person only behaved with brutality: and that was the painter David, who was recognized by the King as he looked at him from the entrance. Louis asked him if he should soon have completed his portrait. "I will never for the future paint the portrait of a tyrant," replied David, "until his head lies before me on the scaffold. [Je ne ferai désormais le portrait d'un tyran, que quand sa tête posera devant moi sur un échafaud.]" The King looked down and was silent at this brutal insult. David mistook his moment: a bold word before tyranny becomes cowardice in the presence of a reversal of fortune . . . [A. de Lamartine, *Histoire des Girondins* (1847; ed. 1908), 2:359; *History of the Girondists* (tr. Ryde, 1847), p. 68]

72. *Memoirs of Romilly*, 2:45, 253.

73. Earl of Selkirk, *A Letter addressed to John Cartwright, Esq . . . . on the Subject of Parliamentary Reform* (London, 1809), pp. 1–22.

74. William Hazlitt, *The Life of Thomas Holcroft* (1816; ed. Colby, 1925), vol. 2, pp. 92–93.

75. Henry W. Meikle, *Scotland and the French Revolution* (1912), p. 222 n.

76. Jeremy Bentham, *Plan of Parliamentary Reform, in the Form of a Catechism, with Reasons for Each Article: with an Introduction, showing the necessity of Radical, and the Inadequacy of Moderate, Reform* (1817), and *Radicalism Not Dangerous* (MS., 1819–20) in *The Works of Jeremy Bentham* (ed. Bowring, 1843), 3:450, 452, 599.

77. Thomas Smith, *The Law of the Revolution* (1872), in *The English Defence of the Commune 1871* (ed. Harrison, 1971), pp. 261–70. *The Letters of John Stuart Mill* (ed. Elliot, 1910), 2:346–48.

78. Brown, *The French Revolution in English History*, p. 153. *Life of Cartwright*, 2:4; 1:240.

79. *Life and Correspondence of Major Cartwright*, 1:300.

80. Edward Dowden, *The Life of Percy Bysshe Shelley* (1909), 1:103–7.

Chapter 16

1. *Bagehot's Historical Essays* (1965), pp. 401–33; *Physics and Politics* (1872), ch. 6; and, generally, Alastair Buchan, *The Spare Chancellor: The Life of Walter Bagehot* (1959), and Norman St. John-Stevas, *Walter Bagehot* (1959).

2. J. S. Mill, *Autobiography* (1873; Oxford ed., 1940), pp. 246–47; Michael St. John Packe, *The Life of John Stuart Mill* (1954), pp. 459–60.

3. Alexis de Tocqueville, *The Old Regime and the French Revolution* (1856; tr. Gilbert, 1955), pp. 141, 162–65.

4. R. R. Palmer, *The Age of the Democratic Revolution* (1959), 1:470.

5. Antoine Nicholas de Condorcet, *Esquisse d'un tableau historique des progrès de l'espirit humain* (1795), pp. 270–71. There was an English translation printed in London in the same year; I have used the London edition (1955, tr. Barraclough), pp. 143–44.

6. Condorcet, *Esquisse*, pp. 331–32; *Sketch for a Historical Picture of the Progress of the Human Mind*, p. 175.

7. See the introduction by O. H. Prior to his edition of the *Esquisse* (1938); J. Salwyn Schapiro, *Cordorcet and the Rise of Liberalism* (1934); Alexander Koyré, "Condorcet," *Journal of the History of Ideas* (April 1948), pp. 131–52; Joseph Fabre, *Les Pères de la Révolution: de Bayle à Condorcet* (1910); and, especially, Léon Cahen, *Condorcet et la Révolution Française* (1904), pp. 516–48. For a hostile viewpoint of Condorcet's "progressive" sins, see Friedrich Hayek, "The Counter-Revolution of Science," *Economica* (February, May, August 1941), and Eric Voegelin, *From Enlightenment to Revolution* (1975, ed. Hallowell), pp. 125–35. Hayek cites the following remark by Condorcet, from a discourse celebrating the destruction of papers relating to the history of noble families in France: "Today Reason burns the innumerable volumes which attest the vanity of a caste. Other vestiges remain in public and private libraries. They must be involved in a common destruction." Voegelin goes on

from there to build a simple case against Condorcet as a "totalitarian" from whose theories "not much" differs in the base techniques of Nazi and Communist dictatorships.

8. Cahen, *Condorcet et la Révolution Française*, pp. 519–20; Condorcet, *Oeuvres* (ed. A. Condorcet-O'Connor and F. Arago [1847–49]), 12:643: "Faisons des lois révolutionnaires, mais pour accélérer le moment ou nous cesserons d'avoir besoin d'en faire. Adoptons des mesures révolutionnaires, non pour prolonger ou ensanglanter la révolution, mais pour la completer et en précipiter le terme."

9. I am following here the valuable research in the dissertation of Rolf Reichardt, *Reform und Revolution bei Condorcet* (Bonn, 1973), especially pp. 312–63.

10. Brissot and Robespierre, *Discours aux Jacobins*, 23 April 1792; in Condorcet, *Esquisse d'un tableau historique* (1971, ed. Hincker), pp. 58–59.

11. Albert Soboul, *Le Procès de Louis XVI* (1966), p. 27.

12. Immanuel Kant, *Zum ewigen Frieden* (1795 ed.), pp. 103–4. *Metaphysik der Sitten* (1787), in Kant, *Werke* (ed. Weischedel, 1956), 4:479. *Perpetual Peace* (ed. Beck, 1957), pp. 53, 59.

13. *Zum ewigen Frieden*, pp. 87, 91; *Perpetual Peace*, pp. 44, 46. *Kant* (ed. Rabel, 1963), pp. 62, 317. *Werke*, 4:586–88.

14. Kant, *Werke*, 4:786, 862–63 n; *Religion within the Limits of Reason Alone* (1793; ed. Greene-Hudson, 1960), pp. 112–13, 176 n. *Werke*, 6:55; *What is Enlightenment?* (1784), in Kant, *On History* (ed. Beck, 1963), p. 4. Edmund Wilson, "The Documents on De Sade," in *The Bit between My Teeth* (1966), p. 217; Marquis de Sade, *Selected Letters* (ed. Lély, 1965), pp. 168–88.

15. *Metaphysik der Sitten* (1797), in *Werke*, 4:599; *The Metaphysical Principles of Virtue* (tr. Ellington, 1964), p. 126.

16. *Kant*, p. 288. *Zum ewigen Frieden*, pp. 71–74; *Perpetual Peace*, pp. 38–39. *Die Religion innerhalb der Grenzen der blossen Vernunft* (1793), in *Werke*, 4:665–99; *Religion within the Limits of Reason Alone* (tr. Greene-Hudson), pp. 15–43.

17. *Über Pädagogik* (1803), in *Werke*, 6:700–701; *Education* (tr. Churton, 1960), p. 8.

18. *Der Streit der Facultäten* (1798) in *Werke*, 6:35–68; *The Strife of the Faculties* (1798), in *On History*, pp. 137–54.

19. Bruce Mazlish, *The Riddle of History* (1966), p. 119. See, generally, Kurt Borries, *Kant als Politiker* (1928); Hans Saner, *Kants Weg von Krieg zum Frieden* (1967), vol. 1; and Hans Reiss's edition of *Kant's Political Writings* (tr. Nisbet, 1970).

20. Kant, *Gesammelte Schriften* (1922), 9:436–37; *Philosophical Correspondence* (ed. Zweig, 1967), p. 207. Reinhold Aris, *History of Political Thought in Germany: 1789–1815* (1936), p. 73 n.

21. *The Strife of the Faculties, Idea for a Universal History from a Cosmopolitan Point of View* (1784), and *Conjectural Beginning of Human History* (1786), in Kant, *On History*, pp. 16–17, 59–60, 153; *Werke*, 6:39–92, 367.

22. For the views of J. L. Talmon, see his illuminating (if not completely persuasive) studies, *The Origins of Totalitarian Democracy* (1952) and *Political Messianism* (1960). In his lecture on *Utopianism and Politics* (published by the Conservative Political Centre, London 1957), he writes: "The tragic paradox of Utopianism has been that instead of bringing about, as it promises, a system of final and permanent stability, it gave rise to utter restlessness, and in place of a reconciliation between human freedom and social cohesion, *it brought* totalitarian coercion."

My italics; for one is put off by so simplistic a notion of historical causation, where "tended to contribute to the development of" would seem to be so much nearer the truth. Critical readers have also pointed out how ironical it is that these brilliant tirades against apocalyptic and utopian politics should come to us, in the apocalyptic tones of Professor Talmon, out of Israel, "the greatest single product of modern utopianism."

For the view of Friedrich A. Hayek, see *The Constitution of Liberty* (1960), and also *The Road to Serfdom* (1944), in which the motto to ch. 2, "The Great Utopia," sets this thesis: "What has always made the state a hell on earth has been precisely that man has tried to make it his heaven" (Hölderlin).

What this school misses is the whole traditional hold of the perfectionist ideal on men's minds, quite apart from its late appearance in secular utopian thought. Surely a glance at the literature of both primitive and Christian religiosity ("Be ye therefore perfect," Matthew 5:48; "Let us go on to perfection," Hebrews 6:1; St. Thomas Aquinas's doctrine of *Status Perfectionis*) would have constituted a reminder that the quest for wholeness and the desire for completeness—the longing for tranquillity and the dream of absolute fulfillment—began neither with the Jacobins nor the Marxists, neither with rationalism nor with romanticism. Progress leading to a utopian state of justice, reason, harmony, or happiness is, as Rudolph Bultmann concedes (*History and Eschatology*, p. 66), "the idea of eschatological perfection retained in a secularised form . . . "

There are, of course, varying and irreconcilable viewpoints as to exactly when, if at all, the process of modern secularization translated an other-worldly schedule into an earthly timetable. On this point, see the excellent study of *The Idea of Perfection in Christian Theology* by R. N. Flew (1934). Flew's evidence suggests that the great divide between the two conceptions of paradise—which, for the arbitrary purposes of my history of utopia and revolution, I have ascribed to Dante and his *De monarchia*—was rarely so clearly perceived and sustained as is commonly believed. As has been argued throughout this book, these central questions of religious and social thought lie very close together. Should (or can) the ideal of perfection be applied to the present life? Is perfection on earth one of the promised human goals? Can the eternal world be realized in the here and now? Where is the vaunted "better country," and how can it be reached? Is it possible to calculate, and to stimulate, the coming of the full consummation? Or is the bliss to be only in a world to come? Put most simply and unambiguously, is the full and final perfection only in the state beyond the grave? Can it be anything but the reward of the righteous in a life after death?

Dr. Flew tries hard to avoid the contradiction in terms contained in a phrase like "relative perfection." For he does believe that, although the ideal attainable in this life can never be the Christian's ultimate goal, nevertheless a certain degree of perfect attainment lies implicit in the human effort to live by the message of the Sermon on the Mount, the Epistles of St. Paul, the Epistle to the Hebrews, etc. But the danger of the concern with the *vita angelica* is the temptation to lose one's heart to temporal goals. Here, again, the *theologia spiritualis* lies close to the *politica perennis*. The strategy and tactics of means and ends pose eternally painful problems.

Thus, Irenaeus tried to modify for the second-century Church the old apocalyptic view, which expected a sudden catastrophe, into a sense of process, involving stages and periods; the perfect state could only be the fulfillment of a development. Perhaps there even were, as St. Ambrose was ingenious enough to argue, two kinds of perfection: "the one availing here, the other hereafter." John Calvin confirmed the idea of "progress in the present life," as posited in St. Augustine's idea of "relative perfection," even though he sternly warned mankind the absolute goal was not reachable by them. The dialecticians stretched their theories to include the protection of irony and paradox. Calvin was pleased to quote Augustine to the effect that part of perfection "consists in the recognition of our imperfection"; or, as it has been put the other way round, that which cannot be perfect is that which claims to be.

And, finally, will the great and good state of (relative) felicity come to men all at once, or bit by bit? It is, *mutatis mutandis*, the ubiquitous debate over "reform or revolution." In the words of St. Basil to a monastic disciple: "It is better to advance a little at a time. Withdraw then by degrees from the pleasures of life, gradually destroying all your wonted habits, lest you bring on yourself a crowd of temptations by irritating all your passions at once." In a homily of Macarius the Egyptian, there is a similar note of theological meliorism, emphasizing "bit by bit, and not all at once." The homilies were needed, for the strategy of perfection was not always clear. John Wesley took the trouble to explain (in 1763) that "Absolute or infallible perfection I never contended for . . . " But, as Dr. Flew points out, in the argument between Wesley and Zinzendorf (in Gray's Inn Garden, 3 September 1741), it was Zinzendorf who said, "I acknowledge no inherent perfection in this life. This is the error of errors. I pursue it through the world with fire and sword"; and Wesley had remarked, "I think we strive about words."

So the path to the perfect was full of imperfections. And indeed the ideal itself did not always embrace only the felicities. In fiery spirits, tempted to take to the sword on behalf of hatred as a higher love, there were always the fighting words of the Psalmist (139:21–22), "Do I not hate them, O Lord, that hate thee? . . . I hate them with a perfect hatred."

23. Sir Thomas More, *The Confutation of Tyndale's Answer* (1532), 2:129; *The Workes of Sir Thomas More, Knyght, sometyme Lord Chauncellour of England, wrytten by him in the Englysh Tonge* (1557), pp. 422–23. There are minor differences in this passage as printed in these two editions in the British Museum.

24. Robert Southey, *Sir Thomas More: or, Colloquies on the Progress and Prospects of Society* (1829) 2:303, 458–59.

25. Marx/Engels, *Selected Works* (ed. Adoratsky, 1951), 2:111–12. *Briefwechsel* (1949 ed.), 2:314.

26. *Werke*, 6:357–67; *The Strife of the Faculties*, in *On History*, pp. 143–52; *Lectures on Ethics* (tr. Infield, 1963), pp. 252–53; *Gesammelte Schriften*, 10:75–77; *Philosophical Correspondence*, p. 158.

27. Marx to Sorge, 10 October 1877, in *Selected Correspondence* (tr. Torr, 1942), p. 350. Marx/Engels, *Werke*, 1:80. Karl Jaspers, "Das radikale Böse bei Kant," in *Rechenschaft und Ausblick* (1951), p. 90.

28. *Werke*, 6:355–58; *The Quarrel between the Faculties* in *Kant* (ed. Rabel), pp. 335–36; and *The Strife of the Faculties*, in *Kant, On History*, pp. 141–44. Arthur O. Lovejoy, *The Great Chain of Being* (1936), p. 4. Kant, *Gesammelte Schriften*, 11:141–43; *Philosophical Correspondence*, pp. 159–61.

29. Letter of E. G. Biester, 5 October 1793, in *Kant* (ed. Rabel), p. 260. *Metaphysik der Sitten*, in *Werke*, 4:477. *Perpetual Peace*, p. 34. *Kant*, p. 278.

30. *Der Streit der Facultäten*, in *Werke*, 6:267–73; *The Quarrel between the Faculties*, in *Kant*, pp. 328–30. Friedrich Paulsen, *Immanuel Kant, His Life and Doctrine* (tr. 1902), p. 50. Kant to Moses Mendelssohn, 8 April 1766, in *Vermischte Schriften und Briefwechsel* (ed. Kirchman, 1873), pp. 384–85.

31. *Gessammelte Schriften*, 11:535–36; *Philosophical Correspondence*, p. 220. *Religion within the Limits of Reason* (Greene-Hudson tr.), p. 178 n.; *Werke*, 4:865 n.

32. Bruce Mazlish, in the Kant chapter of *The Riddle of History* (1966), p. 123. The lack of fairness and generosity of this view is practically conceded when the critic goes out of his way to quote—"purely *ad hominem*," he admits (p. 116 n)—a remark of the Nazi mass murderer Adolph Eichmann, to the effect that he had tried to live as best he could "according to Kant's categorical imperative . . . "

33. Paulsen, *Kant, His Life and Doctrine*, pp. 50–51.

34. Aris, *History of Political Thought in Germany*, p. 100 n.

35. *Anthropologie in pragmatischer Hinsicht* (1798), in *Werke*, 4:485; *Kant*, p. 344.

36. Hannah Arendt, *On Revolution* (1963), p. 203.

37. "A quels signes peut-on connaître quelle est l'opinion de la majorité de la nation?" (1791), in *Madame de Staël* (1964, ed. Berger), pp. 103–4. Thomas Hobbes, *De corpore politico* (1650), pp. 2–3. *The Life Records of John Milton* (ed. French, 1954), 3:217–19.

38. Eric Voegelin, *From Enlightenment to Revolution* (1975), p. viii.

39. *Madame de Staël* (ed. Berger), p. 107.

40. Albert Camus, *L'homme révolté* (1951); *The Rebel* (tr. Bower, 1953). Jean-Paul Sartre, *Baudelaire* (1947), pp. 58–59; (tr. Turnell, 1949), p. 50.

41. Simone de Beauvoir, *Le Force de l'Age* (1960); *The Prime of Life* (tr. Green, 1962), p. 30. The whole passage from this memoir of the 1930s has a certain topical interest in the recent revival of Paris ideological controversy.

> We saw a good deal of Raymond Aron. . . . He was a member of the Socialist Party, an organisation which we despised—firstly on the ground that it was infiltrated by the bourgeoisie, and secondly because we were temperamentally opposed to the idea of reform: society, we felt, could change only as a result of sudden cataclysmic upheaval on a global scale. But we hardly ever talked politics with Aron. Mostly he and Sartre argued bitterly about problems of philosophy. I took no part in these discussions, since my mind moved too slowly for them; nevertheless I found myself more often than not on Aron's side . . . .
>
> Aron enjoyed critical analysis, and set himself to tear Sartre's rash syntheses to bits. He had the knack of getting his opponent in the fork of a dilemma and then crushing him with one sharp hammer stroke. "There are two alternatives, *mon petit camarade*," he would say. "Take your choice." . . . Sartre struggled hard to avoid being cornered, but as there was more imagination than logic in his mental processes, he had his work cut out. I cannot recall one occasion on which he convinced Aron—or on which Aron succeeded in shaking Sartre's own beliefs.

On Sartre's practical politics, see the chapter by François Bondy in *The New Left* (1971, ed. Cranston), pp. 51–82 and Jean Amery's perceptive essay, "Sartre: Grösse und Scheitern," in *Merkur* (December 1974), pp. 1123–37. I have tried to make a brief summary of Sartre's political influence as a contemporary culture-hero in my "Ulrike Meinhof & the Baader-Meinhof Gang," *Encounter* (June 1975), p. 22:

> Sartre had fought Albert Camus' insidious influence on young minds and (after Camus' death in 1960) won the battle to discredit liberal non-Communist humanism; he had devised philosophical rationalisations for the plastic-bombers of Algiers; he had cheered on Fidel Castro and Che Guevara; he had blessed Cohn-Bendit and the Student Revolt of 1968; he had exposed American imperialism in Viet Nam; he hailed the emancipatory impulses of the Pop-&-Drug culture; he was prepared to go to jail for distributing Maoist newspapers on the streets of Paris (but de Gaulle had said, "One does not arrest Voltaire"); and for all his occasional criticisms of Communist and Soviet excesses (Budapest, Prague) he remained inflexibly loyal to the romantic principles of a Revolution which would change things utterly.

See also my "From Sartre to Solzhenitsyn," *Encounter* (July 1975), pp. 94–95.

As for Raymond Aron, his most recent formulation of the intellectual and personal differences between *les petits camarades* is in his analysis of Sartre's *Critique de la Raison dialectique* entitled *Histoire et Dialectique de la Violence* (1973). In the preface to the English edition, Aron refers to "this dialogue between two men who were friends in their youth, who were separated by their quarrels and united by their interests . . . . There were never any political disagreements between Sartre and me of a kind that would compromise our friendship until the united front of the Resistance fell apart in 1946–47 . . . . In any event his meeting Simone de Beauvoir necessarily altered the nature of the ties among those who at the École Normale were called his '*petits camarades*'. In 1938 Sartre was less 'anti-Munich' than I was . . . ." But, with much generosity, Aron declines to go into detail: "There is a chance this book will be interpreted as a balance sheet between two youthful friends who, through the events and the passions of the age, have become opposed to one another. Let me say that in the evening of my life the memory of our friendship remains to me more alive than our polemics. It may happen that when the opportunity arises a new polemic will be stirred up. I doubt it—and besides, what does it matter? We have never separated philosophy and politics.... I think differently, but I accept him as he is—even while opposing him indefinitely with reasons he will never be ready to listen to" (Raymond Aron, *History and the Dialectic of Violence* [tr. Cooper, 1975], pp. ix–xvi).

Index

Aaron, Daniel, 153; 641 nn. 83, 91
Abbott, Wilbur Cortez, 656 n. 10
Abrams, Philip, 410
Abt, Clark, 34
Adam (patriarch), 221, 493
Adami, Tobias, 664 n. 16
Adams, John, 248, 401, 675 nn. 31, 32
Adams, John Quincy, 87
Adler, Viktor, 113
Adorno, T. W., 620 n. 31
Aeschylus, 687 n. 34
Aitzema, Lion, 653 n. 21
Aldridge, A. O., 701 n. 58, 702 nn. 61, 62, 64–67
Alba, F. A. de Toledo, Duke of, 227
Alembert, Jean le Rond d', 581, 584
Alençon, François, duc d', 188
Alexander the Great, 17
Alexander, Henry, 692 n. 23
Alger, John G., 689 n. 15, 690 n. 19
Allen, J. W., 644 n. 6, 680 n. 12
Althaus, Friedrich, 663 n. 8
Ambrose, St., 705 n. 22
Amelung, J. G., 667 n. 9
America, and Hobbes's absolute rule, 318; Milton on, 222; as "New World," 19–20, 26–27; revolution in, 87, 152; slavery abolished, 166; Sprat on, 351
Amery, Jean, 707 n. 41
Anabaptists, 420
Anderson, Robert, 701 n. 57
Andreae, Johann Valentin, attitudes and ideas, 328, 330–34, 371; torch imagery, 479; *Republicae Christianopolitanae Descriptio*, 12, 330, 345, 479
Annenkov, P. V., 634 n. 20
Ants, ant-hills, as hero figure, 5–7; as ideal republic, 8–9
Ant Brotherhood, 4–5, 11

Anthony, H. S., 676 n. 37
Antilia, 376–79, 612 n. 63
Anti-Semitism. *See* Jews
Aphasia, 251
Apocalypse, and Golden Number, 337
Apocalyptic thought, Comenius's utopianism, 357–63, 366–71; as consolation, 371; revolutionary relevance of, 60–61, 65
Aquinas, St. Thomas, 21
Aragon, Louis, 641 n. 80
Arcadia, and realism, 236; Sidney on, 178–86, 194, 209–10
Archer, Henry, 419
Archetypes, 256–59
Arciniegas, German, 610 n. 39
Arendt, Hannah, 88, 600; 622 n. 35, 630 nn. 104–5, 637 n. 52
Ariosto, Lodovico, 198, 205
Aris, Reinhold, 704 n. 20, 706 n. 34
Aristonicus, 16
Aristotle, 17, 24, 168, 211
Armageddon, 384, 389–90, 398, 673 n. 14
Armstrong, John, 608 n. 34
Arnold, Matthew, 145, 325
Aron, Raymond, 288, 602
Arrowsmith, John, 251
Arthur, J. J., 503
Ashley, M. H., 680 nn. 12, 17, 681 n. 40
Ascham, Anthony, 246, 248
Aspinwall, William, 658 n. 24
Astronomy, and revolutionary images, 196–210, 228–29, 231, 392–93
Auber, D. F. E., 660 n. 24
Aubrey, John, 396
Auden, W. H., on "affirming flame," 474; and Brecht, 54–55; on necessary murder, 455; on social change, 152
Augustine, St., 705 n. 22

Austria, 380–81
Axelrod, Pavel, 78

Babeuf, François Noël, 40, 76–77
Bachelard, Gaston, 489–90
Bacon, Francis, and absolute control, 12; and Andreae, 330–31; on innovation, 311; on intellectual attitudes, 170; influenced by Joabin, 300; Mackintosh on, 549; and Marxist-Leninism, 251; Milton on, 222; foresees Royal Society, 666 n. 1; and science, 350; on words, 157; *New Atlantis*, 334–35, 376, 666 n. 1
Bacon, Roger, 610 n. 43
Bagehot, Walter, 10–11, 72, 88, 578–79
Bagwell, William, 648 n. 14, 677 n. 7
Bailey, Nathan, 649 n. 15
Bainton, Roland, 605 n. 7, 635 n. 39
Bakunin, Michael, blood and fire imagery, 481–82; Caussidière on shooting, 633 n. 6; exile, 106; neurosis, 77; on passion for destruction, 473; on coming revolution, 70, 73–74, 81, 106; as Siegfried, 74–76; influenced by Weitling, 106
Bald, R. C., 661 n. 31
Baldwin, James, 140; 686 n. 29
Balfour, A. J., on party conflict, 494; on political system in England, 629 n. 103
Ball, John, 37
Banaster, Thomas, 263
Barbauld, Anna Laetitia, 502, 507–9, 541–43
Barère, Bertrand, 531–32, 560, 585, 699 n. 57
Barker, Arthur E., 673 nn. 1, 2
Barker, Ernest, 607 n. 25
Barlow, Joel, 504–5
Barnikol, A., 634 n. 17
Barnwell, Sarah, 654 n. 4
Baron, Hans, 27, 611 n. 67
Baron, Samuel Haskell, 625 n. 69, 635 n. 26
Barth, Hans, 487 n. 42
Bastille, fall of, 498, 519, 574
Baudet, Henri, 608 n. 35
Bayle, Pierre, on Bruno, 200; attacks Comenius, 358–59, 363–71; opposes extremism, 601; and historical accuracy, 364; on unlearned experience, 320; utopian position, 355; *Dictionnaire*, 363, 365, 369, 601, 667 n. 8, 669 n. 22, 670 n. 28
Beard, Miriam, 625 n. 74
Beauvoir, Simone de, 602
Bebel, August, 104, 119, 632 n. 6
Becker, Carl, 670 n. 27
Beer, Joan, 686 n. 20
Beer, Max, 70
Bees, 380
Bell, Daniel, 635 n. 27
Bellamy, Edward, 9. 153
Bellers, John, 672 n. 51

Belt, Thomas, 605 n. 9
Benda, Julien, 156
Benét, Stephen Vincent, 604 n. 6
Bentham, Jeremy, 89–90, 172, 502–3, 570–71; 630 n. 108
Berlin, Sir Isaiah, 106; 634 n. 18, 635 n. 27, 684 n. 1
Bermuda, 671 n. 44
Berneri, Marie-Louise, 606 nn. 14, 16
Bernstein, Eduard, 78; doctrine and revisionism, 102–6, 118, 127; and Engels, 103; and Leveller moderation, 422–24, 429; Plekhanov on destroying, 112; and seventeenth century, 251; on social miracles, 615 n. 78; 624 nn. 55, 56
Bett, Henry, 610 n. 42
Biester, E. G., 598
Binyon, Laurence, 610 n. 40
Bismarck, Prince Otto von, 6
Black power. *See* Negro revolution
Blake, William, 18, 146, 474, 480, 486
Blank, Louis, 44
Bloch, Ernst, 125–27, 562; *The Principles of Hope*, 125
Blok, Alexander, 70, 482; 625 n. 70
Blood, imagery of, 151, 233, 263, 285, 299, 472–82, 585
Blount, Thomas, 245; 648 n. 15
Blumenberg, Hans, 646 n. 31
Bologna, insurrections in, 460
Bolsheviks, Bolshevism, 102, 105, 315. *See also* Communism
Bonaparte, Joseph, 94
Bonaventura, St., 21
Bond, W. H., 644 n. 15
Bondy, François, 707 n. 41
Boniface VIII, Pope, 25
Bonnell, Samuel, 660 n. 22
Booker, John, 647 n. 1
Boothby, Sir Brooke, 500–501, 517
Borkenau, Franz, 53
Borries, Kurt, 704 n. 19
Bossuet, Jacques Bénigne, 661 n. 30
Botticelli, Sandro, 20
Bourges, Michel de, 473, 683 n. 3
Bourget, Paul, 642 n. 98
Bowle, John, 662 n. 37
Boyle, Robert, 311, 341–46, 357, 371–74, 381
Brandes, Georg, 484; 624 n. 55
Braxfield, Robert MacQueen, Lord, 510–11, 549
Brecht, Bert, 129; 626 n. 84; *Die Massnahme*, 54
Bredvold, Louis I, 437; 681 n. 41
Briggs, Asa, 694 n. 50
Briggs, W. D., 644 n. 12
Brinton, Crane, 615 n. 74, 673 n. 12, 682 n. 74

Brissot, Jean-Pierre, 584
British Revolutionary Club, 502, 504
Bronowski, Jacob, 687 n. 45
Brook Farm (Massachusetts), 44, 73
Brook, Benjamin, 678 n. 8
Brown, Harcourt, 666 n. 38
Brown, Louise Fargo, 657 n. 14, 658 n. 23
Brown, Norman O., 490
Brown, P. A., 689 nn. 2, 6, 9, 10, 694 n. 45, 695 nn. 4, 5, 696 n. 16, 703 n. 78
Bruni, Leonardo (Aretino), 27
Bruno, Giordano, faith and enthusiasm, 388; fire imagery, 479; Florio uses, 242; Hartlib studies, 379; on heavenly order and liberation, 196–217, 229; influence, 200, 458; martyrdom, 216–17; and Sidney, 191, 196, 209, 325, 379, 651 n. 6, 176; *De Immenso*, 200, 217; *De la Causa*, 202; *De l'Infinito Universo et Mondi*, 210, 212; *De Monade*, 217; *Gli Eroici Furori*, 201, 216, 479; *Spaccio de la Bestia Trionfante*, 196, 204
Brustein, Robert, 696 n. 11
Buber, Martin, 44–46, 51, 60; 616 n. 8, 617 nn. 13, 17, 622 n. 45, 626 n. 80; *The Prophetic Faith*, 45, 60
Buchan, Alastair, 703 n. 1
Buchanan, George, *De Jure Regni*, 182, 189–90
Bug-words, 161, 643 n. 104
Bukharin, N. I., 50, 78, 125, 127
Bull, Major (jailer), 265, 279, 479
Bullitt, William C., 152; 632 n. 120
Bulloker, John, 648 n. 15
Bultmann, Rudolph, 254, 622 n. 41, 705 n. 22
Bunyan, John, 142, 281
Buonarroti, Philippe, 40
Burckhardt, Jakob, 43
Burke, Edmund, Boothby refutes, 500; opposes French Revolution, 473, 516, 520; opposes innovation, 311; Mackintosh opposes, 544–47; on moderation and revolution, 86–88, 94–95; debate with Paine, 521, 523, 525, 533; on social change, 17; Wyvill on, 525
Burke, Kenneth, 642 n. 97
Burnet, Gilbert, Bishop of Salisbury, 448–53
Burnet, John, 420, 434
Burnett, George, 652 n. 14
Burrage, Champlin, 658 n. 25
Burridge, Kenelm, 653 n. 34
Butler, Charles, 673 n. 52
Buxton, John, 645 n. 14
Byng, John, Admiral, 131
Byron, George, Lord, 486; *Childe Harold's Pilgrimage*, 51, 146, 158

Cabet, Etienne, 12, 38

Cahen, Leon, 703 n. 7, 704 n. 8
Caillois, Roger, 696 n. 11
Calas, Jean, 131
Calvin, Jean, 122, 132, 200, 231–32, 705 n. 22
"Camelot, Project," 34
Campanella, Tommaso, Andreae on, 331; on Hebrew restlessness, 200; as Prometheus, 486; on reformation as expediency, 217; *City of the Sun*, Boyle on, 345; Comenius reads, 665 n. 36; on dissembling, 120; on messianism, 62; on obedience, 11–12; F. A. Yates on, 646 n. 41
Camus, Albert, on city as ant-heap, 604 n. 5; ideological position, 354, 370, 601–2; on Marx, 103; on revolutionaries, 30, 51, 96; and Sartre, 601–2; 633 n. 8
Canning, George, 465
Capp, B. S., 654 nn. 2–4, 655 nn. 6, 8, 656 n. 9, 657 nn. 15, 16, 658 nn. 20, 23, 24, 29
Carew, John, 285, 288
Carlyle, Thomas, 502, 702 n. 71; 673 n. 51, 697 n. 35
Carmichael, Stokely, 150
Carr, Edward Hallett, 77; 625 nn. 67, 76, 626 nn. 79, 81, 634 n. 19, 635 n. 28, 486 n. 24
Carsten, F. L., 635 n. 33
Cartwright, John, 78, 497–500, 526, 566, 568, 573–74
Case, Thomas, 240, 387
Cassirer, Ernst, 159, 364
Castellio, Sebastian, 122
Castro, Fidel, 140, 142–44
Cate, Curtis, 684 n. 3
Caussidiere, Marc, 633 n. 6
Caute, David, 641 n. 80
Cawdrey, Robert, 648 n. 15
Cestro, C., 682 n. 74
Chain, of hope, 149; Lovejoy and Lenin, 639–40 n. 76
Chaloner, W. H., 659 n. 14
Chamberlain, John, 154
Chambers, R. W., 610 n. 39
Champion, H. H., 633 n. 6
Charles I, King of England, and astronomy, 231; on calamity, 319; and Civil War, 312; concessions, 313–14, 318; executed, 246, 388; hostility to, 300, 309; Milton on, 314, 390, 392; pleads reform, 305–10, 312–14; opposes revolution, 224, 310–11, 393; *Eikon Basilike*, 305, 307–9, 312, 314, 390, 660 n. 26
Charles II, King of England, 246, 379, 398, 425–26, 658 n. 29
Charles, R. H., 674 n. 14
Chartism, 40; "whole hog," 80
Chateaubriand, François René de, vicomte, 71, 473

Ch'en, Jerome, 639 n. 75
Chenier, Marie-Joseph de, 700 n. 57
Cheynell, Francis, 251
Chiang Ching (Mme Mao), 639 nn. 72, 75
China, 49, 101–2, 146, 148
Chronique de Mois, 503
Christ, Jesus, 67, 480; Columbus as Christ figure, 20
Chrysostom, Johann, 661 n. 30
Church, R. W., 611 n. 53
Churchill, Sir Winston S., on principles, 494
Cicero, Marcus Tullius, 668 n. 9, 671 n. 30
Cintra, Wordsworth on, 460–61
Circles, of time, 243; fiery wheel, 477; Howell, 295; Kant, 594; Nedham, 405; Polybius, 246; Weitling and, 111
Clarendon, Edward Hyde, 1st Earl of, on Charles I and popular antipathy, 300; on Charles's concessions, 313; on Fifth Monarchy men, 285; on Hobbes, 317–18; on Lilburne, 425; on reform, 88; Rogers's dedication to, 434; on sectarian extremism, 426; *History of the Rebellion*, 230, 241, 313
Clarke, Samuel, 419
Clarke, T. E. S., 681 n. 37, 682 nn. 60, 61, 64
Clasen, Claus-Peter, 627 n. 91
Cobbett, William, 516, 521–23
Cockeram, Henry, 648 n. 15
Cocteau, Jean, 517
Cohn, Norman, 37
Cohn-Bendit, Daniel, 476
Colcord, Lincoln, 152
Cole, G. D. H., 626 n. 82, 634 n. 17
Coleridge, Samuel Taylor, Bruno influences, 200; on Burke, 86–87; on contagion of passion, 71; on fire, 474; political involvement, 507; on political theories, 615–74; and Wordsworth's convictions, 457, 461, 465–67; 695 n. 5
Coleridge, Sara, 507
Colero, Johann, 660 n. 24
Coles, Elisha, 649 n. 15
Colline, William, 674 n. 27
Collingwood, R. G., 242
Collot d'Herbois, J. M., 69, 503
Colmer, John, 629 n. 99
Columbus, Christopher, 18–20, 26, 197–98, 222
Comenius, Jan Amos (Komensky), Andreae's influence on, 665 n. 36; and apocalyptic revolution, 357–63, 366; and Austrian overthrow, 380–81; attacked by Bayle, 358–59, 363–71; faith, 323; and Hartlib, 330, 342, 360, 371, 380; on human unity, 262; on innovation, 348; Henry

More on, 61–62; reputation, 667 n. 9; on struggle, 324; travels, 325; works burned, 669 n. 18; *Lux e tenebris*, 358; *Via lucis*, 666 n. 36
Comets, 227–29. *See also* Astronomy
Communia (Iowa), 110
Communism, definitions of, 56–57; ethics of, 53–54; as historical solution, 42; anthill life, 8; Marx on, as humanism, 617 n. 10; Marx opposes institutionalization in, 101; and messianism, 62; and religion, 59; and revolution, 52. *See also* Marxism
Communist Journal (London), 632 n. 4, 633 n. 10
Communist League, 106
Condorcet, Antoine Nicolas de, on "chain," 640 n. 76; in French Revolution, 156, 580, 583–84; plea for gradualism, 551; Malesherbes on, 71; on Nedham, 248; on progress, 204, 213, 595; on revolution, 38, 114, 580–85; on sweet hopes, 576; *Esquisse*, 583; *Historical Picture of the Human Mind*, 580
Conference of Revolutionary Youth (London, 1968), 260
Confino, Michael, 625 n. 76
Congregation, Lords of the (Scotland), 37
Conrad, Joseph, 68, 73
Conscience, liberty of, 387, 407
Constant, Benjamin, 160, 573
Constitutional Society, 499
Conway, M. D., 701 n. 58, 702 nn. 63–66, 68
Copernicus, Nicolaus, Bruno and, 196, 198, 212; Heath and, 221; Kant and, 594; Nedham and, 405; *De revolutionibus*, 212, 228, 236
Corday, Charlotte, 76, 503
Corrodi, H. H., 667 n. 9, 668 n. 10
Cotgrave, Randle, 246, 659 n. 7
Courtines, L. P., 670 n. 25
Couthon, Georges, 699 n. 57
Coverdale, Miles, 642 n. 104
Cowley, Abraham, 225–26, 445
Cowley, Malcolm, 154
Cowper, William, 688 n. 1, 694 n. 42, 696 n. 16
Crankshaw, Edward, 633 n. 9
Cranston, Maurice, 249; 643 n. 107, 695 n. 7
Croce, Benedetto, xi, 660 n. 24
Cromwell, Henry, 275
Cromwell, Oliver, and astronomy, 231; on Charles I, 314; as "Committee man," 667 n. 3; Cowley on, 225–26; death, 281; Dryden honors, 438, 444; on France, 92; and Hartlib, 381; Howell and, 292–93; "left-wing" opposition to, 426; and Lilburne, 425; meets Menasseh ben Israel, 262, 327;

pathology of, 78; political balance, 322; puritanism, 193; and revolutionary commitment, 51; and Rogers' millenarianism, 263–65, 268–280

Cromwell, Richard, 281

Crosland, Anthony, 104

Crossley, J., 669 n. 18

Crossman, Richard, 104; 630 n. 103

Culpeper, Sir Cheney, 378, 663 n. 5

Curtius, Ernst Robert, 254

Dahrendorf, Rolf, 606 n. 20

Daily Telegraph (London), 34

Danby, Sir Thomas Osborne, 1st Earl of, 441

Daniel, Book of, 689 n. 17

Dante Alighieri, on adventure, 190; on doubt, 100; imagery, 265, 478, 491; and Joachim, 20–21; and Paradise, 18, 20, 26, 27, 213; challenges pope, 195; political principles, 23–26, 81; adopts sovereignty, 12; *De monarchia*, 23, 705 n. 22; *Divine Comedy*, 23

Danton, Georges-Jacques, 503, 562

Danvers, Harry, 658 n. 20

Darwin, Charles, 632 n. 120

Daunou, P. C. F., 583

David, Jacques-Louis, 532, 551, 558; judgments on, 700 n. 57, 702 nn. 69–71; and Yorke, 563–64, 698 n. 39, 699 n. 57

David, Richard, 651 n. 6

Davis, Walter R., 644 nn. 2, 3

Day Lewis, Cecil, on revolution, 151

Dead Sea Scriptures, 257

Debray, Régis, 142–45

Dell, Floyd, 153

De Quincey, Thomas, 457, 460, 465

Descartes, René, 341, 343

Destruction, 304; passion for, 472–73

Deutscher, Isaac, 114, 620 n. 31, 631 n. 113, 686 n. 24

De Witt brothers, 123

Dewey, John, 129

Dicey, A. V., 683 n. 78

Diderot, Denis, 124, 132, 134, 584

Diels, Hermann, 686 n. 31

Dien Bien Phu, 141

Diggers, 403

Dircks, Henry, 381; 653 n. 1, 662 n. 3

Disenchantment, and language, 155–65

Disraeli, Benjamin, on amelioration, 494; 629 n. 103, 672 n. 51

Djilas, Milovan, 128

Dog, Dante's imagery of, 478

Dogma, in socialism, 100–105

Dohna, Lothar Graf zu, 626 n. 86

Donne, John, 21, 156, 172

Dorp, Martin, 126

Dorsten, J. A. van, 644 n. 14

Dos Passos, John, 153

Dostoyevsky, Fyodor, 7, 112

Douglas, Mary, 697 n. 33

Dowd, David L., 695 n. 3, 698 n. 39, 699 n. 57, 702 n. 65

Dowden, Edward, 689 n. 2, 703 n. 80

Downing, Calybute, 252

Drabicius, Nicholas, 358–60, 362; Bayle attacks, 363–66; death, 669 n. 18; Hartlib on, 371

Drake, Sir Francis, 190

Drama, social functions of, 533–34

Dress, uniformity of, 12

Drucker, Philip, 653 n. 34

Dryden, John, on bug-words, 161; deprived by Revolution, 439, 442, 444–47; on disenchantment, 155; dispute with Burnet, 448–49, 451–52; involvement and changed views, 438–48; metaphors and vocabulary, 443, 448; on moderation, 437

Du Barry, Marie Jeanne, comtesse, 503

Duff, Sir Mountstuart E. Grant, on Marx, 628 n. 96, 629 n. 97

Dunn, John, 676 n. 44

Dunoyer, Alphonse, 701 n. 57

Dürer, Albrecht, 122

Durkheim, Emile, 638 n. 60

Dury, John, 262, 323; and Austrian overthrow, 380–81; letter from Boyle, 374; and Gustavus Adolphus, 327–28, 341; and Hartlib, 329–30, 341, 345; travels, 325, 664 n. 29; *Clavis Apocalyptica*, 324

Dutschke, Rudi, 640 n. 78

Duvignaud, Jean, 637 n. 53

Dyscracy, 393

Earthquake, biblical 233, 384; as revolutionary image, 220, 243, 255, 281, 302, 310

East Germany, 129

Eastman, Max, 152–53

Eclipses, 227–28. *See also* Astronomy

Eden, Garden of. *See* Paradise

Edwards, John, 420

Eichmann, Adolph, 706 n. 32

Eliade, Mircea, 58, 254, 258, 478, 493

Eliot, T. S., 702 n. 60

Elizabeth I, Queen of England, 188, 190, 227

Ellis, Amanda M., 682 n. 74

Encyclopédie, 124

Engels, Friedrich, on Christianity, 66–67; and continuity, 215; and "dreamers," 592; on Lassalle, 64; eulogy on Marx, 57; as revisionist, 102–3; on revolution, 41,

67, 130; on revolution in England, 90–91; on Russian revolution, 68–69; and sociological exactness, 343; and Weitling, 107, 110; *Socialism: Utopian and Scientific,* 99–100

England, and Bernstein's socialism, 104; Fifth Monarchy Men in, 263–85; French on, 91–94; Howell on rebellion in, 298–99; Jews in, 301; national character, 578–79; revolution predicted, 90–91; revolutionary thought in, 85, 90, 92, 251–52, 262–65, 290–316

Enthusiasm, 420–21, 500

Entreves, A. P. d', 611 n. 54

Epimetheus, 315, 316

Eppendorf, Henry of, 671 n. 29

Epstein, Jacob, 640 n. 77

Erasmus, Desiderius, 11, 16, 121–22, 591, 597

Erbury, William, 278

Erikson, Erik H., 626 n. 82

Erskine, Thomas, 506, 510, 549, 691 n. 20, 692 n. 23

Esslin, Martin, 621 nn. 33, 34

Evans, B. and C., 642 n. 104

Evelyn, John, 371, 379–80, 432

Explosions, 253; Engels on, 68–69

Eyre, Sir James, 526

Ezra, Book of, 81

Fabian Society, 118

Fabius Maximus Rullianus, Quintus, 18

Fabre, Joseph, 703 n. 7

Fairfax, Thomas, 3rd Baron, 278

Fanon, Frantz, 140–41; 638 n. 66

Fantastical (word), 244

Faustianism (Faustus), 77, 226

Feake, Christopher, 283, 285, 655 n. 6

Ferguson, Adam, 437

Feria, Jane Dormer, Duchess of, 227

Feuer, Lewis S., 635 n. 40

Fever, as revolutionary image, 310; Landauer, 76; Shelley, 69

Ficino, Marsilio, 210, 645 n. 27

Fifth Monarchy Men, 263–85; Milton associated with, 387; Henry More on, 420; Nedham on, 403

Filgus, Peter, 380

Fire, festivals, 491–92; as love symbol, 261; as revolutionary image, 220, 223–26, 232, 243, 250, 253, 286, 299, 310, 331, 348, 361, 362–63, 423, 464, 474–93, 555

First International, 571–72

Firth, C. H., 654 n. 2, 657 nn. 12, 13, 674 n. 30

Fischer, Louis, 641 n. 86

Fitzgerald, F. Scott, 26

Fixler, Michael, 676 n. 37

Flame, as revolutionary image, 233, 250, 299, 308, 310, 317, 348, 435, 474, 477–78, 486, 490

Flavius, Josephus, 327

Fleming, Robert, 681 n. 34

Flew, R. N., 705 n. 22

Flood, as revolutionary image, 69, 220–21, 226, 243, 256–57, 263

Florence, 27

Florio, John, 229, 241–42, 325, 651 n. 6

Foner, Philip S., 635 n. 25

Foreign (word), 243

Forel, Auguste, 8

Formicary. *See* Ants, Ant-hill

Forset, Edward, 251

Fortune's wheel, 221, 225, 229, 246, 255, 299

Fortune, R. F., 688 n. 49

Fourier, F. C. M., 38, 592

Fox, Charles James, 519

Foxcroft, H. C., 681 nn. 37, 38, 682 nn. 60, 61, 64

Foxe, John, 21

France, Bagehot on national character, 578; Howell on rebellion in, 298; revolutionary action in, 37, 38; revolutionary thought in, 85, 91–92, 316. *See also* French Revolution

France, Anatole, 71

Francis, Sir Philip, 524, 573

Franck, Sebastian, 627 n. 90

Frank, Joseph, 675 n. 30; 680 nn. 12, 13, 15

Frankfurter Allgemeine Zeitung, 603 n. 3

Fraser, Sir William, 631 n. 117

Frazer, Sir James, 491–93

Frederick II, Emperor (1194–1250), 18

Frederick William II of Prussia, 597

Freedom, 7. *See also* Liberty

Freeman, Joseph, 156

Fremantle, Anne, 633 n. 6, 635 n. 34

French Revolution, boredom and, 73; Condorcet's involvement in, 580–85; cruelties, 562–65; effect on English radical reformers, 498–527, 530–75; Kant on, 585, 589, 596; influence of Nedham on, 675 n. 33; Napoleon justifies, 55, 69; Nietzsche on, 58; Paine's disaffection with, 558–62; pathology and, 76–77; Mme de Staël on, 600; Walpole on, 498; Wordsworth and, 454, 461–62

French, J. Milton, 676 n. 37

Freud, Sigmund, 129, 492–93; cited, 632 n. 120

Freyhan, R., 610 n. 43, 611 n. 49

"Friend to the Poor," 510–12

Friends of Parliamentary Reform, 566

Friends of the People, 514–15, 524, 532–33

Fröhlich, Paul, 635 n. 33
Fromm, Erich, 66
Froude, J. A., 648 nn. 8, 9, 697 n. 35
Fussell, Paul, 605 n. 7

Galileo, 222–23
Gallienus, Emperor, 607 n. 25
Garboil (word), 245
Gardiner, S. R., 654 n. 2, 658 n. 19
Garin, Eugenio, 635 n. 36
Garnett, Constance, 684 n. 1
Garrison, William Lloyd, 152
Gaster, Theodore H., 653 n. 36
Gauden, John, 306, 313, 661 n. 27
Gay, Peter, 619 n. 27, 632 n. 2, 636 n. 41, 637 n. 54
Gentz, Friedrich, 87–88
Germany, 90, 99, 105
Giap, General Vo Nguyen, 144
Gibb, M. A., 680 nn. 12, 16, 681 n. 35
Gide, André, 155
Gilson, Etienne, 611 n. 54
Giraffi, Alessandro, 297, 302, 475–76, 651 n. 3
Girondins, 582
Glanvill, Joseph, 421, 666 n. 1
Glasson, T. F., 674 n. 14
Glökler, J. P., 663 n. 14
"Glorious Revolution, The," 432–36, 501
Godwin, William, 9, 513, 519, 524–25, 546, 549; *Enquiry concerning Political Justice*, 619 n. 27
Goethe, J. W. von, 57, 200, 257, 486, 594
Goffman, Ervin, 696 n. 11
Gold, Michael, 62
Gold, golden, Lenin on, 167; golden number, 337; golden time, 259; golden world, 19; Columbus's "gold for paradise," 608 n. 36; Wagner's golden age, 74; 651 n. 3
Goldmann, Lucien, 620 n. 32
Goldsmith, Lewis, 702 n. 61
Gomulka, Wladyslaw, 129
Gooch, G. P., 657 n. 15, 680 n. 12
Goodman, Christopher, 182, 189
Goodman, Paul, 614 n. 68
Goodwin, Thomas, 662 n. 2
Gorky, Maxim, 76, 113–18
Gottschalk, Andreas, 107
Goulemot, J. M., 660 n. 23
Gouzenko, Igor, 635 n. 29
Graham, Cunningham, 633 n. 6
Grant, Michael, 687 n. 34
Grass, Günter, 170–71
Green, Thomas, 547
Green stick, and universal welfare, 4, 5, 11
Greenberg, Sidney, 645 n. 29

Greenblatt, S. J., 647 n. 50
Greenham, Richard, 251
Greenlaw, E. A., 644 n. 12
Gregory, Allene, 689 n. 2
Grenville, William Wyndham, Baron, 524
Greville, Fulke, murdered, 193; orthodoxy, 192–93; on Paradise, 208; on Sidney, 187, 189, 190, 325, 651 n. 6; verses, 191–93
Grieve, George, 503
Griffiths, William, 633 n. 9
Grosclaude, Pierre, 638 n. 58
Grundmann, Herbert, 610 n. 38, 611 n. 51
Guevara, Ché, 67, 70, 140, 143–45, 482
Guicciardini, Francesco, 241, 242, 403
Gustavus Adolphus, King of Sweden, 327–28, 341
Gutenberg, Johann, 338, 652 n. 20. *See also* Journalism; Printing
Guyau, Marie Jean, 491

Hadas, Moses, 652 n. 14
Halifax, George Savile, 1st Marquis, attitude to Burnet, 452; Dryden dedication to, 445; on moderation and balance, 329, 434–36; on third opinion, 169
Hall, Jennifer, 664 n. 16
Hall, John, 342, 365 n. 36, 372
Hall, Joseph, Bishop, 223, 224, 659 n. 11
Hall, W. P., 695 n. 4
Halliday, F. E., 651 n. 6
Hamburger, Joseph, 630 nn. 107, 109
Hamburger, Michael, 618 n. 24
Hamel, Frank, 693 n. 29
Hancock, A. E., 689 n. 2
Hanke, Lewis, 611 n. 62
Happiness, 384, 407–8
Hardy, Thomas, 168, 506, 540, 693 n. 34
Hare, Richard, 113; 635 n. 29, 684 n. 1
Harich, Wolfgang, 127; 620 n. 32, 637 n. 50
Harrington, James, Kant defends, 590, 593; and Milton, 369, 396, 398; on reason and passion, 169; on revolution, 70, 246, 253, 254, 451; and Rota Club, 396, 674 n. 25; in Tower, 376; *Oceana*, 253, 673 n. 54
Harrison, Thomas, 224, 281–85
Hartlib, Samuel, 229–30, 262; and Andreae, 330, 334; on Apocalypse, 337–38; and Boyle, 341–42, 344–46, 374; and Comenius, 330, 342, 360; death, 374–75; and dissolving Parliament, 374; on Drabicius, 371; and Dury's peace, 328–30; Evelyn on, 379–80; faith, 323; life and ideas, 326–46, 356, 374–81; "Office of Addresse," 340–41; papers and correspondence, 375; promises revolution, 324–25; uncertainties, 374–79; on utopian delays, 348; Worthington and, 369, 376–

78; *Macaria,* 334–41, 346; *The Reformed Common-wealth of Bees,* 380, 665 n. 36
Hastings, Warren, 524
Hatto, Arthur, 246; 660 n. 23
Haupt, Helmut, 626 n. 87, 627 n. 88
Hautecoeur, Louis, 702 n. 69
Hawthorne, Nathaniel, 73
Hay, Julius, 128
Hayek, Friedrich, 591; 703 n. 7
Hayley, William, 696 n. 16
Hazard, Paul, 669 nn. 21–23
Hazlitt, William, 91, 520, 532, 537, 546, 568–69
Hearn, Lafcadio, 158
Heath, Robert, 221
Heavenly disorders, 227–29
Heavenly order, 196–210, 217
Hebert, Mme., 522
Hegel, G. W. F., 65–67, 124, 144, 200
Heidegger, Martin, 129
Heine, Heinrich, 64, 594
Held, F. E., 665 n. 36
Henderson, W. D., 659 n. 14
Henry VII, Emperor, 25
Henry VIII, King of England, 17
Henry III, King of France, 200
Henze, Hans Werner, 220
Heraclitus, 172, 483–84, 601–2
Herbert, Robert L., 702 n. 69
Herbert, Zbigniew, 637 n. 49
Herder, J. G., 594, 663 nn. 14, 15
Hermes Trismegistus, 645 n. 27
Herzen, Alexander, 160, 172, 482, 581, 633 n. 6
Hexter, J. H., 15–17
Heywood, John, 642 n. 104
Hill, Christopher, 251, 648 n. 1, 654 n. 1, 661 n. 32, 681 n. 50
History, Bayle on, 364–65; Howell on, 290–91, 294–95
Hitler, Adolf, 55, 536
Hobbes, Thomas, on ambition, 182; on extremism and moderation, 600–601; and Hartlib, 346; on revolution, 245–46; on youthful rebels, 685 n. 9; *Behemoth,* 87, 670 n. 27; *Leviathan,* 6, 157, 316–19, 644 n. 7
Hobhouse, Christopher, 694 n. 45
Ho Chi Minh, 144
Hodgkin, Roger, 285
Hoffer, Eric, 96, 156; 625 n. 74
Hofstadter, Richard, 632 n. 120
Hogg, Quintin (Lord Hailsham), 630 n. 103
Holbein, Hans, 122
Holcroft, Thomas, 513–14, 540, 548, 561
Hölderlin, J. C. Friedrich, 486; 705 n. 22
Holmes, Geoffrey, 681 n. 37

Holt, Anne, 694 n. 50
Holy League (France), 37
Hook, Sidney, 102, 634 n. 15
Hooker, Richard, 161, 412
Hope, and French Revolution, 562
Hopton, Sir Ralph, 535
Horwitz, Henry, 680 n. 32, 681 n. 36
Hotman, François, 182
House, Edward Mandell, 152
Howard of Escrick, William, 3rd Baron, 680 n. 18
Howell, James, epitaph on Charles I, 319; Hartlib on, 338; historical ideas and revolution, 290–305, 312, 344, 411; imprisonment, 291–92; on Masaniello, 297, 302–3, 369, 476; on reform, 305; on Scotland, 302; translates *Le Rivoluzioni di Napoli,* 475; on tyranny, 393; vocabulary, 228–29, 242–45, 247, 249, 293; *Lexicon tetraglotton,* 659 n. 7
Howell, Roger, 645 n. 14
Hubris, 68
Hughes, Merritt Y., 673 n. 12
Hugo, Victor, 146–47, 160, 258
Huguenots, 37
Huizinga, J., 635 n. 37, 644 n. 14, 697 n. 11
Humanism, 27
Hume, David, 29, 169, 537
Humor, and revolutionary grimness, 101; 632 n. 6
Hungary, 128–30
Hus, Jan, 82, 132
Hutten, Ulrich von, 121
Huxley, Aldous, 8
Hyde, H. Montgomery, 693 n. 33
Hyman, Stanley Edgar, 650 n. 23

Iambulus, 16
Iglesia, Ramon, 609 n. 35
Imagery. *See* Metaphors; Similes; Words
Imerti, Arthur D., 646 n. 42
Incendiarism. *See* Fire
Independents, 299
Indians (N. American), 255–56
Indonesia, 196–98
Industry, defined, 672 n. 51; Hartlib advocates, 379–80
Infinity, infinite 215–16, 307
Inge, W. R., 607 n. 25
Innovation, 234–36, 310–12, 348, 353, 357, 372
Invention, 352
Invisible College, 344–45, 375
Ireland, as Jewish refuge, 673 n. 54
Irenaeus, 705 n. 22
Ireton, Henry, 314, 386
Italy, 242, 298

Jacobin Club, 503, 584
Jacobs, Joseph, 659 n. 4
Jakubec, Jan, 667 n. 9
James I, King of England, 393
James II, King of England, 433
James, William, 659 n. 11
Jaspers, Karl, 129, 706 n. 27
Jaurès, Jean, 128
Jebb, John, 499–500
Jefferson, Thomas, 562, 631 n. 120, 675 nn. 31–32
Jeffreys, George, 693 n. 33
Jews: English puritans and, 301; Howell on, 301; in Bacon's *New Atlantis*, 300; Joachim as "converted Jew," 21; residence in England, 301, 327; in Ireland, 673 n. 54; and revolution, 63, 299–300; suspected, 92; and utopianism, 200–231; "white Jew," 302; Calvin and "foolish Jewish fantasies," 200, 231; Columbus, 19, 609 n. 36; "perfidious" Judaism, 612 n. 63
Joabin of Bensalem, 300
Joachim of Flora, Abbot, 18–22, 81, 84, 266
Johnson, Douglas, 684 n. 2
Johnson, F. R., 647 n. 53
Johnson, J. W., 605 n. 7
Johnson, Lyndon Baines, 604 n. 5
Johnson, Samuel, 246; 642 n. 104, 649 n. 15
Joll, James, 617 n. 13, 619 n. 27
Jones, Ernest, 688 n. 46
Jones, Howard Mumford, 611 n. 62
Jonson, Ben, 187, 268; 659 n. 11
Journal d'Instruction Sociale, 581
Journalism, 652 n. 20
Jove, 204–10
Joyce, J., 540
Justice, 388–89, 393–94

Kaminsky, Howard, 627 n. 91
Kant, Immanuel, Bruno's influence on, 200; disenchantment, 160; on French Revolution, 585, 589, 593, 596; on government, 596–97; on man's imperfection, 576; personal compromise and integrity, 597–99; on pragmatism, 659 n. 11; on revolution, 142, 585–91, 593, 596; on terroristic history, 483; utopianism, 354, 593–95
Kantorowicz, Ernst, 608 n. 34
Kautsky, Karl, criticises Bernstein, 104; and dogma, 101, 103–5; Harich on, 128; on insoluble problems, 125; on opportunism, 429; and seventeenth century, 251; letter from Trotsky, on Rosa Luxembourg, 118; 623 n. 51
Kazin, Alfred, 154
Kecskemeti, Paul, 637 n. 52
Keep, J. L. H., 623 n. 51, 626 n. 83

Kepler, Johann, 217, 648 n. 11
Kerenyi, Karl, 620 n. 31, 662 n. 35, 687 n. 34
Kermode, Frank, 620 n. 32
Kestenberg-Gladstein, Ruth, 610 n. 44, 611 nn. 50, 51
Keynes, John Maynard, 58, 129
Kiddle, Martin, 674 n. 14
Kierkegaard, Søren, 43, 56, 58, 480
Kindersley, Richard, 615 n. 78, 632 n. 2
King, Lord, 676 n. 48
Kinloch, T. F., 648 n. 4
Knachel, Philip A., 675 n. 30
Knox, John, 37, 78, 182, 233, 252
Knox, Ronald A., 617 n. 14
Koenigsberger, H. G., 616 n. 2
Koestler, Arthur, 595, 641 n. 86
Kolakowski, Leszek, 622 n. 44, 627 n. 91
Kotterus, Christoph, 358, 359, 365
Koyré, Alexander, 647 n. 53, 703 n. 7
Kozik, Frantisek, 668 n. 9
Krakeur, L. G., 638 n. 58
Kristeller, Paul Oskar, 645 n. 28
Kropotkin, Prince Peter A., 45
Krupskaya, Nadejda Konstantinovna (Mme Lenin), 114
Kugelmann, Ludwig, 52
Kuhn, Thomas S., 650 n. 24
Kvacsala, Johann, 667 n. 9

La Barre, chevalier de, 131
Labedz, Leopold, 637 n. 48
Lafayette, marquis de, 455
Lally, Thomas, baron de Tollendal, 131
Lamartine, A. de, 507, 702 n. 71
Landauer, Gustave, 45, 76
Landor, Walter Savage, 146
Language, and disenchantment, 157–65; and English reformist ideology, 514–20; power of, 157; and revolution, 134–50; Tooke on, 514. *See also* Words
Languet, Hubert, 187–89
Lanham, R. A., cited, 644 nn. 2, 3
Las Cases, marquis de la Caussade, 61
Lasch, Christopher, 641 n. 82
Laski, Prince, 645 n. 26
Lasky, Melvin J., 620 n. 31, 637 n. 52
Lassal, Heyman, 64
Lassalle, Ferdinand, 63–65, 81, 484, 624 n. 55
Lasswell, Harold D., 626 n. 82
Lava, Marx's "glowing," 70; Wagner, 75; golden, 84. *See also* Earthquake; Storm; Explosions
League of Nations, 8
Leavis, F. R., 138, 253
Le Bon, Gustave, 101
Lecky, W. E. H., 682 n. 65

Leff, Gordon, 610 n. 46
Leith, James A., 702 n. 69
Lenin, V. I., and censorship, 114; on "chain," 640 n. 76; Debray on, 144; on democratic principle, 111; Gorky criticizes, 115–17; on Leveller cynicism, 429; on music, 76; protects Plekhanov, 635 n. 28; on revolution and reformism, 166–67; and revolutionary commitment, 51, 633 n. 10; Rosa Luxembourg opposes centralism of, 119–20; on social change, 17, 633 n. 10; on gold, 167; ruining the old, 50
Leroux, Pierre, 51
Leslie, John, Bishop of Ross, 227
L'Estrange, Sir Roger, 293
Levellers, Cromwell and, 425; ideology and moderation, 305, 315, 403, 416, 422–33
Lévi-Strauss, Claude, 255–56
Lewis, C. S., 99, 155, 251
Liberty, denial of, in French Revolution, 560–65; Halifax on, 435–36; Locke on, 408, 412; and Milton's revolutionary utopianism, 387–88; Wordsworth on, 454–56
Lichtheim, George, 620 n. 31, 635 n. 33, 636 n. 47, 659 n. 14
Liebknecht, Karl, 118, 120
Lightning, biblical, 384; as revolutionary image, 256, 258, 285, 405
Lilburne, John, 160, 224, 226, 278; and Cromwell, 425; and Leveller ideals, 423–25, 429–31; on reform, 305; retirement, 433
Linder, Robert D., 605 n. 7
Lindsay, A. D., 47
Lindsay, Jack, 645 n. 29
Llandaff (Landaff), Bishop of, 454–56
Lisbon earthquake, 517
Locke, John, on bugbears, 642 n. 104; interest in Drabicius, 669 n. 19; on happiness, 384, 407, 408; and ideal society, 250; on ideology, 406–14; Masaniello influences, 660 n. 24; on moderation, 329; on orthodoxy, 96; secretiveness, 249; on seeking after truth, 604 n. 5; vocabulary on revolution, 247–50, 254; on words, 162–64, 238, 414; Two Treatises of Government, 249
Lockhart, J. G., 702 n. 71
Lockie, D. M., 648 n. 8
London Corresponding Society (1794), 512, 524, 533, 690 n. 20
Louis XVI, King of France, 531
Love, and fire, 201; and balance, xii
Lovejoy, A. O., x, 155, 254, 595; 603 n. 4, 639 n. 76
Lowie, Robert H., 653 n. 34

Löwith, Karl, 59, 611 n. 51
Lubac, Henri de, 622 n. 40
Lucas (scribe), 21
Luethy, Herbert, 54
Lukacs, George, 53, 124–25, 127; 621 n. 32
Luther, Martin, criticized by Andreae, 334; Bruno on, 646 n. 33; Erasmus and, 121–22; More's polemic against, 14, 591; Proudhon on new theology of, 43; and religious liberty, 497
Lützow, Francis, Count von, 668 n. 10
Luxembourg, Rosa, criticizes Bernstein, 104, 118; death, 119, 120; doctrines, 118–20; Harich on, 127; pathology of, 78; on spilling blood, 632 n. 6; Letters from Prison, 118; The Russian Revolution, 120

Macarius the Egyptian, 705 n. 22
Macaulay, T. B., 682 n. 65
McConnell, Allen, 684 n. 2
McCook, Henry C., 8
McFarquhar, Robert, 618 n. 21
Machiavelli, Niccolo, Comenius on, 360; and fantasia, 535; More and, 15–16; influence on Nedham, 402; Robespierre on, 52; and word "revolution," 241–42
MacInnes, Colin, 640 n. 79
MacIntyre, Alastair, 622 n. 41
Mackintosh, Sir James, opposes Burke 544–47; Carlyle on, 697 n. 35; and French Revolution, 502; ideological position, 354, 528, 530, 543–49, 558; on reform, 523, 525; Vindiciae Gallicae, 544, 547
McLellan, David, 634 n. 20
Madan, Francis F., 661 n. 26
Madariaga, Salvador de, 608 n. 35
Madison, James, 114, 580
Maeterlinck, Maurice, 7
Magarshak, David, 684 n. 1
Magdeburg, Bekenntnis of, 182
Maitland, F. W., 615 n. 74
Malcolm X, 135, 136, 139, 140
Malesherbes, C. G. de L. de, 71, 134
Malinowski, B., 138, 157, 218
Malraux, André, 113
Mandeville, B. de, 53
Manifesto, importance of, 185
Mann, Thomas, 53, 169
Mannheim, Karl, 617 n. 7, 626 n. 80
Manuel, Frank E., 610 n. 45, 611 n. 50, 626 n. 82, 636 n. 45, 653 n. 36, 663 n. 13, 671 n. 35, 673 n. 51
Mao Tse-tung, 47, 49, 102, 144, 148, 625 n. 65
Marat, Jean-Paul, 71, 76
Maravall, Jose Antonio, 611 n. 61
Marcilly, Jean, 686 n. 28

Marcuse, Herbert, 220; 640 n. 78
Maresius, S. (Desmarets), 365
Margarot, Maurice, 549, 690 n. 20, 693 n. 34
Marvell, Andrew, 30
Marx, Karl, anti-utopianism, 591–94; challenge to Tsar, 195; classical learning, 650 n. 23; and Communism, 42, 43, 49, 101, 617 n. 10; and continuity, 215; Debray on, 144; on defense of evil, 53; dogma and revisionism, 100, 102–3, 105, 125, 127, 129–30; Duff describes, 628 n. 96; on farce and tragedy, 536; on good from evil, 124; on Lassalle, 63–64; Lukacs on, 125; on old order, 149; prejudices, 92; on Prometheus, 486; on prophetic reformers, 38, 45; religious content, 58–60, 65–67; on revolution as utopia, 30–31, 38–52, 130; on coming revolution, 70, 81, 86; as scientist, 57–58; and sociological exactness, 343; relations with Weitling, 62, 106–10; womb imagery, 493; *Civil War in France*, 38; *Communist Manifesto*, 16; *Die Deutsche Ideologie*, 46; *Das Kapital*, 52
Marxism, bureaucratic dictatorship in, 120; and Christian ideas, 58–60, 65–66; divergent views of, 57; and reformism, 167; and revisionism, 101–5, 118, 125, 128–30, 154; and revolution from below, 351. *See also* Communism
Masaniello, Tommaso Aniello (called), 242–43; Howell on, 297, 302, 303, 369; influence, 660 n. 24; and Naples revolution, 475–76
Masaryk, Thomas G., 667 n. 9
Masson, David, 398; 625 n. 68
Maude, Aylmer, 604 n. 1
Mazlish, Bruce, 704 n. 19, 706 n. 32
Medawar, Sir Peter, 100
Mede, Joseph, 337, 419, 421–22, 480
Mehnert, Klaus, 633 n. 9
Mehring, Franz, 78
Meikle, Henry W., 694 n. 37, 703 n. 75
Meinicke, Friedrich, 622 n. 49, 635 n. 36, 687 n. 35
Meinhof, Ulrike, 662 n. 1, 707 n. 41
Melville, Herman, 67
Menasseh ben Israel, 262, 301, 327
Mendelssohn, Moses, 597
Mendieta, Geronimo de, 18, 27, 608 n. 33, 612 n. 63
Meray, Tibor, 637 n. 52
Mercurius Anti-Politicus, 224
Mercurius Politicus, 398, 401
Mercurius Pragmaticus, 398
Meredith, George, 484
Méricourt, Théroigne de, 502, 557–58, 689 n. 16

Merleau-Ponty, Maurice, 124, 168
Merriman, R. B., 684 n. 7
Messianism. *See* Prophets and prophetism
Metaphor, 310; Blount defines, 245; Brown on, 490; dangers of, 157–58; and English reform, 516, 519; function, 443; revolutionary, 222–59; 285–86. *See also* individual words
Metaphorics, Curtius on, 254; 653 n. 30
Metaphysics, political, 290
Michael the Scot, 19
Michel, Paul Henri, 645 n. 30, 647 nn. 53, 57
Michelet, Jules, 474
Michels, Roberto, 629 n. 98
Middle way. *See* Moderation; Three, third, triad
Mill, James, 88–90
Mill, John Stuart, on human manner, 72; influences militant workers, 579; on minority view, 614 n. 70; on principles of revolution, 572–73, 581; radicalism, 571–73; *Political Economy*, 128–29
Millenarianism, 263, 337, 419–22. *See also* Fifth Monarchy Men
Millett, Kate, 493
Mills, C. Wright, 140, 638 n. 66
Milton, John, and absolute control, 12; on ant, 5, 6; Blake on, 18, 441; on brotherhood, 236; Dryden praises, 441; on *Eikon Basilike*, 661 n. 27; Hartlib and, 324–25, 327, 342, 345, 376; Harrington on, 369; influence on French Revolution, 675 n. 33; on liberty, 145; influence on Lilburne, 430; and Locke's disillusionment, 411; and Nedham, 401, 403; on new ideals, 30; on overcoming, 384; political balance, 322; and revolutionary utopianism, 386–98, 402, 455; on revolution, 70, 221–23, 233, 241, 247, 257, 259; and Rota Club, 387, 396; dispute with Salmasius, 87; vocabulary, 247, 249, 257, 398, 659 n. 11; *Eikonoklastes*, 314, 390, 392, 395, 661 nn. 28, 34; *Paradise Lost*, 221–22, 257, 259; *The Readie and Easie Way to Establish a Free Commonwealth*, 395, 406; *Samson Agonistes*, 402; *The Spirit of the Phanaticks Dissected*, 398
Minogue, Kenneth, 535
Mirabeau, Honoré G. Riquetti, comte de, 76, 455
Mixed modes, 248
Moderate, The, 422–23
Moderation (middle way), 307, 309, 314–15; Bagehot's "animated moderation," 88; Bayle advocates, 370; Bentham opposes, 570–71; Burke's prudence, 94; Burnet on, 449, 452; Camus and Sartre on, 602; Cart-

wright condemns, 499; Dryden on, 437; Hobbes on, 600; Kant dismisses, 587; Levellers advocate, 422–23; Disraeli, Balfour, Heath, Wilson, 629 n. 103

Molerius, Elias, 648 n. 11

Monarchy: Charles I on, 306–15; Hobbes on, 316–17; Nedham on, 400; revolutionary, 433; Sidney on, 188–89

Monk, George (1st Duke of Albermarle), 396

Montaigne, Michel de, 16–17, 100, 160, 241

Montefiore, Leonard, 628 n. 96

Montesquieu, Charles de Secondat, baron de, 316, 557, 585

Mooney, James, 635 n. 35

Moore, George, 546

Moore, John, 563, 691 n. 21, 701 n. 57, 702 n. 70

More, Hannah, 498

More, Henry, 61–62, 244, 357, 362–63, 420, 655 n. 9

More, Sir Thomas, and Bruno, 207; career, 17; denies heavenly values, 194; letter to Dorp, on change, 126; Erasmus on, 121; executed, 17, 398–99; and high principle, 217; on involvement and instruction, 18; Kant and, 590, 593, 596–97; Milton and, 222, 236; political career, 593; on revolution and reform, 88, 130, 131, 591; self-doubts, 591–94; Southey challenges optimism of, 678 n. 9; ideas of utopia, 8, 9, 11, 15, 17, 26, 28–29, 46, 343; inspired by Vespucci, 20; *Confutation of Tyndale's Answer*, 591; *Utopia*, 23, 121, 335, 398; Burnet's version, 453

Morison, Samuel Eliot, 608 n. 35

Morley, John, 86

Mornet, Daniel, 670 n. 25

Morney, Philippe de, 644 n. 14

Morning Post, 456

Morris, Christopher, 659 n. 31

Morris, William, 9

Mossner, E. C., 696 n. 13

Mount, Ferdinand, 696 n. 11

Mountains, and revolution, 142–48; mountain forest leader, 83; mountain circles, 256; sacred mountains, 259; "mountain-top-ism," 639 n. 72

Mühlmann, Wilhelm E., 627 n. 91, 665 n. 24

Muir, Kenneth, 651 n. 6

Muir, Thomas, 515, 549, 689 n. 17, 697 n. 37

Mumford, Lewis, 10, 11

Münzer, Thomas, 82

Music, and revolution, 75–76

Naipaul, V. S., 641 n. 79

Naples, revolts in (1647–48), 242–43; Howell on Masaniello and, 297, 302–3

Napoleon Bonaparte, on England, 93–94; fire imagery, 481; on French Revolution, 55, 61, 69, 73; Herzen on, 172; and Mackintosh, 547; revolutionary timing, 85; opposes utopians, 42

Nasser, Gamal Abdel, 140; 638 n. 66

Nationalism, and revolution, 92

Nechayev, S. G., 74, 116, 153

Nedham, Marchamont, career and ideological changes, 376, 400–406, 556; "dispatches" from Utopia, 398–401; and Fifth Monarchists, 282; Hartlib recommends, 345; criticizes Levellers, 425; quoted on popular revolution, 384; on revolutionary justice, 388; translates Selden, 294; vocabulary, 247–49, 276, 293, 322; *Excellencie of a Free State*, 401; *A Short History of the English Rebellion*, 405; *True State of the Case of the Commonwealth*, 658 n. 25

Negro Revolution, 141, 148, 150–51

Nettl, J. P., 626 n. 83, 632 n. 6, 634 n. 16, 635 nn. 33–35

New Atlantis, 300

New Harmony (Indiana), 44

New Lanark, 44. *See also* Owen, Robert

New Left, 148

Newman, F. B., 645 n. 18

New Model Army, 658 n. 19

Newton, Sir Isaac, 671 n. 35

New World. *See* America

New York Times, 603 n. 3, 616 n. 1

Nicholas I, Tsar of Russia, 660 n. 24

Nicolaevsky, Boris, 113

Nicolai, Christoph Friedrich, 598

Nicolson, Marjorie, 647 n. 1

Nider, Johannes, 605 n. 7

Niebuhr, Reinhold, 59

Nietzsche, Friedrich, on causes of revolution, 84; on French Revolution, 58; on gradual reform, 167–68; scorns Kant, 598; pessimism, 43; scorns utopianism, 41; on Wagner, 74; on words, 159, 218

Niewenhuis, Domela, 616 n. 5

Nihilism, 472–73

Nisbet, Robert A., 616 n. 1

Nkrumah, Kwame, 6, 136

Noland, Aaron, 686 n. 25

Norris, John, 336

North, Roger, 161

Nottingham, Daniel Finch, 2nd Earl of, 434

Novalis (F. L. von Hardenberg), 51

Novaya Zhizn, 114–15

Novy Luch, 116

Nyerere, Julius, 136

Oakeshott, Michael, 32

Oates, Titus, 693 n. 33

Obedience, 11

"Oberrheinische Revolutionär," 82
O'Brien, Bronterre, 40, 80
O'Brien, Conor Cruise, 140
Obscurity, 238, 249
Ogden, C. K., and Richards, I. A., 162, 639 n. 67, 642 nn. 93, 97, 103, 643 nn. 108, 114
Oldenbarneveldt, J. von, 123
Olschki, Leonardo, 609 n. 37
Olssen, E. A., 65
Oncken, Hermann, 624 nn. 54–55
Orwell, George, 11, 156, 431
Orlov, A., 635 n. 29
Ornstein, Martha, 666 n. 38
Osgood, Charles, 643 n. 114
Oswald, John, 503–4
Overton, Richard, 423–24
Owen, Robert, 17, 38, 44, 77, 343, 592

Packe, Michael St. John, 637 n. 51, 703 n. 2
Paine, Thomas, 152; debate with Burke, 521, 523, 525; disenchantment in and French Revolution, 502–5, 521–23, 532, 558–62; imprisoned in Paris, 522, 560–61, 585; revolutionary extremism, 526; trial, 510; and utopian opportunity, 30; interview with Yorke, 558–59; *Common Sense*, 521
Palmer, R. R., 625 n. 67, 703 n. 4
Panofsky, Erwin, 635 n. 39
Parker, Samuel, 642 n. 96, 677 n. 4
Parker, William Riley, 674 nn. 25, 27
Parliamentary Reform (English), 566–68
Paradise, Hartlib and, 336; Hazlitt on, 532, 537, 568–69; idea of, supplanted by Utopia, 18, 27; location of, 19; Milton and, 390; Wordsworth on, 419
Paris, 1968 disturbances in, 220
Parkes, H. P., 687 n. 34
Parr, Dr. Samuel, 696 n. 28
Pascal, Blaise, 68, 421
Passions, 603 n. 1
Pasternak, Boris, 72–73, 113
Paulhan, Jean, 159
Paulsen, Friedrich, 706 nn. 30, 33
Pavese, Cesare, 65
Peasants' Revolt (England, 1381), 37
Pease, T. C., 680 n. 12
Peel, Robert, 89
Péguy, Charles, 156
Pell, John, 345, 374
Pellegrini, A. M., 645 n. 18
Pembroke, Philip Herbert, 4th Earl of, 301
"People, the," as political factor, 496–506, 542
Pepys, Samuel, 284
Petergorsky, D. W., 654 n. 2
Peter Martyr, 19

Peter, Hugh, 267, 655 n. 7
Peters, Thomas, 278
Petty, Sir William, 343, 375, 674 n. 25
Phelan, John Leddy, 608 n. 33, 609 n. 35, 612 n. 63, 613 n. 64
Philip of Macedon, 607 n. 29
Phillips, Edward, 245, 247, 649 n. 15
Phillips, James E., 644 n. 15
Philo Judaeus of Alexandria, 32
Philosophes, 213, 369
Phin, John, 642 n. 104
Piaget, Jean, 668 n. 9
Piel, Gerald, 605 n. 7
Pitt, William, 523–25, 540–41, 566, 619 n. 27
Plants, as revolutionary image, 240
Plato, Bruno on, 211; Kant defends, 590, 593; on kings and philosophers, 607 n. 29; Milton on, 222; *Phaedo*, 5; *Republic*, 9, 47–48; *Timaios*, 606 n. 20
Plattes, Gabriel, 664 n. 20
Plekhanov, George, 62, 69, 70, 78, 111–13
Plotinus, 607 n. 25
Plummer, Alfred, 617 n. 6, 626 n. 85
Pobedonostsev, K. P., 619 n. 27
Polak, Fred L., 605 n. 11
Poland, 129
"Policy science," 344
Polybius, 246
Ponce de Leon, 609 n. 37
Poniatovia, Christina, 358–59
Pope, Alexander, 8, 605 n. 7
Popper, Sir Karl, 28–29, 483, 613 n. 68, 686 nn. 31–32
Porphyry, 607 n. 25
Potter, Mr., 337
Powell, Enoch, 630 n. 103
Powell, Vavasor, 282, 285, 654 n. 4
Pragmatical, 297, 629 n. 103, 659 n. 11
Pragmaticus, 224
Presbyterians, 299
Price, Richard, 497–98, 507, 516–17
Priestley, Joseph, 500, 502, 516, 519–22
Printing, 293, 338, 652 n. 20
Prior, O. H., 703 n. 7
Prometheus, Prometheans, 315–16, 365, 405; myth of, 485–90, 492–93
Prophets and prophetism, 35–45, 60–66, 81, 88
Protestant ethic, 672 n. 51
Proudhon, Pierre J., on collective supremacy, 50; defines Communism, 42–43; disenchantment, 160; opposes doctrines, 100; fire imagery, 482; on Jacobinism, 78; on Marx as "tapeworm," 618 n. 23; pessimism, 43–44; on politics and religion, 58; prejudices, 92; on revolutionizing, 34; on Rousseau, 480; on words, 163, 626 n. 82; *Confessions of a Revolutionist*, 58; *Gen-*

eral idea of the Revolution in the Nineteenth Century, 138–39; *What is Property?*, 16
Proust, Jacques, 638 n. 58
Purge, as imagery, 251, 263
Pym, John, 252

Qaddafi, Muammar al-, 136, 140
Quicherat, L., 652 n. 13
Quietists, 45
Quiring, Heinrich, 686 n. 31
Quiroga, Vasco de, 18, 26–27

Rabaut de St. Etienne, M., 473
Rabelais, François, 160, 218
Ramsey, R. W., 661 n. 34
Raumer, Friedrich von, 629 n. 98
Rayment, Robert, 504
Reavey, George, 684 n. 1
Redemption, 149, 236, 259, 475
Redhead, Henry. *See* Yorke, Henry Redhead
Reeves, Marjorie, 610 nn. 41, 43, 47, 611 nn. 48–49
Reform Bill (1832), 88–91, 543
Reform League, 140
Reformatio Sigismundi (c. 1438), 81, 83
Reformation, and political change, 81–82
Reformation (renewal), 240–41
Regeneration, 234
Reichardt, Rolf, 704 n. 9
Reincarnation, 236
Reiss, Hans, 704 n. 19
Religion, as revolutionary element, 59–67
Renan, Ernest, 72
Republik der Arbeiter, die, 110
Resurrection, 236
Revelation, Book of, 233
Revolution Society (London), 499, 501–2, 539, 695 n. 4
Revolutionary Club. *See* British Revolutionary Club
Rhetoric. *See* Language; Metaphor; Words
Ribner, Irving, 645 n. 14
Ridolfi, Roberto, 651 n. 5
Robespierre, Augustin, 699 n. 57
Robespierre, Maximilien., debate with Brissot, 584; and Condorcet, 580–81, 584; David and death of, 699 n. 57; on disagreement, 561; on England, 92–93; on fanaticism, 71; health, 76; on Machiavelli, 52; and messianism, 61; rejects *philosophes*, 369; and revolutionary opportunity, 30–31, 51, 130, 585; Remilly on, 531; rebukes Yorke, 557
Robinson, Howard, 670 nn. 25, 29, 671 n. 31
Rochester, Lawrence Hyde, Earl of, 649 n. 16, 650 n. 2, 660 n. 17

Rockingham, Sir Lewis Watson, 1st Baron, 434
Rogers, Edward, 654 n. 5, 685 n. 17
Rogers, John, deposition, 510; flight, 285, 376; imprisonment, 279, 479; later career, 433; millenarianism, 264–83, 327, 654 nn. 4, 6; uncompromising attitude, 323; *Life and Opinions*, 658 n. 22; *Ohel*, 655 n. 8; *Sagrir*, 657 n. 16
Rogers, Nehemiah, 264, 393, 510
Rogers, P. G., 654 n. 2, 658 n. 23, 659 n. 30
Roland, Mme (Jeanne Manon Phlipon), 522
Romilly, Sir Samuel, 521, 530–32, 537, 566
Rooke, Sir Giles, 698 n. 37
Rosenberg, Alfred, 55
Rota Club, 387, 396, 674 n. 25
Roth, Cecil, 660 n. 18
Roth, Léon, 660 n. 24
Roth, Lucien, 660 n. 18
Rousseau, Jean-Jacques, 132, 480, 533–37, 585, 588, 596
Roux, Jacques, 503
Rowley, H. H., 617 n. 16, 622 n. 45
Royal Society of London, 345, 421
Ruge, Arnold, 106
Rühle, Jurgen, 636 n. 44
Rushworth, John, 661 n. 34
Russia, censorship in, 114–16, 619 n. 27; differing views of, 56–57; doctrinal disputes with China, 101–2; Gorky criticizes régime in, 116–18; *Das Kapital* in, 52; propaganda challenged, 172; revolution in, 71, 86; revolutionary thought in, 85; slavery abolished, 166; socialism in, 50

Sacheverell, Dr. Henry, 434–35
Sade, marquis de, 587
Sadler, John Edward, 376; 665 n. 36, 671 nn. 41, 43
Sadovsky, Baron, 381
St. John-Stevas, Norman, 703 n. 1
Saint-Just, Louis Antoine de, 71, 76, 699 n. 57
Saint-Pierre, C. I. Castel de, 596
Saint-Simon, Claude Henri, comte de, 38, 77, 343, 592, 673 n. 73
Salisbury, 3rd Marquis of, 633 n. 6
Salmasius, C., 87, 327
Salutati, Coluccio, 27
Sand, George, 473
Sanford, Charles L., 608 n. 35
Santayana, George, 170
Sarpi, Fra Paolo, 120
Sartre, Jean-Paul, 129, 140, 163, 601–2; *Kean*, 695 n. 2
Savet, L., 649 n. 21
Savile, Sir George, 496, 497
Savonarola, Girolamo, 241

Saxl, Fritz, 635 n. 38
Sayers, Dorothy L., 610 n. 40
Schaff, Adam, 622 n. 44
Schapiro, J. Salwyn, 618 n. 23, 703 n. 7
Schelling, F. W. J. von, 200
Schiller, J. C. Friedrich von, 10, 31, 146–47, 594
Schirokauer, Arno, 623 n. 54, 624 n. 55
Schlechta, Karl, 642 nn. 98, 100
Schlüter, Herman, 635 n. 25
Schneirla, T. C., 605 n. 7
Scholtz, Harald, 663 n. 14
Schorer, Mark, 419
Schram, Stuart, 625 n. 65, 639 n. 75
Schwarzchild, Leopold, 634 n. 17
Science, meanings of, 99, 100. *See also* Royal Society of London
Scotland, 302, 514
Scott, Sir Walter, 146, 442, 447, 702 n. 71
Sedgwick, Obadiah, 278
Sedition, 245
Selden, John, 294
Selkirk, Thomas Douglas, 5th Earl of, 566–68
Semantics. *See* Words
Seneca, 205, 588
Seraphic (word), 277, 657 n. 18
Servetus, Michael, 122, 132
Sewell, George, 450
Shadwell, Thomas, 444–46
Shaftesbury, Anthony Ashley Cooper, 1st Earl of, 248
Shakespeare, William, on earthly disorders, 227; on industry, 672 n. 51; on innovation, 311–12; on revolution, 229–30, 249; quoted, 55, 160, 227
Shaplen, Robert, 638 n. 61
Shaw, E. P., 638 n. 58
Shaw, Goerge Bernard, 74, 633 n. 6
Sheares, John, 557–58
Shelley, Mary, 493
Shelley, Percy Bysshe, and Bruno, 200, 213; on "cancelled cycles," 150; disenchantment, 160; on effects of revolution, 69–70; and Godwin, 575; on mountains, 146; on Prometheus, 486–89; Southey on, 574, 575
Sherfey, Dr. Mary Jane, 688 n. 50
Sheridan, Richard Brinsley, 514
Sickingen, Franz von, 627 n. 90
Sidney, Algernon, 433, 554, 675 n. 33, 693 n. 33
Sidney, Sir Philip, and Bruno, 191, 196, 209, 325, 379, 651 n. 6; circle of acquaintances, 189–93; and compromise, 176, 217; death, 179, 189, 193, 654 n. 6; on images of life, 493; and policy science, 344; political commitment, 179, 187–94, 253, 266, 655

n. 6; *Arcadia,* 178–86, 189, 190, 194–95, 209, 210, 369
Sièyes, comte Emmanuel Joseph (abbé), 432, 581, 587
Silone, Ignazio, 520; 641 n. 86
Similes, autonomous, 253. *See also* Metaphors; Words
Simpkinson, C. H., 654 n. 2
Singer, Dorothy Waley, 645 n. 26, 646 n. 34, 647 n. 51, 670 n. 26
Sirven family, 131
Skinner, B. F., 7
Skirving, A., 515
Slavery, effect of abolition, 166
Smith, Adam, 672 n. 51
Smith, C. I., 686 n. 32
Smith, Sydney, 89–90
Smith, Thomas, 571
Snow, Vernon F., 250; 651 n. 4, 653 n. 24, 660 n. 23
Soboul, Albert, 704 n. 11
Socialism, 8, 50, 99–100, 103–4
Society for Constitutional Information, 513
Socrates, 5
Solt, Leo F., 658 nn. 21, 23
Sorge, Friedrich Albert, 706 n. 27
South, Robert, 164, 353
Southey, Robert, disagreement with Wordsworth, 683 n. 85; on fire, 474; on French Revolution, 507; on More, 592, 678 n. 9; on Shelley, 574–75; on Wordsworth's *Cintra,* 683 n. 78
Spain, 187, 460–61
Spectre, of words, 248
Spencer, John, 234–35, 263
Spender, Stephen, 152; 641 n. 86
Spengler, Oswald, 58
Spiegel, Der, 624 n. 61, 625 n. 67, 640 n. 78
Spinka, Mathew, 667 n. 9, 669 n. 19, 673 n. 53
Spinoza, Benedictus de, 122–23, 590, 597, 603 n. 1, 660 n. 24
Spittlehouse, John, 267, 655 nn. 6, 8
Splendid (word), 225
Sprat, Thomas, on improving English personal habits, 672 n. 51; on extremes; 348; and scientific utopianism, 350–57, 372; on words, 157–58, 244; *History of the Royal Society,* 350, 665 n. 34
Staël, de, family, 93
Staël, Mme de, 354, 370, 581, 600–601
Staël, Holstein Erik Magnus, baron de, 42, 169
Stainer, C. J., 658 n. 30
Stalin, Josef V., 85, 112, 117, 127, 172
Stanhope, Charles, 3rd Earl, 502, 518–19
Stearns, R. P., 655 n. 8
Steffens, Lincoln, 152

Stein, Lorenz, 52
Steiner, George, 620 n. 31, 621 n. 32, 636 n. 44, 642 n. 101
Stephens, Alexander, 696 nn. 17, 18, 21
Sternberg, Fritz, 128
Stevenson, Adlai, 583
Storm, as revolutionary image, 70, 220, 243, 244, 255, 258, 310, 357
Strachey, John, 427
Struve, Peter, 101, 615 n. 78
Stuart, Daniel, 456
Stubbe, Henry, 353
Stühlingen and Lupfen, Articles of Peasants of, 83
Suharto, T. N. J., 638 n. 61
Sukarno, Achmed, 136–38, 140
Sunday Times (London), 685 n. 10
Sun State, 16, 31
Surtz, Edward, 606 n. 19
Sweet Dreamers, 256, 585
Swift, Jonathan, 452, 687 n. 45
Sydney, Algernon. See Sidney, Algernon
Syfret, R. H., 666 n. 38
Symbionese Liberation Army, 603 n. 3
Syms, Christopher, 262
Szamuely, Tibor, 635 n. 30

Tait, William, 689 n. 17
Talleyrand, le prince de, 566
Talmon, J. L., 591; 629 n. 14
Tansillo, Luigi, 208, 216, 242
Tarn, W. W., 16, 608 n. 30
Tasso, Torquato, 208
Tawney, R. H., 672 n. 51
Taylor, G. C., 651 n. 6
Taylor, Harriet, 128
Tennyson, Alfred, Lord, 474
Theatricality, and politics, 533–36; melodramatic tactics, 89; theatrical device, 166
Thelwall, John, 540, 573, 690 n. 20
Thomason, George, collection of tracts, 230, 263
Thompson, J. M., 76; 616 n. 8, 622 n. 46, 626 n. 80, 631 n. 119
Thomson, David, 626 nn. 79, 80
Thoreau, David, 76
Thorndike, Lynn, 608 n. 34, 649 nn. 21, 23
Three, third, triad, Halifax's "third opinion," 169; Hegel, 65; Joachim's pattern, 21; third camp, 87; "third choice," 579, 601; no third way, 101
Thunder, thunderbolts, biblical, 233, 384; Columbus, 19; as revolutionary images, 224, 234, 285, 357, 405; Shelley, 69
Thurloe, John, 281, 283
Tillich, Paul, 641 n. 92
Timon: a play, 643 n. 104
Tocqueville, Alexis de, on causes of revolution, 84, 86; on English and French, 91, 579; on revolutionaries, 37–38, 43, 517, 573; on revolutionary values, 71, 298, 581; on true ideas, 172; on writers and statesmen, 4, 592
Todd, F. M., 682 n. 74, 683 n. 82
Tolstoy, Leo, 4
Tooke, John Horne, bravura, 540; on French Revolution, 519, 533, 538–40; late ideology, 541, 543, 573; and Mackintosh, 544; observed by spies, 539–40; trial, 510, 514, 526, 540
Torch, burning, Dante, 265, 478; Rogers, 479; Andreae, 479
Toynbee, Arnold, 8–9, 58
Trevelyan, G. M., 433
Trevor-Roper, H. R., 262, 263, 324; 618 n. 25, 661 n. 26, 662 n. 3
Trilling, Lionel, 156
Trotsky, Leon, as Benthamite, 631 n. 113; Debray on, 144; denies need for popular majority, 111; fire imagery, 482; on Gorky, 114; Gorky criticizes, 115–17; Harich on, 127; and Mao, 102; on Rosa Luxembourg, 118; Rosa Luxembourg criticizes, 120
Trumbull, G. H., 666 n. 38
Tseretelli, Irakli, 113
Tucker, Robert, 52; 616 n. 80, 617 nn. 13, 18
Turgenev, Ivan, 472
Turgot, Anne Robert Jacques, baron, 126
Turnbull, G. H., 343; 662 n. 3, 663 nn. 8, 10, 11, 665 nn. 25, 33
Tuveson, Ernest Lee, 420; 678 n. 9
Tyndale, William, 591

Ulam, Adam, 633 n. 6
United States, Negro revolution in, 148
Universal Coloured People's Association, 150
Universities, fire ritual in Paris, 477; Hobbes on, 685 n. 9; in Naples, 685 n. 9; rebels and academic reform of, in Berlin, 149–50

Vadier, Marc Guillaume, 560
Van den Ende, F., 123
Vane, Sir Henry, 285
Vaneigem, Raoul, 643 n. 11
Vanity, as revolutionary impulse, 531
Varillas, Antoine, 448–49
Vaughan, Benjamin, 503
Veblen, Thorstein, 351
Vega, Lope de, 20
Veitch, G. S., 695 n. 4
Venner, Thomas, 281–85, 323, 674 n. 25
Vernon, W. W., 685 n. 15
Vertot, René de, 582

Vespucci, Amerigo, 13, 18, 20, 26
Villani, Matteo, 241
Villiers, 188
Viret, Pierre, 605 n. 7
Vocabulary. *See* Words
Voegelin, Eric, 611 n. 51, 661 n. 30, 703 n. 7, 706 n. 38
Volcano, Marx's "lava," 70; Napoleon's "eruption," 69; Wagner's Europe, 75; "snow-capped" (Condorcet), 581
Voltaire, on "chain," 640 n. 76; on Charlemagne, 583; and proscribed *Encyclopédie*, 124; and French Revolution, 534; advocates tolerance, 131–34; *Philosophical Dictionary*, 131, 133
Vossler, Karl, 141

Wagner, Richard, 74–76, 660 n. 24
Waldseemüller, Martin, 26
Walker, D. P., 645 n. 27
Wallace, Malcolm, 644 n. 14
Waller, Edmund, 671 n. 44
Waller, Sir William, 535
Walpole, Horace, 498
Walther, Gérard, 700 n. 57
Walwyn, William, 305, 369, 424, 428–31
Walzer, Michael, 251; 626 n. 83, 649 n. 20
War, 13, 410, 413, 423, 462
Ward, Charles E., 682 n. 59
Ward, Richard, 669 n. 20
Warnock, G. J., 672 n. 44
Watchman, The (Coleridge on Burke), 86
Water Beggars, 37
Watkins, Alan, 629 n. 103
Watnick, Morris, 636 n. 43
Watson, George, 641 n. 81
Wayman, Edward, 654 n. 4
Weber, Max, 4, 17, 58, 672 n. 51
Webster, Charles, 375, 663 n. 5, 364 nn. 16, 20
Weitling, Wilhelm, and absolute control, 12; on coming revolution, 70; doctrines and career, 105–11; on messianism, 62; *Guarantees of Harmony and Freedom*, 106, 108
Wellington, Arthur Wellesley, 1st Duke of, 91, 460
Wells, H. G., 8
Wells, J. E., 683 nn. 77, 78
Wendel, François, 635 n. 39
Wesley, John, 706 n. 22
West, Rebecca, 171
Weydemeyer, Joseph, 110
Wheelwright, Philip, 643 n. 126, 686 n. 32
Whirlwinds, as revolutionary image, 243, 244, 256, 302, 647 n. 57
Whitehead, Alfred North, 96, 300; 632 n. 120

Whitman, Sidney, 604 n. 4
Whole-Hog Chartism, 80
Wilberforce, William, 502, 574
Wildman, Sir John, 425, 433, 674 n. 25
Wilkinson, Henry, 251
William IV, King of England, 433, 434, 452
Williams, G. H., 627 n. 91, 646 n. 35, 647 n. 54
Williams, Raymond, 620 n. 32, 622 n. 44
Williamson, Audrey, 701 n. 58
Williamson, George, 677 n. 3
Wilson, Arthur M., 636 n. 41, 638 n. 58
Wilson, Charles, 661 n. 32
Wilson, Edmund, 107; 623 n. 51, 626 n. 79, 634 nn. 17, 20, 704 n. 14
Wilson, Sir Harold, 634 n. 14
Wilson, Woodrow, 631 n. 120
Winstanley, Gerrard, on change, 232–33; disenchantment, 160; fire imagery, 482; on knowledge and power, 34; on paradise, 336; retirement, 433; on universal freedom, 145; utopian position, 354; Walwyn on, 369; *The Law of Freedom*, 428
Winthrop, John (the younger), 334–35, 379
Wittke, Carl, 625 n. 67, 634 nn. 17, 25
Wolf, wolves, in revolutionary imagery, 265, 296
Wolfe, Bertram D., 114; 623 n. 51, 634 n. 17, 635 n. 31
Wolfe, Don M., 676 n. 2, 680 n. 25
Wolfenstein, Victor, 626 n. 82
Wolff, S. L., 652 n. 14
Wöllner, Johann Christoph, 497
Wollstonecraft, Mary, 517, 521, 522; 688 n. 51
Womb, imagery of, 493; Lassalle's metaphor, 64
Women's rights, 572
Wood, Anthony à, 675 n. 30
Wood, Neal, 641 n. 81
Woodcock, George, 617 n. 13, 486 n. 25
Woodhouse, A. S. P., 673 n. 1
Words, Cromwell on, 269; and English ideology, 514–15; evil, 248; meaning and disenchantment of, 157–65; and revolutionary images, 222–59, 286; spectre, 248; Tooke on, 514. *See also the following individual words:* Bees; Blood; Bug-words; Chain; Circle; Clouds; Comet; Dog; Earthquake; Explosions; Fantastical; Fire; Flame; Flood; Foreign; Garboil; Lightning; Obscurity; Plants; Purge; Roots; Seraphic; Splendid; Storm; Thunder; thunderbolts; Wolf; Womb
Wordsworth, Dorothy, 460, 466
Wordsworth, William, disenchantment, 160; on earthly paradise, 419; fire imagery, 482; on language, 158; political ex-

pression, 453–68, 507, 519; and Southey, 683 n. 85; 681 n. 39; *The Convention of Cintra*, 456, 460–68
Wormald, B. H. G., 630 n. 106
Worsley, Lt.-Col., 272
Worthington, John, on extremists, 442; and Hartlib, 369, 375–79; on revolutions, 419; 669 n. 19, 671 n. 32, 677 n. 8
Wren, Sir Christopher, 341
Wren, Matthew, 246
Wyclif, John, 82
Wyvill, Christopher, 498, 499, 524, 526

Yates, Frances A., 196, 199; 646 nn. 34, 41, 651 n. 6
Yeats, W. B., 68; 604 n. 7
Yellow Dwarf, 547
Yevtushenko, Evgeny A., 171
Yonge, C. D., 652 n. 13
Yorke, Henry Redhead, 504–6, 534; and

David, 563–64; imprisonment and trial, 549–50; and Paine, 558–59; recantation, 550–65; *A Letter to the Reformers*, 550; *Travels in France*, 552
Young, Arthur, 538
Young, Edward, 640 n. 76
Young, R. F., 662 n. 2, 668 n. 14

Zagoria, Donald S., 633 n. 9
Zagorim, Perez, 651 n. 7, 654 nn. 2, 4, 657 n. 15, 675 n. 30, 695 n. 10
Zandvoort, R. W., 644 n. 12
Zasulich, Vera, 46, 624 n. 63
Zavala, Silvio, 609 n. 37, 611 nn. 61, 62
Zeeveld, W. G., 644 n. 12
Zemlya i Volya, 116
Zinner, Paul E., 637 n. 52
Zinoviev, G. E., 125
Zinzendorf, N. L., Graf von, 706 n. 22
Zschäbitz, Gerhard, 627 n. 88

utopia & revolution

*On the Origins of a Metaphor,
or Some Illustrations of the Problem
of Political Temperament and
Intellectual Climate
and
How Ideas, Ideals, and Ideologies
Have Been Historically Related*

MELVIN J. LASKY

There is a fateful moment in human history
when the vision of the perfect society confronts the movement toward violent social
change. In a remarkable feat of scholarship in
intellectual history, Melvin J. Lasky charts
the course of this confrontation over some five
centuries. In so doing he traces the ideological
extension of the human personality through
the writings of political theorists, philosophers, poets, and historians—from Dante to
More, from More to Marx.

Revolutionary vocabulary, Mr. Lasky finds,
was born in archetypal metaphors of spark
and fire, storm and whirlwind, and, above all,
the circles of time and the progressions of
the very planets. The utopian vision has its
origins in the image of a human formicary—
the noble ant hill that is repeatedly celebrated
from Plato's *Republic* to Skinner's *Walden
Two*. As the idea of "revolution" moved from
astronomy to social theory, the idea of utopia
moved from theology to politics. However,
Lasky argues, progressive secularization of
these attitudes is accompanied by the "eschatologization" of the new ideologies. As a result,
the realization of social ideals becomes inseparable from the great incendiary cliché of
"revolution."

Lasky traces a recurring transformation that
turns utopian longing into revolutionary com-